Simply Visual Basic .NET

Deitel Books, Cyber Classrooms, Complete Training Courses and Web-Based Training Courses Published by Prentice Hall

Simply Series

Simply Visual Basic® .NET: An Application-Driven™ Tutorial Approach

Simply C++: An Application-Driven™ Tutorial Approach (coming in 2003)

Simply Java™ Programming: An Application-Driven™ Tutorial Approach (coming in 2003)

How to Program Series

Advanced Java™ 2 Platform How to Program
C How to Program, 3/E
C++ How to Program, 4/E
C# How to Program
e-Business and e-Commerce How to Program
Internet and World Wide Web How to Program, 2/E
Java™ How to Program, 5/E
Perl How to Program
Python How to Program
Visual Basic® 6 How to Program
Visual Basic® .NET How to Program, 2/E
Wireless Internet & Mobile Business How to Program
XML How to Program

.NET How to Program Series

C# How to Program
Visual Basic®.NET How to Program, 2/E

Visual Studio Series

C# How to Program
Visual Basic® .NET How to Program, 2/E
Getting Started with Microsoft® Visual C++® 6 with an Introduction to MFC
Visual Basic® 6 How to Program

For Managers Series

e-Business and e-Commerce for Managers

Developer Series

C# A Programmer's Introduction
C# for Experienced Programmers
Java™ Web Services for Experienced Programmers
Web Services A Technical Introduction
Visual Basic® .NET for Experienced Programmers
Visual C++ .NET for Experienced Programmers

Coming Soon

e-books and e-whitepapers
Premium CourseCompass, WebCT and Blackboard Multimedia Cyber Classroom versions

Multimedia Cyber Classroom Series

C++ Multimedia Cyber Classroom, 4/E
C# Multimedia Cyber Classroom
e-Business and e-Commerce Multimedia Cyber Classroom
Internet and World Wide Web Multimedia Cyber Classroom, 2/E
Java™ 2 Multimedia Cyber Classroom, 5/E
Perl Multimedia Cyber Classroom
Python Multimedia Cyber Classroom
Visual Basic® 6 Multimedia Cyber Classroom
Visual Basic® .NET Multimedia Cyber Classroom, 2/E
Wireless Internet & Mobile Business Programming Multimedia Cyber Classroom
XML Multimedia Cyber Classroom

The Complete Training Course Series

The Complete C++ Training Course, 4/E
The Complete C# Training Course
The Complete e-Business and e-Commerce Programming Training Course
The Complete Internet and World Wide Web Programming Training Course, 2/E
The Complete Java™ 2 Training Course, 5/E
The Complete Perl Training Course
The Complete Python Training Course
The Complete Visual Basic® 6 Training Course
The Complete Visual Basic® .NET Training Course, 2/E
The Complete Wireless Internet & Mobile Business Programming Training Course
The Complete XML Programming Training Course

To communicate with the authors, send e-mail to:

> deitel@deitel.com

For information on corporate on-site seminars and public seminars offered by Deitel & Associates, Inc. worldwide, visit:

> www.deitel.com

For continuing updates on Prentice Hall and Deitel publications visit:

> www.deitel.com,
> www.prenhall.com/deitel or
> www.InformIT.com/deitel

Simply Visual Basic .NET

H. M. Deitel
Deitel & Associates, Inc.

P. J. Deitel
Deitel & Associates, Inc.

T. R. Nieto
Deitel & Associates, Inc.

Prentice
Hall

Upper Saddle River, NJ 07458

Library of Congress Cataloging-in-Publication Data

On file

Vice President and Editorial Director, ECS: *Marcia J. Horton*
Acquisitions Editor: *Petra J. Recter*
Assistant Editor: *Sarah Parker*
Project Manager: *Jennifer Cappello*
Vice President and Director of Production and Manufacturing, ESM: *David W. Riccardi*
Executive Managing Editor: *Vince O'Brien*
Managing Editor: *Tom Manshreck*
Production Editor: *Chirag Thakkar*
Director of Creative Services: *Paul Belfanti*
Creative Director: *Carole Anson*
Chapter Opener and Cover Designer: *Tamara L. Newnam, Dr. Harvey Deitel*
Interior Design: *Jonathan Boylan, John Root, Dr. Harvey Deitel*
Interior Design Assistance: *Geoffrey Cassar*
Manufacturing Manager: *Trudy Pisciotti*
Manufacturing Buyer: *Lisa McDowell*
Marketing Manager: *Pamela Shaffer*
Marketing Assistant: *Barrie Reinhold*

 © 2003 by Pearson Education, Inc.
Upper Saddle River, New Jersey 07458

Printed in the United States of America

10 9 8 7 6 5 4 3 2 1

ISBN 0-13-140553-5

Pearson Education Ltd., *London*
Pearson Education Australia Pty. Ltd., *Sydney*
Pearson Education Singapore, Pte. Ltd.
Pearson Education North Asia Ltd., *Hong Kong*
Pearson Education Canada, Inc., *Toronto*
Pearson Educación de Mexico, S.A. de C.V.
Pearson Education–Japan, *Tokyo*
Pearson Education Malaysia, Pte. Ltd.
Pearson Education, Inc., *Upper Saddle River, New Jersey*

Trademarks:

Microsoft® Visual Studio .NET® are either registered trademarks or trademarks of Microsoft Corporation in the United States and/or other countries.

DEITEL, DIVE INTO, APPLICATION-DRIVEN and LIVE CODE are trademarks of Deitel and Associates, Inc.

In memory of Phyllis Gippetti
whose smile brought joy to her family and friends.

Barbara, Harvey, Paul and Abbey Deitel

Brief Table of Contents

Welcome to Visual Basic .NET and the world of Windows, Internet and World-Wide-Web programming with Visual Studio and the .NET platform! This book, the first in our new *Simply* series, was a joy to create. Our goal was to write a book that focuses on core concepts and features of Visual Basic .NET while keeping the discussion of this highly technical subject as simple as possible.

To achieve these goals, we implemented an innovative teaching methodology. We present the core concepts of leading-edge computing technologies using the tutorial-based, APPLICATION-DRIVEN™ approach, combined with the DEITEL™ signature LIVE-CODE™ approach of teaching programming using complete, working, real-world applications. We merged the notion of a lab manual with that of a conventional textbook, creating a book that is best used by students sitting at computers and building each example application as they read the tutorials.

As students work through the tutorials, they learn about Visual Basic .NET and its fundamental features, such as visual programming concepts, graphical-user-interface (GUI) components, multimedia (audio, images, animation and video), file processing, database processing and Internet and World-Wide-Web-based client/server networking. At the end of most sections, we provide self-review questions with answers so that students receive immediate feedback on their understanding of the material. Hundreds of additional self-review questions with answers are available on this book's Companion Web Site.

Features in Simply Visual Basic .NET

This book is loaded with pedagogic features, including:

- *APPLICATION-DRIVEN™ Tutorial Approach.* Each tutorial uses a contemporary, real-world application to teach programming concepts. The examples and exercises are up-to-the-minute with Internet/Web-related examples and with popular applications, such as ATMs, game playing, graphics, multimedia and even a 3-tier Web-based bookstore. Most examples have a business focus. At the beginning of each tutorial, students "test-drive" the completed application so they can see how it works. Then they build the application by following our step-by-step instructions. The book concentrates on the principles of good software engineering and stresses program clarity.

- *LIVE-CODE™ Approach.* This book is loaded with LIVE-CODE™ examples. Each tutorial ends with the complete, working program code and the students can run the application that they just created. We call this method of teaching and writing the *LIVE-CODE™ Approach.* We feel that this approach is more effective than presenting only snippets of code out of the context of a complete program.

- *Real-World Technologies.* This text incorporates today's technologies to develop useful applications. For example, we use the Unified Modeling Language™ (UML) to replace flowcharts—an older standard. The UML has become the preferred graphical modeling language for designing object-oriented applications. In *Simply Visual Basic .NET*, we use UML to show the flow of control for several applications, so students gain practice reading the type of diagrams that are used in industry.

- **Visual Programming and Graphical User Interface (GUI).** From the first tutorial, we immerse students in visual programming techniques and modifying Visual Basic .NET GUIs. Students who learn these techniques can create graphical programs more quickly and easily. The early tutorials provide students with a foundation for designing GUIs—concepts that they will apply throughout the book as we teach core programming concepts. Many tutorials contain GUI Design Tips that are summarized at the end of the tutorials for easy reference. Additionally, Appendix C compiles all the GUI Design Tips to help students as they prepare for exams.

- **Full-Color Presentation.** This book is in full color so that students can see sample outputs as they would appear on a monitor. Also, we syntax color the Visual Basic .NET code, similar to the way Visual Studio .NET colors the code in its editor window. This way, students can match what they see in the book with what they see on their own screens. Our syntax-coloring conventions are as follows:

  ```
  comments appear in green
  keywords appear in dark blue
  literal values appear in light blue
  text, class, method and variable names appear in black
  errors appear in red
  ```

- **Graphics and Multimedia.** Graphics make applications fun to create and use. In our introduction to graphics, Tutorial 26, we discuss Graphical Device Interface (GDI+)—the Windows service that provides the graphical features used by .NET—to teach students to personalize a bank check. In Tutorial 27, we use a fun technology called Microsoft Agent to add interactive, animated characters to a phone book application. With Microsoft Agent, your applications can speak to users and even respond to their voice commands!

- **Databases.** Databases are crucial to businesses today, and we use real-world applications to teach the fundamentals of database programming. Tutorials 25 and 30 familiarize students with databases, presented in the context of two applications—an ATM and a Web-based bookstore.

- **Case Study.** This book concludes with a sequence of four tutorials in which the student builds a Web-based, bookstore application. Tutorial 28 familiarizes readers with Microsoft's Internet Information Services (which enables Web publishing), multi-tier architecture and simple Web transactions. Tutorials 29–31 use ASP .NET and ADO .NET to build an application that retrieves information from a database and displays the information in a Web page.

- **Object-Oriented Programming.** Object-oriented programming is the most widely employed technique for developing robust, reusable software, and Visual Basic .NET offers advanced object-oriented programming features. This book introduces students to defining classes and using objects, laying a solid foundation for future programming courses.

- **Visual Studio .NET Debugger.** Debuggers are programs that help programmers find and correct logic errors in program code. Visual Studio .NET contains a powerful debugging tool that allows programmers to analyze their programs line-by-line as the programs execute. Throughout the book, we teach the Visual Studio .NET Debugger; we explain how to use its key features, and offer many debugging exercises.

To the Instructor

Focus of the Book

Our goal was clear: Produce a Visual Basic .NET textbook for introductory-level courses in computer programming aimed at students with little or no programming experience. This book teaches computer programming principles and the Visual Basic .NET language, including data types, control structures, object-oriented programming, Visual Basic .NET classes, GUI concepts, event-driven programming and more. After mastering the material in this book, students will be able to program in Visual Basic .NET and to employ many key capabilities of the .NET platform.

Lab Setup

To install some of the required software for this book, students and instructors will need Administrator-level access to the computer. For university computer labs where students do not have Administrator-level access, instructors and system administrators must ensure that the proper software is installed on the lab computers. In Tutorial 27, certain Microsoft Agent software components must be installed to execute and develop the **Phone Book** application. If students are not allowed to install software on lab computers, the Microsoft Agent components discussed in Tutorial 27 must be installed in advance. To configure and execute some of the examples and exercises, such as the **Bookstore** case study in Tutorials 28-31, students will need to have Administrator-level access. In addition, the examples in the book require that students have Debugger or Administrator access to the computer, which is typically required to develop applications in Visual Studio .NET.

A Note Regarding Terminology Used in the Book

In Tutorial 13, we discuss methods as Sub procedures (sometimes called subroutines) and Function procedures (sometimes called functions). We use this terminology for two reasons. First, the keywords Sub and Function are used in procedure definitions, so this naming is logical for students. Second, Visual Basic professionals have used this terminology for years and will continue to do so in the future. We also use the term "function" at certain points in this text to refer to Visual Basic 6 Function procedures that remain in Visual Basic .NET (such as Val and Pmt). When we introduce object-oriented programming concepts in Tutorial 19, we discuss the difference between procedures and methods and indicate that the procedures defined throughout the text are, in fact, methods. We hope our use of terminology helps you present the material in a simple and understandable manner.

Exception Handling: Bonus Tutorial Available Online

Exception Handling is one of the most important topics in Visual Basic .NET for building mission-critical and business-critical applications. Programmers need to know how to recognize the exceptions (errors) that could occur in software components and handle those exceptions effectively, allowing programs to deal with problems and continue executing instead of "crashing." This tutorial overviews the proper use of exception handling, including the termination model of exception handling, throwing and catching exceptions and the library class Exception. To download this tutorial, please go to www.deitel.com/vbnetSIMPLY1/index.html.

Objectives

Each tutorial begins with objectives that inform students of what to expect and give them an opportunity, after reading the tutorial, to determine whether they have met the intended goals.

Outline

The tutorial outline enables students to approach the material in top-down fashion. Along with the tutorial objectives, the outline helps students anticipate future topics and set a comfortable and effective learning pace.

Example Programs (with Program Outputs)

We present Visual Basic .NET features in the context of complete, working Visual Basic .NET programs. We call this our LIVE-CODE™ approach. All examples are available on the CD that accompanies the book or as downloads from our Web site, www.deitel.com/vbnetSIMPLY1/index.html.

Illustrations/Figures

An abundance of charts, line drawings and program outputs are included. The discussion of control structures, for example, features carefully drawn UML activity diagrams. [*Note:* We do not teach UML diagramming as a program-development tool, but we do use UML diagrams to explain the precise operation of many of Visual Basic .NET's control structures.]

Programming Tips

Hundreds of programming tips to help students focus on important aspects of program development. These tips and practices represent the best the authors have gleaned from a combined seven decades of programming and teaching experience.

 Good Programming Practices

Good Programming Practices highlight techniques that help students write programs that are clearer, more understandable and more maintainable.

 Common Programming Errors

Students learning a language—especially in their first programming course—frequently make errors. Pointing out these *Common Programming Errors* in the text reduces the likelihood that students will make the same mistakes.

 Error Prevention Tips

These tips describe aspects of Visual Basic .NET that prevent errors from getting into programs in the first place, which simplifies the testing and debugging process.

 Performance Tips

Teaching students to write clear and understandable programs is the most important goal for a first programming course. But students want to write programs that run the fastest, use the least memory, require the smallest number of keystrokes, etc. *Performance Tips* highlight opportunities for improving program performance.

 Portability Tips

The *Portability Tips* provide insights on how Visual Basic .NET achieves its high degree of portability among .NET platforms.

 Software Design Tips

The *Software Design Tips* highlight architectural and design issues that affect the construction of object-oriented software systems.

 GUI Design Tips

The *GUI Design Tips* highlight graphical-user-interface conventions to help students design attractive, user-friendly GUIs and use GUI features.

Skills Summary

Each tutorial includes a bullet-list-style summary of the new programming concepts presented. This reinforces key actions taken to build the application in each tutorial.

Key Terms

Each tutorial includes a list of important terms defined in the tutorial. These terms also appear in the index and in a book-wide glossary, so the student can locate terms and their definitions quickly.

230 Self-Review Questions and Answers

Self-review multiple-choice questions and answers are included after most sections to build students' confidence with the material and prepare them for the regular exercises. Students should be encouraged to attempt all the self-review exercises and check their answers.

834 Exercises (Solutions in Instructor's Manual)

Each tutorial concludes with exercises. Typical exercises include 10 multiple-choice questions, a "What does this code do?" exercise, a "What's wrong with this code?" exercise and a programming challenge. The questions involve simple recall of important terminology and concepts, writing individual Visual Basic .NET statements, writing small portions of Visual Basic .NET applications and writing complete Visual Basic .NET methods, classes and applications. Every programming exercise uses a step-by-step methodology to suggest how to solve the problems. The solutions for the exercises are *available only to instructors* through their Prentice-Hall representatives. [*NOTE:* **Please do not write to us requesting the instructor's manual. Distribution of this publication is strictly limited to instructors teaching from the book. Instructors may obtain the solutions manual only from their regular Prentice Hall representatives. We regret that we cannot provide the solutions to professionals.**]

GUI Design Guidelines

Consistent and proper graphical user interface design is crucial to visual programming. In each tutorial, we summarize the GUI design guidelines that were introduced. Appendix C, presents a cumulative list of these GUI design guidelines for easy reference.

Controls, Events, Properties & Methods Summaries

Each tutorial includes a summary of the controls, events, properties and methods covered in the tutorial. The summary includes a picture of each control, shows the control "in action" and lists the control's properties, events and methods that were discussed up to and including that tutorial. In addition, Appendix E groups the controls by tutorial for easy reference.

Index

The extensive index includes important terms both under main headings and as separate entries so that students can search for any term or concept by keyword. The code examples and the exercises also are included in the index. For every Visual Basic .NET source-code program in the book, we indexed it both under the appropriate application and as a subindex item under "code examples." We have also double-indexed features such as controls and properties. This makes it easier to find examples using particular features.

Simply Visual Basic .NET Ancillary Package

Simply Visual Basic .NET is accompanied by extensive ancillary materials for instructors, including the following:

- *Instructor's Resource CD (IRCD)* which contains the
  - *Instructor's Manual* with solutions to the end-of-tutorial exercises and
  - *Test-Item File* of multiple-choice questions (approximately two per tutorial section).
- *Customizable PowerPoint® Slides* containing all the code and figures in the text, and bulleted items that summarize the key points in the text. The slides are downloadable from `www.deitel.com/vbnetSIMPLY1/index.html` and are available as part of Prentice Hall's *Companion Web Site* (`www.prenhall.com/deitel`) for *Simply Visual Basic .NET*, which offers resources for both instructors and students.

Companion Web Site

For instructors, the *Companion Web Site* offers a *Syllabus Manager*, which helps instructors plan courses interactively and create online syllabi. Students also benefit from the functionality of the *Companion Web Site*. Book-specific resources for students include:

- PowerPoint® slides
- Example source code
- Reference materials from the book appendices
- Tutorial objectives
- Tutorial summaries
- Tutorial outlines
- Programming tips from each tutorial
- Online Study Guide—contains additional short-answer self-review exercises with answers
- Students can track their results and course performance on quizzes using the *Student Profile* feature, which records and manages all feedback and results from tests taken on the *Companion Web Site*. To access the *Companion Web Site* for *Simply Visual Basic .NET*, visit `www.prenhall.com/deitel`.

Simply Visual Basic .NET Multimedia Cyber Classroom

For the second edition of *Simply Visual Basic .NET*, we are planning to include the *Simply Visual Basic .NET: An APPLICATION-DRIVEN™, Tutorial Approach Multimedia Cyber Classroom* interactive CD. Our *Cyber Classrooms* are loaded with e-Learning features that are ideal for both learning and reference.

Each *Cyber Classroom* CD provides an introduction in which the authors overview the *Cyber Classroom*'s features. The textbook's LIVE-CODE™ examples truly "come alive" in the *Cyber Classrooms*. If you are viewing a program and want to execute it, you just click the lightning-bolt icon, and the program will run. You will see—and hear, when working with audio-based multimedia programs—the program's outputs immediately. If you want to modify a program and see the effects of your changes, click the floppy-disk icon that causes the source code to be "lifted off" the CD and "dropped into" one of your own directories so you can edit the text, recompile the program and try out your new version. Click the audio icon, and one of the authors will discuss the program and "walk you through" the code.

The *Cyber Classrooms* also provide navigational aids, including extensive hyperlinking. The *Cyber Classrooms* are browser based, so they remember sections that you have visited recently and allows you to move forward or backward among them. The thousands of index entries are hyperlinked to their text occurrences. Furthermore, when you key in a term using the "find" feature, the *Cyber Classrooms* locate occurrences of that term throughout the text. The Table of Contents entries are "hot," so clicking a tutorial name takes you immediately to that tutorial.

Course Management Systems

Selected content from *Simply Visual Basic .NET* and other Deitel texts, is available to integrate into various Course Management Systems, including CourseCompass, Blackboard and WebCT.[1] Course Management Systems help faculty create, manage and use sophisticated Web-based educational tools and programs. Blackboard, CourseCompass and WebCT offer:

- Features to create and customize an online course
- Communication tools
- Flexible testing tools
- Support materials

In addition to the tools found in Blackboard and WebCT, CourseCompass from Prentice Hall includes:

- **CourseCompass course home page**, which makes the course as easy to navigate as a book.
- **Hosting on Prentice Hall's centralized servers**, which allows course administrators to avoid separate licensing fees or server-space issues.
- **"How Do I" online-support sections** are available for users who need help personalizing course sites.
- **Instructor Quick Start Guide**

Premium Course Management Systems

For the second edition of *Simply Visual Basic .NET*, we are planning support for Premium Course Management Systems that integrate content from a rich variety of sources, including Deitel books, *Cyber Classrooms* and *Companion Web Sites* with Course Management courseware—providing enhanced content to users. Premium Course Management Systems include:

- **Pre-Loaded DEITEL™ Content in a Customizable Interface**. An instructor can aggregate and customize all course materials. This feature includes the e-Book, a searchable digital version of the book, and downloadable Power-Point® slides.
- **All the Interactivity of the *Cyber Classroom*.** Students can work with code and receive the added benefit of several hours of detailed audio descriptions of thousands of lines of code to help reinforce concepts. Every code example from the books is included.
- **Abundant Self-Assessment and Complete *Test-Item File*.** Use or edit hundreds of pre-loaded assessments, or upload your own. Assessments include self-review exercises, programming exercises (half with answers included) and test questions. Instructors choose which questions to assign, and students receive immediate feedback. Instructors can collect students' work and track their progress in an online gradebook.

To view free online demonstrations and learn more about Course Management Systems that support Deitel content, visit the following Web sites:

- Blackboard: www.blackboard.com and www.prenhall.com/blackboard.
- WebCT: www.webct.com and www.prenhall.com/webct.
- CourseCompass: www.coursecompass.com and www.prenhall.com/coursecompass.

---

1. The entire text of *Simply Visual Basic .NET* will be provided in the e-Book included with Premium CourseCompass for the second edition of the book.

For Students and Instructors: Important Information before You Begin

Please follow the instructions in this section to ensure that you have the proper setup before you begin this book.

Font and Naming Conventions

We use fonts to distinguish between IDE features (such as menu names and menu items) and other elements that appear in the IDE. Our convention is to emphasize IDE features in a sans-serif bold **Helvetica** font (for example, **Properties** window) and to emphasize program text in a serif Lucida font (for example, `Dim x As Boolean`). We use *italics* to emphasize special terms that are associated with Visual Studio .NET features, such as *Intellisense* and *Parameter Info*.

Software Bundled with *Simply Visual Basic .NET*

In the college bookstores, this book is shrink-wrapped with a trial edition of the Microsoft® Visual Studio® .NET integrated development environment. This is a full and complete version of Visual Studio .NET which may be used without charge for 60 days, at which time it becomes inoperable. No technical support accompanies this edition.

Students enrolled in a course at an accredited school who have purchased this book for use in conjunction with that course may purchase Microsoft Visual Basic .NET Standard Edition from Microsoft for $15.00 (US) plus shipping and handling. The standard edition is fully functional and is shipped on 5 CDs. There is no time limit and technical support is available upon registration of the software after installation.

To purchase this software, you must obtain a purchase code from your instructor. This code is supplied to your instructor by Prentice Hall. To order Visual Basic .NET Standard Edition, visit

www.gotdotnet.com/community/student/reference/purchase.aspx

and follow the instructions. A credit card is required to complete the purchase.

Professionals can obtain the 60-day trial edition of Visual Studio .NET from www.msdn.microsoft.com/vstudio/productinfo/trial/default.asp.

Hardware and Software Requirements to Run Visual Basic .NET

To install and run Visual Basic .NET, Microsoft recommends that PCs have these minimum requirements:

- Pentium II 450 MHz processor
- Windows NT 4.0 with Service Pack 6 or later operating system
- 64 megabytes for a Windows NT 4.0 computer; 96 MB for Windows 2000 Professional and 160 MB for Windows XP Professional
- 2.5 gigabytes of available hard drive space
- CD-ROM (DVD for the trial version)
- Super VGA monitor with 256 colors
- Mouse or other Microsoft-compatible pointing device
- **You must install Microsoft's Internet Information Services (IIS) before installing Visual Studio .NET.** Otherwise, the Web-based bookstore application in the case study cannot be created or executed. See Appendix G for detailed instructions on installing IIS.

This book assumes that you are using Windows 2000 or Windows XP, plus Microsoft's Internet Information Services (IIS). Additional setup instructions for

Web servers and other software is available on our Web site along with the examples. [*Note:* This is copyrighted material. Feel free to use it as you study, but you may not republish any portion of it in any form without explicit permission from Prentice Hall and the authors.]

Monitor Display Settings

Simply Visual Basic .NET includes hundreds of screenshots of applications. Your monitor-display settings may need to be adjusted so that the screenshots in the book will match what you see on your computer screen as you develop each application. [*Note:* We refer to single-clicking with the left mouse button as **selecting**, or **clicking.** We refer to double-clicking with the left mouse button simply as **double clicking**.] Follow these steps to set your monitor display correctly:

1. Open the **Control Panel** and double click **Display.**
2. Click the **Settings** tab.
3. Click the **Advanced...** button.
4. In the **General** tab, make sure **Small Fonts** is selected; this should indicate that **96 dpi** is now the setting (if you already have this setting, you do not need to do anything else).
5. Click **Apply.**

If you choose to use different settings, the `Size` and `Location` values we provide for different GUI elements (such as `Buttons` and `Labels`) in each application might not appear correctly on your screen. If so, simply adjust `Size` and `Location` values so the GUI elements in your application appear similar to those in the screenshots in the book.

Theme Settings for Windows XP Users

If you are using Windows XP, we assume that your theme is set to Windows Classic Style. Follow these steps to set Windows XP to display the Windows Classic theme:

1. Open the **Control Panel** and double click **Display.**
2. Click the **Themes** tab. Select **Windows Classic** from the **Theme:** drop-down list.
3. Click **OK** to save the settings.

Copying and Organizing Files

All of the examples for *Simply Visual Basic .NET* are included on the CD-ROM that accompanies this textbook. Follow the steps in the box, *Copying the Book Examples from the CD-ROM*, to copy the examples folder from the CD-ROM onto your hard drive. We suggest that you work from your hard drive rather than your CD drive for two reasons: you cannot save your programs to the book's CD (the CD is read-only), and files can be accessed faster from a hard drive than from a CD. The examples from the book (and our other publications) are also available on the Internet as downloads from the following Web sites:

```
www.deitel.com
www.prenhall.com/deitel
```

Screen shots in the box, *Copying the Book Examples from the CD-ROM*, might differ slightly from what you see on your computer, depending on whether you are using Windows 2000 or Windows XP. We used Windows 2000 to prepare the screenshots for this book.

Copying the Book Examples from the CD-ROM

1. ***Locating the CD-ROM drive.*** Insert the CD that accompanies *Simply Visual Basic .NET* into your computer's CD-ROM drive. The window displayed in Fig. 1 should appear. If the page appears, proceed to *Step 3* of this box. If the page does not appear, proceed to *Step 2*.

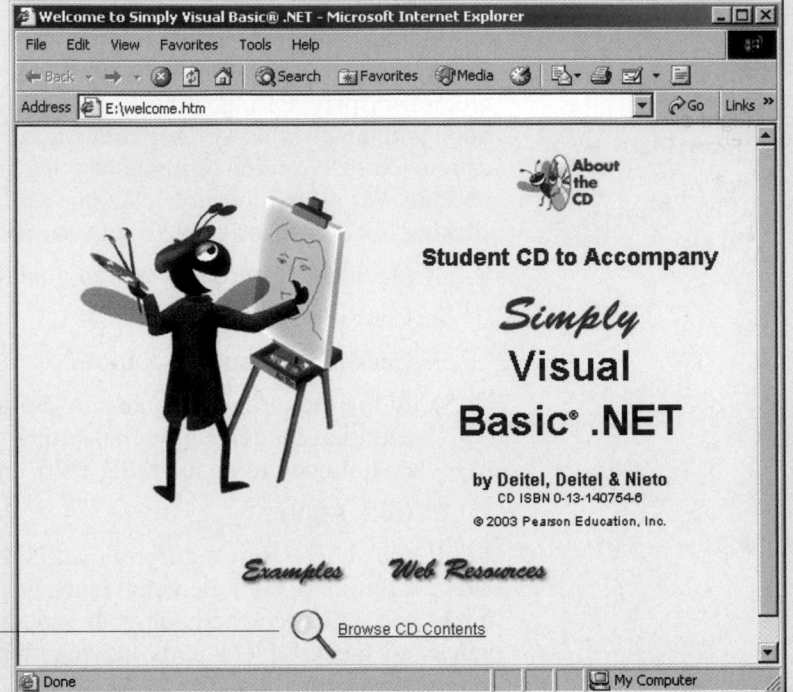

Click the **Browse CD Contents** link to access the CD's contents

Figure 1   Welcome page for Simply Visual Basic .NET CD.

2. ***Opening the CD-ROM directory using My Computer.*** If the page shown in Fig. 1 does not appear, double click the **My Computer** icon on your desktop. In the **My Computer** window, double click your CD-ROM drive (Fig. 2) to access the CD's contents. Proceed to *Step 4*.

Selected CD-ROM drive

Figure 2   Locating the CD-ROM drive.

3. ***Opening the CD-ROM directory.*** If the page in Fig. 1 does appear, click the **Browse CD Contents** link to access the CD's contents.

4. ***Copying the Examples folder.*** Right click the Examples folder (Fig. 3), then select **Copy**. Next, go to **My Computer** and double click the C: drive. Select the **Edit** menu and select **Paste** to copy the folder and its contents from the CD to your C: drive.

(cont.)

[*Note*: We save the examples to the C: drive and refer to this drive throughout the text. You may choose to save your files to a different drive based on your lab setup or personal preferences. Please see your instructor for more information if you are working in a computer lab to confirm where the examples should be saved.]

Right clicking the
Examples folder

Select **Copy**

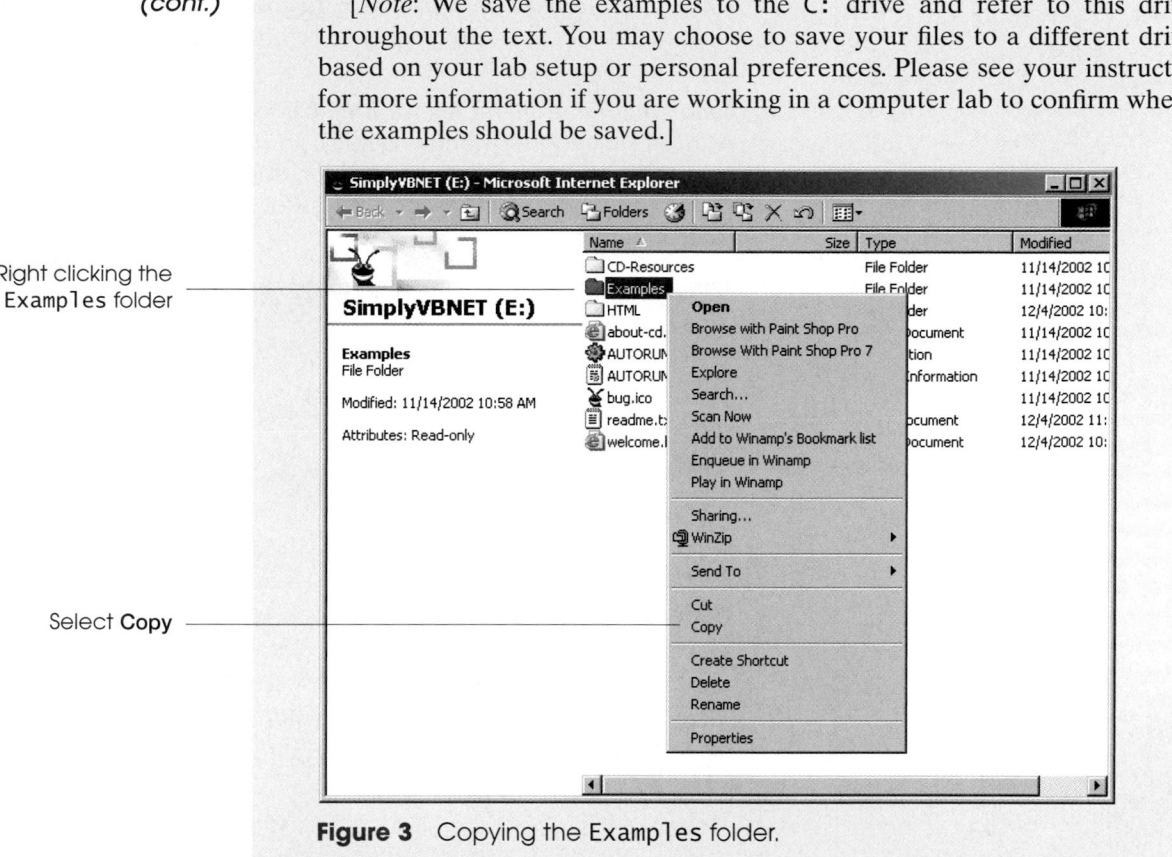

Figure 3   Copying the Examples folder.

The book example files you copied onto your computer from the CD are read-only. To access and modify these files, you must change this property. In the box, *Changing the Read-Only Property of Files*, you change the read-only property so you can run and modify the examples.

Changing the Read-Only Property of Files

1. ***Opening the Properties dialog.*** Right click the Examples folder and select **Properties** from the menu. The **Examples Properties** dialog appears (Fig. 4).

Uncheck the
Read-only attribute

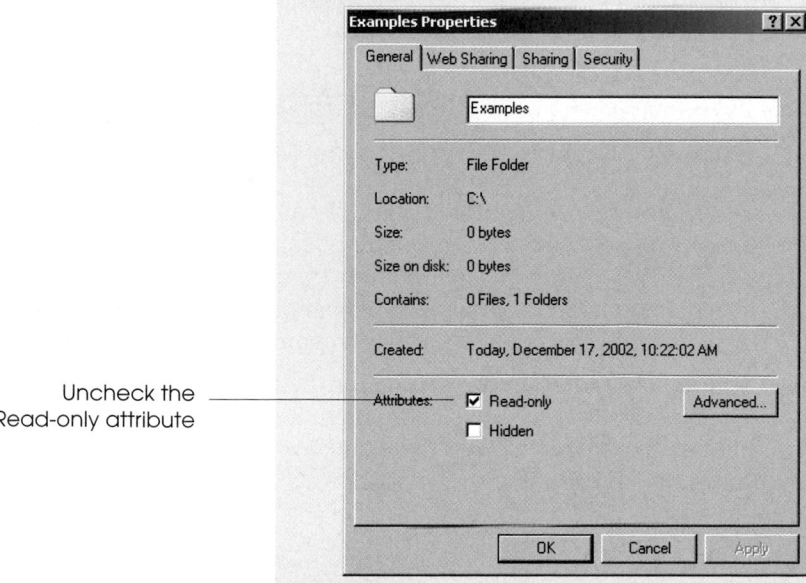

Figure 4   Removing the check in the **Read-only** check box.

(cont.)

2. ***Changing the read-only property.*** In the **Attributes** section of this dialog, click the box next to **Read-only** to remove the check mark. Click **Apply** to apply the changes.

3. ***Changing the property for all files.*** Clicking **Apply** will display the **Confirm Attribute Changes** window (Fig. 5). In this window, click the radio button next to **Apply changes to this folder, subfolders and files** and click **OK** to remove the read-only property for all of the files and folders in the **Examples** folder.

Click this radio button to remove the read-only property for all the files

Figure 5   Removing read-only for all the files in the **Examples** folder.

As you work through this book, you will be developing your own applications. In the box, *Creating a Work Folder*, you create a folder on your C: drive in which you will save all of your applications.

Creating a Work Folder

1. ***Selecting the drive.*** Double click the **My Computer** icon on your desktop to access a list of your computer drives (Fig. 6). Double click the C: drive. The contents of the C: drive are displayed.

Local disk

Figure 6   Computer drives listed under **My Computer**.

2. ***Creating a new folder.*** Select the **File** menu and under the **New** submenu, select **Folder** (Fig. 7). A new, empty folder appears in your C: directory (Fig. 8). [*Note:* From this point onward, we use the > character to indicate the selection of a menu command. For example, we use the notation **File > Open** to indicate the selection of the **Open** command from the **File** menu.]

3. ***Naming the folder.*** Enter a name for the folder. We suggest that you choose a name that you recognize and remember. We chose SimplyVB (Fig. 9). You can use this folder to save the examples from this book, your applications and your exercise solutions.

(cont.)

New folder option
(selected)

New folder

Newly created work folder

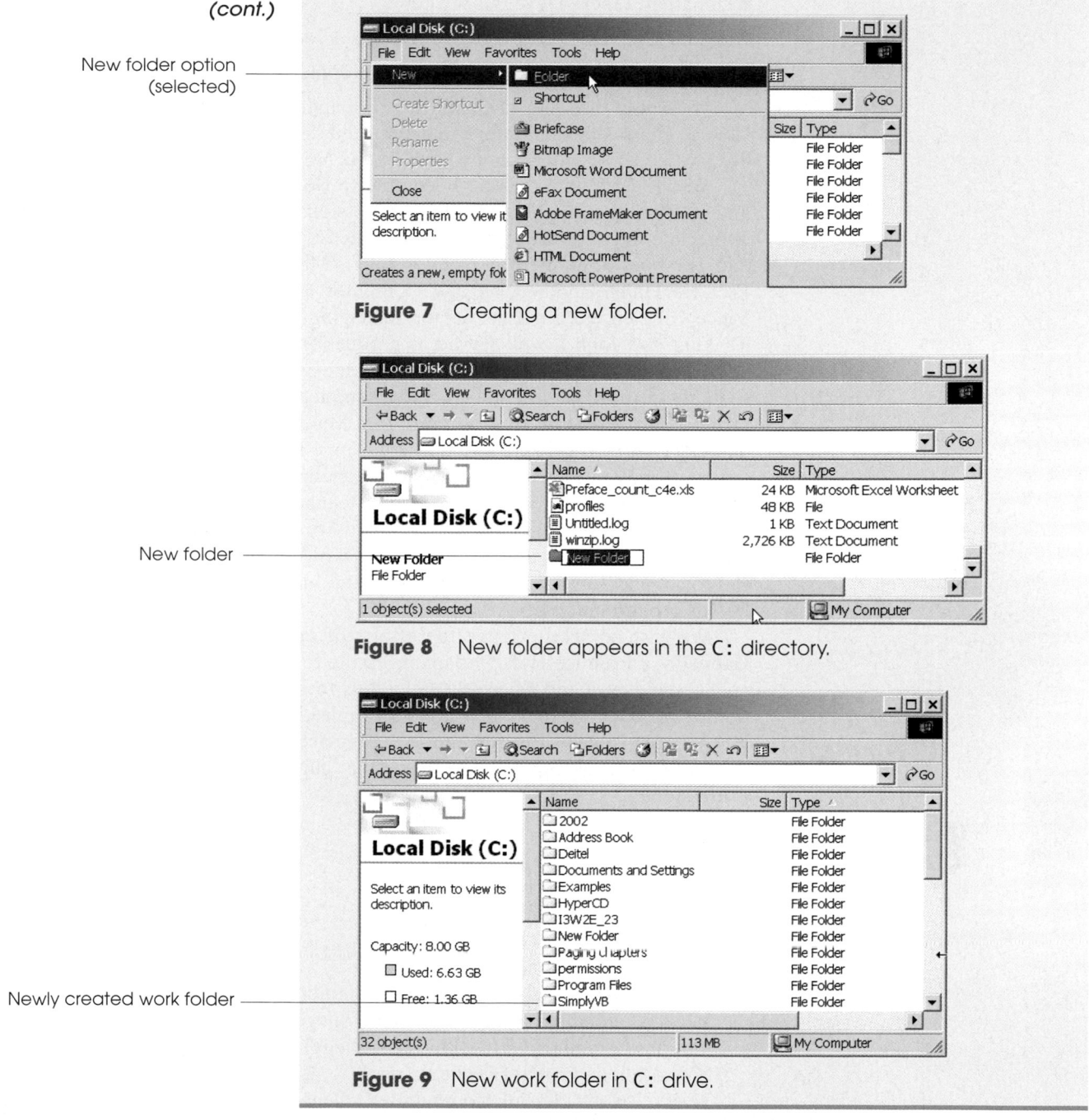

Figure 7 Creating a new folder.

Figure 8 New folder appears in the C: directory.

Figure 9 New work folder in C: drive.

Acknowledgments One of the great pleasures of writing a textbook is acknowledging the efforts of many people whose names may not appear on the cover, but whose hard work, cooperation, friendship and understanding were crucial to the production of the book. Many people at Deitel & Associates, Inc., devoted long hours to this project.

- David Choffnes, Developer
- Christina J. Courtemarche, Developer
- Abbey Deitel, President
- Barbara Deitel, Chief Financial Officer
- Betsy DuWaldt, Editorial Director
- Christi Kelsey, Director of Business Development

- Jonathan Liperi, Developer
- Laura Treibick, Director of Multimedia
- Cheryl Yaeger, Director of .NET Development

We would also like to thank the participants in the Deitel & Associates, Inc., College Internship Program: Emanuel Achildiev, Nicholas Cassie, Thiago Lucas da Silva, Mike Dos'Santos, Jimmy Nguyen and Ngale Truong.[2]

We are fortunate to have been able to work on this project with the talented and dedicated team of publishing professionals at Prentice Hall. We especially appreciate the extraordinary efforts of our Computer Science editor, Petra Recter and her boss—our mentor in publishing—Marcia Horton, Editorial Director of Prentice Hall's Engineering and Computer Science Team. Tom Manshreck and Vince O'Brien did a marvelous job managing the production of the book. Chirag Thakkar and John Lovell served as production editors and Sarah Parker handled editorial responsibilities on the book's extensive ancillary package. We would like to thank the design team that created a completely new look and feel for the *Simply* series—Carole Anson, Paul Belfanti, Tom Manshreck, Jonathan Boylan, John Root and Gary Gray. We would like to thank Carol Trueheart, Editor-in-Chief of Development for Prentice Hall's Engineering, Science and Math Division, and her team of developmental editors—Laura Cheu, Deena Cloud and Susan Cohen.

We owe special thanks to the creativity of Tamara Newnam (`smart_art@earthlink.net`) and illustrator Steve Lefkowitz. They produced the art work for the cover, and Tammy created the delightful bug creature who shares with you the book's programming tips.

We wish to acknowledge the efforts of our reviewers and to thank Jennifer Cappello of Prentice Hall, who managed the review process. The 42 reviewers from colleges, industry and Microsoft helped us to get this book "right." Adhering to a tight time schedule, these reviewers scrutinized the text and the programs, providing countless suggestions for improving the accuracy and completeness of the presentation. It is a privilege to have the guidance of such talented and busy professionals.

Simply Visual Basic .NET reviewers:
Cameron McColl (Microsoft)
Colin Merry (Microsoft)
Jeffrey Welton (Microsoft)
Judith Ashworth (Orillion USA, Inc.)
James Ball (Indiana State University)
Robert Benavides (Collin County Community College)
Chadi Boudiab (Georgia Perimeter College)
Charles Cadenhead (Brookhaven College)
Kunal Cheda (`DotNetExtreme.com`)
Mave Coxon (Lansing Community College)
Chris Crane (Independent Consultant)
Sergio Davalos (University of Washington-Tacoma)
David Fullerton (Yeshiva University)
George Gintowt (William Rainey Harper College)

---

2. The Deitel & Associates, Inc. College Internship Program offers a limited number of salaried positions to college students majoring in Computer Science, Information Technology, Marketing and English. Students work at our corporate headquarters in Maynard, Massachusetts full-time in the summers and (for those attending college in the Boston area) part-time during the academic year. We also offer full-time internship positions for students interested in taking a semester off from school to gain industry experience. Regular full-time positions are available to college graduates. For more information, please contact Abbey Deitel at `deitel@deitel.com`, visit our Web site, `www.deitel.com`, and subscribe to our free e-mail newsletter at `www.deitel.com/newsletter/subscribe.html`.

James Gips (Boston College)
Manu Gupta (Patni Computer Systems)
Richard Hewer (Ferris State University)
James Huddleston (Independent Consultant)
Terrell Hull (Sun Certified Java Architect, Rational Qualified Practitioner)
Jeff Jones (A.D.A.M. Inc.)
Faisal Kaleem (Florida International University)
Yashavant Kanetkar (KICIT Pvt. Ltd.)
Dhananjay Katre (Patni Computer Systems, Ltd.)
Kurt Kominek (Northeast State Technical CC)
Stan Kurkovsky (Columbus State University)
Brian Larson (Modesto Junior College)
Sukan Makmuri (DeVry-Fremont)
Ken McLean (Northern Virginia CC)
Gordon McNorton (Collin County Community College)
Manish Mehta (Independent Consultant)
Marilyn Meyer (Fresno City College)
John Mueller (DataCon Services)
Narayana Rao Surapaneni (Patni Computer Systems)
Michael Rudisill (Northern Michigan University)
Sara Rushinek (University of Miami)
Praveen Sadhu (Infodat Solutions, Inc.)
Kenneth Schoonover (Chubb Technical Institute)
Andrea Shelly (Florida International University)
Robert Taylor (Lansing Community College)
Yateen Thakkar (Syntel India Ltd.)
Catherine Wyman (DeVry-Phoenix)
David Zeng (DeVry-Calgary)

We would sincerely appreciate your comments, criticisms, corrections and suggestions for improving the text. Please address all correspondence to:

deitel@deitel.com

We will respond promptly.

Well, that's it for now. Welcome to the exciting world of Visual Basic .NET programming. We hope you enjoy this look at leading-edge computer applications development. Good luck!

Dr. Harvey M. Deitel
Paul J. Deitel
Tem R. Nieto

About the Authors

Dr. Harvey M. Deitel, Chairman of Deitel & Associates, Inc., has 41 years experience in the computing field, including extensive industry and academic experience. Dr. Deitel earned B.S. and M.S. degrees from the Massachusetts Institute of Technology and a Ph.D. from Boston University. He worked on the pioneering virtual-memory operating-systems projects at IBM and MIT that developed techniques now widely implemented in systems such as UNIX, Linux and Windows NT. He has 20 years of college teaching experience and served as the Chairman of the Computer Science Department at Boston College before founding Deitel & Associates, Inc., with his son, Paul J. Deitel. He is the author or co-author of several dozen books and multimedia packages. With translations published in numerous foreign languages, Dr. Deitel's texts have earned international recognition. Dr. Deitel has delivered professional seminars to major corporations, government organizations and various branches of the military.

Paul J. Deitel, CEO and Chief Technical Officer of Deitel & Associates, Inc., is a graduate of the Massachusetts Institute of Technology's Sloan School of Management, where he studied information technology. Through Deitel & Associates, Inc., he has delivered professional seminars to numerous industry and government clients and has lectured on C++ and Java for the Boston Chapter of the Association for Computing Machinery. He and his father, Dr. Harvey M. Deitel, are the world's best-selling Computer Science textbook authors.

Tem R. Nieto, Director of Product Development of Deitel & Associates, Inc., is a graduate of the Massachusetts Institute of Technology, where he studied engineering and computing. Through Deitel & Associates, Inc., he has delivered courses for numerous industry and government clients. He has co-authored many books and multimedia packages with the Deitels and has contributed to virtually every Deitel & Associates, Inc. publication.

About Deitel & Associates, Inc.

Deitel & Associates, Inc., is an internationally recognized corporate-training and content-creation organization specializing in computer programming languages education, object technology and Internet/World Wide Web software technology. Through its 27-year publishing partnership with Prentice Hall, Deitel & Associates, Inc. publishes leading-edge programming textbooks, professional books, interactive CD-ROM-based multimedia *Cyber Classrooms*, *Complete Training Courses* and course management systems e-content. To learn more about Deitel & Associates, Inc., its publications and its worldwide corporate on-site curriculum, visit:

```
www.deitel.com
```

Individuals wishing to purchase Deitel books, *Cyber Classrooms* and *Complete Training Courses* can do so through bookstores or online booksellers through:

```
www.deitel.com
www.prenhall.com/deitel
www.InformIT.com/deitel
```

Bulk orders by corporations and academic institutions should be placed directly with Prentice Hall. For ordering information, please visit:

```
www.prenhall.com/deitel
```

The Deitel Buzz Online Newsletter

Our free e-mail newsletter includes commentary on industry trends and developments, links to articles and resources from our published books and upcoming publications, information on future publications, product-release schedules and more. For opt-in registration, visit www.deitel.com/newsletter/subscribe.html.

Objectives

In this tutorial, you will learn to:
- Identify the characteristics of low-level and high-level programming languages.
- Apply the basics of object-oriented programming.
- Run your first Visual Basic .NET application.
- Locate additional .NET and Visual Basic .NET information.

Outline

Graphing Application

Introducing Computers, the Internet and Visual Basic .NET

Welcome to Visual Basic .NET! This book uses a straightforward, step-by-step tutorial approach to teach the fundamentals of Visual Basic .NET programming. We hope that you will be informed and entertained as you learn the basics of Visual Basic .NET programming.

The core of the book teaches Visual Basic .NET using our **APPLICATION-DRIVEN™ approach**, which provides step-by-step instructions for creating and interacting with useful, real-world computer applications. With this approach, combined with our signature **LIVE-CODE™ approach**, which shows dozens of complete, working Visual Basic .NET applications and depicts their outputs, you learn basic skills that underlie good programming. You will study bonus tutorials on graphics, multimedia and Web programming. All of the book's examples are available on the CD-ROM that accompanies the book and on our Web site, www.deitel.com.

Computer use is increasing in almost every field. In an era of rising costs, computing costs are actually decreasing dramatically because of rapid developments in both hardware and software technology. Silicon-chip technology has made computing so economical that hundreds of millions of general-purpose computers are in use worldwide, helping people in business, industry, government and their personal lives.

Reading this text will start you on a challenging and rewarding educational path. If you'd like to communicate with us, send an e-mail to deitel@deitel.com, and we will respond promptly. For more information, visit our Web sites at www.deitel.com, www.prenhall.com/deitel and www.InformIT.com/deitel.

1.1 What Is a Computer?

A **computer** is a device capable of performing computations and making logical decisions at speeds millions and even billions of times faster than humans can. For example, many of today's personal computers can perform billions of additions per second. A person operating a desk calculator might require a lifetime to complete the same number of calculations that a powerful personal computer can perform in one second. Today's fastest **supercomputers** can perform hundreds of billions of additions per second. Trillion-instruction-per-second computers are already functioning in research laboratories!

Computers process **data**, using sets of instructions called **computer programs**. These programs guide computers through orderly sets of actions that are specified by people known as **computer programmers**. In this book, we generally use the term "application" instead of the term "program." An application is a program that does something particularly useful. Each tutorial in this book, on average, presents five applications—one in the main example and four in the exercises—for a total of more than 100 applications in the book.

A computer is composed of various devices (such as the keyboard, screen, mouse, hard drive, memory, CD-ROM and processing units) known as **hardware**. The programs that run on a computer are referred to as **software**. Object-oriented programming (which models real-world objects with software counterparts), available in Visual Basic .NET and other programming languages, is a significant breakthrough that can greatly enhance programmers' productivity.

SELF-REVIEW   1. Computers process data, using sets of instructions called _____.

      a) hardware   b) computer programs

      c) processing units   d) programmers

   2. The devices that make up a computer are called _____.

      a) hardware   b) software

      c) programs   d) programmers

Answers: 1) b. 2) a.

1.2 Computer Organization

Computers can be thought of as being divided into six units:

1. **Input unit.** This "receiving" section of the computer obtains information (data and computer programs) from various **input devices**, such as the keyboard and the mouse. Other input devices include microphones (for recording speech to the computer), scanners (for scanning images) and digital cameras (for taking photographs and making videos).

2. **Output unit.** This "shipping" section of the computer takes information that the computer has processed and places it on various **output devices**, making the information available for use outside the computer. Output can be displayed on screens, played on audio/video devices, printed on paper, etc. Output also can be used to control other devices, such as robots used in manufacturing.

3. **Memory unit.** This rapid-access, relatively low-capacity "warehouse" section of the computer stores data temporarily while an application is running. The memory unit retains information that has been entered through input devices, so that information is immediately available for processing. To be executed, computer programs must be in memory. The memory unit also retains processed information until that information can be sent to output devices on which it is made available to users. Often, the memory unit is called either **memory** or **primary memory**. **Random-access memory (RAM)** is an example of primary memory. Primary memory is usually **volatile**, which means that it is erased when the machine is powered off.

4. **Arithmetic and logic unit (ALU).** The ALU is the "manufacturing" section of the computer. It performs calculations such as addition, subtraction, multiplication and division. It also makes decisions, allowing the

computer to perform such tasks as determining whether two items stored in memory are equal.

5. **Central processing unit (CPU).** The CPU serves as the "administrative" section of the computer, supervising the operation of the other sections. The CPU alerts the input unit when information should be read into the memory unit, instructs the ALU when to use information from the memory unit in calculations and tells the output unit when to send information from the memory unit to certain output devices.

6. **Secondary storage unit.** This unit is the long-term, high-capacity "warehousing" section of the computer. Secondary storage devices, such as hard drives, CD-ROM drives, zip drives and floppy disk drives, normally hold programs or data that other units are not actively using; the computer then can retrieve this information when it is needed—hours, days, months or even years later. Information in secondary storage takes much longer to access than information in primary memory. However, secondary storage is much less expensive than primary memory. Secondary storage is nonvolatile, retaining information even when the computer is powered off.

SELF-REVIEW   1. The _____ is responsible for performing calculations, and contains decision-making mechanisms.

    a) central processing unit   b) memory unit
    c) arithmetic and logic unit   d) output unit

2. Information stored in _____ is normally erased when the computer is turned off.

    a) primary memory   b) secondary storage
    c) CD-ROM drives   d) hard drives

Answers: 1) c. 2) a.

1.3 Machine Languages, Assembly Languages and High-Level Languages

Programmers write instructions in various programming languages, some of which are directly understandable by computers and others of which require intermediate translation steps. Although hundreds of computer languages are in use today, the diverse offerings can be divided into three general types:

1. Machine languages

2. Assembly languages

3. High-level languages

A computer can directly understand only its own **machine language**. As the "natural language" of a particular computer, machine language is defined by the computer's hardware design. Machine languages generally consist of streams of numbers (ultimately reduced to 1s and 0s) that instruct computers how to perform their most elementary operations. Machine languages are **machine dependent**, which means that a particular machine language can be used on only one type of computer. The following section of a machine-language program, which adds *overtime pay* to *base pay* and stores the result in *gross pay*, demonstrates the incomprehensibility of machine language to humans:

```
+1300042774
+1400593419
+1200274027
```

As the popularity of computers increased, machine-language programming proved to be slow and error prone. Instead of using the strings of numbers that computers could directly understand, programmers began using English-like abbreviations to represent the basic operations of the computer. These abbreviations formed the basis of **assembly languages**. **Translator programs** called **assemblers** convert assembly-language programs to machine language at computer speeds. The following section of an assembly-language program also adds *overtime pay* to *base pay* and stores the result in *gross pay*, but presents the steps somewhat more clearly to human readers than the machine-language example:

```
LOAD    BASEPAY
ADD     OVERPAY
STORE   GROSSPAY
```

This assembly-language code is clearer to humans, but computers cannot understand it until it is translated into machine language by an assembler program.

Although the speed at which programmers could write programs increased rapidly with the creation of assembly languages, these languages still require many instructions to accomplish even the simplest tasks. To speed up the programming process, **high-level languages**, in which single program statements accomplish more substantial tasks, were developed. Translator programs called **compilers** convert high-level-language programs into machine language. High-level languages enable programmers to write instructions that look almost like everyday English and that contain common mathematical notations. For example, a payroll application written in a high-level language might contain a statement such as

```
grossPay = basePay + overTimePay
```

From these examples, it is clear why programmers prefer high-level languages to either machine languages or assembly languages. Visual Basic is the most popular high-level programming language in the world. In the next section, you will learn about Microsoft's latest version of this language, called Visual Basic .NET.

SELF-REVIEW

1. The only programming language that a computer can directly understand is its own _____.

   a) high-level language
   c) machine language

   b) assembly language
   d) English

2. Programs that translate high-level language programs into machine language are called _____.

   a) assemblers
   c) programmers

   b) compilers
   d) converters

Answers: 1) c. 2) b.

1.4 Visual Basic .NET

Visual Basic .NET evolved from **BASIC** (Beginner's All-Purpose Symbolic Instruction Code), developed in the mid-1960s by Professors John Kemeny and Thomas Kurtz of Dartmouth College as a language for writing simple programs quickly and easily. BASIC's primary purpose was to teach novices fundamental programming techniques.

When Bill Gates founded Microsoft Corporation in the 1970s, he implemented BASIC on several early personal computers. In the late 1980s and the early 1990s, Microsoft developed the Microsoft Windows **graphical user interface (GUI)**—the visual part of the application with which users interact. With the creation of the Windows GUI, the natural evolution of BASIC was to **Visual Basic**, introduced by Microsoft in 1991 to make programming Windows applications easier.

Until Visual Basic appeared, developing Microsoft Windows-based applications was a difficult process. Visual Basic .NET is a so-called object-oriented, event-driven (OOED) visual programming language in which programs are created with the use of a software tool called an **Integrated Development Environment (IDE)**. With Microsoft's **Visual Studio .NET** IDE, a programmer can write, run, test and debug Visual Basic .NET programs quickly and conveniently.

Visual Basic .NET is fully **object oriented**—you will learn some basics of object technology shortly and will study a rich treatment in the remainder of the book. Visual Basic .NET is **event driven**—you will write programs that respond to user-initiated **events** such as mouse clicks and keystrokes. It is a **visual programming** language—instead of writing detailed program statements to build your applications, you will use Visual Studio .NET's graphical user interface in which you conveniently drag and drop predefined objects into place and label and resize them. Visual Studio .NET will write much of the program for you.

Microsoft introduced its **.NET** (pronounced "dot-net") strategy in 2000. The **.NET platform**—the set of software components that enables .NET programs to run—allows Web-based applications to be distributed to a variety of devices (such as cell phones) as well as to desktop computers. The .NET platform offers a new programming model that allows programs created in different programming languages to communicate with each other, whether they reside on the same or on different computers connected to a network such as the Internet.

SELF-REVIEW   1. Microsoft created _____ in 1991 to make it easier to program Windows applications.

      a) Windows   b) BASIC

      c) Visual Basic   d) Visual Basic .NET

2. Visual Basic evolved from _____, which was created as a language for writing simple programs quickly and easily.

      a) .NET   b) Windows

      c) Visual Basic .NET   d) BASIC

Answers: 1) c. 2) d.

1.5 Other High-Level Languages

Although hundreds of high-level languages have been developed, only a few have achieved broad acceptance. IBM Corporation developed **Fortran** in the mid-1950s to create scientific and engineering applications that require complex mathematical computations. Fortran is still widely used.

COBOL was developed in the late 1950s by a group of computer manufacturers in conjunction with government and industrial computer users. COBOL is used primarily for business applications that require the manipulation of large amounts of data. A considerable portion of today's business software is still programmed in COBOL.

The C language, which Dennis Ritchie developed at Bell Laboratories in the early 1970s, gained widespread recognition as a development language of the UNIX operating system. C++, an extension of C, was developed by Bjarne Stroustrup in the early 1980s at Bell Laboratories. C++ provides capabilities for **object-oriented programming (OOP)**. Many of today's major operating systems are written in C or C++.

Objects are reusable software **components** that model items in the real world. Object-oriented programs are often easier to understand, correct and modify than programs developed with previous techniques. Visual Basic .NET provides full object-oriented programming capabilities.

In the early 1990s, many organizations, including Sun Microsystems, predicted that intelligent consumer-electronic devices would be the next major market in which **microprocessors**—the chips that make computers work—would have a profound impact. But the marketplace for intelligent consumer-electronic devices did not develop as quickly as Sun had anticipated. By sheer good fortune, the World Wide Web exploded in popularity in 1993, and Sun saw an immediate potential for using its new **Java** programming language to create **dynamic content** (animated and interactive content) for Web pages. Sun announced Java to the public in 1995, grabbing the immediate attention of the business community because of the widespread interest in the Web. Developers now use Java to create Web pages with dynamic content, to build large-scale enterprise applications, to enhance the functionality of Web servers (the computers that provide the content that is distributed to your Web browser when you browse Web sites), to provide applications for consumer devices (for example, cell phones, pagers and PDAs) and for many other purposes.

In 2000, Microsoft announced **C#** (pronounced "C-Sharp") at the same time the company announced its **.**NET strategy. The C# programming language was designed specifically for the .NET platform. It has roots in C, C++ and Java, adapting the best features of each. Like Visual Basic .NET, C# is object oriented and has access to .NET's powerful library of prebuilt components, enabling programmers to develop applications quickly. C#, Java and Visual Basic .NET have comparable capabilities, so learning Visual Basic .NET may create many opportunities for you.

SELF-REVIEW

1. _____ is an extension of C and offers object-oriented capabilities.
   a) Visual Basic
   b) C++
   c) assembly language
   d) Windows

2. _____ is a programming language originally developed for Microsoft's .NET platform.
   a) C#
   b) Java
   c) C++
   d) Visual Basic

3. _____, developed in the late 1950s, is still used to produce a considerable portion of today's business software.
   a) COBOL
   b) Fortran
   c) Java
   d) C

4. _____, developed in the 1950s, is still used to create scientific and engineering applications that require complex mathematical computations.
   a) Visual Basic
   b) Fortran
   c) COBOL
   d) C#

Answers: 1) b. 2) a. 3) a. 4) b.

1.6 Structured Programming

During the 1960s, software-development efforts often ran behind schedule, costs greatly exceeded budgets and the finished products were unreliable. People began to realize that software development was a far more complex activity than they had imagined. Research activity intended to address these issues resulted in the evolution of **structured programming**—a disciplined approach to the creation of programs that are clear, correct and easy to modify.

One of the results of this research was the development of the **Pascal** programming language in 1971. Pascal, named after the 17th-century mathematician and philosopher Blaise Pascal, was designed for teaching structured programming and rapidly became the preferred introductory programming language in most colleges. Unfortunately, the language lacked many features needed to make it useful in commercial, industrial and government applications. By contrast, C, which also arose from research on structured programming, did not have the limitations of Pascal, and professional programmers quickly adopted it.

The **Ada** programming language was developed under the sponsorship of the U.S. Department of Defense (DOD) during the 1970s and early 1980s. The language was named after **Lady Ada Lovelace**, daughter of the poet Lord Byron. Lady Lovelace is generally credited as being the world's first computer programmer because of an application she wrote in the early 1800s for the Analytical Engine mechanical computing device designed by Charles Babbage.

SELF-REVIEW

1. During the 1960s and 1970s, research to address such software-development problems as running behind schedule, exceeding budgets and creating unreliable products led to the evolution of _____.

    a) multithreading   b) object-oriented programming

    c) Ada   d) structured programming

2. _____ was designed to teach structured programming in academic environments.

    a) C++   b) C

    c) Java   d) Pascal

Answers: 1) d. 2) d.

1.7 Key Software Trend: Object Technology

As the benefits of structured programming were realized in the 1970s, improved software technology began to appear. However, it was not until object-oriented programming became widely used in the 1980s and 1990s that software developers finally felt they had the necessary tools to improve the software-development process dramatically.

What are objects, and why are they special? **Object technology** is a packaging scheme for creating meaningful software units. There are date objects, time objects, paycheck objects, invoice objects, automobile objects, people objects, audio objects, video objects, file objects, record objects and so on. In fact, almost any noun can be reasonably represented as a software object. Objects have **properties** (also called **attributes**), such as color, size and weight; and perform **actions** (also called **behaviors** or **methods**), such as moving, sleeping or drawing. **Classes** are types of related objects. For example, all cars belong to the "car" class, even though individual cars vary in make, model, color and options packages. A class specifies the general format of its objects, and the properties and actions available to an object depend on its class. An object is related to its class in much the same way as a building is related to its blueprint.

Before object-oriented languages appeared, **procedural programming languages** (such as Fortran, Pascal, BASIC and C) focused on actions (verbs) rather than things or objects (nouns). This made programming a bit awkward. However, using today's popular object-oriented languages, such as Visual Basic .NET, C++, Java and C#, programmers can program in an object-oriented manner that more naturally reflects the way in which they perceive the world. This has resulted in significant productivity gains.

With object technology, properly designed classes can be reused on future projects. Using libraries of classes can greatly reduce the amount of effort required to implement new systems. Some organizations report that such software reusability is not, in fact, the key benefit that they get from object-oriented programming. Rather, they indicate that object-oriented programming tends to produce software that is more understandable because it is better organized and has fewer maintenance requirements.

Object orientation allows the programmer to focus on the "big picture." Instead of worrying about the minute details of how reusable objects are implemented, the programmer can focus on the behaviors and interactions of objects. A road map that showed every tree, house and driveway would be difficult, if not

impossible, to read. When such details are removed and only the essential information (roads) remains, the map becomes easier to understand. In the same way, an
application that is divided into objects is easy to understand, modify and update
because it hides much of the detail. It is clear that object-oriented programming will
be the key programming methodology for at least the next decade. Visual Basic
.NET is one of the world's most widely used fully object-oriented languages.

SELF-REVIEW

1. _____ focuses on actions (verbs) rather than things (nouns).

    a) C#   b) Object-oriented programming

    c) Visual Basic .NET   d) Procedural programming

2. In object-oriented programming, _____, which are in a sense like blueprints, are
types of related objects.

    a) classes   b) attributes

    c) behaviors   d) properties

Answers: 1) d. 2) a.

1.8 The Internet and the World Wide Web

In the late 1960s, ARPA—the Advanced Research Projects Agency of the Department of Defense—rolled out the blueprints for networking the main computer systems of approximately a dozen ARPA-funded universities and research institutions.
The computers were to be connected with communications lines operating at a
then-stunning 56 Kbps (1 Kbps is equal to 1,024 bits per second), at a time when
most people (of the few who even had networking access) were connecting over
telephone lines to computers at a rate of 110 bits per second. Academic research
was about to take a giant leap forward. ARPA proceeded to implement what
quickly became called the **ARPAnet**, the grandparent of today's **Internet**.

Things worked out differently from the original plan. Although the ARPAnet
enabled researchers to network their computers, its main benefit proved to be the
capability for quick and easy communication via what came to be known as **electronic mail (e-mail)**. This is true even on today's Internet, with e-mail, instant mes-
saging and file transfer allowing hundreds of millions of people worldwide to
communicate with each other.

The protocol (in other words, the set of rules) for communicating over the
ARPAnet became known as the **Transmission Control Protocol (TCP)**. TCP
ensured that messages, consisting of pieces called "packets," were properly routed
from sender to receiver and that those messages arrived intact.

In parallel with the early evolution of the Internet, organizations worldwide
were implementing their own networks for both intraorganization (that is, within
an organization) and interorganization (that is, between organizations) communication. A huge variety of networking hardware and software appeared. One challenge
was to enable these different networks to communicate with each other. ARPA
accomplished this by developing the **Internet Protocol (IP)**, which created a true
"network of networks," the current architecture of the Internet. The combined set
of protocols is now commonly called **TCP/IP.**

Businesses rapidly realized that, by using the Internet, they could improve their
operations and offer new and better services to their clients. Companies started
spending large amounts of money to develop and enhance their Internet presence.
This generated fierce competition among communications carriers and hardware
and software suppliers to meet the increased infrastructure demand. As a result,
bandwidth—the information-carrying capacity of communications lines—on the
Internet has increased tremendously, while hardware costs have plummeted.

The **World Wide Web** is a collection of hardware and software associated with
the Internet that allows computer users to locate and view multimedia-based docu-

ments (documents with various combinations of text, graphics, animations, audios and videos) on almost any subject. Even though the Internet was developed more than three decades ago, the introduction of the World Wide Web (WWW) was a relatively recent event. In 1989, Tim Berners-Lee of CERN (the European Organization for Nuclear Research) began to develop a technology for sharing information via "hyperlinked" text documents. Berners-Lee called his invention the **HyperText Markup Language (HTML)**. He also wrote communication protocols to form the backbone of his new hypertext information system, which he referred to as the World Wide Web.

In October 1994, Berners-Lee founded an organization, called the **World Wide Web Consortium (W3C, www.w3.org)**, that is devoted to developing technologies for the World Wide Web. One of the W3C's primary goals is to make the Web universally accessible—regardless of a person's disabilities, language or culture.

The Internet and the World Wide Web will surely be listed among the most important creations of humankind. In the past, most computer applications ran on "stand-alone" computers (computers that were not connected to one another). Today's applications can be written with the aim of communicating among the world's hundreds of millions of computers. In fact, this is, as you will see, the focus of Microsoft's .NET strategy. The Internet and World Wide Web make information instantly and conveniently accessible to large numbers of people. They enable even individuals and small businesses to achieve worldwide exposure. They are profoundly changing the way we do business and conduct our personal lives. To highlight the importance of Internet and Web programming, we include four tutorials at the end of the book in which you will actually build and run a Web-based bookstore application.

SELF-REVIEW

1. Today's Internet evolved from the _____, which was a Department of Defense project.

      a) ARPAnet   b) HTML
      c) CERN   d) WWW

2. The combined set of protocols for communicating over the Internet is now commonly called _____.

      a) HTML   b) TCP/IP
      c) ARPA   d) TCP

Answers: 1) a. 2) b.

1.9 Introduction to Microsoft .NET

In June 2000, Microsoft announced its **.NET initiative**, a broad new vision for using the Internet and the Web in the development, engineering, distribution and use of software. Rather than forcing developers to use a single programming language, the .NET initiative permits developers to create .NET applications in any .NET-compatible language (such as Visual Basic .NET, Visual C++ .NET, C# and others). Part of the initiative includes Microsoft's **Active Server Pages (ASP) .NET** technology, which allows programmers to create applications for the Web. You will be introduced to ASP .NET as you build the Web-based bookstore application later in the book.

The .NET strategy extends the idea of software reuse to the Internet, by allowing programmers to concentrate on their specialties without having to implement every component of every application. Instead, companies can buy **Web services**, which are Web-based programs that organizations can incorporate into their systems to speed the Web-application-development process. Visual programming (which you will learn throughout this book) has become popular, because it enables programmers to create applications easily, using such prepackaged graphical components as **buttons**, **textboxes** and **scrollbars** that are so popular today in Windows applications.

The Microsoft **.NET Framework** is at the heart of the .NET strategy. This framework executes applications and Web services, contains a class library (called the **Framework Class Library** or **FCL**) and provides many other programming capabilities that you use to build Visual Basic .NET applications. In this book, you will learn how to develop .NET software with Visual Basic .NET. Steve Ballmer, Microsoft's CEO, stated in May 2001 that Microsoft was "betting the company" on .NET. Such a dramatic commitment surely indicates a bright future for Visual Basic .NET programmers.

SELF-REVIEW

1. _____ is a technology specifically designed for the .NET platform and intended for programmers to create Web-based applications.

   a) Visual Basic   b) C++
   c) HTML   d) Active Server Pages .NET

2. _____ are existing Web-based programs that can be incorporated into other applications.

   a) Web services   b) Wire services
   c) Attributes   d) Properties

3. Programmers use the _____, a part of the .NET Framework, to build Visual Basic .NET applications.

   a) Visual Basic Library (VBL)   b) Framework Class Library (FCL)
   c) Microsoft Class Library (MCL)   d) Visual Basic Framework (VBF)

Answers: 1) d. 2) a. 3) b.

1.10 Test-Driving the Visual Basic .NET Graphing Application

In this section, you will be introduced to a Visual Basic .NET application, using our APPLICATION-DRIVEN™ approach. In each tutorial, you are given a chance to "test-drive" the application. You actually run and interact with the completed application. Then you will learn the Visual Basic .NET features you need to build the application. Finally, you will "put it all together" and actually create your own working version of the application. You begin here in Tutorial 1 simply by running a business application that graphs a fictional company's steel production for each state in which the company has a steel factory. You will actually build a similar application in Tutorial 18.

We created the steel production application because it is often helpful for business managers to view information, such as production data, in the form of a chart rather than a screen full of numbers. The following box, *Test-Driving the Visual Basic .NET Graphing Application*, will show you how the application graphs the production quantities from factories in four different states, so that a manager can visually compare the amounts of steel produced in each state. The elements and functionality you see in this application are typical of what you will learn to program in this text. [*Note*: We use fonts to distinguish between IDE features (such as menu names and menu items) and other elements that appear in the IDE. Our convention is to emphasize IDE features (such as the **File** menu) in a semibold **sans-serif Helvetica** font and to emphasize other elements, such as file names (for example, `Form1.vb`) in a `sans-serif Lucida` font. As you have already noticed, each term that is being defined is set in heavy bold.]

*Test-Driving the Visual
Basic .NET Graphing
Application*

Contents of
C:\Examples\Tutorial01

Double click this file to
execute the application

1. ***Checking your setup.*** Confirm that you have set up your computer properly by reading the *For Students and Instructors: Important Information before You Begin* section in the Preface.

2. ***Locating the application directory.*** Open a Windows Explorer window and navigate to the C:\Examples\Tutorial01 directory (Fig. 1.1).

Figure 1.1   Contents of C:\Examples\Tutorial01.

3. ***Executing the application.*** In that directory, double click the file name SteelProduction.exe to execute the application (Fig. 1.2).

MSChart control

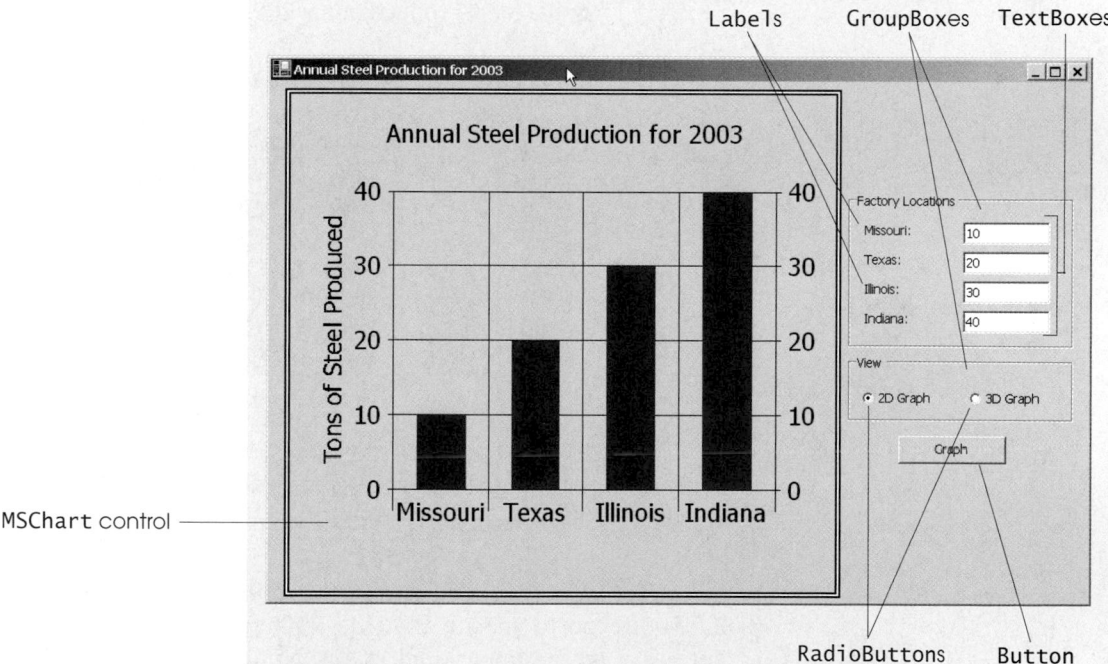

Figure 1.2   A Visual Basic .NET graphing application.

In Fig. 1.2, several graphical elements—called **controls**—are labelled. The controls include GroupBoxes, RadioButtons, Buttons, Labels and an MSChart control. You can use this application to produce an attractive business graph of the values that the user inputs into the TextBoxes. The application allows you to create either a two-dimensional or three-dimensional graph. You will create both in this test-drive.

(cont.)

Because you can use existing controls—which are objects—you can get powerful applications running in Visual Basic .NET much faster than if you had to write all the code yourself. In this text, you will learn how to use many preexisting controls, as well as how to write your own program code to customize your applications.

The graph's initial values (10, 20, 30 and 40) in the TextBoxes are **default** values, the initial values you see when you first run the application. Programmers include default values to provide visual cues for users to enter their own data. You will now customize the chart by entering your own production values.

4. *Changing the sales data.* Type 65 in the TextBox labelled **Missouri:**, 35 in the TextBox labelled **Texas:**, 53 in the TextBox labelled **Illinois:** and 46 in the TextBox labelled **Indiana:**.

5. *Changing the type of graph.* Note the black dot in the RadioButton labelled **2D Graph**. This means that you would like to see a two-dimensional graph. Click the **Graph** Button toward the bottom right of the screen to update the MSChart control as shown in Fig. 1.3.

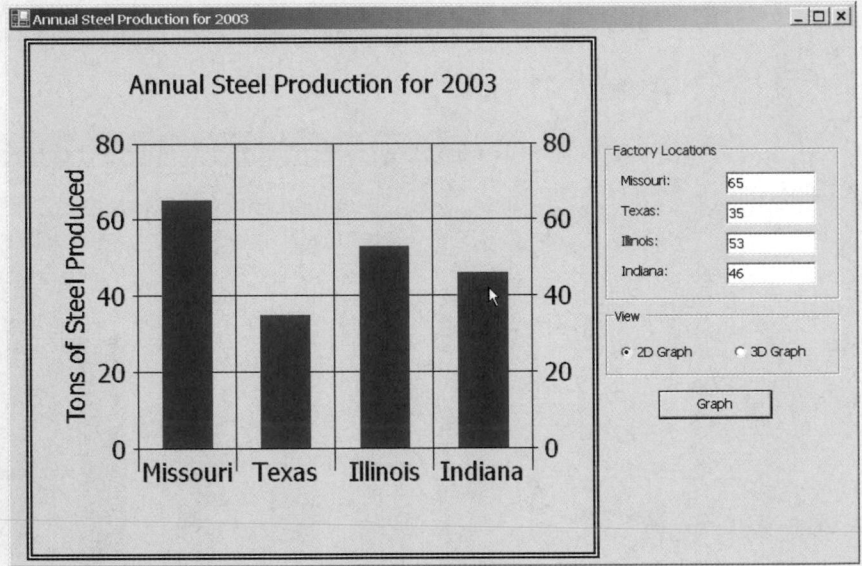

Figure 1.3   New values create a new graph.

6. *Selecting the three-dimensional graph option.* Click the **3D Graph** RadioButton to specify that the MSChart control should now display its data as a three-dimensional graph. Notice that clicking this RadioButton does not update the MSChart control, but it does cause the **2D Graph** RadioButton to become white and the **3D** Button to become black. Only one RadioButton in a group can be selected (black)—all the others automatically will be unselected (white).

7. *Viewing the three-dimensional graph.* Click the **Graph** Button to present the data in a three-dimensional graph (Fig. 1.4).

8. *Closing the application.* Click the **close** box ☒ to close the application.

(cont.)

Figure 1.4   Three-dimensional graph.

Note that the `MSChart` control does most of the work for you. You just type in the numbers, and the control displays a professional-quality bar chart. This is an excellent example of **software reuse**. Microsoft provides this control—which the company no doubt spent a considerable amount of time and money creating—so millions of users worldwide can use the control to prepare professional quality charts without having to do much programming at all!

1.11 Internet and Web Resources

The Internet and Web are extraordinary resources. This section includes links to interesting and informative Web sites. Hot links to all these sites are included on the CD and at www.deitel.com to save you time. Reference sections like this one are included throughout the book where appropriate.

www.deitel.com
Visit this site for updates, corrections and additional resources for Deitel & Associates publications, including *Simply Visual Basic .NET* errata, Frequently Asked Questions (FAQs), hot links, code downloads and PowerPoint® slide downloads.

www.prenhall.com/deitel
The Deitel & Associates page on the Prentice Hall Web site contains information about our publications, code downloads and PowerPoint slides for this book.

www.softlord.com/comp
Visit this site to learn more about the history of computers.

www.elsop.com/wrc/h_comput.htm
This site presents the history of computing. It includes content about famous people in the computer field, the evolution of programming languages and the development of operating systems.

www.w3.org/History.html
Visit this site for the history of the World Wide Web.

www.netvalley.com/intval.html
This site presents the history of the Internet.

`msdn.microsoft.com/vbasic`
This is Microsoft's Visual Basic .NET Web site.

`www.GotDotNet.com`
A site with abundant .NET resources.

1.12 Wrap-Up

In this tutorial, you learned about how computers are organized. You studied the levels of programming languages and which kinds of languages, including Visual Basic .NET, require translators. You became familiar with some of the most popular programming languages. You learned the importance of structured programming and object-oriented programming. You studied a brief history of the Internet and the World Wide Web, were introduced to Microsoft's .NET initiative and learned some key aspects of .NET.

You took a working .NET application out for a "test-drive." In the process of doing this, you learned that .NET provides lots of prebuilt controls that perform useful functions and that, by familiarizing yourself with the capabilities of these controls, you can develop powerful applications much faster than if you tried to build them completely yourself. You were encouraged to explore several Web sites with additional information on this book, computers, the Internet, the Web, .NET and Visual Basic .NET.

In the next tutorial, you will learn about the Visual Studio .NET Integrated Development Environment (IDE). This will help you prepare to create your own Visual Basic .NET applications. You will continue to learn with our APPLICATION-DRIVEN™ approach, in which you will see all Visual Basic .NET features in useful applications and in which you will

1. study the user requirements for an application.

2. test-drive a working version of the application.

3. learn the technologies you'll need to build the application yourself.

4. build your own version of the application.

As you work through the book, if you have any questions about Visual Basic .NET, just send an e-mail to `deitel@deitel.com`, and we will respond promptly. We sincerely hope you enjoy learning the latest version of Microsoft's powerful Visual Basic language—the most widely used programming language in the world—with *Simply Visual Basic .NET*. Good luck!

KEY TERMS

Active Server Pages .NET (ASP .NET)—.NET software that helps programmers create applications for the Web.

assembly language—A type of programming language that uses English-like abbreviations to represent the fundamental operations on the computer.

central processing unit (CPU)—The part of the computer's hardware that is responsible for supervising the operation of the other sections of the computer.

class—The type of a group of related objects. A class specifies the general format of its objects; the properties and actions available to an object depend on its class. An object is to its class much as a house is to its blueprint.

compiler—A translator program that converts high-level-language programs into machine language.

computer—A device capable of performing computations and making logical decisions at speeds millions and even billions of times faster than the speeds at which human beings carry out those same tasks.

computer program—A set of instructions that guides a computer through an orderly series of actions.

computer programmer—A person who writes computer programs in programming languages.

control—A reusable component, such as a GroupBox, RadioButton, Button, Label and an MSChart control.

event-driven program—A program that responds to user-initiated events such as mouse clicks and keystrokes.

Framework Class Library (FCL)—.NET's collection of "prepackaged" classes and methods for performing common mathematical calculations, string manipulations, character manipulations, input/output operations, error checking and many other useful operations.

graphical user interface (GUI)—The visual part of an application with which users interact.

hardware—The various devices that make up a computer, including the keyboard, screen, mouse, hard drive, memory, CD-ROM and processing units.

high-level language—A type of programming language in which a single program statement accomplishes a substantial task. High-level languages use instructions that look almost like everyday English and that contain common mathematical notations.

HyperText Markup Language (HTML)—A language for marking up information to share over the World Wide Web via hyperlinked text documents.

input unit—The "receiving" section of the computer that obtains information (data and computer programs) from various input devices, such as the keyboard and the mouse.

integrated development environment (IDE)—A software tool that enables programmers to write, run, test and debug programs quickly and conveniently.

Internet—A worldwide computer network. Most people today access the Internet through the World Wide Web.

Lady Ada Lovelace—The person credited as being the world's first computer programmer, for work she did in the early 1800s.

machine language—A computer's natural language, generally consisting of streams of numbers that instruct the computer how to perform its most elementary operations.

memory unit—The rapid-access, relatively low-capacity "warehouse" section of the computer, which stores data temporarily while an application is running.

Microsoft .NET—Microsoft's vision for using the Internet and the Web in the development, engineering and use of software. .NET includes tools such as Visual Studio .NET and programming languages such as Visual Basic .NET.

.NET Framework—Microsoft-provided software that executes applications, provides the Framework Class Library (FCL) and supplies many other programming capabilities.

objects—Reusable software components that model items in the real world.

object technology—A packaging scheme for creating meaningful software units. The units are large and are focused on particular application areas. There are date objects, time objects, paycheck objects, file objects and the like.

output device—A device to which information that is processed by the computer can be sent.

output unit—The section of the computer that takes information the computer has processed and places it on various output devices, making the information available for use outside the computer.

procedural programming language—A programming language (such as Fortran, Pascal, BASIC and C) that focuses on actions (verbs) rather than things or objects (nouns).

properties—Object attributes, such as size, color and weight.

software—The set of applications that run on computers.

software reuse—The reuse of existing pieces of software, an approach that enables programmers to avoid "reinventing the wheel," helping them develop new applications faster.

structured programming—A disciplined approach to creating programs that are clear, correct and easy to modify.

visual programming with Visual Basic .NET—Instead of writing detailed program statements, the programmer uses Visual Studio .NET's graphical user interface to conveniently drag and drop predefined objects into place, and to label and resize them. Visual Studio .NET writes much of the Visual Basic .NET program, saving the programmer considerable effort.

World Wide Consortium (W3C)—A forum through which qualified individuals and companies cooperate to develop and standardize technologies for the World Wide Web.

World Wide Web (WWW)—A communications system that allows computer users to locate and view multimedia documents (such as documents with text, graphics, animations, audios and videos).

MULTIPLE-CHOICE QUESTIONS

1.1 The World Wide Web was developed _____.

    a) by ARPA   b) at CERN by Tim Berners-Lee

    c) before the Internet   d) as a replacement for the Internet

1.2 Microsoft's _____ initiative integrates the Internet and the Web into software development.

    a) .NET   b) BASIC

    c) Windows   d) W3C

1.3 `TextBoxes`, `Buttons` and `RadioButtons` are examples of _____.

    a) platforms   b) high-level languages

    c) IDEs   d) controls

1.4 _____ is an example of primary memory.

    a) TCP   b) RAM

    c) ALU   d) CD-ROM

1.5 Visual Basic .NET is an example of a(n) _____ language, in which single program statements accomplish more substantial tasks.

    a) machine   b) intermediate-level

    c) high-level   d) assembly

1.6 Which protocol is primarily intended to create a "network of networks?"

    a) TCP   b) IP

    c) OOP   d) FCL

1.7 A major benefit of _____ programming is that it produces software that is more understandable and better organized than software produced with previously used techniques.

    a) object-oriented   b) centralized

    c) procedural   d) HTML

1.8 .NET's collection of prepackaged classes and methods is called _____.

    a) NCL   b) WCL

    c) FCL   d) PPCM

1.9 The information-carrying capacity of communications lines is called _____.

    a) networking   b) secondary storage

    c) traffic   d) bandwidth

1.10 Which of these programming languages was specifically created for .NET?

    a) C#   b) C++

    c) BASIC   d) Visual Basic

EXERCISES

1.11 Categorize each of the following items as either hardware or software:

    a) CPU   b) Compiler

    c) Input unit   d) A word-processor program

    e) A Visual Basic .NET program

1.12 Translator programs, such as assemblers and compilers, convert programs from one language (referred to as the source language) to another language (referred to as the target language). Determine which of the following statements are *true* and which are *false*:

    a) A compiler translates high-level-language programs into target-language programs.

    b) An assembler translates source-language programs into machine-language programs.

    c) A compiler translates source-language programs into target-language programs.

    d) High-level languages are generally machine dependent.

    e) A machine-language program requires translation before it can be run on a computer.

1.13 Computers can be thought of as being divided into six units.

    a) Which unit can be thought of as "the boss" of the other units?

    b) Which unit is the high-capacity "warehouse" and retains information even when the computer is powered off?

    c) Which unit might determine whether two items stored in memory are identical?

    d) Which unit obtains information from devices like the keyboard and mouse?

1.14 Expand each of the following acronyms:

    a) W3C   b) TCP/IP

    c) OOP   d) FCL

    e) HTML

1.15 What are the advantages to using object-oriented programming techniques?

T U T O R I A L

Welcome Application

Introducing the Visual Studio® .NET IDE

V*isual Studio*® *.NET* is Microsoft's Integrated Development Environment (IDE) for creating and running applications written in .NET programming languages, such as Visual Basic .NET. The IDE allows you to create applications by dragging and dropping existing building blocks into place—a technique, called visual programming—greatly simplifying application development. In this tutorial, you will learn the Visual Studio .NET IDE features that you will need to create Visual Basic .NET applications.

2.1 Test-Driving the **Welcome** Application

In this section, you continue learning with our APPLICATION-DRIVEN™ approach as you prepare to build an application that displays a welcome message and a picture. Your application must meet the following requirements:

> **Application Requirements**
>
> *A software company (Deitel & Associates) has asked you to develop a Visual Basic .NET application that will display the message "Welcome to Visual Basic .NET!" and a picture of the company's bug mascot. To build this application, you must first familiarize yourself with the Visual Studio .NET IDE.*

In this tutorial, you will begin to develop the **Welcome** application. Then, in Tutorial 3, you will "put it all together" and create the **Welcome** application by following our step-by-step boxes. [*Note*: Our convention is to display application names in the **Helvetica** font.] You begin by test-driving the completed **Welcome** application.

Test-Driving the Welcome
Application

1. ***Checking your setup.*** Confirm that you have set up your computer properly by reading the *For Students and Instructors: Important Information before You Begin* section in the Preface.

2. ***Locating the Welcome application.*** Open Windows Explorer, and navigate to the C:\Examples\Tutorial02 folder (Fig. 2.1).

Figure 2.1   Contents of C:\Examples\Tutorial02.

3. ***Executing the application.*** Double click Welcome.exe (Fig. 2.1) to execute the application. Figure 2.2 shows the application executing.

Figure 2.2   Welcome application executing.

4. ***Closing the application.*** Close the executing application by clicking the close box, ☒.

2.2 Overview of the Visual Studio .NET IDE

This section introduces you to the Visual Studio .NET IDE. To begin, be certain that you have Visual Studio .NET installed on your computer. Then, find Visual Studio .NET, and open it; the **Start Page** displays (Fig. 2.3).

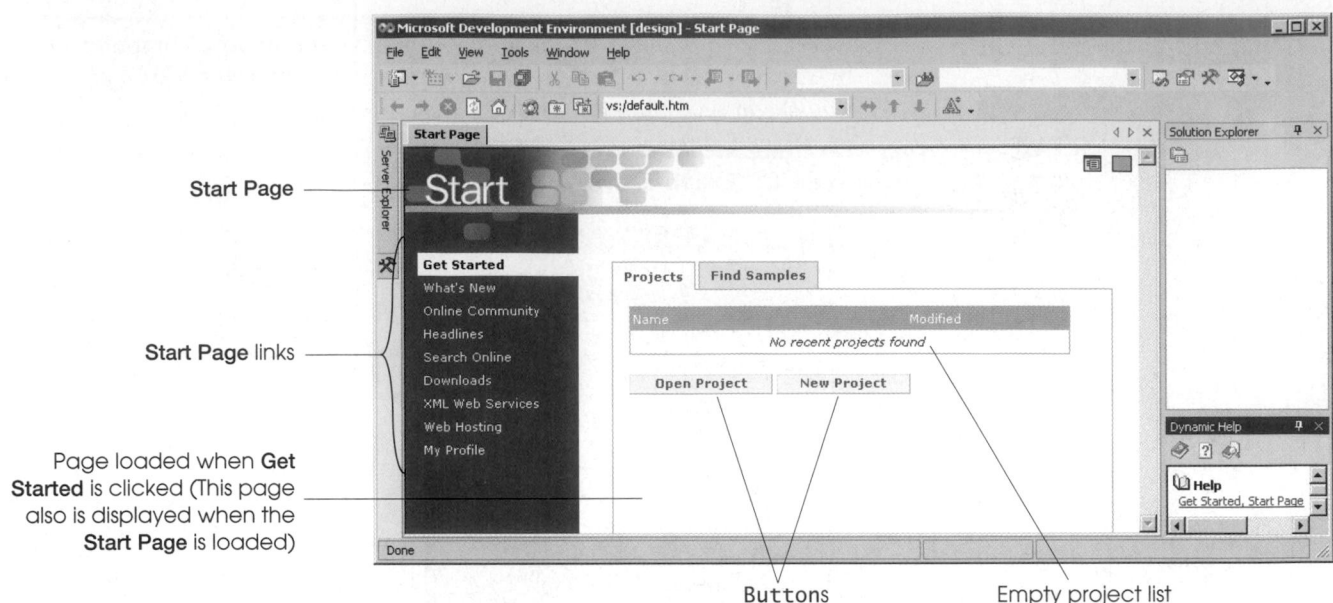

Start Page

Start Page links

Page loaded when **Get Started** is clicked (This page also is displayed when the **Start Page** is loaded)

Buttons   Empty project list

Figure 2.3 Start Page in Visual Studio .NET.

Depending upon your version of Visual Studio .NET, the **Start Page** might look different from the image in Fig. 2.3. The left side of the **Start Page** contains some helpful links, such as **Get Started**, **What's New** and **Online Community**. When you click a link, your computer will display information related to that link. The vast majority of the topics in these links will be more useful to you once you have gained some programming experience. For this book, you use only the **Get Started** link. Many of the **Start Page** links require that your computer be connected to the Internet. The following items describe each of the links on the **Start Page**:

■ Clicking the **Get Started** link loads a page that contains a table listing the names of recent projects (such as **WageCalculator** and **ASimpleProgram** in Fig. 2.4), along with the dates on which these projects were last changed (modified). A **project** is a group of related files and images that make up an application. When you load Visual Studio .NET for the first time, the list of recent projects is empty. There are two **Button**s on the page—**Open Project** and **New Project**, which are used to open existing projects (such as the ones in the table of recent projects) and to create projects, respectively.

Figure 2.4   **Start Page** in Visual Studio .NET.

- Clicking the **What's New** link displays a page that lists new features and updates for Visual Studio .NET, including downloads for Visual Basic .NET samples and programming tools. Information is updated frequently on this page.

- **Online Community** links to online resources for contacting other software developers through **newsgroups** (organized message boards on the Internet), user groups and Web sites.

- Clicking **Headlines** displays a page for browsing articles, news and tips for developing applications using Microsoft technologies.

- To access more extensive information, you can select **Search Online** and begin browsing through the **Microsoft Developer Network (MSDN)** online library, which contains articles and tutorials on technologies of interest to Visual Basic .NET programmers.

- When clicked, **Downloads** displays a page that provides you with access to product updates, code samples and reference materials.

- The **XML Web Services** page provides you with information about **Web services**, which are reusable pieces of Web-based software available on the Internet.

- The **Web Hosting** page allows you to post software (such as Web services) online for public use.

- Clicking the **My Profile** link loads a page where you can adjust and customize various Visual Studio .NET settings, such as the location where various windows should appear in the IDE.

You also can browse the Web from Visual Studio .NET by using Microsoft's Internet Explorer (also called the **internal Web browser** in Visual Studio .NET). For example, type www.deitel.com into the **location bar** (Fig. 2.5), and press the *Enter* key. This causes the DEITEL™ home page to be displayed within the Visual Studio .NET IDE (Fig. 2.6). Click the left-arrow Button (in the set of navigation Buttons from Fig. 2.4) to return to the **Start Page**. Other windows appear in the IDE in addition to the **Start Page**; we discuss several of them later in this tutorial.

Entering www.deitel.com in
the location bar

Figure 2.5 Web site (www.deitel.com) being entered in the location bar.

Figure 2.6 DEITEL™ home page displayed in the Visual Studio .NET IDE. (Courtesy of Deitel & Associates, Inc.)

SELF-REVIEW
1. When you first open Visual Studio .NET, the _____ displays.

    a) **What's New Page**   b) **Start Page**

    c) **Welcome Page**   d) none of the above

2. Clicking the _____ link in the Visual Studio .NET **Start Page** loads a page that contains a table listing the names of recent projects.

    a) **My Profile**   b) **Web Hosting**

    c) **Get Started**   d) **What's New**

Answers: 1) b. 2) c.

2.3 Creating a Project for the Welcome Application

In this section, you will create a simple Visual Basic .NET Windows application. The Visual Studio .NET IDE organizes applications into projects and **solutions**, which contain one or more projects. Every application always contains exactly one solution. Large-scale applications can contain many projects, in which each project performs a single, well-defined task (Fig. 2.7). In this book, each solution you build will contain only one project.

Figure 2.7   Solutions can contain one or more projects.

Creating a Project for the Welcome Application

1. *Creating a new project.* If you have not already done so, start Visual Studio .NET. On the **Start Page**, click the **New Project** Button (Fig. 2.8), causing the **New Project** dialog to display (Fig. 2.9). **Dialogs** are windows that can display information for, and gather information from, the application's user. Like other windows, dialogs are identified by the text in their **title bar**.

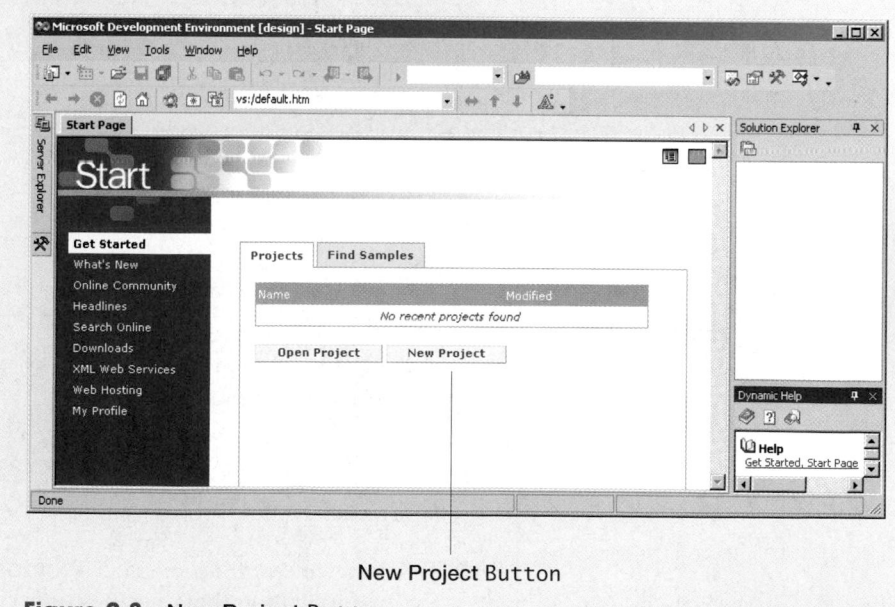

New Project Button

Figure 2.8 **New Project** Button.

(cont.)

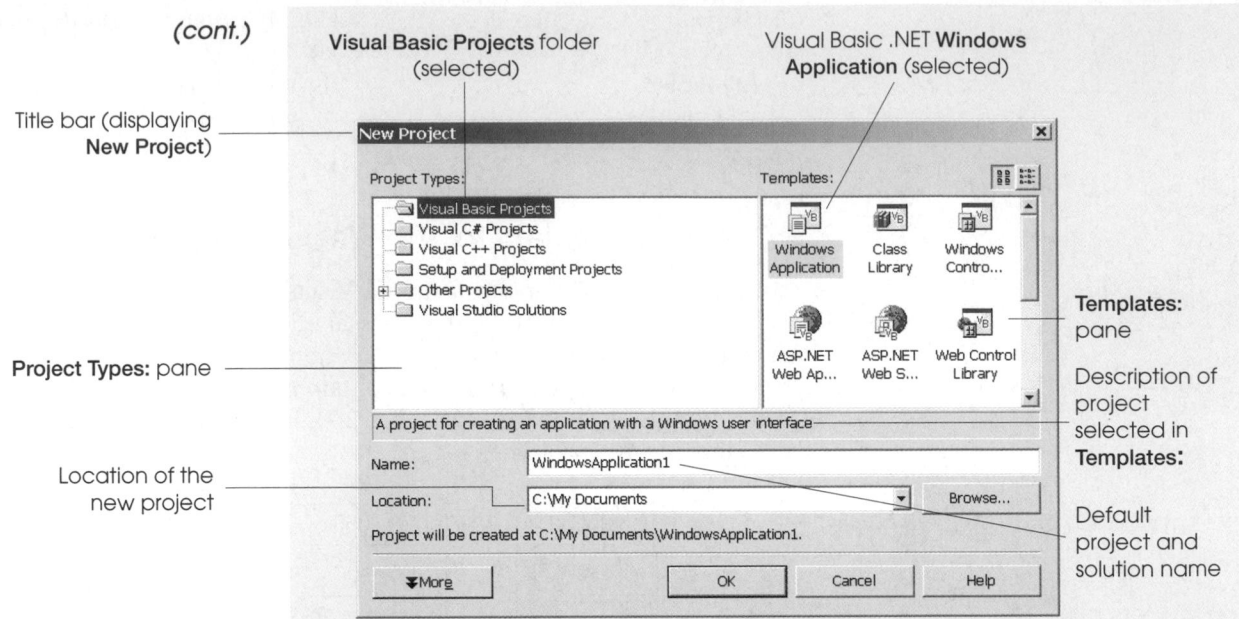

Figure 2.9 **New Project** dialog.

2. ***Selecting the project type.*** The Visual Studio .NET IDE allows you to choose from one of several languages (Visual Basic .NET, Visual C# and Visual C++ .NET) in which to program. Click the **Visual Basic Projects** folder in the **Project Types:** pane (Fig. 2.10) to display the list of Visual Basic .NET project types in the **Templates:** pane. (**Templates** are building blocks for different types of Visual Basic .NET applications.) [*Note*: Depending on your version of Visual Studio .NET, the names and number of items shown in the **Project Types:** and **Templates:** panes could differ.]

Figure 2.10 **New Project** dialog with updated project information.

3. ***Selecting the template.*** Select **Windows Application**, which is a template for an application that executes on machines running Microsoft® Windows. Examples of Windows applications include computer games and software products like Microsoft Word, Internet Explorer and Visual Studio .NET. In this book, you concentrate on **Windows Application**s. In the last tutorials, you will also build **ASP .NET Web Application**s.

(cont.)

4. ***Changing the name of the project.*** By default, the Visual Studio .NET IDE assigns the name WindowsApplication1 to the project and solution (Fig. 2.9) and places these files in a folder named WindowsApplication1. When a project is created in Visual Studio .NET for the first time, Visual Studio .NET places the WindowsApplication1 folder in the C:\My Documents directory. You can change both the project's name and location. To rename the project, type Welcome in the **Name:** TextBox (Fig. 2.10).

5. ***Changing the location of the project.*** Save this project in your SimplyVB directory. To change the project's location, click the **Browse...** Button (Fig. 2.10) to display the **Project Location** dialog (Fig. 2.11). In this dialog, locate your SimplyVB directory, and click **Open**. After providing the project's name and location in the **New Project** dialog, click **OK**. This displays the IDE in **design view** (Fig. 2.12), which contains the features you need to begin creating a Windows application.

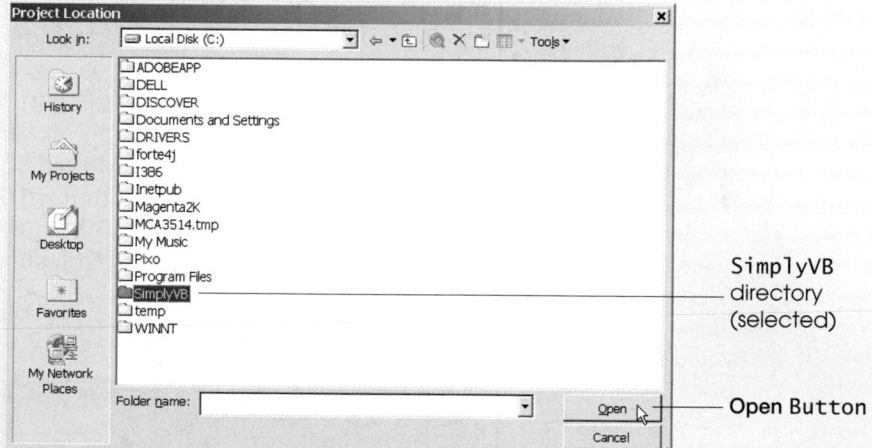

Figure 2.11   **Project Location** dialog.

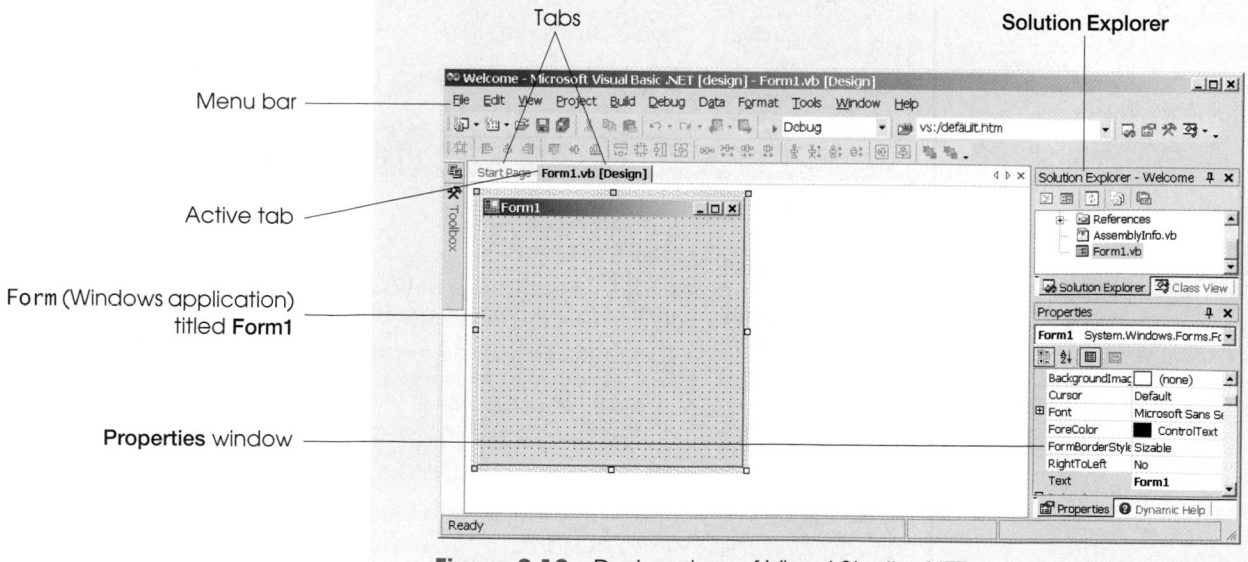

Figure 2.12   Design view of Visual Studio .NET.

The name of each open file is listed on a **tab** (**Start Page** and **Form1.vb [Design]** in Fig. 2.12). To view a file, click its tab. Tabs provide easy access to multiple files. The **active tab** is displayed in bold text (**Form1.vb [Design]** in Fig. 2.12).

The contents of the **Form1.vb [Design]** tab, which includes the gray rectangle (called a **Form**), is the **Windows Form Designer**. The Form (titled **Form1**) represents the Windows application that you are creating. Forms can be enhanced by adding controls such as Buttons. Together, the Form and controls make up the application's **graphical user interface** (**GUI**), which is the visual part of the application. Users enter data (**inputs**) into the application by typing at the keyboard, by clicking the mouse buttons and in a variety of other ways. Applications display instructions and other information (**outputs**) for users to read in the GUI. For example, the **New Project** dialog in Fig. 2.9 is a GUI in which users click with the mouse to select project types and input project names and locations from the keyboard.

GUI controls (such as Buttons) aid both (1) in data entry by users and (2) in formatting and presenting data outputs to users. For example, Internet Explorer (Fig. 2.13) displays Web pages requested by users. Internet Explorer's GUI has a menu bar that contains six menus: **File**, **Edit**, **View**, **Favorites**, **Tools** and **Help**. These menus allow users to print files, save files and more. Below the menu bar is a **toolbar** that contains Buttons. Each Button contains an image (called an **icon**) that identifies the Button. When clicked, toolbar Buttons execute tasks (such as printing and searching). Beneath the toolbar is a ComboBox in which users can type the locations of Web sites to visit. Users also can click the ComboBox's drop-down arrow to select Web sites that they have visited previously. To the left of the ComboBox is a Label (**Address**) that identifies the purpose of the ComboBox. The menus, Buttons and Label are part of Internet Explorer's GUI; they allow users to interact with the Internet Explorer application. Although not part of Internet Explorer's GUI, the Web page's TextBox at the bottom of Fig. 2.13 displays the text **<e-mail>** and allows users to input data. Using Visual Basic .NET, you can create your own applications that have all the GUI controls shown in Fig. 2.13 and many more.

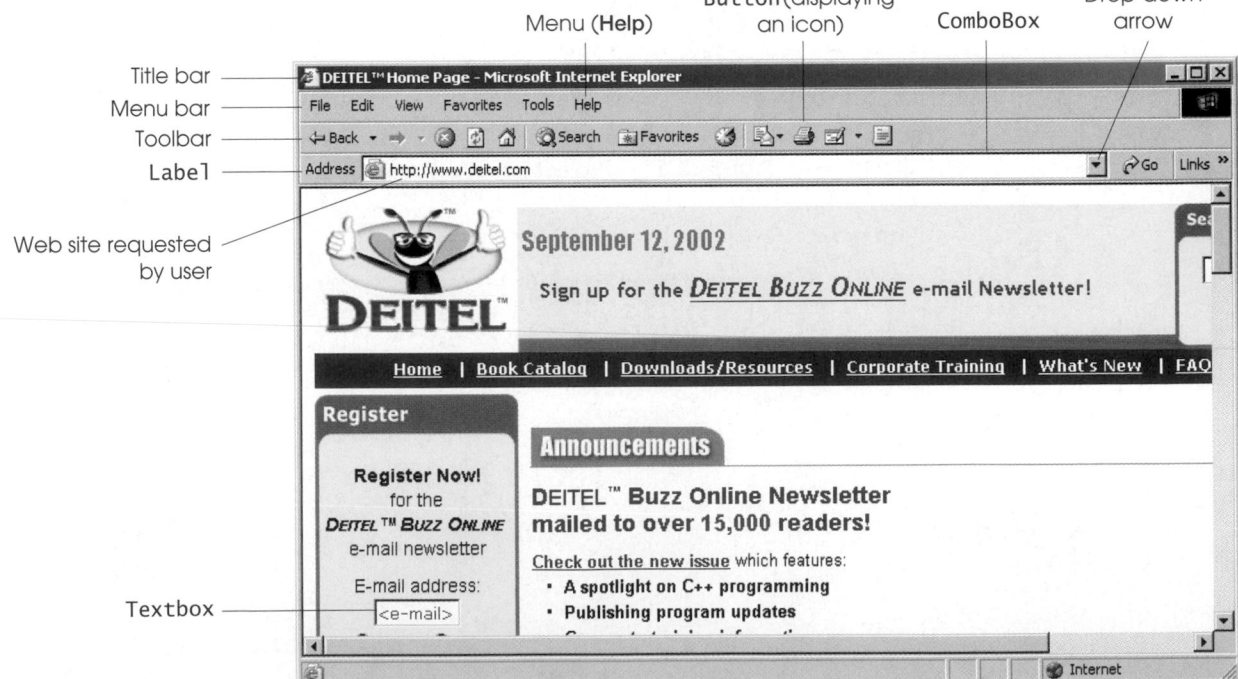

Figure 2.13 Internet Explorer window with GUI controls labeled. (Web site content courtesy of Deitel & Associates, Inc.)

SELF-REVIEW
1. The visual part of the application with which users interact is the application's _____.

    a) graphical user interface   b) project

    c) solution   d) title bar

2. A _____ contains one or more projects that collectively form a Visual Basic .NET application.

 a) dialog b) Form
 c) solution d) GUI

Answers: 1) a. 2) c.

2.4 Menu Bar and Toolbar

Visual Basic .NET programmers use **menus** (located on the Visual Studio .NET IDE menu bar shown in Fig. 2.14) that contain commands for managing the IDE and for developing and executing applications. Each menu has a group of related **commands** (also called **menu items**) that, when selected, cause the IDE to perform specific actions such as opening windows, saving files, printing files and executing applications. For example, to display the **Toolbox** window, select **View > Toolbox**. The menus in Fig. 2.14 are summarized in Fig. 2.15—you will learn to use many of these menus throughout the book. In Tutorial 22, **Typing** Application (Introducing Keyboard Events, Menus and Dialogs), you learn how to create and add your own menus and menu items to your applications.

File Edit View Project Build Debug Data Format Tools Window Help

Figure 2.14 Visual Studio .NET IDE menu bar.

Menu	Description
File	Contains commands for opening and closing projects, printing project data, etc.
Edit	Contains commands such as **Cut**, **Paste**, **Undo**, etc.
View	Contains commands for displaying IDE windows and toolbars.
Project	Contains commands for managing a solution's projects and their files.
Build	Contains commands for compiling a Visual Basic .NET application.
Debug	Contains commands for identifying and correcting problems in applications. Also contains commands for running applications.
Data	Contains commands for interacting with **databases**, which store the data that an application processes. [*Note*: You will learn database concepts in Tutorial 25, **ATM** Application.]
Format	Contains commands for aligning and spacing a Form's controls.
Tools	Contains commands for accessing additional IDE tools and options that enable customization of the IDE.
Window	Contains commands for hiding, opening, closing and displaying IDE windows.
Help	Contains commands for accessing the IDE's help features.

Figure 2.15 Visual Studio .NET IDE menu summary.

Rather than navigating the menus for certain commonly used commands, you can access those same commands from the IDE toolbar (Fig. 2.16). To execute a command via the IDE toolbar, simply click its icon. Some icons have associated down arrows that, when clicked, display additional commands.

Toolbar icon indicates a
command to open a
project or solution

Down arrow indicates
additional commands
are available

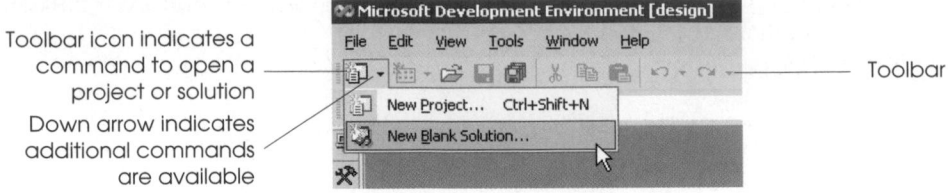

Figure 2.16 IDE toolbar.

Positioning the mouse pointer over an icon highlights the icon and, after a few seconds, displays a description called a **tool tip** (Fig. 2.17). Tool tips help you become familiar with the IDE's features.

Tool tip displayed
when the mouse
pointer has rested
on the icon for a
few seconds

Figure 2.17 Tool-tip demonstration.

SELF-REVIEW
1. _____ contain groups of related commands.

    a) Menu items   b) Menus

    c) Tool tips   d) None of the above

2. When the mouse pointer is positioned over an IDE toolbar icon for a few seconds, a _____ is displayed.

    a) toolbox   b) toolbar

    c) menu   d) tool tip

Answers: 1) b. 2) d.

2.5 Visual Studio .NET IDE Windows

The IDE provides windows for accessing project files and for customizing forms and controls by changing their attributes (names, colors, etc.). These windows provide visual aids for common programming tasks, such as managing files in a project. In this section, you will become familiar with several windows—**Solution Explorer**, **Properties** and **Toolbox**—that are essential for creating Visual Basic .NET applications. You can access these windows by using the IDE toolbar icons (Fig. 2.18) or by selecting the window name, using the **View** menu.

Properties icon

Solution Explorer icon

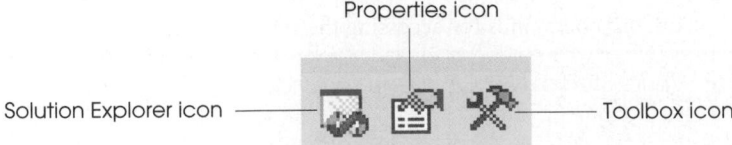

Toolbox icon

Figure 2.18 Toolbar icons for three Visual Studio .NET IDE windows.

Solution Explorer

The **Solution Explorer** window (located on the right side of the IDE as shown in Fig. 2.12) provides access to solution files. This window allows you to manage files visually. The **Solution Explorer** window displays a list of all the files in a project and all projects in a solution. (Remember that a Visual Basic .NET solution can contain one or more projects.) When the Visual Studio .NET IDE is first loaded, the **Solu-**

tion **Explorer** window is empty; there are no files to display. Once a solution is open, the **Solution Explorer** window displays that solution's contents. Figure 2.19 displays the solution contents for the **Welcome** application.

Figure 2.19 **Solution Explorer** with an open solution.

For your single-project solution, **Welcome** is the only project. The file, which corresponds to the Form shown in Fig. 2.12, is named Form1.vb. (Visual Basic .NET Form files use the .vb file name extension, which is short for "Visual Basic.")

The **plus** and **minus** boxes to the left of both the project name and the **References** folder are called **nodes**. The plus and minus boxes expand and collapse information, respectively. (See the box, *Navigating a Project with the* **Solution Explorer**.)

Navigating a Project with the Solution Explorer

1. *Collapsing a node.* Click the minus box to the left of the project name to collapse the node (Fig. 2.20). The minus box now becomes a plus box (Fig. 2.21).

Figure 2.20 Expanded node.

Figure 2.21 Collapsed node.

2. *Expanding a node.* Click the plus box to the left of the project name to expand the node. The **Solution Explorer** window should again look like Fig. 2.20.

Toolbox

Using visual programming, you can "drag and drop" controls onto the Form quickly and easily instead of building them from "scratch," which is a slow and complex process. Just as you do not need to know how to build an engine to drive a car, you do not need to know how to build controls to create effective GUIs. The **Toolbox** (Fig. 2.22) contains a wide variety of controls for building GUIs. You will use the

Toolbox as you finish creating the **Welcome** application in Tutorial 3. If the **Toolbox** is not visible, select **View > Toolbox**.

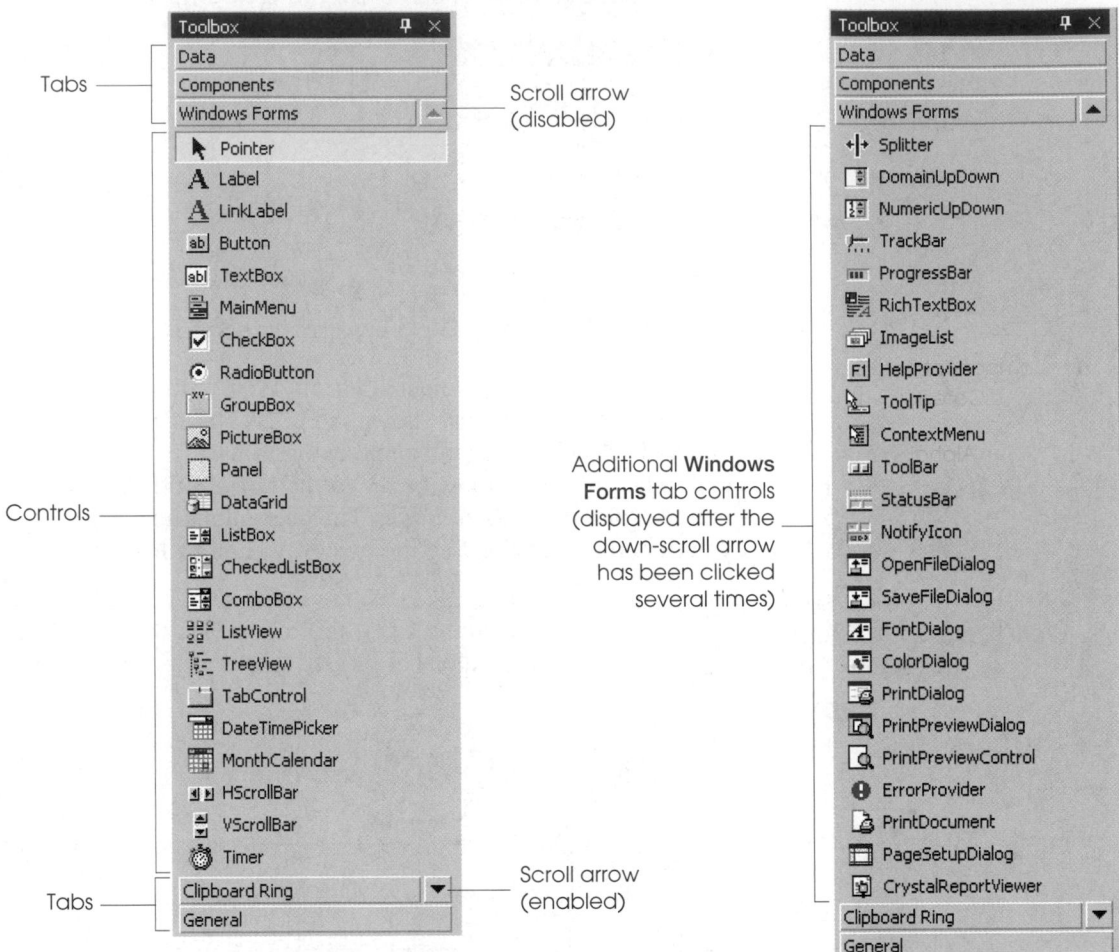

Figure 2.22 **Toolbox** displaying the contents of the **Windows Forms** tab.

The **Toolbox** contains five tabs (three at the top and two at the bottom) that group related controls: **Data, Components, Windows Forms, Clipboard Ring** and **General**. In this book, you will use only the **Windows Forms** tab controls and **Data** tab controls. When you click a tab, the **Toolbox** displays all of the controls in that group. You can scroll through the controls using the black **scroll arrows** to the right of the **Windows Forms** and **Clipboard Ring** tabs. When there are no more controls to display, the scroll arrow becomes gray, meaning that it is **disabled**. (It will not perform its normal function if clicked or held down.) The first item in the group is not a control—it is the **mouse pointer**. You will use the mouse pointer to navigate the IDE and to manipulate the Form and its controls. In the remaining tutorials, you will use approximately 20 of the **Toolbox**'s 47 controls.

Properties **Window**

One of the windows you will use frequently is the **Properties** window, which displays the **properties** for Form and control objects. Properties specify an object's attributes, such as the size, color and position of a control object.

The **Properties** window allows you to set object properties visually, without writing code. Setting properties visually provides a number of benefits:

■ You can see which properties can be modified and, in many cases, you can learn the acceptable values for a given property.

- You do not have to remember or search the Visual Studio .NET documentation (see Section 2.7) for a property's settings.

- This window displays a brief description of the selected property, so you can understand the property's purpose.

- A property can be set quickly.

All of these features are designed to help you ensure that settings are correct and consistent throughout the project. If the **Properties** window is not visible, select **View > Properties Window**. Figure 2.23 shows a Form's **Properties** window:

Figure 2.23 **Properties** window displaying a Form's properties.

- Each Form or control object has its own set of properties. At the top of the **Properties** window is the **component object box**, which allows you to select the object whose properties you wish to display in the **Properties** window.

- You can confirm that you are manipulating the correct object's properties because the object's name and class type are displayed in the component object box. Form objects have class type System.Windows.Forms.Form and are assigned generic names (such as Form1) by Visual Studio .NET. You will learn about the class types for controls in the next tutorial. Icons on the toolbar sort the properties either alphabetically (if you click the **alphabetic icon**) or categorically (if you click the **categorized icon**). Figure 2.23 shows the **Properties** window with its properties sorted categorically. Each gray horizontal bar to the left of the scrollbar is a category that groups related properties. For example, the **Design** category groups five related properties. The categories visible in Fig. 2.23 are **Behavior**, **Configurations**, **Data**, **Design**, **Focus** and **Layout**. Notice that each category is a node.

- The left column of the **Properties** window lists the object's property names; the right column displays each property's value. In the next tutorial, you will learn how to set properties for objects.

- You can scroll through the list of properties by dragging the scrollbar's scrollbox up or down.

- Whenever you select a property, a description of the property displays at the bottom of the **Properties** window.

SELF-REVIEW

1. The _____ allows you to add controls to the Form in a visual manner.
   a) **Solution Explorer**   b) **Properties** window
   c) **Toolbox**   d) **Dynamic Help** window

2. The _____ window allows you to view a solution's files.
   a) **Properties**   b) **Solution Explorer**
   c) **Toolbox**   d) None of the above.

Answers: 1) c. 2) b.

2.6 Auto Hide

Visual Studio .NET provides a space-saving feature used for the **Toolbox**, **Properties** and **Dynamic Help** (Section 2.7) windows, called **Auto Hide**. When Auto Hide is enabled for one or more of these windows, a toolbar appears along one of the edges of the IDE. (See the box, *Using Auto Hide*.)

Using Auto Hide

1. ***Displaying a hidden window.*** When Auto Hide is enabled, the toolbar along one of the edges of the IDE contains one or more tabs, each of which identifies a hidden window (Fig. 2.24). Place the mouse pointer over the **Toolbox** tab to display the **Toolbox** (Fig. 2.25).

Tabs for hidden windows

Figure 2.24 Hidden-window tabs.

Title bar

Horizontal pin icon (Auto Hide enabled)

Mouse pointer over the tab for the **Toolbox**

Toolbox is displayed when the mouse pointer is placed on the tab for the **Toolbox**

Figure 2.25 Displaying a hidden window with Auto Hide enabled.

2. ***Hiding a window.*** Move the mouse pointer outside the **Toolbox** window's area to hide the **Toolbox** (Fig. 2.26).

(cont.)

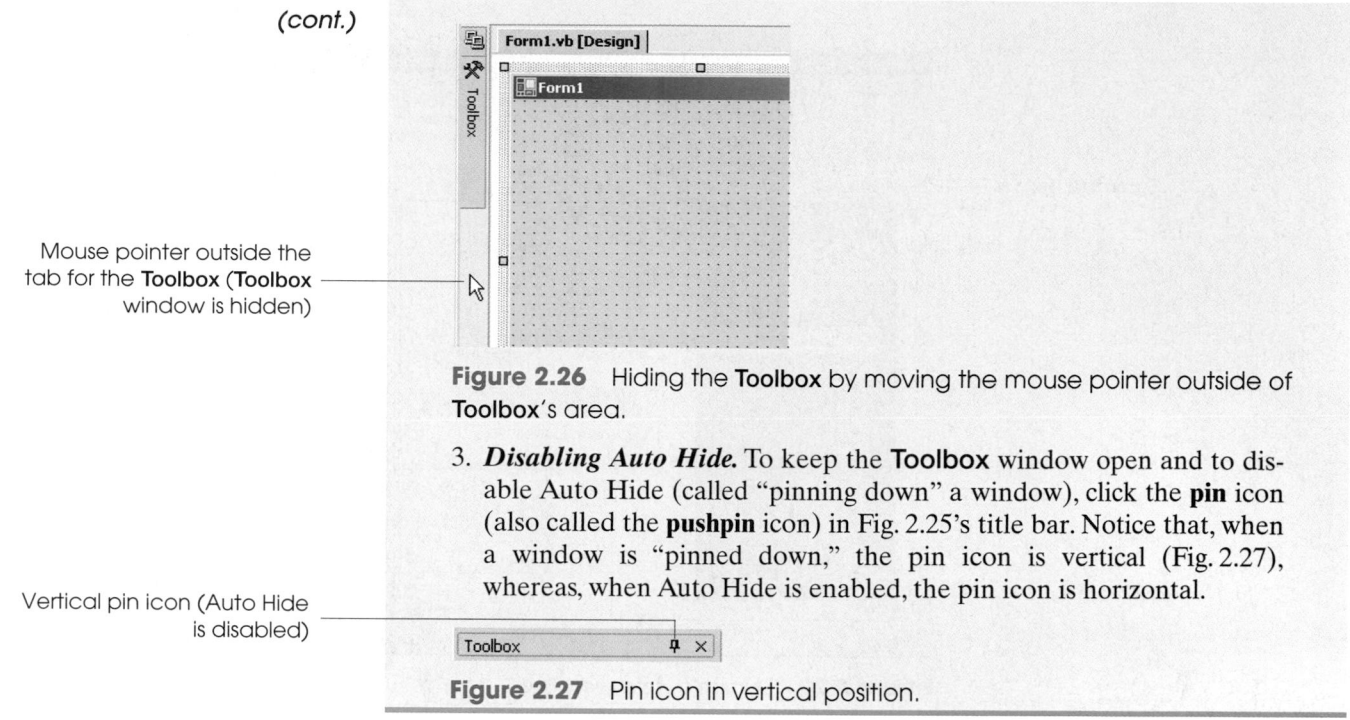

Mouse pointer outside the tab for the **Toolbox** (**Toolbox** window is hidden)

Figure 2.26   Hiding the **Toolbox** by moving the mouse pointer outside of **Toolbox**'s area.

3. ***Disabling Auto Hide.*** To keep the **Toolbox** window open and to disable Auto Hide (called "pinning down" a window), click the **pin** icon (also called the **pushpin** icon) in Fig. 2.25's title bar. Notice that, when a window is "pinned down," the pin icon is vertical (Fig. 2.27), whereas, when Auto Hide is enabled, the pin icon is horizontal.

Vertical pin icon (Auto Hide is disabled)

Figure 2.27   Pin icon in vertical position.

SELF-REVIEW

1. Visual Studio .NET provides a space-saving feature used for the _____ window(s).

    a) **Toolbox**　　　　　　　　　　　　b) **Properties**

    c) **Dynamic Help**　　　　　　　　　　d) All of the above.

2. When Auto Hide is enabled its pin icon is _____.

    a) horizontal　　　　　　　　　　　　b) vertical

    c) down　　　　　　　　　　　　　　　d) diagonal

Answers: 1) d. 2) a.

2.7 Using Help

The Visual Studio .NET IDE provides extensive help features. The **Help** menu commands are summarized in Fig. 2.28. **Dynamic help** (Fig. 2.29) provides links to articles that apply to the current content (that is, the item selected with the mouse pointer). For example, if you have the **Start Page** open, **Dynamic Help** provides links to articles about the **Start Page**, customizing **Dynamic Help** and many other topics. To open the **Dynamic Help** window, select **Help > Dynamic Help**. Then, when you click a word or object (such as a `Form` or a control), links to relevant help articles appear in the **Dynamic Help** window. The window lists help topics, samples and "Getting Started" information. When you click a link, the help topic appears in a new window. This new window also contains a toolbar that provides access to the **Contents...**, **Index...** and **Search...** help features.

Command	Description
Contents...	Displays a categorized table of contents in which help articles are organized by topic.
Index...	Displays an alphabetized list of topics through which you can browse.
Search...	Allows you to find help articles based on search keywords.

Figure 2.28   **Help** menu commands.

Figure 2.29 Dynamic Help window.

1. _____ displays relevant help articles, based on the selected object.

    a) Internal help   b) Dynamic help

    c) External help   d) Context-driven help

2. **Help** command _____ displays an alphabetized list of topics through which you can browse.

    a) **Search...**   b) **Browse...**

    c) **Contents...**   d) **Index...**

Answers: 1) b. 2) d.

2.8 Saving and Closing Solutions in Visual Studio .NET

Once you are finished with a solution, you will want to save the solution's files and close the solution.

Closing the Solution for the Welcome Application

1. ***Saving the Solution files.*** Before closing the solution for the **Welcome** application, you will want to save the solution's files, ensuring that any changes made to the solution's files are not lost. Although you did not make any changes to the solution's files for this particular tutorial, you will be making such changes in most of the tutorials so, for practice, save your solution files by selecting **File > Save All**.

2. ***Closing the Solution.*** To close the solution, select **File > Close Solution**.

2.9 Internet and Web Resources

Please take a moment to visit each of these sites briefly. To save typing time, use the hot links on the enclosed CD or at www.deitel.com.

www.msdn.microsoft.com/vstudio
This site is the home page for Microsoft Visual Studio .NET. This site includes news, documentation, downloads and other resources.

`www.worldofdotnet.net`

This site offers a wide variety of information on .NET, including articles, news and links to newsgroups and other resources.

`www.vbi.org`

This site has Visual Basic articles, reviews of books and software, documentation, downloads, links and more.

`www.msdn.microsoft.com/library/default.asp?url=/library/en-us/`
`vbcon/html/vbconselectingwfcclientcontrol.asp`

This Microsoft site summarizes **Toolbox** controls by function. Each control has a link to a page that contains additional resources for that control.

2.10 Wrap-Up

In this tutorial, you were introduced to the Visual Studio .NET integrated development environment (IDE). You learned key features, including tabs, menus, menu bars, toolbars, icons, Auto Hide and much more.

You created a Visual Basic .NET Windows application. The application contained one `Form` object named `Form1`. `Form` objects represent the application's graphical user interface (GUI).

You worked with the **Solution Explorer, Toolbox** and **Properties** windows that are essential to developing Visual Basic .NET applications. The **Solution Explorer** window allows you to manage your solution's files visually. The **Toolbox** window contains a rich collection of controls (organized on tabs) that allow you to create GUIs. The **Properties** window allows you to set the attributes of the `Form` and controls.

You explored Visual Studio .NET's help features, including the **Dynamic Help** window and the **Help** menu. The **Dynamic Help** window displays links related to the item you select with the mouse pointer. You learned about Web sites that provide additional Visual Basic .NET information.

In the next tutorial, you will begin creating Visual Basic .NET applications. You will follow step-by-step instructions for completing the **Welcome** application by using visual programming and the IDE features you learned in this tutorial.

SKILLS SUMMARY

Viewing a Page that Contains a Table Listing Names of Recent Projects

■ Click the **Start Page**'s **Get Started** link.

Viewing a Page that Lists New Features and Updates for Visual Studio .NET

■ Click the **Start Page**'s **What's New** link.

Viewing a Page that Lists Online Resources for Contacting Other Software Developers

■ Click the **Start Page**'s **Online Community** link.

Viewing a Page that Lists News, Articles and Tips for Developing Microsoft Applications

■ Click the **Start Page**'s **Headlines** link.

Viewing a Page that Allows Browsing of the Microsoft Developer Network (MSDN) Web Site

■ Click the **Start Page**'s **Search Online** link.

Viewing a Page that Lists Product Updates, Code Samples and Reference Materials

■ Click the **Start Page**'s **Downloads** link.

Viewing a Page that Allows You to Customize Visual Studio .NET Settings

■ Click the **Start Page**'s **My Profile** link.

Creating a New Project

■ Click the **Start Page**'s **New Project** `Button` to display the **New Project** dialog.

- Select **Visual Basic Projects** in the **Project Types:** pane.
- Select **Windows Application** in the **Templates:** pane.
- Provide the project's name in the **Name:** TextBox.
- Provide the project's directory information in the **Location:** TextBox.
- Click the OK Button.

Saving a Project

- Select **File > Save All**.

Viewing a Tool Tip for a Visual Studio .NET Icon

- Place the mouse pointer on the icon, and keep it there until the tool tip appears.

Collapsing a Node in the Solution Explorer

- Click the node's minus box.

Expanding a Node in the Solution Explorer

- Click the node's plus box.

Scrolling Through the List of Windows Forms Controls in the Toolbox

- Click the scroll arrows.

Viewing the Properties Window

- Select **View > Properties Window**.

Displaying a Hidden Window

- Place the mouse pointer over the hidden window's tab.

Disabling Auto Hide and "Pinning Down" a Window

- Click the window's horizontal pin icon to change it to a vertical pin icon.

Enabling Auto Hide

- Click the window's vertical pin icon to change it to a horizontal pin icon.

Opening the Dynamic Help Window

- Select **Help > Dynamic Help**.

KEY TERMS

active tab—The tab of the document displayed in the IDE.

alphabetic icon—The icon in the **Properties** window that, when clicked, sorts properties alphabetically.

Auto Hide—A space-saving IDE feature used for windows such as **Toolbox**, **Properties** and **Dynamic Help** that hides a window until the mouse pointer is placed on the hidden window's tab.

categorized icon—The icon in the **Properties** window that, when clicked, sorts properties categorically.

component object box—The ComboBox at the top of the **Properties** window that allows you to select the Form or control object whose properties you want set.

Contents... command—The command that displays a categorized table of contents in which help articles are organized by topic.

Data menu—The menu that contains commands for interacting with databases.

Debug menu—The menu that contains commands for debugging and running an application.

design view—The Visual Studio .NET view that contains the features necessary to begin creating Windows applications.

dialog—A window that can display and gather information.

dynamic help—A help option that provides links to articles that apply to the current content (that is, the item selected with the mouse pointer).

Form—The object that represents the Windows application's graphical user interface (GUI).

graphical user interface (GUI)—The visual components through which users interact with applications.

icon—The graphical representation of commands in the Visual Studio .NET IDE.

Integrated Development Environment (IDE)—The software used to create, document, run and debug applications.

internal Web browser—Web browser (Internet Explorer) included in Visual Studio .NET, with which you can browse the Web.

location bar—The ComboBox in Visual Studio .NET where you can enter the name of a Web site to visit.

menu—A group of related commands.

menu item—A command located in a menu that, when selected, causes an application to perform a specific action.

Microsoft Developer Network (MSDN)—An online library that contains articles, downloads and tutorials on technologies of interest to Visual Studio .NET developers.

minus box—The icon that, when clicked, collapses a node.

New Project dialog—A dialog that allows you to choose which type of application you wish to create.

pin icon—An icon that enables or disables the Auto Hide feature.

plus box—An icon that, when clicked, expands a node.

project—A group of related files that compose an application.

Properties window—The window that displays the properties for a Form or control object.

property—Specifies a control or Form object's attributes, such as size, color and position.

solution—Contains one or more projects.

Solution Explorer—A window that provides access to all the files in a solution.

Start Page—The initial page displayed when Visual Studio .NET is opened.

tool tip—The description of an icon that appears when the mouse pointer is held over that icon for a few seconds.

toolbar—A bar that contains Buttons that execute commands.

toolbar icon—A picture on a toolbar Button.

Toolbox—A window that contains controls used to customize Forms.

Tools menu—A menu that contains commands for accessing additional IDE tools and options that enable customization of the IDE.

Visual Studio .NET—Microsoft's integrated development environment (IDE), which allows developers to create applications in a variety of .NET programming languages.

Windows application—An application that executes on a Windows operating system.

MULTIPLE-CHOICE QUESTIONS

2.1 The _____ integrated development environment is used for creating applications written in .NET programming languages such as Visual Basic.NET.

    a) **Solution Explorer**   b) Gates

    c) Visual Studio .NET   d) Microsoft

2.2 The .vb file name extension indicates a _____.

    a) Visual Basic file   b) dynamic help file

    c) help file   d) very big file

2.3 The pictures on toolbar Buttons are called _____.

    a) prototypes   b) icons

    c) tool tips   d) tabs

2.4 The _____ allows programmers to modify controls visually, without writing code.

    a) **Properties** window   b) **Solution Explorer**

    c) menu bar   d) **Toolbox**

2.5 The _____ hides the **Toolbox** when the mouse pointer is moved outside the Tool-Box's area.

    a) component-selection feature   b) Auto Hide feature

    c) pinned command   d) minimize command

2.6 A _____ appears when the mouse pointer is positioned over an IDE toolbar icon for a few seconds.

    a) drop-down list   b) menu

    c) tool tip   d) down arrow

2.7 The Visual Studio .NET IDE provides _____.

    a) help documentation   b) a toolbar

    c) windows for accessing project files   d) All of the above

2.8 The _____ contains a list of helpful links, such as **Get Started** and **Online Community**.

    a) **Solution Explorer** window   b) **Properties** window

    c) **Start Page**   d) **Toolbox** link

2.9 The **Properties** window contains _____.

    a) the component object box   b) a **Solution Explorer**

    c) menus   d) a menu bar

2.10 A _____ can be enhanced by adding reusable components such as `Buttons`.

    a) control   b) `Form`

    c) tab   d) property

2.11 For Web browsing, Visual Studio .NET includes _____.

    a) Web View   b) Excel

    c) a **Web** tab   d) Internet Explorer

2.12 An application's GUI can include _____.

    a) toolbars   b) icons

    c) menus   d) All of the above

2.13 The _____ does not contain a pin icon.

    a) **Dynamic Help** window   b) **Solution Explorer** window

    c) **Toolbox** window   d) active tab

2.14 When clicked, _____ in the **Solution Explorer** window will expand nodes and _____ will collapse nodes.

    a) minus boxes; plus boxes   b) plus boxes; minus boxes

    c) up arrows; down arrows   d) left arrows; right arrows

2.15 Form _____ specify attributes such as size and position.

    a) nodes   b) inputs

    c) properties   d) title bars

EXERCISES

2.16 (*Closing and Opening the Start Page*) In this exercise, you will learn how to close and reopen the **Start Page**. To accomplish this task, perform the following steps:

    a) Close Visual Studio .NET if it is open by selecting **File > Exit**.

    b) Start Visual Studio .NET.

    c) Close the **Start Page** by clicking its close box (Fig. 2.30).

Figure 2.30 Closing the **Start Page**.

d) Select **Help > Show Start Page** to display the **Start Page**.

2.17 (*Enabling Auto Hide for the Solution Explorer Window*) In this exercise, you will learn how to use the **Solution Explorer** window's Auto-Hide feature by performing the following steps:

a) Open the **Start Page**.

b) In the **Get Started** page (displayed by default), click the **Open Project** Button to display the **Open Project** dialog. You can skip to step e) if the **Welcome** application is already open.

c) In the **Open Project** dialog, navigate to C:\SimplyVB\Welcome, and click **Open**.

d) In the **Open Project** dialog, select Welcome.sln, and click **Open**.

e) Position the mouse pointer on the vertical pin icon in the **Solution Explorer** window's title bar. After a few seconds, a tool tip appears displaying the words **Auto Hide** (Fig. 2.31).

Figure 2.31 Enabling Auto Hide.

f) Click the vertical pin icon. This action causes a **Solution Explorer** tab to appear on the right side of the IDE. The vertical pin icon changes to a horizontal pin icon (Fig. 2.32). Auto Hide has now been enabled for the **Solution Explorer** window.

Figure 2.32 **Solution Explorer** window with Auto Hide enabled.

g) Position the mouse pointer outside the **Solution Explorer** window to hide the window.

h) Position the mouse pointer on the **Solution Explorer** tab to view the **Solution Explorer** window.

2.18 (*Sorting Properties Alphabetically in the Properties Window*) In this exercise, you will learn how to sort the **Properties** window's properties alphabetically by performing the following steps:

a) Open the **Welcome** application by performing steps a) through d) of Exercise 2.17. If the **Welcome** application is already open, you can skip this step.

b) Locate the **Properties** window. If it is not visible, select **View > Properties Window** to display the **Properties** window.

c) To sort properties alphabetically, click the **Properties** window's alphabetic icon (Fig. 2.33). The properties will display in alphabetic order.

Alphabetic icon ———

Figure 2.33   Sorting properties alphabetically.

Objectives

In this tutorial, you will learn to:
- Set the text in the **Form**'s title bar.
- Change the **Form**'s background color.
- Place a **Label** control on the **Form**.
- Display text in a **Label** control.
- Place a **PictureBox** control on the **Form**.
- Display an image in a **PictureBox** control.
- Execute an application.

Outline

Welcome Application

Introduction to Visual Programming

Today, users prefer software with interactive graphical user interfaces (GUIs) that respond to actions such as **Button** clicks, data input and much more. As a result, the vast majority of Windows applications, such as Microsoft Word and Internet Explorer, are GUI based. With Visual Basic .NET, you can create Windows applications that input and output information in a variety of ways, which you will learn throughout the book.

In this tutorial, you use visual programming to complete the **Welcome** application you began creating in Tutorial 2. You will build the application's GUI by placing two controls—a **Label** and a **PictureBox**—on the **Form**. You will use the **Label** control to display text and the **PictureBox** control to display an image. You will customize the appearance of the **Form**, **Label** and **PictureBox** objects by setting their values in the **Properties** window. You will set many property values including the **Form**'s background color, the **PictureBox**'s image and the **Label**'s text. You also will learn how to execute your application from within the Visual Studio .NET IDE.

3.1 Test-Driving the Welcome Application

The last tutorial introduced you to the Visual Studio .NET IDE. In this tutorial, you will use Visual Studio .NET to build the **Welcome** application mentioned in Tutorial 2. Your application must meet the following requirements:

Application Requirements

*Recall that a software company (Deitel & Associates) has asked you to develop a simple **Welcome** application that includes the greeting "Welcome to Visual Basic .NET!" and a picture of the company's bug mascot. Now that you are familiar with the Visual Studio .NET IDE, your task is to develop this application to satisfy the company's request.*

You begin by test-driving the completed **Welcome** application from within the Visual Studio .NET IDE.

Test-Driving the Welcome Application

1. ***Opening the completed Welcome application.*** Start Visual Studio .NET and select **File > Open Solution...** (Fig. 3.1) to display the **Open Solution** dialog (Fig. 3.2). Select the `C:\Examples\Tutorial03\CompletedAppli-cation\Welcome` directory from the **Look in:** ComboBox. Select the **Welcome** solution file and click the **Open** Button. Figure 3.3 shows the **Welcome** application's Form in design view.

Open Solution command
(selected) opens an existing
solution

Figure 3.1   Opening an existing solution with the **File** menu's **Open Solu-tion...** command.

Open Solution dialog

Look in: ComboBox

Welcome solution file
(may display
`Welcome.sln`
depending on your
settings)

Figure 3.2   **Open Solution** dialog displaying the contents of the **Welcome** solution.

2. ***Executing the Welcome application.*** Select **Debug > Start** (Fig. 3.4). The **Start** command runs (executes) the application. Figure 3.5 displays the running application.

3. ***Closing the running application.*** Close the executing application (Fig. 3.5) by clicking the window's close box, ☒.

4. ***Closing the Welcome solution.*** Select **File > Close Solution** in the Visual Studio .NET IDE to close the **Welcome** solution.

(cont.)

Figure 3.3 **Welcome** application's **Form** in design view.

Start command (selected) executes the application

Figure 3.4 Executing the **Welcome** application using the **Debug** menu's **Start** command.

Close box

Figure 3.5 **Welcome** application executing.

3.2 Constructing the Welcome Application

In this section, you perform the steps necessary to develop the **Welcome** application. The application consists of a single `Form` that uses a `Label` control and a `Pic-tureBox` control. A **Label** control displays text that the user cannot change. A **PictureBox** control displays an image that the user cannot change. You will not write a single line of code to create this application. Instead, you will use the technique called **visual programming**, in which Visual Studio .NET processes your programming actions (such as clicking, dragging and dropping controls) and actually writes the program for you! The box, *Changing the Form's File Name and Title Bar Text*, shows you how to begin constructing the **Welcome** application, using the solution you created in Tutorial 2 as a starting point.

Changing the Form's File Name and Title Bar Text

1. ***Opening the Welcome application's solution.*** Select **File > Open Solution...**. Open the **Welcome** solution file (`Welcome.sln`) in the `C:\SimplyVB\Welcome` directory. Double click `Form1.vb` in the **Solution Explorer** window to display the blank `Form`. Figure 3.6 shows the **Welcome** application solution open in Visual Studio .NET.

IDE title bar

Toolbar

Form title bar

Blank `Form`

Solution Explorer window

Solution name

Project name

Form file name

Figure 3.6 Blank `Form`.

2. ***Changing the Form's file name.*** When a Windows application is created, Visual Studio .NET names the `Form` file `Form1.vb`. Select `Form1.vb` in the **Solution Explorer** window (Fig. 3.6) to display the file's properties in the **Properties** window (the window on the left in Fig. 3.7). If either window is not visible, you can select **View > Properties Window** or **View > Solution Explorer** to display the appropriate window. Double click the field to the right of the `File Name` property's box, and type `Welcome.vb` (Fig. 3.7). Press the *Enter* key to update the `Form`'s file name. Notice that the file name changes in the **Solution Explorer** window (the window on the right in Fig. 3.7) and in the **Properties** window.

Good Programming Practice

Change your application's `Form` file name (`Form1.vb`) to a name that describes the application's purpose.

File properties

Selected property

Selected property description

New property value

New file name

GUI Design Tip

Choose short and descriptive `Form` titles. Capitalize words that are not articles, prepositions or conjunctions. Do not use punctuation.

Figure 3.7 Changing the `Form`'s file name.

(cont.)   3. ***Setting the text in the Form's title bar.*** The title bar is the top portion of the window that contains the window's title. To change the text in the Form's title bar from **Form1** to **Welcome**, use the **Properties** window (Fig. 3.8). Click the Form. As in Fig. 3.7, double click the field to the right of the Text property in the **Properties** window, and type `Welcome`. Press the *Enter* key to update the Form's title bar (Fig. 3.9).

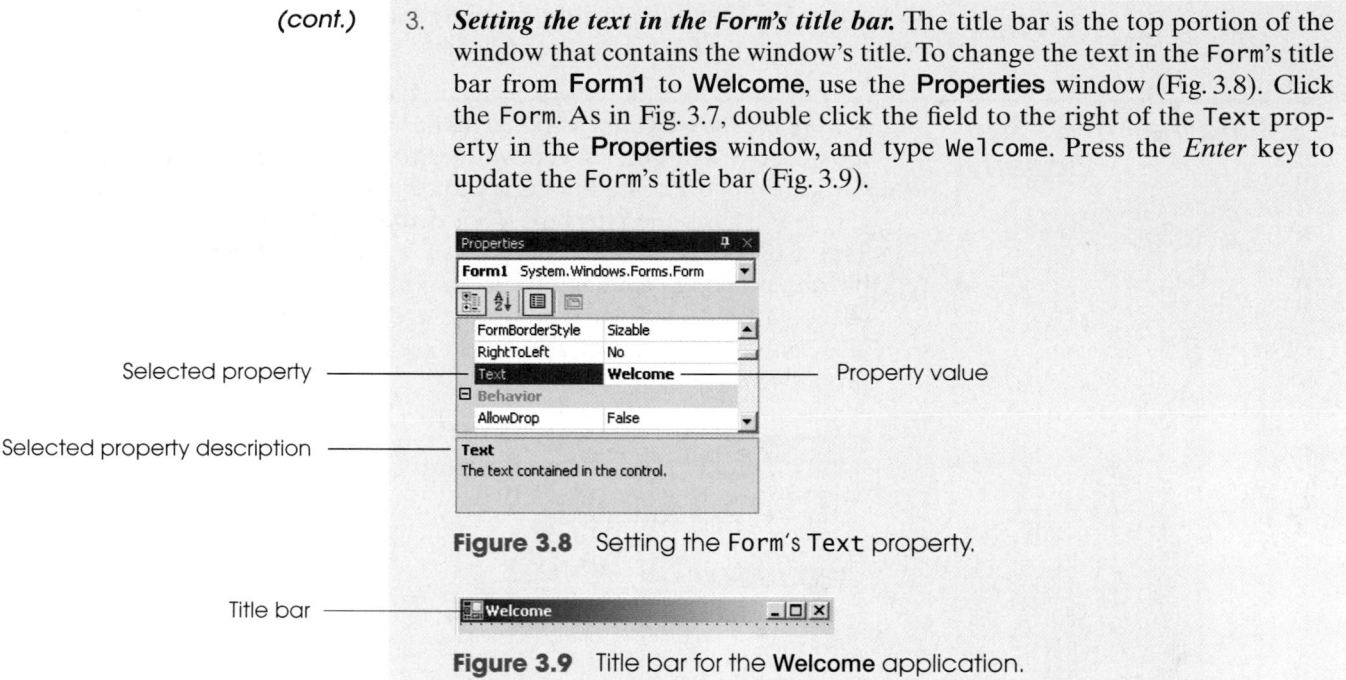

Selected property ──── Property value

Selected property description ────

Figure 3.8 Setting the Form's **Text** property.

Title bar ────

Figure 3.9 Title bar for the **Welcome** application.

There are several ways to resize the Form. If the resizing does not have to be precise, you can click and drag one of the Form's enabled **sizing handles** (the small white squares that appear along the Form's edges, as shown in Fig. 3.10). The appearance of the mouse pointer changes (that is, it becomes a pointer with one or more arrows) when it is over an enabled sizing handle. The new pointer indicates the direction(s) in which resizing is allowed. Disabled **sizing handles** appear in gray and cannot be used to resize the Form.

The dots on the background of the Form are called a **grid**. You use the grid to align controls that you place on the Form. The grid is not visible when the application is running (Fig. 3.5).

Width

Disabled sizing handle

Grid

Height

Mouse pointer over an enabled sizing handle

Enabled sizing handle

Figure 3.10 **Form** with sizing handles.

Forms also can be resized by using the **Size** property, which specifies the Form's width and height in units called **pixels** (*pic*ture *el*ements). A pixel is a tiny point on your computer screen that displays a color. The Size property has two members—the **Width** and the **Height** properties. The Width property indicates the width of the Form in pixels, and the Height property specifies the height in pixels. Next, you learn how to set the Form's width and height.

Setting the *Form's* Size Property

1. **Setting the Form's width and height.** For your **Welcome** application GUI to look exactly like Fig. 3.5, you will need to resize the Form and its controls. Click the Form. Locate the Form's Size property in the **Properties** window (Fig. 3.11). Click the plus box, ⊞, next to this property to expand the node. Type 616 for the Width property value, and press *Enter*. Type 440 for the Height property value and press *Enter*. Note that the Size property value (616, 440) updated when either the Width or the Height is changed. You also can enter the width and height (separated by a comma) in the Size property's value field.

Figure 3.11 Size property values for the Form.

Now that you have set the Form's size, you will customize the Form further by changing its background color from gray to yellow.

Setting the *Form's* Background Color

1. **Exploring the available colors.** Click the Form to display its properties in the **Properties** window. The **BackColor** property specifies an object's background color. When you click the **BackColor** property's value in the **Properties** window, a down-arrow (▾) Button appears (Fig. 3.12). When clicked, the down-arrow Button displays three tabs: **System** (the default), **Web** and **Custom**. Each tab offers a series of colors called a **palette**. The **System** tab displays a palette containing the colors used in the Microsoft Windows GUI. This palette includes the colors for Windows controls and the Windows desktop. The **System** tab's colors are based on the Windows 2000/XP settings in the **Display Properties** dialog. To access this dialog in Windows 2000, right click the desktop and select **Properties**. Click the **Appearance** tab to view the colors used by Windows. The **Web** tab displays a palette of **Web-safe colors**—colors that display the same on different computers. The **Custom** tab palette allows you to choose from a series of predefined colors or to create your own color. Click the **Custom** tab to display its palette as shown in Fig. 3.12.

GUI Design Tip

Use colors in your applications, but not to the point of distracting the user.

2. **Changing the Form's background color.** Right click any one of the 16 white boxes at the bottom of the **Custom** palette to display the **Define Color** dialog (Fig. 3.13). Colors can be created either by entering three values in the **Hue:**, **Sat:** and **Lum:** TextBoxes or by providing values for the **Red:**, **Green:** and **Blue:** TextBoxes. The values for the **Red:**, **Green:** and **Blue:** TextBoxes describe the amount of red, green and blue needed to create the custom color and are commonly called **RGB values**. Each red, green and blue value is in the range 0–255, inclusive. We use RGB values in this book. Set the **Red:** value to 255, the **Green:** value to 237 and the **Blue:** value to 169. Clicking the **Add Color** Button closes the dialog, changes the Form's background color and adds the color to the **Custom** palette (Fig. 3.14).

(cont.)

Tabs

Current color

Down-arrow **Button**

Custom palette

Custom colors can be added to the white boxes

Figure 3.12   Viewing the **Custom** palette in the **Form**'s **BackColor** property value field.

Color preview

Adds a color to **Custom** palette

Red component (255)
Green component (237)
Blue component (169)

Figure 3.13   Adding a color to the **Custom** palette.

Form background set to new custom color

Custom color added to palette

Figure 3.14   **Properties** window after the new custom color has been added.

Now that you have finished customizing the Form, you can add a control to the Form. The box, *Adding a Label to the Form*, guides you through adding and customizing a Label that displays a greeting.

Adding a *Label* to the *Form*

GUI Design Tip

Use Labels to display text that users cannot change.

1. ***Adding a Label control to the Form.*** Click the **Windows Forms** tab in the **Toolbox** (Fig. 3.15). If the **Toolbox** is not visible, select **View > Toolbox**. Double click the Label control in the **Toolbox**. A Label will appear in the upper-left corner of the Form (Fig. 3.16). You also can "drag" the Label from the **Toolbox** and drop it on the Form. You will use this Label control to display the welcome message. The Label displays the text **Label1** by default.

Notice that the Label's background color is the same as the Form's background color. When a control is added to the Form, the control's BackColor property value initially is set to the Form's BackColor property value by the Visual Studio .NET IDE.

Figure 3.15   Clicking the **Windows Forms** tab in the **Toolbox**.

Figure 3.16   Adding a Label to the Form.

GUI Design Tip

Ensure that all Label controls are large enough to display their text.

2. ***Customizing the Label's appearance.*** Click the Label to select it. You will notice that the Label's properties now appear in the **Properties** window. The Label's Text property specifies the text (**Label1**) that the Label displays. Type Welcome to Visual Basic .NET! for the Label's Text property value and press *Enter*. Notice that this text does not fit in the Label (Fig. 3.17). Enlarge the Label (by using the sizing handles) until all the text is displayed (Fig. 3.18).

Figure 3.17   Label after updating its Text property.

Figure 3.18   Label after it has been resized.

3. ***Aligning the Label.*** Drag the Label to the top center of the Form. You also can center the Label by clicking the Label and selecting **Format > Center In Form > Horizontally**. After centering the Label, the Form should look like Fig. 3.19.

(cont.)

Centered Label ————

Figure 3.19   Centered Label.

GUI Design Tip

Use Tahoma font to improve read-ability for controls that display text.

4. **Setting the Label's font.** Click the value of the **Font** property to cause an **ellipsis** Button to appear (Fig. 3.20). If you click the ellipsis Button, the **Font** dialog displays (Fig. 3.21). In this dialog, you can select the font name (**Tahoma**, **Times New Roman**, etc.), font style (**Regular**, **Italic**, etc.) and font size (**16**, **18**, etc.) in points (one point equals 1/72 of an inch). The text in the **Sample** Label displays the selected font. Under the **Size:** category, select **24** points. Under the **Font** category, select **Tahoma**, and click **OK**. If the Label's text does not fit on a single line, it wraps to the next line. Use the sizing handles to enlarge the Label vertically so that the text appears on two lines and looks like the Label in Fig. 3.3.

Figure 3.20   **Properties** window displaying the Label's properties.

Font dialog ————

Current font ————

Font sample

Figure 3.21   **Font** dialog for selecting fonts, styles and sizes.

5. **Aligning the Label's text.** To align text inside a Label, you will need to use the Label's **TextAlign** property. Clicking the TextAlign property displays a down-arrow Button. Click the down-arrow Button to display a three-by-three grid of Buttons (Fig. 3.22). The position of each Button shows where the text will appear in the Label. Click the top-center Button in the three-by-three grid to align the text at the top-center position in the Label. The value TopCenter is assigned to property TextAlign.

(cont.)

Figure 3.22   Centering the Label's text.

To finish this first Visual Basic .NET Windows application, you need to insert an image and execute the application. We use a PictureBox control to add an image to the Form before running the application. The box, *Inserting an Image and Running the **Welcome** Application*, guides you step by step through the process of adding an image to your Form.

Inserting an Image and Running the Welcome Application

1. ***Adding a PictureBox control to the Form.*** The PictureBox allows you to display an image. To add a PictureBox control to the Form, double click the PictureBox control icon

   in the ToolBox. When the PictureBox appears, click and drag it to a position centered below the Label (Fig. 3.23).

GUI Design Tip

Use PictureBoxes to enhance GUIs with graphics that users cannot change.

Figure 3.23   Inserting and aligning the PictureBox.

2. ***Setting the Image property.*** Click the PictureBox to display its properties in the **Properties** window. Locate the **Image** property, which displays a preview of the image (if one exists). No picture has yet been assigned to the Image property, so its value is (none) (Fig. 3.24). You can use any of several popular image formats, including

   - *PNG (Portable Network Graphics)*
   - *GIF (Graphic Interchange Format)*
   - *JPEG (Joint Photographic Experts Group)*
   - *BMP (Windows Bitmap)*

(cont.)

For this application, you will use a PNG-format image. Creating new images requires image-editing software, such as Jasc® Paint Shop Pro™ (www.jasc.com), Adobe® Photoshop™ (www.adobe.com), Microsoft Picture It!® (photos.msn.com) or Microsoft Paint (provided with Windows). You will not create images in this book; instead, you will be provided with the images used in the tutorials.

Figure 3.24   Image property of the PictureBox.

3. ***Displaying an image.*** In the **Properties** window, click the value of the PictureBox's Image property to display an ellipsis Button (Fig. 3.24). Click the ellipsis Button to display the **Open** dialog (Fig. 3.25). Navigate to the C:\Examples\Tutorial03\CompletedApplication\Welcome directory. Click bug.png and click the **Open** Button. Once the image has been selected, the PictureBox displays the image (Fig. 3.26), and the Image property displays a preview of the image (Fig. 3.27). Notice that the PictureBox does not display the entire image (Fig. 3.26). You will solve this problem in the next step.

Figure 3.25   Open dialog used to browse for a PictureBox image.

Figure 3.26   Newly inserted image.

(cont.)

Figure 3.27 Image previewed in the `Image` property value field.

4. ***Sizing the image to fit the PictureBox.*** We want the image to fit in the `PictureBox`. `PictureBox` property **SizeMode** specifies how an image is displayed in a `PictureBox`. To size the image to fit in the `PictureBox`, change the `SizeMode` property to **StretchImage**, which **scales** the image (changes its width and height) to the size of the `PictureBox`. To resize the `PictureBox`, double click the `Size` property and enter 500, 250. Center the image horizontally by clicking the `PictureBox` and selecting **Format > Center in Form > Horizontally**. The Form should now look like Fig. 3.28.

Newly inserted image

Figure 3.28 `PictureBox` displaying an image.

5. ***Locking the Form controls.*** Often, programmers accidentally alter the size and location of controls on the Form. To ensure that the controls remain in position, use the **Lock Controls** feature. First, select all the controls by using the **Edit > Select All** command. Next, select **Format > Lock Controls** (Fig. 3.29).

Lock Controls option

Figure 3.29 Locking controls by using the **Format** menu.

6. ***Saving your solution.*** Select **File > Save All** to save all the files in the solution. The solution file (`.sln`) contains the name(s) and location(s) of its project(s); the project file (`.vbproj`) contains the names and locations of all the files in the project. You should save your solution files to your `C:\Sim-plyVB` directory frequently.

(cont.)   7. ***Running your Welcome application.*** The text **Microsoft Visual Basic .NET [design]** in the IDE's title bar (Fig. 3.6) indicates that we have been working in the IDE **design mode**. (That is, the application being created is not executing.) While in design mode, programmers have access to all the IDE windows (for example, **Toolbox**, **Properties**, etc.), menus and toolbars. In **run mode**, the application is executing, and programmers can interact with fewer IDE features. Features that are not available are disabled ("grayed out"). Select **Debug > Start** to execute the application. Figure 3.30 shows the IDE in run mode. Note that many toolbar icons and menus are disabled.

IDE title bar displaying **[run]** ——

Form (with grid) ——

Running application ——

Figure 3.30   IDE in run mode, with the application running in the foreground.

8. ***Terminating execution and closing the application.*** To terminate the application, click the running application's close box, ⊠. This action terminates execution and returns the IDE to design mode.

SELF-REVIEW   1. The Form's _____ property specifies the text that is displayed in the Form's title bar.

    a) `Title`   b) `Text`

    c) `(Name)`   d) `Name`

    2. Property _____ specifies how text is aligned within a `Label`'s boundaries.

    a) `Alignment`   b) `AlignText`

    c) `Align`   d) `TextAlign`

Answers: 1) b. 2) d.

3.3 Objects used in the Welcome Application

In Tutorials 1 and 2, you learned that controls are reusable software components called objects. The **Welcome** application used a `Form` object, a `Label` object and a `PictureBox` object to create a GUI that displayed text and an image. Each of these objects is an instance of a class defined in the .NET Framework Class Library (FCL). The `Form` object was created by the Visual Studio .NET IDE. The `Label` and `PictureBox` objects were created when you double clicked their respective icons in the **Toolbox**.

We used the **Properties** window to set the properties (attributes) for each object. Recall that the ComboBox—also called the component object box—at the top of the **Properties** window displays the names and class types of Form and control objects (Fig. 3.31). In Fig. 3.32, the component object box displays the name (Form1) and class type (Form) of the Form object. In the FCL, classes are organized by functionality into directory-like entities called **namespaces**. The class types used in this application have namespace System.Windows.Forms. This namespace contains control classes and the Form class. You will be introduced to additional namespaces in later tutorials. Close the solution by selecting **File > Close Solution**.

Figure 3.31   Component object box expanded to show the **Welcome** application's objects.

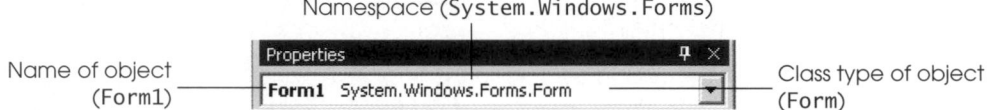

Figure 3.32   The name and class type of an object are displayed in the **Properties** window's component object box.

---

1. The ComboBox at the top of the **Properties** window is the _____.

   a) component object box   b) control box

   c) control object box   d) component box

2. The Framework Class Library (FCL) organizes classes into _____.

   a) collections   b) name boxes

   c) namespaces   d) class spaces

Answers: 1) a. 2) c.

3.4 Wrap-Up

This tutorial introduced you to visual programming in Visual Basic .NET. You learned that visual programming helps you to design and create the graphical user interface portions of applications quickly and easily, by dragging and dropping controls onto Forms.

In creating your **Welcome** application, you used the **Properties** window to set the Form's title-bar text, size (width and height) and background color using properties Text, Size and BackColor, respectively. You learned that Labels are controls that display text and that PictureBoxes are controls that display images. You displayed text in a Label by setting its Text and TextAlign properties, and you displayed an image by setting a PictureBox control's Image and SizeMode properties.

You also examined the relationship between controls and classes. You learned that FCL classes are grouped into directory-like entities called namespaces and that controls are instances (objects) of FCL classes. The FCL classes used in this tutorial (Form, Label and PictureBox) belong to namespace System.Windows.Forms. You used the **Properties** window's component object box to view an object's name, namespace and class type.

In the next tutorial, you continue learning visual programming. In particular, you will create an application with controls that are designed to accept user input.

SKILLS SUMMARY

Creating GUIs Quickly and Efficiently
- Use visual programming techniques.

Placing a Control on the Form
- Double click the control in the **Toolbox** to place the control in the upper-left corner of the Form, or drag the control from the **Toolbox** onto the Form.

Aligning Controls
- Use the Form's background grid for alignment. You also can use the **Format** menu's commands.

Resizing the Form or Control with Sizing Handles
- Click and drag one of the object's enabled sizing handles.

Setting the Dimensions of the Form or Control by Using Property Size
- Enter the height and width of the Form or control in the Size field.

Setting the Width and Height of the Form or Control
- Enter values in the Width and Height property fields (or use the Size property field).

Setting the Form's Background Color
- Set the Form's BackColor property.

Adding a Label Control to the Form
- Double click the Label control in the **Toolbox** to place the control in the upper-left corner of the Form.

Setting a Label's Text Property
- Set the Label's Text property.

Setting a Label's Font Property
- Click the value of the Font property, which causes an ellipsis Button to appear next to the value. When the ellipsis Button is clicked, the **Font** dialog is displayed; it allows programmers to change the font name, style and size of the Label's text.

Aligning Text in a Label
- Use the Label's TextAlign property.

Adding an Image to the Form
- Use a PictureBox control to display the image. Click the ellipsis Button next to the PictureBox Image property's value to browse for an image to insert.
- Scale the image to the size of the PictureBox by setting property SizeMode to value StretchImage.

Displaying a Form or Control's Properties in the Properties Window
- Click the Form or a control on the Form.

KEY TERMS

BackColor property—Property of a Form or control that specifies its background color.

design mode—IDE mode that allows you to create applications using Visual Studio .NET's windows, toolbars and menu bar.

Font property—Property that specifies the font name, style and size of any displayed text in the Form or one of its controls.

Height property—This property, a member of property Size, indicates the height of the Form or one of its controls in pixels.

Image property—Property that indicates the file name of the image displayed in a PictureBox.

Label—Control that displays text the user cannot modify.

namespace—Classes in the FCL are organized by functionality into these directory-like entities.

palette—A set of colors.

PictureBox—Control that displays an image.

pixel—A tiny point on your computer screen that displays a color.

RGB value—The amount of red, green and blue needed to create a color.

run mode—IDE mode indicating that the application is executing.

Size property—Property that specifies the height and width, in pixels, of the Form or one of its controls.

SizeMode property—Property that specifies how an image is displayed in a PictureBox.

sizing handle—Square that, when enabled, can be used to resize the Form or one of its controls.

StretchImage—Value of PictureBox property SizeMode that scales an image to fill the PictureBox.

Text property—Property that specifies the text displayed by the Form or a Label.

TextAlign property—Property that specifies how text is aligned within a Label.

Web-safe colors—Colors that display the same on different computers.

Width property—This setting, a member of property Size, indicates the width of the Form or one of its controls, in pixels.

GUI DESIGN GUIDELINES

Overall Design

- Use colors in your applications, but not to the point of distracting the user.

Forms

- Choose short and descriptive Form titles. Capitalize words that are not articles, prepositions or conjunctions. Do not use punctuation.
- Use Tahoma font to improve readability for controls that display text.

Labels

- Use Labels to display text that users cannot change.
- Ensure that all Label controls are large enough to display their text.

PictureBoxes

- Use PictureBoxes to enhance GUIs with graphics that users cannot change.
- Images should fit inside their PictureBoxes. This can be achieved by setting PictureBox property SizeMode to StretchImage.

CONTROLS, EVENTS, PROPERTIES & METHODS

Label   A Label   This control displays on the Form text that the user cannot modify.

- *In action*

Welcome to Visual Basic .NET!

- *Properties*

  Text—This property specifies the text displayed on the Label.

  Font—This property specifies the font name, style and size of the text displayed in the Label.

  TextAlign—This property determines how the text is aligned within the Label.

PictureBox   PictureBox   This control displays an image on the Form.

- *In action*

■ *Properties*

`Image`—This property specifies the file path of the image.
`SizeMode`—This property specifies the image that is displayed in the `PictureBox`.
`Size`—This property specifies the height and width (in pixels) of the `PictureBox`.

MULTIPLE-CHOICE QUESTIONS

3.1 Property _____ determines the Form's background color.

    a) `BackColor`   b) `BackgroundColor`

    c) `RGB`   d) `Color`

3.2 To save all the solution's files, select _____.

    a) **Save > Solution > Save Files**   b) **File > Save**

    c) **File > Save All**   d) **File > Save As...**

3.3 When the ellipsis `Button` to the right of the **Font** property value is clicked, the _____ is displayed.

    a) **Font Property** dialog   b) **New Font** dialog

    c) **Font Settings** dialog   d) **Font** dialog

3.4 `PictureBox` property _____ contains a preview of the image displayed in the `PictureBox`.

    a) `Picture`   b) `ImageName`

    c) `Image`   d) `PictureName`

3.5 The _____ tab allows you to create your own color.

    a) **Custom**   b) **Web**

    c) **System**   d) **User**

3.6 The `PictureBox` class has namespace _____.

    a) `System.Windows.Forms`   b) `System.Form.Form`

    c) `System.Form.Font`   d) `System.Form.Control`

3.7 A `Label` control displays the text specified by property _____.

    a) `Caption`   b) `Data`

    c) `Text`   d) `Name`

3.8 In _____ mode, the application is executing.

    a) start   b) run

    c) break   d) design

3.9 The _____ command prevents programmers from accidentally altering the size and location of the Form's controls.

    a) **Lock Controls**   b) **Anchor Controls**

    c) **Lock**   d) **Bind Controls**

3.10 Pixels are _____.

    a) picture elements   b) controls in the **Toolbox**

    c) a set of fonts   d) a set of colors on the **Web** tab

---

EXERCISES

For Exercises 3.11–3.16, you are asked to create the GUI shown in each exercise. You will use the visual programming techniques presented in this tutorial to create a variety of GUIs. Because you are creating only GUIs, your applications will not be fully operational. For example, the **Calculator** *GUI in Exercise 3.11 will not behave like a calculator when its* `Buttons` *are clicked. You will learn how to make your applications fully operational in later tutorials. Create each application as a separate project.*

3.11 *(Calculator GUI)* Create the GUI for the calculator shown in Fig. 3.33.

TextBox

Panel (contains 11 Buttons for the numeric keys)

Subtraction Button
Panel (contains 2 Buttons)
Panel (contains 6 Buttons)
Button

Decimal point Button

Figure 3.33 Calculator GUI.

a) *Renaming the Form file.* Name the Form file Calculator.vb.

b) *Manipulating the Form's properties.* Change the Size property of the Form to 272, 192. Change the Text property of the Form to Calculator. Change the Font property to Tahoma.

c) *Adding a TextBox to the Form.* Add a TextBox control by double clicking it in the **Toolbox**. A TextBox control is used to enter input into applications. Set the TextBox's Text property in the **Properties** window to 0. Change the Size property to 240, 21. Set the TextAlign property to Right; this right aligns text displayed in the TextBox. Finally, set the TextBox's Location property to 8, 16.

d) *Adding the first Panel to the Form.* Panel controls are used to group other controls. Double click the Panel icon (☐ Panel) in the **Toolbox** to add a Panel to the Form. Change the Panel's BorderStyle property to Fixed3D to make the inside of the Panel appear recessed. Change the Size property to 88, 112. Finally, set the Location property to 8, 48. This Panel contains the calculator's numeric keys.

e) *Adding the second Panel to the Form.* Click the Form. Double click the Panel icon in the **Toolbox** to add another Panel to the Form. Change the Panel's BorderStyle property to Fixed3D. Change the Size property to 72, 112. Finally, set the Location property to 112, 48. This Panel contains the calculator's operator keys.

f) *Adding the third (and last) Panel to the Form.* Click the Form. Double click the Panel icon in the **Toolbox** to add another Panel to the Form. Change the Panel's BorderStyle property to Fixed3D. Change the Size property to 48, 72. Finally, set the Location property to 200, 48. This Panel contains the calculator's **C** (clear) and **C/A** (clear all) keys.

g) *Adding Buttons to the Form.* There are 20 Buttons on the calculator. To add a Button to a Panel, double click the Button control (abl Button) in the **Toolbox**. Then add the Button to the Panel by dragging and dropping it on the Panel. Change the Text property of each Button to the calculator key it represents. The value you enter in the Text property will appear on the face of the Button. Finally, resize the Buttons, using their Size properties. Each Button labeled 0–9, x, /, -, = and . should have a size of 24, 24. The **00** and **OFF** Buttons have size 48, 24. The **+** Button is sized 24, 64. The **C** (clear) and **C/A** (clear all) Buttons are sized 32, 24.

3.12 *(Alarm Clock GUI)* Create the GUI for the alarm clock in Fig. 3.34.

RadioButton

GroupBox

Buttons

Label

Figure 3.34 Alarm Clock GUI.

a) *Renaming the Form file.* Name the Form file AlarmClock.vb.

b) *Manipulating the Form's properties.* Change the Size property of the Form to 256, 176. Change the Text property of the Form to Alarm Clock. Change the Font property to Tahoma.

c) *Adding Buttons to the Form.* Add six Buttons to the Form. Change the Text property of each Button to the appropriate text. Change the Size properties of the **Hour**, **Minute** and **Second** Buttons to 56, 23. The **ON** and **OFF** Buttons get size 40, 23. The **Timer** Button gets size 48, 32. Align the Buttons as shown in Fig. 3.34.

d) *Adding a Label to the Form.* Add a Label to the Form. Change the Text property to **Snooze**. Set its Size to 248, 23. Set the Label's TextAlign property to Middle-Center. Finally, to draw a border around the edge of the **Snooze** Label, change the BorderStyle property of the **Snooze** Label to FixedSingle.

e) *Adding a GroupBox to the Form.* GroupBoxes are like Panels, except that GroupBoxes can display a title. To add a GroupBox to the Form, double click the GroupBox control ([xy] GroupBox) in the **Toolbox**. Change the Text property to **AM/PM**, and set the Size property to 72, 72. To place the GroupBox in the correct location on the Form, set the Location property to 104, 38.

f) *Adding AM/PM RadioButtons to the GroupBox.* Add two RadioButtons to the Form by dragging the RadioButton control (⊙ RadioButton) in the **Toolbox** and dropping it onto the GroupBox twice. Change the Text property of one RadioButton to AM and the other to PM. Then place the RadioButtons as shown in Fig. 3.34 by setting the Location of the **AM** RadioButton to 16, 16 and that of the **PM** RadioButton to 16, 40. Set their Size properties to 48, 24.

g) *Adding the time Label to the Form.* Add a Label to the Form and change its Text property to 00:00:00. Change the BorderStyle property to Fixed3D and the Back-Color to Black. Set the Size property to 64, 23. Use the Font property to make the time bold. Change the ForeColor to Silver (located in the **Web** tab) to make the time stand out against the black background. Set TextAlign to MiddleCenter to center the text in the Label. Position the Label as shown in Fig. 3.34.

3.13 *(Microwave Oven GUI)* Create the GUI for the microwave oven shown in Fig. 3.35.

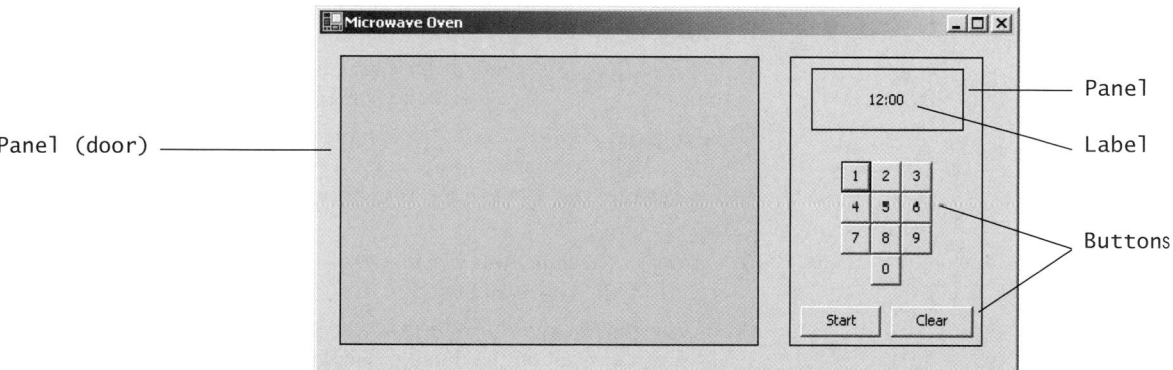

Figure 3.35 Microwave Oven GUI.

a) *Renaming the Form file.* Name the Form file Microwave.vb.

b) *Manipulating the Form's properties.* Change the Size property of the Form to 552, 288. Change the Text property of the Form to Microwave Oven. Change the Font property to Tahoma.

c) *Adding the microwave oven door.* Add a Panel to the Form by double clicking the Panel (☐ Panel) in the **Toolbox**. Select the Panel and change the BackColor property to Silver (located in the **Web** tab) in the **Properties** window. Then change the Size to 328, 224. Next, change the BorderStyle property to FixedSingle.

d) *Adding another Panel.* Add another Panel and change its Size to 152, 224 and its BorderStyle to FixedSingle. Place the Panel to the right of the door Panel, as shown in Fig. 3.35.

e) *Adding the microwave oven clock.* Add a Label to the right Panel by clicking the Label in the **Toolbox** once, then clicking once inside the right Panel. Change the

Label's Text to 12:00, BorderStyle to FixedSingle and Size to 120, 48. Change TextAlign to MiddleCenter. Place the clock as shown in Fig. 3.35.

f) *Adding a keypad to the microwave oven.* Place a Button in the right Panel by clicking the Button control in the Toolbox once, then clicking inside the Panel. Change the Text to 1 and the Size to 24, 24. Repeat this process for nine more Buttons, changing the Text property in each to the next number in the keypad. Then add the **Start** and **Clear** Buttons, each of Size 64, 24. Do not forget to set the Text properties for each of these Buttons. Finally, arrange the Buttons as shown in Fig. 3.35. The **1** Button is located at 40, 80 and the **Start** Button is located at 8, 192.

3.14 *(Cell Phone GUI)* Create the GUI for the cell phone shown in Fig. 3.36.

Figure 3.36 Cell **Phone** GUI.

a) *Renaming the Form file.* Name the Form file Phone.vb.

b) *Manipulating the Form's properties.* Change the Form's Text property to Phone and the Size to 160, 488. Change the Font property to Tahoma.

c) *Adding the display Label.* Add a Label to the Form. Change its BackColor to Aqua (in the **Web** tab palette), the Text to Welcome to Deitel Mobile Phone! and the Size to 136, 184. Change the TextAlign property to MiddleCenter. Then place the Label as shown in Fig. 3.36.

d) *Adding the keypad Panel.* Add a Panel to the Form. Change its BorderStyle property to FixedSingle and its Size to 104, 136.

e) *Adding the keypad Buttons.* Add the keypad Buttons to the Form (12 Buttons in all). Each Button on the number pad should be of Size 24, 24 and should be placed in the Panel. Change the Text property of each Button such that numbers 0–9, the pound (#) and the star (*) keys are represented. Then add the final two Buttons such that the Text property for one is Talk and the other is End. Change the Size of each Button to 24, 80, and notice how the small Size causes the Text to align vertically. Also change each Button's Font size to 12 points.

f) *Placing the controls.* Arrange all the controls so that your GUI looks like Fig. 3.36.

3.15 *(Vending Machine GUI)* Create the GUI for the vending machine in Fig. 3.37.

a) *Renaming the Form file.* Name the Form file VendingMachine.vb.

b) *Manipulating the Form's properties.* Set the Text property of the Form to Vending Machine and the Size to 560, 488. Change the Font property to Tahoma.

c) *Adding the food selection Panel.* Add a Panel to the Form, and change its Size to 312, 344 and BorderStyle to Fixed3D. Add a PictureBox to the Panel, and change its Size to 50, 50. Then set the Image property by clicking the ellipsis Button and choosing a file from the C:\Examples\Tutorial03\ExerciseImages\VendingMachine folder. Repeat this process for 11 more PictureBoxes.

Figure 3.37 Vending Machine GUI.

d) *Adding Labels for each vending item.* Add a Label under each PictureBox. Change the Text property of the Label to A1, the TextAlign property to TopCenter and the Size to 56, 16. Place the Label so that it is located as in Fig. 3.37. Repeat this process for A2 through C4 (11 Labels).

e) *Creating the vending machine door (as a Button).* Add a Button to the Form by dragging the Button control in the **Toolbox** and dropping it below the Panel. Change the Button's Text property to PUSH, its Font Size to 36 and its Size to 312, 56. Then place the Button on the Form as shown in Fig. 3.37.

f) *Adding the selection display Label.* Add a Label to the Form, and change the Text property to B2, BorderStyle to FixedSingle, Font Size to 36, TextAlign to MiddleCenter and Size to 160, 72.

g) *Grouping the input Buttons.* Add a GroupBox below the Label, and change the Text property to Please make selection and the Size to 160, 136.

h) *Adding the input Buttons.* Finally, add Buttons to the GroupBox. For the seven Buttons, change the Size property to 24, 24. Then change the Text property of the Buttons such that each Button has one of the values A, B, C, 1, 2, 3 or 4, as shown in Fig. 3.37. When you are done, move the controls on the Form so that they are aligned as shown in the figure.

Programming Challenge ▶   **3.16** *(Radio GUI)* Create the GUI for the radio in Fig. 3.38. [*Note:* All colors used in this exercises are from the **Web** palette.]

Figure 3.38 Radio GUI.

In this exercise, you will create this GUI on your own. Feel free to experiment with different control properties. For the image in the PictureBox, use the file (MusicNote.gif) found at C:\Examples\Tutorial03\ExerciseImages\Radio.

a) *Renaming the Form file.* Name the Form file Radio.vb.

b) *Manipulating the Form's properties.* Change the Form's Text property to Radio and the Size to 576, 240. Change the Font property to Tahoma. Set BackColor to Peach-Puff.

c) *Adding the Pre-set Stations GroupBox and Buttons.* Add a GroupBox to the Form. Set its Size to 232, 64, its Text to Pre-set Stations, its ForeColor to Black and its BackColor to RosyBrown. Change its Font to bold. Finally, set its Location to 24, 16. Add six Buttons to the GroupBox. Set each BackColor to PeachPuff and each Size to 24, 23. Change the Buttons' Text properties to 1, 2, 3, 4, 5, 6, respectively.

d) *Adding the Speakers GroupBox and CheckBoxes.* Add a GroupBox to the Form. Set its Size to 160, 72, its Text to Speakers and its ForeColor to Black. Set its Location to 280, 16. Add two CheckBoxes to the Form. Set each CheckBox's Size to 56, 24. Set the Text properties for the CheckBoxes to Rear and Front.

e) *Adding the Power On/Off Button.* Add a Button to the Form. Set its Text to Power On/Off, its BackColor to RosyBrown, its ForeColor to Black and its Size to 72, 64. Change its Font style to Bold.

f) *Adding the Volume Control GroupBox, the Mute CheckBox and the Volume Track-Bar.* Add a GroupBox to the Form. Set its Text to Volume Control, its BackColor to RosyBrown, its ForeColor to Black and its Size to 200, 80. Set its Font style to Bold. Add a CheckBox to the GroupBox. Set its Text to Mute and its Size to 56, 24. Add a TrackBar to the GroupBox.

g) *Adding the Tuning GroupBox, the radio station Label and the AM/FM RadioButtons.* Add a GroupBox to the Form. Set its Text to Tuning, its ForeColor to Black and its BackColor to RosyBrown. Set its Font style to Bold and its Size to 216, 80. Add a Label to the Form. Set its BackColor to PeachPuff, its ForeColor to Black, its BorderStyle to FixedSingle, its Font style to Bold, its TextAlign to Middle-Center and its Size to 56, 23. Set its Text to 92.9. Place the Label as shown in the figure. Add two RadioButtons to the GroupBox. Change the BackColor to Peach-Puff and change the Size to 40, 24. Set one's Text to AM and the other's Text to FM.

h) *Adding the image.* Add a PictureBox to the Form. Set its BackColor to Transparent, its SizeMode to StretchImage and its Size to 56, 72. Set its Image property to C:\Examples\Tutorial03\ExerciseImages\Radio\MusicNote.gif.

Objectives

In this tutorial, you will learn to:
- Visually program, using GUI design guidelines.
- Rename the Form and set the Form as the startup object.
- Add Labels, TextBoxes and a Button to the Form.
- Use the TextAlign and BorderStyle properties for Labels.

Outline

Designing the Inventory Application

Introducing TextBoxes and Buttons

This tutorial introduces you to the fundamentals of visual programming. You will design the graphical user interface for a simple inventory application. Through each set of steps, you will enhance the application's user interface by adding controls. You will design a Form on which you place Labels, TextBoxes and a Button. You will learn new properties for Labels and TextBoxes, and you will learn how to add a Button to the Form. At the end of the tutorial, you will find a list of new GUI design guidelines to help you create appealing and easy-to-use graphical user interfaces.

4.1 Test-Driving the Inventory Application

In this tutorial, you will create an inventory application that calculates the number of textbooks received by a college bookstore. This application must meet the following requirements:

Application Requirements

A college bookstore receives cartons of textbooks. In each shipment, each carton contains the same number of textbooks. The inventory manager wants to use a computer to calculate the total number of textbooks arriving at the bookstore for each shipment quickly, from the number of cartons and the number of textbooks in each carton. The inventory manager will enter the number of cartons received and the fixed number of textbooks in each carton for each shipment; then the application will calculate the total number of textbooks in a shipment.

This application performs a simple calculation. The user (the inventory manager) inputs into TextBoxes the number of cartons and number of items in each carton. The user then clicks a Button, which causes the application to multiply the two numbers and display the result—the total number of textbooks received. You begin by test-driving the application.

1. ***Opening the application.*** Open the C:\Examples\Tutorial04\Com-pletedApplication\Inventory folder to locate the Inventory application. Double click Inventory.sln to open the application in Visual Studio .NET. Depending on your system configuration, you may not see the .sln file name extension. In this case, double click the file named Inventory that contains a solution file icon, .

2. ***Running the application.*** Select **Debug > Start** to execute the application. The Form shown in Fig. 4.1 appears.

TextBoxes —

Label

Button

Figure 4.1 Inventory application Form with default data displayed by the application.

Notice that there are two controls that you did not use in the **Welcome** application—the TextBox and Button controls. A **TextBox** is a control that the user can enter data into from the keyboard and that can display data to the user. A **Button** is a control that allows the application to perform an action when clicked.

3. ***Entering quantities in the application.*** Some controls (such as TextBoxes) are not used to display descriptive text for other controls; therefore, we refer to these controls by using the Labels that identify them. For example, we will refer to the TextBox to the right of the **Cartons per shipment:** Label as the **Cartons per shipment:** TextBox. Enter 3 in the **Cartons per shipment:** TextBox. Enter 15 in the **Items per carton:** TextBox. Figure 4.2 shows the Form after these values have been entered.

Figure 4.2 Inventory application with new quantities entered.

4. ***Calculating the total number of items received.*** Click the **Calculate Total** Button. This causes the application to multiply the two numbers you entered and to display the result (45) in the Label to the right of **Total:** (Fig. 4.3).

Result of calculation

Figure 4.3 Result of clicking the **Calculate Total** Button in the **Inventory** application.

5. ***Terminating the application.*** Click the running application's close box to terminate the application.

6. ***Closing the solution.*** Select **File > Close Solution**.

4.2 Constructing the Inventory Application

Now that you have test-driven the completed application, you will begin creating your own version of the application. In the box, *Creating a New Application*, you will create a new project that contains the Form on which you will place the controls required for the **Inventory** application. Then, you will save the solution containing the Form to your work folder, C:\SimplyVB (ensuring that you will know which directory contains your solution if you take a break from building the application). Finally, the initial steps conclude with instructions for renaming the Form.

Creating a New Application

1. ***Creating the new project.*** To create a Windows application, select **File > New > Project…**, to display the **New Project** dialog (Fig. 4.4). Click the **Visual Basic Projects** folder in the **Project Types:** pane to retrieve the list of Visual Basic .NET project types in the **Templates:** pane. From this list, select **Windows Application**. Type Inventory in the **Name:** Textbox, and leave the dialog open.

Project Types: pane with
Visual Basic Projects folder
selected
(your folder list might differ)

Name: TextBox

Location: TextBox

Templates:
pane with
**Windows
Application**
selected

Browse…
Button

Figure 4.4 **New Project** dialog for creating new applications.

2. ***Saving the project to your work folder.*** To save the project to your work folder, click the **Browse…** Button (Fig. 4.4) and the **Project Location** dialog appears (Fig. 4.5). Because you already created the SimplyVB folder, navigate to the C:\SimplyVB directory. Click **Open** to select the folder and dismiss the dialog. The selected folder will then appear in the **Location:** TextBox.

3. ***Viewing the Form.*** Click the **OK** Button (Fig. 4.4) to close the **New Project** dialog. The IDE will then load the new application, containing a Form named **Form1** (Fig. 4.6). If the Form does not appear as in Fig. 4.6, select **View > Designer**. Then click the Form in the IDE to select it.

(cont.)

Figure 4.5 **Project Location** dialog used to specify the folder in which the project files reside.

Work folder

Form title bar (for **Form1**)

Form file name (**Form1.vb**)

Form

Figure 4.6 New Windows application (**Form1**) in Visual Studio .NET.

(cont.)

4. ***Renaming the Form file.*** It is a good practice to change the Form file name to a name more meaningful for your application. To change the Form file name (Fig. 4.7), click its name (Form1.vb) in the **Solution Explorer**. Then select File Name in the **Properties** window, and type Inventory.vb in the field to the right. Press the *Enter* key to update the file name. Unless otherwise noted, you need to press the *Enter* key for changes to take effect.

Form's file name after property change

File Name property

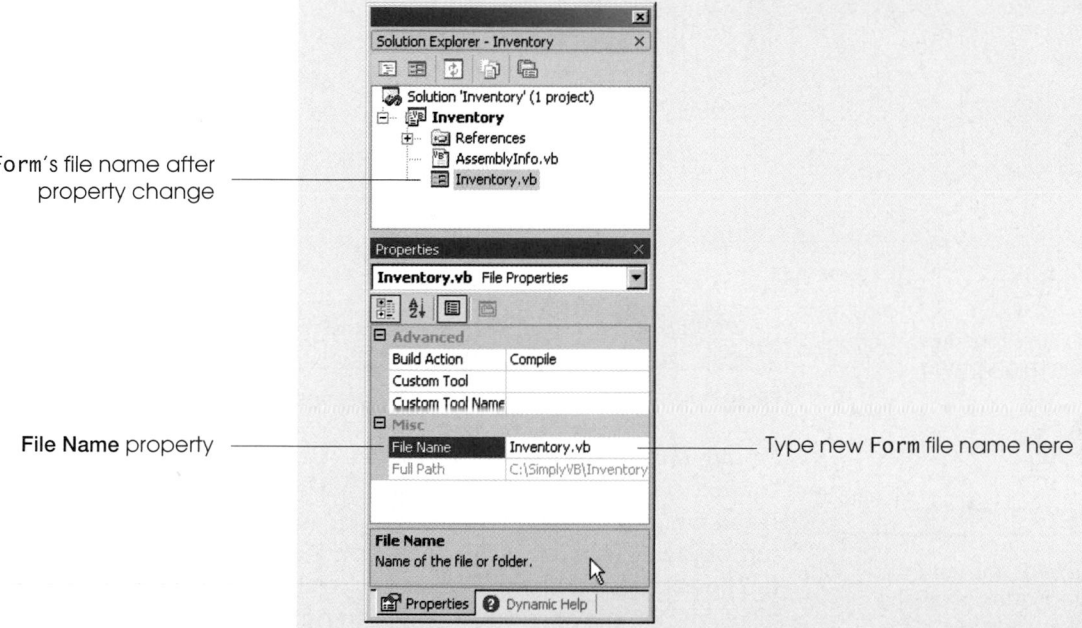

Type new Form file name here

Figure 4.7 Renaming a file in the **Solution Explorer** and **Properties** windows.

5. ***Renaming the Form object.*** Each Form object needs a unique and meaningful name for easy identification. In Visual Studio .NET, you set the Form's name by using the **Name** property. By default, the Visual Studio .NET IDE names the Form **Form1**. Click the Form in the Windows Form Designer. In the **Properties** window, click the field to the right of the Name property, listed as (Name). Type FrmInventory, and press *Enter* to update the name.

6. ***Saving the project.*** Select **File > Save All** to save all the solution's files. Saving your work often will prevent losing changes to the application.

Good Programming Practice

Change the Form name to a unique and meaningful name for easy identification.

Good Programming Practice

Use standard prefixes for names of objects (controls and Forms) so that you can easily tell them apart. Prefix Form names with Frm. Capitalize the first letter of the Form name because Form is a class. Objects (such as controls) should be prefixed with lowercase letters.

When the application executes, it should begin by displaying the FrmInventory Form. For this to happen, you must set FrmInventory as the **startup object**. The startup object defines which object (in this case, the Form) loads when the program begins to run. Normally, the startup object is set as Form1, the default name for a new Form. (In the last tutorial, you did not rename the Form, so the startup object did not need to be changed.) Because you have renamed your Form, use the box, *Setting the Form as the Startup Object,* to set the startup object to the Form's new name.

Setting the *Form* as the Startup Object

1. ***Selecting the project name in the Solution Explorer.*** Right click the project name (**Inventory**) in the **Solution Explorer**, causing a **context menu** (Fig. 4.8) to appear.

2. ***Selecting Properties from the context menu.*** Select the **Properties** menu item (Fig. 4.8).

(cont.)

You also can click the **Properties** icon to access the project's properties

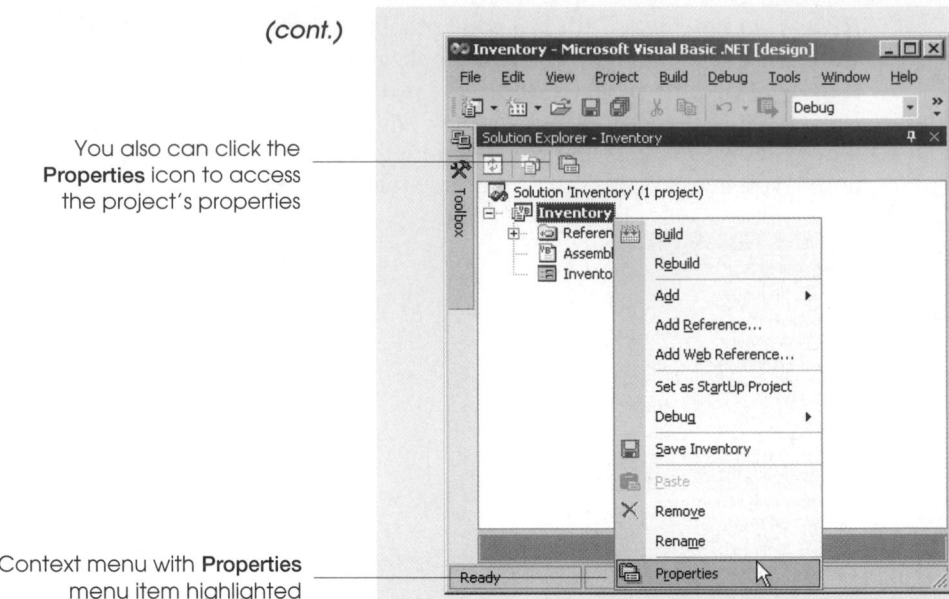

Context menu with **Properties** menu item highlighted

Figure 4.8 Context menu with **Properties** menu item highlighted.

3. *Setting the Form as the startup object.* After you select **Properties** from the context menu, the **Inventory Property Pages** dialog (Fig. 4.9) will appear. If it is not selected already, select FrmInventory as the value in the **Startup object:** ComboBox. Click the **Apply** Button to set the Form as the startup object. Then click the **OK** Button to close the dialog. The Form will now display when the application begins to run.

Error-Prevention Tip

You should update the startup object immediately after changing the name of your **Form** to avoid the **'Sub Main' not found** error when the program attempts to run.

Startup object defines which **Form** executes (select FrmInventory)

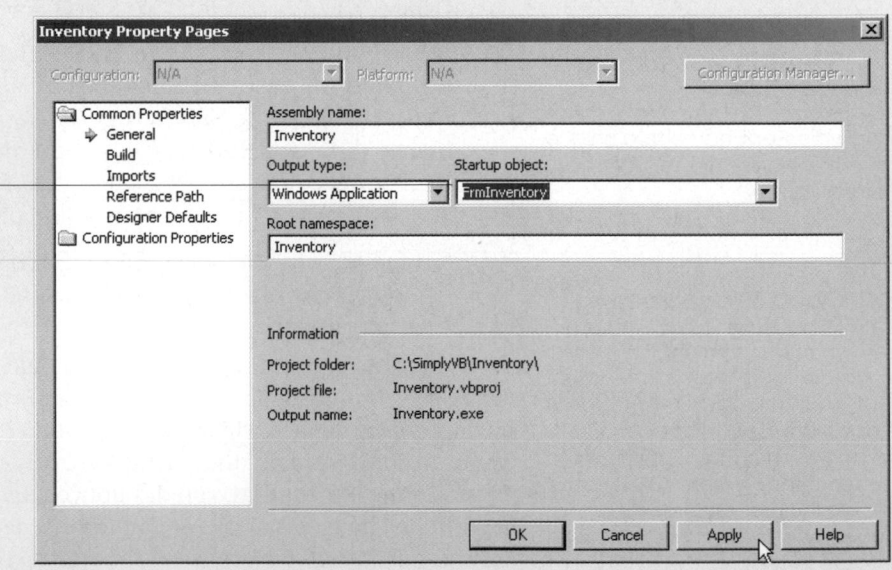

Figure 4.9 Inventory Property Pages dialog.

4. *Saving the project.* Select **File > Save All** to save all of the solution's files.

In the box, *Customizing the Form*, you learn how to modify your Form by setting its font. As in all our examples, you should set the Form's font to Tahoma, the Microsoft-recommended font for GUIs. Changing the Form's font to Tahoma ensures that controls added to the Form use the Tahoma font. You will also learn how to change the Form's title and size. Although you already changed the file name to Inventory.vb, you still need to change the title bar text to help users identify

 GUI Design Tip

Change the Form's font to Tahoma to be consistent with Microsoft's recommended font for Windows.

the Form's purpose. Changing the Form's size to be more appropriate for its content improves its appearance.

Customizing the Form

1. ***Setting the Form's font.*** In the previous tutorial, you used the **Font** dialog to change the font. You will now use the **Properties** window to change the Form's font. Select the Form in the Windows Form Designer. If the **Properties** window is not already open, click the properties icon in the IDE toolbar or select **View > Properties Window**. To change the Form's font to Tahoma, click the plus box ⊞ to the left of the **Font** property in the **Properties** window (Fig. 4.10). This causes other properties related to the Form's Font to be displayed. In the list that appears, select the font's Name property, and click the down arrow to the right of property value. In the list that appears, select Tahoma.

    You will notice that several properties, such as Font, have a plus box ⊞ next to the property name to indicate that there are additional properties available for this node. For example, the Font Name, Size and Bold properties of a Font each have their own listings in the **Properties** window when you click the plus box.

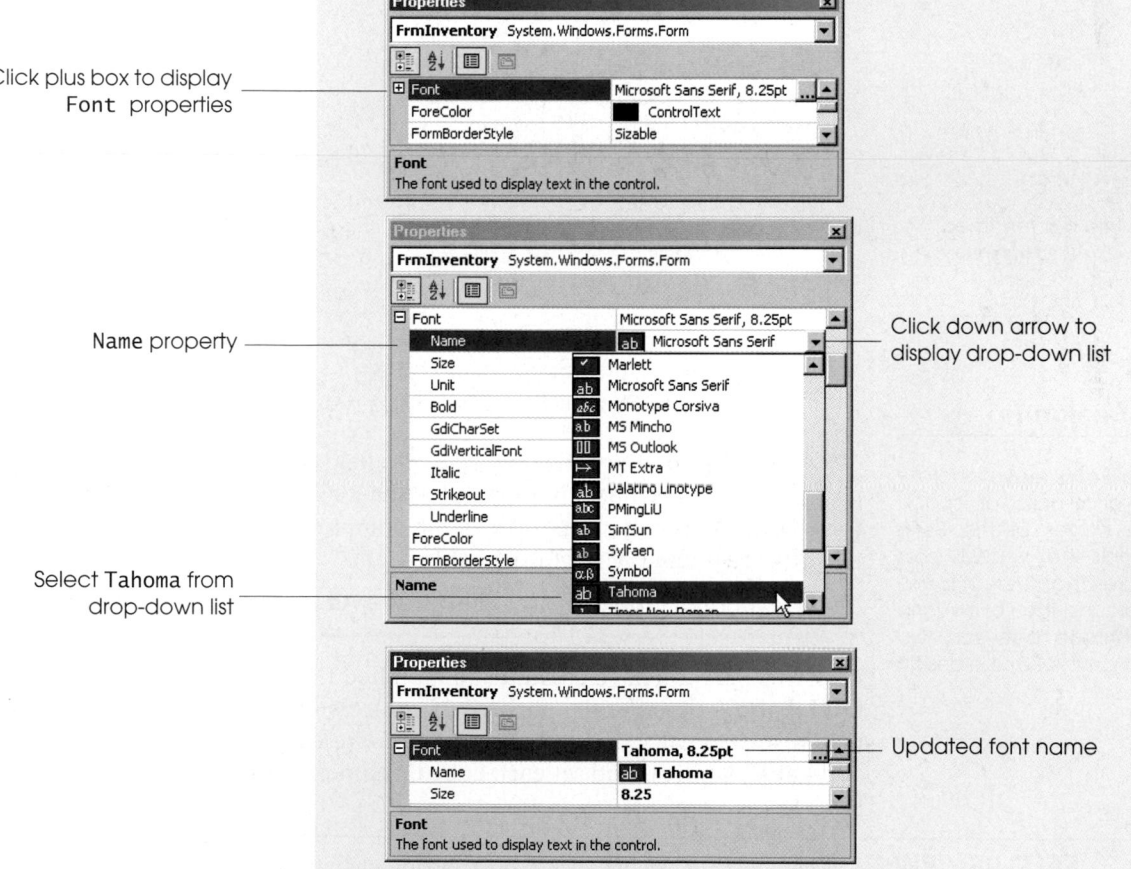

Click plus box to display
Font properties

Name property

Click down arrow to
display drop-down list

Select Tahoma from
drop-down list

Updated font name

Figure 4.10 Setting a Form's font to Tahoma.

(cont.)

GUI Design Tip

Changing the Form's title allows users to identify the application's purpose.

GUI Design Tip

Form titles should use book-title capitalization.

2. ***Setting the text in the Form's title bar.*** The text in the Form's title bar is determined by the Form's **Text** property. To display the Form's properties in the **Properties** window, click the Form in the Windows Form Designer. Double click the field to the right of the Text property in the **Properties** window and type Inventory (Fig. 4.11). Form titles should use book-title capitalization. **Book-title capitalization** is a style that capitalizes the first letter of each significant word in the text and does not end with any punctuation (for example, *Capitalization in a Book Title*). The updated title bar is shown in Fig. 4.12.

Text property ——————

—————— New value for **Text** property

Figure 4.11   Setting the Text property of a Form.

Title bar renamed to **Inventory** ——————

One grid unit ——————

Figure 4.12   Resized Form displaying new title bar text.

GUI Design Tip

When sizing a Form, leave approximately two grid units of space between the edges of the Form and the controls that you will later add. This ensures that there is a uniform border around the Form. A grid unit is the distance between two adjacent dots on the Form in design view.

3. ***Resizing the Form.*** Double click the field to the right of the Size property in the **Properties** window, and enter 296, 112 (Fig. 4.11). Notice that the Form is now the same size as the completed application you test-drove at the beginning of the tutorial (Fig. 4.12).

4. ***Saving the project.*** Select **File > Save All** to save all the solution's files.

Now that you have created and modified the Form, you will add controls to the GUI. Labels describe the purpose of controls on the Form and can be used to display results of calculations. In the box, *Adding Labels to the Form*, you learn how to add Label controls and set each Label's name, text and position on the Form.

SELF-REVIEW

1. The _____ defines which object loads when the application runs.

   a) object box
   c) startup object

   b) load object
   d) context menu

2. When you right click the project name in the **Solution Explorer**, a _____ appears.

   a) context menu
   c) startup object

   b) **Properties** menu
   d) **New Project** dialog

Answers: 1) c. 2) a.

4.3 Adding Labels to the Inventory Application

Although you might not have noticed it, there are four Labels in this application. You can easily recognize three of the Labels from the application you designed in Tutorial 3. The fourth Label, however, has a border and contains no text until the user clicks the **Calculate Total** Button (Fig. 4.13). As the control's name indicates, Labels are often used to identify other controls on the Form. **Descriptive Labels** help the user understand each control's purpose and **output Labels** are used to display program output.

Descriptive Labels

Descriptive Label

Output Label (recessed appearance)

Figure 4.13 Labels used in the **Inventory** application.

Adding Labels to the Form

1. *Adding a Label control to the Form.* Click the **Windows Forms** tab in the **Toolbox**. Then, double click the **Label** control in the **Toolbox** to place a Label on the Form (Fig. 4.14).

Location value 0, 0

Label control

Figure 4.14 Adding a Label to the Form.

2. *Setting the Label's size and location.* If the **Properties** window is not open, select **View > Properties Window**. In the **Properties** window, set the Label's Size property to 120, 21. Similarly, set the Label's Location property to 16, 18. Using these numbers ensures that the controls will align properly when you have added all of the controls to the Form. As you learned in the previous tutorial, you also can click and drag a control to place it on the Form and use sizing handles to resize it.

The Label's **Location** property specifies the position of the upper-left corner of the control on the Form. Visual Studio .NET assigns the value 0, 0 to the top-left corner of the Form, not including the title bar (Fig. 4.14). A control's Location property is set according to its distance from that point on the Form. As the first number of the Location property increases, the control moves to the right. As the second number of the Location property increases, the control moves toward the bottom of the Form. In this case, the value of 16, 18 indicates that the Label is placed 16 pixels to the right of the top-left corner of the Form and 18 pixels down from the top-left corner of the Form (Fig. 4.16). A Location value of 16, 48 would indicate that the Label is placed 16 pixels to the right of the top-left corner of the Form and 48 pixels down from the top-left corner of the Form

3. *Setting the Label's Name and Text properties.* In the **Properties** window, click the field to the right of the Text property, and type Cartons per shipment:. Set the Name property to lblCartons.

When entering values for a Label's Text property, you should use sentence-style capitalization. **Sentence-style capitalization** means that you capitalize the first letter of the first word in the text. Every other letter in the text is lowercase unless it is the first letter of a proper noun (for example, *Deitel*).

GUI Design Tip

Although you can drag a Label control to a location on the Form, the Location property can be used to specify a precise position.

Good Programming Practice

Prefix all Label control names with lbl.

(cont.)

4. **Modifying the Label's text alignment.** Select the TextAlign property in the **Properties** window; then, in the field to the right, click the down arrow (Fig. 4.15). Property **TextAlign** sets the alignment of text within a control such as a Label. Clicking the down arrow opens a window in which you can select the alignment of the text in the Label (Fig. 4.15). In this window, select the middle-left rectangle, which indicates that the Label's text aligns to the middle, vertically, and to the left, horizontally in the control. The value of the property changes to MiddleLeft. Figure 4.16 displays the Label after you set its properties.

TextAlign property

MiddleLeft TextAlign property value

Value of TextAlign property (MiddleLeft)

Down arrow

Window displayed when down arrow is clicked

Figure 4.15 Changing the TextAlign property of a Label.

Location 16, 16

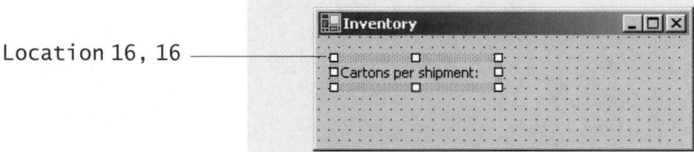

Figure 4.16 GUI after the Label has been customized.

5. **Saving the project.** Select **File > Save All** to save all the solution's files.

Now you will add the remaining Labels to the Form. They will help the user understand what inputs to provide and interpret the application's output. These Labels will identify the controls that you will add to the Form later.

Placing Additional Labels on the Form

1. **Adding a second descriptive Label.** Double click the Label control on the **Toolbox** to add a second Label. Set the Label's Size property to 104, 21 and the Label's Location property to 16, 48. Set the Label's Text property to Items per carton:, and change the Name property of this Label to lblItems. Then set the Label's TextAlign property to MiddleLeft.

2. **Adding a third descriptive Label.** Double click the Label control on the **Toolbox** to add a third Label. Set the Label's Size property to 40, 21 and the Label's Location property to 184, 16. Set the Label's Text property to Total: and change the Name property of this Label to lblTotal. Then set the Label's TextAlign property to MiddleLeft.

(cont.)

GUI Design Tip

Use a descriptive Label to identify an output Label.

GUI Design Tip

Place an application's output below and/or to the right of the Form's input controls.

3. **Adding an output Label.** To add the fourth Label, double click the Label control on the **Toolbox**. Set the Label's Size property to 48, 21 and the Label's Location property to 224, 16. Then name this Label lblTotalResult. Set the Label's TextAlign property to MiddleCenter. For the previous Labels, you set this property to MiddleLeft. To select value MiddleCenter, follow the same actions as in *Step 2*, but select the center rectangle shown in Fig. 4.17. You should use MiddleCenter text alignment to display results of calculations because it distinguishes the value in the output Label from the values in the descriptive Labels (whose TextAlign property is set to MiddleLeft).

MiddleCenter TextAlign property value

Figure 4.17 Setting the TextAlign property to MiddleCenter.

GUI Design Tip

Output Labels should be distinguishable from descriptive Labels. This can be done by setting the BorderStyle property of an output Label to Fixed3D.

GUI Design Tip

If several output Labels are arranged vertically to display numbers used in a mathematical calculation (such as in an invoice), use the MiddleRight TextAlign property.

4. **Changing a Label's BorderStyle property.** Label lblTotalResult displays the result of the application's calculation; therefore, you should make this Label appear different from the other Labels. To do this, you will change the appearance of the Label's border by changing the value of the **BorderStyle** property. Assign the value Fixed3D (Fig. 4.18) to lblTotal-Result's BorderStyle property to make the Label seem as if it is three dimensional (Fig. 4.19). [*Note*: If selected, FixedSingle displays a single dark line as a border.]

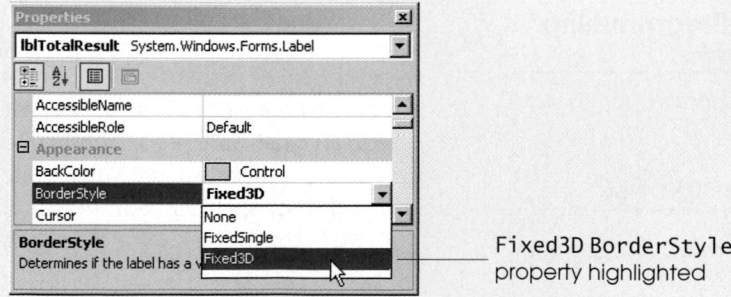

Fixed3D BorderStyle property highlighted

Figure 4.18 Changing a Label's BorderStyle property to Fixed3D.

Good Programming Practice

Clear the value of output Labels initially. When the application performs the calculation for that value, the Label's Text property should be updated to the new value. You will learn how to do this in the next tutorial.

5. **Clearing a Label's Text property.** When a Label is added to a Form, the Text property is assigned the default name of the Label. In this case, you should clear the text of the Label because you will not be adding meaningful text to Label lblTotalResult until later. To do this, delete the text to the right of the Text property in the **Properties** window. Figure 4.19 displays the GUI with all Labels added.

(cont.)

Figure 4.19 GUI with all Labels added.

6. *Saving the project.* Select **File > Save All** to save all the solution's files.

SELF-REVIEW

1. The value _____ for the Location property indicates the top-left corner (not including the title bar) of the Form.

   a) 1, 1   b) 0, 0

   c) 1, 0   d) 0, 1

2. An output Label should _____.

   a) be distinguishable from other Labels   b) initially have an empty Text property

   c) use Fixed3D for the BorderStyle property

   d) All of the above.

Answers: 1) b. 2) d.

4.4 Adding TextBoxes and a Button to the Form

The **Inventory** application requires user input to calculate the total number of textbooks that have arrived per shipment. Specifically, the user types in the number of cartons and the fixed number of books per carton. Because this type of data is entered from the keyboard, you use a TextBox control. Next, you will learn how to add TextBoxes to your Form and set their properties. Then, you will add a Button control to complete your GUI.

Adding *TextBoxes* to the *Form*

1. *Adding a TextBox to the Form.* Double click the TextBox control,

in the **Toolbox** to add a TextBox to the Form. Setting properties for a TextBox is similar to setting the properties for a Label. To name a TextBox, select the Name property in the **Properties** window, and enter txtCartons in the field to the right of the property (Fig. 4.20). Set the TextBox's Size property to 40, 21 and Location property to 128, 16. These size and location properties will cause the top of the TextBox to align with the top of the Label that describes it. Set the TextBox's Text property to 0 (Fig. 4.21). This will cause the value for your TextBox to be initially 0 when the application runs.

Good Programming Practice

Prefix TextBox control names with txt.

GUI Design Tip

Use TextBoxes to input data from the keyboard.

2. *Changing the TextAlign property of a TextBox.* Change txtCartons's TextAlign property to Right. Notice that, when you click the down arrow to the right of this property, the window in Fig. 4.15 does not appear. This is because TextBoxes have fewer TextAlign options, which are displayed simply as a list. Select Right from this list (Fig. 4.21).

(cont.)

GUI Design Tip

Each TextBox should have a descriptive Label indicating the input expected from the user.

GUI Design Tip

Place each descriptive Label either above or to the left of the control (for instance, a TextBox) that it identifies.

GUI Design Tip

Make TextBoxes wide enough for their expected inputs.

GUI Design Tip

A descriptive Label and the control it identifies should be aligned on the left if they are arranged vertically.

GUI Design Tip

A descriptive Label should have the same height as the TextBox it describes if the controls are arranged horizontally.

GUI Design Tip

A descriptive Label and the control it identifies should be aligned on the top if they are arranged horizontally.

GUI Design Tip

Leave at least two grid units between each group of controls on the Form.

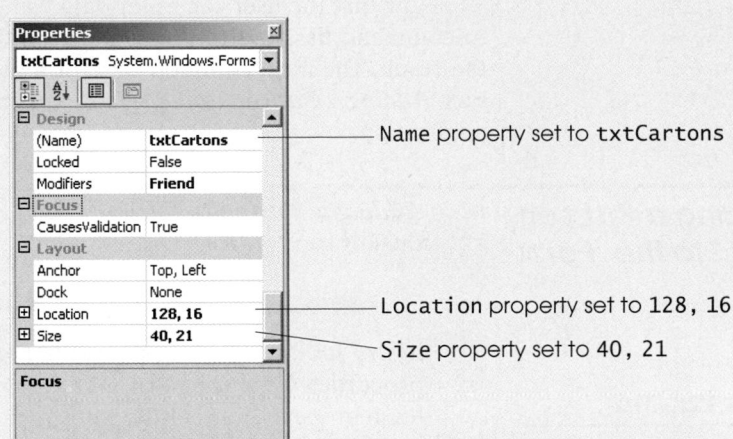

Name property set to txtCartons

Location property set to 128, 16

Size property set to 40, 21

Figure 4.20   Properties window for the txtCartons TextBox.

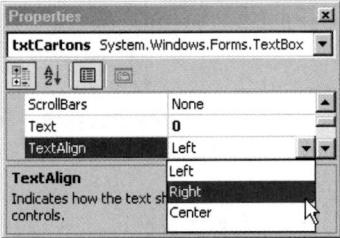

Figure 4.21   Selecting value Right of the TextAlign property of a Text-Box control.

3. ***Adding a second TextBox to the Form.*** Double click the TextBox control in the **Toolbox**. Name the TextBox txtItems. Set the Size property to 40, 21 and the Location property to 128, 48. These settings ensure that the left sides of the two TextBoxes align. The settings also align the top of the TextBox and the top of the Label that describes it. Set the Text property to 0 and the TextAlign property to Right. Figure 4.22 shows the Form after the TextBoxes have been added and their properties have been set.

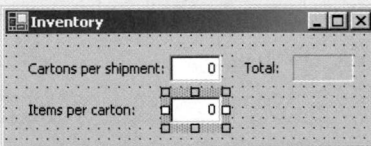

Figure 4.22   GUI after TextBoxes have been added and modified.

4. ***Saving the project.*** Select **File > Save All** to save all the solution's files.

Notice that your controls are aligning horizontally and vertically. In general, you should place each descriptive Label above or to the left of the control it describes (for instance, a TextBox). If you are arranging your controls on the same line, the descriptive Label and the control it describes should be the same height. However, if you arrange your controls vertically, the Label should be placed above the control it describes and the left sides of the controls should align. Also, leave at least two grid units between each group of controls on your Form. A **grid unit** is the space between two adjacent horizontal (or two adjacent vertical) dots on the Form in design view (Fig. 4.12). Following these simple guidelines will make your applications more appealing visually and easier to use by making the controls on the application less crowded.

Now that the user can enter data using a TextBox, you need a way for the user to command the application to perform the multiplication calculation and display the result. The most common way for a user to do this is by clicking a Button. The box, *Adding a Button to the Form*, explains how to add a Button to the **Inventory** application.

Adding a *Button* to the *Form*

GUI Design Tip

Buttons should be stacked downward from the top right of a Form or arranged on the same line starting from the bottom right of a Form.

Good Programming Practice

Prefix Button control names with btn.

GUI Design Tip

Buttons are labeled via their Text property. These labels should use book-title capitalization and be as short as possible while still being meaningful to the user.

1. ***Adding a Button to the Form.*** Add a Button to the Form by double clicking the Button control,

   in the **Toolbox**. Setting the properties for a Button is similar to setting the properties for a Label or a TextBox. Enter btnCalculate in the Button's Name property. For clarity, you should use btn (short for Button) as the prefix for Buttons.

   Set the Button's Size to 88, 24 and Location to 184, 48. Notice that these settings cause the left and right sides of the Button to align with the Labels above it (Fig. 4.23). Enter Calculate Total in the Button's Text property. A Button's Text property displays its value on the face of the Button. You should use book-title capitalization in a Button's Text property. When labelling Buttons, keep the Text as short as possible while still clearly indicating the Button's function.

2. ***Running the application.*** Select **Debug > Start** to run the application. Figure 4.23 shows the running application. Notice that no action occurs if you click the **Calculate Total** Button. This is because you have not written code that tells the application how to respond to your click. In Tutorial 5, you will write code to display (in lblTotalResult) the total number of books in the shipment when you click the Button. Click the Form's close box when you are finished viewing the application.

    ——— Close box

   Figure 4.23 Running the application after completing its design.

3. ***Saving the project.*** By running the application, any modified files were saved.

SELF-REVIEW

1. A Button's _____ property sets the value on the face of the Button.
   a) Name
   b) Text
   c) Title
   d) Face

2. Buttons should be _____ of the Form.
   a) on the same line, from the bottom right
   b) stacked from the top left
   c) aligned with the title bar text
   d) Either a or c.

Answers: 1) b. 2) a.

4.5 Wrap-Up

In this tutorial, you began constructing your **Inventory** application by designing its graphical user interface. You learned how to use Labels to describe controls and how to set a Label's TextAlign and BorderStyle properties. You used these properties to distinguish between descriptive and output Labels.

After labelling your Form, you added TextBoxes to allow users to input data from the keyboard. Finally, you added a Button to the **Inventory** application, allowing a user to signal the application to perform an action (in this case, to multiply two numbers and display the result). While you added controls to the Form, you also learned some GUI design tips to help you create appealing and intuitive graphical user interfaces.

The next tutorial teaches you to program code in Visual Basic .NET that will run when the user clicks the **Calculate Total** Button. When the Button is clicked, the application receives a signal called an event. You will learn how to program your application to respond to that event by performing the multiplication calculation and displaying the result.

SKILLS SUMMARY

Creating a New Project
- Select **File > New > Project…** to create a project
- Save a project to your work folder (C:\SimplyVB) by selecting it from the **Project Location** dialog.

Setting the Application's Font to Tahoma
- Select Tahoma from the Font Name property ComboBox in the Form's **Properties** window.

Creating a Descriptive Label
- Add a Label to your Form, then change the TextAlign property to MiddleLeft.

Creating an Output Label
- Add a Label to your Form, and change the BorderStyle property to Fixed3D and the TextAlign property to MiddleCenter.

Enabling User Input from the Keyboard
- Add a TextBox control to your Form.

Signaling that the Application Should Perform an Action
- Add a Button to the Form, and write program code to perform that action. (You learn how to add program code in Tutorial 5.)

KEY TERMS

book-title capitalization—A style that capitalizes the first letter of the each word in the text (for example, **Calculate Total**).

BorderStyle property—The property that specifies the appearance of a Label's border, which allows you to distinguish one control from another visually. The BorderStyle property can be set to None (no border), FixedSingle (a single dark line as a border), or Fixed3D (giving the Label a "sunken" appearance).

Button control—A control used to command the application to perform an action.

context menu—A menu that appears when you right click an object.

descriptive Label—A Label used to describe another control on the Form. This helps users understand a control's purpose.

Font property—The property that determines the font used to display text on a Form or control.

grid unit—The space between two adjacent horizontal (or two adjacent vertical) dots on the Form in design view.

Location property—The property that specifies the location of the upper-left corner of a control. This property is used to place a control on the Form precisely.

output Label—A Label used to display calculation results.

sentence-style capitalization—A style that capitalizes the first letter of the first word in the text. Every other letter in the text is lowercase, unless it is the first letter of a proper noun (for example, **Cartons per shipment**).

startup object—The object (for example, a Form) displayed when the application executes.

Tahoma font—The Microsoft-recommended font for use in Windows applications.

TextAlign property—The property that specifies how text is aligned in the control.

TextBox control—A control used to retrieve user input from the keyboard.

<table>
<tr><td align="right">**GUI DESIGN**
GUIDELINES</td><td>

Overall Design

- Arrange groups of controls at least two grid units apart on a Form.
- Leave at least two grid units of space between the edges of the Form and the controls nearest each edge.
- Use a control's Location property to precisely specify its position on the Form.
- Place an application's output below and/or to the right of the Form's input controls.

Buttons

- Buttons are labelled using their Text property. These labels should use book-title capitalization and be as short as possible while still being meaningful to the user.
- Buttons should be stacked downward from the top right of a Form or arranged on the same line starting from the bottom right of a Form.

Forms

- Changing the Form's title allows users to identify the application's purpose.
- Form titles should use book-title capitalization.
- Change the Form font to Tahoma to be consistent with Microsoft's recommended font for Windows.

Labels

- The TextAlign property of a descriptive Label should be set to MiddleLeft. This ensures that text within groups of Labels align.
- A descriptive Label should be placed above or to the left of the control that it identifies.
- A descriptive Label should have the same height as the TextBox it describes if the controls are arranged horizontally.
- A descriptive Label and the control it identifies should be aligned on the left if they are arranged vertically.
- Align the left sides of a group of descriptive Labels if the Labels are arranged vertically.
- A Label can be used to display output to the user. Use a descriptive Label to identify each output Label.
- Output Labels should look different from descriptive Labels to focus the user's attention. This can be done by setting the BorderStyle property to Fixed3D and the TextAlign property to MiddleCenter.
- If several output Labels are arranged vertically to display numbers used in a mathematical calculation (such as in an invoice), use the MiddleRight TextAlign property.
- A descriptive Label and the control it identifies should be aligned on the top if they are arranged horizontally.

TextBoxes

- Use TextBoxes to input data from the keyboard.
- TextBoxes should have descriptive Labels indicating the input expected from the user.
- Make TextBoxes wide enough for expected input.

</td></tr>
</table>

<table>
<tr><td align="right">**CONTROLS, EVENTS,**
PROPERTIES &
METHODS</td><td>

Button   `ab| Button`   This control allows the user to raise an action or event.

- ***In action***

  `Calculate Total`

- ***Properties***

  Name—This property specifies the name used to access the Button programmatically. The name should be prefixed with btn.

</td></tr>
</table>

`Size`—This property specifies the height and width (in pixels) of the `Button`.

`Text`—This property specifies the text displayed on the `Button`.

Label   **A** Label   This control displays text that the user cannot modify.

■ *In action*

Total: [   ]

■ *Properties*

`BorderStyle`—This property specifies the appearance of the `Label`'s border.

`Font`—This property specifies the font name, style and size of the text displayed in the `Label`.

`Location`—This property specifies the location of the `Label` on the `Form` relative to the `Form`'s top-left corner.

`Name`—This property specifies the name used to access the `Label` programmatically. The name should be prefixed with `lbl`.

`Size`—This property specifies the height and width (in pixels) of the `Label`.

`Text`—This property specifies the text displayed in the `Label`.

`TextAlign`—This property determines how the text is aligned within the `Label`.

TextBox   [abl] TextBox   This control allows user to input data from the keyboard.

■ *In action*

[0]

■ *Properties*

`Name`—This property specifies the name used to access the `TextBox` programmatically. The name should be prefixed with `txt`.

`Size`—This property specifies the height and width (in pixels) of the `TextBox`.

`Text`—This property specifies the text displayed in the `TextBox`.

`TextAlign`—This property specifies how the text is aligned within the `TextBox`.

MULTIPLE-CHOICE QUESTIONS

4.1 A new Windows application is created by selecting _____ from the **File** menu.

    a) **New > Program**   b) **New > File...**

    c) **New > Project...**   d) **New > Application**

4.2 A `Label`'s `BorderStyle` property can be set to _____.

    a) `Fixed3D`   b) `Single`

    c) `3D`   d) All of the above.

4.3 When creating a `Label`, you can specify the _____ of that `Label`.

    a) alignment of the text   b) border style

    c) size   d) All of the above.

4.4 Changing the value stored in the _____ property will change the name of the `Form` file.

    a) `Name`   b) `File`

    c) `File Name`   d) `Full Path`

4.5 _____ should be used to prefix all `TextBox` names.

    a) `txt`   b) `tbx`

    c) `Frm`   d) `tbn`

4.6 A(n) _____ helps the user understand a control's purpose.

    a) `Button`   b) descriptive `Label`

    c) output `Label`   d) title bar

4.7 A _____ is a control in which the user can enter data from a keyboard.

  a) Button   b) TextBox

  c) Label   d) PictureBox

4.8 A descriptive Label uses _____.

  a) sentence-style capitalization   b) book-title capitalization

  c) a colon at the end of its text   d) Both a and c.

4.9 You should use the _____ font in your Windows applications.

  a) Tahoma   b) MS Sans Serif

  c) Times   d) Palatino

4.10 _____ should be used to prefix all Button names.

  a) but   b) lbl

  c) Frm   d) btn

EXERCISES

At the end of each tutorial, you will find a summary of new GUI design tips listed in the GUI Design Guidelines section. A cumulative list of GUI design guidelines, organized by control, appears in Appendix C. In these exercises, you will find Visual Basic .NET Forms that do not follow the GUI design guidelines presented in this tutorial. For each exercise, you must modify control properties so that your end result is consistent with the guidelines presented in the tutorial. Note that these applications do not provide any functionality.

4.11 *(Address Book GUI)* In this exercise, you apply the GUI design guidelines you have learned to a graphical user interface for an address book (Fig. 4.24).

  a) *Copying the exercise application.* Copy the template application from C:\Examples\Tutorial04\Exercises\AddressBook to your work folder.

  b) *Opening the application.* In your work folder, double click AddressBook.sln to open the exercise in Visual Studio .NET.

  c) *Applying GUI design guidelines.* Rearrange the controls and modify properties so that the GUI conforms to the design guidelines you have learned.

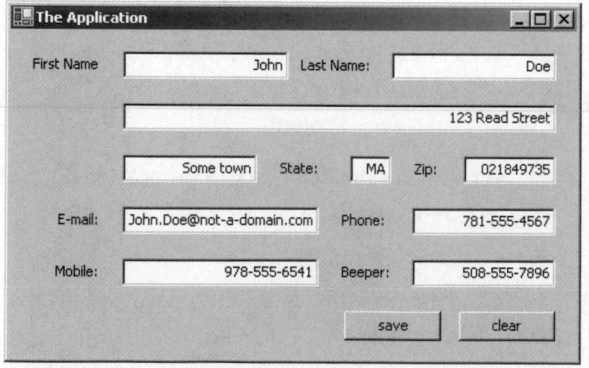

Figure 4.24 **Address Book** application without GUI design guidelines applied.

4.12 *(Mortgage Calculator GUI)* In this exercise, you apply the GUI design guidelines you have learned to a graphical user interface for a mortgage calculator (Fig. 4.25).

  a) *Copying the exercise application.* Copy the template application from C:\Examples\Tutorial04\Exercises\MortgageCalculator to your work folder.

  b) *Opening the application.* In your work folder, double click MortgageCalculator.sln to open the exercise in Visual Studio .NET.

  c) *Applying GUI design guidelines.* Rearrange the controls and modify properties so that the GUI conforms to the design guidelines you have learned.

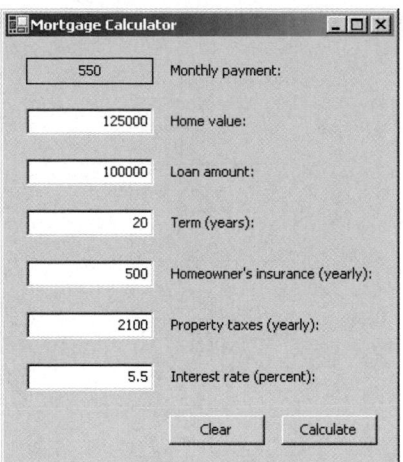

Figure 4.25 **Mortgage Calculator** application without GUI design guidelines applied.

4.13 *(Password GUI)* In this exercise, you apply the GUI design guidelines you have learned to a graphical user interface for a password-protected message application (Fig. 4.26).

a) *Copying the exercise application.* Copy the template application from `C:\Examples\Tutorial04\Exercises\Password` to your work folder.

b) *Opening the application.* In your work folder, double click `AddressBook.sln` to open the exercise in Visual Studio .NET.

c) *Applying GUI design guidelines.* Rearrange the controls and modify properties so that the GUI conforms to the design guidelines you have learned.

Multiline `TextBox` (you will learn how to create these in later tutorials)

Figure 4.26 **Password** application without GUI design guidelines applied.

Programming Challenge ▶

4.14 *(Invoice GUI)* In this exercise, you apply the GUI design guidelines you have learned to a graphical user interface for an invoice application (Fig. 4.27).

a) *Copying the exercise application.* Copy the template application from `C:\Examples\Tutorial04\Exercises\MonitorInvoice` to your work folder.

b) *Opening the application.* In your work folder, double click `MonitorInvoice.sln` to open the exercise in Visual Studio .NET.

c) *Applying GUI design guidelines.* Rearrange the controls and modify properties so that the GUI conforms to the design guidelines you have learned.

Figure 4.27 **Invoice** application without GUI design guidelines applied.

Objectives

In this tutorial, you will learn to:
- Add an event handler for a **Button** control.
- Insert code into an event handler.
- Access a property's value by using Visual Basic .NET code.
- Use the assignment and multiplication operators.

Outline

Completing the Inventory Application

Introducing Programming

This tutorial introduces fundamentals of nonvisual programming to create an application with which users can interact. You will learn these concepts as you add functionality (with Visual Basic .NET code) to the **Inventory** application you designed in Tutorial 4. The term **functionality** describes the actions an application can execute. In this tutorial, you will examine **events**, which represent user actions, such as clicking a **Button** or altering a value in a **TextBox**, and **event handlers**, which are pieces of code that are executed (called) when such events occur (that is, when the events are **raised**). You will learn why events and event handlers are crucial to programming Windows applications.

5.1 Test-Driving the Inventory Application

In this tutorial, you will complete the **Inventory** application you designed in Tutorial 4. Recall that the application must meet the following requirements:

Application Requirements

A college bookstore receives cartons of textbooks. In each shipment, each carton contains the same number of textbooks. However, cartons from different shipments can have a different number of textbooks. The inventory manager wants to use a computer to calculate the total number of textbooks arriving at the bookstore for each shipment quickly, from the number of cartons and the fixed number of textbooks in each carton. Create an application that first allows the inventory manager to enter the number of cartons received and the number of textbooks in each carton and that then calculates the total number of textbooks in a shipment.

The inventory manager has reviewed and approved your design. Now you must add code that, when the user clicks a **Button**, will make the application multiply the number of cartons by the number of textbooks per carton and display the result—the total number of textbooks received. You begin by test-driving the application. Next, you learn the additional Visual Basic .NET technologies you will need to complete the application. Finally, you will create and run the application.

Test-Driving the Completed Inventory Application

1. ***Opening the application.*** Double click the file `Inventory.sln` in directory `C:\Examples\Tutorial05\CompletedApplication\Inventory2` to open this application in Visual Studio .NET.

2. ***Running the application.*** Select **Debug > Start** to execute the application. Enter 3 in the **Cartons per shipment:** TextBox. Enter 15 in the **Items per carton:** TextBox. Figure 5.1 shows the Form after these values have been entered.

Figure 5.1   **Inventory** application with quantities entered.

3. ***Calculating the total number of items received.*** Click the **Calculate Total** Button. The application multiplies the two numbers you entered and displays the result (45) in the Label to the right of **Total:** (Fig. 5.2).

Result of calculation

Figure 5.2   Result of clicking the **Calculate Total** Button in the **Inventory** application.

4. ***Terminating the application.*** Click the running application's close box to terminate the application.

5. ***Closing the solution.*** Select **File > Close Solution**.

5.2 Introduction to Visual Basic .NET Code

In Tutorials 3 and 4, you were introduced to a concept called visual programming, which allows you to create GUIs without writing any program code. In this section, you will combine visual programming with conventional programming techniques to enhance the **Inventory** application.

Before you begin to view and edit code, you should customize the way Visual Studio .NET displays and formats your code. In the box, *Customizing the IDE*, you open the template application and change display and format settings to make it easy for you to work with code and follow our discussions. Adding line numbers, adjusting tab sizes and setting fonts and colors help you to navigate your code more easily.

Customizing the IDE

1. ***Copying the template to your work folder.*** Copy the `C:\Examples\Tutorial05\TemplateApplication\Inventory2` folder to `C:\SimplyVB`. This folder contains the application created by following the steps in the previous tutorial.

(cont.)

2. ***Opening the template application.*** Double click `Inventory.sln` in the `Inventory2` folder to open the solution in Visual Studio .NET.

   This is the first tutorial in which you will use our template applications. If an error occurs when you try to copy or modify the template, please consult your system administrator to ensure that you have proper privileges to edit these applications.

3. ***Displaying line numbers.*** In all of our programming discussions, we refer to specific code elements by line number. To help you locate where you will insert code in the examples, you need to enable Visual Studio .NET's capability to show line numbers in your code.

   Select **Tools > Options…**, and, in the **Options** dialog that appears (Fig. 5.3), click the **Text Editor** folder icon. Then click the **Basic** folder icon (Fig. 5.4) to expand the options for Visual Basic .NET. If the arrow is not pointing to the **General** option after you click the **Basic** folder, click **General** to display the page in Fig. 5.4. Locate the **Display** header. If the Checkbox next to **Line numbers** is not checked, click inside the box to add a checkmark. If the box is already checked, you need not do anything; however, do not close the dialog.

Figure 5.3   **Options** dialog.

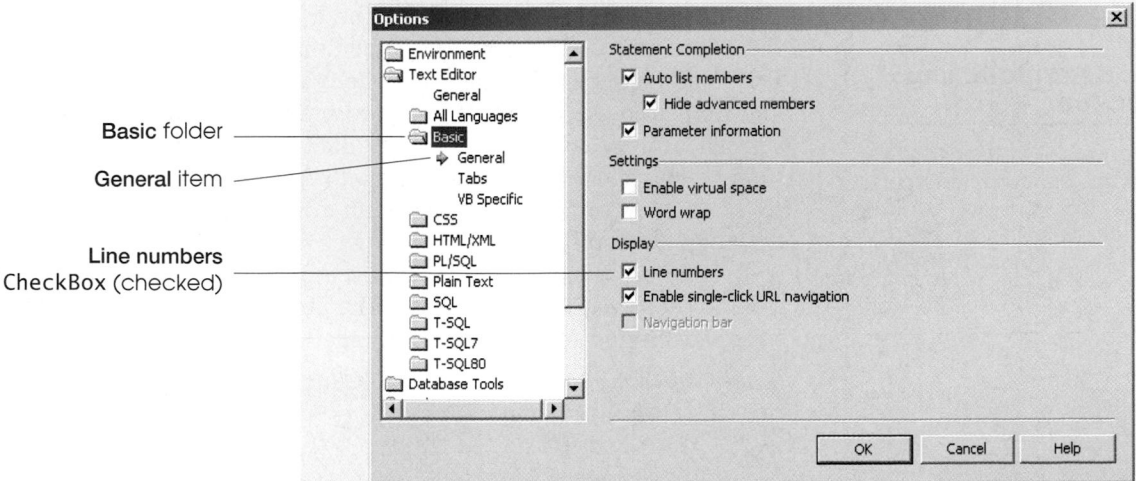

Figure 5.4   **General** settings page for Visual Basic .NET text editor.

(cont.)

4. ***Setting the tab size.*** Just as you indent the first line of each paragraph when writing a letter, it is important to use proper spacing when writing code. Indenting code improves program readability. You can control indents with tabs. Click the **Tabs** item under the **Basic** folder (Fig. 5.5). The **Smart** RadioButton, under the **Indenting** header, should be selected by default. If it is not, select the **Smart** RadioButton by clicking inside the white circle. Using this setting, Visual Studio .NET will indent code for you.

Smart Indenting (selected) ——————

Tabs item ——————

Insert spaces (selected) ——————

Figure 5.5 Setting the **Tabs** options.

Set **Tab size:** to 3 and **Indent size:** to 3. The **Tab size:** setting indicates the number of spaces each tab character (inserted when you press the *Tab* key) represents. The **Indent size:** setting determines the number of spaces each indent inserted by Visual Studio .NET represents. Visual Studio .NET will now insert 3 spaces for you if you are using the **Smart** indenting feature; you can insert them yourself with one keystroke by pressing the *Tab* key.

Then make sure the **Insert spaces** RadioButton is selected (Fig. 5.5), so Visual Studio .NET will insert three one-character spaces (instead of one tab character) to indent lines. If you select the **Keep tabs** RadioButton, each tab or indent will be represented by one tab character. We suggest you select the **Insert spaces** RadioButton.

5. ***Exploring fonts and colors.*** Click the **Environment** folder icon; then click the **Fonts and Colors** item. The screen that appears allows you to customize fonts and colors used to display code. Visual Studio .NET can apply colors and fonts to make it easier for you to read and edit code. Note that, if your settings are not consistent with the default settings, what you see on your screen will appear different from what is presented in this book. If you need to reset your settings to the default for fonts and colors, click the **Use Defaults** Button (Fig. 5.6).

In the book's examples, you will see code with the **Selected Text** background set to yellow for emphasis. The default setting for **Selected Text** is a blue background. You should use the default settings on your machine.

6. ***Applying your changes.*** Click the **OK** Button to apply your changes and dismiss the **Options** dialog.

Good Programming Practice

You can change the font and color settings if you prefer a different appearance for your code. To remain consistent with this book, however, we recommend that you not change the default font and color settings.

(cont.)

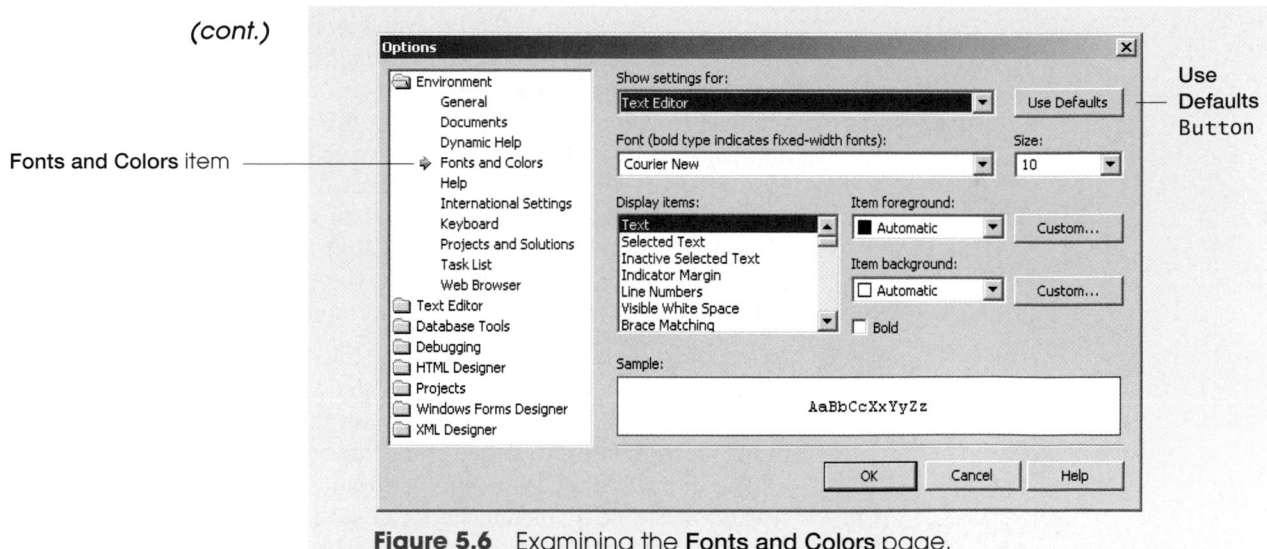

Figure 5.6 Examining the **Fonts and Colors** page.

Fonts and Colors item

Use Defaults Button

Visual programming is fun and saves time, but it is insufficient for the vast majority of applications. While you've been programming in a completely visual environment when adding Labels and TextBoxes, Visual Studio .NET has actually been writing code for you in the background. Behind the scenes, everything that your application will do is performed by code written either by you or by the IDE. The key is to develop the right mix of visual programming with code writing ("non-visual" programming) for each application. In the box, *Introducing Visual Basic .NET Code*, you will take your first peek at Visual Basic .NET code.

Introducing Visual Basic .NET Code

1. ***Viewing application code.*** If the Windows Form Designer is not open, double click the Inventory.vb file in the **Solutions Explorer** window. Then switch to **code view** (where the application's code is displayed in an editor window), by selecting **View > Code**. The tabbed window (Inventory.vb) in Fig. 5.7, also called a **code editor**, appears. Note that when you are asked to select **View > Code**, the Inventory.vb file must be selected in the **Solutions Explorer**.

    You will notice that the IDE through which we present code to you may appear different than your IDE. To improve readability, we have hidden the **Toolbox** and closed any extra windows, such as the **Solutions Explorer**, **Properties** and **Task List** windows.

Inventory.vb tabbed window

Class definition

Figure 5.7 IDE showing code for the **Inventory** application.

(cont.)

Most Visual Basic .NET programs consist of pieces called classes, which simplify application organization. Recall from Tutorial 1 that classes contain groups of code statements that perform tasks and return information when the tasks are completed. The code in this application defines your **Inventory** application class. (These lines collectively are called a **class definition**.) Most Visual Basic .NET applications consist of a combination of code written by programmers (like you) and preexisting classes written and provided by Microsoft in the Framework Class Library (FCL). Again, the key to successful Visual Basic .NET application development is achieving the right mix of the two. You will learn how to use both techniques in your programs.

2. *Examining class definitions.* Line 1 (Fig. 5.7) begins the class definition. The **Class keyword** introduces a class definition in Visual Basic .NET and is immediately followed by the **class name** (FrmInventory in this application, the value you entered in the Form's Name property).

The name of the class is an **identifier**, which is a series of characters consisting of letters, digits and underscores (_). Identifiers cannot begin with a digit and cannot contain spaces. Examples of valid identifiers are intValue1, intLabel_Value and btnExit. The name 7welcome is not a valid identifier, because it begins with a digit, and the name input field is not a valid identifier, because it contains a space. The class definition ends on line 125 with the keywords **End Class**. **Keywords** (or **reserved words**) are reserved for use by Visual Basic .NET (you will learn the various keywords throughout the text). Notice that keywords appear in blue by default in the IDE. A complete list of Visual Basic .NET keywords can be found in Appendix F.

The Class keyword is preceded by the Public keyword. The code for every Form you design in Visual Studio .NET begins with the Public keyword. You will learn about this keyword in Tutorial 19.

Visual Basic .NET keywords and identifiers are not **case sensitive**. This means that uppercase and lowercase letters are considered to be identical; that practice causes FrmInventory and frminventory to be understood by Visual Basic .NET as the same identifier. Although the first letter of every keyword is capitalized, keywords are nevertheless not case sensitive. Visual Studio .NET applies the correct case to each letter of a keyword and identifier, so, when you type clasS, it is changed to Class when the *Enter* key is pressed.

3. *Understanding inheriting from class Form.* Every visual Windows application consists of at least one class that Inherits from class Form (Fig. 5.7, line 2) in the FCL. The keyword **Inherits** indicates that the class FrmInventory inherits members from another class. By inheriting from System.Windows.Forms.Form, your application uses class Form as a "template." A key benefit of inheriting from class Form is that the FCL previously has defined "what it means to be a Form." The Windows operating system expects every window (for example, a Form) to have certain capabilities. However, because class Form already provides those capabilities, programmers do not need to "reinvent the wheel" by defining all those capabilities themselves. The use of Inherits to derive from class Form enables programmers to create Forms quickly and easily.

Good Programming Practice

Capitalize the first letter of each class identifier, such as the Form name.

Good Programming Practice

Always type a keyword with the correct capitalization, even though Visual Studio .NET will correct any capitalization errors.

In the editor window (Fig. 5.7), notice the text Windows Form Designer generated code on line 4, which is surrounded by a gray rectangle and has a plus box ⊞ next to it. The plus box indicates that this section of code, called a **region**, is collapsed, as discussed in Tutorial 2. Notice that the line numbers in Fig. 5.7 jump from 4 to 124. The missing line numbers correspond to code hidden from you by Visual Studio .NET. Although collapsed code is not visible, it is still part of the application.

Code collapsing allows you to hide code in the editor, so that you can focus on key code segments. Notice that the entire class definition also can be collapsed by clicking the minus box ⊟ to the left of `Public`. In Fig. 5.7, the description to the right of the plus box indicates that the collapsed code was created by the Windows `Form` Designer. This collapsed code contains the code, inserted by the IDE, that creates the `Form` and its controls. In the box, *Examining Windows* `Form` *Designer Generated Code*, you explore the code generated by the IDE.

Examining Windows `Form` *Designer Generated Code*

1. ***Viewing the generated code.*** In this step, you will view other code that is part of your application. You will not be expected to understand the code. Visual programming saves development time by allowing you to build applications without needing to know how every component works "under the hood," just as you don't need to know how an engine works in order to drive a car.

   Click the plus box on line 4 to view the generated code. The **expanded code** (Fig. 5.8) certainly appears to be complex. The vast majority of the code shown has not been introduced yet. Again, you are not expected to understand how it works.

   This code is created by the IDE and normally is not edited by the programmer. This is Microsoft's intent—you can develop powerful applications without having to worry about the IDE-generated code. This type of code is present in *every* Windows application developed with Visual Studio .NET, saving you a considerable amount of development time. As you read this book, the purpose of much of this code will become clearer.

Figure 5.8 Windows `Form` Designer generated code, when expanded.

   Collapse the code by clicking the node at line 6. Your code should now appear exactly as in Fig. 5.8. A box containing an ellipses appears in place of the code in that region. This area is called **outlined code**. Placing the cursor over the outlined code displays a portion of the collapsed code.

(cont.)

2. **Viewing the generated code for a specific control.** Click and drag the scrollbar downward until you reach the code in Fig. 5.9. This region contains code generated by the IDE for setting Label lblCarton's properties, including the Label's Location, Name, Size, Text and TextAlign properties.

When you designed this application in Tutorial 4, you used the **Properties** window to set properties for the Form, Labels, TextBoxes and Buttons. Once a property was set, the object was updated immediately. Objects (Forms and controls) have **default properties**, which are displayed initially in the **Properties** window when an object is created. These default properties provide the initial characteristics of an object. When a control, such as a Label, is placed on the Form, the IDE adds code to the class (in this case, FrmInventory) that creates the control and sets some of the control's property values, such as the name of the control and its location on the Form.

Property values for lblCartons

Click tab for design view

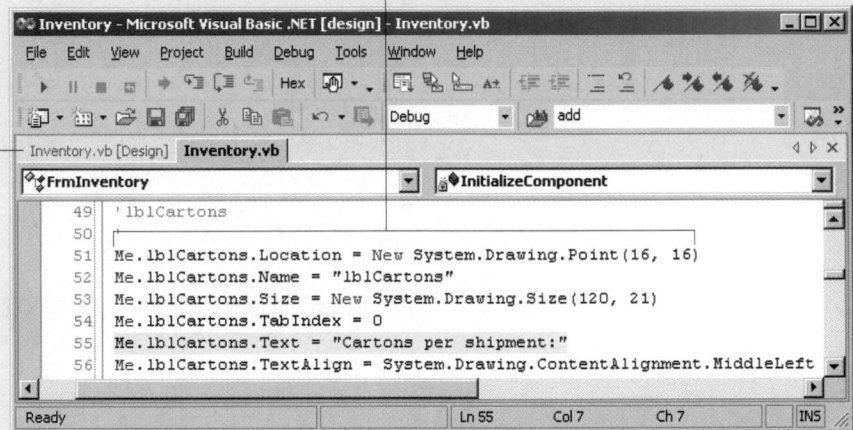

Figure 5.9 Code generated by the IDE for lblCartons (with the code setting the Text property highlighted).

The values in the code in Fig. 5.9 correspond to what you entered in the **Properties** window in the Windows Form Designer in Tutorial 4. Notice that the Label's Text property is assigned the text that you entered in the **Properties** window (line 55). When you change a property in design view, the Windows Form Designer updates the appropriate line of code in the class to reflect the new value.

3. **Collapsing code.** Collapse this application's generated code by clicking the node at line 4.

SELF-REVIEW 1. Identifiers _____.

    a) can begin with any character, but cannot contain spaces

    b) must begin with a digit, but cannot contain spaces

    c) cannot begin with a digit or contain spaces

    d) cannot begin with a digit, but can contain spaces

2. In code view, the plus box shown to the left of a line of code indicates that this region is _____.

    a) positive   b) closed

    c) expanded   d) collapsed

Answers: 1) c. 2) d.

5.3 Inserting an Event Handler

Now that you have finalized the GUI, you are ready to modify your application so it will respond to user input. You will do this by inserting code manually. Most of the Visual Basic .NET applications in this book provide functionality in the form of event handlers. Recall that an event handler is executed when an event occurs, such as the clicking of a Button. The box, *Adding a Button's Click Event Handler*, shows you how to add an event handler to your application.

Adding a *Button's* Click *Event Handler*

1. ***Adding an event handler for the Button.*** In this step, you use the Windows Form Designer to create an event handler and enter code view. Begin by clicking the Inventory.vb [Design] tab to enter the Windows Form Designer. Then double click the Form's Button to enter code view. Notice that the code for the application, which now includes the new event handler on lines 125–127 of Fig. 5.10, is displayed.

Asterisks indicate unsaved changes to application

Empty event handler

Figure 5.10 Event handler btnCalculate_Click before you add your program code.

Double clicking the Button in design view caused Visual Studio .NET to generate the Button's Click event handler—the code that will execute when the user clicks the **Calculate Total** Button. When any control is double clicked in design view, Visual Studio .NET inserts an event handler for that control. The event that the handler is associated with may differ based on the control that is double clicked. For instance, double clicking Button controls causes Click event handlers to be created. Double clicking other types of controls will cause other types of event handlers to be generated. Each control has a default type of event handler that is generated when that control is clicked in design view.

In Visual Basic .NET, event handlers by convention follow the naming scheme *controlName_eventName*. The word *controlName* refers to the name of the control provided in its Name property (in this case, btnCalculate). The name of the event raised by the control (in this case, Click) is represented by *eventName*. When event *eventName* occurs, event handler *controlName_eventName* executes. In this application, btnCalculate_Click handles the **Calculate Total** Button's Click events—in other words, the code in btnCalculate_Click executes when the user clicks the **Calculate Total** Button.

(cont.)

2. ***Running the application.*** Select **Debug > Start** to run the application. Figure 5.11 shows the running application. Click the **Calculate Total** Button.

Figure 5.11 Running application without functionality.

Notice that, although you have added an event handler for the Button's Click event, no action occurs when you click the Button because you haven't added any code to the event handler yet. In the box, *Adding Code to an Empty Event Handler*, you add code to the event handler so that, when a user clicks the Button, text displays in the output Label (lblTotalResult). Click the running application's close box to terminate the application.

3. ***Saving the application.*** Select **File > Save All** to save all the solution's files.

Now that you have created an event handler for the **Calculate Total** Button, you need to insert code to perform an action. Specifically, you need to make the application multiply the number of cartons in a shipment by the fixed number of items per carton when a user clicks the **Calculate Total** Button. You write your first Visual Basic .NET statement in the box, *Adding Code to an Empty Event Handler*.

Adding Code to an Empty Event Handler

1. ***Changing to code view.*** If you are not already in code view, select **View > Code** to view the application's code.

2. ***Adding code to the event handler.*** In the body of the event handler, insert lines 127–128 of Fig. 5.12 by typing the text on the screen.

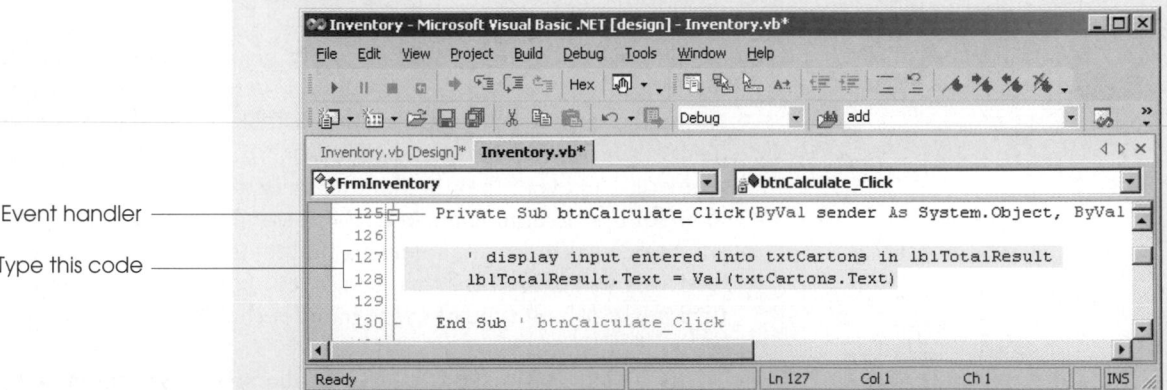

Figure 5.12 Code added to the **Calculate Total** Button's event handler.

Line 127 of Fig. 5.12 begins with a **single-quote character** (`'`), which indicates that the remainder of the line is a **comment**. Programmers insert comments in programs to improve the readability of their code. These comments explain the code so that other programmers who need to work with the application can understand it more easily.

Comments also help you read your own code, especially when you haven't looked at it for a while. Comments can be placed either on their own lines (these are called "full-line comments") or at the end of a line of Visual Basic .NET code (these are called "end-of-line comments").

Good Programming Practice

Comments written at the end of a line should be preceded by one or more spaces, to enhance program readability.

(cont.)

The Visual Basic .NET compiler ignores comments, which means that comments do not cause the computer to perform any actions when your applications run. The comment used in line 127 simply indicates that the next line displays the value entered into the **Cartons per shipment:** TextBox in the **Total:** Label. Comments appear in green when displayed in the code editor of Visual Studio .NET.

Line 128 of Fig. 5.12 presents your first executable Visual Basic .NET **statement**, which performs an action. By default, statements end when the current line ends. Later in this tutorial, you will see how to continue a statement past one line. This statement (line 128) accesses the Text properties of txtCartons and lblTotalResult. In Visual Basic .NET, properties are accessed in code by placing a period between the control name (for example, lblTotalResult) and property name (for example, Text). This period, which is placed to the right of the control name, is called the **member access operator (.)**, or the **dot operator**. Notice that, when the control name and member access operator are typed, a window appears listing that object's members (Fig. 5.13). This is known as Visual Studio .NET's *IntelliSense* feature, which displays all the members in a class for your convenience. You scroll to the member you are interested in and select it. Click the member name once to display a description of that member; double click it to add the name of the member to your application. *IntelliSense* can be useful in discovering a class's members and their purpose.

Good Programming Practice

Precede every full-line comment or group of full-line comments with a blank line. The blank line makes the comments stand out and improves program readability.

Description of selected member

Selected member

IntelliSense

Figure 5.13   *IntelliSense* activating while entering code.

Let's examine line 128 of Fig. 5.12 more closely. Reading the line from left to right, we see lblTotalResult's Text property, followed by an "equals" sign (=), followed by txtCartons' Text property value. The "=" symbol, as used here, is known as the **assignment operator**. The expressions on either side of the assignment operator are referred to as its **operands**. This assignment operator assigns the value on the right of the operator (the **right operand**) to the variable on the left of the operator (the **left operand**). The assignment operator is known as a **binary operator**, because it has two operands—lblTotalResult.Text and txtCartons.Text.

(cont.)

The entire statement is called an **assignment statement**, because it assigns a value to the left operand. In this example, you are assigning the value of `txtCartons'` Text property to `lblTotalResult`'s Text property. The statement is read as, "The Text property of `lblTotalResult` *gets* the value of `txtCarton`'s Text property." Note that the right operand is unchanged by the assignment statement.

When the user clicks the **Calculate Total** Button, the event handler will execute, displaying the value the user entered in the **Cartons per shipment:** TextBox in the output Label `lblTotalResult`. Clearly, this is not the correct result—the correct result is the number of items per carton times the number of cartons per shipment. In the box, *Completing the Inventory Application*, you correct this error. Notice that we have added a comment on line 130 of Fig. 5.12, indicating the end of our event handler.

3. *Running the application.* Select **Debug > Start** to run the application. Figure 5.14 shows the running application. Type 5 into the **Cartons per shipment:** TextBox and 10 into the **Items per carton:** TextBox, then click the **Calculate Total** Button. Notice that the text of `lblTotalResult` now incorrectly displays the data, 5, that was entered into the **Cartons per shipment:** TextBox, rather than displaying the correct result, 50. Click the close box in the upper-right corner of the window to terminate the application.

Result of clicking **Calculate Total** Button

Figure 5.14 Execution of application with event handler.

4. *Saving the application.* Select **File > Save All** to save your work. The next section will explain how to perform a calculation and display its result.

SELF-REVIEW

1. Event handlers generated by Visual Studio .NET follow the naming convention _____.

   a) *controlName_eventName*   b) *eventName_controlName*

   c) *eventNameControlName*   d) *controlNameEventName*

2. The expressions on either side of the assignment operator are referred to as its _____.

   a) operator values   b) results

   c) operands   d) arguments

Answers: 1) a. 2) c.

5.4 Performing a Calculation and Displaying the Result

Now that you are familiar with displaying output in a Label, you will complete the **Inventory** application by displaying the product of the number of cartons per shipment and the number of items per carton. In the box, *Completing the Inventory Application*, you will learn how to perform mathematical operations in Visual Basic .NET.

Completing the Inventory Application

Common Programming Error

Placing anything, including comments, to the right of a line-continuation character is a syntax error. Syntax errors are introduced in the box, *Using the Debugger: Syntax Errors*.

1. *Changing the event handler.* If you are not already in code view, select **View > Code** or click the Inventory.vb tab. Insert underscore (_) characters as shown at the right of lines 125–126. Indent lines 126–127 as shown in Fig. 5.15 by placing the cursor at the beginning of each line's text and pressing the *Tab* key. Then replace the body of btnCalculate_Click with the code in lines 129–131 of Fig. 5.15.

Modified **Inventory** appilcation code

Figure 5.15   Using multiplication in the **Inventory** application.

The comment in line 129 indicates that you will be multiplying the two values input by the user and displaying the result in a Label.

Good Programming Practice

A lengthy statement may be spread over several lines. If a single statement must be split across lines, choose breaking points that make sense, such as after an operator. If a statement is split across two or more lines, indent all subsequent lines with one "level" of indentation.

Common Programming Error

Splitting a statement over several lines without including the line-continuation character is a syntax error.

2. *Adding multiline code.* Lines 130–131 perform the multiplication and assignment. You again use the assignment operator to assign a value to lblTotalResult.Text in line 130. To the right of the assignment operator is a space followed by an underscore (_), known as the **line-continuation character**. This character indicates that the next line is a continuation of the previous line. A single statement can contain as many line-continuation characters as necessary. However, at least one whitespace character must precede each line-continuation character. A **whitespace character** is a space, tab or newline (the character inserted by pressing the *Enter* key). Because this statement has been continued past the current line, look to the next line for the assignment operator's right operand. We have also used the line-continuation character on lines 125–126 to split the first line of the event handler into three lines; this enables all the program code to fit in the window. The line-continuation character has no effect when placed at the end of a comment.

The assignment operator in line 130 assigns the result of multiplying the numbers input by the user to lblTotalResult.Text. On line 131, Val(txtCartons.Text) is followed by an asterisk (*) and then Val(txtItems.Text). The asterisk is known as the **multiplication operator**—the operator's left and right operands are multiplied together.

(cont.)

Your **Inventory** application cannot prevent users from accidentally entering nonnumeric input such as letters and special characters like $ and @. Line 131 uses the **Val function** to prevent inputs like this from terminating the application. A function is a portion of code that performs a task when **called** (executed) and sends, or **returns**, a value to the location from which it was called. In this case, the values returned by Val become the values used to perform multiplication (line 131). We call functions (as in line 131) by typing their name followed by parentheses. Any values inside the parentheses (for example, `txtCartons.Text`) are known as function **arguments**. Arguments are inputs to the function that provide information that the function needs to perform its task. In this case, the argument specifies which value you want to send to function Val. You will learn how to create your own functions (called procedures) in Tutorial 13.

Function Val can be used to obtain a value from a string of characters (keyboard input) that is guaranteed to be a number. We use Val because this application is not intended to perform arithmetic calculations with characters that are not numbers. Val reads its argument one character at a time until it encounters a character that is not a number. Once a nonnumeric character is read, Val returns the number it has read up to that point. Val ignores whitespace characters (for example, "33 5" will be converted to 335). Figure 5.16 presents samples of Val calls and their results. Val recognizes the decimal point as a numeric character, and the plus and minus signs when they appear at the beginning of the string (to indicate that a number is positive or negative). Val does not recognize such symbols as commas and dollar signs. If function Val receives an argument that cannot be converted to a number (for example, "b35", which begins with a nonnumeric character), it returns 0. The result is assigned to `lblTotalResult.Text` (line 130), to display the result to the user.

You should be careful when using Val, however. Though the value returned is a number, it is not always the value the user intended (see Fig. 5.16). If incorrect data is entered from the user, Val makes no indication of the error. The function returns a value (usually not the value intended by the user) and the application continues, possibly using the incorrect input in calculations. For example, someone entering a monetary amount may enter the text `$10.23`, which Val will evaluate to 0. Notice how a common mistake causes an application to execute incorrectly. Visual Basic .NET provides two ways to handle invalid input. One way is to use Visual Basic .NET's string processing capabilities to examine input. You will learn about such capabilities as you read this book. The other form of handling invalid input is called exception handling, where you write code to handle errors that may be raised as the application executes. You can learn about exception-handling at our Web site, `www.deitel.com`.

3. ***Running the application.*** Select **Debug > Start** to run the application. Now the user can enter data in both TextBoxes. When the **Calculate Total** Button is clicked, the application will multiply the two numbers entered and display the result in `lblTotalResult`. Click the application's close box to terminate the application.

4. ***Saving the project.*** Select **File > Save All** to save all the solution's files.

Val **Function Call Samples**	**Results**
`Val("16" )`	16
`Val("-3" )`	-3

Figure 5.16 Val function call examples. (Part 1 of 2.)

Val **Function Call Samples**	**Results**
Val("1.5")	1.5
Val("67a4")	67
Val("8+5")	8
Val("14 Main St.")	14
Val("+1 2 3 4 5")	12345
Val("hello")	0

Figure 5.16 Val function call examples. (Part 2 of 2.)

Figure 5.17 presents the applications code. [*Note*: In code listings such as Fig. 5.17, we don't display the Visual Studio .NET generated code. We simply provide a comment (line 4) as a place holder. The line numbers shown in these figures are not intended to match those shown in the IDE.]

```
1   Public Class FrmInventory
2      Inherits System.Windows.Forms.Form
3
4      ' Windows Form Designer generated code
5
6      Private Sub btnCalculate_Click(ByVal sender As _
7         System.Object, ByVal e As System.EventArgs) _
8         Handles btnCalculate.Click
9
10        ' multiply values input and display result in Label
11        lblTotalResult.Text = _
12           Val(txtCartons.Text) * Val(txtItems.Text)
13
14     End Sub ' btnCalculate_Click
15
16  End Class ' FrmInventory
```

Figure 5.17 **Inventory** application code.

SELF-REVIEW

1. _____ provide information that functions need to perform their tasks.

   a) Inputs   b) Arguments
   c) Outputs   d) Both a and b.

2. What is the result of Val("%5")?

   a) 5   b) 0
   c) 500   d) 0.05

Answers: 1) d. 2) b.

5.5 Using the Debugger: Syntax Errors

So far in this book, you have executed the applications by selecting **Debug > Start**. This compiles and runs the application. If you do not write your code correctly, errors appear in a window known as the **Task List** when the application is compiled. **Debugging** is the process of fixing errors in an application. There are two types of errors: syntax errors and logic errors.

Syntax errors (or compilation errors) occur when code statements violate the grammatical rules of the programming language. Examples of syntax errors include misspellings of keywords or identifiers and failure to use the line-continuation character when splitting a statement across multiple lines. An application cannot be executed until all of its syntax errors are corrected.

Logic errors do not prevent the application from compiling successfully, but do cause the application to produce erroneous results. Visual Studio .NET contains software called a **debugger**, which allows you to analyze the behavior of your application to determine that it is executing correctly.

You can compile an application without executing it by selecting **Build > Build Solution**. Programmers frequently do this when they wish to determine whether there are any syntax errors in their code. Using either **Debug > Start** or **Build > Build Solution** will display any syntax errors in the **Task List** window. The **Output** window will display the result of the compilation. Figure 5.18 displays the output window for an application with no errors.

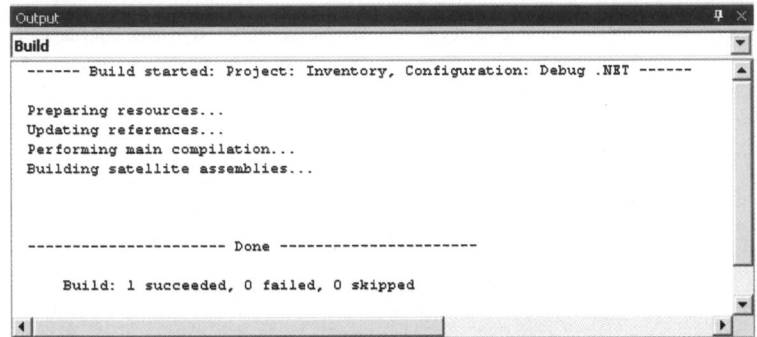

Figure 5.18 Results of successful build in the **Output** window.

In Visual Studio .NET, syntax errors appear in the **Task List** window along with a description of each error. Figure 5.19 displays the error that appears when the line-continuation character is left out of a multiple-line statement. For additional information on a syntax error, right click the error statement in the **Task List** window, and select **Show Task Help**. This displays a help page explaining the error message and suggests corrections.

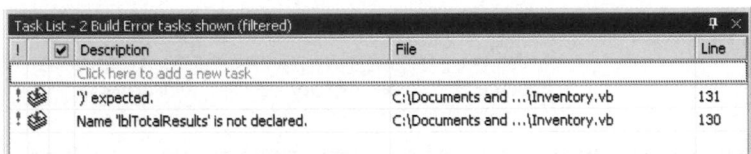

Figure 5.19 **Task List** lists syntax errors.

In the box, *Using the Debugger: Syntax Errors*, you will create syntax errors, view the results and fix the errors.

Using the Debugger: Syntax Errors

1. *Opening the application.* If the **Inventory** application is not currently open, locate the `Inventory.sln` file and double click it to load your application in the IDE.

2. *Creating your own syntax errors.* You will now create your own syntax errors, for demonstration purposes. If you are not in code view, select **View > Code**. Add an additional character (s) to Label `lblTotalResult` on line 130 and delete the right parenthesis at the end of the assignment statement on line 131. Notice the changes to the IDE (Fig. 5.20).

The Visual Studio .NET IDE provides **real-time error checking**. While you were manipulating the code in the code editor, you might have noticed that violations of Visual Basic .NET syntax is immediately reported in the **Task List**. The precise location of the syntax error in your code is also emphasized by a blue jagged line. Unrecognized identifier `lblTotalResults` and the missing parenthesis are reported in the **Task List** (Fig. 5.21).

(cont.)

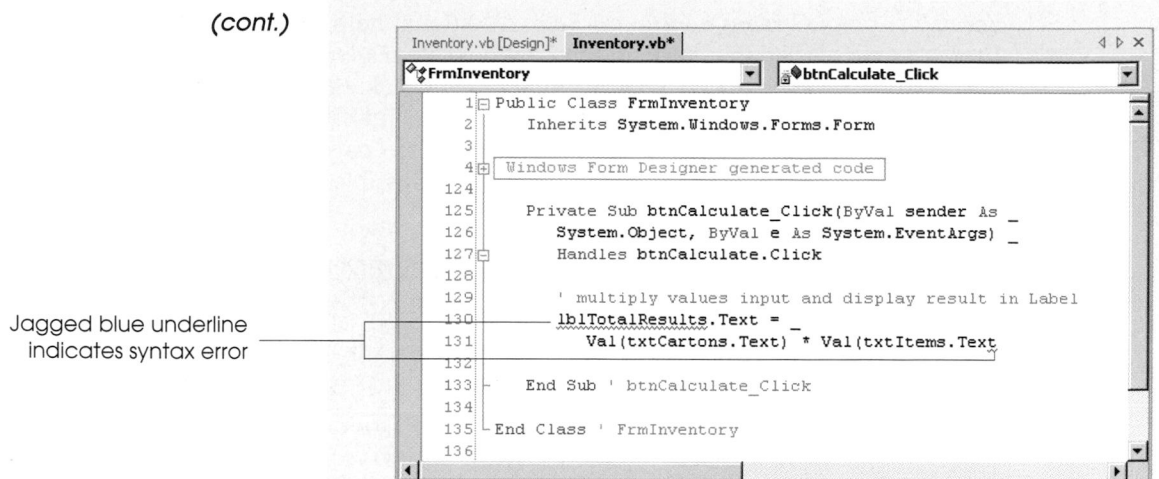

Figure 5.20 IDE with syntax errors.

These features notify you of possible errors and give you the chance to fix the error before compiling the application. The IDE will refuse to run your modified application until *all* syntax errors have been corrected.

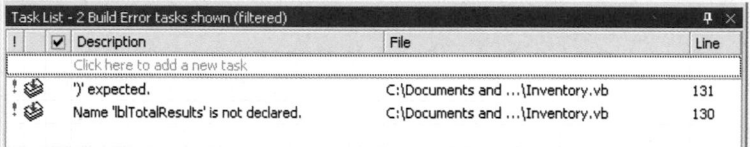

Figure 5.21 **Task List** displaying the syntax errors.

3. ***Locating the syntax errors***. Double clicking an error in the **Task List** window selects the code containing that error. Double click the **')' expected.** error to highlight the error on line 131 (Fig. 5.22).

Figure 5.22 Highlighting the portion of code where a syntax error occurs.

(cont.)

4. ***Getting additional help.*** Additional help regarding the syntax error is also available through the **Task List** item's context menu, which you can access by right clicking an item. Right click the **Name 'lblTotalResults' is not declared** error message from the **Task List**, and select **Show Task Help** (Fig. 5.23). This displays a reference page with information regarding the general form of the syntax error, possible solutions and links to other documentation (Fig. 5.24).

Context help

Figure 5.23 Getting additional help.

Suggested solution to misspelled keyword (Note that the debugger interprets the misspelling as a new, undeclared identifier)

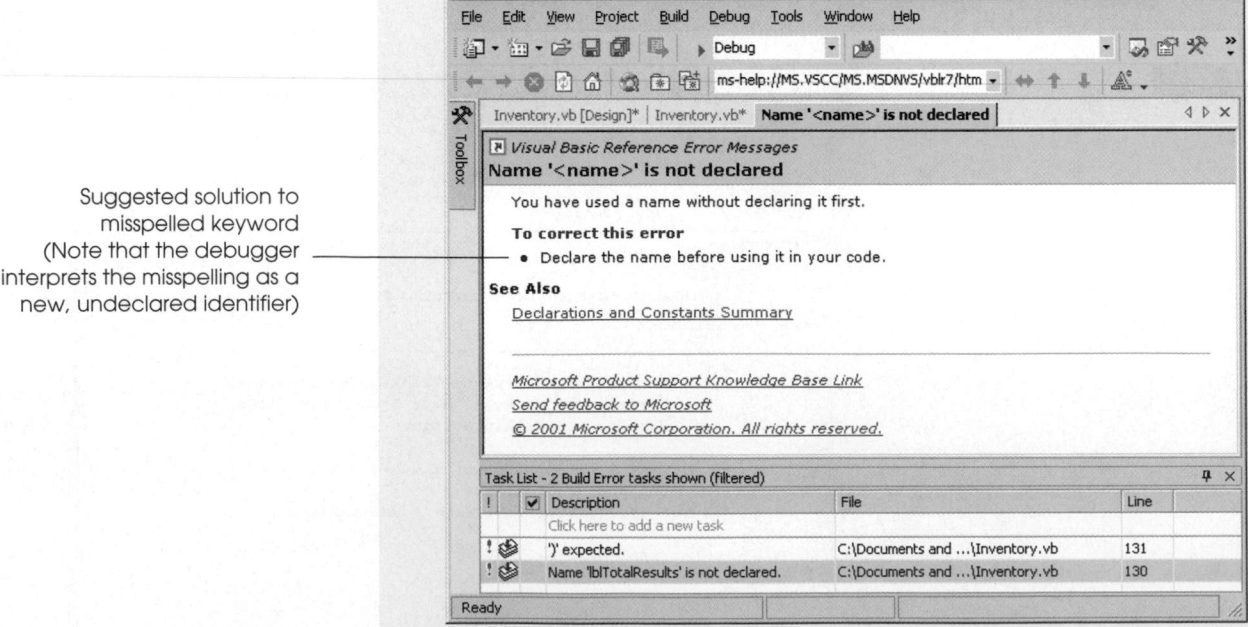

Figure 5.24 **Task Help** window.

(cont.)

5. ***Fixing the syntax error.*** Now that you know how to locate and fix the syntax error, go back to code view and correct the two errors you created in *Step 2*. Note, when you correct the errors, that the jagged lines do not disappear immediately. However, when you move the cursor to another line, the debugger rechecks the code for errors and removes the jagged underline for each corrected syntax error.

6. ***Saving the application.*** Select **File > Save All**. Notice that the error will be removed from the **Task List** window. The application is now ready to be compiled and executed.

In this section, you learned about syntax errors and how to find and correct them. In later tutorials, you will learn to detect and remove logic errors by using the Visual Studio .NET run-time debugger.

SELF-REVIEW

1. If there are syntax errors in an application, they will appear in a window known as the _____ when the application is compiled.

   a) **Task List**   b) **Output**
   c) **Properties**   d) **Error List**

2. A syntax error occurs when _____.

   a) the application terminates unexpectedly   b) a statement breaks over several lines
   c) a parenthesis is omitted   d) All of the above.

Answers: 1) a. 2) c.

5.6 Wrap-Up

In this tutorial, you were introduced to Visual Basic .NET programming. You learned how to use a `TextBox` control to allow users to input data and how to use a `Button` control to signal to your running application that it should perform a particular action. You were introduced to the code generated by Visual Studio .NET that creates an application's GUI. Though you are not yet expected to understand the meaning of the Windows Form Designer generated code, you learned that the key to good programming is to achieve the right balance between employing visual programming (in which Visual Studio .NET writes code for you) and writing your own code (nonvisual programming).

After learning about operators in Visual Basic .NET, you wrote a few lines of code as you added an event handler to your application to perform a simple multiplication calculation and display the result to the user. You also used comments to improve the readability of your code. You learned that placing code in an event handler allows an application to respond to that type of event, such as a click of a `Button`.

Finally, you learned about syntax errors and how to use the Visual Studio .NET debugger to reduce the number of errors you see when you try to run an application. In the next tutorial, you continue the developing of your **Inventory** application by using identifiers to create variables. You will also enhance your **Inventory** application by using the `TextChanged` event, which is raised when the user changes the value in a `TextBox`. After applying your knowledge of variables, you will use the debugger while an application runs to remove a logic error from that application.

SKILLS SUMMARY **Accessing a Property's Value by Using Visual Basic .NET Code**

■ Place the property name after the control name and the member access operator (`.`). For example, to access the `Text` property of a `TextBox` named `txtCartons`, use `txtCartons.Text`.

Inserting Visual Basic .NET Comments in Code

■ Begin the comment with a single-quote character ('). A comment can be placed either on its own line (full-line comment) or at the end of a line of code (end-of-line comment).

Continuing a Code Statement Over More Than One Line

■ Insert a line-continuation character (_), preceded by one or more whitespace characters, to indicate that the next line is a continuation of the previous line. Only whitespace characters may follow a line-continuation character.

Naming an Event Handler

■ Use the format for an event handler, *controlName_eventName*, where *controlName* is the name of the control that the event is related to and *eventName* is the name of the event. When event *eventName* is raised on control *controlName*, event handler *controlName_eventName* executes.

Inserting an Event Handler for a Button Control's Click Event

■ Double click the Button in design view to create an empty event handler; then, insert the code that will execute when the event occurs.

Using an Assignment Statement

■ Use the = ("equals" sign) to assign the value of its right operand to its left operand. The entire statement is called an assignment statement, because it assigns a value to the left operand (for example, a property).

Using the Multiplication Operator

■ Use an asterisk (*) between the two expressions to be multiplied. The multiplication operator multiplies the right and left operands if both operands contain numeric values or variables of numeric data types. It is a syntax error to use the multiplication operator on values of nonnumeric data types.

Obtaining a Numeric Value from a TextBox

■ Access the TextBox's Text property from within a call to function Val.

Finding a Syntax Error

■ Double click the error message in the **Task List** window, or locate the jagged blue underlined text in your code.

Obtaining Help for a Syntax Error

■ Right click the error message in the **Task List** window, and select **Show Task Help** from the context menu.

KEY TERMS

assignment statement—A statement that copies one value to another. An assignment statement contains an "equals"-sign (=) operator that causes the value of its right operand to be copied to its left operand.

binary operator—An operator that requires two operands.

case sensitive—The instance where two words that are spelled identically are treated differently if the capitalization of the two words differs.

class definition—The code that belongs to a class, beginning with keyword Class and ending with keywords End Class.

class name—The identifier used to identify the name of a class in code.

Class keyword—The keyword used to begin a class definition.

Click event—An event raised when a user clicks a control.

comment—A line of code that follows a single-quote character (') and is inserted to improve an application's readability.

debugging—The process of fixing errors in an application.

dot operator—See member access operator.

event—A user action that can trigger an event handler.

event handler—A section of code that is executed (called) when a certain event is raised (occurs).

functionality—The actions an application can execute.

identifier—A series of characters consisting of letters, digits and underscores used to name program units such as classes, controls and variables.

***IntelliSense* feature**—Visual Studio .NET feature that aids the programmer during development by providing windows listing available class members and pop-up descriptions for those members.

keyword—A word in code reserved for a specific purpose. These words appear in blue in the IDE and cannot be used as identifiers.

line-continuation character—An underscore character (_) preceded by one or more spaces, used to continue a statement to the next line of code.

logic error—An error that does not prevent the application from compiling successfully, but does cause the application to produce erroneous results.

member access operator—Also known as the dot operator (.). Allows programmers to access a control's properties using code.

multiplication operator—The asterisk (*) used to multiply its two operands, producing their product as a result.

operand—An expression subject to an operator.

region—A portion of code that can be collapsed or expanded.

statement—A unit of code that, when compiled and executed, performs an action.

syntax error—An error that occurs when program statements violate the grammatical rules of a programming language.

`Val` function—A function that filters a number from its argument if possible. This avoids errors introduced by the entering of nonnumeric data when only numbers are expected. However, the result of the `Val` function is not always what the programmer intended.

whitespace character—A space, tab or newline character.

CONTROLS, EVENTS, PROPERTIES & METHODS

Button `ab| Button`   This control allows user to raise an action or event.

- ***In action***

  `Calculate Total`

- ***Events***

  `Click`—This event is raised when the user clicks the `Button`.

- ***Properties***

  `Location`—This property specifies the location of the `Button` on the `Form` relative to the top-left corner.

  `Name`—This property specifies the name used to access the `Button` programmatically. The name should be prefixed with `btn`.

  `Size`—This property specifies the height and width (in pixels) of the `Button`.

  `Text`—This property specifies the text displayed on the `Button`.

MULTIPLE-CHOICE QUESTIONS

5.1 A(n) _____ represents a user action, such as clicking a `Button`.

a) statement   b) event

c) application   d) function

5.2 To switch to code view, select _____.

a) **Code > View**   b) **Design > Code**

c) **View > Code**   d) **View > File Code**

5.3 Code that performs the functionality of an application _____.

a) normally is provided by the programmer

b) can never be in the form of an event handler

c) always creates a graphical user interface

d) is always generated by the IDE

5.4 Comments _____.

    a) help improve program readability

    b) are preceded by the single-quote character

    c) are ignored by the compiler   d) All of the above.

5.5 The _____ allows a statement to continue past one line (when that character is preceded by one or more whitespace characters).

    a) single-quote (') character   b) hyphen (-) character

    c) underscore (_) character   d) plus (+) character

5.6 A(n) _____ causes an application to produce erroneous results.

    a) logic error   b) event

    c) assignment statement   d) syntax error

5.7 A portion of code that performs a specific task and returns a value is known as a(n) _____.

    a) variable   b) function

    c) operand   d) identifier

5.8 Visual Basic .NET keywords are _____.

    a) identifiers   b) reserved words

    c) case sensitive   d) properties

5.9 Visual Studio .NET allows you to organize code into _____, which you can expand or collapse to facilitate code editing.

    a) statements   b) operators

    c) regions   d) keywords

5.10 An example of a whitespace character is a _____ character.

    a) space   b) tab

    c) newline   d) All of the above.

EXERCISES

5.11 (*Inventory Enhancement*) Extend the **Inventory** application to include a TextBox in which the user can enter the number of shipments received in a week. Assume every shipment has the same number of cartons (each of which has the same number of items). Then modify the code so that the **Inventory** application uses that value in its calculation.

    a) *Copying the template application.* Copy the template application from `C:\Examples\Tutorial05\Exercises\InventoryEnhancement` to your work folder. Open the application by clicking `Inventory.sln` in the `InventoryEnhancement` folder.

    b) *Resizing the Form.* Resize the Form you used in this tutorial by setting the Size property to `296, 144`. Move the Button toward the bottom of the Form, as shown in Fig. 5.25. Its new location should be `184, 78`.

    c) *Adding a Label.* Add a Label to the Form and change the Text property to `Shipments this week:`. Set the Location property to `16, 80`. Resize the Label so that the entire text displays. Set the Label's Name property to `lblShipments`.

    d) *Adding a TextBox.* Add a TextBox to the right of the Label. Set its Text property to `0` and the Location property to `128, 80`. Set the TextAlign and Size properties to the same values as for the other TextBoxes in this tutorial's example. Set the TextBox's Name property to `txtShipments`.

    e) *Modifying the code.* Modify the **Calculate Total** Click event handler so that it multiplies the number of shipments per week with the product of the number of cartons in a shipment and the number of items in a carton.

Figure 5.25 Enhanced **Inventory** application GUI.

5.12 *(Counter Application)* Create a counter application. Your counter application will consist of a Label and Button on the Form. The Label initially displays 0, but, each time a user clicks the Button, the value in the Label is increased by 1. When incrementing the Label, you will need to write a statement such as lblTotal.Text = Val(lblTotal.Text) + 1.

a) *Modifying a new Form.* Create a new Form and change its Size property to 168, 144. Modify the Form so that the title reads **Counter**.

b) *Adding a Label.* Add a Label to the Form, and place it as shown in Fig. 5.26. Make sure that the Label's Text property is set to 0 and that TextAlign property is set so that any text will appear in the middle (both horizontally and vertically) of the Label. This can be done by using the MiddleCenter TextAlign property. Also set the BorderStyle property to Fixed3D. Set the Label's Name property to lblCountTotal.

c) *Adding a Button.* Add a Button to the Form. Set the Button's Text property to contain the text **Count**. Set the Button's Name property to btnCount.

d) *Creating an event handler.* Add an event handler to the **Count** Button such that the value in the Label increases by 1 each time the user clicks the **Count** Button.

Label ——————

Button ——————

Figure 5.26 **Counter** GUI.

5.13 *(Account Information Application)* Create an application that allows a user to input a name, account number and deposit amount. The user then clicks the **Enter** Button, which causes the name and account number to be copied and displayed in two output Labels. The deposit amount entered will be added to the deposit amount displayed in another output Label. The result is displayed in the same output Label. Every time the **Enter** Button is clicked, the deposit amount entered is added to the deposit amount displayed in the output Label, keeping a cumulative total. When updating the Label, you will need to write a statement such as lblDeposits.Text = Val(lblDeposits.Text) + Val(txtDepositAmount).

a) *Copying the template application.* Copy the template application from C:\Examples\Tutorial05\Exercises\AccountInformation to your work folder. Open the application by clicking AccountInformation.sln in the AccountInformation folder.

b) *Creating an event handler.* Add an event handler for the **Enter** Button's Click event.

c) *Coding the event handler.* Code the event handler to copy information from the **Name:** and **Account number:** TextBoxes to their corresponding output Labels. Then add the value in the **Deposit amount:** TextBox to the **Deposit amount:** output Label, and display the result in the **Deposit amount:** output Label.

d) *Testing the application.* Begin with the values in Fig. 5.27 when you test your application.

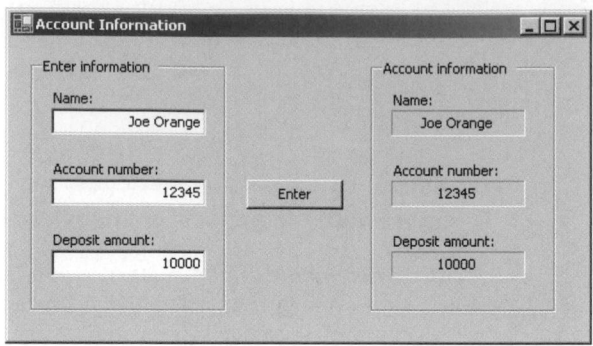

Figure 5.27 Account Information GUI.

What does this code do? ▶

5.14 After entering 10 in the `txtPrice` TextBox and 1.05 in the `txtTax` TextBox, a user clicks the `Button` named `btnEnter`. What is the result of the click, given the following code?

```
1   Private Sub btnEnter_Click(ByVal sender As _
2       System.Object, ByVal e As System.EventArgs) _
3       Handles btnCalculate.Click
4
5       lblOutput.Text = Val(txtPrice.Text) * Val(txtTax.Text)
6
7   End Sub ' btnEnter_Click
```

What's wrong with this code? ▶

5.15 The following event handler should execute when the user clicks a **Calculate** Button. Identify the error(s) in its code.

```
1   Private Sub btnCalculate_Click(ByVal sender As
2       System.Object, ByVal e As System.EventArgs) _   ' second line
3       Handles btnCalculate.Click
4
5       lblResult.Text = txtPrice.Text * txtTax.Text
6   End Sub ' btnCalculate_Click
```

Using the Debugger ▶

5.16 *(Account Information Debugging Exercise)* Copy the folder from `C:\Examples\Tutorial05\Exercises\DebuggingExercise` to your work folder, `C:\SimplyVB`, and run the **Account Information** application. Remove any syntax errors, so that the application runs correctly.

Programming Challenge ▶

5.17 *(Account Information Enhancement)* Modify Exercise 5.13 so that it no longer asks for the user's name and account number, but rather asks the user for a withdrawal or deposit amount. The user can enter both a withdrawal and deposit amount at the same time. When the **Enter** Button is clicked, the balance is updated appropriately.

   a) *Copying the template application.* If you have not already done so, copy the template application from `C:\Examples\Tutorial05\Exercises\AccountInformation` to your work folder.

   b) *Modifying the GUI.* Modify the GUI so that it appears as in Fig. 5.28.

   c) *Setting the default values.* Set the default name and account number to the values shown in Fig. 5.32 using the **Properties** window.

   d) *Writing code to add functionality.* Update the account balance for every withdrawal (which decreases the balance) and every deposit (which increases the balance). When the balance is updated, reset the TextBoxes to zero.

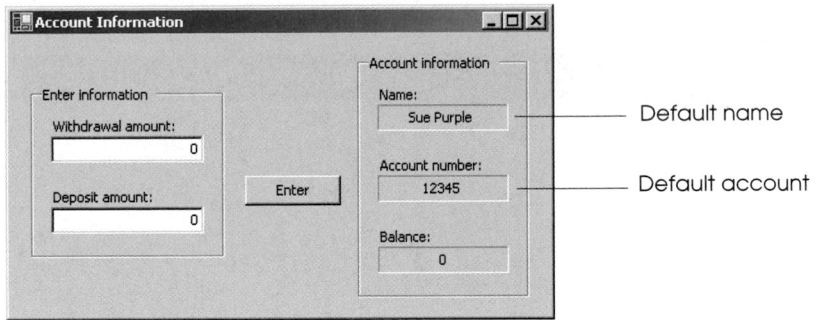

Figure 5.28   Modified **Account Information** GUI.

Objectives

In this tutorial, you will learn to:
- Create variables.
- Handle the **TextChanged** event.
- Apply basic memory concepts using variables.
- Use the precedence rules of arithmetic operators.
- Set breakpoints to debug applications.

Outline

T U T O R I A L

Enhancing the Inventory Application

Introducing Variables, Memory Concepts and Arithmetic

In the previous tutorial, you developed an **Inventory** application that performed a multiplication calculation to calculate the number of items received into inventory. You learned how to create TextBoxes to read user input from the keyboard. You also added a Button to a Form and programmed that Button to respond to a user's click. In this tutorial, you will enhance your **Inventory** application using additional programming concepts, including variables, events and arithmetic.

6.1 Test-Driving the Enhanced Inventory Application

In this tutorial, you will enhance the previous tutorial's **Inventory** application by inserting code rather than dragging and dropping Visual Basic .NET controls. You will use variables to perform arithmetic in Visual Basic .NET and you will study memory concepts, to help you understand how applications run on computers. Recall that your **Inventory** application from Tutorial 5 calculated the number of items received, from information supplied by the user—the number of cartons and the number of textbooks per carton. The enhanced application must meet the following requirements:

> **Application Requirements**
>
> *The inventory manager notices a flaw in your **Inventory** application. Although the application calculates the correct result, that result continues to display even after new data is entered. The only time the output changes is when the inventory manager clicks the **Calculate Button** again. You need to alter the **Inventory** application to clear the result as soon as the user enters new information into either of the TextBoxes, to avoid any confusion over the accuracy of your calculated result.*

You begin by test-driving the completed application. At first glance, the application does not seem to operate any differently from the application in the previous tutorial. However, you should notice that the **Total:** Label clears when you enter new data into either of the TextBoxes.

1. ***Opening the completed application.*** Double click `Inventory.sln` in the directory that contains this tutorial's completed application—`C:\Examples\Tutorial06\CompletedApplication\Inventory3` to open the completed application in Visual Studio .NET. If the `Form` does not appear in design view, double click `Inventory.vb` in the **Solutions Explorer** window. In general, if Visual Studio .NET does not open the `Form` in design view, you will need to double click the `Form`'s file name in the **Solution Explorer** window.

2. ***Running the application.*** Select **Debug > Start** to build and run the application. The application in Fig. 6.1 will appear.

Figure 6.1   **Inventory** application GUI displayed when the application is executed.

3. ***Calculating the number of items in the shipment.*** Enter 5 in the **Cartons per shipment:** TextBox and 6 in the **Items per carton:** TextBox. Click the **Calculate Total** Button. The result will be displayed in the **Total:** output Label (Fig. 6.2).

Figure 6.2   Running the **Inventory** application.

4. ***Entering new quantities.*** After you modify the application, the result displayed in the **Total:** Label will be removed when the user enters a new quantity in either TextBox. Enter 13 as the new number of cartons—the last calculation's result is cleared (Fig. 6.3). This will be explained in the box, *Handling the TextChanged Event.*

Figure 6.3   Modified **Inventory** application clears output Label after new input.

5. ***Terminating the application.*** Click the running application's close box to terminate the application.

6. ***Closing the solution.*** Select **File > Close Solution**.

6.2 Variables

Good Programming Practice

Typically, variable-name identifiers begin with a lowercase letter. Every word in the name after the first word should begin with a capital letter, for example, `intFirstNumber`.

Good Programming Practice

Use only letters and digits as characters for your variable names.

A variable holds data for your application, much as the `Text` property of a `Label` holds the text to be displayed to the user. Unlike the `Text` property of a `Label`, however, variable values are not shown to the user by default. Using variables in an application allows you to store and manipulate data without necessarily showing the data to the user and to store data without adding or using controls. Variables store such data as numbers, the date, the time and so on. However, each variable used in Visual Basic .NET corresponds to exactly one type of information. For example, a variable that stores a number cannot be used to store text.

In Visual Basic .NET, all variables must be **declared**, or reported, to the compiler by using program code. All **declarations** that you will make within event handlers begin with the keyword **Dim**. Recall that keywords are reserved for use by Visual Basic .NET. (A complete list of Visual Basic .NET keywords is presented in Appendix F.)

The box, *Using Variables in the Inventory Application*, introduces programming with variables. A variable name can be any valid identifier, which, as you learned in Tutorial 5, is a name that the compiler will recognize (and is not a keyword). As you also learned in the last tutorial, there are many valid characters for identifiers.

Using Variables in the Inventory Application

1. *Copying the template to your work folder.* Copy the `C:\Examples\Tutorial06\TemplateApplication\Inventory3` folder to `C:\SimplyVB` directory.

2. *Opening the template application.* Double click `Inventory.sln` in the `Inventory3` folder to open the application in Visual Studio .NET.

3. *Adding variable declarations to event handler `btnCalculate_Click`.* If you are in design view, enter code view by selecting **View > Code**. Add lines 130–133 of Fig. 6.4 to event handler `btnCalculate_Click`. Lines 131–133 are declarations, which begin with keyword `Dim`. Notice that, when you type the word `Dim`, as with all keywords, Visual Studio .NET colors it blue by default. The words `intCartons`, `intItems` and `intResult` are the names of variables. Lines 131–133 declare that variables `intCartons`, `intItems` and `intResult` store data of type **Integer**, using the **As** keyword. The As keyword indicates that the following word (in this case `Integer`) is the variable type. `Integer` variables store integer values (whole numbers such as 919, 0 and –11). Data types already defined in Visual Basic .NET, such as `Integer`, are known as **built-in data types** or **primitive data types**. Primitive data type names are also keywords. The 10 primitive data types are listed in Fig. 6.6. You will use some of these data types throughout the book.

Good Programming Practice

Prefix all `Integer` variable names with `int`. Using prefixes that indicate a variable's data type makes your code clearer, especially when you are first learning to program.

4. *Retrieving input from TextBoxes.* Skip one line after the variable declarations, and add lines 135–137 of Fig. 6.5 in event handler `btnCalculate_Click`. Once the user enters numbers and clicks **Calculate Total**, the values found in the `Text` property of the `TextBox` controls are converted to numerical values by the `Val` function. Then the numbers are assigned to variables `intCartons` (line 136) and `intItems` (line 137) with the assignment operator, `=`. Line 136 is read as "`intCartons` *gets* the result of the `Val` function applied to `txtCartons.Text`."

5. *Saving the application.* Select **File > Save All** to save all the solution's files.

(cont.)

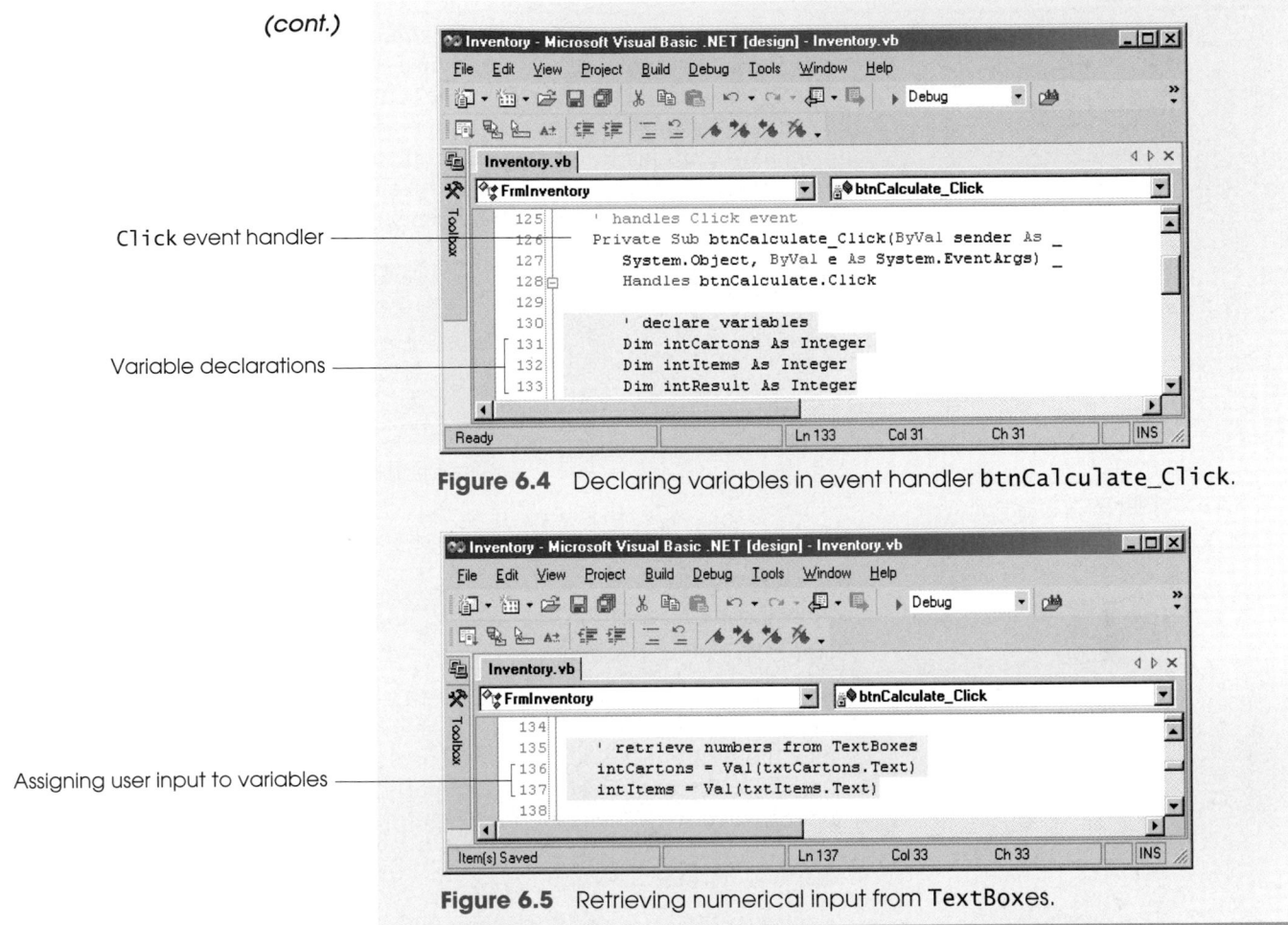

Figure 6.4   Declaring variables in event handler `btnCalculate_Click`.

Figure 6.5   Retrieving numerical input from `TextBoxes`.

The `Val` function returns a numerical value as data type **Double** when converting a value retrieved from a `TextBox`'s `Text` property. Data type `Double` is used to store both whole and fractional numbers. Normally, `Doubles` store floating-point numbers, which are numbers with decimal points such as 2.3456 and –845.4680. Variables of data type `Double` can hold values that are much larger than variables of data type `Integer`.

After `Val` converts the two values typed by the user to `Doubles`, lines 136–137 implicitly convert the `Doubles` to `Integer` values. Likewise, the integer value obtained by converting the `Double` in line 137 is assigned to variable `intItems`. Because `Doubles` and `Integers` are different types of variables, Visual Basic .NET performs a conversion from one type to the other. This process is called **implicit conversion** because the conversion takes place without any additional code. Now that you have assigned values to your new variables, you use the variables to calculate the number of textbooks received.

Built-in (primitive) data types				
Boolean	Date	Integer	Short	Char
Byte	Decimal	Long	Single	Double

Figure 6.6   Visual Basic .NET built-in data types.

Using Variables in a Calculation

1. **Performing the multiplication operation.** Skip one line from the end of the last statement you inserted and insert lines 139–140 in event handler `btnCalculate_Click` (Fig. 6.7). The statement on line 140 will multiply the `Integer` variable `intCartons` by `intItems` and assign the result to variable `intResult`, using the assignment operator `=`. The statement is read as, "`intResult` *gets* the value of `intCartons * intItems`." (Most calculations are performed in assignment statements.)

Calculating and displaying the result

Figure 6.7   Multiplication, using variables in `btnCalculate_Click`.

2. **Displaying the result.** Add lines 142–143 of Fig. 6.7 to event handler `btnCalculate_Click`. After the calculation is completed, line 143 will display the result of the multiplication operation. The number sets the value of Label `lblTotalResult`'s `Text` property. Once the property is updated, the Label will display the result of the multiplication operation (Fig. 6.8).

Result of calculation

Figure 6.8   Displaying the multiplication result using variables.

3. **Saving the application.** Select **File > Save All** to save all the solution's files.

4. **Running the application.** Select **Debug > Start** to run the application. Your application should appear as in Fig. 6.1. Enter 5 in the **Cartons per shipment:** TextBox and 6 in the **Items per carton:** TextBox. Then click the **Calculate Total** Button to test your application.

5. **Terminating the application.** Click the running application's close box to terminate the application.

SELF-REVIEW

1. When Visual Basic .NET converts a `Double` to an `Integer` without requiring any code, this is referred to as a(n) _____.

   a) explicit conversion   b) implicit conversion

   c) data-type change   d) transformation

2. Data types already defined in Visual Basic .NET, such as `Integer`, are known as _____ data types.

   a) provided   b) existing

   c) defined   d) built-in

Answers: 1) b. 2) d.

6.3 Handling the TextChanged Event

You might have noticed that the flaw, or **bug**, mentioned in the application requirements at the beginning of this tutorial remains in your application. Although the Label `lblTotalResult` displays the current result, once you enter a new number into a TextBox, that result is no longer valid. However, the result displayed does not change again until you click the **Calculate Total** Button, potentially confusing anyone using the application. Visual Studio .NET provides a convenient way to deal with this problem.

Handling the
TextChanged Event

1. ***Adding an event handler for txtCartons's TextChanged event.*** Double click the **Cartons per shipment:** TextBox, `txtCartons` to generate an event handler for the **TextChanged** event, which is raised when the TextBox's text changes. Visual Studio .NET will then generate an event handler with an empty body (no additional code) and place the cursor in the body. Insert line 151 of Fig. 6.9 into your code. Remember to add a comment (line 146) before the event handler. According to the application requirements for this tutorial, the application should clear the value in `lblTotalResult` every time users change the text in either TextBox. Line 151 clears the value in `lblTotalResult`.

TextChanged event handler ——

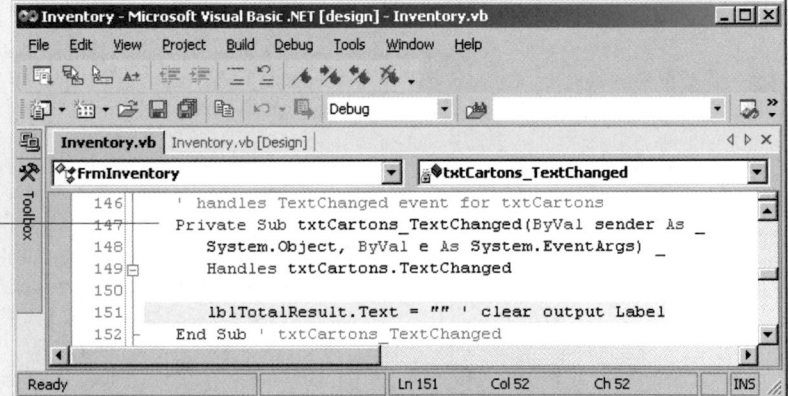

Figure 6.9 TextChanged event handler for **Cartons per shipment:** TextBox.

The notation "" (side-by-side double quotes) in line 151 is called an **empty string**, which is a value that does not contain any characters. This empty string replaces whatever is stored in `lblTotalResult.Text`. Note the line-continuation characters (_) at the ends of lines 147 and 148 of this code. Recall from Tutorial 5 that using line-continuation characters increases code readability by avoiding long lines that don't fit in the window.

2. ***Adding an event handler for txtItems's TextChanged event.*** We want the result cleared regardless of which TextBox changes value first. Return to design view by clicking the **Inventory.vb [Design]** tab. Then, double click the **Items per carton:** TextBox, and insert line 159 from Fig. 6.10 into the new event handler. Notice that these lines perform the same task as line 151—we want the same action, namely the clearing of a TextBox, to occur.

3. ***Saving the application.*** Select **File > Save All** to save all the solution's files.

4. ***Running the application.*** Select **Debug > Start** to run the application. To test the application, enter 8 in the **Cartons per shipment:** TextBox and 7 in the **Items per carton:** TextBox. When you click the **Calculate Total** Button, the number 56 should appear in the output Label. Then enter 9 in the **Items per carton:** TextBox to ensure that the TextChanged event handler clears the output Label.

Good Programming
Practice

If a statement is wider than the code editor window, use the line-continuation character within the statement to continue it on the next line.

(cont.)

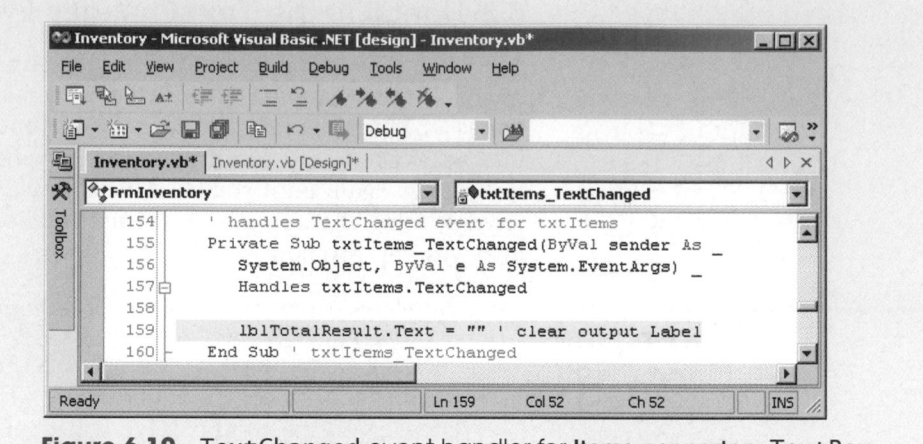

Figure 6.10   TextChanged event handler for **Items per carton:** TextBox.

Figure 6.11 presents our changes to class FrmInventory's event handlers. Notice that the class's name is the value of the Form's Name property, as you learned in Tutorial 4. New programming concepts are highlighted in yellow.

```
1    Public Class FrmInventory
2        Inherits System.Windows.Forms.Form
3
4        ' Windows Form Designer generated code
5
6        ' handles Click event
7        Private Sub btnCalculate_Click(ByVal sender As _
8            System.Object, ByVal e As System.EventArgs) _
9            Handles btnCalculate.Click
10
11           ' declare variables
12           Dim intCartons As Integer
13           Dim intItems As Integer
14           Dim intResult As Integer
15
16           ' retrieve numbers from TextBoxes
17           intCartons = Val(txtCartons.Text)
18           intItems = Val(txtItems.Text)
19
20           ' multiply two numbers
21           intResult = intCartons * intItems
22
23           ' display result in Label
24           lblTotalResult.Text = intResult
25        End Sub ' btnCalculate_Click
26
27        ' handles TextChanged event for txtCartons
28        Private Sub txtCartons_TextChanged(ByVal sender As _
29            System.Object, ByVal e As System.EventArgs) _
30            Handles txtCartons.TextChanged
31
32           lblTotalResult.Text = ""   ' clear output Label
33        End Sub ' txtCartons_TextChanged
34
```

Use keyword **Dim** to declare variables inside an event handler

Assigning a property's value to a variable

Assigning a variable to a property

Setting a TextBox's Text property to an empty string

Figure 6.11   **Inventory** application code. (Part 1 of 2.)

```
35        ' retrieve numbers from TextBoxes
36        Private Sub txtItems_TextChanged(ByVal sender As _
37          System.Object, ByVal e As System.EventArgs) _
38          Handles txtItems.TextChanged
39
40            lblTotalResult.Text = ""   ' clear output Label
41        End Sub ' txtItems_TextChanged
42
43    End Class ' FrmInventory
```

Figure 6.11   **Inventory** application code. (Part 2 of 2.)

1. The _____ is represented by `""` in Visual Basic .NET.

a) empty character   b) empty string

c) empty value   d) None of the above.

2. Use property _____ to remove any text displayed in a TextBox.

a) `ClearText`   b) `Remove`

c) `Display`   d) `Text`

Answers: 1) b. 2) d.

6.4 Memory Concepts

Variable names—such as `intCartons`, `intItems` and `intResult`—correspond to actual **locations** in the computer's memory. Every variable has a **name**, **type**, **size** and **value**. In the **Inventory** application code listing in Fig. 6.11, when the assignment statement (line 16)

```
intCartons = Val(txtCartons.Text)
```

executes, the user input stored in `txtCartons.Text` is converted to an `Integer`. This `Integer` is placed into the memory location to which the name `intCartons` has been assigned by the compiler. Suppose that the user enters the characters 12 in the **Cartons per shipment:** TextBox. This input is stored in `txtCartons.Text`. When the user clicks **Calculate Total**, Visual Basic .NET then converts the user input to an `Integer` and places the `Integer` value 12 into location `intCartons`, as shown in Fig. 6.12.

`intCartons` | 12 |

Figure 6.12   Memory location showing name and value of variable `intCartons`.

Whenever a value is placed in a memory location, this value replaces the value previously stored in that location. The previous value is overwritten (lost).

Suppose that the user then enters the characters 10 in the **Items per carton:** TextBox and clicks **Calculate Total**. Line 17 of Fig. 6.11

```
intItems = Val(txtItems.Text)
```

converts `txtItems.Text` to an `Integer`, placing the `Integer` value 10 into location `intItems`, and memory appears as shown in Fig. 6.13.

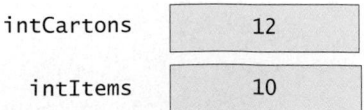

`intCartons` | 12 |

`intItems` | 10 |

Figure 6.13   Memory locations after values for variables `intCartons` and `intItems` have been input.

Once the **Calculate Total** Button is clicked, line 20 multiplies these values and places their total into variable `intResult`. The statement

```
intResult = intCartons * intItems
```

performs the multiplication and replaces (that is, overwrites) `intResult`'s previous value. After `intResult` is calculated, the memory appears as shown in Fig. 6.14. Note that the values of `intCartons` and `intItems` appear exactly as they did before they were used in the calculation of `intResult`. Although these values were used when the computer performed the calculation, they were not destroyed. This illustrates that, when a value is read from a memory location, the process is **non-destructive** (meaning that the value is not overwritten).

intCartons	12
intItems	10
intResult	120

Figure 6.14   Memory locations after a multiplication operation.

SELF-REVIEW

1. When a value is placed into a memory location, the value _____ the previous value into that location.

   a) copies
   b) replaces
   c) adds itself to
   d) moves

2. When a value is read from memory, that value is _____.

   a) overwritten
   b) replaced with a new value
   c) moved to a new location in memory
   d) not overwritten

Answers: 1) b. 2) d.

6.5 Arithmetic

Most programs perform arithmetic calculations. In the last tutorial, you performed the arithmetic operation multiplication by using the multiplication operator (*). The **arithmetic operators** are summarized in Fig. 6.15. Note the use of various special symbols not used in algebra. For example, the **asterisk** (*) indicates multiplication, the keyword **Mod** represents the **modulus operator**, the **backslash** (\) represents integer division and the **caret** (^) represents exponentiation. The majority of arithmetic operators in Fig. 6.15 are binary operators, each requiring two operands.

Visual Basic .NET operation	Arithmetic operator	Algebraic expression	Visual Basic .NET expression
Addition	+	$f + 7$	f + 7
Subtraction	–	$p - c$	p - c
Multiplication	*	bm	b * m
Division (float)	/	x/y or $\frac{x}{y}$ or $x \div y$	x / y
Division (integer)	\	none	v \ u
Modulus	Mod	r modulo s	r Mod s
Exponentiation	^	q^p	q ^ p
Unary Negative	–	$-e$	-e
Unary Positive	+	$+g$	+g

Figure 6.15   Arithmetic operators.

For example, the expression `intSum + intValue` contains the binary operator `+` and the two operands `intSum` and `intValue`. Visual Basic .NET also provides **unary operators**, which are operators that take only one operand. For example, unary versions of plus (+) and minus (–) are provided so that programmers can write expressions such as +9 (a positive number) and –19 (a negative number).

Visual Basic .NET has separate operators for **integer division** (the backslash, \) and **floating-point division** (the forward slash, /). Floating-point division divides two numbers (whole or fractional) and returns a floating-point number (a number with a decimal point). The operator for integer division treats its operands as integers and returns an integer result. `Integer` division takes two `Integer` operands and yields an `Integer` result; for example, the expression 7 \ 4 evaluates to 1, and the expression 17 \ 5 evaluates to 3. Note that any fractional part in the `Integer` division result simply is discarded (also called truncated)—no rounding occurs. When floating-point numbers (numbers with decimal points) are used with the integer-division operator, the numbers are first rounded to the nearest whole number, then divided. This means that, although 7.1 \ 4 evaluates to 1 as expected, the statement 7.7 \ 4 evaluates to 2, because 7.7 is rounded to 8 before the division occurs. Neither division operator allows division by zero. If your code divides by zero, a run-time error occurs. By default, this error will terminate the application.

The modulus operator, `Mod`, yields the remainder after division. The expression x `Mod` y yields the remainder after x is divided by y. Thus, 7 `Mod` 4 yields 3, and 17 `Mod` 5 yields 2. This operator is used most commonly with `Integer` operands, but also can be used with other types. The modulus operator can be applied to several interesting problems, such as discovering whether one number is a multiple of another. If a and b are numbers, a `Mod` b yields 0 if a is a multiple of b. 8 `Mod` 3 yields 2, so 8 is not a multiple of 3. But 8 `Mod` 2 and 8 `Mod` 4 each yield 0, because 8 is a multiple both of 2 and of 4.

Arithmetic expressions in Visual Basic .NET must be written in **straight-line form** so that you can type them into a computer. For example, the division of 7.1 by 4.3 cannot be written

$$\frac{7.1}{4.3}$$

but is written in straight-line form as 7.1 / 4.3. Raising 3 to the 2nd power cannot be written as 3^2, but is written in straight line form as 3 ^ 2.

Parentheses are used in Visual Basic .NET expressions in the same manner as in algebraic expressions. For example, to multiply *a* times the quantity *b* + *c*, you write

```
a * ( b + c )
```

Visual Basic .NET applies the operators in arithmetic expressions in a precise sequence, determined by the **rules of operator precedence,** which are generally the same as those followed in algebra. These rules enable Visual Basic .NET to apply operators in the correct order.

Common Programming Error

Attempting to divide by zero is a **run-time error** (that is, an error that has its effect while the application executes). Dividing by zero terminates an application.

Rules of Operator Precedence

1. *Operators in expressions contained within a pair of parentheses are evaluated first.* Thus, *parentheses can be used to force the order of evaluation to occur in any sequence desired by the programmer.* Parentheses are at the highest level of precedence. With **nested** (or **embedded**) parentheses, the operators contained in the innermost pair of parentheses are applied first.

2. *Exponentiation is applied next.* If an expression contains several exponentiation operations, operators are applied from left to right.

3. *Unary positive and negative, + and -, are applied next.* If an expression contains several sign operations, operators are applied from left to right.

(cont.)

4. ***Multiplication and floating-point division operations are applied next.*** If an expression contains several multiplication and floating-point division operations, operators are applied from left to right.

5. ***Integer division is applied next.*** If an expression contains several `Integer` division operations, operators are applied from left to right.

6. ***Modulus operations are applied next.*** If an expression contains several modulus operations, operators are applied from left to right.

7. ***Addition and subtraction operations are applied last.*** If an expression contains several addition and subtraction operations, operators are applied from left to right.

Notice in the box, *Rules of Operator Precedence*, that we mention nested parentheses. Not all expressions with several pairs of parentheses contain nested parentheses. For example, although the expression

```
a * ( b + c ) + c * ( d + e )
```

contains multiple pairs of parentheses, none of the parentheses are nested. Rather, these sets are referred to as being "on the same level" and are evaluated from left to right.

Let's consider several expressions in light of the rules of operator precedence. Each example lists an algebraic expression and its Visual Basic .NET equivalent.

The following calculates the average of three numbers:

Algebra: $m = \dfrac{(a + b + c)}{3}$

Visual Basic .NET: `m = ( a + b + c ) / 3`

The parentheses are required, because floating-point division has higher precedence than addition. The entire quantity (a + b + c) is to be divided by 3. If the parentheses are omitted, erroneously, we obtain a + b + c / 3, which evaluates as

$a + b + \dfrac{c}{3}$

The following is the equation of a straight line:

Algebra: $y = mx + b$

Visual Basic .NET: `y = m * x + b`

No parentheses are required. The multiplication is applied first, because multiplication has a higher precedence than addition. The assignment occurs last because it has a lower precedence than multiplication and addition.

To develop a better understanding of the rules of operator precedence, consider how the expression $y = ax^2 + bx + c$ is evaluated:

Good Programming Practice

The use of redundant parentheses in complex arithmetic expressions can make the expressions easier to read.

The circled numbers under the statement indicate the order in which Visual Basic .NET applies the operators. Remember that, in Visual Basic .NET, x^2 is represented as x ^ 2. Also, note that the assignment operator is applied last because it has a lower precedence than any of the arithmetic operators.

As in algebra, it is acceptable to place unnecessary parentheses in an expression to make the expression easier to read—these parentheses are called **redundant parentheses**. For example, the preceding assignment statement might use redundant parentheses to emphasize terms:

$$y = (a * x \wedge 2) + (b * x) + c$$

SELF-REVIEW

1. Arithmetic expressions in Visual Basic .NET must be written _____ to facilitate entering applications into the computer.

   a) using parentheses   b) on multiple lines

   c) in straight-line form   d) None of the above.

2. The expression to the right of the assignment operator (=) is always evaluated _____ the assignment occurs.

   a) before   b) after

   c) at the same time   d) None of the above.

Answers: 1) c. 2) a.

6.6 Using the Debugger: Breakpoints

The debugger will be one of your most important tools in developing applications, once you become familiar with its features. You were introduced to the debugger in Tutorial 5, where you used it to locate and eliminate syntax errors. In this tutorial, you continue your study of the debugger, learning about breakpoints, which allow you to examine what your application is doing while it is running. A **breakpoint** is a marker that can be set at any executable line of code. When program execution reaches a breakpoint, execution pauses, allowing you to peek inside your application and ensure that there are no logic errors, such as an incorrect calculation. In the box, *Using the Debugger: Breakpoints*, you learn how to use breakpoints in the Visual Studio .NET debugger.

Using the Debugger:
Breakpoints

1. ***Enabling the debugger.*** The debugger is enabled by default. If it is not enabled, you have to change the Solution Configuration ComboBox to **Debug**. To do this, click the ComboBox's down arrow (Fig. 6.16) to access the Solution Configuration ComboBox, and select **Debug**. The IDE toolbar will then display **Debug** in the Solution Configuration ComboBox.

Solution Configuration **ComboBox** ⎯⎯⎯⎯⎯⎯⎯

Figure 6.16 Setting Solution Configuration to **Debug**.

(cont.)

2. ***Inserting breakpoints in Visual Studio .NET.*** To insert a breakpoint in Visual Studio .NET, either click inside the **margin indicator bar** (the gray margin indicator at the left of the code window, Fig. 6.17) next to the line of code at which you wish to break, or right click that line of code and select **Insert Breakpoint**. You can set as many breakpoints as necessary. Set breakpoints at lines 140 and 143 of your code. A solid maroon circle appears where you clicked, indicating that a breakpoint has been set (Fig. 6.17). When the application runs, it suspends execution at any line that contains a breakpoint. The application is said to be in **break mode** when the debugger pauses the application's execution. Breakpoints can be set during design mode, break mode and run mode.

Margin indicator bar

Breakpoints

Figure 6.17 Setting two breakpoints.

3. ***Beginning the debugging process.*** After setting breakpoints in the code editor, select **Debug > Start** to begin the debugging process. During debugging of a Windows application, the application window appears (Fig. 6.18), allowing program interaction (input and output). Enter 10 and 7 into the `Text-boxes` and click **Calculate Total** to continue. The title bar of the IDE will now display **[break]** (Fig. 6.19), indicating that the IDE is in break mode.

Figure 6.18 **Inventory** application running.

Title bar displays **[break]**

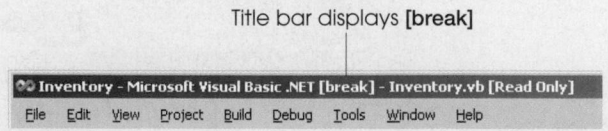

Figure 6.19 Title bar of the IDE displaying **[break]**.

4. ***Examining program execution.*** Program execution suspends at the first breakpoint, and the IDE becomes the active window (Fig. 6.20). The **yellow arrow** to the left of line 140 indicates that this line contains the next statement to execute.

(cont.)

Figure 6.20   Program execution suspended at the first breakpoint.

5. ***Using the Continue command to resume execution.*** To resume execution, select **Debug > Continue**. The application executes until it stops at the next breakpoint on line 143. Notice that, when you place your mouse pointer over the variable name `intResult`, the value that the variable stores is displayed in a ***Quick Info*** box (Fig. 6.21). In a sense, you are peeking inside the computer at the value of one of your variables. As you'll see, this can help you spot logic errors in your applications.

Figure 6.21   Displaying a variable value by placing the mouse pointer over a variable name.

6. ***Finishing program execution.*** Use the **Debug > Continue** command to complete the program execution. When there are no more breakpoints at which to suspend execution, the application will execute to completion and the output will appear in the **Total:** Label (Fig. 6.22).

Figure 6.22   Program output.

(cont.)

7. ***Disabling a breakpoint.*** To **disable a breakpoint**, right click a line of code on which a breakpoint has been set, and select **Disable Breakpoint**. The disabled breakpoint is indicated by a hollow maroon circle (Fig. 6.23). Disabling rather than removing a breakpoint allows you to re-enable the breakpoint (by clicking inside the hollow circle) in an application. This also can be done by right clicking the line marked by the hollow maroon circle and selecting **Enable Breakpoint**.

Disabled breakpoint ——

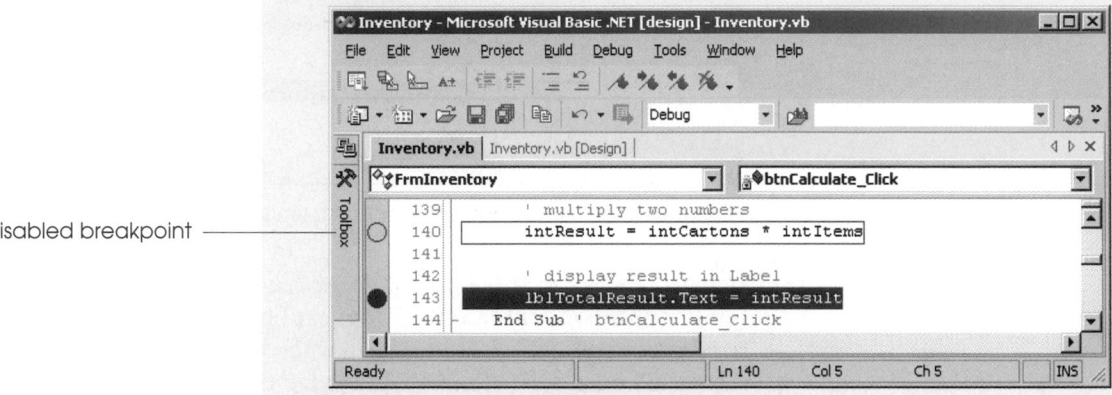

Figure 6.23 Disabled breakpoint.

8. ***Removing a breakpoint.*** To remove a breakpoint that you no longer need, right click a line of code on which a breakpoint has been set and select **Remove Breakpoint**. You also can remove a breakpoint by clicking the maroon circle in the margin indicator bar.

In this section, you learned how to enable the debugger and set breakpoints so that you can examine the results of code while an application is running. You also learned how to continue execution after an application suspends execution at a breakpoint and how to disable and remove breakpoints.

SELF-REVIEW

1. A breakpoint cannot be set at a(n) _____.

    a) comment   b) executable line of code

    c) assignment statement   d) arithmetic statement

2. When program execution suspends at a breakpoint, the next statement to be executed is the statement _____ the breakpoint.

    a) before   b) after

    c) at   d) None of the above.

Answers: 1) a. 2) c.

6.7 Internet and Web Resources

Please take a moment to visit each of these sites briefly. To save typing time, use the hot links on the enclosed CD or at www.deitel.com.

www.devx.com/dotnet
This Web site contains information about the .NET platform, which includes Visual Basic .NET. The site includes links to articles, books and news.

www.vbcity.com
This site lists numerous links to articles, books and tutorials on Visual Basic .NET. The site allows programmers to submit code and have it rated by other developers.

This site also polls visitors on a variety of Visual Basic .NET topics and provides access to archives, which include code listings and news.

www.cyber-matrix.com/vb.htm
This site links to Visual Basic .NET tutorials, books, tips and tricks, controls, programming tools, magazines, news groups and more.

searchvb.techtarget.com
This site offers a search engine designed specifically to discover Visual Basic .NET Web sites.

www.aewnet.com/root/dotnet/vbnet
The site links to demonstrations, articles, tutorials and Visual Basic .NET sites in German and Spanish.

6.8 Wrap-Up

You have now added variables to your **Inventory** application. You began by using variables to produce the same results as your previous **Inventory** application. Then you enhanced the **Inventory** application, using the TextChanged event, which allowed you to execute code that cleared the value in the output Label when the user changed a value in either TextBox.

You learned about memory concepts, including how variables are read and written. You will apply these concepts to the applications that you will build in later tutorials, which rely heavily on the use of variables. You learned how to perform arithmetic in Visual Basic .NET and you studied the rules of operator precedence to evaluate mathematical expressions correctly. Finally, you learned how to insert breakpoints in the debugger. Breakpoints allow you to pause program execution and examine variable values. This capability will prove useful to you in finding and fixing logic errors.

In the next tutorial, you will design a graphical user interface and write code to create a wage calculator. You will use pseudocode, an informal language that will help you design the application. You will learn to use to the debugger's **Watch** window, another useful tool that will help you remove logic errors.

SKILLS SUMMARY

Declaring a Variable
- Use the keyword Dim.
- Use a valid identifier as a variable name.
- Use the keyword As to indicate that the following word specifies the variable's data type.
- Specify a type such as Integer or Double.

Handling a TextBox's TextChanged Event
- Double click a TextBox on a Form to generate an empty event handler.
- Insert code into the event handler, which executes when the text in a TextBox changes.

Reading a Value from a Memory Location
- Use the variable's name (as declared in the variable's Dim statement) on the right side of an assignment statement.

Replacing a Value in a Memory Location
- Use the variable name, followed by the assignment operator (=), followed by an expression giving the new value.

Representing Positive and Negative Numbers
- Use the unary versions of plus (+) and minus (-).

Performing Arithmetic Operations
- Write arithmetic expressions in Visual Basic .NET in straight-line form.
- Use the rules of operator precedence to determine the order in which operators will be applied.

- Use operator + to perform addition.
- Use operator – to perform subtraction.
- Use operator * to perform multiplication.
- Use operator / to perform floating-point division.
- Use operator \ (backslash) to perform Integer division, which treats the operands as Integers and returns an Integer result.
- Use operator ^ to perform exponentiation.
- Use the modulus operator, Mod, to report the remainder after division.

Setting a Breakpoint

- Click the margin indicator bar (the gray margin indicator at the left of the code window) next to the line at which you wish to break, or right click a line of code and select **Insert Breakpoint**.

Resuming Program Execution after Entering Break Mode

- Select **Debug > Continue**.

Disabling a Breakpoint

- Right click a line of code containing a breakpoint, and select **Disable Breakpoint**.

Removing a Breakpoint

- Right click a line of code containing a breakpoint, and select **Remove Breakpoint**.
- You also can remove a breakpoint by clicking the maroon circle in the margin indicator bar.

Enabling a Breakpoint

- Enable a disabled breakpoint by clicking inside the hollow circle in the margin indicator bar.
- You also can enable a disabled breakpoint by right clicking the line marked by the hollow maroon circle and selecting **Enable Breakpoint**.

KEY TERMS

active window—The front-most window on your screen.

arithmetic operators—The operators +, –, *, /, \, ^ and Mod.

break mode—The IDE mode when program execution is suspended. This mode is entered through the debugger.

breakpoint—A statement where execution is to suspend, indicated by a solid maroon circle.

built-in data type—A data type already defined in Visual Basic .NET, such as an Integer (also known as a primitive data type).

Dim keyword—The keyword that indicates the declaration of a variable.

empty string—A string that does not contain any characters.

implicit conversion—A conversion from one data type to another performed by Visual Basic .NET.

integer—A whole number, such as 919, –11, 0 and 138624.

Integer data type—The data type that stores integer values.

margin indicator bar—A margin in the IDE where breakpoints are displayed.

Mod—The modulus operator yields the remainder after division.

primitive data type—A data type already defined in Visual Basic .NET, such as Integer (also known as a built-in data type).

run-time error—An error that has its effect at execution time.

TextChanged event—The event that occurs when the text in a TextBox changes.

variable—A location in the computer's memory where a value can be stored for use by an application.

CONTROLS, EVENTS, PROPERTIES & METHODS

TextBox   `[abl]` `TextBox`   This control allows the user to input data from the keyboard.

■ *In action*

| 0 |

■ *Events*

`TextChanged`—This event is raised when the text in the `TextBox` is changed.

■ *Properties*

`Location`—This property specifies the location of the `Label` on the `Form` relative to the top-left corner.

`Name`—This property specifies the name used to access the `TextBox` programmatically. The name should be prefixed with `txt`.

`Size`—This property specifies the height and width (in pixels) of the `TextBox`.

`Text`—This property specifies the text displayed in the `TextBox`.

`TextAlign`—This property specifies how the text is aligned within the `TextBox`.

MULTIPLE-CHOICE QUESTIONS

6.1 Parentheses that are added to an expression simply to make it easier to read are known as _____ parentheses.

    a) necessary   b) redundant

    c) embedded   d) nested

6.2 The _____ operator performs `Integer` division.

    a) `\`   b) `+`

    c) `Mod`   d) `^`

6.3 Every variable has a _____.

    a) name   b) value

    c) type   d) All of the above.

6.4 In Visual Basic .NET, arithmetic expressions must be written in _____ form.

    a) straight-line   b) top-bottom

    c) left-right   d) right-left

6.5 Arithmetic expressions are evaluated _____.

    a) from right to left   b) from left to right

    c) according to the rules of operator precedence

    d) from the lowest level of precedence to the highest level of precedence

6.6 Variable declarations in event handlers begin with the keyword _____.

    a) `Declare`   b) `Dim`

    c) `Sub`   d) `Integer`

6.7 Entering a value in a `TextBox` raises the _____ event.

    a) `TextAltered`   b) `ValueChanged`

    c) `ValueEntered`   d) `TextChanged`

6.8 The _____ function converts user input from a `TextBox` to a variable of type `Double`.

    a) `Convert`   b) `MakeDouble`

    c) `Val`   d) `WriteDouble`

6.9 Variables to store integer values should be declared with keyword _____.

    a) `Integer`   b) `Int`

    c) `IntVariable`   d) None of the above.

6.10 Keyword _____ in a variable declaration indicates that the data type is the next word.

a) IsA   b) Type

c) Dim   d) As

EXERCISES

6.11 *(Simple Encryption Application)* This application uses a simple technique to encrypt a number. Encryption is the process of modifying data so that only those intended to receive the data can undo the changes and view the original data. The user enters the data to be encrypted via a TextBox. The application then multiplies the number by 7 and adds 5. The application displays the encrypted number in a Label as shown in Fig. 6.24.

a) *Copying the template application.* Copy the folder SimpleEncryption from C:\Examples\Tutorial06\Exercises to C:\SimplyVB.

b) *Opening the template application.* Open the application by double clicking SimpleEncryption.sln.

Figure 6.24 Result of completed **Simple Encryption** application.

c) *Coding the Click event handler.* Encrypt the number in the Click event handler by using the preceding technique. The user input should be stored in an Integer variable (intNumber) before it is encrypted. The event handler then should display the encrypted number.

d) *Clearing the result.* Add an event handler for the **Enter number to encrypt:** TextBox's TextChanged event. This event handler should clear the **Encrypted number:** TextBox whenever the user enters new input.

6.12 *(Temperature Converter Application)* Write an application that converts a Celsius temperature, *C*, to its equivalent Fahrenheit temperature, *F*. Figure 6.25 displays the completed application. Use the following formula:

$$F = \frac{9}{5}C + 32$$

a) *Copying the template application.* Copy the folder TemperatureConversion from C:\Examples\Tutorial06\Exercises to C:\SimplyVB.

b) *Opening the template application.* Open the application by double clicking TemperatureConversion.sln.

Figure 6.25 Completed **Temperature Converter**.

c) *Coding the Click event handler.* Perform the conversion in the **Convert** Button's Click event handler. Define Integer variables to store the user-input Celsius temperature and the result of the conversion. Display the Fahrenheit equivalent of the temperature conversion.

d) *Clearing user input.* Clear the result in the **Enter a Celsius temperature:** TextBox's TextChanged event.

6.13 *(Simple Calculator Application)* In this exercise, you will add functionality to a simple calculator application. The calculator will allow a user to enter two numbers in the TextBoxes. There will be four Buttons labeled +, -, / and *. When the user clicks the Button labeled as addition, subtraction, multiplication or division, the application will perform that operation on the numbers in the TextBoxes and displays the result. The calculator also should clear the calculation result when the user enters new input. Figure 6.26 displays the completed calculator.

a) **Copying the template application.** Copy the folder `SimpleCalculator` from `C:\Examples\Tutorial06\Exercises` to `C:\SimplyVB`.

b) **Opening the template application.** Open the application by double clicking `Simple-Calculator.sln`.

Figure 6.26 Result of **Calculator** application.

c) **Coding the addition `Click` event handler.** This event handler should add the two numbers and display the result.

d) **Coding the subtraction `Click` event handler.** This event handler should subtract the second number from the first number and display the result.

e) **Coding the multiplication `Click` event handler.** This event handler should multiply the two numbers and display the result.

f) **Coding the division `Click` event handler.** This event handler should divide the first number by the second number and display the result.

g) **Clearing the result.** Write event handlers for the TextBoxes' TextChanged events. Write code to clear the result Label (`lblResult`) after the user enters new input into either TextBox.

What does this code do? ▶ **6.14** This code modifies values `intNumber1`, `intNumber2` and `intResult`. What are the final values of these variables?

```
1   Dim intNumber1 As Integer
2   Dim intNumber2 As Integer
3   Dim intResult As Integer
4
5   intNumber1 = 5 * (4 + 6)
6   intNumber2 = 2 ^ 2
7   intResult = intNumber1 \ intNumber2
```

What's wrong with this code? ▶ **6.15** Find the error(s) in the following code, which uses variables to perform a calculation.

```
1   Dim intNumber1 As Integer
2   Dim intNumber2 As Integer
3   Dim intResult As Integer
4
5   intNumber1 = (4 * 6 ^ 4) / (10 Mod 4 - 2)
6   intNumber2 = (16 \ 3) ^ 2 * 6 + 1
7   intResult = intNumber1 - intNumber2
```

Using the Debugger ▶ **6.16** **(Average Three Numbers)** You have just written an application that takes three numbers as input in TextBoxes, stores the three numbers in variables and then finds the average of the numbers. The output is displayed in a Label (Fig. 6.27, which displays the incorrect output). You soon realize, however, that the number displayed in the Label is not the average, but rather a number that does not make sense given the input. Use the debugger to help locate and remove this error.

Figure 6.27 **Average Three Numbers** application for Exercise 6.16.

a) *Copying the template application.* Copy the folder AverageDebugging from C:\Examples\Tutorial06\Exercises to C:\SimplyVB.

b) *Running the template application.* Run the application, and view the output to observe that the output is incorrect.

c) *Closing the application.* Close the application, and view the Average.vb file in code view.

d) *Setting breakpoints.* Set a breakpoint in the btnCalculate_Click event handler. Run the application again, and use the debugger to help find the error(s).

e) *Finding and correcting the error(s).* Once you have found the error(s), modify the application so that it correctly calculates the average of three numbers.

Programming Challenge ▶ **6.17** *(Digit Extraction)* Write an application that allows the user to enter a five-digit number into a TextBox. The application then separates the number into its individual digits and displays each digit in a Label. The application should look and behave similarly to Fig. 6.28. [*Hint:* You can use the Mod operator to extract the ones digit from a number. For instance, 12345 Mod 10 is 5. You can use integer division (\) to "peel off" digits from a number. For instance, 12345 \ 100 is 123. This allows you to treat the 3 in 12345 as a ones digit. Now you can isolate the 3 by using the Mod operator. Apply this technique to the rest of the digits.]

Figure 6.28 **Digit Extractor** application GUI.

Objectives

In this tutorial, you will learn to:
- Understand basic problem-solving techniques.
- Understand control structures.
- Understand and create pseudocode.
- Use the If...Then and If...Then...Else selection statements to choose among alternative actions.
- Use the assignment operators.
- Use the debugger's **Watch** window.

Outline

Wage Calculator Application

Introducing Algorithms, Pseudocode and Program Control

Before writing an application, it is essential to have a thorough understanding of the problem you need to solve. This will allow you to design a carefully planned approach to solving the problem. When writing an application, it is equally important to recognize the types of building blocks that are available and to use proven application-construction principles. In this tutorial, you will learn the theory and principles of **structured programming**. Structured programming is a technique for organizing program control that will help you develop applications that are clear and easier to debug and modify. The techniques presented are applicable to most high-level languages, including Visual Basic .NET.

7.1 Test-Driving the Wage Calculator Application

In this section, we preview this tutorial's **Wage Calculator** application. The application must meet the following requirements:

Application Requirements

A payroll company calculates the gross earnings per week of employees. Employees' weekly salary is based on the number of hours they worked and their hourly wages. Create an application that accepts this information and calculates the employee's total (gross) earnings. The application assumes a standard work week of 40 hours. The wages for forty or fewer hours are calculated by multiplying the employee's hourly salary by the number of hours worked. Any time worked over 40 hours in a week is considered "overtime" and earns time and a half. Salary for time and a half is calculated by multiplying the employee's hourly wage by 1.5 and multiplying the result of that calculation by the number of overtime hours worked. The total overtime earned is added to the user's gross earnings for the regular 40 hours of work to calculate the total earnings for that week.

This application calculates wages from hourly salary and hours worked per week. Normally, if an employee has worked 40 or fewer hours, the employee is paid regular wages. The calculation differs if the employee has worked more than the standard 40-hour work week. In this tutorial, we introduce a programming tool known as a **control structure** that allows us to make this distinction and perform different calculations based on different user inputs. You begin by test-driving the completed application.

Test-Driving the Wage Calculator Application

1. ***Running the application.*** Load the **Wage Calculator** application by double clicking `WageCalculator.sln` in the `C:\Examples\Tutorial07\CompletedApplication\WageCalculator` folder. Select **Debug > Start** to run the application. The Form in Fig. 7.1 will appear. Notice that we have placed the TextBoxes vertically, rather than horizontally, in this application. To make our GUI well-organized, we have aligned the right sides of each TextBox and made the TextBoxes the same size. We have also left aligned the TextBoxes' descriptive Labels.

Figure 7.1 **Wage Calculator** application.

 GUI Design Tip

When using multiple TextBoxes vertically, align the TextBoxes on their right sides, and where possible make the TextBoxes the same size. Left-align the descriptive Labels for such TextBoxes

2. ***Enter the employee's hourly wage.*** Enter **10** in the **Hourly wage:** TextBox.

3. ***Enter the number of hours the employee worked.*** Enter **45** in the **Weekly hours:** TextBox.

4. ***Calculate the employee's gross earnings.*** Click the **Calculate** Button. The result (**$475.00**) is displayed in the **Gross earnings:** TextBox (Fig. 7.2). Notice that the employee's salary is the sum of the wages for the standard 40-hour work week (40 * 10) and the overtime pay (5 * 10 * 1.5).

Figure 7.2 Calculating wages by clicking the **Calculate** Button.

5. ***Terminating the application.*** Click the running application's close box to terminate the application.

6. ***Closing the solution.*** Select **File > Close Solution**.

7.2 Algorithms

Computing problems can be solved by executing a series of actions in a specific order. A procedure for solving a problem, in terms of:

1. the **actions** to be executed and
2. the **order** in which these actions are to be executed

is called an **algorithm**. The following example demonstrates the importance of correctly specifying the order in which the actions are to be executed. Consider the "rise-and-shine algorithm" followed by one junior executive for getting out of bed and going to work: (1) get out of bed, (2) take off pajamas, (3) take a shower, (4) get dressed, (5) eat breakfast and (6) carpool to work. This routine prepares the executive for a productive day at the office.

However, suppose that the same steps are performed in a slightly different order: (1) get out of bed, (2) take off pajamas, (3) get dressed, (4) take a shower, (5) eat breakfast, (6) carpool to work. In this case, our junior executive shows up for work soaking wet.

Indicating the appropriate sequence in which to execute actions is equally crucial in computer programs. **Program control** refers to the task of ordering an application's statements correctly. In this tutorial, you will begin to investigate the program-control capabilities of Visual Basic .NET.

SELF-REVIEW

1. _____ refers to the task of ordering an application's statements correctly.

   a) Actions   b) Program control
   c) Control structures   d) Visual programming

2. A(n) _____ is a plan for solving a problem in terms of the actions to be executed and the order in which these actions are to be executed.

   a) chart   b) control structure
   c) algorithm   d) ordered list

Answers: 1) b. 2) c.

7.3 Pseudocode

Pseudocode is an informal language that helps programmers develop algorithms. The pseudocode we present is particularly useful in the development of algorithms that will be converted to structured portions of Visual Basic .NET applications. Pseudocode resembles everyday English; it is convenient and user-friendly, but it is not an actual computer-programming language.

Software Design Tip

Pseudocode helps the programmer conceptualize an application during the application-design process. The pseudocode statements can be converted to Visual Basic .NET at a later point.

Pseudocode statements are not executed on computers. Rather, pseudocode helps you "think out" an application before attempting to write it in a programming language, such as Visual Basic .NET. In this tutorial, we provide several examples of pseudocode.

The style of pseudocode that we present consists solely of characters, so that you can create and modify pseudocode by using editor programs, such as the Visual Studio .NET code editor or Notepad. A carefully prepared pseudocode program can be converted easily to a corresponding Visual Basic .NET application. Much of this conversion is as simple as replacing pseudocode statements with their Visual Basic .NET equivalents. Let us look at an example of a pseudocode statement:

Assign 0 to the counter

This pseudocode statement provides an easy-to-understand task. You can put several such statements together to form an algorithm that can be used to meet application requirements. When the pseudocode algorithm has been completed, the programmer can then convert pseudocode statements to their equivalent Visual Basic .NET statements. The pseudocode statement above, for instance, can be converted to the following Visual Basic .NET statement:

```
intCounter = 0
```

Pseudocode normally describes only **executable statements**, which are the actions that are performed when the corresponding Visual Basic .NET application is run. An example of a programming statement that is not executed is a declaration. The declaration

```
Dim intNumber As Integer
```

informs the compiler of `intNumber`'s type and instructs the compiler to reserve space in memory for this variable. The declaration does not cause any action, such as input, output or a calculation, to occur when the program executes, so we would not include this information in the pseudocode.

7.4 Control Structures

Normally, statements in an application are executed one after another in the order in which they are written. This is called **sequential execution**. However, Visual Basic .NET allows you to specify that the next statement to be executed might not be the next one in sequence. A **transfer of control** occurs when an executed statement does not directly follow the previously executed statement in the written application. This is common in computer programs.

All programs can be written in terms of only three control structures: the **sequence structure**, the selection structure and the repetition structure. The sequence structure is built into Visual Basic .NET—unless directed to act otherwise, the computer executes Visual Basic .NET statements sequentially—that is, one after the other in the order in which they appear in the application. The **activity diagram** in Fig. 7.3 illustrates a typical sequence structure, in which two calculations are performed in order. We discuss activity diagrams in detail following Fig. 7.3.

Figure 7.3   Sequence structure activity diagram.

Activity diagrams are part of the **Unified Modeling Language (UML)**—an industry standard for modeling software systems. An activity diagram models the **activity** (also called the **workflow**) of a portion of a software system. Such activities may include a portion of an algorithm, such as the sequence structure in Fig. 7.3. Activity diagrams are composed of special-purpose symbols, such as **action-state symbols** (a rectangle with its left and right sides replaced with arcs curving outward), **diamonds** and **small circles**; these symbols are connected by **transition arrows**, which represent the flow of the activity. Figure 7.3 does not include any diamond symbols—these will be used in later activity diagrams, beginning with Fig. 7.6.

Like pseudocode, activity diagrams help programmers develop and represent algorithms, although many programmers prefer pseudocode. Activity diagrams clearly show how control structures operate.

Consider the activity diagram for the sequence structure in Fig. 7.3. The activity diagram contains two **action states** that represent actions to perform. Each action state contains an **action expression**—for example, "add grade to total" or "add 1 to counter"—that specifies a particular action to perform. Other actions might include calculations or input/output operations. The arrows in the activity diagram are called transition arrows. These arrows represent **transitions**, which indicate the order in which the actions represented by the action states occur—the application that implements the activities illustrated by the activity diagram in Fig. 7.3 first adds `intGrade` to `intTotal`, then adds `1` to `intCounter`.

The **solid circle** located at the top of the activity diagram represents the activity's **initial state**—the beginning of the workflow before the application performs the modeled activities. The solid circle surrounded by a hollow circle that appears at the bottom of the activity diagram represents the **final state**—the end of the workflow after the program performs its activities.

Notice, in Fig. 7.3, the rectangles with the upper-right corners folded over. These look like sheets of paper and are called **notes** in the UML. Notes are like comments in Visual Basic .NET applications—they are explanatory remarks that describe the purpose of symbols in the diagram. Figure 7.3 uses UML notes to show the Visual Basic .NET code that the programmer might associate with each action state in the activity diagram. A **dotted line** connects each note with the element that the note describes. Activity diagrams normally do not show the Visual Basic .NET code that implements the activity, but we use notes here to show you how the diagram relates to Visual Basic .NET code.

Visual Basic .NET provides three types of **selection structures**, which we discuss in this tutorial and in Tutorial 11. The **If...Then** selection structure performs (selects) an action (or sequence of actions) based on a condition. A **condition** is an expression with a **true** or **false** value that is used to make a decision. Conditions are **evaluated** (that is, tested) to determine whether their value is true or false. These values are of data type **Boolean** and are specified in Visual Basic .NET code by using the keywords **True** and **False**. Sometimes we refer to a condition as a Boolean expression.

If the condition evaluates to true, the actions specified by the If...Then structure will execute. If the condition evaluates to false, the actions specified by the If...Then structure will be skipped. The **If...Then...Else** selection structure performs an action (or sequence of actions) if a condition is true and performs a different action (or sequence of actions) if the condition is false. The `Select Case` structure, discussed in Tutorial 11, performs one of many actions (or sequences of actions), depending on the value of an expression.

The If...Then structure is called a **single-selection structure** because it selects or ignores a single action (or a sequence of actions). The If...Then...Else structure is called a **double-selection structure** because it selects between two different actions (or sequences of actions). The `Select Case` structure is called a **multiple-selection structure** because it selects among many different actions or sequences of actions.

Visual Basic .NET provides seven types of **repetition structures**—While...End While, Do While...Loop, Do...Loop While, Do Until...Loop, Do...Loop Until, For...Next and For Each...Next. Repetition structures Do While...Loop and Do Until...Loop are covered in Tutorial 8; Do...Loop While and Do...Loop Until are covered in Tutorial 9; For...Next is covered in Tutorial 10; and For Each...Next is covered in Tutorial 20.[1] The words If, Then, Else, End, Select, Case, While, Do, Until, Loop, For, Next and Each are all Visual Basic .NET keywords—Appendix F includes a complete list of Visual Basic .NET keywords. We discuss many of Visual Basic .NET's keywords and their respective purposes throughout this book. Visual Basic .NET has a much larger set of keywords than most other popular programming languages.

Visual Basic .NET has 11 control structures—the sequence structure, three types of selection structures and seven types of repetition structures. Each Visual Basic .NET application is formed by combining as many of each type of control structure as is necessary. As with the sequence structure in Fig. 7.3, each control structure is drawn with two small circle symbols—a solid black one to represent the entry point to the control structure, and a solid black one surrounded by a hollow circle to represent the exit point.

All Visual Basic .NET control structures are **single-entry/single-exit control structures**—each has exactly one entry point and one exit point. Such control structures make it easy to build applications—the control structures are attached to one another by connecting the exit point of one control structure to the entry point of the next. This is similar to stacking building blocks, so, we call it **control-structure stacking**. The only other way to connect control structures is through **control-structure nesting**, whereby one control structure can be placed inside another. Thus, algorithms in Visual Basic .NET applications are constructed from only 11 different types of control structures combined in only two ways—this is a model of simplicity. Control structures in Visual Basic .NET are implemented as statements, so, from this point forward (after the following exercises), we use the term "statement" in preference to the term "structure."

SELF-REVIEW

1. All Visual Basic .NET applications can be written in terms of _____ types of control structures.

   a) one   b) two

   c) three   d) four

2. The process of application statements executing one after another in the order in which they are written is called _____.

   a) transfer of control   b) sequential execution

   c) workflow   d) None of the above.

Answers: 1) c. 2) b.

7.5 If...Then Selection Statement

A selection statement chooses among alternative courses of action in an application. For example, suppose that the passing grade on a test is 60 (out of 100). The pseudocode statement

> If student's grade is greater than or equal to 60
>   Display "Passed"

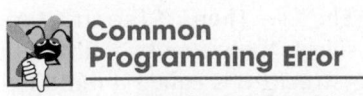

Common Programming Error

Omission of the Then keyword in an If...Then statement is a syntax error.

determines whether the condition "student's grade is greater than or equal to 60" is true or false. If the condition is true, then "Passed" is displayed, and the next pseudocode statement in order is "performed." (Remember that pseudocode is not a real programming language.) If the condition is false, the display statement is ignored, and the next pseudocode statement in order is performed.

---

1. We do not discuss the While...End While loop in this book. This repetition structure behaves identically to the Do While...Loop and is provided for programmers familiar with previous versions of Visual Basic.

The preceding pseudocode *If* statement may be written in Visual Basic .NET as

```
If intStudentGrade >= 60 Then
    lblGradeDisplay.Text = "Passed"
End If
```

Good Programming Practice

Indent the statements of If...Then statements to improve readability.

Notice that the Visual Basic .NET code corresponds closely to the pseudocode, demonstrating the usefulness of pseudocode as a program-development tool. The body (sometimes called a **block**) of the If...Then statement displays the string "Passed" in a Label. The keywords End If close an If...Then statement.

Notice the indentation in the If...Then statement. Such indentation enhances application readability. The Visual Basic .NET compiler ignores whitespace characters, such as spaces, tabs and new lines used for indentation and vertical spacing, unless the whitespace characters are contained in strings.

Common Programming Error

It is a syntax error to add spaces between the symbols in the operators <>, >= and <= (as in < >, > =, < =).

The condition between keywords If and Then determines whether the statement(s) within the If...Then statement will execute. If the condition is true, the body of the If...Then statement executes. If the condition is false, the body is not executed. Conditions in If...Then statements can be formed by using the **equality operators** and **relational operators** (also called **comparison operators**), which are summarized in Fig. 7.4. The relational and equality operators all have the same level of precedence.

Common Programming Error

Reversal of the operators <>, >= and <= (as in ><, =>, =<) is a syntax error.

Algebraic equality or relational operators	Visual Basic .NET equality or relational operator	Example of Visual Basic .NET condition	Meaning of Visual Basic .NET condition
Relational operators			
>	>	intX > intY	intX is greater than intY
<	<	intX < intY	intX is less than intY
≥	>=	intX >= intY	intx is greater than or equal to intY
≤	<=	intX <= intY	intX is less than or equal to intY
Equality operators			
=	=	intX = intY	intX is equal to intY
≠	<>	intX <> intY	intX is not equal to intY

Figure 7.4 Equality and relational operators.

Figure 7.5 shows the **syntax** of the If...Then statement. A statement's syntax specifies how the statement must be formed to execute without syntax errors. Throughout this book, we will describe the syntax of any new control statements. Let's look closely at the syntax of an If...Then statement. The first line of Fig. 7.5 specifies that the statement must begin with the keyword If and be followed by a condition and the keyword Then. Notice that we have italicized *condition*. This indicates that, when creating your own If...Then statement, you should replace the text *condition* with the actual condition that you would like evaluated. The second line indicates that you should replace *statements* with the actual statements that you want to be included in the body of the If...Then statement. These statements make up the body of the If...Then statement. Notice that the text *statements* is placed within square brackets. These brackets do not appear in the actual If...Then statement. Instead, the square brackets indicate that certain portions of the statement are optional. In this example, the square brackets indicate that all statements in the If...Then statement's body are optional. Of course, if there are no statements in the body of the If...Then statement, then no actions will occur as part of that statement, regardless of the condition's value. The final line indicates that the statement ends with the End If keywords.

Syntax

```
If condition Then
   [ statements ]
End If
```

Figure 7.5 If...Then statement syntax.

Figure 7.6 illustrates the single-selection If...Then statement. This activity diagram contains what is perhaps the most important symbol in an activity diagram—the diamond, or **decision symbol**, which indicates that a decision is to be made. Note the two sets of square brackets above or next to the arrows leading from the decision symbol; these are called **guard conditions**. A decision symbol indicates that the workflow will continue along a path determined by the symbol's associated guard conditions, which can be true or false. Each transition arrow emerging from a decision symbol has a guard condition (specified in square brackets above or next to the transition arrow). If a particular guard condition is true, the workflow enters the action state to which that transition arrow points. For example, in Fig. 7.6, if the grade is greater than or equal to 60, the application displays "Passed", then transitions to the final state of this activity. If the grade is less than 60, the application immediately transitions to the final state without displaying a message. Only one guard condition associated with a particular decision symbol can be true at once.

Figure 7.6 If...Then single-selection statement activity diagram.

Note that the If...Then statement (Fig. 7.6), is a single-entry/single-exit statement. The activity diagrams for the remaining control structures also contain (aside from small circle symbols and flowlines called transitions) only action-state symbols, indicating actions to be performed, and diamond symbols, indicating decisions to be made. Representing control structures in this way emphasizes the **action/decision model of programming**. To understand the process of structured programming better, we can envision 11 bins, each containing a different type of the 11 possible control structures. The control structures in each bin are empty, meaning that nothing is written in the action-state symbols and no guard conditions are written next to the decision symbols. The programmer's task is to assemble an application, using as many control structures as the algorithm demands, combining those control statements in only two possible ways (stacking or nesting) and filling in the actions and decisions (with the decisions' guard conditions) in a manner appropriate to the algorithm. Again, each of these control structures is implemented in Visual Basic .NET as a statement.

SELF-REVIEW

1. Which of the following If...Then statements correctly displays that a student received an A on an exam if the score was 90 or above?

```
a) If intStudentGrade <> 90 Then
      lblDisplay.Text = "Student received an A"
   End If
```

```
b) If intStudentGrade > 90 Then
       lblDisplay.Text = "Student received an A"
    End If
c) If intStudentGrade = 90 Then
       lblDisplay.Text = "Student received an A"
    End If
d) If intStudentGrade >= 90 Then
       lblDisplay.Text = "Student received an A"
    End If
```

2. The symbol _____ is not a Visual Basic .NET operator.

   a) *   b) ∧

   c) %   d) <>

Answers: 1) d. 2) c.

7.6 If...Then...Else Selection Statement

As you have learned, the If...Then selection statement performs an indicated action (or sequence of actions) only when the condition evaluates to true; otherwise, the action (or sequence of actions) is skipped. The If...Then...Else selection statement allows the programmer to specify that a different action (or sequence of actions) be performed when the condition is true from when the condition is false. For example, the pseudocode statement

> *If student's grade is greater than or equal to 60*
> > *Display "Passed"*
>
> *Else*
> > *Display "Failed"*

displays "*Passed*" if the student's grade is greater than or equal to 60, but displays "Failed" if the student's grade is less than 60. In either case, after output occurs, the next pseudocode statement in sequence is "performed."

The preceding pseudocode *If...Else* statement may be written in Visual Basic .NET as

```
If intStudentGrade >= 60 Then
    lblDisplay.Text = "Passed"
Else
    lblDisplay.Text = "Failed"
End If
```

Good Programming Practice

Apply a standard indentation convention consistently throughout your applications to enhance readability.

Note that the body of the **Else** clause is indented so that it lines up with the indented body of the If clause. A standard indentation convention should be applied consistently throughout your applications. It is difficult to read programs that do not use uniform spacing conventions. The If...Then...Else selection statement follows the same general syntax as the If...Then statement. The Else keyword and any related statements are placed between the If...Then and closing End If statements as in Fig. 7.7.

Syntax

```
If condition Then
    [ statements ]
Else
    [ statements ]
End If
```

Figure 7.7   If...Then...Else statement syntax.

Figure 7.8 illustrates the flow of control in the If...Then...Else double-selection statement. Once again, note that (besides the initial state, transition arrows and final state) the only other symbols in the activity diagram represent action states and decisions. In this example, the grade is either less than 60 or greater than or equal to 60. If the grade is less than 60, the application displays `"Failed"`. If the grade is equal to or greater than 60, the application displays `"Passed"`. We continue to emphasize this action/decision model of computing. Imagine again a deep bin containing as many empty double-selection statements as might be needed to build any Visual Basic .NET application. Your job as a programmer is to assemble these selection statements (by stacking and nesting) with any other control statements required by the algorithm. You fill in the action states and decision symbols with action expressions and guard conditions appropriate to the algorithm.

Good Programming Practice

Indent both body statements of an `If...Then...Else` statement to improve readability.

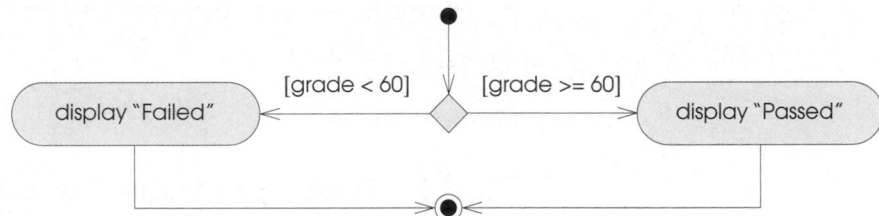

Figure 7.8 `If...Then...Else` double-selection statement activity diagram.

Nested `If...Then...Else` statements test for multiple conditions by placing `If...Then...Else` statements inside other `If...Then...Else` statements. For example, the following pseudocode (Fig. 7.9) will display "A" for exam grades greater than or equal to 90, "B" for grades in the range 80–89, "C" for grades in the range 70–79, "D" for grades in the range 60–69 and "F" for all other grades:

> If student's grade is greater than or equal to 90
>   Display "A"
>
> Else
>   If student's grade is greater than or equal to 80
>   Display "B"
>
>   Else
>   If student's grade is greater than or equal to 70
>   Display "C"
>
>   Else
>   If student's grade is greater than or equal to 60
>   Display "D"
>
>   Else
>   Display "F"

Figure 7.9 Pseudocode for an application that displays a student's grades.

The pseudocode above may be written in Visual Basic .NET as shown in Fig. 7.10.

Good Programming Practice

If there are several levels of indentation, each level should be indented further to the right by the same amount of space.

```
If intStudentGrade >= 90 Then
    lblDisplay.Text = "A"
Else
    If intStudentGrade >= 80 Then
        lblDisplay.Text = "B"
    Else
        If intStudentGrade >= 70 Then
            lblDisplay.Text = "C"
        Else
            If intStudentGrade >= 60 Then
                lblDisplay.Text = "D"
            Else
                lblDisplay.Text = "F"
            End If
        End If
    End If
End If
```

Figure 7.10 Visual Basic .NET code converted from the pseudocode in Fig. 7.9.

If `intStudentGrade` is greater than or equal to 90, the first condition evaluates to `True` and the statement `lblDisplay.Text = "A"` is executed. Notice that, with a value for `intStudentGrade` greater than or equal to 90, the remaining three conditions will evaluate to `True`. These conditions, however, are never evaluated, because they are placed within the `Else` portion of the outer `If...Then...Else` statement. Because the first condition is `True`, all statements within the `Else` clause are skipped. Let's now assume `intStudentGrade` contains the value 75. The first condition is `False`, so the program will execute the statements within the `Else` clause of this statement. This `Else` clause also contains an `If...Then...Else` statement, with the condition `intStudentGrade >= 80`. This condition evaluates to `False`, causing the statements in this `If...Then...Else` statement's `Else` clause to execute. This `Else` clause contains yet another `If...Then...Else` statement, with the condition `intStudentGrade >= 70`. This condition is `True`, causing the statement `lblDisplay.Text = "C"` to execute. The `Else` clause of this `If...Then...Else` statement is then skipped.

Most Visual Basic .NET programmers prefer to write the preceding `If...Then...Else` statement, using the **ElseIf keyword**, as

```
If intStudentGrade >= 90 Then
    lblDisplay.Text = "A"
ElseIf intStudentGrade >= 80 Then
    lblDisplay.Text = "B"
ElseIf intStudentGrade >= 70 Then
    lblDisplay.Text = "C"
ElseIf intStudentGrade >= 60 Then
    lblDisplay.Text = "D"
Else
    lblDisplay.Text = "F"
End If
```

Figure 7.11   `If...Then...Else` statement using the `ElseIf` keyword.

The two statements are equivalent, but the latter statement is popular because it avoids deep indentation of the code. Such deep indentation often leaves little room on a line, forcing lines to be split and decreasing code readability. Notice that the final portion of the `If...Then...Else` statement uses the `Else` keyword to handle all remaining possibilities. The `Else` clause must always be last in an `If...Then...Else` statement—following an `Else` clause with another `Else` or `ElseIf` clause is a syntax error. You should also note that the latter statement requires only one `End If`.

SELF-REVIEW

1. `If...Then...Else` is a _____-selection statement.

   a) single

   b) double

   c) triple

   d) nested

2. Placing an `If...Then...Else` statement inside another `If...Then...Else` statement is an example of _____.

   a) nesting `If...Then...Else` statements

   b) stacking `If...Then...Else` statements

   c) creating sequential `If...Then...Else` statements

   d) None of the above.

Answers: 1) b. 2) a.

7.7 Constructing the Wage Calculator Application

The following section teaches you how to build the **Wage Calculator** by using the `If...Then...Else` statement. The `If...Then...Else` statement allows you to select between calculating regular wages and including overtime pay based on the number of hours worked. The following pseudocode describes the basic operation of the **Wage Calculator** application, which executes when the user clicks **Calculate:**

Input the number of hours worked and hourly wage from the user

If the number of hours worked is less than or equal to 40 hours
　　Gross earnings equals hours worked times hourly wage
Else
　　Gross earnings equals 40 times hourly wage plus hours
　　　above 40 times wage and a half

Display gross earnings

Visual Studio .NET provides many programming tools to aid you in creating powerful and effective applications. Because there are so many tools available, it is often helpful to create a table to organize and choose the best GUI elements. Like pseudocode, these tables simplify the task of creating the application by outlining the application's actions. In addition to listing the application's actions, the table assigns controls and events to the actions described in the pseudocode. Figure 7.12 presents the Action/Control/Event (ACE) table for the **Wage Calculator** application.

Action/Control/Event (ACE) Table for the Wage Calculator Application

Action	Control	Event

Label the application's controls	`lblWage`
	`lblHours`
	`lblEarnings`	

Retrieve user input	`txtWage` `txtHours`	
Calculate employee's pay	`btnCalculate`	`Click`
Display employee's earnings	`lblEarningsResult`	

Figure 7.12　Action/Control/Event table for the **Wage Calculator** application.

The `Label`s in the first row display information about the application to the user. These `Label`s help guide the user through the application. The `Button` control, `btnCalculate`, is used to calculate the employee's wages. Notice that the third column of the table specifies that we will be using this control's `Click` event to perform any calculations. The `TextBox`es will contain input from the user. The final control, `lblEarningsResult`, is a `Label` that displays the application's output.

We now apply our pseudocode and the ACE table to complete the **Wage Calculator** application. The box, *Declaring Variables in the* **Calculate** *Button's Click Event Handler*, will guide you through the process of adding a `Click` event to the **Calculate** `Button` and declaring the variables you'll need to calculate the employee's wages. If you forget to add code to this `Click` event, the program will not respond when the user clicks the **Calculate** `Button`.

Declaring Variables in the Calculate Button's Click Event Handler

1. ***Copying the Wage Calculator template application to your work folder.*** Locate the `WageCalculator` folder in `C:\Examples\Tutorial07\TemplateApplication`. Copy this folder to your work folder (`C:\SimplyVB`).

2. ***Opening the solution.*** Double click `WageCalculator.sln` to open the **Wage Calculator** application in Visual Studio .NET. If the application does not open in design view, double click the **WageCalculator.vb** file in the **Solution Explorer**. If the **Solution Explorer** is not open, select **View > Solution Explorer**.

(cont.)

3. **_Adding the Calculate Button Click event handler._** In this example, the event handler calculates the gross wages when the **Calculate** Button's Click event occurs. Double click the **Calculate** Button. An event handler will be generated, and you will be switched to code view. Lines 127–130 of Fig. 7.13 display the generated event handler. We have formatted the header of the event handler for readability.

Figure 7.13   **Calculate** Button event handler.

Finally, notice that we have added comments on lines 126 and 130. On line 130, the End Sub keywords indicate the end of event handler btnCalculate_Click. On line 132, the End Class keywords indicate the end of class FrmWageCalculator. We often add such comments so that the reader can easily determine which event handler or class is being closed without having to search for the beginning of that event handler or class in the file.

4. **_Declaring variables._** This program introduces two primitive data types, **Double** and **Decimal**. A Double holds numbers with decimal points. Because hours and wages are often fractional numbers, Integers are not appropriate for this application. Add lines 130–133 of Fig. 7.14 into the body of event handler btnCalculate_Click. Line 131 contains a variable declaration for Double dblHours, which holds the number of hours input by the user. Notice that the variable names for Doubles are prefixed with dbl.

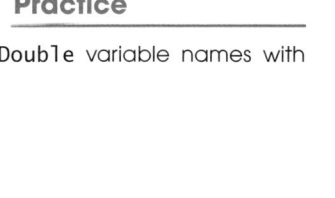

Good Programming Practice

Prefix Double variable names with dbl.

Figure 7.14   Declaring variables of type Double and Decimal.

(cont.)

Type `Decimal` is used to store monetary amounts because this data type ensures rounding accuracy in arithmetic calculations involving monetary amounts. Lines 132–133 declare `decWage`, which stores the hourly wage input by the user, and `decEarnings`, which stores the total amount of earnings for the week. Notice that `Decimal` variable names are prefixed with `dec`.

5. ***Declaring a constant.*** Add line 135 of Fig. 7.15 to the end of event handler `btnCalculate_Click`. Line 135 contains a **constant**, a variable whose value cannot be changed after its initial declaration. Constants are declared with keyword **Const**. In this case, we assign to the constant `intHOUR_LIMIT` the maximum number of hours worked before mandatory overtime pay (40). Notice that we prefix this `Integer` constant with `int` and capitalize the rest of the constant's name to emphasize that it is a constant.

Constant declaration

Figure 7.15 Creating a constant.

6. ***Saving the project.*** Select **File > Save All** to save all the solution's files.

Now that you have declared variables, you can use them to receive input from the user and then use that input to compute and display the user's wages. The box, *Determining the User's Wages*, walks you through using the `If...Then...Else` statement to determine the user's wages.

Determining the User's Wages

1. ***Obtaining inputs from the TextBoxes.*** Add lines 137–139 of Fig. 7.16 to the end of event handler `btnCalculate_Click`. Lines 138–139 assign values to `dblHours` and `decWage` from the `TextBox`es into which the user enters data. The `Val` function returns the user input as `Double`s (lines 138–139). Visual Basic .NET implicitly converts the `Double` result of `Val` to data type `Decimal` in order to assign the result to `decWage` (line 139).

Variable assignment

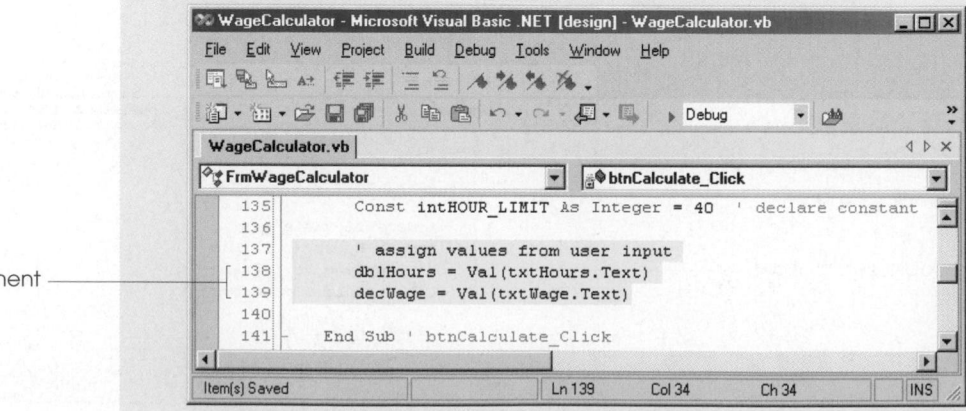

Figure 7.16 Assigning data to variables.

(cont.)

2. ***Determining wages based on hours worked.*** Begin to add the `If...Then...Else` statement shown in lines 141–154 of Fig. 7.17 to the end of event handler `btnCalculate_Click`. First type lines 141–142, and press *Enter*. Notice that the keywords `End If` are added for you by Visual Studio .NET. Continue by adding lines 144–153 to the `If...Then...Else` statement. You might need to indent as you go. This `If...Then...Else` statement determines whether employees earn overtime in addition to their usual wages. Line 142 determines whether the value stored in `dblHours` is less than or equal to `intHOUR_LIMIT`. If it is, then line 145 assigns the value of the product of hours and wage to `decEarnings`. When you multiply a variable of data type `Double` by a variable of data type `Decimal`, Visual Basic .NET implicitly converts the `Decimal` variable to a `Double`. The `Double` result is implicitly converted to a `Decimal` when it is assigned to `decEarnings`.

Error-Prevention Tip

To reduce errors, the IDE sometimes adds keywords for you. One example is the adding of the keywords `End If` when an `If...Then` or an `If...Then...Else` statement is created. This eliminates the possibility that such keywords will be forgotten or misspelled.

Added
`If...Then...Else`
statement

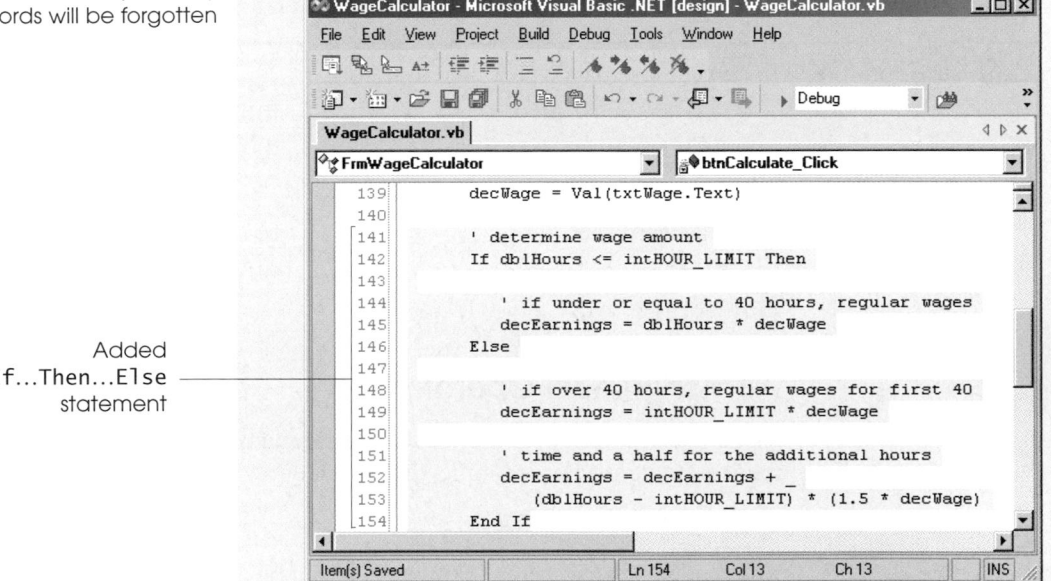

Figure 7.17 `If...Then...Else` statement to determine wages.

If, on the other hand, `dblHours` is not less than or equal to `intHOUR_LIMIT`, then the application proceeds to the `Else` keyword on line 146. Line 149 computes the wage for the hours worked up to the limit set by `intHOUR_LIMIT` and assigns it to `decEarnings`. Lines 152–153 determine how many hours over `intHOUR_LIMIT` there are (by using the expression `dblHours - intHOUR_LIMIT`) and then multiplies that by `1.5` and the user's hourly wages. This calculation results in the user's time-and-a-half pay for overtime hours. The value of this statement is then added to the value of `decEarnings`, and the result is assigned to `decEarnings`.

3. ***Displaying the result.*** Add lines 156–157 of Fig. 7.18 to the end of event handler `btnCalculate_Click`. Line 157 assigns the value in `decEarnings` to the `Text` property of the `Label` `lblEarningsResult`, implicitly converting `decEarnings` from a `Decimal` to a string.

4. ***Running the application.*** Select **Debug > Start** to run the application. Recall that selecting **Debug > Start** also saves any changes made to your application. Notice that the output is not yet formatted as it should be in the completed application. We will demonstrate how to add this functionality in Section 7.9. Once you have finished testing the application, close the running application by clicking its close box.

(cont.)

Displaying output ——

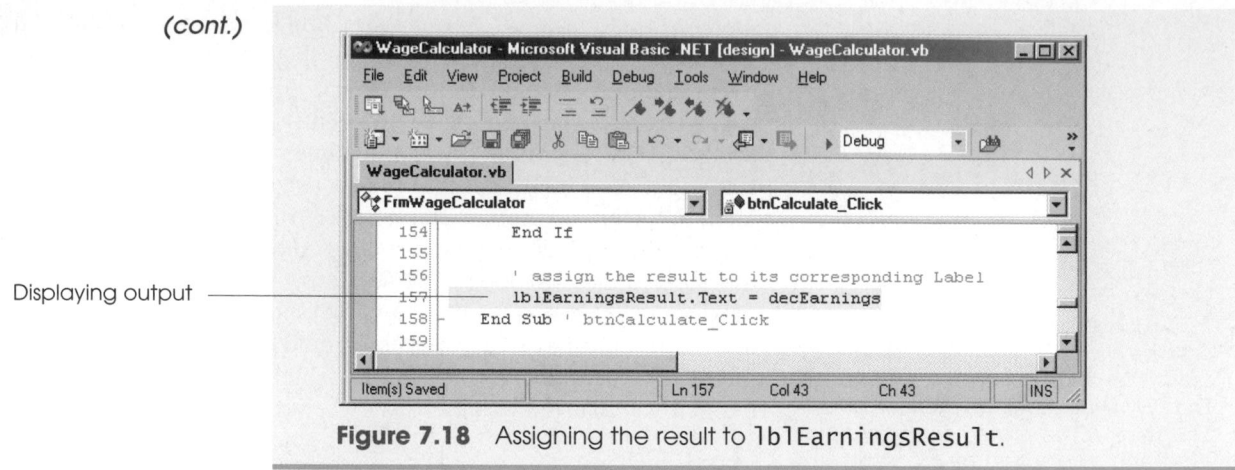

Figure 7.18   Assigning the result to `lblEarningsResult`.

SELF-REVIEW

1. The `Decimal` data type is used to store _____.

     a) letters and digits   b) integers

     c) strings   d) monetary amounts

2. Constants are declared with keyword _____.

     a) `Fixed`   b) `Constant`

     c) `Final`   d) `Const`

Answers: 1) d. 2) d.

7.8 Assignment Operators

Visual Basic .NET provides several **assignment operators** for abbreviating assignment statements. For example, the statement

```
intValue = intValue + 3
```

which adds 3 to the value in `intValue`, can be abbreviated with the addition assignment operator += as

```
intValue += 3
```

The += operator adds the value of the right operand to the value of the left operand and stores the result in the left operand. Visual Basic .NET provides assignment operators for several binary operators, including +, -, *, ^, / or \. When an assignment statement is evaluated, the expression to the right of the operator is always evaluated first, then assigned to the variable on the left. Figure 7.19 includes the assignment operators, sample expressions using these operators and explanations.

Assignment operators	Sample expression	Explanation	Assigns
Assume: `intC = 4`			
+=	`intC += 7`	`intC = intC + 7`	`11` to `intC`
-=	`intC -= 3`	`intC = intC - 3`	`1` to `intC`
*=	`intC *= 4`	`intC = intC * 4`	`16` to `intC`
/=	`intC /= 2`	`intC = intC / 2`	`2` to `intC`
\=	`intC \= 3`	`intC = intC \ 3`	`1` to `intC`
^=	`intC ^= 2`	`intC = intC ^ 2`	`16` to `intC`

Figure 7.19   Assignment operators.

The box, *Using the Addition Assignment Operator*, demonstrates abbreviating our time-and-a-half calculation with the += operator. When you run the application again, you will notice that the program runs the same as before—all that has changed is that one of the longer statements was made shorter.

Using the Addition Assignment Operator

1. **Adding the addition assignment operator.** Replace lines 152–153 of Fig. 7.17 with line 152 of Fig. 7.20.

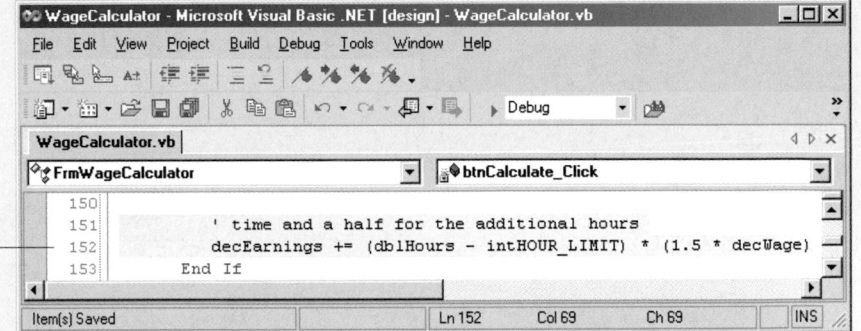

Assignment operator shortens statement

Figure 7.20 Using the addition assignment operator in a calculation.

In this step, we have used the addition assignment operator to make our statement shorter. Notice that the statement still performs the same action—the time-and-a-half pay for the user is calculated and added to the regular wages earned.

2. **Running the application.** Select **Debug > Start** to run the application. Notice that the application executes as it did in the last box. Once you have finished testing the application, close it.

SELF-REVIEW

1. The *= operator _____.
   a) squares the value of the right operand and stores the result in the left operand
   b) adds the value of the right operand to the value of the left operand and stores the result in the left operand
   c) creates a new variable and assigns the value of the right operand to that variable
   d) multiplies the value of the left operand by the value of the right operand and stores the result in the left operand

2. If intX is initialized with the value 5, what value will intX contain after the expression intX -= 3 is executed?
   a) 3   b) 5
   c) 7   d) 2

Answers: 1) d. 2) d.

7.9 Formatting Text

There are several ways to format output in Visual Basic .NET. In this section, we introduce method **String.Format** to control how text displays. Modifying the appearance of text for display purposes is known as text **formatting**. This method takes as an argument a **format control string**, followed by arguments that indicate the values to be formatted. The format control string argument specifies how the remaining arguments are to be formatted.

Recall that your **Wage Calculator** does not display the result of its calculation with the appropriate decimal and dollar sign that you saw when test-driving the application. In the box, *Formatting the Gross Earnings*, you learn how to apply currency formatting to the value in the **Gross earnings:** TextBox.

Formatting the Gross Earnings

1. **Modifying the Calculate *Button's Click event*.** If Visual Studio .NET is not already in code view, select **View > Code**. Replace line 157 of Fig. 7.18 with line 156 of Fig. 7.21.

Formatting output as currency

Figure 7.21 Using the `Format` method to display the result as currency.

Line 156 sends the format control string, "`{0:C}`", and the value to be formatted, `decEarnings`, to the `String.Format` method. The number zero indicates that argument 0 (`decEarnings`—the first argument after the format control string) should take the format specified by the letter after the colon; this letter is called the **format specifier**. In this case, we use the format defined by the uppercase letter C, which represents the **currency format**, used to display values as monetary amounts. The effect of the C format specifier varies, depending on the locale setting of your computer. In our case, the result is preceded with a dollar sign ($) and displayed with two decimal places (representing cents) because we are in the United States.

 GUI Design Tip

Format all monetary amounts using the C (currency) format specifier.

2. **Running the application.** Select **Debug > Start** to run the application. Once you have finished testing the application, close it.

Figure 7.22 shows several format specifiers. All format specifiers are case insensitive, so the uppercase letters may be used interchangeably with their lowercase equivalents. Note that format code D must be used only with `Integers`.

Format Specifier	Description
C	Currency. Formats the currency based on the computer's locale setting. For U.S. currency, precedes the number with $, separates every three digits with commas and sets the number of decimal places to two.
E	Scientific notation. Displays one digit to the left of the decimal point and six digits to the right of the decimal point, followed by the character E and a three-digit integer representing the exponent of a power of 10. For example, `956.2` is formatted as `9.562000E+002`.
F	Fixed point. Sets the number of decimal places to two.
G	General. Visual Basic .NET chooses either E or F for you, depending on which representation generates a shorter string.
D	Decimal integer. Displays an integer as a whole number in standard base-10 format.
N	Number. Separates every three digits with a comma and sets the number of decimal places to two.

Figure 7.22 Format specifiers for strings.

Figure 7.23 shows the completed code for our **Wage Calculator** application. Code that uses new programming concepts is highlighted in yellow.

```
 1   Public Class FrmWageCalculator
 2      Inherits System.Windows.Forms.Form
 3
 4      ' Windows Form Designer generated code
 5
 6      ' handles Click event
 7      Private Sub btnCalculate_Click( ByVal sender As System.Object, _
 8         ByVal e As System.EventArgs) Handles btnCalculate.Click
 9
10         ' declare variables
11         Dim dblHours As Double
12         Dim decWage As Decimal
13         Dim decEarnings As Decimal
14
15         Const intHOUR_LIMIT As Integer = 40   ' declare constant
16
17         ' assign values from user input
18         dblHours = Val(txtHours.Text)
19         decWage = Val(txtWage.Text)
20
21         ' determine wage amount
22         If dblHours <= intHOUR_LIMIT Then
23
24            ' if under 40 hours, regular wages
25            decEarnings = dblHours * decWage
26         Else
27
28            ' if over 40 hours, regular wages for first 40
29            decEarnings = intHOUR_LIMIT * decWage
30
31            ' time and a half for the additional hours
32            decEarnings += (dblHours - intHOUR_LIMIT) * (1.5 * decWage)
33         End If
34
35         ' assign result to its corresponding Label
36         lblEarningsResult.Text = String.Format("{0:C}", decEarnings)
37      End Sub ' btnCalculate_Click
38
39   End Class ' FrmWageCalculator
```

Labels pointing to the code:
- Keyword **Const** specifies constant → line 15
- Condition between keywords **If** and **Then** → line 22
- **Else** body executes when condition evalues to **False** → line 26
- Assignment operator assigns left operand result of adding left and right operands → line 32
- Format result as currency → line 36

Figure 7.23   **Wage Calculator** application code.

SELF-REVIEW   1. Method `String.Format` is used to _____.

      a) create constant variables   b) control how text is formatted

      c) format Visual Basic .NET statements   d) All of the above.

2. The _____ format displays values as monetary amounts.

      a) monetary   b) cash

      c) currency   d) dollar

Answers: 1) b. 2) c.

7.10 Using the Debugger: The Watch Window

Visual Studio .NET includes several debugging windows that are accessible from the **Debug > Windows** submenu. The **Watch window**, which is available only in break mode, allows the programmer to examine the value of a variable or expression. You can use the **Watch** window to view changes in a variable's value as the application executes, or you can change a variable's value yourself by entering the new value directly into the **Watch** window. Each expression or variable that is added to the **Watch** window is called a **watch**. In the box, *Using the Debugger: The Watch Window*, we demonstrate how to add, remove and manipulate watches by using the **Watch** window.

Using the Debugger:
The Watch Window

1. ***Starting debugging.*** If the IDE is not in code view, switch to code view now. Set breakpoints on lines 139 and 145 (Fig. 7.24). Select **Debug > Start** to run the application. The **Wage Calculator** Form appears. Enter 12 into the **Hourly wage:** TextBox and 40 into the **Weekly hours:** TextBox (Fig. 7.25). Click the **Calculate** Button.

Figure 7.24 Breakpoints added to **Wage Calculator** application.

Figure 7.25 **Wage Calculator** application.

2. ***Suspending program execution.*** Clicking the **Calculate** Button will cause event handler btnCalculate_Click to execute until the breakpoint is reached. When the breakpoint is reached, application execution is paused, and the IDE switches into break mode. Notice that the **active window** has been changed from the running application to the IDE. The active window is the window that is currently being used and is sometimes referred to as the window that has the **focus**. The **Wage Calculator** application is still running, but it is hidden behind the IDE.

(cont.)   3.   ***Examining data.*** Once the application has entered break mode, you are free to explore the values of various variables, using the debugger's **Watch** window. To display the **Watch** window, select **Debug > Windows > Watch > Watch 1**. Notice that there are actually four options in the **Debug > Windows > Watch** menu—**Watch 1**, **Watch 2**, **Watch 3** and **Watch 4**. Each window provides the same functionality. The four options simply allow you to have several **Watch** windows open at once. This enables you to display data side by side or to set the different **Watch** windows to display data in different formats. The **Watch** window (Fig. 7.26) is initially empty. To add a watch, you can type an expression into the **Name** column. Single click in the first field of the **Name** column. Type dblHours and press *Enter*. The value and type will be added by the IDE (Fig. 7.26). Notice that this value is 40.0—the value assigned to dblHours on line 138. Type decWage in the next row and press the *Enter* key. The value displayed for decWage is 0D. The D indicates that the number stored in decWage is of type Decimal.

Variable values

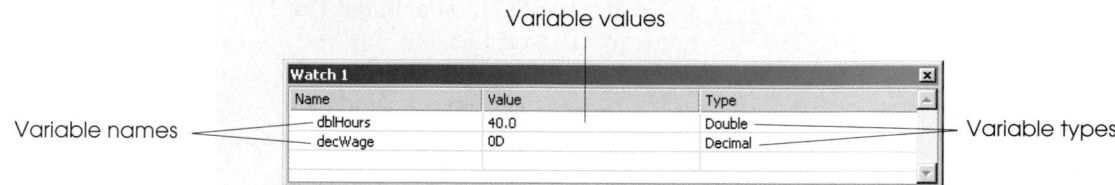

Variable names   Variable types

Figure 7.26   **Watch** window.

4.   ***Examining different expressions.*** Add the expression (decWage + 3) * 5 into the **Watch 1** window. Notice that the **Watch** window can evaluate arithmetic expressions, returning the value **15D**. Add the expression decWage = 3 into the **Watch 1** window. Expressions containing the = symbol are treated as Boolean expressions instead of assignment statements. The value returned is **False**, because decWage does not currently contain the value 3. Add the expression intVariableThatDoesNotExist into the **Watch 1** window. This identifier does not exist in the current application, and therefore cannot be evaluated. An appropriate message is displayed in the **Value** field. Your **Watch** window should look similar to Fig. 7.27.

Complex expression
Boolean expression
Invalid expression

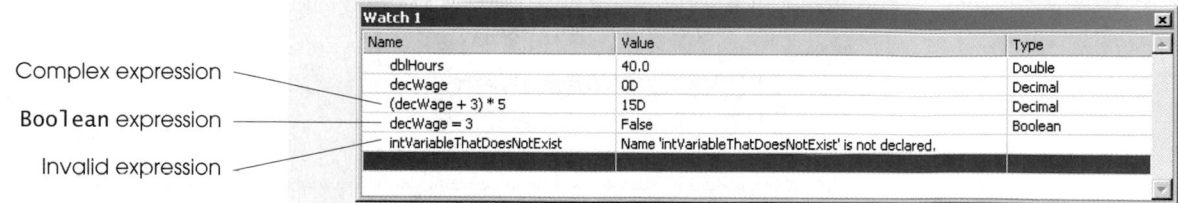

Figure 7.27   Examining expressions.

5.   ***Removing an expression from the Watch window.*** At this point, we would like to clear the final expressions from the **Watch** window. To remove an expression, simply right click the expression in the **Watch** window and select **Delete Watch** (Fig. 7.28). Remove all the expressions that you added in Step 4.

(cont.)

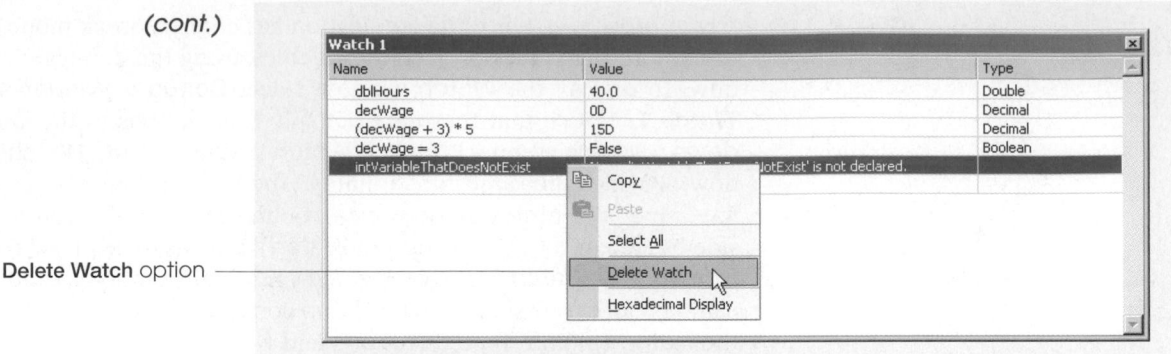

Delete Watch option

Figure 7.28 Deleting a watch.

6. *Viewing modified values in a Watch window.* Continue debugging by selecting **Debug > Continue.** The application will continue to execute until the next breakpoint, on line 145. Line 139 executes, assigning the wage value entered (12) to decWage. The If…Then continuation condition evaluates to True on line 142, and the application is once again suspended on line 145. Notice that the value of decWage has changed not only in the program, but in the **Watch 1** window as well. Because the value has changed since the last time the application was suspended, the modified value is displayed in red (Fig. 7.29).

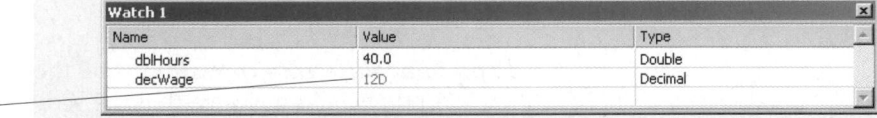

Modified value appears in red

Figure 7.29 Modified values in **Watch** window.

7. *Modifying values directly in a Watch window.* The **Watch** window can be used to change the value of a variable by simply entering the new value in the **Value** column. Click in the **Value** field for dblHours, replace 40.0 with 10.0 and press the *Enter* key. The modified value appears in red (Fig. 7.30). This option enables you to test various values to confirm the behavior of your application. If you repeat this exercise multiple times in the same application, a dialog (Fig. 7.31) might appear. Simply disregard this dialog by clicking the **Continue** Button.

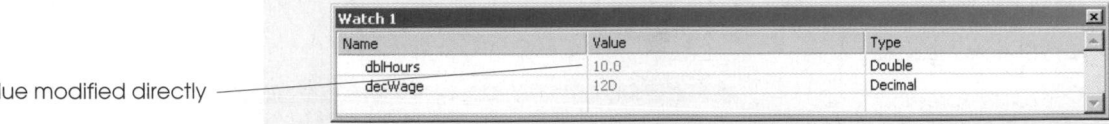

Value modified directly

Figure 7.30 Modifying values in a **Watch** window.

Figure 7.31 Dialog to continue running application after changing values in the **Watch** window.

(cont.)

8. ***Viewing the application result.*** Select **Debug > Continue** to continue program execution. Event handler btnCalculate_Click finishes execution and displays the result in a Label. Notice that the result is $120.00, because we changed dblHours to 10.0 in the last step. The TextBox to the right of **Weekly hours:** still displays the value 40, because we changed the value of dblHours, but not the Text property of either TextBoxes. Once the application has finished executing, the focus is returned to the **Wage Calculator** window, and the final results are displayed (Fig. 7.32).

Earnings result based on altered input

Figure 7.32 Output displayed after the debugging process.

9. ***Closing the application.*** To close the application, either click the running application's close box or select **Debug > Stop Debugging**.

10. ***Saving and closing the project.*** Select **File > Save All** to save all the files in the solution. Close the solution by selecting **File > Close Solution**.

SELF-REVIEW

1. A program enters break mode when _____.
   a) **Debug > Start** is selected   b) a breakpoint is reached
   c) the **Watch** window is used   d) there is a syntax error

2. The **Watch** window allows you to _____.
   a) change variable values   b) view variable type information
   c) evaluate expressions   d) All of the above.

Answers: 1) b. 2) d.

7.11 Wrap-Up

In this tutorial, we discussed techniques of solving programming problems. We introduced algorithms, pseudocode, the UML and control structures. We discussed different types of control structures and when each might be used.

You began by test-driving an application that used the If...Then...Else statement to determine an employee's weekly pay. You studied different control statements and used the UML to diagram the decision-making processes of the If...Then and the If...Then...Else statements.

You learned how to format text by using the method String.Format and how to abbreviate mathematical statements by using the assignment operators.

In the *Using the Debugger* section, you learned how to use the **Watch** window to view an application's data. You learned how to add watches, remove watches and change variable values.

In the next tutorial you will learn how to display message dialogs based on user input. You will study the logical operators, which give you more expressive power for forming the conditions in your control statements. You will use the CheckBox control to allow the user to select from various options in an application.

SKILLS SUMMARY

Choosing Among Alternate Courses of Action

■ Use the If...Then or If...Then...Else control statements.

Conceptualizing the Application Before Using Visual Studio .NET

■ Use pseudocode.

■ Create an Action/Control/Event (ACE) table.

Understanding Control Structures

■ View the control structure's corresponding UML diagram.

Performing Comparisons

■ Use the equality and relational operators.

Creating a Constant

■ Use the Const keyword.

■ Assign a value to the constant in the declaration.

Abbreviating Assignment Expressions

■ Use the assignment operators.

Formatting a Value As a Monetary Amount

■ Use the format code C in method String.Format.

Examining Data During Program Execution

■ Use the debugger to set a breakpoint, and examine the **Watch** window.

KEY TERMS

action/decision model of programming—Representing control statements as UML activity diagrams with rounded rectangles indicating *actions* to be performed and diamond symbols indicating *decisions* to be made.

action state—An action to perform in a UML activity diagram that is represented by an action-state symbol.

action-state symbol—A rectangle with its left and right sides replaced with arcs curving outward that represents an action to perform in a UML activity diagram.

activity diagram—A UML diagram that models the activity (also called the workflow) of a portion of a software system.

algorithm—A procedure for solving a problem, specifying the actions to be executed and the order in which these actions are to be executed.

Boolean data type—A data type that has the value True or False.

condition—An expression with a true or false value that is used to make a decision.

control structure—A program component that specifies the order in which statements execute (also known as the flow of control).

constant—A variable whose value cannot be changed after its initial declaration.

Decimal data type—A data type used to store monetary amounts.

decision symbol—The diamond-shaped symbol in a UML activity diagram that indicates that a decision is to be made.

diamond—A symbol (also known as the decision symbol) in a UML activity diagram; this symbol indicates that a decision is to be made.

dotted line—A UML activity diagram symbol that connects each UML-style note with the element that the note describes.

Double data type—A data type that contains whole numbers and decimal points.

double-selection statement—A statement, such as If...Then...Else, that selects between two different actions or sequences of actions.

fatal logic error—An error that causes an application to fail and terminate prematurely.

format specifier—Code that specifies the type of format that should be applied to a string for output.

final state—Represented by a solid circle surrounded by a hollow circle in a UML activity diagram; the end of the workflow after a program performs its activities.

guard condition—An expression contained in square brackets above or next to the arrows leading from a decision symbol in a UML activity diagram that determines whether workflow continues along a path.

initial state—The beginning of the workflow in a UML activity diagram before the program performs the modeled activities.

multiple-selection statement—A statement that selects from among many different actions or sequences of actions.

nested statement—A statement that is placed inside another control statement.

nonfatal logic error—An error that does not terminate an application's execution but causes a program to produce incorrect results.

note—An explanatory remark (represented by a rectangle with a folded upper-right corner) describing the purpose of a symbol in a UML activity diagram.

pseudocode—An informal language that helps programmers develop algorithms.

single-selection statement—The If...Then statement, which selects or ignores a single action or sequence of actions.

solid circle—A UML activity diagram symbol that represents the activity's initial state.

String.Format method—Method that formats a string.

transition—A change from one action state to another that is represented by transition arrows in a UML activity diagram.

UML (Unified Modeling Language)—An industry standard for modeling software systems graphically.

Watch window—A Visual Studio .NET window that allows you to view variable values as an application is being debugged.

workflow—The activity of a portion of a software system.

GUI DESIGN GUIDELINES

Overall Design

■ Format all monetary amounts using the C (currency) format specifier.

TextBoxes

■ When using multiple TextBoxes vertically, align the TextBoxes on their right sides, and where possible make the TextBoxes the same size. Left-align the descriptive Labels for such TextBoxes.

CONTROLS, EVENTS, PROPERTIES & METHODS

String The String class represents a series of characters treated as a single unit.

■ *Methods*

Format—This method arranges the string in a specified format.

MULTIPLE-CHOICE QUESTIONS

7.1 The _____ operator returns False if the left operand is larger than the right operand.

a) =   b) <

c) <=   d) All of the above.

7.2 A _____ occurs when an executed statement does not directly follow the previously executed statement in the written program.

a) transition   b) flow

c) logical error   d) transfer of control

7.3 A variable or an expression that is added to the **Watch** window is known as a _____.

a) watched variable   b) watched expression

c) watch   d) watched value

7.4 The If...Then statement is called a _____ statement because it selects or ignores one action.

    a) single-selection   b) multiple-selection

    c) double-selection   d) repetition

7.5 The three types of control statements are the sequence statement, the selection statement and the _____ statement.

    a) repeat   b) looping

    c) redo   d) repetition

7.6 In an activity diagram, a rectangle with curved sides represents _____.

    a) a complete algorithm   b) a comment

    c) an action   d) the termination of the application

7.7 The If...Then...Else selection statement ends with the keywords _____.

    a) End If Then Else   b) End If Else

    c) End Else   d) End If

7.8 A variable of data type Boolean can be assigned keyword _____ or keyword _____.

    a) True, False   b) Off, On

    c) True, NotTrue   d) Yes, No

7.9 A variable whose value cannot be changed after its initial declaration is called a _____.

    a) Double   b) constant

    c) standard   d) Boolean

7.10 The _____ operator assigns the result of adding the left and right operands to the left operand.

    a) +   b) =+

    c) +=   d) + =

EXERCISES

7.11 *(Currency Converter Application)* Develop an application that functions as a currency converter as shown in Fig. 7.33. Users must provide a number in the **Dollars:** TextBox and a currency name (as text) in the **Convert from Dollars to:** TextBox. Clicking the **Convert** Button will convert the specified amount into the indicated currency and display it in a Label. Limit yourself to the following currencies as user input: Dollars, Euros, Yen and Pesos. Use the following exchange rates: **1 Dollar = 1.02 Euros, 120 Yen** and **10 Pesos.**

    a) *Copying and opening the template application.* Copy the CurrencyConverter folder in C:\Examples\Tutorial07\Exercises to C:\SimplyVB. Double click CurrencyConverter.sln in C:\SimplyVB\CurrencyConverter to open the template.

    b) *Obtaining the user input.* Use the Val function to convert the user input from the **Dollars:** TextBox to a Double. Assign the Double to a Decimal variable decAmount. Visual Basic .NET implicitly performs this conversion from Double to Decimal.

    c) *Performing the conversion.* Use an If...ElseIf...ElseIf statement to determine which currency the user entered. Assign the result of the conversion to decAmount.

    d) *Displaying the result.* Display the result using method String.Format with format specifier F.

Figure 7.33 Currency Converter GUI.

7.12 *(Wage Calculator that Performs Tax Calculations)* Develop an application that calculates an employee's wages as shown in Fig. 7.34. The user should provide the hourly wage and number of hours worked per week. When the **Calculate** Button is clicked, the gross earnings of the user should display in the **Gross earnings:** TextBox. The **Less FWT:** TextBox should display the amount deducted for Federal taxes and the **Net earnings:** TextBox displays the difference between the gross earnings and the Federal tax amount. Assume overtime wages are 1.5 times the hourly wage and Federal taxes are 15% of gross earnings. The **Clear** Button should clear all fields.

a) *Copying and opening the template application.* Copy the ExpandedWageCalculator folder in C:\Examples\Tutorial07\Exercises to C:\SimplyVB. Double click WageCalculator.sln in C:\SimplyVB\ExpandedWageCalculator to open the template application.

b) *Modifying the* Calculate *Button's* Click *event handler.* Add the code for Steps c–e to btnCalculate_Click.

c) *Adding a new variable.* Declare decFederalTaxes to store the amount deducted for Federal taxes.

d) *Calculating and displaying the Federal taxes deducted.* Multiply the total earnings (decEarnings) by 0.15 (that is, 15%) to determine the amount to be removed for taxes. Assign the result to decFederalTaxes. Display this value using method String.Format with format specifier C.

e) *Calculating and displaying the employee's net pay.* Subtract decFederalTaxes from decEarnings to calculate the employee's net earnings. Display this value using method String.Format with format specifier C.

f) *Creating an event handler for the* Clear *Button.* Double click the **Clear** Button to generate an empty event handler for the Click event. This event handler should clear user input from the two TextBoxes and the results from the three Labels.

Figure 7.34 Wage Calculator GUI.

7.13 *(Customer Charge Account Analyzer Application)* Develop an application (as shown in Fig. 7.35) that determines whether a department-store customer has exceeded the credit limit on a charge account. Each customer enters an account number (an Integer), a balance at the beginning of the month (a Decimal), the total of all items charged this month (a Decimal), the total of all credits applied to the customer's account this month (a Decimal), and the customer's allowed credit limit (a Decimal). The application should input each of these facts, calculate the new balance (= *beginning balance + credits – charges*), display the new balance and determine whether the new balance exceeds the customer's credit limit. If the customer's credit limit is exceeded, the application should display a message (in a Label at the bottom of the Form) informing the customer of this fact.

a) *Copying and opening the template application.* Copy the CreditChecker folder in C:\Examples\Tutorial07\Exercises to C:\SimplyVB. Double click Credit Checker.sln in C:\SimplyVB\CreditChecker to open the template application.

b) *Adding the* Calculate *Button's* Click *event handler.* Double click the **Calculate** Button to generate the empty event handler for the Click event. The code for Steps c–f is added to this event handler.

c) *Declaring variables.* Declare an Integer variable to store the account number. Declare five Decimal variables to store the starting balance, charges, credits and credit limit. Declare a sixth Decimal variable to store the new balance in the account after the credits and charges have been applied.

d) *Obtaining user input.* Obtain the user input from the TextBoxes' Text properties.

e) *Calculating and displaying the new balance.* Calculate the new balance by adding the total credits to the starting balance and subtracting the charges. Assign the result to a variable. Display the result formatted as currency.

f) *Determining if the credit limit has been exceeded.* If the new balance exceeds the specified credit limit, a message should be displayed in lblError.

g) *Handling the Account number: TextBox's TextChanged event.* Double click the **Account number:** TextBox to generate its TextChanged event handler. This event handler should clear the other TextBoxes, the error message Label and the result Label.

Figure 7.35 Credit Checker GUI.

What does this code do? ▶ **7.14** Assume that txtAge is a TextBox control and that the user has entered the value 27 into this TextBox. Determine the action performed by the following code:

```
1   Dim intAge As Integer
2
3   intAge = Val(txtAge.Text)
4
5   If intAge < 0 Then
6       txtAge.Text = "Enter a value greater than or equal to zero."
7   ElseIf intAge < 13 Then
8       txtAge.Text = "Child"
9   ElseIf intAge < 20 Then
10      txtAge.Text = "Teenager"
11  ElseIf intAge < 30 Then
12      txtAge.Text = "Young Adult"
13  ElseIf intAge < 65 Then
14      txtAge.Text = "Adult"
15  Else
16      txtAge.Text = "Senior Citizen"
17  End If
```

What's wrong with this code? ▶

7.15 Assume that lblAMPM is a Label control. Find the error(s) in the following code:

```
1   Dim intHour As Integer
2
3   intHour = 14
4
5   If intHour < 11 Then
6      If intHour > 0 Then
7         lblAMPM.Text = "AM"
8      End If
9   Else
10     lblAMPM.Text = "PM"
11  ElseIf intHour > 23 Then
12     lblAMPM.Text = "Time Error."
13  End If
```

Using the Debugger ▶

7.16 *(Grade Calculator Application)* Copy the C:\Examples\Tutorial07\Debugger folder to your working directory. This folder contains the Grades application, which takes a number from the user and displays the corresponding letter grade. For values 90–100 it should display **A**; for 80–89, **B**, for 70–79, **C**, for 60–69, **D** and for anything lower, an **F**. Run the application. Enter the value 85 in the TextBox and click **Calculate**. Notice that the application displays **D** when it ought to display **B**. Select **View > Code** to enter the code editor and set as many breakpoints as you feel necessary. Select **Debug > Start** to use the debugger to help you find the error(s). Figure 7.36 shows the incorrect output when the value 85 is input.

Figure 7.36 Incorrect output for **Grade** application.

Programming Challenge ▶

7.17 *(Encryption Application)* A company transmits data over the telephone, but it is concerned that its phones could be tapped. All its data is transmitted as four-digit Integers. The company has asked you to write an application that encrypts its data so that it may be transmitted more securely. Encryption is the process of transforming data for security reasons. Create a Form similar to Fig. 7.37. Your program should read four-digits entered by the user and encrypt the information as follows:

a) Replace each digit by *(the sum of that digit plus 7) modulo 10*. We use the term **modulo** to indicate you are to use the modulus (Mod) operator.

b) Swap the first digit with the third, and swap the second digit with the fourth.

Figure 7.37 **Encryption** application.

Objectives

In this tutorial, you will learn to:

- Use **CheckBox**es to allow users to select options.
- Use dialogs to display messages.
- Use logical operators to form more powerful conditions.

Outline

8.1 Test-Driving the Dental Payment Application

8.2 Designing the Dental Payment Application

8.3 Using **CheckBoxes**

8.4 Using a Dialog to Display a Message

8.5 Logical Operators

8.6 Wrap-Up

Dental Payment Application

Introducing CheckBoxes and Message Dialogs

Many Visual Basic .NET applications use **dialogs** (also called **message dialogs**), which are windows that display messages to users. You encounter many dialogs while using a computer, from those that instruct you to select files or enter passwords to others that notify you of problems while using an application. In this tutorial, you will learn how to use message dialogs to inform users of input problems.

You may have noticed that `TextBoxes` allow users to enter nearly any value as input. In some cases, you may want to use controls that provide users with predefined options. One way to do this is by providing `CheckBoxes` in your application. You also will learn about logical operators, which you can use in your applications to make more involved decisions based on user input.

8.1 Test-Driving the Dental Payment Application

When you visit the dentist, there are many procedures that the dentist can perform. The office assistant may present you with a bill generated by a computer. In this tutorial, you will program an application that prepares a bill for some basic dental procedures. This application must meet the following requirements:

> ### Application Requirements
>
> *A dentist's office administrator wishes to create an application that employees can use to bill patients. The application must allow users to enter the patient's name and specify which services were performed during the visit. The application will then calculate the total charges. If a user attempts to calculate a bill before any services are specified, or before the patient's name is entered, a message will be displayed.*

In the **Dental Payment** application, you will use CheckBox controls and a message dialog to assist the user in entering data. You begin by test-driving the completed application.

Test-Driving the
Completed Dental
Payment Application

1. ***Opening the application.*** Open the C:\Examples\Tutorial08\Com-pletedApplication\DentalPayment folder to locate the **Dental Payment** application. Double click DentalPayment.sln to open the application in Visual Studio .NET.

2. ***Running the application.*** Select **Debug > Start** to execute the application. The **Dental Payment** Form shown in Fig. 8.1 will appear.

   Notice that there are three square-shaped controls in the left column of the Form. These are known as **CheckBox** controls. A CheckBox is a small white square that either is blank or contains a check mark. When a Check-Box is selected, a black check mark appears in the box (☑). A CheckBox can be selected by simply clicking within the CheckBox's small white square or by clicking on the text of the CheckBox. A selected CheckBox can be unchecked in the same way. You will learn how to add CheckBox controls to a Form shortly.

CheckBox controls
(unchecked)

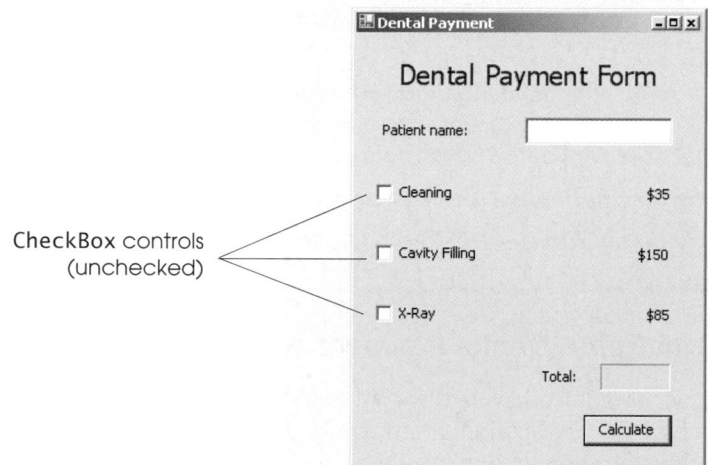

Figure 8.1   **Dental Payment** application without input entered.

3. ***Attempting to calculate a total without entering input.*** Leave the **Patient name** field blank, and deselect any CheckBoxes that you have selected. Click the **Calculate** Button. Notice that a message dialog appears indicating that you must enter data (Fig. 8.2). Close this dialog by clicking its **OK** Button.

Figure 8.2   Message dialog appears when no name is entered and/or no CheckBoxes are selected.

4. ***Entering quantities in the application.*** The **Dental Payment** Form is still displayed. Type Bob Jones in the **Patient name** field. Check all three Check-Boxes by single clicking each one. Notice that a check mark appears in each CheckBox.

5. ***Unchecking the Cavity Filling CheckBox.*** Click the **Cavity Filling** CheckBox to remove its check mark. Only the **Cleaning** and **X-Ray** CheckBoxes should now be selected (Fig. 8.3).

(cont.)

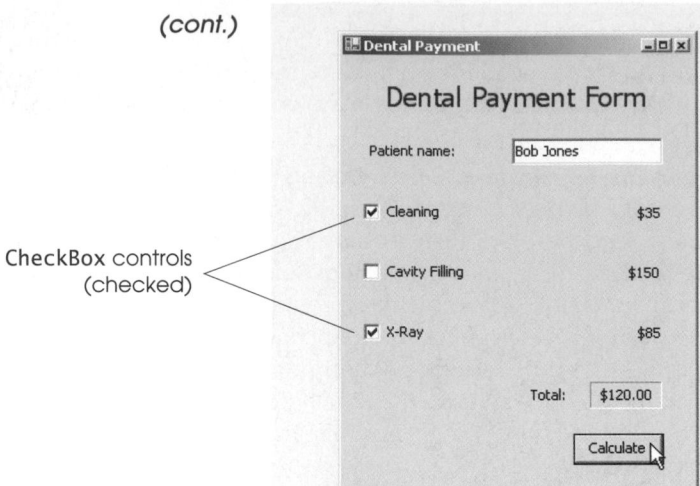

Figure 8.3 Dental Payment application with input entered.

6. *Determining the bill.* Click the **Calculate** Button. This causes the application to total the price of the services performed during the dentist visit. The result is displayed in the **Total:** field.

7. *Closing the application.* Click the close box to terminate execution.

8. *Closing the solution.* Select **File > Close Solution**.

8.2 Designing the Dental Payment Application

Now that you have test-driven the completed **Dental Payment** application, you need to analyze the application components. The following pseudocode describes the actions that your application must execute in order to solve this problem. Recall that pseudocode is an informal language that helps programmers develop algorithms. The pseudocode is as follows:

```
When the user clicks the Calculate Button

    If user has not entered a patient name or has not selected any CheckBoxes
        Display message in dialog
    Else
        Initialize a total to zero

        If "Cleaning" CheckBox is selected
            Add cost of a cleaning to the total

        If "Cavity Filling" CheckBox is selected
            Add cost of receiving a cavity filling to the total

        If "X-Ray" CheckBox is selected
            Add cost of receiving an x-ray to the total

        Format total to be displayed as currency
        Display total
```

The ACE table shown in Fig. 8.4 describes the controls and events that you will use to create the **Dental Payment** application. Data is input via a TextBox (txtName) and CheckBoxes (chkClean, chkCavity and chkXRay). Output is displayed in Label lblTotalResult when a Button (btnCalculate) is clicked. Field names are displayed in the Form's other Labels.

*Action/Control/Event
(ACE) Table for the
Dental Payment
Application*

Action	Control/Object	Event/Method
Label all the application's controls	lblTitle, lblName, lblTotal, lblCleanCost, lblFillingCost, lblXRayCost	
Calculate the bill and display the total	btnCalculate	Click
Retrieve the patient's name	txtName	
Retrieve the services performed	chkClean, chkCavity, chkXRay	
Display a message to the user	MessageBox	Show
Display the amount owed	lblTotalResult	

Figure 8.4   Action/Control/Event table for **Dental Payment** application.

8.3 Using CheckBoxes

As mentioned earlier, a CheckBox is a small white square that either is blank or contains a check mark. (A CheckBox is known as a **state button**, because it can be in the on/off [true/false] state.) When a CheckBox is selected, a black check mark appears in the box. Any number of CheckBoxes can be selected at a time, including none at all. The text that appears alongside a CheckBox is called the **CheckBox label**.

You can determine whether a CheckBox is on (that is, checked) by using the **Checked property**. If the CheckBox is checked, the Checked property returns the Boolean value True when accessed. If the CheckBox is not checked, the Checked property returns False when accessed.

You will now create the **Dental Payment** application from the template provided. The box, *Adding CheckBoxes to the Form*, demonstrates how to add the CheckBoxes to your application. The application you will build in the next two boxes will not display a dialog if the TextBox is empty and/or all the CheckBoxes are unchecked when the **Calculate** Button is clicked. You will learn how to display that dialog in Section 8.4.

GUI Design Tip

A CheckBox's label should be descriptive and as short as possible. When a CheckBox label contains more than one word, use book-title capitalization.

*Adding CheckBoxes to
the Form*

1. ***Copying the template application to your work folder.*** Copy the Dental-Payment folder from C:\Examples\Tutorial08\TemplateApplication to your work folder.

2. ***Opening the template application.*** Open the C:\SimplyVB\Dental-Payment folder. Double click DentalPayment.sln to open the application in Visual Studio .NET. If the Form does not appear, double click Dental-Payment.vb in the **Solution Explorer**. If the **Solution Explorer** is not open, select **View > Solution Explorer**.

3. ***Adding CheckBox controls to the Form.*** Add a CheckBox to the Form by double clicking the

icon in the **Toolbox**. Repeat this process until three CheckBoxes have been added to the Form.

(cont.)

4. ***Customizing the CheckBoxes.*** For this application, you will be modifying the Location, Text, Size and Name properties of each CheckBox. Change the Size property of all three CheckBoxes to 122, 24. Change the Name property of the first CheckBox to chkClean and set its Location property to 16, 112 and its Text property to Cleaning. Change the Name property of the second CheckBox to chkCavity, its Location property to 16, 159 and its Text property to Cavity Filling. Change the Name property of the final CheckBox to chkXRay, its Location property to 16, 206 and its Text property to X-Ray.

After placing the CheckBoxes on the Form and setting their properties, you need to code an event handler to enhance the application's functionality when users select CheckBoxes and click **Calculate**.

Adding the Calculate Button's Event Handler

1. ***Adding an event handler for btnCalculate's Click event.*** Double click the **Calculate** Button on the Form to create an event handler for that control's Click event.

2. ***Adding If...Then statements to calculate the patient's bill.*** Insert the highlighted code of Fig. 8.5 into your application. Be sure to include all blank lines and line-continuation characters shown in Fig. 8.5 to improve code readability and to ensure that your line numbers correspond to the figure's.

Add this highlighted code ⟶

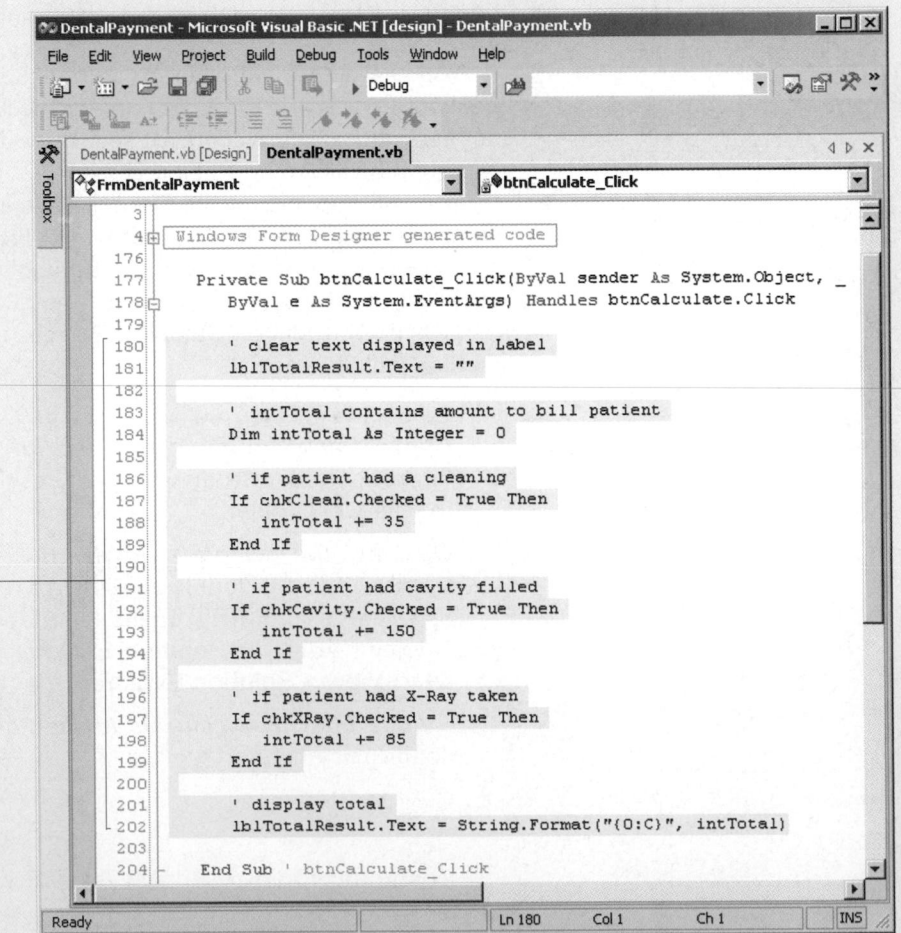

Figure 8.5 Using the Checked property.

(cont.)

Line 181 clears any text in the output `Label` that may be present from a previous calculation. Line 184 declares variable `intTotal`, which stores the total charges for the patient as an `Integer`. This variable is initialized to 0. Lines 186–199 define three `If...Then` statements that determine whether the user has checked any of the Form's `CheckBox`es. Each `If...Then` statement's condition compares a `CheckBox`'s `Checked` property to `True`. For each `If...Then` statement, the dollar value of the service is added to `intTotal` if the current `CheckBox` is checked. The first `If...Then` statement, for example, adds 35 to `intTotal` on line 188 if `CheckBox` `chkClean` is selected (line 187). Notice that the numeric values added to `intTotal` correspond to the monetary values indicated on the GUI, to the right of each service. Line 202 displays the total (formatted as a currency amount) in `lblTotalResult`.

3. ***Running the application.*** Select **Debug > Start** to execute the application. Notice that the user is not required to enter a name or select any Check-Boxes before clicking the **Calculate** `Button`. If no CheckBoxes are selected, the bill displays the value **$0.00** (Fig. 8.6).

Figure 8.6   Application running without input.

4. ***Selecting a CheckBox.*** Select the **Cleaning** CheckBox, and click the **Calculate** `Button`. Notice that the **Total:** field now displays **$35.00**.

5. ***Closing the application.*** Click the application's close box to terminate execution.

SELF-REVIEW

1. The _____ property sets a CheckBox's text.
     a) `Text`   b) `Value`
     c) `Label`   d) `Checked`

2. Which property determines whether a CheckBox is selected?
     a) `Selected`   b) `Checked`
     c) `Clicked`   d) `Check`

Answers: 1.) a. 2.) b.

8.4 Using a Dialog to Display a Message

In the completed application, a message is displayed in a dialog if the user attempts to calculate the total charges without specifying which services were performed and/or without entering a name. In this section, you will learn how to display a dialog when a patient name is not input. In Section 8.5, Logical Operators, you will learn how to write code to determine if at least one CheckBox is checked. When the dialog is closed, control is returned to the application's Form. The message dialog used in your application is displayed in Fig. 8.7.

Title bar — Close box

Icon indicates the tone of the message

OK Button allows the user to close the dialog

Dialog sized to accommodate contents

Figure 8.7 Dialog displayed by the application.

Notice that the message dialog contains a title bar and a close box. This dialog also contains a message (Please enter a name and check at least one item), an **OK** Button that allows the user to **dismiss** (close) the dialog (which the user must do to proceed) and an icon that indicates the tone of the message. (In this case, ⚠ indicates that a problem has occurred.)

Message dialogs are defined by class **MessageBox** and can be displayed by using method **MessageBox.Show**. The message dialog is customized by the arguments passed to method MessageBox.Show. The box, *Displaying a Message Dialog Using MessageBox.Show*, demonstrates displaying a message dialog based on a condition.

GUI Design Tip

Text displayed in a dialog should be descriptive and as short as possible.

Displaying a Message Dialog Using *MessageBox.Show*

1. ***Adding an If...Then statement to the event handler for btnCalculate's Click event.*** The message should display only if the user does not enter the patient's name. Place the cursor on line 182 and press *Enter*. Then insert lines 183–186 of Fig. 8.8 into your event handler. Be sure to include a blank line after the End If statement.

   Line 184 tests whether data was entered in the **Patient name:** TextBox. If no data has been entered, the expression txtName.Text = "" evaluates to True. You will add the body of this If...Then statement in *Step 2*.

Add this highlighted code

Figure 8.8 Adding an If...Then statement to the btnCalculate Click event handler to display a message dialog.

2. ***Adding code to display a message dialog.*** Insert lines 186–190 from Fig. 8.9 into the body of the If...Then statement you created in the previous step. Change the End If (line 186 of Fig. 8.8) to Else (line 192 of Fig. 8.9). Notice that the code you added to the Click event earlier (Fig. 8.5) now composes the body of the Else portion of your If...Else statement. The Else is marked as a syntax error because the If...Else statement is now missing an End If statement. You will add this statement in *Step 3*.

(cont.)

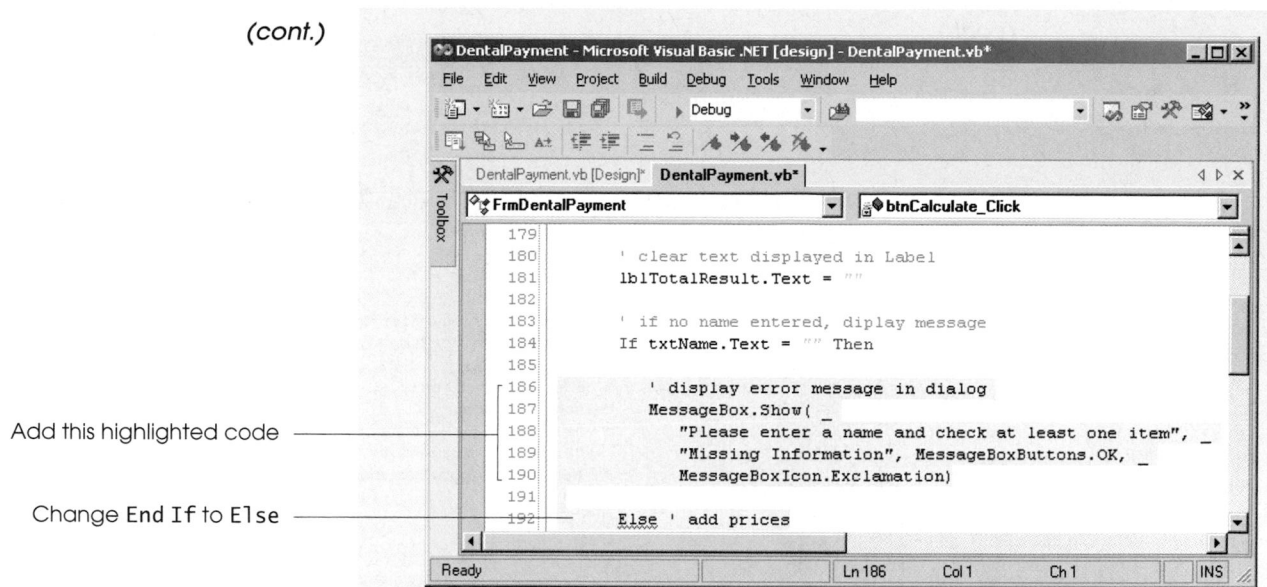

Figure 8.9 Message dialog code that displays a message to users.

Lines 187–190 call method `MessageBox.Show` using four arguments, separated by commas. The first argument specifies the text that displays in the dialog, the second argument specifies the text that appears in its title bar, the third argument indicates which `Button`(s) to display at the bottom of the dialog and the fourth argument indicates which icon appears at the left of the dialog. We discuss the final two arguments in more detail shortly.

3. ***Closing the If...Then statement.*** Scroll to the end of your event handler code. Be sure to close the `If...Else` statement by inserting the keywords `End If` before the end of the event handler (line 215 of Fig. 8.10). Figure 8.11 displays the entire method `btnCalculate_Click` after the new code has been added. Compare this code to your own to ensure that you have added the new code correctly.

Figure 8.10 Ending the `If...Else` statement.

4. ***Running the application.*** Select **Debug > Start** to execute the application. Notice that the user does not have to select any `CheckBoxes` before clicking the **Calculate** `Button`, but the user must enter a name in the **Patient name:** `TextBox`. If none of the `CheckBoxes` is selected, the bill will contain the value **$0.00** (Fig. 8.12). In the next section, you will modify the code to test whether the user has selected any `CheckBoxes`.

5. ***Saving the project.*** Select **File > Save All** to save all the solution's files.

(cont.)

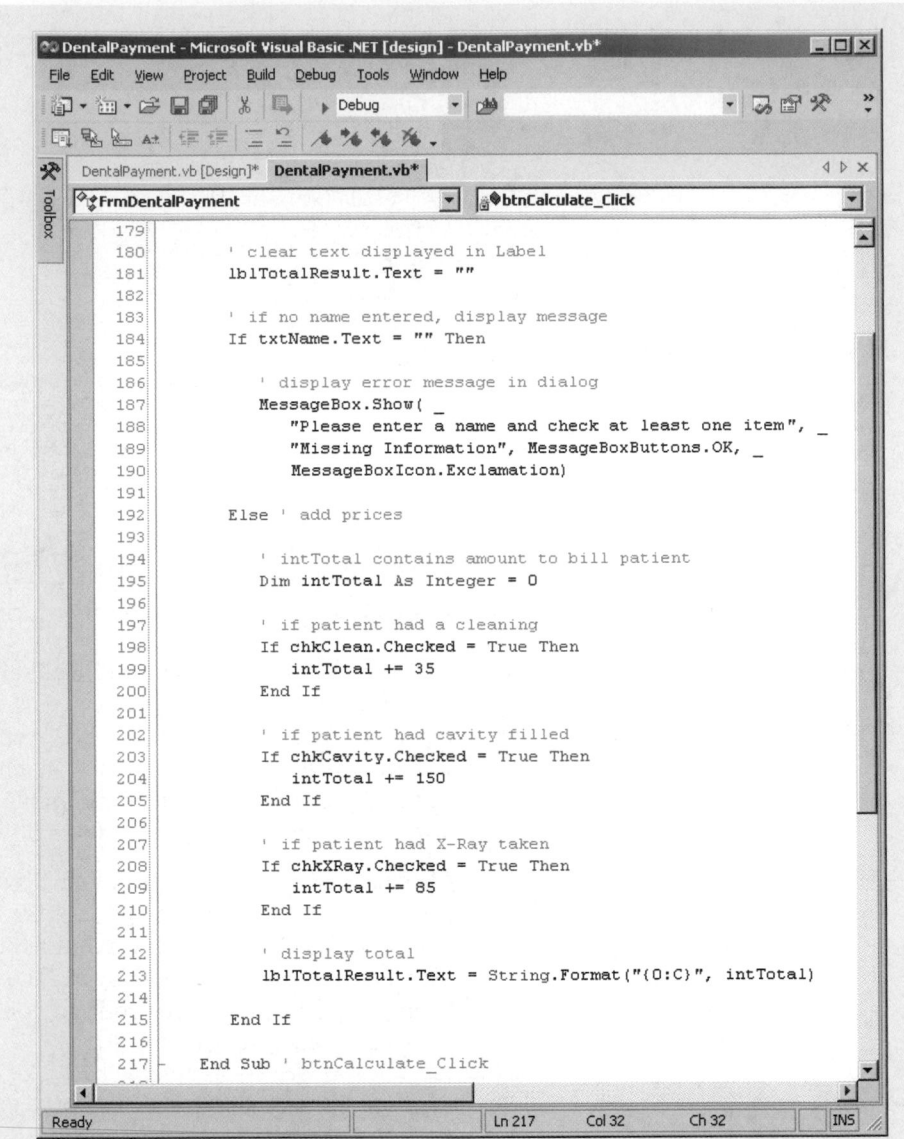

Figure 8.11 Completed `btnCalculate_Click` event handler.

Figure 8.12 Application running without any **CheckBox**es selected.

In this example, you passed four arguments to method `MessageBox.Show`. The first two arguments indicate the text of the dialog's message and the text of the dialog's title bar, respectively. The third argument specifies the `Button` that displays in the dialog. To accomplish this task, you passed one of the FCL's **MessageBoxButtons** constants to method `MessageBox.Show`. You will use only the `MessageBoxButtons.OK` constant in this book. Figure 8.13 lists the available `Button` constants. Note that several `Buttons` can be displayed at once. The fourth argument specifies the icon that displays in the dialog. To set the icon to display, you passed one of .NET's **MessageBoxIcon** constants to method `MessageBox.Show`. The available icon constants are shown in Fig. 8.14.

MessageBoxButtons Constants	Description
`MessageBoxButtons.OK`	**OK** Button. Allows the user to acknowledge a message.
`MessageBoxButtons.OKCancel`	**OK** and **Cancel** Buttons. Allow the user to either continue or cancel an operation.
`MessageBoxButtons.YesNo`	**Yes** and **No** Buttons. Allow the user to respond to a question.
`MessageBoxButtons.YesNoCancel`	**Yes**, **No** and **Cancel** Buttons. Allow the user to respond to a question or cancel an operation.
`MessageBoxButtons.RetryCancel`	**Retry** and **Cancel** Buttons. Typically used to allow the user either to retry or to cancel an operation that has failed.
`MessageBoxButtons.AbortRetryIgnore`	**Abort**, **Retry** and **Ignore** Buttons. When one of a series of operations has failed, these `Buttons` allow the user to abort the entire sequence, retry the failed operation or ignore the failed operation and continue.

Figure 8.13   Message dialog `Button` constants.

MessageBoxIcon Constants	Icon	Description
`MessageBox-Icon.Exclamation`		Icon containing an exclamation point. Typically used to caution the user against potential problems
`MessageBox-Icon.Information`		Icon containing the letter "i." Typically used to display information about the state of the application.
`MessageBox-Icon.Question`		Icon containing a question mark. Typically used to ask the user a question.
`MessageBox-Icon.Error`		Icon containing an ∞ in a red circle. Typically used to alert the user of errors or critical situations.

Figure 8.14   Message dialog icon constants.

SELF-REVIEW

1. Which constant, when passed to method `MessageBox.Show`, indicates that a question is being asked?

   a) `MessageBox.Question`   b) `MessageBoxIcon.QuestionMark`

   c) `MessageBox.QuestionMark`   d) `MessageBoxIcon.Question`

2. What is the message dialog icon containing the letter "i" typically used for?

   a) To display information about the state of the application

   b) To caution the user against potential problems

   c) To ask the user a question   d) To alert the user to critical situations

Answers: 1.) d. 2.) a.

8.5 Logical Operators

So far, you have studied only **simple conditions**, such as `intCount <= 10`, `intTotal > 1000`, and `intNumber <> intValue`. Each selection statement that you used evaluated only one condition with one of the operators >, <, >=, <=, = or <>.

To handle multiple conditions more efficiently, Visual Basic .NET provides **logical operators** that can be used to form complex conditions by combining simple ones. The logical operators are **AndAlso**, **OrElse**, **Xor** and **Not**. We will consider examples that use each of these operators. After you learn about logical operators, you will use them to create a complex condition in your **Dental Payment** application to confirm `CheckBox` entries.

Using AndAlso

Suppose that you wish to ensure that two conditions are *both* true in an application before choosing a certain path of execution. In that case, you can use the logical `AndAlso` operator as follows:

```
If txtGender.Text = "Female" AndAlso intAge >= 65 Then
    intSeniorFemales += 1
End If
```

This `If...Then` statement contains two simple conditions. The condition `txtGender.Text = "Female"` determines whether a person is female, and the condition `intAge >= 65` determines whether a person is a senior citizen. The = and >= operators are always evaluated before the operator `AndAlso` because the = and >= operators have a higher precedence than operator `AndAlso`. In this case, the two simple conditions are evaluated first, then the `AndAlso` operator is evaluated using their result. The `If...Then` statement then considers the combined condition

```
txtGender.Text = "Female" AndAlso intAge >= 65
```

This condition evaluates to true *if and only if* both of the simple conditions are true, meaning that `txtGender.Text` contains the value `"Female"` and `intAge` contains a value greater than or equal to 65. When this combined condition is true, the count of `intSeniorFemales` is incremented by 1. However, if either or both of the simple conditions are false, the application skips the increment and proceeds to the statement following the `If...Then` statement. The readability of the preceding combined condition can be improved by adding redundant (that is, unnecessary) parentheses:

```
(txtGender.Text = "Female") AndAlso (intAge >= 65)
```

Figure 8.15 illustrates the outcome of using the `AndAlso` operator with two expressions. The table lists all four possible combinations of `True` and `False` values for *expression1* and *expression2*, which represent the left operand and the right operand, respectively. Such tables are called **truth tables**. Visual Basic .NET evaluates to `True` or `False` expressions that include relational operators, equality operators and logical operators.

expression1	expression2	expression1 AndAlso expression2
False	False	False
False	True	False
True	False	False
True	True	True

Figure 8.15 Truth table for the `AndAlso` operator.

Error-Prevention Tip

Always write the simplest condition possible by limiting the number of logical operators used. Conditions with many logical operators can be hard to read and can introduce subtle bugs into your applications.

Using OrElse

Now let's consider the OrElse operator. Suppose that you wish to ensure that either *or* both of two conditions are true before you choose a certain path of execution. You would use the OrElse operator as in the following application segment:

```
If (intSemesterAverage >= 90 OrElse intFinalExam >= 90) Then
    MessageBox.Show("Student grade is A", "Student Grade", _
        MessageBoxButtons.OK, MessageBoxIcon.Information)
End If
```

This statement also contains two simple conditions. The condition intSemesterAverage >= 90 is evaluated to determine whether the student deserves an "A" in the course because of an outstanding performance throughout the semester. The condition intFinalExam >= 90 is evaluated to determine whether the student deserves an "A" in the course because of an outstanding performance on the final exam. The If...Then statement then considers the combined condition

```
(intSemesterAverage >= 90 OrElse intFinalExam >= 90)
```

and awards the student an "A" if either or both of the conditions are true, meaning that the student performed well during the semester, performed well on the final exam or both. Note that the text "Student grade is A" is displayed unless both of the conditions are false. Figure 8.16 provides a truth table for the OrElse operator. Note that the AndAlso operator has a higher precedence than the OrElse operator. See Appendix A for a complete listing of operator precedence in Visual Basic .NET.

 Error-Prevention Tip

When writing conditions that contain combinations of AndAlso and OrElse operators, use parentheses to ensure that the conditions evaluate properly. Otherwise, logic errors could occur because AndAlso has higher precedence than OrElse.

expression1	expression2	expression1 OrElse expression2
False	False	False
False	True	True
True	False	True
True	True	True

Figure 8.16   Truth table for the OrElse operator.

An expression containing operator AndAlso is evaluated only until truth or falsity is known. For example, evaluation of the expression

```
(txtGender.Text = "Female" AndAlso intAge >= 65)
```

stops immediately if txtGender.Text is not equal to "Female" (which would mean the entire expression is false). In this case, the evaluation of the second expression is irrelevant; once the first expression is known to be false, the whole expression must be false. Evaluation of the second expression occurs if and only if txtGender.Text is equal to "Female" (which would mean that the entire expression could still be true if the condition intAge >= 65 is true).

Similarly, an expression containing OrElse is evaluated only until truth or falsity is known. For example, evaluation of the expression

```
If (intSemesterAverage >= 90 OrElse intFinalExam >= 90) Then
```

stops immediately if intSemesterAverage is greater than or equal to 90 (which would mean the entire expression is True). In this case, the evaluation of the second expression is irrelevant; once the first expression is known to be true, the whole expression must be true.

This way of evaluating logical expressions can require fewer operations, therefore taking less time. This performance feature for the evaluation of `AndAlso` and `OrElse` expressions is called **short-circuit evaluation**.[1]

Using Xor

A condition containing the **logical exclusive OR (Xor)** operator is `True` *if and only if one of its operands results in a `True` value and the other results in a `False` value.* If both operands are `True` or both are `False`, the entire condition is `False`. Figure 8.17 presents a truth table for the logical exclusive OR operator (`Xor`). This operator always evaluates both of its operands (that is, there is no short-circuit evaluation).

expression1	expression2	expression1 Xor expression2
False	False	False
False	True	True
True	False	True
True	True	False

Figure 8.17   Truth table for the logical exclusive OR (`Xor`) operator.

Using Not

Visual Basic .NET's **Not** (logical negation) operator enables a programmer to "reverse" the meaning of a condition. Unlike the logical operators `AndAlso`, `OrElse` and `Xor`, each of which combines two expressions (that is, these are all binary operators), the logical negation operator is a **unary operator**, requiring only one operand. The logical negation operator is placed before a condition to choose a path of execution if the original condition (without the logical negation operator) is `False`. The logical negation operator is demonstrated by the following application segment:

```
If Not (intGrade = intValue) Then
   lblDisplay.Text = "They are not equal!"
End If
```

The parentheses around the condition `intGrade = intValue` are necessary, because the logical negation operator (`Not`) has a higher precedence than the equality operator. Most programmers prefer to write

```
Not (intGrade = intValue)
```

as

```
(intGrade <> intValue)
```

Figure 8.18 provides a truth table for the logical negation operator. The box, *Using Logical Operators in Complex Expressions*, provides an example of using complex expressions. You will modify your **Dental Payment** application to use a complex expression.

---

1. Visual Basic .NET also provides the `And` and `Or` operators, which do not short-circuit. (They always evaluate their right operand regardless of whether or not the condition's truth or falsity is already known.) In Visual Basic .NET applications, the performance benefit of using `AndAlso` and `OrElse` is negligible. One potential problem of using `AndAlso`/`OrElse` instead of `And`/`Or` is when the right operand contains a **side effect**, such as a function call that modifies a variable. Because such side effects might not occur when using short-circuit evaluation, subtle logic errors could occur. As a good programming practice, most Visual Basic .NET programmers, who prefer to use operators `AndAlso` and `OrElse`, avoid writing conditions that contain side effects.

expression	Not expression
False	True
True	False

Figure 8.18 Truth table for the `Not` operator (logical NOT).

***Using Logical Operators
in Complex Expressions***

1. ***Inserting a complex expression into the `Click` event handler.*** Double click the **Calculate** `Button` on the `Form`. Replace lines 183–184 of Fig. 8.8 with lines 183–187 of Fig. 8.19.

Add the highlighted code —

Figure 8.19 Using the `AndAlso` and `OrElse` logical operators.

Lines 184–187 define a more sophisticated logical expression than others we have used in this book. Notice the use of `OrElse` and `AndAlso`. If the name is blank or if no `CheckBox` is checked, a dialog should appear. After the original expression (`txtName.Text = ""`), you use `OrElse` to indicate that either the expression on the left (`txtName.Text = ""`) or the expression "on the right" (which determines if no `CheckBox` has been checked) needs to be `True` for the entire expression to evaluate to `True` to execute the body of the `If...Then` statement. The complex expression "on the right" uses `AndAlso` twice to determine if all of the `CheckBox`es are unchecked. Note that because `AndAlso` has a higher precedence than `OrElse`, the parentheses on lines 185 and 187 are redundant (unnecessary).

2. ***Running the application.*** Select **Debug > Start** to execute the application. Notice that users must enter a name and select at least one `CheckBox` before they click the **Calculate** `Button`. The application appears the same as in Figs. 8.1 and 8.3. (You have finally corrected the weakness from your earlier implementation of the **Dental Payment** application.)

3. ***Closing the application.*** Click the running application's close box to terminate execution.

4. ***Saving the solution.*** Select **File > Save All** to save the solution's files.

5. ***Closing the solution.*** Select **File > Close Solution** to close the solution.

We present the complete **Dental Payment** application code in Fig. 8.20.

```
1   Public Class FrmDentalPayment
2       Inherits System.Windows.Forms.Form
```

Figure 8.20 Code for the **Dental Payment** application. (Part 1 of 2.)

```
 3
 4        Private Sub btnCalculate_Click(ByVal sender As System.Object, _
 5           ByVal e As System.EventArgs) Handles btnCalculate.Click
 6
 7           ' clear text displayed in Label
 8           lblTotalResult.Text = ""
 9
10           ' if no name entered and no CheckBox checked, display message
11           If (txtName.Text = "") OrElse _
12              (chkClean.Checked = False AndAlso _
13              chkXRay.Checked = False AndAlso _
14              chkCavity.Checked = False) Then
15
16              ' display message in dialog
17              MessageBox.Show( _
18                 "Please enter your name and check at least one item", _
19                 "Missing Information", MessageBoxButtons.OK, _
20                 MessageBoxIcon.Exclamation)
21
22           Else ' add prices
23
24              ' intTotal contains amount to bill patient
25              Dim intTotal As Integer
26
27              ' if patient had a cleaning
28              If chkClean.Checked = True Then
29                 intTotal += 35
30              End If
31
32              ' if patient had cavity filled
33              If chkCavity.Checked = True Then
34                 intTotal += 150
35              End If
36
37              ' if patient had X-Ray taken
38              If chkXRay.Checked = True Then
39                 intTotal += 85
40              End If
41
42              ' display total
43              lblTotalResult.Text = String.Format("{0:C}", intTotal)
44
45           End If
46
47        End Sub ' btnCalculate_Click
48
49     End Class ' FrmDentalPayment
```

Using logical operators and the **Checked** property of a **CheckBox** — (lines 11–14)

Displaying a **MessageBox** — (lines 17–20)

Figure 8.20 Code for the **Dental Payment** application. (Part 2 of 2.)

SELF-REVIEW

1. A unary operator _____.

   a) requires exactly one operand   b) requires two operands

   c) must use the AndAlso keyword   d) can have no operands

2. The _____ operator is used to ensure that two conditions are both true.

   a) Xor   b) AndAlso

   c) Also   d) OrElse

Answers: 1.) a. 2.) b.

8.6 Wrap-Up

In this tutorial, you used CheckBox controls to provide a series of choices to users in the **Dental Payment** application. CheckBoxes provide options that can be selected by clicking them. When a CheckBox is selected, its white square contains a check mark. You can determine whether a CheckBox is selected in your code by accessing its Checked property.

Your **Dental Payment** application also used message dialogs to display messages to the user when information was not entered appropriately. To implement dialogs in your application, you used the MessageBox class, which provides methods and constants necessary to display a dialog containing Buttons and an icon. You used an If...Then...Else statement to calculate the cost of the dental visit or display a message dialog if the user was missing input. Later in this book you will learn to avoid checking for invalid user input by disabling a control (such as a Button) when its events should not cause any action to occur.

You learned to use the logical AndAlso operator when both conditions must be true for the overall condition to be true—if either condition is false, the overall condition is false. You also learned that the logical OrElse operator requires at least one of its conditions to be true for the overall condition to be true—if both conditions are false, the overall condition is false. The logical Xor operator requires that exactly one of its conditions be true for the overall condition to be true—if both conditions are false or if both conditions are true, the overall condition is false. The logical Not operator reverses the Boolean result of a condition—True becomes False, and False becomes True. You then used the AndAlso and OrElse operators to form a complex expression.

In the next tutorial, you will learn more about Visual Basic .NET's control structures. Specifically, you will use **repetition statements**, which allow the programmer to specify that an action or a group of actions should be performed many times.

SKILLS SUMMARY

Adding a CheckBox to a Form

- Double click the CheckBox in the **ToolBox**.

Selecting a CheckBox

- Click the CheckBox, and a check mark will appear in the white box.

Deselecting a CheckBox

- Click a checked CheckBox to remove its check mark.

Determining Whether a CheckBox is Selected

- Access the CheckBox's Checked property.

Displaying a Dialog

- Use method MessageBox.Show.

Combining Multiple Conditions

- Use the logical operators to form complex conditions by combining simple ones.

KEY TERMS

AndAlso operator—A logical operator used to ensure that two conditions are *both* true before choosing a certain path of execution. Performs short-circuit evaluation.

CheckBox control—A small white square GUI element that either is blank or contains a check mark.

CheckBox label—The text that appears alongside a CheckBox.

Checked property of the CheckBox control—Specifies whether the CheckBox is checked (True) or unchecked (False).

dialog (message dialog)—A window that displays messages to users and gathers input from users.

dismiss—Synonym for close.

logical exclusive OR (Xor) operator—A logical operator that is True if and only if one of its operands results in True and the other results in False.

logical operators—The operators (for example, AndAlso, OrElse, Xor and Not) that can be used to form complex conditions by combining simple ones.

MessageBox class—The class that provides a method for displaying message dialogs.

MessageBoxButtons constants—The identifiers that specify Buttons that can be displayed in a MessageBox dialog.

MessageBoxIcon constants—Identifiers that specify icons that can be displayed in a MessageBox dialog.

Not (logical negation) operator—A logical operator that enables a programmer to reverse the meaning of a condition: A True condition, when logically negated, becomes False and a False condition, when logically negated, becomes True.

OrElse operator—A logical operator used to ensure that either *or* both of two conditions are True in an application before a certain path of execution is chosen.

short-circuit evaluation—The evaluation of the right operand in AndAlso and OrElse expressions occurs only if the first condition meets the criteria for the condition.

state button—A button that can be in the on/off (true/false) state.

truth table—A table that displays the boolean result of a logical operator for all possible combinations of True and False values for its operands.

GUI DESIGN GUIDELINES

CheckBoxes

- A CheckBox's label should be descriptive and as short as possible. When a CheckBox label contains more than one word, use book-title capitalization.
- Align groups of CheckBoxes either horizontally or vertically.

Message Dialogs

- Text displayed in a dialog should be descriptive and as short as possible.

CONTROLS, EVENTS, PROPERTIES & METHODS

CheckBox ☑ CheckBox — This control allows user to select an option.

- *In action*

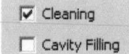

- *Properties*

  Checked—This property specifies whether the CheckBox is checked (True) or unchecked (False).

  Location—This property specifies the location of the CheckBox on the Form.

  Name—This property specifies the name used to access the CheckBox control programmatically. The name should be prefixed with chk.

  Text—This property specifies the text displayed next to the CheckBox.

MULTIPLE-CHOICE QUESTIONS

8.1 How many CheckBoxes in a GUI can be selected at once?

a) 0   b) 1

c) 4   d) any number

8.2 The text that appears alongside a CheckBox is referred to as the _____.

a) CheckBox label   b) CheckBox name

c) CheckBox value   d) CheckBox data

8.3 The first argument passed to method MessageBox.Show is _____.

a) the text displayed in the dialog's title bar

b) a constant representing the Buttons displayed in the dialog

c) the text displayed inside the dialog

d) a constant representing the icon that appears in the dialog

8.4 You can specify the Button(s) and icon to be displayed in a message dialog by using the MessageBoxButtons and _____ constants.

a) MessageIcon   b) MessageBoxImages

c) MessageBoxPicture   d) MessageBoxIcon

8.5 _____ are used to create complex conditions.

a) Assignment operators   b) Activity diagrams

c) Logical operators   d) Formatting codes

8.6 Operator AndAlso _____.

a) performs short-circuit evaluation   b) is not a keyword

c) is a comparison operator

d) evaluates to false if both operands are true

8.7 A CheckBox is selected when its Checked property is set to _____.

a) On   b) True

c) Selected   d) Checked

8.8 The condition *expression1* AndAlso *expression2* evaluates to True when _____.

a) *expression1* is True and *expression2* is False

b) *expression1* is False and *expression2* is True

c) both *expression1* and *expression2* are True

d) both *expression1* and *expression2* are False

8.9 The condition *expression1* OrElse *expression2* evaluates to False when _____.

a) *expression1* is True and *expression2* is False

b) *expression1* is False and *expression2* is True

c) both *expression1* and *expression2* are True

d) both *expression1* and *expression2* are False

8.10 The condition *expression1* Xor *expression2* evaluates to True when _____.

a) *expression1* is True and *expression2* is False

b) *expression1* is False and *expression2* is True

c) both *expression1* and *expression2* are True

d) Both a and b.

EXERCISES

8.11 (*Enhanced Dental Payment Application*) Modify the **Dental Payment** application from this tutorial to include additional services, as shown in Fig. 8.21. Add the proper functionality (using If…Then structures) to determine whether any of the new CheckBoxes are selected and, if so, add the price of the service to the total bill.

a) *Copying and opening the template application.* Copy the C:\Examples\Tutorial08\Exercises\DentalPaymentEnhanced folder to C:\SimplyVB. Double click the DentalPaymentEnhanced.sln file in the DentalPaymentEnhanced folder to open the template application in Visual Studio .NET.

b) *Adding CheckBoxes and Labels and a TextBox.* Add two CheckBoxes and two Labels to the Form. The new CheckBoxes should be labeled **Fluoride** and **Root Canal**, respectively. Add these CheckBoxes and Labels beneath the X-Ray CheckBox and its price Label. The price for a Fluoride treatment is $50; the price for a root canal is $225. Add a CheckBox labeled **Other** and a Label containing a dollar sign (**$**) to the Form, as shown in Fig. 8.21. Then add a TextBox to the right of the $ Label in which the user can enter the cost of the service performed.

c) *Modifying the Click event handler code.* Add code to the btnCalculate_Click event handler that determines whether the new CheckBoxes have been selected. This can be done using If...Then statements that are similar to the ones already in the event handler. Use the If...Then statements to update the bill amount.

d) *Saving and testing the solution.* Save the solution. Test your application by checking one or more of the new services.

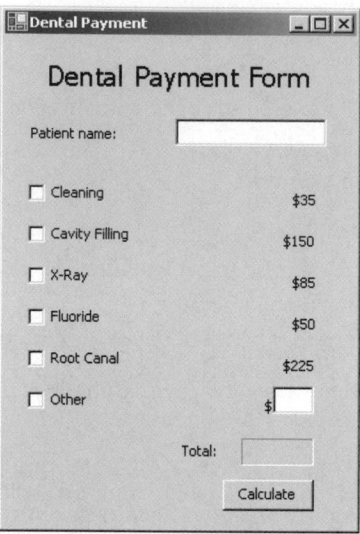

Figure 8.21 Enhanced **Dental Payment** application.

8.12 (*Fuzzy Dice Order Form Application*) Write an application that allows users to process orders for fuzzy dice as shown in Fig. 8.22. The application should calculate the total price of the order, including tax and shipping. TextBoxes for inputting the order number, the customer name and the shipping address are provided. Initially, these fields contain text that describes their purpose. Provide CheckBoxes for selecting the fuzzy-dice color and Text-Boxes for inputting the quantities of fuzzy dice to order. The application should also contain a Button that, when clicked, calculates the subtotals for each type of fuzzy dice ordered and the total of the entire order (including tax and shipping). Use 5% for the tax rate. Shipping charges are $1.50 for up to 20 pairs of dice. If more than 20 pairs of dice are ordered, shipping is free.

a) *Copying and opening the template application.* Copy the C:\Examples\Tutorial08\Exercises\FuzzyDiceOrderForm folder to C:\SimplyVB. Double click the Fuzzy.sln file in the FuzzyDiceOrderForm folder to open the template application in Visual Studio .NET.

b) *Adding CheckBoxes to the Form.* Add three CheckBoxes to the Form. Label the first CheckBox **White/Black**, the second one **Red/Black** and the third **Blue/Black**.

c) *Adding a Click event handler and its code.* Create the Click event handler for the **Calculate** Button. For this application, users should not be allowed to specify an item's quantity unless the item's corresponding CheckBox is checked. For the total to be calculated, the user must enter an order number, a name and a shipping address. Use logical operators to ensure that these terms are met. If they are not, display a message in a dialog.

d) *Calculating the total cost.* Calculate the subtotal, tax, shipping and total, and display the results in their corresponding Labels.

e) *Saving and testing the solution.* Save the solution. Then test the application by providing quantities for checked items. For instance, ensure that your application is calculating 5% sales tax. If more than 20 pairs of dice are ordered, verify that shipping is free. Also, determine whether your code containing the logical operators works correctly by specifying a quantity for an item that is not checked. For instance, in Fig. 8.22, a quantity is specified for **Red/Black** dice, but the corresponding CheckBox is not selected. This should cause the message dialog in Fig. 8.22 to appear.

Figure 8.22 Fuzzy Dice Order Form application.

8.13 (*Modified Fuzzy Dice Order Form Application*) Modify the **Fuzzy Dice Order Form** application from Exercise 8.12 to determine whether customers should receive a 7% discount off their purchase. Customers ordering more than $500 (before tax and shipping) in fuzzy dice are eligible for this discount.

a) *Opening the application.* Open the application you created in Exercise 8.12.

b) *Determining whether the total cost is over $500.* Use an If...Then statement to determine if the amount ordered is greater than $500.

c) *Displaying the discount and subtracting the discount from the total.* If a customer orders more than $500, display a message dialog as shown in Fig. 8.23 that informs the user that the customer is entitled to a 7% discount. The message dialog should contain an Information icon and an **OK** Button. Calculate 7% of the total amount, and display the discount amount in the **Discount:** field. Subtract this amount from the total, and update the **Total:** field.

d) *Saving and testing the solution.* Save the solution. Confirm that your application calculates and displays the discount properly.

What does this code do? ▶   **8.14** Assume that txtName is a TextBox and that chkOther is a CheckBox next to which is a TextBox txtOther, in which the user should specify a value. What does this code segment do?

```
1   If (txtName.Text = "" OrElse _
2      (chkOther.Checked = True AndAlso _
3      txtOther.Text = "") Then
4
5      MessageBox.Show("Please enter a name or value", _
6         "Input Error", MessageBoxButtons.OK, _
7         MessageBoxIcon.Exclamation)
8
9   End If
```

Figure 8.23 Modified **Fuzzy Dice Order Form** application.

What's wrong with this code? ▶ **8.15** Assume that txtName is a TextBox. Find the error(s) in the following code:

```
1  If txtName.Text = "John Doe" Then
2
3      MessageBox.Show("Welcome, John!", _
4          MessageBoxIcon.Exclamation)
5
6  End If
```

Using the Debugger ▶ **8.16** (*Sibling Survey Application*) The **Sibling Survey** application displays the siblings selected by the user in a dialog. If the user checks either the **Brother(s)** or **Sister(s)** Check-Box, and the **No Siblings** CheckBox, the user is asked to verify the selection. Otherwise, the user's selection is displayed in a MessageBox. While testing this application, you noticed that it does not execute properly. Use the debugger to find and correct the logic error(s) in the code. This exercise is located in the C:\Examples\Tutorial08\Debugger\SiblingSurvey folder. Figure 8.24 shows the correct output for the application.

Figure 8.24 Correct output for the **Sibling Survey** application.

Programming Challenge ▶ **8.17** (*Enhanced Fuzzy Dice Order Form Application*) Enhance the **Fuzzy Dice Order Form** application from Exercise 8.12 by replacing the **Calculate** Button with a **Clear** Button.

The application should update the total cost, tax and shipping when the user changes any one of the three **Quantity** field's values (Fig. 8.25). The **Clear** Button should return all fields to their original values. [*Hint*: You will need to use the CheckBox **CheckedChanged** event for each CheckBox. This event is raised when the state of a CheckBox changes. Double click a CheckBox in design view to create an event handler for that CheckBox's CheckedChanged event. You also will need to assign Boolean values to the CheckBoxes' Checked properties to control their states.]

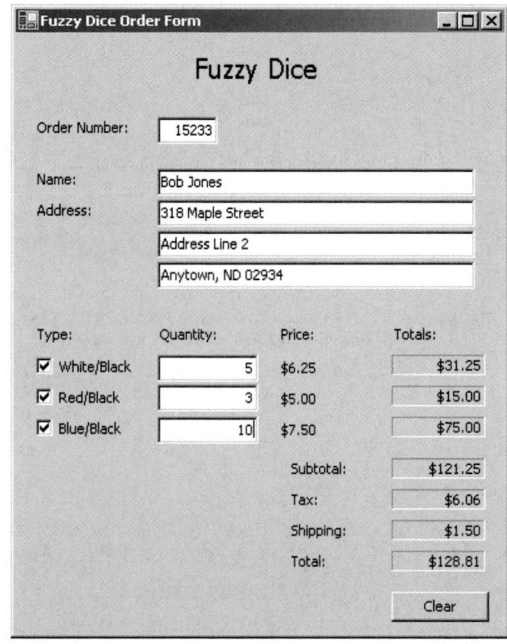

Figure 8.25   Enhanced **Fuzzy Dice Order Form** application.

Objectives

In this tutorial, you will learn to:
- Use the Do While...Loop and Do Until...Loop repetition statements to execute statements in a program repeatedly.
- Use counter-controlled repetition.
- Display information in ListBoxes.

Outline

9.1 Test-Driving the Car Payment Calculator Application

9.2 Do While...Loop Repetition Statement

9.3 Do Until...Loop Repetition Statement

9.4 Constructing the Car Payment Calculator Application

9.5 Wrap-Up

Car Payment Calculator Application

Introducing the Do While...Loop and Do Until...Loop Repetition Statements

This tutorial continues the discussion of structured programming that we began in Tutorial 7. We introduce repetition statements, which are control statements that can repeat actions on the basis of a condition's value. You perform many repetitive tasks based on conditions. For example, each time you turn a page in this book (while there are more pages to read), you are repeating a simple task, namely turning a page, based on a condition, namely that there are more pages to read.

The ability to perform tasks repeatedly is an important part of structured programming. Repetition statements are used in many types of applications. In this tutorial, you will learn to use the Do While...Loop and the Do Until...Loop repetition statements. You will include a repetition statement in the **Car Payment Calculator** application that you build. Later tutorials will introduce additional repetition statements.

9.1 Test-Driving the Car Payment Calculator Application

The following problem statement requires an application that repeats a calculation four times—you will use a repetition statement to solve this problem. This application must fulfill the following requirements:

Application Requirements

Typically, banks offer car loans for periods ranging from two to five years (24 to 60 months). Borrowers repay the loans in monthly installments. The amount of each monthly payment is based on the length of the loan, the amount borrowed and the interest rate. Create an application that allows the customer to enter the price of a car, the down-payment amount and the annual interest rate of the loan. The application should display the loan's duration in months and the monthly payments for two-, three-, four- and five-year loans. The variety of options allows the user to easily compare their options and choose the payment plan that is most convenient for them.

You begin by test-driving the completed application.

Test-Driving the Car Payment Calculator Application

1. ***Opening the application.*** Locate the `CarPaymentCalculator` application in the `C:\Examples\Tutorial09\CompletedApplication\CarPayment-Calculator` directory. Double click `CarPaymentCalculator.sln` to open the application in Visual Studio .NET.

2. ***Running the application.*** Select **Debug > Start** to run the application. The Form shown in Fig. 9.1 appears. Notice a new GUI control—the **ListBox** control, which allows users to view and select from multiple items in a list. Users cannot add items to, or remove items from, a `ListBox` by interacting directly with the `ListBox`. The `ListBox` does not accept keyboard input; users cannot add or delete selected items. You need to add code to your application to add or remove items from a `ListBox`.

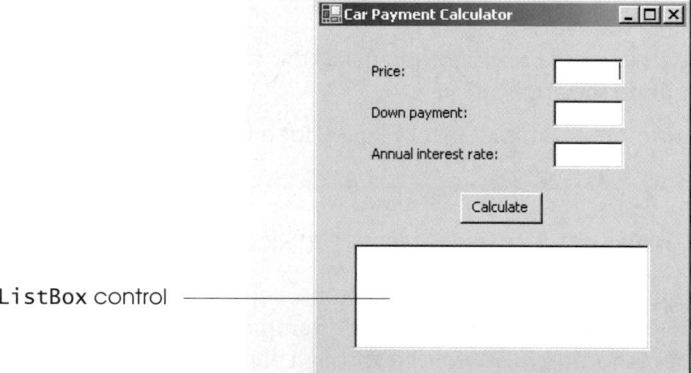

`ListBox` control —

Figure 9.1   **Car Payment Calculator** application before data has been entered.

3. ***Entering quantities in the application.*** Enter 16900 in the **Price:** TextBox. Enter 6000 in the **Down payment:** TextBox. Enter 7.5 in the **Annual interest rate:** TextBox. The Form appears as in Fig. 9.2.

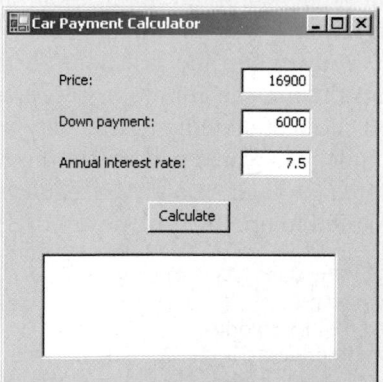

Figure 9.2   **Car Payment Calculator** application after data has been entered.

4. ***Calculating the monthly payment amounts.*** Click the **Calculate** Button. The application displays the monthly payment amounts in the `ListBox` (Fig. 9.3). The information is organized in tabular format.

(cont.)

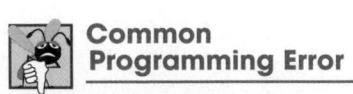

Figure 9.3 **Car Payment Calculator** application displaying calculation results.

5. *Terminating the application.* Click the running application's close box to terminate the application.

6. *Closing the solution.* Select **File > Close Solution**.

9.2 Do While...Loop Repetition Statement

A **repetition statement** can repeat actions, depending on the value of a condition (which can be either true or false). For example, if you go to the grocery store with a list of items to purchase, you go through the list until you have each item. This process is described by the following pseudocode statements:

> Do while there are more items on my shopping list
>   Purchase next item
>   Cross it off my list

These statements describe the repetitive actions that occur during a shopping trip. The condition, "there are more items on my shopping list" can be true or false. If it is true, then the actions, "Purchase next item" and "Cross it off my list" are performed in sequence. In an application, these actions execute repeatedly while the condition remains true. The statement(s) indented in this repetition statement constitute its **body**. When the last item on the shopping list has been purchased and crossed off the list, the condition becomes false. At this point, the repetition terminates, and the first statement after the repetition statement executes. In the shopping example, you would proceed to the checkout station.

As an example of a Do While...Loop statement, let's look at an application segment designed to find the first power of 3 greater than 50.

```
Dim intProduct As Integer = 3

Do While intProduct <= 50
    intProduct *= 3
Loop
```

The application segment initializes variable intProduct to 3, taking advantage of a Visual Basic .NET feature that allows variable initialization to be incorporated into a declaration. The condition in the Do While...Loop statement, intProduct <= 50, is referred to as the **loop-continuation condition**. While the loop-continuation condition remains true, the Do While...Loop statement executes its body repeatedly. When the loop-continuation condition becomes false, the Do While...Loop statement finishes executing, and intProduct contains the first power of 3 larger than 50. Let's examine the execution of the preceding code in detail.

Common Programming Error

Provide in the body of every Do While...Loop statement an action that eventually causes the condition to become false. If you do not, the repetition statement never terminates, causing an error called an **infinite loop**. When an infinite loop occurs in an application running in Visual Studio .NET, use the *Ctrl + Break* key combination to terminate the application.

When the Do While...Loop statement is entered, the value of intProduct is 3. Each time the loop executes, the variable intProduct is multiplied by 3, taking on the values 3, 9, 27 and 81, successively. When intProduct becomes 81, the condition in the Do While...Loop statement, intProduct <= 50, is evaluated to false. When the repetition ends, the final value of intProduct is 81, which is, indeed, the first power of 3 greater than 50. Program execution continues with the next statement after the Do While...Loop statement. Note that, if a Do While...Loop statement's condition is initially false, the body statement(s) are not performed and your application simply continues executing with the next statement after the keyword Loop. The box, *Executing the Do While...Loop Repetition Statement,* describes each step as the above repetition statement executes.

Executing the Do While...Loop ***Repetition Statement***	1. The application declares variable intProduct and sets its value to 3.
	2. The application enters the Do While...Loop repetition statement.
	3. The loop-continuation condition is checked. The condition evaluates to True (intProduct is less than or equal to 50), so the application resumes execution at the next statement.
	4. The number (currently 3) stored in intProduct is multiplied by 3 and the result is assigned to intProduct; intProduct now contains the number 9.
	5. The loop-continuation condition is checked. The condition evaluates to True (intProduct is less than or equal to 50), so the application resumes execution at the next statement.
	6. The number (currently 9) stored in intProduct is multiplied by 3 and the result is assigned to intProduct; intProduct now contains the number 27.
	7. The loop-continuation condition is checked. The condition evaluates to True (intProduct is less than or equal to 50), so the application resumes execution at the next statement.
	8. The number (currently 27) stored in intProduct is multiplied by 3 and the result is assigned to intProduct; intProduct now contains the number 81.
	9. The loop-continuation condition is checked. The condition evaluates to False (intProduct is not less than or equal to 50), so the application exits the Do While...Loop repetition statement and the application resumes execution at the first statement after the Loop statement.

Let's use a UML activity diagram to illustrate the flow of control in the preceding Do While...Loop repetition statement. The UML activity diagram in Fig. 9.4 contains an initial state, transition arrows, a merge, a decision, two guard conditions, three notes and a final state. The oval represents the action state in which the value of intProduct is multiplied by 3.

The activity diagram clearly shows the repetition. The transition arrow emerging from the action state wraps back to the merge, creating a **loop**. The guard conditions are tested each time the loop iterates until the guard condition intProduct > 50 eventually becomes true. At this point, the Do While...Loop statement is exited, and control passes to the next statement in the application following the loop.

Figure 9.4 introduces the UML's **merge symbol**. The UML represents both the merge symbol and the decision symbol as diamonds. The merge symbol joins two flows of activity into one flow of activity. In this diagram, the merge symbol joins the transitions from the initial state and from the action state, so they both flow into the loop-continuation guard decision, which is the decision that determines whether the loop body statement should begin executing (or continue executing). In this case, the UML diagram enters its action state when the loop-continuation guard condition intProduct <= 50 is true.

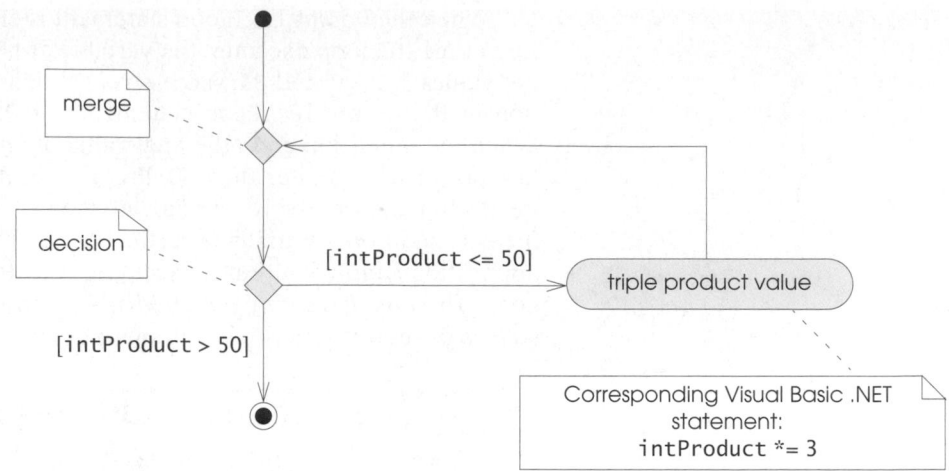

Figure 9.4 `Do While...Loop` repetition statement UML activity diagram.

Although the UML represents both the decision and the merge symbols with the diamond shape, the symbols can be distinguished by the number of "incoming" and "outgoing" transition arrows. A decision symbol has one transition arrow pointing to the diamond and two (or more) transition arrows pointing out from the diamond to indicate possible transitions from that point. In addition, each transition arrow pointing out of a decision symbol has a guard condition next to it. A merge symbol has two (or more) transition arrows pointing to the diamond and only one transition arrow pointing from the diamond, to indicate multiple activity flows merging to continue the activity.

SELF-REVIEW

1. The body of a `Do While...Loop` statement executes _____.

    a) at least once   b) never

    c) if its condition is true   d) if its condition is false

2. The UML represents both the merge symbol and the decision symbol as _____.

    a) rectangles with rounded sides   b) diamonds

    c) small black circles   d) ovals

Answers: 1) c. 2) b.

9.3 Do Until...Loop Repetition Statement

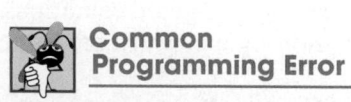

Common Programming Error

Failure to provide the body of a `Do Until...Loop` statement with an action that eventually causes the condition in the `Do Until...Loop` to become true creates an infinite loop.

Unlike the `Do While...Loop` repetition statement, the `Do Until...Loop` repetition statement tests the loop-termination condition for falsity before repetition can continue. For example, you can think of grocery shopping as looping through the list of items until there aren't any left on the list. Note that the condition "there are no more items on my shopping list" must be false for the loop to continue. This process is described by the following pseudocode statements:

> Do until there are no more items on my shopping list
>   Purchase next item
>   Cross it off my list

These statements describe the repetitive actions that occur during a shopping trip. Statements in the body of a `Do Until...Loop` are executed repeatedly for as long as the loop-termination condition remains `False`. As an example of a `Do Until...Loop` repetition statement, let's look again at an application segment designed to find the first power of 3 larger than 50:

```
Dim intProduct As Integer = 3

Do Until intProduct > 50
    intProduct *= 3
Loop
```

The box, *Executing the Do Until...Loop Repetition Statement*, describes each step as the repetition statement executes.

Executing the Do Until...Loop Repetition Statement

1. The application declares variable `intProduct` and sets its value to 3.

2. The application enters the `Do Until...Loop` repetition statement.

3. The loop-termination condition is checked. The condition evaluates to `False` (`intProduct` is not greater than 50), so the application resumes execution at the next statement.

4. The number (3) stored in `intProduct` is multiplied by 3 and the result is assigned to `intProduct`; `intProduct` now contains the number 9.

5. The loop-termination condition is checked. The condition evaluates to `False` (`intProduct` is not greater than 50), so the application resumes execution at the next statement.

6. The number (9) stored in `intProduct` is multiplied by 3 and the result is assigned to `intProduct`; `intProduct` now contains the number 27.

7. The loop-termination condition is checked. The condition evaluates to `False` (`intProduct` is not greater than 50), so the application resumes execution at the next statement.

8. The number (27) stored in `intProduct` is multiplied by 3 and the result is assigned to `intProduct`; `intProduct` now contains the number 81.

9. The loop-termination condition is checked. The condition now evaluates to `True` (`intProduct` is greater than 50), so the application exits the `Do Until...Loop` repetition statement and the application resumes execution at the first statement after the `Loop` statement.

The UML activity diagram in Fig. 9.5 illustrates the flow of control for the Do Until...Loop repetition statement. Once again, note that (besides the initial state, transition arrows, a final state and two notes) the only other symbols in the diagram represent an action state, a decision and a merge.

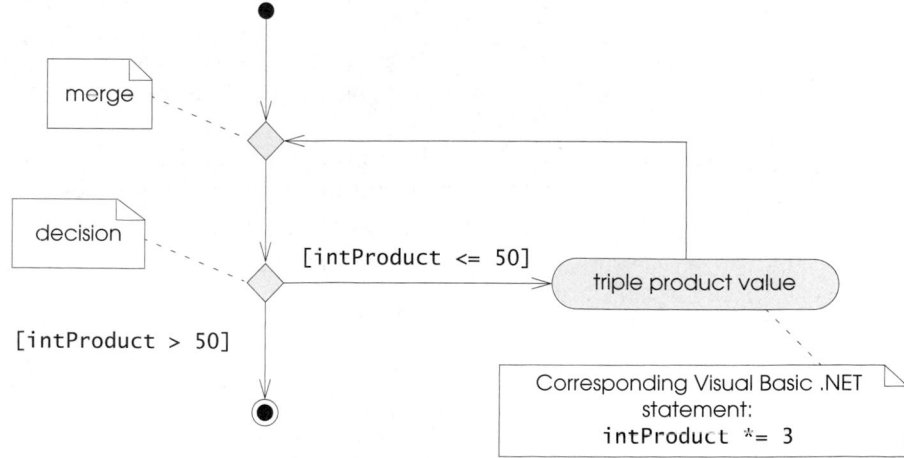

Figure 9.5 Do Until...Loop repetition statement UML activity diagram.

SELF-REVIEW

1. A Do Until...Loop repetition statement differs from a Do While...Loop repetition statement in _____.

   a) that a Do While...Loop repetition statement loops as long as the loop-continuation condition remains False, whereas a Do Until...Loop repetition statement loops as long as the loop-continuation condition remains True

   b) that a Do Until...Loop repetition statement loops as long as the loop-continuation condition remains False, whereas a Do While...Loop repetition statement loops as long as the loop-continuation condition remains True

   c) that a Do Until...Loop repetition statement always executes at least once

   d) no way. There is no difference between the Do Until...Loop and Do While...Loop repetition statements

2. Statements in the body of a Do Until...Loop are executed repeatedly for as long as the _____ remains False.

   a) loop-continuation condition   b) do-loop condition

   c) loop-termination condition   d) until-loop condition

Answer: 1) b. 2) c.

9.4 Constructing the Car Payment Calculator Application

Now that you have learned the Do While...Loop and Do Until...Loop repetition statements, you are ready to construct the **Car Payment Calculator** application.

The following pseudocode describes the tasks that your application must accomplish whenever a user enters information and clicks the **Calculate** Button:

> Clear the ListBox of any previous calculation results
>
> Get sticker price from a TextBox
> Get down payment from a TextBox
> Get interest rate from a TextBox
>
> Calculate loan amount (sticker price – down payment)
> Calculate monthly interest rate (interest rate / 12)
>
> Initialize loan length to two years
>
> Do while loan length is less than or equal to five years
>   Convert the loan length in years to number of months
>
>   Calculate monthly payment based on loan amount, monthly interest rate
>   and loan length in months
>
>   Insert result into ListBox
>   Increment loan length in years by one year

The Action/Control/Event table of Fig. 9.6 lists the GUI elements used in the completed **Car Payment Calculator** application.

Action/Control/Event (ACE) Table for the Car Payment Calculator

Action	Control	Event
Label all the application's controls	lblPrice, lblDownPayment, lblInterest	
Get sticker price	txtStickerPrice	
Get down payment	txtDownPayment	

Figure 9.6 **Car Payment Calculator** application ACE table. (Part 1 of 2.)

Action	Control	Event
Get annual interest rate	txtInterest	
Calculate monthly payments for loans lasting one, two, three, four and five years	btnEnter	Click
Display results	lstPayments	

Figure 9.6   **Car Payment Calculator** application ACE table. (Part 2 of 2.)

Notice in the pseudocode that the retrieval of the user input and the calculations of the loan amount and the monthly interest rate occur before the repetition statement because they need to be performed only once. The statements that have different results in each iteration are included in the repetition statement. The repetition statement's body includes: converting loan length in years to loan length in months, calculating the monthly payment amount, displaying the calculation's result and incrementing the loan length in years.

The application displays the calculation results in a `ListBox`. Next, you will add and customize the `ListBox` that displays the results.

Adding a *ListBox* to the *Car Payment Calculator* **Application**

1. ***Copying the template to your work folder.*** Copy the `C:\Examples\Tutorial09\TemplateApplication\CarPaymentCalculator` folder to `C:\SimplyVB`.

2. ***Opening the template application.*** Double click CarPaymentCalculator.sln to open the application in Visual Studio .NET. To open the Form in design mode, as shown in Fig. 9.7, double click **CarPaymentCalculator.vb** in the **Solution Explorer**. Notice that the TextBoxes for user input and the **Calculate** Button are provided to you.

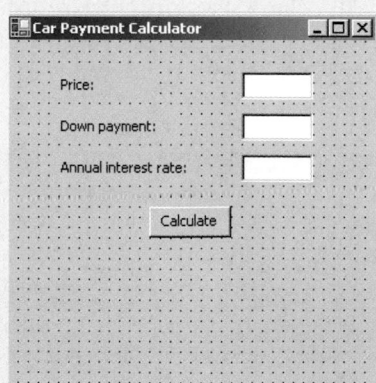

Figure 9.7   **Car Payment Calculator** application's Form in design mode.

3. ***Adding a ListBox control to the Form.*** Double click the ListBox control,

in the **Toolbox**. Change the Name property of the ListBox to lstPayments. Set the Location property to 28, 168 and the Size property to 232, 82. Figure 9.8 shows the Form with the ListBox control. In design view, the ListBox control displays the value of its Name property. This text will not appear when the application executes.

4. ***Saving the solution.*** Select **File > Save All** to save the solution's files.

(cont.)

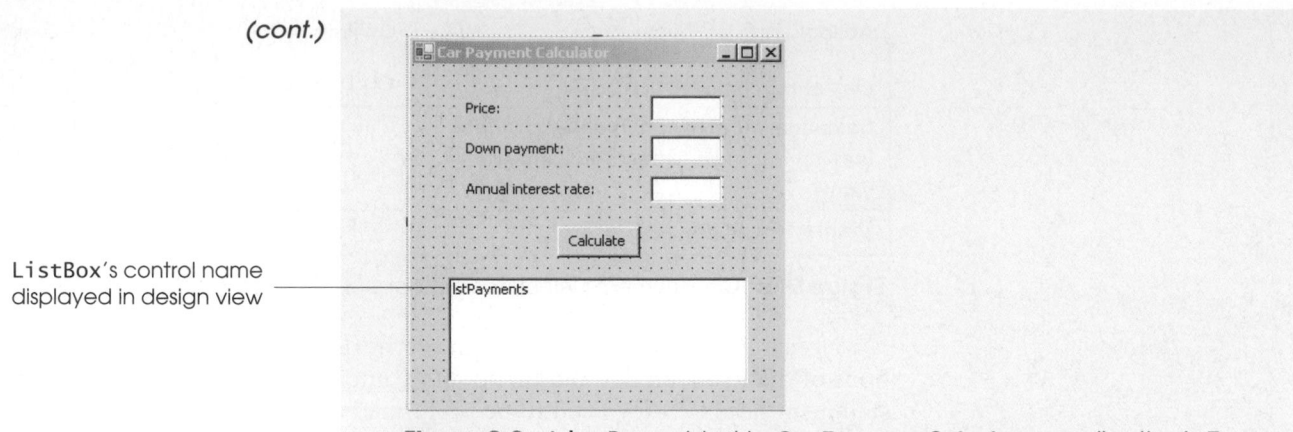

Figure 9.8 ListBox added to **Car Payment Calculator** application's Form.

After adding the ListBox, you must add an event handler to the application so that the application can respond to the user's clicking the **Calculate** Button. Event handler btnCalculate_Click updates the ListBox's contents. The box, *Using Code to Change a ListBox's Contents*, describes how to add items to a ListBox and how to clear a ListBox.

Using Code to Change a ListBox's Contents

1. ***Adding the Calculate Button's event handler.*** Double click the **Calculate** Button to generate the empty event handler btnCalculate_Click.

2. ***Clearing the ListBox control.*** Add lines 145–146 of Fig. 9.9 to btnCalculate_Click. Each time users click the **Calculate** Button, any content previously displayed in the ListBox is removed. To remove all content from the ListBox, call method Clear on property **Items** (line 146). Content can be added and deleted from the ListBox by using its Items property. The Items property returns an object that contains a list of items displayed in the ListBox. Notice that we have added comments on lines 141 and 148, and broken the first line of btnCalculate_Click into two lines for readability.

Figure 9.9 Clearing the contents of a ListBox.

(cont.)

3. ***Adding content to the ListBox control.*** Add lines 148–150 of Fig. 9.10 to btnCalculate_Click. The ListBox displays the number of monthly payments and the amount per payment. To clarify what information is being displayed, a line of text—called a **header**—needs to be added to the ListBox. Method Add (lines 149–150 of Fig. 9.10) adds the header—the column headings "Months" and "Monthly Payment" separated by two tab characters—to the ListBox's Items property.

GUI Design Tip

Use headers in a ListBox when you are displaying tabular data. Adding headers improves readability by indicating the information that will be displayed in the ListBox.

Figure 9.10 Adding a header to a ListBox.

The ampersand symbol (&) is called the **string-concatenation operator**. This operator combines (or concatenates) its two operands into one value. In lines 149–150, the header is created by joining the values "Months" and "Monthly Payments" with two **ControlChars.Tab** constants. The constant ControlChars.Tab inserts a tab character into the string. The application uses two tab characters of separation between the columns (Fig. 9.3).

4. ***Saving the solution.*** Select **File > Save All** to save the solution's files.

Now that you have learned how to change a ListBox's contents, you need to declare variables and obtain user input for the calculation. The box, *Declaring Variables and Receiving User Input*, shows you how to initialize the **Car Payment Calculator** application's variables. The box also guides you through converting the annual interest to the monthly interest rate and shows you how to calculate the amount of the loan.

Declaring Variables and Receiving User Input

1. ***Declaring variables.*** Place the cursor in the blank line immediately preceding the code you added in the box, *Using Code to Change a ListBox's Contents*. Add lines 145–152 of Fig. 9.11 to the application above the code you added in the previous box. Variables intYears and intMonths store the length of the loan in years and months. The calculation requires the length in months, but the loop-continuation condition will use the number of years. Variables intPrice, intDownPayment and dblInterest store the user input from the TextBoxes. Normally intPrice and intDownPayment would be represented as type Decimal, because they represent monetary values. For simplicity in this application, we have used Integers. Variables intLoanAmount and dblMonthlyInterest store calculation results.

2. ***Retrieving user input needed for the calculation.*** Add lines 161–165 of Fig. 9.12 below the code you added in the previous box. Lines 163–165 receive the down payment (intDownPayment), the price (intPrice) and the annual interest rate (dblInterest) provided by the user. Notice that line 165 divides the interest rate by 100 to obtain the decimal equivalent (for example, 5% becomes .05).

(cont.)

Variables to store the length of the loan

Variables to store user input

Variables to store calculation results

Figure 9.11 Variables for the **Car Payment Calculator** application.

Figure 9.12 Retrieving input in the **Car Payment Calculator** application.

3. *Calculating values used in the calculation.* The application computes the amount of the loan by subtracting the down payment from the price. Add lines 167–169 of Fig. 9.13 to calculate the amount borrowed (line 168) and the monthly interest rate (line 169). Because these calculations need to occur only once, they are placed before the Do While...Loop. Variables intLoanAmount and dblMonthlyInterest will be used in the calculation of monthly payments, which will be added to your application shortly.

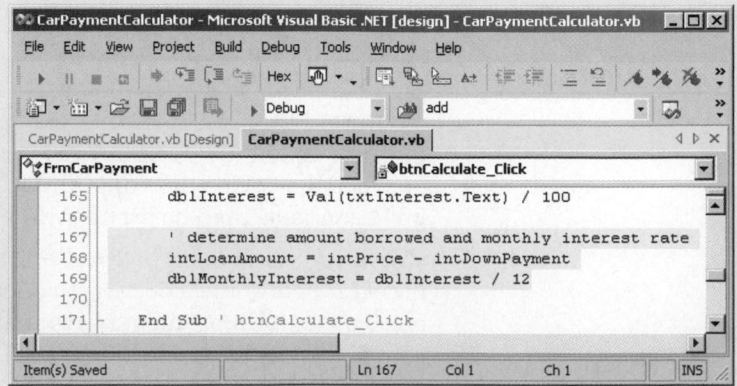

Figure 9.13 Determining amount borrowed and monthly interest rate.

(cont.)   4.   ***Saving the solution.*** Select **File > Save All** to save the solution's files.

The box, *Calculating the Monthly Payment Amounts with a Do While...Loop Repetition Statement*, adds a repetition statement to the application to calculate the monthly payment for four loans. The repetition statement performs this calculation for loans that last two, three, four and five years.

Calculating the Monthly Payment Amounts with a Do While...Loop Repetition Statement

1. ***Setting the loop-continuation condition.*** Place the cursor after the code you entered in the previous box. Add lines 171–172 of Fig. 9.14 to the application below the lines that calculate the amount of the loan (intLoanAmount) and the monthly interest rate (dblMonthlyInterest). After you type line 172 and press *Enter*, Visual Studio .NET closes the repetition statement by adding the keyword Loop on line 174.

Figure 9.14   Loop-continuation condition.

Recall that the shortest loan in this application lasts 2 years, so you initialized intYears to 2 of line 145 (Fig. 9.11). The loop-continuation condition (intYears <= 5) in Fig. 9.14 specifies that the Do While...Loop statement executes while intYears remains less than or equal to 5. This loop is an example of **counter-controlled repetition**. This technique uses a variable called a **counter** (intYears) to control the number of times that a set of statements will execute. Counter-controlled repetition also is called **definite repetition**, because the number of repetitions is known before the loop begins executing. In this example, repetition terminates when the counter (intYears) exceeds 5.

2. ***Calculating the payment period.*** Add lines 174–175 of Fig. 9.15 to the Do While...Loop repetition statement to calculate the number of payments (that is, the length of the loan in months). The number of months changes with each iteration of the loop, and the calculation result changes as the length of the payment period changes. Variable intMonths will have the values 24, 36, 48 and 60, on successive iterations of the loop.

3. ***Computing the monthly payment.*** Add lines 177–179 of Fig. 9.16 to the Do While...Loop repetition statement immediately after the code you just entered. Lines 178–179 (Fig. 9.16) use the Pmt function to calculate the user's monthly payment. The **Pmt** function returns a Double value that specifies the monthly payment amount on a loan for a constant interest rate (dblMonthlyInterest) and a given time period (intMonths).

(cont.)

Figure 9.15 Converting the loan duration from years to months.

Line 179 passes to `Pmt` the interest rate, the total number of payments (equal to the number of months in the payment period) and the amount borrowed. Borrowed amounts are represented by negative values, because they represent a removal of cash from the person or organization that is lending money. Monetary amounts are stored in variables of type `Decimal`. Method **`Convert.ToDecimal`** converts the return value of `Pmt` to type `Decimal` and assigns this value to `decMonthlyPayment`.

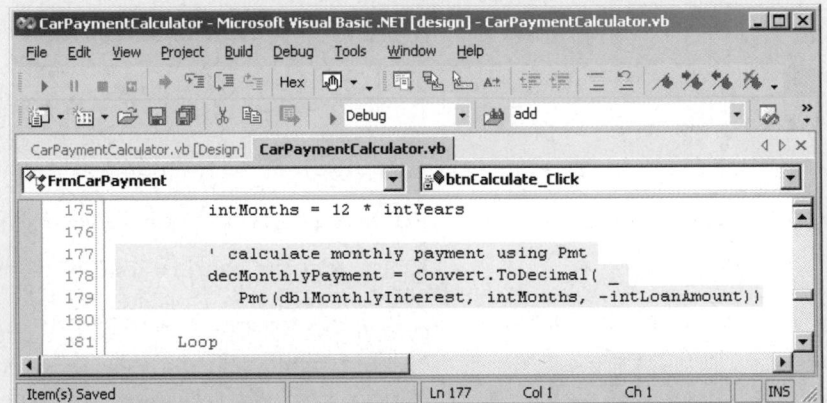

Figure 9.16 `Pmt` function returns monthly payment.

4. ***Displaying the monthly payment amount.*** Add lines 181–184 of Fig. 9.17 to the application. The number of monthly payments and the monthly payment amounts are displayed beneath the header. To add this content to the List-Box, call method `Add` (lines 182–184 of Fig. 9.17). Lines 183–184 use method `String.Format` to display `decMonthlyPayment` in currency format. Notice that the two tab characters ensure that the monthly payment amount is placed in the second column. The space provided by the extra tab character makes the application output more readable.

5. ***Incrementing the counter variable.*** Add line 186 of Fig. 9.18 before the closing statement of the repetition statement. Line 186 increments the counter variable (`intYears`). Variable `intYears` will be incremented until it equals 6. Then the loop-continuation condition (`intYears <= 5`) will evaluate to `False` and the repetition will end.

(cont.)

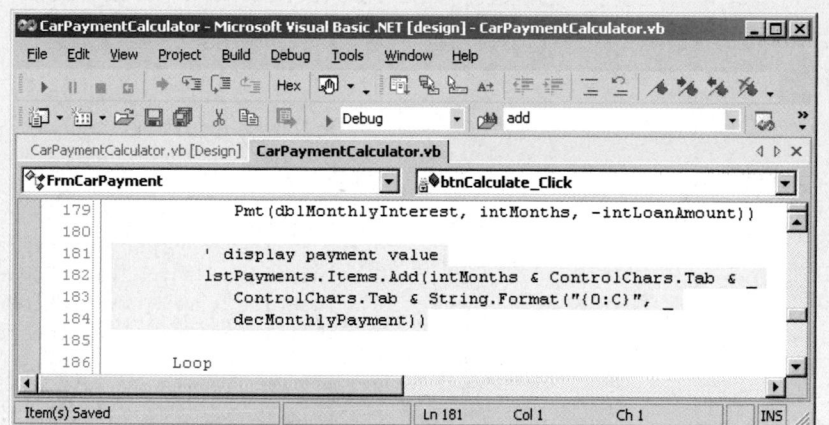

Figure 9.17 Displaying the number of months and the amount of each monthly payment.

Figure 9.18 Incrementing the counter.

6. ***Running the application.*** Select **Debug > Start** to run the application. The application should execute as it did in the test-drive.

Figure 9.19 presents the completed **Car Payment Calculator** application. New programming concepts are highlighted in yellow.

```
1   Public Class FrmCarPayment
2       Inherits System.Windows.Forms.Form
3
4       ' Windows Form Designer generated code
5
6       ' handles Calculate Button's Click event
7       Private Sub btnCalculate_Click(ByVal sender As System.Object, _
8           ByVal e As System.EventArgs) Handles btnCalculate.Click
9
10          Dim intYears As Integer = 2          ' repetition counter
11          Dim intMonths As Integer = 0         ' payment period
12          Dim intPrice As Integer = 0          ' car price
13          Dim intDownPayment As Integer = 0    ' down payment
14          Dim dblInterest As Double = 0        ' interest rate
15          Dim decMonthlyPayment As Decimal = 0 ' monthly payment
16          Dim intLoanAmount As Integer = 0     ' cost after down payment
17          Dim dblMonthlyInterest As Double = 0 ' monthly interest rate
18
```

Figure 9.19 **Car Payment Calculator** application code. (Part 1 of 2.)

```
19      ' remove text displayed in ListBox
20      lstPayments.Items.Clear()
21
22      ' add header to ListBox
23      lstPayments.Items.Add("Months" & ControlChars.Tab & _
24         ControlChars.Tab & "Monthly Payments")
25
26      ' retrieve user input and assign values
27      ' to their respective variables
28      intDownPayment = Val(txtDownPayment.Text)
29      intPrice = Val(txtStickerPrice.Text)
30      dblInterest = Val(txtInterest.Text) / 100
31
32      ' determine amount borrowed and monthly interest rate
33      intLoanAmount = intPrice - intDownPayment
34      dblMonthlyInterest = dblInterest / 12
35
36      ' loop four times
37      Do While intYears <= 5
38
39         ' calculate payment period
40         intMonths = 12 * intYears
41
42         ' calculate monthly payment using Pmt
43         decMonthlyPayment = Convert.ToDecimal( _
44            Pmt(dblMonthlyInterest, intMonths, -intLoanAmount))
45
46         ' display payment value
47         lstPayments.Items.Add(intMonths & ControlChars.Tab & _
48            ControlChars.Tab & String.Format("{0:C}", _
49            decMonthlyPayment))
50
51         intYears += 1  ' increment counter
52      Loop
53
54   End Sub ' btnCalculate_Click
55
56 End Class ' FrmCarPayment
```

Figure 9.19 **Car Payment Calculator** application code. (Part 2 of 2.)

SELF-REVIEW

1. Counter-controlled repetition is also called _____ because the number of repetitions is known before the loop begins executing.

   a) definite repetition   b) known repetition

   c) sequential repetition   d) counter repetition

2. The line of text that is added to a ListBox to clarify the information that will be displayed is called a _____.

   a) title   b) starter

   c) header   d) clarifier

Answers: 1) a. 2) c.

9.5 Wrap-Up

In this tutorial, you began using repetition statements. You used the Do While...Loop and the Do Until...Loop statements to repeat actions in an application, depending on a loop-continuation condition or a loop-termination condition, respectively.

The Do While...Loop repetition statement executes as long as its loop-continuation condition is True. When the loop-continuation condition becomes False, the repetition terminates. An infinite loop occurs if this condition never becomes False.

The Do Until...Loop repetition statement executes as long as its loop-termination condition is False. The repetition terminates when the loop-termination condition becomes True. An infinite loop occurs if this condition never becomes True.

You learned about counter-controlled repetition, in which a repetition statement "knows" the number of times it will iterate because a variable known as a counter precisely counts the number of iterations. You used a repetition statement to develop a **Car Payment Calculator** application in which you calculated the monthly payments for a given loan amount and a given interest rate for loan durations of two, three, four and five years.

In the **Car Payment Calculator** application, you used the ListBox control to display several payment options on a car loan. You learned about the ListBox control, which is used to maintain a list of items. Items can be added and removed from the ListBox programmatically. Values are added to a ListBox control by invoking method Add on the ListBox control's Items property. The Items property returns an object that contains all the values displayed in the ListBox.

In the next tutorial, you will learn two other Do repetition statements and you will continue exploring counter-controlled repetition. The **Car Payment Calculator** application demonstrated one common use of repetition statements—performing a calculation for several different values. The next application introduces another common application of repetition statements—summing a series of numbers.

SKILLS SUMMARY

Displaying Values in a ListBox

- Property Items of the ListBox control returns an object that contains the values to be displayed in a ListBox.
- Invoke method Add to add values to the Items property.

Clearing a ListBox's Contents

- Method Clear of the Items's property deletes (clears) all the values in the ListBox.

Repeating Actions in an Application

- Use a repetition statement that depends on the true or false value of a loop-continuation condition or a loop-termination condition.

Executing a Repetition Statement for a Known Number of Repetitions

- Use counter-controlled repetition with a counter variable to determine the number of times that a set of statements will execute.

Using the Do While...Loop Repetition Statement

- This repetition statement executes while the loop-continuation condition is True.
- An infinite loop occurs if the condition never becomes False.

Using the Do Until...Loop Repetition Statement

- This repetition statement executes while the loop-termination condition is False.
- An infinite loop occurs if the condition never becomes True.

KEY TERMS

Add method of Items—A method that adds an item to a ListBox control.

Clear method of Items—A method that deletes all the values in a ListBox's control.

ControlChar.Tab constant—A constant that represents a tab character.

Convert.ToDecimal method—A method that converts a value to type Decimal, which is appropriate for monetary calculations.

counter—A variable often used to determine the number of times a block of statements in a loop will execute.

counter-controlled repetition—A technique that uses a counter variable to determine the number of times that a block of statements will execute. Also called definite repetition.

definite repetition—See counter-controlled repetition.

diamond symbol—In the UML, represents the decision symbol and the merge symbol, depending on how it is used.

Do Until...Loop repetition statement—A control statement that executes a set of body statements until its loop-termination condition becomes True.

Do While...Loop repetition statement—A control statement that executes a set of body statements while its loop-continuation condition is True.

infinite loop—An error in which a repetition statement never terminates.

Items property of the ListBox control—Returns an object containing all the values in the ListBox.

ListBox control—Allows the user to view items in a list. Items can be added to or removed from the list programmatically.

loop-continuation condition—The condition used in a repetition statement (such as a Do While...Loop) that enables repetition to continue while the condition is True and that causes repetition to terminate when the condition becomes False.

loop-termination condition—The condition used in a repetition statement (such as a Do Until...Loop) that enables repetition to continue while the condition is False and that causes repetition to terminate when the condition becomes True.

merge symbol—A symbol in the UML that joins two flows of activity into one flow of activity.

Pmt function—A function that, given an interest rate, a time period and a monetary loan amount, returns a Double value specifying the payment amount per specified time period.

repetition statement—A statement that allows the programmer to specify that an action or actions should be repeated, depending on the value of a condition.

GUI DESIGN GUIDELINES

ListBox

- A ListBox should be large enough to display all of its content or large enough that scrollbars may be used easily.

- Use headers in a ListBox when you are displaying tabular data. Adding headers improves readability by indicating the information that will be displayed in the ListBox.

CONTROLS, EVENTS, PROPERTIES & METHODS

Convert The Convert class converts the value of a data type to another data type.

- *Methods*

  ToDecimal—This method converts its argument to a Decimal value.

ListBox   ▤▤ ListBox   This control allows the user to view and select from items in a list.

- *In action*

Months	Monthly Payments
24	$490.50
36	$339.06
48	$263.55
60	$218.41

- *Properties*

  Items—This property returns an object that contains the items displayed in the ListBox.
  Location—This property specifies the location of the ListBox on the Form.
  Name—This property specifies the name used to access the properties of the ListBox programatically. The name should be prefixed with lst.
  Size—This property specifies the height and width (in pixels) of the ListBox.

■ *Methods*
Items.Add—This method adds an item to the Items property.
Items.Clear—This method deletes all the values in the ListBox's Items property.

MULTIPLE-CHOICE QUESTIONS

9.1 The _____ statement executes until its continuation condition becomes True.

  a) Do While...Loop   b) Do Until...Loop

  c) Do   d) Loop

9.2 The _____ statement executes until its loop-continuation condition becomes False.

  a) Do While...Loop   b) Do Until...Loop

  c) Do   d) Do While

9.3 A(n) _____ loop occurs when a condition in a Do While...Loop never becomes False.

  a) infinite   b) undefined

  c) nested   d) indefinite

9.4 A _____ is a variable that helps control the number of times that a set of statements will execute.

  a) repeater   b) counter

  c) loop   d) repetition control statement

9.5 The _____ control allows users to add and view items in a list.

  a) ListItems   b) SelectBox

  c) ListBox   d) ViewBox

9.6 In a UML activity diagram, a(n) _____ symbol joins two flows of activity into one flow of activity.

  a) merge   b) combine

  c) action state   d) decision

9.7 Property _____ returns an object containing all the values in a ListBox.

  a) All   b) List

  c) ListItemValues   d) Items

9.8 Method _____ deletes all the values in a ListBox.

  a) Remove   b) Delete

  c) Clear   d) Del

9.9 Items's method _____ adds an item to a ListBox.

  a) Include   b) Append

  c) Add   d) Insert

9.10 Method _____ calculates monthly payments on a loan based on a fixed interest rate.

  a) MonPmt   b) Payment

  c) MonthlyPayment   d) Pmt

EXERCISES

9.11 *(Table of Powers Application)* Write an application that displays a table of numbers from 1 to an upper limit, along with each number's squared value (for example, the number n to the power 2, or n ^ 2) and cubed value (the number n to the power 3, or n ^ 3). The users should specify the upper limit, and the results should be displayed in a ListBox, as in Fig. 9.20.

  a) *Copying the template application to your work folder.* Copy the TableOfPowers folder from C:\Examples\Tutorial09\Exercises to C:\SimplyVB.

  b) *Opening the template application.* Double click TableOfPowers.sln in the C:\SimplyVB\TableOfPowers folder.

c) *Adding a ListBox.* Add a ListBox to the application, as shown in Fig. 9.20. Name the ListBox lstResults.

d) *Adding the Upper limit: TextBox event handler.* Double click the **Upper limit:** TextBox to generate an event handler for this TextBox's TextChanged event. In this event handler, clear the ListBox.

e) *Adding the Calculate Button event handler.* Double click the **Calculate** Button to generate the empty event handler btnCalculate_Click. Add the code specified by the remaining steps to this event handler.

f) *Clearing the ListBox.* Use method Clear on the Items property to clear the List-Box from any previous data.

g) *Obtaining the upper limit supplied by the user.* Assign the value entered by the user in the **Upper limit:** TextBox to a variable. Note that the TextBox's Name property is set to txtInput.

h) *Adding a header.* Use method Add on the Items property to insert a header in the ListBox. The header should label three columns—N, N^2 and N^3. Column headings should be separated by tab characters.

i) *Calculating the powers from 1 to the specified upper limit.* Use a Do Until...Loop to calculate the squared value and the cubed value of each number from 1 to the upper limit, inclusive. Add an item to the ListBox containing the current number being analyzed, its squared value and its cubed value.

j) *Incrementing the counter.* Remember to increment the counter appropriately each time through the loop.

Figure 9.20 Table of Powers application's Form.

9.12 *(Mortgage Calculator Application)* A bank offers mortgages that can be repaid in 5, 10, 15, 20, 25 or 30 years. Write an application that allows a user to enter the price of a house (the amount of the mortgage) and the annual interest rate. When the user clicks a Button, the application displays a table of the mortgage length in years together with the monthly payment, as shown in Fig. 9.21.

a) *Copying the template application to your work folder.* Copy the MortgageCalculator folder from the C:\Examples\Tutorial09\Exercises directory to the C:\SimplyVB folder.

b) *Opening the template application.* Double click MortgageCalculator.sln in the C:\SimplyVB\MortgageCalculator folder.

c) *Adding a ListBox to display the results.* Add a ListBox as shown in Fig. 9.21. Name the ListBox lstResults.

d) *Adding a Calculate Button event handler.* Double click the **Calculate** Button to generate the empty event handler btnCalculate_Click. Add the code specified in the remaining steps to your event handler.

e) *Converting the annual interest rate to the monthly interest rate.* To convert the annual interest rate from a percent value into its Double equivalent, divide the annual rate by 100. Then divide the Double annual rate by 12 to obtain the monthly rate.

f) *Clearing the ListBox.* Use method Clear on the Items property to clear the List-Box from any previous data.

g) *Displaying a header.* Use method Add to display a header in the ListBox. The header should be the column headers "Mortgage Length (Years)" and "Monthly Payment", separated by a tab character.

h) *Using a repetition statement.* Add a Do While...Loop repetition statement to calculate six monthly payment options for the user's mortgage. Each option has a different number of years that the mortgage can last. For this exercise, use the following number of years: 5, 10, 15, 20, 25 and 30.

i) *Converting the length of the mortgage from years to months.* Convert the number of years to months.

j) *Calculating the monthly payments for six different mortgages.* Use the Pmt function to compute the monthly payments. Pass to the function the monthly interest rate, the number of months in the mortgage and the mortgage amount. Remember that the mortgage amount must be negative, as it represents an amount of money being paid out by the lender.

k) *Displaying the results.* Use method Add on the Items property to display the length of the mortgage in years and the monthly payment in the ListBox. You will need to use three tab characters to ensure that the monthly payment appears in the second column.

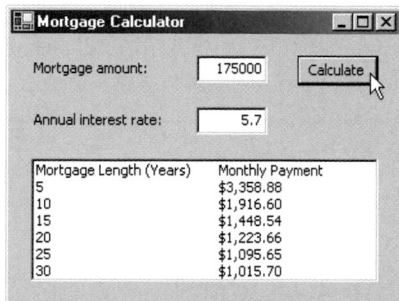

Figure 9.21   Mortgage Calculator application's Form.

9.13 *(Office Supplies Application)* Create an application that allows a user to make a list of office supplies to buy, as shown in Fig. 9.22. The user should enter the supply in a TextBox and click the **Buy** Button to add it to the ListBox. The **Clear** Button removes all the items from the ListBox.

a) *Copying the template application to your work folder.* Copy the OfficeSupplies folder in C:\Examples\Tutorial09\Exercises to C:\SimplyVB.

b) *Opening the template application.* Double click OfficeSupplies.sln in C:\SimplyVB\OfficeSupplies.

c) *Adding a ListBox.* Add a ListBox to the Form. Name the ListBox lstSupplies. Place and size it as shown in Fig. 9.22.

d) *Adding an event handler for the Buy Button.* Double click the **Buy** Button to generate the event handler btnBuy_Click. The event handler should obtain the user input from the TextBox. The user input is then added as an item into the ListBox. After the input is added to the ListBox, clear the **Supply:** TextBox.

e) *Adding an event handler for the Clear Button.* Double click the **Clear** Button to generate the event handler btnClear_Click. The event handler should use the Clear method on the Items property to clear the ListBox.

Figure 9.22   Office Supplies application's Form.

What does this code do? ▶ **9.14** What is the result of the following code?

```
1   Dim intX As Integer = 1
2   Dim intMysteryValue As Integer = 1
3
4   Do While intX < 6
5
6       intMysteryValue *= intX
7       intX += 1
8   Loop
9
10  lblDisplay.Text = intMysteryValue
```

What's wrong with this code? ▶ **9.15** Find the error(s) in the following code:

a) Assume that the variable intX is declared and initialized to 1. The loop should total the numbers from 1 to 10.

```
1   Dim intTotal As Integer = 0
2
3   Do Until intX <= 10
4
5       intTotal += intX
6       intX += 1
7   Loop
```

b) Assume that the variable intCounter is declared and initialized to 1. The loop should sum the numbers from 1 to 100.

```
1   Do While intCounter <= 100
2
3       intTotal += intCounter
4   Loop
5
6   intCounter += 1
```

c) Assume that the variable intCounter is declared and initialized to 1000. The loop should iterate from 1000 to 1.

```
1   Do While intCounter > 0
2
3       lblDisplay.Text = intCounter
4       intCounter += 1
5   Loop
```

d) Assume that the variable intCounter is declared and initialized to 1. The loop should execute five times, adding the numbers 1–5 to a ListBox.

```
1   Do While intCounter < 5
2
3       lstNumbers.Items.Add(intCounter)
4       intCounter += 1
5   Loop
```

Using the Debugger ▶ **9.16** (*Odd Numbers Application*) The **Odd Numbers** application should display all of the odd integers between one and the number input by the user. Copy the **Odd Numbers** application from C:/Examples/Tutorial09/Debugger to your working directory. Run the application. Notice that, after you enter a value into the **Upper limit:** TextBox and click the **View** Button, an infinite loop occurs. Use the debugger to find and fix the error(s) in the application. Figure 9.23 displays the correct output for the application.

Figure 9.23 Correct output for the **Odd Numbers** application.

Programming Challenge ▶ **9.17** *(To Do List Application)* Use a ListBox as a To Do List. Enter each item in a TextBox, and add it to the ListBox by clicking a Button. The item should be displayed in a numbered list as in Fig. 9.24. To do this, we introduce method Count, which returns the number of items in a ListBox's Items property. The following is a sample call to assign the number of items displayed in the lstSample ListBox to an Integer variable:

```
intCount = lstSample.Items.Count()
```

Figure 9.24 **To Do List** application's Form.

T U T O R I A L

10

Objectives

In this tutorial, you will learn to:
- Use the Do...Loop While statement.
- Use the Do...Loop Until statement.
- Understand counter-controlled repetition.
- Transfer the focus to a control.
- Enable and disable Buttons.

Outline

10.1 Test-Driving the Class Average Application

10.2 Do...Loop While Repetition Statement

10.3 Do...Loop Until Repetition Statement

10.4 Creating the Class Average Application

10.5 Wrap-Up

Class Average Application

Introducing the Do...Loop While and Do...Loop Until Repetition Statements

This tutorial continues our discussion of repetition statements that we began in Tutorial 9. In the previous tutorial, we examined Do While...Loop and Do Until...Loop repetition statements, which test their loop-continuation and loop-termination conditions before an iteration. This tutorial introduces two additional repetition statements, Do...Loop While and Do...Loop Until, which perform their tests after each iteration. As a result, the body statements contained in either of these repetition statements are performed at least once.

You will also learn how to disable and enable controls on a Form. When a control, such as a Button, is disabled, it will no longer respond to the user. You will use this feature to prevent the user from causing errors in your applications. This tutorial also introduces the concept of transferring the focus of the application to a control. Proper use of the focus makes an application easier to use.

10.1 Test-Driving the Class Average Application

This application must meet the following requirements:

Application Requirements

A teacher regularly issues quizzes to a class of ten students. The grades on these quizzes are integers in the range from 0 to 100 (0 and 100 are each valid grades). The teacher would like you to develop an application that computes the class average for a quiz.

The class average is equal to the sum of the grades divided by the number of students who took the quiz. The algorithm for solving this problem on a computer must input each of the grades, total the grades, perform the averaging calculation and display the result. You begin by test-driving the completed application.

Test-Driving the Class Average Application

1. ***Opening the completed solution.*** Open the C:\Examples\Tutorial10\CompletedApplication\ClassAverage folder to locate the ClassAverage application. Double click ClassAverage.sln to open the application in Visual Studio .NET.

2. ***Running the completed application.*** Select **Debug > Start** to execute the application. Figure 10.1 displays the running application.

Figure 10.1   **Class Average** application's **Form** in run mode.

3. ***Entering quiz grades.*** Enter 85 as the first quiz grade in the **Enter grade:** TextBox, and click the **Add Grade** Button. The grade entered will display in the ListBox as in Fig. 10.2. Notice that, after you click the **Add Grade** Button, the cursor appears in the **Enter grade:** TextBox. When a control is selected (for example, the **Enter grade:** TextBox), it is said to have the **focus** of the application. You will learn to set the focus to a control as you build this tutorial's application. As a result of the application's focus being transferred to the **Enter grade:** TextBox, you can type another grade without navigating to the TextBox with the mouse or the *Tab* key. Transferring the focus to a particular control tells the user what information the application expects next. [*Note*: If you click the **Average** Button before 10 grades have been input, an error occurs. In the dialog that displays, click **Continue** to return to design mode. Repeat *Step 2*. You will fix this problem in the exercises.]

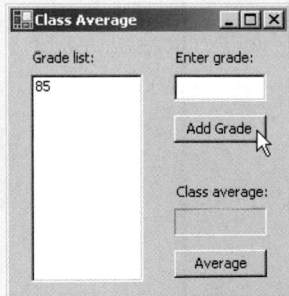

Figure 10.2   Entering grades in the **Class Average** application.

4. ***Repeat*** Step 3 ***nine times.*** Enter nine other grades between 0 and 100, and click the **Add Grade** Button after each entry. After 10 grades are displayed in the **Grade list:** ListBox, the Form will look similar to Fig. 10.3. Notice that, once you have entered 10 grades, the **Add Grade** Button is disabled. That is, its color is gray, and clicking the Button does not invoke its event handler.

(cont.)

Ten quiz grades entered ——————

Disabled **Add Grade** Button

Figure 10.3 **Class Average** application after 10 grades have been input.

5. *Calculating the class average*. Click the **Average** Button to calculate the average of the 10 quizzes. The class average will be displayed in an output Label above the **Average** Button (Fig. 10.4). Notice that the **Add Grade** Button is now enabled.

Label displaying average

Click to calculate class average

Figure 10.4 Displaying the class average.

6. *Entering another set of grades*. You can calculate the class average for another set of 10 grades without restarting the application. Enter a grade in the TextBox, and click the **Add Grade** Button. Notice that the **Grade list:** ListBox and the **Class average:** field are cleared when you start entering another set of grades (Fig. 10.5).

Figure 10.5 Entering a new set of grades.

7. *Terminating the application*. Click the running application's close box.

8. *Closing the solution*. Select **File > Close Solution**.

10.2 Do...Loop While Repetition Statement

The **Do...Loop While** repetition statement is similar to the Do While...Loop statement; both statements iterate while their loop-continuation conditions are True. In the Do While...Loop statement, the loop-continuation condition is tested at the beginning of the loop, before the body of the loop is performed. The Do...Loop

While statement performs the loop-continuation condition *after* the loop body is performed. Therefore, in a Do...Loop While statement, the loop body always executes at least once. Recall that a Do While...Loop executes only if its loop-continuation condition evaluates to true. When a Do...Loop While statement terminates, execution continues with the statement after the Loop While clause.

To illustrate the Do...Loop While repetition style, consider the example of packing a suitcase: Before you begin packing, the suitcase is empty. You place an item in the suitcase and then determine whether the suitcase is full. As long as the suitcase is not full, you continue to put items in the suitcase. As an example of a Do...Loop While statement, let's look at the following program segment designed to display the numbers 1 through 3 in a ListBox:

```
Dim intCounter As Integer = 1

Do
    lstDisplay.Items.Add(intCounter)
    intCounter += 1
Loop While intCounter <= 3
```

The program segment initializes the counter intCounter to 1. The loop-continuation condition in the Do...Loop While statement is intCounter <= 3. While the loop-continuation condition is True, the Do...Loop While statement executes. When the loop-continuation condition becomes False (that is, when intCounter is greater than 3), the Do...Loop While statement finishes executing and lstDisplay contains the numbers 1 through 3. The box, *Executing the Do...Loop While Repetition Statement,* describes each step as the above repetition statement executes.

Common Programming Error

An infinite loop occurs when the loop-continuation condition in a Do...Loop While statement never becomes False.

*Executing the Do...Loop While **Repetition Statement***

1. The application declares variable intCounter and sets its value to 1.

2. The application enters the Do...Loop While repetition statement.

3. The number (currently 1) stored in intCounter is Added to the lstDisplay ListBox's Items property.

4. The value of intCounter is increased by 1; intCounter now contains the number 2.

5. The loop-continuation condition is checked. The condition evaluates to True (intCounter is less than or equal to 3), so the application resumes execution at the first statement after the Do statement.

6. The number (currently 2) stored in intCounter is Added to the lstDisplay ListBox's Items property.

7. The value of intCounter is increased by 1; intCounter now contains the number 3.

8. The loop-continuation condition is checked. The condition evaluates to True (intCounter is less than or equal to 3), so the application resumes execution at the first statement after the Do statement.

9. The number (currently 3) stored in intCounter is Added to the lstDisplay ListBox's Items property.

10. The value of intCounter is increased by 1; intCounter now contains the number 4.

11. The loop-continuation condition is checked. The condition evaluates to False (intCounter is not less than or equal to 3), so the application exits the Do...Loop While repetition statement.

Notice that, if you mistyped the loop-continuation condition as intCounter < 3 or intCounter <= 2, the ListBox would display only 1 and 2. Including an incorrect relational operator (such as the less than sign in intCounter < 3) or an incorrect

Error-Prevention Tip

Including a final value in the condition of a repetition statement (and choosing the appropriate relational operator) can reduce the occurrence of off-by-one errors. For example, in a Do While...Loop statement used to print the values 1–10, the loop-continuation condition should be intCounter <= 10, rather than intCounter < 10 (which is an off-by-one error) or intCounter < 11 (which is correct, but less clear).

final value for a loop counter (such as the 2 in intCounter <= 2) in the condition of any repetition statement can cause **off-by-one errors**, which occur when a loop executes for one more or one fewer iterations than is necessary.

Figure 10.6 illustrates the UML activity diagram for the general Do...Loop While statement. This diagram makes it clear that the loop-continuation guard condition ([intCounter <= 3]) does not evaluate until after the loop performs the action state at least once. Recall that action states can include one or more Visual Basic .NET statements executed one after the other (sequentially) as in the preceding example. When you use a Do...Loop While repetition statement in building an application, you would provide the appropriate action state and the guard conditions for your application.

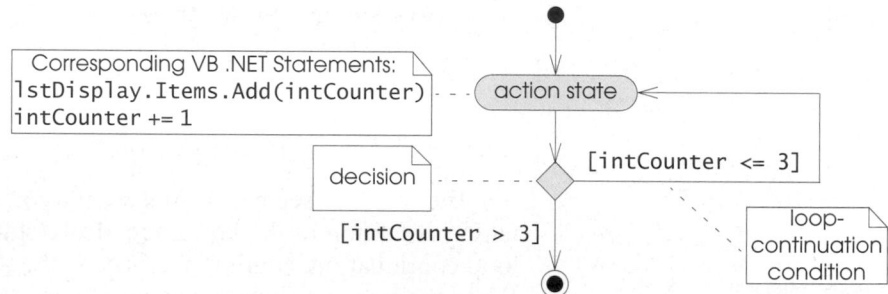

Figure 10.6 Do...Loop While repetition statement UML activity diagram.

SELF-REVIEW

1. The Do...Loop While statement tests the loop-continuation condition _____.
   a) for False after the loop body executes
   b) for False before the loop body executes
   c) for True after the loop body executes
   d) for True before the loop body executes

2. An infinite loop occurs when the loop-continuation condition in a Do While...Loop or Do...Loop While statement _____.
   a) never becomes True
   b) never becomes False
   c) is False
   d) is tested repeatedly

Answers: 1) c. 2) b.

10.3 Do...Loop Until Repetition Statement

The Do...Loop Until statement is similar to the Do Until...Loop statement, except that in the Do...Loop Until statement the loop-continuation condition is tested after the loop body is performed. Therefore, the loop body executes at least once. When a Do...Loop Until terminates, execution continues with the statement after the Loop Until clause.

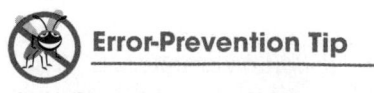

Error-Prevention Tip

An infinite loop occurs when the loop-continuation condition in a Do...Loop Until statement never becomes True.

Again, consider the suitcase-packing example. Before you begin packing, the suitcase is empty. You place an item in the suitcase and then determine whether the suitcase is still empty. As long as the condition "the suitcase is full" is False, you continue to put items into the suitcase.

As an example of a Do...Loop Until statement, let's look at another program segment designed to display the numbers 1 through 3 in a ListBox:

```
Dim intCounter As Integer = 1

Do
    lstDisplay.Items.Add(intCounter)
    intCounter += 1
Loop Until intCounter > 3
```

The application segment initializes the counter intCounter to 1, and the loop-termination condition in the Do...Loop Until statement is intCounter > 3. While the loop-termination condition is False, the Do...Loop Until statement executes.

When the loop-termination condition becomes True, the Do...Loop Until statement finishes executing and lstDisplay contains the numbers 1 through 3. The box, *Executing the Do...Loop Until Repetition Statement*, describes each step as the repetition statement executes.

Executing the Do...Loop Until ***Repetition Statement***	1. The application declares variable intCounter and sets its value to 1.
	2. The application enters the Do...Loop Until repetition statement.
	3. The number (1) stored in intCounter is Added to the lstDisplay List-Box's Items property.
	4. The value of intCounter is increased by 1; intCounter now contains the number 2.
	5. The loop-termination condition is checked. The condition evaluates to False (intCounter is not greater than 3), so the application resumes execution at the first statement after the Do statement.
	6. The number (2) stored in intCounter is Added to the lstDisplay List-Box's Items property.
	7. The value of intCounter is increased by 1; intCounter now contains the number 3.
	8. The loop-termination condition is checked. The condition evaluates to False (intCounter is not greater than 3), so the application resumes execution at the first statement after the Do statement.
	9. The number (3) stored in intCounter is Added to the lstDisplay List-Box's Items property.
	10. The value of intCounter is increased by 1; intCounter now contains the number 4.
	11. The loop-termination condition is checked. The condition now evaluates to True (intCounter is greater than 3), so the application exits the Do...Loop Until repetition statement.

The Do...Loop Until UML activity diagram (Fig. 10.7) makes it clear that the loop-termination guard condition is not evaluated until after the body is executed at least once. This UML diagram indicates the exact same guard conditions as detailed in Fig. 10.6. The only difference for a Do...Loop Until repetition statement is that it continues to execute when the loop-termination guard condition is False. When the guard condition evaluates to True, the repetition ends and program control moves to the next statement following the Loop Until clause.

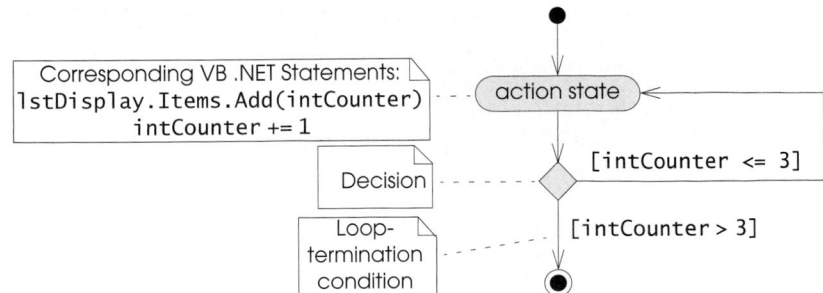

Figure 10.7 Do...Loop Until repetition statement activity diagram.

SELF-REVIEW   1. The Do...Loop Until statement checks the loop-termination condition _____.

a) for False after the loop body executes   b) for False before the loop body executes
c) for True after the loop body executes   d) for True before the loop body executes

2. When a Do...Loop Until terminates, execution continues with the _____.

    a) Loop Until clause   b) statement after the Loop Until clause

    c) statements inside Do and Loop Until   d) Do clause

Answers: 1) c. 2) b.

10.4 Creating the Class Average Application

Now that you have learned the Do...Loop While and Do...Loop Until repetition statements, you can begin to develop the **Class Average** application. First, you will use pseudocode to list the actions to be executed and to specify the order of execution. You will use counter-controlled repetition to input the grades one at a time. Recall that this technique uses a variable called a counter to determine the number of times that a set of statements executes. In this example, repetition terminates when the counter exceeds 10 because we are assuming, for simplicity, that the user will only enter 10 grades. The following is a pseudocode algorithm for the **Class Average** application:

> When the Add Grade Button is clicked,
>
>   If an average has already been calculated for a set of grades
>   Clear the output Label and the ListBox
>
>   Retrieve grade entered by user in the Enter grade: TextBox
>   Display the grade in the ListBox
>   Clear the Enter grade: TextBox
>
> When the Average Button is clicked,
>   Set total to zero
>   Set grade counter to zero
>
>   Do
>   Read the next grade in the ListBox
>   Add the grade to the total
>   Add one to the grade counter
>   Loop until grade counter equals or exceeds 10
>
>   Calculate the class average by dividing the total by 10
>   Display the class average

Before you begin to build the application, it is helpful to create an ACE table for the program. Figure 10.8 lists actions, controls and events required to complete the application.

Action/Control/Event Table for the Class Average Application	Event	Control	Event
	Label all the application's controls	lblPrompt, lblGradeList, lblDescribeOutput	
	User enters grade	txtInput	
	Retrieve grade entered by user in the Enter grade: TextBox	btnAdd	Click
	Display the grades	lstGrades	
	Calculate the class average by reading ListBox values	btnAverage	Click
	Display the class average	lblOutput	

Figure 10.8 ACE table for the **Class Average** application.

We label the application's GUI, using Labels lblPrompt, lblDescribeOut-put and lblGradeList. The user enters grades in the txtInput TextBox and clicks the btnAdd Button. The Click event then Adds the value that the user entered in the txtInput TextBox to the ListBox, using method lstGrades.Items.Add(). When the user has entered 10 grades and clicked the btnAverage Button, the application will retrieve each value from the ListBox, add it to the total and compute the class average by dividing by 10. The class average then will be displayed in the lblOutput Label.

Now that we have formulated an algorithm for solving the **Class Average** problem, we can begin adding functionality to the template application. To display in the **Grade list:** ListBox a grade entered in the **Enter grade:** TextBox, the user clicks the **Add Grade** Button. If the application is already displaying grades in the **Grade list:** ListBox and the class average in the **Class average:** Label, the values are first cleared. The box, *Entering Grades in the **Class Average** Application*, guides you through adding this functionality to the **Add Grade** Button's event handler.

Entering Grades in the Class Average Application	1. **Copying the template to your work folder.** Copy the C:\Examples\Tutorial10\TemplateApplication\ClassAverage directory to C:\SimplyVB. 2. **Opening the template application.** Double click ClassAverage.sln to open the template application in Visual Studio .NET. Double click Class-Average.vb in the **Solution Explorer** to display the Form (Fig. 10.9).

Figure 10.9 **Class Average** application's Form in design view.

3. **Adding an event handler for the Add Grade Button.** Each time users enter grades in the **Class Average** application, they must click the **Add Grade** Button. Double click the Button labeled **Add Grade** to create event handler btnAdd_Click.

4. **Clearing the ListBox and the Class average: Label of any output from a previous calculation.** Add lines 148–152 (Fig. 10.10) to event handler btnAdd_Click. Remember that you should place a comment before each event handler (line 144). To determine whether there was a previous calculation, test whether lblOutput displays any text by comparing the Text property's value to the empty string (line 149). If the lblOutput Label displays the result of a previous calculation, set its Text property to the empty string (line 150). Line 151 clears the grades from the ListBox.

5. **Displaying each grade in the ListBox control.** Add lines 154–156 of Fig. 10.11 to event handler btnAdd_Click below the If...Then statement. Line 155 Adds the grade entered in txtInput to ListBox lstGrades's Items property. The grade is displayed in the ListBox.

6. **Preparing for the next grade to be entered.** Method Clear (line 156 of Fig. 10.11) deletes the grade from the TextBox to prepare the application for the next grade to be entered.

(cont.)

Clearing the grade list and class average

```
144        ' handles Add Grade Button's Click event
145     Private Sub btnAdd_Click(ByVal sender As System.Object, _
146         ByVal e As System.EventArgs) Handles btnAdd.Click
147
148         ' clear previous grades and calculation result
149         If lblOutput.Text <> "" Then
150             lblOutput.Text = ""
151             lstGrades.Items.Clear()
152         End If
```

Figure 10.10   Clearing the ListBox and output Label after a calculation.

Adding a numeric grade to the ListBox and clearing the user input from the TextBox

```
154         ' display grade in ListBox
155         lstGrades.Items.Add(Val(txtInput.Text))
156         txtInput.Clear()   ' clear grade from TextBox
```

Figure 10.11   Adding the grade input to the ListBox and clearing the **Enter grade:** TextBox.

7. ***Saving the solution.*** Select **File > Save All** to save all of the solution's files.

You have added the code to display the grade entered in the **Enter grade:** TextBox in the ListBox when the user clicks the **Add Grade** Button. Now, the box, *Transferring the Focus to a Control and Disabling a Button,* shows you how to transfer the focus to the TextBox for the next grade entry after the user clicks the **Add Grade** Button. The box also shows you how to disable the **Add Grade** Button after 10 grades have been entered, because its functionality is no longer needed.

Transferring the Focus to a Control and Disabling a *Button*

1. ***Transferring the focus to a control.*** Add line 157 (Fig. 10.12) to event handler btnAdd_Click. Line 157 calls txtInput's **Focus** method to place the cursor in the TextBox for the next grade input. This process is called **transferring the focus**. Here the focus is transferred from the Button to the TextBox.

Transferring the focus of the application to the TextBox

```
156         txtInput.Clear()   ' clear grade from TextBox
157         txtInput.Focus()   ' transfer focus to TextBox
```

Figure 10.12   Transferring the focus to the TextBox control.

(cont.)

2. ***Disabling the Add Grade Button to prohibit users from entering more than 10 grades.*** Your application should accept exactly 10 grades. If the number of grades already entered by the user is equal to 10, then the application should prevent the user from entering more grades. Add lines 159–163 of Fig. 10.13 to event handler `btnAdd_Click`. Line 160 determines whether 10 or more grades have been entered, using the `>=` comparison operator. `Items`'s **Count** property returns the number of items displayed in the **Grade list:** `ListBox`. If 10 grades have been entered, line 161 disables `Button` `btnAdd` by setting its **Enabled** property to `False`. Clicking the disabled **Add Grade** `Button` will not cause the `btnAdd_Click` event handler to execute.

GUI Design Tip

Disable `Button`s when their function should not be available to users.

Disabling the **Add grade** `Button` and transferring the focus to the **Average** `Button`

Figure 10.13 Application accepts only 10 grades.

3. ***Transferring the focus to the Average Button after 10 grades have been entered.*** After 10 grades have been entered, it does not make sense for the application to transfer the focus to the `TextBox`. Instead, line 162 invokes method `Focus` to transfer the focus to the **Average** `Button`. This way, you can press *Enter* to invoke **Average** `Button`'s event handler, without navigating to the `Button` or using the mouse pointer.

4. ***Saving the solution.*** Select **File > Save All** to save all of the solution's files.

After 10 grades have been entered and displayed in the `ListBox`, the **Add Grade** `Button`'s event handler transfers the focus to the **Average** `Button`. When the user clicks the **Average** `Button`, the application calculates and displays the average of the 10 grades. The box, *Calculating the Class Average*, shows you how to sum the grades with a `Do…Loop Until` repetition statement before the average calculation. The box also covers displaying the result in the **Class average:** `Label`.

Calculating the Class Average

1. ***Adding an event handler for the Average Button.*** Double click the `Button` labeled **Average** to generate event handler `btnAverage_Click`.

2. ***Initializing variables used in the class-average calculation.*** Add lines 171–175 of Fig. 10.14 to event handler `btnAverage_Click`. Line 172 declares `Integer intTotal`. You will use `intTotal` to calculate the sum of 10 grades (you will need this sum later when you calculate the average grade). Line 173 declares the counter (`intGradeCounter`). It is important that variables used as totals and counters have appropriate initial values before they are used. If a numerical variable is not initialized before its first use, Visual Basic .NET initializes it to a default value of 0. Variable `intGrade` (line 174) temporarily stores each grade read from the `ListBox`. Although the grades entered are `Integer`s, the result of the averaging calculation can be a floating-point value (such as the `81.1` result in Fig. 10.4); therefore, you declare `Double` variable `dblAverage` (line 175) to store the class average.

(cont.)

Initializing variables

Figure 10.14 Initialization phase of class-average calculation.

3. *Summing the grades displayed in the ListBox.* Add lines 177–184 of Fig. 10.15 to event handler btnAverage_Click. The Do...Loop Until statement (lines 178–184) sums the grades that it reads from the ListBox. Line 184 indicates that the statement should iterate until the value of int-GradeCounter is greater than or equal to 10. Line 181 reads the current value from the ListBox, using property **Item** and stores that value in int-Grade. Line 182 adds intGrade to the previous value of intTotal and assigns the result to intTotal, using the += assignment operator. Variable intGradeCounter is incremented (line 183) to indicate that another grade has been processed. (Incrementing the counter ensures that the condition on line 184 eventually becomes True, terminating the loop.)

Using the Do...Loop Until repetition statement to sum grades in the ListBox

Figure 10.15 Do...Loop Until summing grades.

4. *Calculating and displaying the average.* Add lines 186–189 of Fig. 10.16 to event handler btnAverage_Click. Line 186 assigns the result of the average calculation to variable dblAverage. Line 187 displays the value of variable dblAverage. After the average is displayed, another set of 10 grades can be entered. To allow this, you need to enable the **Add Grade** Button, by setting property Enabled to True (line 188). Line 189 transfers the focus to the **Enter grade:** TextBox.

5. *Saving the solution.* Select **File > Save All** to save all of the solution's files.

6. *Running the application.* Select **Debug > Start** to run the application.

7. *Closing the application.* Click the running application's close box.

GUI Design Tip

Enable a disabled **Button** when its function should be available to the user once again.

(cont.)

Calculating the class average, enabling the **Add Grade** Button and transferring the focus to the **Enter grade:** TextBox

Figure 10.16   Displaying the result of the average calculation.

8. *Closing the solution.* Select **File > Close Solution**.

Figure 10.17 presents the completed application's code. Code that uses new programming concepts is highlighted in yellow.

```
1    Public Class FrmClassAverage
2       Inherits System.Windows.Forms.Form
3
4       ' Windows Form Designer generated code
5
6       ' handles Add Grade Button's Click event
7       Private Sub btnAdd_Click(ByVal sender As System.Object, _
8          ByVal e As System.EventArgs) Handles btnAdd.Click
9
10         ' clear previous grades and calculation result
11         If lblOutput.Text <> "" Then
12            lblOutput.Text = ""
13            lstGrades.Items.Clear()
14         End If
15
16         ' display grade in ListBox
17         lstGrades.Items.Add(Val(txtInput.Text))
18         txtInput.Clear()   ' clear grade from TextBox
19         txtInput.Focus()   ' transfer focus to TextBox
20
21         ' prohibit users from entering more than 10 grades
22         If lstGrades.Items.Count >= 10 Then
23            btnAdd.Enabled = False   ' disable Add Grade Button
24            btnAverage.Focus()          ' transfer focus to Average Button
25         End If
26
27      End Sub ' btnAdd_Click
28
29      ' handles Average Button's Click event
30      Private Sub btnAverage_Click(ByVal sender As System.Object, _
31         ByVal e As System.EventArgs) Handles btnAverage.Click
32
33         ' initialization phase
34         Dim intTotal As Integer = 0
35         Dim intGradeCounter As Integer = 0
36         Dim intGrade As Integer = 0
37         Dim dblAverage As Double = 0
38
```

Disabling the **Add Grade** Button and transferring the focus to the **Average** Button

Figure 10.17   **Class Average** application code. (Part 1 of 2.)

Using a Do...Loop Until statement to calculate the class average

Enabling the **Add Grade** Button and transferring the focus to the **Enter grade:** TextBox

```
39          ' sum grades in ListBox
40       Do
41
42          ' read grade from ListBox
43          intGrade = lstGrades.Items.Item(intGradeCounter)
44          intTotal += intGrade     ' add grade to total
45          intGradeCounter += 1     ' increment counter
46       Loop Until intGradeCounter >= 10
47
48       dblAverage = intTotal / 10    ' calculate average
49       lblOutput.Text = String.Format("{0:F}", dblAverage)
50       btnAdd.Enabled = True         ' enable Add Grade Button
51       txtInput.Focus()  ' reset focus to Enter grade: TextBox
52    End Sub ' btnAverage_Click
53
54 End Class ' FrmClassAverage
```

Figure 10.17   **Class Average** application code. (Part 2 of 2.)

SELF-REVIEW   1. If you do not want a Button to call its event handler method when the Button is clicked, set property _____ to _____.

    a) `Enabled, False`   b) `Enabled, True`

    c) `Disabled, True`   d) `Disabled, False`

2. _____ a TextBox selects that TextBox to receive user input.

    a) Enabling   b) Clearing

    c) Transferring the focus to   d) Disabling

Answers: 1) a. 2) c.

10.5 Wrap-Up

In this tutorial, you learned how to use the Do...Loop While and the Do...Loop Until repetition statements. We provided the syntax and included UML activity diagrams that explained how each statement executes. You used the Do...Loop Until statement in the **Class Average** application that you developed.

The Do...Loop While repetition statement executes as long as its loop-continuation condition is True. This repetition statement always executes at least once. When the loop-continuation condition becomes False, the repetition terminates. This repetition statement enters an infinite loop if the loop-continuation condition never becomes False.

The Do...Loop Until repetition statement also executes at least once. It executes as long as its loop-termination condition is False. When the loop-termination condition becomes True, the repetition terminates. The Do...Loop Until statement enters an infinite loop if the loop-termination condition never becomes True.

You also learned more sophisticated techniques for creating more polished graphical user interfaces for your applications. You now know how to invoke method Focus to transfer the focus in an application, indicating that the next action the user takes should involve this control. You also learned how to disable Buttons that should not be available to a user at certain times during an application's execution and you learned how to enable those Buttons again.

In the next tutorial, you will continue studying repetition statements. You will learn how to use the For...Next repetition statement, which is particularly useful for counter-controlled repetition.

SKILLS SUMMARY

Do...Loop While Repetition Statement

■ Iterates while its loop-continuation condition is True.

■ Tests the loop-continuation condition after the loop body is performed.

■ Always executes the loop at least once.

■ Becomes an infinite loop if the loop-continuation condition can never become False.

Do...Loop Until Repetition Statement

■ Iterates until its loop-termination condition becomes True.

■ Tests the loop-termination condition after the loop body is performed.

■ Always executes the loop at least once.

■ Becomes an infinite loop if the loop-termination condition can never become True.

Disabling a Button

■ Set Button property Enabled to False.

Enabling a Button

■ Set Button property Enabled to True.

Transferring the Focus to a Control

■ Call method Focus.

KEY TERMS

Count property of Items—The property that returns the number of ListBox items.

Do...Loop Until repetition statement—A control statement that executes a set of statements until the loop-termination condition becomes True after the loop executes.

Do...Loop While repetition statement—A control statement that executes a set of statements while the loop-continuation condition is True; the condition is tested after the loop executes.

Enabled property—Specifies whether a control such as a Button appears enabled (True) or disabled (False).

Focus method—The method that transfers the focus of the application to the control, on which the method is called.

Item property of Items—The property that returns the value stored in the ListBox at the specified index.

transferring the focus—Selecting a control in an application.

GUI DESIGN GUIDELINES

Button

■ Disable a Button when its function should not be available to users.

■ Enable a disabled Button when its function once again should be available to user.

CONTROLS, EVENTS, PROPERTIES & METHODS

Button   This control allows the user to raise an action or event.

■ *In action*

> Calculate Total

■ *Events*

Click—This event is raised when the user clicks the Button.

■ *Properties*

Enabled—This property determines whether the Buttons event handler executes when the Button is clicked.

Location—This property specifies the location of the Button on the Form relative to the top-left corner.

Name—This property specifies the name used to access the Button programmatically. The name should be prefixed with btn.

Size—This property specifies the height and width (in pixels) of the Button.

Text—This property specifies the text displayed on the Button.

■ *Methods*

Focus—This method transfers the focus of the application to the Button that calls it.

ListBox   ListBox   This control allows the user to view and select from
items in a list.

■ *In action*

Months	Monthly Payments
24	$490.50
36	$339.06
48	$263.55
60	$218.41

■ *Properties*

Items—This property returns an object that contains the items displayed in the ListBox.

Items.Count—This property returns the number of items in the ListBox.

Items.Item—This property returns the values at the specified index in the ListBox.

Location—This property specifies the location of the ListBox on the Form relative to the
top-left corner.

Name—This property specifies the name used to access the ListBox programatically. The
name should be prefixed with lst.

Size—This property specifies the height and width (in pixels) of the ListBox.

■ *Methods*

Items.Add—This method adds an item to the Items property.

Items.Clear—This method deletes all the values in the ListBox's Items property.

TextBox abl TextBox   This control allows the user to input data from the
keyboard.

■ *In action*

0

■ *Event*

TextChanged—This event is raised when the text in the TextBox is changed.

■ *Properties*

Location—This property specifies the location of the TextBox on the Form relative to the
top-left corner.

Name—This property specifies the name used to access the TextBox programmatically.
The name should be prefixed with txt.

Size—This property specifies the height and width (in pixels) of the TextBox.

Text—This property specifies the text displayed in the TextBox.

TextAlign—This property specifies how the text is aligned within the TextBox.

■ *Methods*

Focus—This method transfers the focus of the application to the TextBox that calls it.

MULTIPLE-CHOICE QUESTIONS

10.1 A(n) _____ occurs when a loop-continuation condition in a Do...Loop While never
becomes False.

a) infinite loop   b) counter-controlled loop

c) control statement   d) nested control statement

10.2 Set property _____ to True to enable a Button.

a) Disabled   b) Focus

c) Enabled   d) ButtonEnabled

10.3 The _____ statement executes at least once and continues executing until its loop-termination condition becomes `True`.

   a) `Do While...Loop`   b) `Do...Loop Until`

   c) `Do...Loop While`   d) `Do Until...Loop`

10.4 The _____ statement executes at least once and continues executing until its loop-continuation condition becomes `False`.

   a) `Do...Loop Until`   b) `Do Until...Loop`

   c) `Do While...Loop`   d) `Do...Loop While`

10.5 Method _____ transfers the focus to a control.

   a) `GetFocus`   b) `Focus`

   c) `Transfer`   d) `Activate`

10.6 A _____ contains the sum of a series of values.

   a) total   b) counter

   c) condition   d) loop

10.7 Property _____ of property _____ contains the number of items in a `List-Box`.

   a) `Count, ListBox`   b) `ListCount, Items`

   c) `ListCount, ListBox`   d) `Count, Items`

10.8 A(n) _____ occurs when a loop executes for one more or one less iteration than is necessary.

   a) infinite loop   b) counter-controlled loop

   c) off-by-one error   d) nested control statement

10.9 A `Do...Loop Until` repetition statement's loop-termination condition is evaluated _____.

   a) only the first time the body executes   b) before the body executes

   c) after the body executes   d) None of the above.

10.10 If its continuation condition is initially `False`, a `Do...Loop While` repetition statement _____ .

   a) never executes   b) executes while the condition is `False`

   c) executes until the condition becomes `True`   d) executes only once

---

EXERCISES

10.11 *(Modified Class Average Application)* Modify the **Class Average** application, as in Fig. 10.18, so that **Average** `Button` is disabled until 10 grades have been entered.

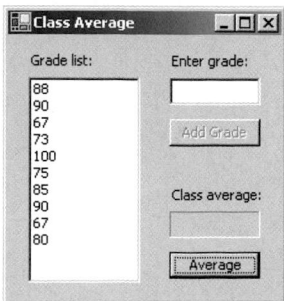

Figure 10.18 Modified **Class Average** application.

   a) ***Copying and opening the template application.*** Copy the `ModifiedClassAverage` folder from `C:\Examples\Tutorial10\Exercises` to `C:\SimplyVB`. Double click the `ClassAverage.sln` file in the `ModifiedClassAverage` folder to open the application in Visual Studio .NET.

b) *Initially disabling the Average Button.* Use the **Properties** window to modify the **Average** Button in the Form so that it is disabled when the application first executes by initially setting its Enabled property to False.

c) *Enabling the Average Button after 10 grades have been entered.* Add code to the btnAdd_Click event handler so that the **Average** Button becomes enabled when 10 grades have been entered.

d) *Disabling the Average Button after the calculation has been performed.* Add code to the btnAverage_Click event handler so that the **Average** Button is disabled once the calculation result has been displayed.

10.12 *(Class Average Application That Handles Any Number of Grades)* Rewrite the **Class Average** application to handle any number of grades, as in Fig. 10.19. Note that, because the application does not know how many grades the user will enter, the Buttons must be enabled at all times.

a) *Copying and opening the template application.* Copy the UndeterminedClassAverage folder from C:\Examples\Tutorial10\Exercises to C:\SimplyVB. Double click the ClassAverage.sln file in the UndeterminedClassAverage folder to open the application in Visual Studio .NET.

b) *Never disabling the Add Grade Button.* Remove code from the btnAdd_Click event handler so that the **Add Grade** Button is not disabled after entering 10 grades.

c) *Summing the grades in the ListBox.* Modify code in the btnAverage_Click event handler so that intGradeCounter is incremented until it is equal to the number of grades entered. Use lstGrades.Items.Count to determine the number of items in the ListBox. The number returned by the Count property will be zero if there are no grades entered. Use an If…Then selection statement to avoid division by zero and display a message dialog to the user if there are no grades entered when the user clicks the **Average** Button.

d) *Calculating the class average.* Modify the code in the btnAverage_Click event handler so that dblAverage is computed by using intGradeCounter rather than the value 10.

Figure 10.19 Modified **Class Average** application handling an unspecified number of grades.

10.13 *(Arithmetic Calculator Application)* Write an application that allows users to enter a series of numbers and manipulate them. The application should provide users with the option of adding or multiplying the numbers. Users should enter each number in a TextBox. After entering each number, users should click a Button and the number should be inserted in a ListBox. The GUI should behave as in Fig. 10.20.

a) *Copying and opening the template application.* Copy the ArithmeticCalculator folder from C:\Examples\Tutorial10\Exercises to C:\SimplyVB. Double click the ArithmeticCalculator.sln file in the ArithmeticCalculator folder to open the application in Visual Studio .NET.

b) *Add a ListBox to display the entered numbers.* Add a ListBox. Place and size it as in Fig. 10.20.

c) *Creating an event handler for the Enter Button.* Create the Click event handler for the **Enter** Button. If the result of a previous calculation is displayed, this event handler should clear the result and disable the addition and multiplication Buttons. It should then insert the current number in the **Operands list:** ListBox. When the

ListBox contains at least two numbers, the event handler should then enable the addition and multiplication Buttons.

d) *Summing the grades in the* ***ListBox.*** Define the Click event handler for the **Add** Button. This event handler should compute the sum of all of the values in the **Operands list:** ListBox and display the result in a Label lblResult.

e) *Define the* ***Click*** *event handler for the Multiply Button.* This event handler should compute the product of all of the values in the **Operands list:** ListBox and display the result in the Label lblResult.

Figure 10.20   **Arithmetic Calculator** application.

What does this code do? ▶   **10.14** What is the result of the following code?

```
1   Dim intY As Integer
2   Dim intX As Integer
3   Dim intMysteryValue As Integer
4
5   intX = 1
6   intMysteryValue = 0
7
8   Do
9       intY = intX ^ 2
10      lstDisplay.Items.Add(intY)
11      intMysteryValue += 1
12      intX += 1
13  Loop While intX <= 10
14
15  lblResult.Text = intMysteryValue
```

What's wrong with this code? ▶   **10.15** Find the error(s) in the following code. This code should add 10 to the value in intY and store it in intZ. It then should reduce the value of intY by one and repeat until intY is less than 10. The output Label lblResult should display the final value of intZ.

```
1   Dim intY As Integer = 10
2   Dim intZ As Integer = 2
3
4   Do
5       intZ = intY + 10
6   Loop Until intY < 10
7
8   intY -= 1
9
10  lblResult.Text = intZ
```

Using the Debugger ▶ **10.16** (*Factorial Application*) The **Factorial** application calculates the factorial of an integer input by the user. The factorial of an integer is the product of the integers from one to that number. For example, the factorial of 3 is 6 ($1 \times 2 \times 3$). While testing the application you noticed that it does not execute correctly. Use the debugger to find and correct the logic error(s) in the application. Figure 10.21 displays the correct output for the **Factorial** application.

Figure 10.21 Correct output for the **Factorial** application.

Programming Challenge ▶ **10.17** (*Restaurant Bill Application*) Develop an application that calculates a restaurant bill. The user should be able to enter the item ordered, the quantity of the item ordered and the price per item. When the user clicks the **Add Item** Button, your application should display the number ordered, the item ordered and the price per unit in three ListBoxes as shown in Fig. 10.22. When the user clicks the **Total Bill** Button, the application should calculate the total cost. For each entry in the ListBox, multiply the cost of each item by the number of items ordered.

Figure 10.22 Restaurant Bill application's Form.

Objectives

In this tutorial, you will learn to:
- Execute statements repeatedly with the **For...Next** repetition statement.
- Obtain user input with the **NumericUpDown** control.
- Display information, using a multiline **TextBox**.

Outline

Interest Calculator Application

Introducing the For...Next Repetition Statement

A s you learned in Tutorials 9 and 10, applications are often required to repeat actions. Using a **Do** repetition statement allowed you to specify a condition and test that condition either before entering the loop or after execution of the body of the loop. In the **Car Payment Calculator** application and the **Class Average** application, a counter was used to determine the number of times the loop should iterate. In fact, the use of counters in repetition statement is so common in applications that Visual Basic .NET provides an additional control statement specially designed for such cases: the **For...Next** repetition statement. In this tutorial, you will use the **For...Next** repetition statement to create an **Interest Calculator** application.

11.1 Test-Driving the Interest Calculator Application

The **Interest Calculator** application calculates the amount of money in your savings account after you begin with a certain amount of money and are paid a certain interest rate for a certain amount of time. Users specify the principal amount (the initial amount of money in the account), the interest rate and the number of years for which interest will be calculated. The application then displays the results. This application must meet the following requirements:

Application Requirements

You are considering investing $1000.00 in a savings account that yields 5% interest and you want to forecast how your investment will grow. Assuming that you will leave all interest on deposit, calculate and print the amount of money in the account at the end of each year over a period of n years. To compute these amounts, use the following formula:

$$a = p (1 + r)^n$$

where

p is the original amount of money invested (the principal)
r is the annual interest rate (for example, .05 is equivalent to 5%)
n is the number of years
a is the amount on deposit at the end of the nth year.

You begin by test-driving the completed application.

Test-Driving the Completed Interest **Calculator Application**

1. *Copying the template to your work folder.* Copy the C:\Examples\Tutorial11\CompletedApplication\InterestCalculator folder to C:\SimplyVB.

2. *Opening the completed application.* Double click InterestCalculator.sln in the InterestCalculator folder to open the application in Visual Studio .NET.

3. *Running the Interest Calculator application.* Select **Debug > Start** to run the application. The Form in Fig. 11.1 is displayed.

NumericUpDown control

Click to increase number of years

Click to decrease number of years

Figure 11.1 Completed **Interest Calculator** application.

4. *Providing a principal value.* Once the application is running, provide a value in the **Principal:** TextBox. Input 1000, as specified in the problem statement.

5. *Providing an interest-rate value.* Next, type a value in the **Interest Rate:** TextBox. We specified the interest rate 5% in the problem statement, so enter 5 in the **Interest Rate:** TextBox.

6. *Providing the duration of the investment.* Now you should choose the number of years for which you want to calculate the amount in the savings account. In this case, select 10 by clicking the up arrow in the **Years:** NumericUpDown control repeatedly until the value reads 10.

7. *Calculating the amount.* After you input the necessary information, click the **Calculate** Button. The amount of money in your account at the end of each year during a period of 10 years displays in the multiline TextBox. The application should look similar to Fig. 11.2.

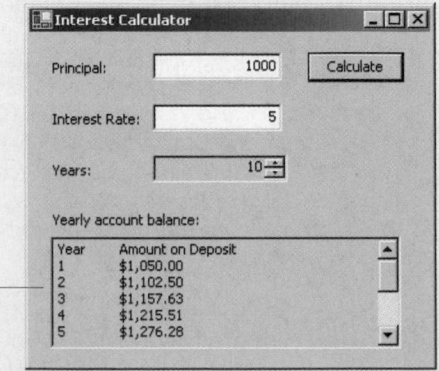

Multiline **TextBox** displays application results

Figure 11.2 Output of completed **Interest Calculator** application.

(cont.)   8. ***Terminating the application.*** Click the running application's close box.

9. ***Closing the solution.*** Select **File > Close Solution**.

11.2 Essentials of Counter-Controlled Repetition

In Tutorial 10, you were introduced to counter-controlled repetition. The four essential elements of counter-controlled repetition are:

1. the *name* of a *control variable* (or loop counter) that is used to determine whether the loop continues to iterate

2. the *initial value* of the control variable

3. the *increment* (or *decrement*) by which the control variable is modified during each iteration of the loop (that is, each time the loop is performed)

4. the condition that tests for the *final value* of the control variable (to determine whether looping should continue).

The example of Fig. 11.3 uses the four elements of counter-controlled repetition. This Do While...Loop is similar to the **Car Payment Calculator** application's loop in Tutorial 9.

```
1     Dim intCounter As Integer = 1 ' repetition counter
2
3     Do While intCounter <= 5
4        intMonths = 12 * (intCounter + 1) ' calculate payment period
5
6        ' calculate payment value
7        decValue = Convert.ToDecimal( _
8           Pmt(dblMonthlyInterest, intMonths, -intLoanAmount))
9
10       ' display payment value
11       lstPayments.Items.Add(intMonths & ControlChars.Tab & _
12          ControlChars.Tab & String.Format("{0:C}", decValue))
13
14       intCounter += 1 ' increment counter
15    Loop
```

Figure 11.3   Counter-controlled repetition example.

Recall that the **Car Payment Calculator** application calculates and displays monthly car payments over periods of 2–5 years. The declaration in line 1 *names* the control variable (intCounter), indicating that it is of data type Integer. This declaration includes an initialization, which sets the variable to an *initial value* of 1.

Consider the Do While...Loop statement (lines 3–15). Line 4 uses the intCounter variable to calculate the number of months over which car payments are to be made. Lines 7–8 use the Pmt function to determine the monthly payment for the car. This value depends on the car's price, the interest rate, the duration of the loan in months and the down-payment amount. Lines 11–12 display the amount in a ListBox. Line 14 increments the control variable intCounter by 1 for each iteration of the loop. The condition in the Do While...Loop statement (line 3) tests for whether the value of the control variable is less than or equal to 5, meaning that 5 is the *final value* for which the condition is true. The body of this Do While...Loop is performed even when the control variable is 5. The loop terminates when the control variable exceeds 5 (that is, when intCounter has a value of 6).

1. The control variable's _____ is not one of the four essential elements of counter-controlled repetition.

    a) name

    b) initial value

    c) type

    d) final value

2. What aspect of the control variable determines whether looping should continue?

    a) name

    b) initial value

    c) type

    d) final value

Answers: 1) c. 2) d.

11.3 Introducing the For...Next Repetition Statement

The **For...Next** repetition statement makes it easier for you to write code to perform counter-controlled repetition. This statement specifies all four elements essential to counter-controlled repetition. The For...Next statement takes less time to code and is easier to read than an equivalent Do repetition statement.

Let's examine the first line of the For...Next repetition statement (Fig. 11.4), which we call the For...Next header. The For...Next header specifies all four essential elements for counter-controlled repetition. The line should be read "*for each value of intCounter starting at 2 and ending at 10, do the following statements and then add (step) two to intCounter.*"

Figure 11.4 For...Next header components.

Each For...Next statement begins with the keyword **For**. Then the statement names and initializes a control variable (in this case, intCounter is set to 2). [*Note:* You must declare (using the Dim keyword) the counter variable before the For statement.] Following the initial value of the control variable is the keyword **To**, followed by the final value of the control variable to be used in the loop. You can then use the **Step** keyword to specify the amount by which to increase (or decrease) the control variable each time the loop body completes execution. If you wish to decrease the value of the control variable each time through the loop, simply use a negative number after the **Step** keyword. The box, *Executing the For...Next Repetition Statement*, describes each step as the above repetition statement executes.

Executing the For...Next Repetition Statement

1. The application sets variable intCounter's value to 2.

2. The application enters the For...Next repetition statement.

3. The value of intCounter is increased by 2; intCounter now contains the number 4.

4. The implied loop-continuation condition is checked. The implied condition evaluates to True (intCounter is less than 10), so the application resumes execution at the first statement after the For statement.

5. The value of intCounter is increased by 2; intCounter now contains the number 6.

(cont.)

6. The implied loop-continuation condition is checked. The implied condition evaluates to `True` (`intCounter` is less than 10), so the application enters the `For...Next` repetition statement.

7. The value of `intCounter` is increased by 2; `intCounter` now contains the number 8.

8. The implied loop-continuation condition is checked. The implied condition evaluates to `True` (`intCounter` is less than 10), so the application resumes execution at the first statement after the `For` statement.

9. The value of `intCounter` is increased by 2; `intCounter` now contains the number 10.

10. The implied loop-continuation condition is checked. The condition evaluates to `False` (`intCounter` is not less than 10), so the application exits the `For...Next` repetition statement.

Good Programming Practice

Place a blank line before and after each control statement to make it stand out in the code.

Using the keyword `Step` is optional. If you omit the `Step` keyword, the control variable is incremented by one after each repetition, by default.

In many cases, the `For...Next` statement can be represented by another repetition statement. For example, an equivalent `Do While...Loop` statement for Fig. 11.4 would be of the form

```
intCounter = 2

Do While intCounter <= 10
    body statement(s)
    intCounter += 2
Loop
```

Notice that the `For...Next` statement's header (Fig. 11.4) implies the loop-continuation condition (`intCounter <= 10`), which is shown explicitly in the preceding `Do While...Loop` statement. The starting value, ending value and increment portions of a `For...Next` statement can contain arithmetic expressions. The expressions are evaluated once (when the `For...Next` statement begins executing) and then used as the starting value, ending value and increment of the `For...Next` header. For example, assume that `intA = 2` and `intB = 10`. The header

```
For intI = intA To (4 * intA * intB) Step (intB \ intA)
```

is equivalent to the header

```
For intI = 2 To 80 Step 5
```

If the implied loop-continuation condition is initially `False` (for example, if the starting value is greater than the ending value and the increment value is positive), the `For...Next`'s body is not performed. Instead, execution proceeds with the statement after the `For...Next` statement.

The control variable frequently is displayed or used in calculations in the `For...Next` body, but it does not have to be. It is common to use the control variable only to control repetition and not use it in the `For...Next` body.

Error-Prevention Tip

Although the value of the control variable can be changed in the body of a `For...Next` loop, avoid doing so, because this practice can lead to subtle errors.

The UML activity diagram for the `For...Next` statement is similar to that of the `Do While...Loop` statement. For example, the UML activity diagram of the `For...Next` statement

```
For intCounter = 1 To 10
    lstDisplay.Items.Add(intCounter * 10)
Next
```

is shown in Fig. 11.5. This activity diagram shows that the initialization occurs only once and that incrementing occurs *after* each execution of the body statement. Note that, besides small circles and flowlines, the activity diagram contains only rounded rectangle symbols and small diamond symbols. The rounded rectangle symbols are filled with the actions, and the flowlines coming out of the small diamond symbols are labeled with the appropriate guard conditions for this algorithm.

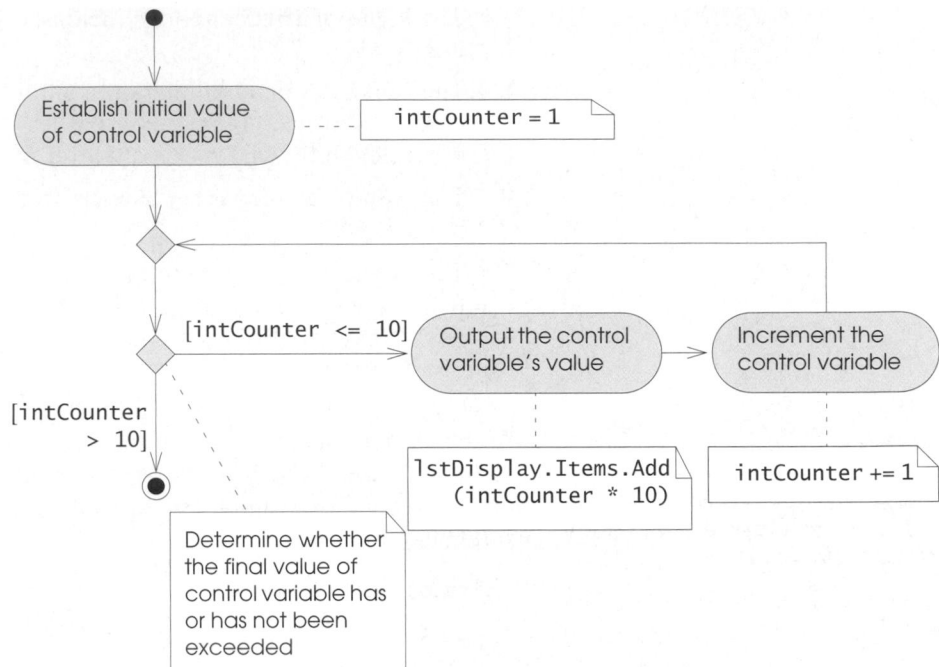

Figure 11.5 For...Next repetition statement UML activity diagram.

Notice that the For...Next header indicates each item needed to conduct counter-controlled repetition with a control variable. To help solidify your understanding of this new repetition statement, you will now learn how the Do While...Loop statement of Fig. 11.3 can be replaced by a For...Next statement.

The converted code is shown in Fig. 11.6. When the For...Next statement begins execution, line 3 of Fig. 11.6 initializes control variable intCounter to 1.

The implied loop-continuation condition intCounter <= 5 (which depends on the counter's final value) is tested in line 3. Keyword To is required in the For...Next statement. The value before this keyword specifies the initial value of intCounter; the value that follows it specifies the value tested for loop continuation (in this case, 5). Keyword Step is optional and is not used here. Step specifies the increment (the amount that is added to intCounter each time the For...Next body is executed.) If Step is not included, then the increment is 1, by default.

The initial value of intCounter is 1, so the implied loop-continuation condition is satisfied and the payment calculations within the For...Next body are executed.

After executing the For...Next body, the Next keyword is reached (line 13). This keyword marks the end of the For...Next repetition statement. When Next is reached, intCounter is incremented by 1 (the default increment amount), and the loop begins again with the implied loop-continuation condition test.

Steps 1–4 repeat until the implied loop-continuation condition becomes False as intCounter becomes greater than 5, then repetition terminates.

```
1   Dim intCounter As Integer
2
3   For intCounter = 1 To 5
4       intMonths = 12 * (intCounter + 1) ' calculate payment period
5
```

Figure 11.6 Code segment for the **Car Payment Calculator** application that demonstrates the For...Next statement. (Part 1 of 2.)

```
6      ' calculate payment value
7      decValue = Convert.ToDecimal( _
8         Pmt(dblMonthlyRate, intMonths, -intLoanAmount))
9
10     ' display payment value
11     lstPayments.Items.Add(intMonths & ControlChars.Tab & _
12        ControlChars.Tab & String.Format("{0:C}", decValue))
13  Next
```

Figure 11.6 Code segment for the **Car Payment Calculator** application that demonstrates the **For...Next** statement. (Part 2 of 2.)

SELF-REVIEW   1. If the Step clause is omitted, the increment of a For...Next statement defaults to _____.

    a) 2   b) 1

    c) 0   d) –1

2. The value before the To keyword in a For...Next statement specifies the _____.

    a) initial value of the counter variable   b) final value of the counter variable

    c) increment   d) number of times the statement iterates

Answers: 1) b. 2) a.

11.4 Examples Using the For...Next Statement

The following examples demonstrate different ways of varying the control variable in a For...Next statement. In each case, we write the appropriate For...Next header:

a) Vary the control variable from 1 to 100 in increments of 1.

```
For intI = 1 To 100
or
For intI = 1 To 100 Step 1
```

b) Vary the control variable from 100 to 1 in increments of -1 (decrements of 1).

```
For intI = 100 To 1 Step -1
```

c) Vary the control variable from 7 to 77 in increments of 7.

```
For intI = 7 To 77 Step 7
```

d) Vary the control variable from 20 to 2 in increments of -2 (decrements of 2).

```
For intI = 20 To 2 Step -2
```

e) Vary the control variable over the sequence of the following values: 2, 5, 8, 11, 14, 17, 20.

```
For intI = 2 To 20 Step 3
```

f) Vary the control variable over the sequence of the following values: 99, 88, 77, 66, 55, 44, 33, 22, 11, 0.

```
For intI = 99 To 0 Step -11
```

SELF-REVIEW   1. Which of the following is the appropriate For...Next header for varying the control variable over the following sequence of values: 25, 20, 15, 10, 5?

    a) For intI = 5 To 25 Step 5   b) For intI = 25 To 5 Step -5

    c) For intI = 5 To 25 Step -5   d) For intI = 25 To 5 Step 5

2. Which of the following statements describes the For…Next header?

    `For intI = 81 To 102?`

    a) Vary the control variable from 81 to 102 in increments of 1.
    b) Vary the control variable from 81 to 102 in increments of 0.
    c) Vary the control variable from 102 to 81 in increments of -1.
    d) Vary the control variable from 81 to 102 in increments of 2.

Answers: 1) b. 2) a.

11.5 Constructing the Interest Calculator Application

Our solution to this tutorial's problem statement computes interest over a given number of years, by using the For…Next statement. This repetition statement will perform the calculation for every year that the money remains on deposit.

The following pseudocode describes the operation of the **Interest Calculator** application when the **Calculate** Button is clicked:

> *Get the values for the principal, interest rate and years entered by the user*
> *Add a header to the TextBox to label the output*
>
> *For each year, starting at 1 and ending with the number of years entered,*
>   *Calculate and display the year*
>   *Calculate and display the current value of the investment*

The template application we provide for this tutorial contains the **Calculate** Button, plus two Labels and their corresponding TextBoxes: for **Principal:** and for **Interest Rate:**. The Form has a **Years:** Label, but you will insert the NumericUp-Down control for this input. The **NumericUpDown** control limits a user's choices for the number of years to a specific range. You will then create a multiline TextBox with a scrollbar and add it to the application's GUI. Finally, you will add functionality with a For…Next statement. The ACE table of Fig. 11.7 lists the actions, controls, objects and events for this application.

Action/Control/Event (ACE) Table for the Interest Calculator Application

Action	Control/Object	Event
Label the application's fields	`lblPrincipal, lblRate, lblYears, lblYearlyAccount`	
Get the values for the principal, interest rate and years entered by user	`txtPrincipal txtRate updYear`	
Control number of years input by user	`updYear`	
Calculate and display account balance	`btnCalculate`	`Click`
Display result of calculation	`txtResult`	

Figure 11.7   ACE table for **Interest Calculator** application.

To begin building the **Interest Calculator** application, follow the steps in the box, *Viewing the Template Application*.

Viewing the Template Application

1. ***Copying the template to your work folder.*** Copy the `C:\Examples\Tutorial11\TemplateApplication\InterestCalculator` folder to your `C:\SimplyVB` directory.

2. ***Opening the template application.*** Double click `InterestCalculator.sln` in the `InterestCalculator` folder to open the application in Visual Studio .NET (Fig. 11.8).

(cont.)

Figure 11.8   Template **Interest Calculator** application **Form** in design view.

First, you will add a **NumericUpDown** control to allow the user to specify the number of years. The NumericUpDown control limits the user to choosing from a range of numbers. This control provides up and down arrows that allow the user to scroll through the control's range of values. The box, *Adding and Customizing a NumericUpDown Control*, shows you how to set the limits of the range (maximum and minimum values). We will use 10 as the maximum value and 1 as the minimum value for this control. The **Increment** property specifies by how much the current number in the NumericUpDown control changes when the user clicks the control's up (for incrementing) or down (for decrementing) arrow. This application uses the Increment property's default value, 1.

Adding and Customizing a *NumericUpDown* Control

1. ***Adding a NumericUpDown control.*** Double click the NumericUpDown control,

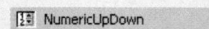

in the **Toolbox** to add it to the Form (Fig. 11.9). Change the control's Name property to updYear. To improve code readability, you should prefix NumericUpDown control names with upd which is short for up-down.

GUI Design Tip

A NumericUpDown control should follow the same GUI Design Guidelines as a TextBox. (See Appendix C.)

Figure 11.9   NumericUpDown control added to **Interest Calculator** application.

2. ***Setting the NumericUpDown control's location and size.*** Set updYear's Location property to 96, 96 and its Size property to 104, 21, so that it aligns horizontally and vertically with the TextBoxes above it.

Good Programming Practice

Prefix NumericUpDown control names with upd.

3. ***Setting property TextAlign.*** Set property TextAlign to Right. The number now appears right-aligned in the control.

(cont.)

4. **Setting property ReadOnly.** To ensure that the user cannot enter invalid values in the **Years:** NumericUpDown control, set the ReadOnly property to True. The ReadOnly property changes the background color of the control to gray, indicating that the user can change its value only by using the up and down arrows.

5. **Setting range limits for the NumericUpDown control.** By default, this control sets 0 as the minimum and 100 as the maximum. You will change these values. Set the **Maximum** property of the **Years:** NumericUpDown control to 10. Then set its **Minimum** property to 1. This (combined with setting its ReadOnly property to True) limits users to selecting values between 1 and 10 for the number of years. Notice that the NumericUpDown control displays 1, the value of its Minimum property. Your Form should now look like Fig. 11.9.

6. **Saving the project.** Select **File > Save All** to save the solution's files.

GUI Design Tip

Use a NumericUpDown control to limit the range of user input.

The **Interest Calculator** application displays the results of its calculations in a multiline TextBox, which is simply a TextBox that can display more than one line of text. You can configure the TextBox to have a scrollbar, so that, if the TextBox is too small to display its contents, the user can scroll up and down to view the entire contents of the box. You will create this TextBox in the box, *Adding and Customizing a Multiline TextBox with a Scrollbar*.

Adding and Customizing a Multiline *TextBox* with a Scrollbar

1. **Adding a TextBox to the Form.** Double click the TextBox control in the **Toolbox** to add a TextBox to the Form. Name the TextBox txtResult.

2. **Creating a multiline TextBox.** Select the TextBox's **Multiline** property, and change its value from False to True. Doing so allows the TextBox to contain multiple lines.

3. **Setting the size and location of the TextBox.** Set the TextBox's Location property to 16, 160 and the Size property to 272, 88, so that it aligns horizontally with the controls above it.

4. **Setting text appearance in the TextBox.** Initially, txtResult should not display any text. Clear the Text property. Then set property TextAlign to Left. This left-aligns text in the TextBox.

5. **Setting property ReadOnly.** To ensure that the user cannot change the output in the **Yearly account balance:** TextBox, set the ReadOnly property to True.

6. **Inserting a vertical scrollbar.** Using scrollbars allows you to keep the size of a TextBox small while still allowing the user to view all the information in that TextBox. Because the length of the text could exceed the height of the TextBox, enable the vertical scrollbar by setting txtResult's **ScrollBars** property to **Vertical**. A vertical scrollbar appears on the right side of the TextBox. By default, property ScrollBars is set to None. Note that the scrollbar is disabled on your Form. A scrollbar is enabled only when it is needed (that is, when there is enough text in the TextBox). Your Form should look like Fig. 11.10.

GUI Design Tip

If a TextBox will display multiple lines of output, set the Multiline property to True and left-align the output by setting the TextAlign property to Left.

GUI Design Tip

If a multiline TextBox will display many lines of output, limit the TextBox height and use a vertical scrollbar to allow users to view additional lines of output.

(cont.)

Figure 11.10 Multiline `TextBox` with vertical scrollbar added to the `Form`.

7. ***Saving the project.*** Select **File > Save All** to save the solution's files.

Now that you have finished designing the GUI, you will add functionality to your application. When the user clicks the **Calculate** `Button`, you want the application to retrieve the input and then output a table containing the amount on deposit at the end of each year. You will do this by adding code to the `Button`'s `Click` event handler.

Adding a *Click* Event Handler

1. ***Creating the event handler.*** Double click the **Calculate** `Button`. The **Calculate** `Button` `Click` event handler appears in the application's code.

2. ***Adding code to event handler btnCalculate_Click.*** Add lines 155–166 of Fig. 11.11 to the `btnCalculate_Click` event handler. Lines 155–161 declare the variables needed to store user inputs, calculation results and the output. Variable `decPrincipal` stores the amount of the principal as entered by the user, `dblRate` stores the interest rate and `intYear` stores the number of years the user selected in the `NumericUpDown` control. Variable `decAmount` stores the result of the interest calculation.

   Line 161 declares a `String` variable `strOutput`. **String** variables store a series of characters. The most commonly used characters are letters and numbers, though characters also include many special characters such as $, *, ^, tabs and newlines. A list of characters you are likely to use is found in Appendix B. You actually have been using `Strings` all along—`Labels` and `TextBoxes` both store values in the `Text` property as values of type `String`. In fact, when you assign a numeric data type, such as an `Integer`, to the `Text` property of a `Label`, the `Integer` value is implicitly converted to a `String`.

   Lines 164–165 retrieve the principal and the interest rate from `TextBoxes`. Line 166 uses the `NumericUpDown` control's `Text` property to obtain the user's selection.

   The multiline `TextBox` displays the results in two columns. Lines 169–170 of Fig. 11.12 assign the header to `strOutput`. The header labels the two columns, as `Year` and `Amount on Deposit`, respectively.

   Recall that you cleared values in a `Label` in Tutorial 6 by setting the `Text` property to the empty string (`""`), which represents a `String` value with no characters. When assigning new text to a `String` variable, you must begin and end the text with a double quotation mark (`"`). For example, if you want to store the word `Year` in the `String` variable `strYear`, you would use the following statement:

   ```
   strYear = "Year"
   ```

Good Programming Practice

We suggest prefixing `String` variable names with `str`.

(cont.)

Input variable declarations

Counter variable declaration

Retrieve user input

Figure 11.11 Application code for retrieving and storing user input.

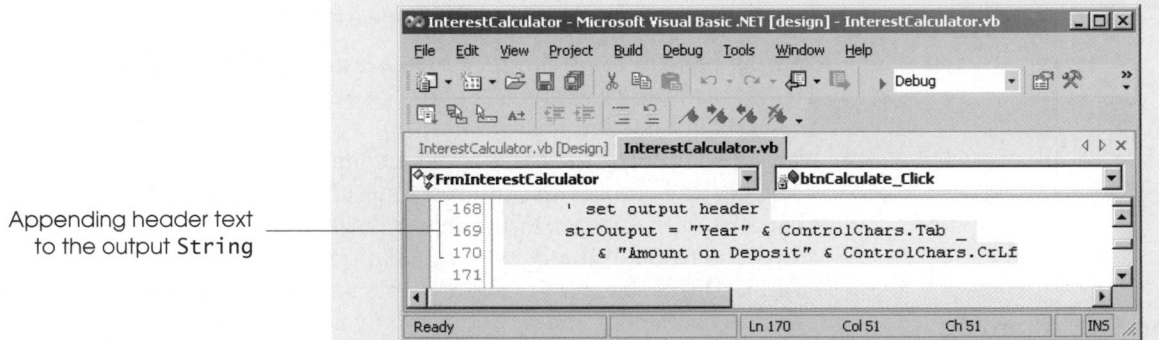

Appending header text to the output `String`

Figure 11.12 Application code for displaying a header in multiline `TextBox`.

You can append a `String` or a character to the end of another `String` by using the concatenation operator (`&`). In lines 169–170 of Fig. 11.12, we use the `ControlChars.Tab` constant to insert a tab character between the word `Year` and the text `Amount on Deposit`. We then insert a newline character (`ControlChars.CrLf`), so that the next series of text will appear on the next line of output.

3. *Saving the project.* Select **File > Save All** to save the solution's files.

The `For...Next` statement in lines 173–180 of Fig. 11.13 performs the interest calculations for the specified number of years. You create the `For...Next` statement in the box, *Calculating Cumulative Interest with a For...Next Statement.*

Calculating Cumulative Interest with a For...Next Statement	1. ***Initializing the control variable and establishing the loop-continuation test.*** Add lines 172–173 of Fig. 11.13 to the `btnCalculate_Click` event handler. Notice that the keyword `Next` appears.

(cont.)

Line 173 is the `For...Next` header which initializes control variable `intYearCounter` to 1. The value after the keyword To sets the implied loop-continuation condition. This loop continues until the control variable is less than or equal to the number of years specified by the user.

Figure 11.13 Application code for `For...Next` statement.

Using the `For...Next` statement to format and append text to the output `String`

2. ***Performing the interest calculation.*** The `For...Next` statement executes its body once for each year up to the value of `intYear`, varying control variable `intYearCounter` from 1 to `intYear` in increments of 1. Add lines 174–175 of Fig. 11.13 to perform the calculation from the formula

$$a = p \, (1 + r)^{\,n}$$

where *a* is `decAmount`, *p* is `decPrincipal`, *r* is `dblRate` and *n* is `intYearCounter`.

Notice that the calculation in line 175 also divides the rate, `dblRate`, by 100. This implies that the user must enter an interest rate value in percentage format (for example, the user should enter the number 5.5 to represent 5.5%).

3. ***Appending the calculation to the output string.*** Add lines 177–178 of Fig. 11.13. These lines append additional text to the end of `strOutput`, using the `&=` operator. The `&=` operator (which behaves much like the `+=` operator) appends the right operand to the text in the left operand. That new value is then assigned to the variable in the left operand. The text includes the current `intYearCounter` value, a tab character (`ControlChars.Tab`) to position to the second column, the result of the call `String.Format("{0:C}", decAmount)` and, finally, a newline character (`ControlChars.CrLf`) to start the next output on the next line. Recall that the `C` (for "currency") formatting code indicates that its corresponding argument (`decAmount`) should be displayed in monetary format.

4. ***Reaching the Next keyword.*** After the body of the loop is performed, program execution reaches keyword `Next` which is now on line 180. The counter (`intYearCounter`) is incremented by 1, and the loop begins again with the implied loop-continuation test.

5. ***Terminating the For...Next statement.*** The `For...Next` statement executes until the control variable exceeds the number of years specified by the user.

6. ***Displaying the result of the calculations.*** After exiting the `For...Next` statement, `strOutput` is ready to be displayed to the user in the `txtResult` TextBox. Add line 182 of Fig. 11.14 to display the header and the results in the multiline TextBox.

(cont.)

Figure 11.14 Application code for displaying calculation results.

7. ***Saving the project.*** Select **File > Save All** to save the solution's files.

Figure 11.15 presents the completed code for your **Interest Calculator** application.

```
1    Public Class FrmInterestCalculator
2       Inherits System.Windows.Forms.Form
3
4       ' Visual Studio .NET generated code
5
6       ' handles Calculate button's Click event
7       Private Sub btnCalculate_Click(ByVal sender As System.Object, _
8          ByVal e As System.EventArgs) Handles btnCalculate.Click
9
10         ' declare variables to store user input
11         Dim decPrincipal As Decimal
12         Dim dblRate As Double
13         Dim intYear As Integer
14         Dim intYearCounter As Integer
15         Dim decAmount As Decimal ' store each calculation
16         Dim strOutput As String ' store output
17
18         ' retrieve user input
19         decPrincipal = Val(txtPrincipal.Text)
20         dblRate = Val(txtRate.Text)
21         intYear = updYear.Text
22
23         ' set output header
24         strOutput = "Year" & ControlChars.Tab _
25            & "Amount on Deposit" & ControlChars.CrLf
26
27         ' calculate amount after each year and append to string
28         For intYearCounter = 1 To intYear
29            decAmount = _
30               decPrincipal * ((1 + dblRate / 100) ^ intYearCounter)
31
32            strOutput &= (intYearCounter & ControlChars.Tab & _
33               String.Format("{0:C}", decAmount) & ControlChars.CrLf)
34
35         Next
36
```

Displaying in the multiline
TextBox the result of the
calculations performed in the
For…Next statement

Using a **For…Next** statement
to calculate amount on
deposit

Figure 11.15 **Interest Calculator** application. (Part 1 of 2.)

```
37            txtResult.Text = strOutput ' display result
38        End Sub ' btnCalculate_Click
39
40    End Class ' FrmInterestCalculator
```

Figure 11.15 **Interest Calculator** application. (Part 2 of 2.)

SELF-REVIEW

1. The _____ property determines by how much the current number in a `NumericUp-Down` control changes when the user clicks the up arrow or the down arrow.

   a) `Amount`   b) `Step`

   c) `Increment`   d) `Next`

2. Which `For...Next` header alters the control variable from 1 to 50 in increments of 5?

   a) `For intI = 1 To 50 Step 50`   b) `For 1 To 50 Step 5`

   c) `For intI = 1 To 50 Step = 5`   d) `For intI = 1 To 50 Step 5`

Answers: 1) c. 2) d.

11.6 Wrap-Up

In this tutorial, you learned that the essential elements of counter-controlled repetition are the name of a control variable, the initial value of the control variable, the increment (or decrement) by which the control variable is modified each time through the loop and the condition that tests the final value of the control variable. We then explored the `For...Next` repetition statement, which combines these essentials of counter-controlled repetition in its header.

After becoming familiar with the `For...Next` repetition statement, you changed the **Car Payment Calculator** application's `Do While...Loop` statement into a `For...Next` statement. You then built an **Interest Calculator**, after analyzing the pseudocode and ACE table for this application. In the **Interest Calculator**'s GUI, you added new design elements, including a `NumericUpDown` control and a multi-line `TextBox` that contained a scrollbar.

In the next tutorial, you will learn to use the `Select Case` multiple-selection statement. You have learned that the `If...Then...Else` selection statement can be used in code to select between multiple courses of action on the value of a condition. You will see that a `Select Case` multiple selection statement can save development time and improve code readability if the number of conditions is large. You will then use a `Select Case` multiple selection statement to build a **Security Keypad** application.

SKILLS SUMMARY

Using the For...Next Repetition Statement

- Specify the initial value of the control variable before keyword `To`.
- Specify the value tested for loop continuation after keyword `To`.
- Use optional keyword `Step` to specify the increment (or decrement).
- Use keyword `Next` to mark the end of the repetition statement.
- Using the `For...Next` statement helps eliminate off-by-one errors.

Creating a Multiline TextBox With a Vertical Scrollbar

- Insert a `TextBox` onto the `Form`.
- Set `TextBox` property `Multiline` to `True`.
- Set `TextBox` property `ScrollBar` to `Vertical`.

Specifying a NumericUpDown Control's Maximum Value

- Use `NumericUpDown` property `Maximum`.

Specifying a NumericUpDown Control's Minimum Value
- Use NumericUpDown property Minimum.

Changing the Current Number in a NumericUpDown Control
- Click the NumericUpDown control's up or down arrow.

Specifying By How Much The Current Number in a NumericUpDown Control Changes When the User Clicks an Arrow
- Use NumericUpDown property Increment.

KEY TERMS	
	For...Next statement—Repetition statement that handles the details of counter-controlled repetition. The For...Next statement uses all four elements essential to counter-controlled repetition in one line of code (the name of a control variable, the initial value, the increment or decrement value and the final value).

For...Next statement—Repetition statement that handles the details of counter-controlled repetition. The For...Next statement uses all four elements essential to counter-controlled repetition in one line of code (the name of a control variable, the initial value, the increment or decrement value and the final value).

Multiline TextBox control—Control that provides the ability to enter or display multiple lines of text. If the text exceeds the size of the TextBox, the control can be set to display a scrollbar.

Multiline property—Specifies whether the TextBox is capable of displaying multiple lines of text. If the property value is True, the TextBox may contain multiple lines of text; if the value of the property is False, the TextBox can contain only one line of text.

NumericUpDown control—Control that allows you to specify maximum and minimum numeric input values. Also allows you to specify an increment (or decrement) when the user clicks the up (or down) arrow.

ScrollBars property—Specifies whether a TextBox has a scrollbar and, if so, of what type. By default, property ScrollBars is set to None. Setting the value to Vertical places a scrollbar along the right side of the TextBox.

Step keyword—Optional component of the For...Next header that specifies the increment (that is, the amount added to the control variable each time the loop is executed).

GUI DESIGN GUIDELINES

TextBox
- If a TextBox will display multiple lines of output, set the Multiline property to True and left-align the output by setting the TextAlign property to Left.
- If a multiline TextBox will display many lines of output, limit the TextBox height and use a vertical scrollbar to allow users to view additional lines of output.

NumericUpDown
- A NumericUpDown control should follow the same GUI Design Guidelines as a single-line TextBox.

CONTROLS, EVENTS, PROPERTIES & METHODS

NumericUpDown   NumericUpDown   This control allows you to specify maximum and minimum numeric input values.

- *In action*

        [6 ⬍]

- *Properties*

    Location—This property specifies the location of the NumericUpDown control on the Form relative to the top-left corner.

    Maximum—This property determines the maximum input value in a particular NumericUpDown control.

    Minimum—This property determines the minimum input value in a particular NumericUpDown control.

    Name—This property specifies the name used to access the NumericUpDown control programmatically. The name should be prefixed with upd.

    ReadOnly—This property determines whether the input value can be typed by the user.

    Size—This property specifies the height and width (in pixels) of the NumericUpDown control.

TextAlign—This property specifies how the text is aligned within the NumericUpDown control.

TextBox   abl TextBox   This control allows the user to input data from the keyboard.

■ *In action*

| 0 |

■ *Events*

TextChanged—This event is raised when the text in the TextBox is changed.

■ *Properties*

Location—This property specifies the location of the TextBox on the Form relative to the top-left corner.

Multiline—This property specifies whether the TextBox is capable of displaying multiple lines of text.

Name—This property specifies the name used to access the TextBox programmatically. The name should be prefixed with txt.

ReadOnly—This property determines whether the value of a TextBox can be changed.

ScrollBars—This property specifies whether the TextBox contains a scrollbar.

Size—This property specifies the height and width (in pixels) of the TextBox.

Text—This property specifies the text displayed in the TextBox.

TextAlign—This property specifies how the text is aligned within the TextBox.

■ *Methods*

Focus—This method transfers the focus of the application to the TextBox that calls it.

MULTIPLE-CHOICE QUESTIONS

11.1 "Hello" has data type _____.

a) String
b) StringLiteral
c) Character
d) StringText

11.2 A _____ provides the ability to enter or display multiple lines of text in the same control.

a) TextBox
b) NumericUpDown
c) MultilineTextBox
d) multiline NumericUpDown

11.3 The NumericUpDown control allows you to specify _____.

a) a maximum value the user can select
b) a minimum value the user can select
c) an increment for the values presented to the user
d) All of the above.

11.4 _____ is optional in a For...Next header when the control variable's increment is 1.

a) Keyword To
b) The initial value of the control variable
c) Keyword Step
d) The final value of the control variable

11.5 Setting TextBox property ScrollBars to _____ creates a vertical scrollbar.

a) True
b) Vertical
c) Up
d) Both

11.6 _____ is used to determine whether a For...Next loop continues to iterate.

a) The initial value of the control variable
b) Keyword For
c) Keyword Step
d) The control variable

11.7 In a For...Next loop, the control variable is incremented (or decremented) _____.

a) after the body of the loop executes
b) when keyword To is reached
c) while the loop-continuation condition is False
d) while the body of the loop executes

11.8 Setting a NumericUpDown control's _____ property to True ensures that the user cannot enter invalid values in the control.

 a) Increment

 c) ReadOnly

 b) ScrollBars

 d) InValid

11.9 The _____ and _____ properties limit the values users can select in the NumericUpDown control.

 a) Maximum, Minimum

 c) High, Low

 b) Top, Bottom

 d) Max, Min

11.10 For...Next header _____ can be used to vary the control variable over the odd numbers between 1 and 10.

 a) For intI = 1 To 10 Step 1

 c) For intI = 1 To 10 Step -1

 b) For intI = 1 To 10 Step 2

 d) For intI = 1 To 10 Step -2

EXERCISES

11.11 *(Present Value Calculator Application)* A bank wants to show its customers how much they would need to invest to achieve a specified financial goal (future value) in 5, 10, 15, 20, 25 or 30 years. Users must provide their financial goal (the amount of money desired after the specified number of years has elapsed), an interest rate and the length of the investment in years. Create an application that calculates and displays the principal (initial amount to invest) needed to achieve the user's financial goal. Your application should allow the user to invest money for 5, 10, 15, 20, 25 or 30 years. For example, if a customer wants to reach the financial goal of $15,000 over a period of 5 years when the interest rate is 6.6%, the customer would need to invest $10,896.96 as shown in Fig. 11.16.

 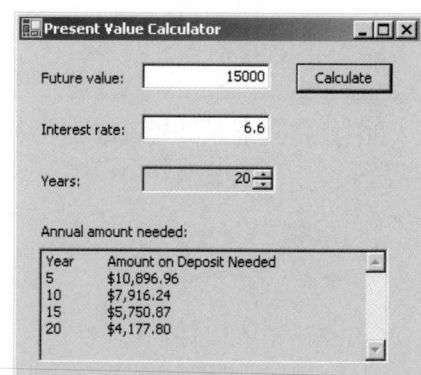

Figure 11.16   Present Value Calculator GUI

 a) *Copying and opening the template application.* Copy the PresentValue folder from C:\Examples\Tutorial11\Exercises to C:\SimplyVB. Double click the PresentValue.sln file to open the application in Visual Studio .NET.

 b) *Adding the NumericUpDown control.* Place and size the NumericUpDown so that it follows the GUI Design Guidelines. Set the NumericUpDown control's Name property to updYear. Set the NumericUpDown control to allow only multiples of five for the number of years. Also, allow the user to select only a duration that is in the specified range of values.

 c) *Adding a multiline TextBox.* Add a TextBox to the Form below the NumericUpDown control. Change the size to 272, 88, and position the TextBox on the Form so that it follows the GUI Design Guidelines. Then set that TextBox to display multiple lines and a scrollbar. Also ensure that the user cannot modify the text in the TextBox.

 d) *Adding a Click event handler and adding code.* Add a Click event handler for the **Calculate** Button. Once in code view, add code to the application such that, when the **Calculate** Button is clicked, the multiline TextBox displays the necessary principal for each five-year interval. Use the following version of the present-value calculation formula:

$$p = a / (1 + r)^n$$

where
p is the amount needed to achieve the future value
r is the annual interest rate (for example, .05 is equivalent to 5%)
n is the number of years
a is the future-value amount.

11.12 *(Compound Interest: Comparing Rates Application)* Write an application that calculates the amount of money in an account after 10 years for interest rate amounts of 5%–10%. For this application, users must provide the initial principal.

    a) ***Copying and opening the template application.*** Copy the ComparingRates folder from C:\Examples\Tutorial11\Exercises to C:\SimplyVB. Double click the ComparingRates.sln file to open the application in Visual Studio .NET.

    b) ***Adding a multiline TextBox.*** Add a TextBox to the Form below the **Result:** Label control. Change the size to 256, 104, and position the TextBox on the Form so that it follows the GUI Design Guidelines (Fig. 11.17). Then set that TextBox to display multiple lines. Also ensure that the user cannot modify the text in the TextBox.

    c) ***Adding a Click event handler and adding code.*** Add a Click event handler for the **Calculate** Button. Once in code view, add code to the application such that, when the **Calculate** Button is clicked, the multiline TextBox displays the amount in the account after 10 years for interest rates of 5, 6, 7, 8, 9 and 10 percent. Use the following version of the interest-calculation formula:

$$a = p \, (1 + r)^{\,n}$$

where
p is the original amount invested (the principal)
r is the annual interest rate (for example, .05 is equivalent to 5%)
n is the number of years
a is the investment's value at the end of the nth year.

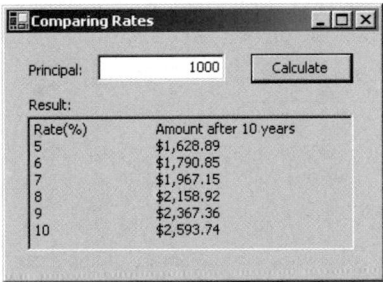

Figure 11.17 Comparing Rates GUI.

11.13 *(Validating Input to the Interest Calculator Application)* Enhance the **Interest Calculator** application with error checking. Test for whether the user has entered valid values for the principal and interest rate. If the user enters an invalid value, display a message in the multiline TextBox. Figure 11.18 demonstrates the application handling an invalid input.

    a) ***Copying and opening the template application.*** Copy the InterestCalculator-Enhancement folder from C:\Examples\Tutorial11\Exercises to C:\SimplyVB. Double click the InterestCalculator.sln file to open the application in Visual Studio .NET.

    b) ***Adding a Click event handler and adding code.*** Add a Click event handler for the **Calculate** Button. Once in code view, modify the code to validate the input. The principal should be a positive amount greater than 0. Also, the interest rate should be greater than 0, but less than 100.

    c) ***Displaying the error message.*** Display the text "The information was not within the correct range of values." in txtResult if the values are not valid.

Figure 11.18   Interest Calculator application with error checking.

What does this code do? ▶ **11.14** What is the value of `intResult` after the following code executes? Assume that `intPower`, `intI`, `intResult` and `intNumber` are all declared as `Integers`.

```
1   intPower = 5
2   intNumber = 10
3   intResult = intNumber
4
5   For intI = 1 To (intPower - 1)
6       intResult *= intNumber
7   Next
```

What's wrong with this code? ▶ **11.15** Assume that the variable `intCounter` is declared as `Integer` for both a and b. Identify and correct the error(s) in each of the following:

a) This statement should display in a `ListBox` all numbers from 100 to 1 in decreasing order.

```
For intCounter = 100 To 1
    lstDisplay.Items.Add(intCounter)
Next
```

b) The following code should display in a `ListBox` the odd `Integers` from 19 to 1 in decreasing order.

```
For intCounter = 19 To 1 By -1
    lstDisplay.Add(intCounter)
Next
```

Using the Debugger ▶ **11.16** (*Savings Calculator Application*) The **Savings Calculator** application calculates the amount that the user will have on deposit after one year. The application gets the initial amount on deposit from the user, and assumes that the user will add $100 dollars to the account every month for the entire year. No interest is added to the account. While testing the application, you noticed that the amount calculated by the application was incorrect. Use the debugger to locate and correct any logic error(s). Figure 11.19 displays the correct output for this application.

Figure 11.19　Correct output for the **Savings Calculator** application.

Programming Challenge ▶ **11.17** *(Pay Raise Calculator Application)* Develop an application that computes the amount of money an employee makes each year over a user-specified number of years. The employee receives an hourly wage and a pay raise once every year. The user specifies the hourly wage and the amount of the raise (in percentages per year) in the application.

　a) *Copying and opening the template application.* Copy the PayRaise folder from C:\Examples\Tutorial11\Exercises to C:\SimplyVB. Double click the PayRaise.sln file to open the application in Visual Studio .NET.

　b) *Adding controls to the Form.* Add two NumericUpDown controls to the Form. The first NumericUpDown control should be provided to allow the user to specify the pay raise percentage. The user should only be able to specify percentages in the range of 3–8 percent. Create the second NumericUpDown control for users to select the number of years in the range 1–50. Then add a multiline TextBox control to the application. Ensure that the user cannot modify the text in the NumericUpDown and TextBox controls. Resize and move the controls you created so that they follow the GUI Design Guidelines as in Fig. 11.20.

　c) *Adding a Click event handler and adding code.* Add a Click event handler for the **Calculate** Button. Once in code view, add code to use the For...Next statement to compute the yearly salary amounts, based on the yearly pay raise.

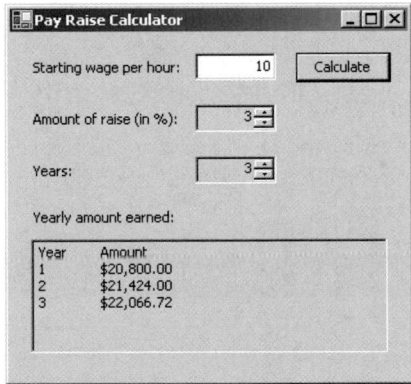

Figure 11.20　**Pay Raise** application's GUI.

Objectives

In this tutorial, you will learn to:
- Use the Select Case multiple-selection statement.
- Use Case statements.
- Use the Is keyword.
- Display a date and time.
- Use TextBox property PasswordChar.

Outline

Security Panel Application

Introducing the Select Case Multiple-Selection Statement

In the last tutorial, you learned how to use the For…Next statement, which is the most concise statement for performing counter-controlled repetition. In this tutorial, you will learn about the Select Case multiple-selection statement. The Select Case statement is used to simplify code that uses several ElseIf statements sequentially when an application must choose among many possible actions to perform.

12.1 Test-Driving the Security Panel Application

In this tutorial, you will use the Select Case multiple-selection statement to construct a **Security Panel** application. This application must meet the following requirements:

Application Requirements

A lab wants to install a security panel outside a laboratory room. Only authorized personnel may enter the lab, using their security codes. The following are valid security codes (also called access codes) and the groups of employees they represent:

Values	Groups
1645–1689	Technicians
8345	Custodians
9998, 1006–1008	Scientists

Once a security code is entered, access is either granted or denied. All access attempts are written to a window below the keypad. If access is granted, the date, time and group (scientists, custodians, etc.) are written to the window. If access is denied, the date, the time and a message, "Access Denied," are written to the window. Furthermore, the user can enter any one-digit access code to summon a security guard for assistance. The date, the time and a message, "Restricted Access," are then written to the window to indicate that the request has been received.

You begin by test-driving the completed application.

Test-Driving the Completed Security Panel Application

1. ***Running   the   Security   Panel   application.*** Open   the `C:\Examples\Tutorial12\CompletedApplication\SecurityPanel` folder. Double click `SecurityPanel.sln` to open the solution in Visual Studio .NET. Select **Debug > Start** to run the application. The Form in Fig. 12.1 will display.

   At the top of the Form, you are provided with a TextBox that displays an asterisk for each digit in the security code enter*ed using the GUI keypad. Notice that the GUI keypad looks much like a real-world keypad. (We will mimic real-world conditions when possible.) The **C** Button clears your current input, and the **#** Button causes the application to process the security code entered. Results are displayed in the ListBox at the bottom of the Form.

Figure 12.1   **Security Panel** application executing.

GUI Design Tip

If your GUI is modeling a real-world object, your GUI design should mimic the physical appearance of the object.

2. ***Entering an invalid security code.*** Use the keypad to enter the invalid security code 1212. Notice that an asterisk (*) is displayed in the TextBox (Fig. 12.2) for each numeric key pressed (by clicking its Button on the Form). These characters do not allow other people to see the code entered. When finished, click the **#** Button. A message indicating that access is denied will appear in the ListBox, as in Fig. 12.3. Notice that the TextBox is cleared when the **#** Button is pressed.

Figure 12.2   Asterisks displayed in **Security code:** field.

(cont.)

Figure 12.3 **Security Panel** displaying **Access Denied** message.

Message indicating that an invalid security code was entered

3. *Using the C Button.* Press a few numeric keys, and then click the **C** Button. Notice that all the asterisks displayed in the TextBox disappear. Users often make mistakes when keystroking or when clicking Buttons, so the **C** Button allows users to make a "fresh start."

4. *Entering a valid security code.* Use the keypad to enter 1006, then click the **#** Button. Notice that a second message appears in the ListBox, as in Fig. 12.4.

Message displayed when a valid security code is entered

Figure 12.4 **Security Panel** application confirming a valid security-code entry.

5. *Terminating the application.* Click the running application's close box.

6. *Closing the solution.* Select **File > Close Solution**.

12.2 Introducing the Select Case Multiple-Selection Statement

In this section, you will learn how to use the **Select Case multiple-selection statement**. For comparison purposes, we will first provide an If...Then...Else multiple-selection statement that displays a text message based on a student's grade:

```
If strGrade = "A" Then
    lblDisplay.Text = "Excellent!"
ElseIf strGrade = "B" Then
    lblDisplay.Text = "Very good!"
ElseIf strGrade = "C" Then
    lblDisplay.Text = "Good."
ElseIf strGrade = "D" Then
    lblDisplay.Text = "Poor."
ElseIf strGrade = "F" Then
    lblDisplay.Text = "Failure."
Else
    lblDisplay.Text = "Invalid grade."
End If
```

This statement can be used to produce the correct output when selecting among multiple values of strGrade. However, by using the Select Case statement, you can simplify every instance like

```
If strGrade = "A" Then
```

to one like

```
Case "A"
```

and eliminate the If and ElseIf keywords.

The following Select Case multiple-selection statement performs the same functionality as the preceding If...Then...Else statement:

```
Select Case strGrade

    Case "A"
        lblDisplay.Text = "Excellent!"

    Case "B"
        lblDisplay.Text = "Very good!"

    Case "C"
        lblDisplay.Text = "Good."

    Case "D"
        lblDisplay.Text = "Poor."

    Case "F"
        lblDisplay.Text = "Failure."

    Case Else
        lblDisplay.Text = "Invalid grade."

End Select
```

Good Programming Practice

Placing a blank line before and after each Case in a Select Case statement improves readability.

Good Programming Practice

Indenting the statements in the body of a Case improves readability.

Common Programming Error

When using the optional Case Else statement in a Select Case statement, failing to place the Case Else as the last Case is a syntax error.

Common Programming Error

Case statements whose controlling expressions result in the same value are logic errors. At run time, only the body of the first matching Case is executed.

The Select Case statement begins with the keywords Select Case followed by a **test expression** (also called a **controlling expression**) and terminates with keywords **End Select**. The preceding Select Case statement contains five **Case statement**s and the optional **Case Else statement**. Each Case contains the keyword Case followed by an **expression list**. The expression list can contain strings such as "A" and numeric values such as 707 and 9.9. Although a Select Case statement can have any number of Cases, it must have at most one Case Else.

Figure 12.5 shows the UML activity diagram for this Select Case multiple-selection statement. The first condition to be evaluated is strGrade = "A". If this condition is True, the text "Excellent!" is displayed, and control proceeds to the first statement after the Select Case statement. If the condition is False (that is, strGrade <> "A"), the statement continues by testing the next condition, strGrade = "B". If this condition is True, the text "Very good!" is displayed, and control proceeds to the first statement after the Select Case statement. If the condition is

False (that is, strGrade <> "B"), the statement continues to test the next condition. This process continues until a matching Case is found or until the final condition evaluates to False (strGrade <> "F"). If the latter occurs, the Case Else's body is executed, and the text "Invalid grade." is displayed. The application then continues with the first statement after the Select Case statement.

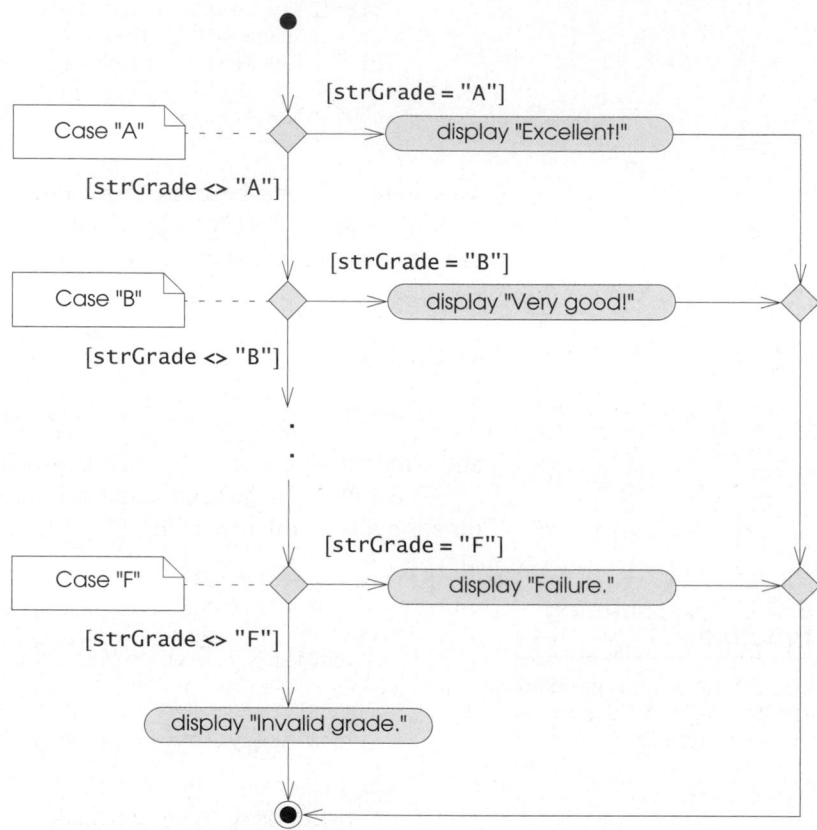

Figure 12.5 Select Case multiple-selection statement UML activity diagram.

SELF-REVIEW

1. Select Case is a _____-selection statement.
   a) multiple
   b) double
   c) single
   d) None of the above.

2. When does the Case Else body execute?
   a) Every time a Select Case statement executes
   b) When more than one Case is matched
   c) When all Cases are matching Case statements in a Select Case statement
   d) None of the above.

Answers: 1) a. 2) b.

12.3 Constructing the Security Panel Application

The **Security Panel** application contains 10 Buttons that display digits. (We call these numeric Buttons.) You will create an event handler for each Button's Click event. These Buttons make up the GUI keypad. The following pseudocode describes the Click event handler for each of these numeric Buttons:

> If a numeric Button is clicked
> Concatenate Button's digit to the TextBox's Text property value

Later in this tutorial, you will convert this pseudocode into the Visual Basic .NET code and create the `Click` event handlers for each numeric `Button`. The user then will be able to use the numeric `Button`s to enter digits and have those digits concatenated to the text in a `TextBox`.

In addition to the numeric `Button`s, this application also contains a **C** `Button` and a **#** `Button`. The **C** `Button` clears the `Form`'s `TextBox`. The pseudocode for the **#** `Button`'s event handler is as follows:

> Store security code input by user (currently in the TextBox) to a variable
> Clear input TextBox
>
> Select correct Case below and execute Case's body statements
>
>   Case where access code is less than 10
>   Store text "Restricted Access" to String variable
>
>   Case where access code is in the range 1645 to 1689
>   Store text "Technicians" to String variable
>
>   Case where access code equals 8345
>   Store text "Custodial Services" to String variable
>
>   Case where access code equals 9998 or is in the range 1006 to 1008
>   Store text "Scientists" to String variable
>
>   Case where none of the preceding Cases match
>   Store text "Access Denied" to String variable
>
> Display message in ListBox with current time and String variable's contents

Now that you have studied the application tasks in pseudocode, you will need to create an ACE table for this application (Fig. 12.6). The first row specifies that you will be using `Label`s to identify the `TextBox` and `ListBox` controls. The second row introduces the `Button`s for the numeric keypad. When these `Button`s are clicked, their values are concatenated to the text in the `TextBox`'s `Text` property. The next row indicates that `TextBox txtSecurityCode` will store the security code that is input by the user. The next two rows specify `Button`s that the user can click to clear the `TextBox` (`btnClear`) and enter the security code (`btnEnter`). The last row indicates the `ListBox` will be used to display a message to the user.

<table>
<tr><td rowspan="7">*Action/Control/Event
(ACE) Table for the
Security Panel
Application*
</td><td>**Action**</td><td>**Control**</td><td>**Event**</td></tr>
<tr><td>Label all the application's controls</td><td>lblSecurityCode,
lblAccessCode</td><td></td></tr>
<tr><td>Enter digits</td><td>btnZero, btnOne, btnTwo,
btnThree, btnFour, btnFive,
btnSix, btnSeven, btnEight,
btnNine</td><td>Click</td></tr>
<tr><td>Store security code as it is being
input digit-by-digit</td><td>txtSecurityCode</td><td></td></tr>
<tr><td>Clear TextBox</td><td>btnClear</td><td>Click</td></tr>
<tr><td>Determine whether security code
stored in TextBox is valid</td><td>btnEnter</td><td>Click</td></tr>
<tr><td>Display message in ListBox</td><td>lstLogEntry</td><td></td></tr>
</table>

Figure 12.6 ACE table for **Security Panel** application.

Now that you are familiar with the Select Case multiple-selection statement, you will use it to build the **Security Panel** application.

Using the *PasswordChar* Property

GUI Design Tip

Mask passwords or other sensitive pieces of information in TextBoxes.

1. *Copying the template application to your work folder.* Copy the Security-Panel folder from C:\Examples\Tutorial12\TemplateApplication to C:\SimplyVB.

2. *Opening the template application.* Double click SecurityPanel.sln in C:\SimplyVB\SecurityPanel. Double click SecurityPanel.vb in the **Solutions Explorer** to open the Form in design view.

3. *Displaying the * character in the TextBox.* Select the **Security code:** Text-Box at the top of the Form, and set this TextBox's PasswordChar property to * in the **Properties** window. Text displayed in a TextBox can be hidden or **masked** with the character specified in property **PasswordChar**. Rather than displaying the actual TextBox text that the user types, **masking characters** are displayed. However, the TextBox's Text property does contain the text the user typed. For example, if a user enters 5469, the TextBox displays ****, yet stores "5469" in its Text property. Now any character displayed in your interface's TextBox displays as the * character.

4. *Disabling the TextBox.* The primary reason for using a TextBox instead of a Label to display the access code is to use the PasswordChar property. To prevent users from modifying the text in the TextBox, set its **Enabled** property to False.

5. *Create the btnEnter_Click event handler.* Double click the # Button to create the btnEnter_Click event handler.

6. *Declaring and initializing variables.* Add lines 215–219 of Fig. 12.7 to the btnEnter_Click event handler. Lines 215–216 declare variables intAccessCode and strMessage. Variable intAccessCode will be used to store the user's security code (access code), and variable strMessage will store the message that will be displayed to the user, one based on the access code entered. Line 218 sets the intAccessCode variable to the security code input by the user. Line 219 clears the **Security code:** TextBox.

Declaring event handler's variables

Figure 12.7 Variable declarations for btnEnter_Click.

7. *Saving the project.* Select **File > Save All** to save all the solution's files.

Now that you have designed the GUI for your application and initialized the variables for your event handler, let's continue by creating your Select Case statement, as shown in the box, *Adding a Select Case Statement to the Application*. This statement will determine the user's access level based on the code input.

<table>
<tr>
<td>

Adding a Select Case Statement to the Application

</td>
<td>

1. **Adding a Select Case statement to btnEnter_Click**. Press *Enter* twice and add line 221 from Fig. 12.8 to the btnEnter_Click event handler, and press *Enter*. Keywords End Select (line 223) immediately appear below the Select Case line that you just added. Line 221 begins the Select Case statement, which contains the controlling expression intAccessCode—the access code entered by the user. Remember that this expression (the value intAccessCode) is compared sequentially with each Case until either a match occurs or the End Select statement is reached. If a matching Case is found, the body of that Case executes and program control proceeds to the first statement after the End Select statement.

</td>
</tr>
</table>

Creating a Select Case statement

Figure 12.8 Select Case statement.

2. **Adding a Case to the Select Case statement**. Press *Enter* and add lines 223–225 from Fig. 12.9 to the Select Case statement. The first Case statement tests whether intAccessCode is less than 10. Keyword **Is** along with the comparison operator < specify a range of values to test. You can use the Is keyword followed by a comparison operator to perform that comparison between the controlling expression and the value to the left of the operator. In this case, if the value in intAccessCode is less than 10, the code in the body of that Case statement will execute and strMessage will be assigned the string "Restricted Access", which will be displayed after the body of the Select Case statement completes.

Is keyword can be used for relational and equality comparisons

Figure 12.9 First Case added to Select Case statement.

(cont.)

3. **Specifying Cases for the remaining access codes.** Press *Enter* twice and add lines 227–238 from Fig. 12.10 to the Select Case statement.

To keyword can be used to specify a range of values to test

Comma used to separate multiple expressions in a Case

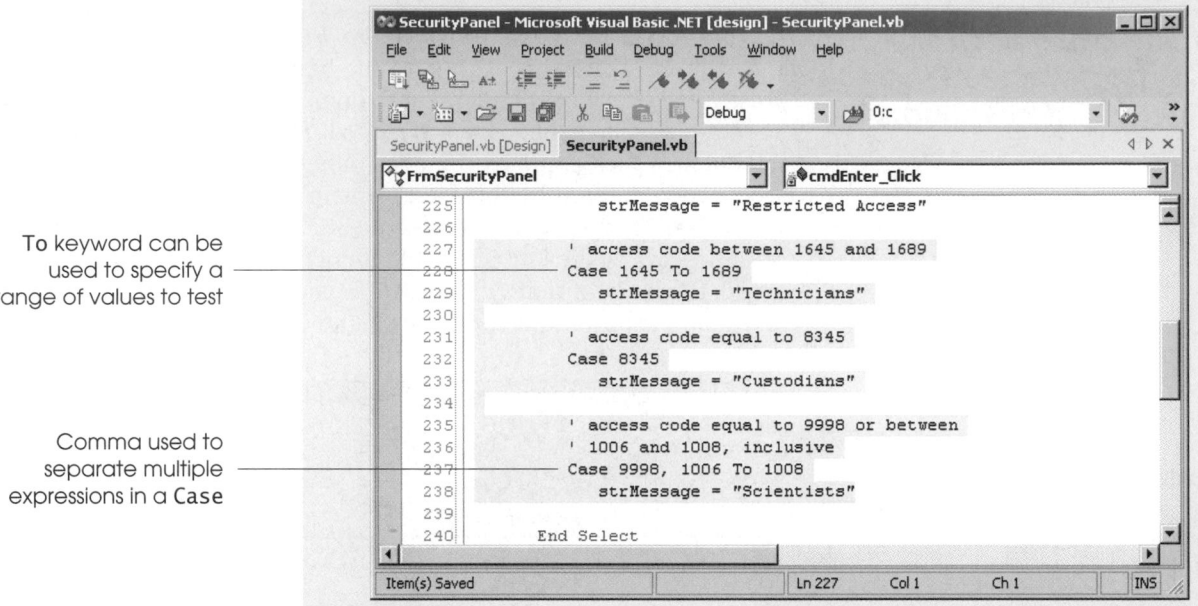

Figure 12.10 Cases specified for remaining access codes.

The Case statement on lines 228–229 determines whether the value of intAccessCode is in the range 1645 to 1689, inclusive. Keyword **To** is used to specify the range. If the user enters an access code in this range, the body of the Case statement sets strMessage to "Technicians".

The next Case statement (lines 231–233) checks for a specific number. If intAccessCode matches the value 8345, then the statement in that Case is executed. Specifying a single value in a Case statement is common.

The next Case statement (lines 235–238) determines whether intAccessCode is 9998 or a number in the range 1006 to 1008, inclusive. Notice that, when multiple values are provided in a Case statement, they are separated by commas.

Common Programming Error

If the value on the left side of the To keyword in a Case statement is larger than the value on the right side, the Case is ignored during program execution, potentially causing a logic error.

4. **Adding a Case Else to the Select Case statement.** Add lines 240–242 from Fig. 12.11 to the Select Case statement. These lines contain the optional Case Else, which is executed when the controlling expression does not match any of the previous Cases. If used, the Case Else must follow all other Case statements. In your application, the body of the Case Else statement sets variable strMessage to "Access Denied".

Case Else statement executes when no other Case matches

Figure 12.11 Case Else of the Select Case statement.

(cont.)

The required keywords End Select (line 244 of Fig. 12.11) terminate the Select Case statement. Note the indentation of the Select Case statement to improve program readability.

5. ***Displaying results in the ListBox.*** Insert lines 246–247 of Fig. 12.12 after the Select Case statement. The statement on line 247 displays a String in lst-LogEntry consisting of the current system date and time, followed by three spaces and the value assigned to strMessage. The first part of method Add's argument contains the expression **Date.Now**. The Framework Class Library (FCL) provides a **Date** structure that can be used to store and display date and time information. A structure is similar to a class. Like objects that you have used in this book, structure members such as properties are accessed by using the dot operator (.). The Date property Now returns the system time and date. Passing this value as a String in the argument to method Add (line 247) causes this value to be converted and displayed as a String. You will learn about how a date is stored using the Date structure in Tutorial 14.

Figure 12.12   Updating the **Security Panel** application's ListBox.

6. ***Saving the project.*** Select **File > Save All** to save all of the solution's files.

Now that you have defined the btnEnter_Click event handler, you will focus on the numeric Buttons. You will create event handlers for each numbered Button and for the C Button in the box, *Programming the Remaining Event Handlers*.

Programming the Remaining Event Handlers

1. ***Create the btnZero_Click event handler.*** In design view, double click the **0** Button (btnZero) to create the btnZero_Click event handler.

2. ***Coding the btnZero_Click event handler.*** Insert line 253 of Fig. 12.13 to the event handler. Line 253 appends the String "0" to the end of txtSecurity-Code's Text property value. You do this to append the numeric Button's value to the access code in the TextBox.

3. ***Define the other numeric Buttons' event handlers.*** Repeat *Steps 1–2* for the remaining numeric Buttons (**1** through **9**). Be sure to substitute the Button's number for the value between the quotes (for example, btnOne_Click sets txtSecurityCode's number as &= "1"). Figure 12.14 shows the event handlers for Buttons btnOne and btnTwo.

4. ***Define the btnClear_Click event handler.*** Double click the **C** Button, and add line 313 as shown in Fig. 12.15. Line 313 clears the **Security code:** Text-Box.

5. ***Saving the project.*** Select **File > Save All** to save all of the solution's files.

6. ***Run the application.*** Select **Debug > Start** to run the application.

(cont.)

Figure 12.13 Event handler `btnZero_Click`.

Figure 12.14 Event handlers `btnOne_Click` and `btnTwo_Click`.

Figure 12.15 Event handler `btnClear_Click` defined.

7. ***Terminating application execution and closing the solution.*** Click the running application's close box. Select **File > Close** solution.

Figure 12.16 displays the code for the entire **Security Panel** application. Look over the code carefully to make sure that you have added all of the event handlers correctly.

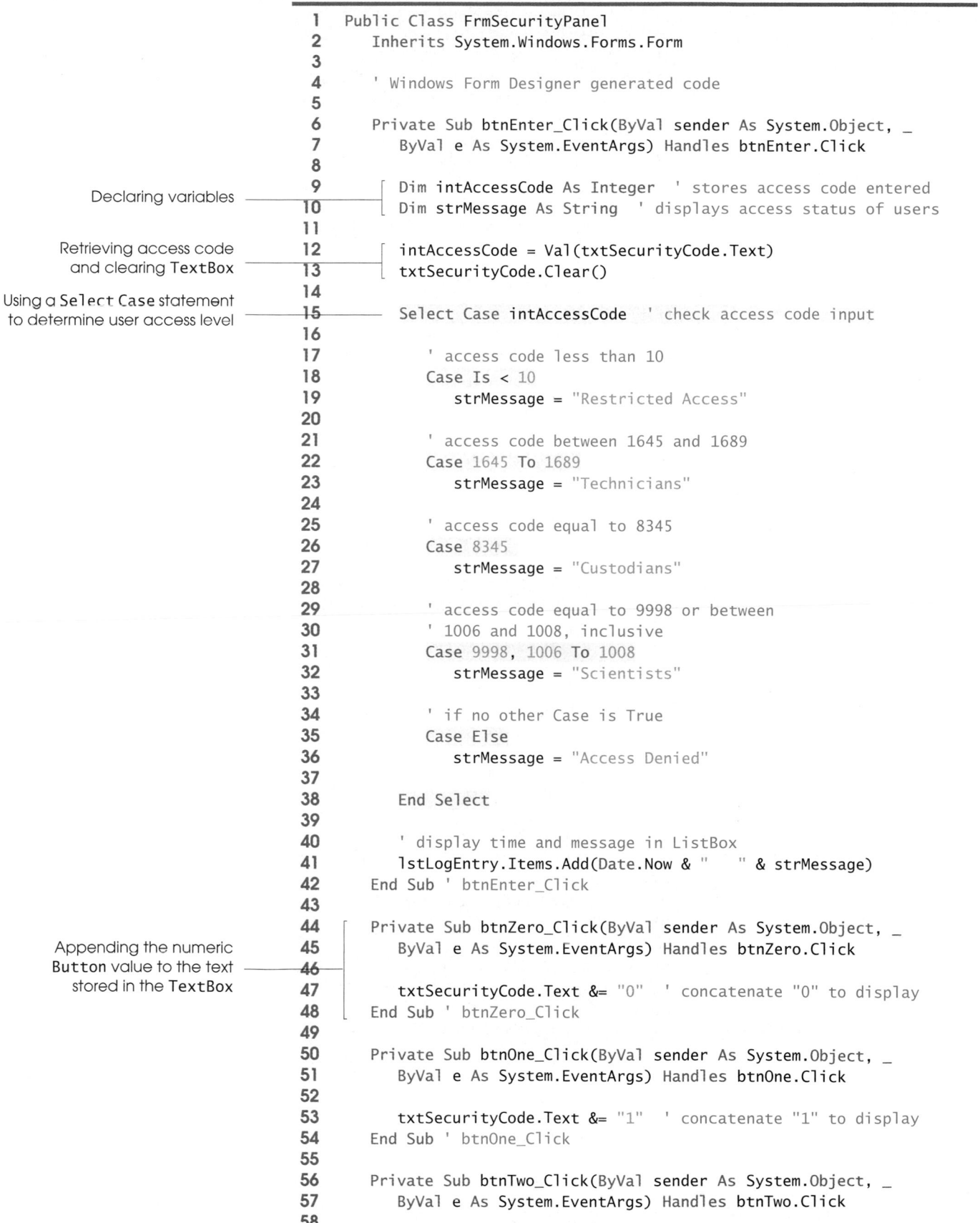

Declaring variables

Retrieving access code
and clearing TextBox

Using a Select Case statement
to determine user access level

Appending the numeric
Button value to the text
stored in the TextBox

```
1    Public Class FrmSecurityPanel
2       Inherits System.Windows.Forms.Form
3
4       ' Windows Form Designer generated code
5
6       Private Sub btnEnter_Click(ByVal sender As System.Object, _
7          ByVal e As System.EventArgs) Handles btnEnter.Click
8
9          Dim intAccessCode As Integer  ' stores access code entered
10         Dim strMessage As String  ' displays access status of users
11
12         intAccessCode = Val(txtSecurityCode.Text)
13         txtSecurityCode.Clear()
14
15         Select Case intAccessCode  ' check access code input
16
17            ' access code less than 10
18            Case Is < 10
19               strMessage = "Restricted Access"
20
21            ' access code between 1645 and 1689
22            Case 1645 To 1689
23               strMessage = "Technicians"
24
25            ' access code equal to 8345
26            Case 8345
27               strMessage = "Custodians"
28
29            ' access code equal to 9998 or between
30            ' 1006 and 1008, inclusive
31            Case 9998, 1006 To 1008
32               strMessage = "Scientists"
33
34            ' if no other Case is True
35            Case Else
36               strMessage = "Access Denied"
37
38         End Select
39
40         ' display time and message in ListBox
41         lstLogEntry.Items.Add(Date.Now & "    " & strMessage)
42      End Sub ' btnEnter_Click
43
44      Private Sub btnZero_Click(ByVal sender As System.Object, _
45         ByVal e As System.EventArgs) Handles btnZero.Click
46
47         txtSecurityCode.Text &= "0"  ' concatenate "0" to display
48      End Sub ' btnZero_Click
49
50      Private Sub btnOne_Click(ByVal sender As System.Object, _
51         ByVal e As System.EventArgs) Handles btnOne.Click
52
53         txtSecurityCode.Text &= "1"  ' concatenate "1" to display
54      End Sub ' btnOne_Click
55
56      Private Sub btnTwo_Click(ByVal sender As System.Object, _
57         ByVal e As System.EventArgs) Handles btnTwo.Click
58
```

Figure 12.16 Security Panel application. (Part 1 of 2.)

```
59                txtSecurityCode.Text &= "2"   ' concatenate "2" to display
60          End Sub ' btnTwo_Click
61
62          Private Sub btnThree_Click(ByVal sender As System.Object, _
63             ByVal e As System.EventArgs) Handles btnThree.Click
64
65                txtSecurityCode.Text &= "3"   ' concatenate "3" to display
66          End Sub ' btnThree_Click
67
68          Private Sub btnFour_Click(ByVal sender As System.Object, _
69             ByVal e As System.EventArgs) Handles btnFour.Click
70
71                txtSecurityCode.Text &= "4"   ' concatenate "4" to display
72          End Sub ' btnFour_Click
73
74          Private Sub btnFive_Click(ByVal sender As System.Object, _
75             ByVal e As System.EventArgs) Handles btnFive.Click
76
77                txtSecurityCode.Text &= "5"   ' concatenate "5" to display
78          End Sub ' btnFive_Click
79
80          Private Sub btnSix_Click(ByVal sender As System.Object, _
81             ByVal e As System.EventArgs) Handles btnSix.Click
82
83                txtSecurityCode.Text &= "6"   ' concatenate "6" to display
84          End Sub ' btnSix_Click
85
86          Private Sub btnSeven_Click(ByVal sender As System.Object, _
87             ByVal e As System.EventArgs) Handles btnSeven.Click
88
89                txtSecurityCode.Text &= "7"   ' concatenate "7" to display
90          End Sub ' btnSeven_Click
91
92          Private Sub btnEight_Click(ByVal sender As System.Object, _
93             ByVal e As System.EventArgs) Handles btnEight.Click
94
95                txtSecurityCode.Text &= "8"   ' concatenate "8" to display
96          End Sub ' btnEight_Click
97
98          Private Sub btnNine_Click(ByVal sender As System.Object, _
99             ByVal e As System.EventArgs) Handles btnNine.Click
100
101                txtSecurityCode.Text &= "9"   ' concatenate "9" to display
102          End Sub ' btnNine_Click
103
104          Private Sub btnClear_Click(ByVal sender As System.Object, _
105             ByVal e As System.EventArgs) Handles btnClear.Click
106
107                txtSecurityCode.Clear()   ' clear text from TextBox
108          End Sub ' btnClear_Click
109
110    End Class ' FrmSecurityPanel
```

Clearing the TextBox — (line 107)

Figure 12.16 **Security Panel** application. (Part 2 of 2.)

SELF-REVIEW   1. A Case that handles all values larger than a specified value must precede the > operator with keyword _____.

    a) Select

    b) Is

    c) Case

    d) All

2. Use a(n) _____ to separate multiple conditions in a Case statement.

   a) period   b) asterisk

   c) comma   d) colon

Answers: 1) b. 2) c.

12.4 Wrap-Up

In this tutorial, you learned how to use the Select Case multiple-selection statement and discovered its similarities to the If...Then...Else statement. You studied a UML activity diagram that illustrates the flow of control in Select Case statements.

You then applied what you learned to create your **Security Panel** application. You used a Select Case statement to determine whether the user inputted a correct security code. You also defined several Cases and included a Case Else statement, which executes if a valid security code is not provided.

In the next tutorial, you will learn how to construct applications from small, manageable pieces of reusable code called procedures. You will use this capability to enhance an example you created earlier in the book.

SKILLS SUMMARY

Creating a Select Case statement

- Use the keywords Select Case followed by a controlling expression.
- Use the keyword Case followed by an expression to compare with the controlling expression.
- Define the statements that execute if the Case's expression matches the controlling expression.
- Use the keywords Case Else followed by statements to execute if the controlling expression does not match any of the provided Cases. Case Else, if used, must be the last Case statement.

Masking User Input in a TextBox

- Set the TextBox's PasswordChar property to the desired character, typically the asterisk (*), to mask the user input.
- Retrieve the value typed by the user in the Text property.

Retrieving the Current Date and Time

- Use property Now of structure Date, which, when converted to a String, displays the current date in the format 12/31/2002 11:59:59 P.M.

KEY TERMS

Case Else statement—Optional statement whose body executes if the Select Case's test expression does not match any of the Cases' expressions.

controlling expression—Value compared sequentially with each Case until either a match occurs or the End Select statement is reached.

Date structure—A structure whose properties can be used to store and display date and time information.

Enabled property of a TextBox—The property that determines whether the TextBox will respond to user input.

End Select keywords—Terminates the Select Case statement.

masking—Hiding text such as passwords or other sensitive pieces of information that should not be observed by other people as they are typed. Masking is achieved by using the PasswordChar property of the TextBox for which you would like to hide data. The actual data entered is retained in the TextBox's Text property.

masking character—Character that is used to replace each character displayed in a TextBox when the TextBox's data is masked for privacy.

multiple-selection statement—A statement that performs one of many actions (or sequences of actions) depending on the value of the controlling expression.

Now property of Date statement—Returns the current system time and date.

PasswordChar property of a TextBox—Specifies the masking character for a TextBox.

Select Case statement—The multiple-selection statement used to make a decision by comparing an expression to a series of conditions. The algorithm then takes different actions based on those values.

GUI DESIGN GUIDELINES

Overall Design

- If your GUI is modeling a real-world object, your GUI design should mimic the physical appearance of the object.

TextBox

- Mask passwords or other sensitive pieces of information in TextBoxes.

CONTROLS, EVENTS, PROPERTIES & METHODS

TextBox This control allows the user to input data from the keyboard.

- *In action*

      | 0 |

- *Events*

  TextChanged—This event is raised when the text in the TextBox is changed.

- *Properties*

  Enabled—This property determines whether the user can enter data (True) in the Text-Box or not (False).

  Location—This property specifies the location of the TextBox on the Form relative to the top-left corner.

  Multiline—This property specifies whether the TextBox is capable of displaying multiple lines of text.

  Name—This property specifies the name used to access the TextBox programmatically. The name should be prefixed with txt.

  PasswordChar—This property specifies the masking character to be used when displaying data in the TextBox.

  ReadOnly—This property determines whether the value of a TextBox can be changed.

  ScrollBars—This property specifies whether the TextBox contains a scrollbar.

  Size—This property specifies the height and width (in pixels) of the TextBox.

  Text—This property specifies the text displayed in the TextBox.

  TextAlign—This property specifies how the text is aligned within the TextBox.

- *Methods*

  Focus—This method transfers the focus of the application to the TextBox that calls it.

MULTIPLE-CHOICE QUESTIONS

12.1 The _____ keywords signify the end of a Select Case statement.

    a) End Case   b) End Select

    c) End Select Case   d) Case End

12.2 The expression _____ returns the current system time and date.

    a) Date.DateTime   b) Date.SystemDateTime

    c) Date.Now   d) Date.SystemTimeDate

12.3 You can hide information entered into a TextBox by setting that TextBox's _____ property to a character; that character will be displayed for every character entered by the user.

    a) PrivateChar   b) Mask

    c) MaskingChar   d) PasswordChar

12.4 Which of the following is a syntax error?

a) Having duplicate `Case` statements in the same `Select Case` statement

b) Having a `Case` statement in which the value to the left of a `To` keyword is larger than the value to the right

c) Preceding a `Case` statement with the `Case Else` statement in a `Select Case` statement

d) Using keyword `Is` in a `Select Case` statement

12.5 Keyword _____ is used to specify a range in a `Case` statement.

a) `Also`   b) `Between`

c) `To`   d) `From`

12.6 _____ separates multiple values tested in a `Case` statement.

a) A comma   b) An underscore

c) Keyword `Also`   d) A semicolon

12.7 The _____ method inserts a value in a `ListBox`.

a) `Append`   b) `Items.Insert`

c) `Insert`   d) `Items.Add`

12.8 If the value on the left of the `To` keyword in a `Case` statement is larger than the value on the right, _____.

a) a syntax error occurs   b) the body of the `Case` statement executes

c) the body of the `Case` statement never executes

d) the statement causes a runtime error

12.9 The expression following the keywords `Select Case` is called a _____.

a) guard condition   b) controlling expression

c) selection expression   d) case expression

12.10 To prevent a user from modifying text in a `TextBox`, set its _____ property to `False`.

a) `Enabled`   b) `Text`

c) `TextChange`   d) `Editable`

EXERCISES

12.11 *(Sales Commission Calculator Application)* Develop an application that calculates a salesperson's commission from the number of items sold (Fig. 12.17). Assume that all items have a fixed price of 10 dollars per unit. Use a `Select Case` statement to implement the following sales commission schedule:

Fewer than 10 items sold = 1% commission
Between 10 and 40 items sold = 2% commission
Between 41 and 100 items sold = 4% commission
More than 100 items sold = 8% commission

a) ***Copying and opening the template application.*** Copy the `SalesCommission-Calculator` folder from `C:\Examples\Tutorial12\Exercises` to `C:\SimplyVB`. Double click the `SalesCommissionCalculator.sln` file in the `SalesCommission-Calculator` folder to open the application in Visual Studio .NET.

b) ***Defining an event handler for the Button's `Click` event.*** Create an event handler for the **Calculate** `Button`'s `Click` event.

c) ***Display the salesperson's gross sales.*** In your new event handler, multiply the number of items that the salesperson has sold by 10, and display the resulting gross sales as a monetary amount.

d) ***Calculate the salesperson's commission percentage.*** Use a `Select Case` statement to compute the salesperson's commission percentage, from the number of items sold. The rate that is selected is applied to all the items the salesperson sold.

e) *Display the salesperson's earnings.* Multiply the salesperson's gross sales by the commission percentage determined in the previous step to calculate the salesperson's earnings. Remember to divide by 100 to obtain the percentage.

Figure 12.17 Sales Commission Calculator GUI.

12.12 *(Cash Register Application)* Use the numeric keypad from the **Security Panel** application to build a **Cash Register** application (Fig. 12.18). In addition to numbers, the cash register should include a decimal point `Button`. Apart from this numeric operation, there should be **Enter**, **Delete**, **Clear** and **Total** `Button`s. Sales tax should be calculated on the amount purchased. Use a `Select Case` statement to compute sales tax. Add the tax amount to the subtotal to calculate the total. Display the tax and total for the user. Use the following sales-tax percentages, which are based on the amount of money spent:

> Amounts under $100 = 5% (.05) sales tax
> Amounts between $100 and $500 = 7.5% (.075) sales tax
> Amounts above $500 = 10% (.10) sales tax

a) *Copying and opening the template application.* Copy the `CashRegister` folder from `C:\Examples\Tutorial12\Exercises` to `C:\SimplyVB`. Double click the `CashRegister.sln` file in the `CashRegister` folder to open the application in Visual Studio .NET.

b) *Define event handlers for the numeric Buttons and decimal point in the keypad.* Create event handlers for each of these `Button`'s `Click` events. Have each event handler concatenate the proper value to the `TextBox` at the top of the `Form`.

c) *Define an event handler for the Enter Button's Click event.* Create an event handler for this `Button`'s `Click` event. Have this event handler add the current amount to the subtotal and display the new subtotal.

d) *Define an event handler for the Total Button's Click event.* Create an event handler for this `Button`'s `Click` event. Have this event handler use the subtotal to compute the tax amount.

e) *Define an event handler for the Clear Button's Click event.* Create an event handler for this `Button`'s `Click` event. Have this event handler clear the user input and display the value $0.00 for the subtotal, sales tax and total.

f) *Define an event handler for the Delete Button's Click event.* Create an event handler for this `Button`'s `Click` event. Have this event handler clear only the data in the `TextBox`.

Figure 12.18   Cash Register GUI.

12.13 *(Income Tax Calculator Application)* Create an application that computes the amount of income tax that a person must pay, depending upon that person's salary. Your application should perform as shown in Fig. 12.19. Use the following income ranges and corresponding tax rates:

Under $20,000 = 2% income tax
$20,000 – $50,000 = 5% income tax
$50,001 – $75,000 = 10% income tax
$75,001 – $100,000 = 15% income tax
Over $100,000 = 20% income tax

a) ***Copying and opening the template application.*** Copy the IncomeTaxCalculator folder from C:\Examples\Tutorial12\Exercises to C:\SimplyVB. Double click the IncomeTaxCalculator.sln file in the IncomeTaxCalculator folder to open the application in Visual Studio .NET.

b) ***Define an event handler for the Calculate Button's Click event.*** Use the designer to create an event handler for this Button's Click event. Have this event handler use a Select Case statement to determine the user's income-tax percentage. For simplicity, this value should then be multiplied by the user's salary and displayed in the output Label.

Figure 12.19   Income Tax Calculator GUI.

What does this code do? ▶ **12.14** What is output by the following code? Assume that btnDonation is a Button, txtDonation is a TextBox and lblMessage is an output Label. [*Note*: Code listing continues at the top of the next page.]

```
1    Private Sub btnDonation_Click(ByVal sender As _
2       System.Object, ByVal e As System.EventArgs) _
3       Handles btnDonation.Click
4
5       Select Case Val(txtDonationAmount.Text)
6
7          Case 0
8             lblMessage.Text = "Please consider donating to our cause."
9
```

(cont.)

```
10          Case 1 To 100
11              lblMessage.Text = "Thank you for your donation."
12
13          Case Is > 100
14              lblMessage.Text = "Thank you very much for your donation!"
15
16          Case Else
17              lblMessage.Text = "Please enter a valid amount."
18
19      End Select
20
21  End Sub
```

What's wrong with this code? ▶ **12.15** This `Select Case` statement should determine whether an `Integer` is even or odd. Find the error(s) in the following code:

```
1  Select Case intValue Mod 2
2
3      Case 0
4          lblOutput.Text = "Odd Integer"
5
6      Case 1
7          lblOutput.Text = "Even Integer"
8
9  End Select
```

Using the Debugger ▶ **12.16** (*Discount Calculator Application*) The **Discount Calculator** application determines the discount the user will receive, based on how much money the user spends. A 15% discount is received for purchases over $200, a 10% discount is received for purchases between $150–$199, a 5% discount is received for purchases between $100–$149 and a 2% discount is received for purchases between $50–$99. While testing your application, you notice that the application is not calculating the discount properly for some values. Use the debugger to find and fix the logic error(s) in the application. Figure 12.20 displays the correct output for the application.

Figure 12.20 Correct output for the **Discount Calculator** application.

Programming Challenge ▶ **12.17** (*Enhanced Cash Register Application*) Modify the **Cash Register** application (Exercise 12.12) to include the operations addition, subtraction and multiplication. Remove the **Enter** `Button`, and replace it with the addition (**+**), subtraction (**–**) and multiplication (***)** `Buttons`. These `Buttons` should take the value displayed in the **Subtotal:** field and the value displayed in the upper `Label` and perform the operation of the clicked `Button`. The result should be displayed in the **Subtotal:** field. Fig. 12.21 displays the enhanced **Cash Register** application GUI.

Figure 12.21   Enhanced Cash Register GUI.

13 TUTORIAL

Objectives

In this tutorial, you will learn to:
- Construct applications modularly from pieces called procedures.
- Work with "built-in" procedures.
- Distinguish between **Function** procedures and **Sub** procedures, and determine when each should be used.
- Create your own **Function** procedures and **Sub** procedures.

Outline

Enhancing the Wage Calculator Application

Introducing *Function* Procedures and *Sub* Procedures

Most software applications that solve real-world problems are much larger than the applications presented in the first few tutorials of this text. Experience has shown that the best way to develop and maintain a large application is to construct it from smaller, more manageable pieces. This technique is known as **divide and conquer**. These manageable pieces include program components, known as **procedures**, that simplify the design, implementation and maintenance of large applications. In this tutorial, you will learn how to create two kinds of procedures—namely, **Function** procedures and **Sub** procedures.

13.1 Test-Driving the Enhanced Wage Calculator Application

Next, you will use procedures to enhance the **Wage Calculator** application that you created in Tutorial 7. This enhanced application must meet the following requirements:

Application Requirements

Recall the problem statement from Tutorial 7: A payroll company calculates the gross earnings per week of employees from the number of hours they worked and their hourly wages. Create an application that takes this information and calculates the gross earnings by multiplying the employee's hourly wages by the number of hours worked. The application assumes a standard work week of 40 hours. Any hours worked over 40 hours in a week are considered overtime and earn time and a half (that is, one and one-half times the hourly wage). Use a procedure to determine whether the employee has earned overtime pay. Salary for time and a half is calculated by multiplying the employee's hourly wage by 1.5 and multiplying the result of that calculation by the number of overtime hours worked. This value is then added to the user's earnings for the regular 40 hours of work to calculate the total earnings for that week. Use another procedure to display the user's pay.

The completed application has the same functionality as that of the application in Tutorial 7, but uses procedures to better organize the code. This application calculates wages that are based on an employee's hourly salary and the number of hours worked per week. Normally, an employee who works 40 or fewer hours earns the hourly wage multiplied by the number of hours worked. The calculation differs if the employee has worked more than the standard 40-hour work week. In this tutorial, you learn about procedures that perform calculations based on input values that may differ with each execution of the application. You begin by test-driving the completed application.

Test-Driving the Wage Calculator Application

1. ***Opening and running the application.*** Open the WageCalculator2.sln file located in the C:\Examples\Tutorial13\CompletedApplication\WageCalculator2 folder. Select **Debug > Start** to run the application.

2. ***Entering the employee's hourly wage.*** Enter 10 in the **Hourly wage:** TextBox (Fig. 13.1).

Figure 13.1   **Wage Calculator** executing.

3. ***Entering the number of hours the employee worked.*** Enter 45 in the **Weekly hours:** TextBox.

4. ***Calculating wages earned.*** Click the **Calculate** Button. The result ($475.00) is displayed in the **Gross earnings:** Label.

5. ***Terminating the application.*** Click the running application's close box to terminate execution.

6. ***Closing the solution.*** Select **File > Close Solution**.

13.2 Classes and Procedures

The key to creating large applications is to break the applications into smaller pieces. In object-oriented programming, these pieces consist primarily of classes, which can be further broken down into methods. In Visual Basic .NET programming, methods are implemented (created) by writing procedures.

Programmers typically combine **programmer-defined** classes and methods with preexisting (also predefined) code available in the FCL. Using preexisting code saves time, effort and money. This concept of **reusing code** increases efficiency for application developers. Figure 13.2 explains and demonstrates several preexisting Visual Basic .NET procedures.

You have already used several preexisting classes and methods in the FCL. For example, all of the GUI controls you have used in your applications are defined in the FCL as classes. You have also used FCL class methods, such as method Format of class String, to display output properly in your applications. Without method String.Format, you would have needed to code this functionality yourself—a task that would have included many lines of code and programming techniques that have not been introduced yet. You will learn many more FCL classes and methods in this book.

Procedure	Description	Example
Math.Max(x, y)	Returns the larger value of x and y	Math.Max(2.3, 12.7) is 12.7 Math.Max(-2.3, -12.7) is -2.3
Math.Min(x, y)	Returns the smaller value of x and y	Math.Min(2.3, 12.7) is 2.3 Math.Min(-2.3, -12.7) is -12.7
Math.Sqrt(x)	Returns the square root of x	Math.Sqrt(9) is 3.0 Math.Sqrt(2) is 1.4142135623731
Pmt(x, y, z)	Calculates loan payments where x specifies the interest rate, y specifies the number of payment periods and z specifies the principal value of the loan	Pmt(0.05, 12, -4000) is 451.301640083261
Val(x)	Returns a numeric value for x	Val("5") is 5 Val("5a8") is 5 Val("a5") is 0
String.Format(x, y)	Returns String values where x is a format string, and y is a value to be formatted as a String	String.Format("{0:C}", 1.23) is "$1.23"

Figure 13.2   Some predefined Visual Basic .NET procedures.

However, the FCL cannot provide every conceivable feature that you might want, so Visual Basic .NET allows you to create your own programmer-defined procedures to meet the unique requirements of your particular applications. Two types of procedures exist: **Function procedures** and **Sub procedures**. In the next section, you will learn about Function procedures; in Section 13.4, you will learn about Sub procedures. Throughout this tutorial, the term "procedure" refers to both Function procedures and Sub procedures, unless otherwise noted.

SELF-REVIEW   1. _____ provides the programmer with preexisting classes that perform common tasks.

    a) The Framework Class Library   b) The PreExisting keyword
    c) The Framework Code Library   d) The Library keyword

2. Programmers normally use _____.

    a) programmer-defined procedures   b) preexisting procedures
    c) both programmer-defined and preexisting procedures
    d) neither programmer-defined nor preexisting procedures

Answers: 1) a. 2) c.

13.3 Function Procedures

The applications presented earlier in this book have called FCL methods (such as String.Format) to help accomplish the applications' tasks. You will now learn how to write your own programmer-defined procedures. You will first learn how to create procedures in the context of two small applications, before you create the enhanced **Wage Calculator** application. The first application uses the Pythagorean Theorem to calculate the length of the hypotenuse of a right triangle, and the second application determines the maximum of three numbers. Let us begin by reviewing the Pythagorean Theorem. A right triangle (which is a triangle with a 90-degree angle) always satisfies the following relationship—the sum of the squares of the two smaller sides of the triangle equal the square of the largest side of the triangle, which is known as the hypotenuse. In this application, the two smaller sides are called sides A and B, and their lengths are used to calculate the length of the hypotenuse. Follow the steps in the box, *Creating the Hypotenuse Calculator Application*, to create the application.

Creating the Hypotenuse Calculator Application	1. ***Copying the template to your work folder.*** Copy the `C:\Examples\Tutorial13\TemplateApplication\HypotenuseCalculator` folder to `C:\SimplyVB`.

2. ***Opening the template application.*** Double click `HypotenuseCalculator.sln` in the `HypotenuseCalculator` folder to open the application in Visual Studio .NET. If the application does not open in design view, switch to design view. You will see the GUI shown in Fig. 13.3. When this application is running, the user enters the lengths of a triangle's two shorter sides into the **Length of side A:** and **Length of side B:** TextBoxes, then clicks the **Calculate Hypotenuse** Button. The completed application will calculate the length of the hypotenuse at this time and display the result in the **Length of hypotenuse:** output Label.

Figure 13.3   Hypotenuse Calculator GUI.

Software Design Tip

Use procedures to increase the clarity and organization of your applications. This not only helps others understand your applications, but it also helps you develop, test and debug your applications.

3. ***Viewing the template application code.*** Switch to code view, and examine the code provided in the template, shown in Fig. 13.4. We have provided an incomplete event handler for the **Calculate Hypotenuse** Button. This event handler contains six declarations (lines 129–134). Variables `dblSideA` and `dblSideB` will contain the lengths of sides A and B, entered by the user. Variable `dblHypotenuse` will contain the length of the hypotenuse, which will be calculated shortly. Variable `dblSquareSideA` will be used to store the length of side A, squared. Similarly, variables `dblSquareSideB` and `dblSquareHypotenuse` will be used to store the squares of the lengths of sides B and the hypotenuse, respectively. Lines 136–137 store the user input for the lengths of sides A and B. Lines 140–146 contain an `If...Then...Else` statement. The `If` statement's body displays a message dialog if a negative value (or zero) is input as the length of side A or side B, or both. The `Else`'s body, which will execute if values greater than zero are entered, will be used to calculate the length of the hypotenuse.

4. ***Creating an empty `Function` procedure.*** Add lines 150–152 of Fig. 13.5 after event handler `btnCalculate_Click`. The keywords `End Function` will appear (line 154). You will learn about these keywords shortly. Notice that we have added a comment (line 154) to identify the procedure being terminated.

(cont.)

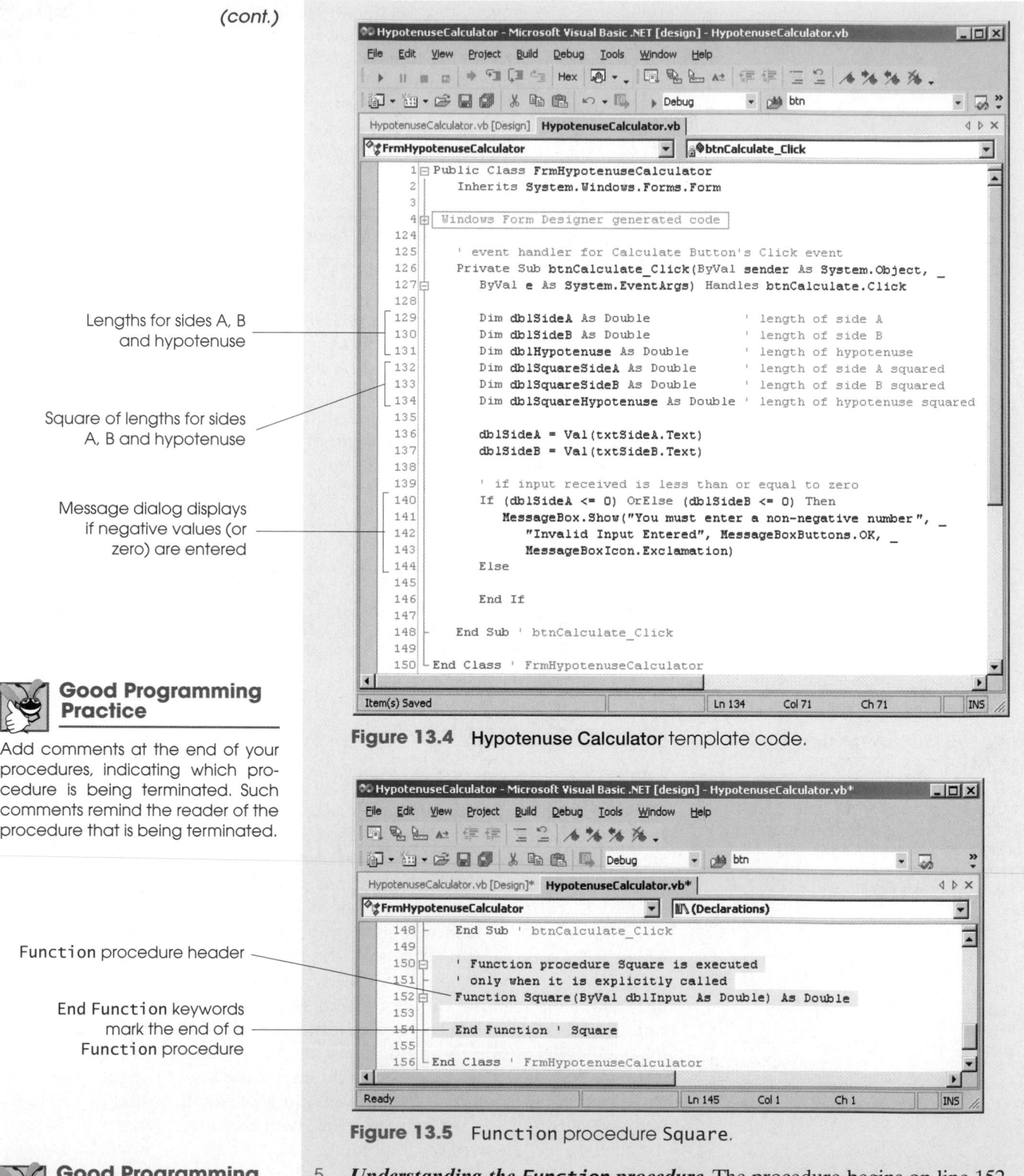

Lengths for sides A, B and hypotenuse

Square of lengths for sides A, B and hypotenuse

Message dialog displays if negative values (or zero) are entered

Figure 13.4 **Hypotenuse Calculator** template code.

Function procedure header

End Function keywords mark the end of a Function procedure

Figure 13.5 Function procedure Square.

Good Programming Practice

Add comments at the end of your procedures, indicating which procedure is being terminated. Such comments remind the reader of the procedure that is being terminated.

Good Programming Practice

Choosing meaningful procedure names and parameter names makes applications more readable and reduces the need for excessive comments.

5. *Understanding the Function procedure.* The procedure begins on line 152 (Fig. 13.5) with keyword **Function**, followed by a **procedure name** (in this case, Square). The procedure name can be any valid identifier. The procedure name is followed by a set of parentheses containing a variable declaration.

(cont.)

Software Design Tip

To promote reusability, each procedure should perform a single, well-defined task, and the procedure name should express that task effectively.

Good Programming Practice

Procedure names should be verbs and should begin with an uppercase first letter. Each subsequent word in the name should begin with an uppercase first letter.

The declaration within the parentheses is known as the **parameter list**, where variables (called **parameters**) are declared. Although this parameter list contains only one declaration, the parameter list can contain multiple declarations separated by commas. This parameter list declares each parameter's name and type. Notice that the declarations of parameter variables here use the keyword ByVal instead of keyword Dim. We will discuss keyword ByVal shortly. Parameter variables are used in the Function procedure body.

The parameter list is followed by the keyword As, which is in turn followed by the data type Double. The type that follows As is known as the **return type**, which indicates the type of the result returned from the Function (in this case, Double). The first line of a procedure (including the keyword Function, the procedure name, the parameter list and the return type) is often called the **procedure header**. The procedure header for Square declares one parameter variable, dblInput, to be of type Double and sets the return type of Square to be Double.

The Function procedure of Fig. 13.5 ends on line 154 with the keywords **End Function**. The declarations and statements that appear after the procedure header but before the keywords End Function form the **procedure body**. The procedure body contains Visual Basic .NET code that performs actions, generally by manipulating or interacting with the parameters from the parameter list. In the next step, you will add statements to the body of procedure Square. The procedure header, the body and the keywords End Function collectively make up the **procedure definition**.

6. **Adding code to the body of a Function procedure.** You want your Function procedure to perform the squaring functionality needed in this application. Add lines 154–155 of Fig. 13.6 to Square's body.

Calculating squares by using the ^ operator ——————

Figure 13.6 Square procedure definition.

Line 155 uses the ^ operator to calculate the square of dblInput—the parameter of this procedure. Line 155 uses a **Return statement** to return this value. This statement begins with the keyword **Return**, followed by an expression. The Return statement returns the result of the expression following keyword Return, in this case dblInput ^ 2, and terminates execution of the procedure. This value is returned to the point at which the procedure was called. You will write the code to call the procedure in the next step.

7. **Calling procedure Square.** Now that you have created your procedure, you will need to call it from your event handler. Add lines 146–148 of Fig. 13.7 to your application, in the Else block of the If...Then...Else statement. These lines call Square by using the procedure name followed by a set of parentheses that contain the procedure's argument. In this case, the arguments are the result of Val(txtSideA.Text) and Val(txtSideB.Text).

Good Programming Practice

Placing a blank line between procedure definitions enhances application readability.

(cont.)

Good Programming Practice

Selecting descriptive parameter names makes the information provided by the *Parameter Info* feature more meaningful.

Notice that typing the opening parenthesis after a procedure name causes Visual Studio .NET to display a window containing the procedure's argument names and types (Fig. 13.8). This is the **Parameter Info** feature of the IDE, which provides you with information about procedures and their arguments. The *Parameter Info* feature displays information for programmer-defined procedures as well as for FCL methods. If the *Parameter Info* window does not appear, it may have been disabled. You can enable *Parameter Info* by selecting **Tools > Options**. In the dialog that appears, select the **Text Editor** folder in the left pane, and then select the **Basic** folder. In the right portion of the dialog, check the **Parameter information** CheckBox.

Calling procedure `Square`

Figure 13.7 Invoking procedure `Square`.

Parameter Info window

Figure 13.8 *Parameter Info* window.

A procedure is **invoked** (that is, made to perform its designated task) by a **procedure call**. The procedure call specifies the procedure name and provides information (**arguments**) that the **callee** (the procedure being called) requires to do its job. When the called procedure completes its task, it returns control to the **caller** (the **calling procedure**). For example, we have typically called function `Val` as follows:

```
intResult = Val(txtInput.Text)
```

where `Val` is the name of the function, and `txtInput.Text`'s value is the argument passed to this function. The procedure uses this value to perform its defined task (returning the value of `txtInput.Text` as a number).

When program control reaches line 147 of Fig. 13.7, the application calls `Function` procedure `Square`. At this point, the application makes a copy of the value entered into the **Length of side A:** TextBox (after this value has been passed to function `Val`), and program control transfers to the first line of `Square`.

(cont.)

Keyword **ByVal**, specified in the header of procedure Square, indicates that a copy of the argument's value (the length of side A) should be passed to Square. Square receives the copy of the value input by the user and stores it in the parameter dblInput. When the Return statement in Square is reached, the value to the right of keyword Return is returned to the point on line 147 where Square was called, and the procedure's execution completes (any remaining statements of the procedure's body will not be executed). Program control will also be transferred to this point, and the application will continue by assigning the return value of Square to variable dblSquareSideA. These same actions will occur again when program control reaches the second call to Square on line 148. With this call, the value passed to Square is the value entered into the **Length of side B:** TextBox (after this value has been passed to function Val), and the value returned is assigned to variable dblSquareSideB.

8. ***Calling a preexisting method of the FCL.*** Add lines 150–158 of Fig. 13.9 to the Else's body of the If...Then...Else statement in your application. Line 152 adds the square of side A and the square of side B, resulting in the square of the hypotenuse, which is assigned to variable dblSquareHypotenuse. Line 156 then calls FCL method Sqrt of class Math (by using the dot operator). This method will calculate the square root of the square of the hypotenuse to find the length of the hypotenuse.

Figure 13.9   Completing the btnCalculate_Click event handler.

9. ***Running the application.*** Select **Debug > Start** to run the application. Enter 3 into the **Length of side A:** TextBox and 4 into the **Length of side B:** TextBox. Click the **Calculate Hypotenuse** Button. The output is shown in Fig. 13.10. Click the running application's close box to terminate execution.

Error-Prevention Tip

Small procedures are easier to test, debug and understand than are large ones.

Figure 13.10   **Hypotenuse Calculator** application executing.

10. ***Closing the solution.*** Select **File > Close Solution**.

You have now successfully created a `Function` procedure. You have also tested this `Function` procedure (by running the application) to confirm that it works correctly. This `Function` procedure can now be used in any Visual Basic .NET application where you wish to calculate the square of a `Double`. All you need to do is include the procedure definition in your application. This is an example of code reuse, which helps programmers create application's faster.

As demonstrated in the **Hypotenuse Calculator** application, the procedure call used to call a `Function` procedure follows the format

name(*argument list*)

There must be one argument in the argument list of the procedure call for each parameter in the parameter list of the procedure header. The arguments also must be compatible with the parameters' types (that is, Visual Basic .NET must be able to assign the value of the argument to its corresponding parameter variable). For example, a parameter of type `Double` could receive the value of 53547.350009, 22 or –.03546, but not `"hello"`, because a `Double` variable cannot contain a `String`. If a procedure does not receive any values, the parameter list is empty (that is, the procedure name is followed by an empty set of parentheses). You will study procedure parameters in detail in Tutorial 15.

As you saw in the previous example, the statement

`Return` *expression*

can occur anywhere in a `Function` procedure body and returns the value of *expression* to the caller. If necessary, Visual Basic .NET attempts to convert the value of *expression* to the `Function` procedure's return type. `Functions` `Return` exactly one value. When a `Return` statement is executed, control returns immediately to the point at which that `Function` procedure was called.

You will now create another `Function` procedure. This procedure, which is part of the **Maximum** application, returns the largest of three numbers input by the user. In the box, *Creating a `Function` Procedure That Returns the Largest of Three Numbers*, you will create the **Maximum** application.

Creating a *Function* Procedure That Returns the Largest of Three Numbers

1. ***Copying the template to your work folder.*** Copy the `C:\Examples\Tutorial13\TemplateApplication\Maximum` folder to `C:\SimplyVB`.

2. ***Opening the template application.*** Double click `Maximum.sln` in the `Maximum` folder to open the application in Visual Studio .NET. Switch to design view. The `Form` will appear as in Fig. 13.11.

Figure 13.11 **Maximum** application in design view.

(cont.)

3. **Creating an event handler for the Maximum Button.** Double click the **Maximum** Button to create an event handler for this Button's `Click` event. Add lines 157–158 of Fig. 13.12 to the event handler. Add the comment on line 153 above your event handler. Lines 157–158 call `Function` procedure `Maximum` and pass it the three values the user has input into the application's `TextBox`es. Notice that `Maximum` has been underlined in blue, indicating a syntax error. This occurs because `Function` procedure `Maximum` has not yet been defined. You will define `Maximum` in the next step. This syntax error will occur whenever you call a procedure that is not recognized by Visual Studio .NET. Misspelling the name of a procedure in a procedure call will likewise cause a syntax error.

Calling a procedure that has not yet been defined is an error

Figure 13.12   Invoking `Function` procedure `Maximum`.

4. **Creating Function procedure Maximum.** Add lines 161–163 of Fig. 13.13 after event handler `btnMaximum_Click` and press *Enter*. Notice that the keywords `End Function` will be added for you by the IDE. The parameter list specifies that the values of the three arguments passed to `Maximum` will be stored in parameters `dblOne`, `dblTwo` and `dblThree`. The parameter list is followed by the keyword `As` and the return type `Double`.

Empty `Function` procedure `Maximum`

Figure 13.13   Maximum `Function` procedure.

(cont.)

5. **Adding functionality to Function procedure Maximum.** Add lines 165–171 of Fig. 13.14 to the body of Maximum. Line 165 creates a variable that will contain the maximum of the first two numbers passed to this procedure. This maximum is determined on line 168 by using the Max method of FCL class Math. This method takes two Doubles and returns the maximum of those two values. The value returned is assigned to variable dblTemporaryMaximum on line 168. You then compare that value to Function procedure Maximum's third parameter, dblThree, on line 169. The maximum determined on this line, dblFinalMaximum, is the maximum of the three values. Line 171 uses a Return statement to return this value. The Return statement terminates execution of the procedure and returns the result of dblFinalMaximum to the calling procedure. The result is returned to the point (line 157 of Fig. 13.12) where Maximum was called and is assigned to lblOutput's Text property.

Calling Math.Max to determine the maximum of two values

Figure 13.14 Math.Max returns the larger of its two arguments.

6. **Run the application.** Select **Debug > Start** to run the application. Enter a numeric value into each TextBox, and click the **Maximum** Button. Notice that the largest of the three values is displayed in the output Label. Terminate the application by clicking the close box. Select **File > Close Solution** to close the solution.

Figure 13.15 **Maximum** application executing.

7. **Closing the solution.** Select **File > Close Solution**.

SELF-REVIEW

1. A procedure is invoked by a(n) _____.

    a) callee   b) caller

    c) argument   d) parameter

2. The _____ statement in a Function procedure sends a value back to the calling procedure.

    a) Return   b) Back

    c) End   d) None of the above.

Answers: 1) b. 2) a.

13.4 Using Sub Procedures in the Wage Calculator Application

The **Calculate** Button's Click event handler in the original version of the **Wage Calculator** application (Tutorial 7) calculated the wages and displayed the result in a Label. In the box, *Creating a Sub Procedure within the **Wage Calculator** Application*, you will write Sub procedure DisplayPay to perform these tasks. **Sub procedures** are similar to Function procedures, with one important difference: Sub procedures do not return a value to the caller. When the user clicks the **Calculate** Button, event handler btnCalculate_Click calls Sub procedure DisplayPay.

Creating a Sub Procedure within the Wage Calculator Application

1. ***Copying the template to your work folder.*** Copy the C:\Examples\Tutorial13\TemplateApplication\WageCalculator2 folder to C:\SimplyVB.

2. ***Opening the template application.*** Double click WageCalculator2.sln in the WageCalculator2 folder to open the application in Visual Studio .NET.

3. ***Creating the btnCalculate_Click event handler.*** View the application's Form in design view. Double click the **Calculate** Button to generate the Click event handler.

4. ***Entering functionality to btnCalculate_Click.*** Add lines 130–139 of Fig. 13.16 to the empty event handler. This code calls procedure DisplayPay to calculate and display the wages. Lines 135–136 retrieve the user input from the TextBoxes and assign the values to variables declared in lines 131–132. Line 139 calls procedure DisplayPay, which you will define shortly. This procedure call takes two arguments: the hours worked (dblUserHours) and the hourly wage (decWage). Notice that the call to DisplayPay is underlined in blue, as the procedure has not yet been defined; for the moment, this is a syntax error. Also notice that the procedure's arguments in this example are variables. Arguments also can be constants or expressions.

Call to DisplayPay

Figure 13.16 btnCalculate_Click calls DisplayPay.

(cont.)

5. **Creating a Sub procedure.** After event handler btnCalculate_Click, add Sub procedure DisplayPay to your application (lines 142–167 of Fig. 13.17).

Add this code ———

```
140        End Sub ' btnCalculate_Click
141
142        ' calculate and display wages
143        Sub DisplayPay(ByVal dblHours As Double, _
144            ByVal decRate As Decimal)
145
146            ' declare variables
147            Dim decEarnings As Decimal
148            Const intHOUR_LIMIT As Integer = 40
149
150            ' determine wage amount
151            If dblHours <= intHOUR_LIMIT Then
152
153                ' earnings for regular wages
154                decEarnings = dblHours * decRate
155            Else
156
157                ' regular wages for first intHOUR_LIMIT hours
158                decEarnings = intHOUR_LIMIT * decRate
159
160                ' time and a half for overtime
161                decEarnings += ((dblHours - intHOUR_LIMIT) * _
162                    (1.5 * decRate))
163            End If
164
165            ' display result
166            lblEarningsResult.Text = String.Format("{0:C}", decEarnings)
167        End Sub ' DisplayPay
168
169        ' determine whether overtime pay has been earned
170        Function CheckOvertime(ByVal dblTotal As Double, _
```

Figure 13.17 Sub procedure DisplayPay definition.

Procedure DisplayPay receives the argument values and stores them in the parameters dblHours and decRate. Notice that the syntax of a Sub procedure is the same as the syntax of a Function procedure, with a few small changes. One change is that the Function keywords are replaced with Sub keywords (lines 143 and 167 of Fig. 13.17). Another difference is that there is no return type, because Sub procedures do not return a value.

Note that the variable decEarnings and the constant intHOUR_LIMIT have been moved to the DisplayPay procedure. (In Fig. 7.14 and 7.15 of Tutorial 7, they were located within the btnCalculate_Click event handler.) Because they are no longer needed in btnCalculate_Click, they should be removed from that event handler.

Lines 151–163 define the If...Then...Else statement that determines whether overtime must be calculated. The condition for this statement determines whether dblHours is less than or equal to constant intHOUR_LIMIT. If it is, then the employee's earnings without overtime are calculated. Otherwise, the employee's earnings including overtime are calculated. Line 166 displays the result (formatted as currency) in a Label.

When the End Sub statement on line 167 is encountered, control is returned to the calling procedure, btnCalculate_Click (line 139 in Fig. 13.16).

6. **Saving the project.** Select **File > Save All** to save all the solution's files.

The box, *Creating a Function Procedure within the* **Wage Calculator** *Application* shows you how to add Function procedure CheckOvertime to the **Wage Calculator** application. CheckOvertime will be used to determine whether an employee has worked overtime.

Creating a Function *Procedure within the* **Wage Calculator** *Application*	1. ***Creating a** Function **procedure header.*** Add Function procedure Check-Overtime (lines 169–179 of Fig. 13.18) to your application, after the DisplayPay procedure definition. Notice that the return type of the procedure is Boolean. This indicates that the value returned by the procedure must be a Boolean (that is constants, variables or expressions that evaluate to True or False).

Add this code ———

Figure 13.18   Function procedure CheckOverTime definition.

When CheckOvertime is called, program control is transferred to the beginning of this procedure at line 170. The arguments passed to this procedure (passed in the procedure call, which you will write in the next step) are stored in the parameter variables dblTotal and intLimit. Line 174 returns the Boolean value True, to indicate that the employee has worked overtime; line 176 returns the Boolean value False, to indicate that the employee has not worked any overtime. Program control and the value (either True or False) are returned to the line where CheckOvertime was initially called.

2. ***Modifying Sub procedure** DisplayPay.* In Sub procedure DisplayPay, replace the statement (line 151 of Fig. 13.17)

```
If dblHours <= intHOUR_LIMIT Then
```

with line 151 from Fig. 13.19. We modify DisplayPay so that it now calls Function procedure CheckOvertime to determine whether the employee qualifies for overtime pay.

Function procedure CheckOvertime is called (line 151) with the procedure call CheckOvertime(dblHours, intHOUR_LIMIT). When program control reaches this expression, the application calls Function procedure CheckOvertime. At this point, the application makes a copy of the value of dblHours and intHOUR_LIMIT (the arguments in the procedure call), and control transfers to the header of Function procedure CheckOvertime.

Common Programming Error

Failure to return a value from a Function procedure (for example, by forgetting to provide a Return statement) causes the procedure to return the default value for the *return-type*, often resulting in logic errors.

(cont.)

Call to procedure
CheckOvertime

Figure 13.19 DisplayPay calls Function procedure CheckOvertime.

The parameter variables in CheckOvertime's header are initialized to copies of dblHours's value and intHOUR_LIMIT's value. The value returned from CheckOvertime is compared to the value False on line 151.

Now when the **Calculate Hypotenuse** Button is clicked, DisplayPay is called and executed. Recall that Function procedure CheckOvertime is called by the DisplayPay Sub procedure. This sequence of calls is repeated every time the user clicks the **Calculate** Button.

3. ***Running the application.*** Select **Debug > Start** to run the application. Notice that the application works as it did in the test-drive.

4. ***Closing the solution.*** Select **File > Close Solution** to close the solution.

Figure 13.20 displays the code for the entire **Wage Calculator** application. Review each procedure's code to ensure that you understand the concepts presented in this tutorial.

```
1   Public Class FrmWageCalculator
2      Inherits System.Windows.Forms.Form
3
4      ' Visual Studio .NET generated code
5
6      ' calculate wages based on hourly pay and hours worked
7      Private Sub btnCalculate_Click(ByVal sender As System.Object, _
8         ByVal e As System.EventArgs) Handles btnCalculate.Click
9
10        ' declare variables
11        Dim dblUserHours As Double
12        Dim decWage As Decimal
13
14        ' assign values from user input
15        dblUserHours = Val(txtHours.Text)
16        decWage = Val(txtWage.Text)
17
18        ' call DisplayPay Sub procedure
19        DisplayPay(dblUserHours, decWage)
20     End Sub ' btnCalculate_Click
21
22     ' calculate and display wages
23     Sub DisplayPay(ByVal dblHours As Double, _
24        ByVal decRate As Decimal)
25
```

Figure 13.20 Code for **Wage Calculator** application. (Part 1 of 2.)

```
26          ' declare variables
27          Dim decEarnings As Decimal
28          Const intHOUR_LIMIT As Integer = 40
29
30          ' determine wage amount
31          If CheckOvertime(dblHours, intHOUR_LIMIT) = False Then
32
33             ' earnings for regular wages
34             decEarnings = dblHours * decRate
35          Else
36
37             ' regular wages for first intHOUR_LIMIT hours
38             decEarnings = intHOUR_LIMIT * decRate
39
40             ' time and a half for overtime
41             decEarnings += ((dblHours - intHOUR_LIMIT) * _
42                (1.5 * decRate))
43          End If
44
45          ' display result
46          lblEarningsResult.Text = String.Format("{0:C}", decEarnings)
47       End Sub ' DisplayPay
48
49       ' determine whether overtime pay has been earned
50       Function CheckOvertime(ByVal dblTotal As Double, _
51          ByVal intLimit As Integer) As Boolean
52
53          If dblTotal > intLimit Then
54             Return True    ' return True if over limit
55          Else
56             Return False  ' return False otherwise
57          End If
58
59       End Function ' CheckOvertime
60
61    End Class ' FrmWageCalculator
```

Figure 13.20 Code for **Wage Calculator** application. (Part 2 of 2.)

SELF-REVIEW

1. Arguments to a procedure can be _____.

   a) constants   b) expressions

   c) variables   d) All of the above.

2. The _____ is a comma-separated list of declarations in a procedure header.

   a) argument list   b) parameter list

   c) value list   d) variable list

Answers: 1) d. 2) b.

13.5 Using the Debugger: Debug Toolbar

Now, you continue your study of the debugger by learning about the debug toolbar, which contains Buttons for controlling the debugging process. These Buttons provide convenient access to actions in the **Debug** menu. In this section, you will learn how to use the debug toolbar's Buttons to verify that a procedure's code is executing correctly. In the box, *Using the Debugger: Debug Toolbar*, we use the debug toolbar Buttons to examine the WageCalculator2 application.

Using the Debugger:
Debug Toolbar

1. **Opening the application.** Open the completed **Wage Calculator** application.

2. **Opening the debug toolbar.** The debug toolbar contains Buttons for controlling the debugging process. These Buttons provide easy access to the **Debug** menu commands. To display the debug toolbar (Fig. 13.21), select **View > Toolbars > Debug**. The debug toolbar appears below the IDE menu bar (Fig. 13.22).

Figure 13.21   Debug toolbar.

3. **Setting a breakpoint.** Set a breakpoint on line 139 by clicking in the margin indicator bar (Fig. 13.22).

Figure 13.22   Setting a breakpoint.

4. **Starting the debugger.** To start the debugger, select **Debug > Start**. The WageCalculator2 application executes. Enter the value 7.50 in the **Hourly wage:** TextBox, and enter 35 in the **Weekly hours:** TextBox. Click the **Calculate** Button.

5. **Using the Step Into Button.** The Step Into Button (Fig. 13.21) executes the next statement (the yellow highlighted line) in the application. If the next statement to execute is a procedure call (Fig. 13.23) and the Step Into Button is clicked, control is transferred to the called procedure. The Step Into Button allows you to enter a procedure and confirm the procedure's execution. Click the Step Into Button to enter procedure DisplayPay (Fig. 13.24).

6. **Clicking the Step Over Button.** Click the Step Over Button to execute the current statement (lines 143–144 in Fig. 13.24) and transfer control to line 151 (Fig. 13.25).

(cont.)

Next statement to execute
is a procedure call

Figure 13.23 Statement calls procedure `DisplayPay`.

Control is transferred to the
procedure definition

Figure 13.24 Using the debug toolbar's Step Into `Button`.

Procedure `CheckOverTime`
will be executed without
stepping into it when the
Step Over `Button` is clicked

Figure 13.25 Using the debug toolbar's Step Over `Button`.

7. *Clicking the Step Over Button again*. Click the Step Over `Button`. This `Button` behaves like the Step Into `Button` when the next statement to execute does not contain a procedure call. If the next statement to execute contains a procedure call, the called procedure executes in its entirety (without transferring control and entering the procedure), and the yellow arrow advances to the next executable line in the current procedure (Fig. 13.26).

(cont.)

Figure 13.26 Using the debug toolbar's Step Over Button again.

8. ***Setting a breakpoint.*** Set a breakpoint at the end of procedure DisplayPay on line 167 (End Sub) of Fig. 13.27. You will make use of this breakpoint in the next step.

9. ***Using the Continue Button.*** Clicking the Continue Button will execute any statements between the next executable statement and the next breakpoint or the end of the current event handler, whichever comes first. Notice that there is one executable statement (line 167) before the breakpoint that was set in Step 8. Click the Continue Button. The next executable statement is now line 167 (Fig. 13.27). This feature is particularly useful when you have many lines of code before the next breakpoint that you do not want to step through line by line.

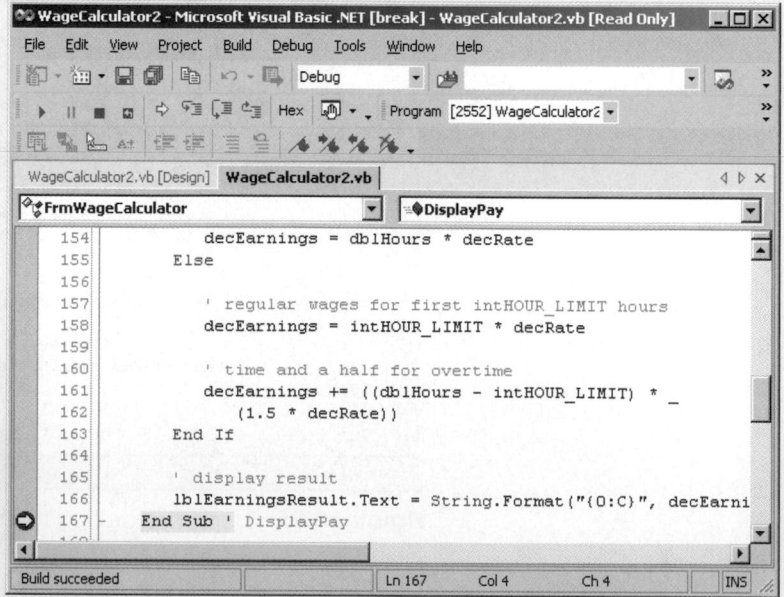

Figure 13.27 Using the debug toolbar's Continue Button.

10. ***Using the Stop Debugging Button.*** The Stop Debugging Button ends the debugging session and returns the IDE to design mode. Click the Stop Debugging Button.

(cont.)

11. ***Starting the debugger.*** We have one last feature we wish to present that will require you to start the debugger again. Start the debugger, as you did in Step 4, entering the same values as input.

12. ***Using the Step Into Button.*** Keep the breakpoint on line 139 (Fig. 13.22) and remove the breakpoint from line 167. Repeat Step 5.

13. ***Clicking the Step Out Button.*** After you have stepped into the `DisplayPay` procedure, click the Step Out `Button` to execute the statements in the procedure and return control to line 139, which contains the procedure call. Often, in lengthy procedures, you will want to look at a few key lines of code and then continue debugging the caller's code. This feature is useful for such situations, where you do not want to continue stepping through the entire procedure line by line.

14. ***Clicking the Stop Debugging Button.*** Click the Stop Debugging `Button` to end the debugging session.

15. ***Close the solution.*** Select **File > Close Solution** to close the solution.

SELF-REVIEW

1. During debugging, the _____ Button executes the remaining statements in the current procedure call and returns program control to the place where the procedure was called.

   a) Step Into   b) Step Out
   c) Step Over   d) Steps

2. The _____ Button behaves like the Step Into `Button` when the next statement to execute does not contain a procedure call.

   a) Step Into   b) Step Out
   c) Step Over   d) Steps

Answers: 1) b. 2) c.

13.6 Wrap-Up

In this tutorial, you learned about the difference between `Function` and `Sub` procedures, and you learned how procedures can be used to better organize an application. This tutorial introduced you to the concept called code reuse, showing how time and effort can be saved by using preexisting code. You used preexisting code provided by the FCL and learned to create your own code that can be used in other applications.

You were introduced to the syntax for creating and invoking the two types of procedures. You learned the components of a procedure, including the procedure header, parameter list and (in the case of `Function` procedures) the `Return` statement. After learning how to develop and write procedures, you learned about the order of execution that occurs from the line where a procedure is called (invoked) to the procedure definition, and returning control back to the point of invocation. In this tutorial's applications, you created three `Function` procedures—`Square`, `Maximum` and `CheckOvertime` and a `Sub` procedure (`DisplayPay`).

After creating the procedures in this tutorial, you learned how to debug the procedures in the application by using the `Buttons` in debug toolbar. These `Buttons` (including the Step Into, Step Out and Step Over `Buttons`) can be used to determine whether a procedure is executing correctly.

In the next tutorial, you learn about such controls as `GroupBoxes` and `DateTimePickers` and use them to build a **Shipping Time** application. This application controls information about a package being shipped from one location to another.

SKILLS SUMMARY

Invoking a Procedure

- Specify the procedure name and any arguments in parentheses.
- Ensure that the arguments passed match the procedure definition's parameters in number, type and order.

Using a Function Procedure

- Use a Function procedure when a value needs to be returned to the caller.
- Use keyword Function to begin the procedure.
- Specify a parameter list declaring each parameter's name and type. In the parameter list, use keyword ByVal in place of keyword Dim.
- Place the keyword As and the return type after the parenthesis that terminates the parameter list.
- Press the *Enter* key to generate the terminating End Function statement.
- Add code to the procedure's body to perform a specific task.
- Return a value with the Return statement.

Returning a Value From a Function Procedure

- Use the Return keyword followed by the value to be returned.

Creating a Sub Procedure

- Start the procedure header with keyword Sub.
- Specify a parameter list declaring each parameter's name and type. In the parameter list, use keyword ByVal in place of keyword Dim.
- Press the *Enter* key to generate the terminating End Sub statement.
- Add code to the procedure's body to perform a specific task.

KEY TERMS

ByVal—The keyword specifying that the calling procedure should pass a copy of its argument's value in the procedure call to the called procedure.

callee—The procedure being called.

caller—The procedure that calls another procedure.

divide-and-conquer technique—Constructing large applications from small, manageable pieces to make development and maintenance of large applications easier.

End Function Keywords—Indicates the end of a Function procedure.

End Sub Keywords—Indicates the end of a Sub procedure.

Function procedure—A procedure similar to a Sub procedure, with one important difference: Function procedures return a value to the caller, whereas Sub procedures do not.

method—A procedure contained in a class.

parameter list—A comma-separated list in which the procedure declares each parameter variable's name and type.

parameter variable—A variable declared in a procedure's parameter list that can be used in the body of the procedure.

procedure—A set of instructions for performing a particular task.

procedure body—The declarations and statements that appear after the procedure header but before the keywords End Sub or End Function. The procedure body contains Visual Basic .NET code that performs actions, generally by manipulating or interacting with the parameters from the parameter list.

procedure call—The procedure call invokes a procedure, and specifies the procedure name and provides information (arguments) that the callee (the procedure being called) requires to perform its task.

procedure definition—The procedure header, body and ending statement.

procedure header—The first line of a procedure (including the keyword Sub or Function, the procedure name, the parameter list and the Function procedure return type).

procedure name—Follows the keyword Sub or Function and distinguishes one procedure from another. A procedure name can be any valid identifier.

programmer-defined procedure—A procedure created by a programmer to meet the unique needs of a particular application.

Return keyword—Signifies the return statement that sends a value back to the procedure's caller.

return type—Data type of the result returned from a Function procedure.

Sub procedure—A procedure similar to a Function procedure, with one important difference: Sub procedures do not return a value to the caller, whereas Function procedures do.

CONTROLS, EVENTS, PROPERTIES & METHODS

Math This class provides methods used to perform common arithmetic calculations.

- **Methods**

  Min—Returns the smaller of two numeric values.
  Max—Returns the larger of two numeric values.
  Sqrt—Returns the square root of a numeric value.

MULTIPLE-CHOICE QUESTIONS

13.1 A procedure defined with keyword Sub _____.

a) must specify a return type   b) does not accept arguments

c) returns a value   d) does not return a value

13.2 The technique of developing large applications from small, manageable pieces is known as _____.

a) divide and conquer   b) returning a value

c) click and mortar   d) a building-block algorithm

13.3 What is the difference between Sub and Function procedures?

a) Sub procedures return values, Function procedures do not.

b) Function procedures return values, Sub procedures do not.

c) Sub procedures accept parameters, Function procedures do not.

d) Function procedures accept parameters, Sub procedures do not.

13.4 What occurs after a procedure call is made?

a) Control is given to the called procedure. After the procedure is run, the application continues execution at the point where the procedure call was made.

b) Control is given to the called procedure. After the procedure is run, the application continues execution with the statement after the called procedure's definition.

c) The statement before the procedure call is executed.

d) The application terminates.

13.5 Functions can return _____ value(s).

a) zero   b) exactly one

c) one or more   d) any number of

13.6 Which of the following must be true when making a procedure call?

a) The number of arguments in the procedure call must match the number of parameters in the procedure header.

b) The argument types must be compatible with their corresponding parameter types.

c) Both a and b.   d) None of the above.

13.7 Which of the following statements correctly returns the variable intValue from a Function procedure?

a) Return Dim intValue   b) Return intValue As Integer

c) intValue Return   d) Return intValue

13.8 The _____ Button executes the next statement in the application.

a) Step Into

b) Step Out

c) Step Over

d) Steps

13.9 The first line of a procedure (including the keyword Sub or Function, the procedure name, the parameter list and the Function procedure return type) is known as the procedure _____.

a) body

b) title

c) caller

d) header

13.10 Method _____ of class Math calculates the square root of the value passed as an argument.

a) SquareRoot

b) Root

c) Sqrt

d) Square

EXERCISES

13.11 (*Temperature Converter Application*) Write an application that performs various temperature conversions. The application should be capable of performing two types of conversions: degrees Fahrenheit to degrees Celsius and degrees Celsius to degrees Fahrenheit.

a) *Copying this application's folder to the work folder.* Copy the TemperatureConversion folder from C:\Examples\Tutorial13\Exercises to C:\SimplyVB.

b) *Convert Fahrenheit to Celsius.* To convert degrees Fahrenheit to degrees Celsius, use this formula:

```
dblCelsius = (5 / 9) * (dblFahrenheit - 32)
```

c) *Convert Celsius to Fahrenheit.* To convert degrees Celsius to degrees Fahrenheit, use this formula:

```
dblFahrenheit = (9 / 5) * dblCelsius + 32
```

d) *Adding event handlers to your application.* Double click each Button to add the proper event handlers to your application. These event handlers will call procedures (that you will define in the next step) to convert the degrees entered to either Fahrenheit or Celsius. Each event handler will display the result in the application's output Label.

e) *Adding Function procedures to your application.* Create Function procedures to perform each conversion, using the formulas above. The user should provide the temperature to convert.

f) *Formatting the temperature output.* To format the temperature information, use the String.Format method. Use F as the formatting code to limit the temperature to two decimal places.

Figure 13.28 Temperature Converter GUI.

13.12 *(Display Square Application)* Write an application that displays a solid square composed of a character input by the user (Fig. 13.29). The user also should input the size.

a) *Copying this application's folder to your work folder.* Copy the folder DisplaySquare from C:\Examples\Tutorial13\Exercises to C:\SimplyVB.

b) *Adding a Sub procedure.* Write a Sub procedure DisplaySquare to display the solid square. The size should be specified by the Integer parameter intSize. The character that fills the square should be specified by the String parameter strFillChar-acter. You should use a For...Next statement nested within another For...Next statement to create the square. The outer For...Next specifies what row is currently being displayed. The inner For...Next appends all the characters that form the row to a display String.

c) *Adding an event handler for your Button's Click event.* Double click the **Display Square** Button to create the event handler. Program the event handler to call procedure DisplaySquare.

d) *Displaying the output.* Use the multiline TextBox provided to display the square. For example, if intSize is 8 and strFillCharacter is #, the application should look similar to Fig. 13.29.

Figure 13.29   **Display Square** application.

13.13 (*Miles Per Gallon Application*) Drivers often want to know the miles per gallon their cars get so they can estimate gasoline costs. Develop an application that allows the user to input the number of miles driven and the number of gallons used for a tank of gas.

a) *Copying this application's folder to the work folder.* Copy the folder MilesPerGal-lon from C:\Examples\Tutorial13\Exercises to C:\SimplyVB.

b) *Calculating the miles per gallon.* Write a Function procedure MilesPerGallon that takes the number of miles driven and gallons used (entered by the user), calculates the amount of miles per gallon and returns the miles per gallon for a tankful of gas.

c) *Displaying the result.* Create a Click event handler for the **Calculate MPG** Button that invokes the Function procedure MilesPerGallon and displays the result returned from the procedure as in Fig. 13.30.

Figure 13.30   **Miles Per Gallon** application.

What does this code do? ▶

13.14 What does the following code do? Assume this procedure is invoked by using Mys-tery(70, 80). [*Note*: Code listing is continued at the top of the next page.]

```
1   Sub Mystery(ByVal intNumber1 As Integer, ByVal _
2       intNumber2 As Integer)
3
4       Dim intX As Integer
5       Dim dblY As Double
```

(cont.)

```
6
7      intX = intNumber1 + intNumber2
8      dblY = intX / 2
9
10     If dblY <= 60 Then
11        lblResult.Text = "<= 60 "
12     Else
13        lblResult.Text = "Result is " & dblY
14     End If
15
16  End Sub ' Mystery
```

What's wrong with this code? ▶ **13.15** Find the error(s) in the following code, which should take an `Integer` value as an argument and return the value of that argument multiplied by two.

```
1   Function TimesTwo(ByVal intNumber As Integer) As Integer
2
3      Dim intResult As Integer
4
5      intResult = intNumber * 2
6   End Function ' CheckValue
```

Using the Debugger ▶ **13.16** (*Gas Pump Application*) The **Gas Pump** application calculates the cost of gas at a local gas station. This gas station charges $1.41 per gallon for **Regular** grade gas, $1.47 per gallon for **Special** grade gas and $1.57 per gallon for **Super+** grade gas. The user enters the number of gallons to purchase and clicks the desired grade. The application calls a Sub procedure to compute the total cost from the number of gallons entered and the selected grade. While testing your application, you noticed that one of your totals was incorrect, given the input.

Figure 13.31 Gas Pump application executing correctly.

a) *Copying the application*. Copy the `GasPumpIncorrect` folder from `C:\Examples\Tutorial13\Debugger` to your `Debugger` folder.

b) *Running the application*. Run the application, and determine which total is incorrect.

c) *Setting a breakpoint*. Set a breakpoint at the beginning of the event handler that is providing incorrect output. For instance, if the **Regular** `Button` is providing incorrect output when clicked, add a breakpoint at the beginning of that `Button`'s `Click` event handler. Use the debugger to help find any logic error(s) in the application.

d) *Modifying the application*. Once you have located the error(s), modify the application so that it behaves correctly.

Programming Challenge ▶ **13.17** (*Prime Numbers Application*) An `Integer` greater than 1 is said to be prime if it is divisible by only 1 and itself. For example, 2, 3, 5 and 7 are prime numbers, but 4, 6, 8 and 9 are not. Write an application that takes two numbers (representing a lower bound and an upper bound) and determines all of the prime numbers within the specified bounds, inclusive.

a) *Creating the application*. Create an application named PrimeNumbers and have its GUI appear as shown in Fig. 13.32. Add an event handler for the **Calculate Primes** Button's Click event.

b) *Checking for prime numbers*. Write a Function procedure Prime that returns True if a number is prime, False otherwise.

c) *Limiting user input*. Allow users to enter a lower bound (intLower) and an upper bound (intUpper). Prevent the user from entering negative bounds, or an upper bound that is smaller than the lower bound.

d) *Displaying the prime numbers*. Call Function procedure Prime from your event handler to determine which numbers between the lower and upper bounds are prime. Then have the event handler display the prime numbers in a multiline, scrollable TextBox, as in Fig. 13.32.

Figure 13.32　**Prime Numbers** application.

14 TUTORIAL

Objectives

In this tutorial, you will learn to:
- Create and manipulate **Date** variables.
- Execute code at regular intervals using a **Timer** control.
- Retrieve **Date** input with a **DateTimePicker** control.
- Group controls using a **GroupBox** control.

Outline

Shipping Time Application

Using Dates and Timers

Many companies rely on date and time information in daily operations, from airlines to shipping companies. These companies often require applications that reliably perform date and time calculations. In this tutorial, you will create an application that performs calculations using the **Date** structure, which allows you to store and manipulate date and time information. You will also learn how to use a **DateTimePicker** control to retrieve date and time information from the user. Finally, you will learn how to use a **Timer**—a Visual Basic .NET control that allows you to execute code at specified time intervals.

14.1 Test-Driving the Shipping Time Application

In this tutorial, you will build the **Shipping Time** application. This application must meet the following requirements:

Application Requirements

A seafood distributor has asked you to create an application that will calculate the delivery time for fresh seafood shipped from Portland, Maine to its distribution center in Las Vegas, Nevada, where only the freshest seafood is accepted. The distributor has arrangements with local airlines to guarantee that seafood will ship on either flights that leave at noon or ones that leave at midnight. However, for security reasons, the airport requires the distributor to drop off the seafood at the airport at least one hour before each flight. When the distributor specifies the drop-off time, the application should display the delivery time in Las Vegas. This application should take into account the 3-hour time difference (it's 3 hours earlier in Las Vegas) and the 6-hour flight time between the two cities. The application should allow the user to select drop-off times within the current day (seafood must be shipped within a day to guarantee freshness). The application should also include a running clock that displays the current time.

This application calculates the shipment's delivery time from the user's drop-off time, taking into account factors such as transit time and time zones. You will use the **DateTimePicker** control to enable the user to enter the drop-off time.

You will use the Date structure properties and methods to calculate the delivery time. You begin by test-driving the completed application.

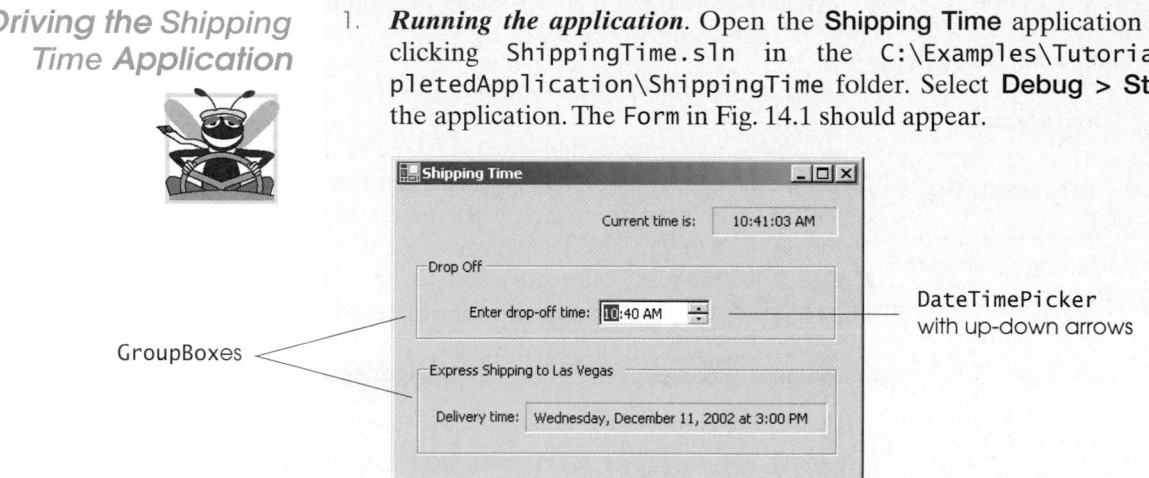

1. ***Running the application.*** Open the **Shipping Time** application by double clicking `ShippingTime.sln` in the `C:\Examples\Tutorial14\Com-pletedApplication\ShippingTime` folder. Select **Debug > Start** to run the application. The Form in Fig. 14.1 should appear.

Figure 14.1 Shipping Time application.

2. ***Entering a drop-off time.*** Notice that the default drop-off time is set to your computer's current time when the application is loaded (opened). When you change the drop-off time, the Label displaying the delivery time will display the delivery time based on the new time. Notice that if you select a time before 11:00 A.M., the shipment will arrive in Las Vegas at 3:00 P.M. If you specify a time between 11:00 A.M. and 11:00 P.M., the shipment will arrive in Las Vegas at 3:00 A.M. the following day. Finally, if you specify a time after 11:00 P.M., the shipment will not arrive until 3:00 P.M. the following day.

   The time displayed in the **Current time is:** Label will update to the current time once each second. However, the drop-off time displayed in the DateTimePicker will change only if you select different values by using the up and down arrows or by typing in a new value.

3. ***Closing the application.*** Click the application's close box to terminate program execution.

4. ***Closing the solution.*** Select **File > Close Solution**.

14.2 Date Variables

Choosing the correct data type in which to store information can decrease development time by simplifying code. For example, if you are counting whole numbers, variables of type Integer are your best choice; if you need to store monetary values, you should use variables of type Decimal. However, if you want to store date information (such as the day, month, year and time), there is no obvious primitive-data type. For example, if you used an Integer to count days, you would also need separate variables to keep track of the month, day of the week, year and other date-related information. Keeping track of all of these variables would be a complicated task and could slow the development of applications that require date and time information.

Declaring a Date Variable

The Date structure in Visual Basic .NET simplifies manipulation, storage and display of date (and time) information. A **Date** variable, which is created from the Date structure, stores information about a point in time (for example, 12:00:00 A.M. on January 1, 2003). Using code, you can access a Date's properties, including the day, the hour and the minute. Your **Shipping Time** application requires calculations involving time, so you will use `Date` variables to store and manipulate this information.

Because the `Date` type is a structure, you must use the **New** keyword when creating a `Date` value. In the code,

Date constructor ────────────

Date variable ──────────

```
Dim dtmDelivery As Date = New Date(2003, 1, 1, 0, 0, 0)
```

a new `Date` variable named `dtmDelivery` is declared. The **New** keyword calls the `Date` structure's constructor. A **constructor** is a procedure that initializes a class object or structure value when it is created. You will use FCL class constructors in Tutorial 16. You will also learn how to write your own constructors in Tutorial 19. Notice that this particular constructor takes six arguments: year, month, day, hour, minute and second. These values are described in Fig. 14.2.

Good Programming Practice

Prefix `Date` variable names with `dtm` (short for date/time).

Argument	Range	Description
Initializing a Date variable using `New Date(`*year*`,` *month*`,` *day*`,` *hour*`,` *minute*`,` *second*`)`		
year	`Integer` values 1–9999	Specifies the year.
month	`Integer` values 1–12	Specifies the month of the year.
day	`Integer` values 1–*number of days in month*	Specifies the day of the month. Each month has 28 to 31 days depending on the month and year.
hour	`Integer` values 0–23	Specifies the hour of the day. The value 0 represents 12:00 A.M.
minute	`Integer` values 0–59	Specifies the minute of the hour.
second	`Integer` values 0–59	Specifies the number of elapsed seconds in the current minute.

Figure 14.2 `Date` constructor arguments.

Using `Date` Members

After assigning a value to a `Date` variable, you can access that variable's properties using the member-access (dot) operator, as follows:

```
intYear = dtmDelivery.Year      ' retrieves Date dtmDelivery's year
intMonth = dtmDelivery.Month    ' retrieves Date dtmDelivery's month
intDay = dtmDelivery.Day        ' retrieves Date dtmDelivery's day
intHour = dtmDelivery.Hour      ' retrieves Date dtmDelivery's hour
intMinute = dtmDelivery.Minute  ' retrieves Date dtmDelivery's minute
intSecond = dtmDelivery.Second  ' retrieves Date dtmDelivery's second
```

In this tutorial, you will use several `Date` properties and methods that can be accessed through the member-access operator.

Values in `Date` variables cannot be added like numeric-primitive-data types such as `Integers` and `Decimals`. Instead of using arithmetic operators to add or subtract values in `Date` variables, you must call the correct method, using the member-access operator. Figure 14.3 demonstrates how to perform various calculations with `Date` variables.

Visual Basic .NET statement	Result
Assume dtmDelivery has been initialized with a Date value.	
`dtmDelivery = dtmDelivery.AddHours(3)`	Add 3 hours.
`dtmDelivery = dtmDelivery.AddMinutes(-5)`	Subtract 5 minutes.
`dtmDelivery = dtmDelivery.AddDays(1)`	Add 1 day.

Figure 14.3 `Date` methods that perform various calculations. (Part 1 of 2.)

Visual Basic .NET statement	Result
`dtmDelivery = dtmDelivery.AddMinutes(30)`	Add 30 minutes.
`dtmDelivery = dtmDelivery.AddHours(-12)`	Subtract 12 hours.

Figure 14.3 Date methods that perform various calculations. (Part 2 of 2.)

Note that each "add" method does not actually change the value of the Date variable on which that method is called. Instead, each "add" method returns a Date value containing the result of the calculation. To change the value of Date variable `dtmDelivery`, you must assign to `dtmDelivery` the value returned by the "add" method.

Visual Basic .NET provides a simple way to assign the current date and time to a Date variable. You can use the Now property to assign your computer's current date and time to a Date variable:

```
Dim dtmCurrentTime As Date = Date.Now
```

Much like methods `MessageBox.Show` and `String.Format`, you can access the Now property of the Date structure by following the name of the structure with the member-access operator and the name of the property. Notice that this assignment does not require keyword New. This is because the `Date.Now` property returns a Date value.

Now that you are familiar with Date variables, you will design the **Shipping Time** application by using two new controls—the GroupBox control and the DateTimePicker control. A **GroupBox** control groups related controls visually by drawing a labeled box around them. The **DateTimePicker** control allows users to enter date and time information.

SELF-REVIEW

1. The _____ property of the Date structure retrieves your computer's current date and time.

    a) `Time`   b) `Now`

    c) `CurrentTime`   d) `DateTime`

2. The fourth argument to the Date constructor specifies the variable's _____.

    a) day   b) year

    c) hour   d) minute

Answers: 1) b. 2) c.

14.3 Building the Shipping Time Application: Design Elements

You are now ready to begin analyzing the problem statement and developing pseudocode. The following pseudocode describes the actions that the **Shipping Time** application needs to execute in order to solve the problem statement:

When the Form loads
    Display the time at which the shipment will arrive in Las Vegas

When the user changes the drop-off time
    Update the time at which the shipment will arrive in Las Vegas

After one second has elapsed
    Update the current time displayed

The ACE table shown in Fig. 14.4 indicates which events will drive this application and lists controls whose properties will be modified while the application runs.

	Action	Control	Event
Action/Control/Event (ACE) Table for the *Shipping Time Application*	Label the application's controls	lblCurrentTimeIs, lblDropOff, lblDeliveryTime	
	Display the time at which the shipment will arrive in Las Vegas	FrmShippingTime, lblLasVegasTime	Load (of Form)
	Update the time at which the shipment will arrive in Las Vegas	dtpDropOff	ValueChanged
	Update and display the current time	tmrClock	Tick

Figure 14.4   ACE table for the **Shipping Time** application.

Now, you will begin building the **Shipping Time** application from the template provided. The box, *Placing Controls in a GroupBox*, demonstrates how to insert a GroupBox control into your application.

Placing Controls in a GroupBox

1. ***Copying the template application to your work folder.*** Copy the Shipping-Time folder from C:\Examples\Tutorial14\TemplateApplication to your SimplyVB folder.

2. ***Opening the template application in your work folder.*** Open the C:\SimplyVB\Tutorial14\ShippingTime folder to locate the template version of the **Shipping Time** application. Double click ShippingTime.sln to open the application in Visual Studio .NET.

3. ***Displaying the template Form.*** Double click ShippingTime.vb in the **Solution Explorer** window to display the Form in Visual Studio .NET.

4. ***Inserting a GroupBox control in the Form.*** The template includes a Group-Box that displays the seafood shipment delivery time. Add a second Group-Box to contain the drop-off time by double clicking the **GroupBox** control,

    in the **Toolbox**. Change the Text property to Drop Off and the Name property to fraDropOff. Change the Location property to 16, 56 and the Size property to 328, 64. After these modifications, your Form should look like Fig. 14.5.

    ![Good Programming Practice icon] **Good Programming Practice**

    Prefix **GroupBox** control names with **fra** (short for frame, the name of **GroupBox**es in earlier versions of Visual Basic).

    Newly created **GroupBox** displaying the text **Drop Off**

    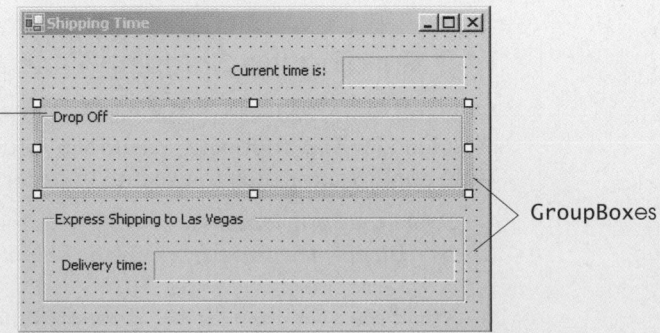

    Figure 14.5   GroupBox controls on the **Shipping Time** Form.

     GUI Design Tip

    GroupBox titles should be concise and should use book-title capitalization.

5. ***Creating Labels inside the GroupBox.*** To place a Label inside the Group-Box, click the **Label** tab in the **Toolbox**, then click inside the GroupBox to place the Label inside the GroupBox (Fig. 14.6).

(cont.)
Change the `Text` property of the `Label` to `Enter drop-off time:` and the `Name` property to `lblDropOff`. Then change the position and size of the `Label` by setting its `Location` property to `40, 32` and the `Size` property to `104, 21`. Change the `Label`'s `TextAlign` property to `MiddleLeft`.

Before clicking inside the `GroupBox`

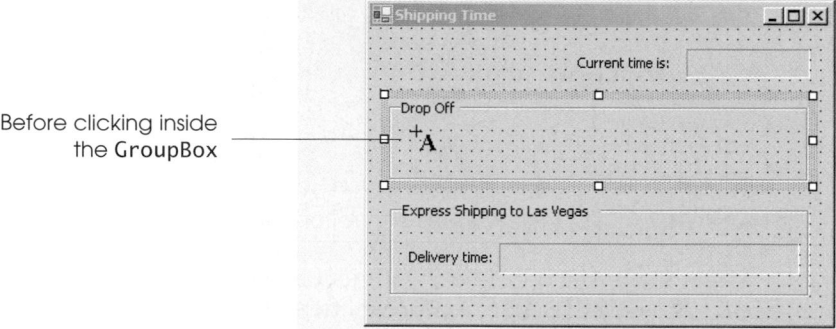

Figure 14.6 Adding a `Label` to a `GroupBox`.

Notice that the `Location` values you entered are measured from the top-left corner of the `GroupBox` and not from the top-left corner of the `Form`. Objects, such as `Forms`, `GroupBoxes` and `Panels` (which you'll use in Tutorial 19), that contain controls are called **containers**. `Location` values for controls in an application are measured from the top-left corner of the object that contains them.

If a `GroupBox` is placed over a control that is already on the `Form`, the control will be behind the `GroupBox` (that is, the `GroupBox` hides the control by covering it). To avoid this problem, remove all controls from the area in which you wish to place the `GroupBox` control before inserting it. You can then either drag and drop existing controls into the `GroupBox` or add new controls as needed by using the method described earlier.

GUI Design Tip

Use `GroupBoxes` to group related controls on the `Form` visually.

6. ***Saving the project.*** Select **File > Save All** to save all the solution's files.

You have now added a `GroupBox` and a `Label` to the **Shipping Time** application to display the drop-off time. In the box, *Creating and Customizing the DateTimePicker*, you will add a `DateTimePicker` control to retrieve the drop-off time from the user.

Recall that the `DateTimePicker` retrieves date and time information from the user. The `DateTimePicker` allows you to select from a variety of predefined date and time formats to present to the user (for example, date formats like 12/31/02 and December 31, 2002; and time formats like 2:00 PM and 14:00) or you can create your own format. The date and time information is then stored in a variable of type `Date`, which you can manipulate using `Date` methods. Note that the format limits the date and/or time information the user can specify. However, the format used to present the date and/or time does not alter the value stored in the `DateTimePicker`.

Creating and Customizing the *DateTimePicker*

1. ***Adding the DateTimePicker.*** To add a `DateTimePicker` to your application, click the **DateTimePicker** control,

in the **Toolbox**, then click to the right of `lblDropOff` to place the `DateTimePicker`. Your `Form` should look similar to Fig. 14.7. (Your control will contain your computer's current date.)

2. ***Modifying the DateTimePicker.*** With the `DateTimePicker` selected, change the `Name` property of the `DateTimePicker` to `dtpDropOff`.

GUI Design Tip

Each `DateTimePicker` should have a corresponding descriptive `Label`.

(cont.)

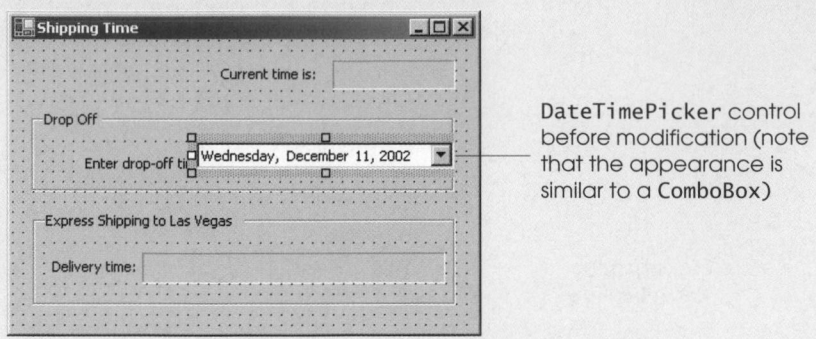

Figure 14.7   `DateTimePicker` control on the Form.

GUI Design Tip

Use a `DateTimePicker` to retrieve date and time information from a user.

Align the `DateTimePicker` with its `Label` by setting its `Size` property to 88, 21 and its `Location` property to 144, 32. Next, change its **Format** property to `Custom`. This indicates that you will specify how the date will appear in the `DateTimePicker`.

3. ***Specifying a custom display format.*** When the `DateTimePicker`'s `Format` property is set to `Custom`, it uses the custom format that you specify in the **CustomFormat** property. Notice that the `DateTimePicker` now displays the date in the format 1/1/2003, the default format when the `CustomFormat` property has not been set.

Good Programming Practice

Prefix `DateTimePicker` control names with `dtp`.

   Set the value of the `CustomFormat` property to `hh:mm tt`. The "hh" displays the hour as a number from 01 to 12, the ":" inserts a colon and the "mm" indicates that the number of minutes from 00 to 59 should follow the colon. The "`tt`" indicates that AM or PM should appear, depending on the time of day. Note that this property eliminates the problem of a user entering a letter or symbol when the application expects a number—the `DateTimePicker` will not allow values in any format other than what you specify in the `CustomFormat` property.

4. ***Using up-down arrows in the DateTimePicker.*** Set the `DateTimePicker`'s **ShowUpDown** property to `True`. This setting allows the user to select the date or time by clicking the up or down arrows that appear on the right side of the control, much like a `NumericUpDown` control. When the property is set to `False` (which is the default), a down arrow will appear on the right side of the control (Fig. 14.7), much like a `ComboBox`. Clicking the down arrow will cause a month calendar to appear, allowing the user to select a date (but not a time). A demonstration of the month calendar is shown in the Controls, Events, Properties & Methods section at the end of this tutorial. Because the user needs to enter only the time of day, you will use up-down arrows to display the time.

GUI Design Tip

If the user should specify a time of day or a date and time, set the `DateTimePicker`'s `ShowUpDown` property to `True`. If the user should specify only a date, set the `DateTimePicker`'s `ShowUpDown` property to `False` to allow the user to select a day from the month calendar.

Error-Prevention Tip

If the user should specify a date and/or time, use a `DateTimePicker` control to prevent the user from entering invalid date and/or time values.

Figure 14.8   Customized `DateTimePicker` control on the Form.

5. ***Saving the project.*** Select **File > Save All** to save all the solution's files.

The final control you will add to the Form is a Timer. In the box, *Creating a Timer Control*, you will use the Timer to place a clock on the Form so that users can see the current time of day while using the application.

<table>
<tr>
<td valign="top">

Creating a Timer Control

</td>
<td valign="top">

1. ***Adding a Timer control.*** A **Timer** control is an object that can "wake up" every millisecond (1/1000 of a second) by generating a Tick event. By default, the Timer "wakes up" every 100 milliseconds (1/10 of a second). Each time the Tick event is generated, its event handler is executed. You can customize the "wake period" (the amount of time between each instance of the Timer's Tick event) and the code that it executes (the event handler for the Tick event) so that a certain task is performed once every "wake up" period.

   Add a Timer to the Form by clicking the **Timer** control,

   in the **Toolbox** and dragging and dropping it anywhere on the Form. Notice that the Timer does not actually appear on the Form; it appears below the Windows Form Designer in an area called the **component tray** (Fig. 14.9). The Timer control is placed in the component tray because it is not part of the graphical user interface—users never see the Timer control.

</td>
</tr>
</table>

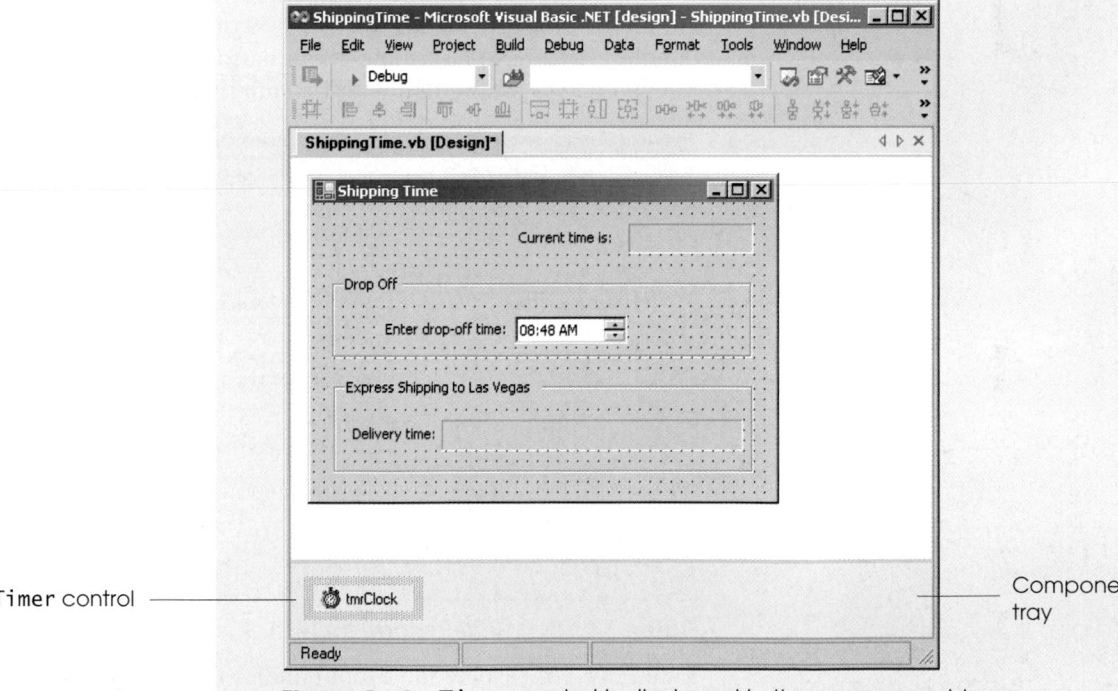

Timer control ⎯⎯⎯⎯⎯⎯⎯⎯⎯ / Component tray

Figure 14.9   Timer control is displayed in the component tray.

> **Good Programming Practice**
>
> Prefix Timer control names with tmr.

2. ***Customizing the Timer control.*** Rename the Timer by setting its Name property to tmrClock. To allow the Timer's Tick event to be raised, set the Timer's Enabled property to True. Then set the Timer's **Interval** property to 1000, which specifies the number of milliseconds between Tick events (1,000 milliseconds = 1 second).

3. ***Saving the project.*** Select **File > Save All** to save all the solution's files.

SELF-REVIEW   1. If a GroupBox is placed over a control that is already on the Form, the control will be
_____ the GroupBox.

      a) replaced by   b) inside

      c) behind   d) in front of

2. Setting the Format property of the DateTimePicker control to _____ indicates that you will specify how the date will appear in the DateTimePicker.

    a) Custom   b) Unique

    c) User   d) Other

Answers: 1) c. 2) a.

14.4 Creating the Shipping Time Application: Inserting Code

Now that you have completed the visual design of the **Shipping Time** application, you will complete the application by inserting code. You will begin coding the application's functionality by inserting code to create a clock on the application that updates the current time every second. You will then write code that displays the delivery time from Portland to Las Vegas. You will implement this feature by inserting code that is executed when the Form loads or whenever the user specifies a new drop-off time. In the box, *Coding the **Shipping Time** Application's Clock*, you will write the code to create the clock.

Coding the Shipping Time Application's Clock

1. ***Inserting code to handle the Timer's Tick event.*** Double click the Timer control in the component tray to generate the empty event handler for the Tick event. (A Tick event is raised once per Interval, as set in the Timer's Interval property.) Add lines 157–159 of Fig. 14.10 to the body of the event handler. Be sure to insert line-continuation and newline characters as shown in Fig. 14.10 to ensure that your line numbers will match those in the text.

Printing the current time

Figure 14.10 Inserting code for a Tick event.

Lines 154–161 display the event handler for the Tick event, which executes every second. Date property Now retrieves your computer's time when it is accessed. The event handler takes this information and formats it to match the format you specify, "hh:mm:ss tt". The Text property of lblCurrentTime is then set to the formatted String for display to the user. Recall that the 0 corresponds to Date.Now and the text following the first colon contains your format information. You are already familiar with the purpose of hh:mm and tt. The :ss following mm indicates that a colon followed by the number of seconds (00–59) should be displayed.

2. ***Saving the application.*** Select **File > Save All** to save your work.

Now that you have coded your application's clock, using the Timer's Tick event handler, you will insert code to display a delivery time when the application opens. You will begin by creating a Load event handler for your application.

Using Code to Display a Delivery Time

1. ***Adding the FrmShippingTime_Load event handler.*** When an application executes, the Form is displayed. However, sometimes you also want a specific action to occur when the application opens but before the Form displays. To execute code when the application first opens, create an event handler for the **Load** event. To create a Load event handler, return to the Windows Form Designer by clicking the **ShippingTime.vb [Design]** tab. Double click an empty area of the Form to generate the Load event handler and enter code view.

2. ***Storing the current date.*** Copy line 168 from Fig. 14.11 into the Load event handler. Line 168 stores the current date in variable dtmCurrentTime. (You will store the date as a variable so that you can preserve information about the current date for use later in the event handler.)

Storing the current time in dtmCurrentTime

Figure 14.11 Storing the current time.

3. ***Setting the drop-off hours.*** Add lines 170–174 of Fig. 14.12 to the FrmShippingTime_Load event handler. These lines set the MinDate and MaxDate properties for dtpDropOff. The **MinDate** property specifies the earliest value that the DateTimePicker will allow the user to enter. The **MaxDate** property specifies the latest value that the DateTimePicker will allow the user to enter. Together, these two properties set the range of drop-off times from which the user can select.

Setting the range of drop-off times

Figure 14.12 Setting the MinDate and MaxDate properties.

(cont.)

To guarantee freshness, the seafood shipment should be dropped off at the airline within the current day; therefore, the earliest drop-off time (Min-Date) is set to 12:00 A.M. of the current day (lines 171–172), and the latest drop-off time (MaxDate) is set to 12:00 A.M. the following day (line 174). Notice that the MaxDate value is calculated by adding one day to the MinDate value using the AddDays method. Recall that the AddDays method does not change the Date value on which it operates—it returns a new Date value. This value is assigned to the MaxDate property on line 174.

The Date constructor (called in line 171) creates a value that stores a time. Recall that the first parameter is the year, the second is the month and the third is the day. The last three parameters specify the hour, minute and number of seconds. A Date variable's Year property returns the value of its year as an Integer (for example, 2003). Its Month property returns the value of the Date variable's month as an Integer (for example, 6 for June). Finally, the Date variable's Day property returns the day of the month (an Integer between 1 and 31, depending on the month and year). You assigned to the dtmCurrentTime variable the value of the current time (using Date.Now); therefore, the first three arguments combine to specify the current date.

4. ***Calling the DisplayDeliveryTime procedure.*** Add lines 176–177 of Fig. 14.13 to call the DisplayDeliveryTime procedure. Notice that DisplayDeliveryTime is underlined in blue. This is due to the syntax error you introduce when you call a procedure that has not yet been written. You will write this procedure in the box, *Coding the DisplayDeliveryTime Procedure*. The DisplayDeliveryTime calculates the delivery time in Las Vegas and displays the result in the **Delivery time:** Label.

Displaying the delivery time ————

Figure 14.13 Calling the DisplayDeliveryTime procedure.

5. ***Saving the application.*** Select **File > Save All** to save your work.

So far, you have added functionality that calculates and displays the delivery time when the application executes initially. However, you should allow a user to select any drop-off time and instantly see when the seafood shipment will be delivered. In the box, *Coding the ValueChanged Event Handler*, you will learn how to handle the DateTimePicker's **ValueChanged** event, which is raised when the user changes the time in the DateTimePicker.

Coding the ValueChanged Event Handler

1. ***Creating the ValueChanged event handler.*** Click the **ShippingTime.vb [Design]** tab. Double click the DateTimePicker control dtpDropOff to generate the ValueChanged event handler.

(cont.)

2. **Inserting code in the event handler.** Insert lines 186–187 of Fig. 14.14 into the event handler. This code will execute when the user changes the time in the DateTimePicker. Note that you need to insert the comment above the event handler in addition to line-continuation characters for your code to match Fig. 14.14.

Calculating and displaying the delivery time

Figure 14.14   Inserting code in the ValueChanged event handler.

The ValueChanged event handler also uses the DisplayDeliveryTime procedure to calculate and display the delivery time in Las Vegas. In the next box, you will write the DisplayDeliveryTime procedure, after which the syntax error will no longer appear.

3. **Saving the solution.** Select **File > Save All** to save all the solution's files.

Though you have called the DisplayDeliveryTime procedure in two event handlers, you still need to write the procedure. Next, you will use Date methods to display the delivery time in an output Label.

Coding the DisplayDeliveryTime Procedure

1. **Creating the DisplayDeliveryTime procedure.** Add lines 191–202 of Fig. 14.15 below the ValueChanged event handler. Line 195 calls the DepartureTime procedure. Notice that DepartureTime is underlined in blue. This is due to the syntax error you introduce when you call a procedure that has not yet been written. You will write this procedure in the box, *Coding the DepartureTime Procedure*. The DepartureTime procedure determines which flight (midnight or noon) the seafood shipment will use. It returns a Date value representing the flight's departure time. Line 195 stores this value in the Date variable dtmDelivery.

2. **Calculating and displaying the delivery time.** Line 198 calculates the delivery time by adding 3 hours to the departure time (see the discussion following this box). Lines 199–200 display the Las Vegas delivery time by calling the Date structure's ToLongDateString and ToShortTimeString methods. A Date variable's **ToLongDateString** method returns the date as a String in the format "Wednesday, October 30, 2002." A Date variable's **ToShortTimeString** returns the time as a String in the format "4:00 PM."

3. **Saving the project.** Select **File > Save All** to save all of the solution's files.

(cont.)

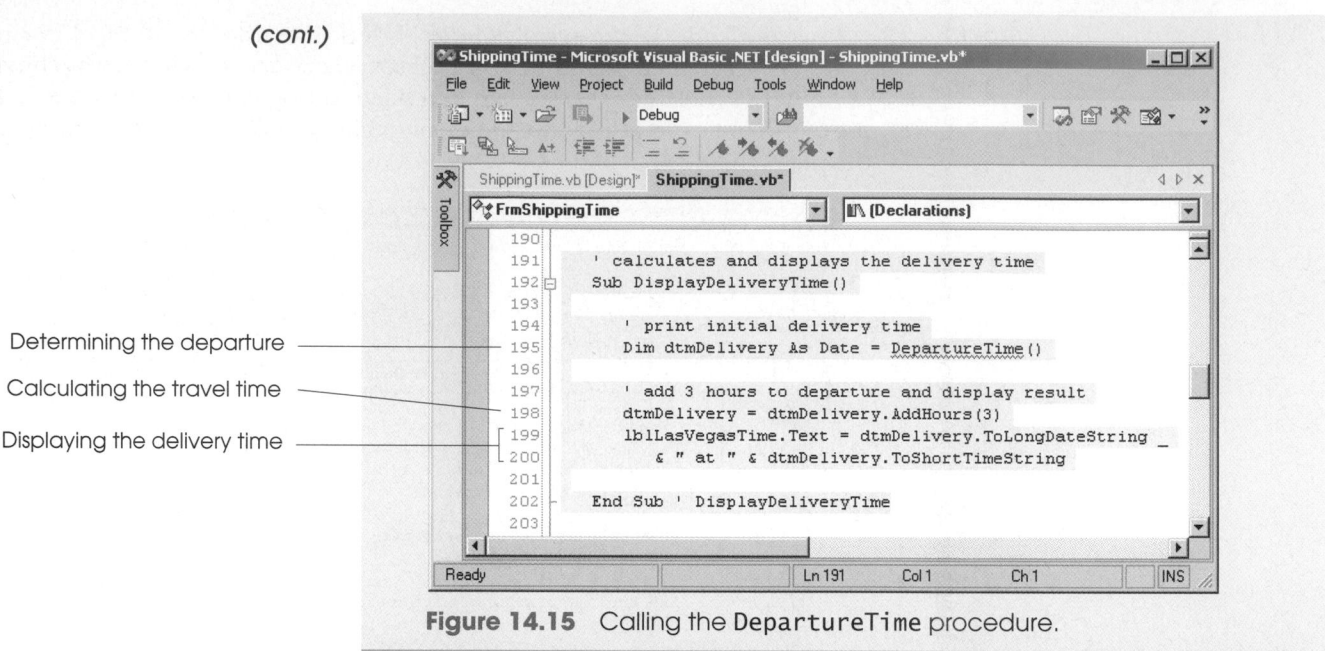

Determining the departure

Calculating the travel time

Displaying the delivery time

Figure 14.15　Calling the `DepartureTime` procedure.

When calculating the shipment's delivery time, you must account for the time-zone difference and the flight time. For instance, if you send a shipment from Portland to Las Vegas, it will travel west three time zones (the time in Las Vegas is 3 hours earlier) and spend 6 hours in transit. If you drop off the shipment at 5:00 P.M. in Portland, the shipment will leave on the midnight flight and arrive in Las Vegas at

12:00 A.M. + (*time zone change* + *flight time*) = 12:00 A.M. + (-3 + 6) *hours,*

which is 3:00 A.M. Las Vegas time. Similarly, if the shipment takes the noon flight to Las Vegas, it will arrive at 3 P.M. in Las Vegas.

To complete the application, you need to code the `DepartureTime` procedure. You will use a `Select Case` statement and `Date` methods to return a `Date` containing the departure time (noon or midnight) for the seafood shipment's flight.

Coding the *DepartureTime* Procedure

1. ***Writing the DepartureTime procedure and declaring variables.*** Insert lines 204–210 of Fig. 14.16 into your code below the `ValueChanged` event handler. Line 207 stores the current date in the `Date` variable `dtmCurrentDate`. Line 208 declares the `Date` variable `dtmDepartureTime`, the variable you will use to store the `DepartureTime Function` procedure's return value.

Declaring variables

Figure 14.16　Inserting procedure `DepartureTime` into the application.

(cont.)   2. ***Determining which flight the shipment uses.*** Insert lines 210–230 of
Fig. 14.17 after the variable declarations and before the End Function statement. The Select Case statement that begins on line 211 uses the hour specified by the user in the DateTimePicker as the controlling expression. The
value selected by the user in the DateTimePicker is located in its **Value**
property. The Date structure's Hour property returns the hour of the Date
stored in the DateTimePicker's Value property.

Using the hour value stored in
the DateTimePicker to
determine departure time

Noon departure time

Noon (the next day)
departure time

Midnight departure time

Figure 14.17   Determining the seafood shipment's flight departure time.

The body of the first Case statement (line 214) executes if the value in the
DateTimePicker is between midnight (Hour = 0) and 10:59 A.M. (Hour =
10). If the drop-off time occurs between midnight and 10:59:59 A.M., the
seafood shipment takes the noon flight to Las Vegas (recall that the shipment leaves for the airport one hour before the flight leaves). The body of
the first Case (lines 215–216) then stores the departure time of noon on the
current day in the return variable dtmDepartureTime.

The body of the next Case statement (line 219) executes if the value in the
DateTimePicker is between 11:00 P.M. and 11:59 P.M. (Hour = 23). If the
drop-off time occurs between 11:00 P.M. and 11:59 P.M, the seafood shipment takes the noon flight to Las Vegas the next day. The body of this Case
(lines 220–222) then stores the departure time of noon on the next day in the
return variable dtmDepartureTime.

The body of the Case Else statement (line 225) executes if the controlling
expression of neither of the other two Case statements evaluates to True
(the value in the DateTimePicker is between 11:00 A.M. and 10:59 P.M.). In
this case, the seafood shipment takes the midnight flight to Las Vegas. The
body of this Case (lines 226–228) then stores the departure time of midnight
in the return variable dtmDepartureTime. Note that because midnight
occurs on the following day, the Date variable representing midnight should
contain a Day property value corresponding to the next day. Line 226
ensures this occurs.

(cont.)

3. ***Returning the delivery time.*** Insert line 232 of Fig. 14.18 into the `DepartureTime` procedure following the `End Select` statement. Line 232 returns the `Date` value containing the flight departure time.

Returning the departure time ——

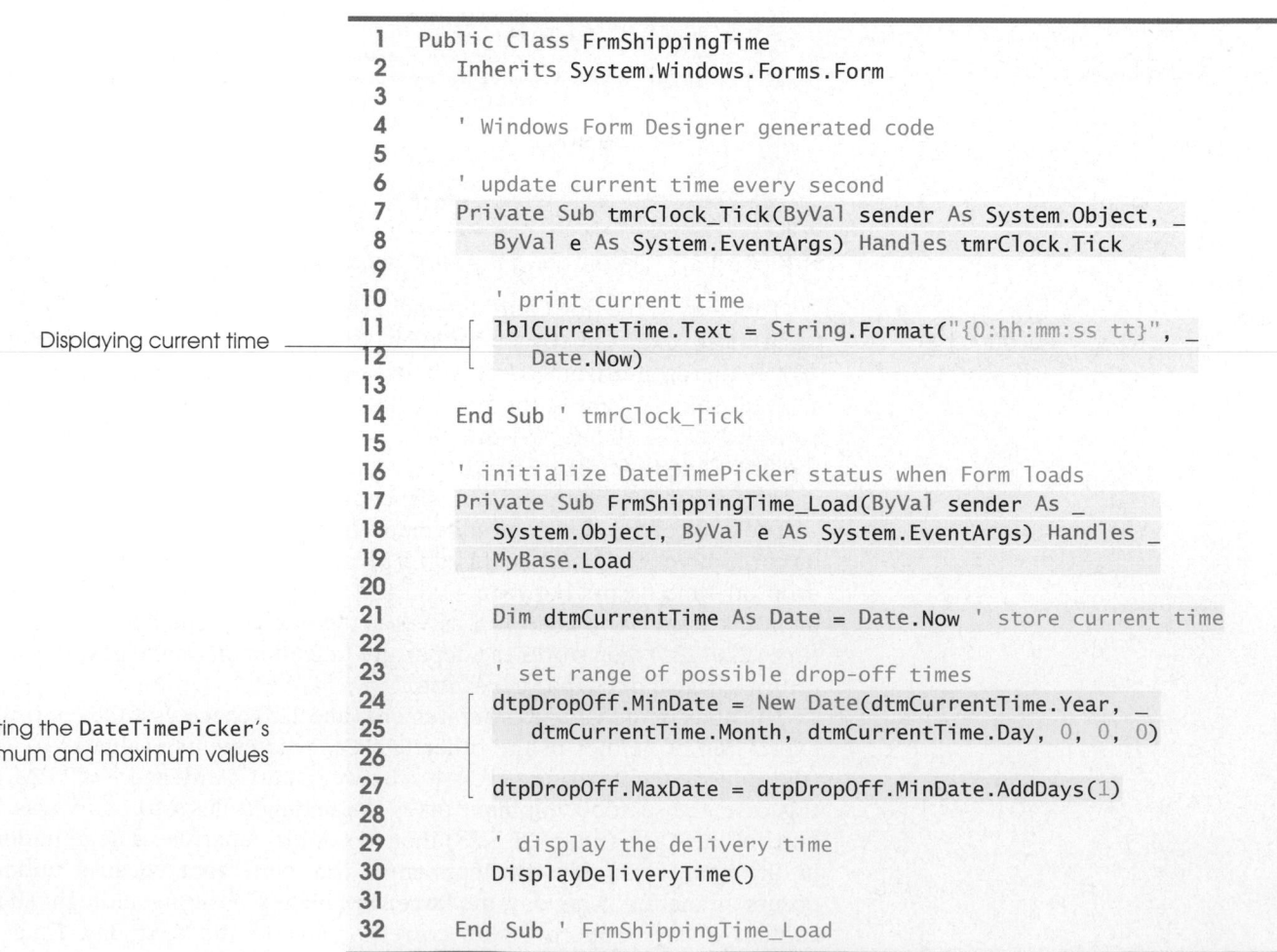

Figure 14.18 Returning the flight departure time.

4. ***Saving the project.*** Select **File > Save All** to save all of the solution's files.

5. ***Run the application.*** Select **Debug > Start** to run the application.

6. ***Terminating application execution and closing the solution.*** Click the running application's close box. Select **File > Close Solution**.

The code for the completed **Shipping Time** application is listed in Fig. 14.19.

```
1    Public Class FrmShippingTime
2       Inherits System.Windows.Forms.Form
3
4       ' Windows Form Designer generated code
5
6       ' update current time every second
7       Private Sub tmrClock_Tick(ByVal sender As System.Object, _
8          ByVal e As System.EventArgs) Handles tmrClock.Tick
9
10         ' print current time
11         lblCurrentTime.Text = String.Format("{0:hh:mm:ss tt}", _
12            Date.Now)
13
14      End Sub ' tmrClock_Tick
15
16      ' initialize DateTimePicker status when Form loads
17      Private Sub FrmShippingTime_Load(ByVal sender As _
18         System.Object, ByVal e As System.EventArgs) Handles _
19         MyBase.Load
20
21         Dim dtmCurrentTime As Date = Date.Now ' store current time
22
23         ' set range of possible drop-off times
24         dtpDropOff.MinDate = New Date(dtmCurrentTime.Year, _
25            dtmCurrentTime.Month, dtmCurrentTime.Day, 0, 0, 0)
26
27         dtpDropOff.MaxDate = dtpDropOff.MinDate.AddDays(1)
28
29         ' display the delivery time
30         DisplayDeliveryTime()
31
32      End Sub ' FrmShippingTime_Load
```

Displaying current time —— (lines 11–12)

Setting the `DateTimePicker`'s minimum and maximum values —— (lines 24–27)

Figure 14.19 **Shipping Time** application code. (Part 1 of 2.)

```
33
34      ' update ship time on change of drop-off time
35      Private Sub dtpDropOff_ValueChanged(ByVal sender As _
36         System.Object, ByVal e As System.EventArgs) Handles _
37         dtpDropOff.ValueChanged
38
39         ' display the delivery time
40         DisplayDeliveryTime()
41
42      End Sub ' dtpDropOff_ValueChanged
43
44      ' calculates and displays the delivery time
45      Sub DisplayDeliveryTime() As Date
46
47         ' print initial delivery time
48         Dim dtmDelivery As Date = DepartureTime()
49
50         ' add 3 hours to departure and display result
51         dtmDelivery = dtmDelivery.AddHours(3)
52         lblLasVegasTime.Text = dtmDelivery.ToLongDateString _
53            & " at " & dtmDelivery.ToShortTimeString
54
55      End Sub ' DisplayDeliveryTime
56
57      ' returns flight departure time for selected drop-off time
58      Function DepartureTime() As Date
59
60         Dim dtmCurrentDate As Date = Date.Now ' store current date
61         Dim dtmDepartureTime As Date          ' store departure time
62
63         ' determine which flight the shipment takes
64         Select Case dtpDropOff.Value.Hour
65
66            ' seafood will be on the noon flight
67            Case 0 To 10
68               dtmDepartureTime = New Date(dtmCurrentDate.Year, _
69                  dtmCurrentDate.Month, dtmCurrentDate.Day, 12, 0, 0)
70
71            ' seafood will be on tomorrow's noon flight
72            Case 23
73               dtmCurrentDate = dtmCurrentDate.AddDays(1)
74               dtmDepartureTime = New Date(dtmCurrentDate.Year, _
75                  dtmCurrentDate.Month, dtmCurrentDate.Day, 12, 0, 0)
76
77            ' seafood will be on midnight flight
78            Case Else
79               dtmCurrentDate = dtmCurrentDate.AddDays(1)
80               dtmDepartureTime = New Date(dtmCurrentDate.Year, _
81                  dtmCurrentDate.Month, dtmCurrentDate.Day, 0, 0, 0)
82
83         End Select
84
85         Return dtmDepartureTime ' return the flight's departure time
86      End Function ' DepartureTime
87
88   End Class ' FrmShippingTime
```

Calculating and displaying the delivery time in Las Vegas — (lines 51–53)

Using a **Select Case** statement to determine departure time — (line 64)

Figure 14.19 Shipping Time application code. (Part 2 of 2.)

1. The ToShortTimeString method is called on a Date variable to return its value in the
    format _____ .

    a) `11 o'clock`   b) `23:00`

    c) `11:00`   d) `11:00 PM`

2. DateTimePicker properties _____ and _____ specify the earliest and latest
    dates that can be selected, respectively.

    a) `MinDate, MaxDate`   b) `Now, Later`

    c) `Minimum, Maximum`   d) `Early, Late`

Answers: 1) d. 2) a.

14.5 Wrap-Up

In this tutorial, you learned how to use the Date type, a structure for manipulating
time and date information. You used variables of this type to calculate and display
delivery times in your **Shipping Time** application. To help users enter date and time
information, you used a DateTimePicker control. You observed how a DateTime-
Picker control can display custom date and time formats and limit user input. To
help you group controls on the Form visually, you used the GroupBox control. You
also learned how to use the Timer control on the Form, which allowed your application to execute code once every second.

      You then learned how to use three new event handlers to help you complete
the **Shipping Time** application. You learned that the Form's Load event handler
allows your application to execute code when the application is opened initially.
You used this event to set initial values in your application. You then learned how
to use the DateTimePicker control's ValueChanged event handler, which allows
you to execute code when the control's value changes. You used this event handler
to update the delivery time each time the user entered a new time. Finally, you
learned about the Timer's Tick event handler, which you used to update and display the current time in a Label that serves as a clock.

      In the next tutorial, you will use the **Fund Raiser** to introduce two program-
ming concepts: arguments and scope rules. Learning these concepts will help you
build more powerful and dependable applications because you will understand how
Visual Basic .NET keeps track of variables throughout your application.

SKILLS SUMMARY   **Storing and Manipulating Date and Time Information**

■ Use a Date variable to store and manipulate date and time information. A Date variable
stores information about a point in time (for example, 12:00:00 A.M. on January 1, 2003).
This information can be formatted for display in predefined long or short formats or in
custom (programmer-defined) formats.

Using Date variables

■ Use keyword New to declare a new Date value.

■ Use property Date.Now to obtain your computer's current date and time.

■ Use the member-access operator to access properties of a Date variable.

■ Use Date methods, such as AddHours and AddDays, to add or subtract time from values in
Date variables. Then assign the value returned by the method to a Date variable.

Using a GroupBox Control

■ Use a GroupBox control to group related controls visually. To add a GroupBox to the Form,
double click the **GroupBox** control in the Toolbox.

Placing Controls Inside a GroupBox

■ Place a control inside the GroupBox by clicking the control's name in the Toolbox and
clicking inside the GroupBox.

Using the `DateTimePicker` Control

■ Use a `DateTimePicker` control to get date and time information from the user.

■ Set property `Format` to `Custom` to indicate that you will specify how the date will appear in the `DateTimePicker`. The format is specified in property `CustomFormat`.

■ Set property `ShowUpDown` to `True` to allow the user to select the date or time by clicking an up or down arrow. If this property's value is `False`, a monthly calendar will drop down, allowing the user to pick a date.

Using the `Timer` Control

■ Use a `Timer` control to execute code (the `Tick` event handler) at specified intervals. To add a `Timer` control to the Form, click **Timer** in the **Windows Forms** tab of the **Toolbox**, and click anywhere on the Form. The `Timer` control will appear in the component tray.

■ Customize the time between `Tick` events by using the `Interval` property, which specifies the number of milliseconds between each `Tick` event.

■ Set the `Enabled` property to `True` so that the `Tick` event is raised once per `Interval`.

KEY TERMS

component tray—The area below the Windows Form Designer that contains controls, such as `Timer`s, that are not part of the graphical user interface.

container—An object that contains controls.

`CustomFormat` property—The `DateTimePicker` property that contains the programmer-specified format string with which to display the date and/or time when `DateTimePicker` `Format` property is set to `Custom`.

Date data type—A type capable of storing date and time data.

`DateTimePicker` control—A control for retrieving date and time information from the user.

`Format` property—The `DateTimePicker` property that allows the programmer to specify a predefined or custom format with which to display the date and/or time.

`GroupBox` control—A control that groups related controls visually.

`Interval` property—The `Timer` property that specifies the number of milliseconds between each `Tick` event.

Load event—The event raised when an application initially executes.

`MaxDate` property—The `DateTimePicker` property that specifies the latest value that the `DateTimePicker` will allow the user to enter.

`MinDate` property—The `DateTimePicker` property that specifies the earliest value that the `DateTimePicker` will allow the user to enter.

Now property—The property of structure `Date` that retrieves your computer's current time.

`ShowUpDown` property—The `DateTimePicker` property that, when true, allows the user to specify the time using up and down arrows.

`Tick` event—The event raised after the number of milliseconds specified in the `Timer` control's `Interval` property has elapsed.

`Timer` control—A control that wakes up at specified intervals to execute code in its `Tick` event handler.

`Value` property—The property that stores the value (such as a time) in a `DateTimePicker` control.

`ValueChanged` event—The event raised when a user selects a new day or time in the `DateTimePicker` control.

GUI DESIGN GUIDELINES

`DateTimePicker`

■ Use a `DateTimePicker` to retrieve date and time information from the user.

■ Each `DateTimePicker` should have a corresponding descriptive `Label`.

■ If the user should specify a time of day or a date and time, set the `DateTimePicker`'s `ShowUpDown` property to `True`. If the user should specify a date, set the `DateTimePicker`'s `ShowUpDown` property to `False` to allow the user to select a day from the month calendar.

GroupBox

- GroupBox titles should be concise and should use book-title capitalization.
- Use GroupBoxes to group related controls on the Form visually.

CONTROLS, EVENTS, PROPERTIES & METHODS

Date This structure provides properties and methods to store and manipulate date and time information.

- *Properties*

  Day—This property returns the day stored in a Date variable.

  Hour—This property returns the hour stored in a Date variable.

  Month—This property returns the month stored in a Date variable.

  Now—This property returns the system's current date and time.

  Year—This property returns the year stored in a Date variable.

- *Methods*

  AddDays—This method creates a new Date value that is the specified number of days later (or earlier) in time.

  AddHours—This method creates a new Date value that is the specified number of hours later (or earlier) in time.

  AddMinutes—This method creates a new Date value that is the specified number of minutes later (or earlier) in time.

  ToLongDateString—This method returns a String containing the date in the format "Wednesday, October 30, 2002."

  ToShortTimeString—This method returns a String containing the time in the format "4:00 PM."

DateTimePicker   This control is used to retrieve date and time information from the user.

- *In action*

DateTimePicker using default format

- *Event*

  ValueChanged—This event is raised when the Value property is changed.

- *Properties*

  CustomFormat—This property sets which format string to use when displaying the date and/or time.

  Format—This property specifies the format in which the date and time are displayed on the control.

    Long—This value specifies that the date should be displayed in the format "Monday, December 09, 2002."

    Short—This value specifies that the date should be displayed in the format "12/ 9/2002."

    Time—This value specifies that the time should be displayed in the format "8:39:53 PM."

    Custom—This value allows the programmer to specify a custom format in which to display the date and/or time.

  Hour—This property stores the hour in the DateTimePicker control.

  Location—This property specifies the location of the DateTimePicker control on its container relative to the container's top-left corner.

MinDate—This property specifies the minimum date and/or time that can be selected when using this control.

MaxDate—This property specifies the maximum date and/or time that can be selected when using this control.

Name—This property specifies the name used to access the DateTimePicker control programmatically. The name should be prefixed with dtp.

ShowUpDown—This property specifies whether the up-down arrows (True) are displayed on the control for time values. If False, a down arrow is displayed for accessing a drop-down calendar.

Value—This property stores the date and/or time in the DateTimePicker control.

GroupBox   This control groups related controls visually.

■ *In action*

■ *Properties*

Name—This property specifies the name used to access the GroupBox control programmatically. The name should be prefixed with fra.

Location—This property specifies the location of the GroupBox control on the Form.

Size—This property specifies the height and width (in pixels) of the GroupBox control.

Text—This property specifies the text displayed on the GroupBox.

Timer   This control wakes up at specified intervals of time to execute code in its Tick event handler.

■ *Event*

Tick—This event is raised after the number of milliseconds specified in the Interval property has elapsed.

■ *Properties*

Enabled—This property determines whether the Timer is running (True). The default is False.

Interval—This property determines the time interval between Tick events.

Name—This property specifies the name used to access the Timer control programmatically. The name should be prefixed with tmr.

MULTIPLE-CHOICE QUESTIONS

14.1 The _____ allows you to store and manipulate date information easily.

    a) Date data type   b) DatePicker control

    c) GroupBox control   d) Now property

14.2 You can _____ to a Date variable.

    a) add hours   b) add days

    c) subtract hours   d) All of the above.

14.3 To subtract one day from Date variable dtmDay's value, assign the value returned by _____ to dtmDay.

    a) dtmDay.AddHours(-24)   b) dtmDay.SubtractDays(1)

    c) dtmDay.AddDays(-1)   d) Both a and c.

14.4 The time 3:45 and 35 seconds in the afternoon would be formatted as 03:45:35 PM according to the format string _____.

    a) "hh:mm:ss"   b) "hh:mm:ss tt"

    c) "hh:mm:ss am:pm"   d) "h:m:s tt"

14.5 A(n) _____ event occurs before the Form is displayed.

    a) `LoadForm`   b) `InitializeForm`

    c) `Load`   d) `FormLoad`

14.6 Timer property `Interval` sets the rate at which `Tick` events occur in _____.

    a) nanoseconds   b) microseconds

    c) milliseconds   d) seconds

14.7 To set Date dtmNow's time five hours earlier, use _____.

    a) `dtmNow = dtmNow.SubtractHours(5)`   b) `dtmNow = dtmNow.AddHours(-5)`

    c) `dtmNow = dtmNow.AddHours(5)`   d) `dtmNow.AddHours(-5)`

14.8 A(n) _____ is a container.

    a) `GroupBox`   b) `Form`

    c) `Timer`   d) Both a and b.

14.9 A Date variable stores hour values in the range _____.

    a) 1 to 12   b) 0 to 12

    c) 0 to 24   d) 0 to 23

14.10 A DateTimePicker's _____ property specifies the format string with which to display the date.

    a) `CustomFormat`   b) `FormatString`

    c) `Format`   d) `Text`

EXERCISES

14.11 (*World Clock Application*) Create an application that displays the current time in Los Angeles, Atlanta, London and Tokyo. Use a `Timer` to update the clock every second. Assume that your local time is the time in Atlanta. Atlanta is three hours later than Los Angeles. London is five hours later than Atlanta. Tokyo is eight hours later than London. The application should look similar to Fig. 14.20.

    a) *Copying and opening the template application.* Copy the `WorldClock` folder from `C:\Examples\Tutorial14\Exercises` to `C:\SimplyVB`. Double click the `WorldClock.sln` file to open the application in Visual Studio .NET.

    b) *Adding a Timer to the Form.* Add a `Timer` control to the **World Clock** application. Set the `Timer` control's name property to `tmrClock`.

    c) *Adding a Tick event handler for tmrClock.* Add a `Tick` event handler for `Timer` `tmrClock`. The event handler should calculate and display the current times for Los Angeles, Atlanta, London and Tokyo. Use the `Date` variable's `ToShortDateString` and `ToLongTimeString` methods to create the display text.

Figure 14.20 World Clock GUI.

14.12 (*Shipping Time Application Enhancement*) During the winter, a distribution center in Denver, Colorado needs to receive seafood shipments to supply the local ski resorts. Enhance the **Shipping Time** application by adding Denver, Colorado as another shipping destination. Denver is two time zones west of Portland, meaning time is two hours earlier than Portland, Maine. Because there are no direct flights to Denver, shipments from Portland will take 8 hours.

a) *Copying and opening the template application.* Copy the ShippingTimeEnhanced folder from C:\Examples\Tutorial14\Exercises to C:\SimplyVB. Double click the ShippingTime.sln file to open the application in Visual Studio .NET.

b) *Inserting a GroupBox.* Resize the Form to fit the **Express Shipping to Denver** GroupBox as shown in Fig. 14.21. Add a GroupBox to the Form. Change the Text property of the GroupBox to indicate that it will contain the delivery time in Denver. Resize and move the GroupBox so that it resembles the GUI shown in Fig. 14.21.

c) *Inserting Labels.* In the GroupBox you just created, add an output Label to display the delivery time for a seafood shipment to Denver and a corresponding descriptive Label.

d) *Inserting code to the DisplayDeliveryTime procedure.* Add code to DisplayDeliveryTime procedure to compute and display the delivery time in Denver.

Figure 14.21   Enhanced Shipping Time GUI.

14.13 (*Alarm Application*) Create an application that allows the user to set an alarm clock. The application should allow the user to set the exact time of the alarm by using a DateTimePicker. While the alarm is set, the user should not be able to modify the DateTimePicker. If the alarm is set and the current time matches or exceeds the time in the DateTimePicker, play the computer's "beep" sound. (Your computer must have the necessary hardware for sound.) The user should be able to cancel an alarm by using a **Reset** Button. This Button is disabled when the application starts.

Figure 14.22   Alarm GUI.

a) *Copying and opening the template application.* Copy the AlarmClock folder from C:\Examples\Tutorial14\Exercises to C:\SimplyVB. Double click the Alarm-Clock.sln file to open the application in Visual Studio .NET.

b) *Inserting a DateTimePicker.* Add a DateTimePicker control to the Form. Set the DateTimePicker to display only the time, as is shown in Fig. 14.22. Set the DateTimePicker control's Size property to 80, 20, and move the control so that it appears as it does in Fig. 14.22.

c) *Coding the Set Button's Click event handler.* Add a Click event handler for the **Set** Button. This event handler should disable the **Set** Button and the DateTimePicker and enable the **Reset** Button.

d) *Coding the Timer's* `Tick` *event handler.* Define the `Tick` event handler for the `Timer`. A `Tick` event should occur every 1000 milliseconds (one second). If the alarm is set and the current time matches or exceeds the time in the `DateTimePicker`, play the computer's "beep" sound by calling the `Beep` function. To call the `Beep` function, type `Beep()` on its own line in your code.

e) *Coding the Reset Button's* `Click` *event handler.* Define the `Click` event handler for the **Reset** Button. When the **Reset** Button is clicked, the GUI should be set back to its original state.

What does this code do? ▶ **14.14** This code creates a `Date` variable. What date does this variable contain?

```
Dim dtmTime As Date = New Date(2003, 1, 2, 3, 4, 5)
```

What's wrong with this code? ▶ **14.15** The following lines of code are supposed to create a `Date` variable and increment its hour value by two. Find the error(s) in the code.

```
Dim dtmNow As Date = Date.Now
dtmNow.AddHours(2)
```

Programming Challenge ▶ **14.16** (*Parking Garage Fee Calculator*) Create an application that computes the fee for parking a car in a parking garage (Fig. 14.23). The user should provide the **Time In:** and **Time Out:** values by using `DateTimePicker`s. The application should calculate the cost of parking in the garage for the specified amount of time. Assume that parking costs three dollars an hour. When calculating the total time spent in the garage, you can ignore the seconds value, but treat the minutes value as a fraction of an hour (1 minute is 1/60 of an hour). For simplicity, assume that no overnight parking is allowed, so each car leaves the garage on the same day in which it arrives.

a) *Copying and opening the template application.* Copy the `ParkingGarageFee-Calculator` folder from `C:\Examples\Tutorial14\Exercises` to `C:\SimplyVB`. Double click the `ParkingGarageFeeCalculator.sln` file to open the application in Visual Studio .NET.

b) *Inserting the* `DateTimePicker` *controls.* Add two `DateTimePicker` controls to the Form. Set the `DateTimePicker`s so that they show the time only. Set the `Size` property of each `DateTimePicker` control to `80, 20`, and move the `DateTimePicker`s so that they are positioned as in Fig. 14.23.

c) *Writing the* `Function` *procedure* `Fee`*.* Define a `Function` procedure `Fee` that accepts four `Integer`s as parameters—the hour value of the **Time In:**, the hour value of the **Time Out:**, the minute value of the **Time In:** and the minute value of the **Time Out:**. Using this information, procedure `Fee` should calculate the fee for parking in the garage. The `Function` procedure should then return this value as a `Decimal`.

d) *Coding the Calculate Button's* `Click` *event handler.* Add the `Click` event handler for the **Calculate** Button. This event handler should call `Fee` to obtain the amount due. It should then display the amount (formatted as currency) in a `Label`.

Figure 14.23   Fee Calculator GUI.

Objectives

In this tutorial, you will learn to:
- Create variables that can be used in all the **Form**'s procedures.
- Pass arguments by reference, using **ByRef**, so that the called procedure can modify the caller's variables.
- Eliminate subtle data-type errors by enabling **Option Strict**.
- Change a value from one data type to another, using methods of class **Convert**.

Outline

Fund Raiser Application

Introducing Scope, Pass-by-Reference and Option Strict

In this tutorial, you will learn several important Visual Basic .NET concepts. First, you will learn how to declare variables that can be referenced from any procedure within your Form's code. Next, you will learn another technique for passing arguments to procedures. In the procedures you have created so far, the application has made a copy of the argument's value, and any changes the called procedure made to the copy did not affect the original variable's value. You will learn how to pass an argument to a procedure—using a technique called pass-by-reference—so that changes made to the parameter's value in the procedure are also made to the original variable in the caller. You will learn how the Visual Basic .NET compiler handles conversions between different data types and how to enable a feature called Option Strict to avoid subtle errors that can occur when a value of one type is assigned to a variable of another type. In addition, you will be introduced to methods from class Convert that allow you to convert data from one type to another.

15.1 Test-Driving the **Fund Raiser** Application

In this tutorial, you will create a fund raiser application that determines how much donated money is available after operating costs. The application must meet the following requirements:

Application Requirements

An organization is hosting a fund raiser to collect donations. A portion of each donation is used to cover the operating expenses of the organization; the rest of the donation goes to the charity. Create an application that allows the organization to keep track of the total amount of money raised. The application should deduct 17% of each donation for operating costs; the remaining 83% is given to the charity. The application should display the amount of each donation after the 17% operating expenses are deducted; it also should display the total amount raised for the charity (that is, the total amount donated less all operating costs) for all donations up to that point.

The user inputs the amount of a donation into a TextBox and clicks a Button to calculate the net amount of that donation the charity receives after operating expenses have been deducted. In addition, the total amount of money raised for charity is updated and displayed. You begin by test-driving the completed application.

Test-Driving the Fund Raiser Application

1. ***Opening the completed application.*** Open the C:\Examples\Tutorial15\CompletedApplication\FundRaiser folder to locate the **Fund Raiser** application. Double click FundRaiser.sln to open the completed application in Visual Studio .NET.

2. ***Running the application.*** Select **Debug > Start** to build and run the application. The Form shown in Fig. 15.1 appears.

Figure 15.1 **Fund Raiser** application's Form.

3. ***Entering a donation in the application.*** Enter 1500 in the **Donation:** Text-Box. Click the **Make Donation** Button. The application calculates the amount of the donation after the operating expenses have been deducted and displays the result ($1245.00) in the **After expenses:** field. Because this is the first donation entered, this amount is repeated in the **Total raised:** field (Fig. 15.2).

Figure 15.2 **Fund Raiser** application's Form with first donation entered.

4. ***Entering additional donations.*** Enter more donations, and click the **Make Donation** Button. Notice that the total raised increases with each additional donation (Fig. 15.3).

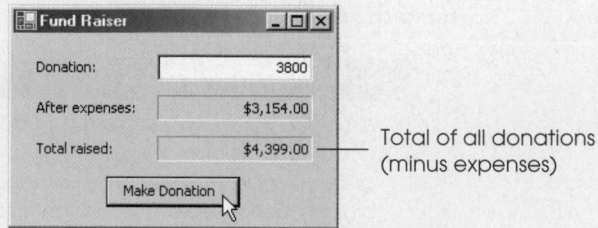

Total of all donations (minus expenses)

Figure 15.3 Making further donations.

5. ***Terminating the application.*** Click the close box to terminate the running application.

6. ***Closing the solution.*** Select **File > Close Solution**.

15.2 Constructing the Fund Raiser Application

Now that you have test-driven the application, you're ready to begin developing the **Fund Raiser** application. The following pseudocode statements describe the functionality of the application:

> When the user changes the current donation amount in the TextBox
>   Clear Label that displays amount of current donation that goes toward
>   charity
>
> When the user clicks the Make Donation Button
>   Obtain amount of current donation from TextBox
>   Calculate amount of current donation that goes toward charity (amount
>   after operating costs)
>   Display amount of current donation that goes toward charity
>   Update total amount raised for charity (from all donations received)
>   Display total amount raised for charity

Now that you've studied the pseudocode, let's examine the application's actions, controls and events. Figure 15.4 presents the ACE table for the **Fund Raiser** application.

Action/Control/Event Table for the Fund Raiser Application

Action	Control	Event
Label all the application's controls	lblDonations, lblDonated, lblTotal	
Clear Label that displays amount of current donation that goes toward charity	txtDonation, lblDonatedValue	TextChanged (of TextBox)
Obtain user donation from TextBox; calculate and display amount of current donation that goes toward charity; update and display total amount raised for charity	btnDonate, txtDonation, lblDonatedValue, lblTotalValue	Click (of Button)

Figure 15.4 **Fund Raiser** application's ACE table.

You're now ready to begin programming the **Fund Raiser** application. First, you will declare the variables needed in the application. In this discussion, you will learn a new concept—scope. The **scope** of a variable identifier is the portion of an application in which the variable's identifier can be referenced. Some identifiers can be referenced throughout an application; others can be referenced only from limited portions of an application (such as within a single procedure). You will now add code to your application to illustrate these various scopes.

Examining Scope with the Fund Raiser Application

1. ***Copying the template application to your work folder.*** Copy the Fund-Raiser folder from `C:\Examples\Tutorial15\TemplateApplication` to `C:\SimplyVB`.

2. ***Opening the template application.*** Double click `FundRaiser.sln` in `C:\SimplyVB\FundRaiser`. Double click `FundRaiser.vb` in the **Solution Explorer** window to display the Form in design view (Fig. 15.5).

3. ***Placing declarations in the code file.*** Select **View > Code**, and add lines 4–5 of Fig. 15.6 to `FundRaiser.vb`. In this application, you need a variable that stores the total amount of money raised for charity.

(cont.)

Figure 15.5   **Fund Raiser** template application's Form.

This variable is initialized when the application first executes and must retain its value while the application executes (that is, it cannot be created each time a procedure is invoked). Variable m_decTotalRaised stores the total amount of money raised. This variable is an **instance variable**—a variable declared inside a class, but outside any procedure definitions of that class. All procedures in class FrmFundRaiser will have access to this variable and will be able to modify its value.

Instance variables have **module scope**. Module scope begins at the identifier after keyword Class and terminates at the End Class statement. This scope enables any procedure in the same class to access all instance variables defined in that class. Form instance variables with module scope are created when the application begins executing.

Good Programming Practice

Prefix instance variables with m_ (for module scope) to distinguish them from other variables.

Figure 15.6   Declaring an instance variable in the application.

4. ***Creating the Click event handler for the Make Donation Button.*** Select **View > Designer** to return to design view. Double click the **Make Donation** Button to generate its Click event handler btnDonate_Click. Split the procedure header over two lines as in lines 155–156 of Fig. 15.7, and place the comments on lines 154 and 158 of Fig. 15.7 around the event handler.

5. ***Declaring local variables in event handler btnDonate_Click.*** Add lines 158–159 of Fig. 15.8 to event handler btnDonate_Click. Variable decDonation (line 158) stores the donation amount. Variable decAfterCosts (line 159) stores the donation amount after the operating expenses have been deducted.

    In Visual Basic. NET, identifiers, such as decDonation and decAfterCosts, that are declared inside a procedure (but outside of a control structure, such as a Do While...Loop) have **procedure scope**. Identifiers with procedure scope cannot be referenced outside of the procedure in which they are declared. Parameters to procedures are also considered to have procedure scope.

(cont.)

Figure 15.7 Adding a `Click` event handler to the application.

Figure 15.8 Declaring local variables in the **Fund Raiser** application.

Identifiers declared inside control structures, such as inside an If...Then statement, have **block scope**. Block scope begins at the identifier's declaration and ends at the block's final statement (for example, End If).

Variables with either procedure scope or block scope are called **local variables**, because they cannot be referenced outside the procedure or block in which they are declared. If a local variable (that is, a variable with either block scope or procedure scope) has the same name as an instance variable (that is, a variable with module scope), the instance variable is hidden in that procedure or block. Any expression containing the variable name will use the local variable's value and not the instance variable's value. The instance variable's value is not destroyed, though—it is still available for access outside that procedure or block.

6. ***Examining the CalculateDonation procedure.*** The template application provides the CalculateDonation Function procedure (lines 131–144 of Fig. 15.9). Line 135 declares constant dblCOSTS, which stores the operating-cost percentage. This constant also is "local" to the procedure and cannot be used elsewhere. The Function procedure accepts one parameter value—the total donation amount (decDonatedAmount). The amount of the donation that goes toward operating costs is 17% of the initial donation. The net donation (the amount that goes toward charity) is calculated by multiplying local constant dblCOSTS, whose value is 0.17, by the initial donation amount.

Error-Prevention Tip

Hidden variable names can sometimes lead to subtle logic errors. Use unique names for all variables, regardless of scope, to prevent an instance variable from becoming hidden.

(cont.)   Procedure `CalculateDonation` subtracts the operating cost from the initial donation amount (`decDonatedAmount`) and assigns the result to `decNetDonation` (lines 139–140). The `Function` procedure then returns the `Decimal` result (line 142).

Parameter `decDonatedAmount` has procedure scope because it is declared in the procedure header

Local variable `decNetDonation` has procedure scope because it is declared in the procedure body

Figure 15.9 `Function` procedure `CalculateDonation` provided by the template application.

7. ***Demonstrating the difference between module scope and procedure scope.***
   Now you are going to demonstrate the limits of procedure scope. Temporarily replace constant `dblCOSTS` with `decDonation`, `btnDonate_Click`'s local variable (line 140 in Fig. 15.10). Notice the jagged line under `decDonation` to indicate an error. Variables with procedure scope can be accessed and modified only in the procedure in which they are defined. The error message displayed when the mouse pointer rests on `decDonation` indicates that `decDonation` is not declared. Because this variable is "local" to `btnDonate_Click`, `Function CalculateDonation` cannot "see" the declaration of `decDonation`. Replace `decDonation` with `dblCOSTS`.

Figure 15.10 Demonstrating procedure scope.

8. ***Obtaining the donation amount.*** Add lines 161–162 of Fig. 15.11 to event handler `btnDonate_Click`. You obtain the total donation amount from TextBox `txtDonation` (line 162).

(cont.)

Figure 15.11   Obtaining the donation amount.

9. ***Calculating and displaying the donation amount after the operating expenses.*** Add lines 164–168 of Fig. 15.12 to the event handler. Line 165 invokes procedure `CalculateDonation` with the amount of the donation (`decDonation`). The result of this procedure—the net amount that goes to charity after the deduction for operating costs—is assigned to variable `decAfterCosts`. The donation amount after expenses is formatted as a currency string and displayed in the **After expenses:** field (line 168).

Figure 15.12   Calculating and displaying the donation amount after operating expenses.

10. ***Updating and displaying the fund raiser total.*** Add lines 170–174 of Fig. 15.13 to the event handler. Line 171 updates instance variable `m_decTotalRaised`, which stores the total amount given to the charity after the operating costs have been deducted. Line 174 displays the total amount raised for charity.

     Notice that `m_decTotalRaised` is not declared as a local variable in this event handler and that `m_decTotalRaised` does not have a jagged line beneath it. Recall that `m_decTotalRaised` is an instance variable, declared on line 5 of Fig. 15.6. Instance variables may be used in any of the class's procedures.

(cont.)

Because `m_decTotalRaised` has module scope, it maintains its value between procedure calls. Variables with procedure scope do not retain their values between procedure calls. Variables with procedure scope, such as `decDonation`, are re-initialized each time their procedure is invoked.

Figure 15.13 Updating and displaying the total amount raised for charity.

11. ***Clearing the After expenses: field to display the next result.*** The template application includes event handler `txtDonation_TextChanged` (lines 146–152 of Fig. 15.14) for the **Donation:** TextBox's TextChanged event. When the user enters data into the TextBox, the TextChanged event occurs and line 151 clears the donation for charity from the **After expenses:** field.

Figure 15.14 Clearing the **Donation:** TextBox.

12. ***Saving the project.*** Select **File > Save All** to save all the solution's files.

13. ***Testing the application.*** Select **Debug > Start** to run the application.

14. ***Terminating the application.*** After successfully testing the application, click the running application's close box.

---

1. Instance variables have _____ scope.

    a) block   b) procedure

    c) module   d) None of the above.

2. Variables with either procedure scope or block scope are called _____.

    a) instance variables   b) local variables

    c) class variables   d) hidden variables

Answers: 1) c. 2) b.

15.3 Passing Arguments: Pass-by-Value vs. Pass-by-Reference

Arguments are passed to procedures in one of two ways: **pass-by-value** and **pass-by-reference** (also called **call-by-value** and **call-by-reference**). The keyword ByVal (which we have used in all our procedures until now, including event handlers generated by Visual Basic .NET) indicates that a variable has been passed by value. When an argument is passed by value, the application makes a copy of the argument's value and passes that copy to the called procedure. Changes made to the copy in the called procedure do not affect the original variable's value in the calling procedure.

In contrast, when an argument is passed by reference (using keyword **ByRef**), the original data can be accessed and modified directly by the called procedure. This is useful in some situations, such as when a procedure needs to produce more than one result. However, it can cause subtle errors and is used largely only by experienced programmers. In the box, *Passing Arguments with ByRef in the **Fund Raiser** Application*, you will learn to use keyword ByRef to pass an argument by reference to the procedure that calculates the donation amount after operating costs.

Passing Arguments with ByRef in the Fund Raiser Application

1. ***Passing variable decAfterCosts by reference.*** Replace line 165 in event handler btnDonate_Click with line 165 of Fig. 15.15. The procedure call in line 165 of Fig. 15.15 passes two variables to procedure CalculateDonation. Notice that because procedure CalculateDonation currently only accepts one argument, the second argument (decAfterCosts) is flagged as a syntax error. In the following steps, we will rewrite procedure CalculateDonation so that it accepts two arguments, resolving the syntax error. The first argument (in this case, decDonation) will be passed by value; the second argument (in this case, decAfterCosts) will be passed by reference. When the CalculateDonation procedure returns, variable decAfterCosts will contain the portion of the donation that the charity receives.

Figure 15.15 Passing variable decAfterCosts by reference.

2. ***Removing the old CalculateDonation Function procedure.*** Delete the CalculateDonation Function procedure (lines 132–144 of Fig. 15.16) from FundRaiser.vb.

3. ***Coding the new CalculateDonation Sub procedure.*** Type lines 132–135 of Fig. 15.17 in the code editor.

(cont.)

Delete these lines of code ———

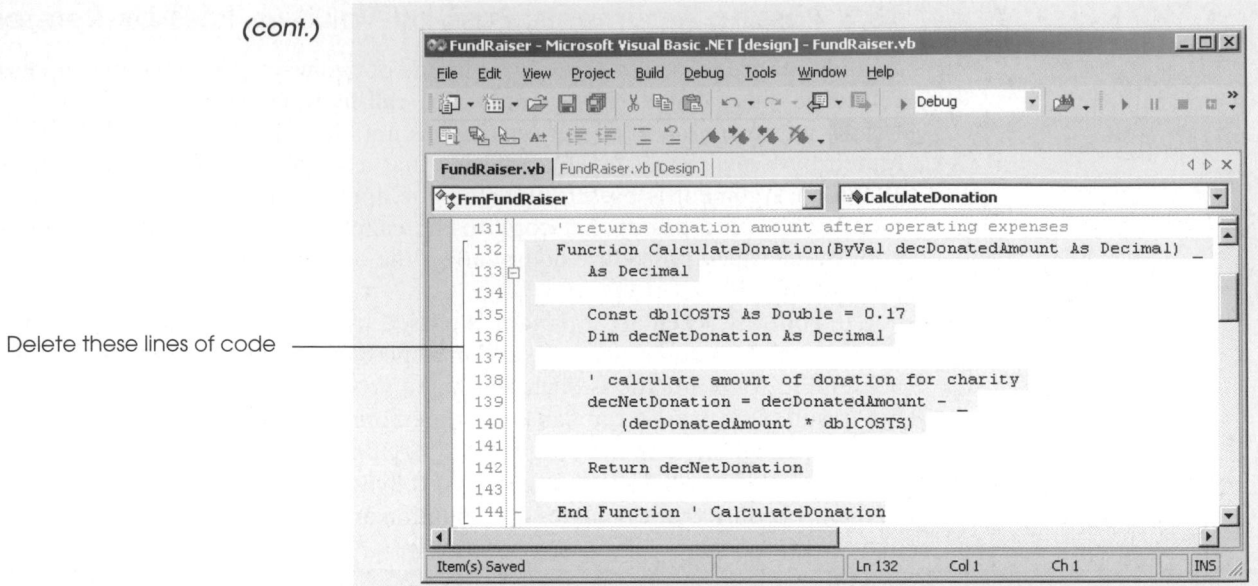

Figure 15.16 Function procedure CalculateDonation to be removed.

Lines 132–133 specify procedure CalculateDonation's header. Keyword ByRef (line 133) indicates that variable decNetDonation is passed by reference. This means that any changes made to variable decNetDonation in CalculateDonation affect btnDonate_Click's local variable decAfterCosts. Because it is no longer necessary for CalculateDonation to return a value, CalculateDonation is now created as a Sub procedure, rather than a Function procedure.

Figure 15.17 CalculateDonation Sub procedure.

4. ***Calculating the donation amount for charity after operating costs.*** Add lines 135–139 of Fig. 15.18 to Sub procedure CalculateDonation. Lines 138–139 calculate the amount of the donation that goes toward charity after operating costs have been deducted. Notice that this is the same calculation that was performed in lines 139–140 of the Function procedure CalculateDonation in Fig. 15.16. The only difference is that assigning the calculation result to variable decNetDonation actually assigns the value to btnDonate_Click's local variable decAfterCosts. You do not need to return the calculation result.

5. ***Saving the project.*** Select **File > Save All** to save all the solution's files.

6. ***Testing the application.*** Select **Debug > Start** to run the application.

7. ***Terminating the application.*** After successfully testing the application, click the running application's close box.

(cont.)

Figure 15.18   Calculating the donation that goes toward charity after operating costs have been deducted.

15.4 Option Strict

When the computer accesses data, it needs to know of what type that data is for the data to make sense. Imagine you are purchasing a book from an online store that ships internationally. You notice that the price for the book is 20, but no currency is associated with the price; it could be dollars, euros, pesos, yen or some other currency. Therefore, it is important to know what type of currency is being used. If the currency is different from the one that you normally use, you will need to perform a conversion to get the price.

Similar conversions occur many times in an application. The computer determines a data type, and, with that knowledge, it adds two Integers or combines two Strings of text. Visual Basic .NET can convert one data type to another, as long as the conversion makes sense. For example, you are allowed to assign an Integer value to a Decimal variable without writing code that tells the application how to do the conversion. These types of assignments perform conversions called **implicit conversions**. When an attempted conversion doesn't make sense, such as assigning "hello" to an Integer variable, an error occurs. Figure 15.19 lists Visual Basic .NET's data types and their allowed implicit conversions. [*Note*: We do not discuss every data type in this book. Consult the Visual Basic .NET documentation to learn more about Visual Basic .NET's types.]

Data Type	Can be implicitly converted to these (larger) types
Boolean	Object
Byte	Short, Integer, Long, Decimal, Single, Double or Object

Figure 15.19   Data types and their allowed conversions. (Part 1 of 2.)

Data Type	Can be implicitly converted to these (larger) types
Char	String or Object
Date	Object
Decimal	Single, Double or Object
Double	Object
Integer	Long, Decimal, Single, Double or Object
Long	Decimal, Single, Double or Object
Object	none
Short	Integer, Long, Decimal, Single, Double or Object
Single	Double or Object
String	Object

Figure 15.19   Data types and their allowed conversions. (Part 2 of 2.)

The types listed in the right column are "larger" types, in that they can store more data than the types in the left column. For example, Integer types (left column) can be converted to Long types (right column, which includes four other data types). An Integer variable can store values in the approximate range ±2.1 billion; a Long variable can store numbers in the approximate range $±9×10^{18}$ (9 followed by 18 zeros). This means that any Integer value can be assigned to a Long variable without losing any data. These kinds of conversions are called implicit **widening conversions**, because the value of a "smaller" type (Integer) is being assigned to a variable of a "larger" type (Long).

When a "larger" type, such as Double, is assigned to a "smaller" type, such as Integer, either a run-time error will occur because the value being assigned is too large to be stored in the "smaller" type or the assignment will be permitted. Consider the following code:

```
Dim dblValue As Double = 4.6
Dim intValue As Integer = dblValue
```

Common Programming Error

Narrowing conversions can result in loss of data, which can cause subtle logic errors.

Variable intValue will be assigned 5—the result of implicitly converting the Double value 4.6 to an Integer. These types of conversions are called implicit **narrowing conversions**. These types of conversions can introduce subtle errors in applications, because the actual value being assigned could have been altered without you being aware of it—a dangerous practice. For example, if the programmer was expecting variable intValue to be assigned a value other than 5 (such as 4.6 or 4), a logic error would occur.

Visual Basic .NET provides a feature called **Option Strict** that, when set to On, disallows implicit narrowing conversions. If you attempt an implicit narrowing conversion, the compiler issues a syntax error. Later, we will show you how programmers can "override" this by performing narrowing conversions explicitly. First, however, you will learn how to enable Option Strict, which is set to Off by default. The box, *Enabling Option Strict*, demonstrates how to set Option Strict to On through the Visual Studio .NET IDE.

Enabling *Option Strict*

1. ***Activating Option Strict.*** In the **Solution Explorer** window, right click the project name (FundRaiser) to display a context menu. Select **Properties** to open the **FundRaiser Property Pages** dialog (Fig. 15.20).

2. ***Selecting the Build option.*** In the left side of the **FundRaiser Property Pages** dialog, select **Build** from the **Common Properties** folder (Fig. 15.21). In the middle of the dialog under **Compiler Defaults** is a ComboBox labeled **Option Strict:**. By default, the option is set to Off.

(cont.)

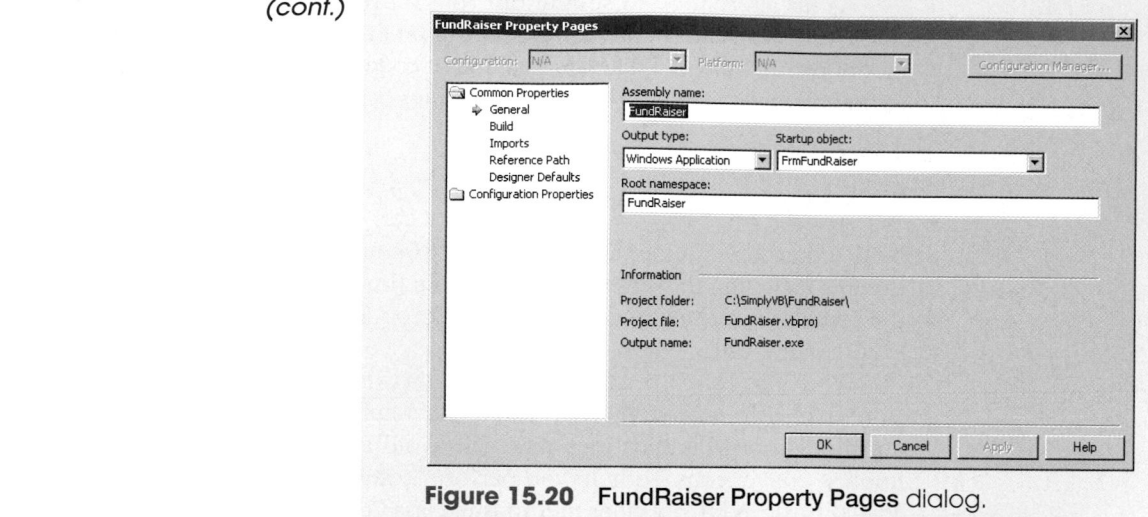

Figure 15.20   FundRaiser **Property Pages** dialog.

Build option ———

ComboBox containing value
for Option Strict, which is ———
set to Off by default

Figure 15.21   Selecting **Build** in the **FundRaiser Property Pages** dialog.

3. ***Setting Option Strict to On.*** Select On in the ComboBox labeled **Option Strict:**. Click **Apply**, then click **OK** to close the dialog. Option Strict is now set to On for this application. You will need to set Option Strict to On for each application you create.

On option for Option Strict ———

Figure 15.22   Setting Option Strict to On.

4. ***Saving the project.*** Select **File > Save All** to save all the solution's files.

As an alternative to setting Option Strict to On through the Visual Studio .NET IDE, you can set Option Strict to On programmatically by writing the statement Option Strict On as the first line of code. For example, to set Option Strict to On in FundRaiser.vb, the first three lines of the file would appear as

```
Option Strict On

Public Class FrmFundRaiser
```

Notice that the statement Option Strict On must appear before any other code in the file, including the class definition. From this point forward, all code examples in the remainder of this book have had Option Strict set to On through the Visual Studio .NET IDE.

When Option Strict is On, you must write code to perform narrowing conversions explicitly. At first, this may seem like a nuisance. However, it will help you create more robust applications that will avoid subtle errors that could result from implicit conversions. To help you perform conversions when Option Strict is On, Visual Basic .NET provides methods in class **Convert** (Fig. 15.23).

Error-Prevention Tip

Set Option Strict to On in every application to avoid subtle errors that can be introduced by implicit narrowing conversions.

Convert To	Use Convert Method	Sample Statement
Integer	ToInt32	intValue = Convert.ToInt32(_ Val(txtInput.Text))
Decimal	ToDecimal	decValue = Convert.ToDecimal(_ Pmt(dblMonthlyInterest, _ intMonths,-intLoanAmount))
Double	ToDouble	dblRate = Convert.ToDouble(_ Val(txtRate.Text)) / 100
String	ToString	strResult = Convert.ToString(intTotal)

Figure 15.23   Four of class Convert's methods.

The name of each conversion method is the word To, followed by the name of the data type to which the method converts its argument. For example, to convert a String input by the user in TextBox txtInput to an Integer (represented in Visual Basic .NET as type **Int32**) use the statement

```
intNumber = Convert.ToInt32(Val(txtInput.Text))
```

Conversions in statements that call Convert methods are called **explicit conversions**. In the box, *Using Class Convert in the **Fund Raiser** Application*, you will learn to use explicit conversions.

Using Class Convert in the Fund Raiser Application

1. ***Converting a Double donation amount to a Decimal value.*** Notice that lines 138–139 in Fig. 15.24 are underlined. Place the mouse pointer over the jagged lines. An error message now displays, indicating that Option Strict prohibits an implicit conversion from Double to Decimal. This is because converting from Double to Decimal could result in data loss.

    Replace the underlined expression with lines 138–139 of Fig. 15.25. Method Convert.ToDecimal converts the Double value to a Decimal value. When the conversion is performed explicitly with a call to method Convert.ToDecimal, the jagged lines disappear.

2. ***Converting the user input from a String to a Decimal.*** Line 158 of Fig. 15.26 is underlined. The error message that appears when the mouse pointer rests on this line indicates that Option Strict prohibits an implicit conversion from Double to Decimal.

(cont.)

Figure 15.24 `Option Strict` prohibits implicit narrowing conversions.

Figure 15.25 Explicitly performing a narrowing conversion with `Convert.ToDecimal`.

Figure 15.26 `Option Strict` prohibits a narrowing conversion from type `Double` to type `Decimal`.

Replace the underlined expression with line 158 of Fig. 15.27. Method `Convert.ToDecimal` explicitly converts the `Double` to a `Decimal`. After this change is made, the jagged lines disappear.

(cont.)

Figure 15.27 Explicitly converting a `Double` to type `Decimal` with `Convert.ToDecimal`.

3. *Running the application.* Select **Debug > Start** to run the application.

4. *Closing the solution.* Select **File > Close Solution**.

Figure 15.28 presents the **Fund Raiser** application's code. Lines that use new programming concepts are highlighted in yellow.

```
1   Public Class FrmFundRaiser
2      Inherits System.Windows.Forms.Form
3
4      ' instance variable stores total raised for charity
5      Dim m_decTotalRaised As Decimal = 0
6
7      ' Windows Form Designer generated code
8
9      ' returns donation amount after operating expenses
10     Sub CalculateDonation(ByVal decDonatedAmount As Decimal, _
11        ByRef decNetDonation As Decimal)
12
13        Const dblCOSTS As Double = 0.17
14
15        ' calculate amount of donation for charity
16        decNetDonation = Convert.ToDecimal(decDonatedAmount - _
17           (decDonatedAmount * dblCOSTS))
18     End Sub ' CalculateDonation
19
20     ' handles Donation: TextBox's TextChanged event
21     Private Sub txtDonation_TextChanged(ByVal sender As _
22        System.Object, ByVal e As System.EventArgs) _
23        Handles txtDonation.TextChanged
24
25        lblDonatedValue.Text = "" ' clear After expenses: field
26     End Sub ' txtDonation_TextChanged
27
28     ' handles Make Donation Button's Click event
29     Private Sub btnDonate_Click(ByVal sender As System.Object, _
30        ByVal e As System.EventArgs) Handles btnDonate.Click
31
32        Dim decDonation As Decimal   ' amount donated
```

Figure 15.28 Fund Raiser application's code. (Part 1 of 2.)

```
33          Dim decAfterCosts As Decimal   ' amount for charity
34
35          ' get donation amount
36          decDonation = Convert.ToDecimal(Val(txtDonation.Text))
37
38          ' obtain donation amount after operating costs deduction
39          CalculateDonation(decDonation, decAfterCosts)
40
41          ' display amount of donation after costs
42          lblDonatedValue.Text = String.Format("{0:C}", decAfterCosts)
43
44          ' update total amount of donations received
45          m_decTotalRaised += decAfterCosts
46
47          ' display total amount collected for charity
48          lblTotalValue.Text = String.Format("{0:C}", m_decTotalRaised)
49       End Sub ' btnDonate_Click
50
51    End Class ' FrmFundRaiser
```

Figure 15.28   Fund Raiser application's code. (Part 2 of 2.)

SELF-REVIEW   1. When Option Strict is set to On, the programmer must explicitly perform _____.

a) narrowing conversions   b) widening conversions

c) all type conversions   d) no conversions

2. The methods in _____ are used to change data types explicitly.

a) class Strict   b) class Change

c) class Convert   d) class Conversion

Answers: 1) a. 2) c.

15.5 Wrap-Up

In this tutorial, you learned concepts about data types and variables, and you built the **Fund Raiser** application to demonstrate these concepts.

You learned how to create instance variables, which are declared inside a class, but outside any procedure definitions. Instance variables have module scope, which means that they are accessible to all procedures in the class in which they are declared. In this tutorial, you declared your instance variable in the Form class. In Tutorial 19, you will learn how to create your own classes and how to declare instance variables in them. Until now, all the variables you have declared have been local variables—that is, variables with either procedure scope or block scope. Variables with procedure scope are modifiable only within the procedure in which they are declared. Variables with block scope are modifiable only within the block (such as the body of an If...Then statement) in which they are declared.

You learned the difference between passing arguments by reference and passing arguments by value. When using pass-by-value, the calling procedure makes a copy of the argument's value and passes the copy to the called procedure. Changes to the called procedure's copy do not affect the original variable value in the calling procedure. When using pass-by-reference, the original data can be accessed and modified directly by the called procedure. You now know to use keyword ByVal to pass arguments by value and keyword ByRef to pass arguments by reference.

You also learned about data-type conversions. You learned that narrowing conversions (such as converting a Double to a Decimal) can result in data loss and that widening conversions (such as a conversion from Integer to Double) don't have this problem. You learned that setting `Option Strict` to `On` causes Visual Basic .NET to flag implicit narrowing conversions as syntax errors and forces the programmer to perform such conversions explicitly.

In the next tutorial, you will learn about random-number generation, and you will create an application that simulates the dice game called Craps.

SKILLS SUMMARY

Setting `Option Strict` to `On`

- Right click the project in the **Solution Explorer**, and select **Properties**.
- Select **Build** from the directory tree in the **Property Pages** dialog.
- Set the **Option Strict:** ComboBox to On.
- Click **Apply**, then click **OK**.

Passing Arguments

- Arguments can be passed in two ways: pass-by-value (`ByVal`) and pass-by-reference (`ByRef`).

Passing Arguments by Value

- In the procedure header, place keyword `ByVal` before the name of each argument that should be passed by value.
- The application makes a copy of the argument's value and passes the copy to the called procedure.
- Changes to the called procedure's copy do not affect the original argument value.

Passing Arguments by Reference

- In the procedure header, place keyword `ByRef` before the name of each argument that should be passed by reference.
- Called procedures can access and modify original arguments directly.

Understanding Scope

- You have learned the differences between module scope, procedure scope and block scope.
- Instance variables have module scope and can be accessed by all procedures in the same class.
- Local variables have either procedure scope or block scope.
- Variables with procedure scope cannot be referenced outside the procedure in which they are declared.
- Variables with block scope cannot be referenced outside the block (such as the body of an `If...Then` statement) in which they are declared.
- Block scope begins at the identifier's declaration and ends at the block's end statement.

KEY TERMS

block scope—Variables declared inside control structures, such as an `If...Then` statement, have block scope. Block scope begins at the identifier's declaration and ends at the block's final statement (for example, `End If`).

call-by-reference—See *pass-by-reference*.

call-by-value—See *pass-by-value*.

Convert class—A class that provides methods for converting data types.

instance variable—A variable declared inside a class but outside any procedure of that class. Instance variables have module scope.

local variable—A variable declared inside a procedure or block, such as the body of an `If...Then` statement. Local variables have either procedure scope or block scope.

module scope—Module scope, which begins at the identifier after keyword `Class` and terminates at the `End Class` statement, enables all procedures in the same class to access all instance variables defined in that class.

Option Strict—When set to `On`, `Option Strict` causes the compiler to check all conversions and requires the programmer to perform an explicit conversion for all narrowing conversions (for example, conversion from Double to Decimal) or application termination (conversion of a String, such as "hello", to type Integer).

pass-by-reference—When an argument is passed by reference, the called procedure can access and modify the caller's original data directly. Keyword ByRef indicates pass-by-reference (also called call-by-reference).

pass-by-value—When an argument is passed by value, the application makes a copy of the argument's value and passes that copy to the called procedure. With pass-by-value, changes to the called procedure's copy do not affect the original variable's value. Keyword ByVal indicates pass-by-value (also called call-by-value).

procedure scope—Variables declared inside a procedure but outside of a control structure, have procedure scope. Variables with procedure scope cannot be referenced outside the procedure in which they are declared.

scope—The portion of an application in which an identifier (such as a variable name) can be referenced. Some identifiers can be referenced throughout an application; others can be referenced only from limited portions of an application (such as within a single procedure or block).

MULTIPLE-CHOICE QUESTIONS

15.1 In the **Property Pages** dialog, _____ must be selected to access Option Strict.

a) **Build**

b) **Designer Defaults**

c) **General**

d) **Imports**

15.2 When Option Strict is set to On, variables _____.

a) are passed by value

b) are passed by reference

c) might need to be converted explicitly to a different type to avoid errors

d) are used only within the block in which the variables are declared

15.3 A variable declared inside a class, but outside a procedure, is called a(n) _____.

a) local variable

b) hidden variable

c) instance variable

d) constant variable

15.4 Visual Basic .NET provides methods in class _____ to convert from one data type to another.

a) ChangeTo

b) Convert

c) ConvertTo

d) ChangeType

15.5 When Option Strict is _____, the conversion attempt intX = dblPercent results in an error.

a) On

b) True

c) Off

d) False

15.6 Keyword _____ indicates pass-by-reference.

a) ByReference

b) ByRef

c) Ref

d) Reference

15.7 With _____, changes made to a parameter variable's value do not affect the value of the variable in the calling procedure.

a) Option Strict

b) pass-by-value

c) pass-by-reference

d) None of the above.

15.8 Instance variables _____.

a) are members of class

b) are prefixed by m_

c) can be accessed by a procedure in the same class

d) All of the above.

15.9 Assigning a "smaller" type to a "larger" type is a _____ conversion.

a) narrowing

b) shortening

c) widening

d) lengthening

15.10 A value of type Boolean can be implicitly converted to _____.

a) Integer

b) String

c) Object

d) Double

EXERCISES

15.11 (*Task List Application*) Create an application that allows users to add items to a daily task list. The application should also display the number of tasks to be performed. Use method Convert.ToString to display the number of tasks in a Label.

a) *Copying the template application to your work folder.* Copy the TaskList folder from C:\Examples\Tutorial15\Exercises to C:\SimplyVB.

b) *Opening the template application.* Double click TaskList.sln in C:\SimplyVB\TaskList. Double click TaskList.vb in the **Solution Explorer** window to open the Form in design view (Fig. 15.29).

c) *Setting Option Strict to On.* Use the directions provided in the box, *Enabling Option Strict*, to set Option Strict to On.

d) *Adding the Add Task Button's Click event handler.* Double click the **Add Task** Button to generate the empty event handler btnAdd_Click. This event handler should display the user input in the ListBox and clear the user input from the TextBox. The event handler should also update the Label that displays the number of tasks. Use method Convert.ToString to display the number of tasks in the Label. Finally, the event handler should transfer the focus to the TextBox.

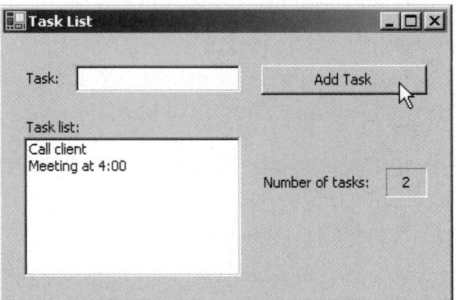

Figure 15.29 **Task List** application's GUI.

15.12 (*Quiz Average Application*) Develop an application that computes a student's average quiz score for all of the quiz scores entered. The application should look like the GUI in Fig. 15.30. Use method Convert.ToInt32 to convert the user input to an Integer. Use instance variables with module scope to keep track of the sum of all the quiz scores entered and the number of quiz scores entered.

Figure 15.30 **Quiz Average** application's GUI.

a) *Copying the exercise template to your work folder.* Copy the QuizAverage folder from C:\Examples\Tutorial15\Exercises to C:\SimplyVB.

b) *Opening the template exercise.* Double click QuizAverage.sln in C:\SimplyVB\QuizAverage.

c) *Setting Option Strict to On.* Use the directions provided in the box, *Enabling Option Strict*, to set Option Strict to On.

d) *Adding instance variables.* Add two instance variables—m_intTotalScore, which keeps track of the sum of all the quiz scores entered, and m_intTaken, which keeps track of the number of quiz scores entered.

e) *Adding the Grade Quiz Button's event handler.* Double click the **Submit Score** Button to generate the empty event handler btnCalculate_Click. The code required in *Steps f–k* should be placed in this event handler.

f) *Obtaining user input.* Use method Convert.ToInt32 to convert the user input from the TextBox to an Integer.

g) *Updating the number of quiz scores entered.* Increment the number of quiz scores entered.

h) *Updating the sum of all the quiz scores entered.* Add the current quiz score to the current total to update the sum of all the quiz scores entered.

i) *Calculating the average score.* Divide the sum of all the quiz scores entered by the number of quiz scores entered to calculate the average score.

j) *Displaying the average score.* Use method Convert.ToString to display the average quiz grade in the **Average:** field.

k) *Displaying the number of quizzes taken.* Use method Convert.ToString to display the number of quiz scores entered in the **Number taken:** field.

15.13 (*Maximum Application*) Modify the **Maximum** application from Chapter 13 (Fig. 15.31) to use keyword ByRef to pass a fourth argument to procedure Maximum by reference. Also, use methods from class Convert to perform any necessary type conversions.

Figure 15.31 **Maximum** application's GUI.

a) *Copying the exercise template to your work folder.* Copy the Maximum folder from C:\Examples\Tutorial15\Exercises to C:\SimplyVB.

b) *Opening the template exercise.* Double click Maximum.sln in C:\SimplyVB\Maximum.

c) *Setting Option Strict to On.* Use the directions provided in the box, *Enabling Option Strict,* to set Option Strict to On.

d) *Adding a local variable.* Add local variable dblMaximum of type Double to event handler btnMaximum_Click. The code required in *Steps d–f* should be placed in this event handler. Variable dblMaximum will store the result of procedure Maximum.

e) *Passing four arguments to procedure Maximum.* Use method Convert.ToDouble to convert the user input from the TextBoxes to Doubles. Pass these three values as the first three arguments to procedure Maximum. Pass local variable dblMaximum as the fourth argument to procedure Maximum.

f) *Displaying the maximum value.* Use method Convert.ToString to display local variable dblMaximum in the **Maximum:** field.

g) *Changing procedure Maximum to a Sub procedure.* Change procedure Maximum to a Sub procedure. Make sure that Sub procedure Maximum no longer returns a value and does not specify a return type. The modifications required in *Steps g–h* should be performed on this Sub procedure.

h) *Adding a fourth parameter to procedure Maximum.* Add a fourth parameter dblFinalMaximum of type Double to Maximum's procedure header. Use keyword ByRef to specify that this argument will be passed by reference. Remove the declaration of variable dblFinalMaximum from the body of procedure Maximum.

What does this code do? ▶ **15.14** What is displayed in Label lblDisplay when the following code is executed?

```
1   Public Class FrmScopeTest
2      Inherits System.Windows.Forms.Form
3
4      Dim intValue2 As Integer = 5
5
6      Private Sub btnEnter_Click(ByVal sender As System.Object, _
7         ByVal e As System.EventArgs) Handles btnEnter.Click
8
9         Dim intValue1 As Integer = 10
10        Dim intValue2 As Integer = 3
11
12        Test(intValue1)
13        lblDisplay.Text = Convert.ToString(intValue1)
14     End Sub ' btnEnter_Click
15
16     Sub Test(ByRef intValue1 As Integer)
17        intValue1 *= intValue2
18     End Sub ' Test
19
20  End Class ' FrmScopeTest
```

What's wrong with this code? ▶ **15.15** Find the error(s) in the following code (the procedure should assign the value 14 to variable intResult).

```
1   Sub Sum()
2      Dim strNumber As String = "4"
3      Dim intNumber As Integer = 10
4      Dim intResult As Integer
5
6      intResult = strNumber + intNumber
7   End Sub ' Sum
```

Programming Challenge ▶ **15.16** (*Schedule Book Application*) Develop an application that allows a user to enter a schedule of appointments and their respective times. Create the Form in Fig. 15.32 and name the application **Schedule Book**. Add a Function procedure called TimeTaken that returns a Boolean value. Each time a user enters a new appointment, Function procedure TimeTaken determines if the user has scheduled more than one appointment at the same time. If Time-Taken returns True, the user will be notified via a message dialog. Otherwise, the appointment should be added to the ListBoxes. Set Option Strict to On and use methods from class Convert as necessary.

Figure 15.32 Schedule Book application's GUI.

Craps Game Application

Introducing Random-Number Generation

Objectives

In this tutorial, you will learn to:
- Code simulation techniques that employ random-number generation.
- Use class **Random** methods.
- Generate random numbers.
- Use enumerations to enhance code readability.

Outline

Y ou will now be introduced to a popular type of application—simulation and game playing. In this tutorial, you will develop a **Craps Game** application. There is something in the air of a gambling casino that invigorates each person—from the high rollers at the plush mahogany-and-felt Craps tables to the quarter-poppers at the one-armed bandits. Many of these individuals are drawn by the element of chance—the possibility that luck will convert a pocketful of money into a mountain of wealth.

The element of chance can be introduced into computer applications using random numbers. This tutorial's **Craps Game** application introduces several new concepts, including random-number generation and enumerations. It also uses important concepts that you learned earlier in this book, including instance variables, procedures and the `Select Case` multiple-selection control structure.

16.1 Test-Driving the Craps Game Application

One of the most popular games of chance is a dice game known as "Craps," played in casinos throughout the world. This application meets the following requirements:

Application Requirements

Create an application that simulates playing the game of "Craps." In this game, a player rolls two dice. Each die has six faces. Each face contains 1, 2, 3, 4, 5 or 6 spots. After the dice have come to rest, the sum of the spots on the two top faces is calculated. If the sum is 7 or 11 on the first throw, the player wins. If the sum is 2, 3 or 12 on the first throw (called "craps"), the player loses (the "house" wins). If the sum is 4, 5, 6, 8, 9 or 10 on the first throw, that sum becomes the player's "point." To win, a player must continue rolling the dice until the player rolls the point value. The player loses by rolling a 7 before rolling the point.

Creating this application will teach you two important concepts; random-number generation and enumerations. You begin by test-driving the completed application.

Test-Driving the Craps Game Application

1. *Copying and opening the completed application.* Copy the C:\Examples\Tutorial16\CompletedApplication\CrapsGame folder to C:\SimplyVB. Double click CrapsGame.sln to open the application in Visual Studio .NET. Select **Debug > Start** to run the application. The Form in Fig. 16.1 will display.

Figure 16.1 **Craps Game** application initial appearance.

2. *Starting the game.* Click the **Play** Button. There are three possible outcomes at this point: The player wins by rolling a 7 or an 11 (Fig. 16.2). The player loses by rolling 2, 3 or 12 (Fig. 16.3). Otherwise, the roll becomes the player's point (4, 5, 6, 8, 9 or 10), which is then displayed for the remainder of the game (Fig. 16.4). Note that unlike the real game of Craps, the value of the roll is computed using the forward-facing die faces instead of the top faces in this application.

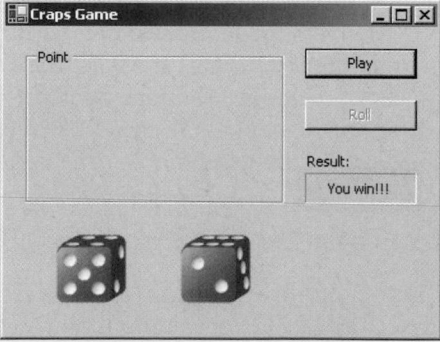

Figure 16.2 Player wins on first roll by rolling 7 or 11.

Figure 16.3 Player loses on first roll by rolling 2, 3 or 12.

(cont.)

Figure 16.4 First roll sets the point that the player must match to win.

3. ***Continuing the game.*** If the application displays **Roll again!**, as in Fig. 16.4, click the **Roll** Button repeatedly until either you win—by matching your point value (Fig. 16.5)—or you lose—by rolling a 7 (Fig. 16.6). When the game ends, you can click **Play** to start over.

Figure 16.5 Winning the game by matching your point before rolling a 7.

Figure 16.6 Losing by rolling a 7 before matching your point.

4. ***Terminating the application.*** Click the running application's close box to terminate the application.

5. ***Closing the solution.*** Select **File > Close Solution**.

16.2 Random-Number Generation

Now you will learn how to use an object of class **Random** to introduce the element of chance into your computer applications. You will learn more about working with objects of existing classes over the next few tutorials, then you will learn to create your own classes and create objects of those classes in Tutorial 19. Consider the following statements:

```
Dim objRandom As Random = New Random()
Dim intRandomNumber As Integer = objRandom.Next()
```

The first statement declares objRandom as a reference of type Random and assigns it a Random object. A **reference** is a variable to which you assign an object. Recall that keyword New creates a new structure value or a new instance of an object in memory.

The second statement declares Integer variable intRandomNumber. It then assigns to it the value returned by calling Random's Next method on object objRandom using the dot operator. The **Next** method generates a positive Integer value between zero and the largest possible Integer, which is the constant **Int32.MaxValue** (2,147,483,647). You can use the Next method to generate random values of type Integer or use the **NextDouble** method to generate random values of type Double. The NextDouble method returns a positive Double value between 0.0 and 1.0 (not including 1.0). Class Random does not contain a Next method for any other data type.

If the Next method were to produce truly random values, then every value in this range would have an equal **chance** (or **probability**) of being chosen when Next is called. However, the values returned by Next are actually **pseudorandom numbers**, a sequence of values produced by a complex mathematical calculation. This mathematical calculation comes close, but is not exactly random in choosing numbers.

The range of values produced by Next (that is, values between 0 and 2,147,483,647) often is different from the range needed in a particular application. For example, an application that simulates coin tossing might require only 0 for "heads" and 1 for "tails." An application that simulates the rolling of a six-sided die would require random Integers from 1 to 6. Similarly, an application that randomly predicts the next type of spaceship (out of four possibilities) that flies across the horizon in a video game might require random Integers from 1 to 4.

By passing an argument to the Next method[1] as follows

```
intValue = 1 + objRandom.Next(6)
```

you can produce integers in the range from 1 to 6. When a single argument is passed to Next, the values returned by Next will be in the range from 0 to (but not including) the value of that argument (that is, 5 in the preceding statement). You can change the range of numbers produced by adding 1 to the previous result, so that the return values are between 1 and 6, rather than 0 and 5. That new range, 1 to 6, corresponds nicely with the roll of a six-sided die, for example.

Visual Basic .NET simplifies this process of setting the range of numbers by allowing the programmer to pass two arguments to Next. For example, the preceding statement also could be written as

```
intValue = objRandom.Next(1, 7)
```

Note that you must use 7 as the second argument to the Next method to produce integers in the range from 1 to 6. The first argument indicates the minimum value in the desired range; the second is equal to *one more than the maximum value desired*.

As with method Next, the range of values produced by method NextDouble (that is, values greater than or equal to 0.0 and less than 1.0) is also usually different from the range needed in a particular application. By multiplying the value returned from method NextDouble as follows

```
dblValue = 6 * objRandom.NextDouble()
```

---

1. In Tutorial 13, you learned that the number, type and order of arguments to a procedure must exactly match the procedure definition. You may notice that the Next method of class Random is called using zero, one and two arguments. There is a sophisticated feature of Visual Basic .NET called procedure overloading that allows multiple procedure definitions of the same name but with different numbers of arguments, types, and/or order.

you can produce Double values in the range from 0.0 to 6.0 (not including 6.0). Figure 16.7 shows examples of the ranges returned by calls to methods Next and NextDouble.

Method call	Resulting range
objRandom.Next()	0 to one less than Int32.MaxValue
objRandom.Next(30)	0 to 29
10 + objRandom.Next(10)	10 to 19
objRandom.Next(10, 20)	10 to 19
objRandom.Next(5, 100)	5 to 99
objRandom.NextDouble()	0.0 to less than 1.0
8 * objRandom.NextDouble()	0.0 to less than 8.0

Figure 16.7 Next and NextDouble method calls with corresponding ranges.

SELF-REVIEW

1. The statement _____ returns a number in the range from 8 to 300.

   a) objRandom.Next(8, 300)   b) objRandom.Next(8, 301)

   c) 1 + objRandom.Next(8, 300)   d) None of the above.

2. The statement _____ returns a number in the range 15 to 35.

   a) objRandom.Next(15, 36)   b) objRandom.Next(15, 35)

   c) 10 + objRandom.Next(5, 26)   d) Both a and c.

Answers: 1) b. 2) d.

16.3 Using Enumerations in the Craps Game Application

Given the problem statement introduced in Section 16.1, you are now ready to study the pseudocode representation for the **Craps Game** application:

```
When the player clicks the Play Button
    Roll the dice using random numbers
    Display images corresponding to the numbers on the rolled dice
    Calculate the sum of both dice
    Select correct case below and execute its body statements

    Case where first roll is 7 or 11
        Display winning message, and allow player to start new game

    Case where first roll is 2, 3 or 12
        Display losing message and allow player to start a new game

    Case where none of the preceding Cases are true
        Set the value of the point to the sum of the dice, and display the value

When the player clicks the Roll Button

    If the player rolls the same value as the point
        Display winning message and allow player to start new game

    If the player rolls a 7
        Display losing message and allow player to start a new game
    Else
        Allow the player to roll again
```

The ACE table in Fig. 16.8 presents the **Craps Game** application's actions and events. These actions and events will guide you as you build the application.

Action/Control/Event (ACE) Table for the Craps Game Application

Action	Control/Object	Event
Label the application's controls	`lblResult`	
Roll the dice using random numbers; calculate and display the value of the point; display images corresponding to the rolled dice; determine if player has won, lost or should continue playing	`btnPlay`, `m_objRandom`, `fraPointDiceGroup`, `picDie1`, `picDie2`, `picPointDie1`, `picPointDie2`,	`Click` (of Button)
Roll the dice using random numbers; display images corresponding to the rolled dice; determine if player has won, lost or should continue playing	`btnPlay`, `m_objRandom`, `picDie1`, `picDie2`, `picPointDie1`, `picPointDie2`,	`Click` (of Button)

Figure 16.8   ACE table for the **Craps Game** application.

In the following boxes, you will create an application to simulate playing the game of Craps. You begin with the box, *Viewing the **Craps Game** Template Application*. The steps that follow show you how to add code to import the `System.IO` namespace. As you have already learned, Visual Basic .NET has access to the Framework Class Library (FCL), which is a rich collection of classes that can be used to enhance applications. The FCL includes classes that provide methods for using files, graphics, multimedia and more. These FCL classes are grouped (by functionality) in units called **namespaces**. The **`System.IO` namespace** provides classes and methods for accessing files (such as images and text) and directories (such as `C:\SimplyVB`). You will need to use code to access image files for the **Craps Game** application; therefore, you import the `System.IO` namespace. Importing a namespace (using keyword **`Imports`**) allows you to access its members.

Viewing the Craps Game Template Application

1. ***Copying the template to your work folder.*** Copy the `CrapsGame` folder from `C:\Examples\Tutorial16\TemplateApplication` to `C:\SimplyVB`.

2. ***Opening the template application.*** Double click `CrapsGame.sln` in `C:\SimplyVB\CrapsGame` to open the application in Visual Studio .NET. Double click `CrapsGame.vb` in the **Solution Explorer** window to open the template application in design view (Fig. 16.9).

Figure 16.9   Template **Craps Game** Form in design view.

3. ***Allowing image-file access.*** The application will display images; therefore, you need to import the `System.IO` namespace to allow access to methods to help you read image files. Select **View > Code**. Add `Imports System.IO` (line 1) into your code before the class definition (Fig. 16.10).

(cont.)

Figure 16.10 Imports statement added in the **Craps Game** application.

4.   *Saving the project.* Select **File > Save All** to save all the solution's files.

Notice that the numbers 2, 3, 7, 11 and 12 have special meanings during a game of Craps. Throughout the course of a Craps game, you will use these numbers (as constants) quite often. In this case, it would be helpful to create a group of related constants and assign them meaningful names for use in your application. Visual Basic .NET allows you to accomplish this by using an **enumeration**. You will learn how to create constant identifiers that describe various significant dice combinations in Craps (such as SNAKE_EYES, TREY, CRAPS, LUCKY_SEVEN, YO_LEVEN and BOX_CARS). By providing descriptive identifiers for a group of related constants, enumerations enhance program readability and ensure that numbers are consistent throughout the application. You will learn how to use enumerations in the box, *Introducing Enumerations and Declaring Instance Variables.*

Introducing Enumerations and Declaring Instance Variables

1.   ***Declaring an enumeration.*** Add lines 155–156 of Fig. 16.11 to your application after the Windows Form Designer generated code and press *Enter.* Notice that keywords End Enum appear. Enumerations begin with the keyword **Enum** (line 156), and end with the keywords **End Enum** (line 163). The name of the enumeration (DiceNames) follows the keyword Enum (line 156). Now add lines 157–162 of Fig. 16.11 into your application between the lines containing keywords Enum and End Enum.

Figure 16.11 Enumeration DiceNames in the **Craps Game** application.

(cont.)

Good Programming Practice

Use enumerations to group related constants and enhance code readability.

Common Programming Error

An enumeration type can be specified after the enumeration name by using the keyword `As` followed by `Byte`, `Integer`, `Long` or `Short`. Enumerations use type `Integer` if no type is specified. Attempting to create enumeration values of type `String`, `Decimal` and `Double` results in a syntax error.

Enumerations are used in this application to make the code easier to read, especially for someone who is unfamiliar with the application. You can refer to the numbers using the enumeration constants and the member-access operator. For instance, use `DiceNames.SNAKE_EYES` for the number 2, `DiceNames.TREY` for the number 3, `DiceNames.CRAPS` and `Dice-Names.LUCKY_SEVEN` for the number 7, `DiceNames.YO_LEVEN` for the number 11 and `DiceNames.BOX_CARS` for the number 12. Notice that you can assign the same value to multiple enumeration constants, as you did in lines 159 and 160.

2. ***Declaring instance variables.*** Several methods will require the use of the same variables throughout the lifetime of the application. You will declare instance variables for this purpose. Add lines 165–172 of Fig. 16.12 below the enumeration definition.

Declaring constants ——

Declaring variable to store point value ——

Creating a **Random** object ——

Figure 16.12   Instance variables added to the **Craps Game** application.

In this application, you will need to access images that display the six faces of a die. For convenience, each file has a name that differs only by one number. For example, the image for the die face displaying 1 is named `die1.png`, and the image for the die face displaying 6 is named `die6.png`. Recall that `png` is an image-file name extension that is short for Portable Network Graphic. These images are stored in the folder named `images` in your project's `bin` directory. As such, the `String images/die1.png` would correctly indicate the location of the die face displaying 1 relative to the `bin` directory. [*Note*: You also can indicate the location of the die face by using the `String images\die1.png`.] To help create a `String` representing the path to the image, `Strings m_strFILE_PREFIX` (`images/die`) and `m_strFILE_SUFFIX` (`.png`) are used (as constants) to store the prefix and suffix of the file name (lines 166–167).

The game of Craps requires that you store the user's point, once established on the first roll, for the duration of the game. Therefore, variable `m_intMyPoint` (line 170 of Fig. 16.12) is declared as an `Integer` to store the value of the dice on the first roll. You will use the `Random` object referenced by `m_objRandom` (line 171) to "roll" the dice and generate those values.

3. ***Saving the project.*** Select **File > Save All** to save all the solution's files.

SELF-REVIEW   1. Use keyword _____ to define groups of related constants.

   a) `ReadOnly`   b) `Enum`

   c) `Constants`   d) `Enumeration`

2. Namespace _____ is used to access files and directories.
   a) `System.File`   b) `System.FileDirectory`
   c) `System.FileAccess`   d) `System.IO`

Answers: 1) b. 2) d.

16.4 Using Random Numbers in the Craps Game Application

Now that you have declared an enumeration and instance variables, you will add code to execute when the user clicks the **Craps Game** application's `Button`s. The box, *Coding the **Play** Button's Click Event Handler* explains how to add the code that executes when the user clicks the **Play** `Button`.

Coding the Play Button's Click Event Handler

1. **Creating the Play Button's Click event handler.** Return to the **Design View** to display the Form. Double click the **Play** `Button` to generate the **Play** Button's `Click` event handler and view the code file. (The **Play** `Button` is used to begin a new game of Craps.)

2. **Removing Images from a PictureBox and rolling dice.** Begin coding the `Click` event handler by adding lines 177–186 from Fig. 16.13 into the `btnPlay_Click` event handler.

Initializing values for a new —

Removing images from `PictureBox`es —

"Rolling" the dice —

Figure 16.13 `btnPlay_Click` event handler definition.

Lines 178–180 initialize variables for a new game. Line 178 sets variable `m_intMyPoint`, the Craps game point value, to 0. Line 179 changes the text displayed on the `GroupBox` to `Point`, using the `GroupBox`'s `Text` property. As you saw in the box, *Test-Driving the Craps Game Application*, the `GroupBox`'s `Text` property will be used to display the point value. Finally, line 180 clears the value of the output `Label` because the user is starting a new game.

Lines 183–184 remove any images from the `PictureBox`es used to display the point die. Though there are no images when the application is first run, if the user chooses to continue playing after completing a game, the images from the previous game must be cleared. Setting the `Image` property to keyword `Nothing` indicates that there is no image to display. Keyword **`Nothing`** is used to clear a reference's value, much as the empty string (`""`) is used to clear a `String`'s value.

(cont.)

Line 186 declares the variable intSum and assigns to it the value returned by rolling the dice. This is accomplished by calling the RollDice procedure, which you will define in the box, *Using Random Numbers to Simulate Rolling Dice.* [*Note*: RollDice() will be underlined in blue because the procedure is not yet defined.] The RollDice procedure will not only roll dice and return the sum of their values, but also will display the die images in the lower two PictureBoxes.

3. ***Using a Select Case statement to determine the result of rolling the dice.*** Recall that if the player rolls 7 or 11 on the first roll, the player wins. However, if the player rolls 2, 3 or 12 on the first roll, the player loses. Add lines 188–189 of Fig. 16.14 to the btnPlay_Click event handler beneath the code you added in the previous step. Press *Enter*. Notice that the keywords End Select are auto-generated. Now add lines 191–202 of Fig. 16.14 into the btnPlay_Click event handler between the Select and End Select keywords.

Winning on the first roll

Losing on the first roll

Figure 16.14 Select Case statement in btnPlay_Click.

The first Case statement (lines 191–195) selects values 7 and 11, using the enumeration values DiceNames.LUCKY_SEVEN and DiceNames.YO_LEVEN. Recall that several expressions can be specified in the same Case statement when they are separated by commas. If the sum of the dice is 7 or 11, the code in lines 194–195 disables the **Roll** Button and displays "You win!!!" in the output Label lblStatus. If the dice add up to 2 (Dice-Names.SNAKE_EYES), 3 (DiceNames.TREY) or 12 (DiceNames.BOX_CARS), the code in the second Case statement executes (lines 197–202). This code disables the **Roll** Button and displays a message in Label lblStatus indicating that the player has lost.

4. ***Using the Case Else statement to continue the game.*** If the player did not roll a 2, 3, 7, 11 or 12, then the value of the dice becomes the point and the player must roll again. Add lines 204–212 of Fig. 16.15 within the Select Case statement to implement this rule.

The first line of the Case Else statement's body (line 205) sets the instance variable m_intMyPoint to the sum of the die values. Next, line 206 changes the text on the GroupBox, using its Text property to display the value of the current point. The Label lblStatus is changed to notify the user to roll again (line 207).

(cont.)

Player must match the point

Display die images

Allow player to roll again

Figure 16.15 Case Else statement in btnPlay_Click.

If the user must match the point, you display the die images corresponding to the result of the dice roll. In Tutorial 3, you learned how to insert an image into a PictureBox in the Windows Form Designer. To set the image for a PictureBox, you used its Image property. You can also use code to set this property as well. To display the die faces for the point in the GroupBox, you should set the Image property of the each PictureBox in the GroupBox to the same Image property value as its corresponding PictureBox below the GroupBox (lines 208–209). Finally, the **Play** Button is disabled (line 210) and the **Roll** Button is enabled (line 211), limiting users to clicking the **Roll** Button for the rest of the game. Line 212 ends the Select Case statement.

5. ***Saving the project.*** Select **File > Save All** to save all the solution's files.

Because the **Roll** Button is enabled after the user clicks **Play**, you must code an event handler for it. You define the event handler in the box, *Coding the **Roll** Button's Click Event Handler.*

Coding the Roll Button's Click Event Handler

1. ***Generating the Roll Button's Click event handler.*** Return to the Windows Form Designer, and double click the **Roll** Button. This generates the **Roll** Button's Click event handler and opens the code window.

2. ***Rolling the dice.*** The user clicks the **Roll** Button to try to match the point, which requires rolling dice. Add line 220 of Fig. 16.16 which will roll the dice, display the die images and store the sum of the dice in variable intSum. [*Note*: RollDice() is underlined in blue because the procedure is not yet defined. You will define it to roll the dice and display the die images, shortly.]

3. ***Determining the output of the roll.*** If the roll matches the point, the user wins and the game ends. However, if the user rolls a 7 (DiceNames.CRAPS), the user loses and the game ends. Add lines 222–231 of Fig. 16.17 into the btnRoll_Click event handler to incorporate this processing into your **Craps Game** application.

The If...Then statement (lines 223–226) determines whether the sum of the dice in the current roll matches the point. If the sum and point match, the program displays a winning message in Label lblStatus. It then allows the user to start a new game, by disabling the **Roll** Button and enabling the **Play** Button.

(cont.)

Figure 16.16 Rolling the dice in `btnRoll_Click`.

Figure 16.17 Determining the outcome of a roll.

The `ElseIf` statement (lines 227–230) determines whether the sum of the dice in the current roll is 7 (`DiceNames.CRAPS`). If so, the application displays a message that the user has lost (in `Label` `lblStatus`) and ends the game by disabling the **Roll** Button and enabling the **Play** Button. If the player neither matches the point nor rolls a 7, then the player is allowed to roll again. The player rolls the dice again by clicking the **Roll** Button.

4. ***Saving the project.*** Select **File > Save All** to save all the solution's files.

In the box, *Using Random Numbers to Simulate Rolling Dice*, you add code into the application to simulate rolling dice and use code to display the dice in the appropriate `PictureBox`es.

Using Random Numbers to Simulate Rolling Dice

1. ***Creating a Random object and simulating die rolling.*** This application will roll and display dice many times as it executes. Therefore, it is a good idea to create two procedures: one to roll the dice (`RollDice`) and one to display the dice (`DisplayDie`). Define `Function` procedure `RollDice` first, by adding lines 235–248 of Fig. 16.18.

This code sets the values of `intDie1` and `intDie2` to the values returned by `m_objRandom.Next(1, 7)`, which is an `Integer` random number between the values 1 to 6 (lines 239 and 240). Remember that the number returned is always less than the second argument.

(cont.)

Getting two random numbers

Displaying die images

Returning sum of dice

Figure 16.18   RollDice procedure definition.

The procedure then makes two calls to DisplayDie (lines 243 and 244), a procedure that displays the image of the die face corresponding to each number. The first parameter in DisplayDie is the PictureBox that will display the image, and the second parameter is the number that appears on the face of the die. The calls to DisplayDie are underlined in blue as syntax errors because the procedure has not yet been defined. You will define the DisplayDie procedure in *Step 2*. Finally, the procedure returns the sum of the values of the dice (line 246), which the application uses to determine the outcome of the Craps game.

2. *Displaying the dice images.* You will now define procedure DisplayDie to display the die images corresponding to the random numbers generated in procedure RollDice. Add lines 250–259 of Fig. 16.19 (after the RollDice procedure) to create the DisplayDie procedure.

Displaying a die image

Figure 16.19   DisplayDie procedure definition.

(cont.)

Line 255 begins the statement that sets the `Image` property for the specified `PictureBox`. Because the `Image` property must be set using an object of type `Image`, you must create an `Image` object.

The `Image` class contains a `FromFile` method to help create `Image` objects. **`Image.FromFile`** returns an `Image` object containing the image located at the path you specify. To specify the location, use the path (as a `String`) as the parameter to the `FromFile` method. In this case, you can begin by using the `Directory.GetCurrentDirectory` method (line 256). The **`Directory.GetCurrentDirectory`** method (contained in the `System.IO` namespace) returns the location of the folder from which your application was loaded (the `bin` directory). In this case, `Directory.GetCurrentDirectory` will return the string `C:\SimplyVB\CrapsGame\bin`.

Now append `m_strFILE_PREFIX & intFace & m_strFILE_SUFFIX` to create the rest of the location of the file (line 257). If the value of `intFace` is 1, the expression would represent the string `images/die1.png`. This is the location of the image of a die face showing 1. If you combine the value of `Directory.GetCurrentDirectory` with the expression mentioned earlier, the result is `C:\SimplyVB\CrapsGame\bin\images\die1.png`, the location of the image on your computer. You can use Windows Explorer to verify that this is the correct location. This image is then displayed in the `PictureBox` by using its `Image` property.

3. ***Saving the project.*** Select **File > Save All** to save all the solution's files.

4. ***Running the application and playing the game.*** Now that you have finished building the application, select **Debug > Start** and enjoy the game!

Figure 16.20 displays the complete code listing for the **Craps Game** application. Note that, as part of the project settings, `Option Strict` is set to `On` (to ensure explicit narrowing conversions).

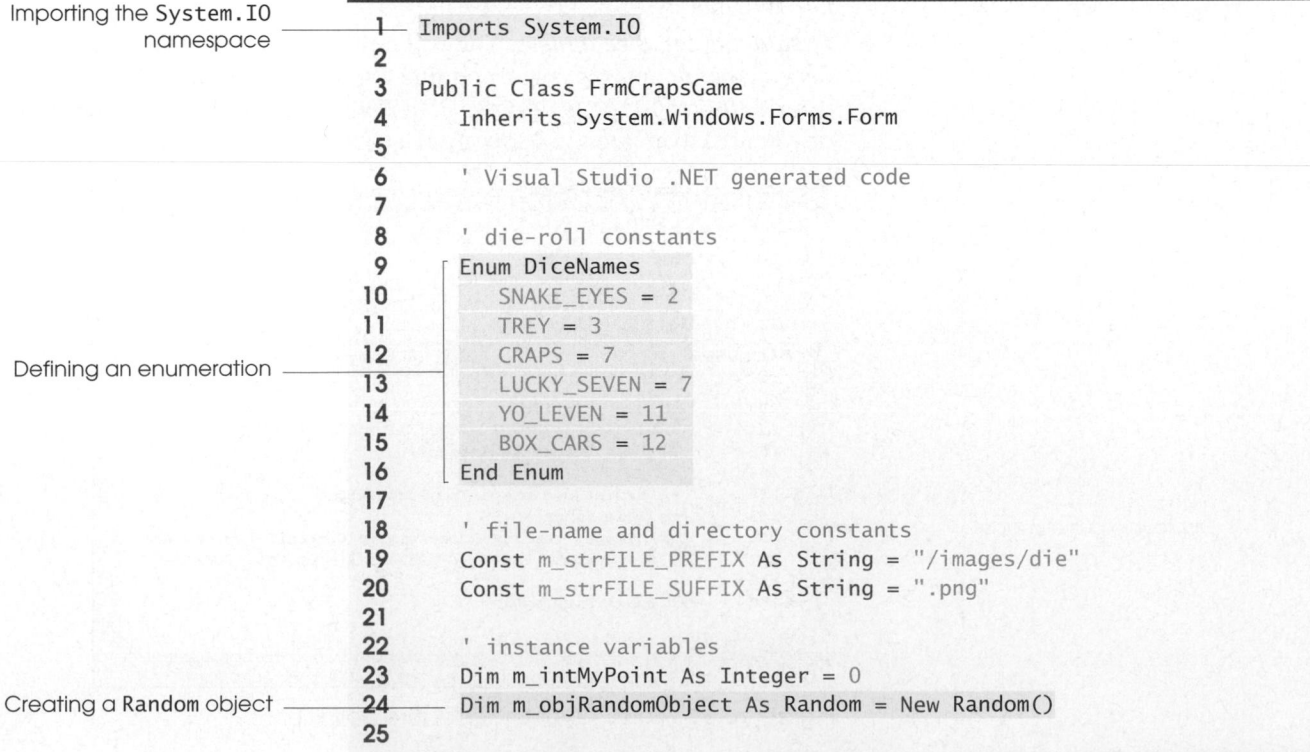

Importing the `System.IO` namespace

Defining an enumeration

Creating a **Random** object

```
1   Imports System.IO
2
3   Public Class FrmCrapsGame
4       Inherits System.Windows.Forms.Form
5
6       ' Visual Studio .NET generated code
7
8       ' die-roll constants
9       Enum DiceNames
10          SNAKE_EYES = 2
11          TREY = 3
12          CRAPS = 7
13          LUCKY_SEVEN = 7
14          YO_LEVEN = 11
15          BOX_CARS = 12
16      End Enum
17
18      ' file-name and directory constants
19      Const m_strFILE_PREFIX As String = "/images/die"
20      Const m_strFILE_SUFFIX As String = ".png"
21
22      ' instance variables
23      Dim m_intMyPoint As Integer = 0
24      Dim m_objRandomObject As Random = New Random()
25
```

Figure 16.20 **Craps Game** application code listing. (Part 1 of 3.)

```
26        ' begin new game and determine point
27        Private Sub btnPlay_Click(ByVal sender As System.Object, _
28           ByVal e As System.EventArgs) Handles btnPlay.Click
29
30           ' initialize variables for new game
31           m_intMyPoint = 0
32           fraPointDiceGroup.Text = "Point"
33           lblStatus.Text = ""
34
35           ' remove point-die images
36           picPointDie1.Image = Nothing
37           picPointDie2.Image = Nothing
38
39           Dim intSum As Integer = RollDice() ' roll dice
40
41           ' check die roll
42           Select Case intSum
43
44              Case DiceNames.LUCKY_SEVEN, _
45                 DiceNames.YO_LEVEN ' win on first roll
46
47                 btnRoll.Enabled = False ' disable Roll Button
48                 lblStatus.Text = "You win!!!"
49
50              Case DiceNames.SNAKE_EYES, _
51                 DiceNames.TREY, _
52                 DiceNames.BOX_CARS ' lose on first roll
53
54                 btnRoll.Enabled = False
55                 lblStatus.Text = "Sorry, you lose."
56
57              Case Else ' player must match point
58                 m_intMyPoint = intSum
59                 fraPointDiceGroup.Text = "Point Is " & intSum
60                 lblStatus.Text = "Roll again!"
61                 picPointDie1.Image = picDie1.Image
62                 picPointDie2.Image = picDie2.Image
63                 btnPlay.Enabled = False ' disable Play Button
64                 btnRoll.Enabled = True  ' enable Roll Button
65           End Select ' intSum
66
67        End Sub ' btnPlay_Click
68
69        ' determine outcome of next roll
70        Private Sub btnRoll_Click(ByVal sender As System.Object, _
71           ByVal e As System.EventArgs) Handles btnRoll.Click
72
73           Dim intSum As Integer = RollDice()
74
75           ' determine outcome of roll
76           If intSum = m_intMyPoint Then ' player matches point
77              lblStatus.Text = "You win!!!"
78              btnRoll.Enabled = False
79              btnPlay.Enabled = True
80           ElseIf intSum = DiceNames.CRAPS Then ' player loses
81              lblStatus.Text = "Sorry, you lose."
82              btnRoll.Enabled = False
83              btnPlay.Enabled = True
84           End If
```

Figure 16.20 Craps Game application code listing. (Part 2 of 3.)

```
85
86        End Sub ' btnRoll_Click
87
88        ' generate random die rolls
89        Function RollDice() As Integer
90
91            ' roll the dice
92            Dim intDie1 As Integer = m_objRandomObject.Next(1, 7)
93            Dim intDie2 As Integer = m_objRandomObject.Next(1, 7)
94
95            ' display image corresponding to each die
96            DisplayDie(picDie1, intDie1)
97            DisplayDie(picDie2, intDie2)
98
99            Return (intDie1 + intDie2) ' return sum of dice values
100
101       End Function ' RollDice
102
103       ' display die image
104       Sub DisplayDie(ByVal picDie As PictureBox, _
105           ByVal intFace As Integer)
106
107           ' assign die images to PictureBox
108           picDie.Image = _
109               Image.FromFile(Directory.GetCurrentDirectory & _
110               m_strFILE_PREFIX & intFace & m_strFILE_SUFFIX)
111
112       End Sub ' DisplayDie
113
114   End Class ' FrmCrapsGame
```

Generating random numbers — (lines 92–93)

Using code to display an image — (lines 108–110)

Figure 16.20 Craps Game application code listing. (Part 3 of 3.)

SELF-REVIEW

1. _____ returns a string that represents the location of the application file.

   a) `Directory.GetWorkingDirectory`   b) `Directory.GetDirectory`

   c) `Directory.GetCurrentDirectory`   d) `Directory.ActiveDirectory`

2. To clear the image in a `PictureBox`, set its `Image` property to _____.

   a) `""` (double quotes)   b) `Nothing`

   c) `None`   d) `Empty`

Answers: 1) c. 2) b.

16.5 Wrap-Up

In this tutorial, you created the **Craps Game** application to simulate playing the popular dice game called Craps. You learned about the Random class and how it can be used to generate random numbers by creating a Random object and calling method Next on it. You then learned how to specify the range of values within which random numbers should be generated by passing various arguments to method Next. You were also introduced to enumerations, which enhance program readability by using descriptive identifiers to represent constants in an application.

Using your knowledge of random-number generation and event handlers, you wrote code that added functionality to your **Craps Game** application. You used random-number generation to simulate the element of chance. In addition to "rolling dice" in code, you learned how to use a `PictureBox` to display an image by using code. You used the `System.IO` namespace to help access images located in a file.

In the next tutorial, you will learn how to use arrays, which allow you to use one name to store many values. You will apply your knowledge of random numbers and arrays to create a **Flag Tutor** application that tests your knowledge of various nations' flags.

SKILLS SUMMARY

Generating Random Numbers

■ Create an object of class Random, and call this object's Next method. Use an argument to specify the maximum value for the random numbers.

Generating Random Numbers within a Specified Range

■ Call the Random class's Next method with two arguments. The first argument represents the minimum possible value; the second argument represents one more than the maximum possible desired value.

Declaring Enumerations

■ Begin an enumeration with keyword Enum; then use a list of descriptive names, and set each one to the value that you want it to represent. End the enumeration with keywords End Enum.

KEY TERMS

Directory.GetCurrentDirectory—A method of class Directory in the System.IO namespace that returns a String containing the path to the directory that contains the application.

Enum keyword—The keyword that begins an enumeration.

enumeration—A group of related, named constants.

Image.FromFile—A method of class Image that returns an Image object containing the image located at the path you specify.

Imports keyword—The keyword used to import namespaces.

namespace—A group of related classes in the Framework Class Library.

Next method—A method of class Random that, when called with no arguments, generates a positive Integer value between zero and the constant Int32.MaxValue.

NextDouble method—A method of class Random that generates a positive Double value that is greater than or equal to 0.0 and less than 1.0.

Nothing keyword—The keyword used to clear a reference's value.

pseudorandom numbers—A sequence of values produced by a complex mathematical calculation that simulates random-number generation.

Random class—A class that contains methods to generate pseudorandom numbers.

reference—A variable to which you assign an object.

System.IO namespace—A namespace containing methods to access files and directories.

CONTROLS, EVENTS, PROPERTIES & METHODS

Directory This class provides functionality to manipulate directories such as creating, moving, and navigating through them.

■ *Method*

GetCurrentDirectory—This method returns the location of the folder from which the application was loaded.

Image This class provides functionality to manipulate images.

■ *Method*

FromFile—This method is used to specify the physical location (path) of the image.

Random This class is used to generate random numbers.

■ *Methods*

Next—This method, when called with no arguments, generates a positive Integer value between zero and the largest possible Integer, which is the constant Int32.MaxValue (2,147,483,647).

NextDouble—This method generates a positive Double value that is greater than or equal to 0.0 and less than 1.0.

MULTIPLE-CHOICE QUESTIONS

16.1 A Random object can generate pseudorandom numbers of type _____.
a) Integer
b) Single
c) Double
d) Both a and c.

16.2 A _____ is a group of related classes in the Framework Class Library.
a) classspace
b) directory
c) namespace
d) library

16.3 Object variable names should be prefixed with _____.
a) var
b) obj
c) ran
d) ojt

16.4 The Next method of class Random can be called using _____.
a) one argument
b) no arguments
c) two arguments
d) All of the above.

16.5 The statement _____ assigns intValue a random number in the range from 5 to 20.
a) intValue = objRandom.Next(5, 21)
b) intValue = objRandom.Next(4, 20)
c) intValue = objRandom.Next(5, 20)
d) intValue = objRandom.Next(4, 21)

16.6 The _____ method specifies the file from which an image is loaded.
a) Next in class Random
b) FromFile in class Image
c) GetCurrentDirectory in class Directory
d) None of the above.

16.7 The System.IO namespace contains classes and methods to _____.
a) access files and directories
b) display graphics in an application
c) insert multimedia into an application
d) All of the above.

16.8 The values returned by the _____ method of class Random are actually pseudorandom numbers.
a) NextRandom
b) Pseudorandom
c) Next
d) Pseudo

16.9 When creating random numbers, the second argument passed to the Next method is _____.
a) equal to the maximum value you wish to be generated
b) equal to one more than the maximum value you wish to be generated
c) equal to one less than the maximum value you wish to be generated
d) equal to the minimum value you wish to be generated

16.10 A(n) _____ is a group of related, named constants.
a) namespace
b) variable
c) enumeration
d) None of the above.

EXERCISES

16.11 (*Guess the Number Application*) Develop an application that generates a random number and prompts the user to guess the number (Fig. 16.21). When the user clicks the **New Game** Button, the application chooses a number in the range 1 to 100 at random. The user enters guesses into the **Guess:** TextBox and clicks the **Enter** Button. If the guess is correct, the game ends, and the user can start a new game. If the guess is not correct, the application should indicate if the guess is higher or lower than the correct number.

a) *Copying and opening the template application.* Copy the GuessNumber folder from C:\Examples\Tutorial16\Exercises to C:\SimplyVB. Double click the Guess-Number.sln file to open the application in Visual Studio .NET. The GUI is displayed in Fig. 16.21.

b) *Creating a Random object.* Create two instance variables. The first variable should store a Random object and the second variable should store a random-generated number.

c) *Adding a Click event handler for the Enter Button.* Add a Click event handler for the **Enter** Button that retrieves the value entered by the user and compares that value to the random-generated number. If the guess is correct, display **Correct!** in the output Label. Then disable the **Enter** Button and enable the **New Game** Button. If the user's guess is higher than the correct answer, display **Too high...** in the output Label. If the user's guess is lower than the correct answer, display **Too low...** in the output Label.

d) *Adding a Click event handler for the New Game Button.* Add a Click event handler for the **New Game** Button that generates a new random number for the instance variable. The event handler should then disable the **New Game** Button, enable the **Enter** Button and clear the **Result:** TextBox.

Figure 16.21   **Guess the Number** application.

16.12 (*Dice Simulator Application*) Develop an application that simulates rolling two six-sided dice. Your application should have a **Roll** Button that, when clicked, displays two dice images corresponding to random numbers. It should also display the number of times each face has appeared. Your application should appear similar to Fig. 16.22.

Figure 16.22   **Dice Simulator** application.

a) *Copying and opening the application.* Copy the DiceSimulator folder from C:\Examples\Tutorial16\Exercises to C:\SimplyVB. Double click DiceSimulator.sln to open the application in Visual Studio .NET.

b) *Displaying the die image.* Create a Sub procedure named DisplayDie that takes a PictureBox control as an argument. This method should generate a random number to simulate a die roll. Then display the die image in the corresponding PictureBox control on the Form. The die image should correspond to the random number that was generated. To set the image, refer to the code presented in Fig. 16.20.

c) *Adding a Click event handler for the Roll Button.* Add a Click event handler for the **Roll** Button. Call method DisplayDie in this event handler to display the images for both dice.

d) *Displaying the frequency.* Add a Sub procedure called DisplayFrequency that uses a Select Case statement to update the number of times each face has appeared. Create an enumeration for the dice faces which will be used in the Select Case statement.

16.13 (*Lottery Picker Application*) A lottery commission offers four different lottery games to play: Three-number, Four-number, Five-number and Five-number + 1 lotteries. Each game has independent numbers. Develop an application that randomly picks numbers for all four games and displays the generated numbers in a GUI (Fig. 16.23). The games are played as follows:

- Three-number lotteries require players to choose three numbers in the range of 0–9.
- Four-number lotteries require players to choose four numbers, in the range of 0–9.
- Five-number lotteries require players to choose five numbers in the range of 1–39.
- Five-number + 1 lotteries require players to choose five numbers in the range of 1–49 and an additional number in the range of 1–42.

a) *Copying and opening the template application.* Copy the LotteryPicker folder from C:\Examples\Tutorial16\Exercises to C:\SimplyVB. Double click LotteryPicker.sln to open the application in Visual Studio .NET.

b) *Generating random numbers.* Create a Function procedure that will generate the random numbers for all four games.

c) *Drawing numbers for the games.* Add code into your application to generate numbers for all four games. To make the applications simple, allow repetition of numbers.

Figure 16.23   Lottery Picker application.

What does this code do? ▶   **16.14** What does this code do?

```
1    Sub PickRandomNumbers()
2
3        Dim intNumber1 As Integer
4        Dim dblNumber As Double
5        Dim intNumber2 As Integer
6        Dim objRandom As Random = New Random()
7
8        intNumber1 = objRandom.Next()
9        dblNumber = 5 * objRandom.NextDouble()
10       intNumber2 = objRandom.Next(1, 10)
11       lblInteger1.Text = Convert.ToString(intNumber1)
12       lblDouble1.Text = Convert.ToString(dblNumber)
13       lblInteger2.Text = Convert.ToString(intNumber2)
14   End Sub ' PickRandomNumbers
```

What's wrong with this code? ▶   **16.15** This Sub procedure should assign a random Decimal number (in the range 0 to Int32.MaxValue) to Decimal decNumber. (Assume that Option Strict is On.) Find the error(s) in the following code.

```
1   Sub RandomDecimal()
2
3       Dim decNumber As Decimal
4       Dim objRandom As Random = New Random()
5
6       decNumber = objRandom.Next()
7       lblDisplay.Text = Convert.ToString(decNumber)
8
9   End Sub ' RandomDecimal
```

Programming Challenge ▶

16.16 (*Multiplication Teacher Application*)   Develop an application that helps children learn multiplication. Use random-number generation to produce two positive one-digit integers that display in a question, such as "How much is 6 times 7?" The student should type the answer into a TextBox. If the answer is correct, then the application randomly displays one of three messages: **Very Good!**, **Excellent!** or **Great Job!** in a Label and displays the next question. If the student is wrong, the Label displays the message **No. Please try again**.

   a) ***Copying and opening the template application.*** Copy the MultiplicationTeacher folder from C:\Examples\Tutorial16\Exercises to C:\SimplyVB. Double click the MultiplicationTeacher.sln file to open the application in Visual Studio .NET.

   b) ***Generating the questions.*** Add a method into your application (Fig. 16.24) to generate each new question.

   c) ***Determining whether the right answer was entered.*** Add code into your application to call the method created in the previous step. After this method has been called, determine whether the student answered the question correctly, and display the appropriate message.

   d) ***Displaying a random message.*** Add a procedure GenerateOutput that displays a random message congratulating the student for answering correctly. This method should be called if the student answered the question correctly.

Figure 16.24   **Multiplication Teacher** application.

17

T U T O R I A L

Objectives

In this tutorial, you will learn to:
- Create and initialize arrays.
- Store information in an array.
- Refer to individual elements of an array.
- Sort arrays.
- Use **ComboBox**es to display options in a drop-down list.
- Determine whether a specific character is in a **String**.
- Remove a character from a **String**.
- Convert a **String** to lowercase characters.

Outline

Flag Quiz Application

Introducing One-Dimensional Arrays and ComboBoxes

This tutorial introduces basic concepts and features of **data structures**. Data structures group together and organize related data. **Arrays** are data structures that consist of data items of the same type. You will learn how to create arrays and how to access the information that they contain. You also will learn how to sort a **String** array's information alphabetically.

This tutorial's **Flag Quiz** application also includes a **ComboBox** control. A **ComboBox** presents user options in a drop-down list. This will be the first time that you will add a **ComboBox** to an application, but you have used them many times before in the Visual Studio .NET environment. For example, when you activated **Option Strict** in Tutorial 15, you selected **On** from a **ComboBox**.

17.1 Test-Driving the Flag Quiz Application

You will now create an application that tests a student's knowledge of the flags of various countries. The application will use arrays to store information, such as the country names and **Boolean** values that determine if a country name has been previously selected by the application as a correct answer. This application must meet the following requirements:

Application Requirements

A geography teacher would like to quiz students on their knowledge of the flags of various countries. The teacher has asked you to write an application that displays a flag and allows the student to select the corresponding country from a list. The application should inform the user of whether the answer is correct and display the next flag. The application should display five flags randomly chosen from the flags of Australia, Brazil, China, Italy, Russia, South Africa, Spain and the United States. When the application is executed, a given flag should be displayed only once.

You begin by test-driving the completed application.

Test-Driving the Flag Quiz Application

1. ***Opening the application.*** Open the C:\Examples\Tutorial17\CompletedApplication\FlagQuiz folder. Double click FlagQuiz.sln to open the application in Visual Studio .NET.

2. ***Running the application.*** Select **Debug > Start** to execute the application. The Form shown in Fig. 17.1 appears. Note that you might see a different flag when you run the application, because the application randomly selects which flag to display.

PictureBox displays flag ——

ComboBox contains answers (country names)

Figure 17.1   Flag Quiz application's Form.

3. ***Selecting an answer.*** The ComboBox contains eight country names. One country name corresponds to the displayed flag and is the correct answer. The scrollbar allows you to browse through the ComboBox's drop-down list. Select an answer from the ComboBox, as shown in Fig. 17.2.

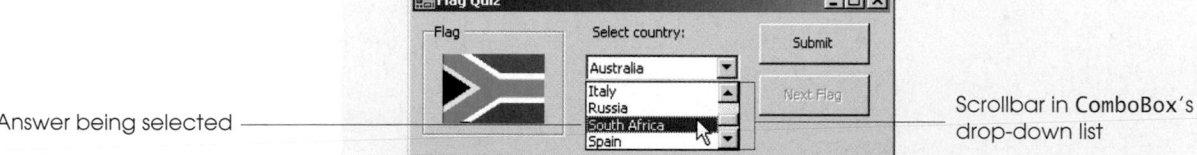

Answer being selected ——

Scrollbar in ComboBox's drop-down list

**Figure 17.2   Selecting an answer from the ComboBox.

4. ***Submitting a correct answer.*** Click the **Submit** Button to check your answer. If it is correct, the message "Correct!" is displayed in an output Label (Fig. 17.3). Notice that the **Submit** Button is now disabled and that the **Next Flag** Button is enabled.

**Figure 17.3   Submitting the correct answer.

5. ***Displaying the next flag.*** Click the **Next Flag** Button to display a different flag (Fig. 17.4). Notice that the **Submit** Button is now enabled, the **Next Flag** Button is disabled, the ComboBox displays **Australia** (the first country listed in the ComboBox) and the output Label is cleared.

**Figure 17.4   Displaying the next flag.

(cont.)

6. ***Submitting an incorrect answer.*** To demonstrate the application's response, select an incorrect answer and click **Submit** as in Fig. 17.5. The application displays "Sorry, incorrect." in the output Label.

Figure 17.5 Submitting an incorrect answer.

7. ***Finishing the quiz.*** After the application displays five flags and the user has submitted five answers, the quiz ends (Fig. 17.6). Notice that the two Buttons and the ComboBox are disabled.

ComboBox is disabled when the quiz ends

Figure 17.6 Finishing the quiz.

8. ***Terminating the application.*** Click the running application's close box to terminate the application.

9. ***Closing the solution.*** Select **File > Close Solution**.

17.2 Introducing Arrays

An array is a group of memory locations all containing data items of the same name and type. Array names follow the same conventions that apply to other identifiers. To refer to a particular location in an array, you specify the name of the array and the **position number** of the location, which is a value that indicates a specific location within an array. Position numbers begin at 0 (zero).

Figure 17.7 depicts an Integer array named intNetUnitsSold. This array contains 13 items, also called **elements**. Each array element represents the net number of "units sold" of a particular book in one month at a bookstore. For example, intNetUnitsSold(1) is the net sales of that book for January (month 1), intNetUnitsSold(2) is the net sales for February, etc. In this example, you simply ignore the first element of the array, because there is no month zero.

Each array element is referred to by providing the name of the array followed by the position number of the element in parentheses (). The position numbers for the elements in an array begin with 0. Thus, the **zeroth element** of array intNetUnitsSold is referred to as intNetUnitsSold(0), element 1 of array intNetUnitsSold is referred to as intNetUnitsSold(1), element 6 of array intNetUnitsSold is referred to as intNetUnitsSold(6) and so on. Element *i* of array intNetUnitsSold is referred to as intNetUnitsSold(i). The position number in parentheses is called an **index** or a **subscript**. An index must be either zero, a positive integer or an integer expression that yields a positive result. If an application uses an expression as an index, the expression is evaluated first to determine the index. For example, if variable intValue1 is equal to 5, and variable intValue2 is equal to 6, then the statement

```
intNetUnitsSold(intValue1 + intValue2) += 2
```

Name of array (note that —— `intNetUnitsSold(0)` | 0 |
all elements of this array
have the same name,
`intNetUnitsSold`) `intNetUnitsSold(1)` | 10 |

`intNetUnitsSold(2)` | 16 |

`intNetUnitsSold(3)` | 72 |

`intNetUnitsSold(4)` | 154 |

`intNetUnitsSold(5)` | 89 |

`intNetUnitsSold(6)` | 0 |

`intNetUnitsSold(7)` | 62 |

`intNetUnitsSold(8)` | -3 |

`intNetUnitsSold(9)` | 90 |

Position number (index `intNetUnitsSold(10)` | 453 |
or subscript) of the
element within array `intNetUnitsSold(11)` | 178 |
`intNetUnitsSold`
`intNetUnitsSold(12)` | 78 |

Figure 17.7   Array consisting of 13 elements.

adds 2 to array element `intNetUnitsSold(11)`. Note that an **indexed array name** (the array name followed by an index enclosed in parentheses)—like any other variable name—can be used on the left side of an assignment statement to place a new value into an array element.

Let's examine array `intNetUnitsSold` in Fig. 17.7 more closely. The **name** of the array is `intNetUnitsSold`. The 13 elements of the array are referred to as `intNetUnitsSold(0)` through `intNetUnitsSold(12)`. The **value** of `intNetUnitsSold(1)` is 10, the value of `intNetUnitsSold(2)` is 16, the value of `intNetUnitsSold(3)` is 72, the value of `intNetUnitsSold(7)` is 62 and the value of `intNetUnitsSold(11)` is 178. A positive value for an element in this array indicates that more books were sold than were returned. A negative value for an element in this array indicates that more books were returned than were sold. A value of zero indicates that the number of books sold was equal to the number of books returned.

Values stored in arrays can be used in various calculations and applications. For example, to determine the net units sold in the first three months of the year and then store the result in variable `intFirstQuarterUnits`, we would write

```
intFirstQuarterUnits = intNetUnitsSold(1) + intNetUnitsSold(2) + _
    intNetUnitsSold(3)
```

You will deal exclusively with **one-dimensional** arrays, such as `intNetUnitsSold`, in this tutorial. The indexed array names of one-dimensional arrays use only one index. In the next tutorial, you will study two-dimensional arrays; their indexed array names use two indices.

SELF-REVIEW

1. The number that refers to a particular element of an array is called its _____.

   a) value   b) size

   c) indexed array name   d) index (or subscript)

2. The indexed array name of one-dimensional array `decUnits`'s element 2 is _____.

   a) `decUnits{2}`   b) `decUnits(2)`

   c) `decUnits[0,2]`   d) `decUnits[2]`

Answers: 1) d. 2) b.

17.3 Declaring and Allocating Arrays

To declare an array, you provide the array's name and data type. The following statement declares the array in Fig. 17.7:

```
Dim intNetUnitsSold As Integer()
```

The parentheses that follow the data type indicate that `intNetUnitsSold` is an array. Arrays can be declared to contain any data type. In an array of primitive data types, every element of the array contains one value of the declared data type. For example, every element of an `Integer` array contains an `Integer` value.

Before you can use an array, you must specify the size of the array and allocate memory for the array, using keyword `New`. Recall from Tutorial 15 that keyword `New` can be used to create an object. Arrays are represented as objects in Visual Basic .NET, so they, too, must be allocated by using keyword `New`. The value stored in the array variable is actually a reference to the array object. To allocate memory for the array `intNetUnitsSold` after it has been declared, the statement

```
intNetUnitsSold = New Integer(12) {}
```

Common Programming Error

Attempting to access elements in the array by using an index outside the array bounds is a run-time error.

is used. **Array bounds** determine what indices can be used to access an element in the array. Here, the array bounds are 0 (which is implicit in the preceding statement) and 12 (one less than the number of elements in the array). Notice that because of array element 0, the actual number of elements in the array (13) is one larger than the upper bound specified in the allocation (12).

The required braces (`{` and `}`) are called an **initializer list** and specify the initial values of the elements in the array. When the initializer list is empty, as it is here, the elements in the array are initialized to the default value for the array's data type. Again, these default values are 0 for numeric primitive-data-type variables (such as `Integer`), `False` for `Boolean` variables and `Nothing` for references. Recall that keyword `Nothing` denotes an empty reference (that is, a value indicating that a reference variable has not been assigned an object). The initializer list also can contain a comma-separated list specifying the initial values of the elements in the array. For example,

```
Dim intSalesPerDay As Integer()
intSalesPerDay = New Integer() {0, 2, 3, 6, 1, 4, 5, 6}
```

declares and allocates an array containing eight `Integer` values. Visual Basic .NET can determine the array bounds from the number of elements in the initializer list. Thus, it is not necessary to specify the size of the array when a nonempty initializer list is present.

You can specify both the upper bound and an initializer list, as in the following statement:

Common Programming Error

If you specify an upper bound when initializing an array, it is a syntax error if you provide too many or too few values.

```
Dim dblTemperatures As Double() = _
    New Double(3) {23.45, 34.98, 78.98, 53.23}
```

Notice that the upper bound is one less than the number of items in the array.

Often, the elements of an array are used in a calculation. The box, *Computing the Sum of an Array's Elements*, demonstrates declaring and initializing an array and accessing the array's elements.

Computing the Sum of an Array's Elements	1. ***Opening the application.*** Double click `SumArray.sln` in the `C:\Examples\Tutorial17\TemplateApplication\SumArray` folder to open the application in Visual Studio .NET.
	2. ***Adding the Button's*** `Click` ***event handler.*** Double click the **Sum Array** `Button` in design view (Fig. 17.8) to generate the empty event handler `btnSum_Click` (Fig. 17.8).

(cont.)

Figure 17.8   **Sum Array** application's `Form` in design view.

3. ***Combining the declaration and allocation of an array.*** Add lines 84–89 of Fig. 17.9 to the event handler. Lines 85–86 combine the declaration and allocation of an array into one statement.

Creating an array of `Integers` ——————

Figure 17.9   Declaring an array in the event handler.

4. ***Calculating the sum.*** Add lines 91–98 (Fig. 17.10) to the event handler. The `For...Next` loop (lines 92–96) retrieves each element's value (one at a time), which is added to `intTotal`. Method **GetUpperBound** returns the index of the last element in the array. Method `GetUpperBound` takes one argument, indicating a dimension of the array. We discuss arrays with two dimensions in Tutorial 18. For one-dimensional arrays, such as `intArray`, the argument passed to `GetUpperBound` is always 0, to indicate the first (and only) dimension (or row) of the array. In this case,

```
intArray.GetUpperBound(0)
```

returns 9.

Every array in Visual Basic .NET "knows" its own length. The **length** (or the number of elements) of the array (10 in this case) is returned by the following expression:

```
intArray.Length
```

We could have set the upper bound in the `For...Next` loop as

```
intArray.Length - 1
```

which returns 9. The value returned by method `GetUpperBound` is one less than the value of the array's `Length` property.

5. ***Displaying the result.*** Line 98 displays the sum of the values of the array's elements.

6. ***Running the application.*** Select **Debug > Start** to run the application. The result of adding the integers from 1 to 10, inclusive, is displayed (Fig. 17.11).

Error-Prevention Tip

Use method `GetUpperBound` when you need to find the largest index in an array. Using an actual numerical value for the upper bound instead could lead to errors if you change the number of array elements.

(cont.)

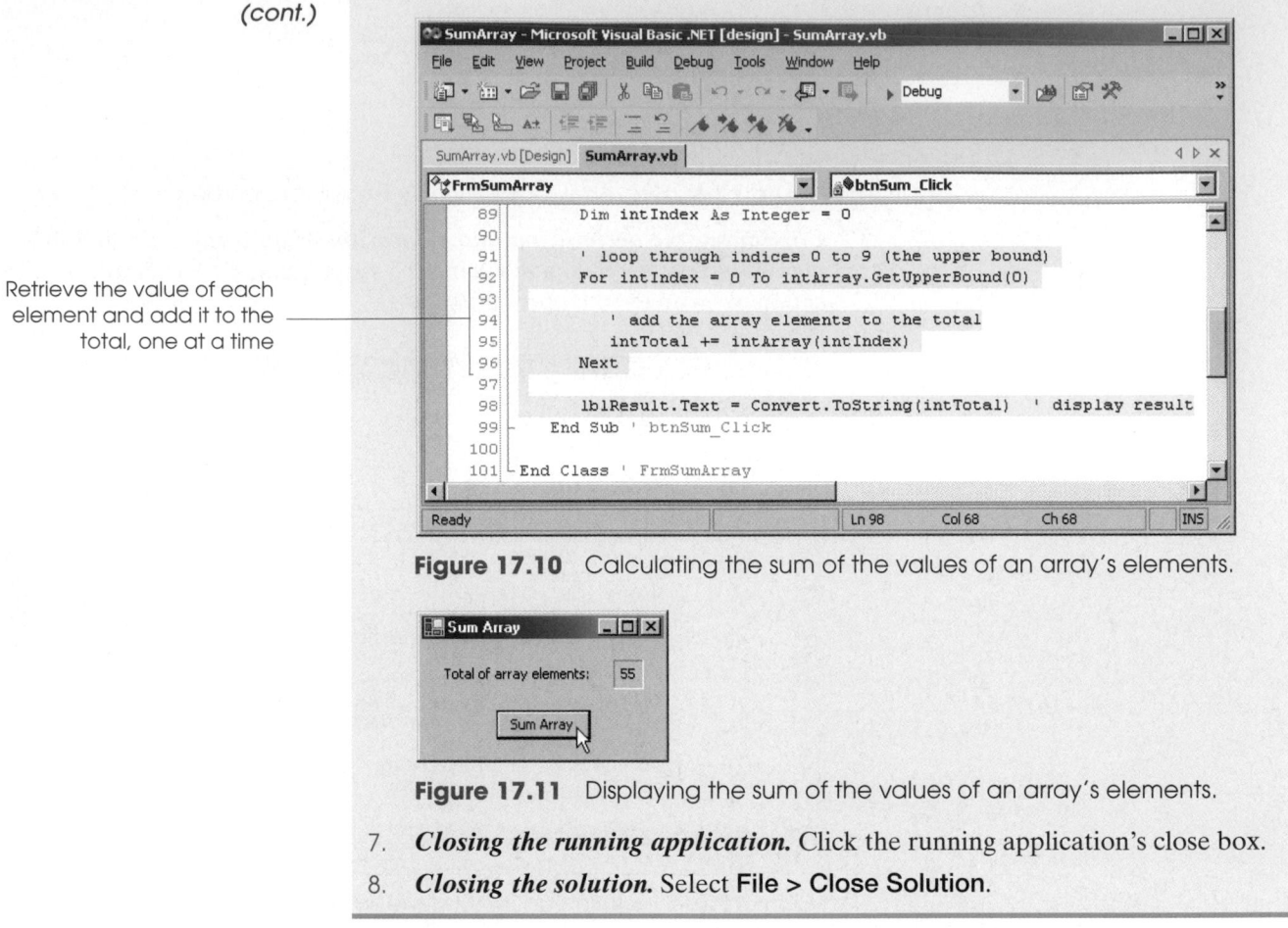

Retrieve the value of each element and add it to the total, one at a time

Figure 17.10 Calculating the sum of the values of an array's elements.

Figure 17.11 Displaying the sum of the values of an array's elements.

7. **Closing the running application.** Click the running application's close box.

8. **Closing the solution.** Select **File > Close Solution**.

SELF-REVIEW

1. Arrays can be allocated using keyword _____.

   a) `Declare`   b) `Create`

   c) `New`   d) `Allocate`

2. An array's length is _____.

   a) one more than the array's last index   b) one less than the array's last index

   c) the same as the array's last index   d) returned by method `GetUpperBound`

Answers: 1) c. 2) a.

17.4 Constructing the Flag Quiz Application

Before you can begin building the **Flag Quiz** application, you will need to develop the application, using pseudocode and an ACE table. The following pseudocode describes the functionality of the **Flag Quiz** application:

> When the Form loads
>   Order country names in the array alphabetically
>   Place country names in ComboBox
>   Randomly select correct answer
>   Display first flag in PictureBox
>
> When the Submit Button is clicked
>   Retrieve selected country name from ComboBox
>
>   If the selected value matches the correct answer
>   Display "Correct!" in the Label

```
                        Else
                              Display "Sorry, incorrect." in the Label

                        If a total of five images has been displayed
                              Append "Done!" to the Label's text
                              Disable the Buttons and ComboBox
                        Else
                              Disable Submit Button
                              Enable Next Flag Button

                  When the Next Flag Button is clicked
                        Randomly select a correct answer that has not been chosen previously
                        Display the new flag in the PictureBox
                        Clear the Label's text
                        Set ComboBox to display the first name in its drop-down list
                        Update counter that contains the number of flags displayed
                        Enable Submit Button
                        Disable Next Flag Button
```

Figure 17.12 shows the ACE table for the **Flag Quiz** application.

Action/Control/Event (ACE) Table for the Flag Quiz Application	Action	Control/Object	Event
	Label the application's controls	`fraFlagGroupBox,` `lblChoose`	

	Order country names in the array alphabetically; Place country names in ComboBox; Randomly select correct answer; Display first flag in PictureBox	`FrmFlagQuiz,`
		`cboOptions,`
		`objRandom,`
		`picFlag`
			Load (of Form)

	Retrieve selected country name from ComboBox; determine if the selected value matches the correct answer; display either "Correct!" or "Sorry, incorrect." in the Label; determine if a total of five images has been displayed; either append "Done!" to the Label's text and disable the Buttons and ComboBox—or disable Submit Button and enable Next Flag Button	`btnSubmit,`
		`cboOptions,`
		`lblFeedback,`
		`btnNext`
			Click (of btnSubmit)

	Randomly select a correct answer that has not been chosen previously; display the new flag in the PictureBox; Clear the Label's text; set ComboBox to display the first name in its drop-down list; update counter that contains the number of flags displayed; enable Submit Button; disable Next Flag Button	`btnNext,`
		`objRandom,`
		`picFlag,`
		`lblFeedback,`
		`cboOptions`
		`btnSubmit`
			Click (of btnNext)

Figure 17.12 **Flag Quiz** application's ACE table.

The box, *Initializing Important Variables*, shows you how to initialize the variables used in the application. In particular, the application requires two one-dimensional arrays.

<table>
<tr>
<td>

Initializing Important Variables

</td>
<td>

1. ***Copying the template application to your work folder.*** Copy the FlagQuiz folder from C:\Examples\Tutorial17\TemplateApplication to C:\SimplyVB.

2. ***Opening the template application.*** Double click FlagQuiz.sln in the C:\SimplyVB\FlagQuiz directory to open the **Flag Quiz** template application in Visual Studio .NET.

3. ***Declaring the array of country names.*** Add lines 4–7 of Fig. 17.13 to the application. Lines 5–7 declare and initialize array m_strOptions. Each element is a String containing the name of a country. These lines assign the initializer list to the array, combining the declaration and initialization into one statement. The compiler allocates the size of the array (in this case, eight elements) to suit the number of items in the initializer list.

</td>
</tr>
</table>

Creating an array of Strings to store country names

Figure 17.13 String array that stores country names.

4. ***Creating a Boolean array.*** The application should not display any flag more than once. Because the application uses random-number generation to pick a flag, the same flag could be selected more than once—just as, when you roll a six-sided die many times, a die face could be repeated. You will use a Boolean array to keep track of which flags have been displayed. Add lines 9–11 of Fig. 17.14 to FlagQuiz.vb. Lines 10–11 declare and create Boolean array m_blnUsed.

Creating an array of Boolean values with the same number of elements as the array of country names

Figure 17.14 Boolean array that keeps track of displayed flags.

(cont.)   Method `GetUpperBound` returns array `m_strOptions`'s largest index, which is used as the upper bound of `m_blnUsed`. Therefore, array `m_blnUsed` has the same size as `m_strOptions`. The elements of `m_blnUsed` correspond to the elements of `m_strOptions`; for example, `m_blnUsed( 0 )` specifies whether the flag corresponding to the country name of `m_strOptions( 0 )` (Russia) has been displayed. Recall that, by default, each uninitialized element in a `Boolean` array is `False`. The application will set an element of `m_blnUsed` to `True` if its corresponding flag has been displayed.

5. ***Initializing a counter and a variable to store the answer.*** Add lines 13–14 of Fig. 17.15 to `FlagQuiz.vb`. The application ensures that only five flags are displayed by incrementing counter `m_intCount`, which is initialized to 1 (line 13). The correct answer (the name of the country whose flag is displayed) will be stored in `m_strCountry` (line 14).

Creating instance variables ——————

Figure 17.15   Instance variables, used throughout the application.

6. ***Saving the project.*** Select **File > Save All** to save all the solution's files.

GUI Design Tip

Each `ComboBox` should have a descriptive `Label` that describes the `ComboBox`'s contents.

Now you will add another control to the **Flag Quiz** application template. The **Flag Quiz** application allows students to select answers from a *ComboBox*. The ComboBox control combines a `TextBox` and a `ListBox`. A ComboBox usually appears as a `TextBox` with a down arrow to its right. The user can click the down arrow to display a list of predefined items. If a user chooses an item from this list, that item is displayed in the ComboBox. If the list contains more items than the drop-down list can display at one time, a vertical scrollbar appears. The box, *Adding and Customizing a ComboBox*, shows you how to assign an array's elements to a ComboBox before the Form is displayed to users.

Adding and Customizing a ComboBox

1. ***Adding a ComboBox to the Form.*** Double click `FlagQuiz.vb` in the **Solution Explorer** to display the application's Form (Fig. 17.16). Add a ComboBox to the Form by double clicking the

> 🔲 ComboBox

control in the **ToolBox**.

Figure 17.16   **Flag Quiz** template application's Form.

(cont.)

2. ***Customizing the ComboBox.*** Change the Name property of the ComboBox to cboOptions. Clear the ComboBox's Text property, and set the Location property to 136, 32. Leave the Size property at its default setting, 121, 21. The Form should look like Fig. 17.17.

Figure 17.17 ComboBox added to **Flag Quiz** application's Form.

Good Programming Practice

Prefix ComboBox control names with cbo.

GUI Design Tip

If a ComboBox's content should not be editable, set its DropDownStyle property to DropDownList.

3. ***Setting the appearance of ComboBox.*** Property **DropDownStyle** determines the ComboBox's appearance. Value **DropDownList** specifies that the ComboBox is not editable (the user cannot type text in its TextBox portion). You can click the arrow button to display a drop-down list from which you can select an item. In this style of ComboBox, if you press the key that corresponds to the first letter of an item in the ComboBox, that item is selected and displayed in the ComboBox's TextBox portion. Set the DropDownStyle property of the ComboBox to DropDownList. Finally, set the **MaxDropDownItems** property of cboOptions to 4, so that the drop-down list can display a maximum of four items at one time. A vertical scrollbar will be added to the drop-down list, to allow users to select the remaining items.

4. ***Generating an event handler to add items to the ComboBox during the Load event.*** The ComboBox should contain a list of country names when the Form is displayed. The Form's Load event occurs before the Form is displayed; as a result, you should add the items to the ComboBox in the Form's Load event handler. Double click the Form to generate the empty event handler FrmFlagQuiz_Load.

5. ***Displaying items in the ComboBox.*** Add lines 148–149 of Fig. 17.18 to the FrmFlagQuiz_Load. ComboBox property **DataSource** specifies the source of the items displayed in the ComboBox. In this case, the source is array m_strOptions (discussed shortly).

Specifying the source of the ComboBox items

Figure 17.18 Assigning the String elements of an array to a ComboBox.

6. ***Saving the project.*** Select **File > Save All** to save all the solution's files.

Recall that, to specify the image displayed in a PictureBox, you need to set its Image property to the image's file name. The flag images are stored in C:\SimplyVB\FlagQuiz\bin\images. The name of each flag-image file is of the form *countryname*.png, where *countryname* has no whitespace. The box, *Building a*

Flag-Image File's Path Name, shows how the application constructs the full path name needed to locate and display each flag.

Building a Flag-Image File's Path Name

1. ***Creating a procedure to build the flag-image file's path name.*** Add lines 153–157 of Fig. 17.19 to the **Flag Quiz** application after event handler FrmFlagQuiz_Load. Procedure BuildPathName constructs a full path name for a flag-image file, beginning with the country name. The country name is retrieved from instance variable m_strCountry (the correct answer) and stored in local variable strOutput.

Removing whitespace from country names

Figure 17.19 Removing whitespace from the country name.

2. ***Removing whitespace from the country name.*** Some countries—for example, South Africa and the United States—have a space character in their names, but the flag-image file names do not allow whitespace characters. Add lines 158–165 of Fig. 17.19 to procedure BuildPathName. Line 160 uses String method **IndexOf** to assign to intSpace the index where the space character (" ") in the country name occurs. For instance, if strOutput were "South Africa", intSpace would be 5, because the space appears at index 5 of the name, counting from position zero. If the country does not have a space character, method IndexOf returns –1. Line 163 tests for whether intSpace is a positive number. In this application, method IndexOf returns a number greater than 0 if the country name is "South Africa" or "United States."

    If a space is found (line 164), the **Remove** method is called to eliminate the space character. Method Remove receives an index as its first argument and the number of characters to remove as its second argument. For example, the words "South Africa" would become the word "SouthAfrica". Method Remove returns a copy of the String without the space character. The copy is assigned to variable strOutput. [*Note:* String methods, such as Remove, do not modify the String object for which they are called. The String object returned by these methods contains a copy of the modified String.]

3. ***Ensuring that all characters are lowercase.*** Add line 167 of Fig. 17.20 to procedure BuildPathName. Now that strOutput contains a country name without whitespace, line 167 invokes method **ToLower**, which returns a copy of the String with any uppercase letters in the name converted to lowercase. All the flag-image file names are in lowercase, for consistency.

(cont.)

Constructing full path name
for flag images

Returning full path name of
flag images

Figure 17.20 Building the flag-image file path name.

4. *Adding the file extension.* Add line 168 of Fig. 17.20 to procedure Build-PathName. The flag-image files are in PNG format. Line 168 appends the file extension ".png" to strOutput.

5. *Adding the fully qualified path name.* Add lines 170–174 of Fig. 17.20 to procedure BuildPathName. The flag-image files are stored in an images folder in the directory containing the application's executable. Property **CurrentDirectory** of class **System.Environment** (line 172) returns the directory from which the application is executing as a fully qualified path name (for example, C:\SimplyVB\FlagQuiz\bin). Method **Insert** combines this path name and "\images\" to *countryname*.png. The first argument to Insert specifies at what index the String will be added, and the second argument is the String to insert. Method Insert returns a copy of the string with the inserted characters. This copy is assigned to strOutput.

6. *Returning the full path name.* Add line 174 of Fig. 17.20 to procedure BuildPathName. Line 174 returns the fully qualified path name of the specified country's flag image file.

7. *Saving the project.* Select **File > Save All** to save all the solution's files.

To ensure that the user is not asked the same question twice, a flag must be displayed no more than once when running the application. The application uses Boolean array m_blnUsed to track which flags have been displayed. The box, *Selecting a Unique Flag to Display,* shows you how to ensure that the application displays a flag no more than once.

Selecting a Unique Flag to Display

1. *Creating the GetUniqueRandomNumber procedure.* Add lines 177–178 of Fig. 17.21 to the **Flag Quiz** application after procedure BuildPathName. Line 178 is the header for the GetUniqueRandomNumber procedure. Get-UniqueRandomNumber returns the index of a country name whose flag has not been displayed.

2. *Generating a random index.* Add line 180 of Fig. 17.21 to the procedure GetUniqueRandomNumber. To select the next flag to display, you create a reference, objRandom (line 180), to a Random object.

(cont.)

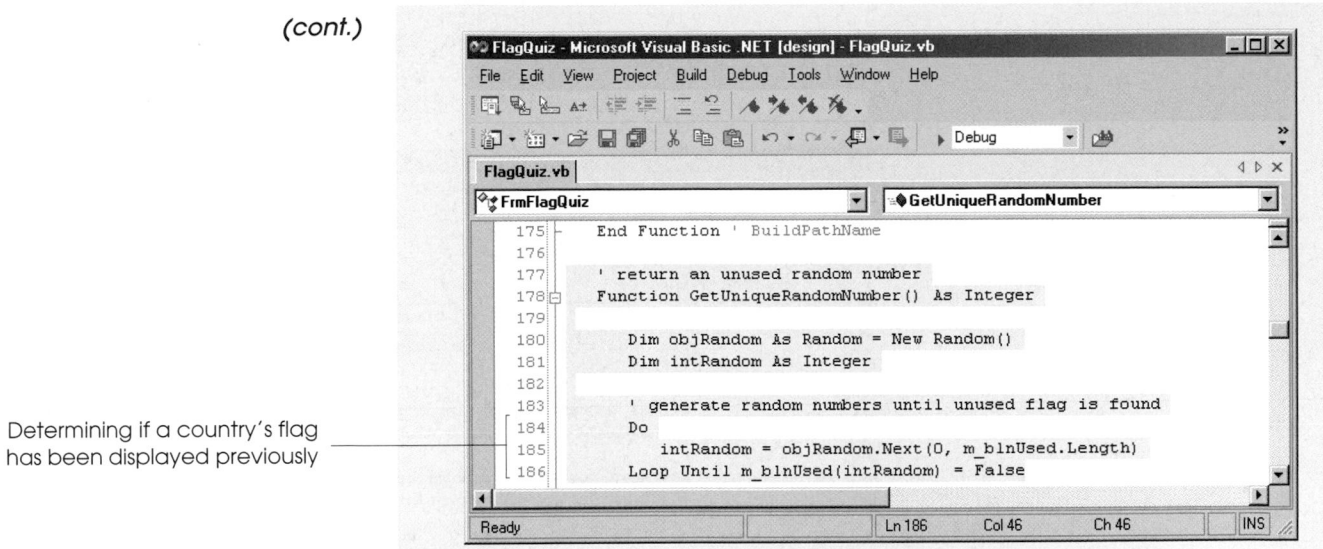

Figure 17.21   Generating a unique index.

3. ***Ensuring that each flag displays only once.*** Add lines 181–186 of Fig. 17.21 to GetUniqueRandomNumber. Method Next (line 185) of class Random generates a random index between 0 and m_blnUsed.Length (the number of country names). If the index has been selected previously, the element of m_blnUsed at the generated index is True. The Do...Loop Until statement (lines 184–186) iterates until it finds a unique index (that is, until m_blnUsed(intRandom) is False).

4. ***Indicating that the index has been used.*** Add lines 188–189 of Fig. 17.22 to the GetUniqueRandomNumber procedure. Line 189 sets the element at the selected index of m_blnUsed to True. This indicates that the flag has been used. Checking the values in this array ensures that the index will not be used again in the application.

Figure 17.22   Returning the unique index.

5. ***Returning the unique random number.*** Add line 191 of Fig. 17.22 to the GetUniqueRandomNumber procedure. Line 191 returns the unique random index.

6. ***Saving the project.*** Select **File > Save All** to save all the solution's files.

With the full path name and a unique flag selected, the application can display that flag. The box, *Displaying a Flag,* shows how to display the selected flag.

Displaying a Flag

1. *Creating the* `DisplayFlag` *procedure.* Add lines 194–195 of Fig. 17.23 to the **Flag Quiz** application after procedure `GetUniqueRandomNumber`. Procedure `DisplayFlag` selects a random country name and displays that country's flag.

Getting index of unused flag

Retrieving the flag's corresponding country name

Figure 17.23 Choosing a random country name.

2. *Obtaining a unique index.* Add lines 197–198 of Fig. 17.23 to the `Display-Flag` procedure. Line 198 invokes `GetUniqueRandomNumber` to find an index of a flag that has not been displayed during the application's execution and assigns it to `intRandom`.

3. *Retrieving a country name.* Add lines 200–201 of Fig. 17.23 to the `Display-Flag` procedure. Line 201 assigns to `m_strCountry` the flag's corresponding country name at index `intRandom` of `String` array `m_strOptions`.

4. *Building the flag image's path name.* Add lines 203–204 of Fig. 17.24 to the `DisplayFlag` procedure. Line 204 invokes procedure `BuildPathName`. The procedure returns the flag image's path name, which is assigned to `strPath`.

Getting the path name of the flag and displaying the flag image

Figure 17.24 Displaying a flag image.

5. *Displaying the flag image.* Add line 205 of Fig. 17.24 to the `DisplayFlag` procedure. Line 205 sets `PictureBox` `picFlag`'s `Image` property to the **Image** object returned by method `Image.FromFile`. Method **Image.From-File** returns an `Image` object from the specified file.

6. *Displaying a flag when the application is run.* When the `Form` loads, the first flag image in the quiz is displayed. The `Form Load` event handler should invoke procedure `DisplayFlag`. Add line 151 of Fig. 17.25 to event handler `FrmFlagQuiz_Load`.

7. *Saving the project.* Select **File > Save All** to save all the solution's files.

(cont.)

Displaying a flag when application is first run

Figure 17.25   Displaying a flag when the **Form** is loaded.

The user submits an answer by selecting a country name from the ComboBox and clicking the **Submit** Button. The application displays whether the user's answer is correct. If the application is finished (that is, five flags have been displayed), the application informs the user that the quiz is done; otherwise, the application enables the user to view the next flag. The box, *Processing a User's Answer,* implements this functionality.

Processing a User's Answer

1. ***Adding the Submit Button's Click event handler.*** Return to design view (**View > Designer**). Double click the **Submit** Button to generate the Click event handler btnSubmit_Click.

2. ***Retrieving the selected ComboBox item.*** Add lines 213–215 of Fig. 17.26 to the empty event handler. Lines 214–215 retrieve the user's answer, convert it to a String and assign it to strResponse. Property **SelectedValue** returns the value of the ComboBox's selected item. Visual Basic .NET method Convert.ToString converts the selected item to a String. Recall that we now use Option Strict, which requires explicit conversions. Variable strResponse contains the selected country's name.

3. ***Verifying the user's answer.*** Add lines 217–222 of Fig. 17.26 to btnSubmit_Click. The If...Then...Else statement (lines 218–222) determines whether the user's response matches the correct answer. Line 219 displays "Correct!" in the Label if the user's response matches the correct answer. Otherwise, line 221 displays "Sorry, incorrect.".

4. ***Informing the user that the quiz is over, when five flags have been displayed.*** Add lines 224–233 of Fig. 17.27 to the btnSubmit_Click event handler. If five flags have been displayed (lines 225–229), the Label displays text informing the user that the quiz is over, and both Buttons are disabled. The ComboBox is also disabled, by setting its **Enabled** property to False.

5. ***Continuing the quiz while fewer than five flags have been shown.*** If the quiz is not finished (that is, m_intCount is less than 5), the application disables the **Submit** Button and enables the **Next Flag** Button (lines 231–232). The functionality of the **Next Flag** Button will be discussed shortly.

6. ***Saving the project.*** Select **File > Save All** to save all the solution's files.

(cont.)

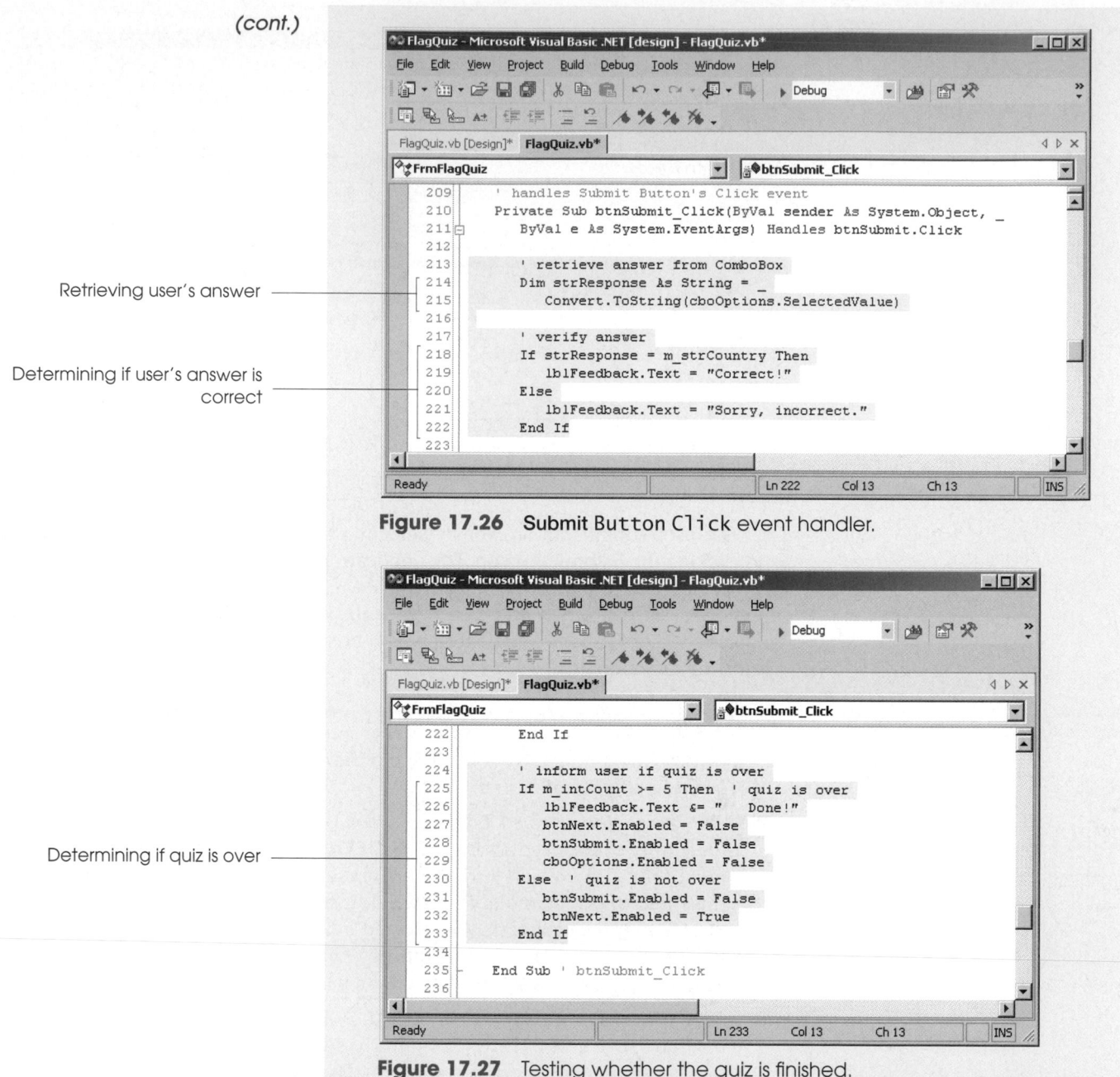

Retrieving user's answer

Determining if user's answer is correct

Figure 17.26 Submit `Button` `Click` event handler.

Determining if quiz is over

Figure 17.27 Testing whether the quiz is finished.

The user requests the next flag in the quiz by clicking the **Next Flag** Button. The application then displays the next flag and increments the number of flags shown. In the box, *Displaying the Next Flag,* you will implement this functionality.

Displaying the Next Flag

1. ***Adding the Next Flag Button's*** `Click` ***event handler to the application.*** Return to design view (**View > Designer**). Double click the **Next Flag** Button to generate the `Click` event handler `btnNext_Click`.

2. ***Displaying the next flag.*** Add line 241 of Fig. 17.28 to the empty event handler. This line calls procedure `DisplayFlag` to place the next flag in the PictureBox.

3. ***Clearing the previous results.*** Add line 242 of Fig. 17.28 to `btnNext_Click` to clear the output `Label`, deleting the results of the previous question.

(cont.)

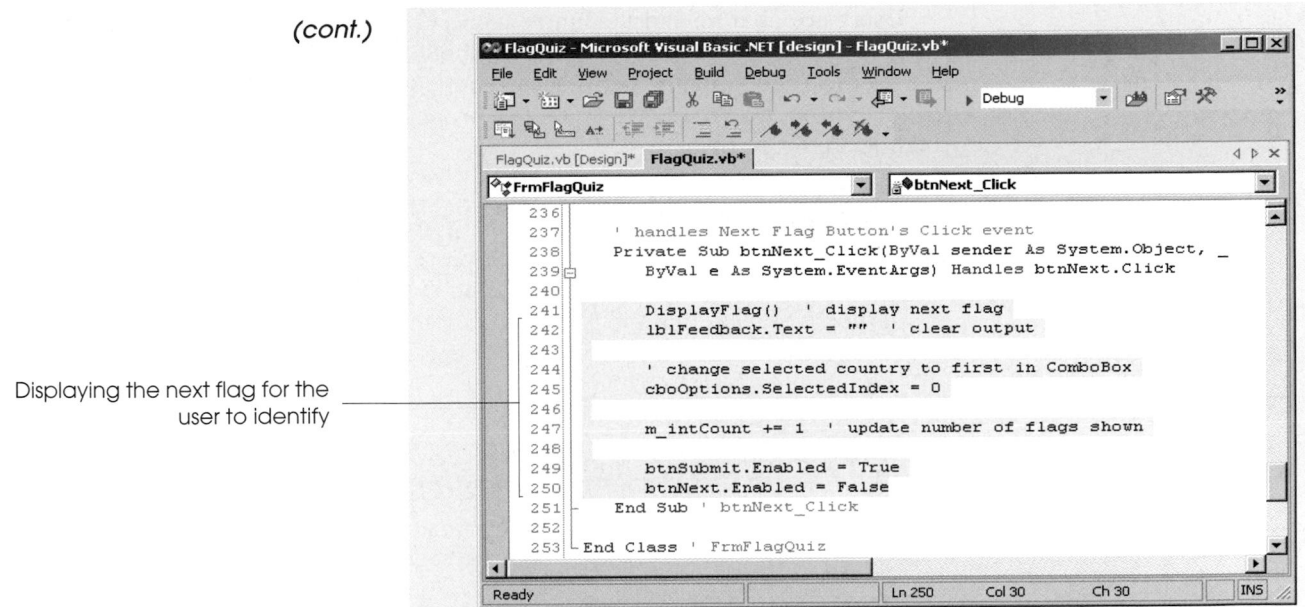

Figure 17.28 Next Flag Button Click event handler.

4. **Resetting the ComboBox.** Add lines 244–245 of Fig. 17.28 to btnNext_Click. Line 245 sets property **SelectedIndex** of ComboBox cboOptions to 0, the first item in the ComboBox's drop-down list.

5. **Updating the number of flags shown.** Add line 247 of Fig. 17.28 to btnNext_Click to update m_intCount to indicate that one more flag has been shown.

6. **Enabling the Submit Button and disabling the Next Flag Button.** Add lines 249–250 of Fig. 17.28 to btnNext_Click. Line 250 enables the **Submit** Button; line 250 disables the **Next Flag** Button. This is a visual reminder to the user that an answer must be submitted before another flag can be displayed.

7. **Saving the project.** Select **File > Save All** to save all of the solution's files.

SELF-REVIEW

1. Property _____ specifies the source of the data displayed in the ComboBox.

   a) ComboData   b) Source

   c) DataList   d) DataSource

2. ComboBox property _____ is 0 when the first ComboBox item is selected.

   a) SelectedIndex   b) SelectedValue

   c) Index   d) SelectedNumber

Answers: 1) d. 2) a.

17.5 Sorting Arrays

Sorting data refers to arranging the data into some particular order, such as ascending or descending order. Sorting is one of the most popular computing capabilities. For example, a bank sorts checks by account number, so that it can prepare individual bank statements at the end of each month. Telephone companies sort account information by last name and, within last-name listings, by first name, to make it easy to find phone numbers. Virtually every organization must sort some data, and often, massive amounts of it. In this section, you learn how to sort the values in an array so that you can alphabetize the list of countries in the **Flag Quiz** application.

Users are able to find a country name in the ComboBox faster if the country names are alphabetized. [*Note*: Class ComboBox contains property **Sorted**, which, when set to True, sorts the items in the ComboBox alphabetically. Because this tutorial focuses on arrays, we do not use this property.] The *Sorting an Array* box shows you how to sort an array.

Sorting an Array

1. ***Sorting the array of country names.*** Add line 148 of Fig. 17.29 to event handler FrmFlagQuiz_Load. Line 148 passes array m_strOptions to method **Array.Sort**, which sorts the values in the array into ascending alphabetical order. Note that this line is placed prior to the assigning of m_strOptions to property DataSource, so that the items in the ComboBox are displayed in alphabetical order.

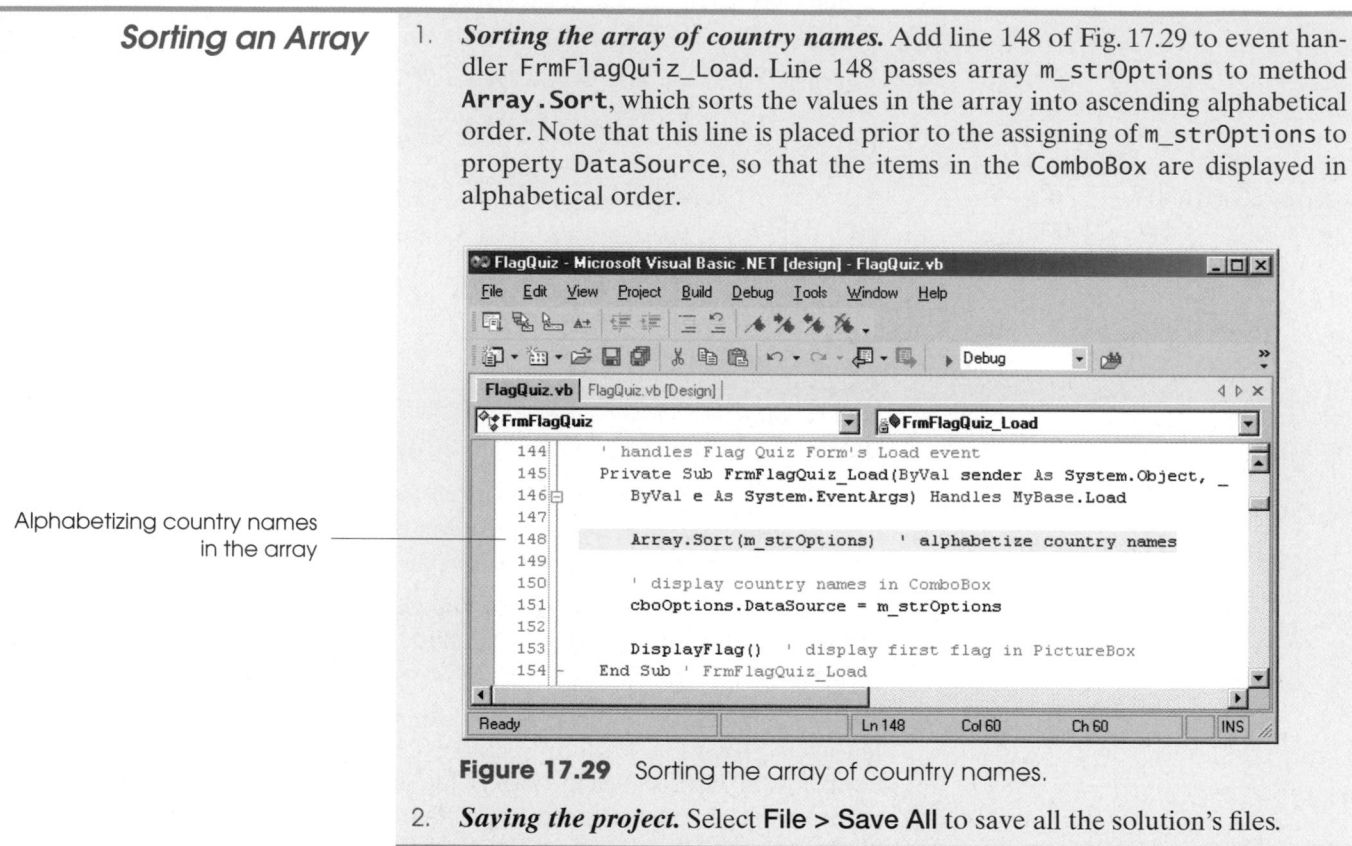

Alphabetizing country names in the array

Figure 17.29 Sorting the array of country names.

2. ***Saving the project.*** Select **File > Save All** to save all the solution's files.

The code for the completed **Flag Quiz** application is listed in Fig. 17.30.

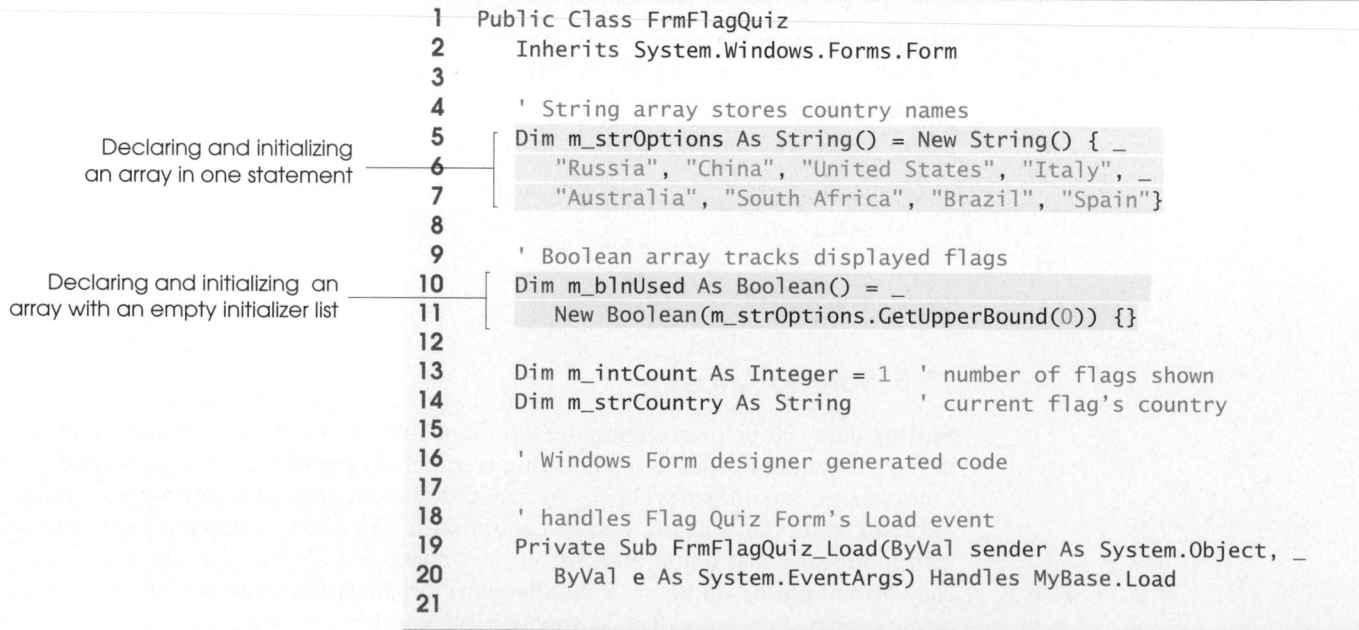

Declaring and initializing an array in one statement

Declaring and initializing an array with an empty initializer list

```
1   Public Class FrmFlagQuiz
2       Inherits System.Windows.Forms.Form
3
4       ' String array stores country names
5       Dim m_strOptions As String() = New String() { _
6           "Russia", "China", "United States", "Italy", _
7           "Australia", "South Africa", "Brazil", "Spain"}
8
9       ' Boolean array tracks displayed flags
10      Dim m_blnUsed As Boolean() = _
11          New Boolean(m_strOptions.GetUpperBound(0)) {}
12
13      Dim m_intCount As Integer = 1  ' number of flags shown
14      Dim m_strCountry As String     ' current flag's country
15
16      ' Windows Form designer generated code
17
18      ' handles Flag Quiz Form's Load event
19      Private Sub FrmFlagQuiz_Load(ByVal sender As System.Object, _
20          ByVal e As System.EventArgs) Handles MyBase.Load
21
```

Figure 17.30 **Flag Quiz** application's code. (Part 1 of 3.)

Sorting an array

Displaying array elements in a **ComboBox**

Locating a space character in a **String**

Removing a character from a **String**

Converting a **String** to lowercase

Inserting characters into a **String**

Assigning a value to an array element

Retrieving a value from an array

```
22          Array.Sort(m_strOptions)   ' alphabetize country names
23
24          ' display country names in ComboBox
25          cboOptions.DataSource = m_strOptions
26
27          DisplayFlag()  ' display first flag in PictureBox
28       End Sub ' FrmFlagQuiz_Load
29
30       ' return full path name of image file as a String
31       Function BuildPathName() As String
32
33          ' begin with country name
34          Dim strOutput As String = m_strCountry
35
36          ' locate space character if there is one
37          Dim intSpace As Integer = strOutput.IndexOf(" ")
38
39          ' remove space from country name if there is one
40          If intSpace > 0 Then
41             strOutput = strOutput.Remove(intSpace, 1)
42          End If
43
44          strOutput = strOutput.ToLower() ' make characters lowercase
45          strOutput &= ".png" ' add file extension
46
47          ' add path name
48          strOutput = strOutput.Insert(0, _
49             System.Environment.CurrentDirectory & "\images\")
50
51          Return strOutput  ' return full path name
52       End Function ' BuildPathName
53
54       ' return an unused random number
55       Function GetUniqueRandomNumber() As Integer
56
57          Dim objRandom As Random = New Random()
58          Dim intRandom As Integer
59
60          ' generate random numbers until unused flag is found
61          Do
62             intRandom = objRandom.Next(0, m_blnUsed.Length)
63          Loop Until m_blnUsed(intRandom) = False
64
65          ' indicate that flag has been used
66          m_blnUsed(intRandom) = True
67
68          Return intRandom  ' return index for new flag
69
70       End Function ' GetUniqueRandomNumber
71
72       ' display random flag in PictureBox
73       Sub DisplayFlag()
74
75          ' unique index ensures that a flag is used no more than once
76          Dim intRandom As Integer = GetUniqueRandomNumber()
77
78          ' retrieve country name from array m_strOptions
79          m_strCountry = m_strOptions(intRandom)
80
```

Figure 17.30 Flag Quiz application's code. (Part 2 of 3.)

```
81            ' get image's full path name
82            Dim strPath As String = BuildPathName()
83
84            picFlag.Image = Image.FromFile(strPath) ' display image
85         End Sub ' DisplayFlag
86
87         ' handles Submit Button's Click event
88         Private Sub btnSubmit_Click(ByVal sender As System.Object, _
89            ByVal e As System.EventArgs) Handles btnSubmit.Click
90
91            ' retrieve answer from ComboBox
92            Dim strResponse As String = _
93               Convert.ToString(cboOptions.SelectedValue)
94
95            ' verify answer
96            If strResponse = m_strCountry Then
97               lblFeedback.Text = "Correct!"
98            Else
99               lblFeedback.Text = "Sorry, incorrect."
100           End If
101
102           ' inform user if quiz is over
103           If m_intCount >= 5 Then  ' quiz is over
104              lblFeedback.Text &= "   Done!"
105              btnNext.Enabled = False
106              btnSubmit.Enabled = False
107              cboOptions.Enabled = False
108           Else   ' quiz is not over
109              btnSubmit.Enabled = False
110              btnNext.Enabled = True
111           End If
112
113        End Sub ' btnSubmit_Click
114
115        ' handles Next Flag Button's Click event
116        Private Sub btnNext_Click(ByVal sender As System.Object, _
117           ByVal e As System.EventArgs) Handles btnNext.Click
118
119           DisplayFlag()  ' display next flag
120           lblFeedback.Text = ""   ' clear output
121
122           ' change selected country to first in ComboBox
123           cboOptions.SelectedIndex = 0
124
125           m_intCount += 1  ' update number of flags shown
126
127           btnSubmit.Enabled = True
128           btnNext.Enabled = False
129        End Sub ' btnNext_Click
130
131     End Class ' FrmFlagQuiz
```

Converting the selected value from the **ComboBox** into a **String** *(annotation pointing to lines 92–93)*

Setting the selected **ComboBox** item *(annotation pointing to line 123)*

Figure 17.30 **Flag Quiz** application's code. (Part 3 of 3.)

SELF-REVIEW
1. The process of ordering the elements of an array is called _____ the array.

a) allocating   b) sorting

c) declaring   d) initializing

2. Which of the following sorts array `dblAverageRainfall`?

    a) `Array(dblAverageRainfall).Sort()` b) `Sort.Array(dblAverageRainfall)`

    c) `Sort(dblAverageRainfall)`   d) `Array.Sort(dblAverageRainfall)`

Answers: 1) b. 2) d.

17.6 Wrap-Up

In this tutorial, you learned about data structures called arrays, which contain elements of the same type. You then learned how to create, initialize and access one-dimensional arrays. You created a simple application called **SumArray**, which calculated the sum of the `Integer` values stored in an array. You studied pseudocode and an ACE table to help you begin creating the **Flag Quiz** application.

In building the **Flag Quiz** application, you were introduced to the `ComboBox` control. You learned how to add a `ComboBox` to the `Form` and modify the `ComboBox`'s appearance. You then populated the `ComboBox` with data from an array. You reviewed how to display images in a `PictureBox` and how to generate random numbers by using an object of class `Random`.

You were introduced to several new `String` methods, including method `Insert` (for inserting characters), method `Remove` (for removing characters), method `ToLower` (for converting uppercase letters to lowercase letters) and method `IndexOf` (for returning the index of a character in a `String`). You learned how to sort an array alphabetically by using method `Array.Sort`.

In the next tutorial, you will learn how to create more sophisticated arrays, ones having two dimensions, and you will use them to implement a graphing application. You will see that two-dimensional arrays are like tables organized in rows and columns.

SKILLS SUMMARY

Creating an Array

- Declare the array using the format:

    `Dim` *arrayName* `As` *arrayType*`()`

    where *arrayName* is the reference name of the array and *arrayType* is the type of data that will be stored in the array.

Assigning an Object to an Array Reference

- Use keyword `New` as in the statement:

    arrayName `= New` *arrayType*`()` `{`*arrayInitializerList*`}`

    where *arrayInitializerList* is a comma-separated list of the items that will initialize the elements of the array.

Referring to Element *n* of an Array

- Use index *n*.
- Enclose the index in parentheses after the array name.

Obtaining the Length of an Array

- Use property `Length`.

Obtaining the Index of the Last Element in a One-Dimensional Array

- Invoke method `GetUpperBound` with 0 as its argument.

Combining `TextBox` Features With `ListBox` Features

- Use a `ComboBox` control.

Setting the Maximum Number of Drop-Down Items a ComboBox's List Displays

- Use property `MaxDropDownItems`.

Specifying the Source of Data Displayed in a ComboBox

- Use property `DataSource`.

Obtaining a User's Selection in a ComboBox

- Use property `SelectedValue`.

Sorting an Array

- Invoke method `Array.Sort`.

Determining Whether a `String` Contains a Specified Character

- Method `IndexOf` returns the index of a specified character in a `String`.
- If the character is not in the `String`, method `IndexOf` returns –1.

Converting a `String` to Lowercase

- Method `ToLower` returns a copy of a `String` with all uppercase characters converted to lowercase.

Inserting Characters into a `String`

- Method `Insert` returns a copy of a `String` with specified characters added at a specified index.

Removing Characters from a `String`

- Method `Remove` returns a copy of the `String` with a specified number of characters removed.

KEY TERMS

array—A data structure containing data items of the same type.

array bounds—Integers that determine what indices can be used to access an element in the array. The lower bound is 0; the upper bound is the length of the array minus one.

ComboBox control—A control that combines a `TextBox` with a `ListBox`.

DropDownStyle property—Property of the `ComboBox` control that specifies the appearance of the `ComboBox`.

element—An item in an array.

index—An array element's position number, also called a subscript. An index must be zero, a positive integer or an integer expression. If an application uses an expression as an index, the expression is evaluated first, to determine the index.

indexed array name—The array name followed by an index enclosed in parentheses. The indexed array name can be used on the left side of an assignment statement to place a new value into an array element. The indexed array name can be used in the right side of an assignment to retrieve the value of that array element.

IndexOf method—`String` method that accepts as an argument a character to search for in a `String`. The method returns the index of a specified character in a `String`. If the `String` does not contain the character, the method returns –1.

initializer list—The required braces ({ and }) surrounding the initial values of the elements in the array. When the initializer list is empty, the elements in the array are initialized to the default value for the array's data type.

Insert method—`String` method that inserts its second argument (a `String`) at the position specified by the first argument.

Length property—Contains the number of elements in an array.

MaxDropDownItems property—Property of the `ComboBox` class that specifies how many items can be displayed in the drop-down list.

one-dimensional array—An array that uses only one index.

Remove method—`String` method that deletes a specified number of characters (the second argument) starting at the index specified by the first argument.

subscript—See index.

zeroth element—The first element in an array.

GUI DESIGN GUIDELINES	**ComboBoxes**

- ■ Each ComboBox should have a descriptive Label that describes the ComboBox's contents.
- ■ If a ComboBox's content should not be editable, set its DropDownStyle property to Drop-DownList.

CONTROLS, EVENTS, PROPERTIES & METHODS

ComboBox 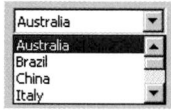 This control allows users to select from a drop-down list of options.

- ■ *In action*

- ■ *Properties*

  DataSource—This property specifies the source of items listed in a ComboBox.

  DropDownStyle—This property specifies a ComboBox's appearance.

  Enabled—This property specifies whether a user can select an item from the ComboBox.

  Location—This property specifies the location of the ComboBox control on the container control relative to the top-left corner.

  MaxDropDownItems—Property that specifies the maximum number of items the ComboBox can display in its drop-down list.

  Name—This property specifies the name used to access the ComboBox control programmatically. The name should be prefixed with cbo.

  SelectedIndex—This property specifies the index of the selected item. Returns –1 if no item is selected.

  SelectedValue—This property specifies the selected item.

  Size—This property specifies the height and width (in pixels) of the ComboBox control.

  Sorted—This property, when set to True, displays the ComboBox options in alphabetical order or ascending order.

Array This data structure stores a fixed number of elements of the same type.

- ■ *Property*

  Length—This property specifies the number of elements in the array.

- ■ *Methods*

  GetUpperBound—This method returns the largest index of the array.

  Sort—This method orders an array's elements. An array of numerical values would be organized in ascending order and an array of Strings would be organized in alphabetical order.

String The String class represents a series of characters treated as a single unit.

- ■ *Methods*

  Format—This method arranges the String in a specified format.

  IndexOf—This method returns the index of the specified character(s) in a String.

  Insert—This method returns a copy of the String for which it is called with the specified character(s) inserted.

  Remove—This method returns a copy of the String for which it is called with the specified character(s) removed.

  ToLower—This method returns a copy of the String for which it is called with any uppercase letters converted to lowercase letters.

MULTIPLE-CHOICE QUESTIONS

17.1 Arrays can be declared to hold values of _____.

   a) type `Double`   b) type `Integer`

   c) type `String`   d) any data type

17.2 The elements of an array are related by the fact that they have the same name and _____.

   a) constant value   b) subscript

   c) type   d) value

17.3 Method _____ returns the largest index in the array.

   a) `GetUpperBound`   b) `GetUpperLimit`

   c) `GetLargestIndex`   d) `GetUpperSubscript`

17.4 The first element in every array is the _____.

   a) subscript   b) zeroth element

   c) length of the array   d) smallest value in the array

17.5 Arrays _____.

   a) are controls   b) always have one dimension

   c) keep data in sorted order at all times   d) are objects

17.6 The initializer list can _____.

   a) be used to determine the size of the array

   b) contain a comma-separated list of initial values for the array elements

   c) be empty   d) All of the above.

17.7 Which method call sorts array `strWords` in ascending order?

   a) `Array.Sort(strWords)`   b) `strWords.SortArray()`

   c) `Array.Sort(strWords, 1)`   d) `Sort(strWords)`

17.8 The `ComboBox` control combines a `TextBox` with a _____ control.

   a) `DateTimePicker`   b) `ListBox`

   c) `NumericUpDown`   d) `Label`

17.9 To search for a period (.) in a `String` called `strTest`, call method _____.

   a) `String.Search(strTest, ".")`   b) `String.IndexOf(strTest, ".")`

   c) `strTest.IndexOf(".")`   d) `strTest.Search(".")`

17.10 Property _____ contains the size of an array.

   a) `Elements`   b) `ArraySize`

   c) `Length`   d) `Size`

EXERCISES

17.11 *(Enhanced Flag Quiz Application)* Enhance the **Flag Quiz** application by counting the number of questions that were answered correctly. After all the questions have been answered, display a message in a `Label` that describes how well the user performed. The following table shows which messages to display:

Number of correct answers	Message
5	`Excellent!`
4	`Very good`
3	`Good`
2	`Poor`
1 or 0	`Fail`

a) *Copying the template application.* Copy the `FlagQuiz2` folder in the `C:\Exam-ples\Tutorial17\Exercises` directory to `C:\SimplyVB`.

b) *Opening the template application.* Open the **Flag Quiz** application by double click-ing `FlagQuiz.sln` in `C:\SimplyVB\FlagQuiz2`.

c) *Adding a variable to count the number of correct answers.* Add an instance variable `m_intNumberCorrect`, and initialize it to 0. You will use this variable to count the number of correct answer submitted by the user.

d) *Counting the correct answers.* Increment `m_intNumberCorrect` in the **Submit** But-ton's event handler whenever the submitted answer is correct.

e) *Displaying the message.* Write a procedure `DisplayMessage` that displays a message in `lblScore` depending on the value of `m_intNumberCorrect`. Call this procedure from the **Submit** Button's event handler when the quiz is completed. The finished application should behave like Fig. 17.31.

Figure 17.31   Enhanced **Flag Quiz** application's GUI.

17.12 (*Salary Survey Application*) Use a one-dimensional array to solve the following problem: A company pays its salespeople on a commission basis. The salespeople receive $200 per week, plus 9% of their gross sales for that week. For example, a salesperson who grosses $5000 in sales in a week receives $200 plus 9% of $5000, a total of $650. Write an application (using an array of counters) that determines how many of the salespeople earned salaries in each of the following ranges (assuming that each salesperson's salary is truncated to an integer amount): $200–299, $300–399, $400–499, $500–599, $600–699, $700–799, $800–899, $900–999 and over $999.

Allow the user to enter the sales for each employee in a TextBox. The user should click the **Calculate** Button to calculate that salesperson's salary. When the user is done entering this information, clicking the **Show Totals** Button should display how many of the salespeo-ple earned salaries in each of the above ranges. The finished application should behave like Fig. 17.32.

a) *Copying the template application to your work folder.* Copy the `SalarySurvey` folder from `C:\Examples\Tutorial17\Exercises` to `C:\SimplyVB`.

b) *Opening the template application.* Double click `SalarySurvey.sln` in `C:\Sim-plyVB\SalarySurvey` to open the application.

c) *Creating an array of salary ranges.* Create a `String` array, and initialize it to con-tain the salary ranges (the `Strings` displayed in the `ListBox`'s first column).

d) *Create an array that represents the number of salaries in each range.* Create an empty `Decimal` array to store the number of employees who earn salaries in each range.

e) *Creating an event handler for the Calculate Button.* Write event handler `btnCalculate_Click`. Obtain the user input from the **Enter sales:** TextBox. Calcu-late the commission due to the employee and add that amount to the base salary. Increment the element in array `decSalaries` that corresponds to the employee's sal-ary range. This event handler should also display the employee's salary in the **Total salary:** Label.

f) *Writing an event handler for the Show Totals Button.* Create event handler `btnShowTotals_Click` to display the salary distribution in the `ListBox`. Use a For...Next statement to display the range (an element in `strSalaryRanges`) and the number of employees whose salary falls in that range (an element in `decSalaries`).

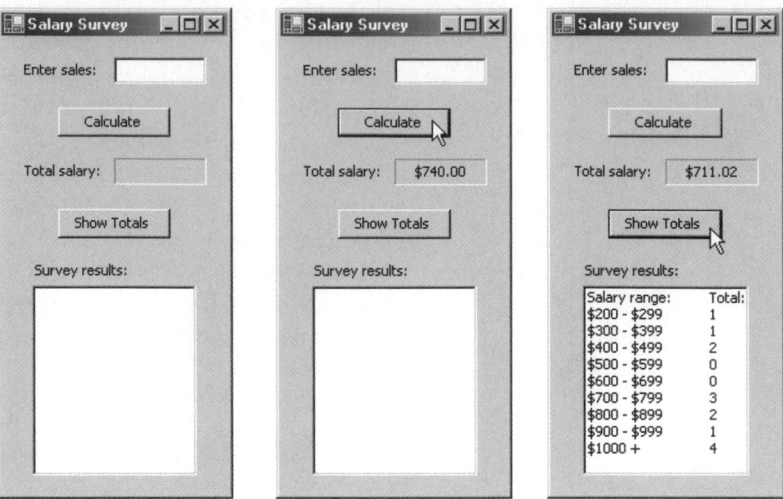

Figure 17.32 **Salary Survey** application's GUI.

17.13 (*Cafeteria Survey Application*) Twenty students were asked to rate, on the scale from 1 to 10, the quality of the food in the student cafeteria, with 1 being "awful" and 10 being "excellent." Allow the user input to be entered using a ComboBox. Place the 20 responses in an Integer array, and determine the frequency of each rating. Display the frequencies as a histogram in a multiline, scrollable TextBox. Figure 17.33 demonstrates the completed application.

Figure 17.33 Cafeteria Survey GUI.

a) *Copying the template application.* Copy the CafeteriaSurvey folder from C:\Examples\Tutorial17\Exercises to C:\SimplyVB.

b) *Opening the template application.* To open the application, double click Cafeteria-Survey.sln in C:\SimplyVB\CafeteriaSurvey.

c) *Creating an array of the possible ratings.* Create an array of 10 consecutive integers, called m_intChoices to contain the integers in the range 1–10, inclusive.

d) *Adding a ComboBox.* Add a ComboBox to the GUI as in Fig. 17.33. The ComboBox will display the possible ratings. Set property DropDownStyle to DropDownList.

e) *Displaying the possible ratings when the application starts.* Write the event handler for the Load event so that the DataSource of the ComboBox is set to intChoices when the application starts.

f) *Creating an array to store the responses.* Create an Integer array of length 11 named m_intResponses. This will be used to store the number of responses in each of the 10 categories (element 0 will not be used).

g) *Counting the number of responses.* Create an Integer variable named m_intResponseCounter to keep track of how many responses have been input.

h) *Storing the responses.* Write the event handler btnSubmit_Click to increment m_intResponseCounter. Store the response in array m_intResponses. Call procedure DisplayHistogram to display the results.

i) *Creating procedure DisplayHistogram.* Add a header to the TextBox. Use nested For...Next loops to display the ratings in the first column. The second column uses asterisks to indicate how many students surveyed submitted the corresponding rating.

What does this code do? ▶ **17.14** This procedure declares intNumbers as its parameter. What does it return?

```
1   Function Mystery(ByVal intNumbers As Integer()) As Integer()
2
3      Dim intI As Integer
4      Dim intLength As Integer = intNumbers.Length - 1
5      Dim intTempArray As Integer() = _
6         New Integer(intLength) {}
7
8      For intI = intLength To 0 Step -1
9         intTempArray(intLength - intI) = intNumbers(intI)
10     Next
11
12     Return intTempArray
13  End Function ' Mystery
```

What's wrong with this code? ▶ **17.15** The code that follows uses a For...Next loop to sum the elements in an array. Find the error(s) in the following code:

```
1   Sub SumArray()
2      Dim intSum As Integer
3      Dim intCounter As Integer
4      Dim intNumbers As Integer() = _
5         New Integer() {1, 2, 3, 4, 5, 6, 7, 8}
6
7      For intCounter = 0 To intNumbers.Length
8         intSum += intNumbers(intCounter)
9      Next
10
11  End Sub ' SumArray
```

Programming Challenge ▶ **17.16** (*Road Sign Test Application*) Write an application that will test the user's knowledge of road signs. Your application should display a random sign image and ask the user to select the sign name from a ComboBox. This application should look like Fig. 17.34. *Hint:* The application is similar to the **Flag Quiz** application. You can find the images in C:\Examples\Tutorial17\Exercises\images. Remember to set Option Strict to On.

Figure 17.34   Road Sign Test GUI.

Objectives

In this tutorial, you will learn to:
- Understand the differences between one-dimensional and two-dimensional arrays.
- Declare and manipulate two-dimensional arrays.
- Understand the usefulness of two-dimensional arrays.
- Use RadioButtons to enable users to select exactly one option out of several.
- Use an MSChart control to graph data.

Outline

Sales Data Application

Introducing Two-Dimensional Arrays, RadioButtons and the MSChart Control

Using graphs to display data enhances the effectiveness of business presentations. It often is easier for the audience to read and understand data from a colorful, well-organized chart than from a large table of data values. In this tutorial, you will learn to use Microsoft's MSChart control to create and display graphs for your **Sales Data** application. You will use the MSChart control's properties to customize the graph. You will also learn about two-dimensional arrays, which, like one-dimensional arrays, store multiple values. However, with two-dimensional arrays, you will learn to store multiple rows of values and display them in a graph. Finally, you will learn about the RadioButton control, which you will employ to enable users to customize the appearance of your application's graph.

18.1 Test-Driving the Sales Data Application

In this tutorial, you will complete the **Sales Data** application by using a two-dimensional array. The application must meet the following requirements:

Application Requirements

The CEO of a steel company is giving a presentation that details recent sales. The presentation requires a chart that displays the number of tons of steel produced by the company's factories in Missouri, Texas, Illinois and Indiana. The application should allow a user to input the annual steel production (in thousands of tons) for each factory and to view the chart produced as either a two-dimensional or a three-dimensional bar graph. The chart should display as a two-dimensional chart by default.

You begin by test-driving the completed application.

Test-Driving the Sales Data Application

1. ***Opening the application.*** Open the C:\Examples\Tutorial18\Com-pletedApplication\SalesData folder to locate the **Sales Data** application. Double click SalesData.sln to open the application in Visual Studio .NET.

2. ***Running the application.*** Select **Debug > Start** to execute the application. The application will display the chart in Fig. 18.1.

Graph title

Axis labels

MSChart control

Axis titles

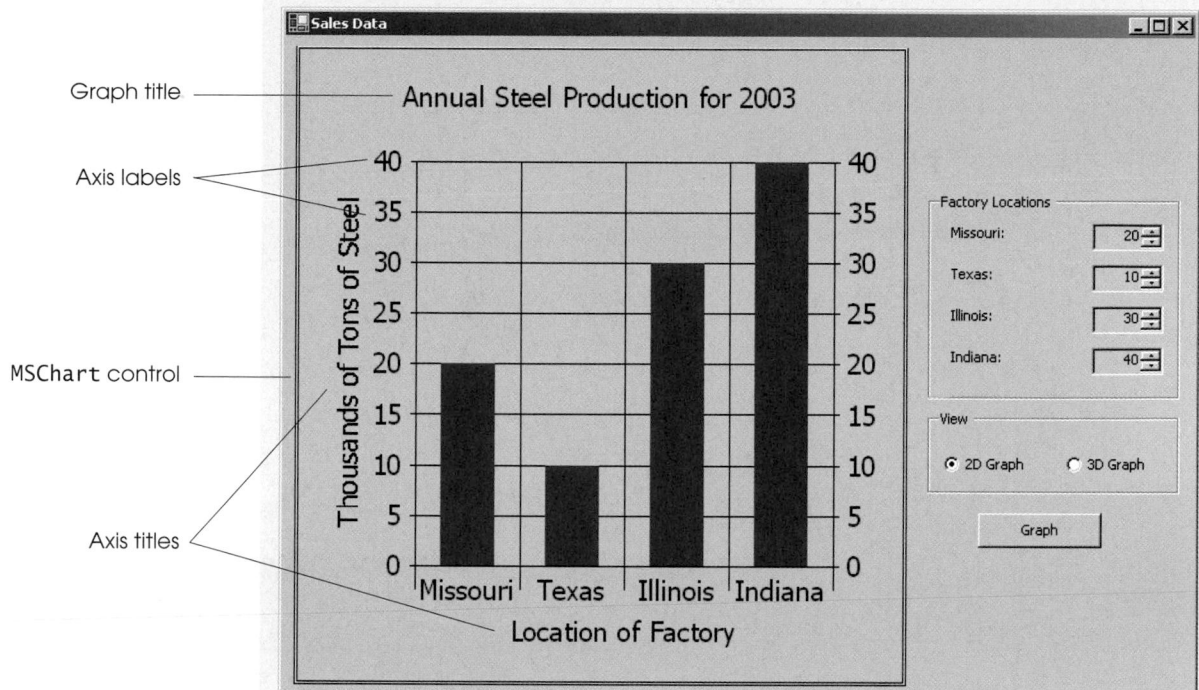

Figure 18.1   Completed **Sales Data** application.

3. ***Entering data.*** By default, the **Sales Data** application graphs the data shown in Fig. 18.1. You will add this functionality when you create the application. Use the NumericUpDown controls' up and down arrows to set the number of thousands of tons of steel produced in each factory. Enter 30 in the **Missouri:** NumericUpDown control, 20 in the **Texas:** NumericUpDown control, 25 in the **Illinois:** NumericUpDown control and 65 in the **Indiana:** NumericUpDown control. Click the **Graph** Button to display the new data in the MSChart control (Fig. 18.2).

4. ***Selecting the graph's appearance.*** Change the graph's appearance by clicking the **3D Graph** RadioButton (Fig. 18.3). The graph will display the data in a 3D bar graph. Click the **2D Graph** RadioButton to once again display the graph in a 2D bar graph (Fig. 18.2).

5. ***Terminating the application.*** Click the running application's close box to terminate the application, and close the solution by selecting **File > Close Solution**.

(cont.)

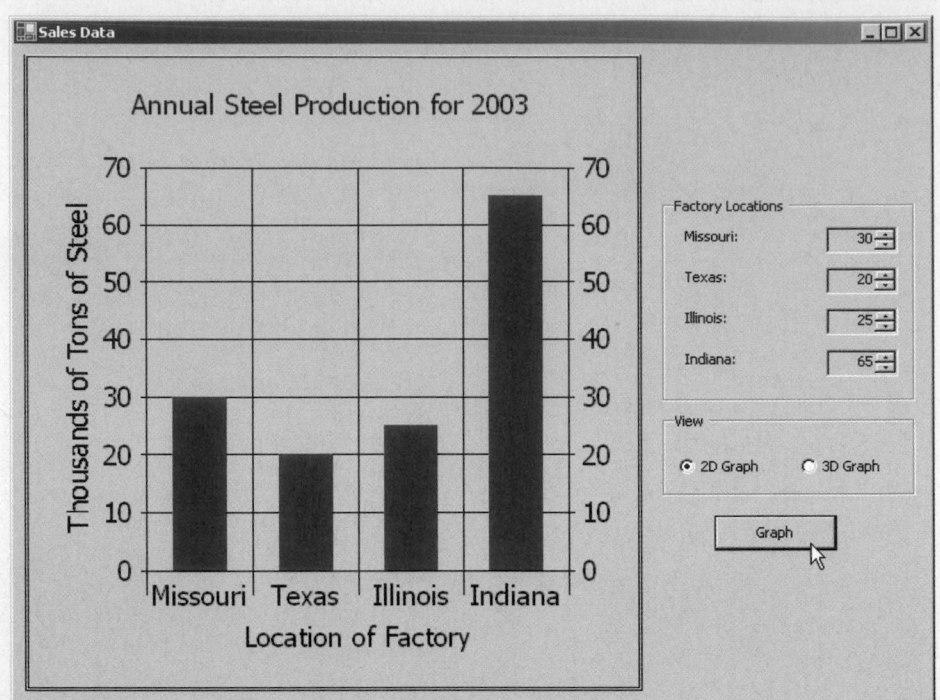

Figure 18.2 Updated graph in the **Sales Data** application.

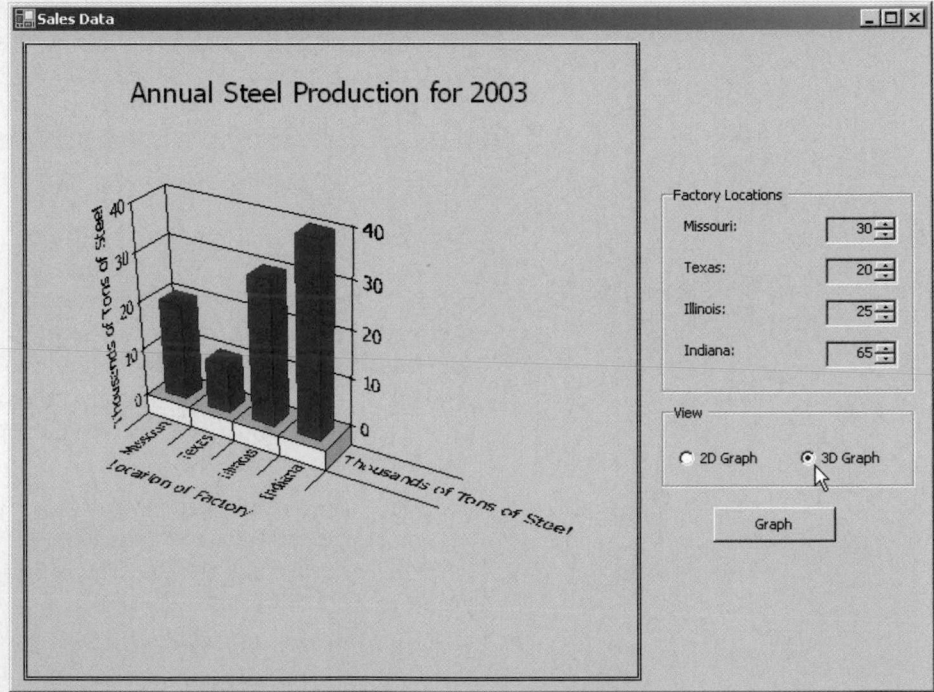

Figure 18.3 Displaying chart data as a 3D bar graph.

18.2 Two-Dimensional Rectangular Arrays

So far, you have studied one-dimensional arrays, which contain one sequence (or row) of values. In this section, we introduce **two-dimensional arrays** (often called **double-subscripted arrays**), which require two indices to identify particular elements. **Rectangular arrays** with two indices are two-dimensional arrays that are often used to represent **tables** of values consisting of information arranged in **rows** and **columns**. Each row is the same size and therefore has the same number of columns (hence, the term "rectangular"). To identify a particular table element, you must specify the two indices—by convention, the first identifies the element's row and the second identifies the element's column. Figure 18.4 illustrates a two-dimensional rectangular array, `intArray`, which contains three rows and four columns. A rectangular two-dimensional array with *m* rows and *n* columns is called an **m-by-n array**; therefore, the array in Fig. 18.4 is a 3-by-4 array.

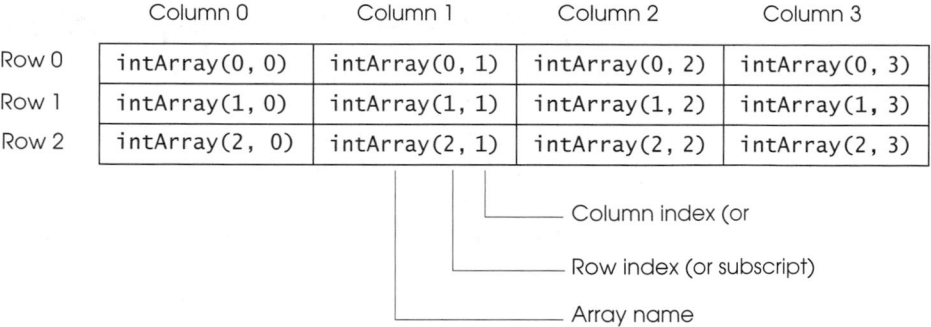

Figure 18.4   Two-dimensional rectangular array with three rows and four columns.

Every element in array `intArray` is identified in Fig. 18.4 by an element name of the form `intArray(intI, intJ)`, where `intArray` is the name of the array and `intI` and `intJ` are the indices that uniquely identify the row and column of each element in array `intArray`. Notice that, because row numbers and column numbers in two-dimensional arrays each begin with zero, the names of the elements in the first row each have a first index of 0; the names of the elements in the last column each have a second index of 3 (Fig. 18.4).

Two-dimensional arrays are initialized in declarations through the same process and notations employed for one-dimensional arrays. For example, a two-dimensional rectangular array, `intNumbers`, with two rows and two columns, could be declared and initialized with

```
Dim intNumbers As Integer(,) = New Integer(1, 1) {}
intNumbers(0, 0) = 1
intNumbers(0, 1) = 2
intNumbers(1, 0) = 3
intNumbers(1, 1) = 4
```

Notice that the values of the arguments in the array declaration (in this case, 1) always indicate *one less than* the number of elements in the row or column. Alternatively, the preceding initialization could be written on one line:

```
Dim intNumbers As Integer(,) = New Integer(,) {{1, 2}, {3, 4}}
```

The values are grouped by row in braces, with 1 and 2 initializing `intNumbers(0,0)` and `intNumbers(0,1)`, respectively, and 3 and 4 initializing `intNumbers(1,0)` and `intNumbers(1,1)`, respectively.

SELF-REVIEW

1. Arrays that use two indices are referred to as _____ arrays.

   a) single-subscripted   b) two-dimensional

   c) `Double`   d) one-dimensional

2. _____ creates an `Integer` array of two rows and five columns.

   a) `New Integer(2, 5){}`   b) `New Integer(1, 5){}`

   c) `New Integer(1, 4){}`   d) `New Integer(2, 4){}`

Answers: 1) b. 2) c.

18.3 Creating and Customizing a Chart Graphic by Using the MSChart Control

The Microsoft Chart control (also known as the **MSChart** control) uses two-dimensional arrays to graph and display data on a Form. Using the MSChart control, you can create a chart on the Form and customize its appearance. Such a chart can be used to display statistical information in a visual format that is easy to read and analyze.

When you view charts, you often refer to their *x*- and *y*-axes. As in Fig. 18.5, the *y*-axis is the vertically oriented line and the *x*-axis is the horizontally oriented line.

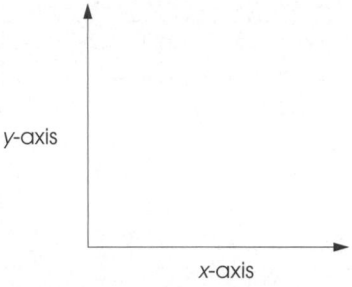

Figure 18.5 Chart axes.

The following pseudocode describes the operation of the **Sales Data** application:

```
When the Form loads
    Retrieve graphing data from the NumericUpDown controls
    Display the chart in the MSChart control

When the user clicks the Graph Button
    Retrieve graphing data from the NumericUpDown controls
    Display the chart in the MSChart control

When the user selects the 2D Graph RadioButton
    Display the chart as a 2D bar graph

When the user selects the 3D Graph RadioButton
    Display the chart as a 3D bar graph
```

Your **Sales Data** application will use NumericUpDown controls to retrieve graphing data from the user and update the chart when the user clicks the **Graph Button**. This application also uses the RadioButton control's CheckChanged event to update the chart when the user selects either a 2D or a 3D graph. The ACE table of Fig. 18.6 lists the actions, controls and events for this application.

Action/Control/Event (ACE) Table for the Sales Data Application

Action	Control	Event
Label the application's controls	fraLocations, fraView, lblMissouri, lblTexas, lblIllinois, lblIndiana	
Retrieve graphing data from the NumericUpDown controls; Display the chart in the MSChart control	FrmSalesData, chSales, updMissouri, updTexas, updIllinois, updIndiana	Load (of Form)
Retrieve graphing data from the NumericUpDown controls; Display the chart in the MSChart control	btnGraph, chSales, updMissouri, updTexas, updIllinois, updIndiana	Click (of Button)

Figure 18.6 ACE table for the **Sales Data** application. (Part 1 of 2.)

Action	Control	Event
Display chart as a 2D bar graph	rad2D, chSales	CheckedChanged (of RadioButton)
Display chart as a 3D bar graph	rad3D, chSales	CheckedChanged (of RadioButton)

Figure 18.6   ACE table for the **Sales Data** application. (Part 2 of 2.)

The MSChart control is not in the Visual Studio .NET **Toolbox**. The box, *Adding the MSChart Control to the **Toolbox***, demonstrates how to place the MSChart control in the **Toolbox** so that you can use the control into your application.

Adding the MSChart **Control to the Toolbox**

1. *Copying the template into your work folder.* Copy the C:\Examples\Tutorial18\TemplateApplication\SalesData folder to C:\SimplyVB.

2. *Opening the template application.* Double click SalesData.sln in the SalesData folder to open the application in Visual Studio .NET. Double click SalesData.vb in the **Solution Explorer** to open the application in design view.

3. *Opening the Customize Toolbox dialog.* If the **Toolbox** is not currently open, go to **View > Toolbox**. Right click the **Windows Forms** tab of the **Toolbox**. Click **Customize Toolbox...** in the context menu that appears (Fig. 18.7). After a pause, the **Customize Toolbox** dialog will appear (Fig. 18.8).

Figure 18.7   Customize Toolbox... context menu.

4. *Selecting the Microsoft Chart Control.* Select the **COM Components** tab in the **Customize Toolbox** dialog if it is not already selected. Scroll down until the option **Microsoft Chart Control 6.0 (SP4) (OLEDB)** appears, as shown in Fig. 18.8. Note that the text in the parentheses of the Microsoft Chart Control option may differ on your system. Also note that the names and number of controls listed in your **Customize Toolbox** dialog may differ from Fig. 18.8. Click that option's CheckBox to select the Microsoft Chart control, and click the **OK** Button to add the MSChart control to the **Toolbox**.

5. *Viewing the Microsoft Chart control in the Toolbox.* Select the **MSChart** control,

from the **Windows Forms** tab of the **Toolbox**. Note that it could be the last control in the list.

(cont.)

COM Components tab ——

Selected control ——

Figure 18.8   Customize Toolbox dialog showing **Microsoft Chart Control**.

Now that you have added the MSChart control to the **Toolbox**, you can create an MSChart control in the **Sales Data** application to take advantage of MSChart's many features. You will begin creating the application in the box, *Placing the MSChart Control on the Form*.

Placing the *MSChart* Control on the *Form*

1. ***Inserting the MSChart control.*** With the MSChart control selected in the **Toolbox**, click near the upper left corner of the Form. An MSChart control will appear (Fig. 18.9).

Figure 18.9   MSChart control placed on the Form.

2. ***Resizing and positioning the MSChart.*** In the **Properties** window, set the Location property to 8, 8. Set the Size property to 480, 495, so that the chart is large enough to display all its data clearly. The data that appears on the chart merely indicates how data will be formatted in the chart and does not represent actual values in your application. The initial values for the chart will be set when the application loads.

3. ***Renaming the chart.*** In the **Properties** window, set the Name property to chSales.

4. ***Disabling the chart.*** In the **Properties** window, set property Enabled to False, so users cannot change the size or position of the chart within the MSChart control while the application is running.

5. ***Saving the project.*** Select **File > Save All** to save all of the solution's files.

Now that you have added an MSChart control to your Form, you will customize the control. You will change the properties and the appearance of the chart in the box, *Customizing the MSChart Control Using the **Properties** Window*.

GUI Design Tip

Resize an MSChart control so that all the data is clearly visible.

Good Programming Practice

Prefix MSChart control names with ch (for chart).

GUI Design Tip

Set the MSChart control's Enabled property to False to prevent users from repositioning the chart within the MSChart control.

<table>
<tr><td></td><td>Customizing the</td></tr>
</table>

Customizing the
*MSChart **Control Using***
the Properties Window

1. ***Viewing the Properties dialog.*** Select chSales from the **Properties** window component object box to access the MSChart's properties. Notice the hyperlink named **ActiveX -Properties** appears above the description pane of the **Properties** window (Fig. 18.10), regardless of which MSChart control property is selected. Click this hyperlink to display the **Properties** dialog (Fig. 18.11). Though you can set the MSChart control's properties via the **Properties** window, the **Properties** dialog simplifies this process by grouping related settings in a tabbed interface.

ActiveX -Properties hyperlink
displays **Properties** dialog

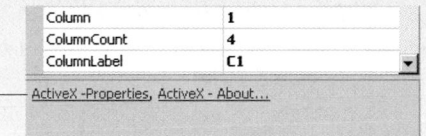

Figure 18.10 **ActiveX -Properties** hyperlink in the **Properties** window.

2. ***Creating a two-dimensional bar/pictograph.*** In the **Properties** dialog (Fig. 18.11), the **Chart** tab should be selected by default. If it is not, click the **Chart** tab. In the **Chart Type** GroupBox, make sure that the **2D** RadioButton is selected and that option **Bar/Pictograph** is selected in the ListBox.

Chart tab

Sets chart's appearance

Sets chart type

Figure 18.11 **Chart** tab in MSChart control **Properties** dialog.

3. ***Changing the color of the data in the graph.*** The MSChart control can graph data in a variety of colors. To change the color of your bar graph, click the **Series Color** tab in the **Properties** dialog (Fig. 18.12). In the **Interior** Groupbox, click the **Color:** ComboBox to display a palette of colors. Select the blue color shown in Fig. 18.12.

Figure 18.12 **Series Color** tab in the MSChart control's **Properties** dialog.

(cont.)

GUI Design Tip

Assign meaningful descriptions in the MSChart graph's title and axis labels. Use book-title capitalization for these descriptions.

4. ***Setting the MSChart control's title***. The MSChart title contains text that appears above the graph. This title, much like the Form's Text property, is used to describe the purpose of the chart. Click the **Text** tab in the **Properties** dialog (Fig. 18.13). If it is not already selected, select **Title** from the **Property Name:** ComboBox. In the **Text:** TextBox, type Annual Steel Production for 2003. Click the **Apply** Button to apply the new settings to the MSChart control. Note that the **Apply** Button is disabled until you change the MSChart control settings again.

Text tab ——————

Property Name: ComboBox ——

Text: TextBox ——————

Apply Button sets the property ——

Figure 18.13 **Text** tab in MSChart control **Properties** dialog.

5. ***Labeling the x- and y-axes***. In the **Text** tab of the **Properties** dialog, select **X Axis Title** from the **Property Name:** ComboBox. In the **Text:** TextBox, type Location of Factory. Click the **Apply** Button to set the *x*-axis label to the value you typed in the TextBox. Your *y*-axis indicates the thousands of tons of steel produced at each location. To label the *y*-axis, select **Y Axis Title** from the ComboBox and type Thousands of Tons of Steel in the TextBox. Click the **Apply** Button to set the *y*-axis label.

Labeling chart axes allows users to easily interpret the data presented. As you saw in the box, *Test-Driving the **Sales Data** Application*, the *x*-axis (that is, the horizontal line) in your MSChart will be divided into four sections, one for each state. A state name (Missouri, Texas, Illinois or Indiana) is displayed below each bar in the graph. To help the user read the graph, you should include a descriptive label below the *x*-axis.

GUI Design Tip

Increase the MSChart graph's title and axis label font sizes to enhance readability.

6. ***Changing the font properties of the title and axis labels***. The graph's title describes the purpose of the chart, so it should be large enough to draw the user's attention. Click the **Fonts** tab in the **Properties** dialog (Fig. 18.14). The default font for the title should be Tahoma. If it is not, select **Title** from the **Property Name:** ComboBox and change the font of the chart title by selecting **Tahoma** from the **Font:** ComboBox. Then change the size of the title to 16 points by changing the value to 16 in the **Size:** ComboBox. A **point** is a measurement that determines the height of the font (1 point is 1/72 of an inch).

The text that labels the axes is difficult to read on a graph of this size; therefore, you should also increase the text's font size. Choose **Axis Labels** in the **Property Name:** ComboBox, and make sure the **Font:** ComboBox is set to **Tahoma** and change the **Size:** to 16. **Axis labels** display the values associated with data in the graph. Finally, select **Axis Title** from the **Property Name:** ComboBox, and make sure the **Font:** ComboBox is set to **Tahoma** and change its **Size:** to 16. (**Axis titles** describe the meaning of the values on an axis.) Click **Apply** to apply the changes to the chart.

(cont.)

Figure 18.14   Changing font properties of an MSChart control.

7. **Creating a border around the chart.** To enhance your chart's appearance, create a border around it. Select the **Backdrop** tab in the **Properties** dialog (Fig. 18.15). **Chart** should be selected by default in the **Property Name:** ComboBox. In the **Border** GroupBox, select **Double Line** from the **Style:** ComboBox, and make sure **1pt** (for 1 point of width) is the value in the **Width:** TextBox, and select black from the **Color:** ComboBox as shown in Fig. 18.15. This creates a double-line border around your chart and helps distinguish it from the rest of the Form. Click **OK** to apply the changes and close the dialog.

Figure 18.15   BackDrop tab of the MSChart **Properties** dialog.

8. **Saving the project.** Select **File > Save All** to save all the solution's files.

Now that you have set the MSChart control's properties, you are ready to insert additional design elements into your application. You will use RadioButton controls to allow the user to change the appearance of the graph.

1. The *x*-axis in a chart is the _____ oriented line.

   a) vertically   b) horizontally

   c) diagonally   d) None of the above.

2. To use the MSChart control, it must be added to the Visual Studio .NET _____.

   a) **Toolbox**   b) **Solution Explorer**

   c) **Properties** window   d) code file

Answers: 1) b. 2) a.

18.4 Using RadioButtons

A **RadioButton** is a small white circle that either is blank or contains a smaller black dot. When a RadioButton is selected, a black dot appears in the circle. A RadioButton is known as a **state button** because it can be only in the "on" state or in the "off" state. (The other state button you have learned is the CheckBox, which was introduced in Tutorial 8.)

RadioButtons are similar to CheckBoxes in that they are state buttons, but RadioButtons normally appear as a group; only one RadioButton in the group can be selected at a time. Similar to car-radio preset buttons, in which only one station can be selected at a time, RadioButtons are used to represent a set of mutually exclusive options. **Mutually exclusive options** are a set of options in which only one can be selected at a time. By default, all RadioButtons added to the Form become part of the same group. To separate RadioButtons into several groups, each RadioButton group must be in a different container (such as a GroupBox).

The RadioButton control's **Checked** property indicates whether the RadioButton is checked (contains a small black dot) or unchecked (blank). If the RadioButton is checked, property Checked returns the Boolean value True. If the RadioButton is not checked, property Checked returns False.

A RadioButton also generates an event when its checked state changes. Event **CheckedChanged** is generated when a RadioButton is either selected or deselected. You now learn how to insert RadioButtons in the **Sales Data** application in the box, *Placing RadioButtons in the GroupBox*.

GUI Design Tip

Use RadioButtons when the user should choose only one option from a group.

GUI Design Tip

Always place each group of RadioButtons in a separate container (such as a GroupBox).

Placing RadioButtons in the GroupBox

1. *Creating RadioButtons in the GroupBox.* Create a RadioButton on the Form by clicking the **RadioButton** control,

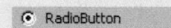

in the **Toolbox** and then clicking inside the **View** GroupBox located to the right of the MSChart control (Fig. 18.16). Repeat this process until two RadioButtons have been added to the GroupBox. Notice that, as with CheckBoxes, each RadioButton control contains a label.

2. *Customizing the RadioButtons.* To align the RadioButtons horizontally, set the Location property of one RadioButton to 13, 29, and set the other RadioButton's Location property to 108, 29. Then resize the RadioButton labels by setting each RadioButton's Size property to 76, 28. Rename the left RadioButton by changing its Name property to rad2D and set its Text property to 2D Graph. Then set the right RadioButton control's Name property to rad3D, and set its Text property to 3D Graph. Your GroupBox should now look similar to Fig. 18.16.

Good Programming Practice

We suggest prefixing RadioButton controls with rad.

GUI Design Tip

Align groups of RadioButtons either horizontally or vertically.

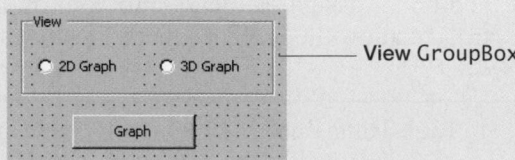

Figure 18.16 RadioButtons placed in the GroupBox.

3. *Saving the project.* Select **File > Save All** to save all the solution's files.

SELF-REVIEW

1. Which property determines whether a RadioButton is selected?

a) Selected   b) Clicked

c) Checked   d) Enabled

2. The _____ event is raised when a RadioButton is either selected or deselected.

    a) CheckedChanged   b) Changed

    c) SelectedChanged   d) None of the above.

Answers: 1) c. 2) a.

18.5 Inserting Code into the Sales Data Application

Now that you have placed the controls on the Form, you are now ready to write code to display data in the chart when the application first executes. You can accomplish this task by using the Form's Load event handler. Recall that the Form's Load event occurs before the application is displayed for the first time. You will write code to display data in the chart while completing the box, *Coding the Form's Load Event Handler.*

Coding the *Form's* Load Event Handler

1. ***Creating the Load event handler.*** Double click an empty area of the Form to enter code view and generate the event handler FrmSalesData_Load.

2. ***Inserting code into the event handler.*** Insert lines 223–232 of Fig. 18.17 in event handler FrmSalesData_Load. Be sure to add the comments and line-continuation characters as shown in Fig. 18.17 so that the line numbers in your code match those presented in this tutorial.

    Setting initial data

    Checking the **2D Graph** RadioButton

    Graphing the data

Figure 18.17 **Sales Data** application's Load event handler.

Lines 224–227 assign default values to the NumericUpDown controls by using their Text properties. These values will be used to draw the initial graph. Line 230 selects the **2D Graph** RadioButton, because the initial chart type will be a 2D bar graph.

Line 232 calls the GraphData procedure. The GraphData procedure will use the data in the NumericUpDown controls to create a graph. You will define the procedure in the box, *Coding the GraphData Procedure.*

3. ***Saving the project.*** Select **File > Save All** to save all the solution's files.

Error-Prevention Tip

To avoid subtle logic errors, one RadioButton in a group should be selected by default by setting its Checked property to True. This can be done using code (as shown) or by setting the value using the **Properties** window.

When the user clicks the **Graph** Button, the application should read the chart data entered by the user and update the graph. You will add this capability in the box, *Coding the **Graph** Button's Click Event Handler.*

Coding the Graph Button's `Click` Event Handler

1. ***Switching to design view.*** Click the **SalesData.vb [Design]** tab to switch to design view.

2. ***Adding the `Click` event handler.*** Double click the **Graph** Button to enter code view and generate the event handler `btnGraph_Click`.

3. ***Inserting code in the event handler.*** Insert line 239 of Fig. 18.18 into event handler `btnGraph_Click`.

Graphing the data

Figure 18.18 **Sales Data** application's **Load** event handler.

The `GraphData` procedure will use the data in the `NumericUpDown` controls to create a graph (line 239). You will define the procedure in the next box.

4. ***Saving the project.*** Select **File > Save All** to save all the solution's files.

The `MSChart` control uses two-dimensional arrays as input to display data. In the box, *Coding the GraphData Procedure*, you will write code that creates an array in which you will store user input. You will then use code to enable the `MSChart` control to display that data.

Coding the `GraphData` Procedure

1. ***Writing the `GraphData` procedure code.*** Add lines 242–261 of Fig. 18.19 below your `btnGraph_Click` event handler.

Lines 246–249 retrieve user input from the `NumericUpDown` controls by using their `Text` properties and store the values in `String` variables. Lines 253–258 create and initialize a 5-by-2 `String` array `strSales`. Array `strSales` contains the data that will be displayed in the chart.

The `MSChart` control does not use the first element of the array (`"Location"`) to display data. In this case, we use the first element to label our array. The second column of the first row (`"Thousands of Tons of Steel"`) contains a label that displays to the right of the graph in the 3D bar graph (Fig. 18.3).

The *x*-axis is divided into four factory locations. The first column (the first elements in the last four rows)—`strSales(1,0)`, `strSales(2,0)`, `strSales(3,0)` and `strSales(4,0)`—contains the axis labels for the *x*-axis categories, as seen on lines 254–258. Each label (that is, `Missouri`, `Texas`, `Illinois` and `Indiana`) appears below the values in its column.

The `String` variables (which represent numbers) in array `strSales` indicate the value associated with each state. For instance, if `strMissouri` contains the value `"30"`, then line 255 indicates that the Missouri factory produced 30 thousand tons of steel. As a result, the chart displays a blue bar of height 30 above the **Missouri** label on the *x*-axis, as shown in Fig. 18.2.

(cont.)

Retrieving user input

Declaring a two-dimensional array and setting its values

Setting the ChartData property updates the graph

Figure 18.19 GraphData procedure code.

Lines 254–258 follow this pattern as well. Notice that you do not have to specify the values along the *y*-axis. The MSChart control uses the data in the chart to place the values on the *y*-axis in such a way that the values fit the range of data. The *y*-axis in your chart in Fig. 18.2 extends from 0 to 70, because this includes the range of values (20–65) that you specified in the NumericUpDown controls.

Line 260 sets the data displayed in MSChart chSales to be the data contained in array strSales. Property **ChartData** stores the two-dimensional array of data displayed by an MSChart.

2. *Saving the project.* Select **File > Save All** to save all the solution's files.

3. *Running the application.* Select **Debug > Start** to run the application. Notice that you can select new values in the NumericUpDown control and update the graph by clicking the **Graph** Button, but the RadioButtons do not change the appearance of the graph. You will add this functionality in the next box.

4. *Closing the application.* Click the running application's close box to terminate the application.

You will now code an event handler to enhance the application's functionality by allowing users to select whether they want to view the chart in two dimensions or in three dimensions. You will learn how to code this functionality in the box, *Coding Event Handlers for the RadioButtons.*

Coding Event Handlers for the RadioButtons

1. *Creating event handlers for RadioButtons CheckedChanged events.* While in design mode, double click the rad2D RadioButton on the Form. This will generate an event handler for that RadioButton control's CheckedChanged event.

(cont.)

2. **Coding the 2D Chart RadioButton's CheckedChanged event.** Insert lines 268–270 from Fig. 18.20 into the rad2D_CheckedChanged event handler. Lines 269–270 set the chSales MSChart control's **ChartType** property to a two-dimensional bar graph. The VtChChartType2dBar property (line 270) specifies a two-dimensional bar graph.

Setting the MSChart control to display a 2D bar graph

Figure 18.20 rad2D_CheckedChanged event handler.

3. **Coding the 3D Chart RadioButton's CheckedChanged event.** In the Windows Form Designer, double click the rad3D RadioButton to generate its CheckedChanged event handler, and enter code view. Then insert lines 279–281 of Fig. 18.21 into the event handler. This code will set the chSales control's ChartType property to a three-dimensional bar graph. Value VtChChartType3dBar (line 281) specifies a three-dimensional bar graph.

Setting the MSChart control to display a 3D bar graph

Figure 18.21 rad3D_CheckedChanged event handler.

4. **Saving the project.** Before saving the project, verify that your code matches the code listed in Fig. 18.22 (although line numbers will differ). Then select **File > Save All** to save all of the solution's files.

5. **Running the application.** Select **Debug > Start** to execute the application. Notice that the chart appearance now changes when you change the RadioButton selection.

(cont.) 6. ***Terminating application execution and closing the solution.*** Click the running application's close box. Select **File > Close Solution**.

Figure 18.22 contains the code listing for the completed **Sales Data** application. New programming concepts are highlighted in yellow.

```
1    Public Class FrmSalesData
2        Inherits System.Windows.Forms.Form
3
4        ' Windows Form Designer generated code
5
6        ' handles Form's Load event
7        Private Sub FrmSalesData_Load(ByVal sender As System.Object, _
8            ByVal e As System.EventArgs) Handles MyBase.Load
9
10           ' set NumericUpDown control default values
11           updMissouri.Text = "20"
12           updTexas.Text = "10"
13           updIllinois.Text = "30"
14           updIndiana.Text = "40"
15
16           ' set RadioButton rad2D's Checked property to True
17           rad2D.Checked = True
18
19           GraphData() ' update the graph
20       End Sub ' FrmSalesData_Load
21
22       ' handles Graph Button's Click event
23       Private Sub btnGraph_Click(ByVal sender As System.Object, _
24           ByVal e As System.EventArgs) Handles btnGraph.Click
25
26           GraphData() ' update the graph
27       End Sub ' btnGraph_Click
28
29       ' procedure to display data in Chart control
30       Sub GraphData()
31
32           ' declare String variables and input user data
33           Dim strMissouri As String = updMissouri.Text
34           Dim strTexas As String = updTexas.Text
35           Dim strIllinois As String = updIllinois.Text
36           Dim strIndiana As String = updIndiana.Text
37
38           ' first row contains Labels for the columns
39           ' first column contains x-axis values
40           Dim strSales(,) As String = New String(,) _
41               {{"Location", "Thousands of Tons of Steel"}, _
42               {"Missouri", strMissouri}, _
43               {"Texas", strTexas}, _
44               {"Illinois", strIllinois}, _
45               {"Indiana", strIndiana}}
46
47           chSales.ChartData = strSales ' set the Chart's data
48       End Sub ' GraphData
49
```

Using code to select a RadioButton control *(points to line 17)*

Declaring a 5-by-2 String array to store values for graphing *(points to lines 40–45)*

Sets the data for the MSChart control to graph *(points to line 47)*

Figure 18.22 Completed **Sales Data** application code. (Part 1 of 2.)

Event raised when user checks or unchecks the RadioButton

Using the ChartType property to display a 2D bar graph

Using the ChartType property to display a 3D bar graph

```
50    ' handles rad2D RadioButton's CheckedChanged event
51    Private Sub rad2D_CheckedChanged(ByVal sender As _
52        System.Object, ByVal e As System.EventArgs) _
53        Handles rad2D.CheckedChanged
54
55        ' displays Chart as 2D bar graph
56        chSales.ChartType = _
57            MSChart20Lib.VtChChartType.VtChChartType2dBar
58
59    End Sub ' rad2D_CheckedChanged
60
61    ' handles rad3D RadioButton's CheckedChanged event
62    Private Sub rad3D_CheckedChanged(ByVal sender As _
63        System.Object, ByVal e As System.EventArgs) _
64        Handles rad3D.CheckedChanged
65
66        ' displays Chart as 3D bar graph
67        chSales.ChartType = _
68            MSChart20Lib.VtChChartType.VtChChartType3dBar
69
70    End Sub ' rad3D_CheckedChanged
71
72 End Class ' FrmSalesData
```

Figure 18.22 Completed **Sales Data** application code. (Part 2 of 2.)

SELF-REVIEW

1. The _____ of an array used to store data for an MSChart control contains values that will display as the *x*-axis labels.

    a) first row
    b) second row
    c) first column
    d) second column

2. The _____ property of an MSChart control stores the data values it will graph.

    a) DataSouce
    b) ChartSource
    c) ChartDataSource
    d) ChartData

Answers: 1.) c. 2.) d.

18.6 Wrap-Up

In this tutorial, you learned how to use two-dimensional arrays to display chart data in an MSChart control. You studied two-dimensional arrays and learned how to declare and assign values to a rectangular array.

To help complete the **Sales Data** application, you used the RadioButton control and the MSChart control. You learned that RadioButtons are used to represent a set of mutually exclusive options—one RadioButton in a group of RadioButtons can be checked. You also learned that you must group related RadioButtons by placing them in separate containers.

The MSChart control is not in the **Toolbox** by default, so you learned how to place this control in the **Toolbox**. You then created an MSChart control on your Form and used its properties to set display options, including the graph's title, border and axes labels.

After learning about RadioButtons and the MSChart control, you used code to store user input in a two-dimensional array and you assigned that array to the MSChart control's ChartData property to graph that data. You also learned how to use the RadioButton's CheckedChanged event handler to change a graph's appearance when the user selects a display option.

In the next tutorial, you will learn about classes. (Recall that you have been using classes all along, from the Form class that represents the application's GUI to the Random class that you use to generate random numbers.) You will learn how to create your own classes for use in your applications.

SKILLS SUMMARY

Using Two-Dimensional Arrays

■ Declare a rectangular array to create a table of values (each row will contain the same number of columns).

Adding the MSChart Control to the Visual Studio .NET Toolbox.

■ Right click the **Windows Forms** tab in the **Toolbox** and select **Customize Toolbox...** to display the **Customize Toolbox** dialog.

■ Then check the **Microsoft Chart Control 6.0 (SP4) (OLEDB)** CheckBox within the **COM Components** tab.

■ Click **OK** to add the control to the **Toolbox**.

Displaying the Properties Dialog to Customize the MSChart Control

■ Select the MSChart control on the Form, and click the **ActiveX -Properties** link at the bottom of the **Properties** window.

Setting the Title of an MSChart Control

■ Select the **Text** tab in the **Properties** dialog of the MSChart control.

■ Then select the **Title** option in the **Property Name:** ComboBox and type the desired title in the **Text:** TextBox.

Labeling the X- (or Y-) Axis of the MSChart Control

■ Select the **Text** tab in the **Properties** dialog of the MSChart control.

■ Then select the **X Axis Title** (or **Y Axis Title**) option in the **Property Name:** ComboBox, and type the desired title in the **Text:** TextBox.

Changing the Font Properties of the Text in an MSChart Control

■ Select the **Fonts** tab in the **Properties** dialog of the MSChart control.

■ Then select from the **Property Name:** ComboBox the desired option that you wish to change.

■ You can then specify a font in the **Font:** ComboBox and a font size in the **Size:** ComboBox.

Using a RadioButton

■ Use a RadioButton in an application to present the user with mutually exclusive options.

Selecting a RadioButton at Runtime

■ Click the white circle of the RadioButton. (A small black dot will appear inside the white circle.)

Determining Whether a RadioButton Is Selected

■ Access the RadioButton's Checked property.

Executing Code When a RadioButton's State Has Changed

■ Use the CheckedChanged event handler, which executes when a RadioButton is selected or deselected.

KEY TERMS

ActiveX -Properties—A hyperlink at the bottom-left of the **Properties** window for the MSChart control. When clicked, it displays a dialog with which you can set the MSChart properties.

ChartData property—The MSChart property that stores the array containing the data to be displayed as a graph.

ChartType property—The MSChart property that determines the type of graph the control uses to display its data.

Checked property—The RadioButton property that, when True, displays a small black dot in the control. When False, the control displays an empty white circle.

CheckedChanged event—The event raised when a `RadioButton`'s state (checked or unchecked) changes.

MSChart control— A control that allows you to display data as a graph on the `Form`.

RadioButton control—A control that appears as a small white circle that is either blank (unchecked) or contains a smaller black dot (checked). Usually these controls appear in groups of two or more. Exactly one `RadioButton` in a group is selected at once.

rectangular array—A type of two-dimensional array that can represent tables of values consisting of information arranged in rows and columns. Each row contains the same number of columns.

two-dimensional array—A double-subscripted array that contains multiple rows of values.

GUI DESIGN GUIDELINES

MSChart Control

- Resize an `MSChart` control so that all the data is clearly visible.
- Set the `MSChart` control's `Enabled` property to `False` to prevent users from repositioning the chart within the `MSChart` control.
- Assign meaningful descriptions in the `MSChart` graph's title and axis labels. Use book-title capitalization for these descriptions.
- Increase the `MSChart` graph's title and axis label font sizes to enhance readability.

RadioButton

- Use `RadioButton`s when the user should choose only one option in a group.
- Always place each group of `RadioButton`s in a separate container (such as a `GroupBox`).
- Align groups of `RadioButton`s either horizontally or vertically.

CONTROLS, EVENTS, PROPERTIES & METHODS

MSChart   `MSChart`   This control is used to display data in graphs.

- *In action*

- *Properties*

  `ChartData`—This property contains the data to be graphed.

  `ChartType`—This property determines the appearance of the graph.

  `Location`—This property specifies the location of the `MSChart` control on the container control relative to the top-left corner.

  `Name`—This property specifies the name used to access the `MSChart` control programmatically. The name should be prefixed with `ch`.

  `Size`—This property specifies the height and width (in pixels) of the `MSChart` control.

RadioButton   `RadioButton`   This control is used to enable users to select exactly one option from several.

- *In action*

  ⦿ 3D Graph

- *Event*

  `CheckedChanged`—This event is raised when the control is either selected or deselected.

■ *Properties*

Checked—This property is True if control is selected and False if it is not selected.

Location—This property specifies the location of the RadioButton control on the container control relative to the top-left corner.

Name—This property specifies the name used to access the RadioButton control programmatically. The name should be prefixed with rad.

Size—This property specifies the height and width (in pixels) of the RadioButton control.

Text—This property specifies the text displayed in the label to the right of the RadioButton.

MULTIPLE-CHOICE QUESTIONS

18.1 RadioButton controls should be prefixed with _____.

a) rad

b) rbn

c) btn

d) radbtn

18.2 A two-dimensional array in which each row contains the same number of columns is called a _____ array.

a) data

b) rectangular

c) tabular

d) All of the above.

18.3 In an *m*-by-*n* array, the *m* stands for _____.

a) the number of columns in the array

b) the total number of array elements

c) the number of rows in the array

d) the number of elements in each row

18.4 The statement _____ assigns an array of three columns and five rows to two-dimensional Integer array intArray.

a) intArray = New Integer(5, 3)

b) intArray = New Integer(4, 2)

c) intArray = New Integer(4, 3)

d) intArray = New Integer(5, 2)

18.5 To change the MSChart graph's title size, use the _____ tab of the MSChart **Properties** dialog.

a) **Size**

b) **Title**

c) **Fonts**

d) **Font Size**

18.6 Use a _____ to group RadioButtons on the Form.

a) GroupBox control

b) ComboBox control

c) ListBox control

d) None of the above.

18.7 Use the _____ tab of the MSChart **Properties** dialog to access properties to include a border around your chart.

a) **Border**

b) **Backdrop**

c) **BorderStyle**

d) **Background**

18.8 A point of height is approximately equal to _____.

a) 1/72"

b) 1"

c) 1/4"

d) 1/36"

18.9 The **Chart Type** GroupBox of the MSChart control's **Properties** dialog is located in the _____ tab.

a) **Chart**

b) **Graph**

c) **Series**

d) **ChartType**

18.10 The **Fonts** tab of the MSChart control's **Properties** dialog allows you to change the font _____.

a) **Style**

b) **Width**

c) **Color**

d) All of the above.

EXERCISES

18.11 (*Stock Price Application*) It is often useful to track a company's stock price over time by using a line graph. You will learn to create a line graph by using an MSChart control in this exercise. Create an application that allows users to enter values for a company's stock price at the end of six consecutive quarters and graph that data, using an MSChart control (Fig. 18.23).

a) *Copying and opening the template application.* Copy the StockPrice folder from C:\Examples\Tutorial18\Exercises to C:\SimplyVB. Double click the Stock-Price.sln file in the StockPrice folder to open the application in Visual Studio .NET.

b) *Changing the graph type and color.* To change the graph type and color, click the chart in **Design View** and select the **ActiveX -Properties** hyperlink from the **Properties** window to display the **Properties** dialog. In the **Chart** tab's **Chart Type** Group-Box, select **Line**, and make sure the RadioButton is set to **2D**. Click the **Series Color** tab, and, in the **Edge/Line** GroupBox, change the color to red.

c) *Inserting code in the Graph Button's Click event handler.* Double click the **Graph** Button in **Design** view to generate the **Graph** Button Click event handler. Insert an If...Then statement that verifies that the user entered a stock name. If the value in the TextBox is the empty string, the application should display a message dialog.

d) *Checking the remaining TextBoxes.* For the chart to function properly, the user must enter values in all TextBoxes. Add If...ElseIf...Else statements to verify that there is a value greater than zero in each NumericUpDown (using the Value property), and display an error message in a MessageBox if any values are missing (contain the zero).

e) *Calculating the average.* Calculate the average of all of the values from the Numeric-UpDowns, and output the result in the output Label lblAverage.

f) *Inserting data into an array.* Create a 6-by-2 array from the data that will display the week number on the *x*-axis and prices on the *y*-axis. (The week number should be in the first column, and the stock price should be in the second column.) Use the Numer-icUpDown's Text property to retrieve the value stored in the control as a String.

g) *Displaying the chart.* Assign the array to the ChartData property to display the data in the array. Remember to set Label lblMessage's Visible property to False and set the MSChart control's Visible property to True. A control's **Visible** property determines if the control is displayed on the Form (True) or hidden (False).

Figure 18.23 Stock Price application GUI.

18.12 (*Enhanced Lottery Picker*) A lottery commission offers four different lottery games to play: three-number, four-number, five-number and five-number + 1 lotteries. In Tutorial 16, your **Lottery Picker** application could select duplicate numbers for each lottery. In this exercise, you enhance the **Lottery Picker** to prevent duplicate numbers for the five-number and five-number + 1 lotteries (Fig. 18.24). According to this new requirement the games are now played as follows:

- Three-number lotteries require players to choose three numbers in the range of 0–9.
- Four-number lotteries require players to choose four numbers, in the range of 0–9.
- Five-number lotteries require players to choose five unique numbers in the range of 1–39.
- Five-number + 1 lotteries require players to choose five unique numbers in the range of 1–49 and an additional unique number in the range of 1–42.

Figure 18.24   Enhanced **Lottery Numbers Picker** application.

a) *Copying and opening the template application.* Copy the EnhancedLotteryPicker folder from C:\Examples\Tutorial18\Exercises to C:\SimplyVB. Double click LotteryPicker.sln to open the application in Visual Studio .NET.

b) *Declaring a two-dimensional array to maintain unique random numbers.* Declare an instance variable m_blnNumbers that stores a 2-by-50 Boolean array. You will use this array later in this exercise to test whether a lottery number has already been chosen.

c) *Initializing the array.* Each time the user clicks the **Generate** Button, the application should initialize the array by declaring its rows and setting the initial values. Write a ClearArray procedure that uses a For...Next statement to assign each value in the m_blnNumbers array to False.

d) *Modifying the Generate Function procedure.* You will modify the Generate Function procedure to use the Boolean array to pick unique random numbers. Begin by writing a statement that generates a random number and assigns its value to an Integer variable intNumber.

e) *Determining whether the random number has already been selected.* Use an If...Then statement to determine whether the maximum lottery number is less than 40. (This happens when the upper limit on the random number equals 40.) In this case, you will examine the first row of the array. To maintain unique numbers, you will set the value of the element in that row whose index equals the random number to True (indicating that it has been picked). For example, if the random number 34 has been picked, blnNumbers(0)(34) would contain the value True. To test whether a number has been picked, use a Do While...Loop statement inside the If...Then statement to access that element of the array. If the array element's value is True, use the body of the loop to assign a new random number to intNumber. If the value in the array is False, use the condition in the Do While...Loop header to ignore the body of the loop. Just outside the Do While...Loop, include a statement that modifies the array to indicate that the number has now been picked.

f) *Completing the application.* Use a second If...Then statement to determine whether the maximum lottery number is greater than 40. In this case, you will examine the second row of the array. Repeat the process in the previous step. Remember to return the value stored in intNumber at the end of the Generate Function procedure.

18.13 (*Student Grades Application*) A teacher needs an application that computes each student's grade average (on a scale of 0 to 100 points) and the class average for ten students. The application should add a student's name and test average (separated by a tab character) to a ListBox and calculate the class grade average each time the user clicks the **Submit Grades** Button (Fig. 18.25). The **Submit Grades** Button should be disabled after ten grades have been entered.

a) *Copying and opening the template application.* Copy the StudentGrades folder from C:\Examples\Tutorial18\Exercises to C:\SimplyVB. Double click StudentGrades.sln to open the application in Visual Studio .NET.

b) *Declare instance variables.* Declare an Integer counter and a 10-by-2 String array as instance variables.

c) *Coding the Submit Grades Button's Click event handler.* Double click the **Submit Grades** Button to generate its Click event handler. Write code in the event handler to retrieve input from the TextBoxes. Then store the student's name in the first column of the two-dimensional String array and the student's test average in the second column of the array. Use a Function procedure to calculate the student's test average.

d) *Computing the class average.* Add the student's name and the student's test average (separated by a tab character) to the ListBox. Then calculate and display the class average, using a Function procedure. [*Hint:* You should use the two-dimensional String array and the Integer counter to calculate the class average.]

e) *Completing the event handler.* Increment the counter by one after calculating the class average. If ten students' grades have been entered, disable the **Submit Grades** Button.

Figure 18.25 Student Grades application.

What does this code do? ▶

18.14 What is returned by the following code? Assume that GetStockPrices is a Function procedure that returns a 2-by-31 array, with the first row containing the stock price at the beginning of the day and the last row containing the stock price at the end of the day, for each day of the month.

```
1   Function Mystery() As Integer()
2       Dim intPrices As Integer(,) = New Integer(1, 30){}
3
4       intPrices = GetStockPrices()
5
6       Dim intResult As Integer() = New Integer(30){}
7       Dim intI As Integer
8
9       For intI = 0 To 30
10          intResult(intI) = intPrices(0, intI) - intPrices(1, intI)
11      Next
12
13      Return intResult
14  End Function ' Mystery
```

What's wrong with this code? ▶

18.15 Find the error(s) in the following code. The TwoDArrays procedure should create a two-dimensional array and initialize all its values to one. [Note: Code listing continues on the top of the next page.]

```
1   Sub TwoDArrays()
2       Dim intArray As Integer(,)
```

(cont.)

```
3
4       intArray = New Integer(3, 3){}
5
6       Dim intI As Integer
7
8       ' assign 1 to all cell values
9       For intI = 0 To 3
10          intArray(intI, intI) = 1
11      Next
12
13  End Sub ' TwoDArrays
```

Programming Challenge ▶

18.16 (*Enhanced Student Grades Application*) Modify the application in Exercise 18.13 to include a bar graph that displays each student's grade and the class average. The chart should display only after the user enters the grades for ten students (Fig. 18.26). Until then, a Label should display the text, "Enter ten grades to display the chart." Student names and the text Class Average should display on the *x*-axis, and grades should display on the *y*-axis. Also write code that ensures that the user has entered values in each TextBox when the **Submit Grades** Button is clicked.

a) *Copying and opening the template application.* Copy the EnhancedStudentGrades folder from C:\Examples\Tutorial18\Exercises to C:\SimplyVB. Double click StudentGrades.sln to open the application in Visual Studio .NET. If you have not completed Exercise 18.13, follow the steps in Exercise 18.13 before proceeding to the next step. If you have completed Exercise 18.13, copy the code you wrote into this application.

b) *Completing the application design.* Place a Label on the Form that reads "Enter ten grades to display the chart." Then insert an MSChart control at the bottom of the Form. Set its Visible property to False to hide the graph initially. A control's Visible property determines if the control is displayed on the Form (True) or hidden (False). Open the MSChart control's **Properties** dialog, set the **Chart Type** to a 2D Bar/PictoGraph and set the **Series Interior Color** property (under the **Series Color** tab) to yellow.

c) *Inserting code to check input.* Write code that determines whether the user has entered values in each TextBox. If the student name is missing, display a MessageBox indicating that the user must enter a student name. If any grades are missing, display a MessageBox indicating that three grades are required.

d) *Enhancing the user interface.* Write code to clear each TextBox after the user clicks the **Submit Grades** Button. Then insert code to set the focus of the application to the **Student name:** TextBox.

e) *Displaying the chart.* Write a procedure that displays each of the ten students' test averages and the class average in the MSChart control. Recall that student names and the text Class Average should display on the *x*-axis, and grades should display on the *y*-axis. Finally, set the chart's Visible property to True, and set the Visible property of the Label you added in *Step b* to False.

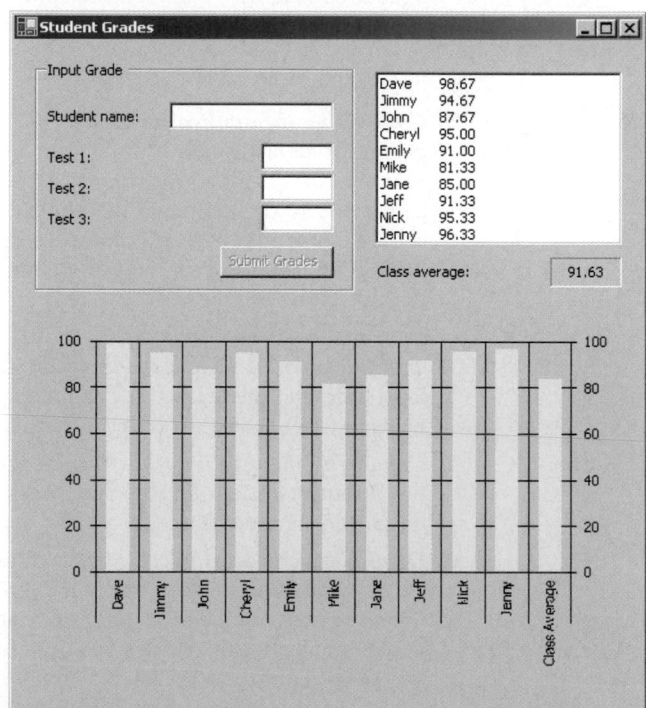

Figure 18.26 Enhanced **Student Grades** application.

Objectives

In this tutorial, you will learn to:
- Create your own classes.
- Create and use objects of your own classes.
- Control access to object instance variables.
- Use keyword `Private`.
- Create your own properties.
- Use the `Panel` control.
- Use `String` methods `PadLeft` and `Substring`.

Outline

Microwave Oven Application

Building Your Own Classes and Objects

In earlier tutorials, you used the following application-development methodology: You analyzed many typical problems that required an application to be built and determined what classes from the FCL were needed to implement each application. You then selected appropriate methods from these classes and created any necessary procedures to complete each application.

You have now seen several FCL classes. Each GUI control is defined as a class. When you add a control to your application from the **Toolbox**, an object (also known as an **instance**) of that class is created and added to your application. You have also seen FCL classes that are not GUI controls. Classes `String` and `Random`, for example, have been used to create `String` objects (for textual data) and `Random` objects (for generating random numbers), respectively. When you create and use an object of a class in an application, your application is known as a **client** of that class.

In this tutorial, you will learn to create and use your own classes (sometimes known as **programmer-defined classes**, or **programmer-defined types**). Creating your own classes is a key part of object-oriented programming (OOP). As with procedures, classes can be reused. In the world of Visual Basic .NET programming, applications are created by using a combination of FCL classes and methods and programmer-defined classes and procedures. You have already created several procedures in this book. Note that all of these procedures were created within classes, because all of your applications have been defined as classes. In this tutorial (and for the remainder of the book), you will refer to a class's procedures as methods, which is the industry-preferred term for procedures located within a class.

You will create a microwave-oven simulator where the user will enter an amount of time for the microwave to cook food. To handle the time data, you will create a class called `Time`. This class will store a number of minutes and seconds (which your **Microwave Oven** application will use to keep track of the remaining cook time) and provide properties whereby clients of this class can change the number of minutes and seconds.

19.1 Test-Driving the Microwave Oven Application

In this tutorial you will build your own class as you construct your **Microwave Oven** application. This application must meet the following requirements:

Application Requirements

An electronics company is considering building microwave ovens. The company has asked you to develop an application that simulates a microwave oven. The oven will contain a keypad that allows the user to specify the microwave cook time, which is displayed for the user. Once a time is entered, the user clicks the Start Button to begin the cooking process. The microwave's glass window changes color (from gray to yellow) to simulate the oven's light that remains on while the food cooks, and a timer counts down one second at a time. Once the time expires, the color of the microwave's glass window returns to gray (indicating that the microwave's light is now off) and the microwave displays the text "Done!". The user can click the Clear Button at any time to stop the microwave and enter a new time. The user should be able to enter a number of minutes no larger than 59 and a number of seconds no larger than 59; otherwise, the invalid cook time will be set to zero. A beep will be sounded whenever a Button is clicked, and when the microwave oven has finished a countdown.

You begin by test-driving the completed **Microwave Oven** application.

Test-Driving the Microwave Oven Application

1. *Opening the Microwave Oven application.* Open `C:\Examples\Tutorial19\CompletedApplication\MicrowaveOven`. Double click `MicrowaveOven.sln` to open the solution in Visual Studio .NET.

2. *Running the Microwave Oven application.* Select **Debug > Start** to run the application. The Form in Fig. 19.1 is displayed. The application contains a large rectangle on the left (representing the microwave oven's glass window) and a keypad on the right, including a Label with the text **Microwave Oven**. The numeric Buttons are used to enter the cook time, which will be displayed in the Label on the top right. Notice that the keypad Buttons appear flat, to give the application a more "real-world" appearance. To create this appearance, the Buttons' **FlatStyle** property has been set to **Flat**. Similarly, the Label's **BorderStyle** property has been set to **FixedSingle**.

Microwave's glass window ——————

Numeric keypad (Buttons appear flat)

Figure 19.1 **Microwave Oven** application's Form.

3. *Entering a time.* Click the following numeric Buttons in order: **1, 2, 3, 4** and **5**. Each time you click a keypad Button, you will hear a beeping sound. (If you do not hear a beeping sound, please check your computer settings to ensure that the volume of your machine's speaker has not been lowered or muted.)

(cont.)

Notice that you can enter no more than four digits (the first two for the minutes and the second two for the seconds)—any extra digits will not appear (Fig. 19.2). The number of minutes and the number of seconds must each be 59 or less. If the user enters an invalid number of minutes or seconds (such as 89), the invalid amount will be set to zero.

Figure 19.2 **Microwave Oven** application accepts only four digits.

4. ***Entering invalid data.*** Click the **Clear** Button to clear your input. Click the following numeric Buttons in order: **7**, **2**, **3** and **5** (Fig. 19.3). This input is invalid because the number of minutes, 72, is larger than the maximum allowed value, 59, so the number of minutes is reset to zero when the **Start** Button is clicked. Click the **Start** Button now. Notice that the number of minutes has been reset to **00** (Fig. 19.4). Also notice that the microwave oven's window has changed to yellow, to simulate the light that goes on inside the oven so that the user can watch the food cooking.

Figure 19.3 **Microwave Oven** application with invalid input.

5. ***Entering valid data.*** Click the **Clear** Button to enter a new cook time. Click Button **5** (to indicate 5 seconds); then, click **Start** (Fig. 19.5).

6. ***Viewing the application after the cooking time has expired.*** Wait five seconds. Notice that the display Label shows the time counting down by 1 each second. When the time has reached zero, the oven beeps, the display Label changes to contain the text **Done!** and the microwave oven's window changes back to the same color as the Form (Fig. 19.6).

7. ***Closing the application.*** Close the application by clicking the close box in the upper-right corner of the Form.

8. ***Closing the solution.*** Select **File > Close Solution** to save all the solution's files.

(cont.)

Figure 19.4 **Microwave Oven** application after invalid input has been entered and the **Start** Button clicked.

Color yellow simulates microwave light

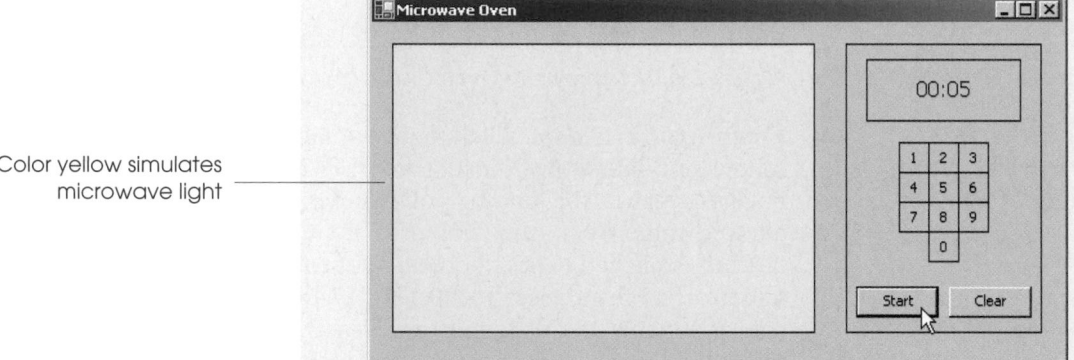

Figure 19.5 **Microwave Oven** application with valid time entered and inside light turned on (it's now cooking).

Label displays **Done!** when cooking is finished

Color returns to default color to simulate that cooking has finished

Figure 19.6 **Microwave Oven** application after the cooking time has elapsed.

GUI Design Tip

Use Panels to organize groups of related controls, where the purpose of those controls is obvious. If the purpose of the controls is not obvious, use a GroupBox in place of a Panel, because GroupBoxes can contain captions.

19.2 Designing the Microwave Oven Application

In Tutorial 14, you learned to use GroupBoxes to group various controls. The **Microwave Oven** application also groups controls, using a **Panel control**. The main difference between Panels and GroupBoxes is that GroupBoxes can display a caption, and Panels cannot. The **Microwave Oven** application requires two Panels—one to contain the controls of the application, and the other to represent the microwave oven's glass window. The template application provided for you contains one of these Panels.

The **Microwave Oven** application contains a class (called Time) whose objects store the cook time in minutes and seconds. All of the controls you have used (including the Form itself) are defined as classes. You will create the Time class before you create the class for the **Microwave Oven**. The following pseudocode describes the operation of class Time:

> When time object is created
>   Assign input to variables for number of minutes and number of seconds
>
> When data is assigned to variables for number of minutes and number of seconds
>   Ensure time is valid
>   If number of minutes is over 59, set time to 0 minutes
>   If number of seconds is over 59, set time to 0 seconds

When an object of class Time is created, the number of minutes and number of seconds will be initialized. Invalid data will cause both the number of minutes and the number of seconds to be set to 0. The following pseudocode describes the operation of your **Microwave Oven** class:

> When the user clicks a numeric Button
>   Sound beep
>   Retrieve input from user
>
>   If less than four digits have been displayed
>   Append digit to display
>
> When the user clicks the Start Button
>   Sound beep
>   Begin countdown—Start timer
>   Turn microwave light on
>
> When the timer ticks (once per second)
>   Decrease time by one second
>   Display new time
>
>   If new time is zero
>   Stop timer
>   Sound beep
>   Display text "Done!"
>   Turn microwave light off
>
> When the user clicks the Clear Button
>   Sound beep
>   Display text "Microwave Oven"
>   Clear input
>   Turn microwave light off

The user enters input by clicking the numeric Buttons. Each time a numeric Button is clicked, the number on that Button is appended to the end of the cook time that is displayed in the GUI's Label. At most, four digits can be displayed. After entering the cook time, the user can click the **Start** Button to begin the cooking process or click the **Clear** Button and enter a new time. Each Button makes a beeping sound when clicked. If the **Start** Button is clicked, a countdown using a Timer control begins, and the microwave oven's window changes to yellow, indicating that the microwave oven's light is on (so that the user can watch the food cook). Each second, the display is updated to show the remaining cooking time. When the countdown finishes, another beep is sounded, the display Label displays the text **Done!** and the microwave oven's "light" is turned off, by changing the window's color back to its default gray. Figure 19.7 lists the actions, controls and events for this application.

*Action/Control/Event
(ACE) Table for the
Microwave Oven
Application*

Action	Control	Event
Retrieve input from user	btnOne, btnTwo, btnThree, btnFour, btnFive, btnSix, btnSeven, btnEight, btnNine, btnZero	Click
Display cooking time and output	lblDisplay	
Begin countdown (enable timer) and turn microwave light on/off	btnStart, tmrClock, pnlWindow	Click (of Button)
Perform countdown	tmrClock	Tick
Clear input	btnClear	Click

Figure 19.7 ACE table for the **Microwave Oven** application.

Input is sent to the application when the user clicks one of the numeric Buttons. Values are displayed in lblDisplay as they are entered. Once all input has been entered, the user clicks the **Start** Button to begin the countdown. The pnlWindow Panel's background color is set to yellow to simulate the microwave oven's light being turned on, and Timer tmrClock will update lblDisplay each second during the countdown. To clear the input and start over, the user can click the **Clear** Button. In the box, *Adding a Panel Control to the* **Microwave Oven** *Application*, you begin creating your **Microwave Oven** application by adding the second Panel to the Form and viewing the template code.

*Adding a Panel Control
to the Microwave Oven
Application*

GUI Design Tip

Although it is possible to have a Panel without a border (by setting the BorderStyle property to None), use borders on your Panels to improve readability and organization.

1. ***Copying the template to your work folder.*** Copy the C:\Examples\Tutorial19\TemplateApplication\MicrowaveOven folder to C:\SimplyVB. Double click MicrowaveOven.sln (located in the MicrowaveOven folder) to open the application.

2. ***Adding a Panel to the Form.*** Add a Panel control to the Form by double clicking the **Panel** control (□ Panel) in the **Toolbox**. Name the control pnlWindow as this Panel will represent your microwave oven's window. Set the Panel's Size property to 328, 224 and its Location property to 16, 16. Set the BorderStyle property to FixedSingle, to display a thin black rectangle surrounding your Panel.

3. ***Viewing the template code.*** Before you add code to this application, open the file MicrowaveOven.vb in code view, and examine the code provided. Line 5 of Fig. 19.8 declares variable m_strTime, a String that will store user input.

   The template code also contains event handlers for the numeric Buttons' Click events. Each Button is clicked when the user wants to append the current Button's digit to the amount of cooking time. Let's look at one of these event handlers closely (Fig. 19.9). Line 229 calls function **Beep**, which causes your computer to make a beep sound. Each event handler for the numeric keypad Buttons begins with a call to Beep, appends the current Button's number to m_strTime (line 230) and calls method DisplayTime (line 231), which displays the remaining cook time in the application's Label. There are ten of these event handlers—one for each digit from 0 to 9.

(cont.)

Good Programming Practice

We recommend you use prefix pnl when naming your Panel controls.

Figure 19.8 Variable m_strTime contains the user's input.

When a number is entered, play a beep, add the number to the input and display the new time

Figure 19.9 Typical numeric event handler.

MicrowaveOven.vb contains four more methods that you will define in this tutorial. The first is the btnStart_Click event handler on lines 315–319 of Fig. 19.10. This event handler will be used to start the microwave oven's cooking process, which in this simulation consists of a time countdown and a change in the window's color to yellow, simulating the oven's light being on.

Event handler btnClear_Click (lines 321–325) will be used to clear the time entered. The **Clear** Button is used to change the time entered or terminate cooking early. The event handler resets the time to all zeros and displays the text **Microwave Oven**. Method DisplayTime (lines 327–330) will be used to display the cooking time as it is being entered. Event handler tmrClock_Tick (lines 332–336) will be used to change the application's Label during the countdown.

4. ***Saving the solution.*** Select **File > Save All** to save all the solution's files.

GUI Design Tip

A Panel can display scrollbars for use when the Panel is not large enough to display all of its controls at once. To increase readability, we suggest avoiding the use of scrollbars on Panels. If a Panel is not large enough to display all of its contents, increase the size of the Panel.

(cont.)

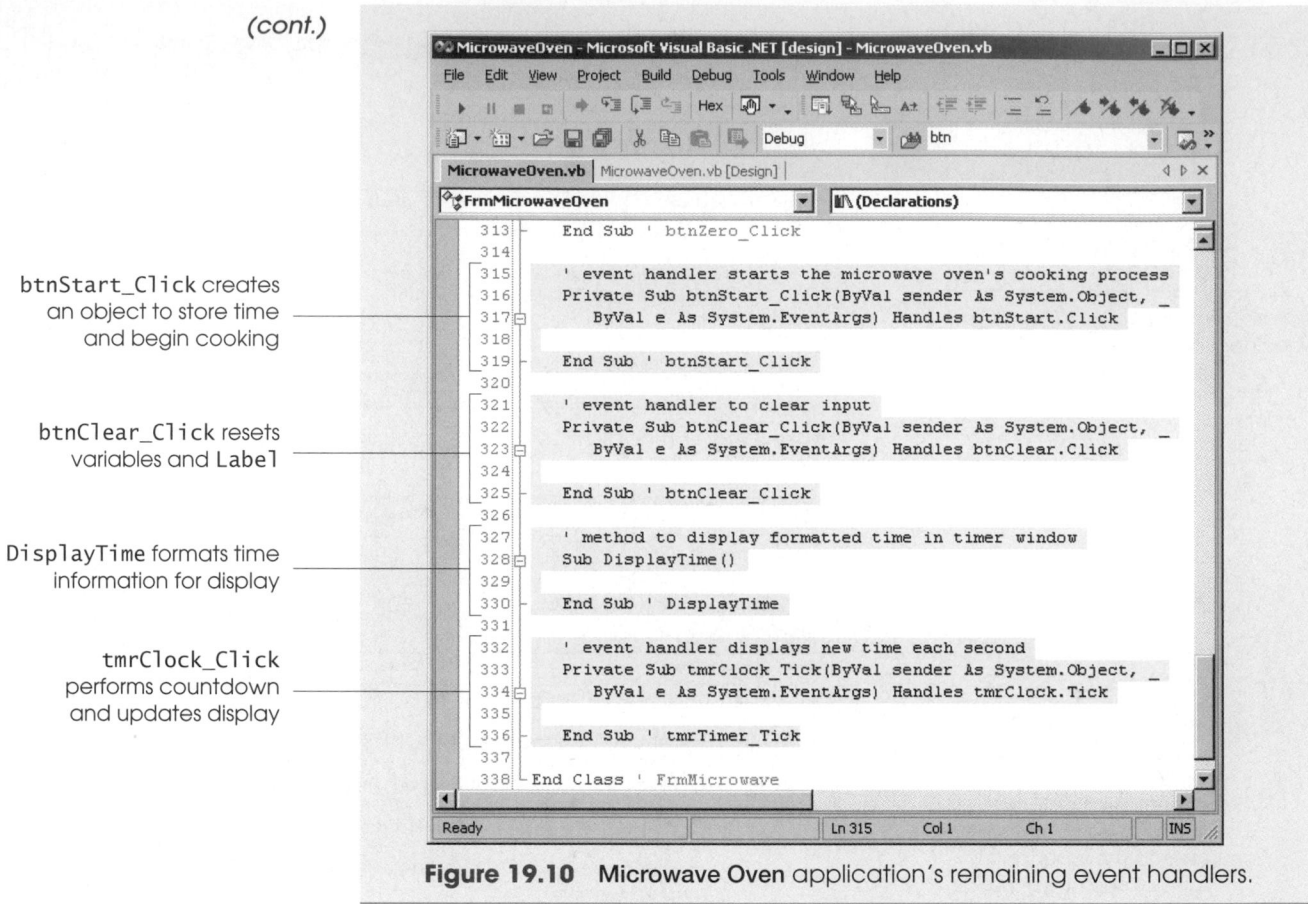

btnStart_Click creates an object to store time and begin cooking

btnClear_Click resets variables and Label

DisplayTime formats time information for display

tmrClock_Click performs countdown and updates display

Figure 19.10 Microwave Oven application's remaining event handlers.

SELF-REVIEW

1. A Panel is different from a GroupBox in that a _____.

   a) GroupBox can be used to organize controls, whereas a Panel cannot

   b) Panel contains a caption, whereas a GroupBox does not

   c) GroupBox contains a caption, whereas a Panel does not

   d) Panel can be used to organize controls, whereas a GroupBox cannot

2. Function Beep causes the computer to _____.

   a) display a message dialog and make a beeping sound

   b) set off the system alarm and pause the application

   c) make three beeping sounds in sequence

   d) make a beeping sound

Answers: 1) c. 2) d.

19.3 Adding a New Class to the Project

Next, you will learn how to add a class to your application. This class will be used to create objects that contain the time in minutes and seconds.

Adding a Class to the Microwave Oven Application

1. ***Adding a new class to the project.*** Select **Project > Add Class**. In the dialog that appears (Fig. 19.11), enter the class name (Time) in the **Name:** field and click the **Open** Button. Note that the class name (ending with the .vb file extension) appears in the **Solution Explorer** below the project name (Fig. 19.12).

(cont.)

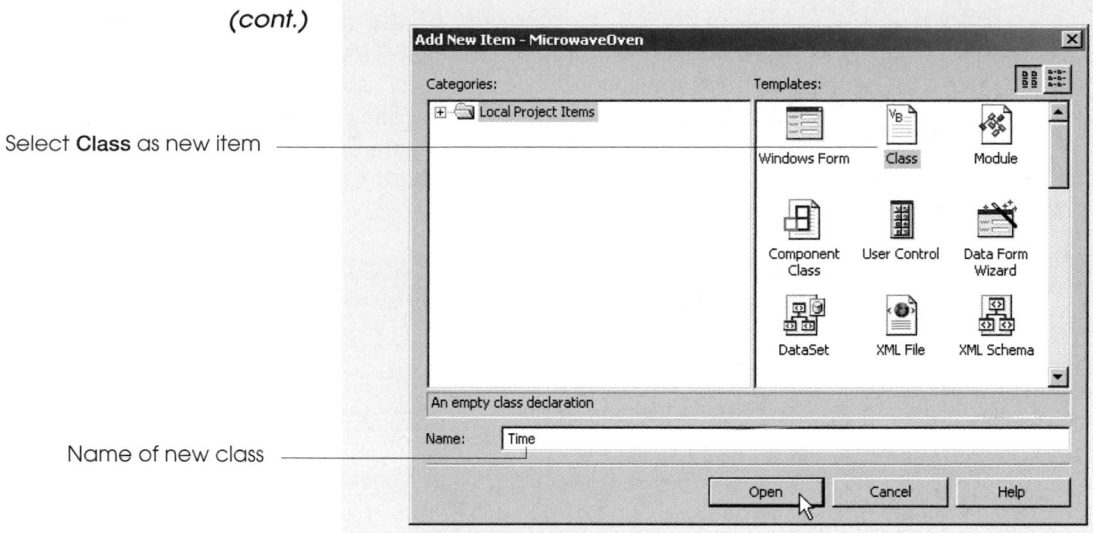

Figure 19.11 **Add New Item** dialog allows you to create a new class.

Select **Class** as new item

Name of new class

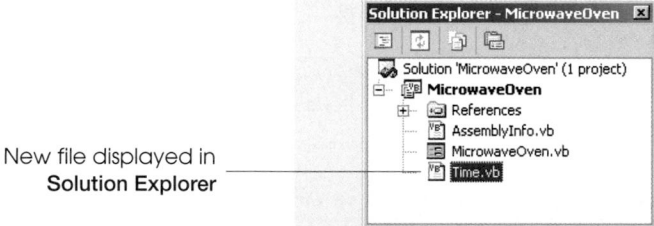

Figure 19.12 **Solution Explorer** displaying new class file.

New file displayed in
Solution Explorer

2. *Viewing the code that has been added to this class.* If Time.vb does not open for you when it is created, double click the file in the **Solution Explorer**. Notice that a few lines of code have been added for you (Fig. 19.13). Line 1, which begins the Time class definition, contains the keywords Public and Class, followed by the name of the class (in this case, Time). Keyword **Class** indicates that what follows is a class definition. You will learn about keyword Public in Section 19.7. The keywords **End Class** (line 3) indicate the end of the class definition. Any code placed between these two lines form the class definition's body. Any methods or variables defined in the body of a class are considered to be **members** of that class.

Figure 19.13 Empty class definition.

Empty class definition
added by Visual Studio .NET

3. *Adding instance variables to your application.* Add lines 1–2 of Fig. 19.14 to Time.vb, above the class definition. You should add comments indicating the name and purpose of your class files. Add lines 6–8 to the Time class definition.

(cont.)

Lines 7 and 8 declare each of the two Integer instance variables—m_intMinute and m_intSecond. The Time class will store a time value containing minutes and seconds—the value for minutes is stored in m_intMinute and the value for seconds is stored in m_intSecond. Recall from Tutorial 15 that our member-naming preference is to prefix an 'm_' to each instance variable. Finally, be sure to add a comment on line 10 where the class definition is terminated.

> **Good Programming Practice**
>
> Add comments at the beginning of programmer-defined classes to increase readability. The comments should indicate the name of the file that contains the class and the purpose of the class being defined.

Instance variables store minute and second information

Figure 19.14 Time's instance variables.

4. ***Saving the solution.*** Select **File > Save All** to save all the solution's files.

19.4 Initializing Class Objects: Constructors

A class can contain methods as well as instance variables. You have already used method Format from class String and method Next from class Random. A constructor is a special method within a class definition that is used to initialize a class's instance variables. In Tutorial 16, you learned how to use constructors to create objects. In the box, *Defining a Constructor*, you will create a constructor for your Time class, allowing clients to create Time objects and initialize those objects' data.

Defining a Constructor

1. ***Adding a constructor to a class.*** Add lines 10–12 of Fig. 19.15 to the body of class Time, and press the *Enter* key. The keywords End Sub will be added for you, just as with the other Sub procedures you created in this text.

   New is the constructor method. You write code for the constructor, which is invoked each time an object of that class is instantiated (created). This constructor method then performs the actions in its body, which you will add in the next few steps. A constructor's actions consist mainly of statements that initialize the class's instance variables.

(cont.)

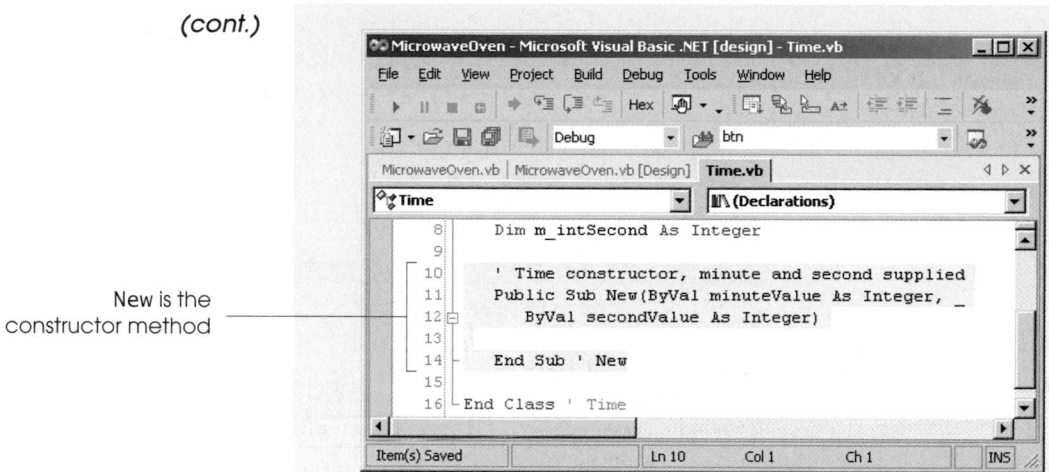

Figure 19.15   Empty constructor.

New is the
constructor method

Constructors can take arguments (you'll see how to provide arguments to constructors momentarily) but cannot return values. An important difference between constructors and other methods is that constructors cannot specify a return data type—for this reason, Visual Basic .NET constructors are implemented as Sub procedures rather than `Function` procedures, because Sub procedures cannot return values. A class's instance variables can be initialized in the constructor, or when those variables are defined in the class definition. Variable `m_intSecond`, for instance, can be initialized where it is declared (line 8) or it can be initialized in `Time`'s constructor.

2. ***Initializing variables in a constructor.*** Add lines 14 and 15 of Fig. 19.16 to the constructor. These lines initialize `Time`'s instance variables to the values of the constructor's parameter variables (lines 11–12 of Fig. 19.15). When an object is created in a client of a class, values are often specified for that object. A `Time` object can now be created with the statement

```
m_objTimeObject = New Time(5, 3)
```

This `Time` object will be created and the constructor will execute. The values 5 and 3 are assigned to the constructor's parameters, which will be used to initialize `m_intSecond` and `m_intMinute`.

Figure 19.16   Constructor initializing instance variables.

Add this code

3. ***Creating a Time object.*** After defining the class, you can use it as a type (just as you would use `Integer` or `Double`) in declarations. View Microwave-Oven.vb by selecting the **MicrowaveOven.vb** tab above the code editor. Add lines 7 and 8 of Fig. 19.17 to your application.

(cont.)

Notice the use of the class name, Time, as a type. Just as you can create many variables from a data type, such as Integer, you can create many objects from class types. You can create your own class types as needed; this is one reason why Visual Basic .NET is known as an **extensible language**—the language can be "extended" with new data types. Notice that, after you type As in line 8, *Intellisense* displays a window of available types. Notice that new class Time will be displayed in the *Intellisense* window (Fig. 19.18).

Declare m_objTime of programmer-defined type Time

Figure 19.17   Declaring an object of type Time.

Time appears as a type in the IDE

Figure 19.18   Time appearing as a type in an *Intellisense* window.

4. ***Saving the solution.*** Select **File > Save All** to save all the solution's files.

---

1. A(n) _____ language is one that can be "extended" with new data types.

   a) data   b) extensible
   c) typeable   d) extended

2. Variables can be initialized _____.

   a) when they are declared   b) to their default values
   c) in a constructor   d) All of the above.

Answers: 1) b. 2) d.

19.5 Properties

Clients of a class usually want to manipulate that class's instance variables. For example, assume a class (`Person`) that stores information about a person, including age information (stored in `Integer` instance variable `intAge`). Clients who create an object of class `Person` could want to modify `intAge`—perhaps incorrectly, by assigning a negative value to `intAge`, for example. Classes often provide **properties** to allow clients to access and modify instance variables safely. You have already seen and used several properties in previous tutorials. For instance, many GUI controls contain a `Text` property, used to retrieve or modify the text displayed by a control. When a value is to be assigned to a property, the code in that property definition is executed. The code in that property typically checks the value to be assigned and rejects invalid data. In this tutorial, you learn how to create your own properties to help clients of a class read and modify the class's instance variables. You will create two properties, `Minute` and `Second`, for your `Time` class. `Minute` allows clients to access variable `m_intMinute` safely, and `Second` allows clients to access variable `m_intSecond` safely.

A **property definition** actually consists of two **accessors**—method-like code units that handle the details of modifying and returning data. The **Set accessor** allows clients to set (that is, assign values to) properties. For example, when the code

```
objTime.Minute = 35
```

executes, the `Set` accessor of the `Minute` property executes. `Set` accessors typically provide data-validation capabilities (such as range checking) to ensure that the value of each instance variable is set properly. In your **Microwave Oven** application, users can specify an amount of minutes only in the range 0 to 59. Values not in this range will be discarded by the `Set` accessor, and `m_intMinute` will be assigned the value 0. The **Get accessor** allows clients to get (that is, obtain the value of) a property. When the code

```
intMinuteValue = objTime.Minute
```

executes, the **Get accessor** of the `Minute` property executes (and returns the value of the `m_intMinute` instance variable).

Each property is typically defined to perform validity checking—to ensure that the data assigned to the property is valid. Keeping an object's data valid is also known as keeping that data in a **consistent state**. Property `Minute` keeps instance variable `m_intMinute` in a consistent state. In the box, *Defining Properties*, you will create properties `Minute` and `Second` for your `Time` class, defining `Get` and `Set` accessors for each.

Defining Properties

1. **Adding property Minute to class Time.** View `Time.vb` by selecting the **Time.vb** tab above the code editor. Type lines 18–19 of Fig. 19.19, and press the *Enter* key to add property `Minute` to class `Time`. Lines 20–26 will be added for you automatically by the IDE. Notice the syntax used in a property definition. You begin on line 19 with the keyword `Public` (which will be discussed in Section 19.7), followed by the keyword **Property**, which indicates that you are defining a property. The keyword `Property` is followed by the name of the property (in this case, `Minute`) and a set of parentheses, which is similar to the way you define methods. The first line of the property then concludes with the keyword `As` followed by a data type (in this case, `Integer`), indicating the data type of any value assigned to, or read from, this property.

(cont.)

Get accessor retrieves data ————

Set accessor stores data ————

Figure 19.19 Empty `Minute` property.

The keyword **Get** on line 20 indicates the beginning of this property's Get accessor. The keywords **End Get** on line 22 indicate the end of the Get accessor. Any code that you insert between these two lines will make up the Get accessor's body and will be executed when a client of this class attempts to read a value from the `Minute` property, such as with the code `intMinuteValue = objTime.Minute`.

The keyword **Set** on line 23 indicates the beginning of this property's Set accessor. The keywords **End Set** on line 25 indicate the end of the Set accessor. Any code that you insert between these two lines will make up the Set accessor's body and will be executed automatically (that's the beauty of properties) when a client of this class attempts to assign a value to the `Minute` property, such as with the code `objTime.Minute = 35`. The value assigned is stored in the parameter specified on line 23, which by default uses the identifier `Value`. This identifier is used to access the value assigned to property `Minute`. The property ends on line 26 with the keywords **End Property**. Notice that we have added a comment to this line, indicating the name of the property being terminated.

Error-Prevention Tip

A property that sets the value of an instance variable should verify that the intended new value is correct. If it is not, the `Set` accessor should place the instance variable into an appropriate consistent state.

2. *Defining the Get accessor.* Add line 23 of Fig. 19.20 to your Get accessor. Also add a blank line (line 20) and a comment (line 21) above the Get accessor, to increase readability. When property `Minute` is referenced, you want your Get accessor to return the value of `m_intMinute` just as you would return a value from a method, so you use the keyword `Return` on line 23, followed by the identifier `m_intMinute`. Finally, you should add a comment on line 24 to indicate the end of the Get accessor.

3. *Defining the Set accessor.* Add lines 29–34 of Fig. 19.21 to your Set accessor. Also add a blank line (line 25) and a comment (line 26) above the Set accessor, to increase readability. When property `Minute` is assigned a value, you want to test whether the value to be assigned is valid. You do not want to accept a minutes value greater than 59, a condition that is tested on line 30. If the number of minutes is valid, it will be assigned to `m_intMinute` on line 31. Otherwise, the value 0 will be assigned to `m_intMinute` on line 33. Finally, you should add a comment on line 36 to indicate the end of the Set accessor.

4. *Adding property Second to class Time.* Add lines 40–41 of Fig. 19.22 to your application, and press *Enter*. Lines 42–48 are added for you automatically by the IDE. You should add the comments on lines 40 and 48 manually.

(cont.)

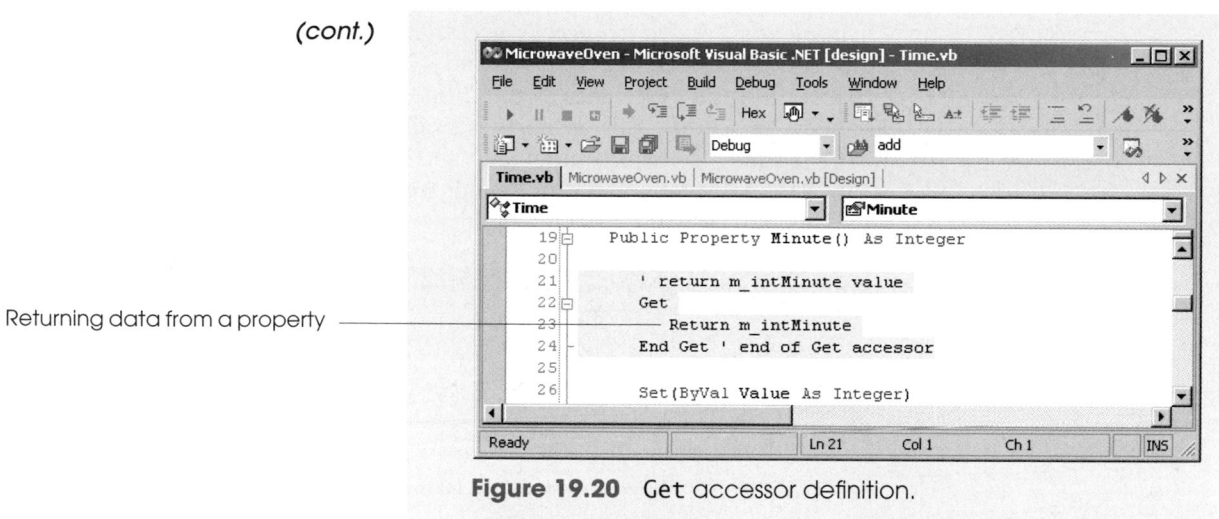

Returning data from a property

Figure 19.20   **Get** accessor definition.

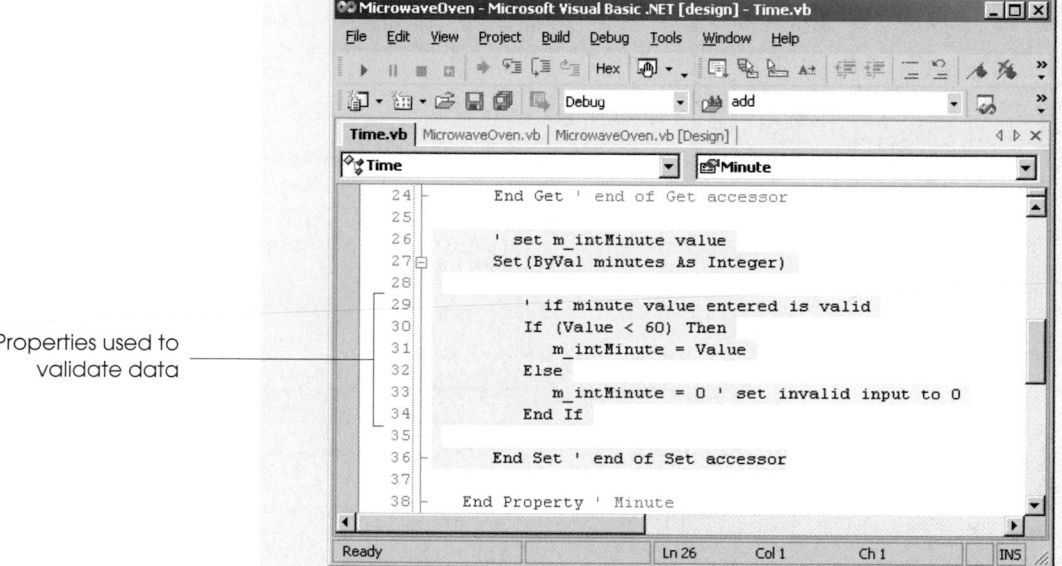

Properties used to validate data

Figure 19.21   **Set** accessor definition.

Add this code

Figure 19.22   **Second** property.

(cont.)

5. ***Defining the Second property's accessors.*** Add blank lines and comments above each accessor (lines 42–43 and 47–48 of Fig. 19.23). Add line 45 to property Second's Get accessor and lines 51–56 to property Second's Set accessor. Notice that this property is similar to Minute, except that variable m_intSecond is being modified and read, as opposed to variable m_intMinute. Finally, you should add comments at the end of each accessor (lines 46 and 58) to increase readability.

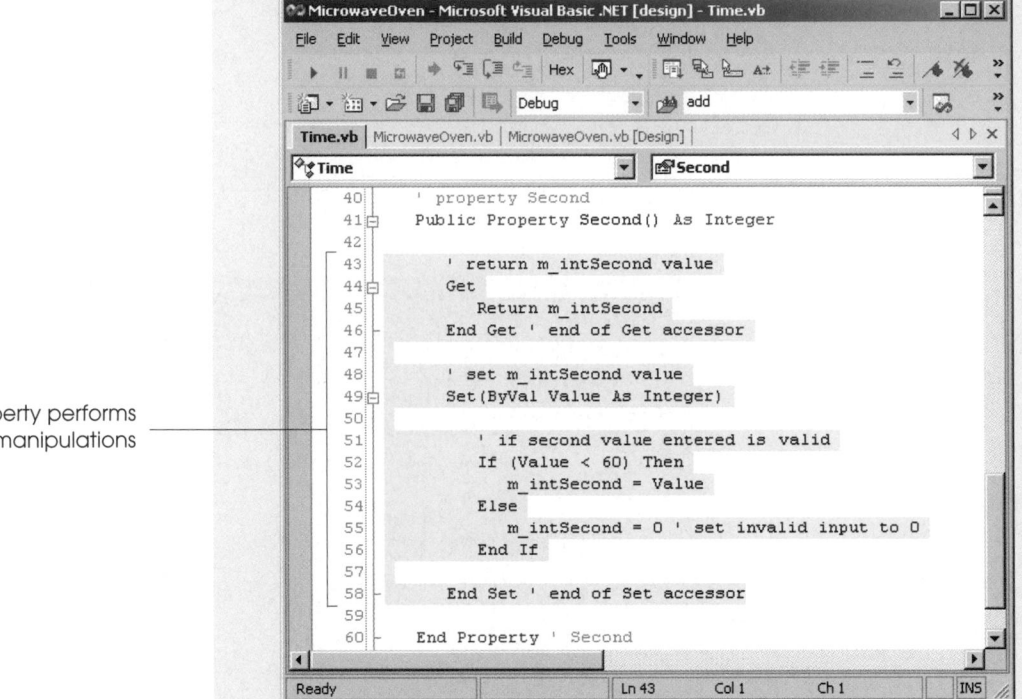

Second property performs similar data manipulations

Figure 19.23 Second property definition.

6. ***Assigning values to properties.*** Change lines 14–15 of Fig. 19.16 to lines 14–15 of Fig. 19.24. Now that you have defined properties to ensure that only valid data will be assigned to m_intMinute and m_intSecond, you can use these properties to safely initialize instance variables in the class's constructor.

Safer to assign data to properties rather than instance variables, because Set accessors perform validity checking

Figure 19.24 Constructor using properties to initialize variables.

7. ***Saving the solution.*** Select **File > Save All** to save all the solution's files.

1. A(n) _____ can ensure that a value is appropriate for a data member, before the data member is assigned that value.

a) `Get` accessor   b) `Access` accessor

c) `Modify` accessor   d) `Set` accessor

2. Properties can contain both _____ accessors.

a) `Return` and `Value`   b) `Get` and `Value`

c) `Get` and `Set`   d) `Return` and `Set`

Answers: 1) d. 2) c.

19.6 Completing the Microwave Oven Application

Now that you have completed your `Time` class, you will use an object of this class to maintain the cook time in your application. Follow the steps in the box, *Completing the **Microwave Oven** Application*, to add this functionality to your application.

Completing the Microwave Oven Application

1. ***Formatting user input.*** View `MicrowaveOven.vb` by selecting the **Micro-waveOven.vb** tab above the code editor. Add lines 322–327 of Fig. 19.25 to event handler `btnStart_Click`. Variables `intSecond` and `intMinute` (lines 322–323) will be used to store the second and minute values entered by the user. Lines 326–327 use `String` method **PadLeft**, which appends characters to the beginning of a `String` based on that `String`'s length. This method can be used to guarantee the length of a `String`—if that `String` has fewer characters than desired, method `PadLeft` will add characters to the beginning of that `String` until the `String` has the proper number of characters. You want `m_strTime` to contain 4 characters (for example, `"0325"` rather than `"325"` for a time of `"3:25"`, representing 3 minutes and 25 seconds). Having four digits makes the conversion to minutes and seconds easier. You can now simply convert the first two digits (03) to a minute value and the last two digits (25) to a second value. The first argument in the `PadLeft` call, 4, specifies the length that `m_strTime` will have after characters have been appended. If `m_strTime` already contains four or more characters, `PadLeft` will not have any effect. The second argument (the character 0) specifies the character that will be appended to the beginning of the `String`. Notice that specifying only `"0"` as the second argument will cause an error, as `"0"` is of type `String`. Method `PadLeft` expects the second argument to be a single character, which is of data type **Char**. You obtain the character 0 by calling method **Convert.ToChar**, which converts your `String` zero to a character zero.

Ensure `m_strTime` has four characters for conversion purposes

Figure 19.25 Declaring variables for second and minute values.

(cont.)

2. ***Converting user input to Integers.*** Add lines 329–331 of Fig. 19.26 to event handler btnStart_Click. Line 330 calls method Convert.ToInt32 to convert the last two characters of m_strTime to an Integer and assign this value to intSecond. The last two characters are selected from m_strTime by using method **Substring**. This is another String method, used to return only a portion of a String from m_strTime. The argument passed to Substring, 2, indicates that the subset of characters returned from this method should begin with the character at position 2, and continue until the end of the string. Remember that the character at position 2 is actually the third character in the String, because the position values of a String being at 0. In the example "0325", calling Substring with the argument 2 returns "25". Line 331 selects the first two characters of m_strTime, converts the value to an Integer, and assigns this value to intMinute. The call to Substring on line 331 takes two arguments. The first argument, 0, indicates that the characters returned from this method start with the first character (at position 0) of m_strTime. The second argument, 2, indicates that only two characters from the starting position should be returned. In the example "0325", calling Substring with the arguments 0 and 2 returns "03".

Figure 19.26 Form minute and second values from input.

3. ***Creating a Time object.*** Add lines 333–334 of Fig. 19.27 to btnStart_Click. Line 334 creates an object of type Time. When the object is instantiated, keyword New allocates the memory in which the Time object will be stored; then, the Time constructor is called (with the values of intMinute and intSecond) to initialize the instance variables of the Time object. The constructor then returns a reference to the newly created object; this reference is assigned to m_objTime.

Figure 19.27 Creating a Time object.

(cont.)   4. ***Accessing a Time object's properties.*** Add lines 336–337 of Fig. 19.28 to
              btnStart_Click. These lines use the newly created Time object and method
              String.Format to display the cook time properly. You want the resulting
              String to contain two digits (for the minute), a colon (:) and finally another
              two digits (for the second). For example, if the time entered was 3 minutes
              and 20 seconds, the String that will display for the user is "03:20". To
              achieve this result, you pass to the method the format control string
              "{0:D2}:{1:D2}", which indicates that arguments 0 and 1 (the first and sec-
              ond arguments after the format String argument) should take the format
              D2 (base 10 decimal number format using two digits) for display purposes—
              thus, 8 would be converted to 08. The colon between the curly braces } and {
              will be included in the output, separating the minutes from the seconds. The
              arguments after the format-control string access m_objTime's minute and
              second values, using the Minute and Second properties. Notice that Time's
              properties appear in the *Intellisense* window (Fig. 19.29) when you try to
              access the object's members (via the dot operator).

Add this code —

Figure 19.28   Displaying time information with separating colon.

Time's properties
appear in *Intellisense*

Figure 19.29   Properties of a programmer-defined type also appear in
Intellisense.

       5. ***Starting the cooking process.*** Add lines 339–343 of Fig. 19.30 to your appli-
           cation. Line 339 clears the user's input, so that the user can enter new input
           at any time. Line 341 starts the Timer by setting its Enabled property to
           True. The Timer's Tick event will now be raised each second. You will
           implement the event handler for this event shortly. Line 343 sets the Panel's
           BackColor property to yellow to simulate the light inside the microwave
           oven. The color yellow is assigned to property BackColor using property
           Yellow of structure **Color**. The Color structure contains several predefined
           colors as properties.

(cont.)

Start timer and turn "light" on to indicate microwave oven is cooking

Figure 19.30 Starting the microwave oven countdown.

6. *Clearing the cook time.* Add lines 351–356 of Fig. 19.31 to event handler btnClear_Click. Line 352 sets the application's Label to **Microwave Oven**. Line 353 clears the input values stored in m_strTime, and line 354 resets the Time object to zero minutes and zero seconds. Line 355 disables the Timer, which stops the countdown. Line 356 sets the Panel's background back to the Panel's original color to simulate turning off the light inside the microwave oven. Notice that we set the Panel's color using the **DefaultBackColor** property. This property contains the default background color for a Panel control. When a Panel is added to a Form, its background takes on the default background color of the Panel.

Add this code

Figure 19.31 Clearing the **Microwave Oven** input.

7. *Displaying data as it is being input.* Add lines 362–370 of Fig. 19.32 to method DisplayTime. This method will be called each time the user enters another digit for the cook time. Lines 362–363 declare variables intSecond and intMinute, which will store the current number of seconds and minutes. Line 365 declares strDisplay, which will store the user's current input in the proper display format. Lines 368–370 remove any extra digits entered by the user. (Recall that the user may enter a maximum of four digits.) Line 368 uses String property **Length**, which returns the number of characters in a String, to determine whether m_strTime has more than four digits.

(cont.)   If it does, line 369 uses `String` method `Substring` to remove the extra digits. The arguments (0 followed by 4) indicate that the substring returned should begin with the first character in `m_strTime` and continue for four characters. The result is assigned back to `m_strTime`, ensuring that any characters appended past the first four will be removed.

Figure 19.32   Modifying invalid user input.

8. ***Completing the `DisplayTime` method.*** Add lines 372–380 of Fig. 19.33 to method `DisplayTime`. These lines are similar to those of event handler `btnStart_Click`. Line 372 appends zeros to the front of `m_strTime` if fewer than four digits were entered. Lines 375–376 use method `Substring` to isolate the number of seconds and minutes currently entered. Lines 379–380 then use method `Format` to display the input correctly.

Figure 19.33   Display current input.

9. ***Performing the countdown.*** Add lines 387–403 of Fig. 19.34 to event handler `tmrTimer_Tick`. Remember that this event handler executes every second for as long as the `Timer` is enabled. Lines 388–400 modify the display `Label` once per second so that the time remaining is shown to the user.

(cont.)

If the value of seconds is larger than zero (line 388), the number of seconds is decremented by one (line 389). If the value of seconds is zero but the value of minutes is greater than zero (line 390), the number of minutes is decremented by one (line 391) and the number of seconds is reset to 59 for the new minute (line 392). If the number of seconds is zero and the number of minutes is zero, the cooking process is stopped—the Timer is disabled (line 394), a beep is sounded (line 395), the display Label is set to **Done!** (line 396) and the window Panel's background color is set back to its default background color.

Modify time appropriately during countdown

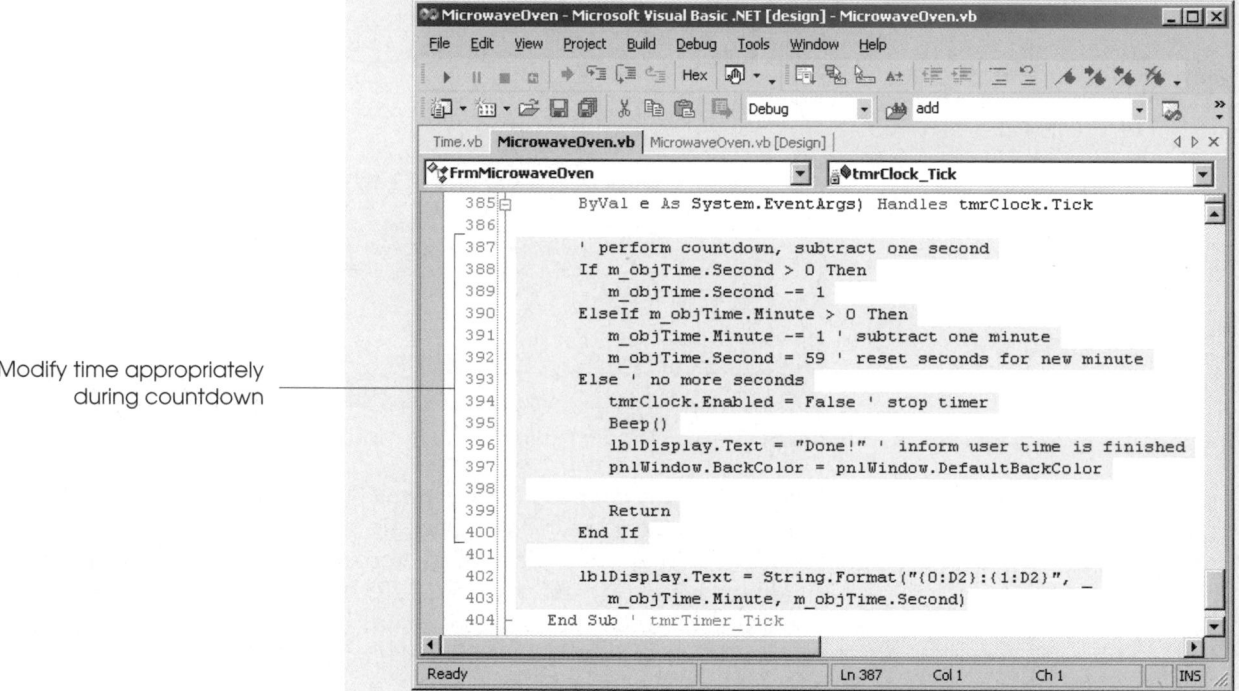

Figure 19.34 Modifying the display during countdown.

10. *Running the Microwave Oven application*. Select **Debug > Start** to run the application. Notice that the application performs as it did in the test-drive.

SELF-REVIEW

1. The _____ property returns the number of characters in a String.

    a) Length   b) Size

    c) Char   d) Width

2. The expression strExample.Substring(0, 7) returns the character(s) _____.

    a) that begin at position seven and run backward to position zero

    b) that begin at position zero and continue for seven characters

    c) at position zero and position seven   d) at position 0, repeated 7 times

Answers: 1) a. 2) b.

19.7 Controlling Access to Members

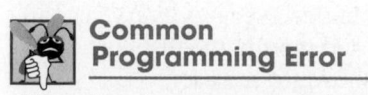

Common Programming Error

Attempting to access a Private class member from outside that class is a syntax error.

Keywords **Public** and **Private** are called **member-access modifiers**. You defined properties with member access modifier Public earlier in this tutorial. Class members that are declared with access modifier Public are available to any Time object. The declaration of instance variables or properties with member-access modifier Private makes them available only to methods, properties and events of the class. Attempting to access a class's Private data from outside the class definition is a compilation error. Normally, instance variables are declared `Private`, whereas methods and properties are declared `Public`. In the box, *Controlling Access to Members*, you will declare this application's instance variables as `Private`.

Controlling Access to Members

Good Programming Practice

Group all `Private` class members in a class definition, followed by all `Public` class members. This helps enhance clarity and readability.

1. ***Declaring Time's instance variables as Private.*** View `Time.vb` by selecting the **Time.vb** tab above the code editor. Replace keyword `Dim` on lines 7 and 8 with keyword `Private` (as in Fig. 19.35), indicating that these instance variables are accessible only to members of class `Time`. A class's `Private` instance variables may be accessed by methods, properties and events of that class.

Figure 19.35　Time's instance variables are `Private`.

2. ***Declaring FrmMicrowaveOven's instance variables as Private.*** View `MicrowaveOven.vb` by selecting the **MicrowaveOven.vb** tab above the code editor. Replace keyword `Dim` on lines 5 and 8 with keyword `Private` (as in Fig. 19.36), indicating that these instance variables are accessible only to members of class `FrmMicrowaveOven`. When an object of the class contains such instance variables, only methods, properties and events of that object's class can access the variables.

Good Programming Practice

For clarity, every instance variable or property definition should be preceded by a member-access modifier.

Figure 19.36　Microwave Oven's instance variables are `Private`.

3. ***Setting method DisplayTime as Private.*** Add keyword `Private` to the beginning of method `DisplayTime` (line 360 of Fig. 19.37). As with variables, methods are declared `Private` when they should only be accessible to other members of the current class. In this example only the class that defines your **Microwave Oven** uses method `DisplayTime`, so you should make this method `Private`.

(cont.)

Notice that the event handlers you have created throughout this book have the keyword `Private` automatically added to their headers. You now know that this occurs because event handlers are specific to the `Form`'s class, and not the entire application, which includes class `Time`.

Figure 19.37 Microwave Oven's methods are `Private`.

4. ***Running your Microwave Oven application.*** Select **Debug > Start** to run your application. Notice that the application performs as it did in the test-drive. This occurs because when instance variables are declared by using keyword `Dim`, they are by default `Private` variables. For example, recall that the instance variables of `Time` did not appear in the *Intellisense* window of Fig. 19.29. These variables were `Private` by default, and therefore not accessible outside of class `Time`. Inaccessible variables do not appear in the *Intellisense* window. It is a good practice always to precede instance variables with a member-access modifier (usually `Private`). Changing `DisplayTime` to be `Private` did not affect the application either, because your code does not attempt to access this method from outside the class in which it is defined.

Software Design Tip

Declare all instance variables of a class as `Private`. When necessary, provide `Public` properties to set and get the values of `Private` instance variables.

Now that you have completed the **Microwave Oven** application, you should review the completed code. Compare your application to the code shown in Fig. 19.38 and Fig. 19.39 to ensure that you have successfully completed the application.

```
1   Public Class FrmMicrowaveOven
2      Inherits System.Windows.Forms.Form
3
4      ' contains time entered as a String
5      Private m_strTime As String = ""
6
7      ' contains time entered
8      Private m_objTime As Time
9
10     ' event handler appends 1 to time string
11     Private Sub btnOne_Click(ByVal sender As System.Object, _
12        ByVal e As System.EventArgs) Handles btnOne.Click
13
14        Beep()                ' sound beep
15        m_strTime &= "1"      ' append digit to time input
16        DisplayTime()         ' display time input properly
17     End Sub ' btnOne_Click
18
```

Figure 19.38 Microwave Oven application code. (Part 1 of 4.)

```
19      ' event handler appends 2 to time string
20      Private Sub btnTwo_Click(ByVal sender As System.Object, _
21         ByVal e As System.EventArgs) Handles btnTwo.Click
22
23         Beep()              ' sound beep
24         m_strTime &= "2"    ' append digit to time input
25         DisplayTime()       ' display time input properly
26      End Sub ' btnTwo_Click
27
28      ' event handler appends 3 to time string
29      Private Sub btnThree_Click(ByVal sender As System.Object, _
30         ByVal e As System.EventArgs) Handles btnThree.Click
31
32         Beep()              ' sound beep
33         m_strTime &= "3"    ' append digit to time input
34         DisplayTime()       ' display time input properly
35      End Sub ' btnThree_Click
36
37      ' event handler appends 4 to time string
38      Private Sub btnFour_Click(ByVal sender As System.Object, _
39         ByVal e As System.EventArgs) Handles btnFour.Click
40
41         Beep()              ' sound beep
42         m_strTime &= "4"    ' append digit to time input
43         DisplayTime()       ' display time input properly
44      End Sub ' btnFour_Click
45
46      ' event handler appends 5 to time string
47      Private Sub btnFive_Click(ByVal sender As System.Object, _
48         ByVal e As System.EventArgs) Handles btnFive.Click
49
50         Beep()              ' sound beep
51         m_strTime &= "5"    ' append digit to time input
52         DisplayTime()       ' display time input properly
53      End Sub ' btnFive_Click
54
55      ' event handler appends 6 to time string
56      Private Sub btnSix_Click(ByVal sender As System.Object, _
57         ByVal e As System.EventArgs) Handles btnSix.Click
58
59         Beep()              ' sound beep
60         m_strTime &= "6"    ' append digit to time input
61         DisplayTime()       ' display time input properly
62      End Sub ' btnSix_Click
63
64      ' event handler appends 7 to time string
65      Private Sub btnSeven_Click(ByVal sender As System.Object, _
66         ByVal e As System.EventArgs) Handles btnSeven.Click
67
68         Beep()              ' sound beep
69         m_strTime &= "7"    ' append digit to time input
70         DisplayTime()       ' display time input properly
71      End Sub ' btnSeven_Click
72
73      ' event handler appends 8 to time string
74      Private Sub btnEight_Click(ByVal sender As System.Object, _
75         ByVal e As System.EventArgs) Handles btnEight.Click
76
```

Figure 19.38 Microwave Oven application code. (Part 2 of 4.)

```
77        Beep()              ' sound beep
78        m_strTime &= "8"    ' append digit to time input
79        DisplayTime()       ' display time input properly
80      End Sub ' btnEight_Click
81
82      ' event handler appends 9 to time string
83      Private Sub btnNine_Click(ByVal sender As System.Object, _
84        ByVal e As System.EventArgs) Handles btnNine.Click
85
86        Beep()              ' sound beep
87        m_strTime &= "9"    ' append digit to time input
88        DisplayTime()       ' display time input properly
89      End Sub ' btnNine_Click
90
91      ' event handler appends 0 to time string
92      Private Sub btnZero_Click(ByVal sender As System.Object, _
93        ByVal e As System.EventArgs) Handles btnZero.Click
94
95        Beep()              ' sound beep
96        m_strTime &= "0"    ' append digit to time input
97        DisplayTime()       ' display time input properly
98      End Sub ' btnZero_Click
99
100     ' event handler starts the microwave oven's cooking process
101     Private Sub btnStart_Click(ByVal sender As System.Object, _
102       ByVal e As System.EventArgs) Handles btnStart.Click
103
104       Dim intSecond As Integer
105       Dim intMinute As Integer
106
107       ' ensure that m_strTime has 4 characters
108       m_strTime = m_strTime.PadLeft(4, _
109         Convert.ToChar("0"))
110
111       ' extract seconds and minutes
112       intSecond = Convert.ToInt32(m_strTime.Substring(2))
113       intMinute = Convert.ToInt32(m_strTime.Substring(0, 2))
114
115       ' create Time object to contain time entered by user
116       m_objTime = New Time(intMinute, intSecond)
117
118       lblDisplay.Text = String.Format("{0:D2}:{1:D2}", _
119         m_objTime.Minute, m_objTime.Second)
120
121       m_strTime = "" ' clear m_strTime for future input
122
123       tmrClock.Enabled = True ' start timer
124
125       pnlWindow.BackColor = Color.Yellow ' turn "light" on
126
127     End Sub ' btnStart_Click
128
129     ' event handler to clear input
130     Private Sub btnClear_Click(ByVal sender As System.Object, _
131       ByVal e As System.EventArgs) Handles btnClear.Click
132
133       ' reset each property or variable to its initial setting
134       lblDisplay.Text = "Microwave Oven"
```

Creating a new object of a programmer-defined type

Accessing properties of a programmer-defined type

Start timer to begin countdown

Use property **BackColor** to change the **Panel**'s color

Figure 19.38   Microwave Oven application code. (Part 3 of 4.)

```
135        m_strTime = ""
136        m_objTime = New Time(0, 0)
137        tmrClock.Enabled = False
138        pnlWindow.BackColor = pnlWindow.DefaultBackColor
139     End Sub ' btnClear_Click
140
141     ' method to display formatted time in timer window
142     Private Sub DisplayTime()
143
144        Dim intSecond As Integer
145        Dim intMinute As Integer
146
147        Dim strDisplay As String ' String displays current input
148
149        ' if too much input entered
150        If m_strTime.Length > 4 Then
151           m_strTime = m_strTime.Substring(0, 4)
152        End If
153
154        strDisplay = m_strTime.PadLeft(4, Convert.ToChar("0"))
155
156        ' extract seconds and minutes
157        intSecond = Convert.ToInt32(strDisplay.Substring(2))
158        intMinute = Convert.ToInt32(strDisplay.Substring(0, 2))
159
160        ' display number of minutes, ":" and number of seconds
161        lblDisplay.Text = String.Format("{0:D2}:{1:D2}", _
162           intMinute, intSecond)
163     End Sub ' DisplayTime
164
165     ' event handler displays new time each second
166     Private Sub tmrClock_Tick(ByVal sender As System.Object, _
167        ByVal e As System.EventArgs) Handles tmrClock.Tick
168
169        ' perform countdown, subtract one second
170        If m_objTime.Second > 0 Then
171           m_objTime.Second -= 1
172        ElseIf m_objTime.Minute > 0 Then
173           m_objTime.Minute -= 1 ' subtract one minute
174           m_objTime.Second = 59 ' reset seconds for new minute
175        Else ' no more seconds
176           tmrClock.Enabled = False ' stop timer
177           Beep()
178           lblDisplay.Text = "Done!" ' inform user time is finished
179           pnlWindow.BackColor = pnlWindow.DefaultBackColor
180
181           Return
182        End If
183
184        lblDisplay.Text = String.Format("{0:D2}:{1:D2}", _
185           m_objTime.Minute, m_objTime.Second)
186     End Sub ' tmrTimer_Tick
187
188  End Class ' FrmMicrowave
```

Property **Length** returns number of characters in a **String**

Method **Substring** returns a subset of characters in a **String**

Method **PadLeft** appends characters to the beginning of a **String**

Figure 19.38   Microwave Oven application code. (Part 4 of 4.)

Keyword **Class** used to define a class

New is the constructor

Assign data to properties, rather than to instance variables directly

End Sub keywords end the constructor definition

Keyword **Property** used to define a property

Get accessor returns data

Set accessor modifies data

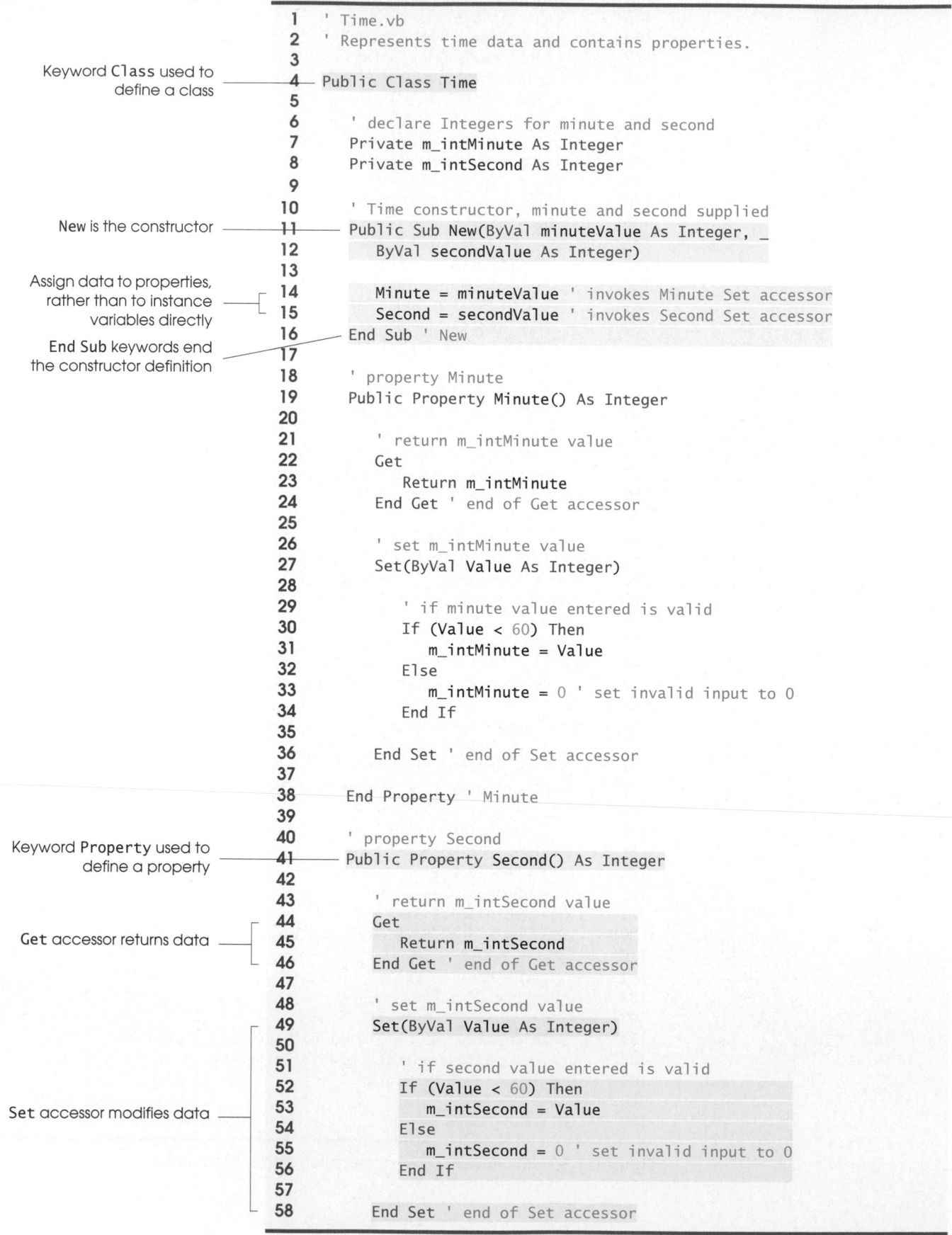

```vb
1   ' Time.vb
2   ' Represents time data and contains properties.
3
4   Public Class Time
5
6      ' declare Integers for minute and second
7      Private m_intMinute As Integer
8      Private m_intSecond As Integer
9
10     ' Time constructor, minute and second supplied
11     Public Sub New(ByVal minuteValue As Integer, _
12        ByVal secondValue As Integer)
13
14        Minute = minuteValue ' invokes Minute Set accessor
15        Second = secondValue ' invokes Second Set accessor
16     End Sub ' New
17
18     ' property Minute
19     Public Property Minute() As Integer
20
21        ' return m_intMinute value
22        Get
23           Return m_intMinute
24        End Get ' end of Get accessor
25
26        ' set m_intMinute value
27        Set(ByVal Value As Integer)
28
29           ' if minute value entered is valid
30           If (Value < 60) Then
31              m_intMinute = Value
32           Else
33              m_intMinute = 0 ' set invalid input to 0
34           End If
35
36        End Set ' end of Set accessor
37
38     End Property ' Minute
39
40     ' property Second
41     Public Property Second() As Integer
42
43        ' return m_intSecond value
44        Get
45           Return m_intSecond
46        End Get ' end of Get accessor
47
48        ' set m_intSecond value
49        Set(ByVal Value As Integer)
50
51           ' if second value entered is valid
52           If (Value < 60) Then
53              m_intSecond = Value
54           Else
55              m_intSecond = 0 ' set invalid input to 0
56           End If
57
58        End Set ' end of Set accessor
```

Figure 19.39   Class Time. (Part 1 of 2.)

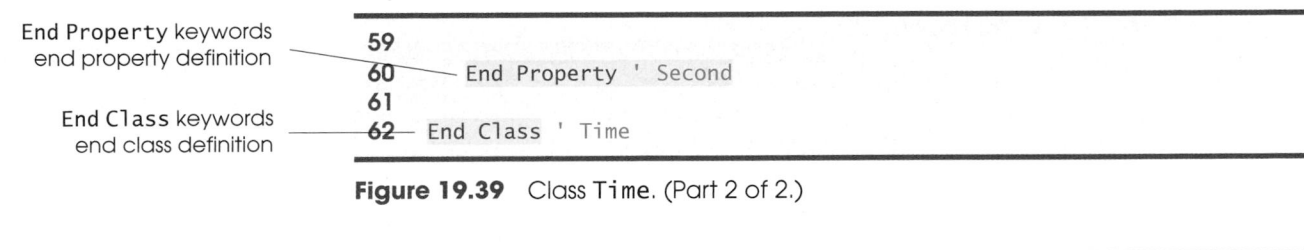

End Property keywords
end property definition

```
59
60    End Property ' Second
61
62    End Class ' Time
```

End Class keywords
end class definition

Figure 19.39   Class Time. (Part 2 of 2.)

SELF-REVIEW

1. Instance variable declarations must be preceded by which of the following keywords?

   a) `Dim`   b) `Private`
   c) `Public`   d) Any of the above.

2. Instance variables are considered _____ by default.

   a) `Private`   b) `Public`
   c) `Dimensional`   d) None of the above.

Answers: 1) d. 2) a.

19.8 Using the Debugger: The Autos and Locals Windows

Now you will enhance your knowledge of the debugger by studying the capabilities of the **Autos** and **Locals** windows. These windows allow you to view the values stored in an object's instance variables. In this section, you will learn how to view the contents of the Time object m_objTime's instance variables to verify that your application is executing correctly. In the box, *Using the Debugger: Using the **Autos** and **Locals** Windows*, you use these windows to examine the state of the Time object in the **Microwave Oven** application.

---

*Using the Debugger:
Using the Autos and
Locals Windows*

1. ***Viewing the application code.*** View MicrowaveOven.vb by selecting the **MicrowaveOven.vb** tab above the code editor.

2. ***Setting breakpoints.*** Set breakpoints at lines 388 and 397 by clicking in the margin indicator bar (Fig. 19.40). You can set breakpoints in your application to examine an object's instance variables at certain places during execution. In the **Microwave Oven** application, the tmrClock's Tick event handler modifies the properties of m_objTime. Setting breakpoints at lines 388 and 397 allows you to suspend execution before and after certain properties have been modified, ensuring that data is being modified properly.

3. ***Starting the debugger.*** Start the debugger by selecting **Debug > Start**.

4. ***Opening the Autos window.*** Open the **Autos** window (Fig. 19.41) by selecting **Debug > Windows > Autos** while the debugger is running. The **Autos** window allows you to view the contents of the properties used in the last statement that was executed. This allows you to verify that the previous statement executed correctly. The **Autos** window also lists the values in the next statement to be executed.

5. ***Opening the Locals window.*** Open the **Locals** window (Fig. 19.42) by selecting **Debug > Windows > Locals** while the debugger is running. The **Locals** window allows you to view the state of the variables in the current scope. Recall that the scope of a variable's identifier is the portion of an application in which that identifier can be referenced. Because the Timer's Tick event is a method of the Form class, all of the instance variables and controls of the Form are viewable in the **Locals** window. This means that you will be able to view the values of the properties of m_objTime, because m_objTime is an instance variable of the Form class.

(cont.)

Figure 19.40 **Microwave Oven** application with breakpoints added.

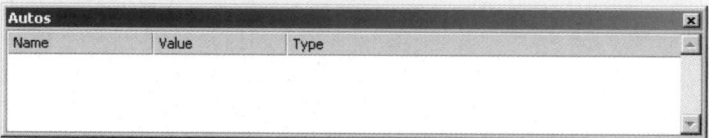

Figure 19.41 Empty **Autos** window.

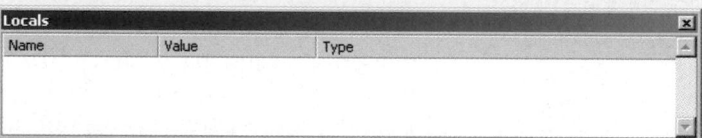

Figure 19.42 Empty **Locals** window.

6. **Setting the time.** Set the microwave oven's time to 1:01, and click the **Start** Button.

7. **Using the Autos window.** When execution halts at the breakpoint on line 388, view the **Autos** window (Fig. 19.43). If the **Autos** window is now hidden, reselect **Debug > Windows > Autos**. Notice that the **Autos** window lists the Minute and Second properties of m_objTime, their values (returned from each property's Get accessor) and their types. Viewing the values stored in an object lets you verify that your application is manipulating these variables correctly.

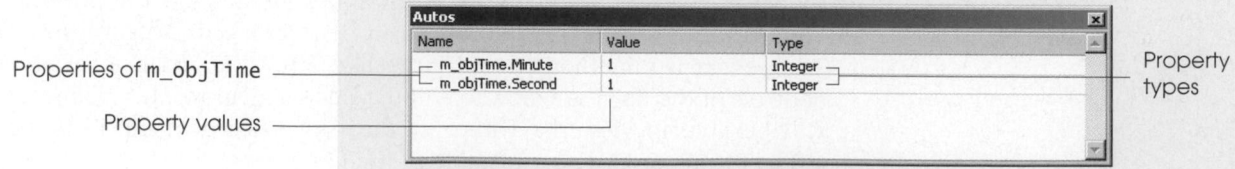

Figure 19.43 **Autos** window displaying the state of m_objTime.

(cont.)

8. ***Using the Locals window.*** While execution is still halted, look at the **Locals** window. If the **Locals** window is now hidden, reselect **Debug > Windows > Locals**. The **Locals** window lists all the variables that are in the scope of the Timer's Tick event handler. To view the contents of m_objTime, click the plus box next to the word **Me**. Scroll down until you reach m_objTime, and click the plus box next to it. This will show all of the members of m_objTime, their current values and their types (Fig. 19.44). Notice that the values for minute and second are the same as they were in the **Autos** window.

Instance variables of m_objTime

Figure 19.44 **Locals** window displaying the state of m_objTime.

9. ***Continuing program execution.*** Click the debug toolbar's Continue Button, and view the values of the m_objTime's members in both the **Autos** and **Locals** windows. Notice that the value for the amount of seconds (as represented by variable m_intSecond and property Second) is now shown in red, indicating that it has changed. Click the Continue Button again. Notice that both the amount of seconds and minutes have changed, so that the values of m_intSecond, m_intMinute and properties Second and Minute are shown in red (Fig. 19.45 and Fig. 19.46).

Changed values shown in red

Figure 19.45 **Autos** window displaying changed variables in red.

Changed values shown in red

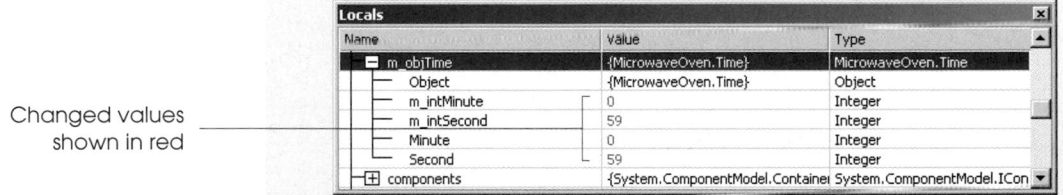

Figure 19.46 **Locals** window displaying changed variables in red.

10. ***Changing the value of a variable.*** In the **Autos** window, double click the value for property Second. Type 0 and press *Enter* to set the microwave oven's time to zero (Fig. 19.47). The **Autos** and **Locals** windows allow you to change the values of variables to verify that program execution is correct at certain points without having to run the program again for each value.

Value changed by user

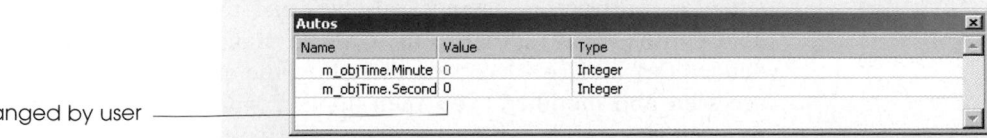

Figure 19.47 Changing the value of a variable in the **Autos** window.

(cont.)

11. ***Continuing execution.*** Click the Continue Button. Execution continues until the breakpoint on line 397 is reached.

12. ***Viewing the Autos and Locals window.*** View the **Autos** window, and notice that the variables listed have now changed (Fig. 19.48). This happened because execution is now at a new statement that uses new variables. View the **Locals** window. Notice that the **Locals** window still lets you view the state of m_objTime.

New variables shown
in **Autos** window

Figure 19.48   New variables listed in the **Autos** window.

13. ***Stopping the debugger.*** Click the Stop Debugging Button to end the debugging session.

14. ***Closing the application.*** Select **File > Close Solution** to close the solution.

In this section, you learned how to use the **Autos** and **Locals** windows to view the state of an object and verify that your application is executing correctly.

SELF-REVIEW

1. The **Locals** window allows you to _____.

    a) change the value stored in an instance variable of an object

    b) view all of the variables in the current scope

    c) view the values stored in all of the variables in the current scope

    d) All of the above.

2. When a variable's value is changed, it becomes _____ in the **Autos** and **Locals** windows.

    a) red   b) italic

    c) blue   d) bold

Answers: 1) d. 2) a.

19.9 Wrap-Up

In previous tutorials, you used FCL classes and methods to add functionality to your applications. In this tutorial, you learned how to create your own classes, also known as programmer-defined classes, to provide functionality not available in the FCL. In the world of Visual Basic .NET programming, applications are created by using a combination of FCL classes and methods and programmer-defined classes and methods.

You created a microwave-oven simulator using a programmer-defined class called Time. You added a file to your application to create the Time class; then, you added a constructor, instance variables and properties to that class. You defined your constructor to initialize the class's instance variables. For each property, you defined Get and Set accessors that allow the class's instance variables to be safely accessed and modified. You then applied what you have already learned about using classes and properties to create a Time object. You used the properties of class Time to access and display the number of minutes and number of seconds that the user has specified as the microwave oven's cook time. You also learned how Panels can organize controls (much like GroupBoxes), and used a Panel to simulate the microwave oven's door. You concluded the tutorial by learning how to view an application's values using the debugger's **Autos** and **Locals** windows.

In the next tutorial, you will learn about collections. The FCL provides several collection classes, which enable you to store collections of data in an organized way. A collection can be thought of as a group of items. You will use collections to create a **Shipping Hub** application that stores information about several packages that are being shipped to various states. Each package will be defined by using a `Package` programmer-defined class. Several `Package` objects will be maintained by using collections.

SKILLS SUMMARY

Defining a Property

- Use keyword `Public` and `Property` followed by the name of the property and a set of parentheses.
- After the parentheses, specify the property's type with the `As` keyword.
- Press *Enter*. Empty `Get` and `Set` accessors will be added for you by the IDE, followed by the keywords `End Property`. The `Get` accessor begins with keyword `Get` and ends with keywords `End Get`. The `Set` accessor begins with keyword `Set` and ends with keywords `End Set`.
- In the `Get` accessor, provide code to return the requested data.
- In the `Set` accessor, provide code to modify the relevant data. Be sure to do validity checking.

Adding a Class File to Your Project

- Select **Project > Add Class**.
- In the **Add New Item** dialog, select **Class**, and enter a name for the class.

Creating a Constructor

- Use keywords `Public Sub New`, followed by a set of parentheses enclosing any parameter variables for the constructor.
- Press *Enter*. The keywords `End Sub` will be provided by the IDE.
- Add code to initialize the object's data.

Adding a `Panel` to Your Application

- Double click the `Panel` control in the **Toolbox**, or drag the `Panel` control from the **Toolbox** to the Form. We recommend prefixing `Panel` names with `pnl`.

KEY TERMS

constructor—A special class method that initializes a class's variables.

Get accessor—Used to retrieve a value of an instance variable.

instantiate an object—Create an object of a class.

Length property of class `String`—Returns the number of characters in a `String`.

New keyword—Allocates memory in which an object will be stored.

PadLeft method of class `String`—Adds characters to the beginning of the string until the length of a string equals the specified length.

Panel control—Used to group controls. Unlike `GroupBoxes`, `Panels` do not have captions.

Private keyword—Member-access modifier that makes instance variables or methods accessible only to that class.

property—Contains accessors—portions of code that handle the details of modifying and returning data.

Public keyword—Member-access modifier that makes instance variables or methods accessible wherever the application has a reference to that object.

Set accessor—Provides data-validation capabilities to ensure that the value is set properly.

Substring method of class `String`—Returns characters from a string that correspond to the arguments passed by the user that indicate the start and the end positions within a `String`.

<table>
<tr><td>

GUI DESIGN GUIDELINES

</td><td>

Panel

- Use Panels to organize groups of related controls where the purpose of those controls is obvious. If the purpose of the controls is not obvious, use a GroupBox in place of a Panel, because GroupBoxes can contain captions.

- A Panel can display scrollbars if that Panel is not large enough to display all of its controls at once. To increase readability, we suggest avoiding the use of scrollbars on a Panel. If the Panel is not large enough to display all of its contents, increase the size of the Panel.

- Although it is possible to have a Panel without a border (by setting the BorderStyle property to None), use borders on your Panels whenever possible. The helps to increase readability and organization.

</td></tr>
</table>

CONTROLS, EVENTS, PROPERTIES & METHODS

Button   This control allows the user to raise an action or event.

- *In action*

  Calculate Total

- *Event*

  Click—This event is raised when the user clicks the Button.

- *Properties*

  Enabled—This property determines whether the Button's event handler is executed when the Button is clicked.

  FlatStyle—This property determines whether the Button will appear flat or three-dimensional.

      Flat—This value specifies that a Button will appear flat.

  Location—This property specifies the location of the Button on the Form relative to the top-left corner.

  Name—This property specifies the name used to access the Button programmatically. The name should be prefixed with btn.

  Size—This property specifies the height and width (in pixels) of the Button.

  Text—This property specifies the text displayed on the Button.

- *Method*

  Focus—This method transfers the focus of the application to the Button that calls it.

Convert   The Convert class converts the value of a data type to another data type.

- *Methods*

  ToChar—This method converts a value into a character (of data type Char).

  ToDecimal—This method converts the value from another data type to type Decimal.

Label   This control displays text on the Form that the user cannot modify.

- *In action*

  Total: [   ]

- *Properties*

  BorderStyle—This property specifies the appearance of the Label's border.

      FixedSingle—This value specifies that the Label will display a thin, black border.

  Font—This property specifies the font name, style and size of the text displayed in the Label.

  Location—This property specifies the location of the Label on the Form relative to the top-left corner.

Name—This property specifies the name used to access the Label programmatically. The name should be prefixed with lbl.

Size—This property specifies the height and width (in pixels) of the Label.

Text—This property specifies the text displayed on the Label.

TextAlign—This property specifies how the text is aligned within the Label.

Panel   ☐ Panel   This control is used to organize various controls. Unlike a GroupBox control, the Panel control does not display a caption.

■ *In action*

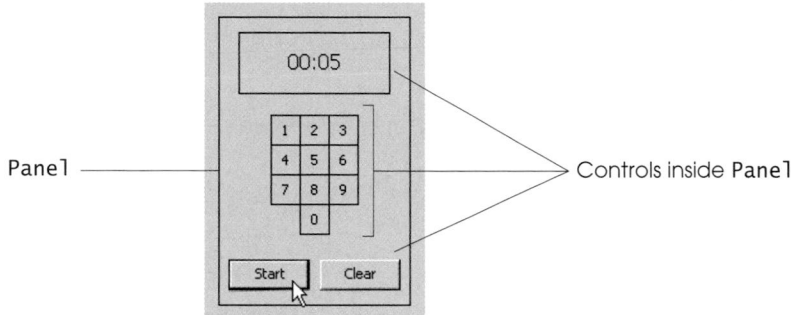

Panel ——————————— → Controls inside Panel

■ *Properties*

DefaultBackColor—This property returns the default background color of a Panel control.

Name—This property specifies the name of the Panel.

Size—This property specifies the size of the Panel.

Location—This property specifies the Panel's location on the Form.

BorderStyle—This property specifies the Panel's border style. Options include None (displaying no border), FixedSingle (a single-line border) and Fixed3D (a three-dimensional border).

    None—This value specifies that the Panel's will not display a border.

    FixedSingle—This value specifies that the Panel will display a thin, black border.

    Fixed3D—This value specifies that the Panel will display a three-dimensional border.

BackColor—This property specifies the background color of the Panel.

String The String class represents a series of characters treated as a single unit.

■ *Property*

Length—This property returns the number of characters in the String.

■ *Methods*

Format—This method arranges the string in a specified format.

IndexOf—This method returns the index of the specified character(s) in a String.

Insert—This method returns a copy of the String for which it is called with the specified character(s) inserted.

PadLeft—This method inserts characters at the beginning of a String.

Remove—This method returns a copy of the String for which it is called with the specified character(s) removed.

Substring—This method returns a substring from a String.

ToLower—This method returns a copy of the String for which it is called with any uppercase letters converted to lowercase letters.

MULTIPLE-CHOICE QUESTIONS

19.1 A Button appears flat if its _____ property is set to Flat.

  a) BorderStyle   b) FlatStyle

  c) Style   d) BackStyle

19.2 Keyword _____ introduces a class definition.
a) `NewClass`   b) `ClassDef`
c) `VBClass`   d) `Class`

19.3 Keyword _____ is used to create an object.
a) `CreateObject`   b) `Instantiate`
c) `Create`   d) `New`

19.4 String characters are of data type _____.
a) `Char`   b) `StringCharacter`
c) `Character`   d) `strCharacter`

19.5 The _____ is used to retrieve the value of an instance variable.
a) `Get` accessor of a property   b) `Retrieve` method of a class
c) `Client` method of a class   d) `Set` accessor of a property

19.6 When you enter the header for a constructor in Visual Studio .NET and press *Enter*, the keywords _____ are created for you.
a) `End Public Class`   b) `End Procedure`
c) `End Sub`   d) `End`

19.7 An important difference between constructors and other methods is that _____.
a) constructors cannot specify a return data type
b) constructors cannot specify any parameters
c) other methods are implemented as Sub procedures
d) constructors can assign values to instance variables

19.8 A class can yield many _____, just as a primitive data type can yield many variables.
a) names   b) objects
c) values   d) types

19.9 The Set accessor enables you to _____.
a) provide range checking   b) modify data
c) provide data validation   d) All of the above.

19.10 Instance variables declared `Private` are not accessible _____.
a) outside the class   b) by other methods of the same class
c) by other members of the same class   d) inside the same class

EXERCISES

19.11 (*Triangle Creator Application*) Create an application that allows the user to enter the lengths for the three sides of a triangle as `Integers`. The application should then determine whether the triangle is a right triangle (two sides of the triangle form a 90-degree angle), an equilateral triangle (all sides of equal length) or neither. The application's GUI is completed for you (Fig. 19.49). You must create a class to represent a triangle object and define the event handler for the **Create** Button.

a) *Copying and opening the template application.* Copy the `Triangle` folder from `C:\Examples\Tutorial19\Exercises` to `C:\SimplyVB`. Double click the `Triangle.sln` file in the `Triangle` folder to open the application in Visual Studio .NET.

b) *Creating the Triangle class.* Add a class to the project, and name it `Triangle`. This is where you will define the properties of the `Triangle` class.

c) *Defining the necessary properties.* Define a constructor that will take the lengths of the three sides of the triangle as arguments. Create three properties that enable clients to access and modify the lengths of the three sides. If the user enters a negative value, that side should be assigned the value zero.

d) *Adding additional features.* Create two more properties in the `Triangle` class: One determines whether the sides form a right triangle, the other an equilateral triangle. These properties are considered **read-only**, because you would naturally define only the `Get` accessor. There is no simple `Set` accessor that can make a triangle a right triangle or an equilateral triangle without first modifying the lengths of the triangle's sides. To create a read-only property (where the Set accessor is omitted), precede keyword Property with the keyword **ReadOnly**.

e) *Adding code to event handler.* Now that you have created your Triangle class, you can use it to create objects in your application. Double click the **Create** Button in **Design View** to generate the event handler. Create new variables to store the three lengths from the TextBoxes; then, use those values to create a new Triangle object.

f) *Displaying the result.* Use an If...ElseIf statement to determine if the triangle is a right triangle, an equilateral triangle or neither. Display the result in a Label.

Figure 19.49   Triangle Creator application with all possible outputs.

19.12 (*Modified Microwave Oven Application*) Modify the tutorial's **Microwave Oven** application to include an additional digit, which would represent the hour. Allow the user to enter up to 9 hours, 59 minutes, and 59 seconds (Fig. 19.50).

a) *Copying and opening the template application.* Copy the MicrowaveOven2 folder from C:\Examples\Tutorial19\Exercises to C:\SimplyVB. Double click the MicrowaveOven.sln file in the MicrowaveOven folder to open the application in Visual Studio .NET.

b) *Adding the hour variable.* To allow cooking time that includes the hour digit, you will need to modify the Time class. Define a new Private instance variable to represent the hour. Change the Time constructor to take in as its first argument (now Time should have three arguments) the hour amount. You will also have to modify the **Start** Button event handler and the DisplayTime method to include an hour variable.

c) *Adding the Hour property.* Use the Minute and Second properties as your template to create the property for the hour. Remember, we are allowing an additional digit to represent the hour (hour < 10).

d) *Changing the padding amount.* Change the calls to the PadLeft method to be consistent with the new time format.

e) *Extracting the hour.* Add a call to the Substring method so that hour gets the first digit in the m_strTime String. Also, change the calls to the Substring method for minute and second so that they extract the proper digits from the m_strTime String.

f) *Accessing the first five digits.* Change the If...Then statement from the DisplayTime method to take and display the first five digits entered by the user.

g) *Edit the Timer object.* Edit the tmrClock_Tick event handler to provide changes to hours and its corresponding minutes and seconds.

h) *Displaying the time.* Edit the Format String so that the display Label includes the hour.

Figure 19.50 **Microwave Oven** application's GUI.

19.13 (*Account Information Application*) The local bank wants you to create an application that will allow them to view their clients' information. The interface is created for you; you need to implement the class (Fig. 19.51). Once the application is completed, the bank manager should be able to click the **Next** or **Previous** Button to run through each client's information. The information is stored in four arrays containing first names, last names, account numbers and account balances.

a) *Copying and opening the template application.* Copy the AccountInformation folder from C:\Examples\Tutorial19\Exercises to C:\SimplyVB. Double click the AccountInformation.sln file in the AccountInformation folder to open the application in Visual Studio .NET.

b) *Determining variables for the class.* Examine the code from AccountInformation.vb, including all the properties that the Client object uses to retrieve the information.

c) *Creating the Client class.* Create a new class, and call it Client. Add this class to the project. Define four Private instance variables to represent each property value, to ensure that each Client object contains all the required information about each client. Use those variables to define a constructor.

d) *Defining each property.* Each Private variable should have a corresponding property, allowing the user to set or get each Private variable's value.

e) *Adding more information.* In the FrmAccountInformation_Load event handler, add two more accounts. Include names, account numbers, and balances for each corresponding array.

Figure 19.51 **Account Information** application GUI.

What does this code do? ▶ **19.14** What does the following code do? The first code listing contains the definition of class Shape. Each Shape object represents a closed shape with a number of sides. The second code listing contains a method (Mystery) created by a client of class Shape. What does this method do?

```
1   Public Class Shape
2
3      Private m_intSides As Integer
4
5      ' constructor with number of sides
6      Public Sub New(ByVal intSides As Integer)
7         Side = intSides
8      End Sub ' New
9
10     ' set and get side value
11     Public Property Side() As Integer
12
13        ' return m_intSides
14        Get
15           Return m_intSides
16        End Get ' end of Get accessor
17
18        ' set m_intSides
19        Set(ByVal Value As Integer)
20
21           If Value > 0 Then
22              m_intSides = Value
23           Else
24              m_intSides = 0
25           End If
26
27        End Set ' end of Set accessor
28
29     End Property ' Side
30
31  End Class ' Shape
```

```
1   Public Function Mystery(ByVal objShape As Shape) As String
2      Dim strShape As String
3
4      ' determine case with objShape.Side
5      Select Case objShape.Side
6
7         Case Is < 3
8            strShape = "Not a Shape"
9
10        Case 3
11           strShape = "Triangle"
12
13        Case 4
14           strShape = "Square"
15
16        Case Else
17           strShape = "Polygon"
18
19     End Select
20
21     Return strShape
22  End Function ' Mystery
```

What's wrong with this code? ▶   **19.15** Find the error(s) in the following code. The following method should create a new Shape object with `intNumberSides` sides. Assume the Shape class from Exercise 19.14.

```
1   Private Sub ManipulateShape(ByVal intNumberSides As Integer)
2      Dim objShape As Shape = New Shape(3)
3
4      Shape.m_intSides = intNumberSides
5   End Sub ' ManipulateShape
```

Using the Debugger ▶

19.16 (*View Name Application*) The **View Name** application allows the user to enter the user's first and last name. When the user clicks the **View Name** Button, a MessageBox that displays the user's first and last name appears. The application creates an instance of Class Name. This class uses its property definitions to set the first-name and last-name instance variables. Copy the Names folder from C:\Examples\Tutorial19\Exercises\Debugger to your Debugger folder. Open and run the application. While testing your application, you noticed that the MessageBox did not display the correct output. Use the debugger to find the logic error(s) in the application. The application with the correct output is displayed in Fig. 19.52.

Figure 19.52   **View Name** application with correct output.

Programming Challenge ▶

19.17 (*DVD Burner Application*) Create an application that simulates a DVD burner. Users create a DVD with their choice of title and bonus materials. The GUI is provided for you (Fig. 19.53). You will create a class (DVDObject) to represent the DVD object and another class (Bonus) to represent bonus materials for a DVD object.

a) ***Copying and opening the template application.*** Copy the DVDBurner folder from C:\Examples\Tutorial19\Exercises to C:\SimplyVB. Double click the DVD-Burner.sln file in the DVDBurner folder to open the application in Visual Studio .NET.

b) ***Creating the bonus material object.*** Create a class, and name it Bonus. The class's objects will each represent one bonus-material item on the DVD. Each Bonus object should have a name (description) and a length (in minutes). Use this tutorial's Time class as your guide in creating the properties for the name and length of each bonus material.

c) ***Creating the DVD class.*** Create a class, and name it DVDObject. This class contains the movie title and the length of the movie. The class should also include an array of three Bonus items.

d) ***Creating the necessary variables.*** Before you define the **Create** Button's event handler, create an DVDObject class instance variable. Inside the **Create** Button's event handler, create the necessary variables to store the information from the TextBoxes on the GUI. Also, this is where you need to create the array of Bonus objects to store the bonus materials.

e) ***Adding bonus-material information.*** Add the description and length of each bonus item to the Bonus array you created from the previous step.

f) ***Creating a DVD object.*** Use information about the movie, its title, length and the array of bonus materials to make your DVD object.

g) ***Displaying the output.*** The **Information** Button's Click event is already defined for you. Locate the event handler, add a String containing the complete information on the DVD object that you created earlier and display this String to a MessageBox.

Figure 19.53   **DVD Burner** application's GUI.

T U T O R I A L

Objectives

In this tutorial, you will learn to:
- Create and manipulate an `ArrayList` object.
- Set the `TabStop` and `TabIndex` properties of a control.
- Create an access key for a control.
- Use a `For Each...Next` loop to iterate through an `ArrayList`.

Outline

Shipping Hub Application

Introducing Collections, the For Each...Next Statement and Access Keys

Though most business can be conducted over phone lines and using e-mail messages, often it is necessary to send documents using a shipping company. As the pace of business increases, it is essential that shipping companies develop an efficient means to transfer packages from one location to another. To accomplish this task, many shipping companies send packages to a central location (a hub) before the packages reach their final destination. In this tutorial, you will develop a **Shipping Hub** application to simulate package processing at a shipping warehouse. You will develop the application by using collections, which provide you with a quick and easy way to organize and manipulate the data used by your application. This tutorial focuses on the `ArrayList` collection, which includes data storage capabilities of an array, but with much greater flexibility. You will also learn to use the `For Each...Next` repetition statement to iterate through the objects in a collection.

20.1 Test-Driving the **Shipping Hub** Application

In this section, you will test-drive the **Shipping Hub** application. This application must meet the following requirements:

Application Requirements

A shipping company receives packages at its headquarters, which functions as its shipping hub. After receiving the packages the company ships them to a distribution center in one of the following states: Alabama, Florida, Georgia, Kentucky, Mississippi, North Carolina, South Carolina, Tennessee, West Virginia or Virginia. The company needs an application to track the packages that pass through its shipping hub. The application generates a package ID number for each package that arrives at the shipping hub when the user clicks the application's Scan New Button. Once a package has been scanned, the user should be able to enter the shipping address for the package. The user should be able to navigate through the list of scanned packages by using < BACK or NEXT > Buttons and by viewing a list of all packages destined for a particular state.

This application stores a list of packages in an `ArrayList`. You will use the `For Each...Next` repetition statement to access the objects stored in the `ArrayList`. You begin by test-driving the completed application.

Test-Driving the Shipping Hub Application

1. ***Copying and opening the application***. Copy the `C:\Examples\Tutorial20\CompletedApplication\ShippingHub` folder to `C:\SimplyVB`. Double click the `ShippingHub.sln` file to open the application in Visual Studio .NET.

2. ***Running the Shipping Hub application***. Select **Debug > Start** to run the application. The application will display as shown in Fig. 20.1.

Figure 20.1   **Shipping Hub** application when first run.

3. ***Scanning a new package***. Click the **Scan New** `Button`. The application displays a package ID number, enables the `TextBoxes` and allows the user to enter the package information (Fig. 20.2).

Figure 20.2   Scanning a new package.

4. ***Using the* Tab *key***. Click in the **Address:** `TextBox` to transfer the focus of the application to that field so that you can enter data. Type `318 Some Street`, and press the *Tab* key. Notice that the cursor moves to the **City:** `TextBox` (Fig. 20.3).

5. ***Adding a package to the list of packages***. Type `Point Pleasant` in the **City:** field, and press the *Tab* key. Select **WV** from the **State:** `ComboBox`, and press the *Tab* key. Type `25550` in the **Zip:** field, and click the **Add** `Button` to add the package to the application's `ArrayList`.

(cont.)

Cursor now appears in the **City:** TextBox

Figure 20.3 Pressing the *Tab* key moves the cursor to the next TextBox.

Note that you cannot enter more than five numbers in the **Zip:** field because the **Zip:** TextBox's MaxLength property is set to 5. The value in the **MaxLength** property determines the maximum number of characters that the user can enter into a TextBox. The values in the **State:** ComboBox were added using its **Items** property in the Windows Form Designer. When you open the template application, examine the values stored in the Items property to see how this is accomplished.

6. ***Removing*, *editing and browsing packages*.** The application's **NEXT >** and **< BACK** Buttons allow the user to navigate the list of packages. The **Remove** Button allows the user to delete packages and the **Edit** Button allows the user to update a particular package's information. Experiment with the various Buttons by adding, removing and editing packages. We suggest using the following sample data:

- 9 Some Road, Goose Creek, SC, 29445
- 234 Some Place, Tamassee, SC, 29686
- 46 Some Avenue, Mammoth Cave, KY, 42259
- 3 Some Street, Yazoo City, MS, 39194

7. ***Viewing all packages going to a state*.** The ComboBox on the right side of the application allows the user to select a state. When a state is selected, all of the package ID numbers of packages destined for that state are displayed in the ListBox (Fig. 20.4). If the ListBox contains more package numbers than it can display, a vertical scrollbar will be added to the ListBox.

![Shipping Hub window showing package information for Yazoo City, MS, and Packages by State list for SC showing 49295 and 49296]

Figure 20.4 Viewing all packages going to South Carolina.

8. ***Closing the application*.** Click the running application's close box. Then select **File > Close Solution**.

20.2 Package Class

Your application must store data retrieved from the packages' shipping information. Each package ships to one location with an address, city, state and zip code. However, since multiple packages can be shipped to the same location, each package will need a unique identification number to distinguish it from other packages. As you learned in Tutorial 19, a convenient way to group related information is by creating instances of a class. The `Package` class included with the template application provides the necessary properties to keep track of package information. It also provides properties that ensure that only methods of class `Package` can access the instance variables of the class. The table in Fig. 20.5 describes the properties for class `Package`.

Property	Description
Address	Provides access to instance variable m_strAddress. Represents the package's address as a String.
City	Provides access to instance variable m_strCity, which represents the package's city as a String.
State	Provides access to m_strState, which stores the package's state as a String. It uses the standard two-letter state abbreviations. For example, NC is used for North Carolina.
Zip	Provides access to m_intZip. Represents the zip code as a five-digit Integer.
PackageNumber	Provides access to m_intPackageNumber, which stores the package's identification number as a String.

Figure 20.5   Properties listing for class `Package`.

The `Package` class must be added to the **Shipping Hub** application before objects of this class can be created. You will learn how to add the `Package` class to the **Shipping Hub** application in the box, *Adding a Class to an Application.*

Adding a Class to an Application	1. ***Copying and opening the application.*** Copy the C:\Examples\Tutorial20\TemplateApplication\ShippingHub folder to C:\SimplyVB. Double click the ShippingHub.sln file to open the application in Visual Studio .NET.
	2. ***Adding class Package.*** In the **Solution Explorer**, right click the **ShippingHub** project. Select **Add > Add Existing Item...** from the context menu that appears. When the **Add Existing Item** dialog appears, select the Package.vb file and click **Open**. The `Package` class is now included in the application and shown in the **Solution Explorer** (Fig. 20.6).

Package class added to the
ShippingHub project

Figure 20.6   **Solution Explorer** with Package.vb added.

20.3 Using Properties TabIndex and TabStop

Many applications require users to enter information into multiple TextBoxes. It is awkward for users to have to select each TextBox using the mouse. It is often easier to allow the user to use the *Tab* key to navigate the controls on the Form. To ensure ease of use, the focus must be transferred to the proper control when the *Tab* key is pressed. The **TabIndex** property allows you to specify the order in which focus is transferred to controls when *Tab* is pressed. However, some controls, such as a read-only TextBox, should not be selected using the *Tab* key. The **TabStop** property specifies whether the user can select the control using the *Tab* key. Setting this property to **False** prevents the control from being selected using the *Tab* key. You set both of these properties in the *Setting Properties TabIndex and TabStop* box.

Setting Properties *TabIndex* and *TabStop*

1. ***Opening ShippingHub.vb.*** Double click ShippingHub.vb in the **Solution Explorer** to open the file in design view.

   The **Shipping Hub** application requires that the user enter the package information into these TextBoxes. To ensure the user can easily enter the data, you should allow the user to press the *Tab* key to access the proper control.

2. ***Setting property TabStop.*** The TabStop property defaults to True for controls that receive user input. Ensure that this is the case by setting the TabStop properties to True for the **Address:**, **City:**, and **Zip:** TextBoxes, the **State:** and **Packages by State** ComboBox and the **Scan New** Button if they are not already set to True.

3. ***Disabling property TabStop.*** Set the TabStop property for the other controls on the Form to False. The user should be given access only to certain controls; therefore, you must prevent the *Tab* key from transferring the focus to an improper control, such as a disabled TextBox.

4. ***Using the Tab Order view in the Windows Form Designer.*** To help visualize the tab order, Visual Studio .NET provides a view called **Tab Order**. To use the **Tab Order** view, select the Form by clicking it, then select **View > Tab Order**. White numbers indicating the TabIndex appear in blue boxes in the upper-left corner of the control (Fig. 20.7). The first time you click a control in this view, its TabIndex value will be set to zero, as displayed in the TabIndex box (Fig. 20.7). Subsequent clicks will increment the value by one.

   Begin by clicking the **Package Information** GroupBox. Notice its value becomes 0 and the background of the surrounding box changes to white (Fig. 20.7). Then click the **Address:** TextBox and notice that the value changes to 0.0. The first zero refers to the TabIndex of the container (in this case, the GroupBox) and the second zero refers to the TabIndex for that control within the container.

   Continue setting the tab indices by clicking the **City:** TextBox, then the **State:** ComboBox and finally the **Zip:** TextBox. Complete setting the tab indices for the GroupBox by clicking each control that has not been changed. Controls that have not been changed display a box with a blue background.

GUI Design Tip

Set a control's TabStop property to True only if the control is used to receive user input.

GUI Design Tip

Use the TabIndex property to define the logical order in which the user should enter data. Usually the order transfers the focus of the application from top to bottom and left to right.

TabIndex box set to zero ———

TabIndex boxes (not modified) ———

Figure 20.7   Setting the TabIndex properties using the **Tab Order** view of the **Shipping Hub** application.

(cont.)   5. ***Setting the TabIndex properties for the rest of the application.*** Continue setting the `TabIndex` properties by clicking the **Scan New** Button. Then click the remaining unchanged controls in the order indicated in Fig. 20.8. Exit the **Tab Order** view by selecting **View > Tab Order.**

Figure 20.8   Tab Order view of the **Shipping Hub** application.

Using the `TabIndex` and `TabStop` properties properly improves the speed at which the user enters data into an application. Most controls have `TabIndex` and `TabStop` properties. `TabIndex` values on a `Form` or within a `GroupBox` must be unique—two controls cannot receive the focus at the same time. By default, the first control added to the `Form` has a value of 0 for its `TabIndex` property. The second control added has a value of 1 for its `TabIndex` property. The third control has a value of 2 (one more than the last control's value) for its `TabIndex` property, etc.

20.4 Using Access Keys

Applications that require the user to enter a great deal of text data should provide users with the ability to enter data by using only the keyboard. Setting the `TabIndex` and `TabStop` properties, for instance, helps the user enter data in a logical order. **Access keys** (or keyboard shortcuts) allow the user to perform an action on a control using the keyboard.

To specify an access key for a control, insert an & (ampersand) symbol in the `Text` property before the letter you wish to use as an access key. If you wish to use "s" as the access key on the **Scan New** Button, set its `Text` property to `&Scan New`. You can specify many access keys in an application, but each letter used as an access key in a container must be unique. To use the access key, you must press and hold the *Alt* key, then press the access key character on the keyboard (release both keys after pressing the access key character). In this case of the **Scan New** Button, you would press and hold the *Alt* key, then press the *S* key (also written as *Alt+S*) You would then release the *Alt* key.

Access keys are often used on Button controls and on the MainMenu control, which will be introduced in Tutorial 22. If you wish to display an ampersand character on a control, you must type && in its Text property. Follow the steps in the *Creating Access Keys* box to use access keys in your **Shipping Hub** application.

Creating Access Keys

GUI Design Tip

Use access keys to allow users to "click" a control using the keyboard.

Using the & symbol to create an access key (there is no space between & and S)

1. ***Creating an access key for the Scan New Button.*** Insert an & symbol before the letter S in the Text property of the **Scan New** Button (Fig. 20.9). Press *Enter* or click outside the field to update the property. Notice that the letter S is now underlined on the Button (Fig. 20.9). If the user presses *Alt* then *S* during execution, this will have the same effect as if the user "clicks" the **Scan New** Button. (The Click event will be raised.) Note that depending on your system configuration, you may need to press the *Alt* key to display the underline under the access key character.

Access key letter underlined

Figure 20.9 Creating an access key.

2. ***Inserting access keys for the remaining Buttons.*** Use the Text properties of the remaining Buttons to create access keys. Precede the B on the **< BACK** Button with an ampersand. Repeat this process for the A on the **Add** Button, the R on the **Remove** Button, the E on the **Edit** Button and the N on the **NEXT >** Button.

3. ***Saving the project.*** Select **File > Save All** to save all the solution's files.

20.5 Collections

The .NET Framework provides several classes, called **collections**, which you can use to store groups of related objects. These classes provide methods that facilitate the storage and organization of your data without requiring any knowledge of the details of how the objects are being stored. This capability improves your program development time because you do not have to write code to organize your data efficiently—the methods in the collection classes are proven to be reliable and efficient.

In Tutorials 17 and 18, you learned how to declare and use arrays in your applications. You may have noticed a limitation to arrays—once an array is declared, its size will not change to match its data set. This poses a problem if the number of items in an array will change over time.

Class ArrayList (a member of the Collections namespace) provides a convenient solution to this problem. The **ArrayList** collection provides all of the capa-

Software Design Tip

Use an ArrayList to store a group of values when the number of elements in the group varies during the execution of an application.

bilities of an array, but also provides dynamic resizing capabilities. **Dynamic resizing** enables the `ArrayList` object to increase its size to accommodate new elements and to decrease its size when elements are removed.

SELF-REVIEW
1. Collections _____.
    a) force you to focus on how your data is stored
    b) speed up application development
    c) allow you to focus on the details of your application
    d) Both b and c.

2. One limitation of arrays is that _____.
    a) their size cannot change dynamically   b) they can only store primitive data types
    c) `Strings` cannot be placed in them   d) All of the above.

    Answers: 1) d. 2) a.

20.6 Shipping Hub Application: Using Class `ArrayList`

By now, you are familiar with designing GUIs and writing methods and event handlers. This tutorial's template file provides much of the application's functionality so that you may concentrate on using an `ArrayList`. You are encouraged to study the full source code at the end of the tutorial to understand how the application is implemented. The following pseudocode statements describe the operation of your **Shipping Hub** application:

```
When the Form loads
    Generate an initial package ID number
    Create an empty ArrayList

When the user clicks the Scan New Button
    Generate a unique package ID number
    Enable TextBoxes, the ComboBox and the Add Button

When the user clicks the Add Button
    Retrieve address, city, state and zip code values; and disable input controls
    Add the package to the ArrayList
    Add the package number to the ListBox
    Change the ComboBox value to the package's destination state

When the user clicks the < BACK Button
    Display the previous package in the list

When the user clicks the NEXT > Button
    Display the next package in the list

When the user clicks the Remove Button
    Remove the package from the list

When the user clicks the Edit Button
    Change the Button to read Update
    Allow the user to modify package address information

When the user clicks the Update Button
    Update the package's information in the list
    Disable controls that allow user input, and change the Update Button to read
    Edit
```

> *When the user chooses a different state in the ComboBox*
>> *Display the package number for each package destined for that state in the*
>> *ListBox*

The **Shipping Hub** application must store a list of packages through which the user can navigate using the **NEXT >** and **< BACK** Buttons. Each time the application executes, it must allow for any number of packages to be added. Using arrays, you would be limited by the number of values that you could store in the array. The `ArrayList` collection solves this problem by combining the functionality of an array with dynamic resizing capabilities. The ACE table of Fig. 20.10 lists the actions, controls and events for this application.

Action/Control/Event
(ACE) Table for the
Shipping Hub
Application

Action	Control/Object	Event
Label the application's controls	fraAddress, fraListByState, lblArrived, lblPackageID, lblAddress, lblCity, lblState, lblZip	
Generate an initial package ID number; create an empty ArrayList	FrmShippingHub, m_objRandom, m_objList	Load (of Form)
Generate a unique package ID number; enable TextBoxes, the ComboBox and the Add Button	btnNew, btnAdd, txtAddress, txtCity, cboState, txtZip	Click (of Button btnNew)
Retrieve address, city, state and zip code values; disable input controls; add the package to the ArrayList; add the package number to the ListBox; change the ComboBox value to the package's destination state	btnAdd, txtAddress, txtCity, cboState, txtZip, m_objList, lstPackages	Click (of Button)
Display the next package in the ArrayList	btnNext, m_objList	Click
Display the previous package in the ArrayList	btnBack, m_objList	Click
Remove a package from the ArrayList	btnRemove, m_objList	Click
Change the Button to read Update; allow the user to modify package address information	btnEditUpdate, txtAddress, txtCity, cboState, txtZip	Click (of Button)
Update the package's information in the ArrayList; disable controls that allow user input and change the Update Button to read Edit	btnEditUpdate, txtAddress, txtCity, cboState, txtZip, m_objList	Click (of Button)
Display the package number for each package destined for the selected state in the ListBox	cboViewPackages, lstPackages	SelectedIndexChanged (of ComboBox)

Figure 20.10   ACE table for the **Shipping Hub** application.

In this tutorial, you focus on the use of an `ArrayList` in the **Shipping Hub** application. You begin by creating an `ArrayList` object in the box, *Creating a List of Packages*.

Creating a List of Packages

1. **Declaring an ArrayList**. Insert line 4 of Fig. 20.11 into your application to declare `ArrayList m_objList`. Notice the use of the member-access operator (`.`) to gain access to the `ArrayList` class, which is located in namespace `System.Collections`. Alternatively, you could use the `Imports` statement to import the `Collections` namespace such as

   ```
   Imports System.Collections
   ```

   In this case, you would not need to use the member-access operator because the namespace has been imported. In the following discussion, we will refer to the `Collections.ArrayList` object as an `ArrayList`.

Declaring an `ArrayList` reference

Figure 20.11   Declaring the `ArrayList` reference.

2. **Initializing the ArrayList**. To use the `ArrayList` instance variable declared in *Step 1*, you must create a new `ArrayList` object. You will then assign a reference to the `ArrayList` object to the instance variable. Insert line 320 (Fig. 20.12) to the Form's `Load` event handler. This line uses the `New` keyword to create an empty `ArrayList` object when the application loads. Notice that line 319 uses the `ComboBox`'s `Items.Item` property to show the first state in the list. The **`Items.Item`** property retrieves the value stored in the `ComboBox` at the specified index.

Initializing the `ArrayList` reference

Figure 20.12   Creating an `ArrayList` object.

Now that you have created an `ArrayList` object, you will need to insert code that allows the user to add packages to the `ArrayList`. To accomplish this, you will create a reference to an object of class `Package` and use the `ArrayList`'s `Add` method to store the reference in the `ArrayList`. Recall that you added the `Package` class to your application in the *Adding a Class to an Application* box. You will now create packages and add them to your list in the *Adding and Removing Packages* box.

Adding and Removing Packages

1. ***Creating a package.*** The user clicks the **Scan New** Button when a new package arrives at the shipping hub. When this occurs, the application should create a package number and allow the user to enter the shipping address. Insert lines 327–328 from Fig. 20.13 into the **Scan New** Button's Click event handler. Line 327 increments m_intPackageID to ensure that all packages have a unique identification number. Line 328 passes the package number as an argument to the constructor for class Package. The value that you pass to the Package constructor can then be accessed using its PackageNumber property. Note that line 328 uses the same reference, m_objPackage, many times to reference a new Package object. However, the previous Package object will not be destroyed each time the reference is changed. This is because each package reference is stored in the ArrayList.

Create a new Package object with a unique ID

Figure 20.13   Creating a package object.

2. ***Displaying the package number and arrival time.*** After the package has been "scanned," the application should display the new package's arrival time and package number to the user. Insert lines 331–334 of Fig. 20.14 into your application. Lines 331–332 display the package identification number in a Label. The **ToString** method, which is defined for most objects and data types, returns a value representing the object as text (of type String). For instance, a Date structure's ToString method returns the date as a String, in the format 11/11/2002 9:34:00 AM. However, be aware that for many FCL classes, ToString merely returns the class name. The ToString method can be used as an alternative to the Convert.ToString method. Lines 333–334 display the arrival time (the current time) in a Label.

Displaying arrival time and package ID number in Labels

Figure 20.14   Displaying the package's number and arrival time.

(cont.)   3. ***Adding a package to the* ArrayList.** To add the package to the `ArrayList` after entering the package's information, the user clicks the **Add** Button. Copy line 349 of Fig. 20.15 to the **Add** Button's `Click` event handler.

This line stores the package information by adding the `Package` object to the `m_objList` `ArrayList` using the `ArrayList`'s **Add** method.

Adding a `Package` object to an `ArrayList`

Figure 20.15   Adding a package to the `ArrayList`.

Each time you add an object to the `ArrayList` by calling the Add method, the object is added to the end of the `ArrayList`. With arrays, you refer to a value's location by its index. Similarly, in an `ArrayList`, you refer to an object's location in the `ArrayList` as the object's **index**. Much like an array, the index of an object at the beginning of the `ArrayList` is zero and the index of an object at the end of the `ArrayList` is one less than the number of objects in the `ArrayList`.

4. ***Removing a package from the* ArrayList.** When the user selects a package and clicks the **Remove** Button, the application should remove the package from the `ArrayList`. The `ArrayList` class provides a simple way to remove objects from the `ArrayList`. Insert line 404 (Fig. 20.16) into the **Remove** Button's `Click` event handler. This line uses the **RemoveAt** method to remove a package from the `ArrayList`. The argument passed to the `RemoveAt` method is the index of the package in the `ArrayList`, contained in the variable `m_intPosition`. This variable keeps track of the position and is incremented or decremented each time the user clicks the **NEXT >** or **< BACK** Buttons.

Removing the current package from the `ArrayList`

Figure 20.16   Removing a package from the `ArrayList`.

If a package at index 3 is removed from the `ArrayList`, the package that was previously at index 4 will then be located at index 3. Whenever an object is removed from an `ArrayList`, the indices update accordingly. Notice that line 407 of Fig. 20.16 uses the Count property of class `ArrayList`. The **Count** property returns the number of objects contained in the `ArrayList`.

Once a package has been added to the `ArrayList`, the **Shipping Hub** application disables the `TextBoxes` so that the user does not accidentally modify the package information. To allow users to modify any of the package information except for the arrival time and the package identification number, an **Edit** Button is provided. When the user clicks the **Edit** Button, its event handler should enable the controls that allow the user to modify the package data. You add functionality to accomplish this in the *Updating Package Information* box.

Updating Package Information

1. **Changing the Edit Button's Text property.** Add lines 434–435 of Fig. 20.17 to your application. When the **Edit** Button is clicked, line 435 changes the text on the **Edit** Button to &Update (using U as the access key). This indicates that the user should click the same Button, which now is labeled **Update**, to submit changes to the package information.

Using code to change the text displayed on a Button

Figure 20.17 Changing the **Edit** Button to display **Update**.

2. **Updating the package data.** Insert lines 441–442 (Fig. 20.18) into the `btnEditUpdate_Click` event handler. When the user chooses to alter the package information, the package is removed from the `ArrayList` and a new one with the updated address information is added.

Updating the `ArrayList` with new package information

Figure 20.18 Removing and inserting a package to update data.

Line 441 removes the old package object from the `ArrayList`. Line 442 uses class `ArrayList`'s Insert method to add the package to the `ArrayList`. The **Insert** method is like the Add method, but `Insert` allows you to specify the index in the `ArrayList` at which to insert the package. The first argument to the `Insert` method is the index at which to insert the package (in this case, `m_intPosition`), and the second argument contains the package to insert into the `ArrayList` (`m_objPackage`). Using the `Insert` method allows you to place the updated package object at the same index in the `ArrayList` as the package object you just removed.

(cont.)

3. ***Changing the Button's Text property to Edit****. After the user clicks the **Update** Button, the TextBoxes are once again disabled. The user's changes have been applied; therefore, you should reset the text on the **Update** Button to read **Edit**. Insert line 452 of Fig. 20.19 into the event handler to reset the text on the **Button** to **Edit**. Notice once again the use of the & to enable the **Button's** access key.

Using code to display the text on the **Button**

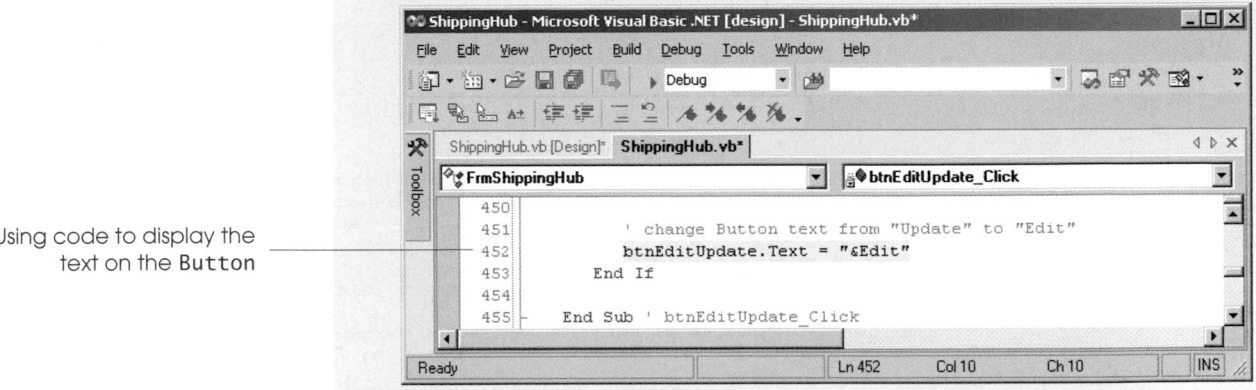

Figure 20.19   Setting the **Button's** **Text** property back to **Edit**.

The user navigates the ArrayList by clicking the **NEXT >** and **< BACK** Buttons. Each time the user chooses to view a different package in the ArrayList, the package information displayed in the Form's controls must be updated. To display a package's information, you must retrieve the information from the ArrayList that you created. You will learn how to do this in the box, *Displaying a Package*.

Displaying a Package

1. ***Retrieving package data****. Insert lines 469–471 from Fig. 20.20 into your application's LoadPackage method. To display the information, you must retrieve the data from the ArrayList using the Item method. The Item method returns the object stored at the index specified by the method's argument. Lines 470–471 assign to m_objPackage the package stored at index m_intPosition.

Retrieving a **Package** object from an ArrayList

Figure 20.20   Retrieving a package from the ArrayList.

Note that the code you inserted explicitly converts the object returned by the ArrayList to an object of type Package. One of the many advantages of using an ArrayList is that it stores references to objects of type Object—which means that it can store *any* object you choose, from predefined objects (like a Random object) to programmer-defined objects (like a Package object). To use and access the properties and methods of a package returned from an ArrayList, you must explicitly convert it to a Package object.

(cont.)

2. ***Displaying the package information***. Insert lines 474–481 of Fig. 20.21 into your application. These lines retrieve the package information from m_objPackage and display the data in the corresponding controls on the Form, using the ToString method.

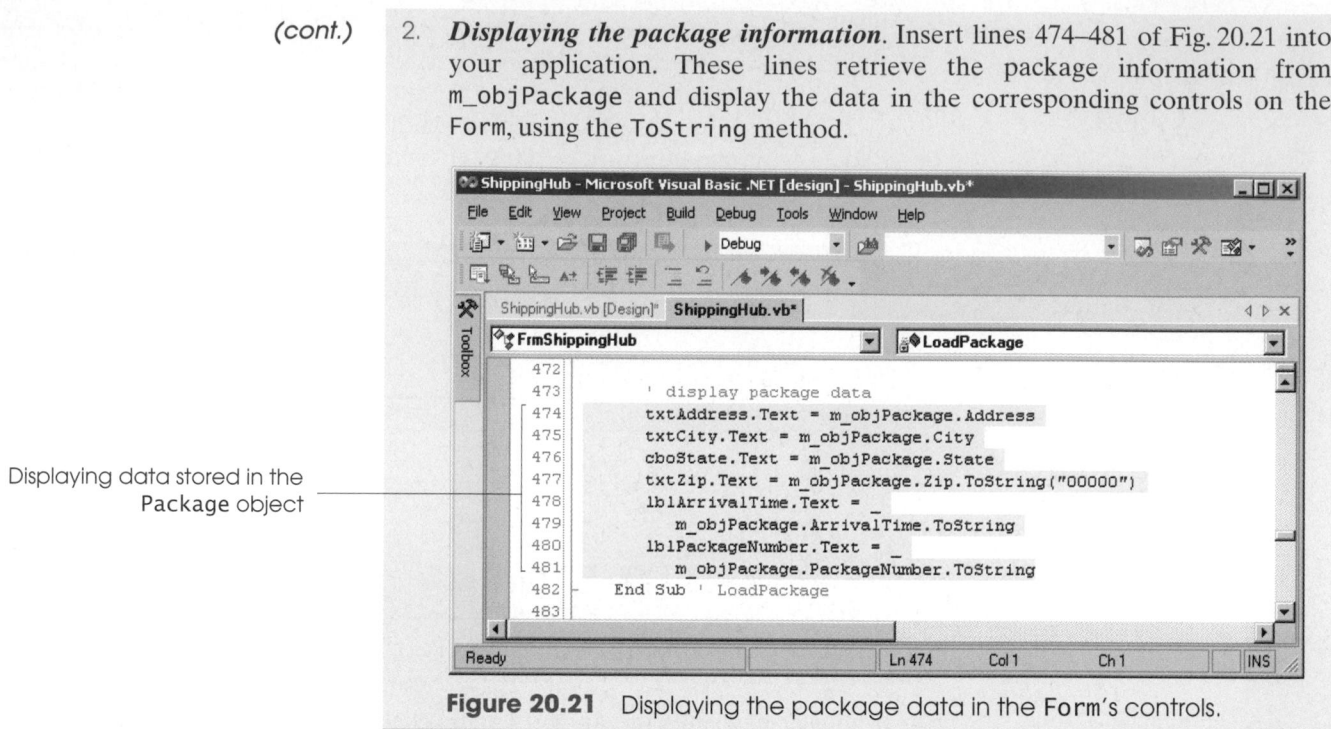

Displaying data stored in the Package object

Figure 20.21 Displaying the package data in the Form's controls.

SELF-REVIEW

1. Method _____ of class ArrayList can be used to add an object at a specific location in the ArrayList.

    a) AddAt
                                 b) Insert

    c) AddObjectAt
                           d) Add

2. The **Shipping Hub** application uses an ArrayList because class ArrayList _____.

    a) can store a variable number of objects

    b) allows the addition and removal of packages

    c) allows the insertion of items into any index in the ArrayList

    d) All of the above.

Answers: 1) b. 2) d.

20.7 For Each...Next Repetition Statement

Visual Basic .NET provides the **For Each...Next** repetition statement for iterating through the values in an array or a collection. Instead of setting initial and final values for a counter variable, the For Each...Next statement uses a control variable (a reference) that can reference each object in the collection. Assuming that you have created an ArrayList objArrayList that contains only Package objects, the code

Good Programming Practice

Use a For Each...Next repetition statement to iterate through values in an array or collection without using a counter variable.

```
Dim objPackage As Package

For Each objPackage In objArrayList
    lstPackages.Items.Add(objPackage.PackageNumber)
Next
```

adds each package's ID number to a ListBox. The For Each...Next statement requires both a collection type and an element. The **collection type** specifies the array or collection (in this case, the ArrayList objArrayList) through which you wish to iterate. The **element** is used to store a reference to a value in the collection type. If the For Each...Next statement contains an element of the same type (or one that can be converted to the same type) as the collection type, the statement assigns the collection type's object to the element (in this case, objPackage). The body of the For Each...Next statement is then executed. Notice that because the For Each...Next statement does not require you to specify initial and final counter values, it simplifies access to groups of values.

The UML activity diagram for the preceding For Each...Next repetition statement is found in Fig. 20.22. Notice that it is similar to the UML diagram for the For...Next statement in Tutorial 11. The only difference is that the For Each...Next continues to execute the body until all elements in the array (or collection) have been accessed.

Common Programming Error

If the element in a For Each...Next statement cannot be converted to the same type as the collection type's objects, a runtime error occurs. For example, if an Array-List contained only Date values, declaring a reference to a Package object as the element would cause a runtime error.

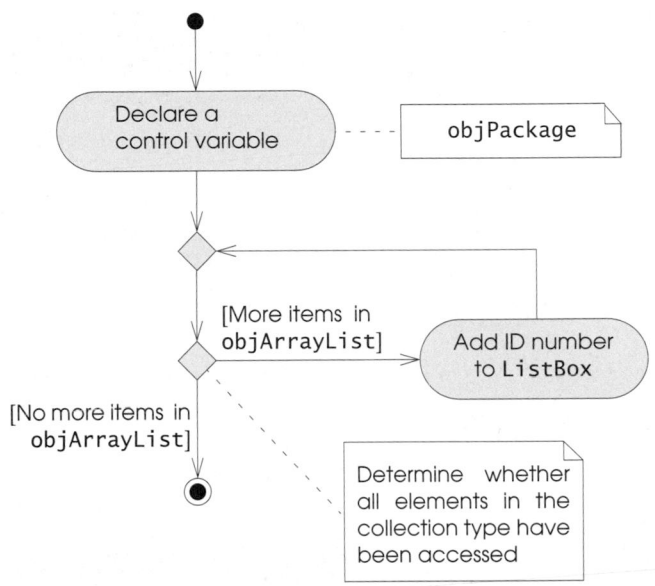

Figure 20.22   UML activity diagram for For Each...Next repetition statement.

When the user selects a state from the ComboBox, the application should display the package number for each package destined for that state. You will use the For Each...Next statement in the **Shipping Hub** application to add this functionality in the box, *Inserting a For Each...Next Statement.*

Inserting a For Each...Next Statement

1. ***Declaring a control variable (reference).*** Copy line 520 of Fig. 20.23 into your application. This line declares reference objViewPackage of type Package. The reference objViewPackage will be used to reference each Package object (one at a time) in your ArrayList as you iterate through the ArrayList of Package objects. Notice that you have added code to a ComboBox's SelectedIndexChanged event handler. The **SelectedIndexChanged** event is raised when the value selected in the ComboBox changes.

Declaring the control variable for the For Each...Next repetition statement

Figure 20.23   Declaring a reference for use in For Each...Next loop.

(cont.)

2. ***Inserting a For Each...Next statement.*** Add line 527 of Fig. 20.24 to your application. This line is the header for the repetition statement. This loop will iterate through `ArrayList m_objList`, assigning the next element in the `ArrayList` (beginning with the first package object) to reference `obj-ViewPackage` before executing the body of the loop. When a new package is reached, the `For Each...Next` body executes.

For Each...Next header

Figure 20.24 Writing a `For Each...Next` statement.

3. ***Determining a package's destination state.*** Insert lines 531–535 of Fig. 20.25 into your application. These lines contain an `If...Then` statement that tests each package's destination state against the state name displayed in the **Packages By State** ComboBox. If the two state names match, line 535 displays the package number in the `ListBox`.

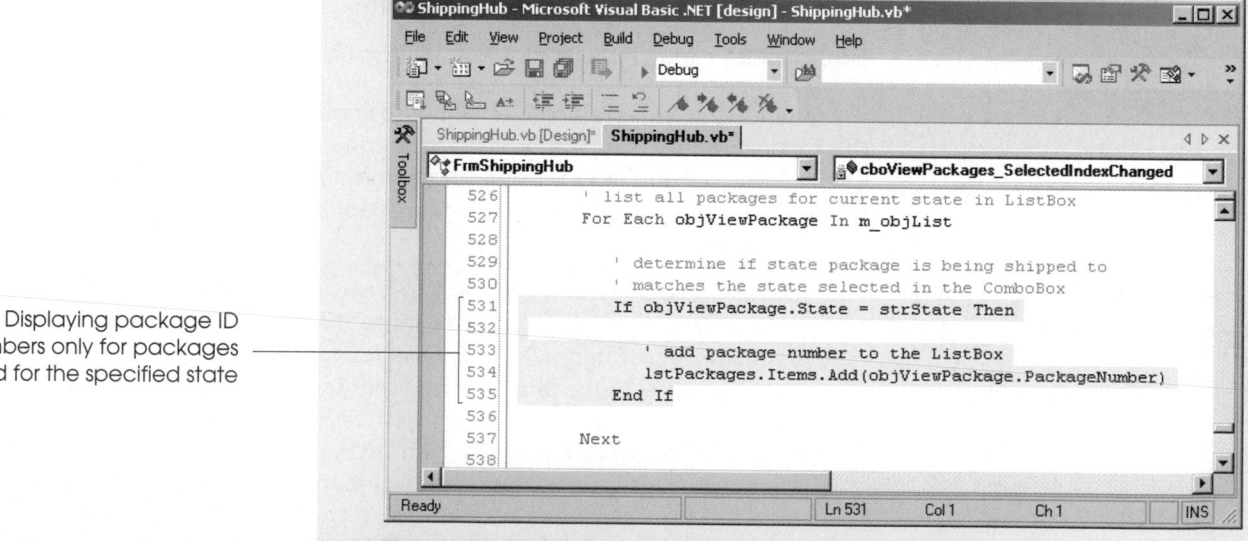

Displaying package ID numbers only for packages destined for the specified state

Figure 20.25 Displaying all packages going to selected state.

4. ***Saving the project.*** Select **File > Save All** to save all the solution's files.

5. ***Running the application.*** Now that you have completed inserting code into the application, select **Debug > Start** to run the completed application.

6. ***Closing the solution.*** Click the running application's close box. Select **File > Close Solution** to close the solution.

Figure 20.26 shows the entire code listing for the **Shipping Hub** application. The portions of code you added are highlighted in yellow.

```
 1   Public Class FrmShippingHub
 2      Inherits System.Windows.Forms.Form
 3
 4      Private m_objList As Collections.ArrayList ' list of packages
 5      Private m_objPackage As Package    ' current package
 6      Private m_intPosition As Integer   ' position of current package
 7      Private m_objRandom As Random       ' random number for package id
 8      Private m_intPackageID As Integer ' individual package number
 9
10      ' Windows Form Designer generated code
11
12      ' Form Load event
13      Private Sub FrmShippingHub_Load(ByVal sender As _
14         System.Object, ByVal e As System.EventArgs) _
15         Handles MyBase.Load
16
17         m_intPosition = 0 ' set initial position to zero
18         m_objRandom = New Random() ' create new Random object
19         m_intPackageID = m_objRandom.Next(1, 100000) ' new package ID
20
21         ' show first state in ComboBox (using the Items property)
22         cboState.Text = Convert.ToString(cboState.Items.Item(0))
23         m_objList = New Collections.ArrayList() ' list of packages
24      End Sub ' FrmShippingHub_Load
25
26      ' Scan New Button Click event
27      Private Sub btnNew_Click(ByVal sender As System.Object, _
28         ByVal e As System.EventArgs) Handles btnNew.Click
29
30         m_intPackageID += 1 ' increment package ID
31         m_objPackage = New Package(m_intPackageID) ' create package
32
33         ClearControls() ' clear fields
34         lblPackageNumber.Text = _
35            m_objPackage.PackageNumber.ToString ' package number
36         lblArrivalTime.Text = _
37            m_objPackage.ArrivalTime.ToString ' display arrival time
38
39         ' only allow user to add package
40         fraAddress.Enabled = True ' disable GroupBox and its controls
41         SetButtons(False) ' enable/disable Buttons
42         btnAdd.Enabled = True   ' enable Add Button
43         btnNew.Enabled = False ' disable Scan New Button
44         txtAddress.Focus() ' transfer the focus to txtAddress TextBox
45      End Sub ' btnNew_Click
46
47      ' Add Button Click event
48      Private Sub btnAdd_Click(ByVal sender As System.Object, _
49         ByVal e As System.EventArgs) Handles btnAdd.Click
50
51         SetPackage() ' set Package properties from TextBoxes
52         m_objList.Add(m_objPackage) ' add package to ArrayList
53
54         fraAddress.Enabled = False ' disable GroupBox and its controls
55         SetButtons(True) ' enable appropriate Buttons
56
57         ' package cannot be added until Scan New is clicked
58         btnAdd.Enabled = False ' disable Add Button
```

Initially, there are no objects in the **ArrayList**, so set the position to zero

Use a **Random** object to generate a random number for package IDs

Figure 20.26   Complete code listing for the **Shipping Hub** application. (Part 1 of 5.)

Display package ID numbers in `ListBox` if the state names match

When the user clicks the < **BACK** Button, decrement the position. If the position was zero, set the position to the last object in the

When the user clicks the **NEXT** > Button, increment the position. If the position was the last object in the array, set the position to zero

Set the position to the next package in the `ArrayList`

```vbnet
59
60          ' if package's state displayed, add ID to ListBox
61          If cboState.Text = cboViewPackages.Text Then
62             lstPackages.Items.Add(m_objPackage.PackageNumber)
63          End If
64
65          cboViewPackages.Text = m_objPackage.State ' list packages
66          btnNew.Enabled = True ' enable Scan New Button
67       End Sub ' btnAdd_Click
68
69       ' Back Button Click event
70       Private Sub btnBack_Click(ByVal sender As System.Object, _
71          ByVal e As System.EventArgs) Handles btnBack.Click
72
73          ' move backward one package in the list
74          If m_intPosition > 0 Then
75             m_intPosition -= 1
76          Else ' wrap to end of list
77             m_intPosition = m_objList.Count - 1
78          End If
79
80          LoadPackage() ' load package data from item in list
81       End Sub ' btnBack_Click
82
83       ' Next Button Click event
84       Private Sub btnNext_Click(ByVal sender As System.Object, _
85          ByVal e As System.EventArgs) Handles btnNext.Click
86
87          ' move forward one package in the list
88          If m_intPosition < m_objList.Count - 1 Then
89             m_intPosition += 1
90          Else
91             m_intPosition = 0 ' wrap to beginning of list
92          End If
93
94          LoadPackage() ' load package data from item in list
95       End Sub ' btnNext_Click
96
97       ' Remove Button click event
98       Private Sub btnRemove_Click(ByVal sender As _
99          System.Object, ByVal e As System.EventArgs) _
100         Handles btnRemove.Click
101
102         ' remove ID from ListBox if state displayed
103         If cboState.Text = cboViewPackages.Text Then
104            lstPackages.Items.Remove(m_objPackage.PackageNumber)
105         End If
106
107         m_objList.RemoveAt(m_intPosition) ' remove package from list
108
109         ' load next package in list if there is one
110         If m_objList.Count > 0 Then
111
112            ' if not at first position, go to previous one
113            If m_intPosition > 0 Then
114               m_intPosition -= 1
115            End If
116
```

Figure 20.26 Complete code listing for the **Shipping Hub** application. (Part 2 of 5.)

```
117              LoadPackage() ' load package data from item in list
118          Else
119              ClearControls() ' clear fields
120          End If
121
122          SetButtons(True) ' enable appropriate Buttons
123      End Sub ' btnRemove_Click
124
125      ' Edit/Update Button Click event
126      Private Sub btnEditUpdate_Click(ByVal sender As _
127          System.Object, ByVal e As System.EventArgs) _
128          Handles btnEditUpdate.Click
129
130          ' when Button reads "Edit", allow user to
131          ' edit package information only
132          If btnEditUpdate.Text = "&Edit" Then
133              fraAddress.Enabled = True
134              SetButtons(False)
135              btnEditUpdate.Enabled = True
136
137              ' change Button text from "Edit" to "Update"
138              btnEditUpdate.Text = "&Update"
139          Else
140
141              ' when Button reads "Update" remove the old package
142              ' data and add new data from TextBoxes
143              SetPackage()
144              m_objList.RemoveAt(m_intPosition)
145              m_objList.Insert(m_intPosition, m_objPackage)
146
147              ' display state in ComboBox
148              cboViewPackages.Text = m_objPackage.State
149
150              ' when done, return to normal operating state
151              fraAddress.Enabled = False  ' disable GroupBox
152              SetButtons(True) ' enable appropriate Buttons
153
154              ' change Button text from "Update" to "Edit"
155              btnEditUpdate.Text = "&Edit"
156          End If
157
158      End Sub ' btnEditUpdate_Click
159
160      ' set package properties
161      Private Sub SetPackage()
162          m_objPackage.Address = txtAddress.Text
163          m_objPackage.City = txtCity.Text
164          m_objPackage.State = _
165              Convert.ToString(cboState.SelectedItem)
166          m_objPackage.Zip = Convert.ToInt32(Val(txtZip.Text))
167      End Sub ' SetPackage
168
169      ' load package information into Form
170      Private Sub LoadPackage()
171
172          ' retrieve package from list
173          m_objPackage = CType(m_objList.Item(m_intPosition), _
174              Package)
```

Retrieve data from user, and store it in the Package object _(annotation pointing to lines 161–166)_

Figure 20.26 Complete code listing for the **Shipping Hub** application. (Part 3 of 5.)

```
175
176            ' display package data
177            txtAddress.Text = m_objPackage.Address
178            txtCity.Text = m_objPackage.City
179            cboState.Text = m_objPackage.State
180            txtZip.Text = m_objPackage.Zip.ToString("00000")
181            lblArrivalTime.Text = _
182               m_objPackage.ArrivalTime.ToString
183            lblPackageNumber.Text = _
184               m_objPackage.PackageNumber.ToString
185         End Sub ' LoadPackage
186
187         ' clear all the input controls on the Form
188         Private Sub ClearControls()
189            txtAddress.Clear()
190            txtCity.Clear()
191            txtZip.Clear()
192            cboState.SelectedText = ""
193            lblArrivalTime.Text = ""
194            lblPackageNumber.Text = ""
195         End Sub ' ClearControls
196
197         ' enable/disable Buttons
198         Private Sub SetButtons(ByVal blnState As Boolean)
199            btnRemove.Enabled = blnState
200            btnEditUpdate.Enabled = blnState
201            btnNext.Enabled = blnState
202            btnBack.Enabled = blnState
203
204            ' disable navigation if not multiple packages
205            If m_objList.Count < 2 Then
206               btnNext.Enabled = False
207               btnBack.Enabled = False
208            End If
209
210            ' if no items, disable Remove and Edit/Update Buttons
211            If m_objList.Count = 0 Then
212               btnEditUpdate.Enabled = False
213               btnRemove.Enabled = False
214            End If
215
216         End Sub ' SetButtons
217
218         ' event raised when user selects a new state in ComboBox
219         Private Sub cboViewPackages_SelectedIndexChanged( _
220            ByVal sender As System.Object, ByVal e As System.EventArgs) _
221            Handles cboViewPackages.SelectedIndexChanged
222
223            Dim objViewPackage As Package ' control variable package
224            Dim strState As String = _
225               Convert.ToString(cboViewPacakges.SelectedItem)
226
227            lstPackages.Items.Clear() ' clear ListBox
228
229            ' list all packages for current state in ListBox
230            For Each objViewPackage In m_objList
231
```

Enable or disable Buttons depending on value of **blnState** *(annotation pointing to lines 199–202)*

Figure 20.26 Complete code listing for the **Shipping Hub** application. (Part 4 of 5.)

```
232            ' determine if state package is being shipped to
233            ' matches the state selected in the ComboBox
234            If objViewPackage.State = strState Then
235
236                ' add package number to the ListBox
237                lstPackages.Items.Add(objViewPackage.PackageNumber)
238            End If
239
240        Next
241
242    End Sub ' cboViewPackages_SelectedIndexChanged
243
244 End Class ' FrmShippingHub
```

Figure 20.26   Complete code listing for the **Shipping Hub** application. (Part 5 of 5.)

SELF-REVIEW   1. The collection type in a For Each...Next repetition statement represents _____.

a) the counter used for iteration   b) the reference used for iteration

c) an array or collection   d) the guard condition

2. The _____ statement provides a convenient way to iterate through values in an array or collection.

a) Do While...Loop   b) For...Next

c) For Each...Next   d) None of the above.

Answers: 1) c. 2) c.

20.8 Wrap-Up

In this tutorial, you learned how to use the TabStop and TabIndex properties to enhance the **Shipping Hub** application's usability. You learned how to determine which controls receive the application's focus when the *Tab* key is pressed using the TabStop property. You then set the TabIndex property, to specify the order in which controls receive the focus of the application when the *Tab* key is pressed. To further enhance the user interface, you created access keys to allow the user to "click" Buttons in the **Shipping Hub** application by pressing the *Alt* key and then the access key for the particular Button.

You learned about using the ArrayList collection. You used ArrayList methods to add a package object to an ArrayList and delete the package from a specific index in an ArrayList. You then wrote code to insert a Package object into the ArrayList at a specific index. These methods helped you store, edit and navigate an ArrayList of packages in the **Shipping Hub** application.

Finally, you learned about the For Each...Next repetition statement. You declared a control variable for use in the loop and used that reference in the For Each...Next statement to iterate through each element in a collection type (which can be an array or a collection). Then you used the For Each...Next statement to iterate through package objects in the ArrayList in your **Shipping Hub** application.

In the next tutorial, you will learn about mouse events, which are events raised when the user moves or clicks the mouse. You will use these mouse events to allow the user to draw art on a Form.

SKILLS SUMMARY   **Using the TabIndex and TabStop Properties**

■ Set the TabIndex properties of controls on your Form using numbers to specify the order in which to transfer the focus of the application when the user presses the *Tab* key.

■ Set the `TabStop` property of a control to `False` if a control is not used by the user to input data. Set the `TabStop` property of a control to `True` if focus should be transferred to the control using the *Tab* key.

Creating Access Keys

■ Insert the & symbol in a control's `Text` property before the character you wish you use as an access key (keyboard shortcut).

Creating an `ArrayList`

■ Assign a reference to an `ArrayList` to an object of type `Collections.ArrayList` using keyword `New`.

Using an `ArrayList`

■ Call `ArrayList` method `Add` on an `ArrayList` object to add the method's argument to the `ArrayList`.

■ Call `ArrayList` method `RemoveAt` on an `ArrayList` object to remove the object from the `ArrayList` at the index specified by the method's argument.

■ Call `ArrayList` method `Insert` on an `ArrayList` object to add the object specified by the second argument to the `ArrayList` at the index specified by the first argument to the method.

Using a For Each...Next Repetition Statement

■ Declare a reference of the same type as elements you wish to access in a collection type (array or collection).

■ Specify the reference as the control variable in the For Each...Next repetition statement and the array or collection through which you wish to iterate. The loop repeats and the body of the For Each...Next repetition statement executes for each element in the collection type. The value accessed at the beginning of each iteration is stored in the element reference for the body of the loop.

KEY TERMS

Add method of class `ArrayList`—A method of class `ArrayList` that adds a specified object to the end of an `ArrayList`.

`ArrayList` class—Performs the same functionality as an array, but has resizing capabilities.

collection—A class used to store groups of related objects.

`Collections` namespace—The namespace that contains collection classes such as `ArrayList`.

For Each...Next repetition statement—The repetition statement that can be used to iterate through elements in an array or collection.

Insert method of class `ArrayList`—A method of class `ArrayList` that inserts a specified object into the specified location of an `ArrayList`.

RemoveAt method of class `ArrayList`—A method of class `ArrayList` that removes the object located at a specified location of an `ArrayList`.

`SelectedIndexChanged` event of `ComboBox`—The event raised when a new value is selected in a `ComboBox`.

TabIndex property—A control property that specifies the order in which focus is transferred to controls on the `Form` when the *Tab* key is pressed.

TabStop property—A control property that specifies whether a control can receive the focus when the *Tab* key is pressed.

ToString method—A method that returns a `String` representation of the object or data type on which the method is called.

GUI DESIGN GUIDELINES

Overall Design

■ Set a control's `TabStop` property to `True` only if the control is used to receive user input.

■ Use the `TabIndex` property to define the logical order in which the user should enter data.

■ Use access keys to allow users to "click" a control using the keyboard.

■ Usually the tab order transfers the focus of the application from top to bottom and left to right.

CONTROLS, EVENTS, PROPERTIES & METHODS

ArrayList This class is used to store a variable number of objects.

■ *Property*

Count—This property returns the number of objects contained in the ArrayList.

■ *Methods*

Add—This method adds an object to the ArrayList object.

Insert—This method adds an object to the ArrayList object at a specific index.

RemoveAt—This method removes an object from the ArrayList object at the specified index.

ComboBox 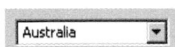 This control allows users to select options from a drop-down list.

■ *In action*

■ *Event*

SelectedIndexChanged—This event is raised when a new value is selected in the ComobBox.

■ *Properties*

DataSource—This property allows you to add items to the ComboBox.

DropDownStyle—This property determines the ComboBox's style.

Enabled—This property determines whether the user can enter data (True) in the ComboBox or not (False).

Items—This property specifies the values the user can select from the ComboBox.

  Item—This property retrieves the value at the specified index.

Location—This property specifies the location of the ComboBox control on its container control relative to the top-left corner.

MaxDropDownItems—This property determines the maximum number of items to be displayed when user clicks the drop-down arrow.

Name—This property specifies the name used to access the ComboBox control programmatically. The name should be prefixed with cbo.

SelectedValue—This property contains the item selected by the user.

Text—This property specifies the text displayed in the ComboBox.

TextBox ab| TextBox This control allows the user to input data from the keyboard.

■ *In action*

■ *Events*

TextChanged—This event is raised when the text in the TextBox is changed.

■ *Properties*

Enabled—This property determines whether the user can enter data (True) in the Text-Box or not (False).

Location—This property specifies the location of the TextBox on its container control relative to the top-left corner.

MaxLength—This property specifies the maximum number of characters that can be input into the TextBox.

Multiline—This property specifies whether the TextBox is capable of displaying multiple lines of text.

Name—This property specifies the name used to access the TextBox programmatically. The name should be prefixed with txt.

PasswordChar—This property specifies the masking character to be used when displaying data in the TextBox.

ReadOnly—This property determines whether the value of a TextBox can be changed.

ScrollBars—This property specifies whether a multiline TextBox contains a scrollbar.

Size—This property specifies the height and width (in pixels) of the TextBox.

Text—This property specifies the text displayed in the TextBox.

TextAlign—This property specifies how the text is aligned within the TextBox.

■ *Method*

Focus—This method transfers the focus of the application to the TextBox that calls it.

MULTIPLE-CHOICE QUESTIONS

20.1 _____ are specifically designed to store groups of values.

a) Collections
b) Properties
c) Accessors
d) None of the above.

20.2 The _____ key provides a quick and convenient way to navigate through controls on a Form.

a) *Tab*
b) *Enter*
c) *Caps Lock*
d) *Alt*

20.3 An ArrayList differs from an array in that an ArrayList can _____.

a) store objects of any type
b) resize dynamically
c) be accessed programmatically
d) All of the above.

20.4 The element in a For Each…Next statement _____.

a) must be of type Integer
b) must be of (or convertible to) the same type as the collection or array type
c) must be of type ArrayList
d) None of the above.

20.5 The control that receives the focus the first time *Tab* is pressed has a TabIndex property set to _____.

a) First
b) 0
c) Next
d) 1

20.6 Users should be able to use the *Tab* key to transfer the focus to _____.

a) only Buttons
b) only TextBoxes
c) only controls that have an AcceptTab property
d) only the controls that receive user input

20.7 To ensure that the proper controls obtain the focus when the *Tab* key is pressed, use the _____.

a) TabIndex property
b) TabStop and TabIndex properties
c) TabStop property
d) Focus property

20.8 To add a value to the end of an ArrayList, call the _____ method.

a) Add
b) AddToEnd
c) AddAt
d) InsertAt

20.9 To remove a value from a specific index in the ArrayList, use method _____.

a) Remove
b) RemoveAt
c) Delete
d) DeleteAt

20.10 To display an ampersand character on a control, type a _____ in its Text property.

a) &_
b) &
c) &&
d) _&

EXERCISES

20.11 (*Modified* **Salary Survey** *Application*) Modify the **Salary Survey** application you created in Exercise 17.12 by using a For Each...Next loop to replace the For...Next loop that is used in Tutorial 17 (Fig. 20.27).

a) *Copying and opening the template application.* Copy the SalarySurveyModified folder from C:\Examples\Tutorial20\Exercises to C:\SimplyVB. Double click the SalarySurvey.sln file in the SalarySurvey folder to open the application in Visual Studio .NET.

b) *Locating the event handler.* In **Design View**, double click the **Show Totals** Button to bring up the event handler. The code to handle the Click event should include two statements, one to clear the items in the ListBox and the other to add a header.

c) *Creating a counter variable.* The For Each...Next loop allows you to loop through each element in a specified collection. The For...Next loop from Exercise 17.12 handles the String (m_strSalaryRanges) and Integer (m_intSalaries) arrays. This presents a problem. You cannot loop through both of these arrays using the same element reference. (One is an Integer, and the other is a String.) To handle this you need to create a common counter variable, one that you will use to loop through the indices of both arrays. This is possible because the lengths of both arrays are the same.

d) *Adding an element reference.* It does not matter which array you decide to use in this exercise, because these arrays are of the same length. Declare an element reference with the correct data type.

e) *Create the For Each...Next loop.* Use the new element reference that you have created along with the array of your choice to create the For Each...Next loop statement.

f) *Adding text to the ListBox.* Adding the statement to output to the ListBox is exactly the same as the one from Exercise 17.12. The only difference will be the name of the counter variable that you decide to use.

g) *Increment the counter variable.* To successfully loop through both arrays and output the data, you need to increment the counter variable. This ensures that the proper data is added to the ListBox through each iteration.

Figure 20.27   Modified **Salary Survey** GUI.

20.12 (*Modified Shipping Hub Application*) Modify the **Shipping Hub** application created in this tutorial, so that the user can double click a package in the lstPackages ListBox. When a package number is double clicked, the package's information should be displayed in a MessageBox (Fig. 20.28).

a) *Copying and opening the template application.* Copy the ShippingHubModified folder from C:\Examples\Tutorial20\Exercises to C:\SimplyVB. Double click the ShippingHub.sln file in the ShippingHubModified folder to open the application in Visual Studio .NET.

b) *Viewing the event handler*. Click **ShippingHub.vb** in the **Solution Explorer** and select **View > Code**. Scroll to the end of code listing to locate the ListBox's Double-Click event handler.

c) *Initializing necessary variables*. To loop through the packages in the ArrayList of Packages, you need to create a reference of type Package. It is also helpful to create a String variable to store the information about the given package. Write code in the DoubleClick event handler to declare the String strPackage. A ListBox's DoubleClick event is raised when the control is double clicked.

d) *Check whether the user has selected a valid item*. To determine whether the user has selected a valid item (and not an empty element in the ListBox), write an If...Then statement to make sure that the ListBox is not empty when the user selected an item. [*Hint*: A SelectedIndex value of –1 means that no item is currently selected.]

e) *Writing a For Each...Next loop*. Use the Package reference you declared in *Step* c to create a For Each...Next loop with the m_objList collection.

f) *Determining whether the current selected package is correct*. Insert an If...Then statement to determine whether the current object that is selected from the m_objList collection matches the selected item from the ListBox. Because the packages are listed in the ListBox by their package number, use that information in your If...Then statement. Once the correct package is matched, store that package's information in the strPackage String.

g) *Inserting the Else statement*. Make sure to notify the user if an invalid item has been selected from the ListBox. If this occurs, add a message to the strPackage String that will be displayed in the MessageBox.

h) *Displaying the MessageBox*. Call the MessageBox's Show method to display the text you have added to the strPackage String. This displays either the information for the package they have selected or the message telling them they have selected an invalid package.

Figure 20.28 Modified **Shipping Hub** application GUI.

20.13 (*Controls* **Collection** *Application*) Visual Basic .NET provides many different types of collections. One such collection is the Controls collection, which is used to provide access to all of the controls on a Form. Create an application that uses the Controls collection and a For Each...Next loop to iterate through each control on the Form. As each control is encountered, add the control's name to a ListBox, and change the control's background color (in Fig. 20.29, Color.Wheat, is used).

a) *Copying and opening the template application*. Copy the ControlsCollection folder from C:\Examples\Tutorial20\Exercises to C:\SimplyVB. Double click the `ControlsCollection.sln` file in the `ControlsCollection` folder to open the application in Visual Studio .NET.

b) *Generating an event handler.* Double click the **Submit** Button in design view to create an event handler for the click event.

c) *Declaring a control variable.* Declare a reference of type `Control`. This reference represents each element in the For Each...Next statement as it iterates through each `Control` on the Form.

d) *Clearing the ListBox.* To ensure that the information in the `ListBox` is updated each time the **Submit** Button is clicked, clear the `ListBox` of all items.

e) *Writing a For Each...Next loop.* To create the For Each...Next loop, use the control variable that you created to iterate through the Form's `Controls` collection.

f) *Adding each control's name to the ListBox.* Use the `ListBox`'s Add method to insert the name of each control on the Form. Recall that a control's `Name` property contains the name of the control.

g) *Changing the control's background color.* Use the `Control`'s `BackColor` property to change the control's background color. Set the property to a new color using a member of the `Color` structure. [*Hint:* Type the word `Color` followed by the member-access operator to display a list of predefined colors using the *Intellisense* feature.] Note that the color of the `PictureBox` does not appear to change because its image displays in the control's foreground.

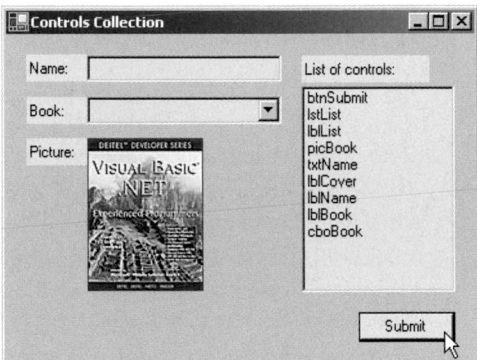

Figure 20.29 *Controls* Collection GUI.

What does this code do? ▶

20.14 What is the result of the following code?

```
1   Dim intList As Collections.ArrayList
2   Dim intListItems As Integer
3   Dim strOutput As String
4
5   intList = New ArrayList()
6   intList.Add(1)
7   intList.Add(3)
8   intList.Add(5)
9
10  For Each intListItems In intList
11      strOutput &= (" " & intListItems.ToString)
12  Next
13
14  MessageBox.Show(strOutput, "Mystery", _
15      MessageBoxButtons.OK, MessageBoxIcon.Information)
```

What's wrong with this code? ▶

20.15 This code should iterate through an array of `Packages` in `ArrayList` `objList` and print each package's number in Label `lblDisplay`. Find the error(s) in the following code.

```
1   Dim objValue As ArrayList
2
3   For Each objValue In objList
4     lblDisplay.Text &= (" " & objValue.PackageNumber)
5   Next
```

Programming Challenge ▶

20.16 (*Enhanced Shipping Hub Application*) Enhance the **Shipping Hub** application created in Exercise 20.12 to allow the user to move a maximum of five packages from the warehouse to a truck for shipping (Fig. 20.30). If you have not completed Exercise 20.12, follow the steps in Exercise 20.12 before proceeding to the next step. If you have completed Exercise 20.12, copy the code you added to the lstPackages ListBox DoubleClick event handler to the same event handler in this application before beginning the exercise.

a) *Copying and opening the template application.* Copy the ShippingHubEnhanced folder from C:\Examples\Tutorial20\Exercises to C:\SimplyVB. Double click the ShippingHub.sln file in the ShippingHubEnhanced folder to open the application in Visual Studio .NET. Notice that there are two GroupBoxes on the right side of the Form.

b) *Enabling the Ship Button.* The **Ship** Button should not be enabled until a package is selected in the lstPackage ListBox. Double click the lstPackage ListBox from design view to define the event handler. Use the Button's Enabled property to enable the Button if the SelectedIndex of the ListBox is not -1. This means that when the user selects a package from the ListBox, the user can send the package to the truck by clicking the **Ship** Button. Also, insert a line of code after the For Each...Next statement in the SelectedIndexChanged event handler to disable the **Ship** Button when a user chooses a different state.

c) *Defining the Ship Button's Click Event.* Double click the **Ship** Button in **Design View** to define the Click event.

d) *Incrementing the counter.* Because you are only allowing five packages to be "shipped," declare an instance variable that will track how many packages have been placed onto the truck. Increment the variable each time the **Ship** Button is clicked.

e) *Creating temporary variables.* Create two temporary Package references to store the correct package's information. Use objTempPackage as the reference to the element in the collection type of a For Each...Next statement, and the objTruckPackage as a reference to the package added to the truck.

f) *Using the If...Then...Else statement.* Use an If...Then...Else statement to allow packages to be placed onto the truck if the number of packages on the truck is less than five.

g) *Using the For Each...Next loop.* Use a For Each...Next loop to iterate through the values in m_objList. Each iteration should determine whether the current package is the one selected from the ListBox.

h) *Adding the package to the truck.* When the For Each...Next loop has located the correct package, add that package to the truck by adding the reference to objTempPackage to the truck's ArrayList, m_objTruckList. Then assign the value in objTempPackage (the package sent to the truck) to objTruckPackage.

i) *Removing the package.* When the For Each...Next loop completes, remove the package meant for the truck from m_objList and the lstPackages ListBox.

j) *Displaying the package in the ListBox.* Use a For Each...Next loop that iterates through each package in the m_objTruckList ArrayList and displays each package in the lstTruck ListBox.

k) *Refreshing the GUI.* Call the ClearControls and SetButtons methods to clear the TextBoxes and enable the appropriate Buttons. Also, set the **Ship** Button's Enabled property to False.

l) *Coding the Else statement.* Display a MessageBox that notifies the user if the number of packages on the truck is already five. Then disable the **Ship** Button.

Figure 20.30   Enhanced **Shipping Hub** GUI.

"Cat and Mouse" Painter Application

Introducing the Graphics Object and Mouse Events

Objectives

In this tutorial, you will learn to:
- Use mouse events to allow user interaction with an application.
- Handle MouseDown, MouseUp and MouseMove events.
- Use the Graphics object to draw circles on the Form.
- Determine which mouse button was pressed.

Outline

21.1 Test-Driving the Painter Application

21.2 Constructing the Painter Application

21.3 Using a Graphics Object

21.4 Handling the MouseDown Event

21.5 Handling the MouseUp Event

21.6 Handling the MouseMove Event

21.7 Distinguishing Between Mouse Buttons

21.8 Wrap-Up

The computer mouse is one of the most important input devices and is essential to the GUIs of Windows applications. With the mouse, the user can point to, click and drag items in applications. Clicking and releasing a mouse button are associated with events, as is moving the mouse. Every time you move the mouse, Windows interprets that event and redraws the mouse pointer as it moves across the screen.

In this tutorial, you create a **Painter** application that handles mouse events. The user clicks the left mouse button over the Form to enable drawing. By moving the mouse pointer over the Form with the left mouse button pressed, the user can create line drawings composed of small circles. In addition to learning how to draw a shape on the Form (a circle), you will learn how to set the shape's color. You will then learn how to stop drawing when the user releases the mouse button. You will also enable the user to erase a drawing by holding down the right mouse button.

21.1 Test-Driving the Painter Application

In this tutorial, you will create a **Painter** application. This application must meet the following requirements:

Application Requirements

The principal of an elementary school wants to introduce computers to children by appealing to their creative side. Many elementary-level applications test skills in mathematics, but the principal wishes to use an application that allows children to express their artistic skills. Develop an application that allows the student to "paint" on a Form, using the mouse. The application should draw when the user moves the mouse with the left mouse button held down and stop drawing when the left mouse button is released. The application draws many small blue-violet circles side by side to trace out lines, curves and shapes. An important part of any drawing application is the ability to erase mistakes or to clear the Form for more drawing room. The user can erase portions of the drawing by moving the mouse with the right mouse button held down.

You begin by test-driving the completed application.

Test-Driving the Painter Application

1. ***Opening the completed application.*** Navigate to the C:\Examples\Tutorial21\CompletedApplication\Painter folder. To open the completed application in Visual Studio .NET, double click `Painter.sln`.

2. ***Running the Painter application.*** Select **Debug > Start** to run the application. Figure 21.1 shows the executing **Painter** application before the user starts to draw.

Figure 21.1   **Painter** application before drawing.

3. ***Drawing with the mouse.*** To draw on the Form using the **Painter** application, press and hold down the left mouse button while the mouse pointer is anywhere over the Form (Fig. 21.2). To stop drawing, release the mouse button. Note that the application draws little blue-violet circles as you move the mouse while pressing the left mouse button. The size of these circles will vary depending on your display settings.

Drawing lines composed of small, colored circles

Figure 21.2   Drawing on the **Painter** application's Form.

4. ***Being creative.*** Draw a cat and a computer mouse, as shown in Fig. 21.3. Be creative and have fun—your drawing need not look like the image shown.

5. ***Using the eraser.*** Hold down the right mouse button and move the mouse pointer over part of your drawing. This "erases" the drawing wherever the mouse pointer comes into contact with the colored line (Fig. 21.4). You will see, when you add code to the application to erase, that you are actually drawing circles in Form's background color.

(cont.)

Figure 21.3   Drawing a cat and a computer mouse on the Form.

Erasing by drawing circles
that are the same color as
the Form's background

Figure 21.4   Erasing part of the drawing.

6. ***Terminating the application***. Click the running application's close box to terminate the application.

7. ***Closing the solution***. Select **File > Close Solution** to close the solution's files.

21.2 Constructing the Painter Application

Before you begin building the **Painter** application, you should review the application's functionality. The following pseudocode describes what happens when the user moves the mouse pointer over the application's Form:

> When a mouse button is pressed
>> If the left mouse button is pressed
>>> Draw a blue-violet circle at the position of the mouse pointer
>
>> Else if the right mouse button is pressed
>>> "Erase" by drawing a circle at the position of the mouse pointer in the Form's background color

The ACE table of Fig. 21.5 describes the mouse events associated with the **Painter** application's Form.

This tutorial starts by showing you how to use two mouse events—the event that occurs when you press a mouse button and the event that occurs when you release that mouse button. At first, your **Painter** application will draw a circle when the user presses or releases any mouse button. The circles drawn by pressing a mouse button will have a larger size than and a different color from the circles drawn by releasing the mouse button. Next, you will modify the application so that it draws when the user moves the mouse with a button pressed. If the user moves the mouse without pressing a mouse button, nothing will be drawn.

Action/Control/Event (ACE) Table for the Painter Application

Action	Control	Event
Draw a blue-violet circle if the left mouse button is pressed; draw a circle in the Form's background color if the right mouse button is pressed	FrmPainter	MouseMove
Set a variable indicating that the application should draw blue-violet circles	FrmPainter	MouseDown (left mouse button)
Set a variable indicating that the application should erase (that is, draw circles with the same color as the Form)	FrmPainter	MouseDown (right mouse button)
Set variables indicating that the application should neither draw nor erase	FrmPainter	MouseUp

Figure 21.5 **Painter** application's ACE table.

To complete the **Painter** application, you will need to add the eraser capability, which requires you to determine which mouse button the user presses. The last section of this tutorial will show you how to assign the drawing capability to the left mouse button and the eraser capability to the right mouse button.

21.3 Using a Graphics Object

Now that you have seen the pseudocode and ACE table, you are ready to begin building the **Painter** application. You will use a **Graphics** object to enable the user to draw on the Form. Class Graphics contains methods used for drawing text, lines, rectangles and other shapes. The box, *Creating a Graphics Object*, shows you how to create the **Painter** application's Graphics object.

Creating a Graphics Object

1. *Copying the template application to your work folder.* Copy the C:\Examples\Tutorial21\TemplateApplication\Painter folder to C:\SimplyVB.

2. *Opening the template application.* Double click the Painter.sln file to open the application in Visual Studio .NET.

3. *Creating a Graphics object.* Add lines 7–8 of Fig. 21.6 into the **Painter** application. Line 8 declares Graphics reference m_objGraphic. The **CreateGraphics** method (which is a member of class Form) creates a Graphics object with which you will draw shapes on the Form. Note that because you are writing code in the Form's class (FrmPainter), you do not need to use the member-access operator to access the Form's CreateGraphics method. Notice that the template already contains a declaration of constant m_intDIAMETER (line 5). We will discuss this constant shortly.

4. *Saving the application.* Select **File > Save All** to save the solution's files.

(cont.)

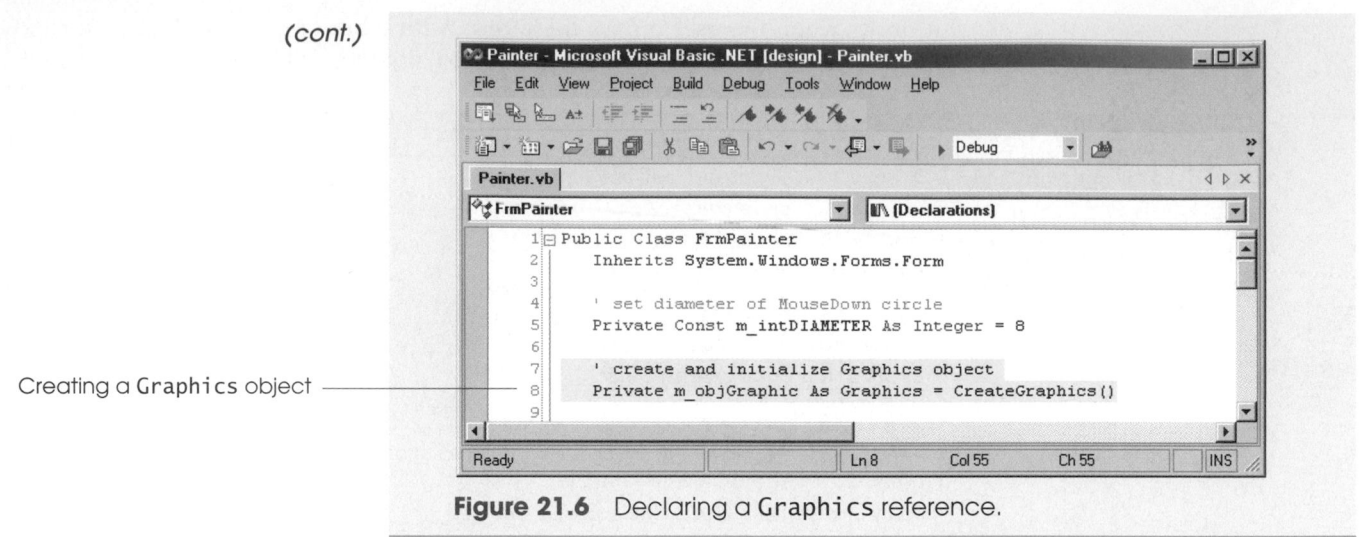

Creating a Graphics object

Figure 21.6 Declaring a Graphics reference.

SELF-REVIEW

1. To draw on a Form, use an object of class _____.

   a) `Graphics`   b) `Drawing`

   c) `Paint`   d) `Sketch`

2. The _____ method creates a Graphics object.

   a) `GetGraphics`   b) `MakeGraphics`

   c) `CreateGraphics`   d) `InitializeGraphics`

Answers: 1) a. 2) c.

21.4 Handling the MouseDown Event

This section begins our discussion of handling **mouse events**, which are generated when the mouse is used to interact with the Form or controls on the Form. In the **Painter** application, the mouse interacts exclusively with the Form. (There are no controls on the Form.)

A Form's **MouseDown** event occurs when a mouse button is pressed while the mouse pointer is over the Form. You will learn how to add a MouseDown event handler to your application in the box, *Handling the MouseDown Event.* You will notice that, when you run your application after following the steps in this box, you can press any mouse button to draw a circle on the Form. When you add the eraser capability to the **Painter** application in Section 21.7, you will learn how to determine which mouse button was pressed.

Handling the MouseDown Event

1. **Generating the MouseDown event handler.** To generate the MouseDown event handler, select **(Base Class Events)** from the Class Name ComboBox (Fig. 21.7). Then select MouseDown from the Method Name ComboBox.

   This generates the event handler FrmPainter_MouseDown (Fig. 21.8). As always, you should add a comment and format your code to improve readability (lines 52–57). The application invokes FrmPainter_MouseDown when the user generates the Form's MouseDown event by pressing a mouse button when the mouse pointer is over the Form FrmPainter.

   Notice that the second argument passed to event handler FrmPainter_MouseDown is a variable of type **MouseEventArgs**. This MouseEventArgs object (referenced by e) contains information about the MouseDown event, including the coordinates of the mouse pointer when the mouse button was pressed on the Form.

(cont.)

Class Name ComboBox with
(Base Class Events) selected

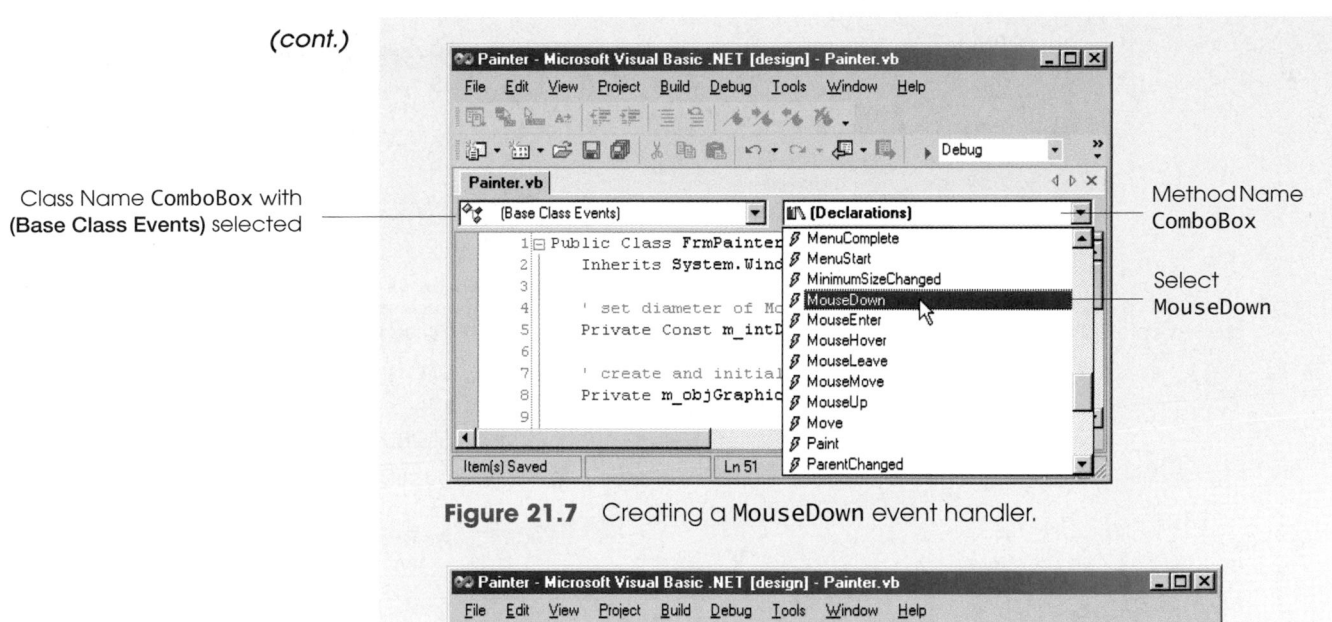

Figure 21.7 Creating a **MouseDown** event handler.

MouseEventArgs argument

Figure 21.8 MouseDown event handler generated for **FrmPainter**.

Note that the *x*- and *y*-coordinates of the MouseEventArgs object are relative to the top-left corner Form or control that raises the event. Point *(0,0)* represents the upper-left corner of the Form. If you wish to access the *x*-coordinate of the mouse, use property **X** of reference e. To access the *y*-coordinate of the mouse, use property **Y** of reference e.

2. ***Drawing on the Form whenever a mouse button is clicked.*** Add lines 57–59 of Fig. 21.9 to the MouseDown event handler. The **FillEllipse** method of class Graphics draws an ellipse on the Form. Recall that you declared m_objGraphic as your Graphics reference in the box, *Creating a Graphics Object*. Figure 21.10 shows a diagram of a general ellipse. The dotted rectangle is known as the ellipse's **bounding box**. The bounding box specifies an ellipse's height, width and location on the Form.

The first argument passed to the FillEllipse method is a **brush**, which can be used to fill shapes with colors. In this case, the **SolidBrush** class, which fills a shape using a single color, is specified as the brush. The color of the brush is specified in the call to the constructor. The color you select (Color.BlueViolet) is a member of the **Color** structure, which contains many predefined colors. For a complete list of predefined colors in Visual Basic .NET, simply type the word Color followed by a dot, and the *Intellisense* feature will provide a drop-down list of over 100 pre-defined colors (Fig. 21.11).

(cont.)

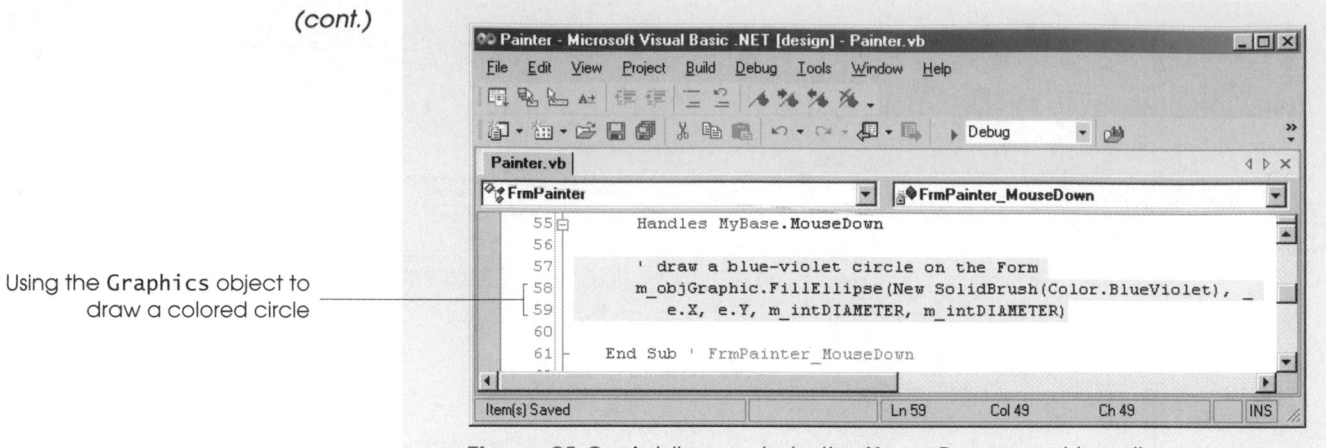

Figure 21.9 Adding code to the **MouseDown** event handler.

Using the **Graphics** object to draw a colored circle

Figure 21.10 General ellipse.

The second and third arguments to the **FillEllipse** method specify the *x*- and *y*-coordinates of the upper-left corner of the bounding box, relative to the upper-left corner of the **Form**. In this application, you use the *x*- and *y*-coordinates of the mouse (returned by properties X and Y of **MouseEventArgs** reference **e**). The fourth and fifth arguments passed to the **FillEllipse** method (constant **m_intDIAMETER**) specify the height and width of the bounding box. An ellipse with equal width and height is a circle—this method call draws a blue-violet circle.

Type **Color** followed by a dot (.) to access *Intellisense*

Figure 21.11 Selecting a color by using *Intellisense*.

(cont.)

The Graphics object provides methods for drawing shapes other than ellipses. You will learn about these methods in Tutorial 26. Note that the *x*- and *y*-coordinates the Graphics object uses to draw a shape are relative to the control or Form that created it. In this case, the Graphics object draws shapes at positions relative to the Form.

3. *Saving the solution.* Select **File > Save All** to save the solution's files.

4. *Run the application.* Select **Debug > Start** to execute the application. Notice that a small blue-violet circle is drawn when a mouse button is pressed while the mouse pointer is over the Form (Fig. 21.12).

Figure 21.12   Running the application.

21.5 Handling the MouseUp Event

Using the application, you can click anywhere on the Form and place a blue-violet circle. To enhance the application further, you will place a green circle on the Form when the user releases the mouse button. A Form's **MouseUp** event is generated when a mouse button is released when the pointer is over the Form. You will add this functionality in the box, *Handling the MouseUp Event*.

Handling the *MouseUp* **Event**

1. *Adding a second diameter.* Add lines 7–8 of Fig. 21.13 to your application (above the initialization of the Graphics reference and below the initialization of constant m_intDIAMETER). These lines declare a second constant that stores the diameter of a smaller circle. A circle with this diameter (in pixels) will be drawn whenever the user releases a mouse button.

2. *Adding the MouseUp event handler.* Select **(Base Class Events)** from the Class Name ComboBox, as you did in Fig. 21.7. Then select MouseUp from the Method Name ComboBox. This creates an empty event handler called FrmPainter_MouseUp (Fig. 21.14).

(cont.)

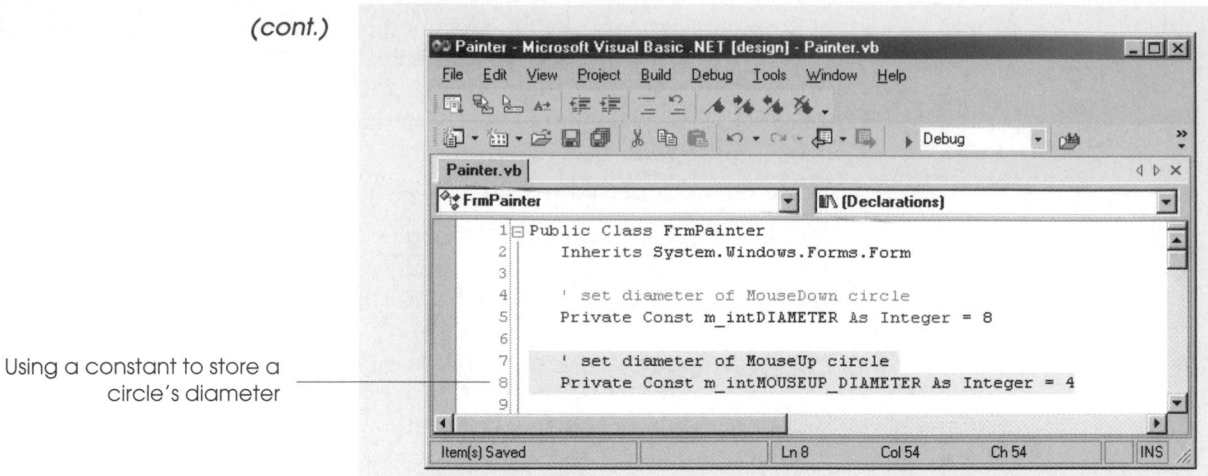

Using a constant to store a circle's diameter

Figure 21.13 Declaring a constant for use in the **MouseUp** event handler.

Add the comments on lines 66 and 71 to your application. This header is similar to the header for the **MouseDown** event handler (the only difference is that the word **Down** is changed to **Up**). The **MouseUp** event handler executes only when a mouse button is released.

MouseUp event handler after commenting and formatting

Figure 21.14 **MouseUp** empty event handler.

3. ***Drawing a circle when the user releases a mouse button.*** Add lines 71–72 of Fig. 21.15 to the **MouseUp** event handler to draw a circle at the position of the mouse pointer on the **Form** whenever the user releases the mouse button. The diameter of each "mouse up" circle is only half the diameter of the **BlueViolet** circles drawn by the **MouseDown** event handler that is called when a mouse button is pressed.

Drawing a green circle with half the diameter of the blue-violet circle

Figure 21.15 **MouseUp** event handler code.

(cont.)   4. ***Running the application.*** Select **Debug > Start** to execute the application. Press a mouse button, move the mouse pointer to a new location and release the button. Notice that a `BlueViolet` circle is drawn when you press any mouse button and that a `Green` circle is drawn when you release the mouse button.

5. ***Saving the solution.*** Select **File > Save All** to save all the solution's files.

Drawing a flower using only `MouseUp` and `MouseDown` event handlers

Pressing the mouse button and releasing it without moving the mouse pointer

Pressing mouse button, then releasing after moving pointer

Figure 21.16   Running the application.

6. ***Closing the application.*** Click the running application's close box.

SELF-REVIEW   1. Releasing a mouse button generates a _____ event.

a) `MouseRelease`   b) `MouseUp`

c) `MouseOff`   d) `MouseClick`

2. The second and third arguments of the `FillEllipse` method specify the *x*- and *y*-coordinates of the _____.

a) ellipse's center   b) bounding box's lower-left corner

c) bounding box's upper-right corner   d) bounding box's upper-left corner

Answers: 1) b. 2) d.

21.6 Handling the `MouseMove` Event

Currently, the application allows you to draw only isolated circles when a mouse button is pressed or released. It does not yet allow you to draw more sophisticated shapes and designs. Next, you will enhance your application to provide more drawing capabilities. The application should continuously draw `BlueViolet` circles as long as the mouse is being dragged (that is, moved with a button pressed). If the mouse button is not pressed, moving the mouse across the `Form` should not draw anything. To add this functionality, you will begin by modifying your two event handlers in the box, *Modifying the **Painter** Application*.

Modifying the Painter Application

1. ***Adding a Boolean variable to specify whether a mouse button is pressed.*** Delete the constant `m_intMOUSEUP_DIAMETER` (lines 7–8 of Fig. 21.13) and add lines 4–5 of Fig. 21.17 to your application (above the initialization of `m_intDIAMETER`). This line declares and initializes the `Boolean` variable `m_blnShouldPaint`. The application must be able to determine whether a mouse button is pressed, because the application should draw on the `Form` only when the mouse button is held down.

(cont.)

You will alter the MouseDown and MouseUp event handlers so that m_blnShouldPaint is True when any mouse button is held down and False when the mouse button is released. When the application is first loaded, it should not "paint" anything, so this instance variable is initialized to False.

Declaring and setting an instance variable to control painting —

Figure 21.17 Boolean instance variable m_blnShouldPaint is declared and set to False.

2. ***Altering the MouseDown event handler.*** Remove the code inside the Mouse-Down event handler, leaving just the procedure header and the End Sub statement (as in Fig. 21.8). Add line 60 of Fig. 21.18 to the MouseDown event handler to set m_blnShouldPaint to True. This indicates that a mouse button is pressed.

Allow drawing when mouse button is pressed —

Figure 21.18 Setting m_blnShouldPaint to True.

3. ***Altering the MouseUp event handler.*** Remove the code inside the MouseUp event handler, leaving just the procedure header and End Sub statement (as in Fig. 21.14). Add line 69 of Fig. 21.19 to set m_blnShouldPaint to False. This indicates that a mouse button has been released.

4. ***Saving the application.*** Select **File > Save All** to save the solution's files.

(cont.)

Disable drawing when
mouse button is released

Figure 21.19 Setting m_blnShouldPaint to False.

You have altered the event handlers to set the value of the m_blnShouldPaint variable to indicate whether a mouse button is pressed. Next, you will handle the **MouseMove** event, which is raised whenever the mouse moves. Whenever you move the mouse over the **Painter** application's Form, the application invokes the Mouse-Move event handler. You define the MouseMove event handler in the box, *Adding the MouseMove Event Handler.*

Adding the *MouseMove* Event Handler

1. ***Adding the *MouseMove* event handler.*** Select **(Base Class Events)** from the Class Name ComboBox as in Fig. 21.7. Then select MouseMove from the Method Name ComboBox. This generates the empty MouseMove event handler FrmPainter_MouseMove (Fig. 21.20). Add comments to lines 73 and 78.

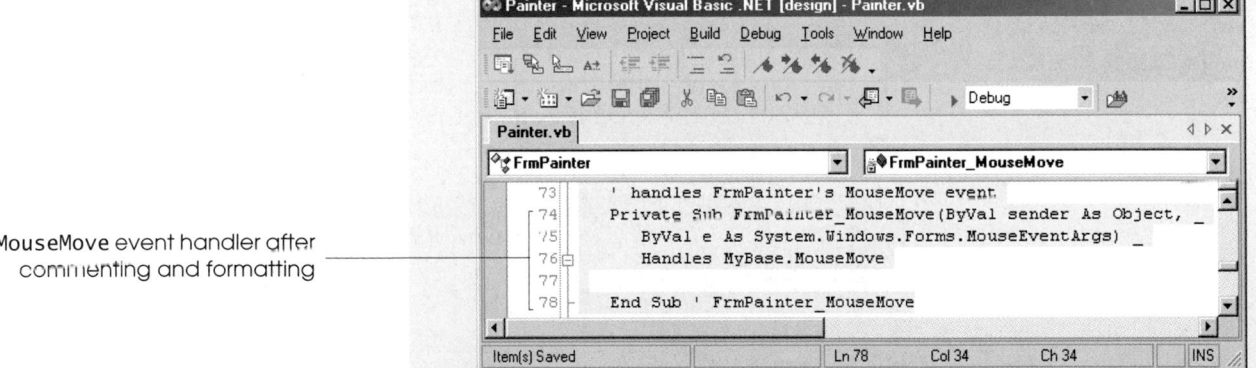

MouseMove event handler after
commenting and formatting

Figure 21.20 MouseMove empty event handler.

2. ***Adding code to the *MouseMove* event handler.*** Add lines 78–82 of Fig. 21.21 to the MouseMove event handler. This event handler executes each time the mouse is moved. The If...Then statement tests the value of m_blnShouldPaint. If this variable contains True (a mouse button is pressed), the FillEllipse method draws a BlueViolet circle on the Form. If m_blnShouldPaint contains False (no mouse button is pressed), then nothing is drawn.

3. ***Saving your application.*** Select **File > Save All** to save the solution's files.

4. ***Running the application.*** Select **Debug > Start** to run the application. Try drawing various shapes and designs on the Form. Note that you can draw lines using any mouse button.

(cont.)

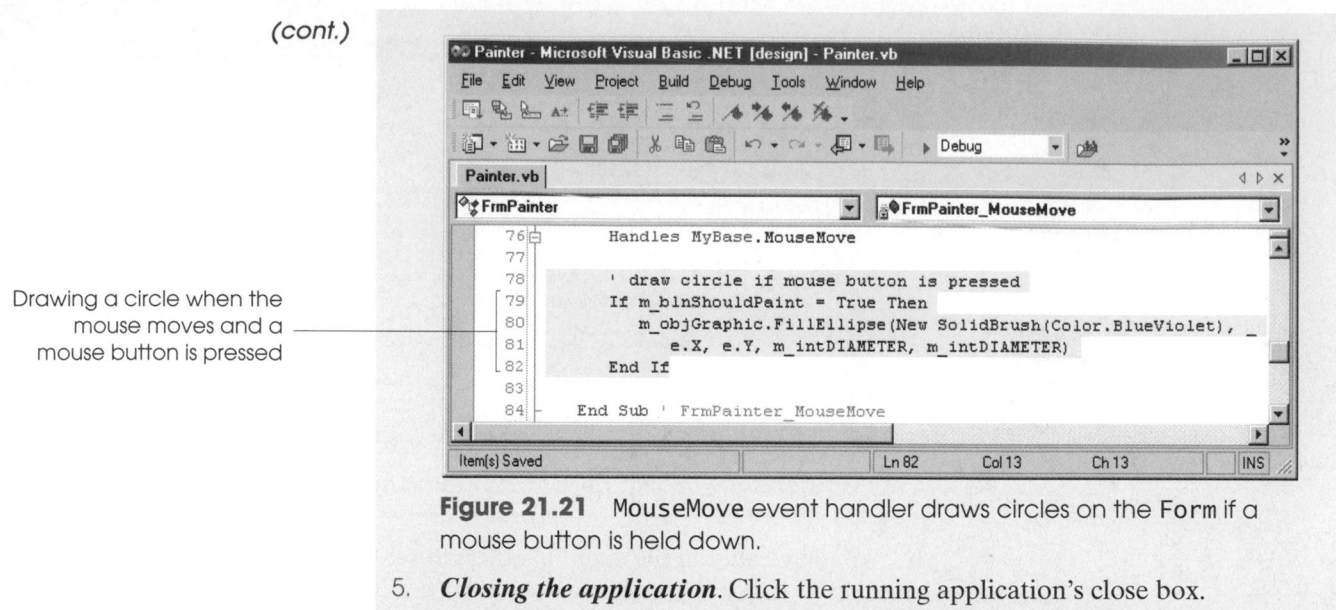

Drawing a circle when the mouse moves and a mouse button is pressed

Figure 21.21 MouseMove event handler draws circles on the Form if a mouse button is held down.

5. *Closing the application*. Click the running application's close box.

21.7 Distinguishing Between Mouse Buttons

Now that your application allows the user to draw using the mouse, you are going to add the code that allows the user to "erase" by moving the mouse over the drawing with the right mouse button pressed. You also will alter the application so that the user draws by moving the mouse with only the left mouse button pressed. To do this, you will need to determine which mouse button was pressed. You learn how to do this in the box, *Distinguishing Between Mouse Buttons*.

Distinguishing Between Mouse Buttons

1. *Adding a* Boolean *variable to specify whether the application should erase while the mouse pointer is moving.* Add lines 4–5 of Fig. 21.22 to your application (above the initialization of m_blnShouldPaint). Instance variable m_blnShouldErase specifies whether moving the mouse pointer should act like an eraser.

Declaring and setting an instance variable to control erasing

Figure 21.22 Boolean instance variable m_blnShouldErase is declared and set to False.

2. *Determining which mouse button was pressed.* Replace the code in event handler FrmPainter_MouseDown with lines 63–70 of Fig. 21.23. The **Button** property of the MouseEventArgs object (referenced by e) specifies which mouse button was pressed. The **MouseButtons** enumeration defines constants that represent the mouse buttons.

(cont.)

The three most common mouse buttons—**Right**, **Left** and **Middle**—are included in MouseButtons. If the left mouse button was pressed (line 64), line 65 sets m_blnShouldPaint to True, which indicates that dragging the mouse should draw. If the right mouse button was pressed (line 68), line 69 sets m_blnShouldErase to True, which indicates that dragging the mouse should erase any blue-violet circles touched by the mouse pointer.

Using the **Button** property to enable drawing

Using the **Button** property to enable erasing

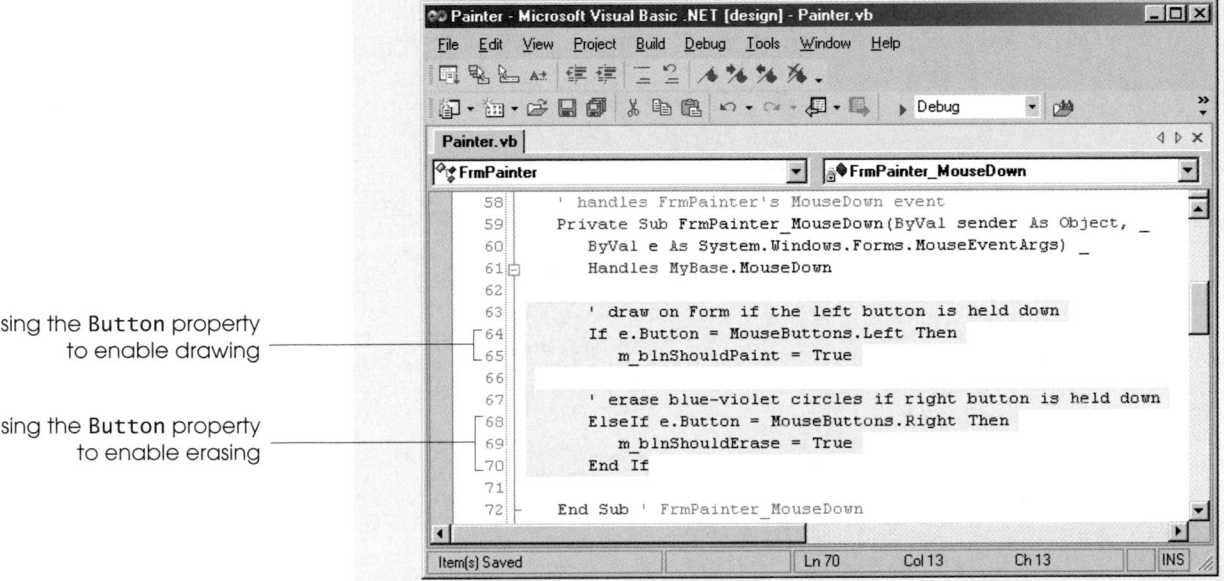

```
58        ' handles FrmPainter's MouseDown event
59        Private Sub FrmPainter_MouseDown(ByVal sender As Object, _
60            ByVal e As System.Windows.Forms.MouseEventArgs) _
61            Handles MyBase.MouseDown
62
63            ' draw on Form if the left button is held down
64            If e.Button = MouseButtons.Left Then
65                m_blnShouldPaint = True
66
67            ' erase blue-violet circles if right button is held down
68            ElseIf e.Button = MouseButtons.Right Then
69                m_blnShouldErase = True
70            End If
71
72        End Sub ' FrmPainter_MouseDown
```

Figure 21.23 Determining which mouse button was pressed.

Notice that only one of the variables can be True at one time. For example, if m_blnShouldPaint is True, then m_blnShouldErase is False. To ensure this, both variables are set to False when the mouse button is released. (See *Step 3*.)

3. ***Changing the MouseUp event handler.*** Add line 80 of Fig. 21.24 to the FrmPainter_MouseUp event handle. The application should not erase or draw when no mouse buttons are pressed. Line 80 sets m_blnShouldErase to False to indicate that the mouse pointer should not act as an eraser. Note that m_blnShouldPaint is also set to False.

Disabling erasing when a mouse button is released

```
74        ' handles FrmPainter's MouseUp event
75        Private Sub FrmPainter_MouseUp(ByVal sender As Object, _
76            ByVal e As System.Windows.Forms.MouseEventArgs) _
77            Handles MyBase.MouseUp
78
79            m_blnShouldPaint = False    ' do not draw on the Form
80            m_blnShouldErase = False    ' do not erase
81
82        End Sub ' FrmPainter_MouseUp
```

Figure 21.24 Setting m_blnShouldErase to False when a mouse button is released.

(cont.)

4. ***Drawing when the left mouse button is pressed.*** Replace the code in event handler FrmPainter_MouseMove with lines 89–99 of Fig. 21.25. If m_blnShouldPaint is True (line 90), lines 91–92 draw a BlueViolet circle. Your changes to the MouseDown event handler make m_blnShouldPaint True when the left mouse button is pressed. As a result, the application only draws BlueViolet circles when the user drags the mouse while pressing the left mouse button.

Drawing circles if right mouse button is pressed while the mouse moves

Erasing by drawing circles with the Form's background color

Figure 21.25   Changing the MouseMove event handler to allow erasing.

5. ***Erasing when the right mouse button is pressed.*** The MouseMove event handler does not actually erase anything. Instead, when m_blnShouldErase is True (line 95 of Fig. 21.25), the FillEllipse method (lines 96–97) draws a circle that is the same size as the BlueViolet circle and has the same color as the Form's background. This allows the mouse pointer to act like an eraser. Notice that the first argument to FillEllipse is BackColor. Much like the CreateGraphics method, the BackColor property of the Form can be accessed without the member-access operator. The **BackColor** property returns the Form's background color as a Color value.

6. ***Saving your application.*** Select **File > Save All** to save the solution's files.

7. ***Running the application.*** Select **Debug > Start** to run the application. Try drawing various shapes and designs on the Form.

8. ***Closing the application.*** Click the running application's close box and select **File > Close Solution**.

Figure 21.26 presents the completed **Painter** application's code.

```
1   Public Class FrmPainter
2       Inherits System.Windows.Forms.Form
3
4       ' specify whether moving the mouse should erase
5       Private m_blnShouldErase As Boolean = False
6
```

Figure 21.26   **Painter** application's code. (Part 1 of 2.)

```
 7    ' specify whether moving the mouse should draw
 8    Private m_blnShouldPaint As Boolean = False
 9
10    ' set diameter of MouseDown circle
11    Private Const m_intDIAMETER As Integer = 8
12
13    ' create and initialize Graphics object
14    Private m_objGraphic As Graphics = CreateGraphics()
15
16    ' Windows Form Designer generated code
17
18    ' handles FrmPainter's MouseDown event
19    Private Sub FrmPainter_MouseDown(ByVal sender As Object, _
20       ByVal e As System.Windows.Forms.MouseEventArgs) _
21       Handles MyBase.MouseDown
22
23       ' draw on Form if the left button is held down
24       If e.Button = MouseButtons.Left Then
25          m_blnShouldPaint = True
26
27       ' erase blue-violet circles if right button is held down
28       ElseIf e.Button = MouseButtons.Right Then
29          m_blnShouldErase = True
30       End If
31
32    End Sub ' FrmPainter_MouseDown
33
34    ' handles FrmPainter's MouseUp event
35    Private Sub FrmPainter_MouseUp(ByVal sender As Object, _
36       ByVal e As System.Windows.Forms.MouseEventArgs) _
37       Handles MyBase.MouseUp
38
39       m_blnShouldPaint = False   ' do not draw on the Form
40       m_blnShouldErase = False   ' do not erase
41
42    End Sub ' FrmPainter_MouseUp
43
44    ' handles FrmPainter's MouseMove event
45    Private Sub FrmPainter_MouseMove(ByVal sender As Object, _
46       ByVal e As System.Windows.Forms.MouseEventArgs) _
47       Handles MyBase.MouseMove
48
49       ' draw circle if left mouse button is pressed
50       If m_blnShouldPaint = True Then
51          m_objGraphic.FillEllipse(New SolidBrush(Color.BlueViolet), _
52             e.X, e.Y, m_intDIAMETER, m_intDIAMETER)
53
54       ' mouse pointer "erases" if right mouse button is pressed
55       ElseIf m_blnShouldErase = True Then
56          m_objGraphic.FillEllipse( New SolidBrush(BackColor), _
57             e.X, e.Y, m_intDIAMETER, m_intDIAMETER)
58
59       End If
60
61    End Sub ' FrmPainter_MouseMove
62
63 End Class ' FrmPainter
```

Property **Button** specifies which button was pressed

Enumeration **MouseButtons** specifies constants for the mouse button

Method **FillEllipse** used to draw a **BlueViolet** ellipse

Create a **Brush** with the Form's background color

Figure 21.26   Painter application's code. (Part 2 of 2.)

SELF-REVIEW

1. Moving the mouse pointer generates a _____ event.

   a) MouseMove
   b) MousePositionChanged
   c) MouseMoved
   d) MouseChanged

2. The _____ enumeration specifies constants for the mouse buttons.

   a) MouseButtons
   b) Buttons
   c) MouseOptions
   d) ButtonOptions

Answers: 1) a. 2) a.

21.8 Wrap-Up

In this tutorial, you learned the essential elements of mouse-event handling. You handled three common mouse events—MouseMove, MouseUp and MouseDown. You learned to create mouse event handlers associated with a Form. You generated these event handlers by selecting the appropriate mouse event from the Method Name ComboBox after selecting **(Base Class Events)** from the Class Name ComboBox.

You used mouse events and a Graphics object in the **Painter** application. You invoked the CreateGraphics method to create a Graphics object. You used the FillEllipse method of the Graphics class to draw a solid circle on the Form. You learned how to use a SolidBrush object to draw a shape in a single, solid color. You used a member of the Color structure to specify the brush's color.

The **Painter** application uses mouse events to determine what the user wants to do. The user moves the mouse with the left mouse button held down to draw on the Form. Moving the mouse across the Form without pressing a button does not draw anything on the Form.

You learned to distinguish which mouse button was pressed. You used this to provide the **Painter** application with an eraser. When users move the mouse with the right mouse button pressed, the **Painter** application draws circles with the same background color as the Form.

To build the **Painter** application, you used MouseEventArgs objects, which are passed to mouse event handlers and provide information about mouse events. Properties X and Y of the MouseEventArgs object specify the *x*- and *y*-coordinates where the mouse event occurred. The Button property specifies which (if any) mouse button was pressed. You used constants defined by the MouseButtons enumeration to determine which button the Button property specified.

In the next tutorial, you will learn how to use event handlers that respond to user interactions with the keyboard. You will then build an application that uses keyboard events. The application will also teach you how to create menus and dialogs.

SKILLS SUMMARY

Raising Events with a Mouse

■ Pressing a mouse's buttons and moving the mouse raise events.

Handling Mouse Events

■ The MouseEventArgs class contains information about mouse events, such as the *x*- and *y*-coordinates where the mouse event occurred. Each mouse-event handler receives an object of class MouseEventArgs as an argument.

■ Moving the mouse raises event MouseMove.

■ Pressing a mouse button raises event MouseDown.

■ Releasing a mouse button raises event MouseUp.

Distinguishing Between Mouse Buttons

■ The Button property of MouseEventArgs specifies which mouse button was pressed.

■ The MouseButtons enumeration specifies the constants Left, Right and Middle for mouse buttons. These are used to determine which button was pressed.

Creating an Event Handler for a Mouse Event Associated with a Form

■ Select **(Base Class Events)** from the Class Name ComboBox. Then select the appropriate event from the Method Name ComboBox.

Drawing on a Form

■ Graphics methods are used to draw shapes on a Form or a control.

■ Create a Graphics object (by invoking the Form's CreateGraphics method) to access methods for drawing shapes.

Drawing a Solid Ellipse

■ Use the Graphics method FillEllipse to draw a solid ellipse.

■ Pass a SolidBrush object to the FillEllipse method to specify the shape's interior color.

■ Specify the color, the height and width of the bounding box and the coordinates of the bounding box's upper-left corner. When the height and width of the bounding box are equal, a circle is drawn.

KEY TERMS

Buttons property—The property of the MouseEventArgs class that specifies which (if any) mouse button is pressed.

Color structure—The structure that specifies the system-defined colors available for drawing.

CreateGraphics method—The method that creates a Graphics object on a Form or control.

BackColor property—The property that returns the Color value used as the background color of the Form or control.

FillEllipse method—The method of the Graphics class that draws an ellipse. This method takes as arguments a brush, a Color, the coordinates of the ellipse's bounding box's upper-left corner and the width and height of the bounding box.

Graphics class—A class that defines methods for drawing shapes.

mouse event—An event that is generated when a user interacts with an application using the computer's mouse.

MouseButtons enumeration—An enumeration that defines constants, such as Left, Right and Middle, to specify mouse buttons.

MouseDown event—An event generated when a mouse button is pressed.

MouseEventArgs class—The class that specifies information about a mouse event.

MouseMove event—The event generated when a mouse pointer is moved.

MouseUp event—The event generated when the mouse button is released.

SolidBrush class—The class that defines a brush that draws with a single color.

X property—The property of class MouseEventArgs that specifies the *x*-coordinate of the mouse event.

Y property—The property of class MouseEventArgs that specifies the *y*-coordinate of the mouse event.

CONTROLS, EVENTS, PROPERTIES & METHODS

Form The class that represents an application's GUI.

■ *Events*

Load—The event raised when an application initially executes.

MouseDown—The event raised when a mouse button is clicked.

MouseMove—The event raised when the mouse pointer is moved.

MouseUp—The event raised when a mouse button is released.

■ *Property*

BackColor—This property specifies the background color of the Form.

■ *Method*

CreateGraphics—This method creates a Graphics object.

Graphics The class that contains methods used to draw text, lines and shapes.

■ *Method*

FillEllipse—This method draws a solid ellipse of a specified size and color at the specified location.

MouseEventArgs The class that contains information about mouse events.

■ *Properties*

Buttons—The property that specifies which (if any) mouse button was pressed.
X—The property that specifies the *x*-coordinate of the mouse event.
Y—The property that specifies the *y*-coordinate of the mouse event.

MULTIPLE-CHOICE QUESTIONS

21.1 The *x*- and *y*-coordinates of the MouseEventArgs object are relative to _____.

a) the screen   b) the application
c) the Form or control that contains the control that raised the event
d) None of the above.

21.2 The _____ method of the Graphics class draws a solid ellipse.

a) FillEllipse   b) Ellipse
c) SolidEllipse   d) DrawEllipse

21.3 The _____ object passed to a mouse event handler contains information about the mouse event that was raised.

a) EventHandler   b) MouseEventHandler
c) MouseEventArgs   d) EventArgs

21.4 The _____ event is raised when a mouse button is pressed.

a) MousePress   b) MouseClick
c) MouseDown   d) MouseButtonDown

21.5 A _____ is used to fill a shape with color using a Graphics object.

a) painter   b) brush
c) paint bucket   d) marker

21.6 A _____ event is raised every time the mouse interacts with a control.

a) control   b) mouse pointer
c) mouse   d) user

21.7 The _____ property of MouseEventArgs specifies which mouse button was pressed.

a) Source   b) Button
c) WhichButton   d) ButtonPressed

21.8 The _____ class contains methods for drawing text, lines, rectangles and other shapes.

a) Pictures   b) Drawings
c) Graphics   d) Illustrations

21.9 An ellipse with its _____ is a circle.

a) height twice the length of its width   b) width set to zero
c) height half the length of its width   d) height equal to its width

21.10 The _____ method creates a Graphics object.

a) NewGraphics

b) CreateGraphics

c) PaintGraphics

d) InitializeGraphics

EXERCISES

21.11 *(Line Length Application)* The **Line Length** application should draw a straight black line on the Form and calculate the length of the line. The line should begin at the coordinates where the mouse button is pressed and should stop at the point where the mouse button is released. The application should display the line's length (that is, the distance between the two endpoints) in the Label **Length =**. Use the following formula to calculate the line's length, where (x_1, y_1) is the first endpoint (the coordinates where the mouse button is pressed) and (x_2, y_2) is the second endpoint (the coordinates where the mouse button is released). To calculate the distance (or length) between the two points, use the following equation:

$$d = \sqrt{(x_1 - x_2)^2 + (y_1 - y_2)^2}$$

To draw a straight line, you need to use the **DrawLine** method on a Graphics object. When drawing lines, you should use a **Pen** object, which is an object used to specify characteristics of lines and curves. Use the following method call to draw a black line between the two points using a Graphics object reference objGraphic:

```
objGraphic.DrawLine(New Pen(Color.Black), x₁, y₁, x₂, y₂)
```

a) *Copying and opening the template application.* Copy the LineLength folder from C:\Examples\Tutorial21\Exercises to C:\SimplyVB. Double click the Line-Length.sln file to open the application in Visual Studio .NET.

b) *Declaring instance variables.* Declare and initialize a reference to a Graphics object that you will use to draw a line. Then declare four Integers in which you will store the *x*- and *y*-coordinates of the two points.

c) *Adding a MouseDown event handler.* Create a MouseDown event handler. Add code to the MouseDown event handler to store the coordinates of the first endpoint of the line.

d) *Creating the Distance method.* Define a Function procedure named Length that returns the distance between two endpoints as a Double. The Function procedure should use the following statement to perform the line length calculation, where intXDistance is the difference between the *x*-coordinates of the two points and intYDistance is the difference between the *y*-coordinates of the two points:

```
Math.Sqrt((intXDistance ^ 2) + (intYDistance ^ 2))
```

e) *Adding a MouseUp event handler.* Create a MouseUp event handler. First store the coordinates of the line's second endpoint. Then call the Length method to obtain the distance between the two endpoints (the line's length). Finally, display the line on the Form and the line's length in the **Length =** Label, as in Fig. 21.27.

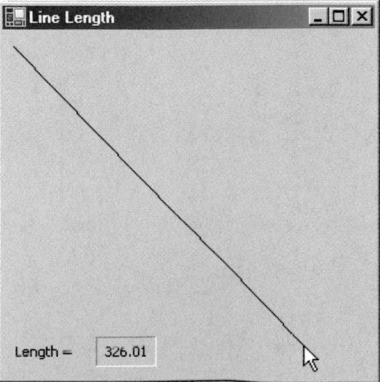

Figure 21.27 **Line Length** application's GUI.

21.12 *(Circle Painter Application)* The **Circle Painter** application should draw a blue circle with a randomly chosen size when the user presses a mouse button anywhere over the Form (Fig. 21.28). The application should randomly select a circle diameter in the range from 5 to 199, inclusive. To draw a blue circle with a given diameter (intDiameter), use the following statement:

```
objGraphic.DrawEllipse(New Pen(Color.Blue), x, y, _
    intDiameter, intDiameter)
```

The DrawEllipse method, when passed a Pen (instead of a brush) as an argument, draws the outline of an ellipse. Recall that an ellipse is a circle if the height and width arguments are the same (in this case, the randomly selected intDiameter). Use the *x*- and *y*-coordinates of the MouseDown event as the *x*- and *y*-coordinates of the circle's bounding box (that is, the second and third arguments to the DrawEllipse method). Notice that the first argument to the DrawEllipse method is a Pen object. See Exercise 21.11 for a description of Pen.

a) *Copying and opening the template application.* Copy the CirclePainter folder from C:\Examples\Tutorial21\Exercises to C:\SimplyVB. Double click the CirclePainter.sln file to open the application in Visual Studio .NET.

b) *Adding a MouseDown event handler.* Create a MouseDown event handler. In the event handler, retrieve the *x*- and *y*-coordinates of the location the mouse pointer when a mouse button was pressed. Then generate a random number to use as the circle's diameter, using a Random object, and store it in a variable. Finally, call the DrawEllipse method on a reference to a Graphics object to draw a blue circle on the Form with the diameter generated by the Random object.

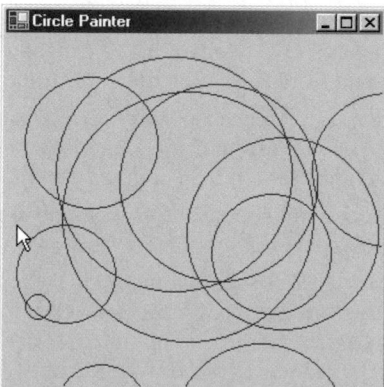

Figure 21.28   **Circle Painter** application's GUI.

21.13 *(Advanced Circle Painter Application)* In this exercise, you will enhance the application you created in Exercise 21.12. The advanced **Circle Painter** application should draw blue circles with a randomly generated diameter when the user presses the left mouse button. When the user presses the right mouse button, the application should draw a red circle with a randomly generated diameter (Fig. 21.29).

Figure 21.29   Advanced **Circle Painter** application's GUI.

a) *Copying and opening the application.* Make a copy of the CirclePainter folder from Exercise 21.12 in C:\SimplyVB. If you have not completed Exercise 21.12, follow the steps in Exercise 21.12 to complete the application. Rename the copy AdvancedCirclePainter. Double click the CirclePainter.sln file in C:\SimplyVB\AdvancedCirclePainter to open the application in Visual Studio .NET.

b) *Drawing the appropriate circle.* Use the Button property of the MouseEventArgs reference, e, to determine which mouse button was pressed. Finally, call the DrawEllipse method on a reference to a Graphics object to draw a blue circle on the Form if the left mouse button was clicked, or a red circle if the right mouse button was clicked.

What does this code do? ▶

21.14 Consider the example in Fig. 21.26. Suppose we change the MouseMove event handler to the code below. What happens when the user moves the mouse? Assume that a Label lblDisplay has been placed on the Form.

```
1   Private Sub FrmPainter_MouseMove(ByVal sender As System.Object, _
2       ByVal e As System.Windows.Forms.MouseEventArgs)
3       Handles MyBase.MouseMove
4
5       lblDisplay.Text = "I'm at " & e.X & ", " & e.Y & "."
6   End Sub ' FrmPainter_MouseMove
```

What's wrong with this code? ▶

21.15 The following code should draw a BlueViolet circle of diameter 4 that corresponds to the movement of the mouse. Find the error(s) in the following code:

```
1   Private Sub FrmPainter_MouseMove(ByVal sender As System.Object, _
2       ByVal e As System.Windows.Forms.MouseEventArgs) _
3       Handles MyBase.MouseMove
4
5       If m_blnshouldPaint = True Then
6          Dim objGraphic As Graphics = Graphics()
7
8          objGraphic.FillEllipse = ( _
9             New SolidBrush(Color.BlueViolet), e.Y, e.X, 5, 4)
10      End If
11  End Sub ' FrmPainter_MouseMove
```

Programming Challenge ▶

21.16 *(Advanced Painter Application)* Extend the Painter application to enable a user to change the size and color of the circles drawn.

a) *Copying and opening the template application.* Copy the AdvancedPainter folder from C:\Examples\Tutorial21\Exercises to C:\SimplyVB. Double click the AdvancedPainter.sln file to open the application in Visual Studio .NET. The template Form looks like Fig. 21.30.

b) *Understanding the provided instance variables.* The template already provides you with four instance variables. Variable m_objBrushColor is a Color value that specifies the color of the brush used in the **Advanced Painter** application. The m_blnShouldPaint and m_blnShouldErase variable perform the same functions as in this tutorial's **Painter** application. The m_intDiameter variable stores the diameter of the circle to be drawn.

c) *Declaring an enumeration to store the circle diameter sizes.* Declare an enumeration Sizes to store the possible values of m_intDiameter. Set constant SMALL to 4, MEDIUM to 8 and LARGE to 10.

d) *Adding event handlers for the Color RadioButtons.* The **Color** RadioButton's event handlers should set m_objBrushColor to their specified colors (Color.Red, Color.Blue, Color.Green or Color.Black).

e) *Adding event handlers for the Size RadioButtons.* The **Size** RadioButton's event handlers should set m_intDiameter to Sizes.SMALL (for the **Small** RadioButton), Sizes.MEDIUM (for the **Medium** RadioButton) or Sizes.LARGE (for the **Large** RadioButton).

f) *Adding a mouse event handler to a Panel.* To associate mouse events with the Panel, select pnlPainter from the (Base Class Events) ComboBox. Then select the appropriate mouse event from the Method Name ComboBox.

g) *Coding the MouseDown and MouseUp event handlers.* The MouseUp and MouseDown event handlers behave exactly as they do in the **Painter** application.

h) *Coding the MouseMove event handler.* The MouseMove event handler behaves as the one in **Painter** application does. The color of the brush that draws the circle when m_blnShouldPaint is True is specified by m_objBrushColor. The eraser color is specified by the Panel's BackColor property.

Figure 21.30 **Advanced Painter** application's GUI.

Objectives

In this tutorial, you will learn to:
- Handle keyboard events.
- Create menus for your Windows applications.
- Use dialogs to display messages.
- Use the **ShowDialog** method of the **Font** and **Color** dialogs.
- Display the **Font** dialog to enable users to choose fonts.
- Display the **Color** dialog to enable users to choose colors.

Outline

Typing Application

Introducing Keyboard Events, Menus and Dialogs

Text editor applications enable you to perform a wide variety of tasks, from writing e-mails to creating business proposals. These applications often use menus and dialogs to help you customize the appearance of your document. They also respond to keys pressed on the keyboard either by displaying characters or performing actions (such as accessing menus or dialogs). In this tutorial, you will learn how to handle **keyboard events**, which occur when keys on the keyboard are pressed and released. Handling keyboard events allows you to specify the action that the application should take when a key is pressed. You will then learn how to add menus to your application. By now, you are familiar with using various menus and dialogs provided by Windows applications. You will learn to create menus, which group related commands and can allow the user to select various actions the application should take. Finally, you will learn about the **Font** and **Color** dialogs, which you will use to allow the user to change the appearance of text in the application.

22.1 Test-Driving the Typing Application

In this tutorial, you will create a **Typing Application** to help students learn how to type. The application must meet the following requirements:

Application Requirements

A high-school course teaches students how to type. The instructor would like to use a Windows application that allows students to watch what they are typing on the screen without looking at the keyboard. You have been asked to create an application that displays what the student types. The application should display a virtual keyboard that highlights any key the student presses on the real keyboard. This application should also contain menu commands for selecting the font style and color of the text displayed, clearing the text displayed and inverting the background and foreground colors of the display.

This application allows the user to type text. As the user presses each key, the application highlights the corresponding key on the GUI and adds the character to a TextBox. The user can select the color and style of the characters the user types, invert the background and foreground colors and clear the TextBox. You will begin by test-driving the completed application.

Test-Driving the *Typing Application*

1. *Opening and running the application.* Copy the C:\Examples\Tutorial22\CompletedApplication\Typing folder to your work folder. Double click Typing.sln to open the application in Visual Studio .NET.

2. *Using the application.* Select **Debug > Start** to execute the application. Once the application has loaded, type the sentence "Programming in Visual Basic .NET is simple." Notice that as you are typing, the corresponding keys light up on the Form's virtual keyboard, and the text is displayed in the TextBox (Fig. 22.1).

Display menu ——————

Virtual keyboard ——————

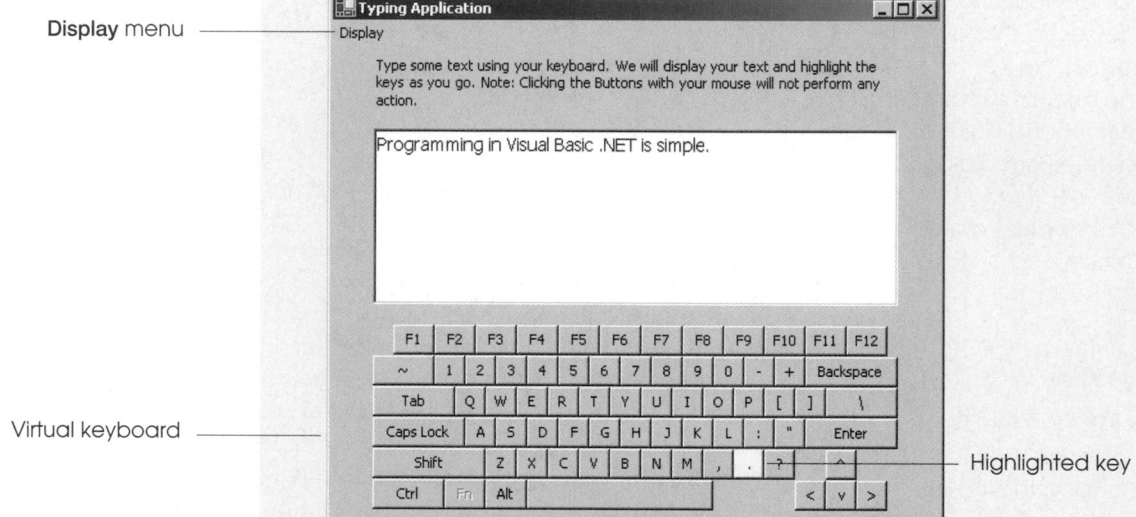

Highlighted key

Figure 22.1 **Typing** application with key pressed.

3. *Changing the font.* Select **Display > Text > Font...** (Fig. 22.2) to open the **Font** dialog shown in Fig. 22.3. The **Font** dialog allows you to choose the font style that should be used to display the application's output. Select Tahoma from the **Font:** ComboBox, select Bold from the **Font style:** ComboBox and select 11 from the **Size:** ComboBox. Click the **OK** Button. Notice that the text you typed in *Step 2* is now bold.

4. *Changing the color of the font.* Select **Display > Text > Color...** to display the **Color** dialog (Fig. 22.4). This dialog is similar to the **Font** dialog, except that it allows you to choose the color of the text displayed. Select a color, and click **OK**.

5. *Inverting the background and foreground colors.* Select **Display > Invert Colors** (Fig. 22.5). This option allows you to swap the background and foreground colors.

(cont.)

Menu item ——————

Submenu ——————

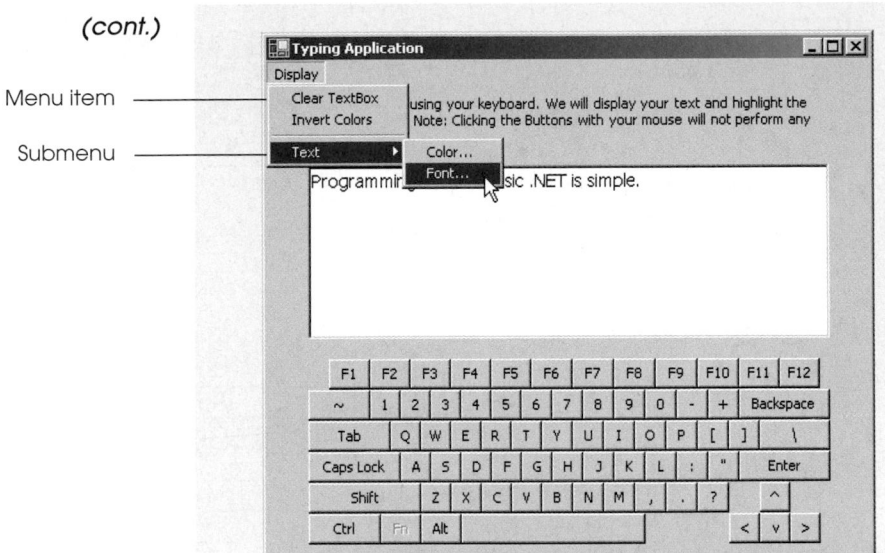

Figure 22.2   Selecting the **Font...** menu item.

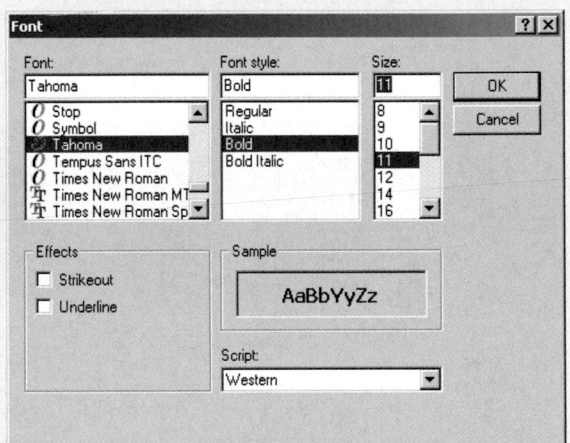

Figure 22.3   **Font** dialog displayed when **Display > Text > Font...** is selected.

Figure 22.4   **Color** dialog displayed when **Display > Text > Color...** is selected.

(cont.)

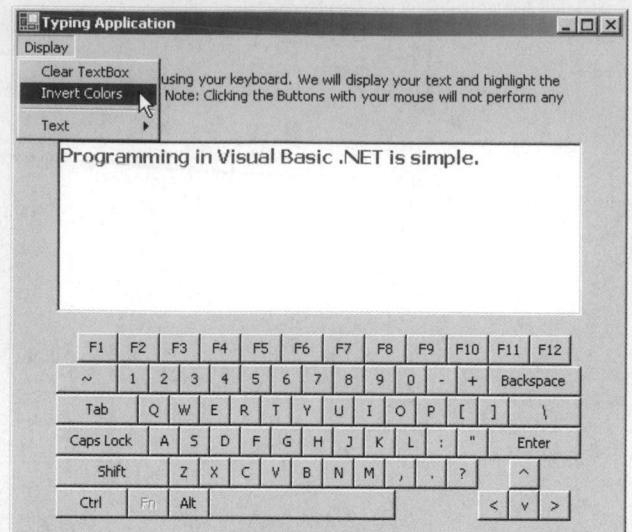

Figure 22.5 Selecting the **Invert Colors** menu item.

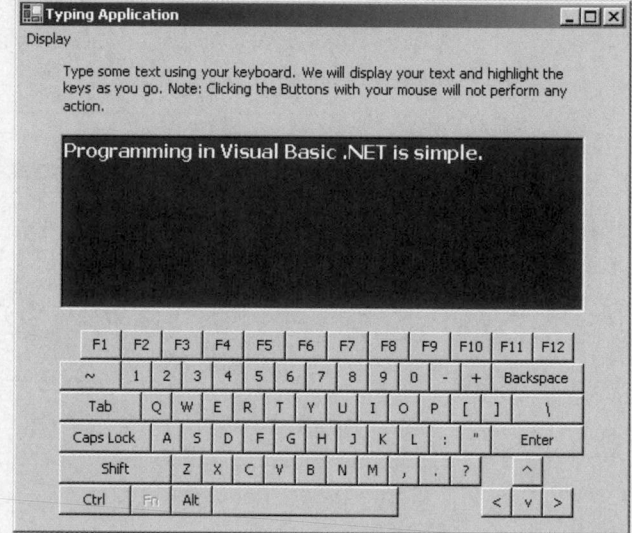

Figure 22.6 Output with colors inverted.

6. *Clearing the TextBox.* Select **Display > Clear TextBox** to remove all of the text from the TextBox.

7. *Closing the application.* Click the application's close box to close the application.

8. *Closing the solution.* Select **File > Close Solution**.

22.2 Analyzing the Typing Application

Before you begin building the **Typing Application**, you should analyze the application's components. The following pseudocode describes the actions that the **Typing Application** must perform to meet the application requirements:

> When the user presses a key
> > Highlight the corresponding Button on the GUI
> > Display the key's value in the TextBox

When the user releases a key
    Reset the corresponding Button's color to the Button's default color

When the user selects the Color... menu item
    Display the Color dialog
    Update the TextBox text's color

When the user selects the Font... menu item
    Display the Font dialog
    Update the TextBox text's font

When the user selects the Clear TextBox menu item
    Clear the TextBox

When the user selects the Invert Colors menu item
    Swap the TextBox's background and foreground colors

The ACE table shown in Fig. 22.7 indicates the events that drive this application and lists controls whose properties are modified when the application runs. [*Note*: The number of Buttons is large and no Button events are used; therefore, the Buttons in the virtual keyboard are not included in the ACE table.]

Action/Control/Event (ACE) Table for the Typing Application

Action	Control	Event
Label the application's controls	lblPrompt	
Highlight the corresponding Button on the GUI; display the key's value in the TextBox	txtOutput	KeyPress, KeyDown
Reset the corresponding Button's color to the Button's default color	txtOutput	KeyUp
Display the Color dialog; update the TextBox text's color	mnuitmColor, txtOutput	Click
Display the Font dialog; update the TextBox text's font	mnuitmFont, txtOutput	Click
Clear the TextBox	mnuitmClear, txtOutput	Click
Swap the TextBox's background and foreground colors	mnuitmInvert, txtOutput	Click

Figure 22.7   ACE table for the **Typing Application**.

22.3 Keyboard Events

This section introduces how to handle keyboard events, which are generated when keys on the keyboard are pressed and released. All keyboard events are raised using the control that currently has the focus. In the **Typing Application**, these events are raised on the TextBox control. The first kind of keyboard event you will learn about is the **KeyDown** event, which is raised when a key is pressed. Since there are many keys on the keyboard, you will find that the template application provides much of the required code. In the box, *Coding the KeyDown Event Handler*, you will insert the remaining code to handle the event when the user presses a key.

Coding the KeyDown
Event Handler

1. *Copying and opening the application.* Copy the `C:\Examples\Tutorial22\TemplateApplication\Typing` folder to `C:\SimplyVB`. Double click the `Typing.sln` file to open the application in Visual Studio .NET. Open `Typing.vb` in code view.

2. *Adding the* **Backspace** *key case.* Add lines 806–814 from Fig. 22.8 to your code. These lines remove a character from the `TextBox` and highlight the **BackSpace** `Button` when the *Backspace* key is pressed.

Testing whether key pressed
was the *Backspace* key

Highlighting the *Backspace*

Removing the last character
in the `TextBox`

Figure 22.8   Removing a character when *Backspace* is pressed.

When a key is pressed, the `KeyDown` event is raised. As you have seen in previous tutorials, many event handlers are passed two arguments: `sender` and `e`. The **sender** `Object` is the GUI component that raised the event (this is also known as the source of the event) and `e` contains data for the event. In this case, `e` (of type **KeyEventArgs**) contains data about which key was pressed. The **KeyData** property of `e` (line 803) contains a value that represents which key was pressed.

Visual Basic .NET provides the **Keys enumeration** to represent keyboard keys using meaningful names. Recall that enumerations are used to assign meaningful names to constant values. In this case, each value in the `Keys` enumeration is an `Integer` that represents a key. `Keys.Back` (line 806) is the `Keys` enumeration's representation of the *Backspace* key. Line 807 calls method `ChangeColor` to highlight the **Backspace** `Button`. The `ChangeColor` method is provided for you in the template. The `If...Then` statement on lines 809–814 tests whether there is text in the `TextBox`. If the `TextBox` contains text, lines 810–812 remove the last character from the `TextBox`. If the `TextBox` is empty, no action is performed.

When invoked `String` method **Remove** deletes characters from a `String`. The first argument contains the index in the `String` at which to begin removing characters, and the second argument specifies the number of characters to remove. The `String` property **Length** returns the number of characters in the `String`. The position of the first character in a `String` is zero; therefore, you must subtract 1 from the value returned by the `Length` property to indicate the position of the last character. Use 1 as the second argument to indicate that you want to remove only one character.

(cont.)   3.   ***Adding the* Enter *key case.*** Add lines 816–819 from Fig. 22.9 to the `Select Case` statement in the KeyDown event handler. `Keys.Enter` (line 817) represents the *Enter* key. Line 818 changes the color of the **Enter** key on the GUI, and line 819 inserts a new line in the `TextBox`.

Testing whether the *Enter* key was pressed

Appending a newline character

Figure 22.9   `Case` that executes when *Enter* key is pressed.

The KeyDown event handler in this application does not test whether any of the letter keys were pressed. It is often inconvenient to use the KeyDown event handler to detect keyboard events because the KeyEventArgs object's KeyData property is case insensitive. If you try to handle letters in the KeyDown event handler, only uppercase letters will be recognized. This is not appropriate for the **Typing Application** because the user should be able to type uppercase and lowercase letters. Visual Basic .NET provides the **KeyPress** event handler, which can be used to recognize both uppercase and lowercase letters. You will learn how to use the KeyPress event handler in the box, *Adding Code to the KeyPress Event Handler*.

Adding Code to the
***KeyPress* Event Handler**

1.   ***Writing the* Select Case *statement.*** Add lines 987–988 from Fig. 22.10 to the KeyPress event handler. Line 988 begins a `Select Case` statement that uses the uppercase equivalent of the pressed key for the controlling expression.

Using the uppercase representation of key pressed

Figure 22.10   Converting the pressed key to an uppercase letter.

(cont.)

The key names in the Keys enumeration are in their uppercase form; therefore, the Case statement must use the uppercase representation of the key that was pressed. Structure **Char** provides methods for manipulating individual characters. Char method **ToUpper** returns the uppercase representation of its argument. Note that the value returned by the ToUpper method does not alter the data in its argument.

In this example, the argument that is passed to the ToUpper method uses the KeyChar property of e. (Type KeyPressEventArgs.) The **KeyChar** property is similar to KeyData property of the KeyEventArgs object, but contains only values representable as characters. Note that parameter e for the Key-Down and KeyPress event handlers are of different types. The KeyChar property can represent both uppercase and lowercase character values.

2. **Inserting the A key case.** Copy lines 990–993 from Fig. 22.11 to the Select Case statement in the KeyPress event handler. These lines highlight the **A** Button in the application and display an **A** in the TextBox when the user presses the *A* key.

Converting to a character to compare key values

Appending a key character

Figure 22.11 Performing actions when the *A* key is pressed.

Line 991 compares the key pressed to the value Keys.A, which represents the *A* key. The Keys enumeration stores numeric values, but the key pressed by the user is passed to the KeyPress event handler as a character; therefore, the Keys enumeration value needs to be converted to a character before a comparison can be made. Line 991 passes the enumeration value to method Convert.ToChar to convert that value into a character. Line 992 changes the color of the **A** Button on the GUI, and line 993 adds either the "a" or "A" character, depending on if *Shift* was pressed, to the end of the text in the TextBox.

3. **Inserting the B key case.** Copy lines 995–997 of Fig. 22.12 to the Select Case statement. These lines will highlight the **B** Button and add a B to the Text-Box when the user presses the *B* key. Notice that for each key pressed, its Button should be highlighted, and the correct output should be displayed in the TextBox.

(cont.)

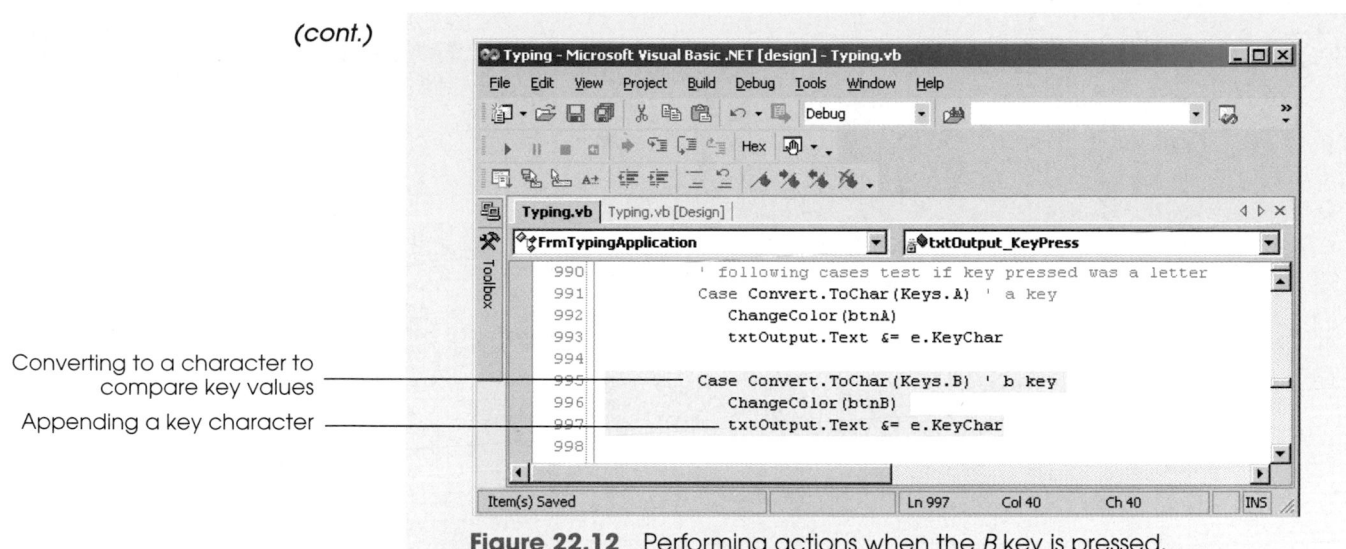

Figure 22.12   Performing actions when the *B* key is pressed.

You may be wondering why you could not just use the **KeyPress** event handler to test for all of the keys on the keyboard. Like the **KeyDown** event handler, the **KeyPress** event handler has its limitations. The **KeyPress** event handler cannot handle the modifier keys (*Ctrl*, *Shift* and *Alt*). **Modifier keys** do not display characters on the keyboard, but can be used to modify the way that applications respond to a keyboard event. For instance, pressing the *Shift* key while pressing a letter in a text editor displays the uppercase form of the letter. You used the **KeyDown** event handler to handle the event raised when a modifier key is pressed. Another reason not to use only the **KeyPress** event handler is that the **KeyChar** property used in this event handler stores the pressed key as a character, requiring an explicit conversion of the **Keys** enumeration values before a comparison can be performed. It is more straightforward to compare the pressed key's numeric value against the numeric values stored in the **Keys** enumeration. The **KeyData** property used in the KeyDown event handler allows you to do this.

Software Design Tip

Use the **KeyPress** event handler for letter key events. Use the **KeyDown** event handler for modifier, number and symbol key events.

The **KeyUp** event is raised whenever a key is released by the user. It is raised regardless of whether the key pressed was handled by the **KeyPress** or the **KeyDown** event handler. The **Typing Application** uses the **KeyUp** event handler to remove the highlight color from the **Buttons** on the GUI when the user releases a key. You will learn how to add the **KeyUp** event handler to your application in the box, *Creating the KeyUp Event Handler*.

Creating the *KeyUp* Event Handler

1. **Creating the KeyUp event handler.** To maintain clarity in the template application, an empty KeyUp event handler is provided for you. However, if you want to generate KeyUp, KeyDown or KeyPress event handlers for other controls, begin by selecting the control for which you wish to add the event handler. In the **Typing Application** select txtOutput from the Class Name ComboBox. Then select the appropriate event handler from the Method Name ComboBox, as shown in Fig. 22.13. When you select an event name from the Method Name ComboBox, that event handler is generated in your code.

(cont.)

Figure 22.13 Generating the KeyUp event handler.

2. **Writing code in the KeyUp event handler.** Insert line 1103 from Fig. 22.14 to your application. The KeyUp event handler executes whenever a key is released; therefore, you need to change the color of the released Button back to that Button's default color. Line 1103 calls procedure ResetColor, provided for you in the template, to perform this action.

Figure 22.14 Resetting a Button's color when its key is released.

Now that you have added code that enables the user to see what they are typing by highlighting the corresponding Buttons and displaying output in a TextBox, you must allow the user to alter the display. To do this, you will use the **MainMenu** control, which creates a menu that allows the user to select various options to format the TextBox.

SELF-REVIEW

1. A _____ event is raised when a key on the keyboard is pressed or released.

    a) keyboard   b) KeyDownEvent

    c) KeyChar   d) KeyUpEvent

2. The _____ event is raised when a key is released.

    a) KeyEventUp   b) KeyRelease

    c) KeyUp   d) None of the above.

Answers: 1) a. 2) c.

22.4 Menus

Menus allow you to group related commands for Windows applications. Although most menus and commands vary among applications, some—such as **Open** and **Save**—are common to many applications. Menus are an important part of GUIs because they organize commands without "cluttering" the GUI. In this section, you will learn how to enhance the **Typing Application** by adding menus that allow the user to control how to display text in the `TextBox`. You will learn how to add menus to the **Typing Application** in the box, *Creating a Menu*.

Creating a Menu

1. *Creating a MainMenu control*. Double click the `MainMenu` control in the **Windows Forms** tab of the **Toolbox** to add a `MainMenu` to your application (Fig. 22.15). Notice that when you do this, a `MainMenu` control appears in the component tray. Recall that controls in the component tray are not part of the graphical user interface. Also, on the top of your `Form`, a box that reads **Type Here** appears. This represents a menu item—a cell of text that the user can select in the `MainMenu` control. Visual Basic .NET uses the `MenuItem` object to store these items. When you type text in the **Type Here** field, Visual Studio .NET creates a `MenuItem`. To edit the menu item, click the **Main-Menu** icon in the component tray. This puts the IDE in **Menu Designer mode**, which allows you to create and edit menus. Change the `Name` property of the `MainMenu` control to `mnuMainMenu`.

MenuItem field

MainMenu control

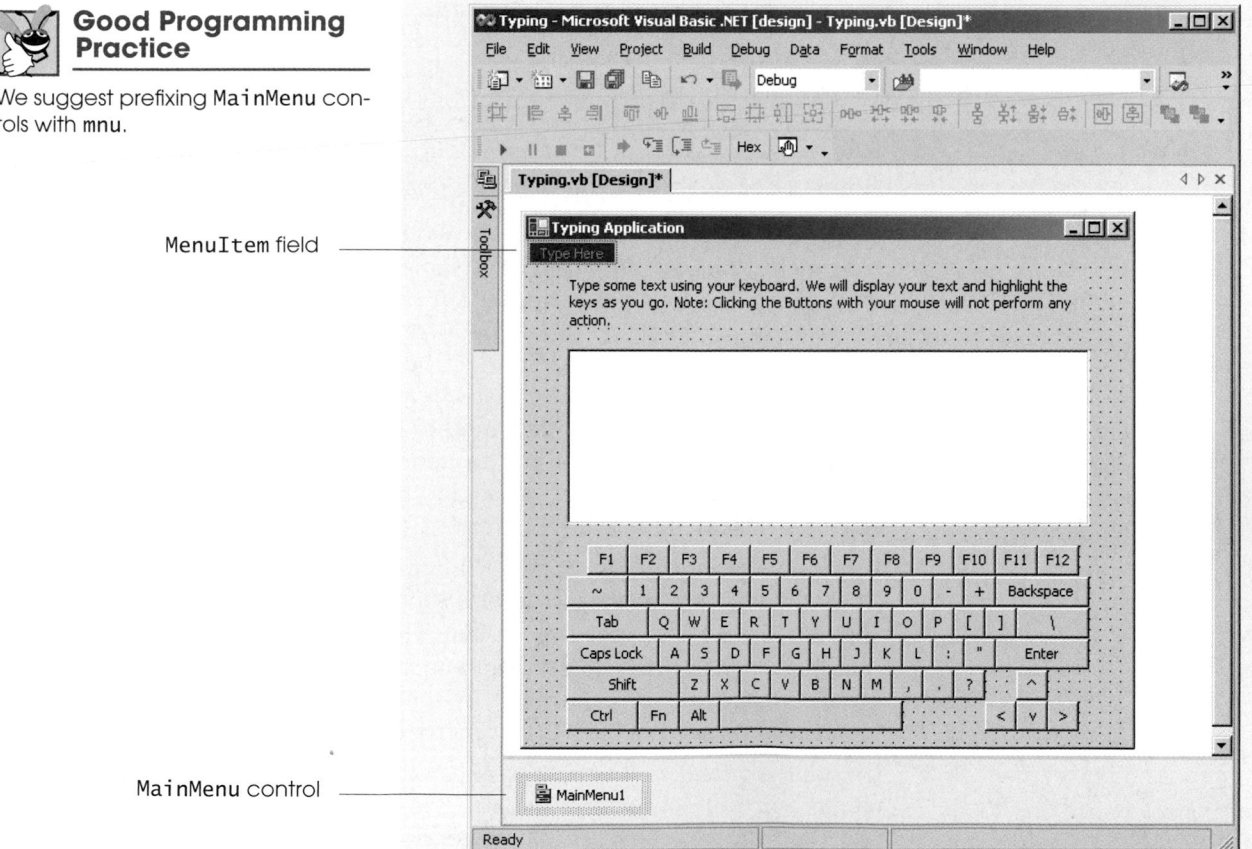

Figure 22.15   `MainMenu` control added to the **Typing Application**.

(cont.)

Good Programming Practice

We suggest prefixing `MenuItem` contols with `mnuitm`.

2. ***Creating the first menu item***. Click inside the **Type Here** box, type `&Display` and press *Enter*. This sets the text to be displayed in that menu item and indicates that the letter D is the access shortcut key. Then change the `Name` property of the `MenuItem` to `mnuitmDisplay`. Notice that when you clicked the **Type Here** field, two more fields appeared (Fig. 22.16). The one on the right represents a new menu item that can be created to the right of the **Display** menu item. The field below the **Display** menu item represents a menu item that will appear when the **Display** menu item is selected. You will use **Display** menu item to display all of the options that allow the user to customize the output displayed in the `TextBox`.

Menu item ——

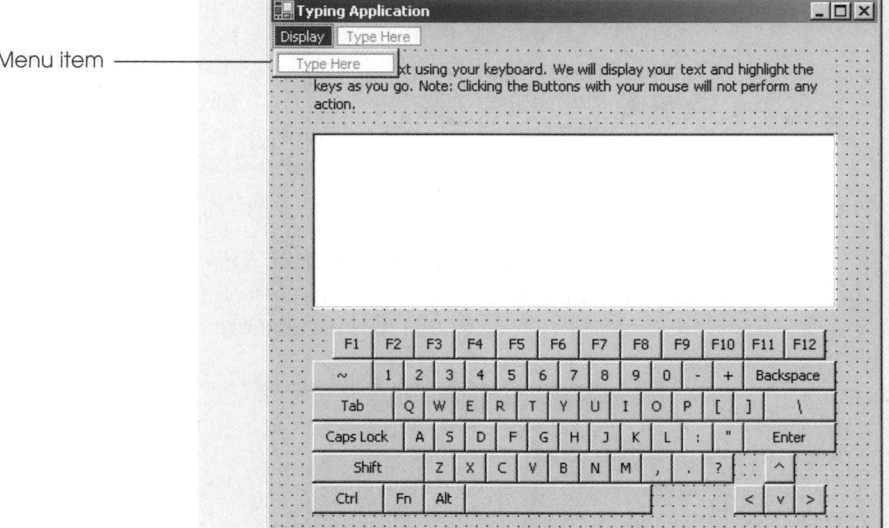

Figure 22.16 Creating the **Display** menu.

GUI Design Tip

Use book-title capitalization in menu item text.

GUI Design Tip

If clicking a menu item opens a dialog, an ellipsis (...) should follow the the menu item's text.

GUI Design Tip

Use separator bars in a menu to group related menu items.

3. ***Creating additional menu items***. In the box that appeared below the **Display** menu, type `&Clear Textbox`. Name this menu item `mnuitmClear` by changing its `Name` property. Notice that once again, two more boxes appear. Every time you add an item to a menu these two boxes will appear (Fig. 22.17). Entering text in the right box turns the menu item on the left into a submenu. The right box is now a menu item of that submenu. Recall that a submenu is a menu within another menu. The box that appears on the bottom of the menu allows you to add another item to that menu. Type `&Invert Colors` in this box to add another menu item. Set the `Name` property of this menu item to `mnuitmInvert`.

4. ***Inserting a separator bar***. Right click the box that appears below the **Invert Colors** menu item, and select **Insert Separator** from the context menu that appears. Notice that a **separator bar**, which is a gray, recessed horizontal rule, appears below the **Invert Colors** menu item. Separator bars are used to group submenus and menu items. A separator bar also can be created by typing a hyphen (-) in the `Text` property of a menu item.

5. ***Creating a submenu***. In the box under the separator bar, type `&Text`. This menu item will contain options to format the appearance of the text displayed in the `TextBox`. All menu items can contain both menu items and submenus. Insert `&Color...` and `&Font...` as menu items in your submenu, naming them `mnuitmColor` and `mnuitmFont`, respectively. (Fig. 22.18)

(cont.)

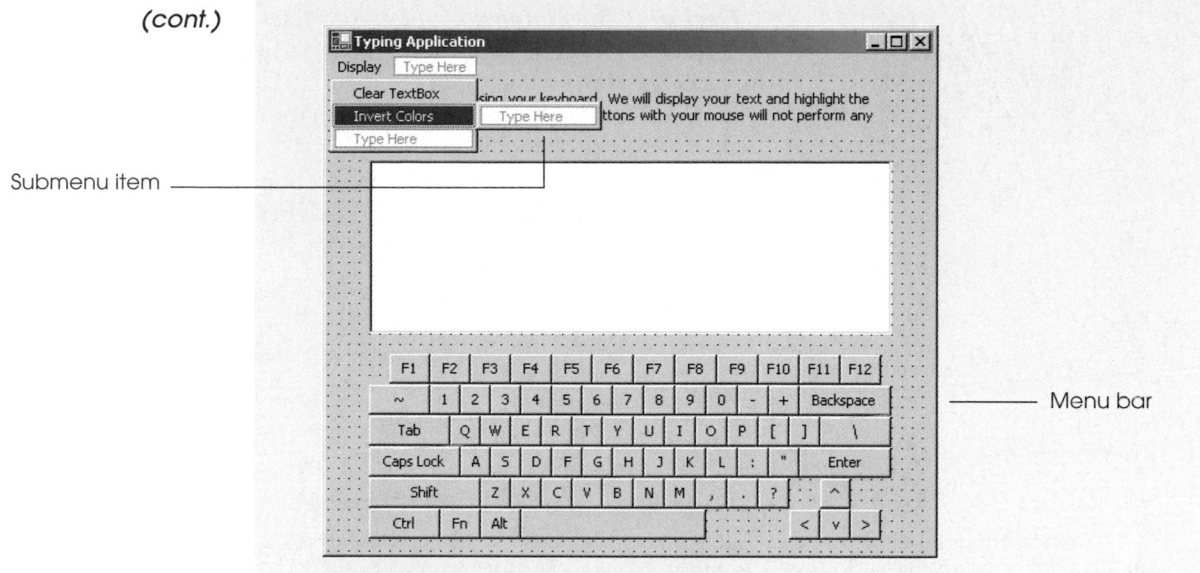

Submenu item ─────

Menu bar

Figure 22.17 Adding items to the menu.

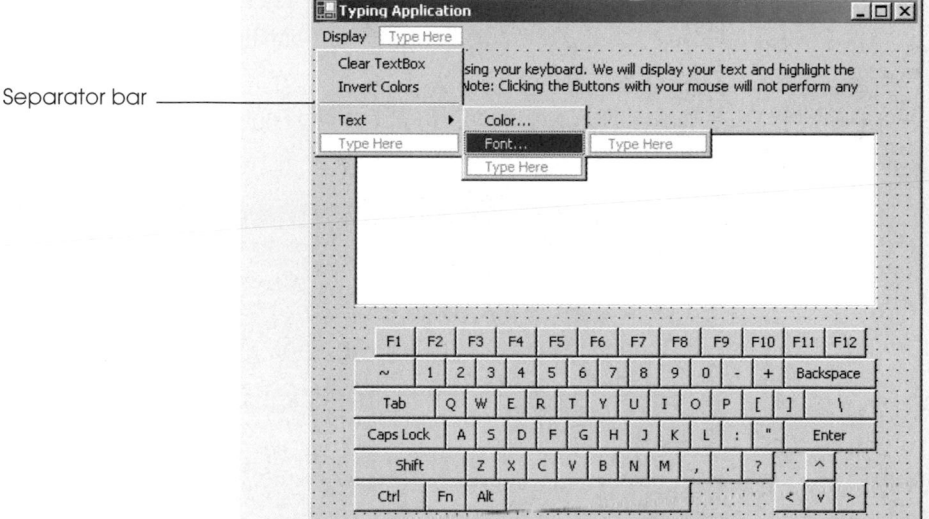

Separator bar ─────

Figure 22.18 Adding a submenu to a menu item.

6. ***Running the application.*** Run the application, and select a menu item. Notice that nothing happens because you have not created event handlers for the menu items. Running the application also saves all of the files in your solution.

For a menu item to perform some action when it is selected, an event handler must be added for that item. The **Typing Application** introduces the **Font** dialog and the **Color** dialog to allow the user to customize the appearance of what is being typed. Dialogs allow you to receive input from and display messages to the user. You will learn how to use the **Font** dialog in the box, *Coding the **Font...** Menu Item's* `Click` *Event Handler.*

Coding the Font... *Menu Item's* Click *Event Handler*

1. ***Creating an event handler.*** In the Windows Form Designer, double click the **Font...** menu item, that you created, to generate an event handler for this menu item.

(cont.)   2. ***Declaring the dialog variables.*** Add lines 1188–1189 from Fig. 22.19 to your code. Line 1188 creates a new **FontDialog** object that will allow the user to select the font style to apply to the text. Line 1189 declares a variable of type `DialogResult` that will store information indicating which `Button` the user clicked to exit the dialog.

Declaration for the
`FontDialog` and its result

Figure 22.19   Declarations for the **FontDialog** and its `DialogResult`.

> **Good Programming Practice**
>
> We suggest prefixing references to dialogs with `dlg`.

3. ***Displaying the dialog.*** Add lines 1191–1192 from Fig. 22.20 to your event handler. These lines call the **ShowDialog** method to display the **Font** dialog to the user.

Showing the dialog and
assigning the result

Figure 22.20   Opening the **Font** dialog.

4. ***Exiting the event handler if the user clicks Cancel.*** Add lines 1194–1197 from Fig. 22.21 to your application. These lines determine whether the user clicked the **Font** dialog's **Cancel** Button. Line 1195 compares the value stored in `result` with the enumeration value **DialogResult.Cancel**. **DialogResult** is an enumeration that contains values corresponding to standard dialog Button names. This provides a convenient way to determine which Button the user clicked. If the user clicks the **Cancel** Button, no action should take place and the method should exit using keyword `Return` (line 1196).

5. ***Setting the font.*** Add lines 1199–1200 from Fig. 22.22 to give the text the style that the user selected from the `FontDialog`. This statement immediately updates the font displayed in the `txtOutput` TextBox.

6. ***Saving the application.*** Select **File > Save All** to save all the solution's files.

(cont.)

Take no action if user cancels ——————

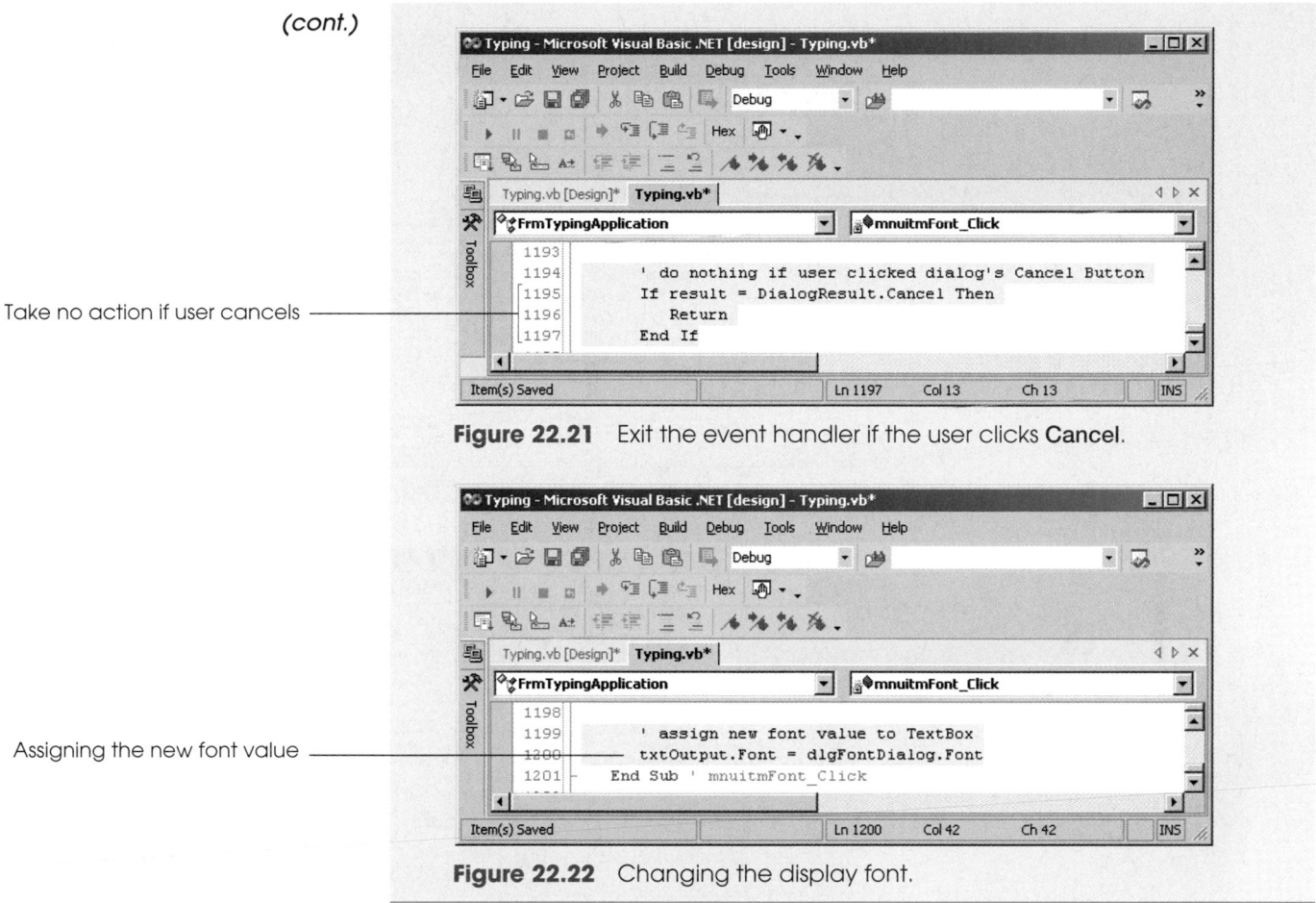

Figure 22.21 Exit the event handler if the user clicks **Cancel**.

Assigning the new font value ——————

Figure 22.22 Changing the display font.

The user of the **Typing Application** should also be able to select the color of the font displayed in the TextBox. You will learn how to display the **Color** dialog in the box, *Coding the* **Color...** *Menu Item's* Click *Event Handler.*

Coding the Color... Menu Item's Click Event Handler

1. **Creating an event handler.** In the Windows Form Designer, double click the **Color...** menu item to generate a Click event handler.

2. **Declaring the dialog variables.** Add lines 1208–1209 from Fig. 22.23 to your application. Line 1208 creates a new ColorDialog object that will allow the user to select the color of the text. Line 1209 declares a DialogResult variable to store the value of the Button clicked by the user.

3. **Setting the ColorDialog's open property.** Add lines 1211–1212 from Fig. 22.24 to your application. The **ColorDialog** object allows you to specify which color options the dialog presents to the user of your application. To display the Color dialog shown in Fig. 22.4, the **FullOpen** option is set to True on line 1211. If this option is set to False, only the left half of the dialog will be displayed. Line 1212 opens the **Color** dialog using the ShowDialog method.

4. **Setting the font color.** Add lines 1214–1220 from Fig. 22.25 to your application. The If...Then statement on lines 1215–1217 prevents the color from being changed if the user clicks **Cancel**. Line 1220 sets the text's color to the color the user selected in the **Color** dialog.

5. **Saving the application.** Select **File > Save All** to save all the solution's files.

(cont.)

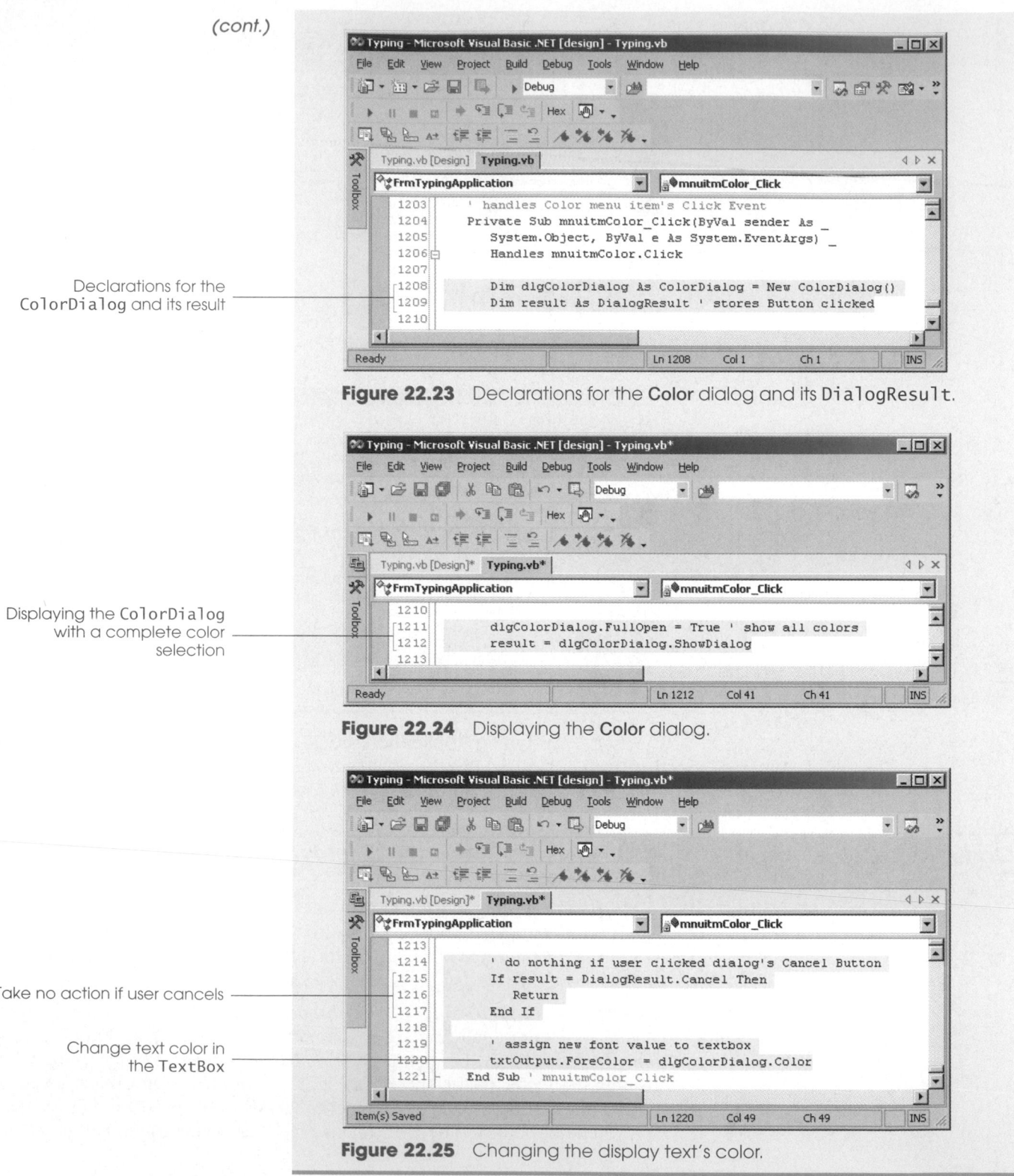

Declarations for the
`ColorDialog` and its result

Figure 22.23 Declarations for the **Color** dialog and its `DialogResult`.

Displaying the `ColorDialog`
with a complete color
selection

Figure 22.24 Displaying the **Color** dialog.

Take no action if user cancels

Change text color in
the TextBox

Figure 22.25 Changing the display text's color.

The user should be able to clear all of the text in the TextBox using the **Clear TextBox** menu item. You will learn how to do this in the box, *Clearing the TextBox.*

Clearing the *TextBox*

1. **Generating an event handler.** Double click the **Clear TextBox** menu item to generate the item's `Click` event.

(cont.)   2. *Clearing the text.* Add line 1228 from Fig. 22.26 to your application. This line calls the `Clear` method to erase the text from the `TextBox`. Calling the `Clear` method on a `TextBox` has the same effect as setting its `Text` property to the empty string.

Figure 22.26   Calling the `Clear` method of class `TextBox` to erase the text.

3. *Saving the application.* Select **File > Save All** to save all the solution's files.

The user should be able to swap the foreground and background colors of the `TextBox`. You will learn how to accomplish this in the box, *Inverting Colors*.

Inverting Colors   1. *Creating an event handler.* Double click the **Invert Colors** menu item in design view. This creates an empty event handler for the **Invert Colors** menu item's `Click` event (Fig. 22.27).

Figure 22.27   Empty event handler for **Invert Color** menu item.

2. *Inverting the colors.* Insert lines 1236–1240 of Fig. 22.28 to your application. Line 1236 declares a `Color` variable. Recall that `Color` variables store color values. To swap colors, you must use a temporary variable to hold one of the colors that you want to swap. A **temporary variable** is used to store data when swapping values. Such a variable is no longer needed after the swap occurs. Without a temporary variable, you would lose the value of one color property (by reassigning its value) before you could assign its color to the other property.

(cont.)

Line 1238 assigns the `Color` variable the background color of the `Text-Box`. Line 1239 then sets the background color to the foreground color. Finally, line 1240 assigns the text color the value stored in the temporary `Color` variable, which contains the `TextBox`'s background color from before the swap.

Using a temporary variable to swap color values

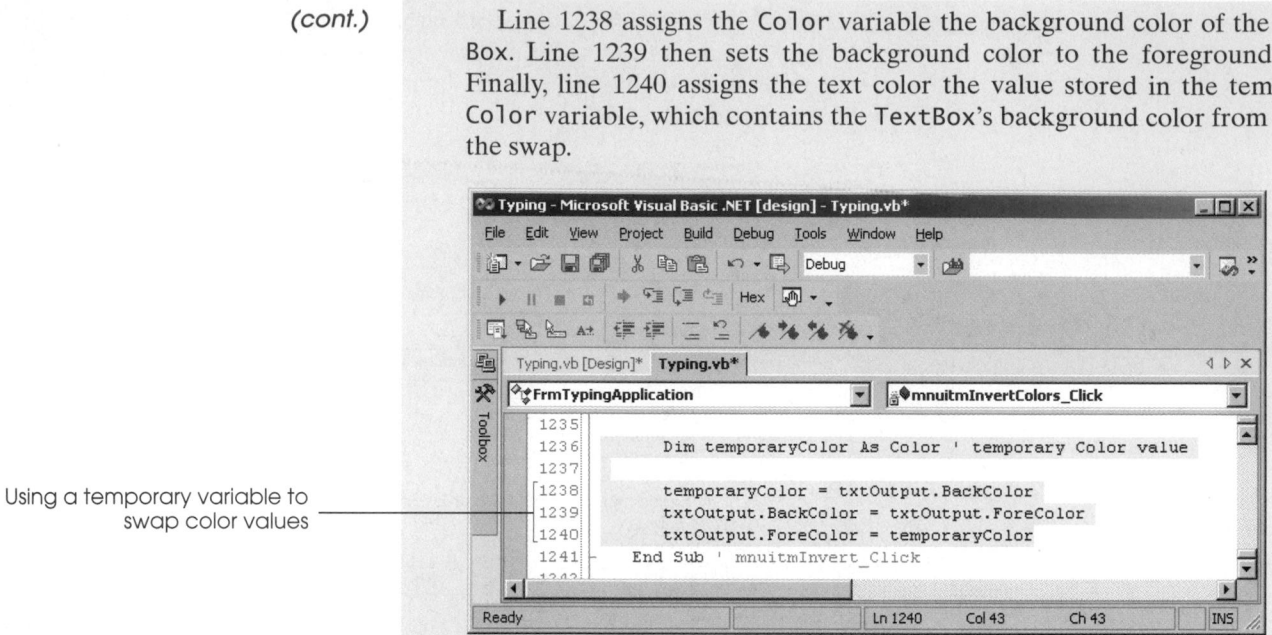

Figure 22.28 Swapping the background and foreground colors.

3. *Saving the application.* Select **File > Save All** to save all the solution's files.

4. *Running the application.* Select **Debug > Start** to execute the application.

5. *Closing the application.* Click the application's close box to terminate execution.

Figure 22.29 displays the complete code listing for the **Typing Application**. New programming concepts are highlighted in yellow.

Instance reference to store which **Button** the user pressed

Select **Case** determines which key was pressed

Handling the case when the *Backspace* key is pressed

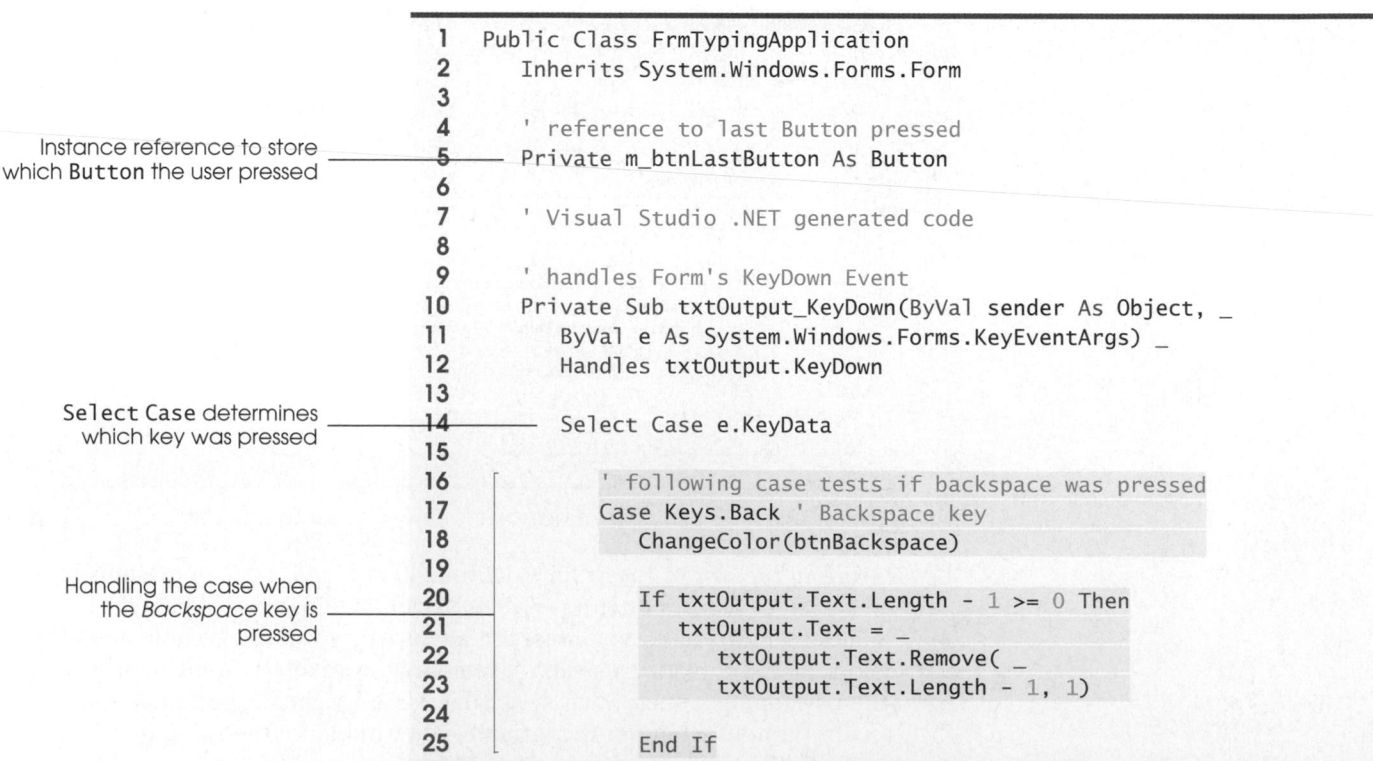

```
1   Public Class FrmTypingApplication
2      Inherits System.Windows.Forms.Form
3
4      ' reference to last Button pressed
5      Private m_btnLastButton As Button
6
7      ' Visual Studio .NET generated code
8
9      ' handles Form's KeyDown Event
10     Private Sub txtOutput_KeyDown(ByVal sender As Object, _
11        ByVal e As System.Windows.Forms.KeyEventArgs) _
12        Handles txtOutput.KeyDown
13
14        Select Case e.KeyData
15
16           ' following case tests if backspace was pressed
17           Case Keys.Back ' Backspace key
18              ChangeColor(btnBackspace)
19
20              If txtOutput.Text.Length - 1 >= 0 Then
21                 txtOutput.Text = _
22                    txtOutput.Text.Remove( _
23                    txtOutput.Text.Length - 1, 1)
24
25              End If
```

Figure 22.29 Typing Application code listing. (Part 1 of 8.)

Handling the case when
the *Enter* key is pressed

```
26
27        ' following cases test if whitespace key was pressed
28        Case Keys.Enter ' Enter key
29            ChangeColor(btnEnter)
30            txtOutput.Text &= ControlChars.CrLf
31
32        Case Keys.Tab ' Tab key
33            ChangeColor(btnTab)
34            txtOutput.Text &= ControlChars.Tab
35
36        Case Keys.Space ' space bar
37            ChangeColor(btnSpace)
38            txtOutput.Text &= " "
39
40        ' following cases test if number key was pressed
41        Case Keys.D0 ' 0 key
42            ChangeColor(btn0)
43            txtOutput.Text &= "0"
44
45        Case Keys.D1
46            ChangeColor(btn1)
47            txtOutput.Text &= "1"
48
49        Case Keys.D2
50            ChangeColor(btn2)
51            txtOutput.Text &= "2"
52
53        Case Keys.D3
54            ChangeColor(btn3)
55            txtOutput.Text &= "3"
56
57        Case Keys.D4
58            ChangeColor(btn4)
59            txtOutput.Text &= "4"
60
61        Case Keys.D5
62            ChangeColor(btn5)
63            txtOutput.Text &= "5"
64
65        Case Keys.D6
66            ChangeColor(btn6)
67            txtOutput.Text &= "6"
68
69        Case Keys.D7
70            ChangeColor(btn7)
71            txtOutput.Text &= "7"
72
73        Case Keys.D8
74            ChangeColor(btn8)
75            txtOutput.Text &= "8"
76
77        Case Keys.D9
78            ChangeColor(btn9)
79            txtOutput.Text &= "9"
80
81        ' following cases test if one of the F keys was pressed
82        Case Keys.F1 ' F1 key
83            ChangeColor(btnF1)
```

Figure 22.29 Typing Application code listing. (Part 2 of 8.)

```
84
85           Case Keys.F2 ' F2 key
86               ChangeColor(btnF2)
87
88           Case Keys.F3 ' F3 key
89               ChangeColor(btnF3)
90
91           Case Keys.F4 ' F4 key
92               ChangeColor(btnF4)
93
94           Case Keys.F5 ' F5 key
95               ChangeColor(btnF5)
96
97           Case Keys.F6 ' F6 key
98               ChangeColor(btnF6)
99
100          Case Keys.F7 ' F7 key
101              ChangeColor(btnF7)
102
103          Case Keys.F8 ' F8 key
104              ChangeColor(btnF8)
105
106          Case Keys.F9 ' F9 key
107              ChangeColor(btnF9)
108
109          Case Keys.F10 ' F10 key
110              ChangeColor(btnF10)
111
112          Case Keys.F11 ' F11 key
113              ChangeColor(btnF11)
114
115          Case Keys.F12 ' F12 key
116              ChangeColor(btnF12)
117
118          ' following cases test if a special character was pressed
119          Case Keys.OemOpenBrackets ' left square bracket
120              ChangeColor(btnLeftBrace)
121              txtOutput.Text &= "["
122
123          Case Keys.OemCloseBrackets ' right square bracket
124              ChangeColor(btnRightBrace)
125              txtOutput.Text &= "]"
126
127          Case Keys.Oemplus ' plus sign
128              ChangeColor(btnPlus)
129              txtOutput.Text &= "+"
130
131          Case Keys.OemMinus ' minus sign
132              ChangeColor(btnHyphen)
133              txtOutput.Text &= "-"
134
135          Case Keys.Oemtilde ' tilde (~)
136              ChangeColor(btnTilde)
137              txtOutput.Text &= "~"
138
139          Case Keys.OemPipe ' backslash
140              ChangeColor(btnSlash)
141              txtOutput.Text &= "\"
```

Figure 22.29 Typing Application code listing. (Part 3 of 8.)

```
142
143        Case Keys.OemSemicolon ' colon
144           ChangeColor(btnColon)
145           txtOutput.Text &= ":"
146
147        Case Keys.OemQuotes ' quotation marks
148           ChangeColor(btnQuote)
149           txtOutput.Text &= ControlChars.Quote
150
151        Case Keys.OemPeriod ' period
152           ChangeColor(btnPeriod)
153           txtOutput.Text &= "."
154
155        Case Keys.Oemcomma ' comma
156           ChangeColor(btnComma)
157           txtOutput.Text &= ","
158
159        Case Keys.OemQuestion ' question mark
160           ChangeColor(btnQuestion)
161           txtOutput.Text &= "?"
162
163        Case Keys.CapsLock ' Caps Lock key
164           ChangeColor(btnCaps)
165
166        ' following cases test if one of the arrow keys was pressed
167        Case Keys.Down ' down arrow
168           ChangeColor(btnDown)
169
170        Case Keys.Up ' up arrow
171           ChangeColor(btnUp)
172
173        Case Keys.Left ' left arrow
174           ChangeColor(btnLeft)
175
176        Case Keys.Right ' right arrow
177           ChangeColor(btnRight)
178
179        ' following cases test if a modifier key was pressed
180        Case CType(65552, Keys) ' Shift key
181           ChangeColor(btnShiftLeft)
182
183        Case CType(131089, Keys) ' Control key
184           ChangeColor(btnCtrlLeft)
185
186        Case CType(262162, Keys) ' Alt key
187           ChangeColor(btnAltLeft)
188
189     End Select
190
191  End Sub ' txtOutput_KeyDown
192
193  ' handles Form KeyPress Event
194  Private Sub txtOutput_KeyPress(ByVal sender As Object, _
195     ByVal e As System.Windows.Forms.KeyPressEventArgs) _
196     Handles txtOutput.KeyPress
197
198        ' convert pressed key to uppercase
199        Select Case Char.ToUpper(e.KeyChar)
```

Using the **KeyChar** property to determine which letter key was pressed

Figure 22.29 Typing Application code listing. (Part 4 of 8.)

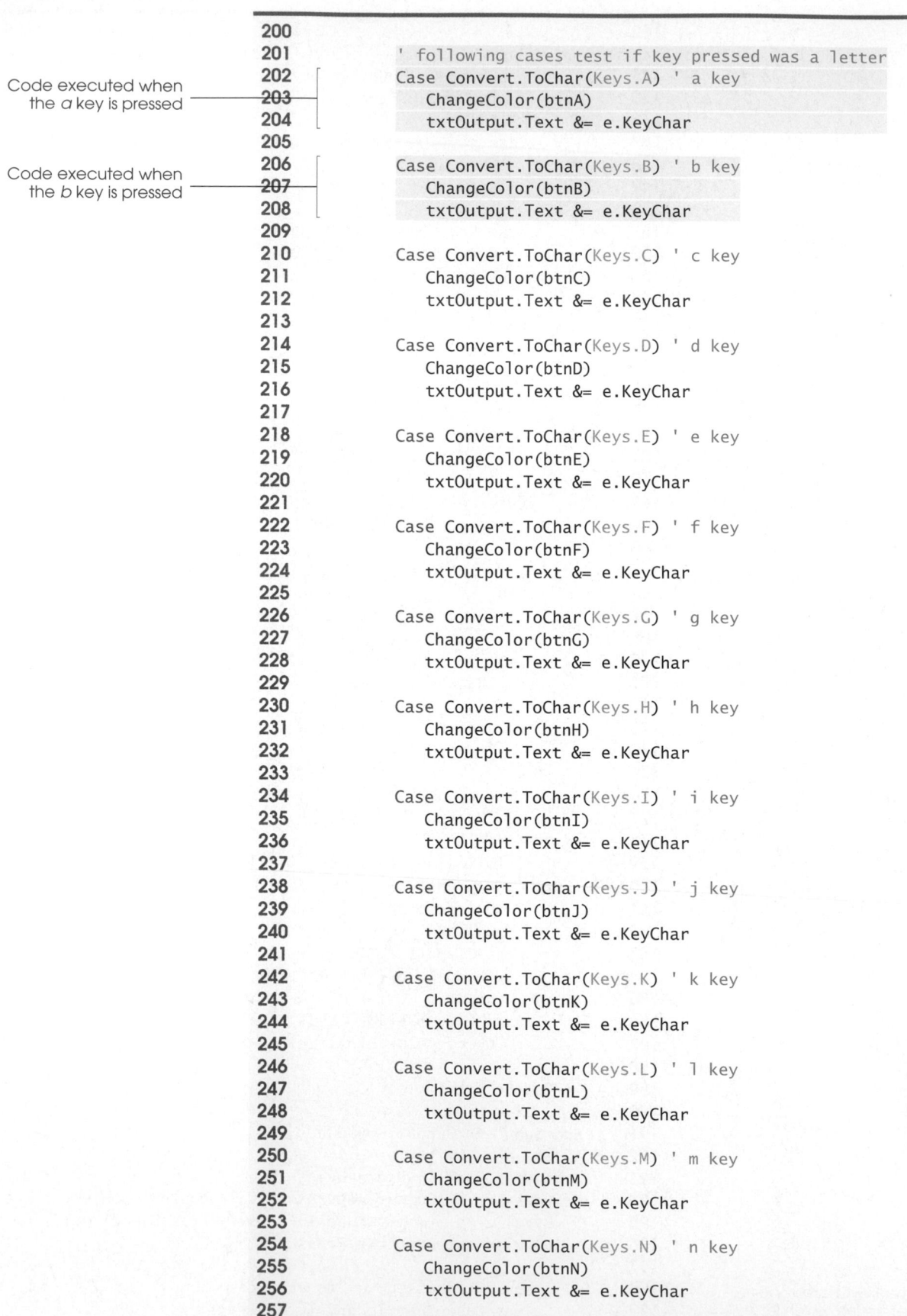

```
200
201              ' following cases test if key pressed was a letter
202              Case Convert.ToChar(Keys.A) ' a key
203                 ChangeColor(btnA)
204                 txtOutput.Text &= e.KeyChar
205
206              Case Convert.ToChar(Keys.B) ' b key
207                 ChangeColor(btnB)
208                 txtOutput.Text &= e.KeyChar
209
210              Case Convert.ToChar(Keys.C) ' c key
211                 ChangeColor(btnC)
212                 txtOutput.Text &= e.KeyChar
213
214              Case Convert.ToChar(Keys.D) ' d key
215                 ChangeColor(btnD)
216                 txtOutput.Text &= e.KeyChar
217
218              Case Convert.ToChar(Keys.E) ' e key
219                 ChangeColor(btnE)
220                 txtOutput.Text &= e.KeyChar
221
222              Case Convert.ToChar(Keys.F) ' f key
223                 ChangeColor(btnF)
224                 txtOutput.Text &= e.KeyChar
225
226              Case Convert.ToChar(Keys.G) ' g key
227                 ChangeColor(btnG)
228                 txtOutput.Text &= e.KeyChar
229
230              Case Convert.ToChar(Keys.H) ' h key
231                 ChangeColor(btnH)
232                 txtOutput.Text &= e.KeyChar
233
234              Case Convert.ToChar(Keys.I) ' i key
235                 ChangeColor(btnI)
236                 txtOutput.Text &= e.KeyChar
237
238              Case Convert.ToChar(Keys.J) ' j key
239                 ChangeColor(btnJ)
240                 txtOutput.Text &= e.KeyChar
241
242              Case Convert.ToChar(Keys.K) ' k key
243                 ChangeColor(btnK)
244                 txtOutput.Text &= e.KeyChar
245
246              Case Convert.ToChar(Keys.L) ' l key
247                 ChangeColor(btnL)
248                 txtOutput.Text &= e.KeyChar
249
250              Case Convert.ToChar(Keys.M) ' m key
251                 ChangeColor(btnM)
252                 txtOutput.Text &= e.KeyChar
253
254              Case Convert.ToChar(Keys.N) ' n key
255                 ChangeColor(btnN)
256                 txtOutput.Text &= e.KeyChar
257
```

Code executed when the *a* key is pressed

Code executed when the *b* key is pressed

Figure 22.29 Typing Application code listing. (Part 5 of 8.)

```
258              Case Convert.ToChar(Keys.O) ' o key
259                  ChangeColor(btnO)
260                  txtOutput.Text &= e.KeyChar
261
262              Case Convert.ToChar(Keys.P) ' p key
263                  ChangeColor(btnP)
264                  txtOutput.Text &= e.KeyChar
265
266              Case Convert.ToChar(Keys.Q) ' q key
267                  ChangeColor(btnQ)
268                  txtOutput.Text &= e.KeyChar
269
270              Case Convert.ToChar(Keys.R) ' r key
271                  ChangeColor(btnR)
272                  txtOutput.Text &= e.KeyChar
273
274              Case Convert.ToChar(Keys.S) ' s key
275                  ChangeColor(btnS)
276                  txtOutput.Text &= e.KeyChar
277
278              Case Convert.ToChar(Keys.T) ' t key
279                  ChangeColor(btnT)
280                  txtOutput.Text &= e.KeyChar
281
282              Case Convert.ToChar(Keys.U) ' u key
283                  ChangeColor(btnU)
284                  txtOutput.Text &= e.KeyChar
285
286              Case Convert.ToChar(Keys.V) ' v key
287                  ChangeColor(btnV)
288                  txtOutput.Text &= e.KeyChar
289
290              Case Convert.ToChar(Keys.W) ' w key
291                  ChangeColor(btnW)
292                  txtOutput.Text &= e.KeyChar
293
294              Case Convert.ToChar(Keys.X) ' x key
295                  ChangeColor(btnX)
296                  txtOutput.Text &= e.KeyChar
297
298              Case Convert.ToChar(Keys.Y) ' y key
299                  ChangeColor(btnY)
300                  txtOutput.Text &= e.KeyChar
301
302              Case Convert.ToChar(Keys.Z) ' z key
303                  ChangeColor(btnZ)
304                  txtOutput.Text &= e.KeyChar
305
306          End Select ' ends test for letters
307
308      End Sub
309
310      Private Sub txtOutput_KeyUp(ByVal sender As Object, _
311          ByVal e As System.Windows.Forms.KeyEventArgs) _
312          Handles txtOutput.KeyUp
313
314          ResetColor()
315      End Sub ' txtOutput_KeyUp
316
```

Resets the **Button** background color ——— 314

Figure 22.29   Typing Application code listing. (Part 6 of 8.)

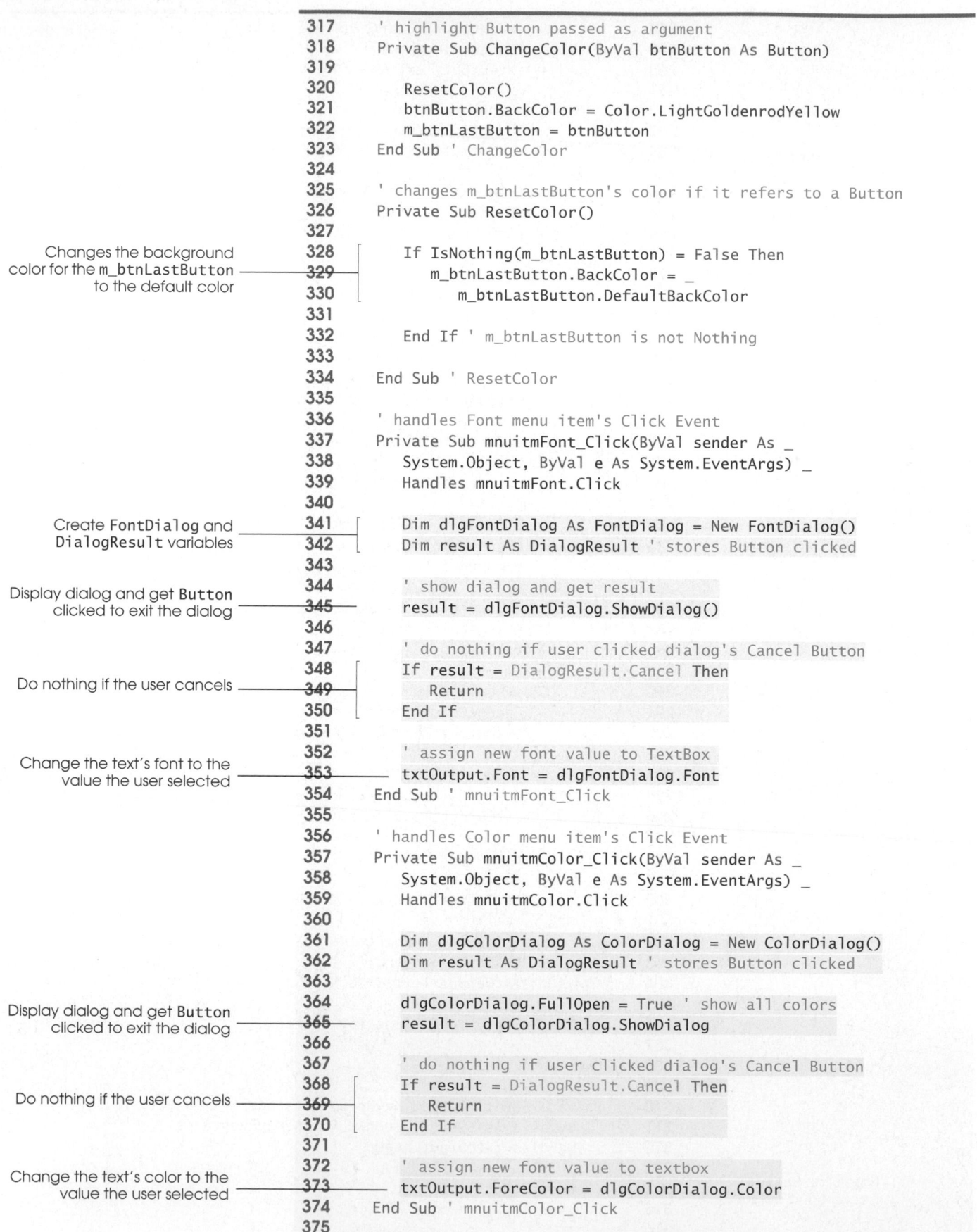

```
317        ' highlight Button passed as argument
318        Private Sub ChangeColor(ByVal btnButton As Button)
319
320            ResetColor()
321            btnButton.BackColor = Color.LightGoldenrodYellow
322            m_btnLastButton = btnButton
323        End Sub ' ChangeColor
324
325        ' changes m_btnLastButton's color if it refers to a Button
326        Private Sub ResetColor()
327
328            If IsNothing(m_btnLastButton) = False Then
329                m_btnLastButton.BackColor = _
330                    m_btnLastButton.DefaultBackColor
331
332            End If ' m_btnLastButton is not Nothing
333
334        End Sub ' ResetColor
335
336        ' handles Font menu item's Click Event
337        Private Sub mnuitmFont_Click(ByVal sender As _
338            System.Object, ByVal e As System.EventArgs) _
339            Handles mnuitmFont.Click
340
341            Dim dlgFontDialog As FontDialog = New FontDialog()
342            Dim result As DialogResult ' stores Button clicked
343
344            ' show dialog and get result
345            result = dlgFontDialog.ShowDialog()
346
347            ' do nothing if user clicked dialog's Cancel Button
348            If result = DialogResult.Cancel Then
349                Return
350            End If
351
352            ' assign new font value to TextBox
353            txtOutput.Font = dlgFontDialog.Font
354        End Sub ' mnuitmFont_Click
355
356        ' handles Color menu item's Click Event
357        Private Sub mnuitmColor_Click(ByVal sender As _
358            System.Object, ByVal e As System.EventArgs) _
359            Handles mnuitmColor.Click
360
361            Dim dlgColorDialog As ColorDialog = New ColorDialog()
362            Dim result As DialogResult ' stores Button clicked
363
364            dlgColorDialog.FullOpen = True ' show all colors
365            result = dlgColorDialog.ShowDialog
366
367            ' do nothing if user clicked dialog's Cancel Button
368            If result = DialogResult.Cancel Then
369                Return
370            End If
371
372            ' assign new font value to textbox
373            txtOutput.ForeColor = dlgColorDialog.Color
374        End Sub ' mnuitmColor_Click
375
```

Changes the background color for the m_btnLastButton to the default color

Create FontDialog and DialogResult variables

Display dialog and get Button clicked to exit the dialog

Do nothing if the user cancels

Change the text's font to the value the user selected

Display dialog and get Button clicked to exit the dialog

Do nothing if the user cancels

Change the text's color to the value the user selected

Figure 22.29 Typing Application code listing. (Part 7 of 8.)

```
376        ' handles Clear TextBox menu item's Click Event
377        Private Sub mnuitmClear_Click(ByVal sender As _
378          System.Object, ByVal e As System.EventArgs) _
379          Handles mnuitmClear.Click
380
381          txtOutput.Clear() ' clear TextBox
382        End Sub ' mnuitmClear_Click
383
384        ' handles Invert Colors menu item's Click Event
385        Private Sub mnuitmInvert_Click(ByVal sender As _
386          System.Object, ByVal e As System.EventArgs) _
387          Handles mnuitmInvert.Click
388
389          Dim temporaryColor As Color ' temporary Color value
390
391          temporaryColor = txtOutput.BackColor
392          txtOutput.BackColor = txtOutput.ForeColor
393          txtOutput.ForeColor = temporaryColor
394        End Sub ' mnuitmInvert_Click
395
396   End Class ' FrmTypingApplication
```

Swap text color and background color — (annotation pointing to lines 391–393)

Figure 22.29 **Typing Application** code listing. (Part 8 of 8.)

SELF-REVIEW

1. Menus can contain _____.

   a) commands that the user can select   b) submenus

   c) separator bars   d) All of the above.

2. _____ allow you to receive input from and display messages to users.

   a) Dialogs   b) Menus

   c) Separator bars   d) Enumerations

Answers: 1) d. 2) a.

22.5 Wrap-Up

In this tutorial, you learned about keyboard events. You learned how to handle the event raised when the user presses a key on the keyboard by using the KeyDown and KeyPress events. You then learned how to use the KeyUp event handler to handle the event raised when the user releases a key.

You added menus to the **Typing Application**. You learned that menus allow you to add controls to your application without cluttering the GUI. You also learned how to code a menu item's Click event handler to alter the displayed text in the **Typing Application**. You learned how to display the **Color** and **Font** dialogs so the user could specify the font style and color of the text in the TextBox. You also learned how to use the DialogResult enumeration to determine which **Button** the user pressed to exit a dialog.

In the next tutorial, you will learn about the methods in the String class that allow you to manipulate Strings. These methods will help you build a screen scraper application that can search text for a particular value.

SKILLS SUMMARY   **Adding Keyboard Event Handlers to Your Application**

■ Select the control for which you want to add the event handler from the Class Name ComboBox.

■ Select the desired event handler from the Method Name ComboBox.

Executing Code When the User Presses a Letter Key on the Keyboard

- Use the KeyPress event handler.
- Use property KeyChar to determine which key was pressed.
- Use method ToUpper to convert the pressed key to an uppercase letter.
- Use a Select Case statement to perform an action depending on what key was pressed.
- Compare the pressed key to a Keys enumeration value in each Case.

Executing Code When the User Presses a Key that is not a Letter

- Use the KeyDown event handler.
- Use property KeyData to determine which key was pressed.

Executing Code When the User Releases a Key

- Use the KeyUp event handler.

Adding Menus to Your Application

- Select the MainMenu control from the tool bar.
- Add menu items to the menu by typing the item's name in the **Type Here** boxes that appear on the bottom of the menu.
- Add submenus by typing a menu item's name in the **Type Here** box that appears to the right of the submenu's name.
- Use a menu item's Click event handler to perform an action when that menu item is selected by the user.

Adding a Font Dialog to Your Application

- Use keyword New to create a new FontDialog object.
- Use a DialogResult variable to store the Button the user clicked to exit the dialog.
- Use method ShowDialog to display the dialog.

Adding a Color Dialog to Your Application

- Use keyword New to create a new FontDialog object.
- Use a DialogResult variable to store the Button the user clicked to exit the dialog.
- Set the FullOpen option to True to provide the user with the full range of colors and to allow custom colors.
- Use method ShowDialog to display the dialog.

KEY TERMS

Char structure—Structure that stores characters (such as letters and symbols).

Click event of class MenuItem—Event generated when an item is clicked or a shortcut key is used.

ColorDialog class—Class that is used to display a dialog containing color options to a use.

e event argument—The event argument that contains data for the event (such as KeyData).

FontDialog class—Class that is used to display a dialog containing font options to a user and record the result.

FullOpen property of class ColorDialog—Property that, when True, enables the Color-Dialog to provide a full range of color options when displayed.

keyboard event—Event that is raised when a key on the keyboard is pressed or released.

KeyChar property of class KeyPressEventArgs—Property containing data about the key that raised the KeyPress event.

KeyData property of class KeyEventArgs—Property containing data about the key that raised the KeyDown event.

KeyDown event—Event generated when a key is initially pressed. Use to handle the event raised when a key that is not a letter key is pressed.

KeyEventArgs class—Class that stores information about special modifier keys.

KeyPress event—The event generated when a key is pressed. Use to handle the event raised when a letter key is pressed.

KeyPressEventArgs class—Class that stores information about character keys.

Keys enumeration—Enumeration containing values representing keyboard keys.

KeyUp event—Event generated when key is released.

MainMenu control—Control that allows you to add menus to your application.

Menu Designer in Visual Studio .NET—Design mode in Visual Studio .NET that allows you to create and edit menus.

menu item—Command located in a menu that, when selected, causes the application to perform a specific action.

menu-access shortcut—*Alt* key shortcut that allows the user to combine the *Alt* key with another key to access a menu item.

menu—Design element that groups related commands for Windows applications. Although these commands depend on the application, some—such as **Open** and **Save**—are common to many applications. Menus are an integral part of GUIs, because they organize commands without cluttering the GUI.

modifier key—Key such as *Shift*, *Alt* or *Control* that modify the way that applications respond to a keyboard event.

sender event argument—Event argument that contains the GUI component that raised the event (also called the source of the event).

separator bar—Bar placed in a menu to separate related menu items.

ShowDialog method of class FontDialog or ColorDialog—Method that displays the dialog on which it is called.

submenu—Menu within another menu.

Text property of class MenuItem—Property that specifies the menu item's text.

ToUpper method of structure Char—Method that returns the uppercase representation of the character passed as a parameter.

GUI DESIGN GUIDELINES

MainMenu

■ Use book-title capitalization in menu item text.

■ Use separator bars in a menu to group related menu items.

■ If clicking a menu item opens a dialog, an ellipsis (...) should follow the menu item's text.

CONTROLS, EVENTS, PROPERTIES & METHODS

Char This structure represents Unicode® characters.

■ *Method*

ToUpper—This method returns the uppercase equivalent of an alphabetic character.

ColorDialog   ColorDialog   This control allows the user to customize the color of what is being typed.

■ *Properties*

Color—This property contains the color selected by the user. The default color is black.

FullOpen—This property, when True, displays an extended color pallete. If this property is set to False, a dialog with less options is displayed.

■ *Methods*

ShowDialog—This method displays the **Color** dialog to the user.

FontDialog   FontDialog   This control allows the user to customize the font, size and style of what is being typed.

■ *Methods*

ShowDialog—This method displays the **Font** dialog to the user.

KeyEventArgs   This class represents arguments passed to the KeyPress event handler.

■ *Property*

KeyData—This property contains data about the key that raised the KeyDown event.

KeyPressEventArgs   This class represents arguments passed to the KeyPress event handler.

■ *Property*

KeyChar—This property contains data about the key that raised the KeyPress event.

MainMenu   This control allows you to group related commands for a Windows application.

■ *In action*

■ *Events*

Click—This event is raised when the user clicks a menu item or presses a shortcut key that represents an item.

TextBox   [abl] TextBox   This control allows the user to input data from the keyboard.

■ *In action*

| 0 |

■ *Events*

KeyDown—This event is raised when a key is pressed. KeyDown is case insensitive. It cannot recognize lowercase letters.

KeyPress—This event is raised when a key is pressed. KeyPress cannot handle modifier keys.

KeyUp—This event is raised when a key is released by the user.

TextChanged—This event is raised when the text in the TextBox is changed.

■ *Properties*

Enabled—This property determines whether the user can enter data (True) in the TextBox or not (False).

Location—This property specifies the location of the TextBox on the container control relative to the top-left corner.

MaxLength—Specifies the maximum number of characters that can be input into the TextBox.

Multiline—This property specifies whether the TextBox is capable of displaying multiple lines of text.

Name—This property specifies the name used to access the TextBox programmatically. The name should be prefixed with txt.

PasswordChar—This property specifies the masking character to be used when displaying data in the TextBox.

ReadOnly—This property determines whether the value of a TextBox can be changed.

ScrollBars—This property specifies whether the TextBox contains a scrollbar.

Size—This property specifies the height and width (in pixels) of the TextBox.

Text—This property specifies the text displayed in the TextBox.

TextAlign—This property specifies how the text is aligned within the TextBox.

■ *Methods*

Focus—This method transfers the focus of the application to the TextBox that calls it.

MULTIPLE-CHOICE QUESTIONS

22.1 When creating a menu, typing a _____ in front of a menu item name will create an access shortcut for that item.

a) &   b) !

c) $ d) #

22.2 *Alt*, *Shift* and *Control* are _____ keys.

a) modifier   b) ASCII

c) function   d) special

22.3 KeyChar is a property of _____.

a) KeyEventArgs   b) Key

c) KeyArgs   d) KeyPressEventArgs

22.4 Typing a hyphen (-) as a menu item's Text property will create a(n) _____.

a) separator bar   b) access shortcut

c) new submenu   d) keyboard shortcut

22.5 A _____ provides a group of related commands for Windows applications.

a) separator bar   b) hot key

c) menu   d) margin indicator bar

22.6 The _____ enumeration specifies key codes and modifiers.

a) Keyboard   b) Key

c) KeyboardTypes   d) Keys

22.7 The _____ event is raised when a key is pressed by the user.

a) KeyPress   b) KeyHeld

c) KeyDown   d) Both a and c.

22.8 Which of the following is not a keyboard event?

a) KeyPress   b) KeyDown

c) KeyUp   d) KeyClicked

22.9 Which of the following is not a structure?

a) Char   b) Color

c) String   d) Date

22.10 The _____ type allows you to determine which Button the user clicked to exit a dialog.

a) DialogButtons   b) DialogResult

c) Buttons   d) ButtonResult

EXERCISES

22.11 (Inventory *Application with Keyboard Events*) Enhance the **Inventory** application that you developed in Tutorial 4 to prevent the user from entering input that is not a number. Use keyboard events to allow the user to press the number keys, the left and right arrows and the *Backspace* keys. If a key other than these is pressed, display a MessageBox instructing the user to enter a number (Fig. 22.30).

a) *Copying an opening the template application*. Copy the KeyEventInventory folder from C:\Examples\Tutorial22\Exercises to C:\SimplyVB. Double click the Inventory.sln file to open the application in Visual Studio .NET.

b) *Adding the KeyDown event handler for the first TextBox*. Add an empty KeyDown event handler for the **Cartons per shipment:** TextBox.

c) *Adding a Select Case statement*. Add a Select Case statement to the KeyDown event handler that determines whether a number key, a left or right arrow or the *Backspace* key was pressed.

d) *Adding the Case Else statement*. Add a Case Else statement that will determine whether a key other than a valid one for this application was pressed. If an invalid key was pressed, display a MessageBox that instructs the user to enter a number.

e) *Adding the KeyDown event handler for the second TextBox.* Repeat *Steps b–d*, only this time create a KeyDown event handler for the **Items per carton:** TextBox. This event handler should perform the same functionality as the one for the **Cartons per shipment:** TextBox.

Figure 22.30 Enhanced **Inventory** application.

22.12 (Bouncing Ball *Game*) Write an application that allows the user to play a game, the goal of which is to prevent a bouncing ball from falling off the bottom of the Form. When the user presses the *S* key, a blue ball will bounce off the top, left and right sides (the "walls") of the Form. There should be a horizontal bar on the bottom of the Form, which serves as a paddle to prevent the ball from hitting the bottom of the Form. (The ball can bounce off the paddle, but not the bottom of the Form.) The user can move the paddle using the left and right arrow keys. If the ball hits the paddle, the ball should bounce up, and the game should continue. If the ball hits the bottom of the Form, the game should end. The paddle's width should decrease every thirty seconds to make the game more challenging. The GUI is provided for you (Fig. 22.31).

Figure 22.31 Bouncing Ball application.

a) *Copying and opening the template application.* Copy the BouncingBall folder from C:\Examples\Tutorial22\Exercises to C:\SimplyVB. Double click the BouncingBall.sln file to open the application in Visual Studio .NET.

b) *Creating the KeyDown event handler.* Insert a KeyDown event handler for the Form.

c) *Writing code to start the game.* Write an If...Then statement in the KeyDown event handler that tests whether the user presses the *S* key. You can use the KeyDown event handler for the *S* key in this case because you do not care whether the user presses an uppercase *S* or a lowercase *S*. If the user presses the *S* key, start the two Timers that are provided in the template.

d) *Inserting code to move the paddle left.* Write an If...Then statement that tests if the user pressed the left-arrow key and if the paddle's horizontal position is greater than zero. If the paddle's horizontal position equals zero, the left edge of the paddle is touching the left wall and the paddle should not be allowed to move farther to the left. If both the conditions in the If...Then are true, decrease the paddle's *x*-position by 10.

e) *Inserting code to move the paddle right.* Write an If...Then statement that tests if the user pressed the right-arrow key and whether the paddle's *x*-coordinate is less than the width of the Form minus the width of the paddle. If the paddle's *x*-coordinate equals the Form's width minus the width of the paddle, the paddle's right edge is touching the right wall and the paddle should not be allowed to move farther to the right. If both the conditions in the If…Then statement are true, increase the paddle's *x*-coordinate by 10.

22.13 (*Modified Painter Application*) Modify the **Painter** application that you developed in Tutorial 21 to include menus that allow the user to select the size and color of the painted ellipses and the color of the Form (Fig. 22.32). (The menus replace the RadioButtons.) Also, add a multiline TextBox that allows the user to type text to accompany the painting. The user should be able to use menus to select the font style and color of the text and the background color of the TextBox.

a) *Copying and opening the template application.* Copy the ModifiedPainter folder from C:\Examples\Tutorial22\Exercises to C:\SimplyVB. Double click the Painter.sln file to open the application in Visual Studio .NET.

b) *Creating the menus.* Create two menus. The first one should be titled **Paint** and should contain a **Paint Color…** menu item, a **Paint Size** submenu that contains menu items **4**, **6**, **8** and **10**, a separator bar and a **Background Color…** menu item. The second menu should be titled **Text** and have **Text Color…** and **Font…** menu items, a separator bar and a **TextBox Color…** menu item.

c) *Changing the paint color.* Add an event handler for the **Paint Color…** menu item. This event handler should display a **Color** dialog that allows the user to change the value stored in m_paintColor.

d) *Changing the paint size.* Add an event handler for each of the **Size** submenu's menu items. Each event handler should change the value stored in m_intDiamter to the value displayed on the menu (that is, clicking the **4** menu item will change the value of m_intDiameter to 4).

e) *Changing the background color.* Add an event handler for the **Background Color…** menu item. This event handler should display a **Color** dialog that allows the user to change the value stored in m_backgroundColor and also change the BackColor property of the Form.

f) *Changing the text color.* Add an event handler for the **Text Color…** menu item. This event handler should display a **Color** dialog that allows the user to change the color of the text displayed in the TextBox.

g) *Changing the text style.* Add an event handler for the **Font…** menu item. This event handler should display a **Font** dialog that allows the user to change the style of the text displayed in the TextBox.

h) *Changing the TextBox's background color.* Add an event handler for the **TextBox Color…** menu item. This event handler should display a **Color** dialog that allows the user to change the background color of the TextBox.

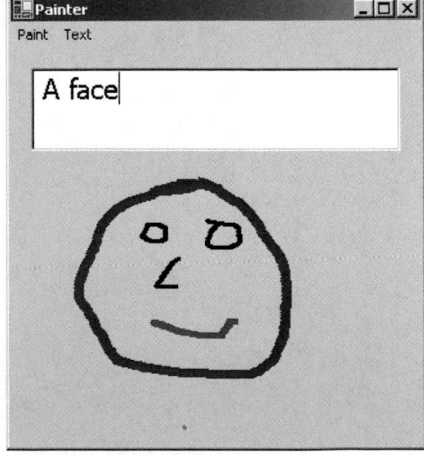

Figure 22.32 Enhanced **Painter** GUI.

What does this code do? ▶ **22.14** What is the result of the following code, assuming that the application's Form is named FrmColoredForm?

```
1   Private Sub mnuitmColor_Click(ByVal sender As _
2      System.Object, ByVal e As System.EventArgs) Handles _
3      mnuitmColor.Click
4
5      Dim dlgColorDialog As ColorDialog = New ColorDialog()
6      Dim result As DialogResult
7
8      dlgColorDialog.FullOpen = True
9
10     result = dlgColorDialog.ShowDialog
11
12     If result = DialogResult.Cancel Then
13       Return
14     End If
15
16     FrmColoredForm.BackColor = dlgColorDialog.Color
17   End Sub ' mnuitmColor_Click
```

What's wrong with this code? ▶ **22.15** This code should allow a user to pick a font from a **Font** and set the text in txtDisplay to that font. Find the error(s) in the following code, assuming that a TextBox named txtDisplay exists on a Form.

```
1   Private Sub Fonts()
2      Dim dlgFontDialog As FontDialog
3
4      dlgFontDialog = New FontDialog()
5      dlgFontDialog.ShowDialog
6      txtDisplay.Font = dlgFontDialog.Font
7   End Sub
```

Programming Challenge ▶ **22.16** (**Dvorak Keyboard** Application) Create an application that simulates the letters on the Dvorak keyboard. A Dvorak keyboard allows faster typing by placing the most commonly used keys in the most accessible locations. Use keyboard events to to create an application similiar to the **Typing** application, except that it simulates the Dvorak keyboard instead of the standard keyboard. The correct Dvorak key should be highlighted on the virtual keyboard and the correct character should be displayed in the TextBox. The keys and characters map as follows:

- On the top row, the *P* key of the Dvorak keyboard maps to the *R* key on a standard keyboard, and the *L* key of the Dvorak keyboard maps to the *P* key on a standard keyboard.
- On the middle row, the *A* key remains in the same position and the *S* key on the Dvorak keyboard maps to the semicolon key on the standard keyboard.
- On the bottom row, the *Q* key on the Dvorak keyboard maps to the *X* key on the standard keyboard and the *Z* key maps to the question mark key.
- All of the other keys on the Dvorak keyboard map to the location shown in Fig. 22.33.

a) *Copying and opening the template application.* Copy the DvorakKeyboard folder from C:\Examples\Tutorial22\Exercises to C:\SimplyVB. Double click the DvorakKeyboard.sln file to open the application in Visual Studio .NET.

b) *Creating the KeyPress event handler.* Add a KeyPress event handler for the TextBox.

c) *Creating a Select Case statement*. Add a Select Case statement to the KeyPress event handler. The Select Case statement should test whether all of the letter keys on the Dvorak keyboard were pressed except for the *S, W, V* and *Z* keys. If a Dvorak key was pressed, highlight it on the GUI and display the character in the TextBox.

d) *Creating a KeyDown event handler*. Add a KeyDown event handler for the TextBox. The *S, W, V* and *Z* keys do not map to a letter key on the standard keyboard; therefore, a KeyDown event handler must be used to determine whether one of these keys was pressed.

e) *Adding a Select Case statement*. Add a Select Case statement to your KeyDown event handler that determines whether *S, W, V* or *Z* was pressed. If one of these keys was pressed, highlight the key, and add the character to the TextBox.

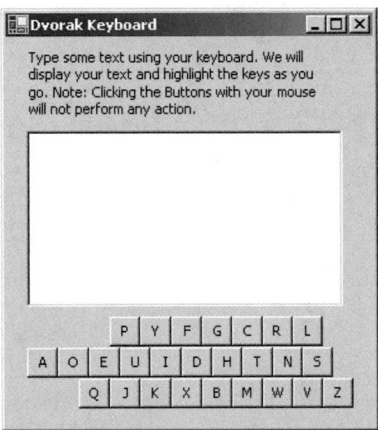

Figure 22.33   Dvorak Keyboard GUI.

23

Objectives

In this tutorial, you will learn to:
- Create and manipulate `String` objects.
- Use properties and methods of class `String`.
- Search for substrings within `Strings`.
- Extract substrings within `Strings`.
- Replace substrings within `Strings`.

Outline

Screen Scraping Application

Introducing *String Processing*

This tutorial introduces Visual Basic .NET's `String`-processing capabilities. The techniques presented in this tutorial can be used to create applications that process text. Earlier tutorials introduced class `String` from the `System` namespace and several of its methods. In this tutorial, you will learn how to search `Strings`, retrieve characters from `String` objects and replace characters in a `String`. You will create an application that uses these `String`-processing capabilities to manipulate a string containing **HTML** (**HyperText Markup Language**). HTML is a technology for describing Web content. Extracting desired information from the HTML that composes a Web page is called **screen scraping**. Applications that perform screen scraping can be used to extract specific information, such as weather conditions or stock prices, from Web pages so that the information can be formatted and manipulated more easily by computer applications. In this tutorial, you will create a simple **Screen Scraping** application.

23.1 Test-Driving the Screen Scraping Application

This application must meet the following requirements:

Application Requirements

An online European auction house wants to expand its business to include bidders from the United States. However, all of the auction house's Web pages currently display their prices in Euros, not dollars. The auction house wants to generate separate Web pages for American bidders that will display the prices of auction items in dollars. These new Web pages will be generated by using screen-scraping techniques on the already existing Web pages. You have been asked to build a prototype application that will test the screen-scraping functionality. The application should search a sample string of HTML and extract information about the price of a specified auction item. For testing purposes, a ComboBox should be provided that contains auction items listed in the HTML. The selected item's amount must then be converted to dollars. For simplicity, assume that the exchange rate is one to one (that is, one Euro is equivalent to one dollar). The price (in dollars) and sample HTML are displayed in Labels.

The **Screen Scraping** application searches for the name of a specified auction item in a string of HTML. Users select the item for which to search from a ComboBox. The application then extracts and displays the price in dollars of this item. You begin by test-driving the completed application.

<table>
<tr>
<td>

***Test-Driving the
Completed Screen
Scraping Application***

</td>
<td>

1. ***Opening the application.*** Open the `C:\Examples\Tutorial23\Com-pletedApplication\ScreenScraping` folder. Double click `ScreenScraping.sln` to open the application in Visual Studio .NET.

2. ***Running the application.*** Select **Debug > Start** to execute the application. The Form shown in Fig. 23.1 appears. Notice that the HTML string is displayed in a Label at the bottom of the Form.

</td>
</tr>
</table>

Label containing HTML —

Figure 23.1   **Screen Scraping** application's Form.

3. ***Selecting an item name.*** The ComboBox contains three item names. Select an item name from the ComboBox as shown in Fig. 23.2.

ComboBox's drop-down list —

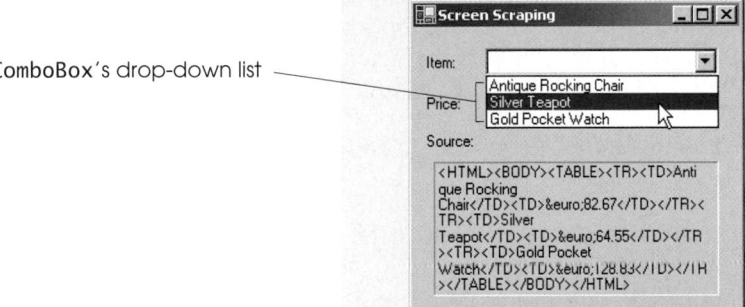

Figure 23.2   Selecting an item name from the ComboBox.

4. ***Searching for an item's price.*** Click the **Search** Button to display the price for the selected item. The extracted price is displayed in a Label (Fig. 23.3).

Extracted price
(converted to dollars) —

Price located in HTML string
(specified in Euros) —

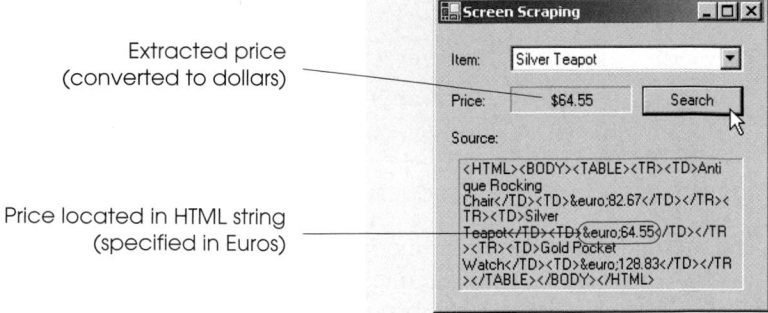

Figure 23.3   Searching for the item's price.

(cont.)   5. ***Terminating the application****. Click the running application's close box to terminate the application.

6. ***Closing the solution.*** Select **File > Close Solution**.

23.2 Fundamentals of `Strings`

A string is a series of characters treated as a single unit. These characters can be uppercase letters, lowercase letters, digits and various **special characters**, such as +, -, *, /, $ and others. A string is an object of class `String` in the `System` namespace. We write **string literals**, or **string constants** (often called **literal `String` objects**), as sequences of characters in double quotation marks, as follows:

```
"This is a string!"
```

You've already created and used `Strings` in previous tutorials. You know that a declaration can assign a `String` literal to a `String` reference. For example, the declaration

```
Dim strColor As String = "blue"
```

initializes `String` reference `strColor` to refer to the `String` literal object `"blue"`.

Like arrays, `Strings` always know their own size. `String` property **Length** returns the length of the `String` (that is, the number of characters in the `String`). For example, the expression `strColor.Length` evaluates to 4 for the `String` `"blue"`.

Another useful property of class `String` is **Chars**, which returns the character located at a specific index in a `String`. Property `Chars` takes an `Integer` argument specifying the index and returns the character at that index. As in arrays, the first element of a `String` is at index 0. For example, the following code

```
If strString1.Chars(0) = strString2.Chars(0) Then
    lblMessage.Text = "The first characters are the same."
```

compares the character at index 0 (that is, the first character) of `strString1` with the character at index 0 of `strString2`.

In earlier tutorials, you used several methods of class `String` to manipulate `String` objects. Figure 23.4 lists some of these methods. You will be introduced to new `String` methods later in this tutorial.

Method	Sample Expression Method Call (assume strText = "My String")	Returns
Insert(*index, string*)	strText.Insert(9,"!")	"My String!"
Remove(*index, count*)	strText.Remove(2,1)	"MyString"
ToLower()	strText.ToLower()	"my string"
ToUpper()	strText.ToUpper()	"MY STRING"

Figure 23.4 `String`-class methods introduced in earlier tutorials.

Any `String` method that appears to modify a `String` actually returns a new `String` that contains the results. For example, `String` method `ToUpper` does not actually modify the original `String`, but instead returns a new `String` in which each lowercase letter has been converted to uppercase. This occurs because `Strings` are **immutable** objects—that is, characters in `Strings` cannot be changed after the `Strings` are created.

SELF-REVIEW

1. The _____ property of the class String returns the number of characters in the String.

   a) MaxChars   b) Length

   c) CharacterCount   d) TotalLength

2. A String can be composed of _____.

   a) digits   b) lowercase letters

   c) special characters   d) All of the above.

Answers: 1) b. 2) d.

23.3 Analyzing the Screen Scraping Application

Before building the **Screen Scraping** application, you must analyze its components. The following pseudocode describes actions that the **Screen Scraping** application performs to solve the problem statement.

> When the Form loads
>   Display the HTML that contains the items' prices in a Label
>
> When the user clicks the Search Button
>   Search the HTML for the item the user selected from the ComboBox
>   Extract the item's price
>   Convert the item's price from Euros to dollars
>   Display the item's price in a Label

The ACE table in Fig. 23.5 indicates which events will drive this application and lists the controls whose properties will be modified while the application runs.

Action/Control/Event (ACE) Table for the Screen Scraping Application

Action	Control	Event
Label the application's controls	lblItem lblPrice lblSource	
When the Form loads	FrmScreenScraping	Load
Display the HTML that contains the items' prices in a Label	lblHTML	
When the user clicks the Search Button	btnSearch	Click
Retrieve selected item from the ComboBox	cboItems	
Display the item's price in a Label	lblResult	

Figure 23.5 ACE table for **Screen Scraping** application.

Now that you've analyzed the **Screen Scraping** application's components, you will learn about the String methods that you will use to construct the application.

23.4 Locating Substrings in Strings

In many applications, it is necessary to search for a character or set of characters in a String. For example, a programmer creating a word-processing application would want to provide capabilities that allow users to search their documents. Class String provides methods that make it possible to search for specified **substrings** (or sequences of characters) in a String. In the box *Locating the Selected Item's Price*, you begin building the **Screen Scraping** application.

1. *Copying the template to your work folder.* Copy the `C:\Examples\Tutorial23\TemplateApplication\ScreenScraping` folder to `C:\SimplyVB`.

2. *Opening the template application.* Double click `ScreenScraping.sln` in the `C:\SimplyVB\ScreenScraping` folder to open the **Screen Scraping** application in Visual Studio .NET.

3. *Displaying the application's Form.* Double click `ScreenScraping.vb` in the **Solution Explorer** to display the application's Form.

4. *Creating a `Click` event handler for the Search Button.* Double click the **Search** Button on the application's Form to generate the event handler `btnSearch_Click`.

5. *Formatting the `Click` event handler.* Add the comments on lines 133 and 137 of Fig. 23.6 around event handler `btnSearch_Click`. Also, split the procedure header over two lines using a line-continuation character (that is, underscore) as in lines 134–135 of Fig. 23.6 to improve its readability.

Figure 23.6 `btnSearch_Click` event handler.

6. *Declaring three `Integer` variables and a `String` reference.* Add lines 137–140 from Fig. 23.7 to the `btnSearch_Click` event handler. These lines declare variables `intItemLocation`, `intPriceBegin` and `intPriceEnd` and `String` reference `strPrice`.

Figure 23.7 `btnSearch_Click` event-handler declarations.

(cont.)   7. ***Locating the specified item name.*** Add lines 142–144 from Fig. 23.8 to event
handler btnSearch_Click. Lines 143–144 call String method **IndexOf** to
locate the first occurrence of the specified item name in the HTML string
(strHTML). There are three versions of IndexOf that search for substrings in
a String. Lines 143–144 use the version of IndexOf that takes a single argument—the substring for which to search. (The specified item name is the
SelectedItem of ComboBox, cboItems.)

Because Option Strict is set to On, we must first convert SelectedItem
to a String, by using method ToString, before passing the selected item to
method IndexOf. If IndexOf finds the specified substring (in this case, the
item name), IndexOf returns the index at which the substring begins in the
String. For example, the return value 0 means that the substring begins at
the first element of the String. If IndexOf does not find the specified substring, IndexOf returns –1. The result is stored in intItemLocation.

Search for the
SelectedItem in the
String strHTML

Figure 23.8   Locating the desired item name.

8. ***Locating the start of the price.*** Add lines 146–148 from Fig. 23.9 to event
handler btnSearch_Click. Lines 147–148 locate the index at which the
item's price begins. Lines 147–148 use a version of method IndexOf that
takes two arguments—the substring to search for and the starting index in
the String at which the search should begin. The method does not examine
any characters that occur prior to the starting index (specified by intItem-
Location). The third version of method IndexOf takes three arguments—
the substring for which to search, the index at which to start searching and
the number of characters to search. We do not use this version of IndexOf in
the **Screen Scraping** application.

Because we know that the first price that follows the specified item name
will be the desired price, we can begin our search at intItemLocation. The
substring we search for is "€". This is the HTML representation of the
Euro symbol, which appears before every price value in the HTML string in
this application. The index returned from method IndexOf is stored in variable intPriceBegin.

9. ***Locating the end of the price.*** Add line 149 from Fig. 23.10 to event handler
btnSearch_Click. Line 149 finds the index at which the desired price ends.
Line 149 calls method IndexOf with the substring "</TD>" and the starting
index intPriceBegin. A </TD> tag directly follows every price (excluding
any spaces) in the HTML string, so the index of the first </TD> tag after
intPriceBegin marks the end of the current price.

(cont.)

Figure 23.9   Locating the desired item price.

Locate the beginning of the price in `strHTML`

The index returned from method `IndexOf` is stored in variable `int-PriceEnd`. In the box, *Retrieving the Desired Item's Price*, We will use `intPriceBegin` and `intPriceEnd` to obtain the price from the string `strHTML`.

Locate the end of the price in `strHTML`

Figure 23.10   Locating the end of the item's price.

10. *Saving the project.* Select **File > Save All** to save all the solution's files.

Another method that is similar to method `IndexOf` is the **LastIndexOf** method. Method `LastIndexOf` locates the last occurrence of a substring in a `String`; it performs the search starting from the end of the `String` and searches toward the beginning of the `String`. If method `LastIndexOf` finds the substring, `LastIndexOf` returns the starting index of the specified substring in the `String`; otherwise, `LastIndexOf` returns –1.

There are three versions of `LastIndexOf` that search for substrings in a `String`. The first version takes a single argument—the substring for which to search. The second version takes two arguments—the substring for which to search and the highest index from which to begin searching backward for the substring. The third version of method `LastIndexOf` takes three arguments—the substring for which to search, the starting index from which to start searching backward and the number of characters to search. Figure 23.11 demonstrates the use of the three versions of `LastIndexOf`.

Method	Example Expression (assume strText = " My String")	Returns
LastIndexOf(*string*)	strText.LastIndexOf("n")	8
LastIndexOf(*string,integer*)	strText.LastIndexOf("n", 6)	-1
LastIndexOf(*string, integer, integer*)	strText.LastIndexOf("m", 7, 3)	-1

Figure 23.11 Demonstration of LastIndexOf methods.

SELF-REVIEW

1. Method _____ locates the first occurrence of a substring.

    a) IndexOf   b) FirstIndexOf

    c) FindFirst   d) Locate

2. The third argument passed to the LastIndexOf method is _____.

    a) the starting index from which to start searching backward

    b) the starting index from which to start searching forward

    c) the length of the substring to locate

    d) the number of characters to search

Answers: 1) a. 2) d.

23.5 Extracting Substrings from Strings

Once you've located a substring in a String, you might want to retrieve the substring from the String. The box *Retrieving the Desired Item's Price* uses the Substring method to retrieve the price of the selected item from the HTML string.

Retrieving the Desired Item's Price

1. ***Extracting the price.*** Add lines 151–153 of Fig. 23.12 to the btnSearch_Click event handler. Class String provides two versions of the **Substring** method, each of which returns a new String object that contains a copy of a part of an existing String object.

Extract price from strHTML ———

Figure 23.12 Retrieving the desired price.

Lines 152–153 extract the price, using the version of the Substring method that takes two Integer arguments. The first argument (intPrice-Begin), specifies the starting index from which the method copies characters from the original String.

(cont.)

> The second argument (`intPriceEnd - intPriceBegin`) specifies the length of the substring to be copied. The substring returned (`strPrice`) contains a copy of the specified characters from the original `String`. In this case, the substring returned is the item's price (in Euros).
>
> The other version of method `Substring` takes one `Integer` argument. The argument specifies the starting index from which the method copies characters in the original `String`.
>
> The substring returned contains a copy of the characters from the starting index to the end of the `String`. We do not use this version of `Substring` in the **Screen Scraping** application.
>
> 2. *Saving the project.* Select **File > Save All** to save all the solution's files.

SELF-REVIEW

1. The `Substring` method _____.

   a) accepts either one or two arguments

   b) returns a new `String` object

   c) creates a `String` object by copying part of an existing `String` object

   d) All of the above.

2. The second argument passed to method `Substring` specifies _____.

   a) the last index of the `String` to copy

   b) the length of the substring to copy

   c) the index from which to begin copying backwards

   d) a character which, when reached, signifies that copying should stop

   Answers: 1) d. 2) b.

23.6 Replacing Substrings in `Strings`

You might want to replace certain characters in `Strings`. Class `String` provides the **Replace** method to replace occurrences of one substring with a different substring. The `Replace` method takes two arguments—a `String` to replace in the original `String` and a `String` with which to replace all occurrences of the first argument. Method `Replace` returns a new `String` with the specified replacements. The original `String` remains unchanged. If there are no occurrences of the first argument in the `String`, the method returns the original `String`. The box *Converting the Price to Dollars* uses method `Replace` to convert the extracted price from Euros to dollars.

Converting the Price to Dollars

1. *Converting the price.* Add lines 155–156 of Fig. 23.13 to `btnSearch_Click`. Line 156 converts the extracted price from Euros to dollars. For simplicity, we assume that dollars are equal to Euros.

   Therefore, to perform the conversion, we need change only the name of the currency. Line 156 uses `String` method `Replace` to return a new `String` object, replacing every occurrence (one in this example) in `strPrice` of substring `"&euro;"` with substring `"$"`. Notice that we assign the value returned from method `Replace` to `lblResult.Text` to display the text in dollars.

2. *Saving the project.* Select **File > Save All** to save all the solution's files.

(cont.)

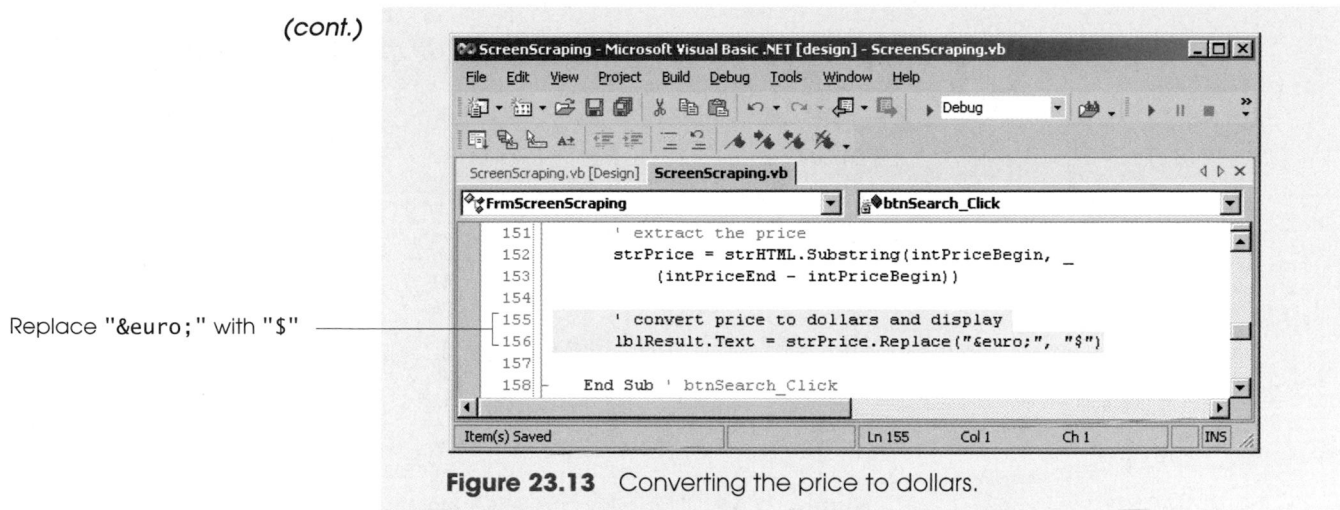

Replace "€" with "$"

Figure 23.13 Converting the price to dollars.

Method `Replace` also is used when the `Form` for the **Screen Scraping** application first loads. The box *Displaying the HTML String* uses method `Replace` to ensure that the HTML string displays correctly in a `Label`.

Displaying the HTML
String

1. ***Creating a Load event handler for the Form.*** In **Design** view (**View > Designer**), double click the `Form` to generate an empty `Load` event handler. This event handler will execute when the application executes.

2. ***Formatting the Load event handler.*** Add the comments on lines 160 and 165 of Fig. 23.14 around event handler `FrmScreenScraping_Load`. Also, split the procedure header over three lines using line-continuation characters (that is, an underscores) as in lines 161–163 of Fig. 23.14 to improve its readability.

Figure 23.14 `Load` event for the `Form`.

3. ***Displaying the HTML string in a Label.*** Add lines 165–166 from Fig. 23.15 to event handler `FrmScreenScraping_Load`. Line 166 calls `String` method `Replace` to replace every occurrence of `"&euro;"` in the HTML string with `"&&euro;"`. As explained previously, the substring `"&euro;"` is the HTML for the Euro symbol. However, for this text to display in a `Label` correctly, we must prefix it with an additional ampersand (&) so the "e" in "euro" is not confused with an access shortcut. The value returned from method `Replace` is displayed in the `lblHTML Label`.

(cont.)

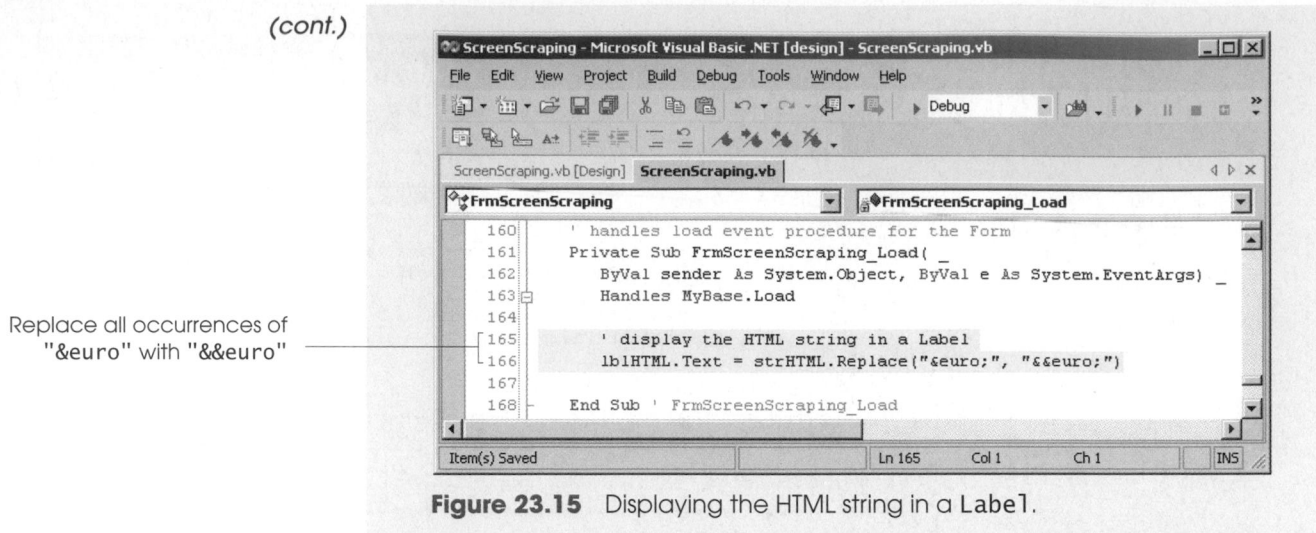

Figure 23.15 Displaying the HTML string in a `Label`.

4. *Saving the project.* Select **File > Save All** to save all the solution's files.
5. *Running the application.* Run the application to confirm its behavior.

1. If there are no occurrences of the substring in the `String`, method `Replace` returns
_____.

    a) `0`   b) `-1`
    c) `Nothing`   d) the original `String`

Answer: 1) d.

23.7 Other `String` Methods

Class `String` provides several additional methods that allow you to manipulate `String`s. Figure 23.16 lists some of these methods and provides a description of what each method does.

Method	Description	Sample Expression (assume `strText = " My String"`)
`EndsWith(`*string*`)`	Returns `True` if a `String` ends with the argument *string*; otherwise, returns `False`.	`strText.EndsWith("ing")` Returns: `True`

`Join(`*separator, array*`)`	Concatenates the elements in a `String` array, separated by the first argument. A new `String` containing the concatenated elements is returned.	`Dim strArray As String() = _`
		  `New String() {"a", "b", "c"}`
		
		`String.Join(";", strArray)`
		
		Returns: `"a;b;c"`

`Split()`	Splits the words in a `String` whenever a space is reached.	`Dim strArray As String() = _`
		  `strText.Split()`
		
		Returns: `"My"` and `"String"` in an array of `String`s

Figure 23.16 Description of other `String` methods. (Part 1 of 2.)

Method	Description	Sample Expression (assume strText = " My String")
StartsWith(*string*)	Returns True if a String starts with argument *string*; otherwise, returns False.	strText.StartsWith("Your") Returns: False
Trim()	Removes any whitespace (that is, blank lines, spaces and tabs) from the beginning and end of a String.	strText.Trim() Returns: "My String"

Figure 23.16 Description of other **String** methods. (Part 2 of 2.)

Figure 23.17 presents the completed code for the **Screen Scraping** application. String methods that were introduced in this tutorial are highlighted in yellow.

```
1   Public Class FrmScreenScraping
2      Inherits System.Windows.Forms.Form
3
4      ' Visual Studio .NET generated code
5
6      ' String of HTML to extract prices from
7      Dim strHTML As String = "<HTML><BODY><TABLE>" & _
8         "<TR><TD>Antique Rocking Chair</TD>" & _
9         "<TD>&&euro;82.67</TD></TR>" & _
10        "<TR><TD>Silver Teapot</TD>" & _
11        "<TD>&&euro;64.55</TD></TR>" & _
12        "<TR><TD>Gold Pocket Watch</TD>" & _
13        "<TD>&&euro;128.83</TD></TR>" & _
14        "</TABLE></BODY></HTML>"
15
16      ' handles Search Button's Click event
17      Private Sub btnSearch_Click(ByVal sender As System.Object, _
18         ByVal e As System.EventArgs) Handles btnSearch.Click
19
20         Dim intItemLocation As Integer  ' index of desired item
21         Dim intPriceBegin As Integer    ' starting index of price
22         Dim intPriceEnd As Integer      ' ending index of price
23         Dim strPrice As String          ' extracted price
24
25         ' locate desired item
26         intItemLocation = strHTML.IndexOf( _
27            cboItems.SelectedItem.ToString())
28
29         ' locate price of item
30         intPriceBegin = strHTML.IndexOf("&euro;", _
31            intItemLocation)
32         intPriceEnd = strHTML.IndexOf("</TD>", intPriceBegin)
33
34         ' extract the price
35         strPrice = strHTML.Substring(intPriceBegin, _
36            (intPriceEnd - intPriceBegin))
37
```

Search for the SelectedItem in the String strHTML — (lines 26–27)

Locate the beginning of the price in strHTML — (lines 30–31)

Locate the end of the price in strHTML — (line 32)

Extract price from strHTML — (lines 35–36)

Figure 23.17 Screen Scraping application. (Part 1 of 2.)

Replace "€" with "$" ————

```
38              ' convert price to dollars and display
39              lblResult.Text = strPrice.Replace("&euro;", "$")
40
41         End Sub ' btnSearch_Click
42
43         ' handles load event procedure for the Form
44         Private Sub FrmScreenScraping_Load( _
45            ByVal sender As System.Object, ByVal e As System.EventArgs) _
46            Handles MyBase.Load
47
48              ' display the HTML string in a Label
49              lblHTML.Text = strHTML.Replace("&euro;", "&&euro;")
50
51         End Sub ' FrmScreenScraping_Load
52
53      End Class ' FrmScreenScraping
```

Replace all occurrences of "&euro" with "&&euro" ————

Figure 23.17   Screen Scraping application. (Part 2 of 2.)

SELF-REVIEW

1. The _____ method removes all whitespace characters that appear at the beginning and end of a String.

   a) RemoveSpaces
   b) NoSpaces
   c) Trim
   d) Truncate

2. The StartsWith method returns _____ if a String begins with the String text passed to StartsWith as an argument.

   a) True
   b) False
   c) 1
   d) the index of the substring

Answers: 1) c. 2) a.

23.8 Wrap-Up

In this tutorial, we introduced you to class String from the System namespace. You learned how to create and manipulate String objects. You learned how to locate, retrieve and replace substrings in Strings. You reviewed several methods from class String and also learned additional methods. You applied your knowledge of Strings in Visual Basic .NET to create a simple **Screen Scraping** application that retrieved the price of an item from an HTML String.

In the next tutorial, you will learn how data is represented in a computer. You will be introduced to the concepts of files and streams. You will learn how to store data in sequential-access files.

SKILLS SUMMARY

Determining the Size of a String

■ Use String property Length.

Locating Substrings in Strings

■ Use String method IndexOf to locate the first occurrence of a substring.

■ Use String method LastIndexOf to locate the last occurrence of a substring.

Retrieving Substrings from Strings

■ Use String method Substring with one argument to obtain a substring that begins at the specified starting index and contains the remainder of the original String.

■ Use String method Substring with two arguments to specify the starting index and the length of the substring.

Replacing Substrings in `Strings`

■ Use `String` method `Replace` to replace occurrences of one substring with another substring.

■ Method `Replace` returns a new `String` containing the replacements.

Comparing Substrings to the Beginning or End of a `String`

■ Use `String` method `StartsWith` to determine whether a `String` starts with a particular substring.

■ Use `String` method `EndsWith` to determine whether a `String` ends with a particular substring.

Removing Whitespace from a `String`

■ Use `String` method `Trim` to remove all whitespace characters that appear at the beginning and end of a `String`.

KEY TERMS

characters—Digits, letters and special symbols.

EndsWith method of class `String`—The method that determines if a `String` ends with a particular substring.

HTML (HyperText Markup Language)—A technology for describing Web content.

IndexOf method of class `String`—Returns the index of the first occurrence of a substring in a `String`. Returns `-1` if the substring is not found.

LastIndexOf method of class `String`—The method that returns the index of the last occurrence of a substring in a `String`. It returns `-1` if the substring is not found.

Length property of class `String`—The property that returns the number of characters in a `String`.

literal `String` objects—A `String` constant written as a sequence of characters in double quotation marks (also called a string literal).

Replace method of class `String`—A method that returns a new `String` object in which every occurrence of a substring is replaced with a different substring.

screen scraping—The process of extracting desired information from the HTML that composes a Web page.

StartsWith method of class `String`—The method that determines if a `String` starts with a particular substring.

string literal—A `String` constant written as a sequence of characters in double quotation marks (also called a literal `String` object).

Substring method of class `String`—A method that creates a new `String` object by copying part of an existing `String` object.

ToLower method of class `String`—A method that creates a new `String` object that replaces every uppercase letter in a `String` with its lowercase equivalent.

ToUpper method of class `String`—A method that creates a new `String` object that replaces every lowercase letter in a `String` with its uppercase equivalent.

Trim method of class `String`—A method that removes all whitespace characters from the beginning and end of a `String`.

CONTROLS, EVENTS, PROPERTIES & METHODS

String The `String` class represents a series of characters treated as a single unit.

■ *Property*

`Length`—This property returns the number of characters in the `String`.

■ *Methods*

`EndsWith`—This method determines if a `String` ends with a particular substring.

`Format`—This method arranges the string in a specified format.

`IndexOf`—This method returns the index of the specified character(s) in a `String`.

`Insert`—This method returns a copy of the `String` for which it is called with the specified character(s) inserted.

`LastIndexOf`—This method returns the index of the last occurrence of a substring in a `String`. It returns `-1` if the substring is not found.

PadLeft—This method inserts characters at the beginning of a String.

Remove—This method returns a copy of the String for which it is called with the specified character(s) removed.

Replace—This method returns a new String object in which every occurrence of a substring is replaced with a different substring.

StartsWith—This method determines if a String starts with a particular substring.

Substring—This method returns a substring from a String.

ToLower—This method returns a copy of the String for which it is called with any uppercase letters converted to lowercase letters.

ToUpper—This method creates a new String object that replaces every lowercase letter in a String with its uppercase equivalent.

Trim—This method removes all whitespace characters from the beginning and end of a String.

MULTIPLE-CHOICE QUESTIONS

23.1 Extracting desired information from Web pages is called _____.

a) Web crawling
b) screen scraping
c) querying
d) redirection

23.2 If IndexOf method does not find the specified substring, it returns _____.

a) False
b) 0
c) -1
d) None of the above.

23.3 The String class allows you to _____ Strings.

a) search
b) retrieve characters from
c) replace characters in
d) All of the above.

23.4 _____ is a technology for describing Web content.

a) Class String
b) A String literal
c) HTML
d) A screen scraper

23.5 The String class is located in the _____ namespace.

a) String
b) System.Strings
c) System.IO
d) System

23.6 The _____ method creates a new String object by copying part of an existing String object.

a) StringCopy
b) Substring
c) CopyString
d) CopySubString

23.7 All String objects are _____.

a) the same size
b) always equal to each other
c) preceded by at least one whitespace character
d) immutable

23.8 The IndexOf method does not examine any characters that occur prior to the _____.

a) starting index
b) first match
c) last character of the String
d) None of the above.

23.9 The _____ method determines whether a String ends with a particular substring.

a) CheckEnd
b) StringEnd
c) EndsWith
d) EndIs

23.10 The Trim method removes all whitespace characters that appear _____ a String.

a) in
b) at the beginning of
c) at the end of
d) at the beginning and end of

EXERCISES

23.11 (*Supply Cost Calculator Application*) Write an application that calculates the cost of all the supplies added to the user's shopping list. The application should contain two List-Boxes. The first ListBox contains all the supplies offered and their respective prices. Users should be able to select the desired supplies from the first ListBox and add them to the second ListBox. Provide a **Calculate** Button that displays the total price for the user's shopping list (the contents of the second ListBox).

a) *Copying and opening the template application.* Copy the SupplyCalculator folder from C:\Examples\Tutorial23\Exercises to C:\SimplyVB. Double click the Sup-plyCalculator.sln file in the SupplyCalculator folder to open the application in Visual Studio .NET.

b) *Adding code to the Add >> Button.* Double click the **Add >>** Button to create an empty event handler. Add code to the event handler that adds the selected item from the first ListBox to the lstStock ListBox. Make sure to check that at least one item is selected in the first ListBox before attempting to add an item to the lstStock ListBox.

c) *Enabling the Buttons.* Once the user adds something to the lstStock ListBox, set the Enabled properties of the **<< Remove** and **Calculate** Buttons to True.

d) *Deselecting the items.* Once the items are added to the lstStock ListBox, make sure that those items are deselected in the lstSupply ListBox. Also, clear the **Total:** Label to indicate to the user that a new total price must be calculated.

e) *Adding code to the Remove Button.* Double click the **<< Remove** Button to create an empty event handler. Use a Do While loop to remove any selected items in the lstStock ListBox. Make sure to check that at least one item is selected before attempting to remove an item. [*Hint*: Method lstStock.Items.RemoveAt(intIndex) will remove the item located at intIndex from the lstStock ListBox.]

f) *Adding code to the Calculate Button.* Double click the **Calculate** Button to create an empty event handler. Use a For...Next statement to loop through all the items in the lstStock ListBox. Convert each item from the ListBox into a String. Then use the String method Substring to extract the price of each item.

g) *Displaying the total.* Convert the String representing each item's price to a Decimal, and add this to the overall total (of type Decimal). Remember to output the value in currency format.

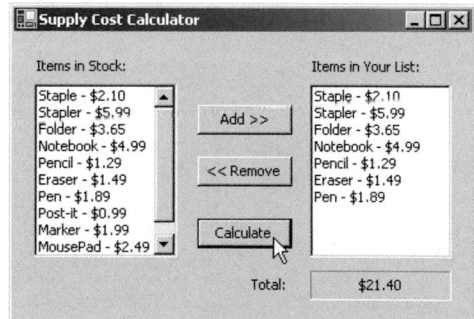

Figure 23.18 Supply Cost Calculator application's GUI.

23.12 (*Encryption Application*) Write an application that encrypts a message from the user. The application should be able to encrypt the message in two different ways: substitution cipher and transposition cipher (both described below). The user should be able to enter the message in a TextBox and select the desired method of encryption. Display the encrypted message in a Label.

In a substitution cipher, every character in the English alphabet is represented by a different character in the substitution alphabet. Every time a letter occurs in the English sentence, it is replaced by the letter in the corresponding index of the substitution string. In a transposition cipher, two Strings are created. The first new String contains all the characters at the even indices of the input String. The second new String contains all of the characters at the odd indices. The new Strings are the encrypted text. For example a substitution cipher for the word "code" would be: "cd oe."

a) *Copying and opening the template application.* Copy the Encryption folder from C:\Examples\Tutorial23\Exercises to C:\SimplyVB. Double click the Encryption.sln file in the Encryption folder to open the application in Visual Studio .NET.

b) *Adding code to the Encrypt Button.* Double click the **Encrypt** Button to create an empty event handler.

c) *Determine the cipher method.* Use If...Then...Else statements to determine which method of encryption the user has selected and call the appropriate procedure.

d) *Locating the SubstitutionCipher method.* Locate the SubstitutionCipher procedure. The English and substitution alphabet Strings have been defined for you in this procedure.

e) *Converting the text input to lowercase.* Add code to the SubstitutionCipher method that uses the ToLower method of class String to make all the characters in the input string (txtPlainText.Text) lowercase.

f) *Performing the substitution encryption.* Use nested For...Next loops to iterate through each character of the input String. When each character from the input String is found in the String holding the English alphabet, replace the character in the input String with the character located at the same index in the substitution String.

g) *Display the String.* Now that the String has been substituted with all the corresponding cipher characters, assign the cipher String to the lblCipherText Label.

h) *Locating the TranspositionCipher method.* Locate the TranspositionCipher method. Define three variables—a counter variable and two Strings (each representing a word).

i) *Extracting the first word.* Use a Do...While...Loop to retrieve all the "even" indices (starting from 0) from the input String. Increment the counter variable by 2 each time, and add the characters located at even indices to the first String created in *Step h.*

j) *Extracting the second word.* Use another Do...While...Loop to retrieve all the "odd" indices (starting from 1) from the same input String. Increment the counter variable by 2, and add the characters at odd indices to the second String that you created in *Step h.*

k) *Output the result.* Add the two Strings together with a space in between, and output the result to the lblCipherText Label.

Figure 23.19 Encryption application's GUI.

23.13 (*Anagram Game Application*) Write an **Anagram Game** that contains an array of pre-set words. The game should randomly select a word and scramble its letters. A Label displays the scrambled word for the user to guess. If the user guesses correctly, display a message, and repeat the process with a different word. If the guess is incorrect, display a message, and let the user try again.

a) *Copying and opening the template application.* Copy the Anagram folder from C:\Examples\Tutorial23\Exercises to C:\SimplyVB. Double click the Anagram.sln file in the Anagram folder to open the application in Visual Studio .NET.

b) *Locating the GenerateAnagram method.* Locate the GenerateAnagram method. It is the first method after the FrmAnagram_Load event handler.

c) *Picking a random word.* Generate a random number to use as the index of the word in the m_strAnagram array. Retrieve word from the m_strAnagram array, using the first random number as an index. Store the word in another `String` variable. Generate a second random number to store the index of a character to be moved.

d) ***Generate the scrambled word.*** Use a For…Next statement to iterate through the word 20 times. Each time the loop executes, pass the second random number created in *Step c* to the Chars property of class `String`. Append the character returned by Chars to the end of the `String`, and remove it from its original position. Next, generate a new random number to move a different character during the next iteration of the loop. Remember to output the final word to the `lblAnagram` Label.

e) ***Defining the Submit Button.*** Double click the **Submit** Button to generate an empty event handler.

f) ***Testing the user's input.*** Use an If…Then…Else statement to determine whether the user's input matches the actual word. If the user is correct, clear and place the focus on the TextBox and generate a new word. Otherwise, select the user's text and place focus on the TextBox.

Figure 23.20 **Anagram Game** application's GUI.

What does this code do? ▶ **23.14** What is assigned to `strResult` when the following code executes?

```
1   Dim strWord1 As String = "CHORUS"
2   Dim strWord2 As String = "d i n o s a u r"
3   Dim strWord3 As String = "The theme is string."
4   Dim strResult As String
5
6   strResult = strWord1.ToLower()
7   strResult = strResult.Substring(4)
8   strWord2 = strWord2.Replace(" ", "")
9   strWord2 = strWord2.Substring(4, 4)
10  strResult = strWord2 & strResult
11
12  strWord3 = strWord3.Substring(strWord3.IndexOf(" ") + 1, 3)
13
14  strResult = strWord3.Insert(3, strResult)
```

What's wrong with this code? ▶ **23.15** This code should remove all commas from `strTest`. Find the error(s) in the following code.

```
1   Dim strTest As String = "Bug,2,Bug"
2
3   strTest = strWord1.ToUpper()
4   strTest = strTest.Replace("")
```

Programming Challenge ▶ **23.16** (***Pig Latin Application***) Write an application that encodes English language phrases into pig Latin (Fig. 23.21). Pig Latin is a form of coded language often used for amusement.

Many variations exist in the methods used to form pig Latin phrases. For simplicity, use the following method to form the pig Latin words:

> *To form a pig Latin word from an English-language phrase, the translation proceeds one word at a time. To translate an English word into a pig Latin word, place the first letter of the English word (if it is not a vowel) at the end of the English word and add the letters "ay." If the first letter of the English word is a vowel, place it at the end of the word and add "y." Using this method, the word "jump" becomes "umpjay," the word "the" becomes "hetay" and the word "ace" becomes "ceay." Blanks between words remain blanks.*

Assume the following: The English phrase consists of words separated by blanks, there are no punctuation marks and all words have two or more letters. Enable the user to input a sentence. The `TranslateToPigLatin` method should translate the sentence into pig Latin, word by word. [*Hint*: You will need to use the `Join` and `Split` methods of class `String` demonstrated in Fig. 23.16 to form the pig Latin phrases].

a) ***Copying and opening the template application***. Copy the `PigLatin` folder from `C:\Examples\Tutorial23\Exercises` to `C:\SimplyVB`. Double click the `Pig-Latin.sln` file in the `PigLatin` folder to open the application in Visual Studio .NET.

b) ***Splitting the sentence***. Use method `Split` on the `String` passed to the `TranslateToPigLatin` method. Assign the result of this operation to `strWords`.

c) ***Retrieving the word's first letter***. Declare a `For…Next` loop that iterates through your array of words. As you iterate through the array, store each word's first letter in `strTemporary`.

d) ***Determining the suffix***. Use `If…Then…Else` statements to determine the suffix for each word. Store this suffix in `strSuffix`.

e) ***Generating new words***. Generate the new words by arranging each word's pieces in the proper order.

f) ***Returning the new sentence***. When the `For…Next` loop finishes, use method `Join` to combine all of the elements in `strWords`, and `Return` the new pig Latin sentence.

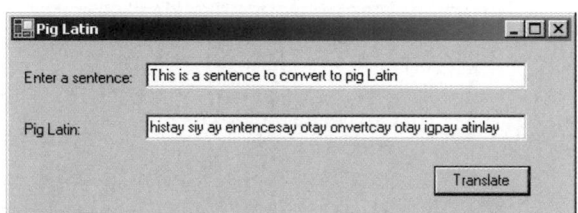

Figure 23.21 Pig Latin application.

TUTORIAL

Objectives

In this tutorial, you will learn to:
- Create, read from, write to and update files.
- Understand a computer's data hierarchy.
- Become familiar with sequential-access file processing.
- Use `StreamReader` and `StreamWriter` classes to read from, and write to, sequential-access files.
- Add and configure a `MonthCalendar` control.

Outline

Ticket Information Application

Introducing Sequential-Access Files

You have used variables and arrays to store data temporarily—the data is lost when a method or program terminates. When you want to store data for a longer period of time, you can use **files**, which are collections of data that are given a name such as `data.txt` or `Welcome.sln`. Data in files exists even after the program that created the data terminates. Such data often is called **persistent data**. Computers store these files on **secondary storage media**, including magnetic disks (for example, the hard drive of your computer), optical disks (for instance, CD-ROMs or DVDs) and magnetic tapes (which are similar to music cassette tapes).

File processing, which includes creating, reading from, writing to and updating files, is an important capability of Visual Basic .NET. It enables Visual Basic .NET to support commercial applications that typically process massive amounts of persistent data. In this tutorial, you will learn about **sequential-access files**, which contain information that is read from a file in the order that it was originally written to the file. You will learn how to create, open and write to a sequential-access file by building a **Write Event** application. This application allows the user to create or open a **text file** (a file containing human-readable characters) and to input the date, time and description of a community event (such as a concert or a sporting match).

You will then learn how to read data from a file by building the **Ticket Information** application. This application displays data from a file called `calendar.txt` created by the **Write Event** application.

24.1 Test-Driving the Ticket Information Application

Many communities and businesses use computer applications to allow their members and customers to view information about upcoming events, such as movies, concerts, sports and other activities. The **Write Event** application that you build in Section 24.4 writes the community event information to a sequential-access file. The **Ticket Information** application that you build in Section 24.5 displays the data stored in the file generated by the **Write Event** application. The **Ticket Information** application must meet the following requirements:

Your application will allow a user to select a date from a **MonthCalendar** control. Then the application will open the calendar.txt file and read its contents to display information about events scheduled for the selected date. You begin by test-driving the completed application.

Test-Driving the Ticket Information Application

1. *Opening the completed application.* Double click TicketInformation.sln in the C:\Examples\Tutorial24\CompletedApplication\TicketInformation folder.

2. *Running the application and viewing the Form.* Select **Debug > Start** to execute the program. The Form shown in Fig. 24.1 will appear. The calendar will look different, depending on the date that you test-drive this application. The calendar should reflect the day and month on which you actually run the application. The MonthCalendar control is similar to the DateTimePicker control (Tutorial 14), except that MonthCalendar allows you to select a range of dates, whereas the DateTimePicker allows you to select the time, but no more than one date. For simplicity, users of this application should select only one date. In addition, the application deals only with the current month, but the MonthCalendar control does allow the user to view calendars of previous or future months by using the arrow buttons.

Arrow buttons allow user to scroll through months

MonthCalendar control

ComboBox lists any events

TextBox displays event details

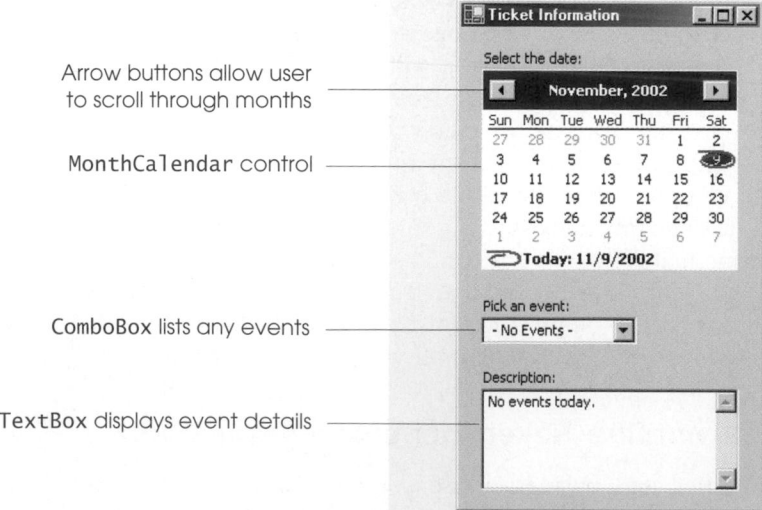

Figure 24.1 Ticket Information application's GUI.

(cont.)   3. **Getting event information.** Select the 18th day of the current month in the MonthCalendar. Notice that the ComboBox displays the message "- No Events -" (Fig. 24.2). This is because there are no events scheduled for the 18th. Select the 19th day of the month. Notice that the ComboBox now displays "- Events -". Click the ComboBox to view the scheduled events and select **Comedy club**. The time, price and description of the event appear in the **Description:** TextBox (Fig. 24.2).

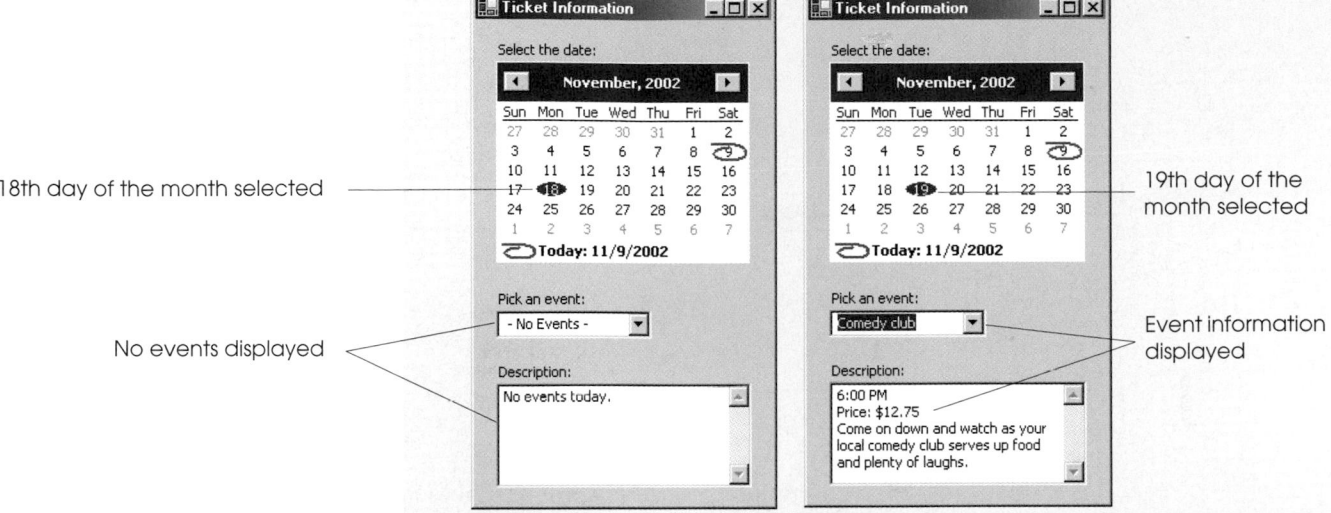

18th day of the month selected

No events displayed

19th day of the month selected

Event information displayed

Figure 24.2 **Ticket Information** application displaying event information.

4. **Testing the application.** Select other dates (such as 1, 12 and 30) and view the results.

5. **Terminating the application.** Click the application's close box to terminate the application.

6. **Closing the solution.** Select **File > Close Solution**.

SELF-REVIEW   1. The _____ control allows a user to select a range of dates.
   a) DateTimePicker   b) MonthCalendar
   c) ComboBox   d) TextBox

2. The MonthCalendar control is similar to the _____ control.
   a) DateTimePicker   b) ComboBox
   c) TextBox   d) Timer

Answers: 1) b. 2) a.

24.2 Data Hierarchy

Data items processed by computers form a **data hierarchy** (Fig. 24.3) in which data items become larger and more complex in structure as they progress from bits, to characters, to fields and to larger data structures.

Throughout this book, you have been manipulating data in your programs. The data has been in several forms: **decimal digits** (0, 1, 2, 3, 4, 5, 6, 7, 8 and 9), **letters** (A–Z and a–z) and **special symbols** ($, @, %, &, *, (,), -, +, ", :, ?, / and many others). Digits, letters and special symbols are referred to as **characters**. The set of all characters used to write programs and represent data items on a particular computer is called that computer's **character set**.

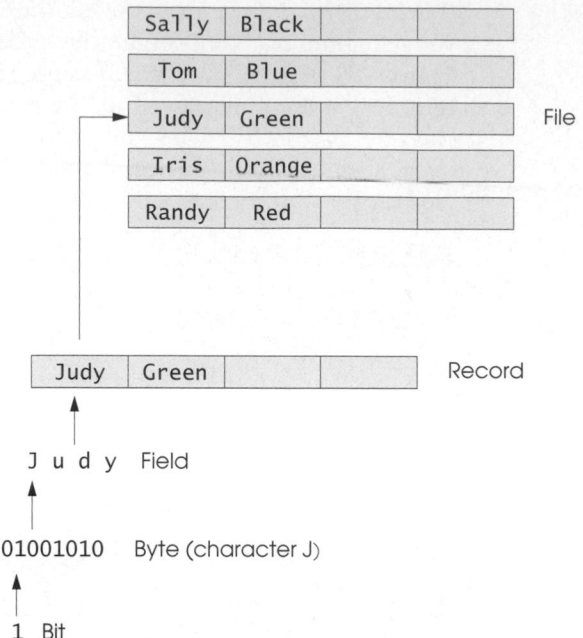

Figure 24.3 Data hierarchy.

The computer's character set is readable and understandable by humans. Ultimately, however, all data items processed by a computer are reduced to combinations of zeros and ones. The smallest data item that computers support is called a **bit**. "Bit" is short for "**binary digit**"—a digit that can be one of two values. Each data item, or bit, can be set only to the value 0 or the value 1. Computer circuitry performs various simple bit manipulations, such as examining the value of a bit, setting the value of a bit and reversing the value of a bit (from 1 to 0 or from 0 to 1). This approach has been adopted because it is simple and economical to build electronic devices that can assume two stable states—0 representing one state and 1 representing the other. It is remarkable that the extensive functions performed by computers involve only the most fundamental manipulations of 0s and 1s.

Because computers can process only 0s and 1s, every character in a computer's character set is represented as a pattern of 0s and 1s. **Bytes** are composed of 8 bits. Characters in Visual Basic .NET are **Unicode** characters, which are composed of 2 bytes. Programming with data in the low-level form of bits is difficult, so programmers create programs and data items with characters, and computers manipulate and process these characters as patterns of bits.

Just as characters are composed of bits, **fields** are composed of characters. A field is a group of characters that conveys some meaning. For example, a field consisting of uppercase and lowercase letters can represent a person's name.

Typically, a **record** (which usually is represented as a `Class` in Visual Basic .NET) is a collection of several related fields (called member variables in Visual Basic .NET). In a payroll system, for example, a record for a particular employee might include the following fields:

1. Employee identification number

2. Name

3. Address

4. Hourly pay rate

5. Number of exemptions claimed

6. Year-to-date earnings

7. Amount of taxes withheld

Thus, a record is a group of related fields. In the preceding example, each field is associated with the same employee. A **file** is a group of related records. A company's payroll file normally contains one record for each employee. Hence, a payroll file for a small company might contain only 22 records, whereas a payroll file for a large company might contain 100,000 records. It is not unusual for a company to have many files, some containing millions, billions or even trillions of characters of information.

To facilitate the retrieval of specific records from a file, at least one field in each record is chosen as a **record key**. A record key identifies a record as belonging to a particular person or entity and distinguishes that record from all other records. Therefore, the record key must be unique. In the payroll record just described, the employee identification number normally would be chosen as the record key because each employee's identification number is different.

There are many ways to organize records in a file. The most common type of organization is called a **sequential file**, in which records typically are stored in order by a record-key field. In a payroll file, records usually are placed in order by employee identification number. The first employee record in the file contains the lowest employee identification number, and subsequent records contain increasingly higher employee identification numbers.

Most businesses use many different files to store data. For example, a company might have payroll files, accounts receivable files (listing money due from clients), accounts payable files (listing money due to suppliers), inventory files (listing facts about all the items handled by the business) and many other types of files. Sometimes, a group of related files is called a **database**. A collection of programs designed to create and manage databases is called a **database management system** (DBMS). You will learn about databases in Tutorial 25.

SELF-REVIEW

1. The smallest data item a computer can process is called a _____.

   a) database   b) byte

   c) file   d) bit

2. A _____ is a group of related records.

   a) file   b) field

   c) bit   d) byte

Answers: 1) d. 2) a.

24.3 Files and Streams

Visual Basic .NET actually views each file as a sequential **stream** of bytes (Fig. 24.4). When a file is opened, Visual Basic .NET creates an object and associates a stream with that object.

Figure 24.4   Visual Basic .NET's conceptual view of an *n-byte* file.

Common Programming Error

Having a `StreamReader` and `StreamWriter` object open for the same file at the same time causes an error because both objects are attempting to access the same file.

To perform file processing in Visual Basic .NET, namespace `System.IO` must be imported. This namespace includes definitions of stream classes such as **StreamReader** (for text input from a file) and **StreamWriter** (for text output to a file).

24.4 Writing to a File: Creating the Write Event Application

An important aspect of the **Ticket Information** application is its ability to read data sequentially from a file. You will need to create the file from which the **Ticket Infor-**

mation application will read its data. Therefore, before you create the **Ticket Information** application, you must learn how to write to a file sequentially.

The **Write Event** application should enable the user to create a new file or open an existing file. The user might want to create a new file for events or update an existing file by adding more event information. You will add this functionality in the box, *Adding a Dialog to Open or Create a File.*

Adding a Dialog to Open or Create a File

1. ***Copying the template application to your work folder.*** Copy the `C:\Examples\Tutorial24\TemplateApplication\WriteEvent` folder to `C:\SimplyVB`.

2. ***Opening the template application.*** Double click `WriteEvent.sln` in the `C:\SimplyVB\WriteEvent` folder to open the application in Visual Studio .NET.

3. ***Adding a dialog to the Form.*** The application uses the **OpenFileDialog** control to customize the **Open** dialog. To add an `OpenFileDialog` component to the application, double click the `OpenFileDialog` control

                    | OpenFileDialog |

in the **Windows Forms** tab of the **Toolbox**. Change the control's `Name` property to `objOpenFileDialog`. Change its **FileName** property to `calendar.txt`, which will be the default file name displayed in the **Open** dialog. [*Note:* This is the name of the file from which the **Ticket Information** application retrieves information.] The **Open** dialog normally allows the user to open only existing files, but you also want the user to be able to create a file. For this reason, set property **CheckFileExists** to `False` so that the **Open** dialog allows the user to specify a new file name. If the user specifies a file that does not exist, the file is created and opened. Figure 24.5 shows the application in design view after the `OpenFileDialog` control has been added and renamed.

`OpenFileDialog` control ⎯⎯

Figure 24.5   `OpenFileDialog` added and renamed.

4. ***Saving the solution.*** Select **File > Save All** to save all the solution's files.

The **Write Event** application stores the user-input information in a text file. It expects the user to open or create a file with the extension .txt. If the user does not do so, the application displays an error message. The box, *Determining Whether a File Name Is Valid*, guides you through adding this functionality.

Determining Whether a File Name Is Valid

1. **Adding the header for method `CheckValidity`.** Add lines 202–206 of Fig. 24.6 to the application. Method `CheckValidity` receives a file name as a String and returns a Boolean value. If the file name is valid, the Function returns True. Otherwise, the Function returns False.

CheckValidity Function procedure header

Figure 24.6 Method `CheckValidity` header.

2. **Displaying a `MessageBox` to indicate an invalid file name.** Add lines 206–213 of Fig. 24.7 to method `CheckValidity`. String method `EndsWith` (line 207) returns False if strName does not end with .txt, the extension that indicates a text file. Lines 208–210 display a MessageBox informing the user that the application expects a text file.

Displaying error message if incorrect file type is provided

Figure 24.7 Displaying an error message indicating an invalid file name.

3. **Receiving a valid file name.** Add lines 213–218 of Fig. 24.8 to the If...Then statement. If a valid file name is entered, method `CheckValidity` should return True. The GUI should indicate that the user cannot create or open another file, but the user may enter data into the file or close the file. For this reason, line 215 disables the **Open File...** Button, while lines 216–217 enable the **Enter** and **Close File** Buttons, respectively. The method returns True (line 218) to indicate that the user entered a valid file name.

4. **Saving the solution.** Select **File > Save All** to save all the solution's files.

(cont.)

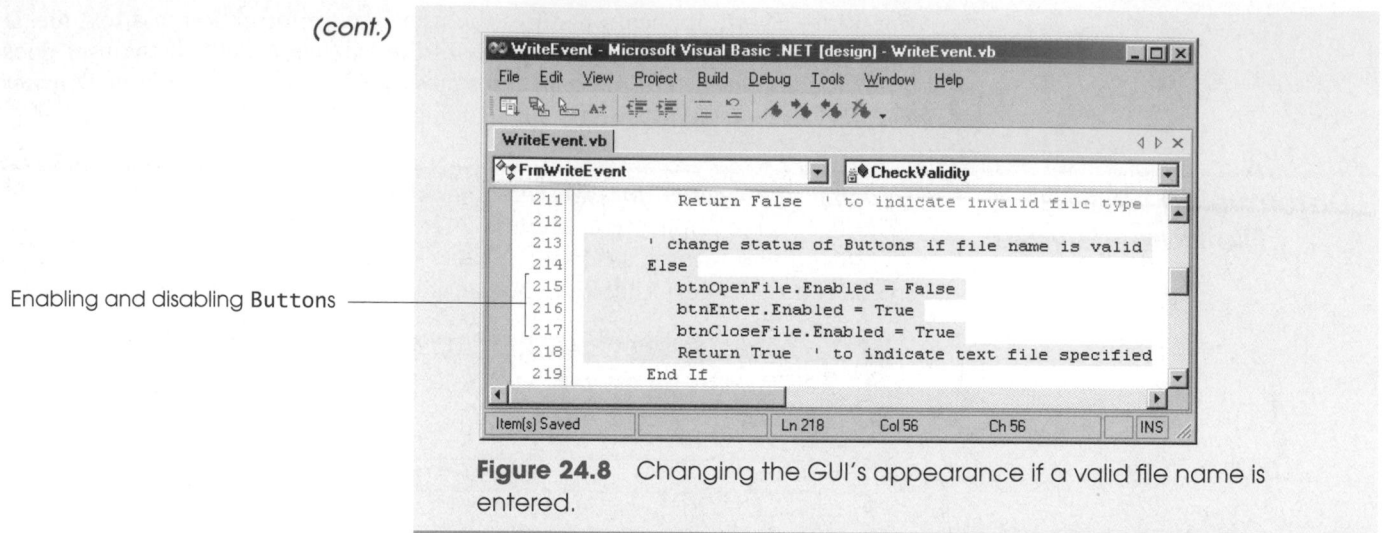

Figure 24.8 Changing the GUI's appearance if a valid file name is entered.

You have added the OpenFileDialog control to allow users to open a file and a method that determines whether the user has entered a valid file name. Now you will add code that associates the specified file with a stream.

Creating a StreamWriter Object

1. ***Importing namespace System.IO to enable file processing.*** To access the classes and methods that will enable you to perform file processing with sequential-access files, you must import namespace System.IO. Accordingly, add line 1 of Fig. 24.9.

Figure 24.9 System.IO namespace imported into FrmWriteEvent class.

2. ***Declaring a StreamWriter variable.*** Namespace System.IO includes class StreamWriter, which is used to create objects for writing text to a file. You will use a StreamWriter to write data into the file created or opened by the user. Add line 6 of Fig. 24.10 to the FrmWriteEvent class definition to declare the variable that will be assigned a StreamWriter object.

3. ***Creating the Open File... Button's Click event handler.*** Double click the **Open File...** Button on the **Write Event** application's Form (Fig. 24.11) to create the empty btnOpenFile_Click event handler.

4. ***Displaying the Open dialog.*** Add lines 231–240 of Fig. 24.12 to the event handler. When the user clicks the **Open File...** Button, the **ShowDialog** method of the OpenFileDialog control displays the **Open** dialog to allow the user to open a file (line 232). If the user specifies a file that does not exist, it will be created. The user can use the default file name (calendar.txt) or specify another file name. Line 232 assigns the return value of method ShowDialog to a DialogResult variable named result.

(cont.)

Figure 24.10 Declaring a `StreamWriter` object.

Declaring `StreamWriter` object

Open File... Button

objOpenFileDialog

Figure 24.11 **Write Event** application `Form` in design view.

5. ***Exiting event handler if the user clicks the Cancel Button.*** The value of the `DialogResult` variable specifies whether the user clicked the **Cancel** `Button` in the **Open** dialog. If the user did so, the event handler exits (line 236). At this point, the user can still open or create a file by clicking the enabled **Open File...** `Button` again.

6. ***Retrieving the file name.*** Property `FileName` of `OpenFileDialog` specifies the file name that the user selected (line 240). The application stores the path and file name in `strFileName`. The file name will be tested to determine whether it is valid and then used to initialize the `StreamWriter` object.

7. ***Checking for a valid file type.*** Add lines 242–247 of Fig. 24.13 to the event handler. Line 243 invokes method `CheckValidity` (which you defined in the box, *Determining Whether a File Name is Valid*) to determine whether the specified file is a text file (that is, the file name ends with `".txt"`).

(cont.)

Displaying **Open** dialog

If the user clicks **Cancel** the event handler exits

Setting variable to user-specified file name

Figure 24.12 Displaying the **Open** dialog and retrieving the result.

Check for valid filename

Create **StreamWriter** object

Figure 24.13 Validating the filename and initializing a **StreamWriter** object.

Common Programming Error

When you open an existing file by invoking the **StreamWriter** constructor with a **False** second argument, data previously contained in the file will be lost.

8. *Initializing a StreamWriter object.* The call to the StreamWriter constructor (line 246) initializes StreamWriter object m_objOutput, which will be used to write to the new file specified by the user. Notice that the StreamWriter constructor takes two arguments. The first indicates the name of the file (specified by variable strFileName) to which you will write information. The second is a Boolean value that determines whether the StreamWriter will append information to the end of the file. You pass value True, so that any information written to the file will be appended to the end of the file.

9. *Saving the solution.* Select **File > Save All** to save all the solution's files.

Now that the application can open a file, the user can input information that will be written to that file. In the box, *Writing Information to a Sequential-Access File,* you will add code that makes the **Enter** Button's Click event handler write the data to the text file.

Writing Information to a Sequential-Access File

1. *Clearing user input from the TextBoxes and resetting the NumericUpDown control.* Add lines 251–257 of Fig. 24.14 to the application below the btnOpenFile_Click event handler. After the user's input is processed, the **Enter** Button's event handler will invoke method ClearUserInput to clear the TextBoxes and to reset the NumericUpDown control's value to 1 (the first day of the month).

Clearing user input

Figure 24.14   Clearing user input.

2. *Creating the btnEnter_Click event handler.* In design view, double click the **Enter** Button to add the btnEnter_Click event handler.

3. *Defining the btnEnter_Click event handler.* Add lines 263–269 of Fig. 24.15 to the event handler. Lines 263–269 write the user input line by line to the file by using the StreamWriter's **WriteLine** method. The Write-Line method writes its argument to the file, followed by a newline character. The information is written to the file in the following order: day of the event, time, price, event name and description. Each piece of information is written on a separate line of the file. Line 269 invokes the ClearUserInput procedure that you defined in *Step 1* of this box.

Writing information to file

Figure 24.15   StreamWriter writing to a file.

4. *Saving the solution.* Select **File > Save All** to save all the solution's files.

You should close the connection to the file after you have finished processing it. You will add this capability to the **Close File** Button's Click event handler in the box, *Closing the StreamWriter.*

1. **Create the btnClose_Click event handler.** Double click the **Close File** Button of the **Write Event** application's Form. The btnClose_Click event handler appears in the WriteEvent.vb file.

2. **Defining the btnClose_Click event handler.** Add lines 276–281 of Fig. 24.16 to the event handler. Line 276 uses the StreamWriter's **Close** method to close the stream. Line 279 reenables the **Open File...** Button in case the user would like to create or update another sequential-access file. Lines 280–281 disable the **Enter** and **Close File** Buttons because users should not be able to click these Buttons when a file is not open.

Closing StreamWriter object

Figure 24.16 Closing the StreamWriter.

3. **Saving the solution.** Select **File > Save All** to save all the solution's files.

You have now successfully created the **Write Event** application. You will test this application to see how it works and will view the file contents in the box, *Writing Event Information to a File.*

1. **Running the Write Event application.** Double click the WriteEvent.sln in the C:\SimplyVB\WriteEvent folder. Select **Debug > Start** to execute the **Write Event** application. The Form displayed in Fig. 24.17 should appear.

Figure 24.17 **Write Event** application executing.

(cont.)

2. ***Creating a file.*** Click the **Open File...** Button to create the file to which you will write. The **Open** dialog appears. Browse to the folder `C:\Examples\ Tutorial24\TemplateApplication\TicketInformation\bin`. [*Note*: An existing `calendar.txt` file should appear in the **Open** dialog.] The file name `calendar.txt` should be displayed in the **File name:** field, as in Fig. 24.18. Click the **Open** Button. This will open the existing `calendar.txt` file.

Figure 24.18   **Open** dialog displaying contents of the template **Ticket Information** application's `bin` folder.

3. ***Inputting event information.*** In the **Day:** NumericUpDown control, select 4 to indicate that the event is scheduled on the fourth day of the month. Enter `2:30 PM` in the **Time:** DateTimePicker. Type `12.50` in the **Price:** TextBox. Enter `Arts and Crafts Fair` in the **Event:** TextBox. In the **Description:** TextBox, enter the information `Take part in creating various types of arts and crafts at this fair`. Click the **Enter** Button to add this event's information to the `calendar.txt` file.

4. ***Inputting more event information.*** Write more event information to the file by repeating *Step 3* with your own set of events.

5. ***Closing the file.*** When you have entered all the events you wish, click the **Close File** Button. This closes the `calendar.txt` file and prevents any more events from being written.

6. ***Terminating the executing application.*** Click the application's close box.

7. ***Opening and closing the sequential-access file.*** Use Visual Studio .NET to open `calendar.txt`. Select **File > Open > File...** to display the **Open** dialog. Select the `calendar.txt` file that you created and click **Open**. Scroll down towards the bottom of the file. The information you entered in *Step 3* should appear in the file, similar to Fig. 24.19. Close the `calendar.txt` file.

8. ***Closing the solution.*** Select **File > Close Solution**.

Day and time of event, ticket price, event name and description

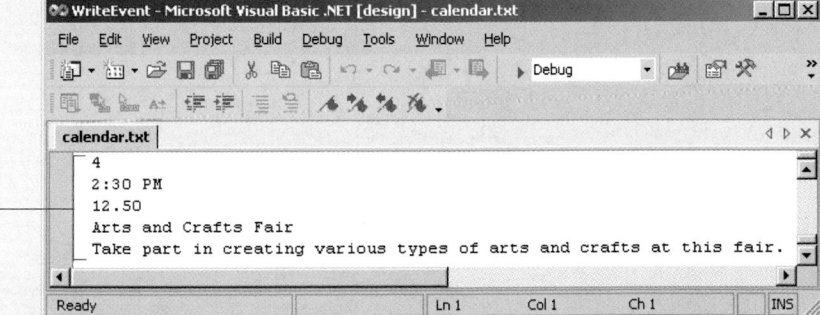

Figure 24.19   Sequential-access file generated by **Write Event** application.

Figure 24.20 presents the **Write Event** application's code.

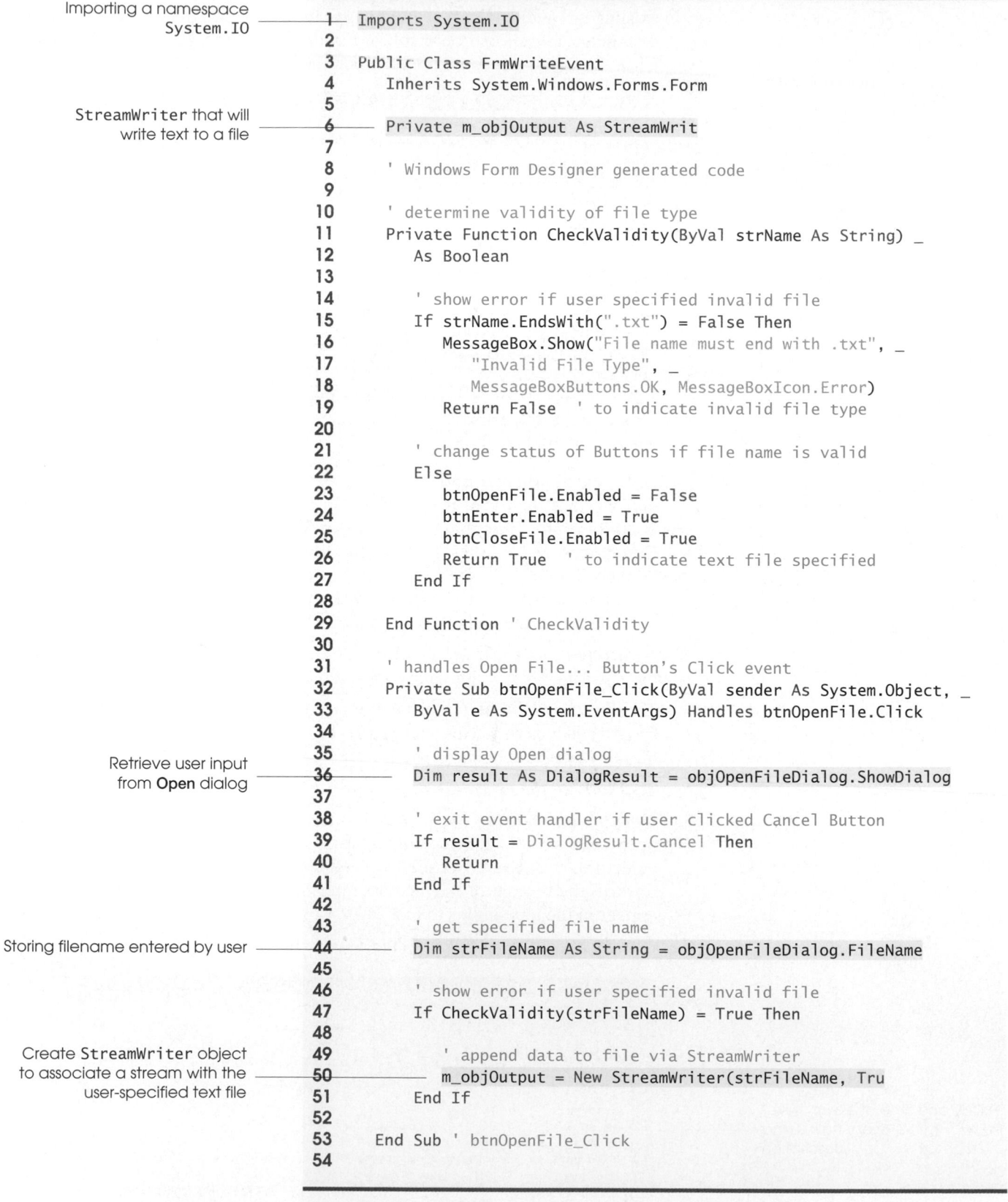

Importing a namespace
System.IO

StreamWriter that will
write text to a file

Retrieve user input
from **Open** dialog

Storing filename entered by user

Create **StreamWriter** object
to associate a stream with the
user-specified text file

```
1    Imports System.IO
2
3    Public Class FrmWriteEvent
4        Inherits System.Windows.Forms.Form
5
6        Private m_objOutput As StreamWrit
7
8        ' Windows Form Designer generated code
9
10       ' determine validity of file type
11       Private Function CheckValidity(ByVal strName As String) _
12          As Boolean
13
14          ' show error if user specified invalid file
15          If strName.EndsWith(".txt") = False Then
16             MessageBox.Show("File name must end with .txt", _
17                "Invalid File Type", _
18                MessageBoxButtons.OK, MessageBoxIcon.Error)
19             Return False  ' to indicate invalid file type
20
21          ' change status of Buttons if file name is valid
22          Else
23             btnOpenFile.Enabled = False
24             btnEnter.Enabled = True
25             btnCloseFile.Enabled = True
26             Return True   ' to indicate text file specified
27          End If
28
29       End Function ' CheckValidity
30
31       ' handles Open File... Button's Click event
32       Private Sub btnOpenFile_Click(ByVal sender As System.Object, _
33          ByVal e As System.EventArgs) Handles btnOpenFile.Click
34
35          ' display Open dialog
36          Dim result As DialogResult = objOpenFileDialog.ShowDialog
37
38          ' exit event handler if user clicked Cancel Button
39          If result = DialogResult.Cancel Then
40             Return
41          End If
42
43          ' get specified file name
44          Dim strFileName As String = objOpenFileDialog.FileName
45
46          ' show error if user specified invalid file
47          If CheckValidity(strFileName) = True Then
48
49             ' append data to file via StreamWriter
50             m_objOutput = New StreamWriter(strFileName, Tru
51          End If
52
53       End Sub ' btnOpenFile_Click
54
```

Figure 24.20 **Write Event** application's code. (Part 1 of 2.)

```
55        ' clear TextBoxes and reset NumericUpDown control
56        Private Sub ClearUserInput()
57           updDay.Value = 1
58           txtPrice.Clear()
59           txtEvent.Clear()
60           txtDescription.Clear()
61        End Sub ' ClearUserInput
62
63        ' handles Enter Button's Click event
64        Private Sub btnEnter_Click(ByVal sender As System.Object, _
65           ByVal e As System.EventArgs) Handles btnEnter.Click
66
67           ' using StreamWriter to write data to file
68           m_objOutput.WriteLine(updDay.Text)
69           m_objOutput.WriteLine(dtpTime.Text)
70           m_objOutput.WriteLine(txtPrice.Text)
71           m_objOutput.WriteLine(txtEvent.Text)
72           m_objOutput.WriteLine(txtDescription.Text
73           ClearUserInput()  ' prepare GUI for more user input
74        End Sub ' btnEnter_Click
75
76        ' handles Close File Button's Click event
77        Private Sub btnCloseFile_Click(ByVal sender As System.Object, _
78           ByVal e As System.EventArgs) Handles btnCloseFile.Click
79
80           m_objOutput.Close()  ' close StreamWrit
81
82           ' allow user to open another file
83           btnOpenFile.Enabled = True
84           btnEnter.Enabled = False
85           btnCloseFile.Enabled = False
86        End Sub ' btnCloseFile_Click
87
88   End Class ' FrmWriteEvent
```

Append data to end of file ——— (lines 68–72)

Closing the file's associated stream ——— (line 80)

Figure 24.20   Write Event application's code. (Part 2 of 2.)

24.5 Building the Ticket Information Application

Now that you have created the **Write Event** application to enable a user to write community-event information to a sequential-access text file, you will create the **Ticket Information** application you test-drove at the beginning of the tutorial. First you need to analyze the application. The following pseudocode describes the actions that the application needs to perform to solve the problem:

> When the user selects a date on the calendar
>> Check whether events are scheduled for that day
>>
>> If events are scheduled for that day
>>> Display list of events in the ComboBox
>>>
>>> If the user selects an event from the list
>>>> Display event information in the TextBox
>> Else
>>> Display "-No Events-" in the ComboBox
>>> Display "No events today." in the TextBox

The ACE table in Fig. 24.21 presents the **Ticket Information** application's actions and events. These actions and events will guide you as you build the application.

Action/Control/Event (ACE) Table for the Ticket Information Application

Action	Control	Event
Label the application's controls	lblDay, lblTime, lblPrice, lblEvent, lblDescription	
Specify date for which information should be displayed	mvwDate	DateChanged
Display events for the selected day in TextBox	cboEvent, txtDescription	SelectedIndexChanged (of ComboBox)

Figure 24.21   ACE table for the **Ticket Information** application.

The **Ticket Information** application allows the user to view the information for a specific date by selecting the date from a MonthCalendar control. The box, *Adding a MonthCalendar Control*, guides you through configuring the MonthCalendar control.

*Adding a MonthCalendar **Control***

1. ***Copying the template to your work folder.*** Copy the C:\Examples\Tutorial24\TemplateApplication\TicketInformation folder to C:\SimplyVB.

2. ***Opening the template application.*** Double click TicketInformation.sln in the C:\SimplyVB\TicketInformation folder to open the application in Visual Studio .NET. The template Form in design view looks like Fig. 24.22. The template also provides the empty methods CreateEventList and ExtractData. You will add code to these methods later.

Figure 24.22   MonthCalendar template application's Form.

3. ***Add a MonthCalendar control to the Form.*** Double click the MonthCalendar control

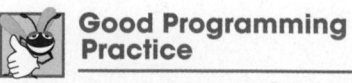

in the **Windows Form** tab of the **Toolbox**. Click the MonthCalendar control on the Form. The **Properties** window should display the control's properties. Change the Name property to mvwDate. Set the Location of the MonthCalendar control to 16, 32.

4. ***Saving the solution.*** Select **File > Save All** to save all the solution's files.

Good Programming Practice

Prefix the names of MonthCalendar controls with mvw.

Now that you have added the MonthCalendar control, you can begin writing code for the **Ticket Information** application. For this application, you will create two Sub procedures named CreateEventList and ExtractData. The template for this application provides the Sub procedure headers for both CreateEventList and ExtractData. You will define these Sub procedures in the boxes, *Defining the CreateEventList Method* and *Reading a Sequential-Access File*. Before adding any functionality to the application, you will import System.IO and create two instance variables in the box, *Beginning to Build the **Ticket Information** Application.*

Beginning to Build the *Ticket Information Application*	1. ***Importing namespace System.IO.*** You must import namespace System.IO to allow the application to use class StreamReader to read information from a sequential-access file. Accordingly, add line 1 of Fig. 24.23 before the class definition.

Figure 24.23   System.IO namespace imported to FrmEvents.

2. ***Adding instance variables.*** Add lines 6–10 of Fig. 24.24 to the application. To keep track of information, you will store the event information read from the file in array m_strData (line 7) and the number of events for a specified day in m_intNumberOfEvents (line 10). For simplicity, the array m_strData is initialized with ten rows of five items each (allowing up to ten total events per day).

Creating an array of Strings —

Figure 24.24   Instance variables declared in the **Ticket Information** application.

3. ***Saving the solution.*** Select **File > Save All** to save all the files in the solution.

When you execute the **Ticket Information** application, by default, the current day should be selected in the MonthCalendar control. The application should show the list of the day's events in the ComboBox. Recall that, if there are no events for the day, the ComboBox displays "- No Events -". In the box, *Handling the Form's Load Event*, you will invoke a method from the Form's Load event handler to set the display in the ComboBox appropriately.

Handling the *Form's* Load Event

1. ***Defining the Form's Load event.*** Double click the Form in design view to generate the event handler FrmEvents_Load. Add lines 138–139 of Fig. 24.25 to the Load event handler. Line 139 invokes method CreateEventList. You will soon add code to CreateEventList to populate the ComboBox with any events scheduled for the current day.

You will add code to
CreateEventList later

Figure 24.25 Load event handler calling method CreateEventList.

2. ***Saving the solution.*** Select **File > Save All** to save all the solution's files.

When the user selects a date in the MonthCalendar control, the **DateChanged** event is raised. You add code to the event handler that invokes the CreateEventList method in the box, *Handling the MonthCalendar's DateChanged Event*.

Handling the MonthCalendar's DateChanged Event

1. ***Creating the MonthCalendar's DateChanged event handler.*** In design view, double click the MonthCalendar to generate the empty event handler mvwDate_DateChanged.

2. ***Invoking the CreateEventList method.*** Add lines 147–148 of Fig. 24.26 to the mvwDate_DateChanged event handler. Line 148 invokes method CreateEventList, which you will define in the next box.

Calling the CreateEventList
method

Figure 24.26 MonthCalendar's DateChanged event handler.

3. ***Saving the solution.*** Select **File > Save All** to save all the solution's files.

The application invokes method `CreateEventList` during the Form's Load event and the `MonthCalendar`'s `DateChanged` event. The `CreateEventList` method will populate the `ComboBox` with event names if there are any events for the date the user chooses, or it will indicate that the event list is empty if there are no events for that day. You define this functionality in the box, *Defining the Create-EventList Method*.

Defining the CreateEventList Method

1. **Setting variables and clearing the ComboBox in the CreateEventList method.** Add lines 126–133 of Fig. 24.27 to the `CreateEventList` method. The `CreateEventList` method first declares a counter, `intCount` (line 126) that will be used to iterate through the events. Line 130 invokes the `Extract-Data` method defined in the next box, passing the `Date` that is currently selected in the `MonthCalendar`. This date is specified by the `MonthCalendar` control's **SelectionStart** property. You will define the `ExtractData` method in the box, *Reading a Sequential-Access File*. The `ExtractData` method will store event information in array `m_strData` and assign the number of events scheduled for the specified date to `m_intNumberOfEvents`. The `Items.Clear` method removes any events currently displayed in the ComboBox (line 133).

You will add code to ExtractData in the next box

```
123    ' Populates ComboBox with current day's events (if any)
124    Private Sub CreateEventList()
125
126        Dim intCount As Integer    ' counter
127
128        ' stores event information in array m_strData
129        ' and assigns number of events to m_intNumberOfEvents
130        ExtractData(mvwDate.SelectionStart)
131
132        ' remove any items in ComboBox
133        cboEvent.Items.Clear()
```

Figure 24.27 `CreateEventList` modified to call method `ExtractData` and clear the `ComboBox`.

2. **Setting events displayed in the ComboBox.** Add lines 135–152 of Fig. 24.28 to the `CreateEventList` method. If there are events scheduled for the chosen day (line 136), then the `For...Next` statement iterates through array `m_strData` and adds the name of each event to the `ComboBox` (lines 138–142). The `CreateEventList` method informs the user that there are events scheduled for the specified day by using the `Text` properties of the ComboBox and TextBox (lines 145–146). If there are events for the chosen day, then the ComboBox displays `"- Events -"` and the Textbox displays `"Pick an event."`. If there are no events for the chosen day, the ComboBox displays `"- No events -"` and the Textbox displays `"No events today."` (lines 150–151).

3. **Saving the solution.** Select **File > Save All** to save all the solution's files.

(cont.)

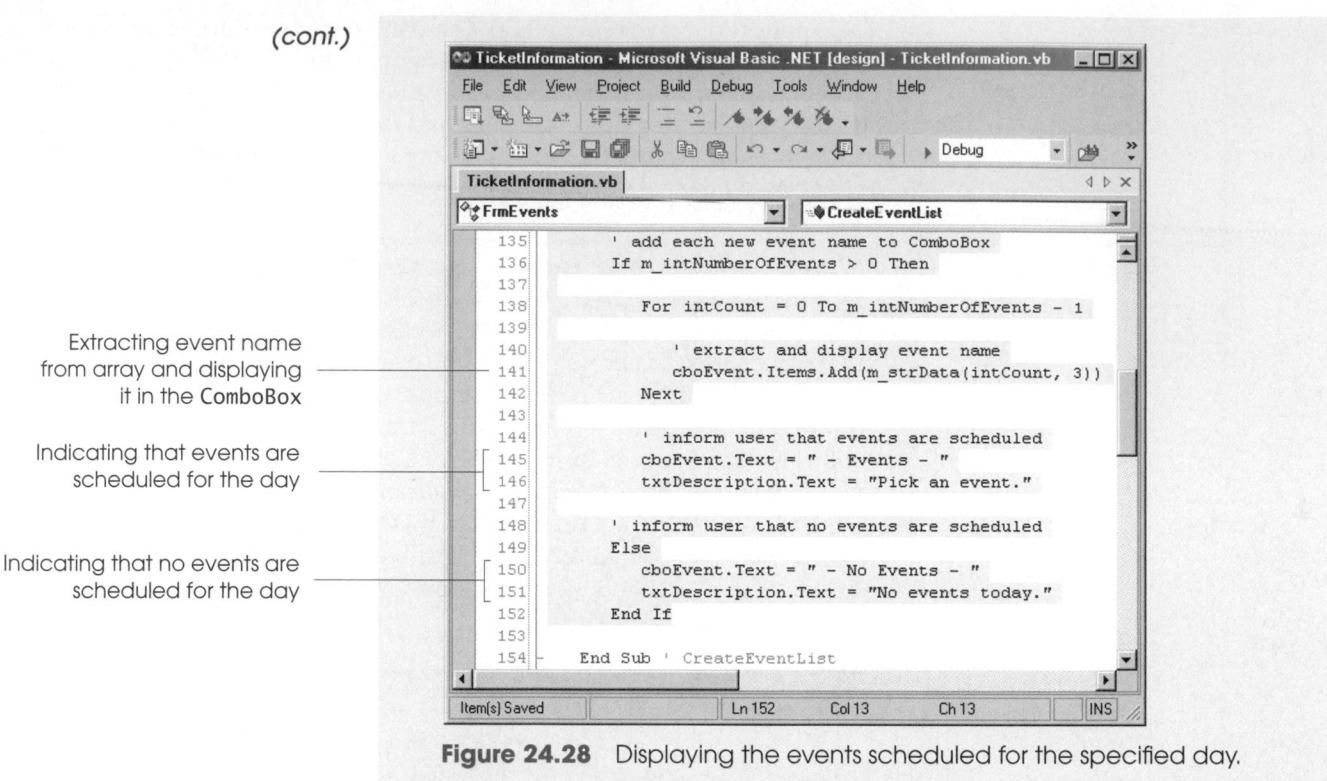

Extracting event name from array and displaying it in the **ComboBox**

Indicating that events are scheduled for the day

Indicating that no events are scheduled for the day

Figure 24.28 Displaying the events scheduled for the specified day.

As described in Step 1 of the previous box, the ExtractData method uses a variable of type Date (dtmDay) as its only parameter. The ExtractData method assigns the information about any events scheduled for that day to the m_strData array and assigns the number of events for that day to the m_intNumberOfEvents variable. You define the ExtractData method in the box, *Reading a Sequential-Access File.*

Reading a Sequential-Access File

1. ***Adding variables to the ExtractData method***. Add lines 160–165 of Fig. 24.29 to the ExtractData method. The Date selected in the MonthCalendar control is passed to the ExtractData method as the parameter dtmDay. Variable intChosenDay (line 161) stores the day selected using the Day property of the Date variable dtmDay. The intFileDay variable (line 162) will store the day of the event read from the file. The intLineNumbers variable (line 163) will store the number of lines to skip between events in the file. The ExtractData method will assign the number of events scheduled for the specified date to the variable m_intNumberOfEvents, which is initialized to 0 in line 165.

2. ***Using a StreamReader to read from the file.*** Add lines 167–171 of Fig. 24.30 to the method. To read from the file, ExtractData creates a new StreamReader object (line 168), passing the name of the file to be read ("calendar.txt"). Recall that you wrote information to this file using the **Write Event** application in the box, *Writing Event Information to a File.* [*Note*: Because the data file is in the same directory as the application's executable (C:\SimplyVB\TicketInformation\bin), you do not need to use the full path name.]

   The **ReadLine** method (line 171) of the StreamReader reads a line of characters up to and including a newline character from the specified stream (objInput) and returns the characters as a String. Line 171 assigns the first line of the file to strLine.

(cont.)

Figure 24.29 ExtractData method's variable declarations.

Creating a StreamReader object to read the calendar.txt file

Figure 24.30 Using StreamReader to read data from a sequential-access file.

3. ***Extracting the day from an event in the file.*** Add lines 173–178 of Fig. 24.31 to the ExtractData method. The Do While...Loop determines whether there is more information to read in the file. This condition ensures that the end of the file has not been reached, at which point looping should stop. This is done by using the StreamReader object's **Peek** method, which returns -1 if there are no more characters to read in the file (that is, the end of the file has been reached). The condition also ensures that no more than 10 events for the specified day are read from the file (that is, m_intNumberOfEvents is less than 10). This constraint is necessary due to the fixed size of the array m_strData. If these conditions are met, the body of the Do While...Loop executes. Line 176 converts the line read from the file (that is, the day of the event) to an Integer and assigns that value to intFileDay. The first time the loop executes, strLine contains the first line in the file.

4. ***Reading event information from the sequential-access file.*** Add lines 178–196 of Fig. 24.32 to the ExtractData method's Do While...Loop. The loop reads each event sequentially from the file. If the day of the event read from the file (intFileDay) and the specified day (intChosenDay) are the same (line 179), then the event information (day, time, ticket price, name and description) is read from the file and is stored in array m_strData (lines 180–184).

(cont.)

Recall that when you created the **Write Event** application, each piece of data (day, time, price, event and description) was written to `calendar.txt` on a separate line, so the event data is retrieved using the `ReadLine` method. Each event for the chosen day is placed in its own row of the array (indicated by `m_intNumberOfEvents`), and each piece of event information is placed in its own column of the array. Line 185 increments `m_intNumberOfEvents` to indicate that an event has been scheduled for that date.

If `intFileDay` and the selected day do not match, then the **Stream-Reader** skips to the next event, using a `For...Next` loop (lines 189–191). Line 196 then reads the next line in the file that contains an event's date. This entire process is repeated until the end of the file is reached or until 10 events have been added to the `m_strData` array.

5. *Saving the solution*. Select **File > Save All** to save all the solution's files.

Verify that end of file has not been reached and less than 10 events are stored in the array

```
172
173            ' loop through lines in file
174            Do While objInput.Peek > -1 AndAlso m_intNumberOfEvents < 10
175
176               intFileDay = Convert.ToInt32(strLine)  ' extract day
177
178            Loop ' End Do While
179
```

Figure 24.31 Extracting the day from an event entry in the file.

Store event information in a row of the array

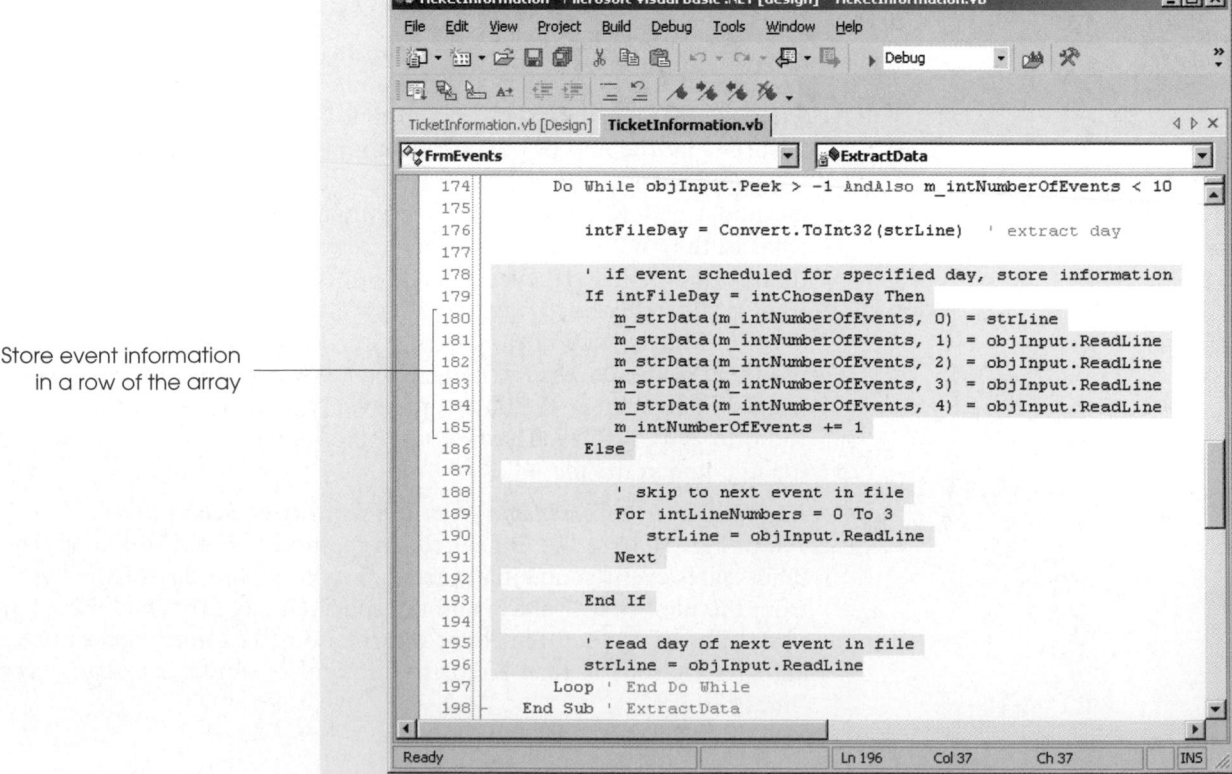

```
174            Do While objInput.Peek > -1 AndAlso m_intNumberOfEvents < 10
175
176               intFileDay = Convert.ToInt32(strLine)  ' extract day
177
178               ' if event scheduled for specified day, store information
179               If intFileDay = intChosenDay Then
180                  m_strData(m_intNumberOfEvents, 0) = strLine
181                  m_strData(m_intNumberOfEvents, 1) = objInput.ReadLine
182                  m_strData(m_intNumberOfEvents, 2) = objInput.ReadLine
183                  m_strData(m_intNumberOfEvents, 3) = objInput.ReadLine
184                  m_strData(m_intNumberOfEvents, 4) = objInput.ReadLine
185                  m_intNumberOfEvents += 1
186               Else
187
188                  ' skip to next event in file
189                  For intLineNumbers = 0 To 3
190                     strLine = objInput.ReadLine
191                  Next
192
193               End If
194
195               ' read day of next event in file
196               strLine = objInput.ReadLine
197            Loop ' End Do While
198         End Sub ' ExtractData
```

Figure 24.32 Sequentially reading event entries from the file.

The ComboBox displays the names of any events scheduled for the date specified in the MonthCalendar control. When the user selects the community event from the ComboBox, the **SelectedIndexChanged** event is raised and the description of the community event is displayed in the TextBox. The box, *Handling the SelectedIndexChanged Event*, explains how to add this functionality.

Handling the SelectedIndex- Changed Event	1. ***Creating the ComboBox's SelectedIndexChanged event handler.*** Double click the ComboBox in design view to generate the empty event handler cboEvent_SelectedIndexChanged. 2. ***Displaying event information.*** Add lines 222–228 of Fig. 24.33 to the event handler. When the user selects an event in the ComboBox, the cboEvent_SelectedIndexChanged event handler displays information about the event in the TextBox txtDescription. The SelectedIndex property of the ComboBox returns the index number of the selected event, which is equivalent to the row number of the event in the m_strData array. The event handler appends descriptive text, newline characters, the time that the event starts (line 223), the ticket price (lines 225–226) and the event's description (line 228) to the TextBox's Text property.

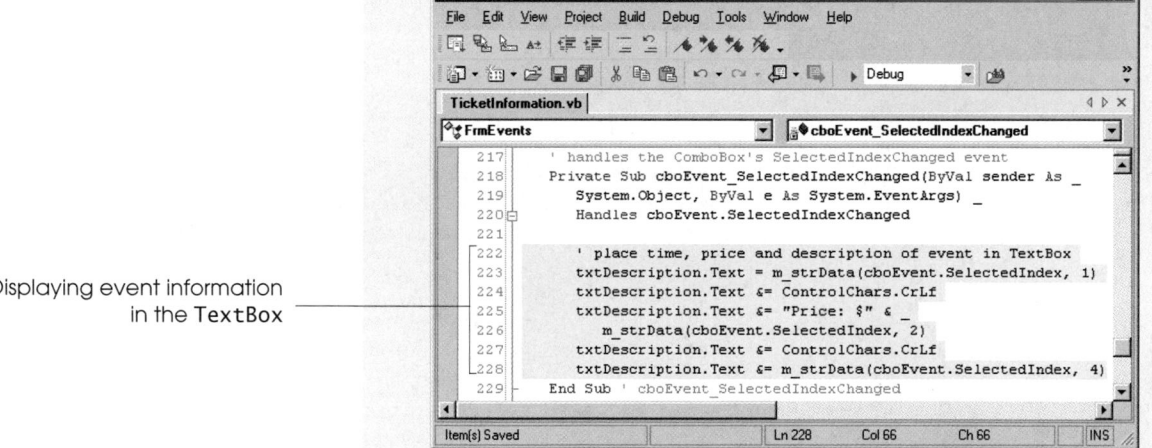

Displaying event information in the TextBox

Figure 24.33 cboEvent_SelectedIndexChanged defined to display event information.

3. ***Saving the solution.*** Select **File > Save All** to save all the solution's files.

Figure 24.34 presents the **Ticket Information** application's code.

Importing namespace System.IO

```
1   Imports System.IO
2
3   Public Class FrmEvents
4      Inherits System.Windows.Forms.Form
5
6      ' stores information for up to 10 events
7      Private m_strData As String(,) = New String(9, 4) {}
8
9      ' number of events on a given day
10     Private m_intNumberOfEvents As Integer
11
12     ' Windows Form Designer generated code
13
```

Figure 24.34 **Ticket Information** application's code. (Part 1 of 3.)

```
14        ' populate ComboBox with current day's events (if any)
15        Private Sub CreateEventList()
16
17           Dim intCount As Integer   ' counter
18
19           ' stores event information in array m_strData
20           ' and assigns number of events to m_intNumberOfEvents
21           ExtractData(mvwDate.SelectionStart)
22
23           ' remove any items in ComboBox
24           cboEvent.Items.Clear()
25
26           ' add each new event name to ComboBox
27           If m_intNumberOfEvents > 0 Then
28
29              For intCount = 0 To m_intNumberOfEvents - 1
30
31                 ' extract and display event name
32                 cboEvent.Items.Add(m_strData(intCount, 3))
33              Next
34
35              ' inform user that events are scheduled
36              cboEvent.Text = " - Events - "
37              txtDescription.Text = "Pick an event."
38
39              ' inform user that no events are scheduled
40           Else
41              cboEvent.Text = " - No Events - "
42              txtDescription.Text = "No events today."
43           End If
44
45        End Sub ' CreateEventList
46
47        ' extracts event data for a specified day from calendar.txt
48        ' and returns number of events during that day
49        Private Sub ExtractData(ByVal dtmDay As Date)
50
51           ' set to selected date in MonthCalendar control
52           Dim intChosenDay As Integer = dtmDay.Day
53           Dim intFileDay As Integer       ' day of event from file
54           Dim intLineNumbers As Integer   ' counts lines to skip
55
56           m_intNumberOfEvents = 0          ' set number of events to 0
57
58           ' initialize StreamReader to read lines from file
59           Dim objInput As StreamReader = New StreamReader("calendar.txt")
60
61           ' read first line before entering loop
62           Dim strLine As String = objInput.ReadLine
63
64           ' loop through lines in file
65           Do While objInput.Peek > -1 AndAlso m_intNumberOfEvents < 10
66
67              intFileDay = Convert.ToInt32(strLine)  ' extract day
68
69              ' if event scheduled for specified day, store information
70              If intFileDay = intChosenDay Then
71                 m_strData(m_intNumberOfEvents, 0) = strLine
```

Creating **StreamReader** object ⎯⎯⎯ *(line 59)*

Using method **ReadLine** to read the first line of the file *(line 62)*

Ensuring that the end of the file has not been reached *(line 65)*

Figure 24.34 **Ticket Information** application's code. (Part 2 of 3.)

Reading information from a file and storing the data in an array

```
72          m_strData(m_intNumberOfEvents, 1) = objInput.ReadLine
73          m_strData(m_intNumberOfEvents, 2) = objInput.ReadLine
74          m_strData(m_intNumberOfEvents, 3) = objInput.ReadLine
75          m_strData(m_intNumberOfEvents, 4) = objInput.ReadLine
76          m_intNumberOfEvents += 1
77       Else
78
79          ' skip to next event in file
80          For intLineNumbers = 0 To 3
81             strLine = objInput.ReadLine
82          Next
83
84       End If
85
86       ' read day of next event in file
87       strLine = objInput.ReadLine
88    Loop ' End Do While
89
90    End Sub ' ExtractData
91
92    ' handle Form's Load event
93    Private Sub FrmEvents_Load(ByVal sender As System.Object, _
94       ByVal e As System.EventArgs) Handles MyBase.Load
95
96       ' display any events scheduled for today in ComboBox
97       CreateEventList()
98    End Sub ' FrmEvents_Load
99
100   ' handle MonthCalendar's DateChanged event
101   Private Sub mvwDate_DateChanged(ByVal sender As System.Object, _
102      ByVal e As System.Windows.Forms.DateRangeEventArgs) _
103      Handles mvwDate.DateChanged
104
105      ' display any events for the specified date in ComboBox
106      CreateEventList()
107   End Sub ' mvwDate_DateChanged
108
109   ' handle ComboBox's SelectedIndexChanged event
110   Private Sub cboEvent_SelectedIndexChanged(ByVal sender As _
111      System.Object, ByVal e As System.EventArgs) _
112      Handles cboEvent.SelectedIndexChanged
113
114      ' place time, price and description of event in TextBox
115      txtDescription.Text = m_strData(cboEvent.SelectedIndex, 1)
116      txtDescription.Text &= ControlChars.CrLf
117      txtDescription.Text &= "Price: $" & _
118         m_strData(cboEvent.SelectedIndex, 2)
119      txtDescription.Text &= ControlChars.CrLf
120      txtDescription.Text &= m_strData(cboEvent.SelectedIndex, 4)
121   End Sub ' cboEvent_SelectedIndexChanged
122
123 End Class ' FrmEvents
```

Using method **ReadLine** to skip to the next event in the file

Using method **ReadLine** to read the day of the next event

Figure 24.34   Ticket Information application's code. (Part 3 of 3.)

24.6 Wrap-Up

In this tutorial, you learned how to store data in sequential-access files. Data in files is called persistent data because the data is maintained after the application that generates the data terminates. Computers store files on secondary storage devices.

Sequential-access files store data items in the order that they are written to the file. They are part of the data hierarchy in which computers process data items. These files are composed of records, which are collections of related fields. Fields are made up of characters, which are composed of bytes. Bytes are composed of the smallest data items that computers can support—bits.

You learned how Visual Basic .NET views each file as a sequential stream of bytes with an end-of-file marker. You learned how to create a sequential-access file in the **Write Event** application by associating a `StreamWriter` object with a specified file name. You used `StreamWriter` to add information to that file. After creating a file of community events with the **Write Event** application, you developed the **Ticket Information** application, which uses a `StreamReader` object to read information from that file sequentially. The user selects a date in the **Ticket Information** application's `MonthCalendar` control and extracts event information from a sequential-access file about any events scheduled for the specified date.

In the next tutorial, you will be introduced to databases, which were briefly mentioned earlier in this tutorial. Databases provide another common mechanism for maintaining persistent data.

SKILLS SUMMARY

Displaying the Open Dialog

■ Add an `OpenFileDialog` object to your application by double clicking the `OpenFileDialog` tab in the **ToolBox**.

■ Invoke the `OpenFileDialog`'s `ShowDialog` method.

Retrieving the Filename From the Open Dialog

■ Use the `Filename` property of the `OpenFileDialog` object.

Writing to a Sequential-Access File

■ Import namespace `System.IO`.

■ Create a `StreamWriter` object by passing two arguments to the constructor: the name of the file to open for writing and a `Boolean` value that determines whether information will be appended to the file.

■ Use the `WriteLine` method of `StreamWriter` to write information to the file.

Reading from a Sequential-Access File

■ Import namespace `System.IO`.

■ Create a `StreamReader` object by passing the name of the file to open for reading to the constructor.

■ Use the `ReadLine` method of `StreamReader` to read information from the file.

Adding a MonthCalendar Control

■ Double click the `MonthCalendar` control's tab in the **ToolBox** to add a `MonthCalendar` to the application.

Handling a MonthCalendar Control's DateChanged Event

■ Double click the `MonthCalendar` control to generate the `DateChanged` event handler.

■ Property `SelectionStart` returns the first (or only) date selected.

Handling a ComboBox Control's SelectedIndexChanged Event

■ Double click the `ComboBox` control to generate the `SelectedIndexChanged` event handler.

KEY TERMS

bit—Short for "binary digit." A digit that can assume one of two values.

byte—Eight bits.

character—A digit, letter or special symbol (characters in Visual Basic .NET are Unicode characters, which are composed of 2 bytes).

character set—The set of all characters used to write applications and represent data items on a particular computer. Visual Basic .NET uses the Unicode character set.

database—Can be a group of related files.

database management system (DBMS)—Collection of programs designed to create and manage databases.

data hierarchy—Collection of data items processed by computers that become larger and more complex in structure as you progress from bits, to characters, to fields and up to larger data structures.

field—Group of characters that conveys some meaning. For example, a field consisting of uppercase and lowercase letters can represent a person's name.

file—Collection of data that is assigned a name. Used for long-term persistence of large amounts of data, even after the program that created the data terminates.

MonthCalendar control—Control that displays a calendar from which a user can select a range of dates.

persistent data—Data maintained in files.

ReadLine method—Method of class StreamReader that reads a line from a file and returns it as a String.

record—A collection of related fields. Usually a Class in Visual Basic .NET composed of several fields (called member variables in Visual Basic .NET).

record key—Identifies a record and distinguishes that record from all other records.

secondary storage media—Devices such as magnetic disks, optical disks and magnetic tapes on which computers store files.

sequential-access file—File which contains data that is read in the order that it was written to the file.

StreamReader class—Class that provides methods for reading information from a file.

StreamWriter class—Class that provides methods for writing information to a file.

WriteLine method—Method of class StreamWriter that writes a String and a line terminator to a file.

CONTROLS, EVENTS, PROPERTIES & METHODS

ComboBox   📇 ComboBox   This control allows users to select options from a drop-down list.

- *In action*

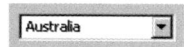

- *Events*

SelectedIndexChanged—This event is raised when a new value is selected in the ComobBox.

- *Properties*

DataSource—This property allows you to add items to the ComboBox.

DropDownStyle—This property determines the ComboBox's style.

Enabled—This property determines whether the user can enter data (True) in the ComboBox or not (False).

Items—This property specifies the values the user can select from the ComboBox.

Item—This property retrieves the value at the specified index.

Location—This property specifies the location of the ComboBox control on its container control relative to the top-left corner.

MaxDropDownItems—This property determines the maximum number of items to be displayed when user clicks the drop-down arrow.

Name—This property specifies the name used to access the ComboBox control programmatically. The name should be prefixed with cbo.

SelectedIndex—This property specifies the index of the item selected.

SelectedValue—This property contains the item selected by the user.

Text—This property specifies the text displayed in the ComboBox.

■ *Methods*

`Items.Add`—This method adds an item to the `ComboBox`.

`Items.Clear`—This method deletes all the values in the `ComboBox`.

MonthCalendar   This control displays a calendar from which the user can select a date or a range of dates.

■ *In action*

■ *Events*

`DateChanged`—Event raised when a new date (or a range of dates) is selected.

■ *Properties*

`Location`—This property specifies the location of the `MonthCalendar` control on the `Form`.

`Name`—This property specifies the name used to access the properties of the `MonthCalendar` control in program code. The name should be prefixed with `mvw`.

`SelectionStart`—This property returns the first (or only) date selected.

OpenFileDialog   OpenFileDialog   This object enables an application to use the **Open** dialog.

■ *Properties*

`CheckFileExists`—This property enables the user to display a warning if a specified file does not exist.

`FileName`—This property sets the default file name displayed in the dialog. It can also be used to retrieve the name of the user-entered file.

`Name`—This property specifies the name that will be used to reference the control's properties and methods.

■ *Method*

`ShowDialog`—This method displays the **Open** dialog and returns the result of the user interaction with the dialog.

StreamWriter   This class is used to write data to a file.

■ *Methods*

`Close`—This method is used to close the stream.

`WriteLine`—This method writes the data specified in its argument, followed by a new line character.

StreamReader   This class is used to read data from a file.

■ *Methods*

`Close`—This method closes the stream.

`ReadLine`—This method reads a line of data from a particular file.

MULTIPLE-CHOICE QUESTIONS

24.1 Data maintained in a file is called _____.

a) persistent data   b) bits

c) secondary data   d) databases

24.2 Methods from the _____ class can be used to write data to a file.
a) `StreamReader`   b) `FileWriter`
c) `StreamWriter`   d) `WriteFile`

24.3 Namespace _____ provides the classes and methods that you need to use to perform file processing.
a) `System.IO`   b) `System.Files`
c) `System.Stream`   d) `System.Windows.Forms`

24.4 Sometimes a group of related files is called a _____.
a) field   b) database
c) collection   d) byte

24.5 A(n) _____ allows the user to select a file to open.
a) `CreateFileDialog`   b) `OpenFileDialog`
c) `MessageBox`   d) None of the above.

24.6 Digits, letters and special symbols are referred to as _____.
a) constants   b) `Integers`
c) `Strings`   d) characters

24.7 The _____ method reads a line from a file.
a) `ReadLine`   b) `Read`
c) `ReadAll`   d) `ReadToNewline`

24.8 A _____ contains information that is read in the order that it was written to the file.
a) sequential-access file   b) text file
c) `StreamReader`   d) `StreamWriter`

24.9 The smallest data item that a computer can support is called a _____.
a) character set   b) character
c) special symbol   d) bit

24.10 Methods from the _____ class can be used to read data from a file.
a) `StreamWriter`   b) `FileReader`
c) `StreamReader`   d) `ReadFile`

EXERCISES

24.11 (_Birthday Saver Application_) Create an application that stores people's names and birthdays in a file. The user creates a file and inputs each person's first name, last name and birthday on the Form. The information is then written to the file.

a) _**Copying and opening the template application.**_ Copy the `BirthdaySaver` folder from `C:\Examples\Tutorial24\Exercises` to `C:\SimplyVB`. Double click the `BirthdaySaver.sln` file to open the template application in Visual Studio .NET. The template Form looks like Fig. 24.35.

b) _**Adding and customizing an `OpenFileDialog` component.**_ Add an `OpenFileDialog` component to the Form. Change its `Name` property to `objOpenFileDialog`. Set the `CheckFileExists` property to `False`.

c) _**Importing namespace `System.IO`.**_ Import `System.IO` to allow file processing.

d) _**Declaring a `StreamWriter` object.**_ Declare a `StreamWriter` object that can be used throughout the entire class.

e) _**Defining the Open File... Button's `Click` event handler.**_ Double click the **Open File...** Button to create the `btnOpen_Click` event handler. Write code to display the **Open** dialog. If the user clicks the **Cancel** Button in the dialog, then the event handler should perform no further actions. Otherwise, determine whether the user provided a file name that has the `.txt` extension (indicating a text file). If the user did not, display a `MessageBox` asking the user to select an appropriate file. If the user specified a valid file name, perform _Step f._

f) *Initializing the StreamWriter.* Initialize the StreamWriter in the event handler btnOpenFile_Click, passing the user-input file name as an argument. Allow the user to append information to the file by passing the Boolean value True as the second argument to the StreamWriter.

g) *Defining the Enter Button's Click event handler.* Double click the **Enter** Button to create the event handler btnEnter_Click. This event handler should write the entire name of the person on one line in the file. Then the person's birthday should be written on the next line in the file. Finally, the TextBoxes on the Form should be cleared, and the DateTimePicker's value should be set back to the current date.

h) *Defining the Close File Button's Click event handler.* Double click the **Close File** Button to create the btnClose_Click event handler. Close the StreamWriter connection in this event handler.

Figure 24.35 Birthday Saver application's GUI.

24.12 (*Photo Album Application*) Create an application that displays images for the user, as shown in Fig. 24.36. This application should display the current image in a large Picture-Box and display the previous and next images in smaller PictureBoxes. A description of the book represented by the large image should be displayed in a multiline TextBox. The application should use the Directory class's methods to facilitate the displaying of the images.

a) *Copying and opening the template application.* Copy the PhotoAlbum folder from C:\Examples\Tutorial24\Exercises to C:\SimplyVB. Double click the PhotoAlbum.sln file to open the application in Visual Studio .NET.

b) *Creating instance variables.* Create instance variable m_intCurrent to represent the current image that is displayed, and set it to 0. Create the m_strLargeImage array (to store the path names of five large images), the m_strSmallImage array (to store the path names of five small images) and the m_strDescriptions array (to store the descriptions of the five books represented by the images).

c) *Defining the RetrieveData procedure.* Create a Sub procedure named RetrieveData to store the path names of the larger images in m_strLargeImages and the path names of the smaller images in m_strSmallImage. Use the Directory class's GetCurrentDirectory method to determine the directory path for the images\large and images\small folders. Sequential-access file books.txt stores the file name of each image. The file is organized such that the file name of the small and large images are on the first line. These files have similar names. The small image's file name ends with _thumb.jpg (that is, *filename*_thumb.jpg) while the large image's file name ends with _large.jpg (that is, *filename*_large.jpg). The description of the book, which should be stored in array m_strDescriptions, follows the file name.

d) *Defining the DisplayPicture procedure.* Create a Sub procedure named DisplayPicture to display the current image in the large PictureBox and to display the previous and next images in the smaller PictureBoxes.

e) *Using If...Then...Else in the DisplayPicture procedure.* Use an If...Then...Else statement to display the images on the Form. If the Integer instance variable is 0, display the image of the first book. Also, display the next book's image in the next image PictureBox. However, because there is no previous image, nothing should be displayed in the previous image PictureBox, and the **Previous Image** Button should be disabled. If the last image is displayed in the large PictureBox, then disable the **Next Image** Button, and do not display anything in the next image PictureBox. Otherwise, all three PictureBoxes should display their corresponding images, and the **Previous Image** and **Next Image** Buttons should be enabled.

f) *Defining the FrmPhotoAlbum_Load event handler.* Double click the Form to create the FrmPhotoAlbum_Load event handler. Invoke methods RetrieveData and DisplayPicture in this event handler.

g) *Defining the `btnPrevious_Click` event handler*. Double click the **Previous Image** Button to create the `btnPrevious_Click` event handler. In this event handler, decrease the `Integer` instance variable by 1 and invoke procedure `DisplayPicture`.

h) *Defining the `btnNext_Click` event handler*. Double click the **Next Image** Button to create the `btnNext_Click` event handler. In this event handler, increment the `Integer` instance variable by 1 and invoke the `DisplayPicture` procedure.

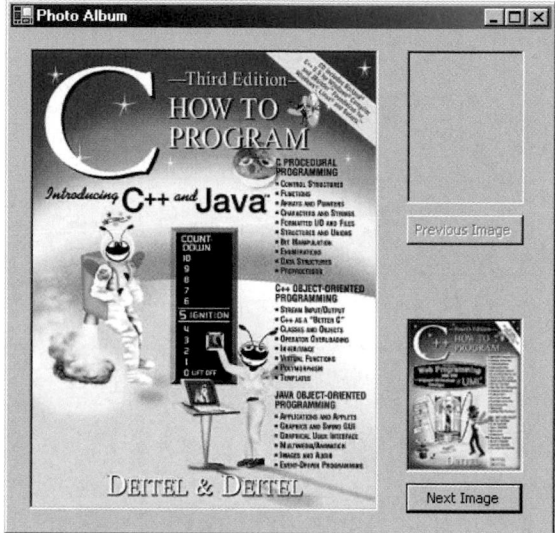

Figure 24.36 **Photo Album** application GUI.

24.13 (*Car Reservation Application*) Create an application that allows a user to reserve a car for the specified day (Fig. 24.37). The small car reservation company can rent out only four cars per day. Let the application allow the user to specify a certain day. If four cars have already been reserved for that day, then indicate to the user that no vehicles are available.

a) *Copying and opening the template application.* Copy the `CarReservation` folder from `C:\Examples\Tutorial24\Exercises` to `C:\SimplyVB`. Double click the `CarReservation.sln` file to open the application in Visual Studio .NET.

b) *Adding a `MonthCalendar` control to the Form.* Drag and drop a `MonthCalendar` control on the Form. Set the `Location` property of the control to 16, 32.

c) *Importing `System.IO` namespace.* Import namespace `System.IO` to allow file processing.

d) *Defining the `FrmReserve_Load` event handler*. Double click the Form to create the `FrmReserve_Load` event handler.

e) *Defining a method*. Create a method named `NumberOfReservations` that takes one argument of type `Date`. The procedure should create a `StreamReader` that reads from the `reservations.txt` file. Use a `Do While Loop` to allow the `StreamReader` to search through the entire `reservations.txt` file to see how many cars have been rented for the day selected by the user. The procedure should close the `StreamReader` connection and return the number of cars rented for the day selected.

f) *Defining a Sub procedure*. Create a Sub procedure named `CheckReservations`. This procedure should invoke the `NumberOfReservations` method, passing in the user-selected day as an argument. The `CheckReservations` method should then retrieve the number returned by `NumberOfReservations` and determine if four cars have been rented for that day. If four cars have been rented, then display a message dialog to the user stating that no cars are available that day for rental. If fewer than four cars have been rented for that day, create a `StreamWriter` object, passing `reservations.txt` as the first argument `True` as the second argument. Write the day and the user's name to the `reservations.txt` file and display a message dialog to the user stating that a car has been reserved.

g) *Defining the `btnReserve_Click` event handler*. Double click the **Reserve Car** Button to create the `btnReserve_Click` event handler. In this event handler, invoke the `CheckReservations` procedure and clear the **Name:** TextBox.

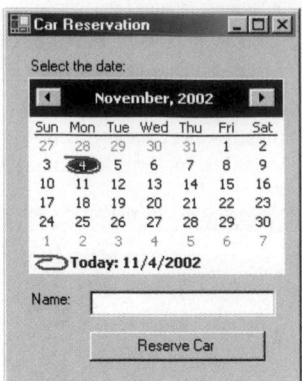

Figure 24.37 **Car Reservation** application GUI.

What does this code do? ▶ **24.14** What is the result of the following code?

```
1   Dim strPath1 As String = "oldfile.txt"
2   Dim strPath2 As String = "newfile.txt"
3   Dim strLine As String
4
5   Dim objStreamWriter As StreamWriter
6   objStreamWriter = New StreamWriter(strPath2)
7
8   Dim objStreamReader As StreamReader
9   objStreamReader = New StreamReader(strPath1)
10
11  strLine = objStreamReader.ReadLine()
12
13  Do While strLine <> ""
14     objStreamWriter.WriteLine(strLine)
15     strLine = objStreamReader.ReadLine()
16  Loop
17
18  objStreamWriter.Close()
19  objStreamReader.Close()
```

What's wrong with this code? ▶ **24.15** Find the error(s) in the following code, which is supposed to read a line from some-file.txt, convert the line to uppercase and then append it to somefile.txt.

```
1   Dim strPath As String = "somefile.txt"
2   Dim strContents As String
3
4   Dim objStreamWriter As StreamWriter
5   objStreamWriter = New StreamWriter(strPath, True)
6
7   Dim objStreamReader As StreamReader
8   objStreamReader = New StreamReader(strPath)
9
10  strContents = objStreamReader.ReadLine()
11
12  strContents = strContents.ToUpper()
13
14  objStreamWriter.Write(strContents)
15
16  objStreamWriter.Close()
17  objStreamReader.Close()
```

Programming Challenge

24.16 (*File Scrape Application*) Create an application similar to the screen scraping application of Tutorial 23, that opens a user-specified file and searches the file for the price of a book, returning it to the user. [*Hints*: You will need to use the ReadToEnd method of class StreamReader to retrieve the entire contents of the files. The book price appears, for example, in the sample booklist.htm file as Our Price: $59.99.]

a) *Copying and opening the template application.* Copy the C:\Examples\Tutorial24 \Exercises\FileScrape folder to C:\SimplyVB. Notice that two HTML files— booklist.htm and bookpool.htm—are provided for you.

b) *Creating an event handler.* Create an event handler for the **Open...** Button that allows the user to select a file to search for prices.

c) *Creating a second event handler.* Create an event handler for the **Search** Button. This event handler should search the specified HTML file for the book price. When the price is found, display it in the output Label.

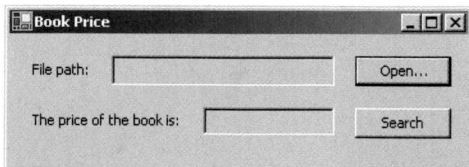

Figure 24.38   **File Scrape** application GUI.

T U T O R I A L

ATM Application

Introducing Database Programming

Objectives

In this tutorial, you will learn to:
- Connect to databases.
- View the contents of an Access database.
- Add database controls to Windows Forms.
- Use the **Server Explorer** window.
- Use the **Query Builder** dialog.
- Read information from and update information in databases.

Outline

In the last tutorial, you learned how to create sequential-access files and how to search through such files to locate information. Sequential-access files are inappropriate for so-called **instant-access applications**, in which information must be located immediately. Popular instant-access applications include airline-reservation systems, banking systems, point-of-sale systems, automated teller machines (ATMs) and other transaction-processing systems that require rapid access to specific data. The bank at which an individual has an account might have hundreds of thousands or even millions of other customers; however, when that individual uses an ATM, the appropriate account is checked for sufficient funds in seconds. This type of instant access is made possible by databases. Individual database records can be accessed directly (and quickly) without sequentially searching through large numbers of other records, as is required with sequential-access files. In this tutorial, you will be introduced to databases and the part of Microsoft .NET—called **ADO .NET**—used for interacting with databases. You will learn about databases and ADO .NET as you create this tutorial's **ATM** application.

25.1 Test-Driving the ATM Application

Many banks offer ATMs to provide their customers with quick and easy access to their bank accounts. When customers use these machines, their account information is updated immediately to reflect the actions they perform (for example, withdrawals). This application must meet the following requirements:

Application Requirements

A local bank has asked you to create a prototype automated teller machine (ATM) application to access a database that contains fictitious customer records. Each record consists of an account number, Personal Identification Number (PIN), first name and balance amount. For testing purposes, valid account numbers will be provided in a ComboBox. The ATM application should allow the user to log in to an account by providing a valid PIN. Once logged in, the user can view the account balance and withdraw money from the account (if the account contains sufficient funds). If money is withdrawn, the application should update the database.

Your **ATM** application will allow the user to enter a PIN number. If the user provides a correct PIN number, then the ATM will retrieve information about the requested account, such as the account holder's name and balance, from the database. If the PIN number entered is invalid, a message is displayed asking the user to reenter the PIN number. You begin by test-driving the completed application.

Test-Driving the ATM Application

1. ***Copying the template to your work folder.*** Copy the `C:\Examples\Tutorial25\CompletedApplication\ATM` folder to `C:\SimplyVB`.

2. ***Opening the template application.*** Double click `ATM.sln` in the ATM folder to open the application in Visual Studio .NET.

3. ***Running the application.*** Select **Debug > Start** to execute the application. The Form shown in Fig. 25.1 will appear with the **OK**, **Balance**, **Withdraw** and **Done** Buttons disabled.

Displays instructions and messages to the user ——

Keypad for entering PIN and withdrawal amount ——

—— Disabled **Buttons**

—— **ComboBox** that displays account numbers

Figure 25.1　ATM application Form.

4. ***Selecting an account number.*** The Label at the top of the ATM displays a message informing the user to select an account number. Use the ComboBox at the bottom of the Form to choose an account number. Select account number `12548693`. Notice that the Label now prompts the user to provide a PIN number (Fig. 25.2). The **Done** Button has also been enabled allowing the user to restart the ATM transaction.

5. ***Entering a PIN number.*** Use the keypad to input the PIN number 1234. As you enter the PIN number, your entry is displayed as an *, to conceal the input. The **OK** Button should be enabled now. Click **OK**. The Label at the top of the ATM displays a welcome message telling the user to select a transaction (Fig. 25.3). Notice that the **Balance** and **Withdraw** Buttons have been enabled, allowing the user to perform these types of transactions.

6. ***Viewing balance information.*** Click the **Balance** Button to view the account balance. The amount displays in the Label at the top of the Form.

7. ***Withdrawing money from the account.*** Click the **Withdraw** Button to perform a withdrawal. The Label at the top of the Form asks you to input the amount you want to withdraw. Use the keypad to input 20 for the amount. Click **OK**. The Label displays your new account balance after deducting the 20 dollars (Fig. 25.4).

(cont.)

Asterisk is displayed here for each keypad **Button** pressed for the PIN numbers

Account number selected

Figure 25.2 Providing PIN number for the selected account.

Welcome message displays in **Label** when user enters correct PIN number

Figure 25.3 ATM displaying welcome message.

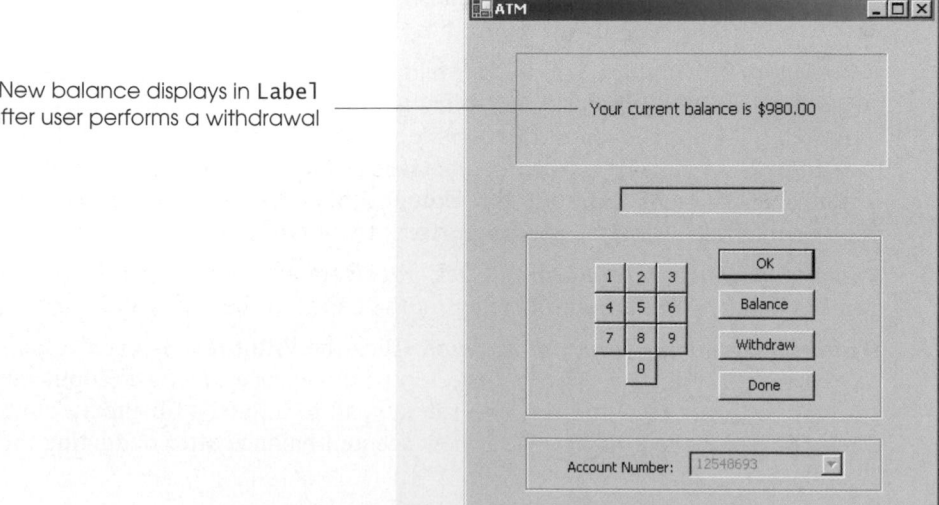

New balance displays in **Label** after user performs a withdrawal

Figure 25.4 **ATM** application displaying balance after withdrawal.

(cont.)   8. ***Ending the transaction.*** Click the **Done** Button to complete the ATM transaction. The transaction ends, and the `Label` prompts for the next customer's
account number. The **Balance**, **Withdraw** and **OK** Buttons are disabled.

9. ***Checking on whether the account information has been updated.*** Click the
running application's close box to terminate the application. Repeat *Steps* 3–
6 to check the balance of the same account. Notice that the balance amount
reflects the withdrawal you performed in *Step* 7. This shows that the account
balance has been updated.

10. ***Terminating the application.*** Click the running application's close box to
terminate the application.

11. ***Closing the solution.*** Select **File > Close Solution**.

25.2 Planning the ATM Application

Now that you have test-driven the **ATM** application, you will begin by analyzing the
application. The following pseudocode describes the actions that the application
needs to execute to solve the problem statement.

> When the user selects an account number from the ComboBox
>
> > Enable the Done Button
> >
> > If the user inputs a PIN number
> > > Enable the OK Button
> >
> > If the user clicks OK
> > > Search database for the account number's corresponding account
> > > information
> > >
> > > If the user provided a correct PIN number
> > > > Enable the Balance and the Withdraw Buttons
> > > > Disable the ComboBox
> > > > Display the user's name and prompt the user to select a transaction
> > > >
> > > > If the user clicks the Balance Button
> > > > > Display the balance amount
> > > >
> > > > If the user clicks the Withdraw Button
> > > > > Prompt the user for the amount to withdraw
> > > > >
> > > > > If the withdrawal amount is greater than the balance
> > > > > > Indicate that the amount is too large
> > > > >
> > > > > Else
> > > > > > Calculate the new balance and update the database
> > > Else
> > > > Prompt for a valid PIN number in the Label
> >
> > If the user clicks the Done Button
> > > Disable the OK, Balance and Withdraw Buttons
> > > Enable the ComboBox

The ACE table in Fig. 25.5 presents the **ATM** application's actions and events.
These actions and events will guide you as you build the application.

Action	Control	Event
Display account numbers	cboAccountNumbers	
Display numbers as asterisks in the TextBox of the ATM	btnZero, btnOne, btnTwo, btnThree, btnFour, btnFive, btnSix, btnSeven, btnEight, btnNine	Click
Submit number input to ATM	btnOK	Click
Display information to user	lblDisplay	
Display balance amount in Label	btnBalance	Click
Withdraw from account and display balance amount in Label	btnWithdraw	Click
Disable Buttons	btnDone	Click

Figure 25.5 ACE table for the **ATM** application.

25.3 Creating Database Connections

In this tutorial, you use Visual Studio .NET's **Server Explorer** window to connect to a database. A **database** is an organized collection of data. Many different strategies exist for organizing data in databases to allow easy access to and manipulation of the data. A **database management system** (**DBMS**) enables you to access and store data without worrying about how the data is organized. In this tutorial, you use a Microsoft Access database. You connect to the database in the box, *Adding a Database Connection to the **ATM** Application.*

*Adding a Database
Connection to the ATM
Application*

1. ***Copying the template application to your work folder.*** Copy the C:\Examples\Tutorial25\TemplateApplication\ATM folder to C:\SimplyVB.

2. ***Opening the template application.*** Double click ATM.sln in the ATM folder to open the application' solution in Visual Studio .NET.

3. ***Displaying the Server Explorer window.*** Select **View > Server Explorer** to display the **Server Explorer** window.

4. ***Adding a database connection.*** To access and manipulate data in a database, you must first establish a connection to the database. Click the **Server Explorer** window's Connect to Database **Button** (Fig. 25.6) to display the **Data Link Properties** dialog (Fig. 25.7). [*Note*: The contents of your **Server Explorer** window will differ.]

Click the Connect to
Database **Button**

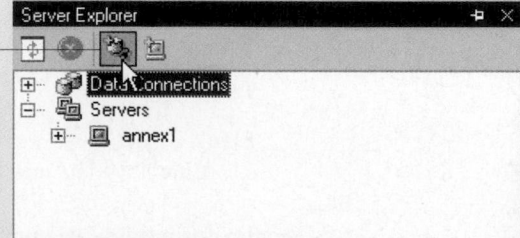

Figure 25.6 **Server Explorer** window.

5. ***Selecting the type of database to access.*** Click the **Provider** tab in the **Data Link Properties** dialog, and select the **Microsoft Jet 4.0 OLE DB Provider** item in the **OLE DB Provider(s)** box as in Fig. 25.7. This selection corresponds to a Microsoft Access database. Click **Next >>**. [*Note*: The number of items displayed in Fig. 25.7 might vary on your system.]

(cont.)

Provider tab ——————————

Select this provider ——————————

Click to continue ——————————

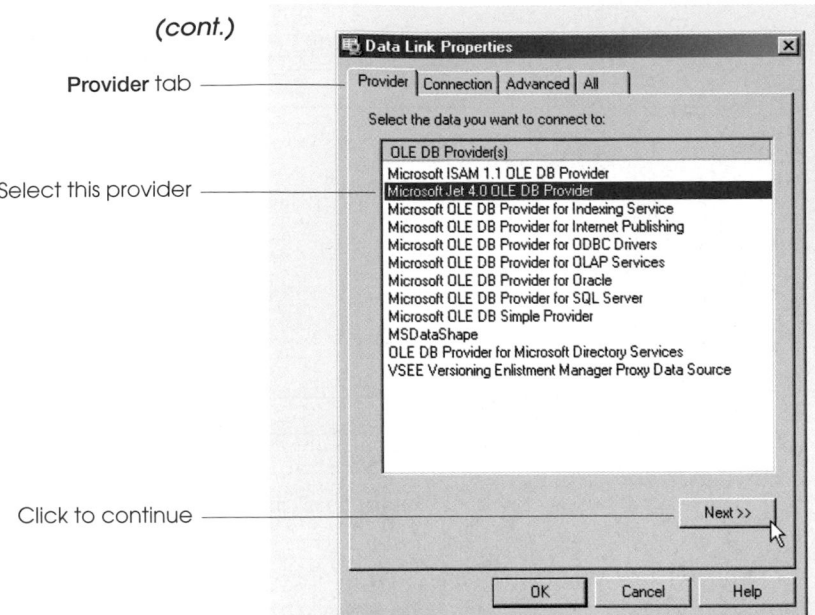

Figure 25.7 **Provider** tab in the **Data Link Properties** dialog.

6. ***Specifying the database connection.*** Before you can manipulate the database, you must first use Visual Studio .NET to connect to the database. After clicking **Next >>**, you are brought to the **Connection** tab of the **Data Link Properties** dialog (Fig. 25.8). Here, you create a **connection object** for the Visual Studio .NET IDE. A connection object maintains a connection to a database. Click the ellipsis (**...**) Button to the right of the **Select or enter a database name:** field, shown in Fig. 25.8, to display the **Select Access Database** dialog (Fig. 25.9).

Connection tab ——————————

Click to select a database

Figure 25.8 **Connection** tab of the **Data Link Properties** dialog.

7. ***Using the Select Access Database dialog.*** In the **Select Access Database** dialog, select the db_ATM.mdb database in C:\SimplyVB\ATM folder as in Fig. 25.9. Click **Open**. You will be redirected back to the **Connection** tab of the **Data Link Properties** dialog.

(cont.)

Select the `db_ATM.mdb` file

Figure 25.9 Select Access Database dialog.

8. ***Testing the database connection.*** Notice that the path of the database is now displayed in the **Select or enter a database name:** field (Fig. 25.10). The database that you will be using does not require a password in order to access its information. Under the **Enter information to log on to the database:** section, make sure the **Blank password** CheckBox is checked. Also make sure that the **User name:** TextBox contains `Admin`. Click the **Test Connection** Button. The **Microsoft Data Link** dialog will appear, indicating a successful connection (Fig. 25.10). However, if the connection fails, make sure that you followed all the instructions in *Steps 5–8*. Click the **Microsoft Data Link** dialog's **OK** Button to close the dialog. Click **OK** to close the **Data Link Properties** dialog.

Database path displayed

User name should be `Admin`

This should be checked

Click to test the connection

Figure 25.10 Connection tab containing selected database path.

9. ***Viewing the database connection in the Server Explorer window.*** Notice that a data connection to the `db_ATM.mdb` database appears in the **Server Explorer** window (Fig. 25.11). You will use the **Server Explorer**'s data connection to add a data connection to the **ATM** application in the next step.

(cont.)

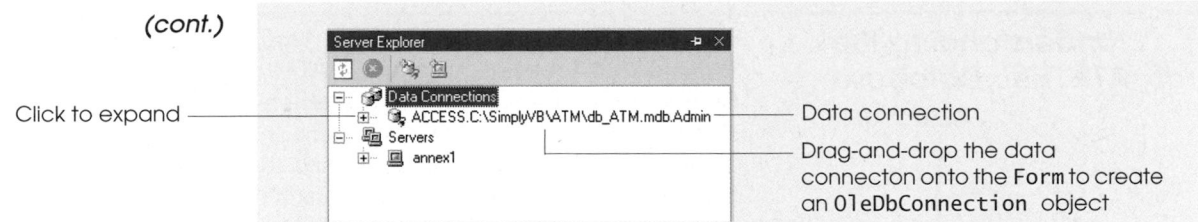

Click to expand ———

Data connection

Drag-and-drop the data connecton onto the **Form** to create an **OleDbConnection** object

Figure 25.11   Database connection shown in the **Server Explorer** window.

10. *Adding the database-connection object to the Form*. Select the data connection in the **Server Explorer** window, and drag-and-drop it onto the Form. An ADO .NET **OleDbConnection** object appears in the component tray (Fig. 25.12). You now have established a connection between the **ATM** application and the db_ATM.mdb database. The **OleDbConnection** object maintains a connection to the database. Class **OleDbConnection** provides methods, such as **Open** and **Close**, which allow you to open and close the connection to the database. You will use these methods shortly.

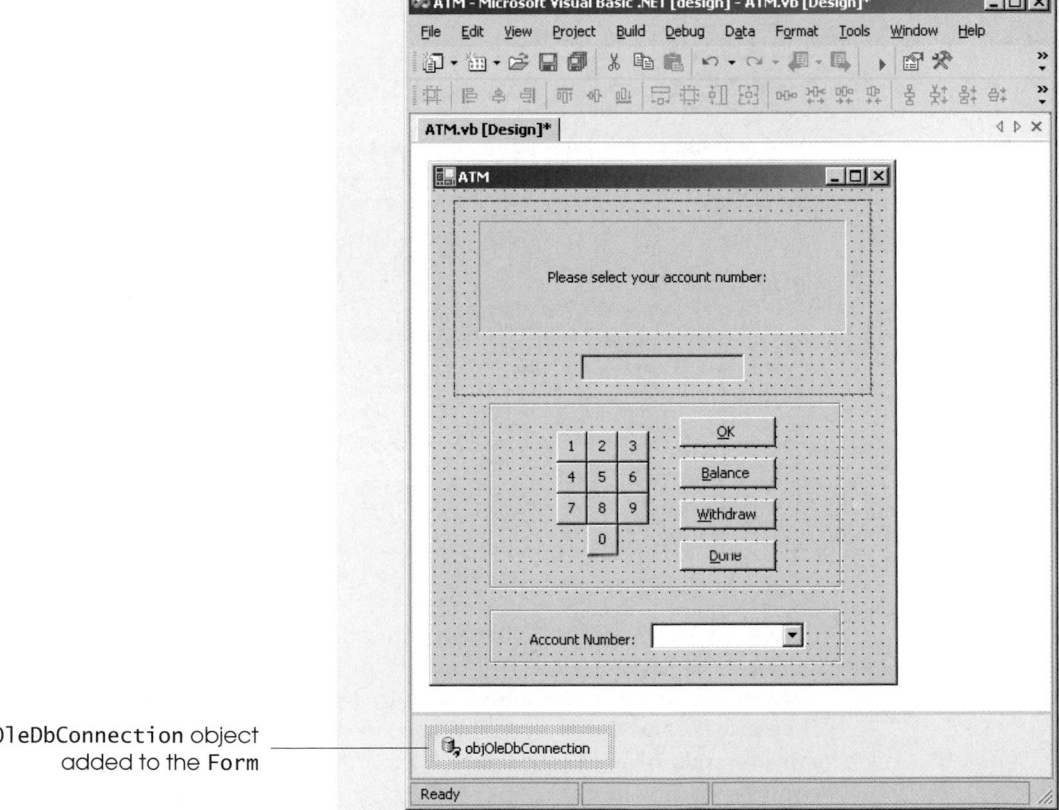

OleDbConnection object added to the **Form**

Figure 25.12   **OleDbConnection** object added to the **Form**.

11. *Setting the OleDbConnection object's properties*. Click the **OleDbConnection** object to view its properties in the **Properties** window. Change the name to **objOleDbConnection**.

12. *Saving the project*. Select **File > Save All** to save all the solution's files.

Now that you have established a connection to the database by using the **Server Explorer** window, you will need to understand how the db_ATM.mdb database organizes its data. You will use the **Server Explorer** window to view the database information in the Visual Studio .NET IDE. You will learn about the database in the box, *Understanding the db_ATM.mdb Database Structure*.

Understanding the db_ATM.mdb Database Structure

1. *Viewing the AccountInformation table of the db_ATM.mdb database.* Expand the **Access.C:\SimplyVB\ATM\db_ATM.mdb.Admin** node in the **Server Explorer**, then expand the **Tables** node to display the **AccountInformation** node (Fig. 25.13). AccountInformation is a table in the db_ATM.mdb database. A **table** is used to store related information in rows and columns. Relational databases, such as Microsoft Access, are composed of one or more tables. Right click **AccountInformation**, and select **Retrieve Data from Table** (Fig. 25.13). The contents of the AccountInformation table display in Visual Studio .NET (Fig. 25.14).

Click to display the **Tables** node

Right click the **AccountInformation** node

Select to view the table's contents

Figure 25.13 Viewing the AccountInformation table.

Fields (columns)

Records (rows)

Collectively, fields and records form a table

Figure 25.14 AccountInformation table's content.

2. *Understanding the database.* Figure 25.14 displays the entire database (because it consists of one table) used in the **ATM** application. This table contains ten **records** and four **fields**. A record is a table row, and a field is a table column. For example, in this table, the row containing the 12548693, 1234, John and 1000 is considered a single record, and the AccountNumber, PIN, FirstName and BalanceAmount columns are fields that represent the data in each record.

In addition to records and fields, a table should contain a **primary key**, which is a field (or combination of fields) that contains unique values that are used to distinguish records from one another. In this table, the Account-Number field is the primary key for referencing the data. Because no two account number values are the same, the AccountNumber field can act as the primary key.

3. *Closing the AccountInformation window.* Right click the **AccountInformation** tab and select **Close**.

Now that you have established a connection to the database and examined the contents of the database, you will add three **data command objects** to the Form. These objects will be used to retrieve information from and update information in the database. You create these objects in the box, *Adding Data Command Objects to the Form*.

Adding Data Command Objects to the Form	1. ***Adding a data command object to the Form.*** Select the **Data** tab in the **Toolbox**. Drag-and-drop an ADO .NET **OleDbCommand** control from the **Data** tab onto the Form to create a data command object. You will use this particular data command object to retrieve information from the database.

2. ***Setting the Name and Connection properties of the data command object.*** Set the Name property of the OleDbCommand object to objSelectAccount. Because the OleDbCommand object will interact with the database, it must be provided with an existing data connection. Select the OleDbCommand's Connection property. Click the down-arrow Button that appears next to the Connection property field. Expand the **Existing** node and select the name of the connection object (objOleDbConnection) you created in *Steps 10–11* of the box, *Adding a Database to the **ATM** Application* (as in Fig. 25.15). |

Connection property —

Figure 25.15   Properties of objSelectAccount.

Click to specify connection object

Select the existing connection (objOleDbConnection)

3. ***Setting the CommandText property of the data command object.*** Select the CommandText property of the data command object in the **Properties** window. Click the ellipsis (...) Button that appears next to the CommandText property field. The **Query Builder** and **Add Table** dialogs appear (Fig. 25.16). **Query Builder** is a Visual Studio .NET tool that allows you to specify the commands that retrieve information from and modify information in databases.

4. ***Adding a table to the Query Builder.*** Notice that the AccountInformation table name appears in the **Add Table** dialog. The **Add Table** dialog displays all of the database's tables. This table appears in the dialog because you set the OleDbConnection object's Connection property, which connects to the db_ATM.mdb database. Select AccountInformation in the **Tables** tab of the **Add Table** dialog and click the **Add** Button. Notice that a window containing the AccountInformation table's fields now appears in the **Query Builder** dialog (Fig. 25.17). Click the **Close** Button in the **Add Table** dialog.

(cont.)

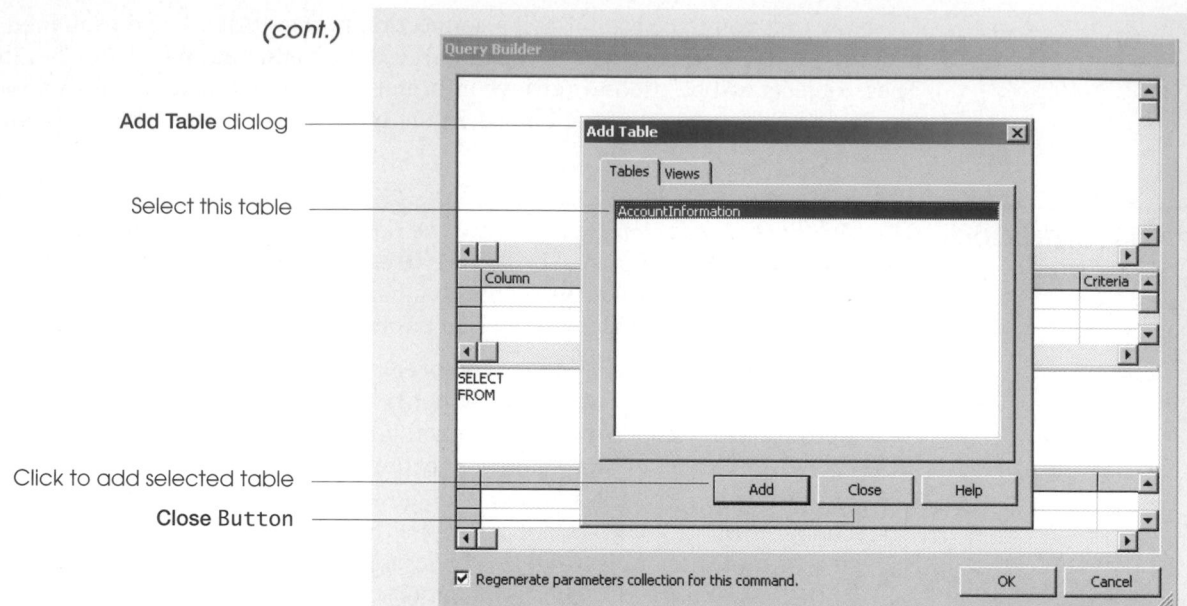

Add Table dialog

Select this table

Click to add selected table

Close Button

Figure 25.16 **Query Builder** and **Add Table** dialogs.

AccountInformation window appears once AccountInformation is added in the **Add Table** dialog

Primary-key-field name displayed in bold

Partial SQL statement

Figure 25.17 AccountInformation table added to the **Query Builder** dialog.

5. *Specifying the fields from which to retrieve data.* You want this data command object to retrieve information from the database. Notice that the lower portion of the **Query Builder** dialog contains the words SELECT, FROM and AccountInformation. This represents the **Structured Query Language (SQL)** statement that will be used to select information from the database. SQL is a language often used to perform database queries (requests for specified information) and to manipulate data. The FROM AccountInformation portion of the SQL statement indicates that the information you will select will be from the database's AccountInformation table.

(cont.)   In the **AccountInformation** window of the **Query Builder**, place a checkmark in the **AccountNumber** CheckBox. Notice that AccountNumber appears in the table beneath the AccountInformation window (Fig. 25.18). The AccountNumber field also appears next to the SELECT keyword. This indicates that the data command object will retrieve the data from the AccountNumber field in the database. Click **OK** in the **Query Builder** dialog.

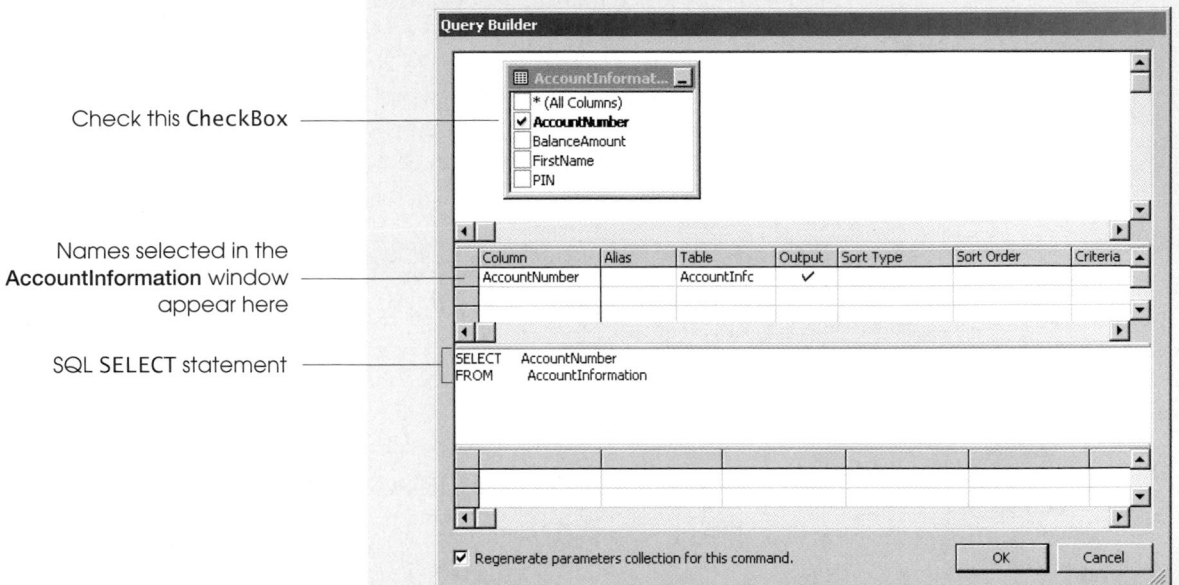

Check this **CheckBox**

Names selected in the
AccountInformation window
appear here

SQL **SELECT** statement

Figure 25.18   Selecting fields in the **Query Builder** dialog.

6. *Adding another data command object*. Add another data command object to the Form. Set its Name property to objSelectAccountData and set the Connection property to the connection object objOleDbConnection. Click the ellipsis (...) Button that appears next to the CommandText property field to display the **Add Table** and **Query Builder** dialogs.

7. *Adding a table to the Query Builder*. Add the AccountInformation table to the **Query Builder** dialog and click the **Add Table** dialog's **Close** Button.

8. *Specifying the fields from which to retrieve data*. You want this data command object to retrieve information from the database, as well. In the **AccountInformation** window of the **Query Builder**, place a checkmark in the **PIN**, **BalanceAmount** and **FirstName** CheckBoxes. These names appear in the table beneath the **AccountInformation** window. The names PIN, BalanceAmount and FirstName fields also should appear next to the SELECT keyword to indicate that the data command object will retrieve the data from these three fields in the database.

9. *Specifying where to retrieve the information*. Check the **AccountNumber** CheckBox in the **AccountInformation** window of the **Query Builder** dialog. AccountNumber appears in the table below the **AccountInformation** window and the word AccountNumber has been added to the SELECT portion of the SQL statement. In the **Criteria** column of the AccountNumber row, type =?. Notice that the words WHERE (AccountNumber=?) have been added to the end of the SQL statement (Fig. 25.19). The **WHERE** clause specifies the selection criteria for the statement (in this case, the AccountNumber field having a specific value). The **criteria** of the command indicates from which specific record data will be retrieved or manipulated. The (AccountNumber=?) portion of the statement indicates that the application will search for the AccountNumber value (which you do not yet know, because the user provides it when the application runs) in the database.

(cont.)

Also notice that a funnel icon appears to the right of the **AccountNumber** CheckBox in the **AccountInformation** window. This funnel icon indicates that you have specified a value in the **Criteria** column of the AccountNumber row. In the **Output** column, uncheck the **AccountNumber**'s CheckBox to remove AccountNumber from the SELECT portion of the statement. This means the result of the SELECT statement should not contain the Account-Number field. Notice that the **AccountNumber** CheckBox in the **AccountIn-formation** window has been unchecked as well. The SQL statement should now look like the statement in Fig. 25.20. This SQL statement will retrieve the PIN, BalanceAmount and FirstName values from the AccountInforma-tion table, where the AccountNumber value equals a value that you will specify shortly. Click the **OK** Button to accept the SQL statement, and close the **Query Builder** dialog.

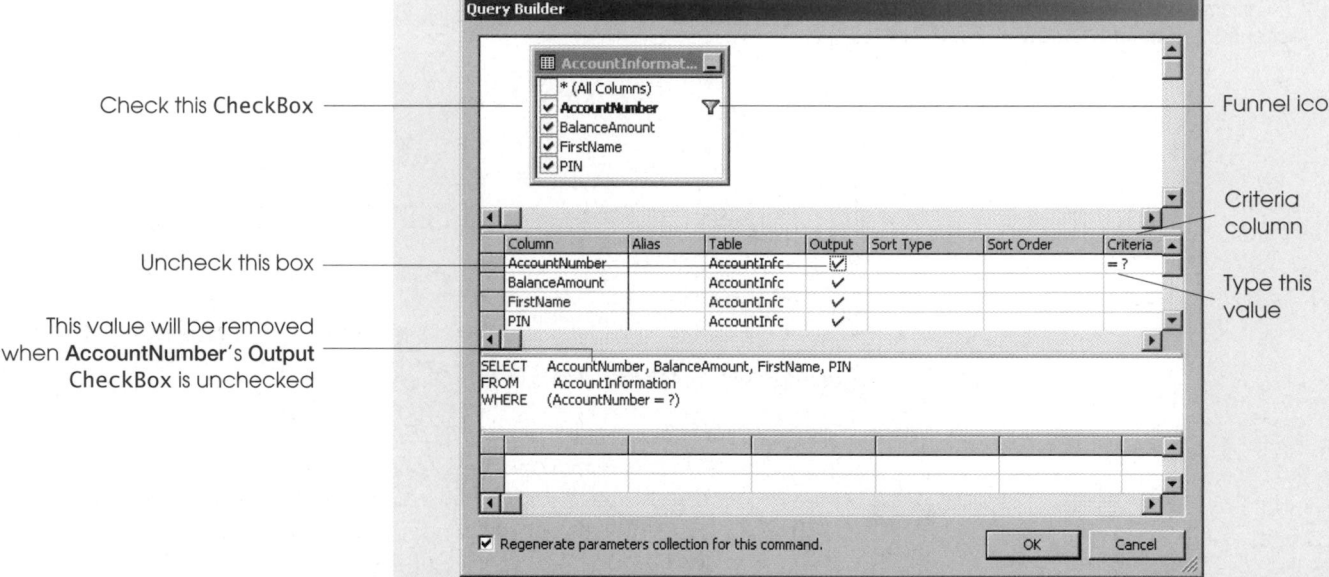

Figure 25.19 WHERE SQL keyword added to the SQL statement.

Figure 25.20 Complete SQL SELECT statement.

(cont.)

10. ***Creating a parameter.*** After clicking the **OK** Button in the **Query Builder** dialog, the **Microsoft Development Environment** dialog (Fig. 25.21) should appear, asking if you want to apply a new parameter configuration. Click the **Yes** Button to create a parameter. This dialog appears only when you need to specify a value to complete the SQL statement (which is why it did not appear when you created the SQL statement for the first data command object).

Figure 25.21 Microsoft Development Environment dialog.

11. ***Viewing the Parameters property of the data command object.*** Select the data command object's `Parameters` property in the **Properties** window, and click the ellipsis (**...**) Button that appears in the **Parameters** property field (Fig. 25.22). The **OleDbParameter Collection Editor** dialog appears (Fig. 25.23). Notice that an `AccountNumber` parameter appears in the collection. Although you do not need to change any settings in this dialog, you will use the `AccountNumber` parameter in the code file to specify the value that will replace the ? in the SQL statement (created in *Step 9*). You will write Visual Basic .NET code to specify the value for this parameter, because you will not know the `AccountNumber` value until the user selects it from the ComboBox in the application's GUI. Click **OK** to close the dialog.

Parameters property —————

————— Click to view collection

Figure 25.22 Parameters property of a data command object.

12. ***Adding a third data command object.*** Drag and drop another `OleDbCommand` object on the Form. Name the object `objUpdateBalance` and set the `Connection` property to `objOleDbConnection`. The command objects should appear in the component tray as in Fig. 25.24. Repeat *Steps 3–4* in this box to display the **Query Builder** dialog.

13. ***Changing the command to update the database.*** After you have added the `AccountInformation` table to the **Query Builder** dialog, right click the **Column** column in the table beneath the **AccountInformation** window (Fig. 25.25). Select **Change Type > Update**. Notice that the SELECT statement in the lower portion of the **Query Builder** dialog has been changed to an UPDATE command. You will use this UPDATE command to modify (that is, update) data in the database.

(cont.)

AccountNumber parameter

Parameter name which you will use in Visual Basic .NET code to complete the SQL statement

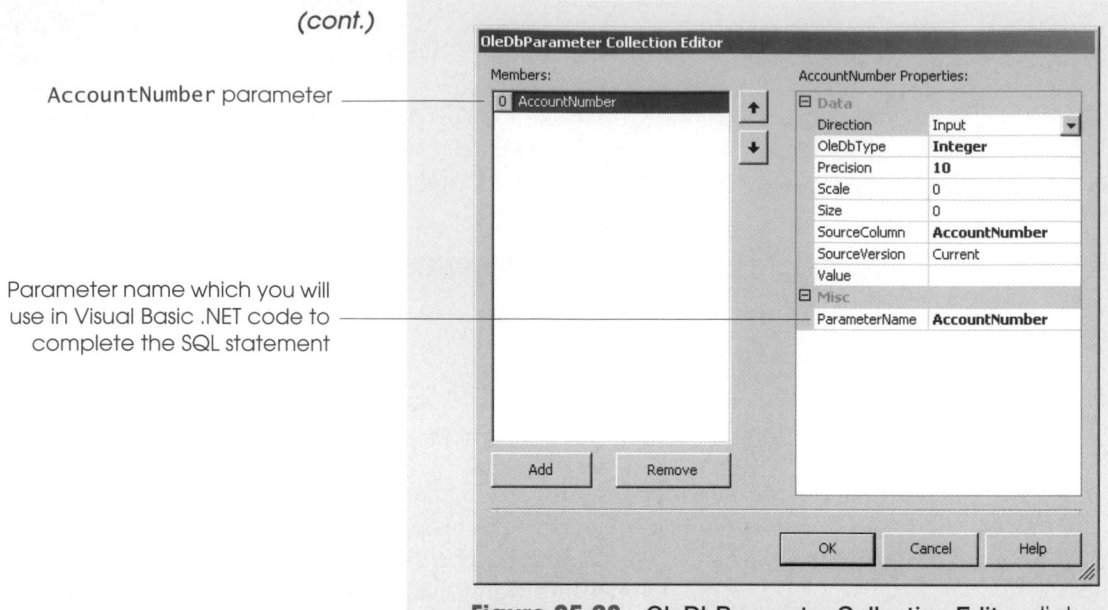

Figure 25.23 **OleDbParameter Collection Editor** dialog.

OleDbCommand object

Figure 25.24 OleDbCommands displayed in the component tray.

14. *Specifying a value to update.* Check the **BalanceAmount** CheckBox in the **AccountInformation** window. Notice that the BalanceAmount field name appears in the UPDATE statement after the SQL keyword SET. In the **New Value** column of the table beneath the **AccountInformation** window, type ? to indicate that the new value is not yet known. The SQL statement in the **Query Builder** dialog now appears as Fig. 25.26. This indicates that the BalanceAmount field in the AccountInformation table will be updated to a new value that you will specify when the application runs.

(cont.)

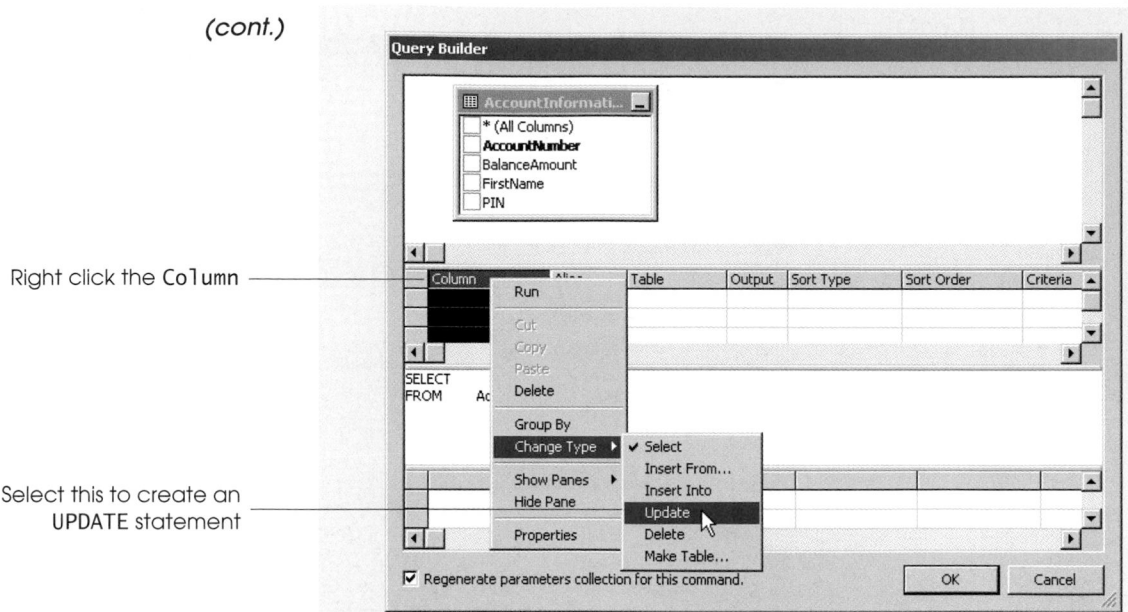

Figure 25.25   Specifying an **UPDATE** command.

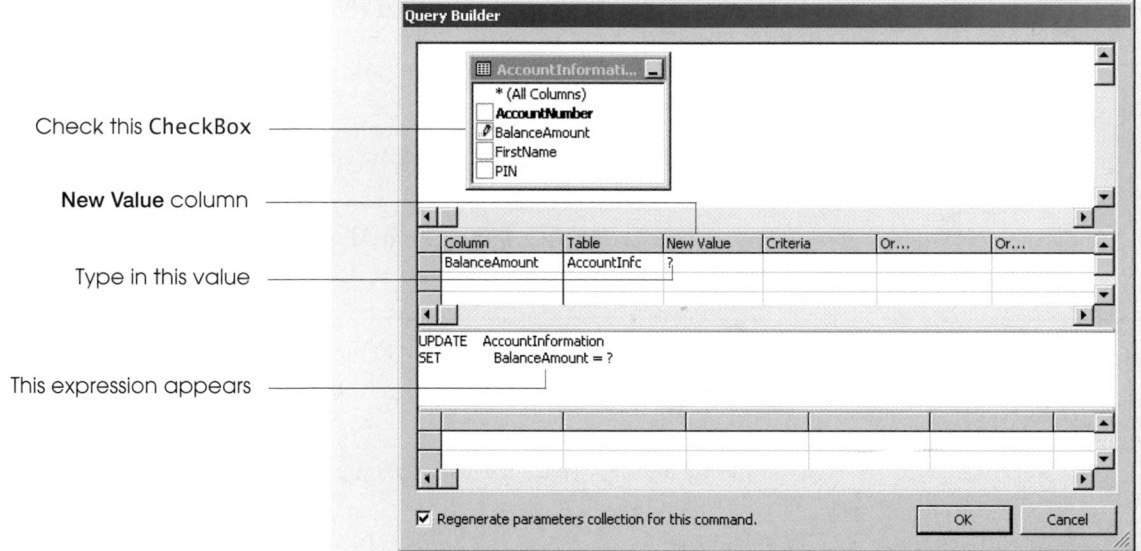

Figure 25.26   Specifying the `BalanceAmount` field in the UPDATE command.

15. ***Specifying which account to update.*** Specify which account to update by checking the **AccountNumber** CheckBox in the **AccountInformation** window. In the table beneath the **AccountInformation** window, type =? in the **Criteria** field of the AccountNumber row to indicate that the account number to update is not yet known. Now uncheck the **AccountNumber** CheckBox in the **AccountInformation** window to remove the AccountNumber value from the SET clause of the SQL command. The UPDATE command should now appear as shown in Fig. 25.27. This SQL command will update the `BalanceAmount` to a value that you will specify by writing Visual Basic .NET code. Click the **Yes** Button to dismiss the **Query Builder** dialog and click **OK** in the **Microsoft Development Environment** dialog to create parameters.

(cont.)

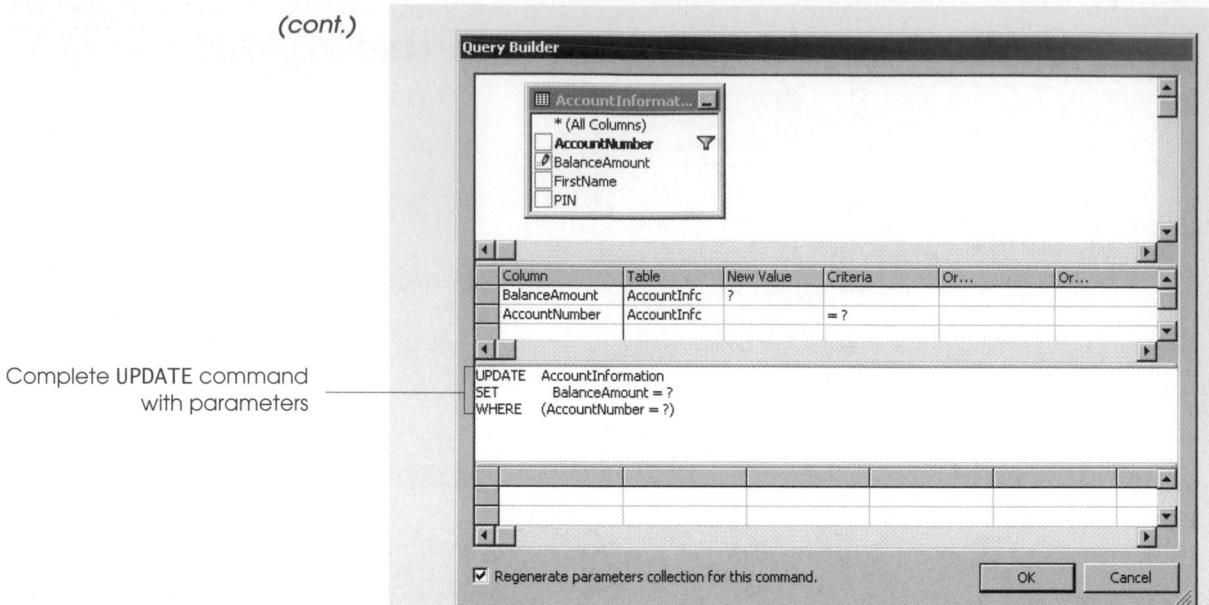

Complete UPDATE command
with parameters

Figure 25.27 UPDATE command displayed in the **Query Builder** dialog.

16. *Viewing the Parameters property*. View the parameters created for this data command as you did in *Step 11*. Notice that there are two parameters: `BalanceAmount` and `ORIGINAL_AccountNumber`. The parameter name `ORIGINAL_AccountNumber` was created by Visual Studio .NET. This value will represent the `AccountNumber` value that will be specified when the user selects an account number from the `ComboBox`. You will use both these parameters in the code file shortly.

17. *Saving the project*. Select **File > Save All** to save all the solution's files.

SELF-REVIEW

1. The _____ object maintains a connection to the database.

    a) `OleDbCommand`   b) `OleDbAdapter`

    c) `OleDbConnection`   d) None of the above.

2. You can specify the value of a parameter by using the `Parameters` property of an _____ object.

    a) `OleDbCommand`   b) `OleDbConnection`

    c) `OleDbParameter`   d) None of the above.

Answers: 1) c. 2) a.

25.4 Programming the ATM Application

When you view the code file (`ATM.vb`), you will notice that code has been provided for you. This code defines the basic functionality of the ATM; however, you will be defining the `FrmATM_Load` event handler and the `RetrieveAccountInformation` and `UpdateBalance` methods that will access the database. The empty `FrmATM_Load` event handler and method headers for these have been provided for you. Your task will be to code their functionality. Now that you have established a connection to the `db_ATM.mdb` database and have created data commands, you will write the necessary code to complete the application. You import an ADO .NET namespace into the application in the box, *Importing Namespace System.Data.OleDb* to provide access to the `OleDb` database objects.

<table>
<tr>
<td valign="top">

Importing Namespace
`System.Data.OleDb`
</td>
<td valign="top">

1. ***Viewing the application code.*** Select **View > Code** to display the **ATM** application code file.

2. ***Importing namespace*** `System.Data.OleDb`. Add line 1 of Fig. 25.28 to import `System.Data.OleDb`. Importing this namespace will allow you to perform database processing and omit typing `System.Data.OleDb` when referring to the classes in this namespace.
</td>
</tr>
</table>

Importing namespace
`System.Data.OleDb`

Figure 25.28   `System.Data.OleDb` imported to ATM.vb.

3. ***Saving the project.*** Select **File > Save All** to save all the solution's files.

Now you will define the FrmATM_Load event handler to fill the ComboBox with a list of account numbers from the database. This will allow the user to select an existing account number when the **ATM** application is executed. You do this in the box, *Displaying Existing Account Numbers in the ComboBox.*

<table>
<tr>
<td valign="top">

Displaying Existing Account Numbers in the ComboBox
</td>
<td valign="top">

1. ***Connecting to the database.*** Locate the FrmATM_Load event handler near the bottom of the code file. Add lines 555–559 of Fig. 25.29 to the FrmATM_Load event handler. Because the OleDbConnection object's connection to the database is not open by default, you must open it. Line 555 opens the connection to the database by invoking the Open method of the OleDbConnection object. Lines 558–559 create an **OleDbDataReader** object (called a **data reader** object) and assign it to reference objReader. Data readers are used to read data from a database. These objects only retrieve data and cannot modify data. The data reader is created by invoking method **ExecuteReader** for the object referenced by objSelectAccount (an OleDbCommand object). This method executes the SQL statement and makes the result of the query available in the data reader.

2. ***Filling the ComboBox with account numbers.*** Add lines 561–566 of Fig. 25.30 to the FrmATM_Load event handler. Lines 562–564 are a Do While...Loop that fills the ComboBox with account numbers.

   Line 562 invokes the data reader object's **Read** method to begin reading information from the database. You must call method Read to position the data reader to the table's first record. Line 563 retrieves the value stored in the AccountNumber field and adds it to the ComboBox. To retrieve the data from the database, you simply provide the name of the field (in double-quotes) in parentheses after the reference name of the data reader. Thus, the objReader("AccountNumber") expression retrieves the value stored in the AccountNumber field. The Do While...Loop will continue to execute as long as the data reader has information to read. Line 566 invokes the Close method of OleDbConnection to close the database connection.
</td>
</tr>
</table>

(cont.)

Figure 25.29 Opening the connection to the database and creating a data reader.

Figure 25.30 Filling the **ComboBox** with account numbers.

Now you are ready to define the `RetrieveAccountInformation` method, which will be used to determine whether the PIN number provided by the user is valid. You create this method in the box, *Retrieving Account Information from the Database.*

Retrieving Account Information from the Database

1. ***Connecting to the database.*** Locate the method header for `RetrieveAccountInformation` near the bottom of the code file. Add lines 572–577 of Fig. 25.31 to the `RetrieveAccountInformation` method. Line 574–575 set the `AccountNumber` parameter value of the `objSelectAccountData` data command to the value of `cboAccountNumber.SelectedItem` (the account number selected by the user). This statement completes the SQL query by providing the missing piece of information—the account number. This will set the command to perform a `SELECT` query on the `AccountInformation` table of the database. The `PIN`, `BalanceAmount` and `FirstName` values associated with the provided account number (specified through the `ComboBox`) are selected from the database. Line 577 opens a connection to the database by invoking the `Open` method of the `OleDbConnection` object.

(cont.)

Setting the AccountNumber parameter value of the command object

Opening the database connection

Figure 25.31 Specifying the `AccountNumber` parameter value of the data command object and connecting to the database.

2. ***Creating and using a data reader.*** You are now ready to read information from the database. Add lines 579–592 of Fig. 25.32 to the `Retrieve-AccountInformation` method. Lines 580–581 create an `OleDbData-Reader` object and assign it to reference `objReader`.

Creating the data reader

Use data reader to read from database

Setting instance variable values to values retrieved from the databse

Closing the reader

Closing the database connection

Figure 25.32 `OleDbDataReader` for reading a record's data.

Line 583 invokes the data reader object's `Read` method to begin reading information from the database. Recall that the `Read` method must be called to position the data reader to the table's first record. Lines 587–589 set the instance variables `m_strPIN`, `m_decBalance` and `m_strFirstName` to the PIN number, balance amount and first name stored in the database for the requested account, respectively. Each account number is unique, so we know there is only one record from which this information is being read. The data reader returns items as `Objects`, so conversions are needed before the assignment in lines 587–589 can be performed. Convert methods `ToDecimal` and `ToString` are used to convert the information retrieved from the database to a `Decimal` and a `String`, respectively.

(cont.)

Line 591 invokes the reader's `Close` method to close the data-reader connection. While the data reader is being used, the connection object is busy and cannot be used for any other actions, besides closing the connection. Calling the `Close` method of the data reader allows the data connection to be used for other operations. You did not need to call this method when you filled the `ComboBox` because you used the `Do While...Loop` which kept the data reader open until no more data could be read. Line 592 uses the `Close` method of `OleDbConnection` to close the database connection.

3. ***Saving the project.*** Select **File > Save All** to save all the solution's files.

After defining the `RetrieveAccountInformation` method, you will need to create the `UpdateBalance` method. This method is invoked if the user-requested withdrawal amount can be deducted from the account balance. The `UpdateBalance` method updates the account balance in the database by writing to the database. You define this method in the box, *Updating the Balance Amount in the Database.*

Updating the Balance Amount in the Database

1. ***Connecting to the database and creating an update statement.*** Locate the `UpdateBalance` method. Add lines 598–604 of Fig. 25.33 to the `UpdateBalance` method. Lines 599–600 set a value for the `BalanceAmount` parameter of the `objUpdateBalance` data command object equal to the value of the variable `m_decBalance`. The value stored in this variable reflects any withdrawals made by the user. Lines 603–604 set the `ORIGINAL_AccountNumber` parameter value of the `objUpdateBalance` data command object equal to the value of the selected account number from the `ComboBox`. Now the `UPDATE` command you created for the `objUpdateBalance` data command object is complete. The SQL command will update the `BalanceAmount` field for the record containing the `AccountNumber` field value of the selected account. The new value of the `BalanceAmount` for that record will be set to the value of `m_decBalance`.

Specifying `objUpdateBalance`'s `BalanceAmount` parameter value

Specifying `objUpdateBalance`'s `ORIGINAL_AccountNumber` parameter value

Figure 25.33 Connecting to the database to update a field.

2. ***Executing the update command.*** Add lines 606–611 of Fig. 25.34 to the `UpdateBalance` method. Line 606 opens the connection to the database. Line 609 executes the update command by using the **ExecuteNonQuery** method of the `objUpdateBalance` data command object. The database has now been updated. Line 611 closes the database connection by using the `Close` method.

(cont.)

Figure 25.34 Executing an UPDATE command before closing the database connection.

3. *Saving the project*. Select **File > Save All** to save all the solution's files.

4. *Executing the application*. Select **Debug > Start** to run the application. Confirm that your application behaves as expected.

Figure 25.35 displays the complete code listing for the **ATM** application. The new programming concepts are highlighted in yellow.

```
1   Imports System.Data.OleDb
2
3   Public Class FrmATM
4      Inherits System.Windows.Forms.Form
5
6      ' variables to store user-entered PIN number
7      Private m_strUserPIN As String
8
9      ' variables to store account balance and user's first name
10     Private m_decBalance As Decimal
11     Private m_strFirstName As String
12     Private m_strPIN As String
13
14     ' variable to indicate action being performed
15     Private m_strAction As String = "Account"
16
17     ' Windows Form Designer generated code
18
19     ' invoke when 0 Button is clicked
20     Private Sub btnZero_Click(ByVal sender As System.Object, _
21        ByVal e As System.EventArgs) Handles btnZero.Click
22
23        InputNumber("0") ' invoke method with argument 0
24     End Sub ' btnZero_Click
25
26     ' invoke when 1 Button is clicked
27     Private Sub btnOne_Click(ByVal sender As System.Object, _
28        ByVal e As System.EventArgs) Handles btnOne.Click
29
30        InputNumber("1") ' invoke method with argument 1
31     End Sub ' btnOne_Click
```

Figure 25.35 ATM application code. (Part 1 of 6.)

```
32
33        ' invoke when 2 Button is clicked
34        Private Sub btnTwo_Click(ByVal sender As System.Object, _
35           ByVal e As System.EventArgs) Handles btnTwo.Click
36
37           InputNumber("2") ' invoke method with argument 2
38        End Sub ' btnTwo_Click
39
40        ' invoke when 3 Button is clicked
41        Private Sub btnThree_Click(ByVal sender As System.Object, _
42           ByVal e As System.EventArgs) Handles btnThree.Click
43
44           InputNumber("3") ' invoke method with argument 3
45        End Sub ' btnThree_Click
46
47        ' invoke when 4 Button is clicked
48        Private Sub btnFour_Click(ByVal sender As System.Object, _
49           ByVal e As System.EventArgs) Handles btnFour.Click
50
51           InputNumber("4") ' invoke method with argument 4
52        End Sub ' btnFour_Click
53
54        ' invoke when 5 Button is clicked
55        Private Sub btnFive_Click(ByVal sender As System.Object, _
56           ByVal e As System.EventArgs) Handles btnFive.Click
57
58           InputNumber("5") ' invoke method with argument 5
59        End Sub ' btnFive_Click
60
61        ' invoke when 6 Button is clicked
62        Private Sub btnSix_Click(ByVal sender As System.Object, _
63           ByVal e As System.EventArgs) Handles btnSix.Click
64
65           InputNumber("6") ' invoke method with argument 6
66        End Sub ' btnSix_Click
67
68        ' invoke when 7 Button is clicked
69        Private Sub btnSeven_Click(ByVal sender As System.Object, _
70           ByVal e As System.EventArgs) Handles btnSeven.Click
71
72           InputNumber("7") ' invoke method with argument 7
73        End Sub ' btnSeven_Click
74
75        ' invoke when 8 Button is clicked
76        Private Sub btnEight_Click(ByVal sender As System.Object, _
77           ByVal e As System.EventArgs) Handles btnEight.Click
78
79           InputNumber("8") ' invoke method with argument 8
80        End Sub ' btnEight_Click
81
82        ' invoke when 9 Button is clicked
83        Private Sub btnNine_Click(ByVal sender As System.Object, _
84           ByVal e As System.EventArgs) Handles btnNine.Click
85
86           InputNumber("9") ' invoke method with argument 9
87        End Sub ' btnNine_Click
88
```

Figure 25.35 ATM application code. (Part 2 of 6.)

```
89      ' determines what text will display in TextBox
90      Private Sub InputNumber(ByVal strNumber As String)
91
92         ' if user is entering PIN number display * to
93         ' conceal PIN entry; store entered PIN in variable
94         If m_strAction = "PIN" Then
95            txtInput.Text &= "*"
96            m_strUserPIN &= strNumber
97
98         Else ' otherwise display number
99            txtInput.Text &= strNumber
100        End If
101
102     End Sub ' InputNumber
103
104     ' invoke when OK Button is clicked
105     Private Sub btnOK_Click(ByVal sender As System.Object, _
106        ByVal e As System.EventArgs) Handles btnOK.Click
107
108        ' determine what action to perform
109        Select Case m_strAction
110
111           ' if user provided PIN number
112        Case "PIN"
113
114              RetrieveAccountInformation() ' invoke method
115
116              ' determine if PIN number is within valid range
117              If m_strUserPIN = m_strPIN Then
118
119                 ' enable Buttons and disable ComboBox
120                 btnBalance.Enabled = True
121                 btnWithdraw.Enabled = True
122                 cboAccountNumber.Enabled = False
123
124                 ' display status to user
125                 lblDisplay.Text = "Welcome " & m_strFirstName & _
126                    ", select a transaction."
127
128                 ' change action to indicate that no user-action
129                 ' is expected
130                 m_strAction = "NoAction"
131              Else
132
133                 ' indicate that incorrect PIN was provided
134                 lblDisplay.Text = "Sorry, PIN number is incorrect." _
135                    & "Please re-enter the PIN number."
136
137                 ' clear user's previous PIN entry
138                 m_strUserPIN = ""
139
140              End If
141
142              txtInput.Clear() ' clear TextBox
143
144           ' if user provided withdrawal amount
145        Case "Withdrawal"
146
```

Figure 25.35   ATM application code. (Part 3 of 6.)

```
147                    ' invoke Withdrawal method with decimal argument
148                    Withdrawal(Convert.ToDecimal(txtInput.Text))
149                    txtInput.Clear()
150                    m_strAction = "NoAction"
151           End Select
152
153        End Sub ' btnOK_Click
154
155        ' invoke when Withdraw Button is clicked
156        Private Sub btnWithdraw_Click(ByVal sender As System.Object, _
157           ByVal e As System.EventArgs) Handles btnWithdraw.Click
158
159           ' display message to user
160           lblDisplay.Text = _
161              "Enter the amount you would like to withdraw."
162
163           ' change action to indicate user will
164           ' provide withdrawal amount
165           m_strAction = "Withdrawal"
166        End Sub ' btnWithdraw_Click
167
168        ' determine new balance amount
169        Private Sub Withdrawal(ByVal decWithdrawAmount As Decimal)
170
171           ' determine if amount can be withdrawn
172           If decWithdrawAmount <= m_decBalance Then
173
174              ' determine new balance amount after withdrawal
175              m_decBalance -= decWithdrawAmount
176
177              UpdateBalance() ' invoke method to update database
178
179              ' display balance information to user
180              lblDisplay.Text = "Your current balance is " & _
181                    String.Format("{0:C}", m_decBalance)
182           Else
183
184              ' indicate amount cannot be withdrawn
185              lblDisplay.Text = "The withdrawal amount is too large." & _
186                    " Select Withdraw and enter a different amount."
187
188           End If
189
190        End Sub ' Withdrawal
191
192        ' invoke when Balance Button is clicked
193        Private Sub btnBalance_Click(ByVal sender As System.Object, _
194           ByVal e As System.EventArgs) Handles btnBalance.Click
195
196           ' display user's balance
197           lblDisplay.Text = "Your current balance is " & _
198              String.Format("{0:C}", m_decBalance)
199
200        End Sub ' btnBalance_Click
201
202        ' invoke when Cancel Button is clicked
203        Private Sub btnDone_Click(ByVal sender As System.Object, _
204           ByVal e As System.EventArgs) Handles btnDone.Click
```

Figure 25.35 ATM application code. (Part 4 of 6.)

```
205
206            lblDisplay.Text = "Please select your account number."
207
208            ' change action to indicate that user will
209            ' provide account number
210            m_strAction = "Account"
211            m_strUserPIN = ""
212
213            txtInput.Clear() ' clear TextBox
214            btnOK.Enabled = False ' disable OK Button
215            btnBalance.Enabled = False ' disable Balance Button
216            btnWithdraw.Enabled = False ' disable Withdraw Button
217            btnDone.Enabled = False ' disable Done Button
218            cboAccountNumber.Enabled = True ' enable ComboBox
219            cboAccountNumber.Text = "" ' clear selected account
220         End Sub ' btnDone_Click
221
222         ' invoke when user inputs information in TextBox
223         Private Sub txtInput_TextChanged(ByVal sender As _
224            System.Object, ByVal e As System.EventArgs) _
225            Handles txtInput.TextChanged
226
227            btnOK.Enabled = True ' enable OK Button
228         End Sub ' txtInput_TextChanged
229
230         ' invoke when selection is made in ComboBox
231         Private Sub cboAccountNumber_SelectedIndexChanged(ByVal _
232            sender As System.Object, ByVal e As System.EventArgs) _
233            Handles cboAccountNumber.SelectedIndexChanged
234
235            ' change action to indicate that user will
236            ' provide account number
237            m_strAction = "PIN"
238
239            ' prompt user to enter PIN number
240            lblDisplay.Text = "Please enter your PIN number."
241            btnDone.Enabled = True ' enable Done Button
242            txtInput.Clear() ' clear TextBox
243         End Sub ' cboAccountNumber_SelectedIndexChanged
244
245         ' load application Form
246         Private Sub FrmATM_Load(ByVal sender As System.Object, _
247            ByVal e As System.EventArgs) Handles MyBase.Load
248
249            objOleDbConnection.Open() ' open database connection
250
251            ' create database reader to read information from database
252            Dim objReader As OleDbDataReader = _
253               objSelectAccount.ExecuteReader
254
255            ' fill ComboBox with account numbers
256            Do While objReader.Read()
257               cboAccountNumbers.Items.Add(objReader("AccountNumber"))
258            Loop
259
260            objOleDbConnection.Close() ' close database connection
261         End Sub ' FrmATM_Load
262
```

Opens database connection — line 249
Creates data reader — lines 252–253
*Fills **ComboBox** with account numbers* — lines 256–258
Closes database connection — line 260

Figure 25.35 ATM application code. (Part 5 of 6.)

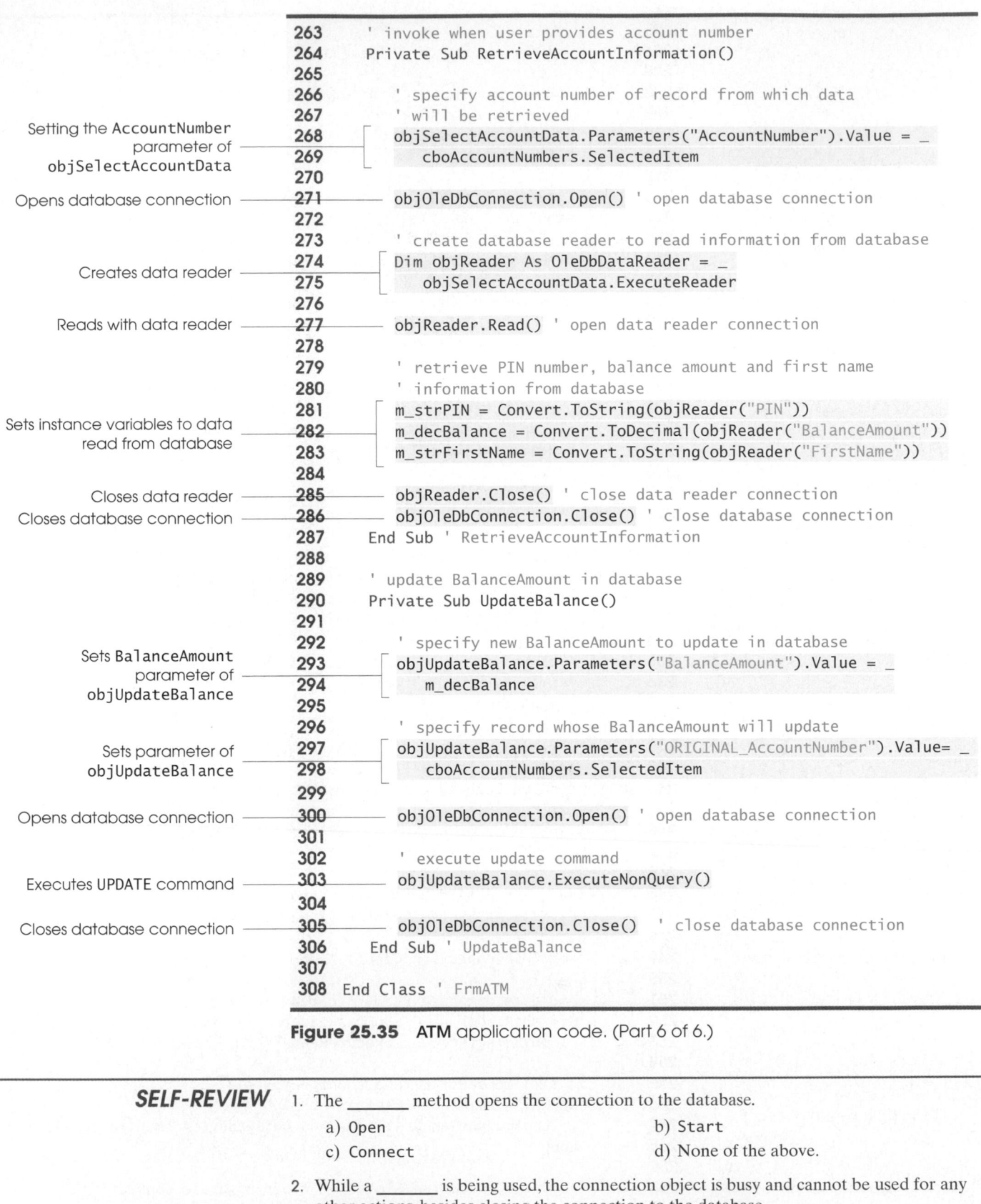

```
263        ' invoke when user provides account number
264        Private Sub RetrieveAccountInformation()
265
266           ' specify account number of record from which data
267           ' will be retrieved
268           objSelectAccountData.Parameters("AccountNumber").Value = _
269              cboAccountNumbers.SelectedItem
270
271           objOleDbConnection.Open() ' open database connection
272
273           ' create database reader to read information from database
274           Dim objReader As OleDbDataReader = _
275              objSelectAccountData.ExecuteReader
276
277           objReader.Read() ' open data reader connection
278
279           ' retrieve PIN number, balance amount and first name
280           ' information from database
281           m_strPIN = Convert.ToString(objReader("PIN"))
282           m_decBalance = Convert.ToDecimal(objReader("BalanceAmount"))
283           m_strFirstName = Convert.ToString(objReader("FirstName"))
284
285           objReader.Close() ' close data reader connection
286           objOleDbConnection.Close() ' close database connection
287        End Sub ' RetrieveAccountInformation
288
289        ' update BalanceAmount in database
290        Private Sub UpdateBalance()
291
292           ' specify new BalanceAmount to update in database
293           objUpdateBalance.Parameters("BalanceAmount").Value = _
294              m_decBalance
295
296           ' specify record whose BalanceAmount will update
297           objUpdateBalance.Parameters("ORIGINAL_AccountNumber").Value= _
298              cboAccountNumbers.SelectedItem
299
300           objOleDbConnection.Open() ' open database connection
301
302           ' execute update command
303           objUpdateBalance.ExecuteNonQuery()
304
305           objOleDbConnection.Close()   ' close database connection
306        End Sub ' UpdateBalance
307
308    End Class ' FrmATM
```

Labels:
- Setting the AccountNumber parameter of objSelectAccountData
- Opens database connection
- Creates data reader
- Reads with data reader
- Sets instance variables to data read from database
- Closes data reader
- Closes database connection
- Sets BalanceAmount parameter of objUpdateBalance
- Sets parameter of objUpdateBalance
- Opens database connection
- Executes UPDATE command
- Closes database connection

Figure 25.35 ATM application code. (Part 6 of 6.)

SELF-REVIEW

1. The _____ method opens the connection to the database.

   a) Open
   b) Start
   c) Connect
   d) None of the above.

2. While a _____ is being used, the connection object is busy and cannot be used for any other actions, besides closing the connection to the database.

   a) data command object
   b) connection object
   c) database
   d) data reader.

Answers: 1) a. 2) d.

25.5 Wrap-Up

In this tutorial, you learned that a database is an organized collection of data and that database management systems provide mechanisms for storing and organizing data in a format consistent with that of a database. You then examined the contents of the Microsoft Access database that was used in the **ATM** application. While examining the db_ATM.mdb database, you learned that a field in a database table is a column and that a record is an entire table row. You also learned that each record must contain a primary key, which is used to distinguish one record from another.

After learning about the Access database, you used ADO .NET objects to communicate with the database. You learned how to create a connection to the database by using the **Server Explorer** and also how to create data command objects by using the **Toolbox**. You then were introduced to the database objects that you used in the **ATM** application. You learned about connection objects that are used to establish connections to databases, and about data command objects that allow you to access and manipulate database data. By creating the data command objects, you learned how to use Visual Studio .NET's **Query Builder** tool to build Structured Query Language (SQL) statements. These statements allowed you to retrieve and update information in the database. Using **Query Builder**, you created SELECT and UPDATE commands. You also learned about data readers that allowed you to retrieve information from a database.

In the next tutorial, you will learn about graphics. In particular, you will learn about coordinate systems and how to create colors and draw shapes. You will then use the concepts and techniques presented in the tutorial to create an application that can draw and print payroll checks.

SKILLS SUMMARY

Adding a Database Connection by Using the Server Explorer Window

- Click the Connect to Database Button to display the **Data Link Properties** dialog.
- Click the **Provider** tab in the **Data Link Properties** dialog.
- Select **Microsoft Jet 4.0 OLE DB Provider** in the **OLE DB Provider(s)** box.
- Click **Next**; then, click the ellipsis (...) Button next to the **Select or enter a database name:** field.
- Choose the desired database, and click **Open**.
- Click the **Test Connection** Button. Click **OK** in the dialog that appears; then, click **OK** in the **Data Link Properties** dialog.

Adding a Connection Object to the Form

- Select the desired database connection in the **Server Explorer** window.
- Drag-and-drop the connection on the Form.

Adding a Data Command Object to the Form

- Select the OleDbCommand icon from the **Data** tab in the **Toolbox**.
- Drag-and-drop the icon on the Form.
- Select the Connection property in the **Properties** window, and specify the name of the connection object created for the Form previously.
- Select the CommandText property, and click the ellipsis Button to display the **Add Table** and **Query Builder** dialogs.
- Add a table to the **Query Builder** dialog by using the **Add Table** dialog.
- Set the desired command statement by right clicking the **Column** field and selecting **Change Type**.
- Check desired field CheckBoxes, and use the **Criteria** column if necessary.

Opening the Database Connection

- Use the Open method of the connection object.

Closing the Database Connection

■ Use the `Close` method of the connection object.

Using a Data Reader

■ Invoke the `ExecuteReader` method of the data command object to create the data reader object.

■ Invoke the data reader object's `Read` method.

■ Retrieve the necessary information.

■ Invoke the data reader object's `Close` method to close the data reader.

KEY TERMS

ADO .NET—Part of Microsoft .NET that is used to interact with databases.

connection object—Used to establish a connection to a database.

data command object—Executes commands that retrieve or modify data in a database.

data reader—Reads data from a database.

database—Organized collection of data.

database management system (DBMS)—Provides mechanisms for storing and organizing data in a manner that is consistent with the database's format.

field—Column in a table of a database.

FROM SQL keyword—Specifies table from which to get data.

instant-access application—Application where a particular record of information must be located immediately.

primary key—Field (or combination of fields) in a database table that contains unique values used to distinguish records from one another.

record—An entire table row in a database.

SELECT SQL keyword—Used to request specified information from a database.

Structured Query Language (SQL)—Language often used by relational databases to perform queries and manipulate data in relational databases.

UPDATE SQL keyword—Used to modify data in a database table.

WHERE SQL keyword—Specifies criteria that determine the rows to retrieve.

CONTROLS, EVENTS, PROPERTIES & METHODS

`OleDbConnection`   ⌧ OleDbConnection   This object establishes connection to a database.

■ *Property*

`ConnectionString`—This property is used to specify to which database to connect.

■ *Methods*

`Close`—This method is used to close the connection to the database.

`Open`—This method is used to open the connection to the database.

`OleDbCommand`   ⌧ OleDbCommand   This object is used to execute a command on a database.

■ *Properties*

`CommandText`—This property is used to specify an SQL statement.

`Connection`—This property is used to specify the connection to a database.

`Parameters`—This property is used to specify an unknown value for the SQL statement.

■ *Methods*

`ExecuteNonQuery`—This method is used to execute nonquery command statements, such as UPDATEs.

`ExecuteReader`—This method is used to create a data reader by executing a database query.

OleDbDataReader This object is used to read data from a database.

■ *Methods*

Read—This method is used to retrieve information from the data reader.

Close—This method is used to close the data reader.

MULTIPLE-CHOICE QUESTIONS

25.1 A _____ provides mechanisms for storing and organizing data in a manner that is consistent with a database's format.

a) relational database
b) connection object
c) data command
d) database management system

25.2 An entire row in a database table is known as a _____.

a) record
b) field
c) column
d) primary key

25.3 A primary key is used to _____.

a) create rows in a database
b) identify fields in a database
c) distinguish between records in a table
d) read information from a database

25.4 A data command object allows you to _____.

a) connect to a database
b) read information from a database
c) execute a command to retrieve or modify a database
d) create a database

25.5 A data reader can _____.

a) retrieve information from a database
b) modify information stored in a database
c) establish a connection to a database
d) close a connection to a database

25.6 In a SELECT statement, what follows the SELECT keyword?

a) the name of the table
b) the name of the field
c) the name of the database
d) the criteria that the record must meet

25.7 What does the following SELECT statement do?

```
SELECT Age FROM People WHERE LastName = 'Purple'
```

a) It selects the age of the person (or people) with the last name Purple from the People table.
b) It selects the value Purple from the Age table of the People database.
c) It selects the age of the person with the last name Purple from the People database.
d) It selects the People field from the Age table with the LastName value Purple.

25.8 The SQL _____ modifies information in a database.

a) SELECT command
b) MODIFY command
c) CHANGE command
d) UPDATE command

25.9 Assuming the account number is 2, which of the following statements modifies the PIN field in the Accounts table?

a) SELECT PIN FROM Accounts WHERE AccountNumber = 2
b) SELECT Accounts FROM AccountNumber – 2 WHERE PIN
c) UPDATE Accounts SET PIN=1243 WHERE AccountNumber = 2
d) UPDATE PIN=1243 SET AccountNumber = 2 WHERE Accounts

25.10 A _____ is an organized collection of data.

a) record
b) database
c) data reader
d) primary key

EXERCISES

25.11 *(Stock Portfolio Application)* A stock broker wants an application that will display a client's stock portfolio (Fig. 25.36). All the companies that the user holds stock in should be displayed in a ComboBox when the application is loaded. When the user selects a company from the ComboBox and clicks the **Stock Information** Button, the stock information for that company should be displayed in Labels.

a) *Copying and opening the template application.* Copy the StockPortfolio folder from C:\Examples\Tutorial25\Exercises to C:\SimplyVB. Double click the StockPortfolio.sln file to open the application in Visual Studio .NET.

b) *Copying the database to your work folder.* Copy the stocks.mdb database from C:\Examples\Tutorial25\Exercises\Databases to your C:\SimplyVB\Stock-Portfolio folder.

c) *Adding a data connection to the Server Explorer.* Click the Connect to Database icon in the **Server Explorer**, and add a data connection to the stock.mdb database. Add an OleDbConnection object to the Form.

d) *Adding command objects to the Form.* Add two command objects to the Form, and set both their Connection properties to the database connection object. Name the command objects objSelectStockNameCommand and objSelectStockInformationCommand.

e) *Adding a Load event to the Form.* Add a Load event handler for the Form. Add code to this event handler that opens a connection to the database. Use the objSelectStockNameCommand to retrieve the StockNames, and add them to the ComboBox.

f) *Adding a Click event handler for the btnStockInformation Button.* Add a Click event handler for the **Stock Information** Button. Add code to the event handler that passes the SelectedItem to the StockData method as a String. Then close the connection.

g) *Defining the StockData method.* Create a StockData method that takes a String representing the name of the stock as an argument. Connect to the database, and retrieve the information for the stock passed as an argument. Display the information in the corresponding Labels and close the connection to the database. Call the ComputeTotalValueString method, which you define in the next step, to calculate the total value.

h) *Defining the ComputeTotalValueString method.* Create the ComputeTotalValueString method to compute the total value by multiplying the number of shares by the price per share.

Figure 25.36 Stock Portfolio application.

25.12 *(Restaurant Bill Calculator Application)* A restaurant wants you to develop an application that calculates a table's bill (Fig. 25.37). The application should display all the menu items from the restaurant's database in four ComboBoxes. Each ComboBox should contain a category of food offered by the restaurant (**Beverage**, **Appetizer**, **Main course** and **Dessert**). The user can choose from one of these ComboBoxes to add an item to a table's bill.

When the table is finished ordering, the user can click the **Calculate Bill** Button to display the **Subtotal:**, **Tax:** and **Total:** for the table.

Figure 25.37   Restaurant Bill Calculator application.

a) *Copying and opening the template application.* Copy the RestaurantBillCalculator folder from C:\Examples\Tutorial25\Exercises to C:\SimplyVB. Double click the RestaurantBillCalculator.sln file in the RestaurantBillCalculator folder to open the application in Visual Studio .NET.

b) *Copying the database to your work folder.* Copy the menu.mdb database from C:\Examples\Tutorial25\Exercises\Databases to your C:\SimplyVB\RestaurantBillCalculator folder.

c) *Adding a data connection to the Server Explorer.* Click the Connect to Database icon in the **Server Explorer**, and add a data connection to the menu.mdb database. Add an OleDbConnection object to the Form.

d) *Adding command objects to the Form.* Add two command objects to the Form, and set both their Connection properties to the database connection object. Name the command objects objSelectNameCommand and objSelectPriceCommand.

e) *Adding a Load event to the Form.* Create the Load event handler for the Form. Add code to the event handler that opens a connection to the database. Call the LoadCategory method four times, each time passing a different category and ComboBox as arguments. Close the connection to the database.

f) *Coding the LoadCategory method.* Create a method LoadCategory that takes a String representing the Category to load and the name of the ComboBox to add items to as arguments. Because the Form's Load event handler is calling this method before it closes the connection to the database, the connection should still be open. Create a data reader to read all the items from the database for the specified Category. Close the reader before exiting the method, so that a new reader can be created when the method is invoked again.

g) *Adding SelectedIndexChanged event handler for the ComboBoxes.* Add a SelectedIndexChanged event handler for all the ComboBoxes. Add code to the event handler that adds the String representation of the SelectedItem to the ArrayList.

h) *Adding a Click event handler for the btnCalculateBill Button.* Add a Click event handler for the **Calculate Bill** Button. Add code to the event handler that ensures that a table number and waiter name have been entered. If one of these fields is empty, display a MessageBox informing the user that both fields must contain information. The event handler should then call the CalculateSubtotal method to calculate the subtotal of the bill. Display the subtotal, tax and total of the bill in the appropriate `Labels`.

i) *Coding the `CalculateSubtotal` method*. The `CalculateSubtotal` method should open a connection to the database and retrieve the `Price` field for all the menu items in the `m_objBillItems ArrayList`. This method should then calculate the total price of all the items in the `ArrayList` and return this value as a `Decimal`. Remember to close the connection to the database.

25.13 *(Airline Reservation Application)* An airline company wants you to develop an application that displays flight information (Fig. 25.38). The database contains two tables, one containing information about the flights, the other containing passenger information. The user should be able to choose a flight number from a ComboBox. When the **View Flight Information** Button is clicked, the application should display the date of the flight, the flight's departure and arrival cities and the names of the passengers schedule to take the flight.

a) *Copying and opening the template application.* Copy the `AirlineReservation` folder from `C:\Examples\Tutorial25\Exercises` to `C:\SimplyVB`. Double click the `AirlineReservation.sln` file in the `AirlineReservation` folder to open the application in Visual Studio .NET.

b) *Copying the database to your work folder.* Copy the `reservations.mdb` database from `C:\Examples\Tutorial25\Exercises\Databases` to the `C:\SimplyVB\AirlineReservation` folder.

c) *Adding a data connection to the Server Explorer.* Click the Connect to Database icon in the **Server Explorer**, and add a data connection to the `reservations.mdb` database. Add an `OleDbConnection` object to the `Form`.

d) *Adding command objects to the Form.* Add three command objects to the `Form`, and set all their `Connection` properties to the database connection object. Name the command objects `objSelectFlightNumberCommand`, `objSelectFlightInformationCommand` and `objSelectPassengerInformationCommand`.

e) *Adding a Load event to the Form.* Create a `Load` event handler for the `Form` that opens a connection to the database. Retrieve all the `FlightNumbers` from the `Flights` table in the `reservations.mdb` database, and add those `FlightNumbers` to the `ComboBox`.

f) *Adding a `Click` event handler for the `btnViewFlightInformation` Button.* Add a `Click` event handler for the **View Flight Information** Button. Add code to the event handler to pass the `SelectedItem` to the `DisplayFlightInformation` method.

g) *Defining the `DisplayFlightInformation` method.* The `DisplayFlightInformation` method should take as an argument a `String` representing the flight number chosen. You will need to define two readers in this method, to read from the two tables in the database. Once you open the connection to the database, create a reader that reads the specified flight information from the `flights` table. Display the flight information in the correct `Label`. Close this reader, and create a second reader that reads passenger information from the `reservations` table. Retrieve from the table all the passengers scheduled to take the specified flight. Clear any old items from the `ListBox`, and display passengers' names in the `ListBox`.

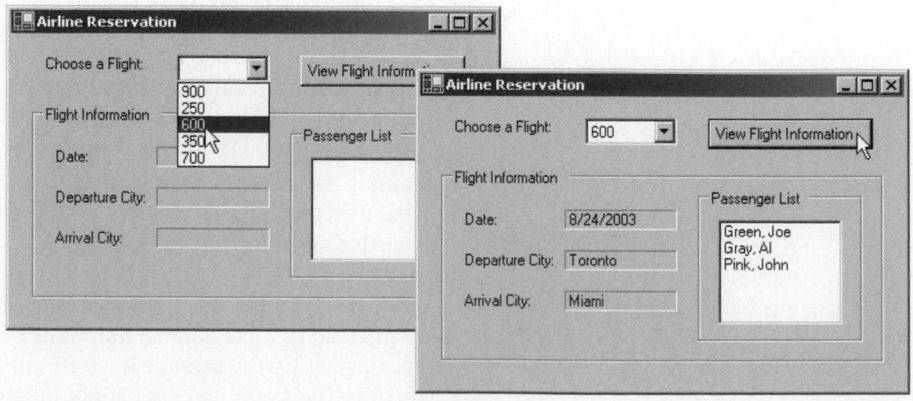

Figure 25.38 Airline Reservation application.

What does this code do? ▶ **25.14** What is the result of executing the following code?

```
 1  objSelectAgeData.Parameters("Name").Value = "Bob"
 2
 3  objOleDbConnection.Open()
 4
 5  Dim objReader As OleDbDataReader = _
 6     objSelectAgeData.ExecuteReader
 7
 8  objReader.Read()
 9
10  m_intAge = Convert.ToInt32(objReader("Age"))
11
12  objReader.Close()
13  objOleDbConnection.Close()
```

What's wrong with this code? ▶ **25.15** Find the error(s) in the following code. This method should modify the Age field of strUserName.

```
1  objUpdateAge("Age").Value = _
2     intAge
3
4  objUpdateBalance.Parameters("ORIGINAL_NAME").Value = _
5     strUserName
6
7  objUpdateAge.ExecuteNonQuery()
8
9  objOleDbConnection.Close()
```

Programming Challenge ▶ **25.16** *(Enhanced Restaurant Bill Calculator Application)* Modify the application you developed in Exercise 25.12 to keep track of multiple table bills at the same time. The user should be able to calculate a bill for a table and save that table's subtotal and waiter's name. The user should also be able to retrieve that information at a later time. [*Hint*: This database contains two tables, one for the menu items, as before, and another for all the tables in the restaurant.] Sample outputs are shown in Fig. 25.39.

a) *Copying the template application.* Copy the RestaurantVBillCalculatorEnhanced folder from C:\Examples\Tutorial25\Exercises to C:\SimplyVB. Double click the RestaurantBillCalculatorEnhanced.sln file in the RestaurantBillCalculatorEnhanced folder to open the application in Visual Studio .NET. Also, copy the database for this application, menu2.mdb, from C:\Examples\Tutorial25\Exercises\Databases to your C:\SimplyVB\RestaurantBillCalculator folder.

b) *Copying your existing code.* Copy the code for the application you created in Exercise 25.12 into the template application for this exercise.

c) *Adding an instance variable.* Add an instance variable to your class, called m_decSubtotal, that will hold the subtotal for each table when it is loaded in the application.

d) *Creating a method.* Create method LoadTables that read the table numbers from the database and add them to the **Table number**: ComboBox. This method should be called when the Form is loaded.

e) *Adding an event handler.* Add an event handler for the **Table number**: ComboBox. When a table is selected from the ComboBox, that table's data should be loaded from the database.

f) *Creating an event handler for the Save Table Button.* Create an event handler for the **Save Table** Button. This event handler should calculate the subtotal for the selected table. The event handler should then call method UpdateTable, passing the subtotal and table number as arguments.

g) *Creating method **UpdateTable***. Create a method UpdateTable that takes the subtotal and table number as arguments. This method should save the table data in the database.

Figure 25.39 Enhanced **Restaurant Bill Calculator** application's GUI.

Objectives

In this tutorial, you will learn to:
- Draw two-dimensional shapes.
- Control the colors and patterns of filled shapes.
- Use Graphics objects.
- Draw shapes on an object.
- Create an application to write checks.

Outline

CheckWriter Application

Introducing Graphics and Printing

In this tutorial, you will learn about Visual Basic .NET's tools for drawing two-dimensional shapes and for controlling colors and fonts. Visual Basic .NET supports graphics that allow you to visually enhance Windows applications. To build the **CheckWriter** application, you will take advantage of the GDI+ Application Programming Interface (API). An **API** is the interface used by a program to access the operating system and various services on the computer. **GDI+** is a graphics API that provides classes for creating and manipulating two-dimensional vector graphics, fonts and images. A **vector graphic** is not represented as a grid of pixels, but is instead represented by a set of mathematical properties called vectors, which describe a graphic's dimensions, attributes and position. Using the GDI+ API, you can create robust graphics without worrying about the specific details of graphics hardware.

The Framework Class Library contains many sophisticated drawing capabilities as part of the System.Drawing namespace and the other namespaces that comprise GDI+. The System.Drawing.Printing namespace will be used in the **CheckWriter** application to specify how the check will be printed on the page.

As you will see, GDI+ graphics capabilities will help you preview and print a check using the **CheckWriter** application. To complete the application, you will learn some more powerful drawing capabilities, such as changing the styles of lines used to draw shapes and controlling the colors of filled shapes. You will also learn how to specify a text style using fonts.

26.1 Test-Driving the CheckWriter Application

Before test-driving the completed **CheckWriter** application, you should understand the purpose of the application. The application must meet the following requirements:

> ### Application Requirements
>
> *A local business is responsible for distributing paychecks to its employees. The human-resources department needs a way to generate and print the paychecks. You have been asked to create an application that allows the human-resources department to input all information necessary for a valid check, which includes the employee's name, the date, the amount that the employee should be paid and the company's address information. Your application should graphically draw the check so that it can be printed.*

This application prints a paycheck. The user inputs the check number, the date, the numeric amount of the check, the employee's name, the amount of the check written in words and the company's address information. The user can press the **Preview** Button, which displays the format of the check. The user can then press the **Print** Button if the format is acceptable, causing the check to print from the printer. You begin by test-driving the completed application.

Test-Driving the CheckWriter Application

1. *Opening the application.* Open the C:\Examples\Tutorial26\CompletedApplication\CheckWriter folder to locate the **CheckWriter** application. Double click CheckWriter.sln to open the application in Visual Studio .NET.

2. *Running the application.* Select **Debug > Start** to run the program. The Form displaying a check appears as shown in Fig. 26.1.

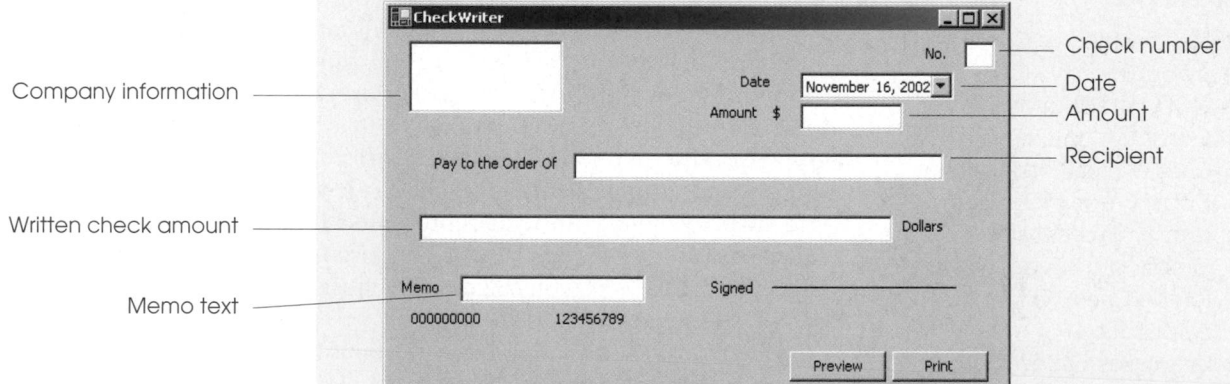

Figure 26.1 CheckWriter application displaying an empty check.

3. *Providing inputs for the company information.* In the company information TextBox, type The Company and press *Enter* to proceed to the next line of the TextBox. Type 123 Fake Street. Press *Enter* to proceed to the third line of the TextBox. Type AnyTown, MA 11111.

4. *Providing values for the remaining information.* For the **No.** field, input the check number 100. Leave the **Date** field (represented by a DateTimePicker control) as today's date, which is the default. Input 1,000.00 as the check amount. Enter John Smith as the recipient, and type One Thousand and 00/100 in the TextBox to the left of **Dollars**. In the **Memo** field, type PayCheck. The check should appear as shown in Fig. 26.2.

(cont.)

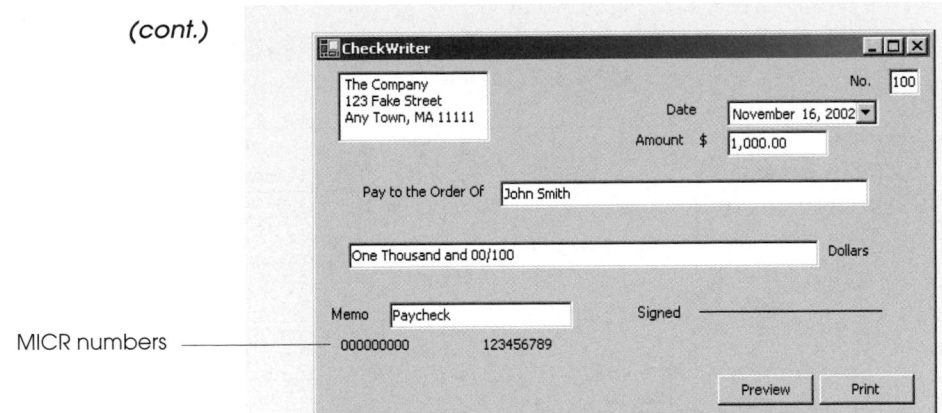

Figure 26.2 **CheckWriter** application displaying a completed check.

You may have noticed that at the bottom left side of all bank checks is a string of numbers and symbols. These are called Magnetic Ink Character Recognition (MICR) numbers. MICR numbers are broken into three components. The first nine digits are the bank's routing number, followed by the account number and then the check number. Banks have special machines that read these numbers and route the check to the appropriate account. Using the MICR font, you can create MICR numbers in your check-writing application. To download the MICR font, visit `http://new-freeware.com/publishers/1561/`.

5. *Previewing the check.* Click the **Preview** Button. A **Print preview** dialog appears, displaying the completed check as shown in Fig. 26.3. This dialog is actually a control of type `PrintPreviewDialog`, which is used to display how a document appears before it is printed.

The **Print preview** dialog contains several toolbar Buttons. The first Button is the print Button (🖨), which allows users to print the document. The next Button (🔍) zooms in and out, allowing users to view the document at different sizes. The next five Buttons allow users to specify the number of pages that can be displayed in the dialog at one time. Users can view 1, 2, 3, 4 or 6 pages at a time in the dialog box. The **Close** Button closes the dialog box. Finally, the right-most control in the dialog box allows users to specify which page of the document they wish to view. The `PrintPreviewDialog` control is discussed in detail in Section 26.4. The document that displays in this dialog box is the `PrintDocument`, an object that you will create when coding the application.

Click **Close** to close the **Print preview** dialog. [*Note:* Printing or previewing the document is not possible when there is no printer installed on your computer.]

6. *Printing the check.* To print the check, your computer must be connected to a printer. Click the **Print** Button. The check prints from the default printer of your computer.

7. *Terminating the application.* After the check prints, click the running application's **Close** Button to terminate the application.

8. *Closing the solution.* Select **File > Close Solution**.

(cont.)

Print

Zoom

Displays three pages

Page to view

Close

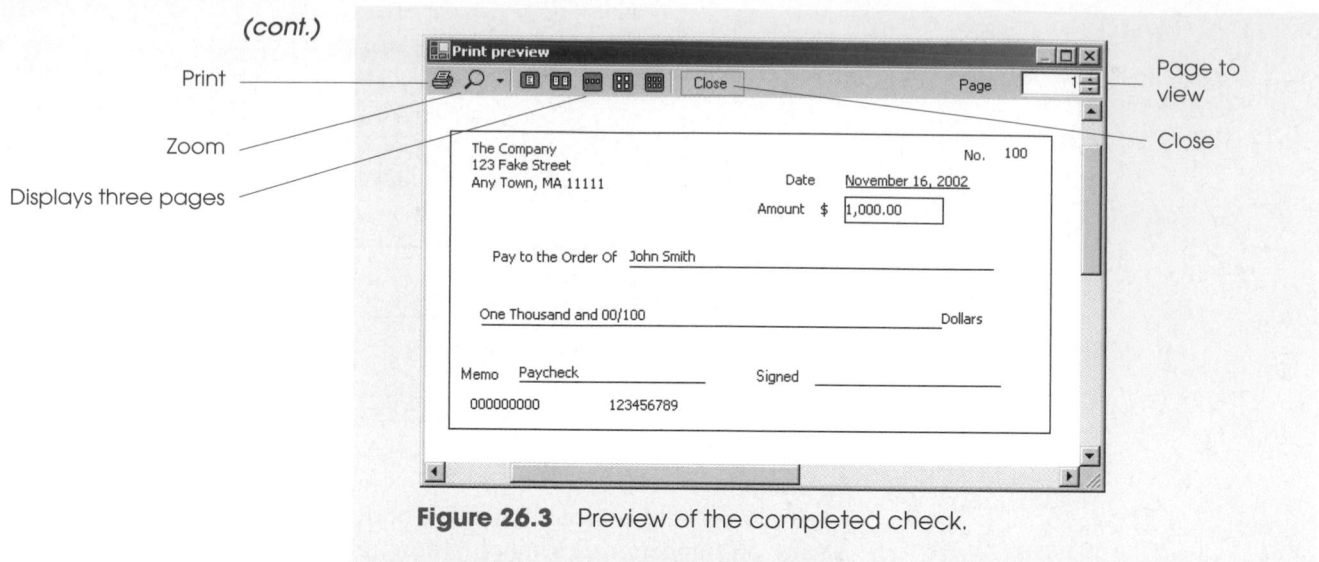

Figure 26.3 Preview of the completed check.

26.2 GDI+ Introduction

This section introduces the graphics classes and structures used in this tutorial and discusses GDI+ graphics programming. Graphics typically consist of lines, shapes, colors and text drawn on the background of a control.

Objects of the `Pen` and `Brush` classes affect the appearances of the lines and shapes you draw. A **Pen** specifies the line style used to draw a shape (for example, line thickness, solid lines, dashed lines, etc.). A **Brush** specifies how to fill a shape (for example, solid color or pattern). As you learned in Tutorial 21, the `Graphics` class contains methods used for drawing. The drawing methods of the `Graphics` class usually require a `Pen` or `Brush` object to render a specified shape.

The `Color` structure contains predefined colors that can be used for the graphics in an application. The `Color` structure also contains methods that allow users to create new colors.

Objects of the `Font` class affect the appearance of text. The **Font** class contains properties (such as **Bold**, **Italic** and **Size**) that describe font characteristics. The **FontFamily** class contains methods for obtaining font information (such as **GetName** and **GetType**).

GDI+ uses a **coordinate system** (Fig. 26.4) to identify every point on the screen. A coordinate pair has both an **x-coordinate** (the **horizontal coordinate**) and a **y-coordinate** (the **vertical coordinate**). The *x*-coordinate is the horizontal distance from zero at the left of the drawing area, which increases as you move to the right. The *y*-coordinate is the vertical distance from zero at the top of the drawing area, which increases as you move down.

The **x-axis** defines every horizontal coordinate, and the **y-axis** defines every vertical coordinate. Programmers position text and shapes on the screen by specifying their (x, y) coordinates. The upper left corner of a GUI component (such as a `Panel` or the `Form`) has the coordinates $(0, 0)$. In the diagram in Fig. 26.4, the red point at position (x, y) is x pixels from the left of position $(0, 0)$ along the *x*-axis and y pixels from the top of position $(0, 0)$ along the *y*-axis. Coordinate units are measured in pixels, which are the smallest units of resolution on a computer monitor.

Portability Tip

Different computer monitors have different resolutions, so the density of pixels on various monitors will vary. This may cause graphics to appear in different sizes on different monitors.

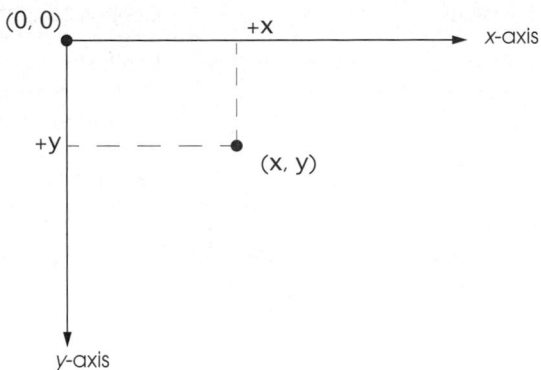

Figure 26.4 GDI+ coordinate system.

SELF-REVIEW

1. The _____ class contains properties that describe font characteristics.
   a) `Font`   b) `GDIFont`
   c) `SystemFont`   d) `FontStyle`

2. The _____ corner of a GUI component has the coordinate *(0, 0)*.
   a) lower left   b) upper right
   c) upper left   d) lower right

Answers: 1) a. 2) c.

26.3 Constructing the CheckWriter Application

Now that you have learned about the features that you will use in your **Check-Writer** application, you need to analyze the application. The following pseudocode describes the actions that the application performs to solve the problem:

> **When the user clicks the Preview Button**
> > Retrieve input from the user
> > Display the check in a Print preview dialog
>
> **When the user clicks the Print Button**
> > Retrieve input from the user
> > Print the check on the printer

The **CheckWriter** application will print a check using information entered by the user. The ACE table of Fig. 26.5 lists the actions, controls, objects and events for this application.

Action/Control/Event (ACE) Table for the CheckWriter Application

Action	Control/Object	Event
Label the application's controls	`lblNumber, lblDate, lblAmount, lblPayee, lblDollars, lblMemo, lblSigned`	
Retrieve input from the user Display the check in a Print preview dialog	`btnPreview, txtNumber, dtpDate, txtAmount, txtPayee, txtPayment, txtMemo, txtPayer, objPreview`	`Click (of Button)`

Figure 26.5 ACE table for the **CheckWriter** application in Design view with PrintPreviewDialog. (Part 1 of 2.)

Action	Control/Object	Event

Retrieve input from the user
Print the check on the printer
	`btnPrint,`
	`objPrintDocument,`
	`txtNumber, dtpDate,`
	`txtAmount, txtPayee,`
	`txtPayment, txtMemo,`
	`txtPayer`
		`Click` (of Button)
		`PrintPage` (of
		`objPrintDocument`)

Figure 26.5 ACE table for the **CheckWriter** application in Design view with PrintPreviewDialog. (Part 2 of 2.)

Now that you have an understanding of the **CheckWriter** application, you can begin to create it. A template application is provided that contains many of the GUI's controls. You might notice that the application does not follow some GUI design guidelines. This is because the controls must be placed near or sometimes overlapping one another for the printed check to appear correctly. You begin writing code for this application by creating a `PrintPreviewDialog` object in the *Adding a `PrintPreviewDialog` in the* **CheckWriter** *Application* box.

Adding a
PrintPreviewDialog
in the *CheckWriter*
Application

1. ***Opening the template application.*** Open the `C:\Examples\Tutorial26\` `TemplateApplication\CheckWriter` folder to locate the **CheckWriter** application. Double click `CheckWriter.sln`.

2. ***Adding the*** ***PrintPreviewDialog.*** In the **Toolbox**, locate the **PrintPreview-Dialog** control

in the **Windows Forms** group, and add it to the Form. The control should appear in the component tray as shown in Fig. 26.6.

Added `PrintPreviewDialog` —

Figure 26.6 **CheckWriter** application in **Design** view with `PrintPreview-Dialog`.

(cont.)

The **PrintPreviewDialog** control uses a dialog to allow users to view a document of different sizes, print a document and display multiple pages of a document before printing. Click the `PrintPreviewDialog` object that you just created and change its `Name` property to `objPreview`. This object has a `Document` property that specifies the document to preview. The document must be a `PrintDocument` object, which will be discussed later in the tutorial. For now, do not specify the document.

3. ***Running the application.*** Select **Debug > Start** to run the program. The executed application displays the `Form` as shown in Fig. 26.7. Click the **Preview** Button, then click the **Print** Button. Currently, the application does nothing because you have not yet added event handlers for the Buttons. You will add functionality to the application in the next series of boxes.

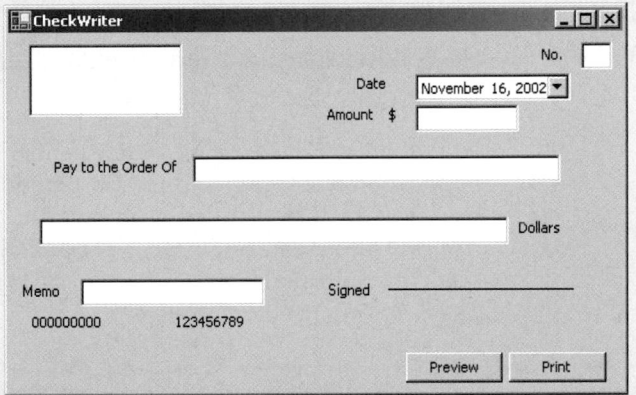

Figure 26.7 Running template application.

4. ***Saving the solution.*** Select **File > Save All** to save all the solution's files.

1. Use a _____ control to preview a document before it is printed.

   a) `PrintDialog`   b) `PrintPreviewDialog`
   c) `PrintPreviewControl`   d) `PrintDocument`

2. A `PrintPreviewDialog` object has a _____ property that specifies the document to preview.

   a) `Preview`   b) `PreviewDocument`
   c) `View`   d) `Document`

Answers: 1) b. 2) d.

26.4 PrintPreviewDialogs and PrintDocuments

In the **CheckWriter** application, you use an object of the `PrintPreviewDialog` class. As previously mentioned, this object displays a dialog that will show a document as it will appear when it is printed. Recall that the dialog object contains the **Document** property, which allows you to specify the document to preview and that the object specified in the `Document` property must be of type `PrintDocument`. `PrintPreviewDialog` also contains the **UseAntiAlias** property, which makes the text in the dialog appear smoother on the screen. To accomplish this, set the `UseAntiAlias` property to `True`. The `PrintPreviewDialog`'s `ShowDialog` method displays the preview dialog. You will use this method later in the application.

The **PrintDocument** object allows you to specify how to print a specified document. The object can raise a **PrintPage** event, which occurs when the data required to print the current page is needed (that is, when the `Print` method is called). You can define this object's `PrintPage` event handler to specify what you want to print.

This object also contains a **Print** method, which uses a Graphics object to print the document. You will use method Print later in the program.

---

1. The object in the Document property must be of type _____.

    a) PrintPreviewDialog   b) PrintDocument

    c) PrintPreviewControl   d) PrintDialog

2. The _____ method of object PrintDocument uses a graphics object to print the document.

    a) Graphics   b) Document

    c) Print   d) None of the above.

Answers: 1) b. 2) c.

26.5 Creating an Event Handler for the CheckWriter Application

Now that you have created the PrintPreviewDialog object in the **CheckWriter** application, you can begin to add functionality to the application. Before you can use print features, you must import the System.Drawing.Printing namespace. You will also create an instance variable that will be used by several different methods. You will implement these features in the box, *Importing a Namespace and Declaring an Instance Variable*.

Importing a Namespace and Declaring an Instance Variable

1. ***Switching to code view.*** Select **View > Code** to view the CheckWriter.vb code.

2. ***Importing namespaces.*** Add line 1 before the class FrmCheckWriter definition, as shown in Fig. 26.8 to import the **System.Drawing.Printing** namespace. This statement allows your applications to access all services related to printing. After you import the namespace, the application can use PrintDocument objects. The namespace also enables access to the PrintPageEventArgs.Graphics property, which you will use to draw the graphics that will appear on the printed page.

Importing the System.Drawing.Printing namespace

Figure 26.8 Import namespaces to class FrmCheckWriter.

3. ***Declaring the instance variable.*** You will declare reference m_objFont, which is used to specify the text font. To accomplish this, add line 6 (Fig. 26.9) to the application. This statement declares a Font reference named m_objFont that you will use shortly to reference a font object.

(cont.)

Declaring a Font object

Figure 26.9 m_objFont created.

4. ***Saving the solution.*** Select **File > Save All** to save all the solution's files.

Now that you have imported a namespace for the **CheckWriter** application and declared the Font reference, you can write code to enable printing and previewing. You will begin by defining the objPrintDocument_PrintPage method, which will specify what to print. When printing the check, you want the printed document to resemble the application's Form. This can be completed using a For Each...Next statement that draws the contents of each control in a Graphics object. You can then print the check using this Graphics object. You will begin writing code to perform these actions in the box, *Defining an Event Handler to Print Pages.*

Defining an Event Handler to Print Pages

1. ***Creating the objPrintDocument_PrintPage method.*** Add lines 301–305 into the application code below the Windows Form Designer Generated Code as in Fig. 26.10. These lines create the event handler for the PrintPage event. You need to type these lines to create the event handler because the PrintDocument object has not yet been created. You will create this object in the box, *Defining the btnPrint_Click Event Handler.*

Empty PrintPage
event handler

Figure 26.10 objPrintDocument_PrintPage event handler.

2. ***Declaring the variables.*** Add lines 305–314 from Fig. 26.11 to the event handler. Lines 305–306 declare Single variables that represent the *x*- and *y*-coordinates where controls appear on the Form. **Single** is a data type that stores floating-point values. Single is similar to Double, but is less precise and require less memory. Lines 309 and 312 declare Single variables, which specify the coordinates of the left and top margins of the page to be printed. These values are determined by using the **MarginBounds.Left** and **MarginBounds.Top** properties of the **PrintPageEventArgs** object (e from line 303) that is passed when the PrintPage event is raised.

(cont.)

Line 313 declares the String variable strLine, which will be used to store text from the controls. Line 314 declares a **Control** reference (an object that represents a control on the Form), which you will use as the control variable in your For Each...Next statement.

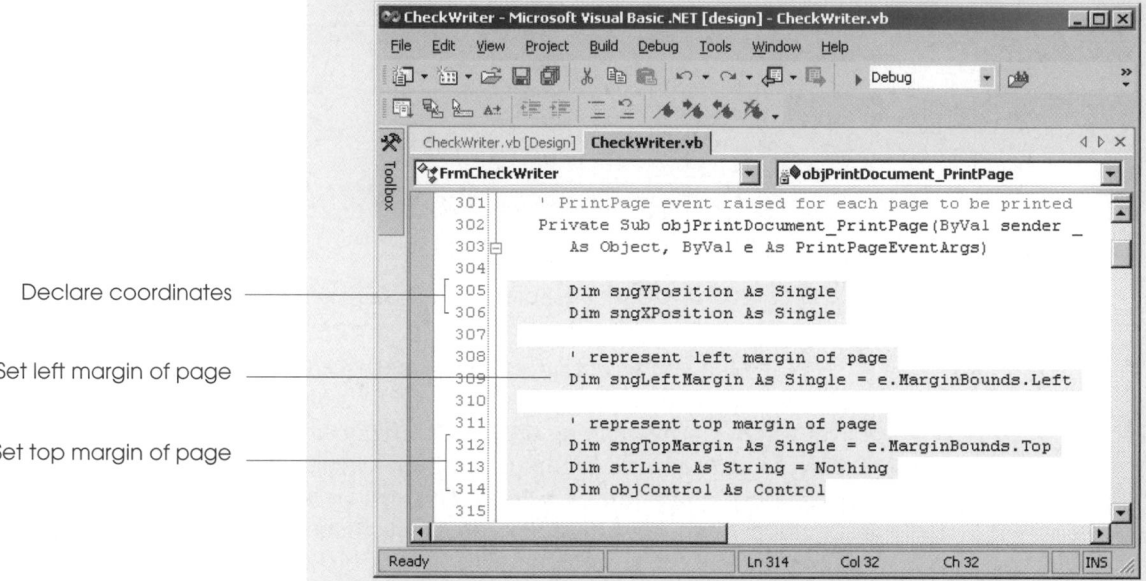

Declare coordinates
Set left margin of page
Set top margin of page

Figure 26.11 Variables created for objPrintDocument_PrintPage.

3. *Iterating through the controls on the Form.* Add lines 316–319 from Fig. 26.12 to the method. This For Each...Next statement iterates through each control on the Form to print the check. You will define the body of this statement in the next box.

Declaring a For Each...Next statement

Figure 26.12 For Each...Next statement used for iteration.

4. *Drawing the check's border.* Add lines 321–323 from Fig. 26.13 into the event handler. The Form's border is not contained in a control; therefore, you must use a Graphics object to draw a rectangle around the check to be printed. These lines of code draw the rectangle.

To draw the rectangle around the check, use the **PrintPageEventArgs** object (e from line 303) that is passed when the PrintPage event is raised. The Graphics property of this object allows you to specify what you want to print. By calling the **DrawRectangle** method on the Graphics object, you can specify the properties of the rectangle to draw.

(cont.)

Draw border of check

Figure 26.13 Event handler `objPrintDocument_PrintPage` modified to draw border of check.

The first argument you pass to the method is the `Pens.Black` object. This is a `Pen` object that uses a black color to draw the rectangle's border. The second argument specifies the *x*-coordinate that defines the left side of the rectangle you wish to draw. Use the `sngLeftMargin` variable that you created in *Step* 2 to represent the position of the left margin of the page on which the check will print. This value ensures that the rectangle will align with the left margin. The third argument in the method specifies the *y*-coordinate that defines the top of the rectangle. Use the `sngTopMargin` variable that you created in *Step* 2 to represent the position of the top margin of the page on which the check will print. Together, the *x*- and *y*-coordinates in the second and third arguments define the upper left corner of the rectangle.

The fourth and fifth arguments specify the width and height of the rectangle. The width is set to `Me.Width`, which returns the width of the `Form`. Keyword **Me** references the current object—in this case, the `Form`. The height, on the other hand, is set to `Me.Height - 60`. This value is the height of the `Form` minus 60 pixels. You subtract 60 pixels because you do not want to print the `Buttons` on the bottom of the `Form`. These `Buttons` were created to allow users to print and preview the checks. (They were not intended to be printed on the checks.)

5. ***Indicating that there are no more pages to print.*** Add lines 325–326 from Fig. 26.14 to the method. Line 326 indicates that there are no more pages to print by setting the event argument's **HasMorePages** property to `False`.

Indicate no more pages to print

Figure 26.14 Event handler `objPrintDocument_PrintPage` modified to indicate that there are no more pages to print.

6. ***Saving the solution.*** Select **File > Save All** to save all the solution's files.

1. Importing the System._____ namespace gives you access to print-related functions.
   a) Windows
   b) Printing
   c) Drawing.Printing
   d) Drawing

2. The _____ keyword references the current object.
   a) Me
   b) Current
   c) Form
   d) None of the above.

Answers: 1) c. 2) a.

26.6 Graphics Objects: Colors, Lines and Shapes

A **Graphics** object controls how information is drawn. In addition to providing methods for drawing various shapes, Graphics objects contain methods for font manipulation, color manipulation and other graphics-related actions. You can draw on many controls, such as Labels and Buttons, which have their own drawing areas. To draw on a control, first obtain a Graphics object for that control by invoking the control's CreateGraphics method as in

```
Dim objGraphics As Graphics = pnlDisplay.CreateGraphics()
```

Now you can use the methods provided in class Graphics to draw on the pnlDisplay Panel. You will see many Graphics methods throughout this tutorial.

Colors

Colors can enhance a program's appearance and help convey meaning. For example, a red traffic light indicates stop, yellow indicates caution and green indicates go. The Color structure defines methods and constants used to manipulate colors.

Every color can be created from a combination of alpha, red, green and blue components. The alpha value determines the **opacity** (amount of transparency) of the color. For example, the alpha value 0 specifies a transparent color, and the value 255 specifies an opaque color. Alpha values between 0 and 255 (inclusive) result in a blending of the color's RGB value with that of any background color, causing a semitransparent effect. All three RGB components are Bytes that represent integer values in the range 0–255. The first number in the RGB value defines the amount of red in the color, the second defines the amount of green and the third defines the amount of blue. The larger the value for a particular color, the greater the amount of that particular color. Visual Basic .NET enables you to choose from almost 17 million colors. If a particular computer monitor cannot display all of these colors, it displays the color closest to the one specified, or the computer attempts to imitate it using **dithering** (using small dots of existing colors to form a pattern that simulates the desired color). Figure 26.15 summarizes some predefined Color constants. You can also find a list of various RGB values and their corresponding colors at http://www.pitt.edu/~nisg/cis/web/cgi/rgb.html.

Good Programming Practice

When working with color, keep in mind that many people are color blind or have varying difficulties perceiving and distinguishing colors.

Constant	RGB value	Constant	RGB value
Color.Orange	255, 200, 0	Color.White	255, 255, 255
Color.Pink	255, 175, 175	Color.Gray	128, 128, 128
Color.Cyan	0, 255, 255	Color.DarkGray	64, 64, 64
Color.Magenta	255, 0, 255	Color.Red	255, 0, 0
Color.Yellow	255, 255, 0	Color.Green	0, 255, 0
Color.Black	0, 0, 0	Color.Blue	0, 0, 255

Figure 26.15   Color structure constants and their RGB values.

You can use pre-existing colors, or you can create your own by using the FromArgb method. The following demonstrates how to create a color:

```
Dim colorSilver As Color
colorSilver = Color.FromArgb(192, 192, 192)
```

These statements create a silver color and assign it to variable colorSilver. Now you can use colorSilver whenever you need a silver color. The Color method FromArgb is used to create this color and other colors by specifying the RGB values as arguments. The method sets the alpha value to 255 (that is, opaque) by default.

Drawing Lines, Rectangles and Ovals

This section presents several Graphics methods for drawing lines, rectangles and ovals. To draw shapes and Strings, you must specify the type of Brushes and Pens to use. A Pen, which functions much like an ordinary pen, is used to specify characteristics such as the color and width of the shape's lines. Most drawing methods require a Pen object. To fill the interior of objects, you must specify a Brush. All classes derived from the abstract class Brush define objects that fill the interiors of shapes with color patterns or images. For example, a SolidBrush specifies the Color that fills the interior of a shape. The following statement creates a Solid-Brush with the color orange:

```
Dim objBrush As SolidBrush = New SolidBrush(Color.Orange)
```

Many drawing methods have multiple versions. When employing methods that draw outlined hollow shapes, use versions that take a Pen argument. When employing methods that draw shapes filled with colors, patterns or images, use versions that take a Brush argument. Many of these methods require x, y, width and height arguments. The x and y arguments represent the shape's upper-left corner coordinate. The width and height arguments represent the width and height of the shape in pixels, respectively. Figure 26.16 summarizes several Graphics methods and their parameters.

Graphics Drawing Methods and Descriptions

Note: Many of these methods have multiple versions.

```
DrawLine(ByVal p As Pen, ByVal x1 As Single, ByVal y1 As Single,
    ByVal x2 As Single, ByVal y2 As Single)
```
Draws a line from the point (x1, y1) to the point (x2, y2). The Pen determines the color, style and width of the line.

```
DrawRectangle(ByVal p As Pen, ByVal x As Single, ByVal y As Single,
    ByVal width As Single, ByVal height As Single)
```
Draws a rectangle of the specified width and height. The top-left corner of the rectangle is at the point (x, y). The Pen determines the rectangle's color, style and border width.

```
FillRectangle(ByVal b As Brush, ByVal x As Single, ByVal y As Single,
    ByVal width As Single, ByVal height As Single)
```
Draws a solid rectangle of the specified width and height. The top-left corner of the rectangle is at the point (x, y). The Brush determines the fill pattern inside the rectangle.

```
DrawEllipse(ByVal p As Pen, ByVal x As Single, ByVal y As Single,
    ByVal width As Single, ByVal height As Single)
```
Draws an ellipse inside a rectangular area of the specified width and height. The top-left corner of the rectangular area is at the point (x, y) and the Pen determines the color, style and border width of the ellipse.

```
FillEllipse(ByVal b As Brush, ByVal x As Single, ByVal y As Single,
    ByVal width As Single, ByVal height As Single)
```
Draws a filled ellipse inside a rectangular area of the specified width and height. The top-left corner of the rectangular area is at the point (x, y) and the Brush determines the pattern inside the ellipse.

Figure 26.16 Graphics methods that draw lines, rectangles and ovals.

1. The RGB value of a Color represents _____.

    a) the index number of a color

    b) the amount of red, green and blue in a color

    c) the thickness of the drawing object   d) the type of shape to draw

2. The _____ method is used to draw solid rectangles.

    a) `DrawRectangle`   b) `FillRectangle`

    c) `SolidRectangle`   d) `OpaqueRectangle`

Answers: 1) b. 2) b.

26.7 Printing Each Control of the CheckWriter Application

Recall earlier that you created the empty For Each...Next structure, in *Step 3* of the box, *Defining an Event Handler to Print Pages* to iterate through all the controls on the Form. Now you will write code for the body of the For Each...Next structure to print all controls on the Form, except for the Buttons. You do this in the box, *Iterating through All the Objects of the Form to Print Each Control.*

Iterating through All the Objects of the *Form* to Print Each Control

1. ***Checking for Buttons.*** In the body of the For Each...Next statement of `objPrintDocument_PrintPage`, add lines 319–322 from Fig. 26.17. Adding this If...Then statement determines whether the current control is a Button. If the control is not a Button, then the body of the If...Then statement executes. However, if the control is a Button, the For Each...Next statement continues to the next control on the Form.

Ensure current control is not a Button ───

Figure 26.17 Code to determine whether the current control is a Button.

2. ***Defining the body of the If...Then statement.*** Now you must add code that properly prints the value that appears in each control on the check. Add lines 321–342 from Fig. 26.18 into the body of the If...Then statement.

Line 321 sets the `strLine` variable that you created earlier to `objControl.Text`. This property contains the value contained in the control's Text property (text displayed to the user or entered by the user). The Select Case statement (lines 323–342) specifies how each control prints. The controlling expression is set to the value `objControl.Name`. This is the Name property of the control. You can use the Name property to select specific controls that need to be treated differently when printed.

(cont.)

Set `strLine` to control's text

Determine current control

Underline the text if displaying
date from `DateTimePicker`

Draw box around dollar amount

Set the default font

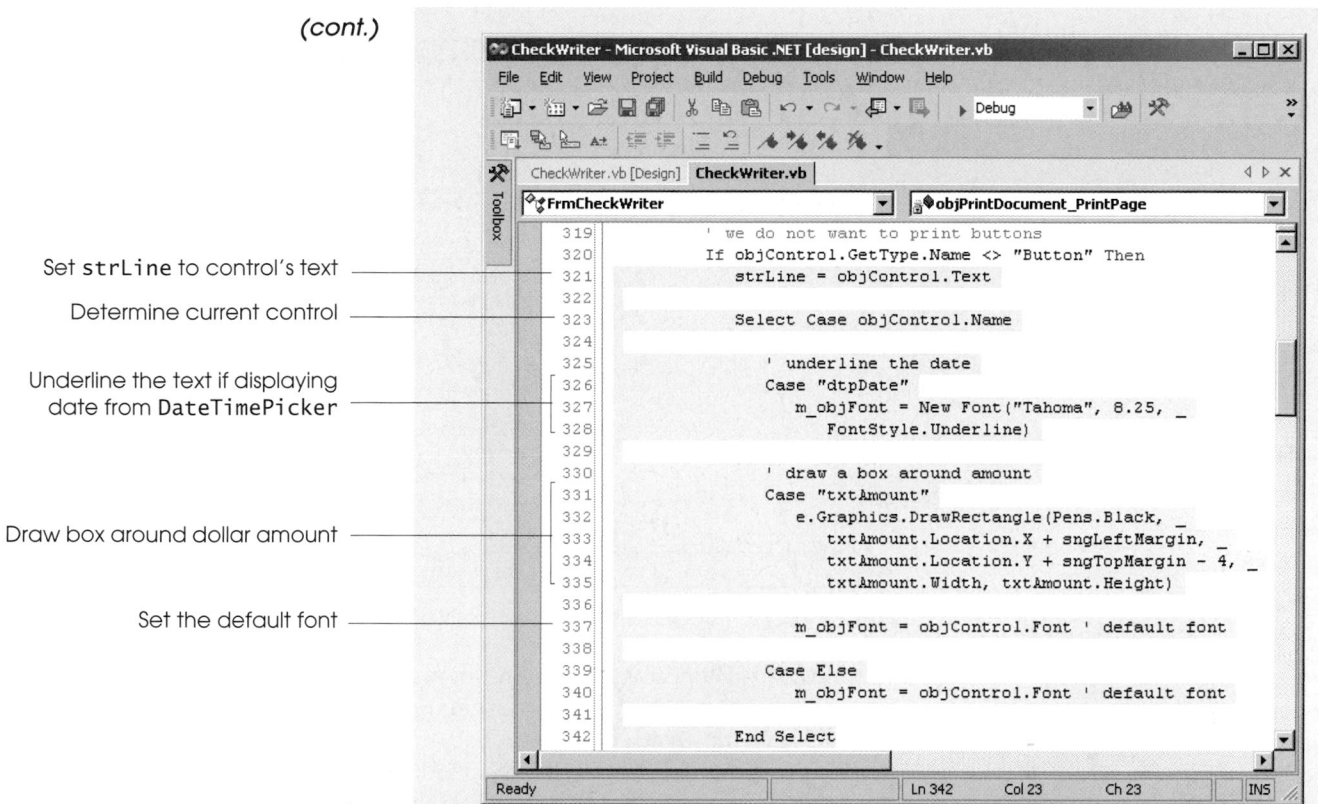

Figure 26.18 Select Case statement to print controls.

The first `Case` (lines 326–328) determines what happens when the current control is the `dtpDate DateTimePicker`. This `Case` sets the `m_objFont` reference to the font style of the date—an underlined Tahoma font, with a size of `8.25` (the same size as the text in the control). So, the date on the check will be underlined and will appear in `8.25` points in Tahoma font. Fonts are discussed in detail later in this tutorial.

The second `Case` (lines 331–337) executes if the control is the `txt-Amount TextBox`. This `Case` draws the box that surrounds the decimal amount of the check. `DrawRectangle` (a `Graphics` method) is invoked by using the `e.Graphics` property. The outline of the rectangle prints in black, indicated by `Pens.Black`. The *x*- and *y*-coordinates are specified by adding the `TextBox`'s *x-y* location on the `Form` to the `sngLeftMargin` and `sng-TopMargin` variables, respectively. Recall that we begin printing the check at the corner of the top and left margins. Adding the margin values to the `Location` properties ensures that the `txtAmount TextBox` prints in the same position as it appears on the `Form`. (Line 334 subtracts four points of space to center the box on the text.) Line 337 sets the font of the text to draw to the same value as the font used to display text in the control.

The third `Case` (lines 339–340) executes for all the other controls. This `Case` sets the `m_objFont` font style to the same value as the font used to display text in the control. Line 342 ends the `Select Case` statement.

3. ***Setting the positions of the text of each control.*** Add lines 344–353 from Fig. 26.19 to the body of the `If...Then` statement. Lines 345–346 set the `sngXPosition` variable to `sngLeftMargin + objControl.Location.X`. By adding the *x*-coordinate of the current control (represented by `objControl.Location.X`) to the left margin, you ensure that the check will not draw outside the margins of the page.

(cont.)

Set horizontal location of current control

Set vertical location of current control

Print current control's text

Figure 26.19 Code to set `String` positions of the controls.

Lines 348–349 perform a similar operation, setting `sngYPosition` to the sum of the top margin and *y*-coordinate of the control's location. Lines 352–353 call the `DrawString` method on the `e.Graphics` property. The **DrawString** method draws the specified `String` of text in the `Graphics` object. The first argument is the `String` to draw, in this case `strLine`. Recall earlier that you set `strLine` to the `Text` property of the current control. The second argument is the font, which is specified by `m_objFont`. The third argument specifies a `Brush`. You pass the value `Brushes.Black`, which creates a black brush object to draw the text. The fourth and fifth arguments are the *x*- and *y*-coordinates where the first character of the `String` prints. Use the `sngXPosition` and `sngYPosition` variables that you set in lines 345–349 to print the text at the correct location on the page.

4. ***Saving the project.*** Select **File > Save All** to save all the files in the solution.

SELF-REVIEW

1. The _____ method draws a specified `String` of text.

   a) `String`
       b) `PrintString`

   c) `DrawString`
       d) `Draw`

2. Typing `Brushes.Black` _____.

   a) obtains a black `Brush` object
       b) retrieves the color of a brush

   c) paints the screen black
       d) creates a `Pen` object

Answers: 1) c. 2) a.

26.8 Font Class

In the **CheckWriter** application, you used a `Font` object to specify the style of the text printed on a page. This section introduces the methods and constants contained in the `Font` class. Note that once a `Font` has been created, its properties cannot be modified. That means that if you require a different `Font`, you must create a new `Font` object with the appropriate settings. There are many versions of the `Font` constructor for creating custom `Font`s to help you do this. Some properties of the `Font` class are summarized in Fig. 26.20.

Property	Description
Bold	Sets a font to a bold font style if value is set to True.
FontFamily	Represents the FontFamily of the Font (a grouping structure to organize fonts with similar properties).
Height	Represents the height of the font.
Italic	Sets a font to an italic font style if value is set to True.
Name	Sets the font's name to the specified String.
Size	Represents a Single value indicating the current font size measured in design units. (Design units are any specified units of measurement for the font.)
SizeInPoints	Represents a Single value indicating the current font size measured in points.
Strikeout	Sets a font to the strikeout font style if value is set to True (for example, ~~Deitel~~).
Underline	Sets a font to the underline font style if the value is set to True.

Figure 26.20 Font class read-only properties.

Common Programming Error

Specifying a font that is not available on a system is a logic error. If this occurs, that system's default font will be used instead.

Note that the Size property returns the font size as measured in **design units**, whereas SizeInPoints returns the font size as measured in points (a more common measurement). The Size property can be specified in a variety of ways, such as inches or millimeters. Some versions of the Font constructor accept a Graphics-Unit argument—an enumeration that allows users to specify the unit of measurement used to describe the font size. Members of the GraphicsUnit enumeration include Point (1/72 inch), Display (1/75 inch), Document (1/300 inch), Millimeter, Inch and Pixel. If this argument is provided, the Size property contains the size of the font as measured in the specified design unit, and the SizeInPoints property contains the size of the font in points. For example, if you create a Font having size 1 and specify that GraphicsUnit.Inch will be used to measure the font, the Size property will be 1, and the SizeInPoints property will be 72 because there are 72 points in an inch. If you create a new Font object without specifying a GraphicsUnit, the default measurement for the font size is Graphics-Unit.Point (thus, the Size and SizeInPoints properties will be equal). [*Note*: There is no way to change the properties of a Font object—to use a different font, you must create a new Font object.]

The Font class has a number of constructors. Most require a **font name**, which is a String representing a font currently supported by the system. Common fonts include *SansSerif* and *Serif*. Constructors also require the **font size** as an argument. Lastly, Font constructors usually require a **font style**, specified by an element of the **FontStyle** enumeration: Fontstyle.Bold, Fontstyle.Italic, Fontstyle.Regular, Fontstyle.Strikeout and Fontstyle.Underline.

SELF-REVIEW

1. The most common measurement of font size is _____.

    a) points   b) inches

    c) pixels   d) millimeters

2. _____ is an example of a font style.

    a) Bold   b) Italic

    c) StrikeOut   d) All of the above.

Answers: 1) a. 2) d.

26.9 Previewing and Printing the Check

After defining how objects are printed in the `objPrintDocument_PrintPage` event handler, you must define what occurs when each **Button** is clicked. You begin with the `btnPrint_Click` event handler to specify the functionality when clicking the **Print** Button. You will write this event handler in the box, *Defining the btnPrint_Click Event Handler*.

Defining the btnPrint_Click Event Handler

1. ***Creating the btnPrint_Click event handler.*** In the Windows Form Designer, double click the **Print** Button. The `btnPrint_Click` event handler appears in the `CheckWriter.vb` file.

2. ***Creating a PrintDocument object.*** Add lines 373–374 from Fig. 26.21 into the event handler. The `PrintDocument` object is used to help print the check.

Declaring a PrintDocument object

Figure 26.21 Code that creates the `PrintDocument` object.

3. ***Specifying the PrintPage event handler.*** Add lines 376–378 from Fig. 26.22 into the event handler. These lines specify the event handler called when the `PrintPage` event is raised. Lines 377-378 use keyword **AddHandler** to associate the `PrintPage` event of the `objPrintDocument` object with the event handler specified after the **AddressOf** keyword (the `objPrintDocument_PrintPage` event handler that you created in the box, *Defining an Event Handler to Print Pages*). To execute the code in the event handler, you must provide the name of the event handler you created to handle the event after keyword `AddressOf`.

Adding an event handler for the PrintDocument object

Figure 26.22 Code that adds an event handler to the `PrintDocument` object.

(cont.)

4. ***Verifying that the user has a printer.*** Add lines 380–384 from Fig. 26.23 to the btnPrint_Click event handler. Line 381 uses the property **Printer-Settings.InstalledPrinters.Count** to determine how many printers the user has installed on the computer. If there are no printers installed (that is, if the Count property returns 0), the user cannot print or preview the document. Line 382 in the body of the If...Then statement displays an error message by calling procedure ErrorMessage, which you will define in the next box. Line 383 exits the event handler using the Return keyword.

Take no action if there are no printers installed

```
379
380          ' if no printers installed, display error message
381     If PrinterSettings.InstalledPrinters.Count = 0 Then
382          ErrorMessage()
383          Return ' exit event handler
384     End If
385
```

Figure 26.23 Exiting the event handler if no printers are installed.

5. ***Printing the document.*** Add lines 386–387 from Fig. 26.24 to the btnPrint_Click event handler. Line 387 calls the Print method of the PrintDocument object. The Print method, in turn, raises the PrintPage event each time it needs output for printing. Your PrintPage event handler then executes and uses a Graphics object to draw. The Graphics object is obtained from the Graphics property of the PrintPageEventArgs class. In this case, the PrintPageEventArgs object was passed as argument e. The objPrintDocument_PrintPage method uses this PrintPageEventArgs' Graphics object to call the DrawRectangle and DrawString methods.

Printing the check

```
385
386          ' print the document
387          objPrintDocument.Print()
388
389     End Sub ' btnPrint_Click
```

Figure 26.24 Event handler btnPrint_Click modified to print the document.

6. ***Saving the project.*** Select **File > Save All** to save all the files in the solution.

Now that you have defined the btnPrint_Click method, you will complete the application by coding the Click event handler for the **Preview** Button. When this Button is clicked, a dialog appears allowing users to preview the check before printing it. You will create the btnPreview_Click event handler to enable this feature in the box, *Defining the btnPreview_Click Event Handler.*

Defining the
btnPreview_Click
Event Handler

1. ***Creating the btnPreview_Click event handler.*** In the Windows Form Designer, double click the btnPreview Button. The btnPreview_Click event handler appears in the CheckWriter.vb file.

2. ***Creating the PrintDocument object and adding the PrintPage handler.*** Add lines 396–401 from Fig. 26.25 into the event handler. As in the btnPrint_Click event handler, line 397 creates a new PrintDocument object named objPrintDocument. Lines 400–401 specify that the PrintDocument object's PrintPage event handler is method objPrintDocument_PrintPage.

Creating a
PrintDocument object

Adding an event handler
for the PrintDocument

Figure 26.25 Event handler btnPreview_Click modified to create PrintDocument and add PrintPage event handler.

3. ***Verifying that the user has a printer.*** Add lines 403–407 from Fig. 26.26 to the btnPrint_Click event handler. These lines of code are exactly the same as the code from *Step 4* of the box, *Defining the btnPrint_Click Event Handler.* An error message is displayed if there are no installed printers.

Figure 26.26 Exiting the print preview event handler if no printers are installed.

(cont.)   4.   ***Specifying the PrintPreviewDialog object's Document property.*** Add line 409 from Fig. 26.27 into the event handler. Recall earlier when you created the `PrintPreviewDialog` object, that you learned that its `Document` property specifies the document to preview. This property requires that its value be of type `PrintDocument`, the same class you use to print the check. This line sets `objPreview`'s `Document` property to `objPrintDocument` (the `PrintDocument` you created on line 397).

Setting the document
to preview

```
408
409          objPreview.Document = objPrintDocument ' specify document
410
411      End Sub ' btnPreview_Click
```

Figure 26.27   Event handler `btnPreview_Click` modified to set the `PrintPreviewDialog` object's `Document` property.

5.   ***Showing the Print preview dialog.*** Add line 410 into the event handler, as shown in Fig. 26.28. This line invokes the `PrintPreviewDialog` object's `ShowDialog` method to display the **Print preview** dialog that displays how the `PrintDocument` will appear when printed. To display the document, the `PrintPreviewControl` of the `PrintPreviewDialog` raises the `PrintPage` event. Rather than using the `Graphics` object to print a page using your printer, the `PrintPreviewDialog` uses the `Graphics` object to display the page on the screen.

Displaying the preview dialog

```
408
409          objPreview.Document = objPrintDocument ' specify document
410          objPreview.ShowDialog() ' show print preview
411
412      End Sub ' btnPreview_Click
```

Figure 26.28   Event handler `btnPreview_Click` modified to show preview dialog.

6.   ***Defining the ErrorMessage procedure.*** Add lines 414–422 from Fig. 26.29 into your application. Lines 417–420 display an error message to the user indicating that printing and print previewing the check is not possible if there are no printers installed on the computer.

7.   ***Saving the project.*** Select **File > Save All** to save all the files in the solution.

(cont.)

Method to display error message

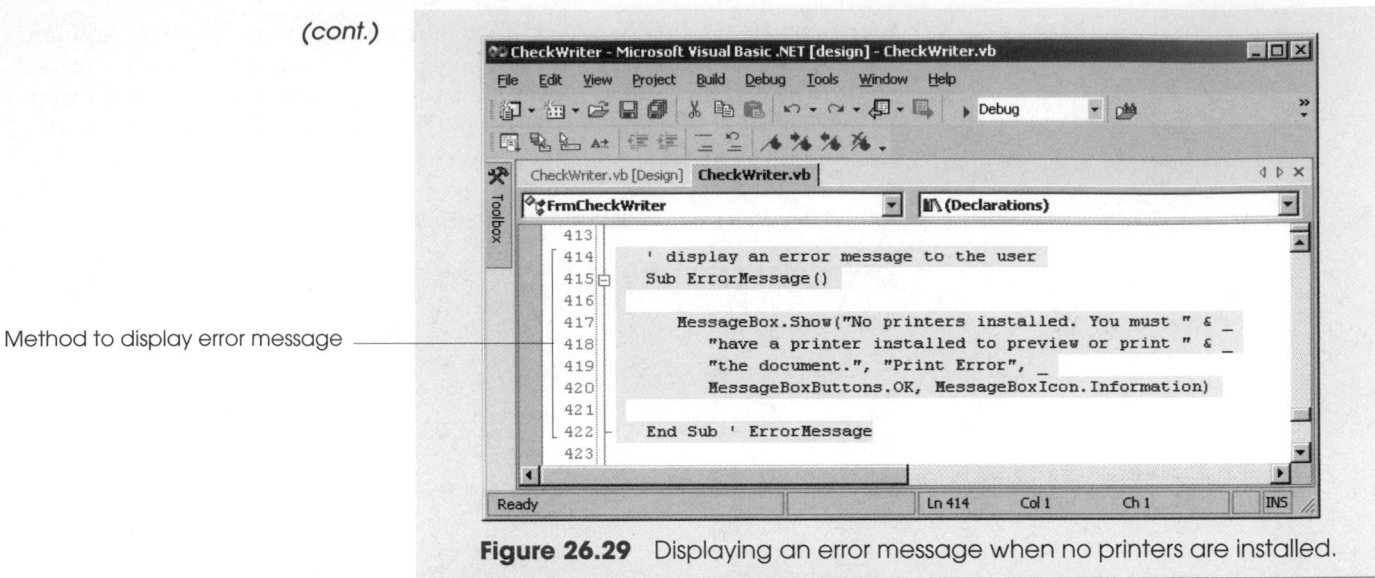

Figure 26.29 Displaying an error message when no printers are installed.

Figure 26.30 contains the entire code listing for the **CheckWriter** application. New concepts are highlighted in yellow.

```
1   Imports System.Drawing.Printing
2
3   Public Class FrmCheckWriter
4       Inherits System.Windows.Forms.Form
5
6       Private m_objFont As Font ' instance variable to stor
7
8       ' Windows Form Designer generated code
9
10      ' PrintPage event raised for each page to be printed
11      Private Sub objPrintDocument_PrintPage(ByVal sender _
12          As Object, ByVal e As PrintPageEventArgs)
13
14          Dim sngYPosition As Single
15          Dim sngXPosition As Single
16
17          ' represent left margin of page
18          Dim sngLeftMargin As Single = e.MarginBounds.Left
19
20          ' represent top margin of page
21          Dim sngTopMargin As Single = e.MarginBounds.Top
22
23          Dim strLine As String = Nothing
24          Dim objControl As Control
25
26          ' iterate over the form, printing each control
27          For Each objControl In Me.Controls
28
29              ' we do not want to print Buttons
30              If objControl.GetType.Name <> "Button" Then
31                  strLine = objControl.Text
32
33                  Select Case objControl.Name
34
```

Instance variable to store font — line 6

Event handler indicating what to print — lines 11–12

Variable to store left margin value — line 18

Variable to store top margin value — line 21

Looping through each control on the Form — line 27

Figure 26.30 **CheckWriter** application code. (Part 1 of 3.)

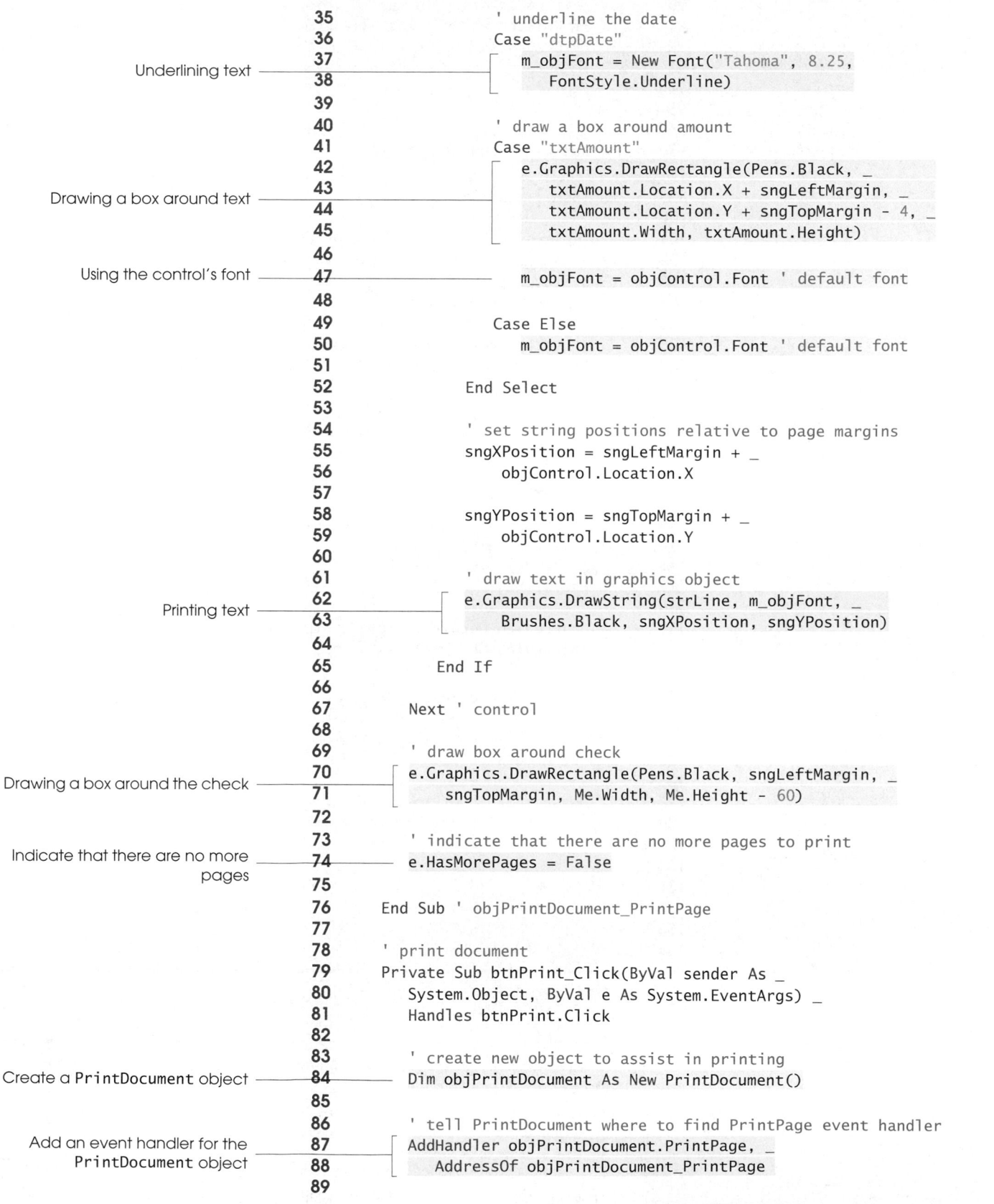

```
35                          ' underline the date
36                          Case "dtpDate"
37                             m_objFont = New Font("Tahoma", 8.25, _
38                                FontStyle.Underline)
39
40                          ' draw a box around amount
41                          Case "txtAmount"
42                             e.Graphics.DrawRectangle(Pens.Black, _
43                                txtAmount.Location.X + sngLeftMargin, _
44                                txtAmount.Location.Y + sngTopMargin - 4, _
45                                txtAmount.Width, txtAmount.Height)
46
47                             m_objFont = objControl.Font ' default font
48
49                          Case Else
50                             m_objFont = objControl.Font ' default font
51
52                       End Select
53
54                       ' set string positions relative to page margins
55                       sngXPosition = sngLeftMargin + _
56                          objControl.Location.X
57
58                       sngYPosition = sngTopMargin + _
59                          objControl.Location.Y
60
61                       ' draw text in graphics object
62                       e.Graphics.DrawString(strLine, m_objFont, _
63                          Brushes.Black, sngXPosition, sngYPosition)
64
65                    End If
66
67                 Next ' control
68
69                 ' draw box around check
70                 e.Graphics.DrawRectangle(Pens.Black, sngLeftMargin, _
71                    sngTopMargin, Me.Width, Me.Height - 60)
72
73                 ' indicate that there are no more pages to print
74                 e.HasMorePages = False
75
76              End Sub ' objPrintDocument_PrintPage
77
78           ' print document
79           Private Sub btnPrint_Click(ByVal sender As _
80              System.Object, ByVal e As System.EventArgs) _
81              Handles btnPrint.Click
82
83              ' create new object to assist in printing
84              Dim objPrintDocument As New PrintDocument()
85
86              ' tell PrintDocument where to find PrintPage event handler
87              AddHandler objPrintDocument.PrintPage, _
88                 AddressOf objPrintDocument_PrintPage
89
```

Labels (left margin):
- Underlining text → lines 37–38
- Drawing a box around text → lines 42–45
- Using the control's font → line 47
- Printing text → lines 62–63
- Drawing a box around the check → lines 70–71
- Indicate that there are no more pages → line 74
- Create a `PrintDocument` object → line 84
- Add an event handler for the `PrintDocument` object → lines 87–88

Figure 26.30 **CheckWriter** application code. (Part 2 of 3.)

```
 90              ' if no printers installed, display error message
 91              If PrinterSettings.InstalledPrinters.Count = 0 Then
 92                 ErrorMessage()
 93                 Return ' exit event handler
 94              End If
 95
 96              ' print the document
 97              objPrintDocument.Print()
 98
 99           End Sub ' btnPrint_Click
100
101           ' display document in print preview dialog
102           Private Sub btnPreview_Click(ByVal sender As _
103              System.Object, ByVal e As System.EventArgs) _
104              Handles btnPreview.Click
105
106              ' create new object to assist in previewing
107              Dim objPrintDocument As New PrintDocument()
108
109              ' tell PrintDocument where to find PrintPage event handler
110              AddHandler objPrintDocument.PrintPage, _
111                 AddressOf objPrintDocument_PrintPage
112
113              ' if no printers installed, display error message
114              If PrinterSettings.InstalledPrinters.Count = 0 Then
115                 ErrorMessage()
116                 Return ' exit event handler
117              End If
118
119              objPreview.Document = objPrintDocument ' specify document
120              objPreview.ShowDialog() ' show print preview
121
122           End Sub ' btnPreview_Click
123
124           ' display an error message to the user
125           Sub ErrorMessage()
126
127              MessageBox.Show("No printers installed. You must " & _
128                 "have a printer installed to preview or print " & _
129                 "the document.", "Print Error", _
130                 MessageBoxButtons.OK, MessageBoxIcon.Information)
131
132           End Sub ' ErrorMessage
133
134        End Class ' FrmCheckWriter
```

Display an error message if no printers are installed — *(lines 91–93)*

Print the check — *(line 97)*

Create a `PrintDocument` object — *(line 107)*

Add an event handler for the `PrintDocument` object — *(lines 110–111)*

Display error message if no printers are installed — *(lines 114–116)*

Show preview in dialog — *(lines 119–120)*

Figure 26.30 CheckWriter application code. (Part 3 of 3.)

SELF-REVIEW

1. When you associate an event with an event handler, the _____ keyword is used to specify the location of the event handler.

   a) `AddHandler`   b) `AddressOf`

   c) `HandlerEvent`   d) Both a and b.

2. The _____ object contains the `PrintPage` event.

   a) `PrintDocument`   b) `PrintPreviewDialog`

   c) `PrintPreviewControl`   d) `PrintDialog`

Answers: 1) b. 2) a.

26.10 Wrap-Up

In this tutorial, you were introduced to the topic of graphics and printing. You created a **CheckWriter** application, which allows you to enter data in a check and print it using the printer installed on your computer. You learned how to use the `Graphics` object and its members. While building the **CheckWriter** application, you used these concepts to draw shapes and `String`s using graphics objects such as `Pen`s and `Brush`es. You also learned how to use code to create fonts to apply to text you wish to display or print.

You also learned about several new classes, which included `PrintPreviewDialog`, `PrintPreviewControl` and `PrintDocument`. You used the `PrintDocument` class to create a `PrintDocument` object. You then used its `PrintPage` event to execute code that draws and prints the check when the user clicks the **Print** Button. You also added a `PrintPreviewDialog` in your application, allowing the user to preview a check before printing it.

In the next tutorial, you will learn how to use multimedia in your applications. In particular, you will be introduced to Microsoft Agent, a technology used to add three-dimensional, animated characters to a program. You will use this technology to create a phone book application.

SKILLS SUMMARY

Printing a Rectangle

- Use the `PrintPageEventArgs` object's `Graphics` property.
- Use the `Graphics` property to invoke the `DrawRectangle` method.
- Specify the five parameters: A `Brush` (or `Pen`) object, the *x*-coordinate, the *y*-coordinate, the width and the height.

Printing a `String`

- Use the `PrintPageEventArgs` object's `Graphics` property.
- Use the `Graphics` property to invoke the `DrawString` method.
- Specify the five parameters: the string to print, the font style, the `Brush` object, the *x*-coordinate and the *y*-coordinate.

Associating an Event with a Defined Event Handler

- Follow the format `AddHandler` *objectName*`.`*eventName*`,` `AddressOf` *eventHandlerName* where *objectName* represents the name of the object with which the event will be associated, *eventName* represents the name of a valid event and *eventHandlerName* represents the name of the defined event handler to be associated with the specified event.

Printing a Document

- Create a new `PrintDocument` object.
- Define the `PrintDocument`'s `PrintPage` event handler to specify what to print.
- Use the `PrintDocument` to invoke the `Print` method.

Displaying a Print Preview Dialog

- Create a `PrintPreviewDialog` object.
- Specify the `PrintDocument` to preview in the `PrintPreviewDialog`'s `Document` property.
- Invoke the `PrintPreviewDialog`'s `ShowDialog` method.

KEY TERMS

AddHandler keyword—Keyword used to add an event handler for a specific event.

AddressOf keyword—Keyword that specifies the location of an event handler associated with an event.

API (application programming interface)—The interface used by a program to access the operating system and various services on the computer.

ARGB values—A combination of alpha, red, green and blue components from which every color is created.

Brush object—An object used to specify drawing parameters when drawing solid shapes.

dithering—Process that uses small dots of existing colors to form a pattern that simulates a desired color.

Document property—Property of the `PrintPreviewDialog` that allows you to specify the document that will be displayed in the dialog.

DrawString method—`Graphics` method that draws the specified `String`.

Font class—Class that contains properties that define unique fonts.

FontFamily class—Class that contains methods for obtaining font information, such as `GetName` and `GetType`.

GDI+—An application programming interface (API) that provides classes for creating two-dimensional vector graphics

Graphics object—An object used to draw two-dimensional images.

Image class—Class used to store and manipulate images from various file formats.

Me keyword—A keyword that references the current object.

Pen object—An object used to specify drawing parameters when drawing shape outlines.

Print method—`PrintDocument` method used to print a document.

PrintDocument class—Class that allows users to describe how to print a document.

PrintPage event—Event that occurs when the data required to print the current page is needed.

PrintPreviewDialog class—Class that previews a document before it prints in a dialog box.

Rectangle structure—Structure that enables you to define rectangular shapes and their dimensions.

Single data type—A data type that stores floating-point values. `Single` is similar to `Double`, but is less precise and requires less memory.

System.Drawing.Printing namespace—Namespace that allows your applications to access all services related to printing.

UseAntiAlias property—Property of class `PrintPreviewDialog` that makes the text in the `PrintPreviewDialog` appear smoother on the screen.

vector graphics—Graphics created by a set of mathematical properties called vectors, which include the graphics' dimensions, attributes and positions.

_x_-coordinate—Horizontal distance (increasing to the right) from the left of the drawing area.

_y_-coordinate—Vertical distance (increasing downward) from the top of the drawing area.

CONTROLS, EVENTS, PROPERTIES & METHODS

Font This class is used to define the font face, size and style of text throughout an application.

■ *Properties*

`Bold`—This property sets the weight of the text.

`Italic`—This property sets the angle of the text.

`Size`—This property sets the size of the text.

`FontFamily`—This property contains a `FontFamily` object, which is used to store font face information.

`FontSyle`—This property specifies the style applied to a `Font` object.

Graphics The class that contains methods used to draw text, lines and shapes.

■ *Methods*

`DrawLine`—This method draws a line of a specified size and color.

`DrawEllipse`—This method draws the outline of an ellipse of a specified size and color at a specified location.

`DrawRectangle`—This method draws the outline of a rectangle of a specified size and color at a specified location.

`DrawEllipse`—This method draws a `String` in a specified font and color at a specified position.

FillEllipse—This method draws a solid ellipse of a specified size and color at the specified location.

FillRectangle—This method draws a solid rectangle of a specified size and color at the specified location.

PrintDocument This class allows you to specify how to print a document.

■ *Event*

PrintPage—This event is raised when data required to print a page is needed.

■ *Method*

Print—This method uses a Graphics object to print a page.

PrinterSettings This class stores information the system's printer settings.

■ *Property*

Count—This property returns the number of printers installed on the system.

PrintPageEventArgs This class contains data passed to a PrintPage event.

■ *Properties*

HasMorePages—This property specifies if there are more pages to print. When False, the PrintPage event is no longer raised.

MarginBounds—This property specifies the margin of the printed page.

  Left—This property specifies the left margin of the page.

  Top—This property specifies the top margin of the page.

PrintPreviewDialog   PrintPreviewDialog   This control is used to display how a document will look when it is printed.

■ *Properties*

Document—This property specifies the document that the control will preview. The document must be of type PrintDocument.

Name—This property specifies the name used to access the PrintPreviewDialog control programmatically. The name should be prefixed with obj.

UseAntiAlias—This property specifies whether the dialog will display a smoothed image.

■ *Method*

ShowDialog—This method is used to display the PrintPreviewDialog to the user.

MULTIPLE-CHOICE QUESTIONS

26.1 The RGB value (0, 0, 255) represents _____.

a) Color.Red   b) Color.Green

c) Color.Blue   d) Color.Yellow

26.2 The _____ property of the PrintPreviewDialog object makes text appear smoother.

a) AntiAlias   b) UseAntiAlias

c) Alias   d) UseAlias

26.3 Use a _____ object to allow the users to preview a document before it is printed.

a) PrintPreviewDialog   b) PrintDocument

c) Print   d) PrintPreviewControl

26.4 The _____ event handler specifies what will be printed.

a) OnPaint   b) Print

c) Document   d) PrintPage

26.5 To display the preview dialog of the _____ object, call method `ShowDialog`.

   a) `PrintPreviewDialog`   b) `PrintDocument`

   c) `PrintDialog`   d) Both a and b.

26.6 Set the _____ property to `False` to indicate that there are no more pages to print.

   a) `Document`   b) `HasMorePages`

   c) `TerminatePrint`   d) Both a and b.

26.7 The `Print` method sends a _____ object to the printer for printing.

   a) `Graphics`   b) `PrintDocument`

   c) `PrintPreviewDialog`   d) `Brush`

26.8 Keyword _____ references the current object.

   a) `This`   b) `Class`

   c) `Me`   d) `Property`

26.9 Opacity is the _____ value of a color.

   a) red   b) transparency

   c) dithering   d) blue

26.10 Design units are used to specify the _____ of a `Font`.

   a) `Size`   b) `Name`

   c) `FontFamily`   d) `Style`

EXERCISES

26.11 (*CheckWriter Modified to Print Background Images*) Modify the **CheckWriter** application to display and print a background for the check. The GUI should look similar to Fig. 26.31. Users can select a background image. The image should appear in the **Print preview** dialog box and also should print as a background to the check.

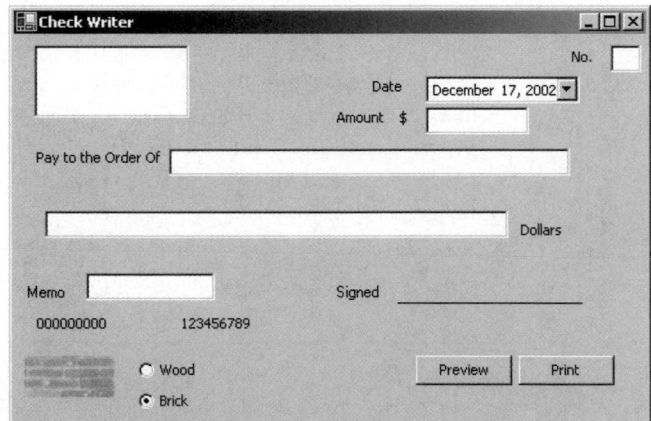

Figure 26.31 Modified **CheckWriter** GUI.

  a) *Copying and opening the template application.* Copy the `ModifiedCheckWriter` folder from `C:\Examples\Tutorial26\Exercises` to `C:\SimplyVB`. Double click the `CheckWriter.sln` file to open the application in Visual Studio .NET.

  b) *Create the CheckedChanged event handler.* Double click the **Wood** `RadioButton` to create its `CheckedChanged` event handler.

  c) *Defining the CheckedChanged event handler.* Define the `RadioButton`'s `CheckedChanged` event handler to notify the application when users have made a background selection. If the **Wood** `RadioButton` is selected, then a preview of the wooden background should display in the `picPreview` `PictureBox`. Otherwise, if the **Brick** `RadioButton` is selected, then a preview of the brick background should display in the `picPreview` `PictureBox`.

  d) *Modifying the objPrintDocument_PrintPage event handler.* Modify event handler `objPrintDocument_PrintPage` to print the background image. (*Hint*: Use the Draw-

Image method to display the background image to print. DrawImage takes five arguments: The image file, the *x*-coordinate, the *y*-coordinate, the width and the height.) To print the image in the background, the DrawImage method must be the first method called on the Graphics object.

26.12 (*Company Logo Designer Application*) Develop a **Company Logo** application that allows users to design a company logo.

a) ***Copying and opening the template application.*** Copy the CompanyLogo folder from C:\Examples\Tutorial26\Exercises to C:\SimplyVB. Double click the Company-Logo.sln file to open the application in Visual Studio .NET.

b) ***Defining the Add Button's Click event handler.*** Create the **Add** Button's Click event handler. Define the event handler so that the shape that users specify is drawn on the PictureBox. Use the CreateGraphics method on the PictureBox to retrieve the Graphics object used to draw on the PictureBox.

c) ***Defining the Clear Button's Click event handler.*** Create the **Clear** Button's Click event handler, and define it so that the PictureBox is cleared. [*Hint*: To clear the entire PictureBox, use the PictureBox's Invalidate method. The Invalidate method is often used to refresh (update) graphics of a control. By using the Invalidate method without specifying a graphic to draw, the PictureBox clears.] Also ensure that all TextBoxes are cleared when the **Clear** Button is clicked.

Figure 26.32   Company Logo GUI.

26.13 (*Letter Head Designer Application*) Create a **Letter Head** application that allows users to design stationery for company documents. Allow users to specify the image that will serve as the letterhead.

a) ***Copying and opening the template application.*** Copy the LetterHead folder from C:\Examples\Tutorial26\Exercises to C:\SimplyVB. Double click the Letter-Head.sln file to open the application in Visual Studio .NET.

b) ***Creating a PrintPreviewDialog control.*** Add a PrintPreviewDialog control to allow users to preview the letterhead before it is printed.

c) ***Defining the PrintPage event handler.*** Allow users to print the document by defining the PrintPage event handler as you did in the **CheckWriter** application.

d) ***Defining the btnPrint_Click event handler.*** The btnPrint_Click event handler should tell the PrintDocument where to find the PrintPage event handler, as in the **CheckWriter** application, and print the document.

e) ***Defining the btnPreview_Click event handler.*** The btnPreview_Click event handler should tell the PrintDocument where to find the PrintPage event handler, as in the **CheckWriter** application, and then show the preview dialog.

f) *Testing the application.* The Letterhead.png image file, located in C:\Examples\Tutorial26\Exercises\Images has been provided for you to test the application's letter head image capability.

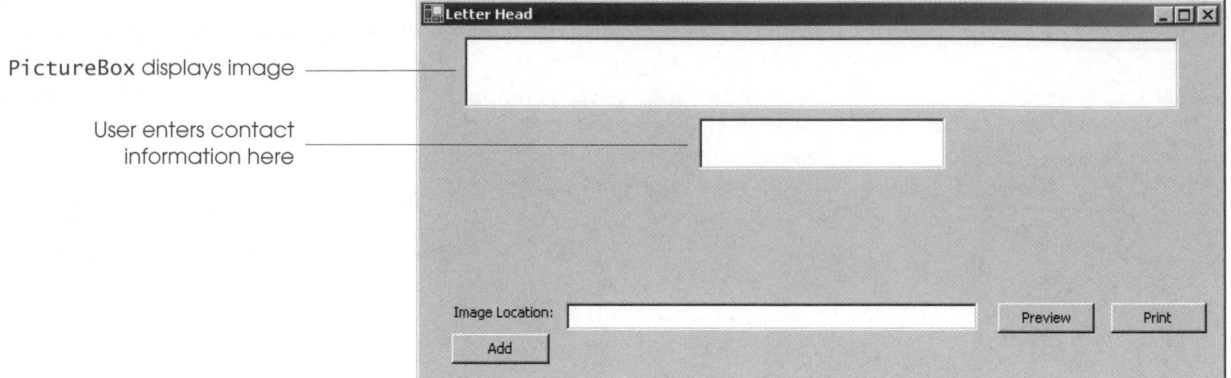

PictureBox displays image

User enters contact information here

Figure 26.33 Letter Head GUI.

What does this code do? ▶

26.14 What is the result of the following code? Assume that objOutput_PrintPage is defined.

```
1   Private Sub btnPrint_Click(ByVal sender As System.Object, _
2      ByVal e As System.EventArgs) Handles btnPrint.Click
3
4      Dim objOutput As New PrintDocument()
5
6      AddHandler objOutput.PrintPage, _
7         AddressOf objOutput_PrintPage
8
9      objPrintOutput.Print()
10
11  End Sub ' btnPrint_Click
```

What's wrong with this code? ▶

26.15 Find the error(s) in the following code. This is the definition for a Click event handler for a Button. This event handler should draw a rectangle on a PictureBox control.

```
1   Private Sub btnDrawImage_Click(ByVal sender As System.Object, _
2      ByVal ev As System.EventArgs) Handles btnDrawImage.Click
3
4      ' create an orange colored brush
5      Dim objBrush As SolidBrush = New SolidBrush(Orange)
6
7      ' create a Graphics object to draw on the PictureBox
8      Dim objGraphics As Graphics = picPictureBox.AcquireGraphics
9
10     ' draw a filled rectangle
11     objGraphics.FillRectangle(objBrush, 2, 3, 40, 30)
12
13  End Sub ' btnDrawImage_Click
```

Programming Challenge ▶

26.16 (*Screen Saver Simulator Application*) Develop an application that simulates a screen saver. This application should add random-colored, random-sized, solid and hollow shapes at different positions of the screen. Copy the C:\Exercises\Tutorial26\ScreenSaver folder, and place it in C:\SimplyVB. The design of the Form has been created, which consists of a black Form and a Timer control. In the ScreenSaver.vb code view, the DisplayShape method has been provided and the Timer's tick event handler has already been defined for you.

You must write the rest of the DisplayShape method code. Create the Graphics object from the Form using the Form's CreateGraphics method, and specify random colors, sizes and positions for the filled and hollow shapes that will be displayed on the screen. The width and height of the shapes should be no larger than 100 pixels.

26.17 (*Screen Saver Simulator Enhancement Application*) Enhance the **Screen Saver Simulator** application from Exercise 26.16 by modifying the Timer control's Tick event handler. Add code to this event handler so that after a specified amount of time, the screen should clear the displayed shapes. After the screen clears, random shapes should continue to display. Also, use the FromArgs method so that you can specify random opacity (alpha values) for the colors. You should pass four arguments to this method. The first argument is the alpha value, the second is the red value, the third is the green value and the fourth is the blue value.

Objectives

In this tutorial, you will learn to:
- Download components necessary to run Microsoft Agent.
- Enhance Windows applications using multimedia.
- Create applications that interact with users.
- Use Microsoft Agent in a Visual Basic .NET application.

Outline

Phone Book Application

Introducing Multimedia Using Microsoft Agent

When computers were first introduced, they were large and expensive and were used primarily to perform arithmetic calculations. **Multimedia** applications, which use a variety of media including graphics, animation, video and sound, were made impractical by the high cost and slow speed of computers. However, today's affordable, ultrafast processors are making multimedia-based applications commonplace. As the market for multimedia explodes, users are purchasing computers with faster processors, larger amounts of memory and wider communications bandwidths needed to support multimedia applications.

Users are seeing exciting new three-dimensional multimedia applications that interact with the user by means of animation, audio and video. Multimedia programming is an entertaining and innovative field, but one that presents many challenges. Visual Basic .NET enables you to include such multimedia presentations in your applications.

In this tutorial, you will explore the **Microsoft Agent** technology, which uses entertaining, animated three-dimensional cartoon characters to interact with the application user. You will create a phone book application that uses one of the predefined Agent characters.

27.1 Microsoft Agent

In this tutorial, you will create a phone book application that displays people's phone numbers, using Microsoft Agent to interact with users and enhance the application. The application must meet the following requirements:

> **Application Requirements**
>
> *A software company's customer-service department is responsible for calling clients. They need a quick way to access their clients' phone numbers and have asked you to develop an application that stores and retrieves the names and numbers of their clients. The service-department employees want an application that employs multimedia (using the Microsoft Agent character, Peedy the Parrot) to allow them to retrieve the phone numbers by speaking the clients' names and also by selecting clients' names with the mouse.*

Microsoft Agent is a technology used to add **interactive animated characters** to Windows applications or Web pages. Microsoft Agent characters can speak (by using voice synthesis) and respond to user input (by using speech recognition). Microsoft employs its Agent technology in such applications as Word, Excel and PowerPoint, where they help users understand how to use the application.

The Microsoft Agent control provides you with access to four predefined characters—*Genie* (a genie), *Merlin* (a wizard), *Peedy* (a parrot) and *Robby* (a robot). Each character contains unique animations that you can use in their applications to illustrate different instructions and actions. For instance, the Peedy character-animation set includes several flying animations which you can use to move Peedy across the screen. Microsoft provides basic information on Agent technology at:

www.microsoft.com/msagent

Microsoft Agent technology enables users to interact with applications and Web pages by using speech. When the user speaks into a microphone, the control uses a **speech-recognition engine**, an application that translates vocal sound input from a microphone into a language that the computer understands. The Microsoft Agent control also uses a text-to-speech engine, which allows the Microsoft Agent characters to speak lines of text. A **text-to-speech engine** is an application that translates typed words into sound that users hear through headphones or speakers connected to a computer. Microsoft provides speech recognition and text-to-speech engines for several languages at

www.microsoft.com/products/msagent/downloads.htm

SELF-REVIEW

1. A _____ translates typed words into sound.
   a) speech-recognition engine
   b) text-to-speech engine
   c) character-animation set
   d) All of the above.

2. The application that translates vocal sound input from a microphone to a language understood by the computer is called the _____.
   a) speech-recognition engine
   b) text-to-speech engine
   c) character-animation set
   d) All of the above.

Answers: 1) b. 2) a.

27.2 Downloading Microsoft Agent Components

Microsoft Agent characters can be used as visual aids for applications. These Agents also allow users to speak to, listen to and interact with the characters. This tutorial demonstrates how to use the Microsoft Agent characters to build the **Phone Book** application. To run this tutorial's application, you must download and install the Agent control, speech-recognition engine, text-to-speech engine and Peedy character definition from the Microsoft Agent Web site. Begin by visiting:

www.microsoft.com/products/msagent/downloads.htm

This page (Fig. 27.1) displays a list of Microsoft Agent downloads. The first component you need to download is the Agent character file. Click the **Microsoft Agent character files** link (Fig. 27.1).

Clicking this link directs users to the location where the Microsoft Agent character files can be downloaded (Fig. 27.2). Select the Peedy character from the drop-down list and click the **Download selected character** link. Save the file Peedy.exe to your computer, and install the Peedy character files by double clicking this file.

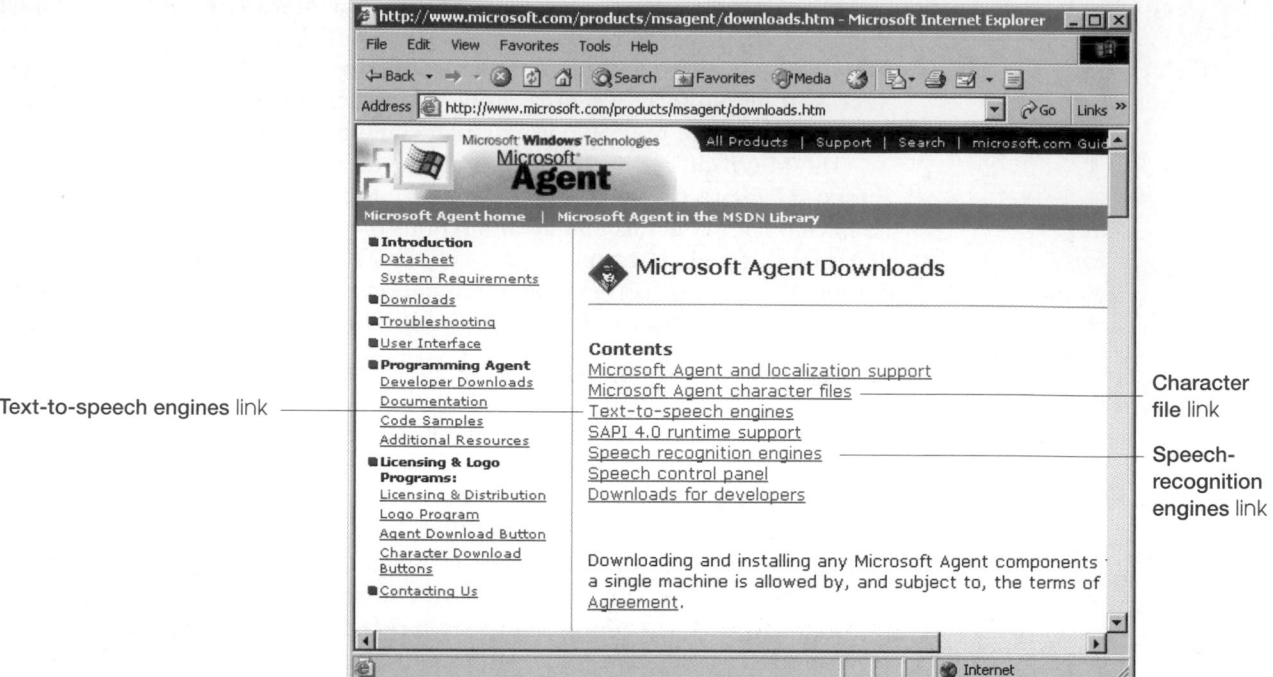

Text-to-speech engines link

Character file link

Speech-recognition engines link

Figure 27.1   Microsoft Web page containing Agent-related downloads.

Select the Peedy character here

Figure 27.2   Location for downloading the Microsoft Agent character.

Next, you should download the text-to-speech engine. Return to the **Microsoft Agent Downloads Contents** list by scrolling to the top of the current page, and click the **Text-to-speech engines** link. Click the ComboBox to display the drop-down list, and select the engine that supports American English. Click the **Download selected engine** link to save the file tv_enua.exe. Double click this file once it has been downloaded to install the text-to-speech engine. You may need to restart your machine after this installation.

You must also download the speech-recognition engine. Return to the **Microsoft Agent Downloads Contents** list by scrolling to the top of the current page, and click the **Speech recognition engines** link. Click the **Download Microsoft Speech Recognition Engine** link to save the file actcnc.exe. Double click this file once it has been downloaded to install the speech-recognition engine. The installation process will walk you through the configuration of your microphone. Once you have downloaded and installed all of the components, you are ready to use Microsoft Agent.

27.3 Test-Driving the Phone Book Application

Recall that you will be creating the **Phone Book** application to allow users to search for a phone number using an interactive Microsoft Agent character. Your **Phone Book** application, which you build in the next section, will contain people's names and phone numbers for the customer-service department. You begin by test-driving the application.

Test-Driving the Phone Book Application

1. ***Opening the application.*** Open the `C:\Examples\Tutorial27\Com-pletedApplication\PhoneBook` folder to locate the **Phone Book** application. Double click `PhoneBook.sln` to open the application in Visual Studio .NET.

2. ***Running the application.*** Select **Debug > Start** to run the application. The application `Form` appears as shown in Fig. 27.3.

Figure 27.3 **Phone Book** application `Form`.

3. ***Calling Peedy.*** Click the **Call Peedy** button to display Peedy. Peedy flies onto the screen into a position beneath the `Form`, waves and speaks the instructions shown in Fig. 27.4. When he is finished speaking, Peedy goes into a resting position (Fig. 27.5).

ComboBox disabled until Peedy arrives

Figure 27.4 Peedy appears after **Call Peedy** button is clicked. (© 1996–1998 Microsoft Corporation. All rights reserved.)

Figure 27.5 Peedy in a resting pose. (© 1996–1998 Microsoft Corporation. All rights reserved.)

4. ***Using the ComboBox to select a name.*** After Peedy appears on the screen, the ComboBox is enabled. Select the name Howard from the list (Fig. 27.6). Notice that the **Call Peedy** Button is disabled, as Peedy is already on the screen. After Howard is selected, Peedy executes several animations. He first appears to be thinking (Fig. 27.7), tells you Howard's number (Fig. 27.8), and then smiles for the user (Fig. 27.9).

(cont.)

Disabled **Call Peedy** Button ——————

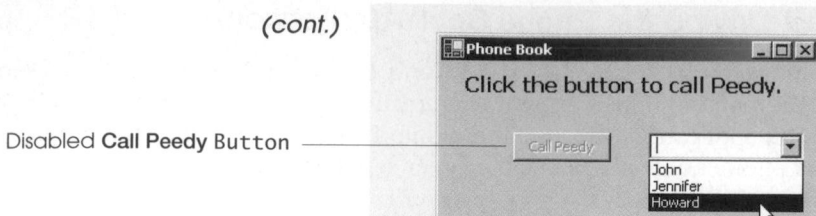

Figure 27.6 Selecting a name from the ComboBox.

Figure 27.7 Peedy thinking. (© 1996–1998 Microsoft Corporation. All rights reserved.)

Figure 27.8 Peedy communicates Howard's phone number. (© 1996–1998 Microsoft Corporation. All rights reserved.)

Figure 27.9 Peedy smiles after speaking phone number. (© 1996–1998 Microsoft Corporation. All rights reserved.)

5. ***Providing a voice command.*** Press the *Scroll Lock* key. A box appears beneath Peedy (called a **status box**) that displays information about Peedy's actions. The status box states that Peedy is listening for your command, as in Fig. 27.10. Speak the name John into your microphone.

Figure 27.10 Peedy listening for a voice command. (© 1996–1998 Microsoft Corporation. All rights reserved.)

If Peedy hears and understands your command, the status box displays the command he heard, as in Fig. 27.11. Otherwise, you must repeat the command clearly, so that Peedy can understand.

(cont.)

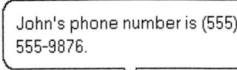

s

Figure 27.11   Peedy heard voice command. (© 1996–1998 Microsoft Corporation. All rights reserved.)

When Peedy successfully hears your command, he gestures as if he is thinking about your request. He then displays John's phone number, as in Fig. 27.12. You will have noticed that Peedy performs several gestures during this application. You will learn how to control these gestures later in the tutorial.

John's phone number is (555) 555-9876.

Figure 27.12   Peedy displays requested phone number. (© 1996–1998 Microsoft Corporation. All rights reserved.)

6. ***Viewing the context menu.*** Right click Peedy and notice that a context menu appears (Fig. 27.13). Selecting one of the names (**John**, **Jennifer** or **Howard**) will cause the same actions to occur as when a name was chosen from the ComboBox.

Commands in pop-up window —————

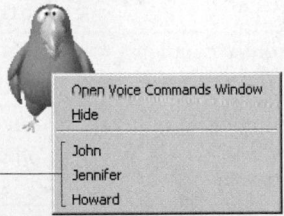

Figure 27.13   Context menu window. (© 1996–1998 Microsoft Corporation. All rights reserved.)

7. ***Terminating the application.*** Click the running application's **Close** button to terminate the application.

8. ***Closing the solution.*** Select **File > Close Solution**.

SELF-REVIEW

1. The _____ displays information about the Microsoft Agent character's actions.
   a) balloon
   b) status box
   c) help window
   d) text window

2. You must press the _____ key for Peedy to listen to your voice commands.
   a) *Shift*
   b) *Number Lock*
   c) *Scroll Lock*
   d) *Insert*

Answers: 1) b. 2) c.

27.4 Constructing the Phone Book Application

Now that you have test-driven the **Phone Book** application, you need to analyze the application, using pseudocode. The Microsoft Agent character, Peedy, helps users search for a specific telephone number. The user can click the ComboBox to select a name and retrieve the specified telephone numbers. However, thanks to the enhancement of the Microsoft Agent character, the user also can communicate verbally with Peedy. The user can retrieve a phone number simply by pressing the *Scroll Lock* key and speaking the name of a person into a microphone connected to the computer. Peedy listens for a name, and, if he recognizes it, displays and speaks the number to the user. The following pseudocode describes the actions that the application needs to execute to meet the application requirements.

> **When the Call Peedy Button is clicked**
> > Display Peedy the Parrot
> > Enable ComboBox containing people's names
>
> **If user selects a name from the ComboBox**
> > Microsoft Agent speaks the phone number of the selected person
>
> **If user presses the Scroll Lock key**
> > Microsoft Agent listens for voice command
> > **If user speaks the name of the person**
> > > Microsoft Agent speaks the phone number of the spoken name

The **Phone Book** application will use Microsoft Agent to help the user quickly find phone numbers. The ACE table of Fig. 27.14 lists the actions, controls, objects and events for this application.

Action/Control/Event (ACE) Table for the Phone Book Application

Action	Control/Object	Event
Label the application's controls	lblInformation	
Display Peedy the Parrot	objMainAgent, btnCall	Click (of Button)
User selects a name from the ComboBox	cboName	SelectedIndexChanged
Peedy speaks a name and number	objMainAgent, cboName	Command (of Microsoft Agent), SelectedIndex-Changed (of ComboBox)
Display instructions to the user	objMainAgent, btnCall	Click (of Button)

Figure 27.14 ACE table for the **Phone Book** application.

Now that you understand the purpose of the **Phone Book** application, you will begin to create it. In the box, *Customizing the Toolbox for the Phone Book Application*, you follow the instructions for adding the Microsoft Agent control to your **Toolbox**.

Customizing the Toolbox for the Phone Book Application

1. ***Copying the template to your work folder.*** Copy the C:\Examples\Tutorial27\TemplateApplication\PhoneBook folder to C:\SimplyVB.

2. ***Opening the template project.*** Double click PhoneBook.sln in the PhoneBook folder to open the application in Visual Studio .NET. If the project does not open in design view, switch to design view at this time.

(cont.)   3. ***Adding the Microsoft Agent to the Toolbox.*** Before you begin designing the
               Form, you must make the Microsoft Agent accessible. To do this, you must
               add the Microsoft Agent control to the **Toolbox** window. Select the **Win-
               dows Forms** tab in the **Toolbox** then select **Tools > Customize Toolbox...**
               as in Fig. 27.15. The **Customize Toolbox** dialog appears (Fig. 27.16). Select
               the **COM Components** tab and search for the **Microsoft Agent Control 2.0**
               item. Then click its CheckBox to select the control as in Fig. 27.16. Click the
               OK Button. The Agent control now appears in the **Windows Forms** group
               in the **Toolbox**, as in Fig. 27.17.

Figure 27.15   **Tools** menu.

Select CheckBox ——

Figure 27.16   **Customize Toolbox** dialog.

           4. ***Saving the project.*** Select **File > Save All** to save all the files in the solution.

(cont.)

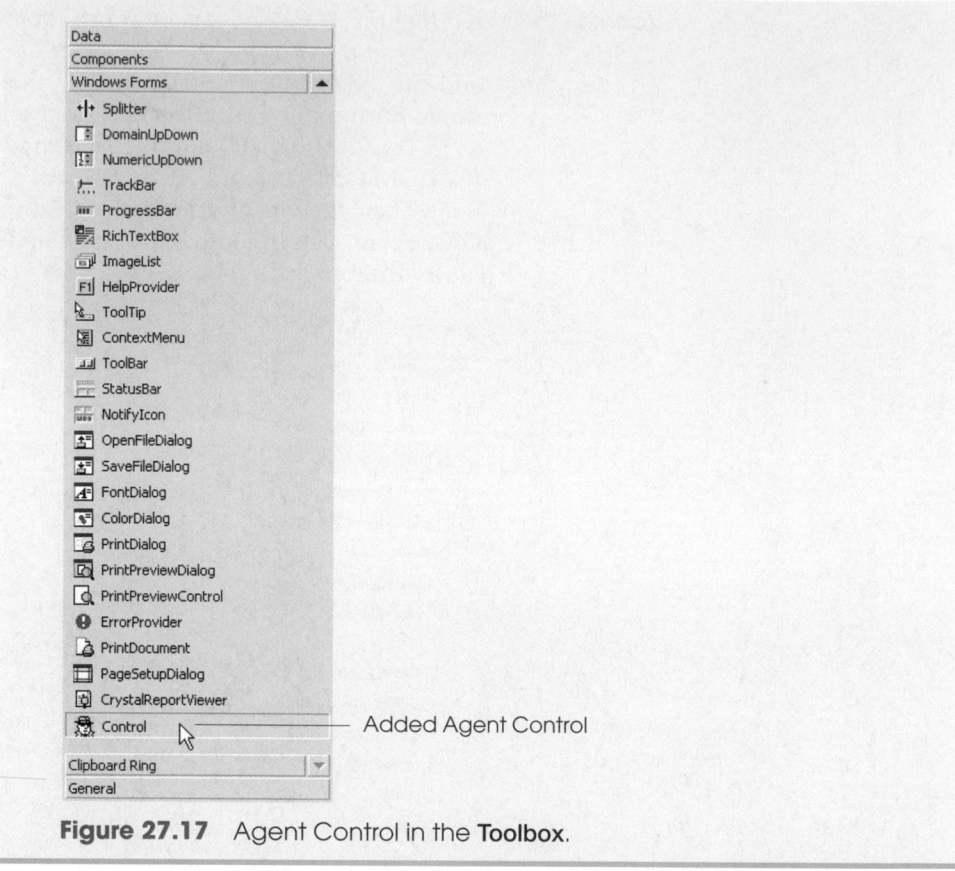

Figure 27.17   Agent Control in the **Toolbox**.

The visual design of the Form (with the exception of the Agent control) is provided in the template application. The next step after adding the Microsoft Agent control to the **Toolbox** is to place a Microsoft Agent control on the Form. The box, *Adding the Microsoft Agent Control to the Application*, demonstrates how to do this.

Adding the Microsoft Agent Control to the Application

 Good Programming Practice

Controls in a container should not overlap. Place your controls so that they are clearly separated from one another, making the design of your application a clean one.

1. ***Placing the Microsoft Agent control on the Form.*** To meet the application requirements, you must add a Microsoft Agent control to your Form, which will be used to display and manage the actions of the Microsoft Agent characters in your application. Drag and drop the Microsoft Agent control from the **Toolbox** onto the Form. Change the Microsoft Agent control's Name property from the default (AxAgent1) to objMainAgent. Change the Microsoft Agent control's Location property to 16, 48 (Fig. 27.18). Because the control icon is not visible when the program executes, the location on the Form does not affect the application's appearance. However, it is good practice to place the control so that it is not overlapping another control on the Form.

    Though you set the Agent control's Location property in this step, you will write code later that will determine where the Agent character appears when the application is running. As you saw in the test drive, the Microsoft Agent character can be displayed outside the application's Form.

2. ***Running the application.*** Select **Debug > Start** to execute the application. The Form appears as shown in Fig. 27.19. The **Call Peedy** Button will be used to make the Agent (in this case, Peedy) appear on the screen. However, clicking the Button does not cause any action to take place yet, because the Button's Click event handler has not been defined. Notice that the ComboBox next to the **Call Peedy** Button is disabled. You will use code to enable and fill the ComboBox with names shortly.

(cont.)

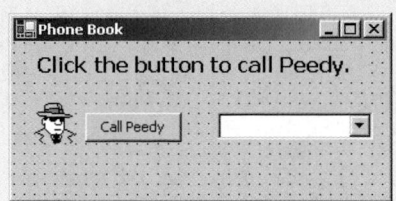

Figure 27.18   Form format of **Phone Book**.

Figure 27.19   **Phone Book** Form with no functionality.

3. *Saving the project.* Select **File > Save All** to save all the files in the solution.

Now that you have placed the Agent control on the application's Form, you will define the event handlers for the **Phone Book** application. These event handlers will define how the Agent responds to user actions. You begin writing code in the box, *Using Code to Display the Peedy Agent Character.*

Using Code to Display the Peedy Agent Character

1. *Declaring instance variables.* To view the code file, select **View > Code**. Declare the instance variables you will use in several event handlers by inserting lines 4–12 of Fig. 27.20 within this Form's class definition.

Create an Agent character variable

List of names in phone book

List of phone numbers

Figure 27.20   Declaring and creating arrays in **Phone Book**.

In addition to the Microsoft Agent object objMainAgent that manages all the application's characters, you also need an object to represent the current character (sometimes referred to as the speaker). In this example, the current character will always be Peedy the Parrot. Line 4 creates a variable to represent this Agent character. The m_objMSpeaker variable is declared as an **AgentObjects.IAgentCtlCharacter** object.

(cont.)

The arrays m_strNameList and m_strNumberList are then declared and filled. The m_strNameList array (lines 7–8) stores the names of people in the phone book (John, Jennifer and Howard), and the m_strNumberList array (lines 11–12) stores the corresponding phone number for each person ((555) 555-9876, (555) 555-1234 and (555) 555-4567).

2. *Writing code that executes when the application loads.* The next step in creating the **Phone Book** application is to use the Form's Load event to execute code before the application becomes available to the user. Double click the Form in the Windows Form Designer to generate the Load event handler, and enter code view. Add the comment on line 104 of Fig. 27.21 above the event handler, and then insert lines 109–114 into the Load event handler. The intCounter variable (line 110) is used to iterate through the m_strNameList array in the For…Next statement (lines 112–114). This statement fills the ComboBox with the contact names that are stored in the m_strNameList array. This allows the user to select names by using the ComboBox instead of speaking the name to Peedy.

Declaring a counter variable

Adding names to the ComboBox

Figure 27.21   Adding items to the ComboBox.

3. *Initializing the Peedy Agent character.* Insert lines 116–120 from Fig. 27.22 into the event handler. Lines 117–118 load the Peedy character into objMainAgent. The first argument of the Load method is a String used to represent the Agent character being loaded. In this case, use the String "Peedy". The second argument is a String representing the file where the character is defined ("Peedy.acs").

Several characters can be loaded into a Microsoft Agent control. In this example, however, we will only be using Peedy the Parrot, so no more characters will be loaded. Line 120 assigns the loaded character to m_objMSpeaker. The character is accessed using the **Characters** property of our Microsoft Agent control. The variable m_objMSpeaker can now be used to represent the Peedy Agent character. It is not necessary to create a separate object of type AgentObjects.IAgentCtlCharacter—the Peedy character can be accessed with the expression objMainAgent.Characters("Peedy"). We have created m_objMSpeaker to increase program clarity.

Good Programming Practice

Use a variable to represent an object when the full reference to the object is long. This improves code readability.

(cont.)

Loading the Peedy character

Assigning Peedy to the Agent character variable

Figure 27.22   Loading the Microsoft Agent character.

4. ***Inserting commands in the Agent Commands context menu.*** Insert lines 122–128 from Fig. 27.23 to your event handler, and add the comment on line 130 to the end of the event handler. This code uses the same counter from the previous step in its For...Next statement (lines 123–128). The header of the For...Next statement resets the counter variable's value to 0. Then, the For...Next statement adds names from the m_strNameList to the Peedy character as voice-enabled commands. The list of valid commands for a character is stored in the **Commands** property of AgentObjects.IAgentCtlCharacter objects.

Creating commands so that Peedy can recognize names when spoken

Figure 27.23   Adding commands to Peedy's context menu.

Method **Add** of the Commands property adds a new command to the command list. The Add method takes five arguments. The first three arguments are Strings and the last two are Boolean values. The first argument identifies the command name. This value enables access to the command from your program. The second argument is a String that appears in a context menu when the user right clicks Peedy. The third String represents the word(s) for which Peedy listens when users make a verbal request. The fourth argument indicates whether the command is enabled. If so, the Agent character will respond to the spoken command. The final argument specifies whether the command is visible in the Commands context menu, which you have already seen in Fig. 27.13.

(cont.)

In this example, you set the first three arguments to the same value in the m_strNameList array and set the last two arguments to True for each name. Now Peedy understands users if they speak any of the names found in the m_strNameList array–John, Jennifer or Howard.

A **Command** event is raised when the user selects the command from the Commands pop-up window or speaks the command into a microphone. Command events are handled by the Command event handler of the Microsoft Agent control (objMainAgent, in this example).

5. ***Defining the btnCall_Click event handler.*** After defining the Form's Load event, you must create an event handler for the **Call Peedy** Button. When this Button is clicked, Peedy should appear and interact with the user. To create the Button's Click event handler, double click the **Call Peedy** Button in the Windows Form Designer. Insert lines 136–141 from Fig. 27.24. Add the comment on line 132 before the event handler.

Line 136 uses the **Show** method to display Peedy on the screen. Specifying 0 as the argument makes Peedy fly onto the screen and land at his default location. However, if 1 is passed to the method, Peedy's image pops onto the screen at his default location (without the flying animation).

Make Peedy fly onto screen ———

Move Peedy ———

Figure 27.24 Displaying the Microsoft Agent character.

After the Show method is called, Peedy appears at (or flies to) the default position on the screen. The command in lines 139–141 causes Peedy to move to a new location. These lines use the **MoveTo** method of the m_objMSpeaker Agent object. Method MoveTo takes two arguments: an *x*-coordinate and a *y*-coordinate, both of type **Short**. The Short data type is similar to the Integer data type, but Short variables occupy less space in memory and therefore cannot hold larger Integer values. **Convert.ToInt16** converts the value of Cursor.Position.X - 100 to a Short value, where **Cursor.Position.X** contains the current position of the mouse pointer. We have subtracted 100 to specify a position that is 100 pixels to the left of the mouse pointer. The same was done for the *y*-coordinate. In this case, the method moves the Agent character 100 pixels to the left and 130 pixels below the mouse pointer at the time the **Call Peedy** Button is clicked. This keeps Peedy near the application Form.

GUI Design Tip

Locate the Microsoft Agent character near the application Form.

6. ***Coding Peedy's greeting.*** Insert lines 143-153 from Fig. 27.25 into your Click event handler. Line 143 uses the **Play** method to command Peedy to perform an action. This method plays the character animation specified by the String argument that is passed. In this line, Peedy's Wave animation is played—he waves hello to the user.

(cont.)

[*Note*: We use only a few of the Peedy character's available animations. To see a listing of the available animations, please visit msdn.microsoft.com/library/default.asp?url=/library/en-us/msagent/peedylst_53xw.asp.]

GUI Design Tip

Use Microsoft Agent character gestures to indicate actions the user should take, or a response to an action the user has already taken.

7. Lines 146–151 call method Speak twice to specify what Peedy says. The argument passed to the Speak method contains the String that Peedy speaks by using the computer's speakers. This String also appears in a conversation bubble above his head. You have already seen an example of this in Fig. 27.4. In this example, you provide the instructions for using the **Phone Book** application. After Peedy displays the instructions, he is positioned in his rest pose (Fig. 27.5) by passing String RestPose (line 153) to the Play method.

Make Peedy wave

Make Peedy speak instructions

Make Peedy rest

Figure 27.25   Code that defines Microsoft Agent's actions when Peedy first appears on the screen.

8. ***Enabling and disabling controls.*** Now that you have made the Agent character available by clicking the **Call Peedy** Button, you should disable the Button and allow the ComboBox to be used. Insert lines 155–156 of Fig. 27.26 into your Click event handler, and add the comment on line 157 to the end of the event handler. These lines set the **Call Peedy** Button's Enabled property to False and cboName's Enabled property to True while the Agent character is shown. Recall that the ComboBox is disabled by default. You disable the **Call Peedy** Button because Peedy is on the screen at this point.

Enable the ComboBox and disable the **Call Peedy** Button

Figure 27.26   Disable btnCall after Peedy has appeared on the screen.

9. ***Saving the project.*** Select **File > Save All** to save all the files in the solution.

Now that you have written code to display Peedy on the screen and have him speak to the user, you must insert code that allows Peedy to respond to user input. Peedy needs to display and read a phone number when the user selects a valid name, either by speaking, by using the context menu or by using the ComboBox. You will enable these features in the box, *Completing the **Phone Book** Application*.

Completing the *Phone Book Application*

1. ***Defining the objMainAgent_Command event handler.*** Event handler objMainAgent_Command executes when the Command event is raised. Recall that this happens when a user speaks a command to the Agent character by using the microphone (while pressing the *Scroll Lock* key). The event is also raised if the user selects a command from Peedy's context menu. You can generate the event handler by selecting objMainAgent from the Class Name ComboBox and Command from the Method Name ComboBox. Insert lines 164–166 from Fig. 27.27 into this event handler. Add the comment on line 159 before the event handler.

Retrieve user input

Figure 27.27   Event handler objMainAgent_Command defined.

Lines 165–166 declare the objCommand variable, which stores values of type **AgentObjects.IAgentCtlUserInput**. This object is used to retrieve the commands that users give Peedy. Notice that you use function **CType** to convert the first argument to the type of object specified by the second argument. This line converts the user input to be of type AgentObjects.IAgentCtlUserInput. You do this to access the name of the command the Agent received.

2. ***Interpreting user input and displaying a phone number.*** Insert lines 168–184 from Fig. 27.28 into your code. Line 168 creates a counter variable that is used in a For...Next statement (lines 173–184). The body of this statement contains an If...Then statement (lines 175–182). The code inside the If...Then statement executes if the user's command matches one of the voice-enabled commands you added earlier by using the m_strNameList array. Using the counter variable, the For...Next statement iterates through each index of the array, comparing the command name (for example, John) to the name in the array. If the names match, the body of the If...Then statement plays Peedy's Think animation (line 176) and uses Peedy to speak and display the requested phone number (lines 177–179). After speaking the phone number, Peedy smiles (the Pleased animation played at line 181). Add the comment on line 186 to the end of your event handler.

(cont.)

Declaring a counter variable

Peedy thinks and speaks
telephone number, if found

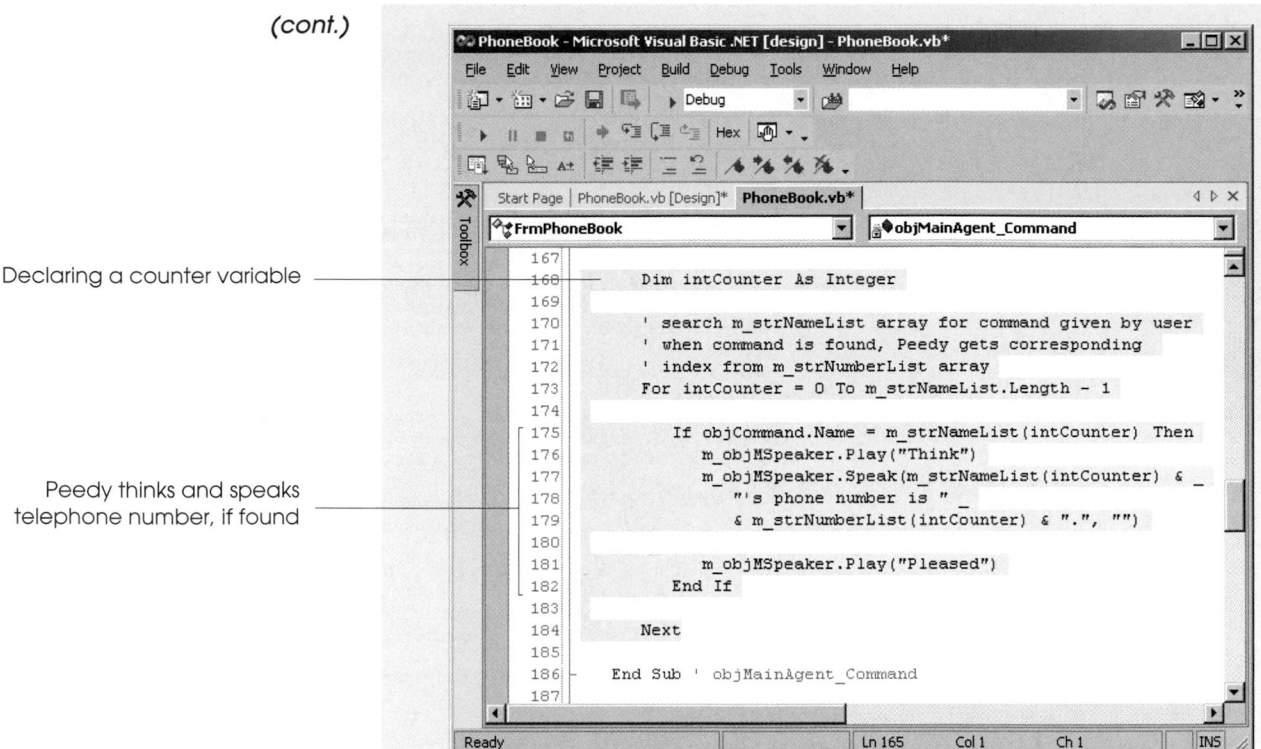

```
167
168         Dim intCounter As Integer
169
170         ' search m_strNameList array for command given by user
171         ' when command is found, Peedy gets corresponding
172         ' index from m_strNumberList array
173         For intCounter = 0 To m_strNameList.Length - 1
174
175             If objCommand.Name = m_strNameList(intCounter) Then
176                 m_objMSpeaker.Play("Think")
177                 m_objMSpeaker.Speak(m_strNameList(intCounter) & _
178                     "'s phone number is " _
179                     & m_strNumberList(intCounter) & ".", "")
180
181                 m_objMSpeaker.Play("Pleased")
182             End If
183
184         Next
185
186     End Sub ' objMainAgent_Command
187
```

Figure 27.28   Finding the spoken or selected name.

3. ***Creating the cboName_SelectedIndexChanged event handler.*** You must
   now write code to display a phone number if the user chooses a name from
   the cboName ComboBox. Double click the cboName ComboBox in the Windows Form Designer to generate the cboName_SelectedIndexChanged
   event handler, and enter code view. Insert lines 193–210 from Fig. 27.29
   into the event handler. Add the comments on lines 188 and 212 to the
   beginning and end of your event handler, respectively.

   This ComboBox allows users who are unable to access the voice-recogni-
   tion engines to use the application. Much as in the Command event handler,
   lines 197–210 search the array for a String that matches the selected item
   in the ComboBox. If a match is found, then Peedy's Think animation plays
   (Fig. 27.7), and the phone number is provided. After Peedy states the number, his Pleased animation plays, indicating that he is content with his ability to provide the user with the correct phone number (Fig. 27.9).

   The cboName_SelectedIndexChanged method executes code similar to
   the objMainAgent_Command event handler. The only difference is that the
   Command method is invoked by verbal requests, whereas this method is
   invoked by selecting items in the cboName.

4. ***Resetting the application's controls when Peedy is hidden.*** You might have
   noticed that you can choose **Hide** from Peedy's context menu (when you
   right click Peedy). When the user hides the Peedy character, you should
   enable the **Call Peedy** Button to allow the user to make Peedy reappear.
   Also, to prevent the user from selecting a name from the ComboBox while
   Peedy is hidden, you should disable the ComboBox.

   When the user selects **Hide**, a **HideEvent** is raised. To generate the
   HideEvent event handler, select objMainAgent from the Class Name ComboBox and HideEvent from the Method Name ComboBox. Then, insert
   lines 219–220 from Fig. 27.30 into the event handler. These lines enable the
   Call Peedy Button and disable the ComboBox. Add the comments on lines
   214 and 221 to the beginning and end of your event handler, respectively.

(cont.)

Declaring a counter variable

Peedy thinks and speaks
telephone number, if found

Figure 27.29 Event handler `cboName_SelectedIndexChanged` defined.

Reset application controls

Figure 27.30 Microsoft Agent `HideEvent` event handler.

5. ***Saving the project***. Select **File > Save All** to save all the files in the solution.

Figure 27.31 contains the complete code listing for the **Phone Book** application. New programming concepts are highlighted in yellow.

```
1   Public Class FrmPhoneBook
2       Inherits System.Windows.Forms.Form
3
4       Private m_objMSpeaker As AgentObjects.IAgentCtlCharacter
5
6       ' fill array with people's names
7       Private m_strNameList As String() = New String() _
8           {"John", "Jennifer", "Howard"}
9
10      ' fill array with people's phone numbers
11      Private m_strNumberList As String() = New String() _
12          {"(555) 555-9876", "(555) 555-1234", "(555) 555-4567"}
13
14      ' called when Form is loaded
15      Private Sub FrmPhoneBook_Load(ByVal sender As _
16          System.Object, ByVal e As System.EventArgs) _
17          Handles MyBase.Load
18
19          ' fill ComboBox with names from objNamelist array
20          Dim intCounter As Integer
21
22          For intCounter = 0 To m_strNameList.Length - 1
23              cboName.Items.Add(m_strNameList(intCounter))
24          Next
25
26          ' load Peedy character into agent object
27          objMainAgent.Characters.Load("Peedy", _
28              "Peedy.acs")
29
30          m_objMSpeaker = objMainAgent.Characters("Peedy")
31
32          ' add names from m_strNameList as enabled commands
33          For intCounter = 0 To m_strNameList.Length - 1
34              m_objMSpeaker.Commands.Add( _
35                  m_strNameList(intCounter), _
36                  m_strNameList(intCounter), _
37                  m_strNameList(intCounter), True, True)
38          Next
39
40      End Sub ' FrmPhoneBook_Load
41
42      ' called when Call Peedy button is clicked
43      Private Sub btnCall_Click(ByVal sender As System.Object, _
44          ByVal e As System.EventArgs) Handles btnCall.Click
45
46          m_objMSpeaker.Show(0) ' show Peedy on the screen
47
48          ' move Peedy to a specified location
49          m_objMSpeaker.MoveTo(Convert.ToInt16 _
50              (Cursor.Position.X - 100), _
51              Convert.ToInt16(Cursor.Position.Y + 130))
52
53          m_objMSpeaker.Play("Wave") ' command Peedy to wave
54
```

Labels:
- Variable to hold Microsoft Agent character → line 4
- Loading Peedy → line 27
- Assigning the Peedy character → line 30
- Adding commands → lines 34–37
- Showing Peedy → line 46
- Moving Peedy → lines 49–51

Figure 27.31   Phone Book application code. (Part 1 of 3.)

```
55          ' tell Peedy what to say
56          m_objMSpeaker.Speak("Hello, I'm Peedy. Please say or select " _
57             & "the name of the person whose phone number you " _
58             & "would like to find.", "")
59
60          m_objMSpeaker.Speak("If you wish to say the name, press " _
61             & "the Scroll Lock key then speak the name.", "")
62
63          m_objMSpeaker.Play("RestPose") ' tell Peedy to rest
64
65          cboName.Enabled = True ' enables ComboBox
66          btnCall.Enabled = False ' disable Button
67       End Sub ' btnCall_Click
68
69       ' called when user gives Peedy a command
70       Private Sub objMainAgent_Command(ByVal sender As System.Object, _
71          ByVal e As AxAgentObjects._AgentEvents_CommandEvent) _
72          Handles objMainAgent.Command
73
74          ' get UserInput object
75          Dim objCommand As AgentObjects.IAgentCtlUserInput = _
76             CType(e.userInput, AgentObjects.IAgentCtlUserInput)
77
78          Dim intCounter As Integer
79
80          ' search m_strNameList array for command given by user
81          ' when command is found, Peedy gets corresponding
82          ' index from m_strNumberList array
83          For intCounter = 0 To m_strNameList.Length - 1
84
85             If objCommand.Name = m_strNameList(intCounter) Then
86                m_objMSpeaker.Play("Think")
87                m_objMSpeaker.Speak(m_strNameList(intCounter) & _
88                   "'s phone number is " _
89                   & m_strNumberList(intCounter) & ".", "")
90
91                m_objMSpeaker.Play("Pleased")
92             End If
93
94          Next
95
96       End Sub ' objMainAgent_Command
97
98       ' called when selection is made in ComboBox
99       Private Sub cboName_SelectedIndexChanged(ByVal sender _
100         As System.Object, ByVal e As System.EventArgs) _
101         Handles cboName.SelectedIndexChanged
102
103         Dim intCounter As Integer
104
105         ' search m_strNameList array for selected
106         ' ComboBox item and speak phone number
107         For intCounter = 0 To m_strNameList.Length - 1
108
109            If Convert.ToString(cboName.SelectedItem) = _
110               m_strNameList(intCounter) Then
111
112               m_objMSpeaker.Play("Think")
```

Annotations:
- Peedy waves and speaks instructions → (lines 55–63)
- Command event handler → (lines 70–72)

Figure 27.31   **Phone Book** application code. (Part 2 of 3.)

```
113              m_objMSpeaker.Speak(m_strNameList(intCounter) & _
114                 "'s phone number is " _
115                 & m_strNumberList(intCounter) & ".", "")
116
117              m_objMSpeaker.Play("Pleased")
118           End If
119
120        Next
121
122     End Sub ' cboName_SelectedIndexChanged
123
124     ' called when user hides Peedy
125     Private Sub objMainAgent_HideEvent(ByVal sender As Object, _
126        ByVal e As AxAgentObjects._AgentEvents_HideEvent) _
127        Handles objMainAgent.HideEvent
128
129        btnCall.Enabled = True  ' enable Button
130        cboName.Enabled = False ' disable ComboBox
131     End Sub ' objMainAgent_HideEvent
132
133  End Class ' FrmPhoneBook
```

HideEvent event handler — (braces point to lines 125–127)

Figure 27.31   Phone Book application code. (Part 3 of 3.)

SELF-REVIEW

1. When Peedy is hidden, you can show him by _____.
   a) using method Show
   b) selecting **Show** from Peedy's tray icon context menu
   c) double clicking Peedy's tray icon   d) All of the above.

2. Method _____ used to relocate the Microsoft Agent character on the screen.
   a) Move   b) Relocate
   c) MoveTo   d) Place

Answers: 1) d. 2) c.

27.5 Wrap-Up

In this tutorial, you were introduced to Microsoft Agent and learned how it can be used to enhance software applications. You learned what Microsoft Agent is used for and how to download all the necessary components. You then wrote code to use a Microsoft Agent character, Peedy the Parrot.

Using Peedy, you created an application that interacts with the user by listening to the user's commands and by answering using speech. You used the Show and MoveTo methods to show Peedy and move him on the screen. You also used Peedy's Speak method to speak instructions and phone numbers to the user. You then learned how to control Peedy's gestures, such as Wave and Think, not only to entertain the user but also to signal visually what the application is doing.

Tutorials 28–31 present you with a Web-based bookstore application case study. You will learn how to build an application that can be accessed by using a Web browser. You will be introduced to the concept of a multi-tier application and you will take your first steps toward building a three-tier application, which you will complete in the subsequent tutorials.

SKILLS SUMMARY   **Displaying The Microsoft Agent to Users**

■ Load the desired Microsoft Agent, using the Characters.Load method.

■ Call the Microsoft Agent object's Show method.

Allowing Verbal Communication With The Agent

- Add voice-enabled commands, using the Microsoft Agent's `Commands.Add` method.
- Define the `Commands` event handler.

Causing The Agent to Speak

- Call the Microsoft Agent's `Speak` method.
- Specify the `String` that Microsoft Agent should speak.

Causing Agent to Perform Actions

- Call the Microsoft Agent character's `Play` method.
- Specify the animation that Microsoft Agent should display.

KEY TERMS

Add method of the Commands property—Method that adds a command to a Microsoft Agent character.

Command event—Event raised when a user speaks a command to a Microsoft Agent character or selects a command from a character's context menu.

Commands property—Property that sets which commands the Microsoft Agent character can understand as input from the user.

Convert.ToInt16 method—Method used to convert data to type `Short`.

CType function—Function that converts the type of its first argument to the type specified by the second argument.

Cursor.Position property—Property containing the x- and y-coordinates of the mouse cursor on the screen (in pixels).

HideEvent event—Event raised when a Microsoft Agent character is hidden.

IAgentCtlCharacter object—Object used to reference a Microsoft Agent character.

IAgentCtlUserInput object—Object used to store the user input retrieved from a Microsoft Agent character.

Microsoft Agent—A technology used to add interactive animated characters to Windows applications and Web pages.

MoveTo method—Method used to relocate the Microsoft Agent character on the screen.

multimedia—The use of various media, such as sound, video and animation, to create content in an application.

Play method—Method used to play a Microsoft Agent character animation.

Short data type—Data type that holds small `Integers`.

Show method—Method used to display a Microsoft Agent character on the screen.

Speak method—Method used to have the Microsoft Agent character speak text to the user.

speech-recognition engine—Application that translates vocal sound input from a microphone into a language that the computer understands.

speech synthesis—The process by which a computer converts text to spoken words.

text-to-speech engine—Application that translates typed words into spoken sound that users hear through headphones or speakers connected to a computer.

GUI DESIGN GUIDELINES

Microsoft Agent Control

- The Microsoft Agent character should be located near the application `Form` when the character is displayed on the screen.
- Use Microsoft Agent character gestures to indicate actions the user should take, or a response to an action the user has already taken.

CONTROLS, EVENTS, PROPERTIES & METHODS

Convert The `Convert` class converts the value of a data type to another data type.
- *Methods*
  ToChar—This method converts a value into a character (of data type `Char`).

ToDecimal—This method converts the value from another data type to type Decimal.

ToInt16—This method converts the value from another data type to type Short.

IAgentCtlCharacter   This class is used to represent the Agent character that is used in the application.

- *Property*

  Commands—This property contains the commands the character will recognize.

- *Methods*

  Show—This method displays the character on the screen.

  MoveTo—This method moves the character to a specified location on the screen.

  Play—This method plays character animations.

  Speak—This method specifies the text to be spoken by the character.

  Commands.Add—Method Add of the Commands property adds a new command to the command list for the Agent object.

IAgentCtlUserInput   This class is used to retrieve commands from users.

- *Property*

  Name—This method retrieves the name of the command given by the user.

Microsoft Agent Control   ⬚ Control   This control is used to create and manipulate the multimedia features of a Microsoft Agent character.

- *In action*

- *Events*

  Command—This event is raised when a user gives the Microsoft Agent character a verbal command or selects an option from the character's context menu.

  HideEvent—This event is raised when a user hides the Microsoft Agent character.

- *Property*

  Location—This property specifies the location of the Microsoft Agent control on the Form.

- *Method*

  Characters.Load—This method loads a character into the Microsoft Agent control.

MULTIPLE-CHOICE QUESTIONS

27.1 The _____ method is used to specify what the Microsoft Agent will say.

   a) Speak   b) Say

   c) Command   d) Voice

27.2 The _____ method is used to activate a Microsoft Agent character's animation.

   a) Show   b) Play

   c) Speak   d) Appear

27.3 Method MoveTo takes two arguments. What do these arguments represent?

   a) The direction in which the Agent should move (left, right, up, down).

   b) The name of the character and its position.

   c) The *x*-coordinate and *y*-coordinate of the location to which the Agent should move.

   d) The name of the character and the direction of movement.

27.4 Which method of IAgentCtlCharacter displays the Microsoft Agent character on the screen?

a) Play
b) Show
c) Speak
d) Appear

27.5 Use the _____ event handler to execute code when users click **Hide** the Agent character context menu.

a) Hide
b) HideEvent
c) Command
d) Disappear

27.6 The Add method of the Commands property _____.

a) adds a new command to the command list
b) joins two commands together
c) displays the Commands pop-up window
d) Both a and c

27.7 The _____ event handler controls what occurs when users speak to the Agent.

a) Command
b) ClickEvent
c) Click
d) SelectedIndexChanged

27.8 _____ specifies the *x*-coordinate of the mouse cursor on the screen.

a) Cursor.Location.X
b) Cursor.Position.X
c) Mouse.Location.X
d) Mouse.Position.X

27.9 Specifying _____ as a parameter to Peedy's Play method causes him to smile.

a) "Think"
b) "Smile"
c) "Pleased"
d) "Happy"

27.10 Specifying _____ as a parameter to Peedy's Play method causes him to rest.

a) "RestPose"
b) "Rest"
c) "Think"
d) "Pose"

EXERCISES

27.11 (*Appointment Book Application Using Microsoft Agent*) Write a program that allows users to add appointments to an appointment book that uses Microsoft Agent. When users speak a person's name, Merlin returns the time and date of the appointment that users have with that person. If users say "Today," Merlin returns a list of the users' appointments for the day.

a) *Copying the template application.* Copy the template application from C:\Examples\Tutorial27\Exercises\AppointmentBook to your work folder, and open the application.

b) *Downloading the Merlin Microsoft Agent.* Download the Merlin.acs character file from the Microsoft Web site.

c) *Adding the Agent Control to the Form.* Add the Microsoft Agent control to the Form.

d) *Creating module-level variables.* Create three module-level variables of type ArrayList to store the date, time and person with which the user has an appointment. Create a module-level variable of type AgentObjects.IAgentCtlCharacter (as you did in the **Phone Book** application).

e) *Defining the FrmAppointments_Load event handler.* Load Merlin's character file, display him on the screen and add the "Today" command to the command list.

f) *Defining the btnAdd_Click event handler.* Define this event handler so that the information provided by the user is added to its corresponding ArrayList. The **Appointment With:** TextBox input should be added to the ArrayList containing the names of people with whom the user has an appointment. The input for the appointment date and time should also be added to their respective ArrayLists. Display an error message if the user leaves the **Appointment With:** or the **Appointment Time:** TextBox empty.

g) *Adding voice-enabled commands.* Within the btnAdd_Click event handler, add a voice-enabled command that allows a user to speak the name of the person with whom the user has an appointment to the command list. This allows a user to check for whether there is an appointment with someone by speaking the person's name. The command should also appear in the Commands context menu.

h) *Defining the Agent's Command event handler.* As you did in the **Phone Book** application, define what occurs when a user speaks or selects a command. If the user specifies the Today command, Merlin should tell the user the names of all the people with whom the user has an appointment today. If the user specifies a specific name, Merlin should state the time and date at which the user has an appointment with this person. If the user did not schedule any appointments, then Merlin should inform the user that no appointments were scheduled.

Figure 27.32   **Appointment Book** GUI. (© 1996–1998 Microsoft Corporation. All rights reserved.)

27.12 (*Craps Game Application Using Microsoft Agent*) Modify the **Craps Game** application from Tutorial 16 to include a Microsoft Agent character.

a) *Copying the template application.* Copy the template application from C:\Examples\Tutorial27\Exercises\CrapsGameEnhancement to your work folder, and open the application.

b) *Downloading the Genie Microsoft Agent.* Download the Genie.acs character file from the Microsoft Web site.

c) *Adding the Agent control to the Form.* Add the Microsoft Agent control to the Form.

d) *Creating a module-level variable.* Create a module-level variable of type AgentObjects.IAgentCtlCharacter (as you did in the **Phone Book** application).

e) *Defining the FrmCrapsGame_Load event handler.* Load Genie's character file, and display him on the screen.

f) *Modifying the btnPlay_Click event handler.* Add code to the btnPlay_Click event handler to control the Agent. When the user wins the game, Genie should play his Pleased animation and congratulate the user. If the user loses, Genie should play his Confused animation and say that the user lost. If the user neither wins nor loses, Genie should tell the user to roll again. Make sure to reset him to his RestPose after he plays any animation.

g) *Defining the btnRoll_Click event handler.* Add code to the btnRoll_Click event handler to control the Agent. If users "make their point," Genie should play his Pleased animation and state that the user won. If the user rolls a 7, Genie should play his Confused animation and say that the user lost. Otherwise, Genie should tell the user to roll again.

h) *Defining the btnInstructions_Click event handler.* Define event handler btnInstructions_Click to make Genie introduce himself to the user. Genie should then explain the rules to the game of craps.

Figure 27.33   Modified **Craps Game** GUI. (© 1996–1998 Microsoft Corporation. All rights reserved.)

27.13 (*Security Panel Application Using Microsoft Agent*) Modify the **Security Panel** application from Tutorial 12 to include Microsoft Agent.

a) *Copying the template application.* Copy the template application from C:\Examples\Tutorial27\Exercises\SecurityPanelEnhancement to your work folder, and open the application.

b) *Downloading the Robby Microsoft Agent.* Download the Robby.acs character file from the Microsoft Web site.

c) *Adding the Agent control to the Form.* Add the Microsoft Agent control to the Form.

d) *Creating a module-level variable.* Create a module-level variable of type AgentObjects.IAgentCtlCharacter (as you did in the **Phone Book** application).

e) *Defining the FrmSecurityPanel_Load event handler.* Load Robby's character file, and display him on the screen. Command Robby to tell users to input their access codes.

f) *Modifying the btnEnter_Click event handler.* Add code to the btnEnter_Click event handler to use the Microsoft Agent. If the user enters a valid access code, Robby should welcome the user and state the type of employee that the access code represents. If the access code is invalid, then Robby should state that an invalid code was provided and that access is denied.

Figure 27.34   Robby from modified **Security Panel** application. (© 1996–1998 Microsoft Corporation. All rights reserved.)

What does this code do? ▶　**27.14** After the user clicks the **Call** Button, what does the following event handler do?

```
1   Private Sub btnCall_Click(ByVal sender As System.Object, _
2       ByVal e As System.EventArgs) Handles btnCall.Click
3
4       objMainAgent.Characters.Load("Genie", "Genie.acs")
5
6       objMSpeaker = objMainAgent.Characters("Genie")
7
8       objMSpeaker.Show(0)
9
10      objMSpeaker.Speak("Hello, I'm Genie the special agent!")
11
12  End Sub
```

What's wrong with this code? ▶　**27.15** Find the error(s) in the following code. The event handler should have an agent object appear and say, "Hello, my name is Merlin." This should happen when the user clicks the **Call** Button.

```
1   Private Sub btnCall_Click(ByVal sender As System.Object, _
2       ByVal e As System.EventArgs) Handles btnCall.Click
3
4       objMainAgent.Characters.Load("Merlin", "Merlin.acs")
5
6       objMSpeaker = objMainAgent.Characters("Merlin")
7
8       Dim intNumber As Integer = 10
9
10      objMSpeaker.Show(intNumber)
11
12      objMSpeaker.Play("Hello, my name is Merlin")
13
14  End Sub
```

Programming Challenge ▶　**27.16** (*Car Payment Application Using Microsoft Agent*) Enhance the **Car Payment Calculator** application from Tutorial 9 to use the Microsoft Agent, Robby. When the application is executed, Robby should appear on the screen and wave to users. He should then explain the purpose of the application. After the user enters information into each field of the **Car Payment Calculator** and clicks the **Calculate** Button, Robby should speak the calculated payment amounts and the period (number of months) over which they were calculated. The C:\Examples\Tutorial27\Exercises\CarPaymentCalculatorEnhancement folder contains the template application for this exercise. Copy it to your work folder and open the application to begin the exercise.

28

Objectives

In this tutorial, you will learn to:
- Use Internet Information Services to serve Web content to Web browser clients.
- Request documents from a Web server.
- Execute an ASP .NET Web application.

Outline

28.1 Multi-Tier Architecture
28.2 Web Servers
28.3 Internet Information Services (IIS)
28.4 Test-Driving the **Bookstore** Application
28.5 Wrap-Up

Bookstore Application: Web Applications

Introducing Internet Information Services

In previous tutorials, you used Visual Basic .NET to develop Windows applications. These applications contained a GUI with which the user interacted. You can also use Visual Studio .NET to create **Web applications**. These applications, also known as Web-based applications, use Visual Basic .NET in combination with Microsoft's **ASP .NET technology** to create Web content (data that can be viewed in a Web browser such as Internet Explorer). This Web content includes HTML (HyperText Markup Language) documents and images.

In this tutorial, you will learn important Web-development concepts in the context of the **Bookstore** application. This application consists of two Web pages. The first page displays a list of books. After selecting a book, the user clicks a Button, which directs the browser to a second Web page. Information about the selected book is then retrieved from a database and displayed for the user. The second Web page also contains a Button that, when clicked, directs the Web browser back to the first Web page, allowing the user to select a different book. Before you create this application, you will be introduced to fundamental Web development concepts that are required to understand the **Bookstore** application. You will then test-drive the **Bookstore** application. In Tutorials 28–31, you will analyze the pseudocode and ACE table and develop the **Bookstore** application.

28.1 Multi-Tier Architecture

Web applications are **multi-tier applications**, sometimes referred to as *n*-tier **applications**. Multi-tier applications divide functionality into separate **tiers** (that is, logical groupings of functionality). The separate tiers of an application can be located on the same computer or on separate computers distributed across any computer network, including the Internet. Figure 28.1 illustrates the basic structure of a multi-tier application.

The **information tier** (also called the **data tier** or the **bottom tier**) maintains data for the application. The information tier for the **Bookstore** application is represented by a database that contains product information, such as book titles, author names, publication dates and edition numbers. The database also contains ISBN numbers, book descriptions and prices.

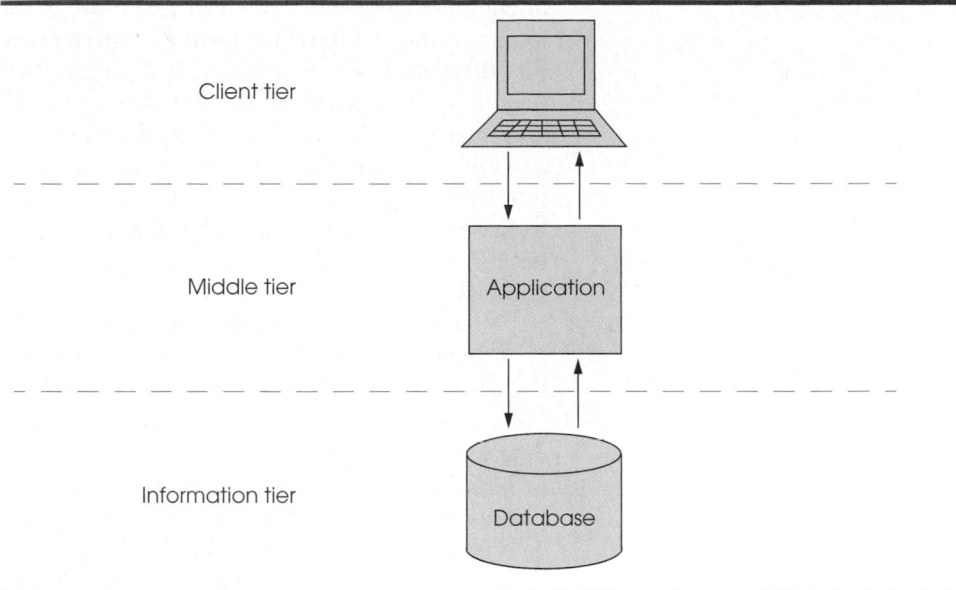

Figure 28.1   Three-tier application model.

The **middle tier** controls interactions between application clients (such as Web browsers) and application data in the information tier. In the **Bookstore** application, the middle-tier code determines which book was selected and which book's information is retrieved from the database. The middle-tier code also determines how the selected book's data will be displayed. The middle tier processes client requests (for example, a request to view a book's information) from the top tier, which we define shortly, and retrieves data from the database (author names, prices, descriptions, etc.) in the information tier. The middle tier then processes data and presents the content to the client. In other words, the middle tier represents the functionality of the Web application.

The **client tier**, or **top tier**, is the application's user interface, which is typically a Web browser. In the **Bookstore** application, the client tier is represented by the pages displayed in the Web browser. The user interacts directly with this application through the client tier (browser) by entering text, selecting from a list, clicking But-tons, etc. The browser reports the user's actions to the middle tier which processes the information. The middle tier can also make requests to and retrieve data from the information tier. The client then displays to the user the data retrieved by the middle tier from the information tier.

SELF-REVIEW

1. A database is located in the _____ tier.
   a) top   b) middle
   c) bottom   d) client

2. The role of the middle tier is to _____.
   a) display the application's user interface   b) provide a database for the application
   c) control the interaction between the client and information tiers
   d) control the interaction between the client and the user interface

Answers: 1) c. 2) c.

28.2 Web Servers

A **Web server** is specialized software that responds to client (Web browser) requests by providing requested resources (such as HTML documents). To request documents from Web servers, users must know the locations at which those documents reside. A **URL** (**Uniform Resource Locator**) can be thought of as an address that directs a browser to a resource on the Web. A URL contains a computer name (called a **host name**) or an IP address (we will discuss IP addresses shortly) that identifies the computer on which the Web server resides.

Once the **Bookstore** application is properly set up, users can run the application by typing its URL into a Web browser. This action is translated into a request to the Web server where the **Bookstore** application resides. The Web server sends back Web content created by the **Bookstore** application. This content is displayed in the Web browser for the user.

When you access the **Bookstore** application, you provide a URL in a browser in order to locate the Web pages of the application. In this tutorial, you will use `localhost` in the URL, which is a special host name that identifies the local computer. You also can use your machine's name. [*Note*: Your computer's name can be determined by right clicking **My Computer** and selecting **Properties** from the context menu to display the **System Properties** dialog. If your operating system is Windows 2000, click the **Network Identification** tab. The **Full computer name:** field in the **System Properties** window displays the computer's name. If your operating system is Windows XP, select the **Computer Name** tab. The **Full computer name:** field in the **Computer Name** tab displays the computer name.]

A **host** is a computer that stores and maintains resources, such as Web pages, databases, multimedia files, etc. In the case of the **Bookstore** application, the host is your computer. A **domain** represents a group of **hosts** on the Internet; it combines with a host name (for example, www for World Wide Web) and a **top-level domain** (**TLD**) to form a **fully qualified domain name** (**FQDN**), which provides a user-friendly way to identify a site on the Internet. In a fully qualified domain name, the TLD often describes the type of organization that owns the domain. For example, the com TLD usually refers to a commercial business, the org TLD usually refers to a nonprofit organization and edu usually refers to an educational institution. In addition, each country has its own TLD, such as cn for China, et for Ethiopia, om for Oman and us for the United States.

Each fully qualified domain name corresponds to a numeric address called an **IP** (**Internet Protocol**) **address**, which is much like the street address of a house. Just as people use street addresses to locate houses or businesses in a city, computers use IP addresses to locate other computers on the Internet. A **domain name system** (**DNS**) **server** is a computer that maintains a database of host names and their corresponding IP addresses. The process of translating fully qualified domain names to IP addresses is called a **DNS lookup**. For example, to access the Deitel Web site, type the fully qualified domain name www.deitel.com into a Web browser. The DNS lookup translates www.deitel.com into the IP address of the Deitel Web server (that is, 63.110.43.82). The IP address of `localhost` is always 127.0.0.1.

SELF-REVIEW
1. A _____ is a computer that stores and maintains resources.
   a) host   b) IP address
   c) domain name   d) domain name system

2. A DNS lookup is a _____.
   a) translation of an IP address to a domain name
   b) translation of a fully qualified domain name to an IP address
   c) translation of a fully qualified domain name to a host name
   d) search for a domain name

Answers: 1) a. 2) b.

28.3 Internet Information Services (IIS)

Microsoft **Internet Information Services** (**IIS**) is the Web server you will use to respond to client requests. IIS must be installed on your machine before you can create Web applications using Visual Studio .NET. To determine if IIS is installed you should read Appendix G. [*Note*: If you encounter problems setting up IIS, please visit www.deitel.com/books/vbnetSIMPLY1. This site contains frequently asked questions (FAQs) from our readers and an errata list. If you cannot find the solution to your problem there, please email us at deitel@deitel.com and we will respond promptly.]

Before you can test-drive the completed application you must specify initial settings for the **Bookstore** application.

Specifying Initial Settings for the Bookstore Application

1. *Copying the Bookstore application files to IIS's root directory.* Copy the C:\Examples\Tutorial28\CompletedApplication\Bookstore folder to IIS's root directory. This directory is usually C:\Inetpub\wwwroot (Fig. 28.2). [*Note*: The folder names and file names in the wwwroot folder may be different on your computer.]

IIS's root directory

Place this folder in the wwwroot directory

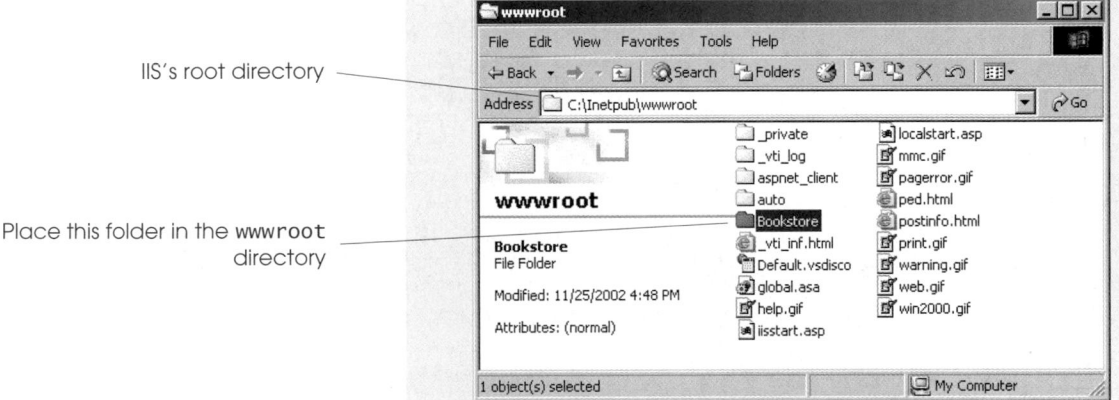

Figure 28.2 Bookstore folder in IIS's root directory.

2. *Opening IIS.* If your operating system is Windows 2000, begin by going to the Windows **Start** menu and selecting **Settings > Control Panel** to display the **Control Panel** dialog. Double click the **Administrative Tools** icon, then double click the **Internet Services Manager** icon to display the **Internet Information Services** dialog (Fig. 28.3). If your operating system is Windows XP, go to the Windows **Start** menu and select **Control Panel**. Click the **Switch to Classic View** link in the upper-left portion of the **Control Panel** dialog to display its contents. Double click the **Administrative Tools** icon, then double click the **Internet Information Services** icon to display the **Internet Information Services** dialog.

Toolbar

Click to expand

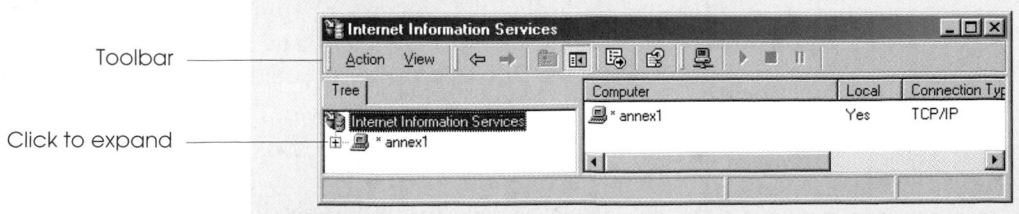

Figure 28.3 Internet Information Services dialog.

(cont.)

3. ***Viewing the Default Web Site.*** Beneath the name **Internet Information Services** (on the **Tree** tab in Windows 2000) is the name of your computer (on which IIS has been installed). Our computer's name is **annex1**. Your computer's name will be different. Expand this node by clicking the plus box. The default sites (Windows 2000 only) set up by IIS should be displayed (Fig. 28.4). The default sites that display in the left pane may differ on your screen. In Windows XP, a node named **Web Sites** appears (Fig. 28.5). Recall that the theme used for the appearance of windows and dialogs is set to **Windows Classic**. The appearance of your windows and dialogs may be different. Expand the **Web Sites** node to display the **Default Web Site** node.

In both Windows 2000 and Windows XP, you will be using only the **Default Web Site**. If no text appears next to **Default Web Site**, then this means that IIS is started and you can proceed to *Step 4*. However, if the text **(Stopped)** appears (Fig. 28.4) then you need to start IIS. To start IIS in either Windows 2000 or Windows XP, select the **Default Web Site** entry and click the Start Item **Button** in the toolbar. IIS will then start allowing IIS to respond to client requests. [*Note*: The contents of the right pane may be different on your system.]

Click Start Item **Button** to start IIS ⎯⎯⎯

Tree tab ⎯⎯⎯

Default Web site node; **(Stopped)** indicates that the IIS Web server is not running ⎯⎯⎯

Click to stop IIS

Right pane

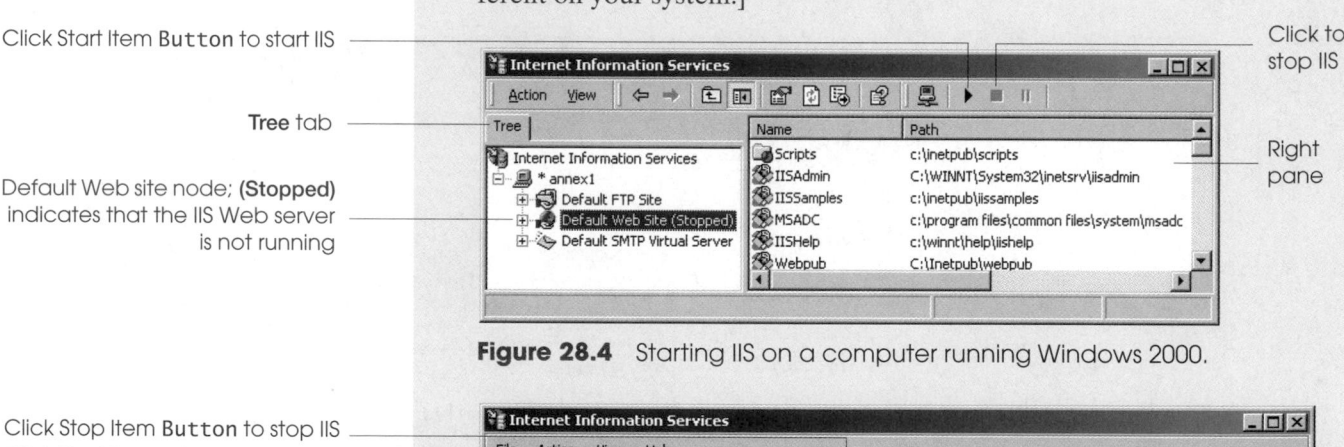

Figure 28.4 Starting IIS on a computer running Windows 2000.

Click Stop Item **Button** to stop IIS ⎯⎯⎯
Click Start Item **Button** to start IIS ⎯⎯⎯

Click to display **Default Web Site** in Windows XP ⎯⎯⎯

Figure 28.5 Location of **Default Web Site** on a Windows XP computer.

4. ***Opening the Bookstore Properties dialog.*** Click **Default Web Site**, in the left pane, to display the contents of your Web site in the right pane. Right click **Bookstore** in the right pane, and select **Properties** (Fig. 28.6). This option opens the **Bookstore Properties** dialog (Fig. 28.7).

5. ***Setting IIS to recognize the Bookstore application.*** To successfully run the application, IIS must recognize the **Bookstore** as a Web application. In the **Directory** tab, click the **Create Button** (Fig. 28.7). The dialog should now look like Fig. 28.8. Click the **OK Button**. This folder is now recognized by IIS as a Web application with the name **Bookstore**. Close the **Internet Information Services** dialog.

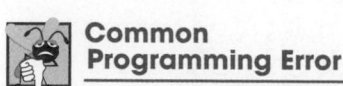

Common Programming Error

Failure to configure IIS to recognize a directory as an application results in an error that prevents the Web application's start page from loading in a Web browser.

(cont.)

Click **Default Web Site** to display the Web site's contents in the right pane

Right click this folder

Contents of **Default Web Site**

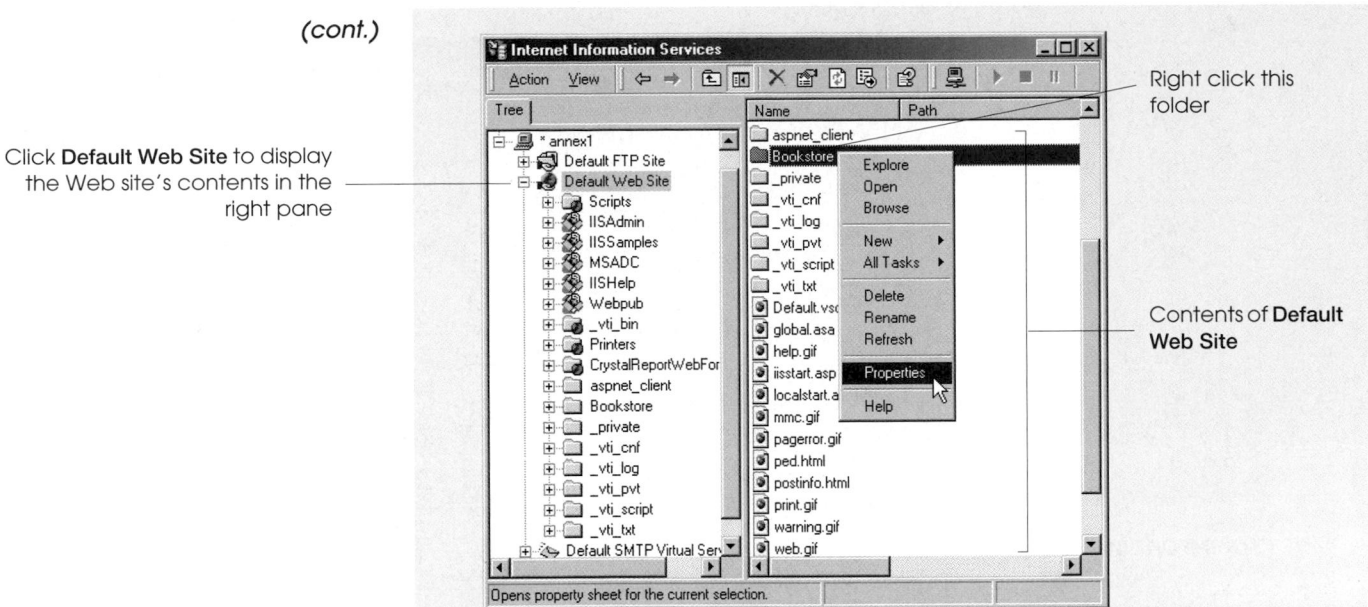

Figure 28.6   `Bookstore` folder in the **Internet Information Services** dialog.

Directory tab

Click to create application

Figure 28.7   **Properties** of the `Bookstore` folder.

6. ***Adding the Databases folder to the wwwroot folder.*** Open a Windows Explorer window, and navigate to the wwwroot folder. Copy the C:\Examples\Tutorial28\Databases folder to the wwwroot folder. This folder contains the database that will be used for the application. This database contains information about various books.

7. ***Changing the settings of the Databases folder.*** Your application will need to open and retrieve information from the database stored in the Databases folder. You must change some settings of this folder. If your operating system is Windows 2000, complete all the instructions presented in *Step 8* and move on to the next section, *Test-Driving the **Bookstore** Application*. (The remaining steps in this box do not apply to Windows 2000.) If your operating system is Windows XP skip *Step 8* and complete the remaining steps (9–12) of this box.

(cont.)

Click the **OK** Button to save settings

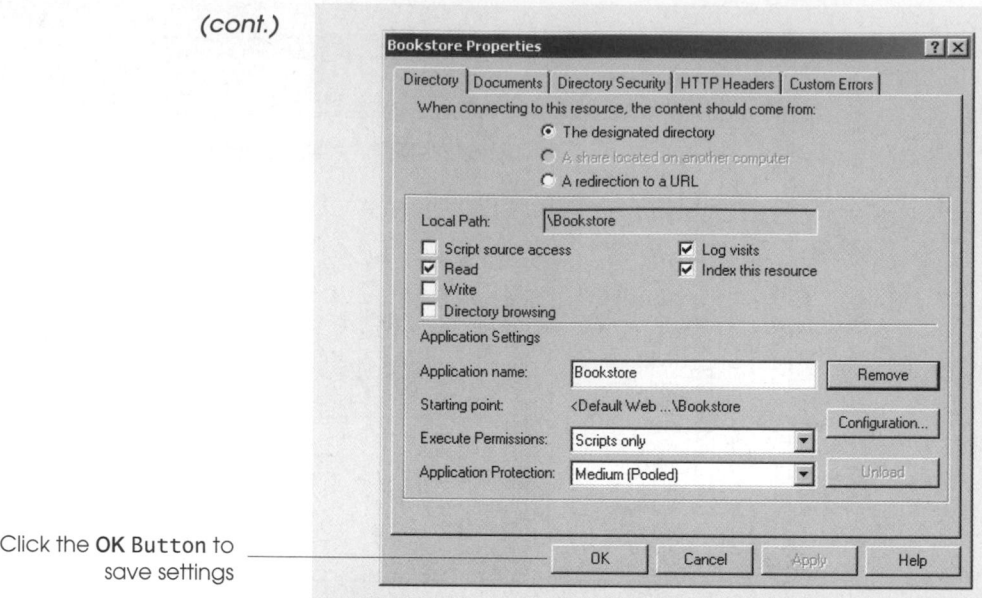

Figure 28.8 Bookstore Properties dialog after clicking **Create** in Fig. 28.7.

8. ***(Windows 2000 only) Changing the security settings of the Databases folder in the Windows Explorer.*** Right click the Databases folder that you placed in the wwwroot folder and select **Properties** (Fig. 28.9). This option opens the **Databases Properties** dialog (Fig. 28.10). You now need to change the security settings of this folder. Select the **Security** tab. Make sure that the **Allow inheritable permissions from parent to propagate to this object** CheckBox is checked. Now click the **Add...** Button (Fig. 28.11). [*Note*: The contents of the **Name** box of the **Security** tab may differ on your computer.]

Right click this folder

Select this item

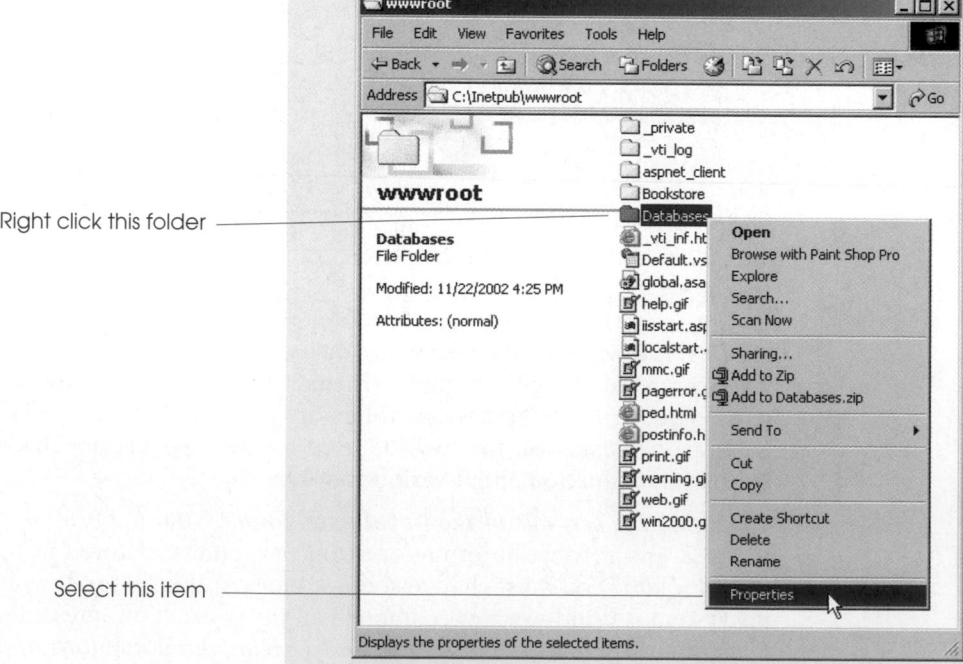

Figure 28.9 Selecting the **Properties** item.

(cont.)

Databases Properties dialog

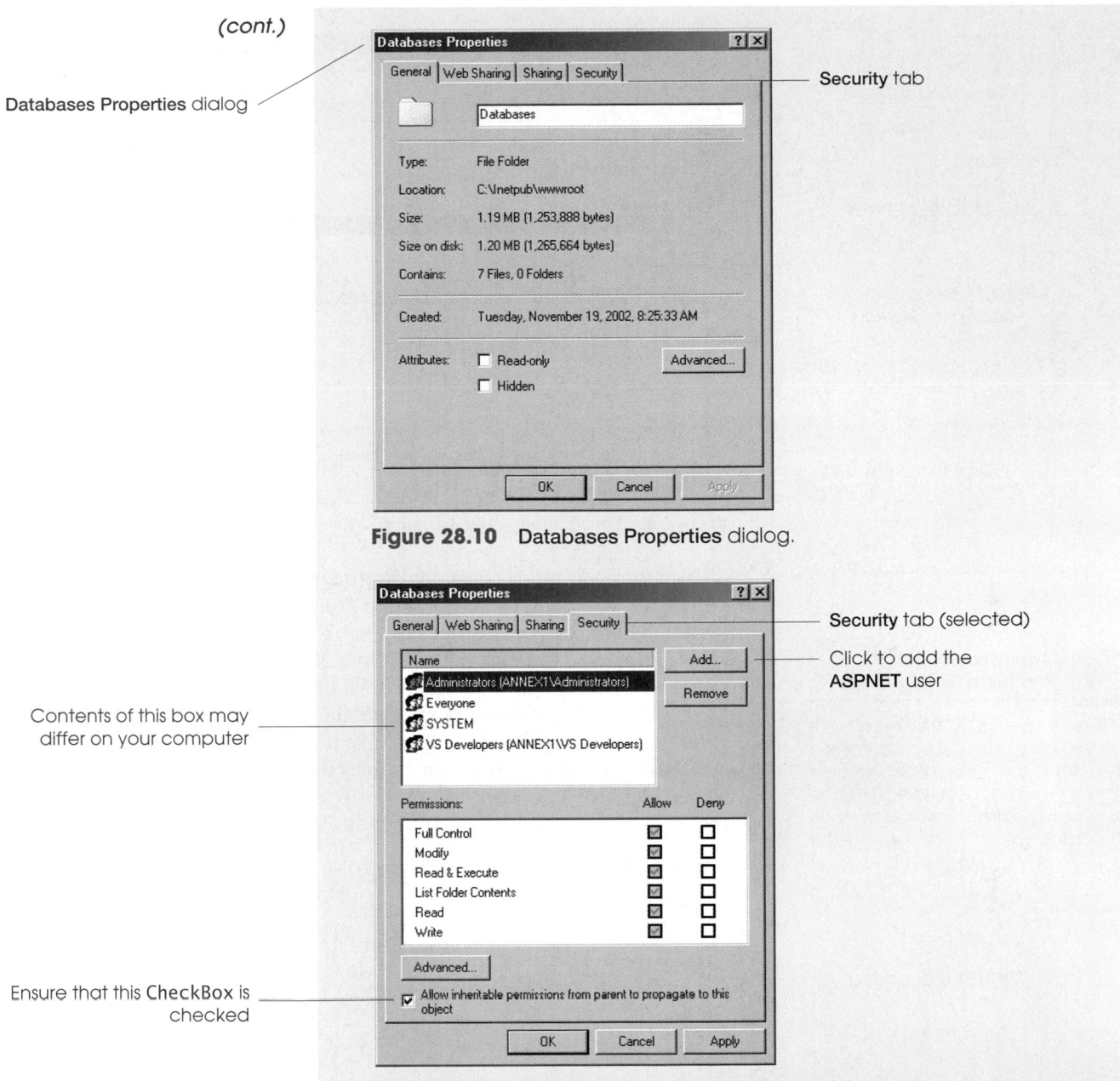

Figure 28.10 **Databases Properties** dialog.

Contents of this box may differ on your computer

Ensure that this **CheckBox** is checked

Figure 28.11 **Security** tab for the Databases folder.

A **Select Users or Groups** dialog (Fig. 28.12) appears, where you can specify the users or groups of users who can access the folder. Make sure that the **Look in:** drop-down list at the top of the dialog displays your computer name. If it does not, search for your computer name in the drop-down list and select it. Locate the **ASPNET** user in the **Name** box. Double click the **ASPNET** user so that it is added to the bottom half of the dialog. The **ASPNET** user represents a user that is configured to run ASP .NET Web applications with the minimum amount of access privileges. Click the **OK** Button.

(cont.)

Make sure your computer name displays here

Name box

Double click the **ASPNET** user

ASPNET user has been added for **ANNEX1**

Click to add user

Click this to select your computer name

Figure 28.12   Adding the **ASPNET** user.

You are then returned to the **Databases Properties** dialog (Fig. 28.13). Select the **ASPNET** user you added from the **Name** box, and check the **Write** CheckBox in the **Permissions:** box to give the **ASPNET** user permission to write to the Databases folder (Fig. 28.13). Any application that opens an Access database writes a **lock file** in the directory to indicate that the database is in use. Only one lock file can be written at a time. Therefore, only one application can modify the database at a time. Giving the **ASPNET** user write permission enables the ASP .NET application to write a lock file in this directory when the application opens the database. Click the **OK** Button to close the **Databases Properties** dialog.

Common Programming Error

Failure to give the **ASPNET** user write permission to the folder containing the database will cause an error when the application executes. The application will not be able to open the database.

ASPNET user added

Permissions: box

Check the **Write CheckBox** to allow **ASPNET** user to have write access

Figure 28.13   Giving the **ASPNET** user write permission.

(cont.)   9. ***(Windows XP Only) Displaying the Security tab of the Databases folder.***
In the wwwroot folder, select **Tools > Folder Options…** (Fig. 28.14) to open
the **Folder Options** dialog (Fig. 28.15). Select the **View** tab, and make sure
that the **Use simple file sharing (Recommended)** CheckBox at the bottom
of the **Advanced settings:** box is unchecked. You need to make sure this
box is unchecked to ensure that the **Security** tab will be displayed in the
Databases Properties dialog, which you access in the next step. If you
changed any of the settings, click **Apply**, then **OK** to save the changes.

Figure 28.14 Displaying the **Folder Options** dialog.

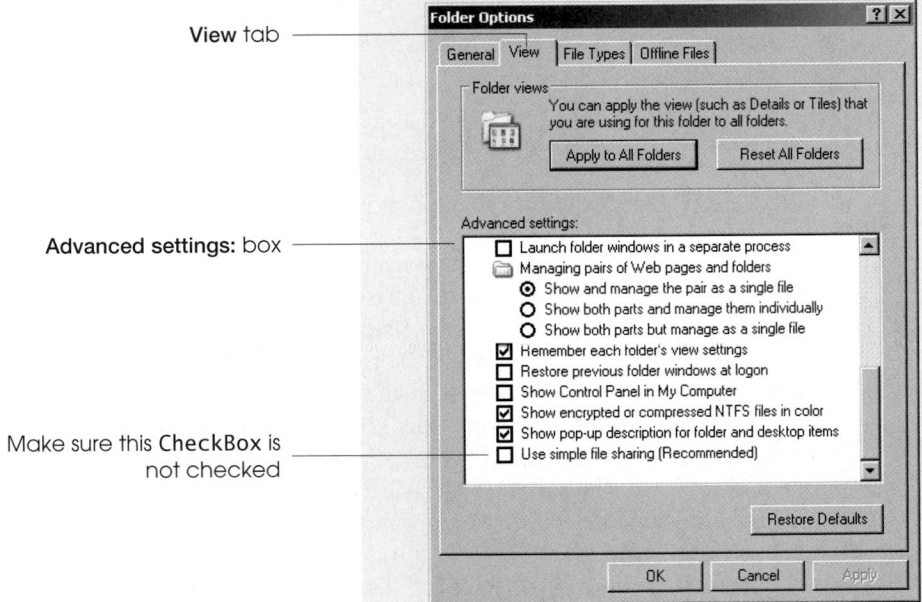

Figure 28.15 Verifying settings in the **Folder Options** dialog.

10. ***(Windows XP Only) Displaying the Databases Properties dialog.*** Right
click the Databases folder, and select **Properties**. The **Databases Properties** dialog appears. Click the **Security** tab; then click the **Advanced** Button
to display the **Advanced Security Settings for Databases** dialog. Make
sure that the **Inherit from parent the permission entries that apply to child
objects. Include these with entries explicitly defined here.** CheckBox contains a checkmark. Click the **OK** Button to return to the **Database Properties** dialog. Click the **Add…** Button to add a user to the folder (Fig. 28.16).
The **Select Users or Groups** dialog appears (Fig. 28.17).

(cont.)

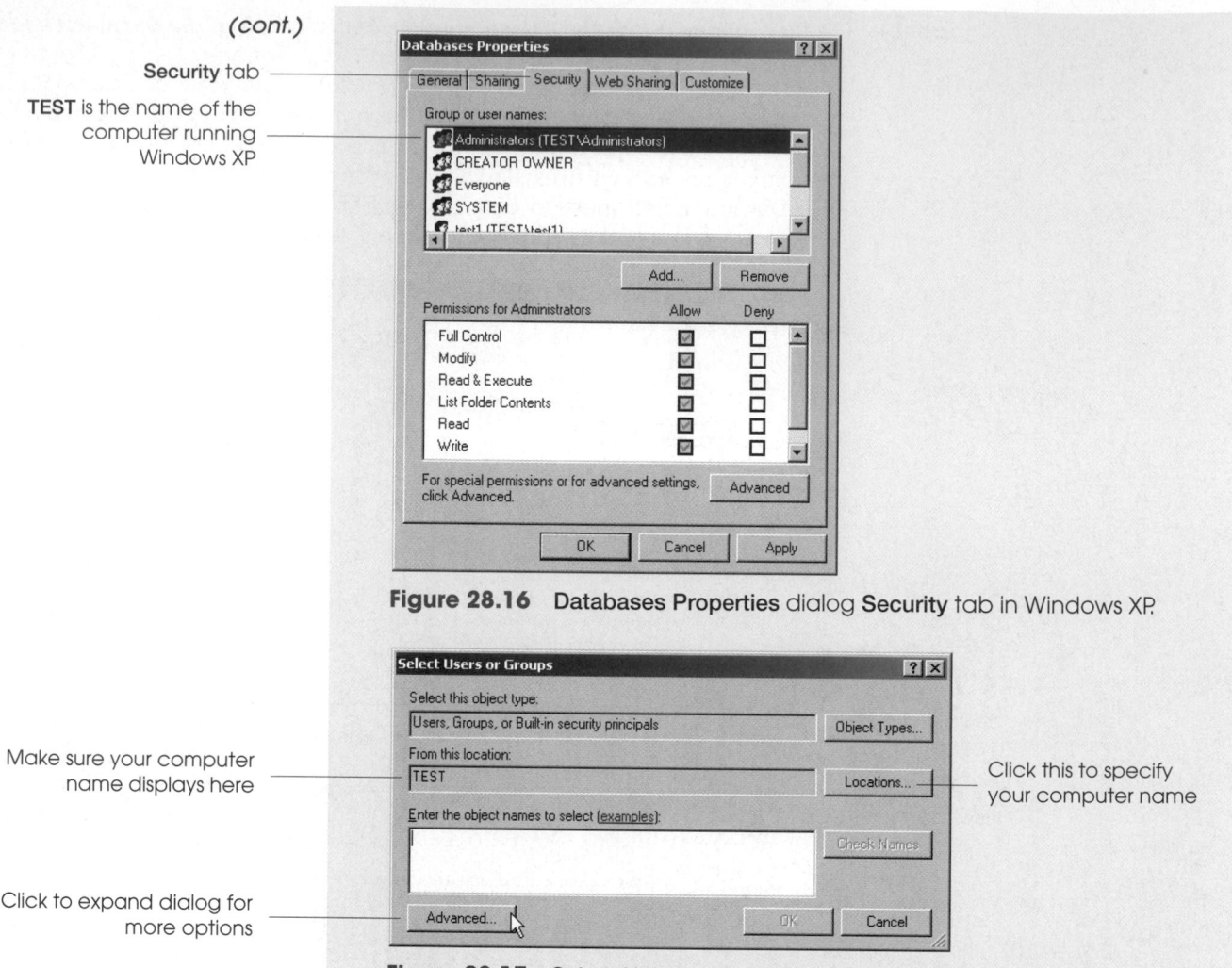

Security tab

TEST is the name of the computer running Windows XP

Figure 28.16 Databases Properties dialog Security tab in Windows XP.

Make sure your computer name displays here

Click this to specify your computer name

Click to expand dialog for more options

Figure 28.17 Select Users or Groups dialog in Windows XP.

11. *(Windows XP Only) Adding a new user to the Databases folder.* In the **Select Users or Groups** dialog, make sure that the **From this location:** field contains your computer name. If it does not, click the **Locations...** Button, select your computer name from the **Location:** box and click the **OK** Button to accept the changes. In the **Select Users or Groups** dialog, click the **Advanced...** Button. This dialog expands to provide more options (Fig. 28.18). Click the **Find Now** Button, select the **ASPNET** user name and click **OK** (Fig. 28.19). The **ASPNET** user represents a user that is configured to run ASP .NET Web applications with the minimum amount of access privileges. User **ASPNET** should now be displayed in the **Select Users or Groups** dialog (Fig. 28.20). Click **OK**.

12. *(Windows XP Only) Giving the ASPNET user write permissions.* The **ASPNET** user should appear in the **Security** tab of the **Databases Proper-ties** dialog. Select the **ASPNET** user and check the **Write** CheckBox to give the user write permission (Fig. 28.21). Any application that opens an Access database writes a **lock file** in the directory to indicate that the data-base is in use. Only one lock file can be written at a time. Therefore, only one application can modify the database at a time. Giving the **ASPNET** user write permission enables the ASP .NET application to write a lock file in this directory when the application opens the database. Click the **OK** Button to close the **Databases Properties** dialog.

(cont.)

Figure 28.18 Expanded **Select Users or Groups** dialog.

Figure 28.19 Adding the **ASPNET** user to the **Databases** folder.

(cont.)

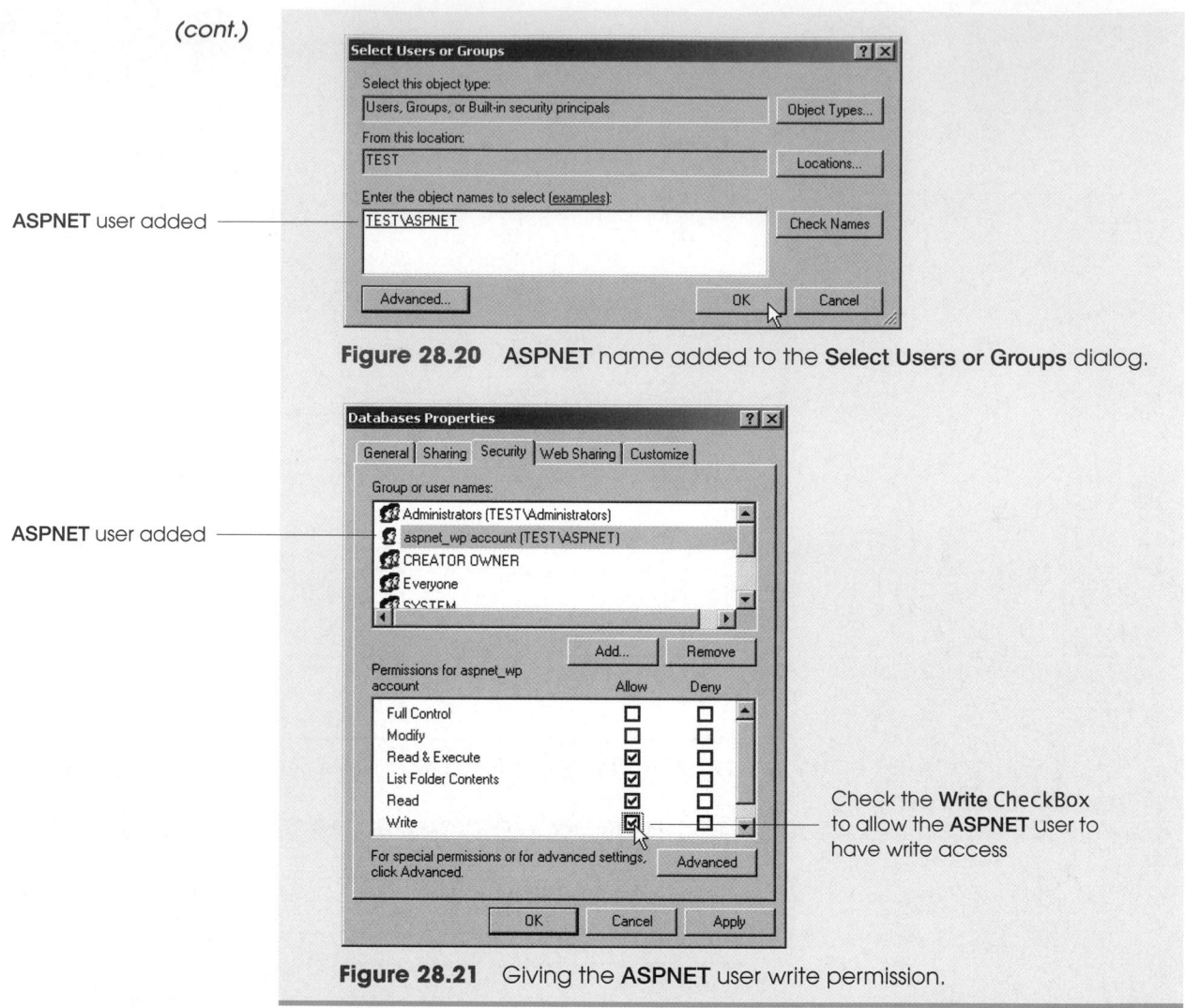

Figure 28.20   **ASPNET** name added to the **Select Users or Groups** dialog.

ASPNET user added

ASPNET user added

Check the **Write** CheckBox to allow the **ASPNET** user to have write access

Figure 28.21   Giving the **ASPNET** user write permission.

SELF-REVIEW

1. The _____ user represents a user that is configured to run ASP .NET Web applications with the minimum amount of access privileges.

   a) **TEST**   b) **WEB**
   c) **ASPNET**   d) **ASPX**

2. To start IIS in the **Internet Information Services** dialog, you must select _____ and click the Start Item Button.

   a) the Web application's folder   b) **Default Web Site**
   c) Both a and b.   d) None of the above.

Answers: 1) c. 2) b.

28.4 Test-Driving the Bookstore Application

In the next three tutorials, you will build an application that displays book information to users upon request. Your **Bookstore** application must meet the following requirements:

Application Requirements

A bookstore employee receives e-mails from customers asking for information pertaining to the books the store provides online. Responding to the numerous e-mails can be a tedious and time-consuming task. The employee has asked you to create a Web application that allows users to view information about various books online. This information includes the author, price, ISBN number, edition number, copyright date and a brief description of the book.

The **Bookstore** application you create uses ASP .NET and is designed to allow users to view various pieces of information about the books offered by the store. You begin by test-driving the completed application.

Test-Driving the Completed Web-Based Bookstore Application

1. *Opening the Bookstore project.* Open the C:\InetPub\wwwroot\Bookstore folder to locate the **Bookstore** application. Double click Bookstore.sln to open the solution in Visual Studio .NET.

2. *Setting the start page.* The start page is the first page that loads when the application is run. To specify the start page, right click the Books.aspx file in the **Solution Explorer**, and select **Set As Start Page** (Fig. 28.22). Files with the extension .aspx (usually referred to as **Web Forms**, **Web Form Pages** or **ASPX pages**) contain the Web page's GUI. The Web Form file represents the Web page that is sent to the client browser. [*Note*: From this point onward, we refer to Web Form files as ASPX pages.] A Web application can contain several ASPX pages. In this example, Books.aspx displays the available books to the user. The BookInformation.aspx page displays information about the book selected. You must set Books.aspx to appear first because you do not know in which book the user is interested until the user makes a selection from the Books.aspx page.

Right click the Books.aspx page

Select this option to set the start page

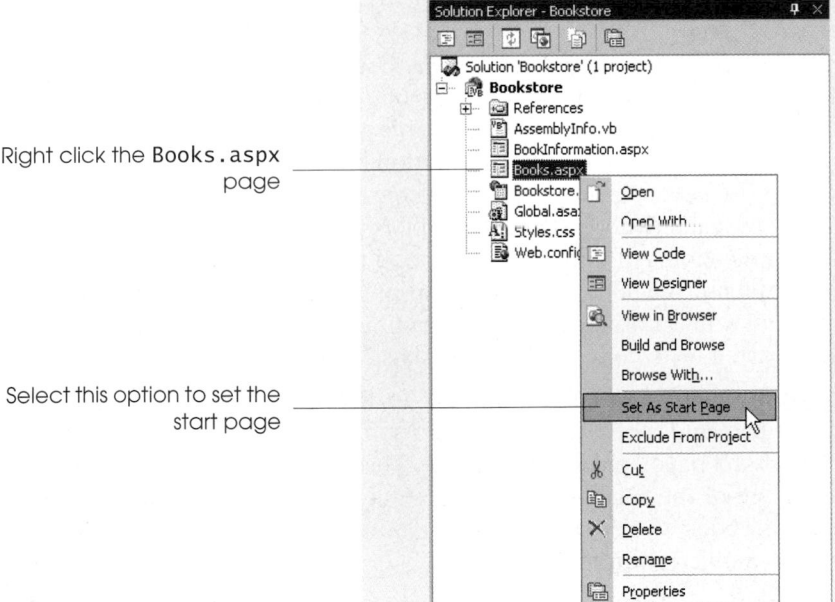

Figure 28.22 Setting Books.aspx as the Web application's start page.

(cont.)

3. **Running the application.** Select **Debug > Start**. The Books.aspx page appears in Internet Explorer, as shown in Fig. 28.23. [*Note:* If you are unable to run the project, make sure that you have followed all of the instructions for copying files, starting IIS and setting the Database folder's properties.] This page displays a ListBox containing the available books. Although this ListBox looks similar to the ListBox control you have used in Windows applications, this ListBox is actually a **Web control** (also called an **ASP .NET server control**). Programmers customize ASPX pages by adding Web controls, such as Labels, TextBoxes, Buttons and other GUI components. As you will learn, Web controls look similar to their Windows application counterparts.

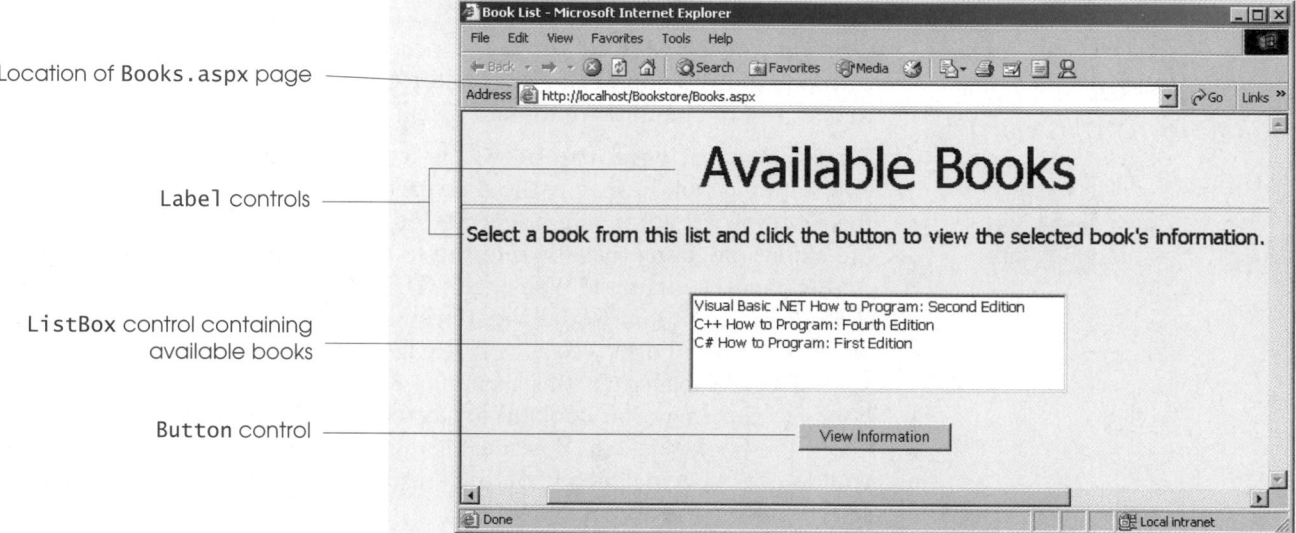

Location of Books.aspx page

Label controls

ListBox control containing available books

Button control

Figure 28.23 Page that displays a list of available books.

Internet Explorer and its HTML content represent the client tier. In Tutorial 29, you will add Web controls, such as Labels to display text, a ListBox to display the list of available books, Buttons to load a different page and a Table to display information on a particular book.

The books displayed in the ListBox are retrieved from a database. The database, named db_bookstore.mdb, is the information tier of this three-tier application. Although only the book titles are displayed in the ListBox, the database includes other information, such as the authors and prices of the books. In Tutorial 30, you will examine the application's information tier and learn how to connect to the database to access the data.

4. **Selecting a book.** Select **C++ How To Program: Fourth Edition** from the book list, and click the **View Information** Button. The BookInforma-tion.aspx page appears (Fig. 28.24). This page displays the title, author and an image of the selected book. This page also contains a table that lists the selected book's price, ISBN number, edition number and copyright date as well as a description of the book.

5. **Returning to Books.aspx.** After viewing a book's information, users can decide whether they wish to view another book's information. The bottom of this page contains a **Book List** Button that, when clicked, redirects the browser back to the Books.aspx page to redisplay the list of book titles.

(cont.)

Location of
`BookInformation.aspx` page

`Table` Web control

When clicked, this `Button`
returns user to `Books.aspx`

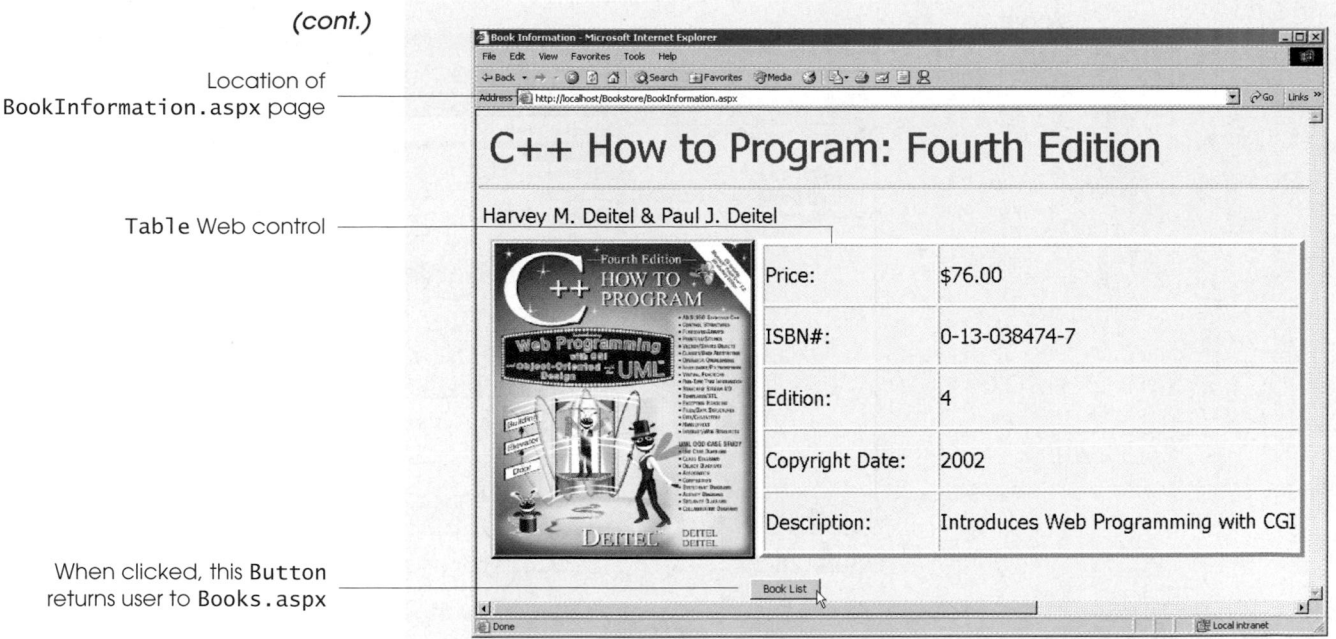

Figure 28.24 Page that displays the selected book's information. (Image courtesy of Deitel & Associates, Inc.)

6. ***Closing the browser.*** Click the browser's close box to close the browser window.

7. ***Closing the solution.*** Select **File > Close Solution**. You have now run the **Bookstore** application from Visual Studio .NET on your local machine. In the next step, you will request the `Books.aspx` Web page, using only Internet Explorer. With real-world ASP .NET applications, clients are browsers that request ASPX pages that reside on remote Web servers.

8. ***Requesting the Books.aspx page from Internet Explorer.*** Open Internet Explorer, type in the URL `http://localhost/Bookstore/Books.aspx` and press the *Enter* key. The URL is the location of the `Books.aspx` page of the **Bookstore** application on your computer. The `Books.aspx` ASPX page should load in the browser. Select a book and click the `Button` to verify that the **Bookstore** application behaves properly.

9. ***Closing the browser.*** Click the browser's close box.

10. ***Removing the completed application from the IIS's root folder.*** Now you will need to remove the completed application from IIS's root folder before you begin developing the application. You cannot have two applications with the same name in the `wwwroot` folder. Therefore, you must delete the completed application so that you can create the **Bookstore** application from scratch over the next three tutorials. Stop IIS by clicking the Stop Item `Button` (the filled square next to the Start Item `Button`) in the **Internet Information Services** dialog. Right click `Bookstore` in the right pane and select **Delete** to remove the completed **Bookstore** application from IIS's root folder (Fig. 28.25).

(cont.)

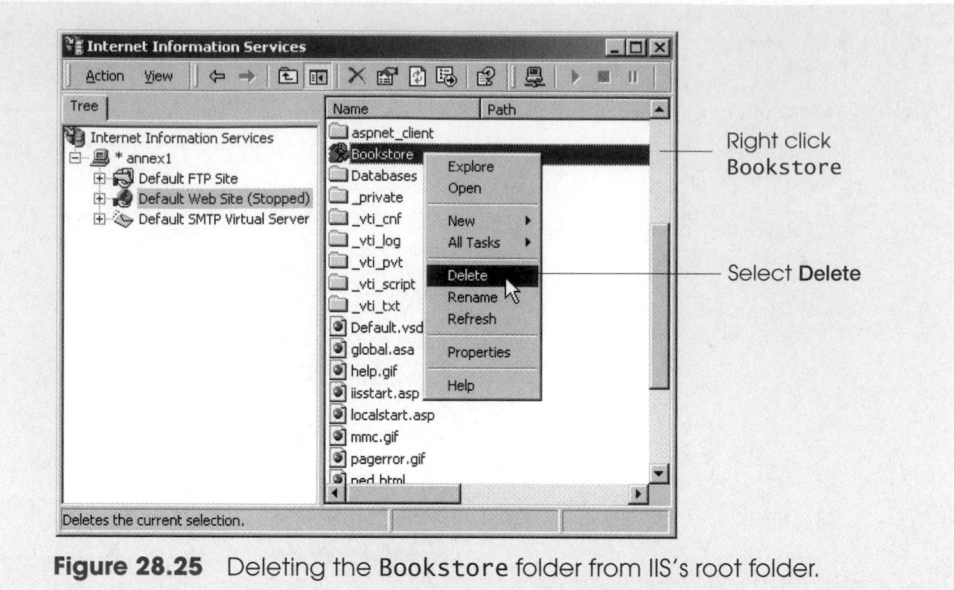

Figure 28.25   Deleting the `Bookstore` folder from IIS's root folder.

Notice that this example uses all three tiers of a three-tier application. The information tier is the database from which the application retrieves information. The middle tier is the code that controls what occurs when users interact with the Web pages. The client tier is represented by the Web pages from which the user views and selects books.

SELF-REVIEW

1. Web controls also are called _____.
   a) ASP .NET server controls   b) ASP controls
   c) HTML controls   d) None of the above.

2. In real-world ASP .NET applications, typically clients are _____ that request ASPX pages that reside on remote Web servers.
   a) Web Form pages   b) Web controls
   c) Web browsers   d) None of the above.

Answers: 1) a. 2) c.

28.5 Wrap-Up

In this tutorial, you learned about the components of a three-tier application. You were introduced to the information tier, which maintains the data for the application. You then learned about the client tier, which displays the application's user interface, and the middle tier, which provides the communication between the information and client tiers. Next, you were introduced to Microsoft Internet Information Services (IIS), which is used for serving Web content such as ASP .NET Web pages. You then test-drove the three-tier **Bookstore** application. In doing this, you learned how to start and stop IIS and how to run ASP .NET Web-based applications. You were also introduced to ASPX pages, and you learned that Web controls are used to customize these pages.

In the next tutorial, Tutorial 29, **Bookstore** Application: Client Tier, you will create the user interface for this application. You will design the Web pages that display the book list and book information. You will then proceed to Tutorial 30, **Bookstore** Application: Information Tier. This tutorial describes the database used in the application and provides a step-by-step discussion of how the application connects to the database. Discussion of the **Bookstore** application will conclude with Tutorial 31, **Bookstore** Application: Middle Tier. In this tutorial, you will write the functionality for the entire **Bookstore** application.

SKILLS SUMMARY

Starting IIS in Windows 2000

- Go to the Windows **Start** menu, and select **Settings > Control Panel**.
- Double click **Administrative Tools**, then double click **Internet Services Manager** to display the **Internet Information Services** dialog.
- Click the plus box next to your computer name's node to display the default sites set up by IIS.
- Click **Default Web Site** in the left pane.
- Click the Start Item `Button` in the toolbar. (This is required only if the **Default Web Site** is stopped.)

Starting IIS in Windows XP

- Go to the Windows **Start** menu, and select **Control Panel**.
- In the **Control Panel** dialog, click the **Switch to Classic View** link.
- Double click **Administrative Tools**, then double click **Internet Information Services** to display the **Internet Information Services** dialog.
- Click the plus box next to your computer name's node to display the **Web Sites** node.
- Click the **Web Sites** node to display the **Default Web Site** node.
- Click **Default Web Site** in the left pane.
- Click the Start Item `Button` in the toolbar. (This is required only if the **Default Web Site** is stopped.)

Stopping IIS in Windows 2000

- Go to the Windows **Start** menu, and select **Settings > Control Panel**.
- Double click **Administrative Tools**, then double click **Internet Services Manager** to display the **Internet Information Services** dialog.
- Click the plus box next to your computer name's node to display the default sites set up by IIS.
- Click **Default Web Site** in the left pane.
- Click the Stop Item `Button` in the toolbar.

Stopping IIS in Windows XP

- Go to the Windows **Start** menu, and select **Control Panel**.
- In the **Control Panel** dialog, click the **Switch to Classic View** link.
- Double click **Administrative Tools**, then double click **Internet Information Services** to display the **Internet Information Services** dialog.
- Click the plus box next to your computer name's node to display the **Web Sites** node.
- Click the **Web Sites** node to display the **Default Web Site** node.
- Click **Default Web Site** in the left pane.
- Click the Stop Item `Button` in the toolbar.

Setting up a Web Application on Your Machine

- Place the Web application's project folder in your Web server's root directory (usually `C:\Inetpub\wwwroot`).
- Start IIS.
- Click **Default Web Site** in **Internet Information Services** dialog to display the contents of the folder in the right pane.
- Right click the desired project's folder, and select **Properties**.
- Click the **Create** `Button`; then click **OK**.
- Open the application, and right click the start page in the **Solution Explorer** window.
- Select **Set As Start Page**.

Enabling Web Applications to use Access Databases in Windows 2000

- Search for the folder containing the database in the wwwroot folder; right click the name of the folder, and select **Properties**.
- Select the **Security** tab.
- Make sure that the **Allow inheritable permissions from parent to propagate to this object** CheckBox is checked, and click the **Add** Button.
- Double click the **ASPNET** user, and click the **OK** Button.
- Give the **ASPNET** user write permission by selecting the **ASPNET** user and checking the **Write** CheckBox.
- Click **OK** to accept the settings.

Enabling Web Applications to use Access Databases in Windows XP

- Select **Tools > Folder Options...** in the wwwroot folder.
- Click the **View** tab; then make sure that the **Use simple file sharing (Recommended)** CheckBox in the **Advanced settings:** tab of the **Folder Options** dialog does not contain a checkmark.
- If you changed any settings, click **OK** to accept the changes.
- Search for the folder containing the database in the wwwroot folder; right click the name of the folder, and select **Properties**.
- Select the **Security** tab, and click the **Add** Button.
- Click the **Advanced...** Button to display more options in the **Select Users or Groups** dialog.
- Click the **Find Now** Button.
- Double click the **ASPNET** user, and click the **OK** Button.
- Click the **OK** Button again to add **ASPNET** as a user.
- Give the **ASPNET** user write permission by selecting the **ASPNET** user and checking the **Write** CheckBox.
- Click **OK** to accept the settings.

Testing the Web Application on localhost, Using Visual Studio .NET

- Open the application in Visual Studio .NET.
- Select **Debug > Start** to run the application.

Testing the Web Application on localhost, Using Internet Explorer

- Open an Internet Explorer browser.
- Type the URL http://localhost/*nameOfProject/nameOfStartPage*, where *nameOfProject* is the name of the project folder and *nameOfStartPage* is the name of the first ASPX page that loads when the application is run.
- Press the *Enter* key to run the application.

KEY TERMS

ASPX page—File that specifies the GUI of a Web page using Web controls.

client tier—Tier containing the user interface of the application.

DNS lookup—Process that translates domain names to IP addresses.

domain—Represents a group of hosts on the Internet.

domain name system (DNS) server—Computer that maintains a database of host names and their corresponding IP addresses.

fully qualified domain name (FQDN)—Host name combined with a domain and top-level domain that provides a user-friendly way to identify a site on the Internet.

host name—Name of a computer where resources reside.

information tier—Tier containing the application data; typically implemented as a database. Also called the bottom tier or database tier.

Internet Information Services (IIS)—A Microsoft Web server.

IP address—Unique address used to locate a computer on the Internet.

`localhost`—Host name that identifies the local computer.

middle tier—Tier that controls interaction between the client and information tiers.

multi-tier application—Application that divides functionality into separate tiers. Typically, each tier performs a specific function.

top-level domain (TLD)—Usually describes the type of organization that owns the domain name.

top tier—Tier containing the application's user interface. Also called the client tier.

uniform resource locator (URL)—Address that can be used to direct a browser to a resource on the Web.

Web controls—Controls, such as `TextBoxes` and `Buttons`, that are used to customize ASPX pages.

Web server—Specialized software that responds to client requests by providing resources.

MULTIPLE-CHOICE QUESTIONS

28.1 ASPX pages have the _____ extension.

   a) `.html`   b) `.wbform`

   c) `.vbaspx`   d) `.aspx`

28.2 _____ applications divide functionality into separate tiers.

   a) *n*-tier   b) Multi-tier

   c) Both a and b.   d) None of the above.

28.3 All tiers of a multi-tier application _____.

   a) must be located on the same computer

   b) must be located on different computers

   c) can be located on the same computer or on different computers

   d) must be arranged so that the client and middle tier are on the same computer and the information tier is on a different computer

28.4 The client tier interacts with the _____ tier to access information from the _____ tier.

   a) middle; information   b) information; middle

   c) information; bottom   d) bottom; information

28.5 A _____ is specialized software that responds to client requests by providing resources.

   a) host   b) host name

   c) DNS server   d) Web server

28.6 A(n) _____ can be thought of as an address that is used to direct a browser to a resource on the Web.

   a) middle tier   b) ASPX page

   c) URL   d) query string

28.7 A _____ represents a group of _____ on the Internet.

   a) domain; hosts   b) host; domain names

   c) host name; hosts   d) None of the above.

28.8 _____ is a Web server.

   a) IIS   b) `localhost`

   c) Visual Studio .NET   d) `wwwroot`

28.9 A _____ is a Web server that is located on a computer across a network such as the Internet.

   a) `localhost`   b) local Web server

   c) remote Web server   d) None of the above.

28.10 The _____ tier is the application's user interface.
a) middle
b) client
c) bottom
d) information

EXERCISES

28.11 (*Phone Book Application*) Over the next three tutorials, you will create a **Phone-Book** application. This phone book should be a Web-based version of the **PhoneBook** application created in Tutorial 27. [*Note*: This Web application will not use Microsoft Agent.] The **PhoneBook** application should consist of two ASPX pages, which will be named PhoneBook and PhoneNumber. The PhoneBook page displays a DropDownList (a Web control similar to a ComboBox Windows Form control) that contains the names of several people. The names are retrieved from the db_Phone.mdb database. When a name is selected and the **Get Number** Button is clicked, the client browser is redirected to the PhoneNumber page. The telephone number of the selected name should be retrieved from a database and displayed in a Label on the PhoneNumber page. For this exercise, you need only organize the components (Phone-Book and PhoneNumber ASPX pages, db_Phone.mdb database and the code that performs the specified functionality) of this Web application into separate tiers. Decide which components belong in which tiers. You will begin building the solution, using Visual Studio .NET, in the next tutorial.

28.12 (*US State Facts Application*) Over the next three tutorials, you will create a **USStateFacts** application. This application is designed to allow users to review their knowledge about specific U.S. states. This application should consist of two ASPX pages. The first page (named States) should display a ListBox containing 10 different state names. These state names are stored in the db_StateFacts.mdb database. The user should be allowed to select a state name and click a Button to retrieve information about the selected state from the database. The information should be displayed on a different ASPX page (named State-Facts). The StateFacts page should display an image of the state flag and list the state capital, state flower, state tree and state bird (retrieved from the database) in a Table. You will be provided with images of the state flags. For this exercise, you need only organize the components (States and StateFacts ASPX pages, db_StateFacts.mdb database and the code that performs the specified functionality) of this Web application into separate tiers. Decide which components belong in which tiers. You will begin building the solution, using Visual Studio .NET, in the next tutorial.

28.13 (*Road Sign Review Application*) Over the next three tutorials, you will create a **RoadSignReview** application. The **RoadSignReview** application should consist of two ASPX pages. This application displays road signs for users to review and allows them to schedule a driving test. The first page (named RoadSigns) should display 15 road signs in a Table. You will be provided images of the road signs. When the mouse pointer is moved over a sign, the name of the sign will appear in a tooltip in the Web browser window. The table should display the images by retrieving their information from the db_RoadSigns.mdb database. This page also will contain two TextBoxes and a Button that allow users to provide their information to register for a driving test. When users click the **Register** Button, the second page (RoadTestRegistered) displays confirmation information that the user has registered for a driving test. For this exercise, you need only organize the components (RoadSigns and RoadTestRegistered ASPX pages, db_RoadSigns.mdb database and the code that performs the specified functionality) of this Web application into separate tiers. Decide which components belong in which tiers. You will begin building the solution, using Visual Studio .NET, in the next tutorial.

Objectives

In this tutorial, you will learn to:

- Create an **ASP .NET** Web **Application** project.
- Create and desi704gn ASPX pages.
- Use Web Form controls.
- Reposition controls, using the `style` attribute.

Outline

Bookstore Application: Client Tier

Introducing Web Controls

I n this tutorial, you will create the client tier (user interface) of your three-tier **Bookstore** application, using visual-programming techniques. You will begin by creating the application's project—an ASP .NET Web application project. You then will learn about Web controls by creating the application's GUI.

29.1 Analyzing the Bookstore Application

Now that you have taken the three-tier **Bookstore** application (in Tutorial 28) for a test-drive, you need to analyze the application components. The following pseudocode describes the actions that the application needs to execute in order to solve the problem (Figure 29.1 displays the ACE table):

> If the Books page is requested
> > Retrieve the book titles from the database
> > Display book titles in a ListBox
>
> If the user selects a book title from the ListBox and clicks the View Information Button
> > Store the selected book in a variable
> > Redirect the user to the BookInformation page
> > Retrieve the selected book's information from a database
> > Display the retrieved information in a Table on the BookInformation page
>
> If the user presses the Book List Button on the BookInformation page
> > Redirect the client browser back to the Books page

Action/Control/Event (ACE) Table for the Web-Based Bookstore Application

Action	Control/Object	Event
Label the Books page	lblAvailable, lblInstructions	
When the Books page loads, retrieve the book titles from the database and display them in the ListBox	Books.aspx, objOleDbConnection, objSelectTitles, lstBookTitles	Load (of Page)
Redirect the client browser to the BookInformation page	btnInformation	Click
When the BookInformation page loads, retrieve the selected book's information from the database and display in a Table	BookInforma-tion.aspx, objOleDbConnection, objSelectBookData, lblBookTitle, lblAuthors, imgBook, tblBook	Load (of Page)
Redirect the client browser back to the Books page	btnBookList	Click

Figure 29.1   ACE table for the Web-based **Bookstore** application.

29.2 Creating ASPX Pages

Now that you have been introduced to IIS and three-tier, Web-based application concepts, you will begin creating the **Bookstore** application that you test-drove in the last tutorial. Before you begin to create the GUI for the **Bookstore** application, you need to set Visual Studio .NET to display line numbers for the ASPX page. You do so in the box, *Configuring Visual Studio .NET to Display Line Numbers For ASPX Pages.*

Configuring Visual Studio .NET to Display Line Numbers For ASPX Pages

1. ***Opening the* Options *dialog.*** Open Visual Studio .NET. Select **Tools > Options...** to display the **Options** dialog.

2. ***Enabling line numbers to be displayed.*** Click **Text Editor** in the left pane of the **Options** dialog; then click **HTML/XML**. Click **General**, and check the **Line Numbers** CheckBox (Fig. 29.2). Click the **OK** Button to save the settings and close the **Options** dialog.

Text Editor (clicked)

HTML/XML (clicked)
General (selected)
Line numbers CheckBox (checked)

Figure 29.2   **Options** dialog.

Now that you have configured Visual Studio .NET to display line numbers for the ASPX page, you can begin creating the **Bookstore** application. This Web-based application allows users to view information about books they select. After viewing a book's information, users can return to the page containing the list of books and select another book. You will create the ASP .NET Web application project for the **Bookstore** in the box, *Creating an ASP .NET Web Application*.

Creating an ASP .NET Web Application	1. ***Starting IIS.*** IIS must be running on the server machine (localhost, in this case) for you to be able to create ASP .NET Web applications in Visual Studio .NET. Start IIS as demonstrated in *Step 3* of the box, *Specifying Initial Settings for the* `Bookstore` *Application* in Tutorial 28.

2. ***Creating the project.*** In Visual Studio .NET, select **File > New > Project...** to display the **New Project** dialog (Fig. 29.3). In this dialog, select **Visual Basic Projects** in the **Project Types:** pane and **ASP .NET Web Application** in the **Templates:** pane. Notice that the **Name:** TextBox for the project name is disabled. Specify the name and location of the project in the **Location:** TextBox. The default value in this TextBox is `http://localhost/WebApplication1`. The files for this application will be stored in a folder called `WebApplication1`, located at `http://localhost`. Recall that this location is really IIS's root directory (usually `C:\Inetpub\wwwroot`).

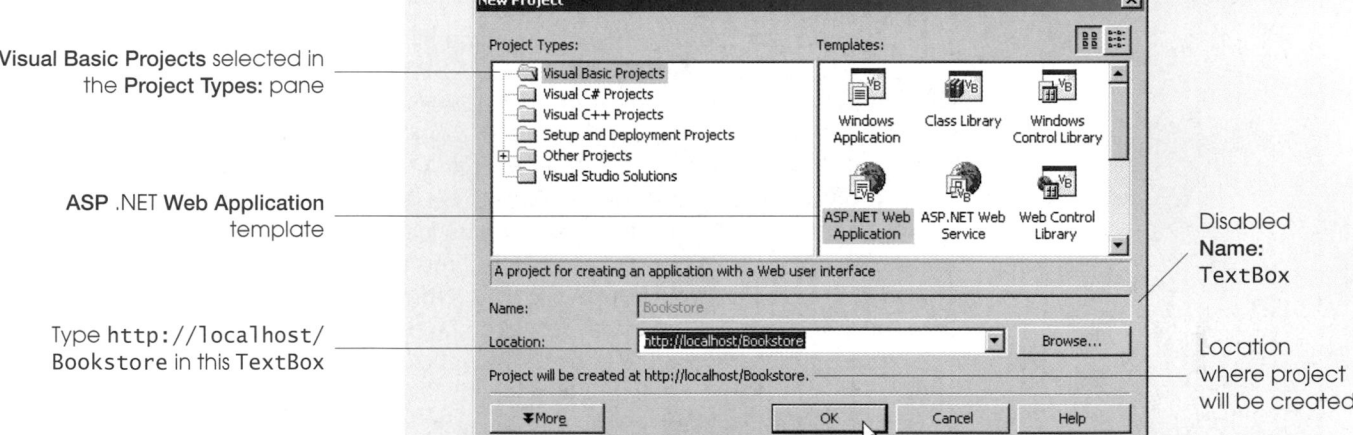

Visual Basic Projects selected in the **Project Types:** pane

ASP .NET Web Application template

Type `http://localhost/Bookstore` in this TextBox

Disabled **Name:** TextBox

Location where project will be created

Figure 29.3   Creating an **ASP** .NET **Web Application** in Visual Studio .NET.

Change `WebApplication1` to `Bookstore`. If the `Bookstore` directory does not yet exist at `http://localhost`, it will be created for you. Below the **Location:** TextBox, the text "**Project will be created at http://localhost/Bookstore.**" appears. When you click **OK**, the project is created. The **Create New Web** dialog displays next, while Visual Studio .NET creates the Web site on the server (Fig. 29.4).

Figure 29.4   Visual Studio .NET creating the **Bookstore** application.

(cont.)   3.   ***Examining the project files.*** The **Solution Explorer** window for the **Bookstore** application is shown in Fig. 29.5. As with Windows applications, Visual Studio .NET creates several files for each new **ASP** .NET **Web Application** project. `WebForm1.aspx` is the default name for the ASPX page.

Project name ——————

Default ASPX page name ——————

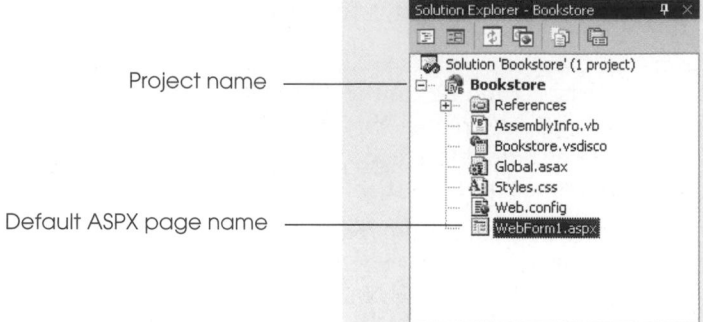

Figure 29.5   **Solution Explorer** window for the `Bookstore` solution.

4.   ***Setting Option Strict to On.*** Right click the `Bookstore` project name in the **Solution Explorer**, and select **Properties**. In the **Bookstore Property Pages** dialog, select **Build** under **Common Properties**, and set `Option Strict` to `On`. Recall that we use Option Strict to avoid subtle errors that may occur in implicit conversions. Click the **OK** Button to close the dialog.

5.   ***Viewing the Toolbox.*** ASPX pages can be customized by using Web controls. These types of controls are used for ASPX pages in a manner similar to how Windows controls are used for Windows Forms. You will be using these controls to create the user interface of your **Bookstore** application. Web controls are located in the **Web Forms** tab of the **Toolbox**. Select **View > Toolbox**, and click the **Web Forms** tab. Figure 29.6 shows the **Web Forms** controls listed in the **Toolbox**. The left part of the figure displays the beginning of the **Web Forms** controls list, and the right part of the figure displays the remaining **Web Forms** controls. Notice that some of the control icons, such as `Label`, `TextBox` and `Button`, are the same as the Windows controls presented earlier in the book. Although some of these control names appear the same, the functionality provided by **Web Forms** controls is different and they can be used only with ASPX pages.

Web Forms tab ——————

Figure 29.6   **Web Forms** tab in **Toolbox**.

(cont.)   6.   ***Viewing the ASPX page in Design mode.*** When you create a Web application, an ASPX page will be displayed in the **Web Form Designer** (Fig. 29.7). [*Note*: We do not apply a `Lucida` font to the word "Form" (in "Web Form Designer"), because Web Forms are not instances of class `Form`.] Unlike the Windows `Form Designer`, the Web Form Designer contains two different viewing modes. The first mode is the **Design mode**. Figure 29.7 shows the ASPX page displayed in **Design** mode for `WebForm1.aspx`. It consists of a grid on which you drag and drop components, such as `Buttons` and `Labels`, from the **Toolbox**. If the **Design** mode for the ASPX page does not display, click the **Design** `Button`, in the lower left corner of the Web Form Designer. **Design** mode should be used when you want to visually create the ASPX page's GUI by dragging and dropping Web controls onto the ASPX page.

HTML `Button`
Design `Button` (selected)

Figure 29.7   **Design** mode of Web Form Designer.

7.   ***Switching to HTML mode.*** The Web Form Designer also can display the ASPX page in **HTML** mode (Fig. 29.8). Click the **HTML** `Button`. ASPX pages are defined using a combination of HTML and ASP markup. ASP markup is the set of instructions processed on the Web server's machine. ASP markup is often converted into HTML and sent to a browser client as part of a response to a client request. When you click the **HTML** `Button` in the Web Form Designer, the Web Form Designer switches to **HTML** mode. You use **HTML mode** when you wish to view your ASPX page's markup. You also can use this mode to edit the markup. When you click the **Design** `Button`, the Web Form Designer switches to **Design** mode. Although you will not be writing markup to create Web controls for this ASPX page, you will be using it to set the locations of the Web controls.

8.   ***Saving the solution file to your Bookstore folder.*** By default, Visual Studio .NET saves solution files for ASP .NET Web applications in a separate directory. For easy access, you will save the solution file in your `Book-store` folder located in the `wwwroot` folder. Click on **Solution 'Bookstore' (1 project)** in the **Solution Explorer**, and then select **File > Save Bookstore.sln As...** to display the **Save File As** dialog.

(cont.)

This portion is highlighted by default in Visual Studio .NET (This is an example of ASP markup)

HTML markup

HTML Button (selected)

Design Button

Figure 29.8   HTML mode of Web Form Designer.

[*Note*: A **Microsoft Development Environment** dialog may appear first asking if you would like to save your changes. No changes should have been made so far, so if this dialog appears we suggest you click the **No** Button and undo any of your changes. If you would instead like to save the changes you've made, click the **Yes** Button to dismiss this dialog.] In this dialog, navigate to the wwwroot folder, and save the solution file in the Bookstore folder.

---

1. _____ mode allows you to view the ASPX page's markup.

   a) **HTML**   b) **Design**
   c) Web control   d) Markup

2. Some Web control names are the same as Windows control names, _____.

   a) because their functionality is the same
   b) but the functionality provided by Web controls is different
   c) because both Web controls and Windows controls can be used in Web applications
   d) None of the above.

Answers: 1) a. 2) b.

29.3 Designing the Books.aspx Page

This **Bookstore** application consists of two ASPX pages, which you create one at a time. The first page of the **Bookstore** application will be named Books.aspx. This page will display the list of available books. You design the first ASPX page in the box, *Creating the Books.aspx Page.*

Creating the Books.aspx Page

1. ***Renaming the ASPX page.*** After you have viewed the contents of the default ASPX page (WebForm1.aspx), you will want to give this ASPX page a meaningful name. Select the WebForm1.aspx file in the **Solution Explorer** window. Change the **File Name** property in the **Properties** window from WebForm1.aspx to Books.aspx (Fig. 29.9).

(cont.)

Now click the Web Form Designer. The properties of the ASPX page should display in the **Properties** window. Notice that ASPX pages are listed with the identifier **DOCUMENT** in the Component Object Box (Fig. 29.10), because they do not have individual names. Select the **title** property, and change WebForm1 to Book List. This step sets the text that is displayed in the requesting browser's title bar.

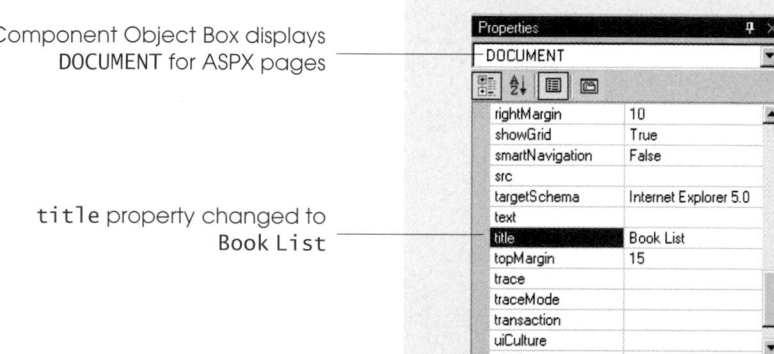

Change the File Name's property value to Books.aspx

Figure 29.9   Setting the **File Name** property of the ASPX page.

Component Object Box displays DOCUMENT for ASPX pages

title property changed to Book List

Figure 29.10   The title property of Books.aspx.

Good Programming Practice

Change the ASPX page's name to a unique and meaningful name for easy identification. The name you choose must end with the .aspx extension for the page to be identified as an ASPX page.

2. *Changing the background color of the ASPX page.* Now you are ready to begin creating the GUI. Make sure you are in **Design** mode of the designer. First change the **bgColor** property of the Books.aspx page so that the background color of Books.aspx is set to light blue. Select bgColor in the **Properties** window, and click the ellipsis (...) Button to display the **Color Picker** dialog (Fig. 29.11). Click the **Web Palette** tab, and select light blue, as shown in Fig. 29.11. Click the **OK** Button. The background color of the Books.aspx page is now light blue.

3. *Creating a Label.* Next, click the Label Web control from the **Web Forms** tab of the **Toolbox**. Drag and drop the control

> **A** Label

onto the Books.aspx page. The Label should appear on the ASPX page (Fig. 29.12). Select the Label in order to view its properties in the **Properties** window. Select the ID property, and change Label1 to lblAvailable. The **ID property** is used to identify controls, much like the Name property in Windows controls. Now change the Label's Text property from Label to Available Books. Set the Label's font size by setting Size, under the Font property to XX-Large (Fig. 29.13). Set the Label's font to Tahoma by clicking the down arrow next to property Name (also under the Font property) and selecting **Tahoma** from the list that appears. To display the words correctly in the Label, you will need to set the height and width of the control. Set the **Height** property of the Label to 56px, and set the **Width** to 335px.

Good Programming Practice

Web controls with similar names and functionality to those of Windows controls should be given the same prefixes recommended in earlier tutorials. For example, prefix the Label Web control with lbl.

(cont.)

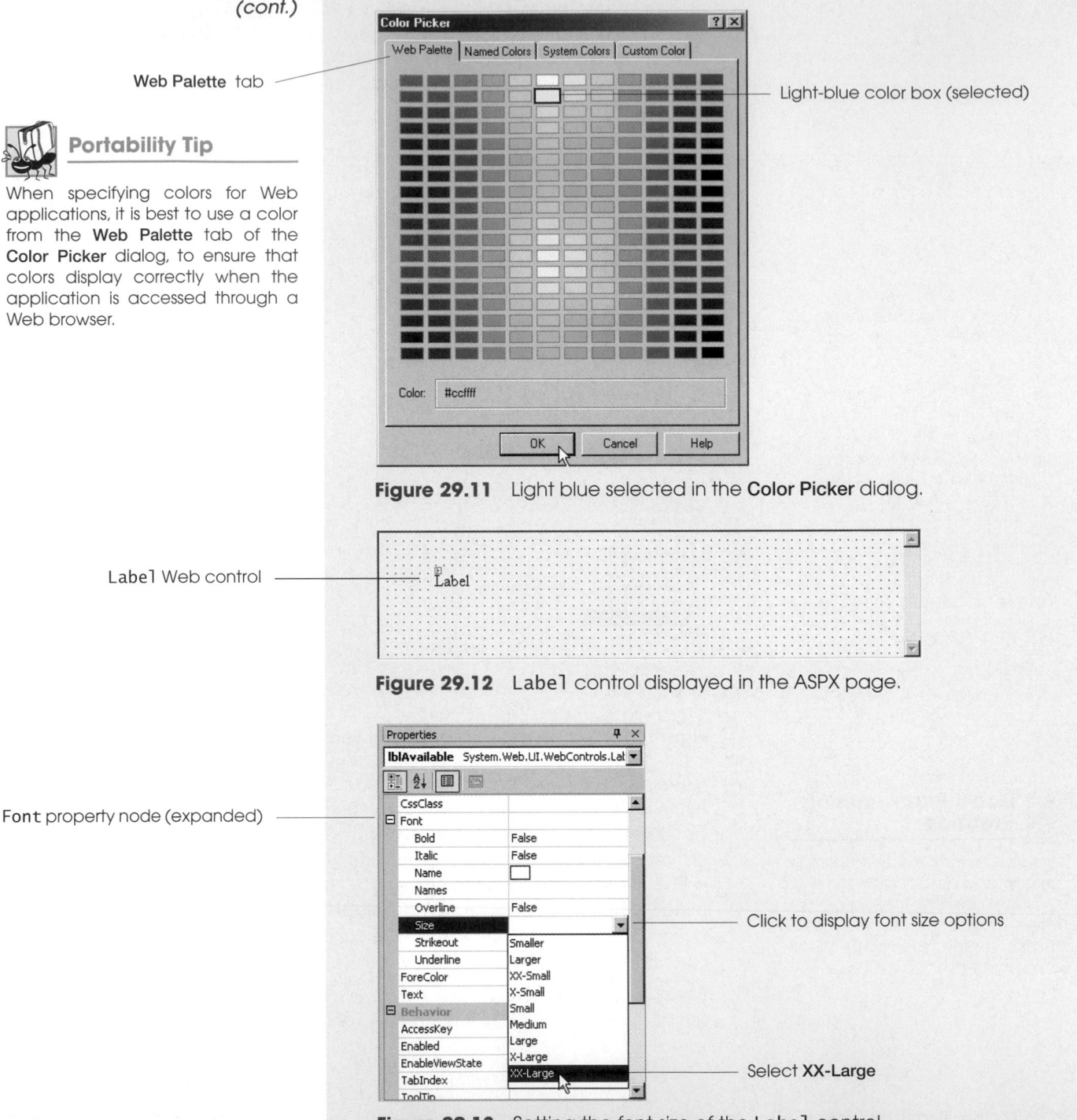

Web Palette tab

Light-blue color box (selected)

Portability Tip

When specifying colors for Web applications, it is best to use a color from the **Web Palette** tab of the **Color Picker** dialog, to ensure that colors display correctly when the application is accessed through a Web browser.

Figure 29.11   Light blue selected in the **Color Picker** dialog.

Label Web control

Figure 29.12   Label control displayed in the ASPX page.

Font property node (expanded)

Click to display font size options

Select **XX-Large**

Figure 29.13   Setting the font size of the Label control.

4. *Positioning the Label.* Place the Label in the top center of the page. To set the exact location of the Label, switch to **HTML** mode. Notice that lines 15–20 of Fig. 29.14 (<asp:label id="lblAvailable"...>) have been added to the markup. Line 16 contains the style attribute, as shown in Fig. 29.14. Set the LEFT: portion of the style attribute value to 295px and the TOP: portion of the attribute value to 16px. The **px** portion of these values specify that the Label will be positioned 295 pixels from the left side of the page and 16 pixels down from the upper left corner of the ASPX page.

(cont.)   Switch back into **Design** mode. The Label should now be repositioned on the page (Fig. 29.15). [*Note*: Your markup may look different from that in Fig. 29.15—we have modified the code slightly for presentation purposes. For example, some of the meta elements may appear in a different order.]

Figure 29.14   Style property for the Label.

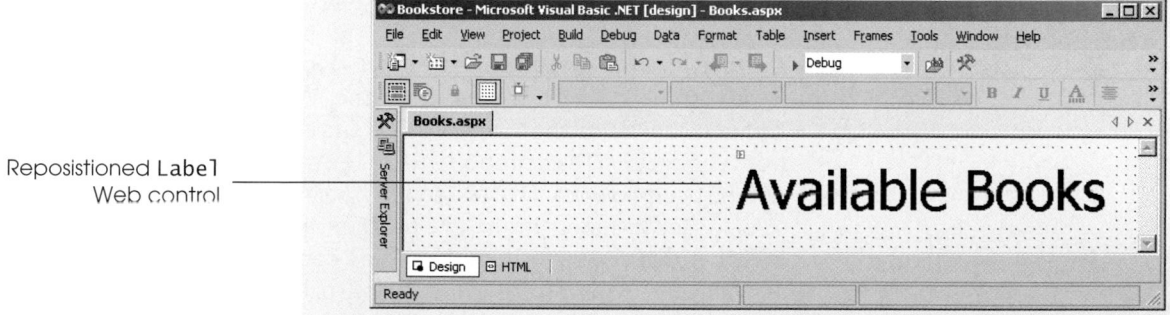

Figure 29.15   Complete Label displayed in **Design** mode.

5. ***Creating a Horizontal Rule.*** Drag and drop the Horizontal Rule control (found in the **HTML** tab in the **Toolbox**),

and place it beneath the lblAvailable Label. A Horizontal Rule provides a horizontal line on a Web page. You use it to separate content on your ASPX page. Horizontal Rules are types of **HTML controls**, which correspond to standard HTML elements. In this case study, we ask you to assume that a control is a Web control, unless we explicitly tell you that it is an HTML control.

Good Programming Practice

When naming a Horizontal Rule control, use the prefix hrz followed by a word that describes the control's use.

(cont.)

In the **Properties** window, set the id property of the Horizontal Rule to hrzBooks. Next, click the style property value in the **Properties** window. Click the ellipsis (...) Button that appears in the style field. The **Style Builder** dialog appears (Fig. 29.16). Click the **Position** Tab in the left pane of the dialog. Set the **Top:** value to 80px, the **Left:** value to 8px, the **Height:** value to 4px and the **Width:** value to 150%. Click **OK**. These settings position the Horizontal Rule 80 pixels from the upper left corner of the page and 8 pixels from the left side of the page. The height of the control is now 4 pixels. Setting the width to 150% ensures that the Horizontal Rule extends to the entire width of the page.

Figure 29.16   **Style Builder** dialog for the Horizontal Rule control.

6. ***Creating another Label.*** After the Horizontal Rule is in place, create another Label control (found in the **Web Forms** tab in the **Toolbox**). Change the ID of the Label to lblInstructions. In the **Properties** window, change the Text property to Select a book from this list and click the button to view the selected book's information. Then set the font size to Medium. Set the height to 18px and the width to 699px. Switch to **HTML** mode and reposition the Label control as you did in *Step 4*. However, set the LEFT: portion of the style attribute value to 152px and the TOP: portion of the attribute value to 95px.

7. ***Creating a ListBox.*** Switch to **Design** mode. The next control you will place on this page is a ListBox. The ListBox will contain a list of the available books offered by the bookstore. In the next two tutorials, you will retrieve information from the database in order to populate the ListBox with book titles. Drag and drop the ListBox control,

and place it below lblInstructions. Change the ID property of the List-Box to lstBookTitles. In the **Properties** window, set the Height to 100 pixels and the Width to 330 pixels. In **HTML** mode, set the LEFT: portion of the style attribute value of the ListBox to 286px and the TOP: portion of the attribute value to 155px.

(cont.)   8. ***Adding a Button control.*** The final control you will add to the page is a Button (found in the **Web Forms** tab in the **Toolbox**). Switch to **Design** mode. Drag and drop the Button control,

|abl Button|

onto the ASPX page. Change the Button's ID to btnInformation, and change its Text property to View Information. Set its Width to 130 pixels in the **Properties** window. Then switch to **HTML** mode. Change the LEFT: portion of the style attribute value to 380px and the TOP: portion of the attribute value to 270px. The Books.aspx page should look like Fig. 29.17. [*Note*: Unbound appears in the ListBox because no items have been added to it.]

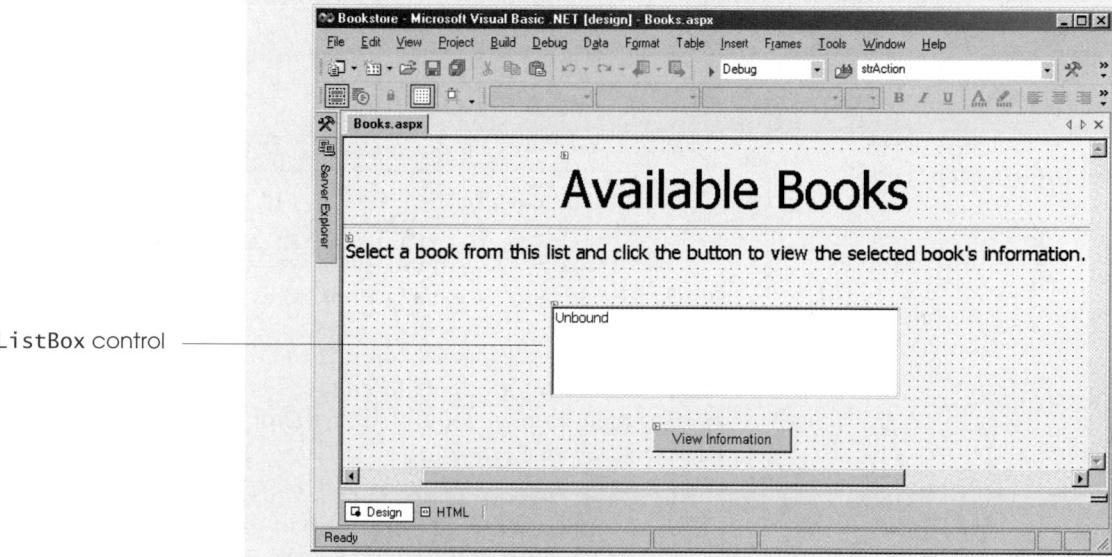

ListBox control

Figure 29.17   **Design** mode of Books.aspx.

   9. ***Saving the project.*** Select **File > Save All** to save the solution's files.

SELF-REVIEW   1. Use the _____ property to change the name of a **Web Forms** control.
       a) Text   b) Name
       c) ID   d) Value

   2. The Horizontal Rule is a(n) _____ control.
       a) **Web Forms**   b) **HTML**
       c) **Data**   d) **Windows Forms**

   Answers: 1) c. 2) b.

29.4 Designing the BookInformation Page

Now that you have designed the Books.aspx page, you will design the BookInformation.aspx page, which displays the information about the book that was selected from the ListBox. You create this page in the box, *Creating the BookInformation.aspx Page*.

Creating the BookInformation Page

1. **Creating a new ASPX page.** Select **File > Add New Item...**, to display the **Add New Item - Bookstore** dialog (Fig. 29.18). Select **Web Form** in the **Templates:** pane, and rename the ASPX page to BookInformation.aspx, using the **Name:** TextBox. Click the **Open** Button. A new ASPX page named BookInformation.aspx appears in the **Solution Explorer** window.

Web Form template

Change this to BookInformation.aspx

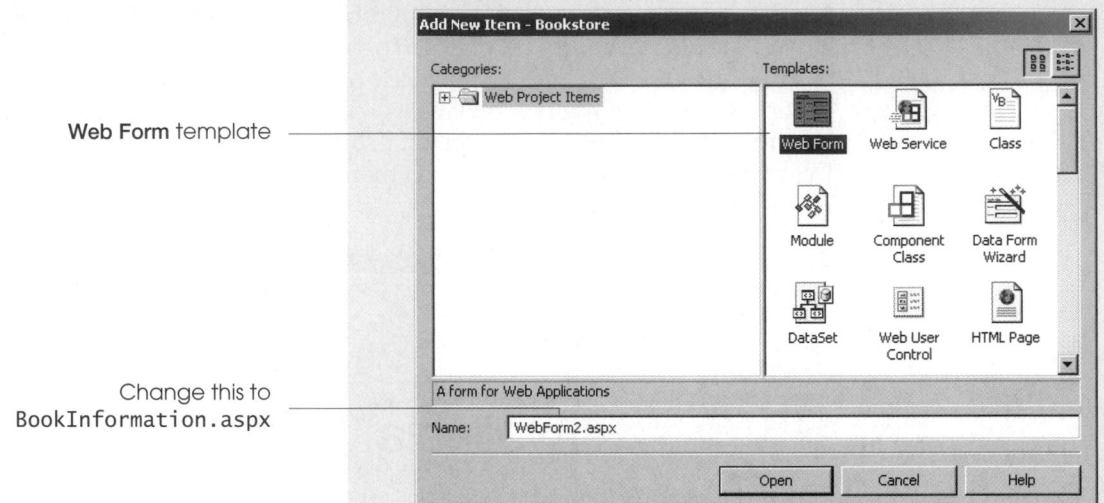

Figure 29.18   **Add New Item - Bookstore** dialog.

2. **Changing the background color.** If the file does not open in **Design** mode, switch to **Design** mode at this time. Change the background color of this page to light blue as you did in *Step 2* of the box, *Creating the Books.aspx Page*.

3. **Creating the lblBookTitle Label.** Create a new Label by double clicking the Label tab in the **Web Forms** tab of the **Toolbox**. This Label will display the title of the book selected by the user. Because you do not yet know what book title will be selected, leave the Text property of this Label blank. The Text property will be set in Tutorial 31. Change the ID property of the Label to lblBookTitle, set the font size to XX-Large and set the Fore-Color to Blue. The ForeColor property specifies the color of the text that displays on the Label. To set the ForeColor, select the ForeColor property in the **Properties** window, and click the down arrow that appears in the ForeColor field. Click the **Web** tab and select Blue to set the forecolor (Fig. 29.19). Set the height to 60px and the width to 1100px. In **HTML** mode, set the LEFT: portion of the style attribute value of the Label to 20px and the TOP: portion of the attribute value to 15px.

4. **Creating the Horizontal Rule.** Switch to **Design** mode. Drag and drop a Horizontal Rule beneath the lblBookTitle Label. Set the id property to hrzBookInformation; then change the style property, setting the **Top:** value to 90px, the **Left:** value to 0px, the **Height:** value to 4px and the **Width:** value to 150%.

5. **Creating the lblAuthors Label.** After adding the Horizontal Rule, create another Label. Name the Label lblAuthors, and change its Font property's Size to Large. Set the height of the Label to 34px and the width to 989px. Do not specify text for this Label, because you do not know which book will be selected. You will set this text in Tutorial 31. In **HTML** mode, set the LEFT: portion of the style attribute value to 20 and the TOP: portion to 110.

(cont.)

ForeColor property

Web tab

Select **Blue**

Figure 29.19 Setting a Label's ForeColor property.

6. **Creating the Image control.** Switch to **Design** mode. Now you must add the **Image control** that displays the cover of the selected book. Drag and drop the Image control,

from the **Web Forms** tab in the **Toolbox** window. Change the Image control's ID property to imgBook. Set the Height and Width properties to 360 and 300 pixels, respectively. Specify the **BorderStyle** as Outset and set the **BorderWidth** to 5 pixels. The BorderStyle property specifies the type of border that displays around the Image. Setting BorderStyle to Outset gives the Image a raised-control appearance. Property BorderWidth specifies the width of the border of the Image control. Setting BorderWidth to 5 causes the border to be 5 pixels thick. Switch to **HTML** mode. Set the LEFT: portion of the style attribute value of the Image to 20px and the TOP: portion to 150px. In Tutorial 31, you will specify the image that will be displayed.

7. **Creating the btnBookList Button.** Switch to **Design** mode. Add a Button to the page. Set the Button's ID to btnBookList, and set its Text to Book List. In the **Properties** window, set the Width property to 80 pixels. Switch to **HTML** mode, then change the LEFT: portion of the style attribute value of the Button to 325px and the TOP: portion to 550px. Switch to **Design** mode. The design of the Bookinformation.aspx page should look like Fig. 29.20.

8. **Saving the project.** Select **File > Save All** to save the solution's files.

(cont.)

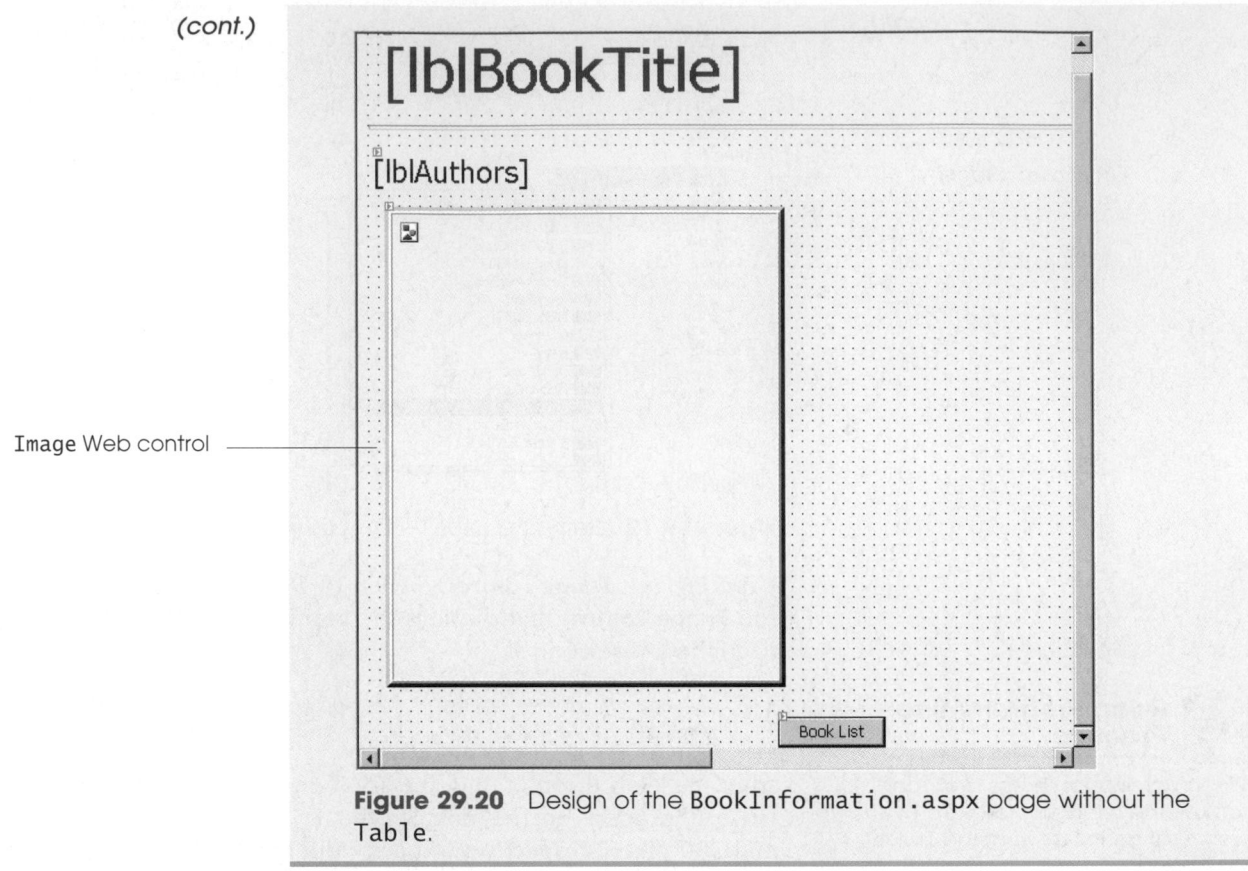

Image Web control ———

Figure 29.20 Design of the `BookInformation.aspx` page without the `Table`.

You are now ready to add the `Table` control to the page. The `Table` is perhaps the most significant control on this page, because it will display the book information in a structured manner. You add the `Table` in the box, *Adding the Table Control*.

Adding the `Table` Control

Good Programming Practice

When naming a `Table` control, use the prefix `tbl` followed by a word that describes what information the `Table` will display.

1. **Creating the `Table` control.** From the **Web Forms** tab of the **Toolbox**, drag and drop the `Table` control,

 Table

onto the page. In the **Properties** window, change the ID of the `Table` to `tblBook`, set the `BorderStyle` to `OutSet` and change the `BorderWidth` to 5 pixels. Also, change the **Gridlines** property to value `Both`. The `Gridlines` property displays separators between the cells (known as **cell borders**) in the `Table`. Setting `Gridlines` to `Both` displays both horizontal and vertical separators between each cell. In **HTML** mode, set the `LEFT:` portion of the `style` attribute value of the `Table` to 335px and change the `TOP:` portion to 150px.

2. **Creating rows in the `Table`.** Switch to **Design** mode. You now must create rows for the `Table`. To do so, select the Rows property in the **Properties** window. Click the ellipsis (...) Button to the right of property Rows. A **Table-Row Collection Editor** dialog appears. Add five rows to the table by clicking the **Add** Button five times (Fig. 29.21). Leave the dialog open so you can customize the `Table`'s rows in the next few steps.

(cont.)

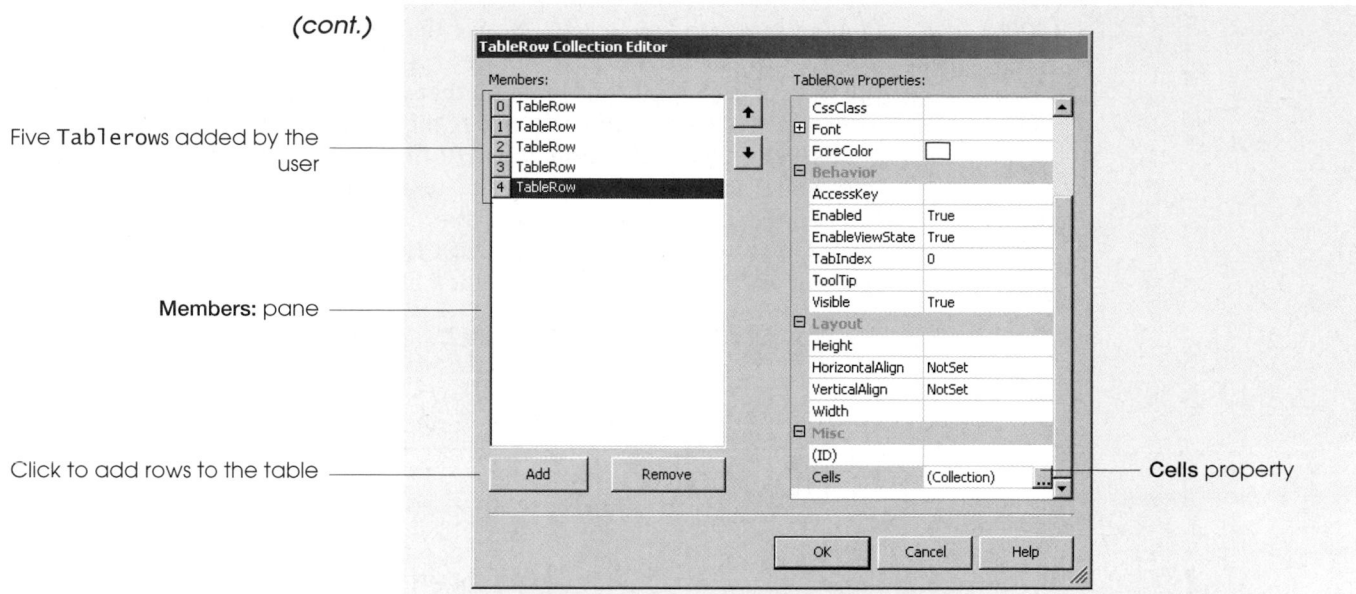

Five `TableRow`s added by the user

Members: pane

Click to add rows to the table

Cells property

Figure 29.21   **TableRow Collection Editor** dialog for the `Table` control.

3. ***Creating cells in the Table.*** `Table` rows contain cells that display data. You will now create each individual cell in each table row. Select `TableRow` 0 in the **Members:** pane. Go to the **TableRow Properties** pane, and click the ellipsis (...) `Button` to the right of the **Cells** property to display the **TableCell Collection Editor** dialog (Fig. 29.22). Add two cells to the row by clicking **Add** twice. Select **TableCell** 0, and set the `Font` property's `Size` to `Large`. Change the `TableCell`'s `Height` property to 70 pixels, `Width` property to 200 pixels and specify the `Text` property as `Price:`. Select the second **TableCell** in the **Members:** box, and set the `Font` property's `Size` to `Large`. Click **OK** in the **TableCell Collection Editor** to accept the settings.

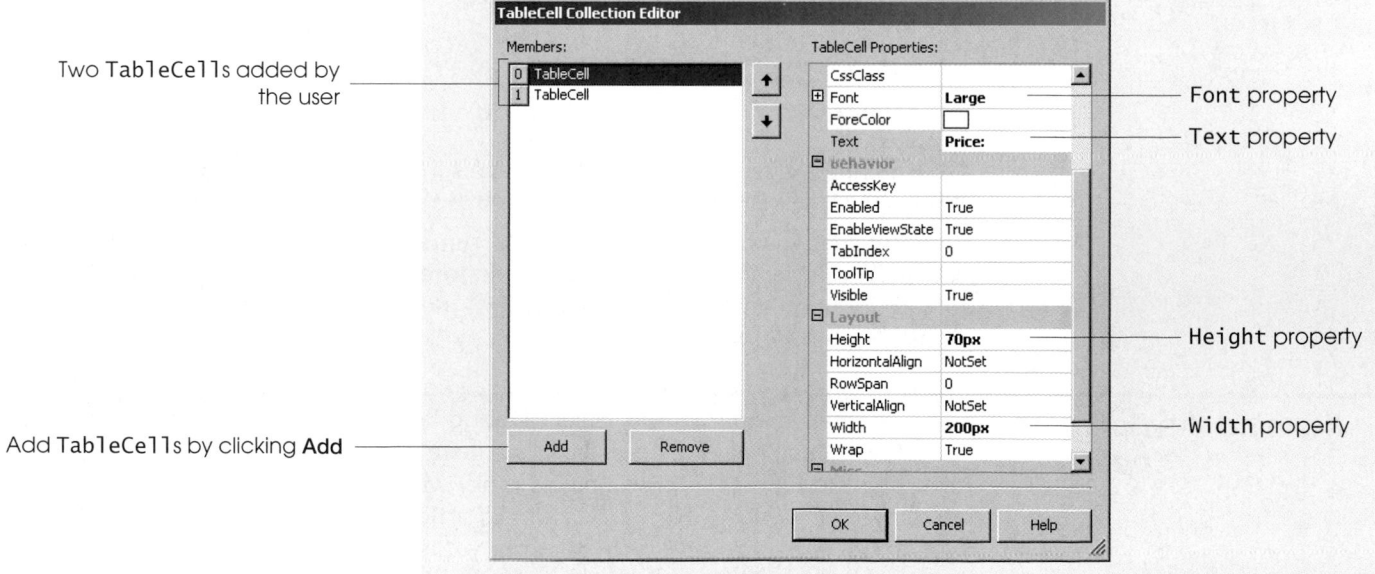

Two `TableCell`s added by the user

Font property

Text property

Add `TableCell`s by clicking **Add**

Height property

Width property

Figure 29.22   **TableCell Collection Editor** dialog of the `Table` control.

(cont.)

4. ***Placing text into Table cells.*** Notice that you set only the font size for the second TableCell. We have not yet set the Text property of the second TableCell because the information that will be displayed in this TableCell is currently unknown. You will specify the information that will be displayed in this TableCell in Tutorial 31. Perform *Step 3* on the rest of the Table-Rows and TableCells, changing the text in the first cells of each row to ISBN#:, Edition:, Copyright Date: and Description:, respectively. Click **OK** in the **TableRow Collection Editor** when you are finished. Your BookInformation.aspx page will look like Fig. 29.23.

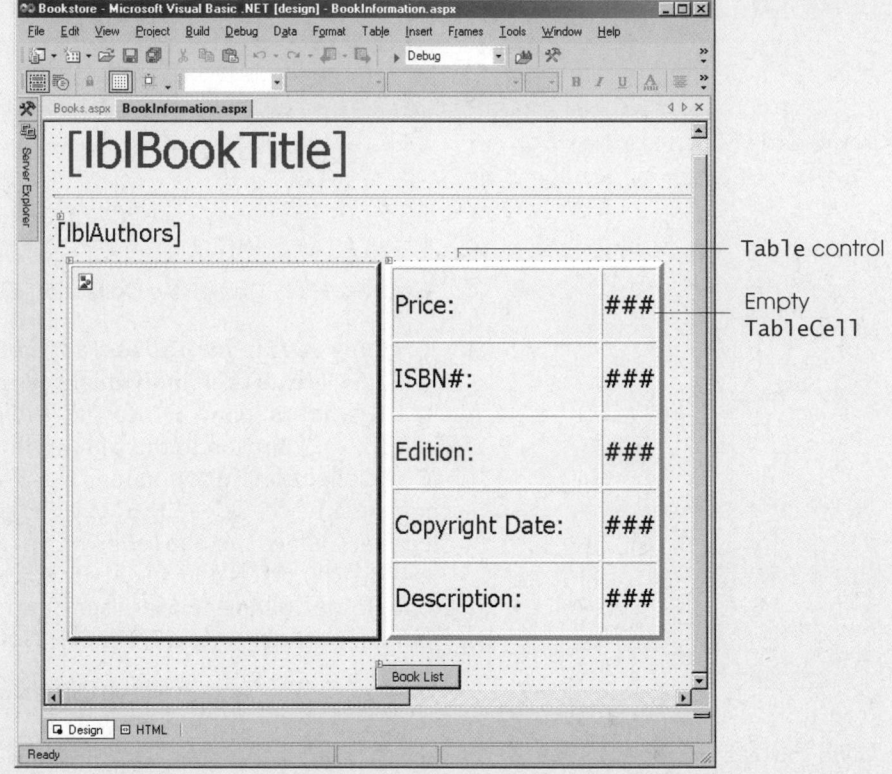

Figure 29.23 Design of the BookInformation.aspx page.

5. ***Saving the project.*** Select **File > Save All** to save the solution's files.

Now that you have completed the user interface design, you will run the application. You have specified only the **Bookstore** application's user interface; therefore, it does not have any functionality. Test the application in the box, *Running the **Bookstore** Application.*

Running the Bookstore Application

1. ***Testing the application.*** Select **Debug > Start** to run the application. The Books.aspx page appears, because the first page you create in an ASP .NET application (in this case, Books.aspx) will be automatically set as the start page (Fig. 29.24). Notice that the ListBox does not yet contain any book titles. This is because you have not yet set up the database connections to retrieve the information. Click the **View Information** Button. Notice that nothing happens. Currently, you have specified only the visual aspects of the page. Thus, users are not forwarded to BookInformation.aspx when the **View Information** Button is clicked.

(cont.)

Empty `ListBox` control ——

Figure 29.24   Empty `ListBox` of the `Books.aspx` page.

2. ***Terminating the application.*** Click the browser's close box to terminate the application.

3. ***Stopping IIS.*** Open the **Internet Information Services** dialog. Select **Default Web Site**, and click the stop `Button` in the toolbar to stop IIS.

4. ***Closing the solution.*** Select **File > Close Solution**.

SELF-REVIEW

1. The _____ property is used to set the width of an `Image` control's border.

    a) `Width`   b) `BorderStyle`

    c) `BorderWidth`   d) None of the above.

2. Use the _____ property to display cell borders between `TableCells` in a `Table`.

    a) `Gridlines`   b) `BorderStyle`

    c) `BorderWidth`   d) `Separator`

Answers: 1) c. 2) a.

29.5 Wrap-Up

In this tutorial, you created the ASPX pages for your three-tier **Bookstore** application. You learned how to create an ASP .NET Web application and how to add Web controls to the ASPX pages. In doing so, you were introduced to the two different modes offered by Visual Studio .NET: **Design** mode and **HTML** mode. You learned that **Design** mode is used to create the user interface by dragging and dropping Web controls on the ASPX page, while **HTML** mode allows you to view and edit the page's markup.

When you added Web controls to the ASPX page, you learned how to set the exact position of the controls by using the `style` attribute in **HTML** mode. You positioned these controls by specifying the `LEFT:` and `TOP:` portions of the `style` attribute values. The Web controls you used in this tutorial included `Labels`, `Buttons`, `ListBoxes`, `Images` and `Tables`. You also set the `Image` control's `BorderStyle` property to `Outset`, which gave the `Image` a raised appearance.

In the next tutorial, you will access the database, or information tier, of the application, which contains information about the books in the bookstore. You will use **Query Builder** to create the necessary SQL statements. You also will create a database connection and data command objects. After you have created these database components, Tutorial 31 will enable you to create the middle tier of the bookstore, which specifies the functionality of the ASPX pages.

SKILLS SUMMARY

Creating an ASP .NET Web Application

- Select **File > New > Project**.
- Select **Visual Basic Projects** in the left pane.
- Select the **ASP .NET Web Application** icon from the **Templates:** pane in the **New Project** dialog.
- Rename the application, and click **OK**.

Adding an ASPX Page to a Web Application

- Right click the project name in the **Solution Explorer**; then select **Add > Add New Item...** to display the **Add New Item** dialog.
- Select the **Web Form** icon in the **Templates:** box, and rename the ASPX page in the **Name:** TextBox.
- Click **Open** to add the new ASPX page to the Web Application.

Creating a `Table` Web Control

- Drag and drop the `Table` control from the **Web Forms** tab of the **Toolbox** onto the page.
- Click the ellipsis (**...**) `Button` in the **Rows** property of the **Properties** window.
- Click the **Add** `Button` to add rows to the `Table`.
- Click the ellipsis (**...**) `Button` in the **Cells** property of the **Properties** window within the **TableRow Collection Editor** dialog.
- Click the **Add** `Button` to add cells to the `TableRow`s.

Setting a Web Control's Location

- Switch to **HTML** mode.
- Use the LEFT: portion of the Web control's style attribute to specify the number of pixels that the Web control will be located from the left side of the Web page.
- Use the TOP: portion of the Web control's style attribute to specify the number of pixels that the Web control will be located from the top of the Web page.

Changing to Design **Mode**

- Click the **Design** mode `Button` beneath the ASPX page in the Web Form Designer.

Changing to HTML **Mode**

- Click the **HTML** mode `Button` beneath the ASPX page in the Web Form Designer.

KEY TERMS

`bgColor`—This property (of an ASPX page) specifies the page's background color.

`BorderStyle`—This property specifies the type of border that displays around an `Image`.

`BorderWidth`—This property specifies the border width of an `Image`.

Button Web control—This Web control allows users to perform an action.

`Cells`—This property allows programmers to create `TableCell`s in a `Table`.

Design mode—Displays the ASPX page's GUI at design time.

`ForeColor`—This property specifies font color for `Label` controls.

`Gridlines`—This property (of a `Table`) specifies whether `TableCell` cell borders display.

`Height`—This property allows you to specify the height of a Web control.

Horizontal Rule HTML control—This HTML control is used to display a line to separate controls on an ASPX page.

HTML mode—This mode displays the ASPX page's markup at design time.

`ID`—This property specifies the name of a Web control.

Image Web control—This Web control is used to display an image in an ASPX page.

Label Web control—This Web control is used to display text on an ASPX page.

ListBox Web control—This Web control is used to display a list of items.

`Rows`—This property allows programmers to create table rows.

`Size`—This property allows you to specify the size of a Web control.

`style`—This property allows you to specify the position of a Web control.

Table Web control—This Web control is used to display a table in an ASPX page.
Text—This property specifies the text that displays on a Web control.
Width—This property allows you to specify the width of a Web control.

CONTROLS, EVENTS, PROPERTIES & METHODS	**ASPX page** The page on which controls are dropped to design the GUI.

■ *Property*

bgColor—This property specifies the ASPX page's background color.

Button   This control allows the user to raise an action or
event.

■ *In action*

> View Information

■ *Properties*

ID—This property that specifies the name of the Label.
Text—This property specifies the text displayed on the Button.
Width—This property specifies the width of the Button.

Horizontal Rule   ☐ Horizontal Rule   This control displays a line on the ASPX page.
It is usually used to separate different areas of the ASPX page.

■ *In action*

――――――――――

■ *Properties*

id—This property specifies the name of the Horizontal Rule.
Style—This property allows you to specify where to position the Horizontal Rule on the
ASPX page.

Image   🖼 Image   This control displays an image on the ASPX page.

■ *In action*

■ *Properties*

BorderStyle—This property specifies the appearance of the Image's border.
BorderWidth—This property specifies the width of the Image's border.
Height—This property specifies the height of the Image control.
ID—This property specifies the name used to access the Image control programmatically.
The name should be prefixed with img.
Width—This property specifies the width of the Image control.

Label This control displays text on the ASPX page that the user cannot modify.

■ *In action*

Books

■ *Properties*

Height—This property specifies the height of the Label.

ID—This property specifies the name used to access the Label programmatically. The name should be prefixed with lbl.

Name (under the expanded Font property in the **Solution Explorer**)—This property specifies the name of the font used for the Label's text.

Size (under the expanded Font property in the **Solution Explorer**)—This property specifies the size of the Label's text.

Text—This property specifies the text displayed on the Label.

Width—This property specifies the width of the Label.

ListBox ListBox This control allows the user to view and select from multiple items in a list.

■ *In action*

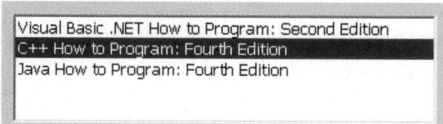

■ *Properties*

Height—This property specifies the height of the ListBox.

ID—This property specifies the name used to access the ListBox control programmatically. The name should be prefixed with lst.

Width—This property specifies the width of the ListBox.

Table Table This control is usually used to organize data in a spreadsheet format.

■ *In action*

Price:	$76.00
ISBN#:	0-13-029363-6
Edition:	2
Copyright Date:	2002
Description:	Microsoft Visual Basic .NET

■ *Properties*

BorderStyle—This property specifies the appearance of the Table's border.

BorderWidth—This property specifies the width of the Table's border.

Cells—This property retrieves or sets the value in the specified table cell.

Gridlines—This property specifies the format in which table cell separators are displayed.

ID—This property specifies the name used to access the Table control programmatically. The name should be prefixed with tbl.

Rows—This property retrieves or sets the value in the specified table cell.

MULTIPLE-CHOICE QUESTIONS

29.1 You change the _____ property of the ASPX page to specify the color that displays in the background of the page.

   a) BackColor

   b) bgColor

   c) BackgroundColor

   d) Color

29.2 Button, Label and Table controls for ASPX pages can be accessed from the _____ tab.

   a) **Web Forms**

   b) **Components**

   c) **Data**

   d) Both a and b.

29.3 The _____ attribute is used to specify the position of a Web control on an ASPX page.

   a) position

   b) location

   c) style

   d) coordinate

29.4 Unlike the Windows Form Designer, the Web Form Designer _____.

   a) does not provide two viewing modes

   b) provides two viewing modes

   c) allows you to design the graphical user interface

   d) does not allow you to design the user interface

29.5 The BorderStyle property of the Image control _____.

   a) specifies the color of the border

   b) specifies the type of border that displays around the Image control

   c) specifies the width of the border

   d) Both a and b.

29.6 Setting the BorderStyle property to OutSet makes a control appear _____.

   a) raised

   b) with a bold border

   c) with the specified border width

   d) with the specified border color

29.7 Every _____ of a Table Web control can contain one or more _____.

   a) TableRow; TableColumns

   b) TableColumn; TableRows

   c) TableRow; TableCells

   d) TableCell; TableRows

29.8 For you to be able to create an **ASP .NET Web** application project, _____ must be running.

   a) IIS

   b) Microsoft Access

   c) Microsoft Word

   d) Internet Explorer

29.9 The _____ mode allows you to create the ASPX page's GUI by dragging and dropping controls on the page.

   a) **HTML**

   b) **Design**

   c) **Visual**

   d) **GUI**

29.10 To specify the position of a Web control, set the _____ and _____ values of the _____ attribute.

   a) X, Y, style

   b) X, Y, position

   c) TOP, LEFT, style

   d) TOP, LEFT, position

EXERCISES

*[Note: In these exercises, we may ask you to set an ASPX page as the application's start page, meaning that this page will appear first when the application is run. You can set an ASPX page as the start page by right clicking the file in the **Solution Explorer** and selecting **Set As Start Page**.]*

29.11 (*Phone Book Application: GUI*) Create the user interface for the **Phone Book** application. The design for the two pages for this application is displayed in Fig. 29.25.

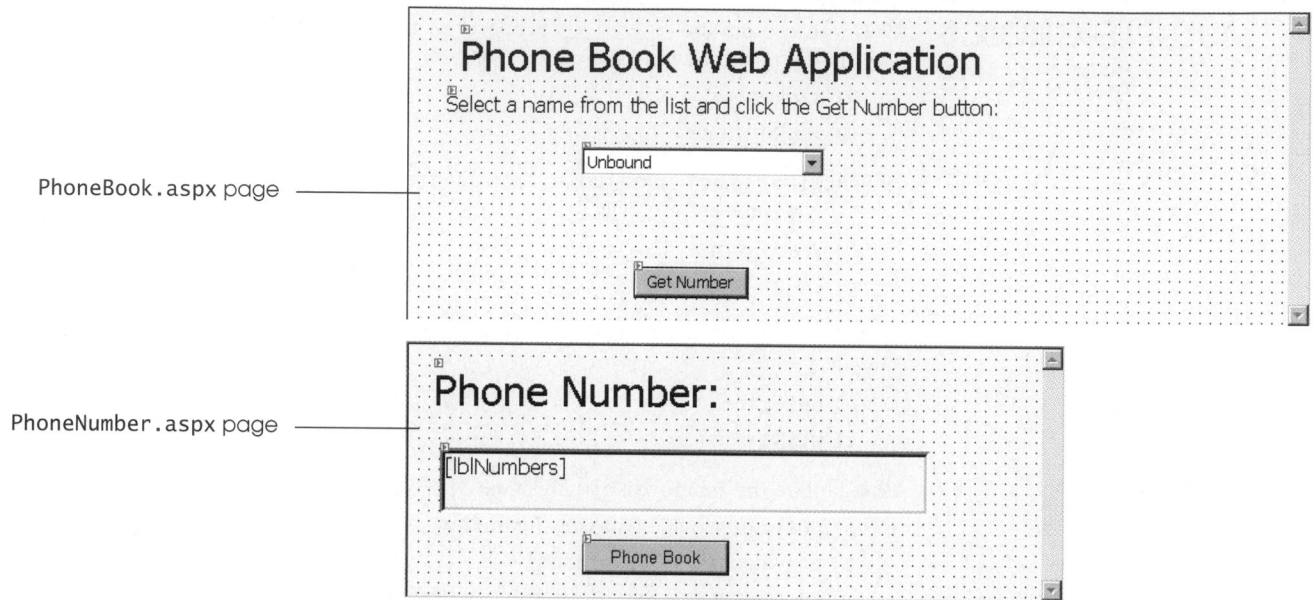

PhoneBook.aspx page

PhoneNumber.aspx page

Figure 29.25 **Phone Book** application ASPX pages' design.

a) *Creating an ASP .NET Web application*. Create an ASP .NET Web application project, and name it PhoneBook. Rename the ASPX page to PhoneBook.aspx, and set Option Strict to On. Set PhoneBook.aspx as the start page.

b) *Changing the background color*. Change the background color of your ASPX page (PhoneBook.aspx) to the light-yellow **Web Palette** color (located in the sixth column of the 12th row) by using the bgColor property as demonstrated in this tutorial. Change the title of the ASPX page to Phone Book.

c) *Adding a Label*. Create a Label, set the font size to X-Large and change the Text property to Phone Book Web Application. Set the LEFT: portion of the style attribute value to 40px and the TOP: portion to 17px. Name the control lblPhoneBook.

d) *Adding another Label*. Create another Label, and set the Text property to Select a name from the list and click the Get Number Button. Set the LEFT: portion of the style attribute value to 30px and the TOP: portion to 65px. Name this Web control lblInstructions.

e) *Adding a DropDownList Web control*. Create a DropDownList Web control by dragging and dropping it from the **Toolbox** onto the ASPX page. The DropDownList Web control looks similar to the ComboBox Windows Form control. Set the width to 190px, and set the LEFT: portion of the style attribute value to 134px and the TOP: portion to 108px. Name the DropDownList cboNames.

f) *Adding a Button*. Create a Button, set its width to 90px and change the Text property to Get Number. Set the LEFT: portion of the style attribute value to 175px and the TOP: portion to 200px. Name the Web control btnGet.

g) *Adding another ASPX page to the Phone Book application*. Add another ASPX page to the **Phone Book** application, name it PhoneNumber.aspx and change the background to the light-yellow color. Change the title property to Phone Number.

h) *Adding a Label to the PhoneNumber.aspx*. Create a Label and name it lblPhoneNumber. Set the font size to X-Large and change the Text property to Phone Number:. Set the LEFT: portion of the style attribute value to 20px and the TOP: portion to 15px.

i) *Adding another Label.* Create another Label, set its BorderStyle to Inset, and set its height and width to 50px and 380px, respectively. Clear the text of the Label. Name the Label lblNumbers, and set the LEFT: portion of the style attribute value to 25px and the TOP: portion to 80px.

j) *Adding a Button to the PhoneNumber.aspx page.* Create a Button, set its width to 115px and change the Text property to Phone Book. Set the LEFT: portion of the style attribute value to 135px and the TOP: portion to 150px. Name the Button btnPhoneBook.

k) *Saving the solution file.* Save the solution file to the PhoneBook folder located in the root directory of your Web server, as you did in *Step 8* of the box, *Creating an ASP .NET Web Application.*

29.12 (*US State Facts Application: GUI*) Create the user interface for the **US State Facts** application. The design for the two pages of this application is displayed in Fig. 29.26.

a) *Creating an ASP .NET Web application.* Create a new ASP .NET Web application project, and name it USStateFacts. Rename the first ASPX page to States.aspx, and set Option Strict to On. Set States.aspx as the start page.

b) *Changing the background color.* Change the background color of the States.aspx page to the light-blue **Web Palette** color (located in the sixth column of the second row) by using the bgColor property as demonstrated in this tutorial. Change the title property of the ASPX page to States.

c) *Adding a Label to States.aspx.* Create a Label Web control, and place it on the page. Set the font size to XX-Large, and change the Text property to States. Change the LEFT: portion of its style attribute value to 390px, and set the TOP: portion to 15px. Name the Web control lblStates.

d) *Adding a Horizontal Rule to States.aspx.* Create a Horizontal Rule, place it on the ASPX page and set its width to 150%. When setting its position, change the TOP: value to 80px, set the LEFT: value to 0px and specify the Height: as 4px. Name the Horizontal Rule hrzStates.

e) *Adding another Label to States.aspx.* Create another Label, and place it beneath the Horizontal Rule. Change the font size to Medium, and set the Text property to Select a state from the list and click the button to view facts about that state. Change the LEFT: portion of its style attribute value to 195px, and set the TOP: portion to 100px. Name this Web control lblInstructions.

f) *Adding a ListBox to States.aspx.* Create a ListBox, and place it on the ASPX page. Set its Height property to 100px and its Width property to 155px. Set the LEFT: portion of the style attribute value to 365px and the TOP: portion to 150px. Name the ListBox lstStates.

g) *Adding a Button to States.aspx.* Create a Button, and place it on the page. Set its Text property to Review Facts and its Width property to 130px. Change the LEFT: portion of the style attribute value to 375px and the TOP: portion to 270px. Name the Button btnFacts.

h) *Adding another ASPX page to the US State Facts application.* Add another ASPX page to the **US State Facts** application, name it StateFacts.aspx and change the background color to light blue.

i) *Adding a Label to StateFacts.aspx.* Create a Label, name it lblStateName, set its font size to XX-Large and change its ForeColor property to Blue. Clear the Label's text. Set its position by setting the LEFT: portion of the style attribute value to 20px and the TOP: portion to 15px.

j) *Adding a Horizontal Rule.* Place the Horizontal Rule beneath the Label and set its TOP: position to 90px, its LEFT: position to 0px and its Height: to 4px. Change the width to 150%. Name the Horizontal Rule hrzStateFacts.

k) *Adding an Image control to StateFacts.aspx.* Create an Image control and set its BorderStyle to Outset. Change the BorderWidth to 5px. Set its height to 200px and its width to 300px. Set the position of the Image by changing the LEFT: portion of the `style` attribute value to 20px and the TOP: portion to 110px. Name the Web control `imgFlag`.

l) *Adding a Table to StateFacts.aspx.* Create a Table with four rows and two columns. Set the `BorderStyle` to `Outset`, the `BorderWidth` to 5px and `GridLines` to `Both`. Set the height and width of each `TableCell` of the first column to 70px and 200px, respectively, and set the `Font` property's `Size` to `Large`. Set the `Text` property of the cells in the first column to `Capital:`, `Flower:`, `Tree:` and `Bird:`, respectively. Change the LEFT: portion of the `style` attribute value to 335px and the TOP: portion to 110px. Name the Table control `tblState`.

m) *Adding a Button to StateFacts.aspx.* Create a Button, change its text to `State List`, and change the LEFT: portion of the `style` attribute value to 285px and the TOP: portion to 425px. Name the Button control `btnStateList`.

n) *Saving the solution file.* Save the solution file to the `USStateFacts` folder located in the root directory of your Web server, as you did in *Step 8* of the box, *Creating an ASP .NET Web Application.*

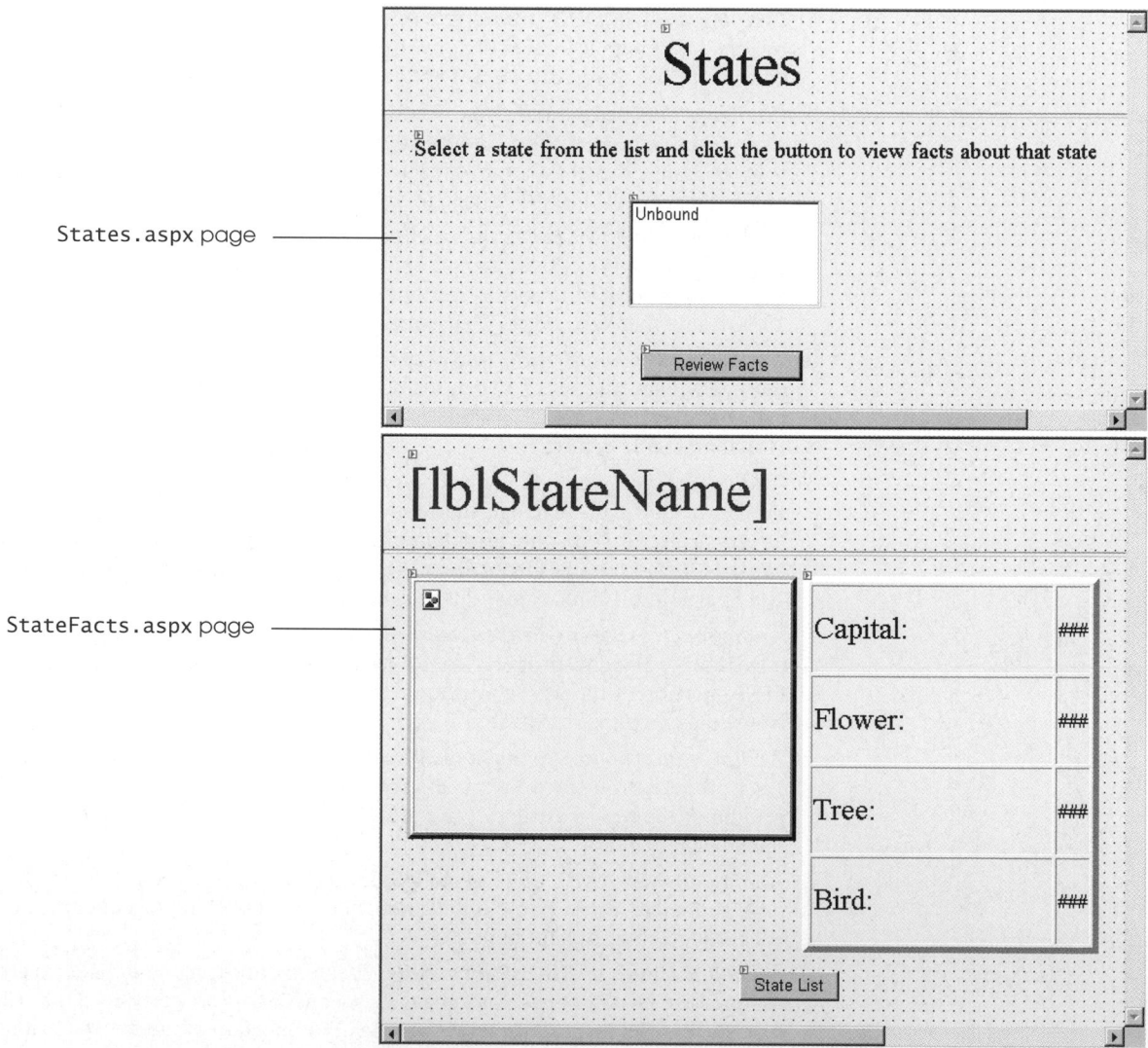

States.aspx page

StateFacts.aspx page

Figure 29.26 US State Facts application ASPX pages' design.

29.13 (*Road Sign Review Application: GUI*) Create the user interface for the **Road Sign Review** application. The design for the two pages of this application is displayed in Fig. 29.27.

a) *Creating an ASP .NET Web application.* Create a new ASP .NET Web application project, and name it `RoadSignReview`. Change the name of the existing ASPX page to `RoadSigns.aspx`, and set `Option Strict` to `On`. Set `RoadSigns.aspx` as the start page.

b) ***Changing the background color.*** Change the background color of RoadSigns.aspx to the light-green **Web Palette** color (located in the sixth column of the 14th row) by using the bgColor property as demonstrated in this tutorial. Change the title of the ASPX page to RoadSigns.

c) ***Adding a Label to RoadSigns.aspx.*** Create a Label, and set its font size to XX-Large. Change the Text property to Road Signs. Set its position by changing the style attribute value's LEFT: portion to 295px and the TOP: portion to 16px. Name the Label control lblRoadSigns.

d) ***Adding a Horizontal Rule to RoadSigns.aspx.*** Create a Horizontal Rule. Set its width to 150%, and set the TOP: position to 80px, the LEFT: position to 0px and the height to 4px. Name the Horizontal Rule hrzRoadSigns.

e) ***Adding a Table to RoadSigns.aspx.*** Create a Table with three rows and five columns. Set the BorderStyle to Outset, the BorderWidth to 5px and the GridLines property to Both. Also, set the Table's Height property to 279px and Width property to 626px. Set each row's height to 50px and each TableCell's width to 20px. Change the style attribute value by setting LEFT: to 70px and TOP: to 150px. Name the Table control tblRoadSigns.

f) ***Adding a Label to RoadSigns.aspx.*** Create a Label, and set its font size to Large. Change the Text property to Register for Your Driving Test. Set its position by changing the style attribute value's LEFT: portion to 70px and TOP: portion to 470px. Name the Web control lblRegister.

g) ***Adding a Label and TextBox to RoadSigns.aspx.*** Create a Label and set its text to Name:. Set its font size to Medium, and change its position to LEFT: 70px and TOP: 520px. Name the Label control lblName. Create a TextBox, and place it next to the **Name:** Label. Set its height to 20px and width to 115px. Change the position to LEFT: 135px and TOP: 520px. Name the TextBox control txtName.

h) ***Adding another Label and TextBox pair to RoadSigns.aspx.*** Create a Label and set its text to Phone Number:. Set its font size to Medium, and change its position to LEFT: 275px and TOP: 520px. Name the Label control lblPhoneNumber. Create a TextBox, and place it next to the **Phone Number:** Label. Set its height to 20px and width to 115px. Change its position to LEFT: 410px and TOP: 520px. Name the TextBox control txtPhoneNumber.

i) ***Adding a Button to RoadSigns.aspx.*** Create a Button, set its Text to Register, and change its height and width to 30px and 120px, respectively. Change the position of the Button by setting the LEFT: portion of the style attribute value to 555px and the TOP: portion to 520px. Name the Button control btnRegister.

j) ***Adding another ASPX page to the Road Sign Review application.*** Add another ASPX page to the application, name it RoadTestRegistered.aspx and change the background color to light green.

k) ***Adding a Label to RoadTestRegistered.aspx.*** Create a Label, setting its font size to XX-Large and its Text property to Registration Complete. Change its position by setting the LEFT: portion of its style attribute value to 200px and the TOP: portion to 15px. Name the Label control lblRegistration.

l) ***Adding a Horizontal Rule to RoadTestRegistered.aspx.*** Create a Horizontal Rule. Set its width to 150%, the TOP: position to 80px, the LEFT: position to 0px and the height to 4px. Name the Horizontal Rule hrzRoadTestRegistered.

m) ***Adding another Label to RoadTestRegistered.aspx.*** Create a Label, name it lblConfirmation and set its font size to Medium. Delete the Text property value, and leave it blank. Change its position by setting the LEFT: portion of its style attribute value to 125px and the TOP: portion to 130px.

n) ***Saving the solution file.*** Save the solution file to the RoadSignReview folder located in the root directory of your Web server, as you did in *Step 8* of the box, *Creating an ASP .NET Web Application.*

RoadSigns.aspx page

RoadTestRegistered.aspx page

Figure 29.27 **Road Signs** application ASPX pages' design.

Objectives

In this tutorial, you will learn to:
- Connect to a database.
- Create SQL statements that retrieve information from a database, using the **Query Builder** tool.

Outline

30.1 Reviewing the Bookstore Application

30.2 Information Tier: Database

30.3 Using the **Server Explorer** and **Query Builder** in ASPX Pages

30.4 Wrap-Up

Bookstore Application: Information Tier

Examining the Database and Creating Database Components

This tutorial focuses on the Web application's information tier, where the application's data resides. In your **Bookstore** application, the information tier is represented by a Microsoft Access database, db_bookstore.mdb, that stores each book's information. Before you begin this tutorial, you should be familiar with the database concepts presented in Tutorial 25.

In this tutorial, you will create the objects that your application will need to connect to the database. You also will define the SQL statements that will retrieve data from that database. Actually, the information tier consists solely of the db_bookstore.mdb database. The connection objects and data command objects created in this tutorial are actually part of the middle tier, as they perform the functionality of retrieving data from the database. You create these objects here because they interact with the information tier and do not require any programming. You will complete the **Bookstore** application by creating the middle tier in the next tutorial.

30.1 Reviewing the Bookstore Application

You have taken the three-tier **Bookstore** application for a test-drive (in Tutorial 28) and have designed the GUI by using Web controls and an HTML control. Now you are ready to create the database components for the application. Before you begin, you should review the pseudocode and the ACE table (Fig. 30.1) for this application:

> If the Books page is requested
> > Retrieve the book titles from the database
> > Display book titles in a ListBox
>
> If the user selects a book title from the ListBox and clicks the View Information Button
> > Store the selected book in a variable
> > Redirect the user to the BookInformation page
> > Retrieve the selected book's information from a database
> > Display the retrieved information in a Table on the BookInformation page

If the user presses the Book List Button on the BookInformation page
Redirect the client browser back to the Books page

Action	Control/Object	Event
Label the Books page	`lblAvailable, lblInstructions`	
When the Books page loads, retrieve the book titles from the database and display them in the ListBox	`Books.aspx, objOleDbConnection, objSelectTitles, lstBookTitles`	`Load` (of Page)
Redirect the client browser to the BookInformation page	`btnInformation`	`Click`
When the BookInformation page loads, retrieve the selected book's information from the database and display in a Table	`BookInforma-tion.aspx, objOleDbConnection, objSelectBookData, lblBookTitle, lblAuthors, imgBook, tblBook`	`Load` (of Page)
Redirect the client browser back to the Books page	`btnBookList`	`Click`

Figure 30.1   ACE table for the Web-based **Bookstore** application.

In this tutorial, you will be creating the objects that are used to retrieve information from the database, including the objects that connect to the database and the objects that execute the command statements.

30.2 Information Tier: Database

The information tier maintains all of the data needed for an application. The database that stores this data might contain product data, such as a description, price and quantity in stock, and customer data, such as a user name and shipping information.

Databases are an integral part of real-world applications, because they provide the ability to update data in **real time**. As soon as a piece of data is entered into the database, it is accessible to users and applications with the proper authorization. Because data is stored electronically, it can be accessed and manipulated much faster than paper copies. Most databases are relational databases—databases where the data is organized in tables. A variety of database products (used to build and modify databases) from Microsoft and other vendors exist, ranging from personal products like Microsoft Access to enterprise products such as Oracle, Sybase and Microsoft SQL Server 2000. Database products also can be used to generate reports from information in a database.

The **Bookstore** application stores the books' data in a Microsoft Access database (`db_bookstore.mdb`). This data is retrieved from the database by using Visual Basic .NET code and ADO .NET objects. The database contains one table, named `Products`, that stores each book's information.

The `Products` table contains nine fields (columns): `productID`, `title`, `authors`, `copyrightDate`, `edition`, `isbn`, `coverart`, `description` and `price`. These fields contain an ID number, the title, authors, copyright date, edition number, ISBN number (a unique number used to reference a book), image name, description and price of each book, respectively. Figure 30.2 displays the `Products` table of `db_bookstore.mdb`, using the **Server Explorer** window.

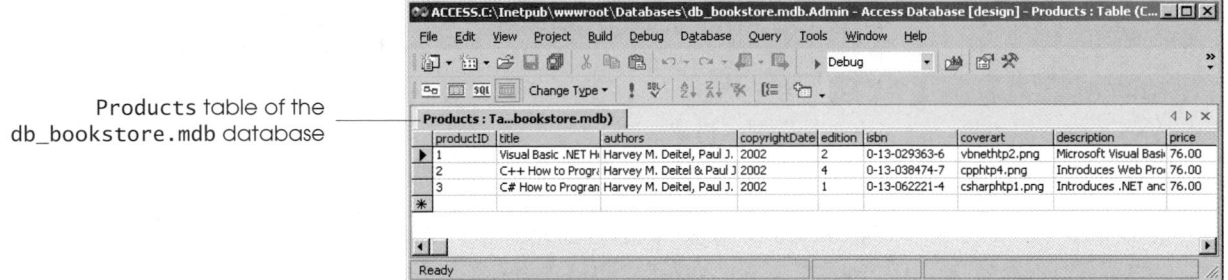

Figure 30.2   Products table of the db_bookstore.mdb database.

SELF-REVIEW

1. Once data is entered into a database, _____.

    a) the data is immediately accessible to users and applications

    b) users must wait until the system reboots in order to access the data

    c) all applications using the database must manually be updated

    d) None of the above.

2. Databases are an integral part of real-world applications because they provide the ability to _____.

    a) store information that cannot be altered

    b) update data in real time

    c) execute applications   d) None of the above.

Answers: 1) a. 2) b.

30.3 Using the Server Explorer and Query Builder in ASPX Pages

Before you begin programming this application's middle tier, you must set up the database connections that retrieve data from the database. Recall that you used the **Server Explorer** window and the **Query Builder** tool in Tutorial 25. You will use these IDE features again to create a database connection and to generate SQL statements to request book information. You add the database connection and data command objects in the box, *Adding Database Components to the Books Page.*

Adding Database Components to the Books Page

1. *Starting IIS.* Make sure that IIS is running for the **Default Web Site**. If it is not running, start it in the **Internet Information Services** dialog, by selecting **Default Web Site** in the left pane and clicking the Start Item Button.

2. *Opening the Bookstore application in Visual Studio .NET.* In Windows Explorer, double click the Bookstore.sln file in the Bookstore folder located in the wwwroot folder in order to open the **Bookstore** application in Visual Studio .NET.

3. *Using the Server Explorer window to add a connection to the database.* You must set up a connection to the database before accessing its data. You will use ADO .NET objects to accomplish this task. This connection will allow you to read information about a book from the database. Select **View > Server Explorer** to display the **Server Explorer** window. Click the Connect to Database icon (Fig. 30.3) to display the **Data Link Properties** dialog.

4. *Specifying provider settings.* You now need to specify the provider of the database software you are using. Click the **Provider** tab to display a list of providers. Because you are using a Microsoft Access database, select the **Microsoft Jet 4.0 OLE DB Provider**, and click the **Next >>** Button (Fig. 30.4). [*Note:* The number of items and the names of the **OLE DB Provider(s)** displayed in the **Provider** tab may be different on your system.]

(cont.)

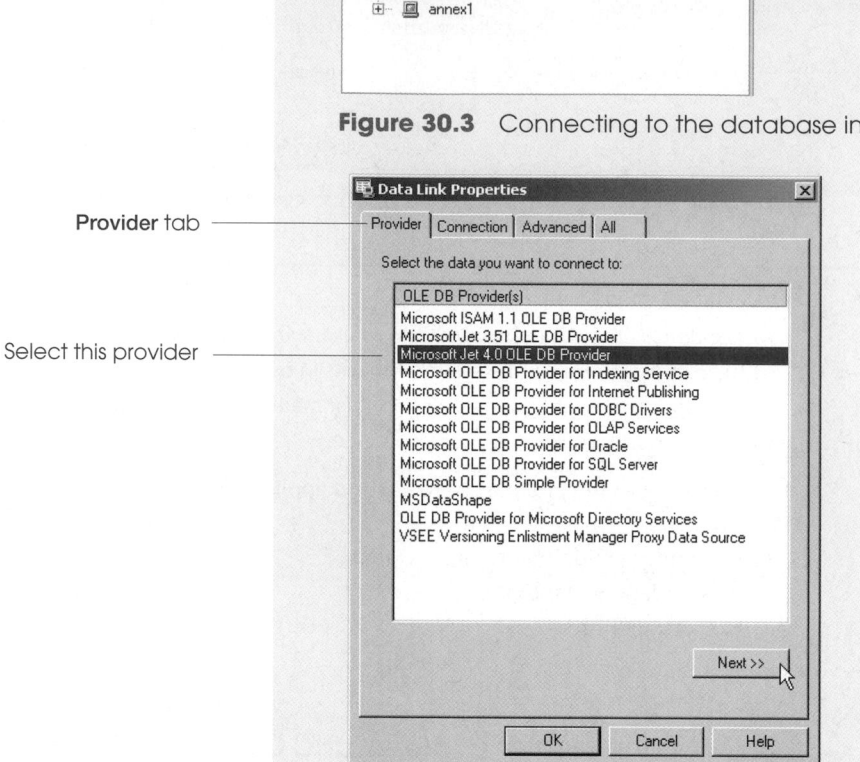

Connect to Database icon

Figure 30.3 Connecting to the database in the **Server Explorer** window.

Provider tab

Select this provider

Figure 30.4 **Data Link Properties** dialog's **Provider** tab.

5. *Specifying connection settings.* When you click the **Next >>** Button, the **Connection** tab (Fig. 30.5) of the **Data Link Properties** dialog is displayed. You are now ready to specify `db_bookstore.mdb` as the database. Click the ellipsis (...) Button next to the **Select or enter a database name:** TextBox.

Connection tab

Click ellipsis Button to select the database

Figure 30.5 **Data Link Properties** dialog's **Connection** tab.

(cont.)   The **Select Access Database** dialog appears as in Fig. 30.6. Locate
db_bookstore.mdb in the C:\InetPub\wwwroot\Databases folder, and
click **Open**.

Select **db_bookstore.mdb**
database (This may display as
db_bookstore, depending on
your Windows settings)

Figure 30.6   **Select Access Database** dialog.

6. ***Testing the connection***. Before proceeding to the next step, you will want to
    ensure that the connection is set up properly. The path of the database should
    now display in the **Select or enter a database name:** TextBox (Fig. 30.7).
    The database that you will be using does not require a password in order to
    access its information. Make sure the **Blank password** CheckBox, under the
    Enter information to log on to the database: section, is checked. Click the
    Test Connection Button to test the database connection. The **Microsoft
    Data Link** dialog should appear, confirming a successful connection. If the
    connection failed, you should make sure you followed all the instructions
    from *Step 2–5* in this box. Click **OK** to close the **Microsoft Data Link** dialog.
    Click **OK** in the **Data Link Properties** dialog. The db_bookstore.mdb con-
    nection has now been added to the **Server Explorer** window.

Location of database

Click to test connection

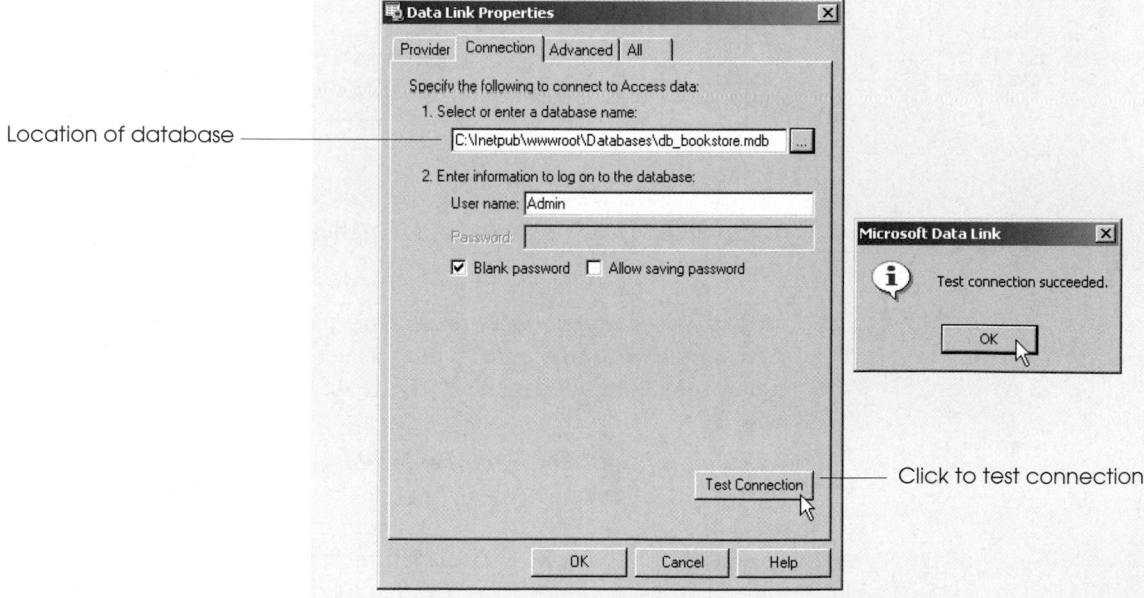

Figure 30.7   Testing the database connection.

(cont.)

7. *Adding a data connection object to the ASPX page.* Double click `Books.aspx` in the **Solution Explorer** window to display the `Books.aspx` page. From the **Server Explorer** window, drag and drop the db_book-store.mdb connection node onto the `Books.aspx` page. An `OleDbConnection` object appears in the component tray. Rename the connection object `objOleDbConnection`. Recall that a connection object is used to maintain a connection to the database.

8. *Adding a data command object to the ASPX page.* From the **Data** tab of the **Toolbox**, drag and drop an `OleDbCommand` object on the ASPX page. Recall that the `OleDbCommand` object allows you to specify SQL statements to retrieve information from the database. Rename the `OleDbCommand` object to `objSelectTitles`. Set the `Connection` property of the data command object to the connection object you created for this page, `objOleDbConnection`. To do this, click the down-arrow `Button` that appears next to the `Connection` property field. Expand the **Existing** node and select the name of the connection object (`objOleDbConnection`) that you created in *Step* 6. You are now ready to create the SQL statements that will retrieve data from the database. Select the `CommandText` property, and click the ellipsis (...) `Button` that appears next to the `CommandText` field. The **Query Builder** and **Add Table** dialogs appear (Fig. 30.8).

Figure 30.8 **Query Builder** and **Add Table** dialogs for the **Bookstore** application.

9. *Adding the Products table to the Query Builder dialog.* Before you can use the **Query Builder** dialog, you must select a database table. In the **Add Table** dialog, select `Products`, and click the **Add** `Button`. Click **Close** to close the **Add Table** dialog.

10. *Selecting information from the database.* You are ready to retrieve the values from the `title` field of the `Products` table. In the **Query Builder** dialog, check the `title` CheckBox in the `Products` window. Your SELECT statement should look like the one displayed in Fig. 30.9. This statement will retrieve the `title` field values from the `Products` table of the database. You will later use this information to populate the `ListBox` in the `Books.aspx` page. Click **OK** to close the **Query Builder** dialog.

11. *Saving the project.* Select **File > Save All** to save all the solution's files.

(cont.)

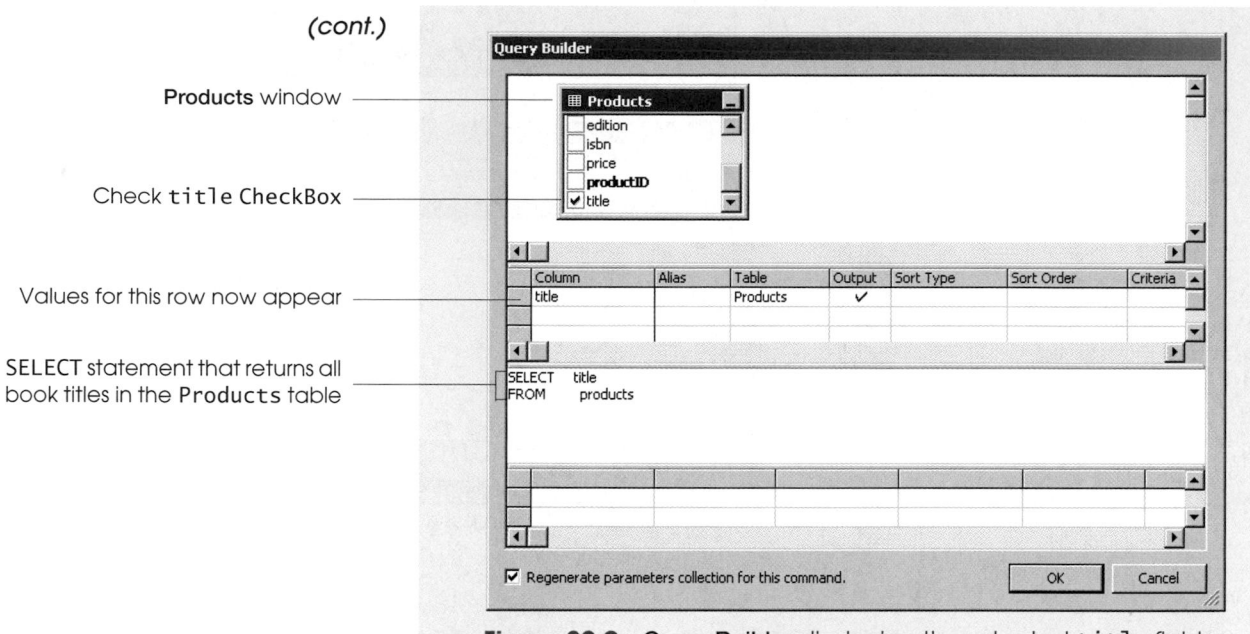

Products window ——

Check `title` CheckBox ——

Values for this row now appear ——

SELECT statement that returns all book titles in the `Products` table ——

Figure 30.9   **Query Builder** displaying the selected `title` field.

Now that you have added database connection and command objects to the `Books.aspx` page, you will do the same for the `BookInformation.aspx` page. The `CommandText` property for the data command object of this page will differ from that of the `Books.aspx` page. In the `BookInformation.aspx` page, you will use the `Parameters` property of the data command object because you do not yet know which record to retrieve—this will be determined when the user selects a book. You will specify the record in the middle tier of the application, which you program in Tutorial 31. For now you will set the database connections and data command objects in the box, *Adding Database Components to the* `BookInformation` *Page*.

Adding Database Components to the `BookInformation` *Page*	1. ***Adding a data connection object to the ASPX page***. From the **Server Explorer** window, drag and drop the db_bookstore.mdb connection node onto the `BookInformation.aspx` page. An `OleDbConnection` object appears in the component tray. Rename the connection object to `objOleDb-Connection`. 2. ***Adding a data command object to the ASPX page***. From the **Data** tab of the **Toolbox**, drag and drop an `OleDbCommand` object on the ASPX page. Rename the `OleDbCommand` object to `objSelectBookData`. Set the `Connection` property of the data command object to the connection object you created for this page, `objOleDbConnection`. Select the `CommandText` property, and click the ellipsis (...) `Button` that appears next to the `CommandText` field. The **Query Builder** and **Add Table** dialogs appear (Fig. 30.10). 3. ***Adding the Products table***. In the **Add Table** dialog, select `Products`, and click the **Add** `Button`. Click **Close** to close the **Add Table** dialog. 4. ***Selecting the fields to retrieve from the database***. Check the `authors`, `coverart`, `description`, `edition`, `isbn`, `price`, `copyrightDate` and `title` CheckBoxes in the `Products` window of the **Query Builder** dialog. Notice that the field names appear after the SELECT keyword in the SELECT statement as well as in the table beneath the `Products` window (Fig. 30.11).

(cont.)

Add Table dialog

Add this table

Figure 30.10   **Query Builder** and **Add Table** dialogs.

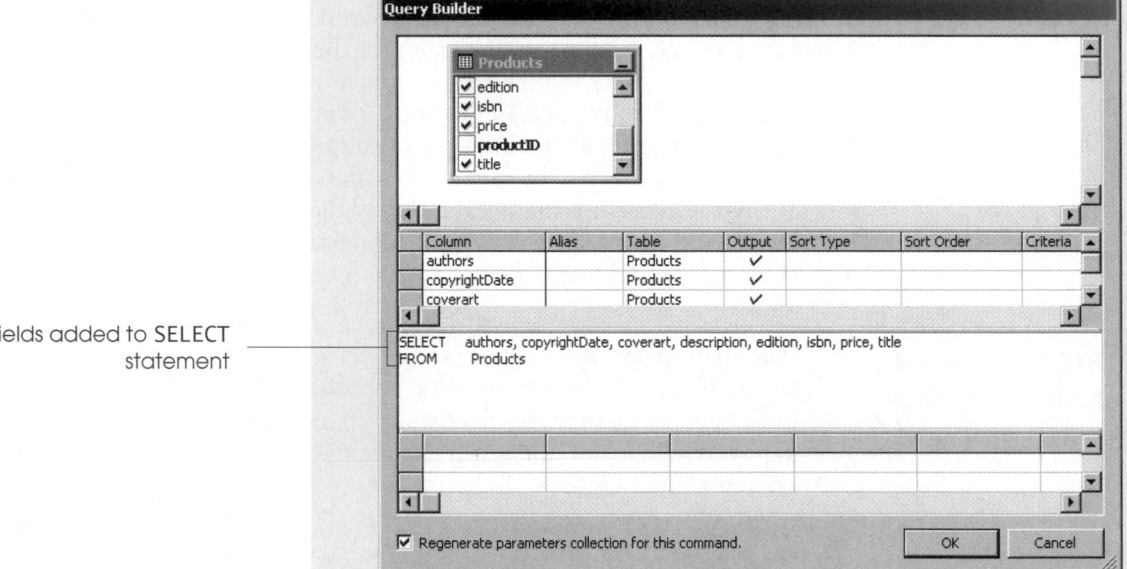

Fields added to SELECT statement

Figure 30.11   Adding fields to the SELECT statement.

5. ***Specifying the record from which information will be retrieved.*** In the table beneath the Products window, type =? in the **Criteria** field of the title row (Fig. 30.12) to indicate that you do not know the record from which the information will be retrieved. Recall that a funnel will appear to the right of the **title** CheckBox, which indicates that a value will be retrieved from the field (title) according to specified criteria.

6. ***Completing the SELECT statement.*** Click the check in the **Output** column of the title row to remove the title field name from the SELECT portion of the SQL statement. You do this step because you do not want to retrieve the title information—the title is used only to locate the appropriate record. The complete SELECT statement should look like the one in Fig. 30.13. Click **OK**. The **Microsoft Development Environment** dialog (Fig. 30.14) appears, asking if you want to apply a new parameter configuration. Click the **Yes** Button to create a title parameter.

(cont.)

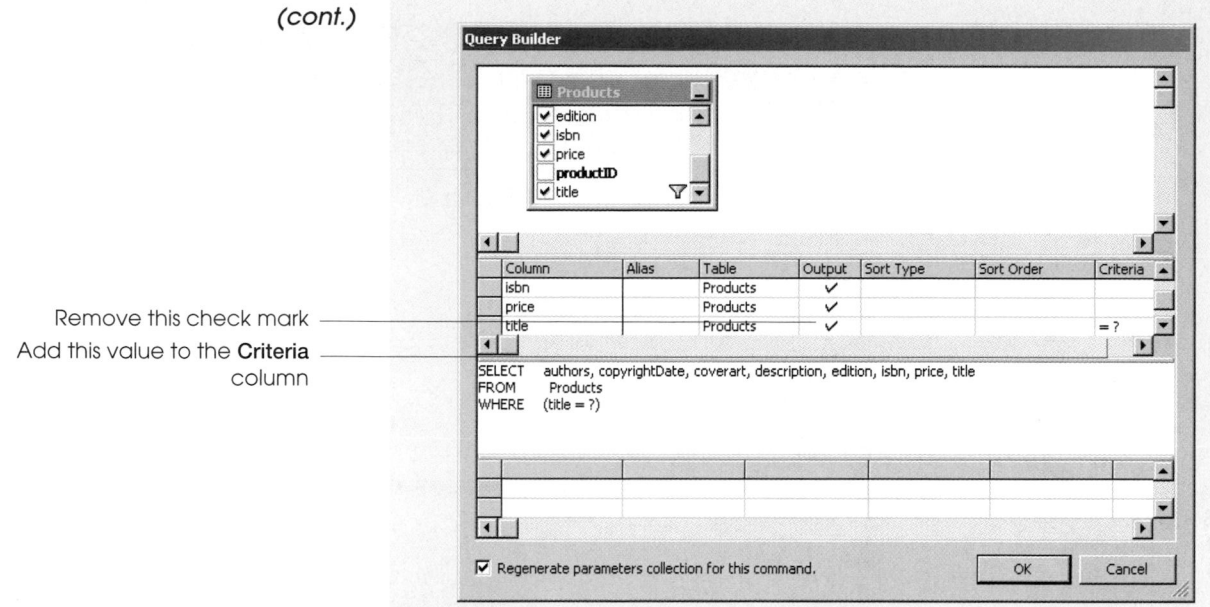

Remove this check mark ⎯⎯⎯⎯

Add this value to the **Criteria** ⎯⎯⎯⎯
column

Figure 30.12 Specifying **Criteria** value for the `title` row.

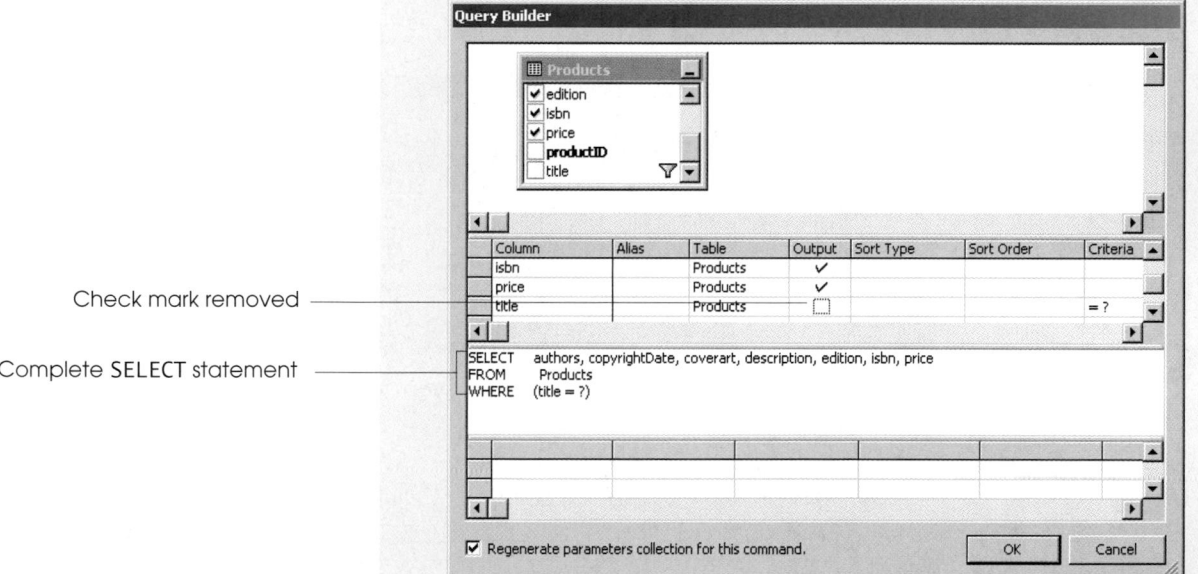

Check mark removed ⎯⎯⎯⎯

Complete **SELECT** statement ⎯⎯⎯⎯

Figure 30.13 Removing the `title` field from the SELECT portion of the SQL statement.

7. ***Viewing the Parameters collection property.*** You will use the `title` parameter you created in *Step* 5 of this box in the next tutorial to specify the record from which you will retrieve information. In this step, you will verify that the parameter was created correctly. Select the `Parameters` property in the **Properties** window of `objSelectBookData`. Click the ellipsis (…) `Button` that appears next to the `Parameters` (Fig. 30.15) field to view the collection of parameters. The **OleDbParameter Collection Editor** dialog appears (Fig. 30.16). This dialog displays the parameters of the data command object. Notice that there is only one parameter, named `title`. Click **OK** to close the dialog.

(cont.)

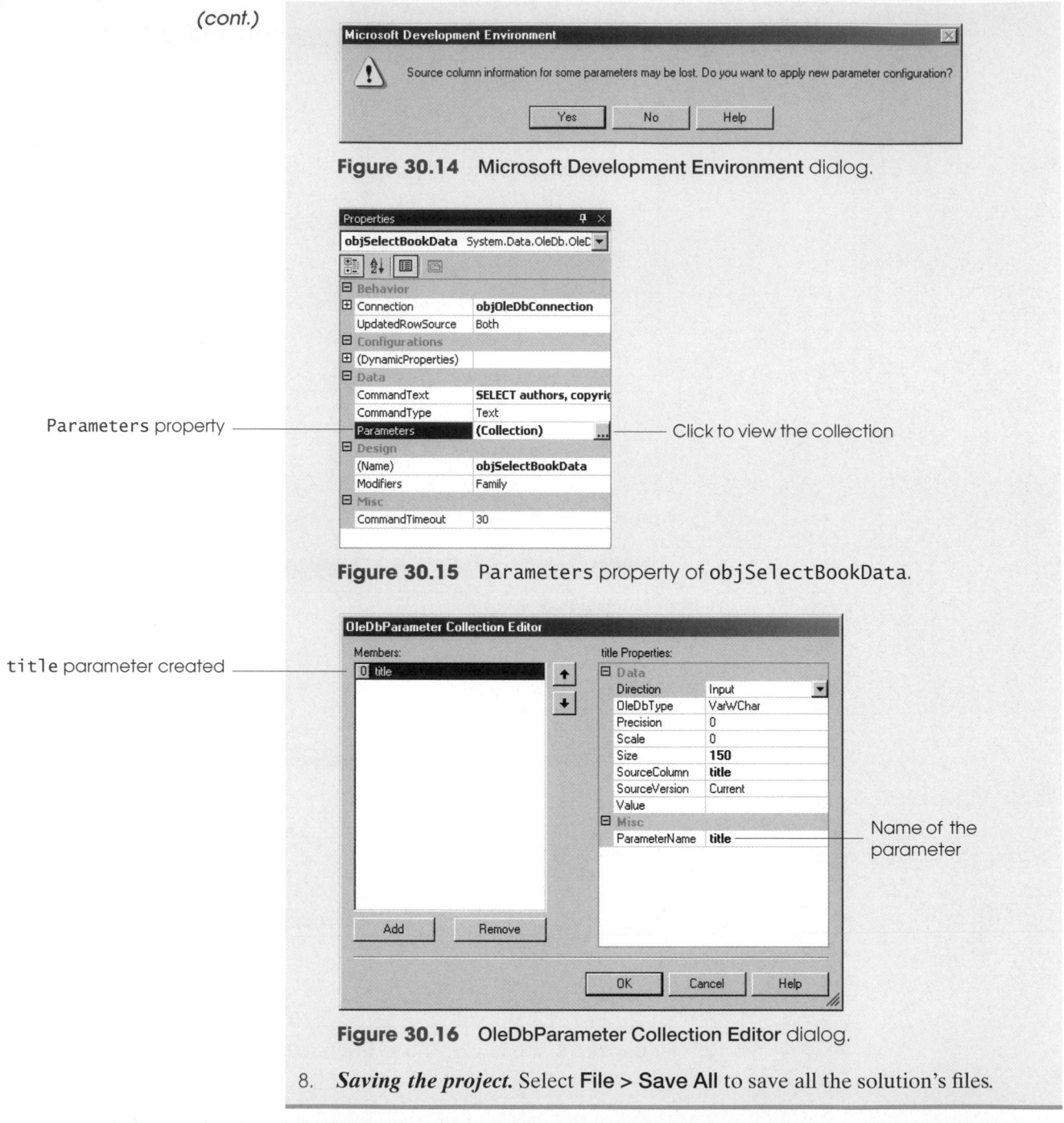

Figure 30.14 Microsoft Development Environment dialog.

Parameters property ——— Click to view the collection

Figure 30.15 Parameters property of objSelectBookData.

title parameter created ———

Name of the parameter

Figure 30.16 OleDbParameter Collection Editor dialog.

8. ***Saving the project.*** Select **File > Save All** to save all the solution's files.

SELF-REVIEW

1. The _____ dialog allows you to select a database table to add to the **Query Builder** dialog.

   a) **Add Table**   b) **Database**

   c) **Database Table**   d) **Data Link Properties**

2. Clicking **Yes** in the **Microsoft Development Environment** dialog after using **Query Builder** _____.

   a) creates the OleDbCommand object   b) creates the SQL statement

   c) creates parameter items in the   d) None of the above.
       Parameters property

Answers: 1) a. 2) c.

30.4 Wrap-Up

In this tutorial, you were introduced to the information tier of the three-tier, Web-based **Bookstore** application. You examined the contents of the db_bookstore.mdb database. You accessed the information tier of the **Bookstore** application by creating database connection objects and data command objects. You used the **Server Explorer** window and the **Query Builder** tool to add a database connection to your ASPX pages and to create SQL statements for the data command objects, respectively. In creating the OleDbCommand object for the BookInformation.aspx page, you used the Parameters property, because you did not know the title of the book for which you would be retrieving information. You will specify the value of this parameter when you program the middle tier.

In the next tutorial, you will create the middle tier of your **Bookstore** application. You will add code to your application to control what data from the database will be displayed on the ASPX page.

SKILLS SUMMARY

Adding a Database Connection Using the Server Explorer Window

- Click the Connect to Database icon to display the **Data Link Properties** dialog.
- Click the **Provider** tab in the **Data Link Properties** dialog.
- Select **Microsoft Jet 4.0 OLE DB Provider** in the **OLE DB Provider(s)** box.
- Click **Next**; then click the ellipsis (...) Button next to the **Select or enter a database name:** field.
- Choose the desired database, and click **Open**.
- Place a checkmark in the **Blank password** CheckBox.
- Click the **Test Connection** Button. Click **OK** in the dialog that appears; then click **OK** in the **Data Link Properties** dialog.

Adding a Connection Object to the ASPX Page

- Select the desired database connection in the **Server Explorer** window.
- Drag and drop the connection onto the ASPX page.

Adding a Data Command to the ASPX Page to Select Information

- Select the OleDbCommand icon from the **Data** tab in the **Toolbox**.
- Drag and drop the icon onto the ASPX page.
- Select the Connection property in the **Properties** window, and specify the name of the connection object created previously.
- Select the CommandText property, and click the ellipsis Button to access the **Query Builder** tool.
- Add a table to the **Query Builder** dialog by using the **Add Table** dialog.
- Check desired-field CheckBoxes, and use the **Criteria** columns if necessary.

MULTIPLE-CHOICE QUESTIONS

30.1 _____ is an example of a database product.

   a) Microsoft Access   b) Microsoft SQL Server

   c) Oracle   d) All of the above.

30.2 An advantage of using information in a database is that _____.

   a) the data can be updated in real time

   b) information that changes need be updated only in one location

   c) Both a and b.

   d) None of the above.

30.3 When a funnel appears to the right of a field's CheckBox in the **Query Builder** dialog, it indicates that _____.

   a) information will be updated in the specified field

b) a value will be retrieved from that field according to specified criteria

c) the field will not be included in the SQL statement

d) None of the above.

30.4 The Parameters property of _____ contains a collection of parameters.

a) OleDbConnection

b) OleDbDataConnection

c) OleDbDataCommand

d) OleDbCommand

30.5 The _____ can be used to create an OleDbConnection.

a) **Server Explorer** window

b) **Query Builder** tool

c) Both a and b.

d) None of the above.

30.6 You use the _____ object to create SQL statements for retrieving data from a database.

a) OleDbConnection

b) OleDbDataReader

c) OleDbCommand

d) None of the above.

30.7 The _____ is used when creating SQL statements visually for the OleDbCommand object's CommandText property.

a) **Server Explorer** window

b) **Query Builder** tool

c) Both a and b.

d) None of the above.

30.8 You use the _____ object to open a connection to the database.

a) OleDbConnection

b) OleDbDataReader

c) OleDbCommand

d) None of the above.

30.9 You use the _____ property of the OleDbCommand object to specify values for information that is not known in advance.

a) Connection

b) Parameters

c) Field

d) Name

30.10 Another name for the database tier is _____.

a) the information tier

b) the bottom tier

c) Both a and b.

d) None of the above.

EXERCISES

30.11 (*Phone Book Application: Database*) Create the database connections and data command objects for the **PhoneBook** application by using the **Server Explorer** window and the **Query Builder** tool.

a) *Opening the application*. Open the **PhoneBook** application that you created in Tutorial 29.

b) *Copying the db_Phone.mdb database to the Databases folder*. Copy C:\Examples\ Tutorial30\Exercises\Databases\db_Phone.mdb to the Databases folder in IIS's wwwroot folder.

c) *Using Server Explorer to add a connection to the database*. In the **Server Explorer** window, add a connection to the db_Phone.mdb database. Drag and drop the connection object onto the PhoneBook.aspx page. Name the connection object objOleDbConnection.

d) *Using Query Builder for the PhoneBook.aspx page*. Add an OleDbCommand to the PhoneBook.aspx page. Set the Connection property to the OleDbConnection object you added to the ASPX page, and use **Query Builder** to set the CommandText property of the OleDbCommand. This command should retrieve all the names of the people from the database. Name this command object objSelectNames.

e) *Adding a connection to the database to the PhoneNumber.aspx page*. Using the **Server Explorer** window, drag and drop a database connection object onto the PhoneNumber.aspx page. Name this connection object objOleDbConnection.

f) *Using Query Builder for PhoneBook.aspx*. Add an OleDbCommand to the PhoneNumber.aspx page. Set the Connection property to the OleDbConnection object you added to the ASPX page, and use **Query Builder** to set the `CommandText` property of the `OleDbCommand`. This configuration should retrieve the phone number of the person whose name will be selected, from the `DropDownList` in the `PhoneBook.aspx` page, by the user. You need to set the criteria to specify which person's phone number will be retrieved from the database. Name this command object `objSelectPhoneNumber`.

g) *Saving the solution.* Select **File > Save All** to save the solution's files.

30.12 (*US State Facts Application: Database*) Create the database connections and data command objects for the **USStateFacts** application by using the **Server Explorer** window and the **Query Builder** tool.

a) *Opening the application.* Open the **USStateFacts** application that you created in Tutorial 29.

b) *Copying the db_StateFacts.mdb database to the Databases folder.* Copy the `C:\Examples\Tutorial30\Exercises\Databases\db_StateFacts.mdb` database to the Databases folder in IIS's wwwroot folder.

c) *Using Server Explorer to add a connection to the database.* In the **Server Explorer** window, add a connection to the db_StateFacts.mdb database. Drag-and-drop the connection object onto the States.aspx page. Name this connection object `objOleDbConnection`.

d) *Using Query Builder for the States.aspx page.* Add an `OleDbCommand` to the States.aspx page. Set the `Connection` property to the `OleDbConnection` object you added to the ASPX page and use **Query Builder** to set the `CommandText` property of the `OleDbCommand`. This command should retrieve the names of the states from the **name** field of the states table in the database. Name this command object `objSelectNames`.

e) *Adding a connection to the database to the StateFacts.aspx page.* Using the **Server Explorer** window, drag-and-drop a database connection object onto the database on the StateFacts.aspx page. Name this connection object `objOleDbConnection`.

f) *Using Query Builder for StateFacts.aspx.* Add an `OleDbCommand` to the StateFacts.aspx page. Set the `Connection` property to the `OleDbConnection` object you added to the ASPX page, and use **Query Builder** to set the `CommandText` property of the `OleDbCommand`. This configuration should retrieve all the information, from the states table of the database, about the state that is selected by the user. You need to set the criteria to specify which state's information will be retrieved from the database. Name this command object `objSelectStateInformation`.

g) *Saving the solution.* Select **File > Save All** to save the solution's files.

30.13 (*Road Sign Review Application: Database*) Create the database connections and data command objects for the **RoadSignReview** application by using the **Server Explorer** window and the **Query Builder** tool.

a) *Opening the application.* Open the **RoadSignReview** application that you created in Tutorial 29.

b) *Copying the db_RoadSigns.mdb database to the Databases folder.* Copy the `C:\Examples\Tutorial30\Exercises\Databases\db_RoadSigns.mdb` database to the Databases folder in IIS's wwwroot folder.

c) *Using Server Explorer to add a connection to the database.* In the **Server Explorer** window add a connection to the db_RoadSigns.mdb database. Drag and drop the connection object onto the RoadSigns.aspx page. Name this command object `objOleDbConnection`.

d) *Using Query Builder for the RoadSigns.aspx page.* Add an `OleDbCommand` to the RoadSigns.aspx page. Set the `Connection` property to the `OleDbConnection` object that you added to the ASPX page, and use **Query Builder** to set the `CommandText` property of the `OleDbCommand`. This configuration should retrieve all the information about all the road signs from the signs table of the database. You will not need to specify a criterion for this exercise, because all the information from the database needs to be retrieved. Name this command object `objSelectSignInformation`.

e) *Saving the solution.* Select **File > Save All** to save the solution's files.

T U T O R I A L

Objectives

In this tutorial, you will learn to:
- Write the functionality for the middle tier, using Visual Basic .NET code.
- Modify code-behind files in a Web application.
- Specify parameters of `OleDbCommand` objects.

Outline

31.1 Reviewing the Bookstore Application

31.2 Programming the Books Page's Code-Behind File

31.3 Coding the `BookInformation` Page's Code-Behind File

31.4 Internet and Web Resources

31.5 Wrap-Up

Bookstore Application: Middle Tier

Introducing Code-Behind Files

I n earlier tutorials, you built the client tier and created connections to the information tier of the **Bookstore** application. Using the Visual Studio .NET IDE, you were able to design the user interface of this Web-based application. In this tutorial, you will learn about the middle tier and complete the **Bookstore** application by programming the middle tier's functionality. Recall that the middle tier is responsible for interacting with the client and information tiers. The middle tier accepts user requests for data from the client tier, retrieves the data from the information tier (that is, the database) and responds to the client's requests with HTML documents.

31.1 Reviewing the Bookstore Application

You have taken the three-tier **Bookstore** application for a test-drive (in Tutorial 28) and have created the Web controls and database components for the application. Now you will need to write code to specify the functionality of the **Bookstore** application. Before you begin to write the code, you should review the pseudocode and the ACE table (Fig. 31.1) for this application:

> If the Books page is requested
> > Retrieve the book titles from the database
> > Display book titles in a ListBox
>
> If the user selects a book title from the ListBox and clicks the View Information Button
> > Store the selected book in a variable
> > Redirect the user to the BookInformation page
> > Retrieve the selected book's information from a database
> > Display the retrieved information in a Table on the BookInformation page
>
> If the user presses the Book List Button on the BookInformation page
> > Redirect the client browser back to the Books page

Action/Control/Event (ACE) Table for the Web-Based Bookstore Application

Action	Control/Object	Event
Label the Books page	`lblAvailable,` `lblInstructions`	

When the Books page loads, retrieve the book titles from the database and display them in the ListBox	`Books.aspx,`
	`objOleDbConnection,`
	`objSelectTitles,`
	`lstBookTitles`
		`Load` (of Page)

Redirect the client browser to the BookInformation page	`btnInformation`	`Click`

When the BookInformation page loads, retrieve the selected book's information from the database and display in a Table	`BookInforma-`
	`tion.aspx,`
	`objOleDbConnection,`
	`objSelectBookData,`
	`lblBookTitle,`
	`lblAuthors,`
	`imgBook,`
	`tblBook`
		`Load` (of Page)

Redirect the client browser back to the Books page	`btnBookList`	`Click`

Figure 31.1   ACE table for the Web-based **Bookstore** application.

In this tutorial, you will implement the interaction between the user interface and the database of the **Bookstore** application. This means that you will write the code that determines which image will be displayed by the `Image` control and which information will be retrieved from the database and displayed in the `Table` control. You also will write the code that redirects the client browser to another page when a `Button` is clicked.

31.2 Programming the Books Page's Code-Behind File

Although you have designed your **Bookstore** application's GUI and have added database connections, the **Bookstore** currently does not have any other functionality. You will now begin programming your application. You start with the `Books.aspx` page in the box, *Defining Page_Load Event Handler for the Books Page.*

Defining the Page_Load Event Handler for the Books Page

1. **Starting IIS.** Make sure that IIS is running for the **Default Web Site**. If it is not running, start it in the **Internet Information Services** dialog, by selecting **Default Web Site** in the left pane and clicking the Start Item `Button`.

2. **Opening the Bookstore application in Visual Studio .NET.** In Windows Explorer, double click the `Bookstore.sln` file in the `Bookstore` folder located in the `wwwroot` folder in order to open the **Bookstore** application in Visual Studio .NET.

3. **Displaying the code-behind file in the Solution Explorer window.** Every ASPX page created in Visual Studio .NET has a corresponding class written in a .NET language, such as Visual Basic .NET. This class includes event handlers, initialization code, methods and other supporting code and represents the middle tier of your application. The Visual Basic .NET file that contains this class is called the **code-behind file** and provides the ASPX page's functionality. It has the file extension `.aspx.vb`. Click the Show All Files `Button` (Fig. 31.2) in the toolbar of the **Solution Explorer**. Click the plus box next to `Books.aspx` to display the code-behind file, `Books.aspx.vb` (Fig. 31.2).

(cont.)

Show All Files **Button**

Click to display the code-behind file

Code-behind file

Figure 31.2   Code-behind file for the `Books.aspx` ASPX page.

4. ***Viewing the code-behind file.*** Figures 31.3 displays `Books.aspx.vb`—the code-behind file for `Books.aspx`. Recall that Visual Studio .NET generates this code-behind file when the project is created; we have reformatted it for presentation purposes. To view this file, double click `Books.aspx.vb` in the **Solution Explorer** window. [*Note*: You also can right click `Books.aspx` and select **View Code** to view the code-behind file.] Click the plus box of `Web Form Designer Generated Code` to display the generated code. Click the minus box of `#Region` to hide the generated code.

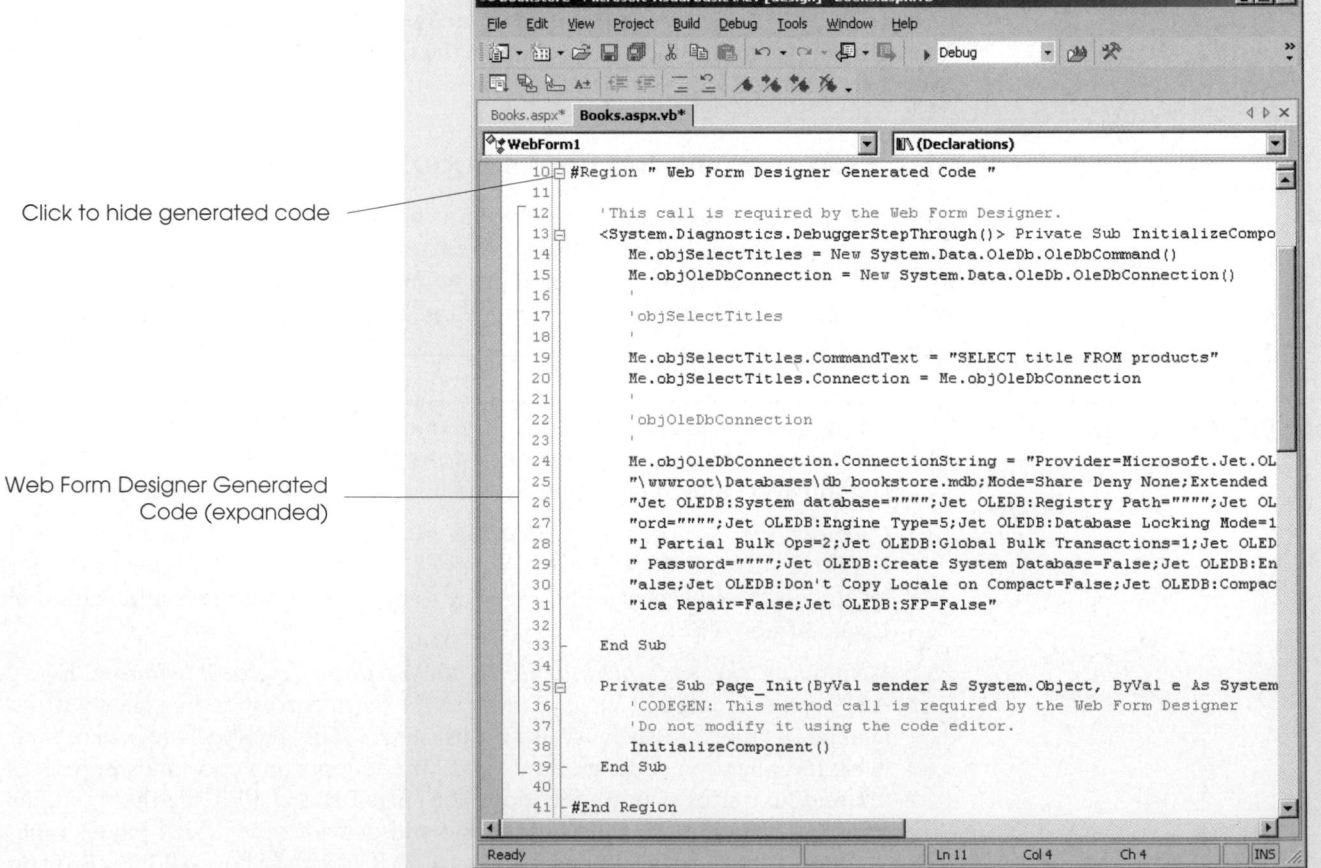

Click to hide generated code

Web Form Designer Generated Code (expanded)

Figure 31.3   `Books.aspx.vb` code-behind file containing code generated by Visual Studio .NET.

(cont.)

5. ***Changing the class name.*** Change the class name on line 1 from WebForm1 to Books (Fig. 31.4). Line 2 indicates that this class inherits from the Page class. The **Page** class defines the basic functionality for an ASPX page, much as the Form class defines the basic functionality for a Windows application Form. The Page class is located in the System.Web.UI namespace. The Page class provides properties, methods and events that are useful for creating Web-based applications.

Figure 31.4   Changing the application's class name.

6. ***Importing a namespace.*** To use database-related objects, you will need to import namespace System.Data.OleDb. Add line 1 of Fig. 31.5 before the Books class definition.

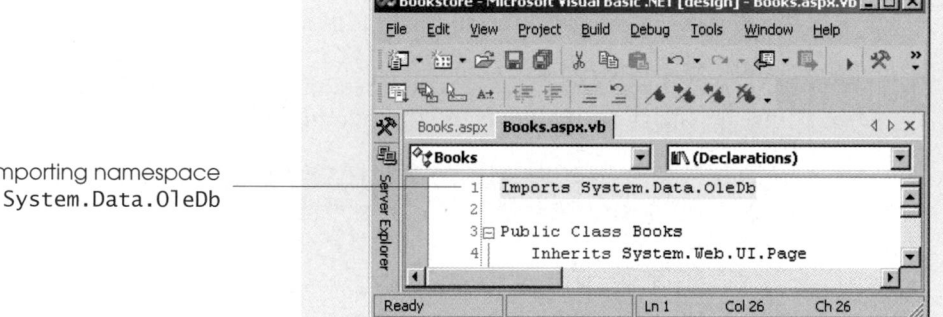

Figure 31.5   Importing namespace System.Data.OleDb.

7. ***Defining the Page_Load event handler.*** **Page_Load** is an event handler that executes any processing necessary to display the page. This event handler is created for you when the ASPX page is created, although it has no code. Add lines 48–52 of Fig. 31.6 to the Page_Load event handler. [*Note*: Initially, the Page_Load event handler contains a comment. We remove this comment from the event handler.] Line 48 opens the connection to the database by invoking the OleDbConnection class method Open. Lines 51–52 create a data reader by invoking the ExecuteReader method of the data command object (objSelectTitles) you created in Tutorial 30.

   The Load event for a Web page is similar to the Load event for a Windows Form. You put code in the Load event handler that is needed to initialize the page or the objects the page uses.

8. ***Using the data reader.*** Add lines 54–62 of Fig. 31.7 to the Page_Load event handler. Lines 55–60 define a Do While...Loop statement that starts the data reader by invoking the Read method. The Do While...Loop statement will terminate when there is no more data to read. Lines 58–59 add the values stored in the database's title field to the ListBox. The title field values will continue to be added to the ListBox until there are no more title field values to read. Line 62 closes the connection to the database by invoking the Close method of class OleDbConnection.

(cont.)

Opening the database connection

Creating a data reader

Figure 31.6 Opening the database connection and creating a data reader.

9. **Using the data reader.** Add lines 54–62 of Fig. 31.7 to the Page_Load event handler. Lines 55–60 define a Do While...Loop statement that starts the data reader by invoking the Read method. The Do While...Loop statement will terminate when there is no more data to read. Lines 58–59 add the values stored in the database's title field to the ListBox. The title field values will continue to be added to the ListBox until there are no more title field values to read. Line 62 closes the connection to the database by invoking the Close method of class OleDbConnection.

Begin reading, using the data reader

Adding book titles from the database to the ListBox

Closing database connection

Figure 31.7 Reading data from a database.

10. **Saving the project.** Select **File > Save All** to save all the solution's files.

Next, you will define the btnInformation_Click event handler. This event handler is invoked when the user clicks the **View Information** Button. The event handler determines the selected book and redirects the client browser to the Book-Information page. You create the event handler in the box, *Defining the Click Event Handler for the Books Page.*

<table>
<tr><td>

Defining the `Click`
Event Handler for the
`Books` ***Page***

</td><td>

1. ***Creating the*** `Click` ***event handler.*** Switch to design mode. Double click the `btnInformation` Button control. The `btnInformation_Click` event handler should appear in the `Books.aspx.vb` file.

2. ***Adding code to the*** `Click` ***event handler.*** Add lines 70–80 of Fig. 31.8 to the event handler.

</td></tr>
</table>

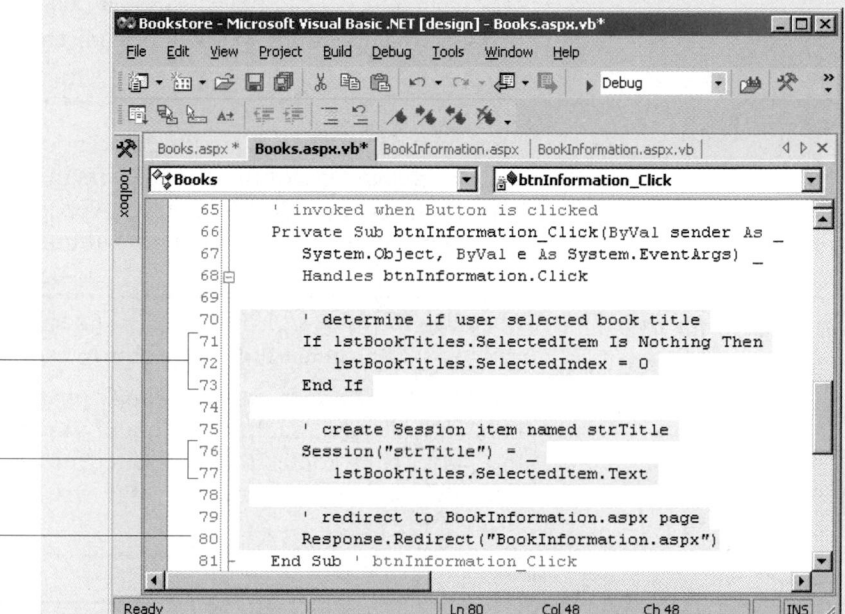

Selecting a title if the user does not make a selection

Creating a `Session` item to store the selected book title

Redirecting the client browser to another Web page

Figure 31.8   `btnInformation_Click` event handler definition.

Lines 71–73 determine if the user selected a book title. You use the List-Box's `SelectedItem` property to determine if a book has been selected. The **`SelectedItem`** property specifies the item that is selected from the `ListBox`. If the user does not select an item, then no value is specified in the `SelectedItem` property (which is what line 71 checks).

If a book title has not been selected, then the first title in the `ListBox` will be set as the default selection. This is accomplished by using the `ListBox`'s `SelectedIndex` property. The **`SelectedIndex`** property specifies the index of the selected item. You set the first title in the `ListBox` as the default selection by setting this property to 0 (line 72), which is the index number of the first item.

Values are not maintained across different ASPX pages. This means that values stored in instance variables cannot be passed from page to page. However, ASP .NET provides **`Session`** items for sharing values among ASPX pages. Lines 76–77 allow information to be maintained across the **Bookstore** application's ASPX pages by adding a **key-value pair** to the session object. A key-value pair associates a value with a corresponding name (key) which identifies the value. In this case, the key is the name `strTitle`, and the value is the title of the selected book, which is determined by `lstBookTitles.SelectedItem.Text`. The storage of key-value pairs across Web pages is made possible by **session state**, which is ASP .NET's built-in support for tracking data. Session state enables the current user's information (including the book the user selected) to be maintained across a browser session.

(cont.)

> When the user selects a book, the title of the selected book is set as the value of key `strTitle`. This information is added to the `Session` object so that it may be used in the `BookInformation` page. After the `strTitle` key has been provided with a value, the page redirects the client browser by calling `Response.Redirect` (line 80). The **Response** object is a predefined ASP .NET object that provides methods for responding to clients. **Redirect** is one of the `Response` object's methods, which is used to specify the Web page to which the client browser will be redirected.
>
> 3. ***Saving the project.*** Select **File > Save All** to save all the solution's files.

Before you begin to program the `BookInformation.aspx.vb` code-behind file, you need to place images of the book covers in the `Bookstore` folder. The `BookInformation.aspx` page will display the cover image of the selected book. You will learn how to place the images in the box, *Adding Images to the* `Bookstore` *Folder*.

Adding Images to the
Bookstore Folder

> 1. ***Locating the images.*** Locate the `C:\Examples\Tutorial31\Images` folder, which contains images of the book covers.
>
> 2. ***Placing the images in the* Bookstore *folder.*** Copy the three images `csharphtp1.png`, `cpphtp4.png` and `vbnethtp2.png`, and paste them into the `Bookstore` folder that is located in the `wwwroot` folder on your computer. These image files will be used when you program the `BookInformation.aspx` page.

SELF-REVIEW

1. The _____ class defines the basic functionality for an ASPX page.

   a) `Form`   b) `WebForm`

   c) `Page`   d) None of the above.

2. The Page class is located in namespace _____.

   a) `System.Web.UI`   b) `System.Data`

   c) `System.WebForm`   d) `System.OleDb`

Answers: 1) c.   2) a.

31.3 Coding the BookInformation Page's Code-Behind File

The next ASPX page in this application is `BookInformation.aspx`. This ASPX page displays information about the book the user selected. In the box, *Defining the Page_Load Event Handler for the BookInformation Page*, you will add the code to the `Page_Load` event handler of the `BookInformation.aspx` page so that you may retrieve the requested book's information from the database.

Defining the Page_Load
Event Handler for the
BookInformation **Page**

> 1. ***Changing the class name.*** Double click `BookInformation.aspx` in the **Solution Explorer** window to view the `BookInformation.aspx` page. Select **View > Code** to view the code-behind file `BookInformation.aspx.vb`. Make sure that the class name is `BookInformation` (Fig. 31.9).
>
> 2. ***Importing a namespace.*** To use database-related objects, you will need to import the `System.Data.OleDb` namespace. Add line 1 of Fig. 31.10 before the `BookInformation` class definition.

(cont.)

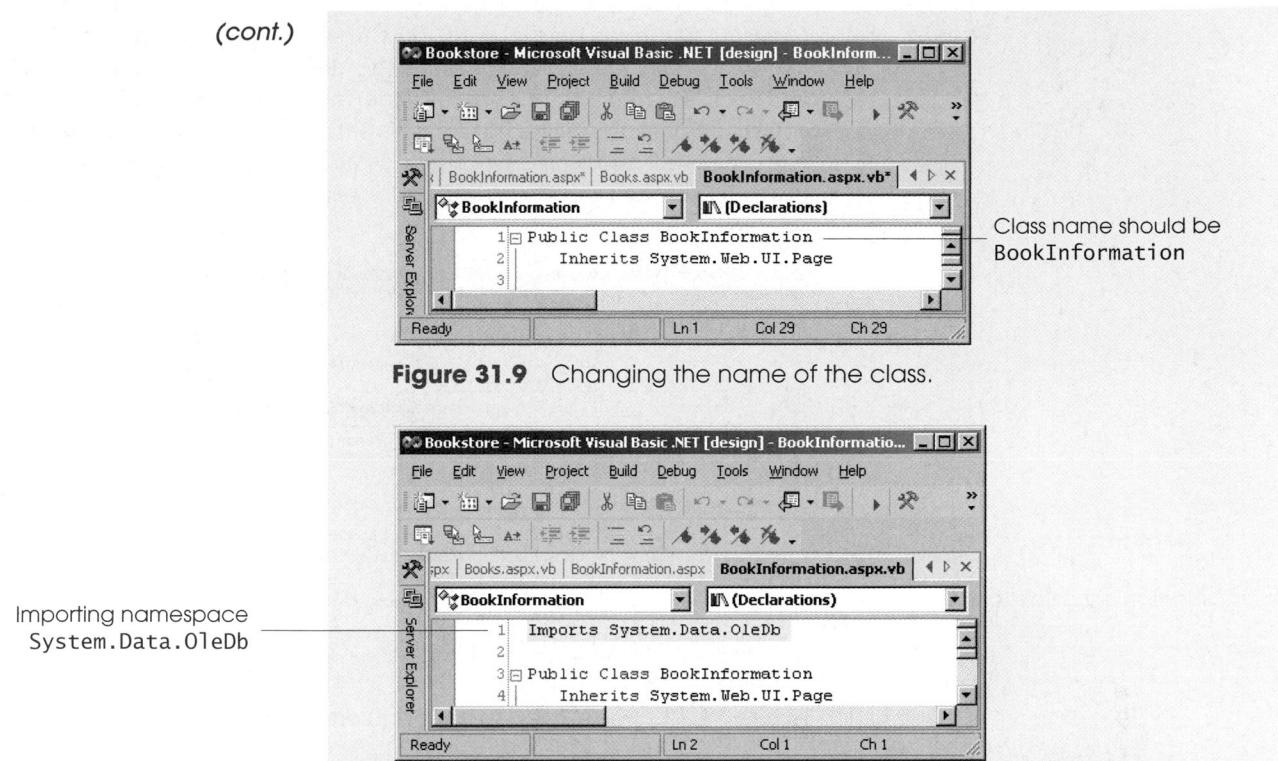

Figure 31.9 Changing the name of the class.

Importing namespace
`System.Data.OleDb`

Figure 31.10 Importing the `System.Data.OleDb` namespace.

3. ***Setting a parameter value and opening the database connection.*** Add lines 52–59 of Fig. 31.11 to the `Page_Load` event handler of the `BookInforma-tion.aspx` page. Line 53 sets the `Text` property of the `lblBookTitle` `Label` to the title of the selected book, using the `Session` item. Recall that, in the `Books.aspx` page, you stored the title of the selected book in the `Session` item with the key `strTitle`. Lines 56–57 set the `title` parameter of the `objSelectBookData` command object to the title of the selected book, which is stored in `Text` property of the `lblBookTitle` `Label`. Line 59 opens the connection to the database by invoking the `Open` method.

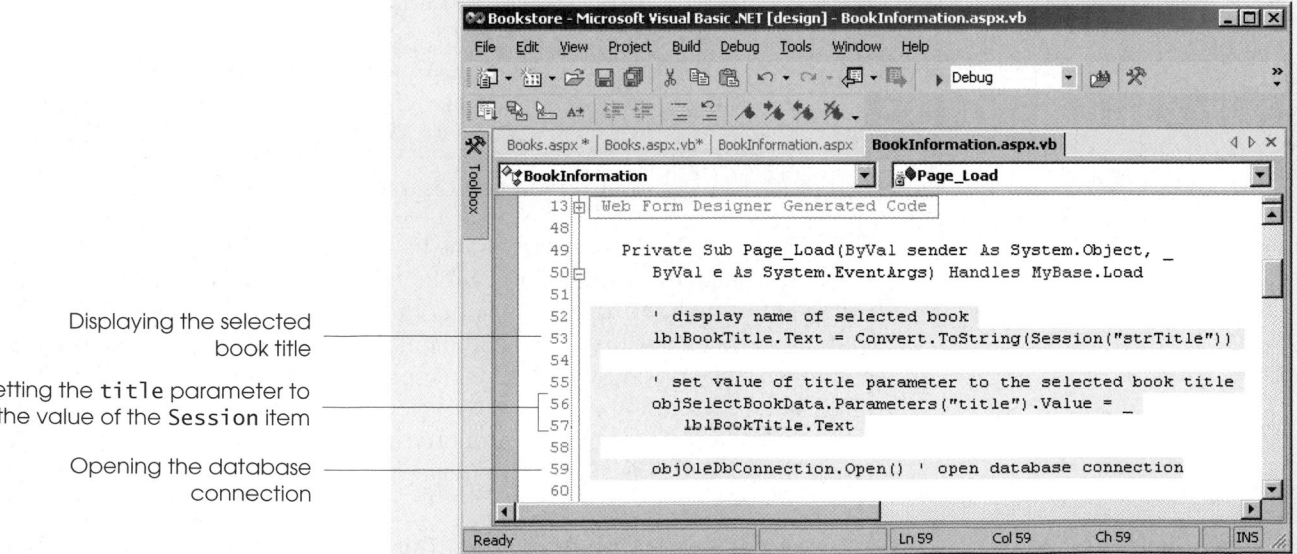

Displaying the selected
book title

Setting the `title` parameter to
the value of the `Session` item

Opening the database
connection

Figure 31.11 `Page_Load` event handler modified to set a parameter value and open a database connection.

(cont.)

4. ***Creating the data reader.*** Add lines 61–65 of Fig. 31.12 to the `Page_Load` event handler. Lines 62–63 create the data reader (of type `OleDbDataReader`) by invoking the `ExecuteReader` method of the `objSelectBookData` command object. Line 65 invokes the data reader's `Read` method to start the data reader. Your query (specified using data command objects) from the previous tutorial will be executed, returning information about the user's selected book.

Figure 31.12 `Page_Load` event handler modified to create a data reader.

5. ***Using the data reader.*** Add lines 67–71 of Fig. 31.13 to the `Page_Load` event handler. Lines 68–71 retrieve data from the database. [*Note*: The `OleDbDataReader` can read, but not modify, information from the database.]

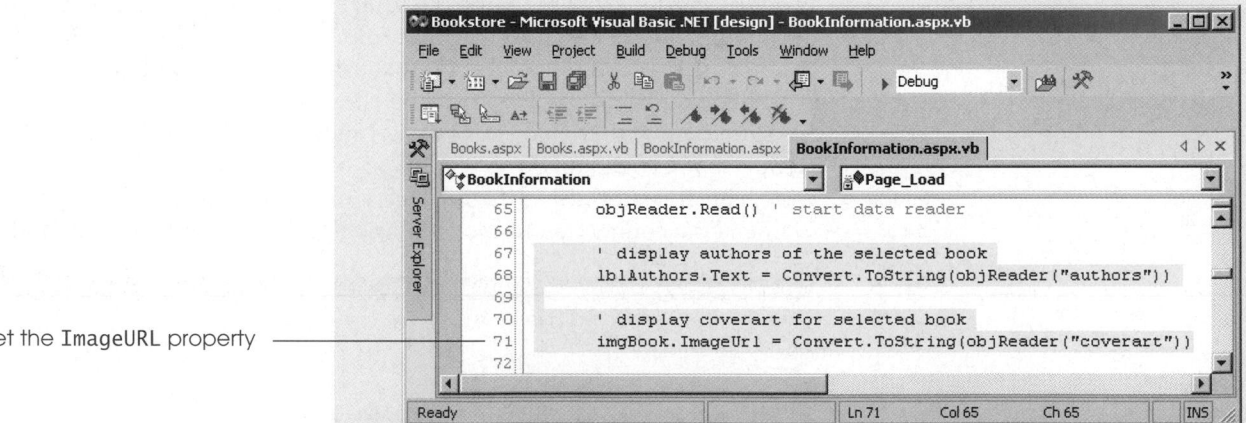

Figure 31.13 Displaying book authors and cover image.

Line 68 sets the `lblAuthors Label`'s text to the authors of the selected book, specified by `objReader("authors")`. This line retrieves the value found in the `authors` field. Remember that the reader is retrieving the information specified by the SQL statement of the `objSelectBookData` data command object. The SQL statement specified only that the selected book and its book information should be retrieved from the database. Line 71 sets the `Image` control's `ImageURL` property to the name of the selected book's cover image, which is specified by using the value of `objReader("coverart")`.

6. ***Displaying book information in the Table.*** Add lines 73–94 of Fig. 31.14 to the `Page_Load` event handler.

(cont.)

Display book information
in the `Table`

```
           71              imgBook.ImageUrl = Convert.ToString(objReader("coverart"))
           72
           73              ' display price in Table
           74              tblBook.Rows(0).Cells(1).Text = _
           75                 "$" & Convert.ToString(objReader("price"))
           76
           77              ' display ISBN number in Table
           78              tblBook.Rows(1).Cells(1).Text = _
           79                 Convert.ToString(objReader("isbn"))
           80
           81              ' display edition number in Table
           82              tblBook.Rows(2).Cells(1).Text = _
           83                 Convert.ToString(objReader("edition"))
           84
           85              ' display copyright date in Table
           86              tblBook.Rows(3).Cells(1).Text = _
           87                 Convert.ToString(objReader("copyrightDate"))
           88
           89              ' display description in Table
           90              tblBook.Rows(4).Cells(1).Text = _
           91                 Convert.ToString(objReader("description"))
           92
           93              objReader.Close()          ' close data reader
           94              objOleDbConnection.Close() ' close database connection
           95         End Sub   ' Page_Load
```

Figure 31.14　Data reader used to retrieve read-only data.

Lines 73–91 display the book information in the `Table` (`tblBook`). Recall that you created a table with five rows that contain two cells each. The second cell in the first row is given the value of the selected book's price. This task is accomplished by using the `Rows` and `Cells` properties. For example, lines 74–75 specify the row number by using property `Rows` of the `Table` control and specifying `0` for the first row. The `Cells` property of `Rows` is then used to specify the second cell in the row by using value `1`. Next, the `Text` property of `Cells` is used to set the text that will display in the second cell of the first row in the `Table`. The `Text` property is assigned the value of the data read by the data reader (`objReader("price")`), which is converted to a `String`. Recall that you need to convert to this to a `String` because the data reader returns items of type `Object`. The rest of the book's information is displayed in the same manner. The second cell in the second row contains the value of the ISBN number. The second cell in the third row displays the edition number. The fourth row contains the copyright date and the fifth row contains the selected book's description.

Line 93 closes the data reader and line 94 closes the database connection by calling the `Close` method. When this application is run, the information is displayed in the format shown in Fig. 31.15.

7. ***Saving the project.*** Select **File > Save All** to save all the solution's files.

(cont.)

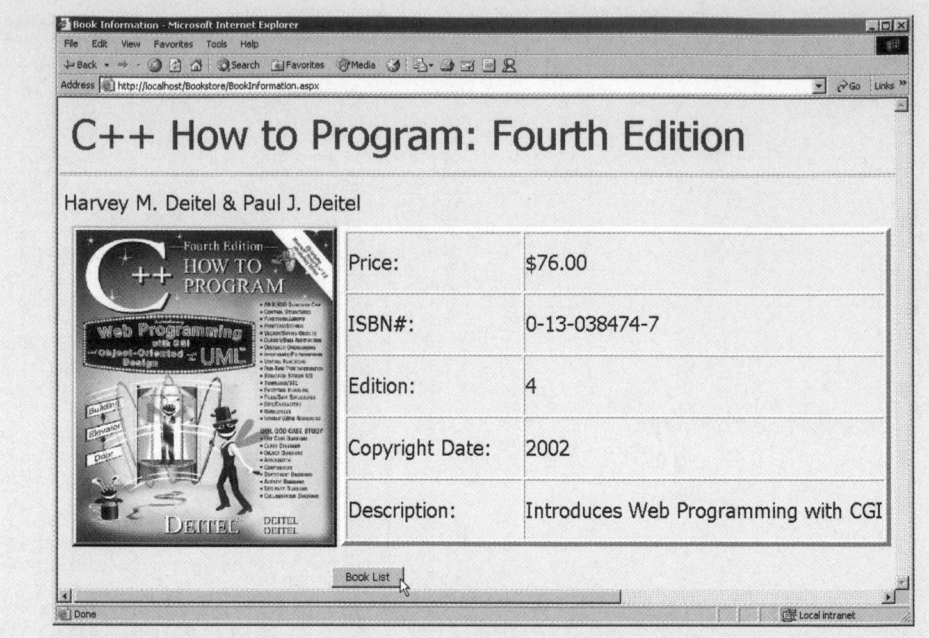

Figure 31.15   `BookInformation.aspx` page displaying book information.

The final event handler you define in the `BookInformation.aspx` page is the `btnBookList_Click` event handler. This event handler allows the user to return to the list of available books. You create this event handler in the box, *Defining the btnBookList_Click Event Handler for the BookInformation Page.*

Defining the
btnBookList_Click
Event Handler for the
BookInformation **Page**

1. ***Creating the btnBookList_Click event handler.*** Now you are ready to define the event handler for the `btnBookList` Button. Select the BookInformation.aspx page, and double click the **Book List** Button. This step creates the `btnBookList_Click` event handler. This Button is used to redirect the client browser to the `Books.aspx` page.

2. ***Adding code to the event handler.*** Add lines 102–103 of Fig. 31.16 to the `btnBookList_Click` event handler. Line 103 redirects the user to the `Books.aspx` page by calling `Response.Redirect`.

Redirecting to the
Books.aspx page

Figure 31.16   Definition of the `btnBookList_Click` event handler.

3. ***Saving the project.*** Select **File > Save All** to save all the solution's files.

Now that you have completed the **Bookstore** application, you will test it to ensure that it is functioning properly in the box, *Testing Your Completed Bookstore Application.*

Testing Your Completed Bookstore Application

1. ***Starting IIS.*** Open the **Internet Information Services** dialog, select **Default Web Site** and click the Start Item **Button** to start IIS.

2. ***Running the application.*** Select **Debug > Start** to run the application. Select a book title from the ListBox, and click the **View Information** Button. Notice that this application performs the same functions as the completed **Bookstore** application that you test-drove in Tutorial 28.

3. ***Terminating the application.*** Click the browser's close box to terminate the application.

4. ***Stopping IIS.*** Open the **Internet Information Services** dialog, select **Default Web Site** and click the stop **Button** to stop IIS.

5. ***Closing the solution.*** Select **File > Close Solution** to close the project.

Figures 31.17 and 31.18 display the complete code listing for the Books.aspx and BookInformation.aspx pages of the **Bookstore** application, respectively. [*Note*: The comment, "control declarations", represents the declaration statements for all controls for the ASPX page.]

```
1    Imports System.Data.OleDb
2
3    Public Class Books
4        Inherits System.Web.UI.Page
5
6        ' control declarations
7
8        ' Web Form Designer generated code
9
10       Private Sub Page_Load(ByVal sender As System.Object, _
11          ByVal e As System.EventArgs) Handles MyBase.Load
12
13          objOleDbConnection.Open() ' open database connection
14
15          ' create data reader
16          Dim objReader As OleDbDataReader = _
17             objSelectTitles.ExecuteReader
18
19          ' perform loop while data reader is reading
20          Do While objReader.Read()
21
22             ' add titles to ListBox while reader is reading
23             lstBookTitles.Items.Add( _
24                Convert.ToString(objReader("title")))
25          Loop
26
27          objOleDbConnection.Close() ' close database connection
28       End Sub  ' Page_Load
29
30       ' invoked when Button is clicked
31       Private Sub btnInformation_Click(ByVal sender As _
32          System.Object, ByVal e As System.EventArgs) _
33          Handles btnInformation.Click
34
```

Figure 31.17   Books.aspx page code. (Part 1 of 2.)

Determining if user made selection from `ListBox`

```
35        ' determine if user selected book title
36        If lstBookTitles.SelectedItem Is Nothing Then
37           lstBookTitles.SelectedIndex = 0
38        End If
39
```

Creating a `Session` item

```
40        ' create Session item named strTitle
41        Session("strTitle") = _
42           lstBookTitles.SelectedItem.Text
43
```

Redirecting client browsers to `BookInformation.aspx` page

```
44        ' redirect to BookInformation.aspx page
45        Response.Redirect("BookInformation.aspx")
46     End Sub ' btnInformation_Click
47
48  End Class ' Books
```

Figure 31.17 Books.aspx page code. (Part 2 of 2.)

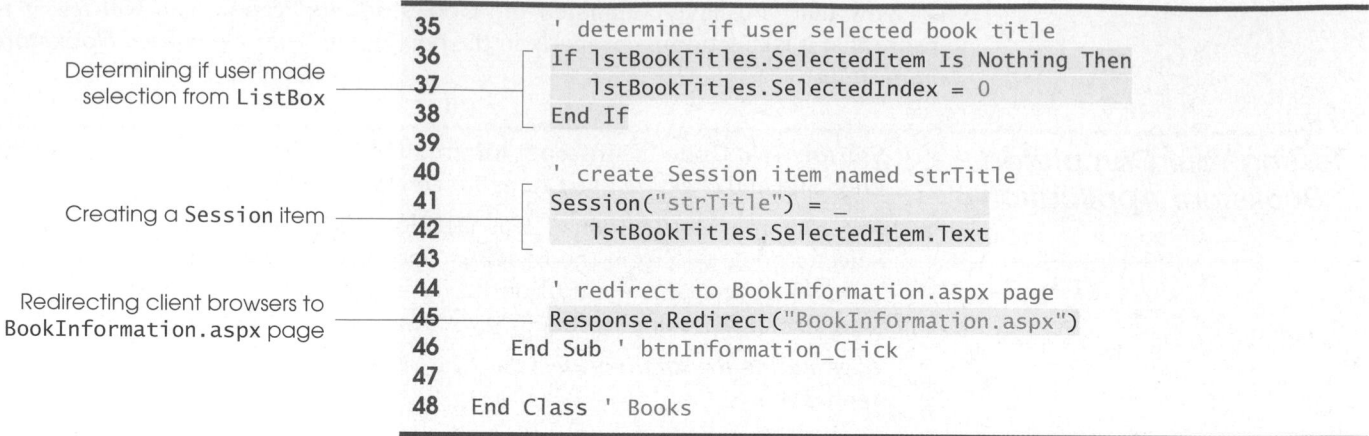

```
1   Imports System.Data.OleDb
2
3   Public Class BookInformation
4      Inherits System.Web.UI.Page
5
6      ' control declarations
7
8      ' Web Form Designer generated code
9
10     Private Sub Page_Load(ByVal sender As System.Object, _
11        ByVal e As System.EventArgs) Handles MyBase.Load
12
13        ' display name of selected book
14        lblBookTitle.Text = Convert.ToString(Session("strTitle"))
15
16        ' set value of title parameter to the selected book title
```

Using a `Session` item to set parameter value

```
17        objSelectBookData.Parameters("title").Value = _
18           lblBookTitle.Text
19
20        objOleDbConnection.Open() ' open database connection
21
22        ' create data reader
23        Dim objReader As OleDbDataReader = _
24           objSelectBookData.ExecuteReader
25
26        objReader.Read() ' start data reader
27
28        ' display authors of the selected book
29        lblAuthors.Text = Convert.ToString(objReader("authors"))
30
31        ' display coverart for selected book
32        imgBook.ImageUrl = Convert.ToString(objReader("coverart"))
33
34        ' display price in Table
35        tblBook.Rows(0).Cells(1).Text = _
36           "$" & Convert.ToString(objReader("price"))
37
38        ' display ISBN number in Table
39        tblBook.Rows(1).Cells(1).Text = _
40           Convert.ToString(objReader("isbn"))
```

Figure 31.18 BookInformation.aspx page code. (Part 1 of 2.)

```
41
42          ' display edition number in Table
43          tblBook.Rows(2).Cells(1).Text = _
44             Convert.ToString(objReader("edition"))
45
46          ' display copyright date in Table
47          tblBook.Rows(3).Cells(1).Text = _
48             Convert.ToString(objReader("copyrightDate"))
49
50          ' display description in Table
51          tblBook.Rows(4).Cells(1).Text = _
52             Convert.ToString(objReader("description"))
53
54          objReader.Close()          ' close data reader
55          objOleDbConnection.Close() ' close database connection
56       End Sub ' Page_Load
57
58       ' invoked when Book List Button is clicked
59       Private Sub btnBookList_Click(ByVal sender As _
60          System.Object, ByVal e As System.EventArgs) _
61          Handles btnBookList.Click
62
63          ' redirects to Books.aspx page
64          Response.Redirect("Books.aspx")
65       End Sub ' btnBookList_Click
66
67    End Class ' BookInformation
```

Figure 31.18 BookInformation.aspx page code. (Part 2 of 2.)

SELF-REVIEW 1. A(n) _____ reads data from a database.

    a) OleDbDataReader   b) OleDbConnection

    c) Query Builder   d) DataSet

2. To specify the third cell in the second row of a Table control called tableName, type

    _____.

    a) tableName.Rows(2).Cells(3)   b) tableName.Rows(1).Cells(2)

    c) tableName.Cells(3).Rows(2)   d) tableName.Cells(2).Rows(1)

Answers: 1) a. 2) b.

31.4 Internet and Web Resources

Please take a moment to visit each of these sites briefly. To save typing time, use the hot links on the enclosed CD or at www.deitel.com.

www.asp.net
This Microsoft site overviews ASP .NET and provides ASP .NET tutorials. This site also includes the IBuySpy e-commerce storefront example that uses ASP .NET and links to Web sites where users can purchase books.

www.asp101.com/aspplus
This site overviews ASP .NET and includes articles, code examples and links to ASP .NET resources.

www.411asp.net
This resource site provides users with ASP .NET tutorials and code samples. The community pages allow users to ask questions, answer questions and post messages.

www.aspfree.com
This site provides free ASP .NET demos and source code. The site also provides a list of articles on various topics and a frequently asked questions (FAQs) page.

31.5 Wrap-Up

In this tutorial, you programmed the middle tier of your three-tier **Bookstore** application. By defining methods and event handlers, you specified the actions that execute when the user interacts with ASPX pages. You learned about Session objects and how they are used to maintain values across ASPX pages. You also learned about the Response.Redirect method, which allows you to redirect the client browser to other ASPX pages.

After learning about Sessions and Response.Redirect, you used them in the **Bookstore** application. You began with the first ASPX page of the application, Books.aspx. This page retrieved the book titles from the database and displayed them in a ListBox control when the ASPX page was loaded. You did this by defining the Page_Load event handler. You then defined the actions that would occur when the user clicks the **View Information** Button. In the Click event handler, you created a Session item to store the title of the book selected by the user. You also used the Response.Redirect method in the Click event handler to direct users from the Books.aspx page to the BookInformation.aspx page.

You then defined the BookInformation.aspx page. You defined event handler Page_Load to display the information about the selected book. Recall that you used the value stored in the Session item to determine the book title selected by the user. You then created a data reader to retrieve the selected book's information and displayed it in the Table control. Through programming, you were able to control the flow of data from the information tier to the client tier, completing the three-tier **Bookstore** application. You also learned about ASP .NET resources available on the Web.

SKILLS SUMMARY

Accessing the Code-Behind File

- Click the Show All Files Button in the **Solution Explorer** window.
- Click the plus box next to the desired ASPX page to display the corresponding code-behind file name.
- Double click the code-behind file name to view the code-behind file.

Creating and Using a Session Item

- Type Session("*nameOfKey*"), where *nameOfKey* represents the key in a key-value pair. Assign this item a value in an assignment statement.
- Use Session("*nameOfKey*") to retrieve the item's value.

Redirecting the Client Browser to Another Web Page

- Type Redirect.Response("*URLOfPage*"), where *URLOfPage* represents the URL of the page to which the client browser redirects.

KEY TERMS

code-behind file—Visual Basic .NET file that contains a class which provides an ASPX page's functionality.

key-value pair—Associates a value with a corresponding key, which is used to identify the value.

Page_Load—An event handler that executes any processing necessary to display a Web page.

Response.Redirect—Method used to redirect the client browser to another Web page.

Session state—ASP .NET's built-in support for tracking data.

Session object—Object that is maintained across several Web pages containing a collection of items (key-value pairs). This variable is specific to each user.

CONTROLS, EVENTS, PROPERTIES & METHODS

ASPX page   Page on which controls are dropped to design the GUI.

■ *Event*

Load—This event is raised when the ASPX page is created.

■ *Property*

bgColor—This property specifies the Web Form's background color.

Image   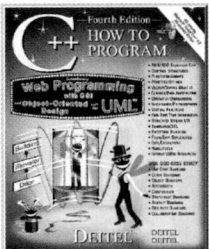 Image   This control displays an image on the ASPX page.

■ *In action*

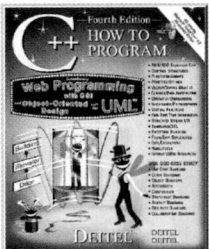

■ *Properties*

BorderStyle—This property specifies the appearance of the Image's border.

BorderWidth—This property specifies the width of the Image's border.

Height—This property specifies the height of the Image control.

ID—This property specifies the name used to access the Image control programmatically. The name should be prefixed with img.

ImageUrl—This property specifies the location of the image file.

Width—This property specifies the width of the Image control.

ListBox   ▤ ListBox   This control allows the user to view and select from multiple items in a list.

■ *In action*

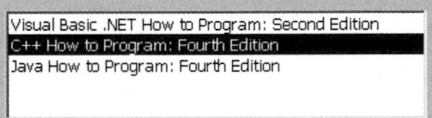

■ *Properties*

Height—This property specifies the height of the ListBox.

ID—This property specifies the name used to access the ListBox control programmatically. The name should be prefixed with lst.

SelectedIndex—This property returns the index of the selected item in the ListBox.

SelectedItem—This property returns the value of the selected item in the ListBox.

Width—This property specifies the width of the ListBox.

Response   This class provides methods for responding to clients.

■ *Method*

Redirect—This method redirects the client browser to the specified location.

MULTIPLE-CHOICE QUESTIONS

31.1 The Page_Load event handler _____.

    a) redirects the client browser to different Web pages

    b) defines the functionality when a Button is clicked

    c) executes any processing necessary to display a Web page

    d) defines the functionality when a Web control is selected

31.2 The `Response.Redirect` method _____.

    a) refreshes the current Web page

    b) sends the client browser to a specified Web page

    c) responds to user input

    d) responds to the click of a `Button`

31.3 `Session` items are used in the **Bookstore** application because _____.

    a) variables in ASP .NET Web applications must be created as `Session` items

    b) values need to be shared among Web pages

    c) `Session` items are simpler to create than instance variables

    d) Both a and b.

31.4 Session state is used for _____ in ASP .NET.

    a) tracking user-specific data   b) running an application

    c) using a database   d) None of the above.

31.5 The file extension for an ASPX code-behind file is _____.

    a) `.asp`   b) `.aspx`

    c) `.aspx.vb`   d) `.code`

31.6 The `Response` object is a predefined ASP .NET object that _____.

    a) connects to a database   b) retrieves information from a database

    c) creates Web controls

    d) provides methods for responding to client requests

31.7 The `Response.Redirect` method takes a(n) _____ as an argument.

    a) URL   b) `Integer` value

    c) `Boolean` value   d) `OleDbConnection` object

31.8 The _____ property specifies the image that an `Image` control displays.

    a) `ImageGIF`   b) `ImageURL`

    c) `Image`   d) `Display`

31.9 The Visual Basic .NET file that contains the ASPX page's corresponding class is called the _____.

    a) ASPX file   b) code-behind file

    c) class file   d) None of the above.

31.10 Information can be maintained across Web pages by adding a _____ to the `Session` object.

    a) key-value pair   b) number

    c) database connection object   d) None of the above.

EXERCISES

31.11 (*Phone Book Application: Functionality*) Define the middle tier for the **Phone Book** application.

    a) ***Opening the application.*** Open the **PhoneBook** application that you created in Tutorial 29 and continued to develop in Tutorial 30.

    b) ***Importing `System.Data.OleDb` in `PhoneBook.aspx.vb`.*** Import namespace `System.Data.OleDb` in `PhoneBook.aspx.vb`.

    c) ***Defining the `Page_Load` event handler of `PhoneBook.aspx` page.*** Use the `Open` method to open the connection to the database. Create a data reader to read the information specified by the data command object.

    d) ***Populating the `DropDownList` with names.*** Add a `Do While...Loop` to `PhoneBook.aspx`'s `Page_Load` method. This loop should add to the `DropDownList` each person's name read by the data reader.

e) ***Closing the reader and connection.*** Close the data reader and the connection to the database by invoking their Close methods.

f) ***Creating the Get Number Button's Click event handler for the PhoneBook.aspx page.*** Double click the **Get Number** Button to create the Click event's event handler.

g) ***Creating a Session item.*** In the Click event handler, create a Session item to store the selected name.

h) ***Redirecting to the PhoneNumber.aspx page.*** In the Click event handler, use the Response.Redirect method to redirect the client browser to the PhoneNumber.aspx page.

i) ***Importing System.Data.OleDb in PhoneNumber.aspx.vb.*** Import namespace System.Data.OleDb in PhoneNumber.aspx.vb.

j) ***Defining the Page_Load event handler for the PhoneNumber.aspx page.*** Use the Open method to open the connection to the database. Access the Session item to retrieve the selected name. Specify this name as the parameter value for the OleDbCommand object. Create a data reader to read the information specified by the data command object.

k) ***Displaying the selected name and phone number.*** In the Page_Load event handler, read the desired phone number from the data reader. Display the selected name and corresponding phone number in the lblNumbers Label.

l) ***Closing the reader and connection.*** Close the data reader and the connection to the database by invoking their Close methods.

m) ***Creating the Phone Book Button's Click event handler for the PhoneNumber.aspx page.*** Double click the **Phone Book** Button to create the Click event's event handler.

n) ***Redirecting to the PhoneBook.aspx page.*** In the Click event handler, use the Response.Redirect method to redirect the client browser to the PhoneBook.aspx page.

31.12 (*US State Facts Application: Functionality*) Define the middle tier for the **US State Facts** application.

a) ***Opening the application.*** Open the **USStateFacts** application that you created in Tutorial 29 and continued to develop in Tutorial 30.

b) ***Copying the FlagImages folder to your project folder.*** Copy the C:\Examples\Tutorial31\Exercises\Images\FlagImages folder to the USStateFacts folder.

c) ***Importing System.Data.OleDb in States.aspx.vb.*** Import namespace System.Data.OleDb in States.aspx.vb before the class definition.

d) ***Defining the Page_Load event handler for the States.aspx page.*** Use the Open method to open the connection to the database. Create a data reader to read the information specified by the data command object.

e) ***Populating the ListBox with state names in the States.aspx page.*** Add a Do While...Loop to States.aspx's Page_Load method. This loop should add to the ListBox the name of each state read by the data reader.

f) ***Creating a Button's Click event handler for the States.aspx page.*** Double click the **Review Facts** Button to create the Click event's event handler.

g) ***Creating a Session item.*** Create a Session item in the Click event handler and assign it to the state name that the user selects from the ListBox.

h) ***Redirecting to the StateFacts.aspx page.*** In the Click event handler, use the Redirect.Response method to redirect the client browser to the StateFacts.aspx page.

i) ***Importing System.Data.OleDb in StateFacts.aspx.vb.*** Import namespace System.Data.OleDb in StateFacts.aspx.vb.

j) ***Defining the Page_Load event handler of StateFacts.aspx page.*** Use the Open method to open the connection to the database. Access the Session object to retrieve the selected state name. Specify this name as a parameter value for the Ole-

DbCommand object. Create a data reader to read the information specified by the data command object.

k) *Displaying the state facts in the Table.* In the Page_Load event handler, use the data reader to retrieve the desired state's facts. Display the selected state's name in the lblStateName Label. Set the ImageURL property of the Image control to the location of the selected state's flag image. Display the name of the state capital, flower, tree and bird in the Table on the StateFacts.aspx page.

l) *Closing the connection.* Close the connection to the database by invoking the Close method.

m) *Creating the State List Button's Click event handler for the StateFacts.aspx page.* Double click the **State List** Button to create the Click event handler.

n) *Redirecting to the States.aspx page.* In the Click event handler use the Redirect.Response method to redirect the client browser to the States.aspx page.

31.13 (*Road Sign Review Application: Functionality*) Define the middle tier for the **Road Sign Review** application.

a) *Opening the application.* Open the **RoadSignReview** application that you created in Tutorial 29 and continued to develop in Tutorial 30.

b) *Copying the SignImages folder to your project folder.* Copy the C:\Examples\ Tutorial31\Exercises\Images\SignImages folder to the RoadSignReview folder.

c) *Importing System.Data.OleDb and System.Web.UI.WebControls to Road-Signs.aspx.vb.* Import the System.Data.OleDb and System.Web.UI.WebControls namespaces to RoadSigns.aspx.vb. You need to import System.Web.UI.WebControls because you will be creating a Web control programmatically in this exercise.

d) *Defining the Page_Load event handler for the RoadSigns.aspx page.* Use the Open method to open the connection to the database. Create a data reader to read the information specified by the data command object.

e) *Populating the Table with sign images in the RoadSigns.aspx page.* Add a Do While...Loop to RoadSigns.aspx's Page_Load method. This loop should display an image of the sign and display the sign name in the ToolTip property. This property specifies the text that displays in a tooltip box when the mouse hovers over the Image. The sign image and name should be retrieved using the data reader. To display an Image in a cell of the Table, you need to create an Image control, specify a cell and use the cell's Controls.Add method to add an image to that cell. For example, to create an Image control programmatically, type Dim imgImageName As Image = New Image(). You then need to set the ImageURL property to the location of the desired image. To display an Image control in the first cell of the first row, you would write the line Table.Rows(0).Cells(0).Controls.Add(imgImageName). Also, if you wish to specify text for a tooltip, you must set the cell's ToolTip property—for example, Table.Rows(0).Cells(0).ToolTip = "This is a tooltip".

f) *Closing the reader and connection.* Close the data reader and the connection to the database by invoking their Close methods.

g) *Creating the Register Button's Click event handler for RoadSigns.aspx.* Double click the **Register** Button of RoadSigns.aspx to create the Click event handler.

h) *Creating Session item.* Create two Session items in the Click event handler, and set the first one equal to the user input for the **Name:** TextBox. The second Session item should equal the user input for the **Phone Number:** TextBox.

i) *Redirecting to the RoadTestRegistered.aspx page.* In the Click event handler, use the Redirect.Response method to redirect the client browser to the RoadTestRegistered.aspx page.

j) *Defining the Page_Load method of RoadTestRegistered.aspx page.* Use the Session items to display a confirmation to the user about the user's registration information. Display the confirmation using Label lblConfirmation. Display the user's name, and display text which states that the user will be contacted shortly at the phone number provided. This information should be displayed in a Label.

Operator Precedence Chart

Operators are shown in decreasing order of precedence from top to bottom with each level of precedence separated by a horizontal line. Visual Basic operators associate from left to right.

Operator	Type
^	exponentiation
+	unary plus
–	unary minus
*	multiplication
/	division
\	integer division
Mod	modulus
+	addition
–	subtraction
&	concatenation
=	relational is equal to
<>	relational is not equal to
<	relational less than
<=	relational less than or equal to
>	relational greater than
>=	relational greater than or equal to
Like	pattern matching
Is	reference comparison
TypeOf	type comparison
Not	logical negation
And	logical AND without short-circuit evaluation
AndAlso	logical AND with short-circuit evaluation
Or	logical inclusive OR without short-circuit evaluation
OrElse	logical inclusive OR with short-circuit evaluation
Xor	logical exclusive OR

Figure A.1   Operator list (in order of operator precedence).

APPENDIX

B

ASCII Character Set

T he digits in the left column of Fig. B.1 are the left digits of the decimal equivalent (0–127) of the character code, and the digits in the top row of Fig. B.1 are the right digits of the character code. For example, the character code for "F" is 70, and the character code for "&" is 38.

Most users of this book are interested in the ASCII character set used to represent English characters on many computers. The ASCII character set is a subset of the Unicode® character set used by Visual Basic .NET to represent characters from most of the world's languages.

	0	1	2	3	4	5	6	7	8	9
0	nul	soh	stx	etx	eot	enq	ack	bel	bs	ht
1	nl	vt	ff	cr	so	si	dle	dc1	dc2	dc3
2	dc4	nak	syn	etb	can	em	sub	esc	fs	gs
3	rs	us	sp	!	"	#	$	%	&	'
4	(	)	*	+	,	-	.	/	0	1
5	2	3	4	5	6	7	8	9	:	;
6	<	=	>	?	@	A	B	C	D	E
7	F	G	H	I	J	K	L	M	N	O
8	P	Q	R	S	T	U	V	W	X	Y
9	Z	[	\	]	^	_	'	a	b	c
10	d	e	f	g	h	i	j	k	l	m
11	n	o	p	q	r	s	t	u	v	w
12	x	y	z	{	|	}	~	del		

Figure B.1   ASCII character set.

GUI Design Guidelines

T his appendix contains a complete list of the GUI design guidelines presented at the end of each tutorial. The guidelines are organized by tutorial; within each tutorial section, they are organized by control.

Tutorial 3: Welcome Application (Introduction to Visual Programming)

Overall Design

■ Use colors in your applications, but not to the point of distracting the user.

Form

■ Choose short and descriptive Form titles. Capitalize words that are not articles, prepositions or conjunctions. Do not use punctuation.

■ Use Tahoma font to improve readability for controls that display text.

Label

■ Use Labels to display text that users cannot change.

■ Ensure that all Label controls are large enough to display their text.

PictureBox

■ Use PictureBoxes to enhance GUIs with graphics that users cannot change.

■ Images should fit inside their PictureBoxes. This can be achieved by setting Picture-Box property SizeMode to StretchImage.

Tutorial 4: Designing the Inventory Application (Introducing TextBoxes and Buttons)

Overall Design

■ Arrange groups of controls at least two grid units apart on a Form.

■ Leave at least two grid units of space between the edges of the Form and the controls nearest each edge.

■ Use a control's Location property to precisely specify its position on the Form.

■ Place an application's output below and/or to the right of the Form's input controls.

Button

■ Buttons are labelled using their Text property. These labels should use book-title capitalization and be as short as possible while still being meaningful to the user.

■ Buttons should be stacked downward from the top right of a Form or arranged on the same line starting from the bottom right of a Form.

Form

■ Changing the Form's title allows users to identify the application's purpose.

■ Form titles should use book-title capitalization.

■ Change the Form font to Tahoma to be consistent with Microsoft's recommended font for Windows.

Label

■ The TextAlign property of a descriptive Label should be set to MiddleLeft. This ensures that text within groups of Labels align.

■ A descriptive Label should be placed above or to the left of the control that it identifies.

■ A descriptive Label should have the same height as the TextBox it describes if the controls are arranged horizontally.

■ A descriptive Label and the control it identifies should be aligned on the left if they are arranged vertically.

■ Align the left sides of a group of descriptive Labels if the Labels are arranged vertically.

■ A Label can be used to display output to the user. Use a descriptive Label to identify each output Label.

■ Output Labels should look different from descriptive Labels to focus the user's attention. This can be done by setting the BorderStyle property to Fixed3D and the TextAlign property to MiddleCenter.

■ If several output Labels are arranged vertically to display numbers used in a mathematical calculation (such as in an invoice), use the MiddleRight TextAlign property.

■ A descriptive Label and the control it identifies should be aligned on the top if they are arranged horizontally.

TextBox

■ Use TextBoxes to input data from the keyboard.

■ TextBoxes should have descriptive Labels indicating the input expected from the user.

■ Make TextBoxes wide enough for expected input.

Tutorial 7: Wage Calculator Application (Introducing Algorithms, Pseudocode and Program Control)

Overall Design

■ Format all monetary amounts using the C (currency) format specifier.

TextBox

■ When using multiple TextBoxes vertically, align the TextBoxes on their right sides, and where possible make the TextBoxes the same size. Left-align the descriptive Labels for such TextBoxes.

Tutorial 8: Dental Payment Application (Introducing CheckBoxes and Message Dialogs)

CheckBox

■ A CheckBox's label should be descriptive and as short as possible. When a CheckBox label contains more than one word, use book-title capitalization.

■ Align groups of CheckBoxes either horizontally or vertically.

Message Dialog

■ Text displayed in a dialog should be descriptive and as short as possible.

Tutorial 9: Car Payment Calculator Application (Introducing the Do While...Loop and Do Until...Loop Repetition Statements)

ListBox

- A ListBox should be large enough to display all of its content or large enough that scrollbars may be used easily.
- Use headers in a ListBox when you are displaying tabular data. Adding headers improves readability by indicating the information that will be displayed in the ListBox.

Tutorial 10: Class Average Application (Introducing the Do...Loop While and Do...Loop Until Repetition Statements)

Button

- Disable a Button when its function should not be available to users.
- Enable a disabled Button when its function once again should be available to users.

Tutorial 11: Interest Calculator Application (Introducing the For...Next Repetition Statement)

NumericUpDown

- A NumericUpDown control should follow the same GUI Design Guidelines as a single-line TextBox.

TextBox

- If a TextBox will display multiple lines of output, set the Multiline property to True and left-align the output by setting the TextAlign property to Left.
- If a multiline TextBox will display many lines of output, limit the TextBox height and use a vertical scrollbar to allow users to view additional lines of output.

Tutorial 12: Security Panel Application (Introducing Select Case Multiple Selection Statement)

Overall Design

- If your GUI is modeling a real-world object, your GUI design should mimic the physical appearance of the object.

TextBox

- Mask passwords or other sensitive pieces of information in TextBoxes.

Tutorial 14: Shipping Time Application (Using Dates and Timers)

DateTimePicker

- Use a DateTimePicker to retrieve date and time information from the user.
- Each DateTimePicker should have a corresponding descriptive Label.
- If the user should specify a time of day or a date and time, set the DateTimePicker's ShowUpDown property to True. If the user should specify a date, set the DateTimePicker's ShowUpDown property to False to allow the user to select a day from the month calendar.

GroupBox

- GroupBox titles should be concise and should use book-title capitalization.
- Use GroupBoxes to group related controls on the Form visually.

Tutorial 17: Flag Quiz Application (Introducing One-Dimensional Arrays and ComboBoxes)

ComboBox

■ Each ComboBox should have a descriptive Label that describes the ComboBox's contents.

■ If a ComboBox's content should not be editable, set its DropDownStyle property to DropDownList.

Tutorial 18: Sales Data Application (Introducing Two-Dimensional Arrays, RadioButtons and the MSChart Control)

MSChart Control

■ Resize an MSChart control so that all the data is clearly visible.

■ Set the MSChart control's Enabled property to False to prevent users from repositioning the chart within the MSChart control.

■ Assign meaningful descriptions in the MSChart graph's title and axis labels. Use book-title capitalization for these descriptions.

■ Increase the MSChart graph's title and axis label font sizes to enhance readability.

RadioButton

■ Use RadioButtons when the user should choose only one option in a group.

■ Always place each group of RadioButtons in a separate container (such as a GroupBox).

■ Align groups of RadioButtons either horizontally or vertically.

Tutorial 19: Microwave Oven Application (Building Your Own Classes and Objects)

Panel

■ Use Panels to organize groups of related controls where the purpose of those controls is obvious. If the purpose of the controls is not obvious, use a GroupBox in place of a Panel, because GroupBoxes can contain captions.

■ A Panel can display scrollbars if that Panel is not large enough to display all of its controls at once. To increase readability, we suggest avoiding the use of scrollbars on a Panel. If the Panel is not large enough to display all of its contents, increase the size of the Panel.

■ Although it is possible to have a Panel without a border (by setting the BorderStyle property to None), use borders on your Panels whenever possible. This helps to increase readability and organization.

Tutorial 20: Shipping Hub Application (Introducing Collections, the For Each...Next Statement and Access Keys)

Overall Design

■ Set a control's TabStop property to True only if the control is used to receive user input.

■ Use the TabIndex property to define the logical order in which the user should enter data.

■ Use access keys to allow users to "click" a control using the keyboard.

■ Usually the tab order transfers the focus of the application from top to bottom and left to right.

Tutorial 22: Typing Application (Introducing Keyboard Events, Menus and Dialogs)

MainMenus

■ Use book-title capitalization in menu item text.

- Use separator bars in a menu to group related menu items.
- If clicking a menu item opens a dialog, an ellipsis (...) should follow the menu item's text.

Tutorial 27: Phone Book Application (Introducing Multimedia Using Microsoft Agent)

Microsoft Agent Control

- The Microsoft Agent character should be located near the application Form when the character is displayed on the screen.
- Use Microsoft Agent character gestures to indicate actions the user should take, or a response to an action the user has already taken.

Visual Studio .NET Windows Form Designer Tools

This book presents some 20 different controls available in Visual Studio .NET. In all, there are 47 items available to you by default in the **Toolbox**. This appendix contains a chart (Fig. D.1) indicating the purpose and usage of each of these controls. A list of Web resources can be found after the chart.

Icon	Item	Purpose	Usage
	Pointer	Allows you to select and modify elements in the IDE. The pointer is not a control.	Used to navigate a GUI.
	Button	Allows users to indicate that an action should be performed.	Most commonly used to execute code when clicked.
	CheckBox	Allows the user to select or deselect an option.	Becomes checked when selected and unchecked when deselected.
	CheckedList-Box	Provides the user with a checkable list of items.	Much like a CheckBox, but all options are contained in a format similar to that of a ListBox.
	ColorDialog	Allows the user to display the Windows **Color** dialog.	Used to retrieve a user's color selection in an application.
	ComboBox	Provides a short list of items in a drop-down menu.	Allow the user to view, enter new text in or search with a search String from multiple items in a list.
	ContextMenu	Displays a menu of programmer-defined options when the user right-clicks an object.	Provide additional options or features as a shortcut.

Figure D.1 Visual Studio .NET Windows **Form** Designer Tools. (Part 1 of 4.)

Icon	Item	Purpose	Usage
	Crystal-ReportViewer	Graphically displays data.	Display a graphic representation of a `DataGrid` object.
	DataGrid	Displays data within a chart.	Represent ADO .NET data in a scrollable chart.
	DateTime-Picker	Allows users to choose the date and time.	Display or allow the selection of a time and date.
	DomainUpDown	Displays string values, using the up and down arrows.	Select strings from an `Object` collection.
	ErrorProvider	Displays errors regarding a control to the user.	Inform the user if there is an error associated with the control.
	FontDialog	Displays a font dialog that includes all available fonts installed on the computer.	Used to retrieve a user-specified font format and size in an application.
	GroupBox	Allows controls to be grouped together.	Organize related controls separately from the rest of the `Form`.
	HelpProvider	Provides additional help features for a specific control.	Create additional help features for a control.
	HScrollBar	A horizontal scrollbar.	Allow users to view text or graphics that may be too large to display horizontally in a control.
	ImageList	A manageable list of images.	Store a list of images for use in other controls, such as a `ListView` or menu.
	Label	Displays text to the user.	Identify specific items on the `Form` or display general-purpose text.
	LinkLabel	Similar to a `Label` control but can include hyperlinks.	Display a hyperlink label that, when clicked, will open a file or Web page.
	ListBox	Provides a list of items.	Allow the user to view and select from multiple items in a list.
	ListView	Displays a group of items with identifiable icons.	Display a list of items (such as files) much like Windows Explorer.
	MainMenu	Creates a menu object on a Form.	Allow users to select options from menus, adding functionality to the application.
	MonthCalendar	Allows the user to select the date and time from a calendar that displays one month at a time.	Retrieve a user's date selection from a calendar.

Figure D.1   Visual Studio .NET Windows **Form** Designer Tools. (Part 2 of 4.)

Icon	Item	Purpose	Usage
	NotifyIcon	Creates icons that are displayed in a status area, usually while an action is performed in the background.	Remind the user that a certain process is running in the background of the application.
	NumericUpDown	Contains a number that is increased or decreased by clicking the up or down arrows.	Allow the user to specify a number in programmer-defined increments.
	OpenFile-Dialog	Displays a dialog to assist the user in selecting a file.	Retrieve user's file-name selection.
	PageSetup-Dialog	Displays a dialog to allow the user to change a document's page properties.	Allow users to modify the page settings and printer options.
	Panel	Similar to a GroupBox, but can include a scrollbar.	Group controls separately on the Form.
	PictureBox	Displays images.	Allow users to view graphics in an application.
	PrintDialog	Allows the user to select a printer and printing options.	Shown to retrieve user selection for printing options.
	PrintDocument	Executes the printing process.	Accessed to print documents.
	PrintPreview-Control	Allows the user to preview a document before printing it.	Display a preview of the document.
	PrintPreview-Dialog	A dialog used to display a PrintPreviewControl.	Display a print-preview dialog.
	ProgressBar	Displays a visual representation of the progress of an action or set of actions.	Inform the user of the completeness of an operation.
	RadioButton	Provides the user with a list of options from which only one or none can be selected.	Allow users to select at most one option from several.
	RichTextBox	Creates a TextBox control with advanced text-editing capabilities.	Allow users to perform more sophisticated editing beyond the features of a TextBox.
	SaveFile-Dialog	Assists the user in selecting a location in which to save a file.	Allow files to be saved.
	Splitter	Allows the user to resize a docked control within an application.	Give the users the ability to change the size of a control.
	StatusBar	Display useful information regarding the Form or objects in the application.	Notify the user of information not intended for the body of a Form.

Figure D.1   Visual Studio .NET Windows **Form** Designer Tools. (Part 3 of 4.)

Icon	Item	Purpose	Usage
	TabControl	Displays available tab pages in which you can place other controls.	Allow multiple tab pages on a **Form**.
	TextBox	Accepts user input from the keyboard. Can also be used to display text.	Used to retrieve user input from the keyboard.
	Timer	Performs an action at programmer-specified intervals. A **Timer** is not visible to the user.	Allow the action of an event through a specific amount of time.
	ToolBar	Contains icons representing specific commands.	Provide the user with options in a toolbar.
	ToolTip	Displays text information about an object when the mouse cursor is over it.	Display additional information to the user.
	TrackBar	Allows the user to set a value from a specified range.	Similar to the scrollbar, but includes a range of values.
	TreeView	Displays a tree structure of objects, using nodes.	Display a hierarchical representation of a collection of objects.
	VScrollBar	Allows users to view text or graphics that may be too large to display vertically in a control.	Enable a vertical scrollbar in the control.

Figure D.1   Visual Studio .NET Windows **Form** Designer Tools. (Part 4 of 4.)

D.1 Internet and Web Resources

A great way to learn about controls not covered in this book is to use them. Several Web sites provide information to help you get started. The following sites should help you as you explore new features of Visual Studio .NET:

http://msdn.microsoft.com/library/default.asp?url=/library/en-us/ vbcon/html/vbconSelectingWFCClientControl.asp
This site provides documentation for the most commonly used Windows **Form** controls, gouped by function.

http://dotnet247.com/247reference/guide/48.aspx
This site provides articles describing features and usage of common controls in .NET. You will also find links to discussions of more advanced topics in .NET.

http://msdn.microsoft.com/library/default.asp?url=/library/en-us/ vbcon/html/vboricontrolsforwinforms.asp
This Web page provides a more technical description of controls you can use on a Windows **Form**.

APPENDIX

Controls, Events, Properties & Methods

This appendix contains a listing of controls and predefined classes used in the text. Each control or class includes a description of its purpose, as well as explanations of events, properties and methods related to that control or class, as covered in the text.

Tutorial 1: Graphing Application (*Introducing Computers, the Internet and Visual Basic .NET*)

No new elements.

Tutorial 2: Welcome Application (*Introducing the Visual Studio® .NET IDE*)

No new elements.

Tutorial 3: Welcome Application (*Introduction to Visual Programming*)

Label   **A** Label   This control displays text on the Form that the user cannot modify.

■ *In action*

■ *Properties*

Font—This property specifies the font name, style and size of the text displayed in the Label.

Text—This property specifies the text displayed on the Label.

TextAlign—This property specifies how the text is aligned within the Label.

PictureBox   PictureBox   This control displays an image on the Form.

■ *In action*

■ *Properties*

Image—This property specifies the file path of the image.

SizeMode—This property specifies how the image is displayed in the PictureBox.

Size—This property specifies the height and width (in pixels) of the PictureBox.

Tutorial 4: Designing the Inventory Application (Introducing TextBoxes and Buttons)

Label   **A** Label   This control displays text on the Form that the user cannot modify.

■ *In action*

Total: [   ]

■ *Properties*

BorderStyle—This property specifies the appearance of the Label's border.

Font—This property specifies the font name, style and size of the text displayed in the Label.

Location—This property specifies the location of the Label on the Form relative to the top-left corner.

Name—This property specifies the name used to access the Label programmatically. The name should be prefixed with lbl.

Size—This property specifies the height and width (in pixels) of the Label.

Text—This property specifies the text displayed on the Label.

TextAlign—This property specifies how the text is aligned within the Label.

TextBox   [abl] TextBox   This control allows the user to input data from the keyboard.

■ *In action*

[0   ]

■ *Properties*

Name—This property specifies the name used to access the TextBox programmatically. The name should be prefixed with txt.

Location—This property specifies the location of the TextBox on the Form relative to the top-left corner.

Size—This property specifies the height and width (in pixels) of the TextBox.

Text—This property specifies the text displayed in the TextBox.

TextAlign—This property specifies how the text is aligned within the TextBox.

Button 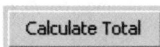 This control allows the user to raise an action or event.

- *In action*

    Calculate Total

- *Properties*

    Location—This property specifies the location of the Button on the Form relative to the top-left corner.

    Name—This property specifies the name used to access the Button programmatically. The name should be prefixed with btn.

    Size—This property specifies the height and width (in pixels) of the Button.

    Text—This property specifies the text displayed on the Button.

Tutorial 5: Completing the Inventory Application (Introducing Programming)

Button This control allows the user to raise an action or event.

- *In action*

    Calculate Total

- *Events*

    Click—This event is raised when the user clicks the Button.

- *Properties*

    Location—This property specifies the location of the Button on the Form relative to the top-left corner.

    Name—This property specifies the name used to access the Button programmatically. The name should be prefixed with btn.

    Size—This property specifies the height and width (in pixels) of the Button.

    Text—This property specifies the text displayed on the Button.

Tutorial 6: Enhancing the Inventory Application (Introducing Variables, Memory Concepts and Arithmetic)

TextBox [abi] TextBox This control allows the user to input data from the keyboard.

- *In action*

    | 0 |

- *Events*

    TextChanged—This event is raised when the text in the TextBox is changed.

- *Properties*

    Location—This property specifies the location of the Label on the Form relative to the top-left corner.

    Name—This property specifies the name used to access the TextBox programmatically. The name should be prefixed with txt.

    Size—This property specifies the height and width (in pixels) of the TextBox.

    Text—This property specifies the text displayed in the TextBox.

    TextAlign—This property specifies how the text is aligned within the TextBox.

Tutorial 7: Wage Calculator Application (Introducing Algorithms, Pseudocode and Program Control)

String The String class represents a series of characters treated as a single unit.

■ *Method*

Format—This method arranges the string in a specified format.

Tutorial 8: Dental Payment Application (Introducing CheckBoxes and Message Dialogs)

CheckBox   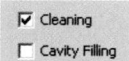   This control allows the user to select an option.

■ *In action*

> ☑ Cleaning
> ☐ Cavity Filling

■ *Properties*

Checked—This property specifies whether the CheckBox is checked (True) or unchecked (False).

Location—This property specifies the location of the CheckBox on the Form.

Name—This property specifies the name used to access the CheckBox control programmatically. The name should be prefixed with chk.

Text—This property specifies the text displayed next to the CheckBox.

Tutorial 9: Car Payment Calculator Application (Introducing the Do While...Loop and Do Until...Loop Repetition Statements)

Convert The Convert class converts the value of a data type to another data type.

■ *Method*

ToDecimal—This method converts the value from another data type to type Decimal.

ListBox   ListBox   This control allows the user to view and select from items in a list.

■ *In action*

Months	Monthly Payments
24	$490.50
36	$339.06
48	$263.55
60	$218.41

■ *Properties*

Items—This property returns an object that contains the items displayed in the ListBox.

Location—This property specifies the location of the ListBox on the Form relative to the top-left corner.

Name—This property specifies the name used to access the ListBox programatically. The name should be prefixed with lst.

Size—This property specifies the height and width (in pixels) of the ListBox.

■ *Methods*

Items.Add—This method adds an item to the Items property.

Items.Clear—This method deletes all the values in the ListBox's Items property.

Tutorial 10: Class Average Application (Introducing the Do...Loop While and Do...Loop Until Repetition Statements)

Button   `ab| Button` This control allows the user to raise an action or event.

- ■ *In action*

  Calculate Total

- ■ *Events*

  Click—This event is raised when the user clicks the Button.

- ■ *Properties*

  Enabled—This property determines whether the Button's event handler is executed when the Button is clicked.

  Location—This property specifies the location of the Button on the Form relative to the top-left corner.

  Name—This property specifies the name used to access the Button programmatically. The name should be prefixed with btn.

  Size—This property specifies the height and width (in pixels) of the Button.

  Text—This property specifies the text displayed on the Button.

- ■ *Methods*

  Focus—This method transfers the focus of the application to the Button that calls it.

ListBox `E| ListBox` This control allows the user to view and select from items in a list.

- ■ *In action*

Months	Monthly Payments
24	$490.50
36	$339.06
48	$263.55
60	$218.41

- ■ *Properties*

  Items—This property returns an object that contains the items displayed in the ListBox.

  Items.Count—This property returns the number of items in the ListBox.

  Items.Item—This property returns the values at the specified index in the ListBox.

  Location—This property specifies the location of the ListBox on the Form relative to the top-left corner.

  Name—This property specifies the name used to access the ListBox programatically. The name should be prefixed with lst.

  Size—This property specifies the height and width (in pixels) of the ListBox.

- ■ *Methods*

  Items.Add—This method adds an item to the Items property.

  Items.Clear—This method deletes all the values in the ListBox's Items property.

TextBox `abl TextBox` This control allows the user to input data from the keyboard.

- ■ *In action*

   0

- ■ *Event*

  TextChanged—This event is raised when the text in the TextBox is changed.

- *Properties*

  Location—This property specifies the location of the TextBox on the Form relative to the top-left corner.

  Name—This property specifies the name used to access the TextBox programmatically. The name should be prefixed with txt.

  Size—This property specifies the height and width (in pixels) of the TextBox.

  Text—This property specifies the text displayed in the TextBox.

  TextAlign—This property specifies how the text is aligned within the TextBox.

- *Methods*

  Focus—This method transfers the focus of the application to the TextBox that calls it.

Tutorial 11: Interest Calculator Application (Introducing the For...Next Repetition Statement)

NumericUpDown   This control allows you to specify maximum and minimum numeric input values.

- *In action*

  6

- *Properties*

  Location—This property specifies the location of the NumericUpDown control on the Form relative to the top-left corner.

  Maximum—This property determines the maximum input value in a particular NumericUp-Down control.

  Minimum—This property determines the minimum input value in a particular NumericUp-Down control.

  Name—This property specifies the name used to access the NumericUpDown control programmatically. The name should be prefixed with upd.

  ReadOnly—This property determines whether the input value can be typed by the user.

  Size—This property specifies the height and width (in pixels) of the NumericUpDown control.

  TextAlign—This property specifies how the text is aligned within the NumericUpDown control.

TextBox   This control allows the user to input data from the keyboard.

- *In action*

  0

- *Events*

  TextChanged—This event is raised when the text in the TextBox is changed.

- *Properties*

  Location—This property specifies the location of the TextBox on the Form relative to the top-left corner.

  Multiline—This property specifies whether the TextBox is capable of displaying multiple lines of text.

  Name—This property specifies the name used to access the TextBox programmatically. The name should be prefixed with txt.

  ReadOnly—This property determines whether the value of a TextBox can be changed.

  ScrollBars—This property specifies whether the TextBox contains a scrollbar.

  Size—This property specifies the height and width (in pixels) of the TextBox.

  Text—This property specifies the text displayed in the TextBox.

TextAlign—This property specifies how the text is aligned within the TextBox.

- *Methods*

   Focus—This method transfers the focus of the application to the TextBox that calls it.

Tutorial 12: Security Panel Application (Introducing the Select Case Multiple-Selection Statement)

TextBox   This control allows the user to input data from the keyboard.

- *In action*

   | 0 |

- *Events*

   TextChanged—This event is raised when the text in the TextBox is changed.

- *Properties*

   Enabled—This property determines whether the user can enter data (True) in the TextBox or not (False).

   Location—This property specifies the location of the TextBox on the Form relative to the top-left corner.

   Multiline—This property specifies whether the TextBox is capable of displaying multiple lines of text.

   Name—This property specifies the name used to access the TextBox programmatically. The name should be prefixed with txt.

   PasswordChar—This property specifies the masking character to be used when displaying data in the TextBox.

   ReadOnly—This property determines whether the value of a TextBox can be changed.

   ScrollBars—This property specifies whether the TextBox contains a scrollbar.

   Size—This property specifies the height and width (in pixels) of the TextBox.

   Text—This property specifies the text displayed in the TextBox.

   TextAlign—This property specifies how the text is aligned within the TextBox.

- *Methods*

   Focus—This method transfers the focus of the application to the TextBox that calls it.

Tutorial 13: Enhancing the Wage Calculator Application (Introducing Function Procedures and Sub Procedures)

Math   This class provides methods used to perform common arithmetic calculations.

- *Methods*

   Min—Returns the smaller of two numeric values.

   Max—Returns the larger of two numeric values.

   Sqrt—Returns the square root of a numeric value.

Tutorial 14: Shipping Time Application (Using Dates and Timers)

Date   This structure provides properties and methods to store and manipulate date and time information.

- *Properties*

   Day—This property returns the day stored in a Date variable.

   Hour—This property returns the hour stored in a Date variable.

   Month—This property returns the month stored in a Date variable.

   Now—This property returns the system's current date and time.

   Year—This property returns the year stored in a Date variable.

- *Methods*

    AddDays—This method creates a new Date value that is the specified number of days later (or earlier) in time.

    AddHours—This method creates a new Date value that is the specified number of hours later (or earlier) in time.

    AddMinutes—This method creates a new Date value that is the specified number of minutes later (or earlier) in time.

    ToLongDateString—This method returns a String containing the date in the format "Wednesday, October 30, 2002."

    ToShortTimeString—This method returns a String containing the time in the format "4:00 PM."

DateTimePicker   This control is used to retrieve date and time information from the user.

- *In action*

DateTimePicker using default format

- *Events*

    ValueChanged—This event is raised when the Value property is changed.

- *Properties*

    CustomFormat—This property sets which format string to use when displaying the date and/or time.

    Format—This property specifies the format in which the date and time are displayed on the control.

    > Long—This value specifies that the date should be displayed in the format "Monday, December 09, 2002."

    > Short—This value specifies that the date should be displayed in the format "12/ 9/2002."

    > Time—This value specifies that the time should be displayed in the format "8:39:53 PM."

    > Custom—This value allows the programmer to specify a custom format in which to display the date and/or time.

    Hour—This property stores the hour in the DateTimePicker control.

    Location—This property specifies the location of the DateTimePicker control on its container relative to the container's top-left corner.

    MinDate—This property specifies the minimum date and/or time that can be selected when using this control.

    MaxDate—This property specifies the maximum date and/or time that can be selected when using this control.

    Name—This property specifies the name used to access the DateTimePicker control programmatically. The name should be prefixed with dtp.

    ShowUpDown—This property specifies whether the up-down arrows (True) are displayed on the control for time values. If False, a down arrow is displayed for accessing a drop-down calendar.

    Value—This property stores the date and/or time in the DateTimePicker control.

GroupBox `[xv] GroupBox`   This control groups related controls visually.

■ *In action*

> Drop Off
>
> Enter drop-off time: `01:00 PM` ⬍

■ *Properties*

Name—This property specifies the name used to access the GroupBox control programmatically. The name should be prefixed with fra.

Location—This property specifies the location of the GroupBox control on the Form.

Size—This property specifies the height and width (in pixels) of the GroupBox control.

Text—This property specifies the text displayed on the GroupBox.

Timer `⏱ Timer`   This control wakes up at specified intervals of time to execute code in its Tick event handler.

■ *Events*

Tick—This event is raised after the number of milliseconds specified in the Interval property has elapsed.

■ *Properties*

Enabled—This property determines whether the Timer is running (True). The default is False.

Interval—This property determines the time interval between Tick events.

Name—This property specifies the name used to access the Timer control programmatically. The name should be prefixed with tmr.

Tutorial 15: Fund Raiser Application (Introducing Scope, Pass-by-Reference and Option Strict)

No new elements.

Tutorial 16: Craps Game Application (Introducing Random-Number Generation)

Directory This class provides functionality to manipulate directories such as creating, moving, and navigating through them.

■ *Method*

GetCurrentDirectory—This method returns the location of the folder from which the application was loaded.

Image This class provides functionality to manipulate images.

■ *Method*

FromFile—This method is used to specify the physical location (path) of the image.

Random This class is used to generate random numbers.

■ *Methods*

Next—This method, when called with no arguments, generates a positive Integer value between zero and the largest possible Integer, which is the constant Int32.MaxValue (2,147,483,647).

NextDouble—This method generates a positive Double value that is greater than or equal to 0.0 and less than 1.0.

Tutorial 17: Flag Quiz Application (Introducing One-Dimensional Arrays and ComboBoxes)

Array This data structure stores a fixed number of elements of the same type.

■ *Property*

Length—This property specifies the number of elements in the array.

■ *Methods*

GetUpperBound—This method returns the largest index of the array.

Sort—This method orders an array's elements. An array of numerical values would be organized in ascending order and an array of Strings would be organized in alphabetical order.

ComboBox This control allows users to select from a drop-down list of options.

■ *In action*

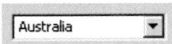

■ *Properties*

DataSource–This property specifies the source of items listed in a ComboBox.

DropDownStyle–This property specifies a ComboBox's appearance.

Enabled–This property specifies whether a user can select an item from the ComboBox.

Location—This property specifies the location of the ComboBox control on the container control relative to the top-left corner.

MaxDropDownItems—Property that specifies the maximum number of items the ComboBox can display in its drop-down list.

Name—This property specifies the name used to access the ComboBox control programmatically. The name should be prefixed with cbo.

SelectedIndex—This property specifies the index of the selected item. Returns –1 if no item is selected.

SelectedValue—This property specifies the selected item.

Size—This property specifies the height and width (in pixels) of the ComboBox control.

Sorted—This property, when set to True, displays the ComboBox options in alphabetical order or ascending order.

String The String class represents a series of characters treated as a single unit.

■ *Methods*

Format—This method arranges the string in a specified format.

IndexOf—This method returns the index of the specified character(s) in a String.

Insert—This method returns a copy of the String for which it is called with the specified character(s) inserted.

Remove—This method returns a copy of the String for which it is called with the specified character(s) removed.

ToLower—This method returns a copy of the String for which it is called with any uppercase letters converted to lowercase letters.

Tutorial 18: Sales Data Application (Introducing Two-Dimensional Arrays, RadioButtons and the MSChart Control)

MSChart MSChart This control is used to display data in graphs.

■ *In action*

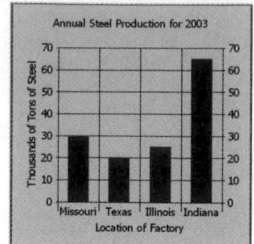

■ *Properties*

ChartData—This property contains the data to be graphed.

ChartType—This property determines the appearance of the graph.

Location—This property specifies the location of the MSChart control on the container control relative to the top-left corner.

Name—This property specifies the name used to access the MSChart control programmatically. The name should be prefixed with ch.

Size—This property specifies the height and width (in pixels) of the MSChart control.

RadioButton   This control is used to enable users to select exactly one option from several.

■ *In action*

■ *Event*

CheckedChanged—This event is raised when the control is either selected or deselected.

■ *Properties*

Checked—This property is True if the control is selected and False if it is not selected.

Location—This property specifies the location of the RadioButton control on the container control relative to the top-left corner.

Name—This property specifies the name used to access the RadioButton control programmatically. The name should be prefixed with rad.

Size—This property specifies the height and width (in pixels) of the RadioButton control.

Text—This property specifies the text displayed in the label to the right of the RadioButton.

Tutorial 19: Microwave Oven Application (Building Your Own Classes and Objects)

Button   ab Button   This control allows the user to raise an action or event.

■ *In action*

Calculate Total

■ *Event*

Click—This event is raised when the user clicks the Button.

■ *Properties*

Enabled—This property determines whether the Button's event handler is executed when the Button is clicked.

FlatStyle—This property determines whether the Button will appear flat or three-dimensional.

  Flat—This value specifies that a Button will appear flat.

Location—This property specifies the location of the Button on the Form relative to the top-left corner.

Name—This property specifies the name used to access the Button programmatically. The name should be prefixed with btn.

Size—This property specifies the height and width (in pixels) of the Button.

Text—This property specifies the text displayed on the Button.

■ *Method*

Focus—This method transfers the focus of the application to the Button that calls it.

Convert The Convert class converts the value of a data type to another data type.

■ *Methods*

ToChar—This method converts a value into a character (of data type Char).

ToDecimal—This method converts the value from another data type to type Decimal.

Label   A Label   This control displays text on the Form that the user cannot modify.

■ *In action*

Total: [   ]

■ *Properties*

BorderStyle—This property specifies the appearance of the Label's border.

  FixedSingle—This value specifies that the Label will display a thin, black border.

Font—This property specifies the font name, style and size of the text displayed in the Label.

Location—This property specifies the location of the Label on the Form relative to the top-left corner.

Name—This property specifies the name used to access the Label programmatically. The name should be prefixed with lbl.

Size—This property specifies the height and width (in pixels) of the Label.

Text—This property specifies the text displayed on the Label.

TextAlign—This property specifies how the text is aligned within the Label.

Panel   ☐ Panel   This control is used to organize various controls. Unlike a GroupBox control, the Panel control does not display a caption.

■ *In action*

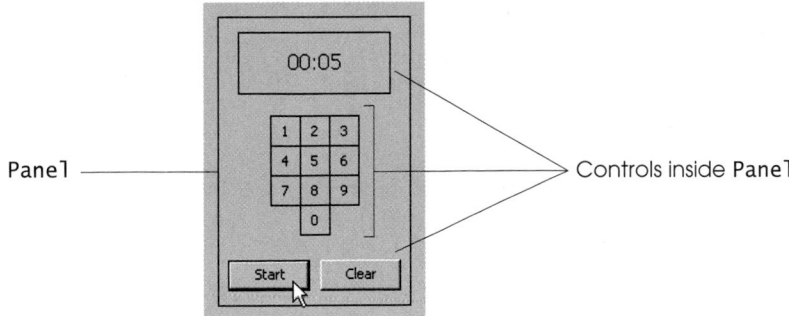

Panel — Controls inside Panel

■ *Properties*

DefaultBackColor—This property returns the default background color of a Panel control.

Name—This property specifies the name of the Panel.

Size—This property specifies the size of the Panel.

Location—This property specifies the Panel's location on the Form.

BorderStyle—This property specifies the Panel's border style. Options include None (displaying no border), FixedSingle (a single-line border) and Fixed3D (a three-dimensional border).

    None—This value specifies that the Panel's will not display a border.

    FixedSingle—This value specifies that the Panel will display a thin, black border.

    Fixed3D—This value specifies that the Panel will display a three-dimensional border.

BackColor—This property specifies the background color of the Panel.

String The String class represents a series of characters treated as a single unit.

- *Property*

Length—This property returns the number of characters in the String.

- *Methods*

Format—This method arranges the string in a specified format.

IndexOf—This method returns the index of the specified character(s) in a String.

Insert—This method returns a copy of the String for which it is called with the specified character(s) inserted.

PadLeft—This method inserts characters at the beginning of a String.

Remove—This method returns a copy of the String for which it is called with the specified character(s) removed.

Substring—This method returns a substring from a String.

ToLower—This method returns a copy of the String for which it is called with any uppercase letters converted to lowercase letters.

Tutorial 20: Shipping Hub Application (Introducing Collections, the For Each...Next Statement and Access Keys)

ArrayList This class is used to store a variable number of objects.

- *Property*

Count—This property returns the number of objects contained in the ArrayList.

- *Methods*

Add—This method adds an object to the ArrayList object.

Insert—This method adds an object to the ArrayList object at a specific index.

RemoveAt—This method removes an object from the ArrayList object at the specified index.

ComboBox 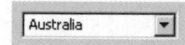 This control allows users to select options from a dropdown list.

- *In action*

    Australia ▾

- *Event*

SelectedIndexChanged—This event is raised when a new value is selected in the ComobBox.

- *Properties*

DataSource—This property allows you to add items to the ComboBox.

DropDownStyle—This property determines the ComboBox's style.

Enabled—This property determines whether the user can enter data (True) in the ComboBox or not (False).

Items—This property specifies the values the user can select from the ComboBox.

    Item—This property retrieves the value at the specified index.

Location—This property specifies the location of the ComboBox control on its container control relative to the top-left corner.

MaxDropDownItems—This property determines the maximum number of items to be displayed when user clicks the drop-down arrow.

Name—This property specifies the name used to access the ComboBox control programmatically. The name should be prefixed with cbo.

SelectedValue—This property contains the item selected by the user.

Text—This property specifies the text displayed in the ComboBox.

TextBox [abl TextBox]   This control allows the user to input data from the keyboard.

- ***In action***

  [0]

- ***Events***

  TextChanged—This event is raised when the text in the TextBox is changed.

- ***Properties***

  Enabled—This property determines whether the user can enter data (True) in the TextBox or not (False).

  Location—This property specifies the location of the TextBox on its container control relative to the top-left corner.

  MaxLength—This property specifies the maximum number of characters that can be input into the TextBox.

  Multiline—This property specifies whether the TextBox is capable of displaying multiple lines of text.

  Name—This property specifies the name used to access the TextBox programmatically. The name should be prefixed with txt.

  PasswordChar—This property specifies the masking character to be used when displaying data in the TextBox.

  ReadOnly—This property determines whether the value of a TextBox can be changed.

  ScrollBars—This property specifies whether a multiline TextBox contains a scrollbar.

  Size—This property specifies the height and width (in pixels) of the TextBox.

  Text—This property specifies the text displayed in the TextBox.

  TextAlign—This property specifies how the text is aligned within the TextBox.

- ***Method***

  Focus—This method transfers the focus of the application to the TextBox that calls it.

Tutorial 21: "Cat and Mouse" Painter Application (Introducing the Graphics Object and Mouse Events)

Form The class that represents an application's GUI.

- ***Events***

  Load—The event raised when an application initially executes.

  MouseDown—The event raised when a mouse button is clicked.

  MouseMove—The event raised when the mouse pointer is moved.

  MouseUp—The event raised when a mouse button is released.

- ***Property***

  BackColor—This property specifies the background color of the Form.

- ***Method***

  CreateGraphics—This method creates a Graphics object.

Graphics The class that contains methods used to draw text, lines and shapes.

■ *Method*

   FillEllipse—This method draws a solid ellipse of a specified size and color at the specified location.

MouseEventArgs The class that contains information about mouse events.

■ *Properties*

   Buttons—The property that specifies which (if any) mouse button was pressed.
   X—The property that specifies the *x*-coordinate of the mouse event.
   Y—The property that specifies the *y*-coordinate of the mouse event.

Tutorial 22: Typing Application (Introducing Keyboard Events, Menus and Dialogs)

Char This structure represents Unicode® characters.

■ *Method*

   ToUpper—This method returns the uppercase equivalent of an alphabetic character.

ColorDialog   [🔲 ColorDialog]   This control allows the user to customize the color of what is being typed.

■ *Properties*

   Color—This property contains the color selected by the user. The default color is black.
   FullOpen—This property, when True, allows the user to see the controls used to create custom colors.

■ *Methods*

   ShowDialog—This method displays the **Color** dialog to the user.

FontDialog   [🅰 FontDialog]   This control allows the user to customize the font, size and style of what is being typed.

■ *Methods*

   ShowDialog—This method displays the **Font** dialog to the user.

KeyEventArgs   This class represents arguments passed to the KeyPress event handler.

■ *Property*

   KeyData—This property contains data about the key that raised the KeyDown event.

KeyPressEventArgs   This class represents arguments passed to the KeyPress event handler.

■ *Property*

   KeyChar—This property contains data about the key that raised the KeyPress event.

MainMenu   [📑 MainMenu]   This control allows you to group related commands for a Windows application.

■ *In action*

■ *Events*

Click—This event is raised when the user clicks a menu item or presses a shortcut key that represents an item.

TextBox   This control allows the user to input data from the keyboard.

■ *In action*

> 0

■ *Events*

KeyDown—This event is raised when a key is pressed. KeyDown is case insensitive. It cannot recognize lowercase letters.

KeyPress—This event is raised when a key is pressed. KeyPress cannot handle modifier keys.

KeyUp—This event is raised when a key is released by the user.

TextChanged—This event is raised when the text in the TextBox is changed.

■ *Properties*

Enabled—This property determines whether the user can enter data (True) in the Text-Box or not (False).

Location—This property specifies the location of the TextBox on the container control relative to the top-left corner.

MaxLength—Specifies the maximum number of characters that can be input into the TextBox.

Multiline—This property specifies whether the TextBox is capable of displaying multiple lines of text.

Name—This property specifies the name used to access the TextBox programmatically. The name should be prefixed with txt.

PasswordChar—This property specifies the masking character to be used when displaying data in the TextBox.

ReadOnly—This property determines whether the value of a TextBox can be changed.

ScrollBars—This property specifies whether the TextBox contains a scrollbar.

Size—This property specifies the height and width (in pixels) of the TextBox.

Text—This property specifies the text displayed in the TextBox.

TextAlign—This property specifies how the text is aligned within the TextBox.

■ *Methods*

Focus—This method transfers the focus of the application to the TextBox that calls it.

Tutorial 23: Screen Scraping Application (Introducing String Processing)

String The String class represents a series of characters treated as a single unit.

■ *Property*

Length—This property returns the number of characters in the String.

■ *Methods*

EndsWith—This method determines if a String ends with a particular substring.

Format—This method arranges the string in a specified format.

IndexOf—This method returns the index of the specified character(s) in a String.

Insert—This method returns a copy of the String for which it is called with the specified character(s) inserted.

LastIndexOf—This method returns the index of the last occurrence of a substring in a String. It returns −1 if the substring is not found.

PadLeft—This method inserts characters at the beginning of a String.

Remove—This method returns a copy of the String for which it is called with the specified character(s) removed.

Replace—This method returns a new String object in which every occurrence of a substring is replaced with a different substring.

StartsWith—This method determines if a String starts with a particular substring.

Substring—This method returns a substring from a String.

ToLower—This method returns a copy of the String for which it is called with any uppercase letters converted to lowercase letters.

ToUpper—This method creates a new String object that replaces every lowercase letter in a String with its uppercase equivalent.

Trim—This method removes all whitespace characters from the beginning and end of a String.

Tutorial 24: Ticket Information Application (Introducing Sequential-Access Files)

ComboBox 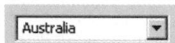 This control allows users to select options from a drop-down list.

- **In action**

  Australia

- **Events**

  SelectedIndexChanged—This event is raised when a new value is selected in the ComboBox.

- **Properties**

  DataSource—This property allows you to add items to the ComboBox.

  DropDownStyle—This property determines the ComboBox's style.

  Enabled—This property determines whether the user can enter data (True) in the ComboBox or not (False).

  Items—This property specifies the values the user can select from the ComboBox.

    Item—This property retrieves the value at the specified index.

  Location—This property specifies the location of the ComboBox control on its container control relative to the top-left corner.

  MaxDropDownItems—This property determines the maximum number of items to be displayed when user clicks the drop-down arrow.

  Name—This property specifies the name used to access the ComboBox control programmatically. The name should be prefixed with cbo.

  SelectedIndex—This property specifies the index of the item selected.

  SelectedValue—This property contains the item selected by the user.

  Text—This property specifies the text displayed in the ComboBox.

- **Methods**

  Items.Add—This method adds an item to the ComboBox.

  Items.Clear—This method deletes all the values in the ComboBox.

MonthCalendar MonthCalendar This control displays a calendar from which the user can select a date or a range of dates.

- **In action**

■ *Events*

DateChanged—Event raised when a new date (or a range of dates) is selected.

■ *Properties*

Location—This property specifies the location of the MonthCalendar control on the Form.

Name—This property specifies the name used to access the properties of the MonthCalendar control in program code. The name should be prefixed with mvw.

SelectionStart—This property returns the first (or only) date selected.

OpenFileDialog [OpenFileDialog] This object enables an application to use the **Open** dialog.

■ *Properties*

CheckFileExists—This property enables the user to display a warning if a specified file does not exist.

FileName—This property sets the default file name displayed in the dialog. It can also be used to retrieve the name of the user-entered file.

Name—This property specifies the name that will be used to reference the control's properties and methods.

■ *Method*

ShowDialog—This method displays the **Open** dialog and returns the result of the user interaction with the dialog.

StreamWriter This class is used to write data to a file.

■ *Methods*

Close—This method is used to close the stream.

WriteLine—This method writes the data specified in its argument, followed by a new line character.

StreamReader This class is used to read data from a file.

■ *Methods*

Close—This method closes the stream.

ReadLine—This method reads a line of data from a particular file.

Tutorial 25: ATM Application (Introducing Database Programming)

OleDbConnection [OleDbConnection] This object establishes connection to a database.

■ *Property*

ConnectionString—This property is used to specify to which database to connect.

■ *Methods*

Close—This method is used to close the connection to the database.

Open—This method is used to open the connection to the database.

OleDbCommand [OleDbCommand] This object is used to execute a command on a database.

■ *Properties*

CommandText—This property is used to specify an SQL statement.

Connection—This property is used to specify the connection to a database.

Parameters—This property is used to specify an unknown value for the SQL statement.

- *Methods*

    ExecuteNonQuery—This method is used to execute nonquery command statements, such as UPDATEs.

    ExecuteReader—This method is used to create a data reader by executing a database query.

OleDbDataReader This object is used to read data from a database.

- *Methods*

    Read—This method is used to retrieve information from the data reader.

    Close—This method is used to close the data reader.

Tutorial 26: CheckWriter Application (Introducing Graphics and Printing)

Font This class is used to define the font face, size and style of text throughout an application.

- *Properties*

    Bold—This property sets the weight of the text.

    Italic—This property sets the angle of the text.

    Size—This property sets the size of the text.

    FontFamily—This property contains a FontFamily object, which is used to store font face information.

    FontSyle—This property specifies the style applied to a Font object.

Graphics The class that contains methods used to draw text, lines and shapes.

- *Methods*

    DrawLine—This method draws a line of a specified size and color.

    DrawEllipse—This method draws the outline of an ellipse of a specified size and color at a specified location.

    DrawRectangle—This method draws the outline of a rectangle of a specified size and color at a specified location.

    DrawEllipse—This method draws a String in a specified font and color at a specified position.

    FillEllipse—This method draws a solid ellipse of a specified size and color at the specified location.

    FillRectangle—This method draws a solid rectangle of a specified size and color at the specified location.

PrintDocument This class allows you to specify how to print a document.

- *Event*

    PrintPage—This event is raised when data required to print a page is needed.

- *Method*

    Print—This method uses a Graphics object to print a page.

PrinterSettings This class stores information the system's printer settings.

- *Property*

    Count—This property returns the number of printers installed on the system.

PrintPageEventArgs This class contains data passed to a `PrintPage` event.

■ *Properties*

`HasMorePages`—This property specifies if there are more pages to print. When `False`, the `PrintPage` event is no longer raised.

`MarginBounds`—This property specifies the margin of the printed page.

    `Left`—This property specifies the left margin of the page.

    `Top`—This property specifies the top margin of the page.

PrintPreviewDialog This control is used to display how a document will look when it is printed.

■ *Properties*

`Document`—This property specifies the document that the control will preview. The document must be of type `PrintDocument`.

`Name`—This property specifies the name used to access the `PrintPreviewDialog` control programmatically. The name should be prefixed with `obj`.

`UseAntiAlias`—This property specifies whether the dialog will display a smoothed image.

■ *Method*

`ShowDialog`—This method is used to display the `PrintPreviewDialog` to the user.

Tutorial 27: Phone Book Application (Introducing Multimedia Using Microsoft Agent)

Convert The `Convert` class converts the value of a data type to another data type.

■ *Methods*

`ToChar`—This method converts a value into a character (of data type `Char`).

`ToDecimal`—This method converts the value from another data type to type `Decimal`.

`ToInt16`—This method converts the value from another data type to type `Short`.

IAgentCtlCharacter This class is used to represent the Agent character that is used in the application.

■ *Property*

`Commands`—This property contains the commands the character will recognize.

■ *Methods*

`Show`—This method displays the character on the screen.

`MoveTo`—This method moves the character to a specified location on the screen.

`Play`—This method plays character animations.

`Speak`—This method specifies the text to be spoken by the character.

`Commands.Add`—Method Add of the `Commands` property adds a new command to the command list for the Agent object.

IAgentCtlUserInput This class is used to retrieve commands from users.

■ *Property*

`Name`—This method retrieves the name of the command given by the user.

Microsoft Agent Control   Control   This control is used to create and
manipulate the multimedia features of a Microsoft Agent character.

- ■ *In action*

- ■ *Events*

  Command—This event is raised when a user gives the Microsoft Agent character a verbal
  command or selects an option from the character's context menu.

  HideEvent—This event is raised when a user hides the Microsoft Agent character.

- ■ *Property*

  Location—This property specifies the location of the Microsoft Agent control on the
  Form.

- ■ *Method*

  Characters.Load—This method loads a character into the Microsoft Agent control.

Tutorial 28: Bookstore Application: Web Applications (Introducing Internet Information Services)

No new elements.

Tutorial 29: Bookstore Application: Client Tier (Introducing Web Controls)

ASPX page   Page on which controls are dropped to design the GUI.

- ■ *Property*

  bgColor—This property specifies the Web Form's background color.

Button   ab| Button   This control allows the user to raise an action or
event.

- ■ *In action*

- ■ *Properties*

  ID—This property that specifies the name of the Label.
  Text—This property specifies the text displayed on the Button.
  Width—This property specifies the width of the Button.

Horizontal Rule   ⊟ Horizontal Rule   This control displays a line on the ASPX page.
It is usually used to separate different areas of the ASPX page.

- ■ *In action*

  _____

- ■ *Properties*

  id—This property specifies the name of the Horizontal Rule.
  Style—This property allows you to specify where to position the Horizontal Rule on the
  ASPX page.

Image   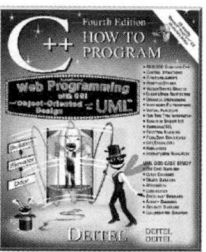 Image   This control displays an image on the ASPX page.

■ *In action*

■ *Properties*

BorderStyle—This property specifies the appearance of the Image's border.

BorderWidth—This property specifies the width of the Image's border.

Height—This property specifies the height of the Image control.

ID—This property specifies the name used to access the Image control programmatically. The name should be prefixed with img.

Width—This property specifies the width of the Image control.

Label   A Label   This control displays text on the ASPX page that the user cannot modify.

■ *In action*

■ *Properties*

Height—This property specifies the height of the Label.

ID—This property specifies the name used to access the Label programmatically. The name should be prefixed with lbl.

Name (under the expanded Font property in the **Solution Explorer**)—This property specifies the name of the font used for the Label's text.

Size (under the expanded Font property in the **Solution Explorer**)—This property specifies the size of the Label's text.

Text—This property specifies the text displayed on the Label.

Width—This property specifies the width of the Label.

ListBox   ListBox   This control allows the user to view and select from multiple items in a list.

■ *In action*

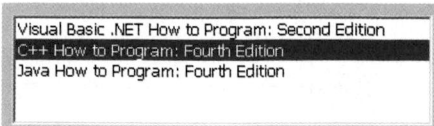

■ *Properties*

Height—This property specifies the height of the ListBox.

ID—This property specifies the name used to access the ListBox control programmatically. The name should be prefixed with lst.

Width—This property specifies the width of the ListBox.

Table   ▦ Table   This control is usually used to organize data in a spreadsheet format.

■ *In action*

Price:	$76.00
ISBN#:	0-13-029363-6
Edition:	2
Copyright Date:	2002
Description:	Microsoft Visual Basic .NET

■ *Properties*

BorderStyle—This property specifies the appearance of the Table's border.

BorderWidth—This property specifies the width of the Table's border.

Cells—This property retrieves or sets the value in the specified table cell.

Gridlines—This property specifies the format in which table cell separators are displayed.

ID—This property specifies the name used to access the Table control programmatically. The name should be prefixed with tbl.

Rows—This property retrieves or sets the value in the specified table cell.

Tutorial 30: Bookstore Application: Information Tier (Examining the Database and Creating Database Components)

No new elements.

Tutorial 31: Bookstore Application: Middle Tier (Introducing Code-Behind Files)

ASPX page   Page on which controls are dropped to design the GUI.

■ *Event*

Load—This event is raised when the ASPX page is created.

■ *Property*

bgColor—This property specifies the Web Form's background color.

Image   ▧ Image   This control displays an image on the ASPX page.

■ *In action*

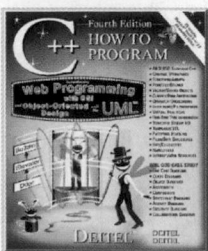

■ *Properties*

BorderStyle—This property specifies the appearance of the Image's border.

BorderWidth—This property specifies the width of the Image's border.

Height—This property specifies the height of the Image control.

ID—This property specifies the name used to access the Image control programmatically. The name should be prefixed with img.

ImageUrl—This property specifies the location of the image file.

Width—This property specifies the width of the Image control.

ListBox 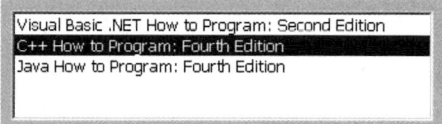 This control allows the user to view and select from multiple items in a list.

■ *In action*

```
Visual Basic .NET How to Program: Second Edition
C++ How to Program: Fourth Edition
Java How to Program: Fourth Edition
```

■ *Properties*

Height—This property specifies the height of the ListBox.

ID—This property specifies the name used to access the ListBox control programmatically. The name should be prefixed with lst.

SelectedIndex—This property returns the index of the selected item in the ListBox.

SelectedItem—This property returns the value of the selected item in the ListBox.

Width—This property specifies the width of the ListBox.

Response This class provides methods for responding to clients.

■ *Method*

Redirect—This method redirects the client browser to the specified location.

Keyword Chart

This table contains a complete listing of Visual Basic .NET keywords is found in Fig. F.1. Many of these keywords are discussed throughout the text.

Visual Basic .NET Keywords

AddHandler	AddressOf	Alias	And
AndAlso	Ansi	As	Assembly
Auto	Boolean	ByRef	Byte
ByVal	Call	Case	Catch
CBool	CByte	CChar	CDate
CDec	CDbl	Char	CInt
Class	CLng	CObj	Const
CShort	CSng	CStr	CType
Date	Decimal	Declare	Default
Delegate	Dim	DirectCast	Do
Double	Each	Else	ElseIf
End	Enum	Erase	Error
Event	Exit	False	Finally
For	Friend	Function	Get
GetType	GoTo	Handles	If
Implements	Imports	In	Inherits
Integer	Interface	Is	Lib
Like	Long	Loop	Me
Mod	Module	MustInherit	MustOverride
MyBase	MyClass	Namespace	New
Next	Not	Nothing	NotInheritable
NotOverridable	Object	On	Option

Figure F.1 Visual Basic .NET keywords. (Part 1 of 2.)

Visual Basic .NET Keywords			
Optional	Or	OrElse	Overloads
Overridable	Overrides	ParamArray	Preserve
Private	Property	Protected	Public
RaiseEvent	ReadOnly	ReDim	REM
RemoveHandler	Resume	Return	Select
Set	Shadows	Shared	Short
Single	Static	Step	Stop
String	Structure	Sub	SyncLock
Then	Throw	To	True
Try	TypeOf	Unicode	Until
When	While	With	WithEvents
WriteOnly	Xor		

The following are keywords, although they are not used in Visual Basic .NET

Let	Variant	Wend

Figure F.1   Visual Basic .NET keywords. (Part 2 of 2.)

APPENDIX

Internet Information Services (IIS) Setup Instructions

To create Web applications using Visual Studio .NET, Internet Information Services (IIS) needs to be installed on your computer. This appendix will guide you through the installation of IIS on computers using either the Windows 2000 or the Windows XP Professional Edition operating system. [*Note*: **IIS cannot be installed on computers using Windows XP Home Edition.**] For Web applications to compile and execute correctly, IIS must be installed before Visual Studio .NET is installed. It is recommended that you follow the steps to determine whether IIS is installed on your computer. If IIS is not installed on your computer and Visual Studio .NET is, you will need to uninstall Visual Studio .NET before continuing with the IIS installation. Once IIS is installed, you will need to reinstall Visual Studio .NET. [*Note*: If you are working in a lab environment and are prompted for a Windows CD, contact your system administrator for assistance.]

G.1 Installing IIS

This section will show you how to determine whether IIS is installed on a computer using the Windows 2000 and Windows XP operating systems. If IIS is not installed, this section will guide you through the installation process.

To begin, open the **Control Panel** by selecting **Start > Settings > Control Panel** in Windows 2000 or **Start > Control Panel** in Windows XP. When the **Control Panel** window opens, double click the **Add/Remove Programs** icon (Fig. G.1) in Windows 2000 or the **Add or Remove Programs** link (Fig. G.2) in Windows XP.

The **Add/Remove Programs** window lists all of the programs that are currently installed on your computer (Fig. G.3). The names and number of items on your computer will be different from those in the figure. In the left column of the **Add/Remove Programs** window, click the **Add/Remove Windows Components** icon (Fig. G.3) to display the **Windows Components Wizard**.

794

Figure G.1   Clicking the **Add/Remove Programs** icon in the **Control Panel** in Windows 2000.

Figure G.2   Clicking the **Add or Remove Programs** link in the **Control Panel** in Windows XP. (The contents of your **Control Panel** may differ.)

Figure G.3   Clicking the **Add/Remove Windows Components** icon.

The **Windows Components Wizard** (Fig. G.4) displays a list of Windows components that can be added to or removed from your computer. Scroll down to the **Internet Information Services (IIS)** component's CheckBox. If there is a check mark in this CheckBox, IIS is already installed, and you can click **Cancel** to exit the wizard. If the CheckBox is empty (Fig. G.4), click in the CheckBox (Fig. G.5), and click the **Next >** Button.

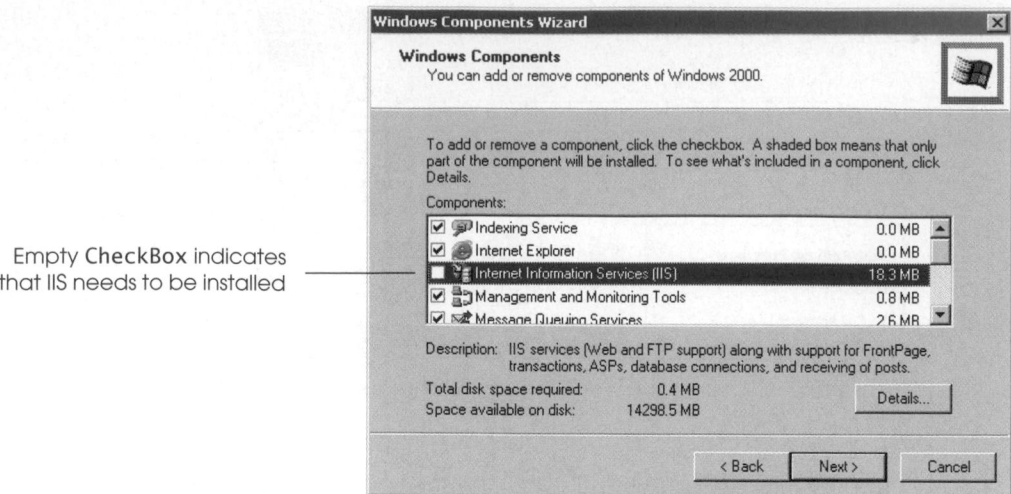

Empty **CheckBox** indicates that IIS needs to be installed

Figure G.4 **Windows Components Wizard** without IIS installed.

Selecting IIS component for installation

Figure G.5 Clicking the **Internet Information Services** CheckBox to install IIS.

Clicking **Next >** will begin the installation process and display the screen shown in Fig. G.6.

Windows may ask for your Windows 2000 CD during the installation proccess

Figure G.6 IIS installing on Windows 2000.

To install IIS, Windows may need to copy files from the Windows 2000 or Windows XP CD. If prompted, insert the CD and click **OK** to continue with the installation. When a dialog informs you that the installation is finished, click **Finish** to complete the installation and close the **Windows Components Wizard** (Fig. G.7).

This dialog appears after a successful installation

Figure G.7   Clicking **Finish** to complete the IIS installation.

A

action state—An action to perform in a UML activity diagram that is represented by an action-state symbol.

action/decision model of programming—Representing control statements as UML activity diagrams with rounded rectangles indicating *actions* to be performed and diamond symbols indicating *decisions* to be made.

action-state symbol—A rectangle with its left and right sides replaced with arcs curving outward that represents an action to perform in a UML activity diagram.

Active Server Pages .NET (ASP .NET)—.NET software that helps programmers create applications for the Web.

active tab—The tab of the document displayed in the IDE.

active window—The front-most window on your screen.

ActiveX -Properties—A hyperlink at the bottom-left of the **Properties** window for the MSChart control. When clicked, it displays a dialog with which you can set the MSChart properties.

activity diagram— A UML diagram that models the activity (also called the workflow) of a portion of a software system.

Add method of class ArrayList—A method of class ArrayList that adds a specified object to the end of an ArrayList.

Add method of Items—A method that adds an item to a ListBox control.

Add method of the Commands property—Method that adds a command to a Microsoft Agent character.

AddHandler keyword—Keyword used to add an event handler for a specific event.

AddressOf keyword—Keyword that specifies the location of an event handler associated with an event.

ADO .NET—Part of Microsoft .NET that is used to interact with databases.

algorithm—A procedure for solving a problem, specifying the actions to be executed and the order in which these actions are to be executed.

alphabetic icon—The icon in the **Properties** window that, when clicked, sorts properties alphabetically.

AndAlso operator—A logical operator used to ensure that two conditions are *both* true before choosing a certain path of execution. Performs short-circuit evaluation.

API (application programming interface)—The interface used by a program to access the operating system and various services on the computer.

ARGB values—A combination of alpha, red, green and blue components from which every color is created.

arithmetic operators—The operators +, -, *, /, \, ^ and Mod.

array—A data structure containing data items of the same type.

array bounds—Integers that determine what indices can be used to access an element in the array. The lower bound is 0; the upper bound is the length of the array minus one.

ArrayList class—Performs the same functionality as an array, but has resizing capabilities.

ASPX page—File that specifies the GUI of a Web page using Web controls.

assembly language—A type of programming language that uses English-like abbreviations to represent the fundamental operations on the computer.

assignment statement—A statement that copies one value to another. An assignment statement contains an "equals"-sign (=) operator that causes the value of its right operand to be copied to its left operand.

Auto Hide—A space-saving IDE feature used for windows such as **Toolbox**, **Properties** and **Dynamic Help** that hides a window until the mouse pointer is placed on the hidden window's tab.

B

BackColor property—Property of a Form or control that specifies its background color.

bgColor—Property of an ASPX page that specifies the page's background color.

binary operator—An operator that requires two operands.

bit—Short for "binary digit." A digit that can assume one of two values.

block scope—Variables declared inside control structures, such as an If...Then statement, have block scope. Block scope begins at the identifier's declaration and ends at the block's final statement (for example, End If).

book-title capitalization—A style that capitalizes the first letter of the each word in the text (for example, **Calculate Total**).

Boolean data type—A data type that has the value True or False.

BorderStyle property—The property that specifies the appearance of a Label's border, which allows you to distinguish one control from another visually. The BorderStyle property can be set to None (no border), FixedSingle (a single dark line as a border), or Fixed3D (giving the Label a "sunken" appearance).

BorderWidth—Property that specifies an Image's border width.

break mode—The IDE mode when program execution is suspended. This mode is entered through the debugger.

breakpoint—A statement where execution is to suspend, indicated by a solid maroon circle.

Brush object—An object used to specify drawing parameters when drawing solid shapes.

built-in data type—A data type already defined in Visual Basic .NET, such as an `Integer` (also known as a primitive data type).

`Button` control—A control used to command the application to perform an action.

`Button` Web control—Web control used to allow users to perform an action.

`Buttons` property—The property of the `MouseEventArgs` class that specifies which (if any) mouse button is pressed.

byte—Eight bits.

`ByVal`—The keyword specifying that the calling procedure should pass a copy of its argument's value in the procedure call to the called procedure.

C

call-by-reference—See *pass-by-reference.*

call-by-value—See *pass-by-value.*

callee—The procedure being called.

caller—The procedure that calls another procedure.

`Case Else` statement—Optional statement whose body executes if the `Select Case`'s test expression does not match any of the `Case`s' expressions.

case sensitive—The instance where two words that are spelled identically are treated differently if the capitalization of the two words differs.

categorized icon—The icon in the **Properties** window that, when clicked, sorts properties categorically.

`Cells`—Property that allows programmers to create `TableCells` in a `Table`.

central processing unit (CPU)—The part of the computer's hardware that is responsible for supervising the operation of the other sections of the computer.

`Char` structure—Structure that stores characters (such as letters and symbols).

character—A digit, letter or special symbol (characters in Visual Basic .NET are Unicode characters, which are composed of 2 bytes).

character set—The set of all characters used to write applications and represent data items on a particular computer. Visual Basic .NET uses the Unicode character set.

`ChartData` property—The `MSChart` property that stores the array containing the data to be displayed as a graph.

`ChartType` property—The `MSChart` property that determines the type of graph the control uses to display its data.

`CheckBox` control—A small white square GUI element that either is blank or contains a check mark.

`CheckBox` label—The text that appears alongside a `CheckBox`.

`Checked` property—The `RadioButton` property that, when `True`, displays a small black dot in the control. When `False`, the control displays an empty white circle.

`Checked` property of the `CheckBox` control—Specifies whether the `CheckBox` is checked (`True`) or unchecked (`False`).

`CheckedChanged` event—The event raised when a `RadioButton`'s state (checked or unchecked) changes.

class—The type of a group of related objects. A class specifies the general format of its objects; the properties and actions available to an object depend on its class. An object is to its class much as a house is to its blueprint.

class definition—The code that belongs to a class, beginning with keyword `Class` and ending with keywords `End Class`.

`Class` keyword—The keyword used to begin a class definition.

class name—The identifier used to identify the name of a class in code.

`Clear` method of `Items`—A method that deletes all the values in a `ListBox`'s control.

`Click` event—An event raised when a user clicks a control.

`Click` event of class `MenuItem`—Event generated when an item is clicked or a shortcut key is used.

client tier—Tier containing the user interface of the application.

code-behind file—Visual Basic .NET file that contains a class which provides an ASPX page's functionality.

collection—A class used to store groups of related objects.

`Collections` namespace—The namespace that contains collection classes such as `ArrayList`.

`Color` structure—The structure that specifies the system-defined colors available for drawing.

`ColorDialog` class—Class that is used to display a dialog containing color options to a use.

`ComboBox` control—A control that combines a `TextBox` with a `ListBox`.

`Command` event—Event raised when a user speaks a command to a Microsoft Agent character or selects a command from a character's context menu.

`Commands` property—Property that sets which commands the Microsoft Agent character can understand as input from the user.

comment—A line of code that follows a single-quote character (`'`) and is inserted to improve an application's readability.

compiler—A translator program that converts high-level-language programs into machine language.

component object box—The `ComboBox` at the top of the **Properties** window that allows you to select the `Form` or control object whose properties you want set.

component tray—The area below the Windows `Form` Designer that contains controls, such as `Timers`, that are not part of the graphical user interface.

computer—A device capable of performing computations and making logical decisions at speeds millions and even billions of times faster than the speeds at which human beings carry out those same tasks.

computer program—A set of instructions that guides a computer through an orderly series of actions.

computer programmer—A person who writes computer programs in programming languages.

condition— An expression with a true or false value that is used to make a decision.

connection object— Used to establish a connection to a database.

constant— A variable whose value cannot be changed after its initial declaration.

container— An object that contains controls.

Contents... command— The command that displays a categorized table of contents in which help articles are organized by topic.

context menu— A menu that appears when you right click an object.

control— A reusable component, such as a `GroupBox`, `RadioButton`, `Button`, `Label` and an `MSChart` control.

control structure— A program component that specifies the order in which statements execute (also known as the flow of control).

ControlChar.Tab constant— A constant that represents a tab character.

controlling expression — Value compared sequentially with each `Case` until either a match occurs or the `End Select` statement is reached.

Convert class— A class that provides methods for converting data types.

Convert.ToDecimal method— A method that converts a value to type `Decimal`, which is appropriate for monetary calculations.

Convert.ToInt16 method— Method used to convert data to type `Short`.

Count property of Items— The property that returns the number of `ListBox` items.

counter— A variable often used to determine the number of times a block of statements in a loop will execute.

counter-controlled repetition— A technique that uses a counter variable to determine the number of times that a block of statements will execute. Also called definite repetition.

CreateGraphics method— The method that creates a `Graphics` object on a `Form` or control.

CType function— Function that converts the type of its first argument to the type specified by the second argument.

Cursor.Position property— Property containing the *x*- and *y*-coordinates of the mouse cursor on the screen (in pixels).

CustomFormat property— The `DateTimePicker` property that contains the programmer-specified format string with which to display the date and/or time when `DateTimePicker` `Format` property is set to `Custom`.

D

data command object— Executes commands that retrieve or modify data in a database.

data hierarchy— Collection of data items processed by computers that become larger and more complex in structure as you progress from bits, to characters, to fields and up to larger data structures.

Data menu— The menu that contains commands for interacting with databases.

data reader— Reads data from a database.

database— Organized collection of data.

database management system (DBMS)— Provides mechanisms for storing and organizing data in a manner that is consistent with the database's format.

Date data type— A type capable of storing date and time data.

Date structure— A structure whose properties can be used to store and display date and time information.

DateTimePicker control— A control for retrieving date and time information from the user.

Debug menu— The menu that contains commands for debugging and running an application.

debugging— The process of fixing errors in an application.

Decimal data type— A data type used to store monetary amounts.

decision symbol— The diamond-shaped symbol in a UML activity diagram that indicates that a decision is to be made.

definite repetition— See counter-controlled repetition.

descriptive Label— A `Label` used to describe another control on the `Form`. This helps users understand a control's purpose.

design mode— IDE mode that allows you to create applications using Visual Studio .NET's windows, toolbars and menu bar.

Design mode— Displays the ASPX page's GUI at design time.

design view— The Visual Studio .NET view that contains the features necessary to begin creating Windows applications.

dialog (message dialog)— A window that displays messages to users and gathers input from users.

diamond symbol— In the UML, represents the decision symbol and the merge symbol, depending on how it is used.

Dim keyword— The keyword that indicates the declaration of a variable.

Directory.GetCurrentDirectory— A method of class `Directory` in the `System.IO` namespace that returns a `String` containing the path to the directory that contains the application.

dismiss— Synonym for close.

dithering— Process that uses small dots of existing colors to form a pattern that simulates a desired color.

divide-and-conquer technique— Constructing large applications from small, manageable pieces to make development and maintenance of large applications easier.

DNS lookup— Process that translates domain names to IP addresses.

Do Until...Loop repetition statement— A control statement that executes a set of body statements until its loop-termination condition becomes `True`.

Do While...Loop repetition statement— A control statement that executes a set of body statements while its loop-continuation condition is `True`.

Do...Loop Until repetition statement— A control statement that executes a set of statements until the loop-termination condition becomes `True` after the loop executes.

Do...Loop While repetition statement— A control statement that executes a set of statements while the loop-continuation condition is True; the condition is tested after the loop executes.

Document property—Property of the PrintPreviewDialog that allows you to specify the document that will be displayed in the dialog.

domain—Represents a group of hosts on the Internet.

domain name system (DNS) server—Computer that maintains a database of host names and their corresponding IP addresses.

dot operator—See member access operator.

dotted line—A UML activity diagram symbol that connects each UML-style note with the element that the note describes.

Double data type—A data type that contains whole numbers and decimal points.

double-selection statement—A statement, such as If...Then... Else, that selects between two different actions or sequences of actions.

DrawString method—Graphics method that draws the specified String.

DropDownStyle property—Property of the ComboBox control that specifies the appearance of the ComboBox.

dynamic help—A help option that provides links to articles that apply to the current content (that is, the item selected with the mouse pointer).

E

e event argument—The event argument that contains data for the event (such as KeyData).

element—An item in an array.

empty string—A string that does not contain any characters.

Enabled property—Specifies whether a control such as a Button appears enabled (True) or disabled (False).

End Function keywords—Indicates the end of a Function procedure.

End Select keywords—Terminates the Select Case statement.

End Sub keywords—Indicates the end of a Sub procedure.

EndsWith method of class String—The method that determines if a String ends with a particular substring.

Enum keyword—The keyword that begins an enumeration.

enumeration—A group of related, named constants.

event—A user action that can trigger an event handler.

event handler—A section of code that is executed (called) when a certain event is raised (occurs).

event-driven program—A program that responds to user-initiated events such as mouse clicks and keystrokes.

F

fatal logic error—An error that causes an application to fail and terminate prematurely.

field—Column in a table of a database.

field—Group of characters that conveys some meaning. For example, a field consisting of uppercase and lowercase letters can represent a person's name.

file—Collection of data that is assigned a name. Used for long-term persistence of large amounts of data, even after the program that created the data terminates.

FillEllipse method—The method of the Graphics class that draws an ellipse. This method takes as arguments a Brush, a Color, the coordinates of the ellipse's bounding box's upper-left corner and the width and height of the bounding box.

final state—Represented by a solid circle surrounded by a hollow circle in a UML activity diagram; the end of the workflow after a program performs its activities.

Focus method—The method that transfers the focus of the application to the control, on which the method is called.

Font class—Class that contains properties that define unique fonts.

Font property—The property that determines the font used to display text on a Form or control.

FontDialog class—Class that is used to display a dialog containing font options to a user and record the result.

FontFamily class—Class that contains methods for obtaining font information, such as GetName and GetType.

For Each...Next repetition statement—The repetition statement that can be used to iterate through elements in an array or collection.

For...Next statement—Repetition statement that handles the details of counter-controlled repetition. The For...Next statement uses all four elements essential to counter-controlled repetition in one line of code (the name of a control variable, the initial value, the increment or decrement value and the final value).

ForeColor—Property that specifies font color for Label controls.

Form—The object that represents the Windows application's graphical user interface (GUI).

Format property—The DateTimePicker property that allows the programmer to specify a predefined or custom format with which to display the date and/or time.

format specifier—Code that specifies the type of format that should be applied to a string for output.

Framework Class Library (FCL)—.NET's collection of "prepackaged" classes and methods for performing common mathematical calculations, string manipulations, character manipulations, input/output operations, error checking and many other useful operations.

FROM SQL keyword—Specifies table from which to get data.

FullOpen property of class ColorDialog—Property that, when True, enables the ColorDialog to provide a full range of color options when displayed.

fully qualified domain name (FQDN)—Host name combined with a domain and top-level domain that provides a user-friendly way to identify a site on the Internet.

Function procedure—A procedure similar to a Sub procedure, with one important difference: Function procedures return a value to the caller, whereas Sub procedures do not.

functionality—The actions an application can execute.

G

GDI+—An application programming interface (API) that provides classes for creating two-dimensional vector graphics

graphical user interface (GUI)—The visual part of an application with which users interact.

Graphics class—A class that defines methods for drawing shapes.

Graphics object—An object used to draw two-dimensional images.

grid unit—The space between two adjacent horizontal (or two adjacent vertical) dots on the Form in design view.

Gridlines—Property of a Table that specifies the format in which TableCell separators display.

GroupBox control—A control that groups related controls visually.

guard condition—An expression contained in square brackets above or next to the arrows leading from a decision symbol in a UML activity diagram that determines whether workflow continues along a path.

H

hardware—The various devices that make up a computer, including the keyboard, screen, mouse, hard drive, memory, CD-ROM and processing units.

Height property—This property, a member of property Size, indicates the height of the Form or one of its controls in pixels.

HideEvent event—Event raised when a Microsoft Agent character is hidden.

high-level language—A type of programming language in which a single program statement accomplishes a substantial task. High-level languages use instructions that look almost like everyday English and that contain common mathematical notations.

Horizontal Rule HTML control—HTML control used to display a line to separate controls on an ASPX page.

host name—Name of a computer where resources reside.

HTML mode—Displays the ASPX page's markup at design time.

HyperText Markup Language (HTML)—A language for marking up information to share over the World Wide Web using hyperlinked text documents.

I

IAgentCtlCharacter object—Object used to reference a Microsoft Agent character.

IAgentCtlUserInput object—Object used to store the user input retrieved from a Microsoft Agent character.

icon—The graphical representation of commands in the Visual Studio .NET IDE.

ID—Property that specifies the name of a Web control.

identifier—A series of characters consisting of letters, digits and underscores used to name program units such as classes, controls and variables.

Image class—Class used to store and manipulate images from various file formats.

Image property—Property that indicates the file name of the image displayed in a PictureBox.

Image Web control—Web control used to display an image in an ASPX page.

Image.FromFile—A method of class Image that returns an Image object containing the image located at the path you specify.

implicit conversion—A conversion from one data type to another performed by Visual Basic .NET.

Imports keyword—The keyword used to import namespaces.

index—An array element's position number, also called a subscript. An index must be zero, a positive integer or an integer expression. If an application uses an expression as an index, the expression is evaluated first, to determine the index.

indexed array name—The array name followed by an index enclosed in parentheses. The indexed array name can be used on the left side of an assignment statement to place a new value into an array element. The indexed array name can be used in the right side of an assignment to retrieve the value of that array element.

IndexOf method—String method that accepts as an argument a character to search for in a String. The method returns the index of a specified character in a String. If the String does not contain the character, the method returns –1.

infinite loop—An error in which a repetition statement never terminates.

information tier—Tier containing the application data; typically implemented as a database. Also called the bottom tier or database tier.

initial state—The beginning of the workflow in a UML activity diagram before the program performs the modeled activities.

initializer list—The required braces ({ and }) surrounding the initial values of the elements in the array. When the initializer list is empty, the elements in the array are initialized to the default value for the array's data type.

input unit—The "receiving" section of the computer that obtains information (data and computer programs) from various input devices, such as the keyboard and the mouse.

Insert method—String method that inserts its second argument (a String) at the position specified by the first argument.

Insert method of class ArrayList—A method of class ArrayList that inserts a specified object into the specified location of an ArrayList.

instance variable—A variable declared inside a class but outside any procedure of that class. Instance variables have module scope.

instant-access application—Application where a particular record of information must be located immediately.

integer—A whole number, such as 919, –11, 0 and 138624.

Integer data type—The data type that stores integer values.

integrated development environment (IDE)—A software tool that enables programmers to write, run, test and debug programs quickly and conveniently.

***IntelliSense* feature**—Visual Studio .NET feature that aids the programmer during development by providing windows listing available class members and pop-up descriptions for those members.

internal Web browser—Web browser (Internet Explorer) included in Visual Studio .NET, with which you can browse the Web.

Internet—A worldwide computer network. Most people today access the Internet through the World Wide Web.

Internet Information Services (IIS)—A Microsoft Web server.

`Interval` property—The `Timer` property that specifies the number of milliseconds between each `Tick` event.

IP address—Unique address used to locate a computer on the Internet.

`Item` property of `Items`—The property that returns the value stored in the `ListBox` at the specified index.

`Items` property of the `ListBox` control—Returns an object containing all the values in the `ListBox`.

K

keyboard event—Event that is raised when a key on the keyboard is pressed or released.

`KeyChar` property of class `KeyPressEventArgs`—Property containing data about the key that raised the `KeyPress` event.

`KeyData` property of class `KeyEventArgs`—Property containing data about the key that raised the `KeyDown` event.

`KeyDown` event—Event generated when a key is initially pressed. Use to handle the event raised when a key that is not a letter key is pressed.

`KeyEventArgs` class—Class that stores information about special modifier keys.

`KeyPress` event—The event generated when a key is pressed. Use to handle the event raised when a letter key is pressed.

`KeyPressEventArgs` class—Class that stores information about character keys.

`Keys` enumeration—Enumeration containing values representing keyboard keys.

`KeyUp` event—Event generated when key is released.

key-value pair—Associates a value with a corresponding key, which is used to identify the value.

keyword—A word in code reserved for a specific purpose. These words appear in blue in the IDE and cannot be used as identifiers.

L

`Label`—Control that displays text the user cannot modify.

`Label` Web control—Web control that is used to display text on an ASPX page.

Lady Ada Lovelace—The person credited as being the world's first computer programmer, for work she did in the early 1800s.

`LastIndexOf` method of class `String`—The method that returns the index of the last occurrence of a substring in a `String`. It returns `-1` if the substring is not found.

`Length` property—Contains the number of elements in an array.

`Length` property of class `String`—The property that returns the number of characters in a `String`.

line-continuation character—An underscore character (`_`) preceded by one or more spaces, used to continue a statement to the next line of code.

`ListBox` control—Allows the user to view items in a list. Items can be added to or removed from the list programmatically.

`ListBox` Web control—Web control used to display a list of items.

literal `String` objects—A `String` constant written as a sequence of characters in double quotation marks (also called a string literal).

`Load` event—The event raised when an application initially executes.

local variable—A variable declared inside a procedure or block, such as the body of an `If...Then` statement. Local variables have either procedure scope or block scope.

`localhost`—Host name that identifies the local computer.

location bar—The `ComboBox` in Visual Studio .NET where you can enter the name of a Web site to visit.

`Location` property—The property that specifies the location of the upper-left corner of a control. This property is used to place a control on the `Form` precisely.

logic error—An error that does not prevent the application from compiling successfully, but does cause the application to produce erroneous results.

logical exclusive OR (`Xor`) operator—A logical operator that is `True` if and only if one of its operands results in `True` and the other results in `False`.

logical operators—The operators (for example, `AndAlso`, `OrElse`, `Xor` and `Not`) that can be used to form complex conditions by combining simple ones.

loop-continuation condition—The condition used in a repetition statement (such as a `Do While...Loop`) that enables repetition to continue while the condition is `True` and that causes repetition to terminate when the condition becomes `False`.

loop-termination condition—The condition used in a repetition statement (such as a `Do Until...Loop`) that enables repetition to continue while the condition is `False` and that causes repetition to terminate when the condition becomes `True`.

M

machine language—A computer's natural language, generally consisting of streams of numbers that instruct the computer how to perform its most elementary operations.

`MainMenu` control—Control that allows you to add menus to your application.

margin indicator bar—A margin in the IDE where breakpoints are displayed.

masking—Hiding text such as passwords or other sensitive pieces of information that should not be observed by other people as they are typed. Masking is achieved by using the `PasswordChar` property of the `TextBox` for which you would like to hide data. The actual data entered is retained in the `TextBox`'s `Text` property.

masking character—Character that is used to replace each character displayed in a `TextBox` when the `TextBox`'s data is masked for privacy.

MaxDate property—The `DateTimePicker` property that specifies the latest value that the `DateTimePicker` will allow the user to enter.

MaxDropDownItems property—Property of the `ComboBox` class that specifies how many items can be displayed in the drop-down list.

Me keyword—A keyword that references the current object.

member access operator—Also known as the dot operator (.). Allows programmers to access a control's properties using code.

memory unit—The rapid-access, relatively low-capacity "warehouse" section of the computer, which stores data temporarily while an application is running.

menu—Design element that groups related commands for Windows applications. Although these commands depend on the application, some—such as **Open** and **Save**—are common to many applications.

Menu Designer in Visual Studio .NET—Design mode in Visual Studio .NET that allows you to create and edit menus.

menu item—Command located in a menu that, when selected, causes the application to perform a specific action.

menu-access shortcut—*Alt* key shortcut that allows the user to combine the *Alt* key with another key to access a menu item.

merge symbol—A symbol in the UML that joins two flows of activity into one flow of activity.

MessageBox class—The class that provides a method for displaying message dialogs.

MessageBoxButtons constants—The identifiers that specify `Buttons` that can be displayed in a `MessageBox` dialog.

MessageBoxIcon constants—Identifiers that specify icons that can be displayed in a `MessageBox` dialog.

method—A procedure contained in a class.

Microsoft .NET—Microsoft's vision for using the Internet and the Web in the development, engineering and use of software. .NET includes tools such as Visual Studio .NET and programming languages such as Visual Basic .NET.

Microsoft Agent—A technology used to add interactive animated characters to Windows applications and Web pages.

Microsoft Developer Network (MSDN)—An online library that contains articles, downloads and tutorials on technologies of interest to Visual Studio .NET developers.

middle tier—Tier that controls interaction between the client and information tiers.

MinDate property—The `DateTimePicker` property that specifies the earliest value that the `DateTimePicker` will allow the user to enter.

minus box—The icon that, when clicked, collapses a node.

Mod—The modulus operator yields the remainder after division.

modifier key—Key such as *Shift*, *Alt* or *Control* that modifies the way that applications respond to a keyboard event.

module scope—Module scope, which begins at the identifier after keyword `Class` and terminates at the `End Class` statement, enables all procedures in the same class to access all instance variables defined in that class.

MonthCalendar control—Control that displays a calendar from which a user can select a range of dates.

mouse event—An event that is generated when a user interacts with an application using the computer's mouse.

MouseButtons enumeration—An enumeration that defines constants, such as `Left`, `Right` and `Middle`, to specify mouse buttons.

MouseDown event—An event generated when a mouse button is pressed.

MouseEventArgs class—The class that specifies information about a mouse event.

MouseMove event—The event generated when a mouse pointer is moved.

MouseUp event—The event generated when the mouse button is released.

MoveTo method—Method used to relocate the Microsoft Agent character on the screen.

MSChart control—A control that allows you to display data as a graph on the `Form`.

Multiline property—Specifies whether the `TextBox` is capable of displaying multiple lines of text. If the property value is True, the `TextBox` may contain multiple lines of text; if the value of the property is `False`, the `TextBox` can contain only one line of text.

Multiline TextBox control—Control that provides the ability to enter or display multiple lines of text. If the text exceeds the size of the `TextBox`, the control can be set to display a scrollbar.

multimedia—The use of various media, such as sound, video and animation, to create content in an application.

multiple-selection statement—A statement that performs one of many actions (or sequences of actions) depending on the value of the controlling expression.

multiplication operator—The asterisk (*) used to multiply its two operands, producing their product as a result.

multi-tier application—Application that divides functionality into separate tiers. Typically, each tier performs a specific function.

N

namespace—Classes in the FCL are organized by functionality into these directory-like entities.

nested statement—A statement that is placed inside another control statement.

.NET Framework—Microsoft-provided software that executes applications, provides the Framework Class Library (FCL) and supplies many other programming capabilities.

New Project dialog—A dialog that allows you to choose which type of application you wish to create.

Next method—A method of class Random that, when called with no arguments, generates a positive Integer value between zero and the constant Int32.MaxValue.

NextDouble method—A method of class Random that generates a positive Double value that is greater than or equal to 0.0 and less than 1.0.

nonfatal logic error—An error that does not terminate an application's execution but causes a program to produce incorrect results.

Not (logical negation) operator—A logical operator that enables a programmer to reverse the meaning of a condition: A True condition, when logically negated, becomes False and a False condition, when logically negated, becomes True.

note—An explanatory remark (represented by a rectangle with a folded upper-right corner) describing the purpose of a symbol in a UML activity diagram.

Nothing keyword—The keyword used to clear a reference's value.

Now property of Date statement—Returns the current system time and date.

NumericUpDown control—Control that allows you to specify maximum and minimum numeric input values. Also allows you to specify an increment (or decrement) when the user clicks the up (or down) arrow.

O

object technology—A packaging scheme for creating meaningful software units. The units are large and are focused on particular application areas. There are date objects, time objects, paycheck objects, file objects and the like.

objects—Reusable software components that model items in the real world.

one-dimensional array—An array that uses only one index.

operand—An expression subject to an operator.

Option Strict—When set to On, Option Strict causes the compiler to check all conversions and requires the programmer to perform an explicit conversion for all narrowing conversions (for example, conversion from Double to Decimal) or application termination (conversion of a String, such as "hello", to type Integer).

OrElse operator—A logical operator used to ensure that either *or* both of two conditions are True in an application before a certain path of execution is chosen.

output device—A device to which information that is processed by the computer can be sent.

output Label—A Label used to display calculation results.

output unit—The section of the computer that takes information the computer has processed and places it on various output devices, making the information available for use outside the computer.

P

Page_Load—An event handler that executes any processing necessary to display a Web page.

parameter list—A comma-separated list in which the procedure declares each parameter variable's name and type.

parameter variable—A variable declared in a procedure's parameter list that can be used in the body of the procedure.

pass-by-reference—When an argument is passed by reference, the called procedure can access and modify the caller's original data directly. Keyword ByRef indicates pass-by-reference (also called call-by-reference).

pass-by-value—When an argument is passed by value, the application makes a copy of the argument's value and passes that copy to the called procedure. With pass-by-value, changes to the called procedure's copy do not affect the original variable's value. Keyword ByVal indicates pass-by-value (also called call-by-value).

PasswordChar property of a TextBox—Specifies the masking character for a TextBox.

Pen object—An object used to specify drawing parameters when drawing shape outlines.

persistent data—Data maintained in files.

PictureBox—Control that displays an image.

pin icon—An icon that enables or disables the Auto Hide feature.

pixel—A tiny point on your computer screen that displays a color.

Play method—Method used to play a Microsoft Agent character animation.

plus box—An icon that, when clicked, expands a node.

Pmt function—A function that, given an interest rate, a time period and a monetary loan amount, returns a Double value specifying the payment amount per specified time period.

Point structure—Structure that represents an (x, y) coordinate pair of a point in a two-dimensional plane.

primary key—Field (or combination of fields) in a database table that contains unique values used to distinguish records from one another.

primitive data type—A data type already defined in Visual Basic .NET, such as Integer (also known as a built-in data type).

Print method—PrintDocument method used to print a document.

PrintDocument class—Class that allows users to describe how to print a document.

PrintPage event—Event that occurs when the data required to print the current page is needed.

PrintPreviewDialog class—Class that previews a document before it prints in a dialog box.

procedural programming language—A programming language (such as Fortran, Pascal, BASIC or C) that focuses on actions (verbs) rather than things or objects (nouns).

procedure—A set of instructions for performing a particular task.

procedure body—The declarations and statements that appear after the procedure header but before the keywords End Sub or End Function. The procedure body contains Visual Basic .NET code that performs actions, generally by manipulating or interacting with the parameters from the parameter list.

procedure call—The procedure call invokes a procedure, and specifies the procedure name and provides information (arguments) that the callee (the procedure being called) requires to perform its task.

procedure definition—The procedure header, body and ending statement.

procedure header—The first line of a procedure (including the keyword Sub or Function, the procedure name, the parameter list and the Function procedure return type).

procedure name—Follows the keyword Sub or Function and distinguishes one procedure from another. A procedure name can be any valid identifier.

procedure scope—Variables declared inside a procedure but outside of a control structure, have procedure scope. Variables with procedure scope cannot be referenced outside the procedure in which they are declared.

programmer-defined procedure—A procedure created by a programmer to meet the unique needs of a particular application.

project—A group of related files that compose an application.

Properties window—The window that displays the properties for a Form or control object.

property—Specifies a control or Form object's attributes, such as size, color and position.

pseudocode—An informal language that helps programmers develop algorithms.

pseudorandom numbers—A sequence of values produced by a complex mathematical calculation that simulates random-number generation.

R

RadioButton control—A control that appears as a small white circle that is either blank (unchecked) or contains a smaller black dot (checked). Usually these controls appear in groups of two or more. Exactly one RadioButton in a group is selected at once.

Random class—A class that contains methods to generate pseudo-random numbers.

ReadLine method—Method of class StreamReader that reads a line from a file and returns it as a String.

record—A collection of related fields. Usually a Class in Visual Basic .NET composed of several fields (called member variables in Visual Basic .NET).

record—An entire table row in a database.

record key—Identifies a record and distinguishes that record from all other records.

Rectangle structure—Structure that enables you to define rectangular shapes and their dimensions.

rectangular array—A type of two-dimensional array that can represent tables of values consisting of information arranged in rows and columns. Each row contains the same number of columns.

reference—A variable to which you assign an object.

region—A portion of code that can be collapsed or expanded.

Remove method—String method that deletes a specified number of characters (the second argument) starting at the index specified by the first argument.

RemoveAt method of class ArrayList—A method of class ArrayList that removes the object located at a specified location of an ArrayList.

repetition statement—A statement that allows the programmer to specify that an action or actions should be repeated, depending on the value of a condition.

Replace method of class String—A method that returns a new String object in which every occurrence of a substring is replaced with a different substring.

Response.Redirect—Method used to redirect the client browser to another Web page.

Return keyword—Signifies the return statement that sends a value back to the procedure's caller.

return type—Data type of the result returned from a Function procedure.

RGB value—The amount of red, green and blue needed to create a color.

Rows—Property that allows programmers to create table rows.

run mode—IDE mode indicating that the application is executing.

run-time error—An error that has its effect at execution time.

S

scope—The portion of an application in which an identifier (such as a variable name) can be referenced. Some identifiers can be referenced throughout an application; others can be referenced only from limited portions of an application (such as within a single procedure or block).

screen scraping—The process of extracting desired information from the HTML that composes a Web page.

ScrollBars property—Specifies whether a TextBox has a scrollbar and, if so, of what type. By default, property ScrollBars is set to None. Setting the value to Vertical places a scrollbar along the right side of the TextBox.

secondary storage media—Devices such as magnetic disks, optical disks and magnetic tapes on which computers store files.

Select Case statement—The multiple-selection statement used to make a decision by comparing an expression to a series of conditions. The algorithm then takes different actions based on those values.

SELECT SQL keyword—Used to request specified information from a database.

SelectedIndexChanged event of ComboBox—The event raised when a new value is selected in a ComboBox.

sender event argument—Event argument that contains the GUI component that raised the event (also called the source of the event).

sentence-style capitalization—A style that capitalizes the first letter of the first word in the text. Every other letter in the text is lowercase, unless it is the first letter of a proper noun (for example, **Cartons per shipment**).

separator bar—Bar placed in a menu to separate related menu items.

sequential-access file—File which contains data that is read in the order that it was written to the file.

Session state—ASP .NET's built-in support for tracking data.

Session object—Object that is maintained across several Web pages containing a collection of items (key-value pairs). This variable is specific to each user.

Short data type—Data type that holds small Integers.

short-circuit evaluation—The evaluation of the right operand in AndAlso and OrElse expressions occurs only if the first condition meets the criteria for the condition.

Show method—Method used to display a Microsoft Agent character on the screen.

ShowDialog method of class FontDialog or ColorDialog—The method that displays the dialog on which it is called.

ShowUpDown property—The DateTimePicker property that, when true, allows the user to specify the time using up and down arrows.

single-selection statement—The If...Then statement, which selects or ignores a single action or sequence of actions.

Size property—Property that specifies the height and width, in pixels, of the Form or one of its controls.

SizeMode property—Property that specifies how an image is displayed in a PictureBox.

sizing handle—Square that, when enabled, can be used to resize the Form or one of its controls.

software—The set of applications that run on computers.

software reuse—The reuse of existing pieces of software, an approach that enables programmers to avoid "reinventing the wheel," helping them develop new applications faster.

solid circle—A UML activity diagram symbol that represents the activity's initial state.

SolidBrush class—The class that defines a Brush that draws with a single color.

solution—Contains one or more projects.

Solution Explorer—A window that provides access to all the files in a solution.

Speak method—Method used to have the Microsoft Agent character speak text to the user.

speech synthesis—The process by which a computer converts text to spoken words.

speech-recognition engine—Application that translates vocal sound input from a microphone into a language that the computer understands.

Start Page—The initial page displayed when Visual Studio .NET is opened.

StartsWith method of class String—The method that determines if a String starts with a particular substring.

startup object—The object (for example, a Form) displayed when the application executes.

state button—A button that can be in the on/off (true/false) state.

statement—A unit of code that, when compiled and executed, performs an action.

Step keyword—Optional component of the For...Next header that specifies the increment (that is, the amount added to the control variable each time the loop is executed).

StreamReader class—Class that provides methods for reading information from a file.

StreamWriter class—Class that provides methods for writing information to a file.

StretchImage—Value of PictureBox property SizeMode that scales an image to fill the PictureBox.

string literal—A String constant written as a sequence of characters in double quotation marks (also called a literal String object).

String.Format method—Method that formats a string.

structured programming—A disciplined approach to creating programs that are clear, correct and easy to modify.

Structured Query Language (SQL)—Language often used by relational databases to perform queries and manipulate data in relational databases.

style—Property that allows you to specify the position of a Web control.

Sub procedure—A procedure similar to a Function procedure, with one important difference: Sub procedures do not return a value to the caller, whereas Function procedures do.

submenu—Menu within another menu.

subscript—See index.

Substring method of class String—A method that creates a new String object by copying part of an existing String object.

syntax error—An error that occurs when program statements violate the grammatical rules of a programming language.

System.Drawing.Printing namespace—Namespace that allows your applications to access to all services related to printing.

System.IO namespace—A namespace containing methods to access files and directories.

T

TabIndex property—A control property that specifies the order in which focus is transferred to controls on the Form when the *Tab* key is pressed.

Table Web control—Web control used to display a table in an ASPX page.

TabStop property—A control property that specifies whether a control can receive the focus when the *Tab* key is pressed.

Tahoma font—The Microsoft-recommended font for use in Windows applications.

Text property—Property that specifies the text displayed by a Form or a control.

Text property of class MenuItem—Property that specifies the menu item's text.

TextAlign property—The property that specifies how text is aligned in the control.

TextBox control—A control used to retrieve user input from the keyboard.

TextChanged event—The event that occurs when the text in a TextBox changes.

text-to-speech engine—Application that translates typed words into spoken sound that users hear through headphones or speakers connected to a computer.

Tick event—The event raised after the number of milliseconds specified in the `Timer` control's `Interval` property has elapsed.

Timer control—A control that wakes up at specified intervals to execute code in its `Tick` event handler.

ToLower method of class String—A method that creates a new `String` object that replaces every uppercase letter in a `String` with its lowercase equivalent.

tool tip—The description of an icon that appears when the mouse pointer is held over that icon for a few seconds.

toolbar—A bar that contains `Buttons` that execute commands.

toolbar icon—A picture on a toolbar `Button`.

Toolbox—A window that contains controls used to customize `Forms`.

Tools menu—A menu that contains commands for accessing additional IDE tools and options that enable customization of the IDE.

top tier—Tier containing the application's user interface. Also called the client tier.

top-level domain (TLD)—Usually describes the type of organization that owns the domain name.

ToString method—A method that returns a `String` representation of the object or data type on which the method is called.

ToUpper method of class String—A method that creates a new `String` object that replaces every lowercase letter in a `String` with its uppercase equivalent.

ToUpper method of structure Char—Method that returns the uppercase representation of the character passed as a parameter.

transferring the focus—Selecting a control in an application.

transition—A change from one action state to another that is represented by transition arrows in a UML activity diagram.

Trim method of class String—A method that removes all whitespace characters from the beginning and end of a `String`.

truth table—A table that displays the boolean result of a logical operator for all possible combinations of `True` and `False` values for its operands.

two-dimensional array—A double-subscripted array that contains multiple rows of values.

U

UML (Unified Modeling Language)—An industry standard for modeling software systems graphically.

uniform resource locator (URL)—Address that can be used to direct a browser to a resource on the Web.

UPDATE SQL keyword—Used to modify data in a database table.

UseAntiAlias property—Property of class `PrintPreviewDialog` that makes the text in the `PrintPreviewDialog` appear smoother on the screen.

V

Val function—A function that filters a number from its argument if possible. This avoids errors introduced by the entering of nonnumeric data when only numbers are expected. However, the result of the `Val` function is not always what the programmer intended.

Value property—The property that stores the value (such as a time) in a `DateTimePicker` control.

ValueChanged event—The event raised when a user selects a new day or time in the `DateTimePicker` control.

variable—A location in the computer's memory where a value can be stored for use by an application.

vector graphics—Graphics created by a set of mathematical properties called vectors, which include the graphics' dimensions, attributes and positions.

visual programming with Visual Basic .NET—Instead of writing detailed program statements, the programmer uses Visual Studio .NET's graphical user interface to conveniently drag and drop predefined objects into place, and to label and resize them. Visual Studio .NET writes much of the Visual Basic .NET program, saving the programmer considerable effort.

Visual Studio .NET—Microsoft's integrated development environment (IDE), which allows developers to create applications in a variety of .NET programming languages.

W

Watch window—A Visual Studio .NET window that allows you to view variable values as an application is being debugged.

Web controls—Controls, such as `TextBoxes` and `Buttons`, that are used to customize ASPX pages.

Web server—Specialized software that responds to client requests by providing resources.

Web-safe colors—Colors that display the same on different computers.

WHERE SQL keyword—Specifies criteria that determine the rows to retrieve.

whitespace character—A space, tab or newline character.

Width property—This setting, a member of property `Size`, indicates the width of the `Form` or one of its controls, in pixels.

Windows application—An application that executes on a Windows operating system.

workflow—The activity of a portion of a software system.

World Wide Consortium (W3C)—A forum through which qualified individuals and companies cooperate to develop and standardize technologies for the World Wide Web.

World Wide Web (WWW)—A communications system that allows computer users to locate and view multimedia documents (such as documents with text, graphics, animations, audios and videos).

WriteLine method—Method of class `StreamWriter` that writes a `String` and a line terminator to a file.

X

X property—The property of class `MouseEventArgs` that specifies the *x*-coordinate of the mouse event.

***x*-coordinate**—Horizontal distance (increasing to the right) from the left of the drawing area.

Y

Y property—The property of class `MouseEventArgs` that specifies the *y*-coordinate of the mouse event.

***y*-coordinate**—Vertical distance (increasing downward) from the top of the drawing area.

Z

zeroth element—The first element in an array.

INDEX

End User License Agreement

PRENTICE HALL LICENSE AGREEMENT AND LIMITED WARRANTY

READ THE FOLLOWING TERMS AND CONDITIONS CAREFULLY BEFORE OPENING THIS SOFTWARE PACKAGE. THIS LEGAL DOCUMENT IS AN AGREEMENT BETWEEN YOU AND PRENTICE-HALL, INC. (THE "COMPANY"). BY OPENING THIS SEALED SOFTWARE PACKAGE, YOU ARE AGREEING TO BE BOUND BY THESE TERMS AND CONDITIONS. IF YOU DO NOT AGREE WITH THESE TERMS AND CONDITIONS, DO NOT OPEN THE SOFTWARE PACKAGE. PROMPTLY RETURN THE UNOPENED SOFTWARE PACKAGE AND ALL ACCOMPANYING ITEMS TO THE PLACE YOU OBTAINED THEM FOR A FULL REFUND OF ANY SUMS YOU HAVE PAID.

1. GRANT OF LICENSE: In consideration of your purchase of this book, and your agreement to abide by the terms and conditions of this Agreement, the Company grants to you a nonexclusive right to use and display the copy of the enclosed software program (hereinafter the "SOFTWARE") on a single computer (i.e., with a single CPU) at a single location so long as you comply with the terms of this Agreement. The Company reserves all rights not expressly granted to you under this Agreement.

2. OWNERSHIP OF SOFTWARE: You own only the magnetic or physical media (the enclosed media) on which the SOFTWARE is recorded or fixed, but the Company and the software developers retain all the rights, title, and ownership to the SOFTWARE recorded on the original media copy(ies) and all subsequent copies of the SOFTWARE, regardless of the form or media on which the original or other copies may exist. This license is not a sale of the original SOFTWARE or any copy to you.

3. COPY RESTRICTIONS: This SOFTWARE and the accompanying printed materials and user manual (the "Documentation") are the subject of copyright. The individual programs on the media are copyrighted by the authors of each program. Some of the programs on the media include separate licensing agreements. If you intend to use one of these programs, you must read and follow its accompanying license agreement. You may not copy the Documentation or the SOFTWARE, except that you may make a single copy of the SOFTWARE for backup or archival purposes only. You may be held legally responsible for any copying or copyright infringement which is caused or encouraged by your failure to abide by the terms of this restriction.

4. USE RESTRICTIONS: You may not network the SOFTWARE or otherwise use it on more than one computer or computer terminal at the same time. You may physically transfer the SOFTWARE from one computer to another provided that the SOFTWARE is used on only one computer at a time. You may not distribute copies of the SOFTWARE or Documentation to others. You may not reverse engineer, disassemble, decompile, modify, adapt, translate, or create derivative works based on the SOFTWARE or the Documentation without the prior written consent of the Company.

5. TRANSFER RESTRICTIONS: The enclosed SOFTWARE is licensed only to you and may not be transferred to any one else without the prior written consent of the Company. Any unauthorized transfer of the SOFTWARE shall result in the immediate termination of this Agreement.

6. TERMINATION: This license is effective until terminated. This license will terminate automatically without notice from the Company and become null and void if you fail to comply with any provisions or limitations of this license. Upon termination, you shall destroy the Documentation and all copies of the SOFTWARE. All provisions of this Agreement as to warranties, limitation of liability, remedies or damages, and our ownership rights shall survive termination.

7. MISCELLANEOUS: This Agreement shall be construed in accordance with the laws of the United States of America and the State of New York and shall benefit the Company, its affiliates, and assignees.

8. LIMITED WARRANTY AND DISCLAIMER OF WARRANTY: The Company warrants that the SOFTWARE, when properly used in accordance with the Documentation, will operate in substantial conformity with the description of the SOFTWARE set forth in the Documentation. The Company does not warrant that the SOFTWARE will meet your requirements or that the operation of the SOFTWARE will be uninterrupted or error-free. The Company warrants that the media on which the SOFTWARE is delivered shall be free from defects in materials and workmanship under normal use for a period of thirty (30) days from the date of your purchase. Your only remedy and the Company's only obligation under these limited warranties is, at the Company's option, return of the warranted item for a refund of any amounts paid by you or replacement of the item. Any replacement of SOFTWARE or media under the warranties shall not extend the original warranty period. The limited warranty set forth above shall not apply to any SOFTWARE which the Company determines in good faith has been subject to misuse, neglect, improper installation, repair, alteration, or damage by you. EXCEPT FOR THE EXPRESSED WARRANTIES SET FORTH ABOVE, THE COMPANY DISCLAIMS ALL

WARRANTIES, EXPRESS OR IMPLIED, INCLUDING WITHOUT LIMITATION, THE IMPLIED WARRANTIES OF MERCHANTABILITY AND FITNESS FOR A PARTICULAR PURPOSE. EXCEPT FOR THE EXPRESS WARRANTY SET FORTH ABOVE, THE COMPANY DOES NOT WARRANT, GUARANTEE, OR MAKE ANY REPRESENTATION REGARDING THE USE OR THE RESULTS OF THE USE OF THE SOFTWARE IN TERMS OF ITS CORRECTNESS, ACCURACY, RELIABILITY, CURRENTNESS, OR OTHERWISE.

IN NO EVENT, SHALL THE COMPANY OR ITS EMPLOYEES, AGENTS, SUPPLIERS, OR CONTRACTORS BE LIABLE FOR ANY INCIDENTAL, INDIRECT, SPECIAL, OR CONSEQUENTIAL DAMAGES ARISING OUT OF OR IN CONNECTION WITH THE LICENSE GRANTED UNDER THIS AGREEMENT, OR FOR LOSS OF USE, LOSS OF DATA, LOSS OF INCOME OR PROFIT, OR OTHER LOSSES, SUSTAINED AS A RESULT OF INJURY TO ANY PERSON, OR LOSS OF OR DAMAGE TO PROPERTY, OR CLAIMS OF THIRD PARTIES, EVEN IF THE COMPANY OR AN AUTHORIZED REPRESENTATIVE OF THE COMPANY HAS BEEN ADVISED OF THE POSSIBILITY OF SUCH DAMAGES. IN NO EVENT SHALL LIABILITY OF THE COMPANY FOR DAMAGES WITH RESPECT TO THE SOFTWARE EXCEED THE AMOUNTS ACTUALLY PAID BY YOU, IF ANY, FOR THE SOFTWARE.

SOME JURISDICTIONS DO NOT ALLOW THE LIMITATION OF IMPLIED WARRANTIES OR LIABILITY FOR INCIDENTAL, INDIRECT, SPECIAL, OR CONSEQUENTIAL DAMAGES, SO THE ABOVE LIMITATIONS MAY NOT ALWAYS APPLY. THE WARRANTIES IN THIS AGREEMENT GIVE YOU SPECIFIC LEGAL RIGHTS AND YOU MAY ALSO HAVE OTHER RIGHTS WHICH VARY IN ACCORDANCE WITH LOCAL LAW.

ACKNOWLEDGMENT

YOU ACKNOWLEDGE THAT YOU HAVE READ THIS AGREEMENT, UNDERSTAND IT, AND AGREE TO BE BOUND BY ITS TERMS AND CONDITIONS. YOU ALSO AGREE THAT THIS AGREEMENT IS THE COMPLETE AND EXCLUSIVE STATEMENT OF THE AGREEMENT BETWEEN YOU AND THE COMPANY AND SUPERSEDES ALL PROPOSALS OR PRIOR AGREEMENTS, ORAL, OR WRITTEN, AND ANY OTHER COMMUNICATIONS BETWEEN YOU AND THE COMPANY OR ANY REPRESENTATIVE OF THE COMPANY RELATING TO THE SUBJECT MATTER OF THIS AGREEMENT.

Should you have any questions concerning this Agreement or if you wish to contact the Company for any reason, please contact in writing at the address below.

Robin Short
Prentice Hall PTR
One Lake Street
Upper Saddle River, New Jersey 07458

The DEITEL™
Suite of Products...

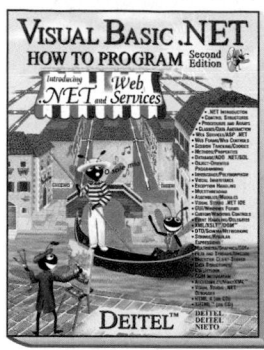

Visual Basic® .NET How to Program Second Edition

BOOK / CD-ROM

*©2002, 1400 pp., paper
(0-13-029363-6)*

This book provides a comprehensive introduction to the next version of Visual Basic—Visual Basic .NET— featuring extensive updates and increased functionality. *Visual Basic .NET How to Program, Second Edition* covers introductory programming techniques as well as more advanced topics, featuring ASP .NET, ADO .NET and developing Web-based applications.

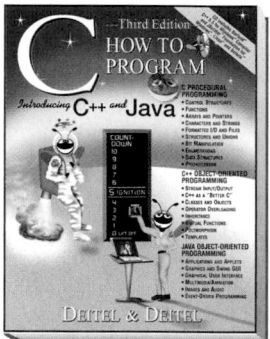

C How to Program Third Edition

BOOK / CD-ROM

*©2001, 1253 pp., paper
(0-13-089572-5)*

Highly practical in approach, the Third Edition of the world's best-selling C textbook introduces the fundamentals of structured programming and software engineering. This comprehensive book not only covers the full C language, but also reviews library functions and introduces object-based and object-oriented programming in C++ and Java and event-driven GUI programming in Java.

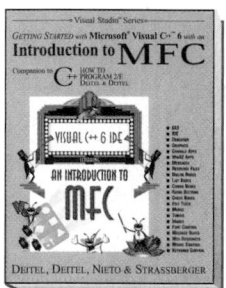

Getting Started with Microsoft® Visual C++™ 6 with an Introduction to MFC

BOOK / CD-ROM

*©2000, 163 pp., paper
(0-13-016147-0)*

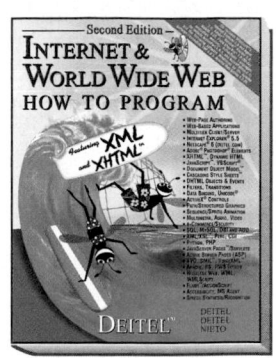

Internet & World Wide Web How to Program Second Edition

BOOK / CD-ROM

*©2002, 1428 pp., paper
(0-13-030897-8)*

Internet & World Wide Web How to Program, Second Edition offers a thorough treatment of programming concepts that yield visible or audible results in Web pages and Web-based applications. This book discusses effective Web-based design, server- and client-side scripting, multitier Web-based applications development, ActiveX® controls and electronic commerce essentials.

Wireless Internet & Mobile Business How to Program

*© 2002, 1292 pp., paper
(0-13-062226-5)*

Wireless Internet & Mobile Business How to Program offers a thorough treatment of both the management and technical aspects of wireless Internet applications development, including coverage of current practices and future trends.

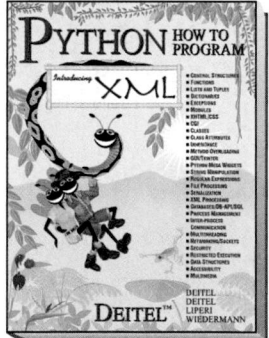

Python How to Program

BOOK / CD-ROM

*©2002, 1376 pp., paper
(0-13-092361-3)*

Python How to Program provides a comprehensive introduction to Python—a powerful object-oriented programming language with clear syntax and the ability to bring together various technologies quickly and easily.

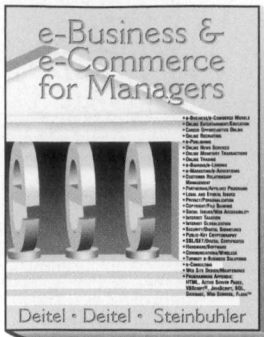

e-Business & e-Commerce for Managers

©2001, 794 pp., cloth (0-13-032364-0)

This comprehensive overview of building and managing e-businesses explores topics such as the decision to bring a business online, choosing a business model, accepting payments, marketing strategies and security, as well as many other important issues (such as career resources).

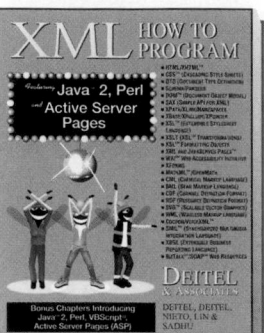

XML How to Program

BOOK / CD-ROM

©2001, 934 pp., paper (0-13-028417-3)

This book is a comprehensive guide to programming in XML. It teaches how to use XML to create customized tags and includes chapters that address markup languages for science and technology, multimedia, commerce and many other fields.

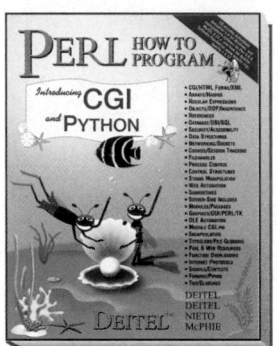

Perl How to Program

BOOK / CD-ROM

©2001, 1057 pp., paper (0-13-028418-1)

This comprehensive guide to Perl programming emphasizes the use of the Common Gateway Interface (CGI) with Perl to create powerful, dynamic multi-tier Web-based client/server applications.

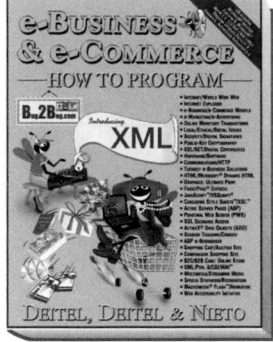

e-Business & e-Commerce How to Program

BOOK / CD-ROM

©2001, 1254 pp., paper (0-13-028419-X)

e-Business & e-Commerce How to Program explores programming technologies for developing Web-based e-business and e-commerce solutions, and covers e-business and e-commerce models and business issues.

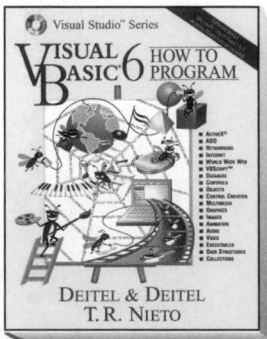

Visual Basic® 6 How to Program

BOOK / CD-ROM

©1999, 1015 pp., paper (0-13-456955-5)

Visual Basic® 6 How to Program was developed in cooperation with Microsoft to cover important topics such as graphical user interfaces (GUIs), multimedia, object-oriented programming, networking, database programming, VBScript®, COM/DCOM and ActiveX®.

Complete Training Courses

Each complete package includes the corresponding *How to Program Series* book and interactive multimedia Windows-based CD-ROM Cyber Classroom. *Complete Training Courses* are perfect for anyone interested in Web and e-commerce programming. They are affordable resources for college students and professionals learning programming for the first time or reinforcing their knowledge.

Intuitive Browser-Based Interface

You'll love the *Complete Training Courses'* browser-based interface, designed to be easy and accessible to anyone who's ever used a Web browser. Every *Complete Training Course* features the full text, illustrations and program listings of its corresponding *How to Program* book—all in full color—with full-text searching and hyperlinking.

Further Enhancements to the Deitels' Signature *Live-Code*™ Approach

Every code sample from the main text can be found in the interactive, multimedia, CD-ROM-based *Cyber Classrooms* included in the *Complete Training Courses*. Syntax coloring of code is included for the *How to Program* books that are published in full color. Even the two-color books use effective syntax shading. The *Cyber Classroom* products are always in full color.

Audio Annotations

Hours of detailed, expert audio descriptions of thousands of lines of code help reinforce concepts.

Easily Executable Code

With one click of the mouse, you can execute the code or save it to your hard drive to manipulate using the programming environment of your choice. With selected *Complete Training Courses*, you can also load all of the code into a development environment such as Microsoft® Visual C++, enabling you to modify and execute the programs with ease.

Abundant Self-Assessment Material

Practice exams test your understanding with hundreds of test questions and answers in addition to those found in the main text. The book include hundreds of programming exercises, while the *Cyber Classrooms* include answers to about half the exercises.

www.phptr.com/phptrinteractive

BOOK/MULTIMEDIA PACKAGES

 The Complete C++ Training Course, Fourth Edition

(0-13-100252-X)

 The Complete Python Training Course

(0-13-067374-9)

 The Complete C# Training Course

(0-13-064584-2)

 The Complete Visual Basic 6 Training Course

(0-13-082929-3)

 The Complete e-Business & e-Commerce Programming Training Course

(0-13-089549-0)

 The Complete Visual Basic .NET Training Course, Second Edition

(0-13-042530-3)

 The Complete Internet & World Wide Web Programming Training Course, Second Edition

(0-13-089550-4)

 The Complete Wireless Internet & Mobile Business Programming Training Course

(0-13-062335-0)

 The Complete Java™ 2 Training Course, Fifth Edition

(0-13-101766-7)

 The Complete XML Programming Training Course

(0-13-089557-1)

The Complete Perl Training Course

(0-13-089552-0)

All of these ISBNs are retail ISBNs. College and university instructors should contact your local Prentice Hall representative or write to cs@prenhall.com for the corresponding student edition ISBNs.